T0182054

IFIP Advances in Information and Communication Technology

633

Editor-in-Chief

Kai Rannenberg, Goethe University Frankfurt, Germany

Editorial Board Members

IFIP – The International Federation for Information Processing

IFIP was founded in 1960 under the auspices of UNESCO, following the first World Computer Congress held in Paris the previous year. A federation for societies working in information processing, IFIP's aim is two-fold: to support information processing in the countries of its members and to encourage technology transfer to developing nations. As its mission statement clearly states:

> IFIP is the global non-profit federation of societies of ICT professionals that aims at achieving a worldwide professional and socially responsible development and application of information and communication technologies.

IFIP is a non-profit-making organization, run almost solely by 2500 volunteers. It operates through a number of technical committees and working groups, which organize events and publications. IFIP's events range from large international open conferences to working conferences and local seminars.

The flagship event is the IFIP World Computer Congress, at which both invited and contributed papers are presented. Contributed papers are rigorously refereed and the rejection rate is high.

As with the Congress, participation in the open conferences is open to all and papers may be invited or submitted. Again, submitted papers are stringently refereed.

The working conferences are structured differently. They are usually run by a working group and attendance is generally smaller and occasionally by invitation only. Their purpose is to create an atmosphere conducive to innovation and development. Refereeing is also rigorous and papers are subjected to extensive group discussion.

Publications arising from IFIP events vary. The papers presented at the IFIP World Computer Congress and at open conferences are published as conference proceedings, while the results of the working conferences are often published as collections of selected and edited papers.

IFIP distinguishes three types of institutional membership: Country Representative Members, Members at Large, and Associate Members. The type of organization that can apply for membership is a wide variety and includes national or international societies of individual computer scientists/ICT professionals, associations or federations of such societies, government institutions/government related organizations, national or international research institutes or consortia, universities, academies of sciences, companies, national or international associations or federations of companies.

More information about this series at http://www.springer.com/series/6102

Alexandre Dolgui · Alain Bernard ·
David Lemoine · Gregor von Cieminski ·
David Romero (Eds.)

Advances in Production Management Systems

Artificial Intelligence for Sustainable and Resilient Production Systems

IFIP WG 5.7 International Conference, APMS 2021
Nantes, France, September 5–9, 2021
Proceedings, Part IV

 Springer

Editors
Alexandre Dolgui (iD)
IMT Atlantique
Nantes, France

David Lemoine (iD)
IMT Atlantique
Nantes, France

David Romero (iD)
Tecnológico de Monterrey
Mexico City, Mexico

Alain Bernard (iD)
Centrale Nantes
Nantes, France

Gregor von Cieminski (iD)
ZF Friedrichshafen AG
Friedrichshafen, Germany

ISSN 1868-4238   ISSN 1868-422X   (electronic)
IFIP Advances in Information and Communication Technology
ISBN 978-3-030-85912-1   ISBN 978-3-030-85910-7   (eBook)
https://doi.org/10.1007/978-3-030-85910-7

This Springer imprint is published by the registered company Springer Nature Switzerland AG
The registered company address is: Gewerbestrasse 11, 6330 Cham, Switzerland

Preface

The scientific and industrial relevance of the development of sustainable and resilient production systems lies in ensuring future-proof manufacturing and service systems, including their supply chains and logistics networks. "Sustainability" and "Resilience" are essential requirements for competitive manufacturing and service provisioning now and in the future. Industry 4.0 technologies, such as artificial intelligence; decision aid models; additive and hybrid manufacturing; augmented, virtual, and mixed reality; industrial, collaborative, mobile, and software robots; advanced simulations and digital twins; and smart sensors and intelligent industrial networks, are key enablers for building new digital and smart capabilities in emerging cyber-physical production systems in support of more efficient and effective operations planning and control. These allow manufacturers and service providers to explore more sustainable and resilient business and operating models. By making innovative use of the aforementioned technologies and their enabled capabilities, they can pursue the triple bottom line of economic, environmental, and social sustainability. Furthermore, industrial companies will be able to withstand and quickly recover from disruptions that pose threats to their operational continuity. This is in the face of disrupted, complex, turbulent, and uncertain business environments, like the one triggered by the COVID-19 pandemic, or environmental pressures calling for decoupling economic growth from resource use and emissions.

The International Conference on Advances in Production Management Systems 2021 (APMS 2021) in Nantes, France, brought together leading international experts on manufacturing, service, supply, and logistics systems from academia, industry, and government to discuss pressing issues and research opportunities mostly in smart manufacturing and cyber-physical production systems; service systems design, engineering, and management; digital lean operations management; and resilient supply chain management in the Industry 4.0 era, with particular focus on artificial intelligence-enabled solutions.

Under the influence of the COVID-19 pandemic, the event was organised as online conference sessions. A large international panel of experts (497 from 50 countries) reviewed all the submissions (with an average of 3.2 reviews per paper) and selected the best 377 papers (70% of the submitted contributions) to be included in these international conference proceedings. The topics of interest at APMS 2021 included artificial intelligence techniques, decision aid, and new and renewed paradigms for sustainable and resilient production systems at four-wall factory and value chain levels, comprising their associated models, frameworks, methods, tools, and technologies for smart and sustainable manufacturing and service systems, as well as resilient digital supply chains. As usual for the APMS conference, the Program Committee was particularly attentive to the cutting-edge problems in production management and the quality of the papers, especially with regard to the applicability of the contributions to industry and services.

The APMS 2021 conference proceedings are organized into five volumes covering a large spectre of research concerning the global topic of the conference: "Artificial Intelligence for Sustainable and Resilient Production Systems".

The conference was supported by the International Federation of Information Processing (IFIP), which is celebrating its 60th Anniversary, and was co-organized by the IFIP Working Group 5.7 on Advances in Production Management Systems, IMT Atlantique (Campus Nantes) as well as the Centrale Nantes, University of Nantes, Rennes Business School, and Audecia Business School. It was also supported by three leading journals in the discipline: Production Planning & Control (PPC), the International Journal of Production Research (IJPR), and the International Journal of Product Lifecycle Management (IJPLM).

Special attention has been given to the International Journal of Production Research on the occasion of its 60th Anniversary. Since its foundation in 1961, IJPR has become one of the flagship journals of our profession. It was the first international journal to bring together papers on all aspects of production research: product/process engineering, production system design and management, operations management, and logistics. Many exceptional scientific results have been published in the journal.

We would like to thank all contributing authors for their high-quality work and for their willingness to share their research findings with the APMS community. We are also grateful to the members of the IFIP Working Group 5.7, the Program Committee, and the Scientific Committee, along with the Special Sessions organizers for their support in the organization of the conference program. Concerning the number of papers, special thanks must be given to the local colleagues who managed the reviewing process as well as the preparation of the conference program and proceedings, particularly Hicham Haddou Benderbal and Maria-Isabel Estrepo-Ruiz from IMT Atlantique.

September 2021

Alexandre Dolgui
Alain Bernard
David Lemoine
Gregor von Cieminski
David Romero

Organization

Conference Chair

Alexandre Dolgui　　　　　IMT Atlantique, Nantes, France

Conference Co-chair

Gregor von Cieminski　　　ZF Friedrichshafen, Germany

Conference Honorary Co-chairs

Dimitris Kiritsis　　　　　EPFL, Switzerland
Kathryn E. Stecke　　　　　University of Texas at Dallas, USA

Program Chair

Alain Bernard　　　　　　Centrale Nantes, France

Program Co-chair

David Romero　　　　　　Tecnológico de Monterrey, Mexico

Program Committee

Alain Bernard　　　　　　Centrale Nantes, France
Gregor von Cieminski　　　ZF Friedrichshafen, Germany
Alexandre Dolgui　　　　　IMT Atlantique, Nantes, France
Dimitris Kiritsis　　　　　EPFL, Switzerland
David Romero　　　　　　Tecnológico de Monterrey, Mexico
Kathryn E. Stecke　　　　　University of Texas at Dallas, USA

International Advisory Committee

Farhad Ameri　　　　　　Texas State University, USA
Ugljesa Marjanovic　　　　University of Novi Sad, Serbia
Ilkyeong Moon　　　　　　Seoul National University, South Korea
Bojan Lalic　　　　　　　University of Novi Sad, Serbia
Hermann Lödding　　　　　Hamburg University of Technology, Germany

Organizing Committee Chair

David Lemoine　　　　　　IMT Atlantique, Nantes, France

Organizing Committee Co-chair

Hichem Haddou Benderbal   IMT Atlantique, Nantes, France

Doctoral Workshop Chairs

Abdelkrim-Ramzi   IMT Atlantique, Nantes, France
  Yelles-Chaouche
Seyyed-Ehsan   IMT Atlantique, Nantes, France
  Hashemi-Petroodi

Award Committee Chairs

Nadjib Brahimi   Rennes School of Business, France
Ramzi Hammami   Rennes School of Business, France

Organizing Committee

Romain Billot   IMT Atlantique, Brest, France
Nadjib Brahimi   Rennes School of Business, France
Olivier Cardin   University of Nantes, France
Catherine Da Cunha   Centrale Nantes, France
Alexandre Dolgui   IMT Atlantique, Nantes, France
Giannakis Mihalis   Audencia, Nantes, France
Evgeny Gurevsky   University of Nantes, France
Hichem Haddou Benderbal   IMT Atlantique, Nantes, France
Ramzi Hammami   Rennes School of Business, France
Oncu Hazir   Rennes School of Business, France
Seyyed-Ehsan   IMT Atlantique, Nantes, France
  Hashemi-Petroodi
David Lemoine   IMT Atlantique, Nantes, France
Nasser Mebarki   University of Nantes, France
Patrick Meyer   IMT Atlantique, Brest, France
Merhdad Mohammadi   IMT Atlantique, Brest, France
Dominique Morel   IMT Atlantique, Nantes, France
Maroua Nouiri   University of Nantes, France
Maria-Isabel Restrepo-Ruiz IMT Atlantique, Nantes, France
Naly Rakoto   IMT Atlantique, Nantes, France
Ilhem Slama   IMT Atlantique, Nantes, France
Simon Thevenin   IMT Atlantique, Nantes, France
Abdelkrim-Ramzi   IMT Atlantique, Nantes, France
  Yelles-Chaouche

Scientific Committee

Erry Yulian Triblas Adesta	International Islamic University Malaysia, Malaysia
El-Houssaine Aghezzaf	Ghent University, Belgium
Erlend Alfnes	Norwegian University of Science and Technology, Norway
Hamid Allaoui	Université d'Artois, France
Thecle Alix	IUT Bordeaux Montesquieu, France
Farhad Ameri	Texas State University, USA
Bjørn Andersen	Norwegian University of Science and Technology, Norway
Eiji Arai	Osaka University, Japan
Jannicke Baalsrud Hauge	KTH Royal Institute of Technology, Sweden/BIBA, Germany
Zied Babai	Kedge Business School, France
Natalia Bakhtadze	Russian Academy of Sciences, Russia
Pierre Baptiste	Polytechnique de Montréal, Canada
Olga Battaïa	Kedge Business School, France
Farouk Belkadi	Centrale Nantes, France
Lyes Benyoucef	Aix-Marseille University, France
Bopaya Bidanda	University of Pittsburgh, USA
Frédérique Biennier	INSA Lyon, France
Jean-Charles Billaut	Université de Tours, France
Umit S. Bititci	Heriot-Watt University, UK
Magali Bosch-Mauchand	Université de Technologie de Compiègne, France
Xavier Boucher	Mines St Etienne, France
Abdelaziz Bouras	Qatar University, Qatar
Jim Browne	University College Dublin, Ireland
Luis Camarinha-Matos	Universidade Nova de Lisboa, Portugal
Olivier Cardin	University of Nantes, France
Sergio Cavalieri	University of Bergamo, Italy
Stephen Childe	Plymouth University, UK
Hyunbo Cho	Pohang University of Science and Technology, South Korea
Chengbin Chu	ESIEE Paris, France
Feng Chu	Paris-Saclay University, France
Byung Do Chung	Yonsei University, South Korea
Gregor von Cieminski	ZF Friedrichshafen, Germany
Catherine Da Cunha	Centrale Nantes, France
Yves Dallery	CentraleSupélec, France
Xavier Delorme	Mines St Etienne, France
Frédéric Demoly	Université de Technologie de Belfort-Montbéliard, France
Mélanie Despeisse	Chalmers University of Technology, Sweden
Alexandre Dolgui	IMT Atlantique, Nantes, France
Slavko Dolinšek	University of Ljubljana, Slovenia

Sang Do Noh	Sungkyunkwan University, South Korea
Heidi Carin Dreyer	Norwegian University of Science and Technology, Norway
Eero Eloranta	Aalto University, Finland
Soumaya El Kadiri	Texelia AG, Switzerland
Christos Emmanouilidis	University of Groningen, The Netherlands
Anton Eremeev	Siberian Branch of Russian Academy of Sciences, Russia
Åsa Fasth-Berglund	Chalmers University of Technology, Sweden
Rosanna Fornasiero	Consiglio Nazionale delle Ricerche, Italy
Xuehao Feng	Zhejiang University, China
Yannick Frein	INP Grenoble, France
Jan Frick	University of Stavanger, Norway
Klaas Gadeyne	Flanders Make, Belgium
Paolo Gaiardelli	University of Bergamo, Italy
Adriana Giret Boggino	Universidad Politécnica de Valencia, Spain
Samuel Gomes	Belfort-Montbéliard University of Technology, France
Bernard Grabot	INP-Toulouse, ENIT, France
Gerhard Gudergan	RWTH Aachen University, Germany
Thomas R. Gulledge Jr.	George Mason University, USA
Nikolai Guschinsky	National Academy of Sciences, Belarus
Slim Hammadi	Centrale Lille, France
Ahmedou Haouba	University of Nouakchott Al-Asriya, Mauritania
Soumaya Henchoz	Logitech AG, Switzerland
Hironori Hibino	Tokyo University of Science, Japan
Hans-Henrik Hvolby	Aalborg University, Denmark
Jan Holmström	Aalto University, Finland
Dmitry Ivanov	Berlin School of Economics and Law, Germany
Harinder Jagdev	National University of Ireland at Galway, Ireland
Jayanth Jayaram	University of South Carolina, USA
Zhibin Jiang	Shanghai Jiao Tong University, China
John Johansen	Aalborg University, Denmark
Hong-Bae Jun	Hongik University, South Korea
Toshiya Kaihara	Kobe University, Japan
Duck Young Kim	Pohang University of Science and Technology, South Korea
Dimitris Kiritsis	EPFL, Switzerland
Tomasz Koch	Wroclaw University of Science and Technology, Poland
Pisut Koomsap	Asian Institute of Technology, Thailand
Vladimir Kotov	Belarusian State University, Belarus
Mikhail Kovalyov	National Academy of Sciences, Belarus
Gül Kremer	Iowa State University, USA
Boonserm Kulvatunyou	National Institute of Standards and Technology, USA
Senthilkumaran Kumaraguru	Indian Institute of Information Technology Design and Manufacturing, India

Thomas R. Kurfess	Georgia Institute of Technology, USA
Andrew Kusiak	University of Iowa, USA
Bojan Lalić	University of Novi Sad, Serbia
Samir Lamouri	ENSAM Paris, France
Lenka Landryova	Technical University of Ostrava, Czech Republic
Alexander Lazarev	Russian Academy of Sciences, Moscow, Russia
Jan-Peter Lechner	First Global Liaison, Germany
Gyu M. Lee	Pusan National University, South Korea
Kangbok Lee	Pohang University of Science and Technology, South Korea
Genrikh Levin	National Academy of Sciences, Belarus
Jingshan Li	University of Wisconsin-Madison, USA
Ming K. Lim	Chongqing University, China
Hermann Lödding	Hamburg University of Technology, Germany
Pierre Lopez	LAAS-CNRS, France
Marco Macchi	Politecnico di Milano, Italy
Ugljesa Marjanovic	University of Novi Sad, Serbia
Muthu Mathirajan	Indian Institute of Science, India
Gökan May	University of North Florida, USA
Khaled Medini	Mines St Etienne, France
Jörn Mehnen	University of Strathclyde, UK
Vidosav D. Majstorovich	University of Belgrade, Serbia
Semyon M. Meerkov	University of Michigan, USA
Joao Gilberto Mendes dos Reis	UNIP Paulista University, Brazil
Hajime Mizuyama	Aoyama Gakuin University, Japan
Ilkyeong Moon	Seoul National University, South Korea
Eiji Morinaga	Osaka Prefecture University, Japan
Dimitris Mourtzis	University of Patras, Greece
Irenilza de Alencar Naas	UNIP Paulista University, Brazil
Masaru Nakano	Keio University, Japan
Torbjörn Netland	ETH Zürich, Switzerland
Gilles Neubert	EMLYON Business School, Saint-Etienne, France
Izabela Nielsen	Aalborg University, Denmark
Tomomi Nonaka	Ritsumeikan University, Japan
Jinwoo Park	Seoul National University, South Korea
François Pérès	INP-Toulouse, ENIT, France
Fredrik Persson	Linköping Institute of Technology, Sweden
Giuditta Pezzotta	University of Bergamo, Italy
Selwyn Piramuthu	University of Florida, USA
Alberto Portioli Staudacher	Politecnico di Milano, Italy
Daryl Powell	Norwegian University of Science and Technology, Norway
Vittaldas V. Prabhu	Pennsylvania State University, USA
Jean-Marie Proth	Inria, France
Ricardo José Rabelo	Federal University of Santa Catarina, Brazil

Agostino Villa	Politecnico di Torino, Italy
Lihui Wang	KTH Royal Institute of Technology, Sweden
Sabine Waschull	University of Groningen, The Netherlands
Hans-Hermann Wiendahl	University of Stuttgart, Germany
Frank Werner	University of Magdeburg, Germany
Shaun West	Lucerne University of Applied Sciences and Arts, Switzerland
Joakim Wikner	Jönköping University, Sweden
Hans Wortmann	University of Groningen, The Netherlands
Desheng Dash Wu	University of Chinese Academy of Sciences, China
Thorsten Wuest	West Virginia University, USA
Farouk Yalaoui	University of Technology of Troyes, France
Noureddine Zerhouni	Université Bourgogne Franche-Comte, France

List of Reviewers

Abbou Rosa
Abdeljaouad Mohamed Amine
Absi Nabil
Acerbi Federica
Aghelinejad Mohsen
Aghezzaf El-Houssaine
Agrawal Rajeev
Agrawal Tarun Kumar
Alexopoulos Kosmas
Alix Thecle
Alkhudary Rami
Altekin F. Tevhide
Alves Anabela
Ameri Farhad
Andersen Ann-Louise
Andersen Bjorn
Anderson Marc
Anderson Matthew
Anholon Rosley
Antosz Katarzyna
Apostolou Dimitris
Arica Emrah
Arlinghaus Julia Christine
Aubry Alexis
Baalsrud Hauge Jannicke
Badulescu Yvonne Gabrielle
Bakhtadze Natalia
Barbosa Christiane Lima
Barni Andrea

Batocchio Antonio
Battaïa Olga
Battini Daria
Behrens Larissa
Ben-Ammar Oussama
Benatia Mohamed Amin
Bentaha M.-Lounes
Benyoucef Lyes
Beraldi Santos Alexandre
Bergmann Ulf
Bernus Peter
Berrah Lamia-Amel
Bertnum Aili Biriita
Bertoni Marco
Bettayeb Belgacem
Bevilacqua Maurizio
Biennier Frédérique
Bititci Umit Sezer
Bocanet Vlad
Bosch-Mauchand Magali
Boucher Xavier
Bourguignon Saulo Cabral
Bousdekis Alexandros
Brahimi Nadjib
Bresler Maggie
Brunoe Thomas Ditlev
Brusset Xavier
Burow Kay
Calado Robisom Damasceno

Calarge Felipe
Camarinha-Matos Luis Manuel
Cameron David
Cannas Violetta Giada
Cao Yifan
Castro Eduardo Lorenzo
Cattaruzza Diego
Cerqueus Audrey
Chang Tai-Woo
Chaves Sandra Maria do Amaral
Chavez Zuhara
Chen Jinwei
Cheng Yongxi
Chiacchio Ferdinando
Chiari da Silva Ethel Cristina
Childe Steve
Cho Hyunbo
Choi SangSu
Chou Shuo-Yan
Christensen Flemming Max Møller
Chung Byung Do
Ciarapica Filippo Emanuele
Cimini Chiara
Clivillé Vincent
Cohen Yuval
Converso Giuseppe
Cosenza Harvey
Costa Helder Gomes
Da Cunha Catherine
Daaboul Joanna
Dahane Mohammed
Dakic Dusanka
Das Dyutimoy Nirupam
Das Jyotirmoy Nirupam
Das Sayan
Davari Morteza
De Arruda Ignacio Paulo Sergio de
De Campos Renato
De Oliveira Costa Neto Pedro Luiz
Delorme Xavier
Deroussi Laurent
Despeisse Mélanie
Di Nardo Mario
Di Pasquale Valentina
Dillinger Fabian
Djedidi Oussama

Dolgui Alexandre
Dolinsek Slavko
Dou Runliang
Drei Samuel Martins
Dreyer Heidi
Dreyfus Paul-Arthur
Dubey Rameshwar
Dümmel Johannes
Eloranta Eero
Emmanouilidis Christos
Ermolova Maria
Eslami Yasamin
Fast-Berglund Åsa
Faveto Alberto
Federico Adrodegari
Feng Xuehao
Finco Serena
Flores-García Erik
Fontaine Pirmin
Fosso Wamba Samuel
Franciosi Chiara
Frank Jana
Franke Susanne
Freitag Mike
Frick Jan
Fruggiero Fabio
Fu Wenhan
Fujii Nobutada
Gahan Padmabati
Gaiardelli Paolo
Gallo Mosè
Ganesan Viswanath Kumar
Gaponov Igor
Gayialis Sotiris P.
Gebennini Elisa
Ghadge Abhijeet
Ghrairi Zied
Gianessi Paolo
Giret Boggino Adriana
Gloeckner Robert
Gogineni Sonika
Gola Arkadiusz
Goodarzian Fariba
Gosling Jon
Gouyon David
Grabot Bernard

Grangeon Nathalie
Grassi Andrea
Grenzfurtner Wolfgang
Guerpinar Tan
Guillaume Romain
Guimarães Neto Abelino Reis
Guizzi Guido
Gupta Sumit
Gurevsky Evgeny
Habibi Muhammad Khoirul Khakim
Haddou Benderbal Hichem
Halse Lise Lillebrygfjeld
Hammami Ramzi
Hani Yasmina
Hashemi-Petroodi S. Ehsan
Havzi Sara
Hazir Oncu
Hedayatinia Pooya
Hemmati Ahmad
Henchoz El Kadiri Soumaya
Heuss Lisa
Hibino Hironori
Himmiche Sara
Hnaien Faicel
Hofer Gernot
Holst Lennard Phillip
Hovelaque Vincent
Hrnjica Bahrudin
Huber Walter
Husniah Hennie
Hvolby Hans-Henrik
Hwang Gyusun
Irohara Takashi
Islam Md Hasibul
Iung Benoit
Ivanov Dmitry
Jacomino Mireille
Jagdev Harinder
Jahn Niklas
Jain Geetika
Jain Vipul
Jasiulewicz-Kaczmarek Małgorzata
Jebali Aida
Jelisic Elena
Jeong Yongkuk
Johansen John

Jones Al
Jun Chi-Hyuck
Jun Hong-Bae
Jun Sungbum
Juned Mohd
Jünge Gabriele
Kaasinen Eija
Kaihara Toshiya
Kalaboukas Kostas
Kang Yong-Shin
Karampatzakis Dimitris
Kayikci Yasanur
Kedad-Sidhoum Safia
Keepers Makenzie
Keivanpour Samira
Keshari Anupam
Kim Byung-In
Kim Duck Young
Kim Hwa-Joong
Kim Hyun-Jung
Kinra Aseem
Kiritsis Dimitris
Kitjacharoenchai Patchara
Kjeldgaard Stefan
Kjersem Kristina
Klimchik Alexandr
Klymenko Olena
Kollberg Thomassen Maria
Kolyubin Sergey
Koomsap Pisut
Kramer Kathrin
Kulvatunyou Boonserm (Serm)
Kumar Ramesh
Kurata Takeshi
Kvadsheim Nina Pereira
Lahaye Sébastien
Lalic Danijela
Lamouri Samir
Lamy Damien
Landryova Lenka
Lechner Jan-Peter
Lee Dong-Ho
Lee Eunji
Lee Kangbok
Lee Kyungsik
Lee Minchul

Lee Seokcheon
Lee Seokgi
Lee Young Hoon
Lehuédé Fabien
Leiber Daria
Lemoine David
Li Haijiao
Li Yuanfu
Lim Dae-Eun
Lim Ming
Lima Adalberto da
Lima Nilsa
Lin Chen-ju
Linares Jean-marc
Linnartz Maria
Listl Franz Georg
Liu Ming
Liu Xin
Liu Zhongzheng
Lödding Hermann
Lodgaard Eirin
Loger Benoit
Lorenz Rafael
Lu Jinzhi
Lu Xingwei
Lu Xuefei
Lucas Flavien
Lüftenegger Egon
Luo Dan
Ma Junhai
Macchi Marco
Machado Brunno Abner
Maier Janine Tatjana
Maihami Reza
Makboul Salma
Makris Sotiris
Malaguti Roney Camargo
Mandal Jasashwi
Mandel Alexander
Manier Hervé
Manier Marie-Ange
Marangé Pascale
Marchesano Maria Grazia
Marek Svenja
Marjanovic Ugljesa
Marmolejo Jose Antonio

Marques Melissa
Marrazzini Leonardo
Masone Adriano
Massonnet Guillaume
Matsuda Michiko
Maxwell Duncan William
Mazzuto Giovanni
Medić Nenad
Medini Khaled
Mehnen Jorn
Mendes dos Reis João Gilberto
Mentzas Gregoris
Metaxa Ifigeneia
Min Li Li
Minner Stefan
Mishra Ashutosh
Mitra Rony
Mizuyama Hajime
Mogale Dnyaneshwar
Mohammadi Mehrdad
Mollo Neto Mario
Montini Elias
Montoya-Torres Jairo R.
Moon Ilkyeong
Moraes Thais De Castro
Morinaga Eiji
Moser Benedikt
Moshref-Javadi Mohammad
Mourtzis Dimitris
Mundt Christopher
Muši Denis
Nääs Irenilza De Alencar
Naim Mohamed
Nakade Koichi
Nakano Masaru
Napoleone Alessia
Nayak Ashutosh
Neroni Mattia
Netland Torbjørn
Neubert Gilles
Nguyen Du Huu
Nguyen Duc-Canh
Nguyen Thi Hien
Nielsen Izabela
Nielsen Kjeld
Nishi Tatsushi

Nogueira Sara
Noh Sang Do
Nonaka Tomomi
Noran Ovidiu
Norre Sylvie
Ortmeier Frank
Ouazene Yassine
Ouzrout Yacine
Özcan Uğur
Paes Graciele Oroski
Pagnoncelli Bernardo
Panigrahi Sibarama
Panıgrahi Swayam Sampurna
Papakostas Nikolaos
Papcun Peter
Pashkevich Anatol
Pattnaik Monalisha
Pels Henk Jan
Pérès François
Persson Fredrik
Pezzotta Giuditta
Phan Dinh Anh
Piétrac Laurent
Pinto Sergio Crespo Coelho da
Pirola Fabiana
Pissardini Paulo Eduardo
Polenghi Adalberto
Popolo Valentina
Portioli Staudacher Alberto
Powell Daryl
Prabhu Vittaldas
Psarommatis Foivos
Rabelo Ricardo
Rakic Slavko
Rapaccini Mario
Reis Milena Estanislau Diniz Dos
Resanovic Daniel
Rey David
Riedel Ralph
Rikalović Aleksandar
Rinaldi Marta
Roda Irene
Rodriguez Aguilar Roman
Romagnoli Giovanni
Romeo Bandinelli
Romero David

Roser Christoph
Rossit Daniel Alejandro
Rudberg Martin
Sabitov Rustem
Sachs Anna-Lena
Sahoo Rosalin
Sala Roberto
Santarek Kszysztof
Satolo Eduardo Guilherme
Satyro Walter
Savin Sergei
Schneider Daniel
Semolić Brane
Shafiq Muhammad
Sharma Rohit
Shin Jong-Ho
Shukla Mayank
Shunk Dan
Siadat Ali
Silva Cristovao
Singgih Ivan Kristianto
Singh Sube
Slama Ilhem
Smaglichenko Alexander
Smeds Riitta Johanna
Soares Paula Metzker
Softic Selver
Sokolov Boris V.
Soleilhac Gauthier
Song Byung Duk
Song Xiaoxiao
Souier Mehdi
Sørensen Daniel Grud Hellerup
Spagnol Gabriela
Srinivasan Vijay
Stavrou Vasileios P.
Steger-Jensen Kenn
Stich Volker
Stipp Marluci Andrade Conceição
Stoll Oliver
Strandhagen Jan Ola
Suh Eun Suk
Suleykin Alexander
Suzanne Elodie
Szirbik Nick B.
Taghvaeipour Afshin

Taisch Marco
Tanimizu Yoshitaka
Tanizaki Takashi
Tasić Nemanja
Tebaldi Letizia
Telles Renato
Thevenin Simon
Thoben Klaus-Dieter
Thurer Matthias
Tiedemann Fredrik
Tisi Massimo
Torres Luis Fernando
Tortorella Guilherme Luz
Troyanovsky Vladimir
Turcin Ioan
Turki Sadok
Ulrich Marco
Unip Solimar
Valdiviezo Viera Luis Enrique
Vallespir Bruno
Vasic Stana
Vaz Paulo
Vespoli Silvestro
Vicente da Silva Ivonaldo
Villeneuve Eric
Viviani Jean-Laurent
Vještica Marko
Vo Thi Le Hoa
Voisin Alexandre
von Cieminski Gregor
Von Stietencron Moritz
Wagner Sarah
Wang Congke
Wang Hongfeng
Wang Yin

Wang Yingli
Wang Yuling
Wang Zhaojie
Wang Zhixin
Wellsandt Stefan
West Shaun
Wiendahl Hans-Hermann
Wiesner Stefan Alexander
Wikner Joakim
Wiktorsson Magnus
Wimmer Manuel
Woo Young-Bin
Wortmann Andreas
Wortmann Johan Casper
Wuest Thorsten
Xu Tiantong
Yadegari Ehsan
Yalaoui Alice
Yang Danqin
Yang Guoqing
Yang Jie
Yang Zhaorui
Yelles Chaouche Abdelkrim Ramzi
Zaeh Michael Friedrich
Zaikin Oleg
Zambetti Michela
Zeba Gordana
Zhang Guoqing
Zhang Ruiyou
Zheng Feifeng
Zheng Xiaochen
Zoitl Alois
Zolotová Iveta
Zouggar Anne

Contents – Part IV

Data-Based Services as Key Enablers for Smart Products, Manufacturing and Assembly

Data-Driven Methods for Supply Chain Optimization

Digital Twins Based on Systems Engineering and Semantic Modeling

**Human-Centered Artificial Intelligence in Smart Manufacturing
for the Operator 4.0**

Operations Management in Engineer-to-Order Manufacturing

Product and Asset Life Cycle Management for Smart and Sustainable Manufacturing Systems

Robotics Technologies for Control, Smart Manufacturing and Logistics

Serious Games Analytics: Improving Games and Learning Support

Smart and Sustainable Production and Supply Chains

Smart Methods and Techniques for Sustainable Supply Chain Management

The New Digital Lean Manufacturing Paradigm

The Role of Emerging Technologies in Disaster Relief Operations: Lessons from COVID-19

AI for Resilience in Global Supply Chain Networks in the Context of Pandemic Disruptions

Modelling COVID-19 Ripple Effect and Global Supply Chain Productivity Impacts Using a Reaction-Diffusion Time-Space SIS Model

Xavier Brusset[1], Morteza Davari[1(✉)], Aseem Kinra[2], and Davide La Torre[1]

[1] SKEMA Business School, Université Côte D'Azur, Nice, France
morteza.davari@skema.edu
[2] Professorship for Global Supply Chain Management,
Universität Bremen, Bremen, Germany

Abstract. As the COVID pandemic shows, infection spreads widely across regions, impacting economic activity in unforeseen ways. We represent here how the geographic spread of the pandemic, by reducing the workers' participation to economic life, undermines the ability of firms and as a result the entire supply networks to satisfy customers' demands. We model the spatio-temporal dynamics of the propagation of Covid-19 infection on population, transport networks, facilities and population flows. The mathematical models will enable prospective analyses to be performed reliably. Such models will be used in what-if scenarios to simulate the impact on both populations and supply chain activities in case of future pandemics. The outcome should be useful tools for policymakers and managers. Results from this research will help in understanding the impact and the spread of a pandemic in a particular region and on supply chains. The data will be from European regions and the expected models will have validity in Europe.

Keywords: Spatial dynamics · Ripple effect · Propagation · Disruption · Graph theory · Network evaluation

1 Introduction

Covid-19 is a highly contagious virus-induced communicable disease, transmitted via droplets and contaminated objects during close unprotected contact between a healthy and an infected person [6]. As such infected people move away from the location in which they were contaminated, uncontaminated locations farther and farther away become centres of infection in their own right.

The Covid-19 pandemic has had huge human and economic consequences. Thus, understanding how to reduce the spread of the disease and which specific policies to implement in order to manage the pandemic is paramount

© IFIP International Federation for Information Processing 2021
Published by Springer Nature Switzerland AG 2021
A. Dolgui et al. (Eds.): APMS 2021, IFIP AICT 633, pp. 3–12, 2021.
https://doi.org/10.1007/978-3-030-85910-7_1

As is well understood, the movement of infected people and the evolution of the virus are fundamental to the spread of the pandemic. The flows of populations are represented depending on the granularity of the data and the level of detail of the maps. When such movements are coupled with the incidence of infection, insights can be obtained about the evolution in time and in space, and causes may be inferred. As the level of detail increases, provided that the corresponding data exists, further insights about the causes of the dispersion of the virus and the corresponding infection intensity in the population can be obtained. Thus, mapping how the infection spreads can shed light both on the type of countermeasures and the impact on economic activity.

The European economy is dependent on international cooperation and on the fact that goods can flow freely. Most of the firms' supply chains are highly interconnected, characterised by a high degree of complexity, long distances, and a large number of intermediaries. According to a study, 75% of European supply chains have been negatively affected by the crisis. The most important bottlenecks are the inward flow of goods from suppliers (62%), lack of insight into customer needs (60%), and the outward flow of goods to customers (50%).

We are therefore now in a largely unknown territory in relation to risk management in the supply chain. The challenge does not only include sharp fluctuations on the part of customers with unknown and highly fluctuating demand but also from supplies which can no longer be produced because specific inputs are produced at slower rates or arrive sporadically.

The purpose of the study is to be able to identify the evolution of the pandemic and model its impact on supply chains. Several models approximating the temporal spread of the pandemic [2] or of the effect of lockdown measures [8] already exist but do not help in understanding the ripple effect on supply chains.

In the following, we present the state of research on the way a pandemic's effects spreads through supply chain networks and the proposed ways for managers to control this impact on their firms' activity. We then present two epidemiological models which explain the infection spread in a homogeneous population and its extension into the spread among various populations. In Sect. 5, we model the impact of a pandemic on the various nodes of a supply network in terms of productivity as workers get infected. We draw some conclusions and present recommendations for future research in Sect. 7.

2   Ripple Effect Visualisation for Global Supply Chains

The phenomenon of the ripple effect has received great research interest in recent years and more and more contributions have tried to model the dynamics of the ripple effect through a supply chain network. The ripple effect occurs when a major disruptive event, such as the lock-downs initiated by Covid-19 virus, trigger a wave of simultaneous disturbances coming from several different directions [7,12,13,15]. It occurs through the propagation of Low Frequency and High Impact unforeseen disturbances [14].

Existing work attempts to understand the effects by modelling the ripple effect [13], and other related supply chain network redesign approaches [22].

Baghersad and Zobel [3] examine the effects of supply chain disruptions on firms' performance by applying a new quantitative measure of a disruption's impact adapted from the systems resilience literature. Li et al. [20] study and examine disruption propagations through simulating simple interaction rules of firms inside the supply chain network by developing an agent-based computational model.

The literature has thus attempted to understand the effects better by ripple effect quantification and other related supply chain mapping approaches [16]. However, there is a niche for exploring other Ripple effect approaches, and our study atemmpts to contribute towards the area of Ripple effect visualizatiou.

3   The Classical SIS Model

The susceptible-infected-susceptible (SIS) epidemiological model represents one of the simplest frameworks to analyze disease dynamics. The population, N, which is assumed to be constant, is composed of two groups: individuals who are infected, I_t, and individuals who are not infected but susceptible to infection, S_t. Infected individuals spontaneously recover from the disease at a speed $\delta > 0$, while susceptible individuals contract the disease at a rate $\alpha > 0$ by interacting through random matching with infected ones. Unhappily, as we now know [23], individuals who have recovered from the infection can be re-infected, that is, after a lapse of time they are susceptible again. This means that we cannot simply use a SIR model (Susceptible, Infected, Recovered) as presented in [1,5,11,21]. The probability with which matching occurs depends on the actual spread of the disease across the population [4,9,10,18,19]. The evolution of the number of infectives and susceptibles is described by the following differential equations:

$$\dot{S}_t = \delta I_t - \alpha \frac{S_t I_t}{N} \tag{1}$$

$$\dot{I}_t = \alpha \frac{S_t I_t}{N} - \delta I_t, \tag{2}$$

The above system can be simply recast in terms of the share of infectives, $i_t = \frac{I_t}{N}$, and the share of susceptibles, $s_t = \frac{S_t}{N}$, as follows:

$$\dot{s}_t = \delta i_t - \alpha i_t s_t \tag{3}$$

$$\dot{i}_t = \alpha i_t s_t - \delta i_t. \tag{4}$$

Since $1 = s_t + i_t$, essentially, the epidemic dynamics can be completely characterized by focusing on one of the two equations as follows:

$$\dot{i}_t = \alpha i_t (1 - i_t) - \delta i_t. \tag{5}$$

The above equation describes the evolution of the disease prevalence in the entire population. Note that analyzing the equilibria for the above model is rather straightforward. As discussed in the epidemiology literature, the long run outcome solely depends on the basic reproduction number, $\mathcal{R}_0$, given by $\mathcal{R}_0 = \frac{\alpha}{\delta}$.

4   A Reaction-Diffusion Time-Space SIS Model

We now focus on an extension of the basic SIS model to allow for geographical heterogeneities and externalities by introducing a spatial dimension. We denote with $S_{x,t}$ and $I_{x,t}$, respectively the susceptibles and infectives in the position $x \in \Omega$, where $\Omega \subset \mathbb{R}^2$ is a compact set at date $t \in \mathbb{R}_+$.

The epidemic dynamics cannot be fully characterized by focusing only on the evolution of the portions of infectives and susceptibles ($i_{x,t}$ and $s_{x,t}$) rather than the numbers of infectives and susceptibles ($I_{x,t}$ and $S_{x,t}$). This is due to the fact that the population is spatially distributed, $N = \int_\Omega N_{x,t}$ with $N_{x,t} = S_{x,t} + I_{x,t}$, and thus it is not necessarily true that the shares of infectives and susceptibles sum up to one in each location x (i.e., they do sum up to one over the whole spatial domain). In particular, the share of infectives, $i_{x,t} = \frac{I_{x,t}}{N}$, and the share of susceptibles, $s_{x,t} = \frac{S_{x,t}}{N}$, in each location x jointly determine the share of the total population residing in that specific location, $n_{x,t}$ with $n_{x,t} = s_{x,t} + i_{x,t}$, while the sum of the shares of the total population residing in all locations is one, $\int_\Omega n_{x,t} dx = 1$.

Therefore, we need to analyze the evolution of the share of infectives and susceptibles over time and across space, and the spatial model can be represented through a system of reaction-diffusion partial differential equations (a similar approach is used, for instance, in [17,24] to describe pollution diffusion) as follows:

$$\frac{\partial s_{x,t}}{\partial t} = d\nabla^2 s_{x,t} + \delta i_{x,t} - \alpha \int_\Omega s_{x',t} i_{x',t} \varphi_{x',x} dx', \tag{6}$$

$$\frac{\partial i_{x,t}}{\partial t} = d\nabla^2 i_{x,t} + \alpha \int_\Omega s_{x',t} i_{x',t} \varphi_{x',x} dx' - \delta i_{x,t}, \tag{7}$$

where the term $\varphi_{x,x'}$ describes the probability that infected people at the location x' could spread the infection at the location x with $x \neq x'$.

By recalling that $n_{x,t} = s_{x,t} + i_{x,t}$, it follows that $n_{x,t}$ solves the summation of Eqs. (6) and (7), that is $\frac{\partial n_{x,t}}{\partial t} = d\nabla^2 n_{x,t}$ with Neumann boundary conditions and initial conditions directly determined from those related to $s_{x,t}$ and $i_{x,t}$. This allows us to consider $n_{x,t}$ as a known exogenous variable, which thus can be substituted in (6) and (7) by writing $s_{x,t} = n_{x,t} - i_{x,t}$.

$$\frac{\partial n_{x,t}}{\partial t} = d\nabla^2 n_{x,t} \tag{8}$$

$$\frac{\partial i_{x,t}}{\partial t} = d\nabla^2 i_{x,t} + \alpha \int_\Omega (n_{x',t} - i_{x',t}) i_{x',t} \varphi_{x',x} dx' - \delta i_{x,t}. \tag{9}$$

Notice that the expression of $n_{x,t}$ is known in closed-form once a specific shape of the set Ω is assumed.

In order to understand the disease dynamics, we can thus analyze the system of partial differential equations (PDEs) given by (8) and (9), which generalizes to a spatial dimension SIS model that accounts for population mobility across locations.

Let us notice that whenever the kernel function $\varphi_{x',x}$ coincides with the Dirac, the above model boils down to:

$$\frac{\partial n_{x,t}}{\partial t} = d\nabla^2 n_{x,t} \tag{10}$$

$$\frac{\partial i_{x,t}}{\partial t} = d\nabla^2 i_{x,t} + \alpha(n_{x,t} - i_{x,t})i_{x,t} - \delta i_{x,t}, \tag{11}$$

with the Neumann boundary conditions $\frac{\partial n_{x,t}}{\partial n} = 0$ and $\frac{\partial i_{x,t}}{\partial n} = 0$.

To conclude, once the configuration of the network is known, the number of infected per node (location) can be evaluated for every location and period of time. Note that this description is computed directly, contrary to [11] which requires an algorithm. When comparing this model with the estimation method in [21], we purport that this one presents numerous advantages as it does not rely on Bayesian mechanics (including having to evaluate multinomial distributions) and yet could be applied using the same Baidu-Qianxi database of population mobility.

5   Supply Chain Network and Total Productivity

The global supply chain is modelled by the means of a graph $G = (V, E)$ with M nodes, where V denotes the node set and $E \subset V \times V$ is the edge set. For simplicity we identify each node $v \in V$ of the network with its geographical coordinates x_v.

Given two nodes $v, u \in V$, $0 \le \phi_{vu} \le 1$ represents the degree of interaction from node v to node u, summarizing the intensity of their reciprocal trade and logistic relationships. The network is then described in compact form by the triplet $G = (V, E, \phi)$ where ϕ is a $M \times M$ weighted matrix with the property that $\phi_{uv} = \phi_{vu}$. The level of infected at each node $v \in V$, is modelled by $i_{x_v,t}$. The local evolution of the infection is depending on both the local evolution of the epidemics as well as the interaction with the adjacent locations.

If $\Gamma(x)$ describes the per capita productivity at location x, the total productivity index $\Gamma_{tot}(t)$ of the supply chain network at time t depends on the susceptible population at each node $v \in V$ of the network and is defined as

$$\Gamma_{tot}(t) = \sum_{v \in V} \Gamma(x_v)s_{x_v,t} = \sum_{v \in V} \Gamma(x_v)(n_{x_v,t} - i_{x_v,t}). \tag{12}$$

Let us notice that, in absence of epidemics,

$$\Gamma_{tot}(t) = \sum_{v \in V} n_{x_v,t}\Gamma(x_v). \tag{13}$$

The combination of the dynamics of the epidemic with the definition of the network productivity leads to the following evolution equation of total $\Gamma_{tot}(t)$:

$$
\begin{aligned}
\dot{\Gamma}_{tot}(t) &= \sum_{v \in V} \Gamma(x_v) \frac{\partial s_{x_v,t}}{\partial t} \\
&= \sum_{v \in V} \Gamma(x_v) \left(d\nabla^2 (n_{x_v,t} - i_{x_v,t}) - \alpha \int_{\Omega} (n_{x',t} - i_{x',t}) i_{x',t} \varphi_{x',x_v} dx' + \delta i_{x_v,t} \right) \\
&= \sum_{v \in V} \Gamma(x_v) \left(d\nabla^2 s_{x_v,t} - \alpha \int_{\Omega} s_{x',t} i_{x',t} \varphi_{x',x_v} dx' + \delta i_{x_v,t} \right).
\end{aligned}
\tag{14}
$$

6   Numerical Simulation

In this section we present a numerical simulation of the dynamic model:

$$
\frac{\partial n_{x,t}}{\partial t} = d\nabla^2 n_{x,t} \tag{15}
$$

$$
\frac{\partial i_{x,t}}{\partial t} = d\nabla^2 i_{x,t} + \alpha \int_{\Omega} (n_{x',t} - i_{x',t}) i_{x',t} \varphi_{x',x} dx' - \delta i_{x,t}. \tag{16}
$$

For simplicity we suppose that Ω is a 1-dimensional domain and it is normalized to $\Omega = [0,1]$ and that $\varphi_{x',x} = \delta_x(x')$ is the Dirac at the point x. We also assume that the diffusion coefficient d is normalized to 1, the initial distribution of infected people i_0 is equal to $0.01x(1-x)$ as shown in Fig. 1, and the initial population $n_{x,0}$ is homogeneous and normalized to 1. The solution to

$$
\frac{\partial n_{x,t}}{\partial t} = d\frac{\partial^2 n_{x,t}}{\partial x^2} \tag{17}
$$

subject to the Neumann condition being known, is provided via the Fourier expansion by:

$$
n_{x,t} = \sum_{n \geq 0} A_n e^{-(n\pi)^2 dt} \cos(n\pi x), \tag{18}
$$

where

$$
A_0 = \int_0^1 n_{x,0} dx = 1, \tag{19}
$$

$$
A_n = 2 \int_0^1 n_{x,0} \cos(n\pi x) \, dx = 0, \tag{20}
$$

which implies that $n_{x,t} = 1$ for any x and t. The above model thus boils down to

$$
\frac{\partial i_{x,t}}{\partial t} = d\frac{\partial^2 i_{x,t}}{\partial x^2} + \alpha(1 - i_{x,t}) i_{x,t} - \delta i_{x,t}. \tag{21}
$$

In this case, for any network G, the total productivity evolves accordingly to:

$$
\Gamma_{tot}(t) = \sum_{v \in V} \Gamma(x_v)(1 - i_{x_v,t}). \tag{22}
$$

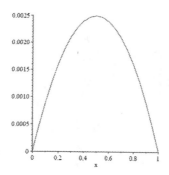

Fig. 1. Initial profile of infected people: $i_0(x) = 0.01x(x-1)$

In the first numerical simulation we suppose that the infection rate α is equal to 0.1328 and the recovery rate $\delta = 0.0476$ (see [18]). The figure shows that after an initial transition phase of growth, the number of infected people converges to a long-run endemic and homogeneous equilibrium $i_{x,\infty}$. In this scenario, the natural recovery rate δ is not big enough to guarantee a decrease of $i_{x,t}$ over time.

In this case, let us observe that due to the presence of the pandemic, the global productivity index Γ_{tot} will converge to (see Fig. 2):

$$\lim_{t \to +\infty} \Gamma_{tot}(t) = (1 - i_{x_v,\infty}) \sum_{v \in V} \Gamma(x_v) < \sum_{v \in V} \Gamma(x_v) \qquad (23)$$

In the second numerical simulation, we suppose that the infection rate α is still equal to 0.1328 but the implementation of treatment has raised the recovery rate δ to 0.1428. In this case, as Fig. 3 shows, the number of infectives decreases over time and it converges to the disease eradication in the long-run. Of course, the interesting part is for intermediate periods where the number of infectives may be non-homogeneous geographically: some locations will be more affected than others.

Let us observe that in this case, instead, the global productivity index Γ_{tot} will converge to:

$$\lim_{t \to +\infty} \Gamma_{tot}(t) = (1 - i_{x_v,\infty}) \sum_{v \in V} \Gamma(x_v) = \sum_{v \in V} \Gamma(x_v) \qquad (24)$$

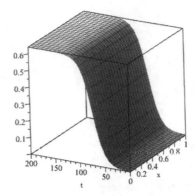

Fig. 2. Long-run behavior of the disease: $d = 1$, $\alpha = 0.1328$, $\delta = 0.0476$

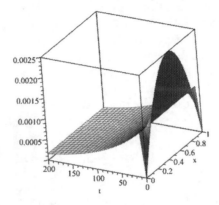

Fig. 3. Long-run behavior of the disease: $d = 1$, $\alpha = 0.1328$, $\delta = 0.1428$

7   Conclusion

In conclusion, we see how a pandemic spreads over regions, countries and continents in continuous time. We have modelled how such a pandemic infects workers and how this effect slows the production in a supply network, thus impacting the productivity of single production units and so the whole supply networks.

In this model, we have considered that the effect on production is simply additive. Of course, in reality, once an upstream partner in a supply network is impacted, all the downstream partners are also impacted. In a later refinement, we could look at a model where the effect of a pandemic is exponential in terms of the position of a node in the network. Another model might take into account the possibility that the infection rate α has different values across regions, or time. It is easy to include this in the model described in (9) as $\alpha_{x,t}$, so accommodating variants to the original virus.

In contrast to other studies of spatial transmission of the pandemic mentioned here, the advantage of the model is to only build from well defined and understood parameters: the infection rate α, recovery rate δ, the layout of the network, and population distribution in the various locations. The model takes into account the fact that people can be re-infected (which means that SIR or SIRD models are inadequate).

In this way, once a new virus is identified, knowing the characteristics of a network, a policy maker (manager) can build a forecasting model to evaluate the spread of the infection in the regions under her purview (supply chain network). Armed with such a model, a calibrated set of measures can be implemented which might impose a lesser burden on populations in the case of public policy or improve the resilience of the supply chain network.

References

1. Aràndiga, F., et al.: A spatial-temporal model for the evolution of the COVID-19 pandemic in spain including mobility. Mathematics **8**(10), 1677 (2020). https://doi.org/10.3390/math8101677
2. Arenas, A., et al.: A mathematical model for the spatiotemporal epidemic spreading of covid19. MedRxiv (2020)
3. Baghersad, M., Zobel, C.W.: Assessing the extended impacts of supply chain disruptions on firms: an empirical study. Int. J. Prod. Econ. **231**, 107862 (2021)
4. Capasso, V., Kunze, H.E., Torre, D.L., Vrscay, E.R.: Solving inverse problems for biological models using the collage method for differential equations. J. Math. Biol. **67**(1), 25–38 (2012)
5. Cooper, I., Mondal, A., Antonopoulos, C.G.: A SIR model assumption for the spread of COVID-19 in different communities. Chaos, Solitons Fractals **139**, 110057 (2020). https://doi.org/10.1016/j.chaos.2020.110057
6. World Health Organization: Coronavirus disease (COVID-19), H.i.i.t. (2020). https://www.who.int/emergencies/diseases/novel-coronavirus-2019/question-and-answers-hub/q-a-detail/coronavirus-disease-covid-19-how-is-it-transmitted. Accessed 19 Mar 2020
7. Dolgui, A., Ivanov, D.: Exploring supply chain structural dynamics: new disruptive technologies and disruption risks. Int. J. Prod. Econ. **229**, 107886 (2020)
8. Gatto, M., Bertuzzo, E., Mari, L., Miccoli, S., Carraro, L., Casagrandi, R., Rinaldo, A.: Spread and dynamics of the covid-19 epidemic in italy: Effects of emergency containment measures. Proc. Nat. Acad. Sci. **117**(19), 10484–10491 (2020)
9. Gersovitz, M., Hammer, J.S.: The economical control of infectious diseases*. Econ. J. **114**(492), 1–27 (2004)
10. Goenka, A., Liu, L., Nguyen, M.H.: Infectious diseases and economic growth. J. Math. Econ. **50**, 34–53 (2014)
11. Gounane, S., Barkouch, Y., Atlas, A., Bendahmane, M., Karami, F., Meskine, D.: An adaptive social distancing SIR model for COVID-19 disease spreading and forecasting. Epidemiologic Methods, vol. 10, no. s1 (2021). https://doi.org/10.1515/em-2020-0044
12. Ivanov, D.: Predicting the impacts of epidemic outbreaks on global supply chains: a simulation-based analysis on the coronavirus outbreak (covid-19/sars-cov-2) case. Transp. Res. Part E: Logistics Transp. Rev. **136**, 101922 (2020)
13. Ivanov, D., Dolgui, A.: Viability of intertwined supply networks: extending the supply chain resilience angles towards survivability. a position paper motivated by COVID-19 outbreak. Int. J. Prod. Res **58**(10), 2904–2915 (2020)

14. Ivanov, D., Sokolov, B., Chen, W., Dolgui, A., Werner, F., Potryasaev, S.: A control approach to scheduling flexibly configurable jobs with dynamic structural-logical constraints. IISE Trans. **53**(1), 1–18 (2020)
15. Kinra, A., Ivanov, D., Das, A., Dolgui, A.: Ripple effect quantification by supplier risk exposure assessment. Int. J. Prod. Res. **58**(18), 5559–5578 (2020). https://doi.org/10.1080/00207543.2019.1675919
16. Kinra, A., Ivanov, D., Das, A., Dolgui, A.: Ripple effect quantification by supplier risk exposure assessment. Int. J. Prod. Res. **58**(18), 5559–5578 (2020)
17. La Torre, D., Liuzzi, D., Marsiglio, S.: Pollution diffusion and abatement activities across space and over time. Math. Soc. Sci. **78**, 48–63 (2015)
18. La Torre, D., Liuzzi, D., Marsiglio, S.: Epidemics and macroeconomic outcomes: Social distancing intensity and duration. J. Math. Econ. **93**, 102473 (2021)
19. La Torre, D., Malik, T., Marsiglio, S.: Optimal control of prevention and treatment in a basic macroeconomic-epidemiological model. Math. Soc. Sci. **108**, 100–108 (2020)
20. Li, Y., Chen, K., Collignon, S., Ivanov, D.: Ripple effect in the supply chain network: Forward and backward disruption propagation, network health and firm vulnerability. European Journal of Operational Research (2020)
21. Oka, T., Wei, W., Zhu, D.: A spatial stochastic sir model for transmission networks with application to covid-19 epidemic in china (2020)
22. Reich, J., Kinra, A., Kotzab, H., Brusset, X.: Strategic global supply chain network design - how decision analysis combining MILP and AHP on a Pareto front can improve decision-making. Int. J. Prod. Res. 0(0), 1–16 (2020)
23. Shayak, B., Sharma, M.M., Gaur, M., Mishra, A.K.: Impact of reproduction number on the multiwave spreading dynamics of COVID-19 with temporary immunity: a mathematical model. Int. J. Infect. Dis. **104**, 649–654 (2021). https://doi.org/10.1016/j.ijid.2021.01.018
24. Wang, T.: Dynamics of an epidemic model with spatial diffusion. Phys. A: Stat. Mech. Appl. **409**, 119–129 (2014)

A Vector Logistic Dynamical Approach to Epidemic Evolution on Interacting Social-Contact and Production-Capacity Graphs

Jan Bart Broekaert[(✉)] and Davide La Torre

AI Institute for Business, SKEMA Business School, Sophia Antipolis, France
{jan.broekaert,davide.latorre}@skema.edu
https://www.skema.edu/faculty-and-research/artificial-intelligence

Abstract. Population inhomogeneity, in the variation of the individual social contact networks and the individual infectious-recovery rates, renders the dynamics of infectious disease spreading uncertain. As a consequence the overlaying economical production network with its proper collaboration components is to extent impacted unpredictably. Our model proposes a *vector logistic* dynamical approach to SIS dynamics in a social contact network interacting with its economic capacity network. The probabilistic interpretation of the graph state in the vector logistic description provides a method to assess the effect of mean and variance of the infected on the production capacity and allows the strategic planning of social connectivity regulation. The impact of the epidemic mean effects and fluctuations on the production capacity is assessed according *cumulative*, *majority* and *fragility* proxy measures.

Keywords: SIS dynamics · Vector logistic equation · Social graph · Production capacity

1 Context and Rationale

Compartmental epidemic models, starting with Kermack and McKendrick [11] and various elaborations reviewed by Hethcote [9], provide a simplified description of the epidemic evolution through transitions between a number of categories in a population, mainly the Susceptible, Infected, and Receptive ('Recovered' or 'Removed') - and in further model extensions, the Exposed (latency of onset), the Deceased (change of population size) and the Maternal (immunity protection from birth), see e.g. [6]. The aspects of socio-spatial distribution of individuals - in terms of inhomogeneity of both the infection-recovery rates and the connectivity of each individual , and the *stochastic* nature of transition events require an extension of the basic compartmental approach. To encompass the effect of socio-spatial structure of the population in the endemic progression, and to cover the

A. Dolgui et al. (Eds.): APMS 2021, IFIP AICT 633, pp. 13–22, 2021.
https://doi.org/10.1007/978-3-030-85910-7_2

resulting fluctuations, complex graph topologies have been implemented [10, 16], and reformulated as the bond percolation problem [14]. Specific graph topologies have been related to epidemic extinction time by Ganesh et al. [7] and the resilience of epidemics related to the diameter of the underlying network (e.g. in the network structures of Facebook, the Internet, Social networks) by Lu et al. [12].

Non-deterministic epidemic models including the effects of fluctuations are based on stochastic diffusion equations, by approximating the continuous time Markov chain model [1], by matching as an epidemic model with multiple hosts [13], or by parameter perturbation [8].

Instead, our model develops a description of the epidemic dynamics immediately at the level of intrinsic infection probability, similar to probabilistic Markov or 'quantum-like' system descriptions, e.g. [3, 5, 18]. In our model we describe the interaction of two networks: the social contact network, as the graph union of all individual 'ego' contact networks, and the production capacity network as the graph union of all production clusters. The nodes spanning both encompassing networks, $\mathscr{G}_A(V, E_A)$ and $\mathscr{G}_B(V, E_B)$, are the individuals of the considered population (filtered for professional activity in the production capacity graph).

We must take care to distinguish the concept of sub graphs - the connected components which do not share any edge with other such components, either in $\mathscr{G}_A(V, E_A)$ or $\mathscr{G}_B(V, E_B)$, and the interacting graphs which are (two) separate implementations - or layers - of functional relations on the same population. While the existence of connected components, or sub graphs, in the social contact network $\mathscr{G}_A(V, E_A)$ has an effect on the dynamics of infectious disease spreading, and can be indirectly influenced by regulated restriction on the degree of social connectivity, such an intervention is not applicable in the economic capacity network. The connected components of the production capacity graph remain fixed over time, since these components represent the economic capacity units of individual businesses, enterprises or service systems. It has been shown that, for interdependent networks failures in one network can percolate in another network on which its optimal performance depends [4]. In this manner, the interaction of the social graph with the production graph will allow an assessment of the production capacity attrition and will allow an analysis for the possible planning of regulatory intervention in the social contact network.

Finally as we have shortly mentioned earlier, in our approach each node of the graph is characterised by its probability of being infected over time, instead of attributing to each node a binary status of "infected" or "not-infected" at each instance of time. The evolution of the node infection probabilities is determined by the N-dimensional *vector logistic* equation. A similar probabilistic infection approach on a graph was proposed by Wang et al. [17], but which applied a Markov-like dynamics (idem, Eq. 13) instead. The usage of the vector logistic equation allows i) to regain the limit of the classic scalar logistic equation for SIS dynamics when the social graph nears the complete graph, $\mathscr{G}_A(V, E_A) = \mathscr{K}_N$ with large N, and ii) a probabilistic interpretation of the graph state vectors of the nodes, $\mathbf{Y}$, in the unit N-hypercube $[0, 1]^N$. This approach hence allows the expression of any infection related expectation quantity $\langle \mathbf{f} \rangle_t = E_t(\mathbf{f}) = \sum_i Y_i(t) f_i$.

2 Probabilistic SIS-dynamic on Social Contact Graphs

In the compartmentalised SIS-model the dynamics of the infected fraction i, is determined by the recovery rate δ over the infected fraction, and the infection rate β on the product of the susceptible, s, and infected, i, fractions:

$$\dot{i} = -\delta i + \beta(1 - i)i, \tag{1}$$

where $1 - i(t) = s(t)$. Two stationary solutions can occur $i_1^* = 0$ and $i_2^* = 1 - \delta/\beta$ (the latter when $\delta < \beta$). In our model, the possible interaction between the individuals - represented by nodes - is controlled by the adjacency matrix A of the graph $\mathcal{G}_A(V, E_A)$, $|V| = N$, $E_A \subset V^2$, representing the social contact network. While the specific realisation of the adjacency matrix in the true social contact network remains unknown, a number of parameters can be estimated or assumed [2]. Some of its properties like the average degree can be regulated as an optimisation parameter, e.g. corresponding with the restricted number of contacts that are allowed in a personal 'social bubble' or 'support circle'.

In order to retain a detailed description at the level of individual agents and to assess fluctuations over the network, a probability based infection-recovery model is constructed on a network. In this approach, a probability Y_i of being infected is attributed to each node i. Conform to the interaction effect by 'contact', we express the exposure of a node i by the product of its proper receptive capacity $1 - Y_i$ and the infective capacity Y_j of an adjacent node j, i.e. $A_{ij} = 1$, weighted by infection rate β_i and moderated by a normalisation factor of the inverse of the node's degree d_i^{-1}.

$$\dot{Y}_i = -\delta_i Y_i + \beta_i d_i^{-1}(1 - Y_i) \sum_j A_{ij} Y_j \tag{2}$$

The dynamical equation of the graph state vectors is written in vector notation by using $\boldsymbol{\delta}$ both for the variable recovery rate vector and likewise $\boldsymbol{\beta}$ for the variable infection rate vector and for the state vector $\mathbf{Y}$. We further need the Hadamard product symbol, $\circ$, to express the *elementwise* multiplication of factors:

$$\dot{\mathbf{Y}} = -\boldsymbol{\delta} \circ \mathbf{Y} + \boldsymbol{\beta}(1 - \mathbf{Y}) \circ \mathbf{d}^{-1} \circ A \, \mathbf{Y} \tag{3}$$

this notation requires that for an isolated node the apparent division '0/0' occurring in $A\mathbf{Y}/\mathbf{d}$ is effectively set equal to 0.

This vector differential equation differs from (the linear form of) the generalized Lotka-Volterra equation by a term proportional to $A\mathbf{Y}$, and from the Replicator equation by its additionally lacking a third order term $\mathbf{Y} \circ (\mathbf{Y}^T A \mathbf{Y})$, and having a first-order term in $\mathbf{Y}$ instead. Essentially the equation differs from these two typical dynamical systems by the first order derivative of the state **not** being a Hadamard product with the state itself. In order to attribute a probabilistic interpretation to the magnitudes Y_i, two observations are made,

- when $Y_i = 1$, the component Y_i decays over time at rate δ_i,
- when $Y_i = 0$, the component Y_i grows at rate $\beta_i/d_i \, \mathbf{A}_i - \mathbf{Y}$, which is non-negative.

With an initial state $0 \leq \mathbf{Y}_0 \leq 1$ at $t = 0$, the component values of $\mathbf{Y}_t$ remain contained in the $[0,1]$ range and hence can be considered as event probabilities (for infection) assigned to the respective nodes of the graph $\mathcal{G}(V, E)$. The state space of the vectors $\mathbf{Y}$ is the unit N-hypercube $[0,1]^N$, allowing each node an infection probability between 0 and 1. We recall that in contrast, in the Replicator system the corresponding state vector $\mathbf{Y}$ would remain on the simplex, $\sum_{i=1}^{N} Y_i = 1$, see e.g. Ohtsuki et al. [15], and in the case of the generalized Lotka-Volterra equation the solution is unconstrained $Y \in \mathbb{R}^{+N}$.

It can be easily shown that the vector logistic system reduces to the standard compartmentalised SIS equation when the graph is complete $\mathcal{G}(V, E) = K_N$ (all nodes have grade $N - 1$), and the recovery and infection rates are considered constant over the graph. With $i = \frac{1}{N} \sum_j Y_j$ and $A\mathbf{Y} = N\mathbf{i} - \mathbf{Y}$, where $\mathbf{i} = i\mathbf{1}$, we recover the SIS equation, Eq. (1), after component-wise summation of Eq. (2), and division by N.

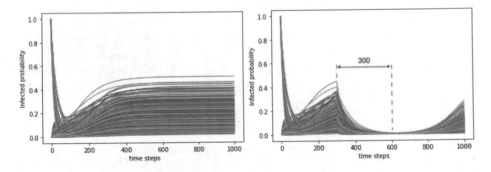

Fig. 1. An illustrative epidemic evolution on a random social contact graph $\mathcal{G}_A(V, E_A)$ with number of nodes N = 1000, number of initially infected nodes $init\_infected = 20$, and average social connectivity $N\_connect\_A = 40$ (left) . The initial number of infected nodes $init\_infected = 10$, the variable infection rate $\beta = 0.6(\mathrm{SD}0.2)$, and the variable recovery rate $\delta = 0.55(\mathrm{SD}0.2)$. During the confinement, the degree-inducing social contacts parameter is reduced to $N\_confinement\_A = 20$. The confinement period, Δt_{conf}, starts at time 300 and is held on for 300 time steps (right).

Finally, with the factor of the social contact graph included in the SIS dynamics, Eq. (3), it is now possible to study the effect on the epidemic progression by changes in the graph structure, see Fig. (2). In particular the effect of diminishing the social person-person contacts by culling edges in $\mathcal{G}(V, E)$, see Fig. 2, while maintaining the degree vector $\mathbf{d}$, allows the dynamical description of confinement efforts in diminishing the epidemic progression.

Concurrently the cost impact from production capacity attrition in the interacting economic graph can be monitored. In the next section, Sect. 3, we

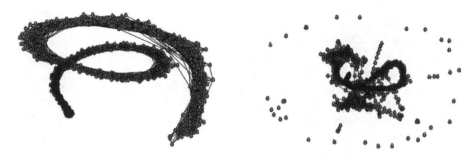

Fig. 2. An unconstrained artificial social contact graph (left) and its confinement rendition (right). In the unconstrained graph ($N = 1000, skew = 4, N\_connect\_A = 40$) the mean degree is 25.82, the mean cluster coefficient is 0.28, and the graph has 4 connected components. In the confined graph ($N = 1000, skew = 4, N\_confinement\_A = 20$) the mean degree has decreased to 8.04, with 88 connected components resulting.

define graph-based objective functions for economic capacity. In relation to the social graph, a social cost can be defined proportional to the contact restrictions and the duration of the confinement, see Fig. 1, through the quantity $(N_{connectA} - N_{confinement_A})\Delta t_{conf}$. The epidemic health cost can be defined proportional to total infection weight on the social graph at each instance of the epidemic through the quantity $\int^T |\mathbf{Y}(t)|_1 dt$.

3 The Interacting Economic Capacity Network

In our present development of the interacting graphs model we build partially sorted random graphs to resemble real-world configurations - both in social connectivity and economic networks. In principle there is no restriction on

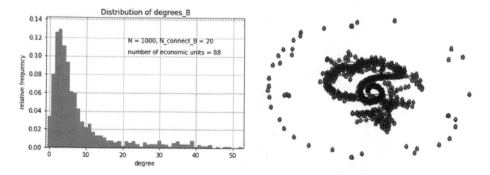

Fig. 3. Construction of the random economic capacity graph $\mathcal{G}_B(V, E_B)$ (right) interacting with the social contact graph $\mathcal{G}_A(V, E_A)$, Fig. 2. The economic capacity network inherits the nodes V_A of the social contact graph (N = 1000), and is parametrized by average connectivity parameter $N\_connect\_B = 20$ to obtain a number of economic capacity units $n_B = 88$ (left).

implementing another topology in either of the interacting graphs. Using the partially sorted random implementation for the economic capacity graph, the Laplace matrix associated to the adjacency matrix B of $\mathcal{G}_B(V, E_B)$ is used to identify the independent economic units, n_B in number. The eigenvectors of the Laplace matrix $\boldsymbol{\delta}_B \circ \mathbf{1} - B$ with 0-eigenvalue correspond to the connected components of the graph. With E_{Bi} the eigenvector of the i-th economic capacity unit, a number of proxy measures for production capacity can be formulated. At each instance of time, the epidemic evolution on the social contact graph $\mathcal{G}_A(V, E_A)$ provides the infected states of all individuals $\mathbf{Y}(t)$. Using a threshold value θ in the range $[0, 1]$ on the infection probability, the drop-out of active individuals can be assessed at all moment of time. Then using the *ceiling* function; $Y_{act}(t) = |ceil(\mathbf{Y}(t) < \theta)|_1$, is the number of healthy individuals. Similarly to identify the active individuals of the i-th graph component in optimal situation (no drop-out), we define its binary vector $\mathbf{W}_{Bi} = ceil(E_{Bi})$. The epidemic repercussions on each of the economic units can be assessed according the nature of the dependence of the economic output on the active nodes in the economic unit:

1. *cumulative metrics*
   The drop-out of individuals on the i-th economic component can impact the capacity of the unit proportionally:

   $$c_{cum.i} = \mathbf{Y}_{act}(t)^T . \mathbf{W}_{Bi}$$

   The total *cumulative* capacity of the full economic network $\mathcal{G}_B(V, E_B)$ is given by $C_{cumB} = \sum_{i=1}^{n_B} c_{cum.i}$.

2. *majority*
   The drop-out of individuals on the i-th economic component can impact the integral capacity of the unit by majority support (or other tip-over value):

   $$c_{maj_i} = ceil \left(\frac{|\mathbf{Y}_{act}(t)^T \circ \mathbf{W}_{Bi}|_1}{|\mathbf{W}_{Bi}|_1} \geq .5 \right)$$

   The total *majority* capacity of the full economic network $\mathcal{G}_B(V, E_B)$ is given by $C_{majB} = \sum_{i=1}^{n_B} c_{maj.i}$.

3. *fragility*
   The drop-out of each single individual of the i-th economic component impacts the integral capacity of the unit:

   $$c_{frag_i} = \Pi_{j=1}^{|\mathbf{W}_{Bi}|} (\mathbf{Y}_{act}(t) \cap \mathbf{W}_{Bi})_j$$

   where we select by intersection strictly the components corresponding to the i-th economic component, and multiply each. The total *fragile* capacity of the full economic network $\mathcal{G}_B(V, E_B)$ is given by $C_{fragB} = \sum_{i=1}^{n_B} c_{frag_i}$.

With the objective functions for economic capacity defined, and a standard expression for social cost of confinement proportional to $(N_{connectA} - N_{confinementA})\Delta t_{conf}$ and a health cost proportional to $\int^T |\mathbf{Y}(t)|_1 dt$, an optimization procedure based on parameters $N_{confinementA}$ and Δt_{conf} can be developed.

4   Implementation and Simulation Results

A partially sorted random-based social contact graph was implemented to reflect more realistic aspects of true person-person networks as reconstructed by e.g. Barrett et al. [2]. In particular the adjacency matrix, A, of a graph on N = 1000 nodes was designed and parametrized (*skew*, *N_connect_A*) to qualitatively approximate the degrees distribution, cluster coefficient distribution and template graph distribution in the communities of Los Angeles, New York City and Seattle [2]. The upper triangular matrix (diag = +1) of an ascending in-row sorted random $N \times N$ matrix in the range $[0, 1]$ was used to construct a symmetric matrix *A_sorted* with the max values in the upper triangle aligning the main 0-diagonal. Its unsorted counterpart *A_base* was retro-fitted by shuffling the row entries right of the main diagonal and restoring symmetry by fitting the lower triangle with the transposed upper triangle matrix. Clearly the sorted proto-adjacency matrix *A_sorted* (still with scalars in the range $[0, 1]$) amasses long linkage and fosters clique formation along the diagonal. In order to tweak this architecture, a parameter *skew* was used to gradually mix in the sorting effect on the random graph. Finally a degree-indicative connectivity parameter, *N_connect_A*, was used to fix the threshold $(N - N\_connect\_A)/N$ for binary adjacency in A:

$$A\_fin = A\_sorted + (A\_base - A\_sorted)/skew$$

$$A = (A\_fin \geq (N - N\_connect\_A)/N) \times 1$$

A number of parameter configurations where repeatedly tested to show for N = 1000 that *skew* = 4 and *N_connect_A* = 40 lead to an average degree of approximately 26 and an average cluster coefficient of .27 approximately, and qualitatively approximates the degrees distribution and cluster coefficient distribution of true social contact graphs [2]. The cluster coefficient distribution can be easily obtained from the adjacency matrix. It is given by the number of unique triangular walks from node ν_i over the number of contacts in the neighbour sub-graph had it formed a clique: $cc(\nu_i) = \frac{A_{ii}^3/2}{\binom{d_i}{2}}$. This sorting and tweaking procedure to construct the artificial social contact network moreover produces cycle and clique template graphs of low degrees. E.g., the particular graph $\mathscr{G}_A(V, E_A)$ in Fig. 2, counts 111216 of 3-cliques, and 1082464 of 4-cliques. The number of 3-cycli is of course the same as the number 3-cliques, and the number of 4-cycli is 4831030.

The node-based perspective of the SIS-dynamics was further deployed to randomly attribute individual infection and recovery rates along a lognormal distribution. In particular for the graph $\mathscr{G}_A(V, E_A)$ in Fig. 2, with infection rate β of mean log(0.6) and 0.2 standard deviation and, recovery rate δ of mean log(0.55) and 0.2 standard deviation, see Fig. 5.

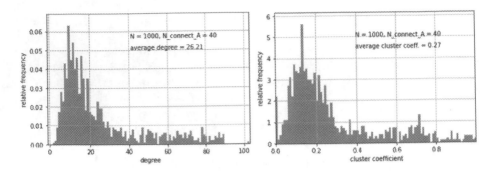

Fig. 4. The degree distribution of the random artificial social contact graph $\mathscr{G}_A(V, E_A)$ (left), and the corresponding cluster coefficient distribution (right).

We reckon that the social planner impacts the social contact graph during the confinement period by bringing about the degree-indicative connectivity parameter to a smaller value $N\_confinement\_A$. This parameter most closely reflects the restriction on the number of contacts that are allowed in a personal social bubble during confinement.

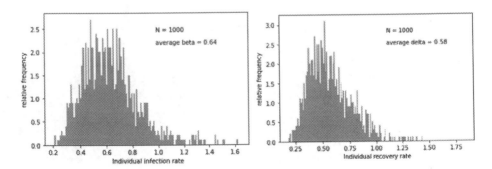

Fig. 5. The lognormal random distributions of infection rate (left) and recovery rate (right) in the random artificial social contact graph $\mathscr{G}_A(V, E_A)$.

Finally the multiplicative structure of the right-hand side of the logistic vector first-order differential equation, Eq. 3,

$$\dot{\mathbf{Y}} = \mathbf{f}(\mathbf{Y})\mathbf{Y}$$

allows a standard solution approach. From the initial state $\mathbf{Y}(0) = \mathbf{Y}_0$ an incrementally updated solution is obtained. The solutions for the full time-range are obtained by the iterated multiplication with a propagator kernel adapted to the previous state;

$$\mathbf{Y}_{t+1} = (1 + \mathbf{f}(\mathbf{Y}_t)dt)\,\mathbf{Y}_t.$$

In the illustrative epidemic evolution on $\mathcal{G}_A(V, E_A)$, Fig. 1, the initial state was randomly seeded with $init\_infected = 10$ nodes. The evolution of the state vector $\mathbf{Y}$ over the full time range was obtained using time increment $dt = 0.1$ for a total number of time $steps = 1000$. At the start of the confinement period the propagator kernel is adapted to the reduced adjacency $A_{confined}$ - with original degrees retained - and applied for next 300 time steps. After the confinement period the original multiplicative kernel based on A is resumed.

5   Discussion and Conclusion

We explored the possibilities of the vector logistic equation on a social contact graph for the description of contagious disease progression and the description of the possible economic impact of sanitary measures of contact regulation. Our main effort focused on the framing of a graph-based probabilistic SIS-dynamical approach through the vector logistic equation, and constructing interactions with an economic capacity graph. A method of partial-sorting based method was found to implement a social contact graph which resembles more closely some properties of true person-person contact graphs.

In real world scenarios the property of social contact is graded. In our present approach the individual's binary adjacencies A_{ij} are only attenuated by the individual's proper infection rate β_i. More realistically this expression should include a parameter to express the contact intensity dependent on each respective contact, i.e. by an infection matrix β_{ij} (e.g. related to the time of mutual exposure).

Future developments of the graph-based vector logistic dynamics for disease spreading and its economic impact will include development of optimal operational control measures for cost and, refinement of the contamination structure.

Acknowledgements. The authors thank the anonymous referees for suggestions on the reciprocal interaction of the economic graph into the social graph.

References

1. Allen, E.: Modeling with Itö Stochastic Differential Equations. Springer-Verlag The Netherlands (2007)
2. Barrett, C.L., et al.: Generation and analysis of large synthetic social contact networks. In: Proceedings of the 2009 Winter Simulation Conference (WSC), pp. 1003–1014 (2009). https://doi.org/10.1109/WSC.2009.5429425
3. Broekaert, J., Busemeyer, J., Pothos, E.: The disjunction effect in two-stage simulated gambles. an experimental study and comparison of a heuristic logistic, markov and quantum-like model. Cogn. Psychol. **117**, 101262 (2020). https://doi.org/10.1016/j.cogpsych.2019.101262, https://www.sciencedirect.com/science/article/pii/S001002851930252X
4. Buldyrev, S., Parshani, R., Paul, G., Stanley, H., Havlin, S.: Catastrophic cascade of failures in interdependent networks. Nature **464**, 1025–1028 (2010). https://doi.org/10.1038/nature08932

5. Busemeyer, J., Bruza, P.: Quantum Models of Cognition and Decision. Cambridge University Press, Cambridge (2012)
6. Choisy, M., Guégan, J.F., Rohani, P.: Mathematical modeling of infectious diseases dynamics. Modern Methodologies, Encyclopedia of Infectious Diseases (2007)
7. Ganesh, A., Massoulie, L., Towsley, D.: The effect of network topology on the spread of epidemics. In: Proceedings IEEE 24th Annual Joint Conference of the IEEE Computer and Communications Societies, vol. 2, pp. 1455–1466 (2005). https://doi.org/10.1109/INFCOM.2005.1498374
8. Gray, A., Greenhalch, D., Hu, L., Mao, X., Pan, J.: A stochastic differential equation sis epidemic model. SIAM J. Appl. Math. **71**(3), 876–902 (2011)
9. Hethcote, H.: The mathematics of infectious diseases. SIAM Rev. **42**(4), 599–653 (2000). https://doi.org/10.1137/S0036144500371907
10. Keeling, M.J., Eames, K.T.: Networks and epidemic models. J. Royal Soc. Interface **2**(4), 295–307 (2005). https://doi.org/10.1098/rsif.2005.0051
11. Kermack, W., McKendrick, A.: A contribution to the mathematical theory of epidemics. Proc. Royal Soc. London Ser. A **115**(772), 700–721 (1927)
12. Lu, D., Yang, S., Zhang, J., Wang, H., Li, D.: Resilience of epidemics for sis model on networks. Chaos **27**, 083105 (2017). https://doi.org/10.1063/1.4997177
13. McCormack, R., Allen, L.: Stochastic sis and sir multihost epidemic models. In: Proceedings of the Conference on Differential and Difference Equations and Applications, pp. 775–78 (2006)
14. Newman, M.E.J.: Spread of epidemic disease on networks. Phys. Rev. E **66**, 016128 (2002). https://doi.org/10.1103/PhysRevE.66.016128
15. Ohtsuki, H., Nowak, M.A.: The replicator equation on graphs. J. Theor. Biol. **243**(1), 86–97 (2006). https://doi.org/10.1016/j.jtbi.2006.06.004, https://www.sciencedirect.com/science/article/pii/S0022519306002426
16. Tao, Z., Zhongqian, F., Binghong, W.: Epidemic dynamics on complex networks. Progress Nat. Sci. **16**(5), 452–457 (2006). https://doi.org/10.1080/10020070612330019
17. Wang, Y., Chakrabarti, D., Wang, C., Faloutsos, C.: Epidemic spreading in real networks: an eigenvalue viewpoint. In: 22nd International Symposium on Reliable Distributed Systems, 2003. Proceedings, pp. 25–34 (2003). https://doi.org/10.1109/RELDIS.2003.1238052
18. Wang, Z., Busemeyer, J., Atmanspacher, H., Pothos, E.: The potential of using quantum theory to build models of cognition. Top. Cogn. Sci. **5**, 672–688 (2013). https://doi.org/10.1111/tops.12043

Modeling Shock Propagation on Supply Chain Networks: A Stochastic Logistic-Type Approach

Cinzia Colapinto[1], Davide La Torre[2], Iside Rita Laganà[3(✉)], and Danilo Liuzzi[4]

[1] Department of Management, Ca' Foscari University of Venice, Venice, Italy
[2] SKEMA Business School, Université Côte d'Azur, Nice, France
[3] Department of Law, Economics, and Human Sciences,
Mediterranea University of Reggio Calabria, Reggio Calabria, Italy
isiderita.lagana@unirc.it
[4] Department of Economics, Management, and Quantitative Methods,
University of Milan, Milan, Italy

Abstract. Supply Chains have been more and more suffering from unexpected industrial, natural events, or epidemics that might disrupt the normal flow of materials, information, and money. The recent pandemic triggered by the outbreak of the new COVID-19 has pointed out the increasing vulnerability of supply chain networks, prompting companies (and governments) to implement specific policies and actions to control and reduce the spread of the disease across the network, and to cope with exogenous shocks. In this paper, we present a stochastic Susceptible-Infected-Susceptible (SIS) framework to model the spread of new epidemics across different distribution networks and determine social distancing/treatment policies in the case of local and global networks. We highlight the relevance of adaptability and flexibility of decisions in unstable and unpredictable scenarios.

Keywords: Networks · Stochastic disruption shocks · Stochastic logistics · COVID-19

1 Introduction

Supply Chains (SCs) have been more and more suffering from unexpected industrial, natural events, or epidemics that might disrupt the normal flow of materials, information, and money [2,3,5]. Indeed, in recent years, studies on supply chain disruptions are getting increased attention to both academics and practitioners. Previous scholars (i.e. [6]) distinguished supply chain risks into operational and disruption risks. While the operational risks relate to ordinary issues in the SC operations (i.e. demand fluctuations), the disruption risks concern mainly events which occur with low frequency but high impacts [4] such as epidemic outbreaks. These are special category of risks in terms of duration

© IFIP International Federation for Information Processing 2021
Published by Springer Nature Switzerland AG 2021
A. Dolgui et al. (Eds.): APMS 2021, IFIP AICT 633, pp. 23–31, 2021.
https://doi.org/10.1007/978-3-030-85910-7_3

(from middle to long term), high uncertainty, and ripple effects' propagation [5]. It has been observed that pandemics can threaten SC resilience and robustness. Resilience concerns the ability of SCs to recover their performance after having absorbed change, disturbance, and the disruption effects [4]. Robustness refers to SCs' ability to maintain its planned performance after a disruption impacts [9]. Both impact on productivity performances. Throughout the history of public health, Cholera Pandemics (1817–1923), Spanish Flu (1918–1919), HIV/AIDS (1981-present), SARS (2002–2003), Ebola (2014–2016), and MERS (2015-present) are some of the most famous and brutal diseases that out-broke across international borders. On March 11, 2020, the World Health Organization officially declared COVID-19 a pandemic, causing 3.881.561 deaths until June 15, 2021 [14]. Scientists, policymakers, and managers all over the world have tried to forecast the pandemic evolution while at the same time keeping it under control by implementing specific policies to manage and reduce the spread of the disease. COVID-19 initially impacted China, which is at the center of many Global Value Chains, thus strong disruptions on supply chains raised. Moreover, the demand side has been affected by lockdown and consumers' physical spending increasing the challenges on the market. The COVID-19 outbreak re-exposes the importance of epidemic researches and the development of mathematical models to describe the behavior of epidemics [11]. Modeling describes the dynamic of epidemics and helps to take informed public health interventions [1]. Although previous research papers have successfully described the mechanism by which epidemics would spread, some control strategies (i.e., vaccination treatment, quarantine, social distancing, etc.) have been often neglected. In this paper, we contribute to the extant literature by adopting a modified Susceptible-Infectious-Susceptible (SIS) framework with a stochastic logistic-type formulation. In this way, we can consider exogenous and external events (i.e. the Indian COVID-19 variant) that might impact on the resilience policy, and thus on the productivity of a supply chain. Our results can help the global supply chain manager to understand the evolution of the epidemics and, therefore, determine the best counteractions to be put in place. The paper is structured as follows. Section 2 presents the Susceptible-Infected-Susceptible (SIS) Model. Section 3 points out the role played by stochastic shocks and Sect. 4 illustrates the shock propagation. In Sect. 5, we present the numerical simulation of our model and Sect. 6 concludes as usual.

2   The Susceptible-Infected-Susceptible Model

The Susceptible-Infected-Susceptible Model is one of the simplest and most widely used framework in mathematical epidemiology. It allows to describe the evolution of a number of infectious diseases which do not confer permanent immunity after recovery as in the case of COVID-19. If we denote by N the total population, by $I(t)$ the number of infected people, and by $S(t) = N - I(t)$ the number of susceptible ones, the model reads as:

$$\begin{cases} \dot{I}(t) = \alpha I(t)S(t) - \delta I(t) \\ \dot{S}(t) = -\alpha I(t)S(t) + \delta I(t) \end{cases} \tag{1}$$

where α is the infection rate and δ is the recovery parameter. By doing the substitution $S(t) = N - I(t)$ the model boils down to:

$$\dot{I}(t) = \alpha I(t)(N - I(t)) - \delta I(t) \tag{2}$$

which is a Bernoulli differential equation whose solution is known and provided by the following expression:

$$I(t) = \frac{(1 - \frac{\delta}{\alpha})Ce^{(\alpha - \delta)t}}{1 + Ce^{(\alpha - \delta)t}} \tag{3}$$

where $C = \frac{1 - \frac{\delta}{\alpha} - I(0)}{I(0)}$ ([7]). The SIS model can be used to analyze the spread of common diseases, such as the seasonal flu and the common cold, but also of emerging diseases. This model also applies to the analysis of as COVID-19 since thus far there exists no evidence that people who have recovered from COVID-19 and have antibodies are protected from a second infection ([12–14]). In the following we suppose that the total population N is normalized to 1. The following Fig. 1 shows the behavior of COVID infected with the following parameters' values: $\alpha = 0.1328$ and the recovery rate $\delta = 0.0476$ (see [7]). In this scenario the amount of infected converges to a plateau representing the long run endemic equilibrium. Figure 2, instead, shows the behavior of COVID-19 infected people with the following parameters' values: $\alpha = 0.1328$ and the recovery rate $\delta = 0.476$. This scenario corresponds to the case in which the adoption of treatment o vaccination campaigns produces an increment of the recovery parameter. As a result we can observe that the number of infected people gets reduced in the long run; we also notice that disease eradication is not possible in finite time.

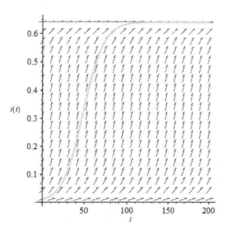

Fig. 1. Deterministic evolution of the number of infected $I(t)$

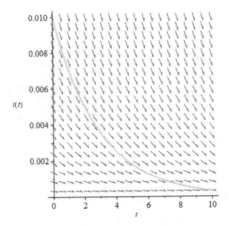

Fig. 2. Deterministic evolution of the number of infected $I(t)$

3   SIS with Stochastic Shocks

The previous section presented a fully deterministic SIS model. In the following paragraph we make an effort to model the effects of exogenous shocks on the epidemic evolution in order to present a more realistic scenario. Therefore we suppose that the number of infected people is subject to exogenous shocks driven by a Wiener process $W(t)$ as follows:

$$dI(t) = [\alpha - \delta - \alpha I(t)] I(t)dt + \sigma I(t)dW(t), \quad I(0) = I^0 \tag{4}$$

Let us recall that a Wiener process is characterized by the following properties:

1. $W(0)$ is deterministic and given,
2. $W(t)$ has independent increments,
3. $W(s) - W(t)$ is normally distributed with zero mean and variance equal to $t - s$

Other stochastic processes could be considered as well. For instance Levy-type or jump processes could be used to model other possible non-continuous shocks. From the perspective of the extant literature, this model can be identified as the geometric stochastic Verhulst diffusion [10]. Verhulst work was built on a previous paper by Malthus [8] who was among the first to notice the existence of two different regimes in the growth of world population. Verhulst model has been at the heart of an interdisciplinary work by researcher coming from many different field. In this context the notion of deterministic equilibrium has to be replaced by the notion of steady state or stationary density. If we denote by

$g[I(s), s; I(t), t]$ the probability density of $I(s)$ at time s, conditional upon its value $I(t)$ at time t, then it is well known that g satisfies the Fokker-Planck equation, which reads as:

$$\frac{\partial g(I,t)}{\partial t} = -\frac{\partial \left(g(I,t)I(\alpha - \delta - \alpha I)\right)}{\partial I} + \frac{1}{2}\sigma^2 \frac{\partial^2 \left(g(I,t)I^2\right)}{\partial I^2}. \tag{5}$$

The steady state density $g(I(\infty), \infty, s; I(t), t)$ can be found by solving the stationary equation $\frac{\partial g(I,t)}{\partial t} = 0$. This yields to a second order ordinary differential equation for g whose solution is provided by:

$$g[I(\infty), \infty, s; I(t), t] = \frac{I^{d-1} e^{-cI} (c)^d}{\Gamma(d)} \tag{6}$$

which is the Gamma distribution. Mean and variance of this distribution are known and provided by $\frac{v-1}{c} = (\theta - \frac{\sigma^2}{2\alpha})$ and $\frac{\theta \sigma^2}{2\alpha} - \frac{\sigma^4}{4\alpha^2}$, respectively. Under the condition that $d = \frac{2(\alpha - \delta)}{\sigma^2} - 1 > 0$ the previous quantities are strictly positive.

Figure 3 shows the stochastic behavior of COVID-19 infected people with the following parameters' values: $\alpha = 0.1328 \, \mathrm{m}$, $\delta = 0.0476$, and $\sigma^2 = 0.01$. This corresponds to the scenario in which the number of infected people fluctuates around an endemic equilibrium. Figure 4 shows the behaviour of $I(t)$ with the following parameters' values: $\alpha = 0.1328 \, \mathrm{m}$, $\delta = 0.0476$, and $\sigma^2 = 0.05$. A greater value of the variance causes more amplified oscillations around the endemic equilibrium and thus more challenges for SC managers.

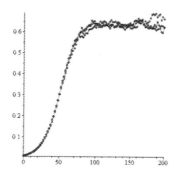

Fig. 3. Stochastic evolution of the number of infected $I(t)$

4   Shock Propagation on a Network

As we are interested in analyzing the epidemic propagation over a supply chain we refer to a network that is modeled by a graph G, composed by N different nodes x_i, $i = 1...N$. Each pair of nodes (i, j) can or cannot be connected through an edge γ_{ij}. γ_{ij} will be zero if the nodes are disconnected and a positive number

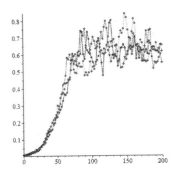

Fig. 4. Stochastic evolution of the number of infected $I(t)$

when the nodes are connected, with the number itself providing the linking intensity. At each node $i \in G$, the total number of infected people is described by:

$$dI_i(t) = \left(\alpha_i - \delta_i - \alpha_i I_i(t) + \sum_{j \neq i} \gamma_{ij} I_j(t) \right) I_i(t) dt + \sigma_i I_i(t) dW_i(t), \quad (7)$$

with initial conditions $I_i(t_0) = I_i^0$. The above system of N stochastic differential equations describes the spread of the epidemic across the network. The amount of infected people at the node i grows as consequence of two effects:

1. the local spread of the epidemics,
2. the immigration of infected people moving from the other nodes j, $j \neq i$, to the node i

The amount of infected is also subject to exogenous shocks, all of them driven by a Geometric Wiener Process W_i where σ_i is the volatility term and the covariance is given by:

$$E(dW_i(t)dW_j(t)) = \rho_{i,j} \quad (8)$$

where $\rho_{i,i} = 1$. The spread of the epidemic causes a loss of productivity. If we define by θ_i, $i = 1...N$ the per-capita productivity at the node i, the total loss of productivity $L(t)$ is given by:

$$L(t) = - \sum_{i=1} \theta_i I_i(t) \quad (9)$$

subject to

$$dI_i(t) = \left(\alpha_i - \delta_i - \alpha_i I_i(t) + \sum_{j \neq i} \gamma_{ij} I_j(t) \right) I_i(t) dt + \sigma_i I_i(t) dW_i(t), \quad I_i(t_0) = I_i^0$$

$$(10)$$

L is a stochastic process that describes the loss of productivity over time.

When a strict lockdown policy is put in place each node of the network is isolated and, therefore, we can assume that $\gamma_{ij} = 0$. We can also suppose that the Wiener processes W_i are independent as the nodes are totally disconnected. In this scenario the above system boils down to:

$$dI_i(t) = (\alpha_i - \delta_i - \alpha_i I_i(t))\, I_i(t)dt + \sigma_i I_i(t)dW_i(t), \quad I_i(t_0) = I_i^0 \tag{11}$$

5   Numerical Simulations

As the number of infected people can affect the productivity level of a supply chain, our model enables decision makers to better understand the impact of lockdown measures. Through a numerical simulation we provide a visual representation of different scenarios. Indeed, the numerical simulations compare the behavior of the number of infected people over medium and large size networks. We consider two scenarios, which correspond either to the presence or to the absence of lockdown restrictions. We also report the average behavior and thus the impact on the supply chain networks. In particular, Figs. 5 and 6 show the behavior over a medium size network with 11 nodes. One can immediately observe that the absence of lockdown restrictions allows internal flows among the different nodes thus it increases, on average, the number of infected people even in presence of exogenous shocks (negative or positive) and localized treatment policies. The same conclusion is supported by Figs. 7 and 8 that show the behavior over a large network with 50 nodes.

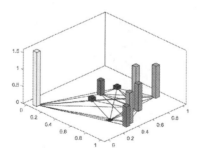

Fig. 5. Evolution of infected people over a connected network with 11 nodes and lockdown restrictions.

This numerical simulation shows the effects of network connectivity on the spread of the disease at the global level. As the spread of exogenous shocks across the network might become relevant and not controllable in the case of connected networks. Thus it is crucial to intervene combing flow barriers between different nodes and local intervention policies. In other words, connectivity might compromise the benefits of implementing local vaccination campaigns.

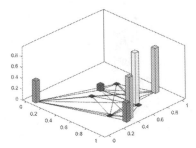

Fig. 6. Evolution of infected people over a disconnected network with 11 nodes and no lockdown restrictions.

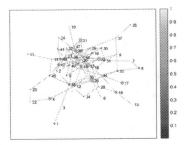

Fig. 7. Evolution of infected people over a connected network with 50 nodes and lockdown restrictions.

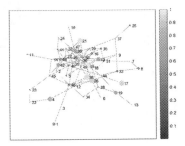

Fig. 8. Evolution of infected people over a connected network with 50 nodes and no lockdown restrictions.

6   Conclusion

As the virus spread and most governments imposed lockdown orders, supply chain disruptions increased. Indeed, COVID-19 illustrated that many companies are not fully aware of the vulnerability of their supply chain relationships to global shocks. SC managers need to balance and combine actions to serve their customers, as well as protect and support their workers. In this paper, we aim at analyzing the stochastic effects of the epidemic spread on a supply chain network. We present a stochastic SIS model which assumes the form of a stochastic logistic differential equation. Exogenous shocks are modeled by means of a stochastic Wiener process. We present a numerical simulation and we draw insights to support local supply chain managers to decide about the social distancing policy: he/she can take into account costs, governmental policies, and infection parameters. We also discuss the flow of infected people from one node to another and we provide some results to control the spread of the epidemics across the network. These results can help the global supply chain manager to understand the evolution of the epidemic and, therefore, determine the best counteractions to put in place: it is evident that lockdown policies and treatment measures have to coexist. Employees around the global supply chain need to receive the vaccine on the same timescale to ensure the best results for everyone. Further research involves the design of a stochastic optimal control model able to identify the best compromise between economic costs of lockdown restrictions and implementation costs of vaccination campaigns.

References

1. Chowell, G., Sattenspiel, L., Bansal, S., Viboud, C.: Mathematical models to characterize early epidemic growth: a review. Phys. Life Rev. **18**, 66–97 (2016)
2. Craighead, C.W., Blackhurst, J., Rungtusanatham, M.J., Handfield, R.B.: The severity of supply chain disruptions: design characteristics and mitigation capabilities. Decis. Sci. **38**(1), 131–156 (2007)
3. Grida, M., Mohamed, R., Zaied, A.N.H.: Evaluate the impact of COVID-19 prevention policies on supply chain aspects under uncertainty. Transportation Research Interdisciplinary Perspectives, vol. 8 (2020)
4. Hosseini, S., Morshedlou, N., Ivanov, D., Sarder, M.D., Barker, K., Al Khaled, A.: Resilient supplier selection and optimal order allocation under disruption risks. Int. J. Prod. Econ. **213**, 124–137 (2019)
5. Ivanov, D., Das, A.: Coronavirus (COVID-19/SARS-CoV-2) and supply chain resilience: a research note. Int. J. Integr. Supply Manag. **13**(1), 90–102 (2020)
6. Ivanov, D.: Structural Dynamics and Resilience in Supply Chain Risk Management. Springer, New York (2018). https://doi.org/10.1007/978-3-319-69305-7
7. La Torre, D., Liuzzi, D., Marsiglio, S.: Epidemics and macroeconomic outcomes: social distancing intensity and duration. J. Math. Econ. **93**, 102473 (2021)
8. Malthus, T.R.: An Essay on the Principle of Population. Cambridge University Press, London (1798)
9. Simchi-Levi, D., Wang, H., Wei, Y.: Increasing supply chain robustness through process flexibility and inventory. Prod. Oper. Manag. **27**(8), 1476–1491 (2018)
10. Verhulst, P.F.: Notice sur la loi que la population suit dans son accroissement. Correspondence Mathematique Physique **10**, 113–121 (1838)
11. Ucakan, Y., Gulen, S., Koklu, K.: Analysing of tuberculosis in Turkey through SIR, SEIR and BSEIR. Math. Models Math. Comput. Model. Dyn. Syst. **27**(1), 179–202 (2021)
12. World Health Organization. https://www.who.int/docs/default-source/coronaviruse/who-china-joint-mission-on-covid-19-final-report.pdf. Accessed 15 Jun 2021
13. World Health Organization. https://www.who.int/news-room/commentaries/detail/immunity-passports-in-the-context-of-covid-19. Accessed 15 Jun 2021
14. World Health Organization. https://www.who.int/emergencies/diseases/novel-coronavirus-2019. Accessed 15 Jun 2021

Towards Explainable Artificial Intelligence (XAI) in Supply Chain Management: A Typology and Research Agenda

Godfrey Mugurusi[1]([⊠]) (iD) and Pross Nagitta Oluka[2] (iD)

[1] Department of Industrial Economics and Technology Management in Gjøvik,
Norwegian University of Science and Technology, Trondheim, Norway
godfrey.mugurusi@ntnu.no
[2] Department of Economics and Managerial Sciences, Uganda Management Institute, Kampala,
Uganda
poluka@umi.ac.ug

Abstract. The potential for artificial intelligence (AI) to drive digital supply chain transformation today is beyond question. However, its full potential to address more complex supply chain management (SCM) problems is still unclear partly due to AI's black-box problem both in practice and in literature. This paper attempts to highlight the significance of explainable AI (XAI) in SCM and shades light on SCM areas where AI's black-box problem remains problematic. The goal of this integrative literature review paper is to provide new insight into the status of XAI as a solution to AI's black-box problem in SCM where AI techniques have made rapid in-roads. The AI techniques in SCM literature and the significance of XAI in SCM are contrasted. We present an integrative research typology for XAI in SCM to better align how SCM literature has conceived AI deployment in SCM this far. The typology should help us understand the gap between what we know about AI deployment in practice, AI maturity in SCM, and the extent of XAI in SCM .

Keywords: Artificial intelligence · Explainable AI · Supply chain management · Supply chains · Integrative literature review

1 Introduction

Supply chains today have increasingly become more information-intensive due to the gradual shift from physical assets management (e.g., inventory, warehouses, transport equipment) to data and information management [1, 2]. As a result, the adoption of artificial intelligence (AI) in supply chain management (SCM) has become one of the most important applications for digital supply chain transformation in the last 10 years [3, 4]. [2, 22] show that AI has the potential to improve SCM through better inventory forecasting, sourcing optimization, asset maintenance, targeted marketing, and better customer experience. [3] cite several examples where AI applications have enhanced

© IFIP International Federation for Information Processing 2021
Published by Springer Nature Switzerland AG 2021
A. Dolgui et al. (Eds.): APMS 2021, IFIP AICT 633, pp. 32–38, 2021.
https://doi.org/10.1007/978-3-030-85910-7_4

supply chain performance including in warehouse automation, demand planning, supplier performance management, transport optimization, predictive risk management etc. [1] predict that AI will become one of the biggest contributors to the digitalization of SCM with a demonstrable impact on cost reduction, revenue, and market growth.

Yet despite the potential for AI, SCM literature has not fully conceptualized the complexity and risks of AIs black-box which has arguably limited AIs adoption in even more complex SCM tasks [1, 23]. The application cases of AI in SCM presented in [2–4] including in demand forecasting, logistics, transport, supplier selection, order-fulfillment, vehicle routing, etc. shows an operational and tactical orientation of AI in SCM. The literature presents limited application cases for more strategic SC processes such as supply chain design, supply chain innovation, strategic sourcing, supply network optimization, etc. This may partly explain AIs low adoption for more complex SCM activities [24]. In the information systems (IS) research, AIs black-box problem has long been associated with the reluctance by users to trust and accept outcomes from algorithms and opaque AI systems [5, 6]. Because SCM decisions have a disruptive impact on firm performance, it is important therefore SC decision markers understand how AI models work, or how AI systems arrive at their decisions [7, 22]. Model comprehensibility and interpretability are critical to AI's ability to solve complex SC problems in the short term as well as for the long-term adoption of AI in complex industrial and SCM processes [3, 22].

Human-machine trust, AI model interpretability, and comprehensibility are well-known characteristics of explainable AI (XAI) [5–7]. The concept XAI is fundamentally about how AI models *must* become more interpretable to humans: to enable humans to understand how AI systems arrive at a specific decision and why a specific action or output should be trusted [6, 7]. XAI is about AI models and systems being understandable, fair, trustworthy, and transparent [5]. Distrust and lack of transparency lead to aversion and decision-making overrides. In SCM this will translate into the reluctance to implement digital SCM which's been touted as a definitive enabler of competitive advantage, better end-to-end SC visibility, better collaboration, advanced decision making, accelerated innovation, and enhanced SC responsiveness [8].

So, this paper examines the view that the potential for AI and its maturity in SCM will be limited by the nuances of the black-box problem in AI. This problem increases exponentially as AI systems become even more complex – from basic algorithms, fuzzy sets, and machine learning to very complex deep learning and convolutional neural networks [9]. The proposed solution, therefore, is to conceptualize the AI application areas in SCM and examine the extent of XAI in those areas currently under-researched. Therefore, the paper answers the research question (RQ): *how significant is XAI in SCM, and where in the application of AI in SCM will black-box risks of AI emerge?* Through a synthesis of few studies on this topic, the paper contributes to a better understanding of XAI in SCM by identifying the weaknesses of XAI in SCM literature.

The paper is organized as follows. The methods are presented in the next section; thereafter the results and discussion are presented. At the tail end of the paper is the conclusion and suggestions for future research.

2   Methods

We conducted an integrative literature review (ILR) following the approach of Torraco [10, 11]. The goal of ILRs is to scour the literature of a specific topic to create preliminary conceptualizations and theoretical models as a basis for further theorizing [11]. We conducted a dummy search (on 24th January 2021) in google scholar (GS) using the search string "artificial intelligence in supply chain management" (with the search operators: "…") and returned 174 results. Despite GS's wide source coverage, the lack of quality controls and clear indexing guidelines makes it problematic compared to other databases like Web of Science (WoS) and Scopus [12].

We retained the same search string and applied it to the Web of Science (WoS) and Scopus databases, which are extensive and renowned for high-quality bibliometric capabilities [9]. The search for articles from 2010 to date resulted in 137 hits for WoS and 101 hits for Scopus hence a total of 238 hits. We filtered the results for only English language and peer-reviewed published articles and controlled for phrases: "AI" and "SCM" in article keywords. This resulted in 50 hits for WoS and 36 articles for Scopus. We divided the 86 articles among the authors and read the abstracts individually, often iterating with each other on select articles to improve interrater reliability. After filtering out the duplicates, we ended up with a total of 18 articles for this review shown in Table 1: two articles [2, 4] were cross listed.

Table 1. Search strings and results from in WoS and Scopus

Database	Search string	Articles for review
Web of science	TOPIC: (Artificial intelligence in supply chain management) Refined by: LANGUAGES: (ENGLISH) AND DOCUMENT TYPES: (ARTICLE) AND DOCUMENT TYPES: (ARTICLE) Timespan: 2010–2020. Indexes: SCI-EXPANDED, SSCI, A&HCI, CPCI-S, CPCI-SSH, ESCI **Total hits 137 (n = 10)**	[2]*[4]*[13–20]
Scopus	"Artificial intelligence in supply-chain-management" AND (LIMIT-TO (DOCTYPE, "ar")) AND (LIMIT-TO (LANGUAGE, "English")) AND (LIMIT-TO (EXACTKEYWORD, "Artificial Intelligence") OR LIMIT-TO (EXACTKEYWORD, "Supply Chain Management")) **Hits total hits 101 (n = 08)**	[21–26]

Cross-listed in both WoS and Scopus

3   Findings and Discussion

Based on the studies reviewed, AI in SCM is a burgeoning research area. Most studies, mainly conceptual papers, report on the potential impact of AI techniques such as agent-based systems (ABS), genetic algorithms(GAs), expert systems (ES) deep learning (DL), multi-agent systems (MAS), artificial neural networks (ANNs), support vector machines (SVMs) in SCM processes including in demand planning and forecasting, supplier selection decisions, supplier performance assessment, make-or-buy decisions, order picking and CRM, SC network design, SC risk analysis, logistics workflow planning, and in transport network optimization [1–4, 20, 24]. Only a couple of studies provide demonstrable use-cases of AI application in SCM. For example, [13] show the application of neural networks (NN) in SC forecasting, [19] demonstrate fuzzy logic (FL) and ML methods use in production planning, [22] apply AI in SC process optimization, [23] report on the use AI in inventory forecasting and fulfillment center optimization, and [25] show the use of ML in replenishment decision making.

Despite the exponential increase in computing power and availability of big data today than has ever been before [14], the big picture in the literature reveals a wait-and-see approach to the strategic adoption of AI within SCM. [21] show that early applications of AI are still predominantly operational than strategic. [22] Demonstrate that AI adoption, especially ML, is still at the developmental stage because of the limited understanding of how ML tools can be applied to SCM processes, the low acceptance in company culture, and the inability to obtain suitable data. In some cases, the models are too complex, while some techniques such as DL make it even harder to understand the intrinsic knowledge emerging from a data set [17, 19]. Complex AI models are meaningless unless they can be manually evaluated or are understood by the practitioners and thus applicable to practical SC problems [2, 14]. This is exactly what XAI must address to enable ease of use for SCM decision-making, especially as AI systems learn and evolve into highly opaque architectures.

XAI must offer a suite of tools to help users understand how AI models work and interpret the recommendations which emerge from AI models [6, 7]. With a slight exception of Zhang et al., [23], all the reviewed articles do not address the role of humans in the AI deployment in SCM processes. Humans and AI are complementary, both contributing cognitive and physical attributes to SCM tasks [23]. In addition, the symbiotic interface between users and AI technologies leads to the development of strong AI capabilities which creates significant business value [22, 23]. Meske et al. [5] citing [27] offer a four-level continuum for explainability which AI models can be based on: Type I for trace and reasoning (how and why decisions were made), Type II for justification or support (to explain the reasoning behind a decision), Type III to explain the systems control behavior and problem-solving strategy, and Type IV to provide terminological detail. This framework for which the typology in Fig. 1 is based, suggests that the level of deep knowledge required for reasoning, audit and trace queries in AI systems tends to increase from Type I to Type IV. We map these into an XAI typology for SCM.

4   Conclusion

In this paper, we set out to explain the significance of XAI in SCM and map where AI's black-box risks will likely emerge in the deployment of AI in SCM. We conclude that AI's potential even if significant in SCM is still limited by capacities of firms to uniquely add humans in the AI decisions loop. At the moment only Type I XAI and Type II XAI are well represented but mainly in operational SCM processes. In these

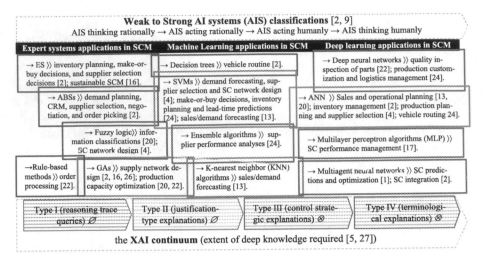

Fig. 1. An XAI typology for SCM ($\emptyset$ = represented: $\otimes$ = not well represented)

processes', humans provide an external layer to monitor, audit, and validate the fidelity of AI decisions. As the literature shows in Fig. 1, the visualized SC structure where AI is deployed, the human side of AI is only considered in "weak-to-moderate" AI systems, where SC processes are still operational. From this ILR and our typology, we can make the following observations:

- XAI is undeveloped and superficially addressed in the AI for SCM literature.
- The link between XAI and SC performance is evident but not well researched.
- AI adoption in SCM is fairly mature but XAI considerations are not researched yet.
- AI in some industries is advanced but deep SCM applications are still not well integrated in typical SCM processes which negatively impacts on XAI deployment.
- As AI systems become ubiquitous and complex, XAI will become a key enabler for digital SC performance.
- The future of AI deployment in SCM is the embedded co-development of AI systems with consideration of the humans e.g. users, regulators, etc. in the loop.
- It appears that true explainability in SCM (currently at Type I & Type II) is difficult to attain due to the gap between the SC skills and AIs rapid development.
- There is a need for the development of metatheories on XAI measures and indicators in SCM as well as to empirically test the XAI typology (Fig. 1) with the existing AI maturity models in SCM

References

1. Hellingrath, B., Lechtenberg, S.: Applications of artificial intelligence in supply chain management and logistics: focusing onto recognition for supply chain execution. In: Bergener, K., Räckers, M., Stein, A. (eds.) The art of structuring, pp. 283–296. Springer, Cham (2019). https://doi.org/10.1007/978-3-030-06234-7_27

2. Min, H.: Artificial intelligence in supply chain management: theory and applications. Int. J. Logistics Res. Appl. **13**(1), 13–39 (2010)
3. Riahi, Y., Saikouk, T., Gunasekaran, A., Badraoui, I.: Artificial intelligence applications in supply chain: a descriptive bibliometric analysis and future research directions. Expert Syst. Appl. **173**, 114702 (2021)
4. Toorajipour, R., Sohrabpour, V., Nazarpour, A., Oghazi, P., Fischl, M.: Artificial intelligence in supply chain management: a systematic literature review. J. Bus. Res. **122**, 502–517 (2021)
5. Meske, C., Bunde, E., Schneider, J., Gersch, M.: Explainable artificial intelligence: objectives, stakeholders, and future research opportunities. Info. Syst. Manage., 1 (2020)
6. Asatiani, A., Malo, P., Nagbøl, P.R., Penttinen, E., Rinta-Kahila, T., Salovaara, A.: Challenges of explaining the behavior of blackbox AI systems. MIS Q. **19**(4), 259–278 (2020)
7. Arrieta, A.B., et al.: Explainable artificial intelligence (XAI): concepts, taxonomies, opportunities, and challenges toward responsible AI. Inf. Fusion **58**, 82–115 (2020)
8. Büyüközkan, G., Göçer, F.: Digital supply chain: literature review and a proposed framework for future research. Comput. Ind. **97**, 157–177 (2018)
9. Wamba, S.F., Bawack, R.E., Guthrie, C., Queiroz, M.M., Carillo, K.D.A.: Are we preparing for a good AI society? A bibliometric review and research agenda. Technol. Forecast. Soc. Change **164**, 120482 (2021)
10. Torraco, R.J.: Writing integrative literature reviews: guidelines and examples. Hum. Resour. Dev. Rev. **4**(3), 356–367 (2005)
11. Snyder, H.: Literature review as a research methodology: an overview and guidelines. J. Bus. Res. **104**, 333–339 (2019)
12. Halevi, G., Moed, H., Bar-Ilan, J.: Suitability of Google Scholar as a source of scientific information and as a source of data for scientific evaluation—review of the literature. J. Informet. **11**(3), 823–834 (2017)
13. Kantasa-ard, A., Bekrar, A., Sallez, Y.: Artificial intelligence for forecasting in supply chain management: a case study of white sugar consumption rate in Thailand. IFAC-PapersOnLine **52**(13), 725–730 (2019)
14. Baryannis, G., Validi, S., Dani, S., Antoniou, G.: Supply chain risk management and artificial intelligence: state of the art and future research directions. Int. J. Prod. Res. **57**(7), 2179–2202 (2019)
15. Gunasekaran, A., Ngai, E.W.: Expert systems and artificial intelligence in the 21st century logistics and supply chain management. Expert Syst. Appl. **41**(1), 1–246 (2014)
16. Annonymous.: Deploying artificial intelligence to augment green supply chain management performance: innovations from South Africa on the road to operational sustainability. Ann. Soc. Responsib. **6**(2), 39–41(2020)
17. Dumitrascu, O., Dumitrascu, M., Dobrotă, D.: Performance evaluation for a sustainable supply chain management system in the automotive industry using artificial intelligence. Processes **8**(11), 1384 (2020)
18. Rodríguez-Espíndola, O., Chowdhury, S., Beltagui, A., Albores, P.: The potential of emergent disruptive technologies for humanitarian supply chains: the integration of blockchain, artificial intelligence and 3D printing. Int. J. Prod. Res. **58**(15), 4610–4630 (2020)
19. Rodríguez, G.G., Gonzalez-Cava, J.M., Pérez, J.A.M.: An intelligent decision support system for production planning based on machine learning. J. Intell. Manuf. **31**, 1–17 (2019)
20. Guo, Z.X., Wong, W.K., Leung, S.Y.S., Li, M.: Applications of artificial intelligence in the apparel industry: a review. Text. Res. J. **81**(18), 1871–1892 (2011)
21. Aguezzoul, A., Pires, S.: Use of artificial intelligence in supply chain management practices and 3PL selection. Syst. Cybern. Inf. **17**(4), 10–12 (2019)
22. Helo, P., Hao, Y.: Artificial intelligence in operations management and supply chain management: an exploratory case study. Prod. Plan. Contro., 1–18 (2021)

23. Zhang, D., Pee, L. G., Cui, L.: Artificial intelligence in e-commerce fulfillment: a case study of resource orchestration at Alibaba's smart warehouse. Int. J. Inf. Manage. **57**, 102304 (2021)
24. Ni, D., Xiao, Z., Lim, M.K.: A systematic review of the research trends of machine learning in supply chain management. Int. J. Mach. Learn. Cybern. **11**(7), 1463–1482 (2019). https://doi.org/10.1007/s13042-019-01050-0
25. Priore, P., Ponte, B., Rosillo, R., de la Fuente, D.: Applying machine learning to the dynamic selection of replenishment policies in fast-changing supply chain environments. Int. J. Prod. Res. **57**(11), 3663–3677 (2019)
26. Min, H.: Genetic algorithm for supply chain modelling: basic concepts and applications. Int. J. Serv. Oper. Manage. **22**(2), 143–164 (2015)
27. Gregor, S., Benbasat, I.: Explanations from intelligent systems: theoretical foundations and implications for practice. MIS Q. **23**, 497–530 (1999)

Distribution of Vaccines During a Pandemic (Covid-19)

Vignesh Dhanapal(✉) ⓘ and Subhash C. Sarin ⓘ

Grado Department of Industrial and Systems Engineering, Virginia Tech,
Blacksburg, VA 24060, USA
{vigneshdhanapal,sarins}@vt.edu

Abstract. Covid-19 has affected the lives of people in different ways. A number of models are available in the literature to study the dynamics of a pandemic. However, there are very few models that study the impact of vaccine distribution among different population groups. In this paper, we use a modified epidemiological model which incorporates relationships between different populations to incorporate the impact of vaccine distribution and present results for different vaccine distribution strategies. We have presented how a sharing-based vaccine distribution strategy could be implemented in the face of the spread of the virus. The main finding of our work is that an effective vaccine distribution may differ depending upon the level of interactions among different population groups and a sharing-based vaccine distribution strategy is the most effective strategy.

Keywords: Pandemic · Epidemiological model · Covid-19 · Population groups

1 Introduction, Background, and Problem Statement

Covid-19, also known as Coronavirus, was first reported in December 2019 [1]. Slowly over time, the virus infections spread worldwide, and the number of cases grew very rapidly. Many people lost their lives and there was scarcity of information about how to control or stop it's spread. Hospitals and other medical facilities were overwhelmed with the number of cases and they lacked resources like respirators, PPEs, healthcare workers and hospital beds. The normal life as we know it got disrupted and the livelihood of a vast number of people worldwide was challenged.

Lockdowns and other measures were implemented to slow down the spread. People were made to stay at home and many businesses were closed. Slowly, more medical centers opened, and the spread rate reduced. More resources like PPEs, respirators and hospital beds became available. As more resources became available, some of the important questions which arose were who/which region needs these resources the most, how many of the resources are needed and what will be the future impact of the actions/strategies implemented.

Different pandemics have devasted humankind over the course of history [2] starting from the earliest recorded pandemic that occurred during the Peloponnesian war around

A. Dolgui et al. (Eds.): APMS 2021, IFIP AICT 633, pp. 39–48, 2021.
https://doi.org/10.1007/978-3-030-85910-7_5

430 B.C [3]. So, when the Covid-19 pandemic surfaced, it was not something completely new. But what makes it different is a higher population size and global travel that it impacted, thereby making it challenging to predict the progress of the pandemic and in making decisions to control its progress.

There have been many different types of forecasting models developed to predict the progress of pandemics. One of the most popular and earliest models is the epidemiological model developed in the year 1927 by Kermack & McKendrick [4]. There have been many additions to this fundamental model over time. After the outbreak of Covid-19, several versions of the epidemiological model have been employed to address the situation [5–13]. A number of recent studies have used deep learning techniques to predict progress of the Covid-19 pandemic [14, 15]. However, there have not been reported works devoted to the use of epidemiological models that study the impact of progression of virus in one group to that in the other, and accordingly, determine effective strategies for the distribution of vaccines in order to mitigate the spread of virus. We have addressed this problem in this paper.

Also, we discuss the different vaccine distribution strategies and their impact in the face of the pandemic. The factors affecting the implementation of different strategies are also discussed. The best strategy for controlling the pandemic globally is suggested.

2 Methodology

This study uses a modified version of the Epidemiological model, which is one of the popular models used to study and predict the progress of pandemics. Epidemiological models are mathematical models which are effective in simulating the spread of many communicable diseases and have been used extensively for the recent Covid-19 research [5–13]. The model consists of multiple compartments with each representing a stage in the progression of the disease. A person moves across different compartments based on requisite transition rates or probabilities. At any point in time, the spread of a pandemic can be represented by the number of people in each compartment. Different models based on the number of compartments can be constructed.

One of the popular models is the SIR (susceptible-infectious-recovered) model. Depending on the intensity of the disease, an individual may move to the susceptible compartment again if they do not develop immunity after the first infection. The SIR model has three compartments namely Susceptible (S), Infectious (I) and Recovered (R). Initially, a person starts in the Susceptible compartment (S) and is not yet infected. Once infected, they move to the Infected compartment (I) at a rate called the disease transmission rate β. Then, they either recover or do not survive and move to the Recovered compartment (R) at a rate called the recovery rate γ. Our primary objective is to track and reduce the number of infected cases. The number of fatalities is proportional to the number of infections. Hence, a reduction in the number of infections will reduce number of fatalities as well. Therefore, we just keep track of the number of infections. If needed, we can further split the R compartment into Recovered and Non-survived compartments and track them separately. The impact resulting from getting the vaccine can be incorporated into the epidemiological model. A person in the Susceptible compartment after getting vaccinated directly moves to the Recovered compartment and cannot get infected. For our study, the effectiveness of the vaccines is assumed to be 100%. Thus, administering, say, v number of vaccines at time t moves v persons from the Susceptible compartment to the Recovered compartment, thereby, reducing the number of people who could further get infected. The dynamics of the model is shown in Fig. 1.

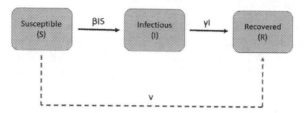

Fig. 1. An epidemiological model including impact resulting from getting a vaccine

The dynamics of movement between different compartments and the differential equations of the model are given below.

$$dS/dt = -\beta IS - v \tag{1}$$

$$dI/dt = \beta IS - \gamma I \tag{2}$$

$$dR/dt = \gamma I + v \tag{3}$$

We can study different population groups separately in order to determine progression of the virus in specific groups. For this study, we consider two groups namely, General population and Healthcare worker population. Each group will entail a separate model with its compartments and transition probabilities. The number of infections and recoveries can be found in each period for both the models. The effect of the pandemic on total population is then the sum of outcomes of both the models.

The above method considers both the population groups to be independent and the progression of the virus in one group not to impact that in the other. Such a method is pertinent to study a situation in which the groups represent regions with no interactions among them because of lockdown. However, we also consider the situation in which the progression of the virus in one group impacts that in the other. Consider the two population groups described above with each group represented by its own model and parameters. Let the ratio of the number of infected healthcare workers to the total number of healthcare population be represented by θ. Also, the number of infections in the healthcare population affects the progress of virus in the general population, because of their essential interactions with general population through activities like testing, caring for the elderly in nursing homes and the patients admitted to the hospital, and for providing consultation to infected persons quarantining at home. This interaction is captured in the model by using a (modification) function that modifies the parameters of the general population model depending on the spread of virus in the healthcare population. The modification function, f(θ) = exp(θ*K) is defined using θ and a constant

K. The β and γ parameters of the general population model are modified as follows:

$$\text{Modified } \beta = \beta * f(\theta) \qquad (4)$$

$$\text{Modified } \gamma = \gamma / f(\theta) \qquad (5)$$

With this modification, the spread of the virus in the healthcare population model (HPM) affects the parameters of the general population model (GPM) and thereby, the general population model itself. An exponential function was chosen for $f(\theta)$ as the impact of the number of infections on the total population is not linear and an exponential function form was found to give the best fit. The constant K can be used to fine tune the model depending on the subtle variations present in the region to which the populations belong. The different parameters of the model could be tuned to the actual data to obtain the best fit. We can use this modified model to evaluate various scenarios and make decisions pertaining to vaccine distribution among different populations, timing of vaccinations, and the sequence in which the vaccinations are given to different populations. Some of the scenarios and their results are discussed in the following sections.

3   Data

Besides the data on general population, we also needed data on the daily number of infected cases among healthcare population for our study. After searching over several available data sources, the Wisconsin state health department was found to provide this data and hence was chosen. Milwaukee country was chosen as it is the most populous country in the state of Wisconsin [16]. The information regarding total population and number of healthcare workers is taken from the datausa website [17]. Data from the Dane country and Waukesha country were used to evaluate different vaccines distribution strategies [16].

4   Results

The different scenarios considered, and their results are discussed in detail in this section. The parameters of the individual population models (healthcare population and general population) are fitted by tuning them to give the best fit with the actual data. Also, our studies showed that parameter tuning with the most recent data makes the model more reactive and accurate in its prediction. The fitted graphs for different population groups are shown in Fig. 2.

We studied several scenarios based on the following:

1. Number of vaccines, 2. Time of vaccination, 3. Ratio of vaccine distribution among populations, 4. Sequence of vaccination, 5. Vaccination times for multiple vaccinations, 6. Independent population groups.

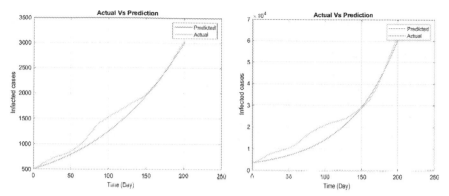

Fig. 2. Fitted model for healthcare population (left) and that for general population (right), that show actual vs predicted number of infected cases.

4.1   Number of Vaccines

In this scenario, the effect of varying the number of vaccines is studied. The model parameters and vaccination introduction time ($t = 10$) are kept the same. The vaccines are allocated fully to one of the population groups. The different iterations (number of vaccines) tried were 5000, 10000, 25000, 50000 and 100000. The results show that the reduction in the number of infections increases with increment in the number of vaccines. The difference in infected cases due to different number of vaccines is non-decreasing in time. The differences vary among the population groups because of their different parameters.

4.2   Time of Vaccination

In this scenario, the effect of varying the time of vaccination is studied. The model parameters and vaccine quantity are kept the same. The vaccines are allocated fully to one of the population groups. The different iterations (vaccination time, day) tried are 10, 25, 50, 100 and 150. As expected, the reduction in the number of infections is higher, when the vaccines are introduced earlier. The differences vary among the population groups because of their different parameters.

4.3   Ratio of Vaccine Distribution among Populations

In this scenario, the effect of varying the ratio of distribution of vaccines among different populations is studied. The model parameters and time of vaccination ($t = 10$) are kept the same. The total number of vaccines available is 25,000, and they are distributed among the population groups. The different iterations (vaccine distribution ratios, healthcare:general) are 0:100, 25:75, 50:50, 75:25 and 100:0. The results show that the reduction in the number of infections is higher when a higher percentage of vaccines is introduced to the healthcare population. Also, note that, the difference in reduction becomes gradually lower with an increased percentage of vaccines being allocated to the healthcare population. Thus, it implies that we should prefer to vaccinate the healthcare population first; however, for overall effectiveness, it would be better to shift towards vaccinating the other populations instead of using all the vaccines on one population.

4.4 Sequence of Vaccination

In this scenario, the effect of the sequence in which different populations are vaccinated is studied. The vaccines are introduced at two points in time, and the number of vaccines introduced is 10,000 each time. Two different combinations of time periods are considered, and the sequence of vaccinations is varied. The model parameters are kept the same. The different iterations (healthcare vaccination time, general vaccination time) are: (50, 10), (10, 50), (100, 10) and (10, 100).

Results show that the reduction in the number of infections is higher when the healthcare population is vaccinated first in the sequence and then the general population. It was observed that vaccinating the healthcare population first would allow longer time before vaccinating the other population when compared to vaccinating general population first. Thus, we can conclude that we should prefer to vaccinate the healthcare population first in a sequence and doing so would allow us more time to delay the next vaccination.

4.5 Vaccination Times for Multiple Vaccinations

In this scenario, the effect of the time of vaccination when vaccinating multiple times is studied. The model parameters are kept the same, and the total number of vaccines to be used is 20,000. The vaccinations are done twice, and iterations consider vaccines to be fully allocated to one of the population groups. The results show that vaccinating a higher quantity during the first period allows us to delay the second vaccination period. Also, moving the first vaccination period by a period p early allows us to delay the second vaccination period by a value more than p. Hence, we can use this model to evaluate different vaccination time and quantity combinations while making vaccine distribution decisions.

4.6 Independent Population Groups

In this scenario, the effect of varying the ratio of distribution of vaccines among different populations, which are considered to be independent, is studied. The model parameters and the time of vaccination (t = 10) are kept the same. The total number of vaccines to be used is 20,000. The different iterations (vaccine distribution ratios- healthcare:general) are 0:100, 25:75, 50:50, 75:25 and 100:0. The results show that the reduction in the number of infections is higher when higher percentage of vaccines are introduced to the general population. This observation is exactly opposite to the case of Sect. 4.3. This is because the general population is significantly larger in size than the healthcare population and a small amount of vaccinations in that population reduces infections by a relatively large number. On the other hand, the healthcare population is smaller in size and the maximum possible reduction in number of cases it can produce is significantly lower than that for the other population group. Also, because the groups are independently administering vaccines, the healthcare population would reduce the number of infections in that group and would not have any impact on the other group. This clearly shows incorporating the relationships between different population groups and the type and scale of relationship makes a significant difference in the decisions made. Moreover, it shows that in case the population groups considered have the least interactions between them, then it will be more effective to distribute vaccines to a larger group first because it would result in greater reductions in infections. Thus, extending this analysis to global level, at the height of pandemic spread, when the countries are essentially locked down, the distribution of vaccines to most populous places first would result in maximum reduction in infections

5   Sharing-Based Distribution of Vaccines

Appropriate steps have been taken to ensure a rapid scale-up of production of vaccines and other supplies. However, it should be noted that there is still a number of countries where the supply of vaccines is way lower than the demand. This uneven availability and inaccess to supplies are major contributors to the struggle in the face of the pandemic. One main reason for this is the hoarding of vaccines and other supplies by a few countries making it less accessible to other countries [18]. [19–22] present the statistics regarding vaccine procurement and reasons for the hoarding. As expected, these countries have procured high volumes of vaccines and a major share of manufacturing happens in these countries as well. It is prudent for a country to have sufficient supplies to vaccinate everyone in its population. However, amassing excessive inventories would leave vaccines away from communities where it can directly help in impeding the spread of the virus. Some of these countries have either procured or had confirmed orders of the vaccines more than enough to vaccinate the entire population. In some cases, this amount had been more than twice the population of those countries only to realize later that this excess inventory may not be needed, and then, starting to redistribute a portion to other nations. However, this delay slowed the global response against the pandemic and a greater impact could have been achieved if the vaccines were made accessible to the needed communities earlier. Having a better and timely redistribution and sharing of vaccines both domestically and internationally to ensure optimal demand-supply dynamics would significantly enhance the impact of vaccinations. To illustrate this, we carried out experiments on the available dataset. Two counties in Wisconsin- Dane and Waukesha were considered and models were fitted to simulate the actual disease dynamics. The total number of vaccinations available per day for both the counties was considered as 500 and vaccinations began on the 10th day and continued till the end of the simulation period (200th day). The total number of infected cases in both the counties was observed at the end of the simulation period. The scenarios tested are shown in Table 1. In the second and sixth scenario, all the vaccines were allocated to the Dane country and Waukesha country respectively. While in Scenarios 3 to 5 this allocation was varied as shown. Scenario 1 is just the base case in which no vaccine is introduced. The last column shows the number of infected cases.

Note that, Scenarios 2–6 are better and give a smaller number of infected cases as expected when compared with the number of infected cases for Scenario 1. Scenario 3

Table 1. Scenarios of experiments on different vaccination strategies in Dane and Waukesha counties in Wisconsin

Scenario number	Number of vaccinations/day in Dane Country	Number of vaccinations/day in Waukesha Country	Total number of infected cases
1	0	0	51811
2	500	0	43101
3	400	100	42289
4	250	250	42680
5	100	400	44500
6	0	500	42309

results in the least total number of infected cases across both the counties. This shows that an appropriate sharing of vaccinations between different regions (Scenario 3) gives a better impact (reduced number of infections) as compared with allocating all the vaccines to one region (Scenario 2 & 6). As the spread of virus is dynamic, ideally the sharing of vaccines should also be implemented dynamically. Note that an equal sharing of vaccines (Scenario 4) does not necessarily give a better result

A question arises as to the implementation of a sharing-based distribution of vaccines. The availability of capacity globally to produce vaccines is well known. Utilization of this capacity would not only enable effective logistics and global distribution of vaccines, but also, would increase the number of vaccines available. However, it demands sharing of patents and requisite materials.

6 Conclusion

In this paper, we have used an epidemiological model to study the impact of different vaccine distribution strategies pertaining to vaccination distribution, vaccinating in multiple stages, and controlling interactions between different groups. This study was carried out with two population groups. Some of the important conclusions from the study are:

- Higher quantities of vaccines and early vaccination produce the best impact.
- Healthcare population should be given a higher priority in administering vaccines and distribution ratio of vaccines.
- It would be more effective to vaccinate a proportion of one group first and then move to the other group instead of trying to completely vaccinate one group before moving to the other.
- The type and scale of relationship between different population groups makes a significant impact on the type of decisions made.
- The strategies for vaccine distribution are different depending upon the level of interaction between population groups.

We also evaluated different vaccine distribution strategies for the maximum impact in controlling the pandemic. The best strategy was found to be sharing of vaccines among different communities. Maintaining a global centralized inventory and distribution system, making vaccine patents accessible to manufacturers in order to enable utilization of available production capacity, and ensuring a free movement of raw materials and products are some of the essential steps needed to enhance the distribution of vaccines and their timely availability in the face of the spread of the virus.

The proposed model could be used to make decisions at both global and local levels. Some ideas for future work include incorporation of additional compartments, population groups, and different relationship functions in the proposed model. Moreover, an overarching optimization model could be formulated to make decisions in view of specified objectives and constraints.

References

1. UC Davis Health. https://health.ucdavis.edu/coronavirus/covid-19-timeline.html
2. Health.com. https://www.health.com/condition/infectious-diseases/worst-pandemics-in-history
3. History.com Information. https://www.history.com/topics/middle-ages/pandemics-timeline
4. Ogilvy, K.W., McKendrick, A.G.: A contribution to the mathematical theory of epidemics. Proc. R. Soc. Lond. A **115**, 700–721 (1927). https://doi.org/10.1098/rspa.1927.0118
5. Chen, T.M., Rui, J., Wang, Q.P., et al.: A mathematical model for simulating the phase-based transmissibility of a novel coronavirus. Infect. Dis. Poverty **9**, 24 (2020). https://doi.org/10.1186/s40249-020-00640-3
6. Lin, Q., et al.: A conceptual model for the coronavirus disease 2019 (COVID-19) outbreak in Wuhan, China with individual reaction and governmental action. Int. J. Infect. Dis. **93**, 211–216 (2020). https://doi.org/10.1016/j.ijid.2020.02.058
7. Anastassopoulou, C., Russo, L., Tsakris, A., Siettos, C.: Data-based analysis, modelling and forecasting of the COVID-19 outbreak. PLoS ONE **15**(3), e0230405 (2020). https://doi.org/10.1371/journal.pone.0230405
8. Wu, J.T., Leung, K.: Nowcasting and forecasting the potential domestic and international spread of the 2019-nCoV outbreak originating in Wuhan, China: a modelling study. Lancet **395**(10225), 689–697 (2020). https://doi.org/10.1016/S0140-6736(20)30260-9
9. Wu, J.T., Leung, K., Bushman, M., et al.: Estimating clinical severity of COVID-19 from the transmission dynamics in Wuhan, China. Nat. Med. **26**, 506–510 (2020). https://doi.org/10.1038/s41591-020-0822-7
10. Kucharski, A.J., Russell, T.W., Diamond, C., Liu, Y., Edmunds, J., Funk, S.: Early dynamics of transmission and control of COVID-19: a mathematical modelling study. Lancet Infect. Dis. **20**(5), 553–558 (2020). https://doi.org/10.1016/S1473-3099(20)30144-4
11. Tang, B., et al.: Estimation of the transmission risk of the 2019-nCoV and its implication for public health interventions. J. Clin. Med. **9**(2), 462 (2020). https://doi.org/10.3390/jcm9020462
12. Khajanchi, S., Sarkar, K., Mondal, J., Perc, M.: Dynamics of the COVID-19 pandemic in India. Res. Square (2020). https://doi.org/10.21203/rs.3.rs-27112/v1
13. Sarkar, K., Khajanchi, S.: Modeling and forecasting the COVID-19 pandemic in India. Chaos Solitons Fractals **139**, 110049 (2020). https://doi.org/10.1016/j.chaos.2020.110049
14. Yan, B., Wang, J., Zhang, Z., Tang, X., Zhou, Y., et al.: An improved method for the fitting and prediction of the number of covid-19 confirmed cases based on lstm. Comput. Mater. Continua **64**(3), 1473–1490 (2020)

15. Martínez-Álvarez, F., et al.: Big Data 308–322 (2020). https://doi.org/10.1089/big.2020.0051
16. Wisconsin Department of Health Services. https://www.dhs.wisconsin.gov/covid-19/hosp-data.htm#HCW%20trend
17. Data USA. https://datausa.io/profile/geo/milwaukee-wi/#about
18. How Rich Countries Are Hoarding The World's Vaccines. Charts. https://www.npr.org/sections/goatsandsoda/2020/12/03/942303736/how-rich-countries-are-hoarding-the-worlds-vaccines-in-charts
19. COVID-19 Vaccination Program Interim Operational Guidance Jurisdiction – CDC. https://www.cdc.gov/vaccines/imz-managers/downloads/Covid-19-Vaccination-Program-Interim_Playbook.pdf
20. Here's Why Distribution of the Vaccine Is Taking Longer than Expected. https://www.nytimes.com/2020/12/31/health/vaccine-distribution-delays.html
21. From the Factory to the Frontlines. https://www.hhs.gov/sites/default/files/strategy-for-distributing-covid-19-vaccine.pdf
22. Emanuel, E.J., Luna, F., Schaefer, G.O., Tan, K.C.: Enhancing the WHO's proposed framework for distributing COVID-19 vaccines among countries. Am. J. Public Health. **111**(3), 371–373 (2021). https://doi.org/10.2105/AJPH.2020.306098

Blockchain in the Operations
and Supply Chain Management

Blockchain-Based Master Data Management in Supply Chains: A Design Science Study

Jacob Lohmer[1(⊠)] , Lasse Bohlen[2], and Rainer Lasch[1]

[1] Chair of Business Management, esp. Logistics, Technische Universität Dresden, Dresden,
Germany
{jacob.lohmer,rainer.lasch}@tu-dresden.de
[2] Chair of Business Informatics, esp. Intelligent Systems and Services,
Technische Universität Dresden, Dresden, Germany
lasse.bohlen@tu-dresden.de

Abstract. Master data management is an essential task for organizations and even more critical when collaborations are pursued. Using centralized platforms to manage master data across business partners is straightforward but also entails risks. Besides the dependency on intermediaries, data sovereignty is limited and a single point of failure persists. With new decentralization trends and the uprising blockchain technology, there is potential for optimized and sovereign master data management across entities. We conduct a design science study to assess blockchain technology's suitability to store and share master data in supply chains. The developed artifact was quantitatively evaluated, focusing on costs and transaction time to further contribute insights to blockchain technology's economic suitability. The Ethereum-based application was implemented in *evan.network* and *Ropsten* test networks. The results substantiate the previous theoretical statements in the literature with reliable numerical data, which indicate that permissioned blockchain networks are more scalable and low-cost than permissionless networks. We also highlight further research opportunities.

Keywords: Blockchain technology · Digital supply chain management · Master data management · Design science research · Technology implementation

1 Introduction

In the modern business world, information systems are the backbone of activities. Business transactions' success depends significantly on data, which have to be maintained and shared while kept up to date at high-quality levels. Effective information flow among supply chain partners enhances the integration of supply chains [1]. Most transactions between entities in supply chains rely heavily on master data stored in individual databases like ERP systems. Therefore, the quality of master data is even more relevant [2]. Ensuring that correct and up-to-date master data is available and integrated into the information systems enables business transactions to be carried out in a time- and resource-efficient manner.

A. Dolgui et al. (Eds.): APMS 2021, IFIP AICT 633, pp. 51–61, 2021.
https://doi.org/10.1007/978-3-030-85910-7_6

Master data is usually created once and regularly re-used, referring to customers, products, or vendors as central business objects [2, 3]. The increasing collaboration of companies in supply chain management (SCM) also makes it necessary to exchange master data more frequently, which is difficult due to individual firms' often isolated data silos. Therefore, concepts such as master data management (MDM) aim to eliminate quality problems and integrate information systems [4, 5]. The mentioned issues have led to central players in the market providing platforms that support data sharing and accessibility for many companies, e.g. *Infor Nexus*, *E2open* or *One Network Enterprises*. However, new problems arise with central data storage or integration of the central interface, such as dependency and a single point of failure. A decentralized solution for MDM offers some advantages, but the technical implementation has been a complicated task until now. Here the aspiring blockchain technology (BCT) comes into play. Initially developed for financial transactions, this decentralized technology enables many participants to agree on a valid state for a distributed system even when malicious agents are involved. No central instance is needed in the process, while BCT promotes high data quality [6, 7]. An application of BCT for collaborative MDM is promising but has not yet been explored. In the context of a design science study, we assess the usefulness of a blockchain master data application and develop a technical artifact to answer the following research questions: **RQ1.** How can blockchain technology improve MDM in supply chains? **RQ2.** What are the economic implications, chances and risks of a blockchain-based MDM application for SCM?

The remainder of this study is structured as follows. We discuss the theoretical background of our study in Sect. 2, focusing on collaborative data management and blockchain technology. Section 3 provides details on the methodology of this article and our approach. Next, we present the MasterData Application as the developed artifact in Sect. 4, followed by the application tests and assessment of results. We discuss the findings in Sect. 5 and conclude with further research opportunities in Sect. 6.

2   Theoretical Background

Many organizations maintain disparate systems with redundant data storage due to historically grown IT landscapes [3]. Master data is used to describe the main entities of business activities, is rarely changed with a constant overall volume and is referenced by transactional data [8, 9]. Virtually all IT processes in a business depend on master data, and they form the basis for cross-company collaboration. Accurate master data is crucial in this context and requires substantial effort, as standardized or automated processes rarely exist [8]. Managing master data is complex due to various requirements, often unclear data ownership and spread management responsibilities [4]. One of the tasks is metadata maintenance, which describes and defines other data's properties, such as reading and writing permissions, modification dates or data origin [5, 9]. Efficient data management is even more challenging in collaboration, as the participating partners' IT departments have to be aligned. Besides, there is a lack of cross-company standards for data models and functionalities [8, 10]. MDM addresses data quality issues through standardization and integration of processes and information systems [4]. Existing architectures for collaborative MDM can be broadly classified into three groups: decentralized synchronization (bilaterally between partners); centralized synchronization via an intermediary (storing and providing metadata and master data in a data pool); and a hybrid form, in which e.g. metadata is stored in a central data pool and master data is exchanged bilaterally [10]. In the last years, a move towards central players as intermediaries is evident due to missing methods for decentralized or hybrid MDM [10]. New problems arise with centralized platforms, such as dependency or single points of failure. Thus, alternatives to centralized systems are worth exploring.

Blockchain is an uprising technology that might lead to a substantial change here. The database operates on a transaction basis rather than a state-based approach. Centered on cryptography and peer-to-peer networks, BCT is one of several distributed ledger technologies (DLT) that immutably log transactions of virtually any form in a chronological chain of blocks [11]. Other forms of DLT that are not in the focus of this study include directed acyclic graphs [12]. Key features of BCT in SCM include transparency, immutability, irreversibility, disintermediation, and smart contract automation potential [6, 13, 14]. Initial research has examined BCT for leak-free and qualitative data sharing in supply chains [15]. Various forms of blockchain systems can be differentiated, e.g. by consensus algorithm and accessibility. Consensus defines how the participants agree on the system's status, with variants differing according to the basic concept of trust creation. The most common variants are Proof-of-Work (PoW) and Proof-of-Authority (PoA). In PoW, the decision-making authority about the system's status is distributed among the network participants according to their committed computing power. As anyone can participate in reaching consensus, these networks are called permissionless [11]. In PoA, the majority of a subset of nodes, called "authorities", decides whether to include or reject a transaction [16]. PoA is especially suited for permissioned networks in which all authorities are known and trusted, and reputation is an important parameter [17]. Therefore, accessibility can be differentiated into permissioned and permissionless networks (writing rights) and public and private systems (reading rights) [6]. Famous examples for public and permissionless systems are cryptocurrencies like Bitcoin or Ethereum, while most proof-of-concepts and industry applications are based on private and permissioned networks. Collaborating entities can automate data management in distributed configurations with BCT by using smart contracts, i.e. a program that runs on the blockchain and blockchain-based identity management.

In SCM, a wide variety of aspects have been considered (see e.g. [15, 17–21]), but the area of master data management has not yet been linked to BCT. Relating the technology features to the theoretical background of data management and the diverse sets of quality criteria for MDM, we focus on three categories of quality criteria that are discussed in the literature to assess the suitability of BCT: data accuracy, data accessibility and data representation [2, 8, 22, 23]. Table 1 shows the criteria that will be used to evaluate BCT for MDM.

Table 1. Quality criteria for MDM

Category	Rationale
Data accuracy	
Timeliness	The time interval between a real-life data change and the corresponding adjustment of the attribute values in the IT system
Completeness	No missing data points, and all relevant data for respective processes available
Accuracy	Match of attribute values of the data objects with the real-life data properties
Reputation	Data source, transport medium and the processing information systems are highly reputable, traceable, and well-known
Data accessibility	
Access security	Describes the reliability of data access (i.e. resilience)
Accessibility and availability	Data accessibility is at a high level if retrievable by users using simple procedures
Processability	Attribute values can be easily adapted and supplemented by authorized users
Flexibility	Basic characteristics can be easily adapted as e.g. requirements change
Data representation	
Identifiability	Data objects should be easily identifiable (i.e. clearly assigned to real-life counterpart)
Metadata	Describe additional data properties - if comprehensive metadata is available and trustworthy, it can support master data management processes
Non-redundancy	Minimal redundancy is targeted to prevent possible data inconsistencies

3   Methodology

We follow the design science research (DSR) methodology for this study [24, 25]. Originating in research on information systems, the DSR aims to create a technical artifact that addresses a relevant problem and evaluate it rigorously [24]. The main stages of DSR include problem identification and motivation, defining objectives of a solution, design and development of the artifact, demonstration, evaluation and communication with iteration steps between the phases [25].

The first DSR stage (problem identification) has been addressed in the first two sections. We assess BCT's suitability to manage master data in supply chains to overcome the issues in centralized, platform-based MDM. Based on insights from centralized platforms and the literature, we derived functionalities that the blockchain-based concept should provide for SCM applications: The concept should comprehensively map master data on the blockchain, replacing a centralized data pool. Thus, firms can create their representations and organizational units (as digital twins) and assign specific master data attributes shared in the network. The ability to represent relationships between individual organizational units should enable the efficient identification of master data objects. Besides, features to rate and digitally sign individual data attributes of other network participants need to be integrated to enable collaborative MDM. Such cross-organizational processes also require basic rights management. Roles should be assigned to individual network participants for each organizational unit. These roles determine who can create, edit, delete, rate, and sign individual data attributes.

In this way, the blockchain-based MDM system can enable minimizing the trust needed for interactions: Data and transactions are stored persistently, digital signatures are enabled, transparency is increased, and smart contracts are integrated. The artifact's objectives are a demonstration of technical feasibility, sufficient scalability and economic applicability. Test runs in varying configurations in different systems are necessary to provide an accurate statement about the expected scalability and costs.

4 Concept

4.1 MasterData Application

The developed technical artifact is a web-based application suitable for collaborative MDM. It includes a backend consisting of smart contracts running on Ethereum and a graphical user interface (GUI) developed on the JavaScript software library *React* as the frontend. The GUI supports the basic functionalities needed for collaborative MDM, e.g. searching or filtering of organizational elements. Communication between the GUI and the backend was established using the Ethereum JavaScript API *web3js* that enables the creation of transactions, signing and generally exchanging data with an Ethereum-based network. The technical architecture of the system is shown in Fig. 1.

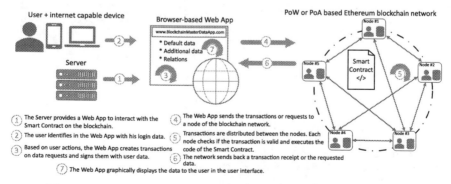

Fig. 1. Technical architecture and workflow of the MasterData application

Smart contracts were developed in *Solidity*. They contain data structures (organizational elements, data fields, data signatures) and functions (rights management, creation and deactivation of organizational elements, management of the respective master

data, management of the relationships between the organizational elements and evaluation and signing of data attributes). The organizational elements, as the main data
objects, represent the individual entities or business objects. They consist of the attributes
ID, *owner/participants/rights*, *orgType* (e.g. corporation or product), *relationTypes*, and
dataKeys. Data fields store attribute values for the appropriate data key. Besides, metadata relating to this value is stored in the specifically defined data structure. Participants
in the blockchain network can digitally sign individual data attributes to increase the
trustworthiness of data and confirm the signed data's validity. The executing user needs
appropriate rights, both in the signing and in the signed element. When the signature is
saved, some metadata is recorded to ensure quick verifiability, including *signingAddress*,
dataHash, *signature* and *validFrom/validTo*.

We provide a brief overview of the smart contracts' functionalities to dive a bit
deeper into the artifact's functionalities (the full source code can be obtained from
the corresponding author). For each organizational element, there are three different
roles, which are hierarchically structured. Each element has exactly one *owner*, but
any number of *admins* and *participants*. So-called function modifiers can be used to
specify which functions can be performed by which role. Two basic functions in the
developed smart contracts are the creation and deactivation of organizational elements.
A new element can be created using the function 'newOrgElement()' and passing on
a suitable ID and the desired element type. The sender of the calling transaction is
defined as the owner. Data management can be handled via 'setData()' to create new
data fields, 'removeData()' to remove fields or 'changeData()'. A relationship between
elements can also be established via 'addRelation()'. Other functions include rating and
signing data attributes via 'rateData()' and 'addSignature()'. The organizational elements
are displayed in the frontend in the form of a simple business card. Figure 2 shows an
example of the authors' university business card, next to an excerpt of the smart contract.

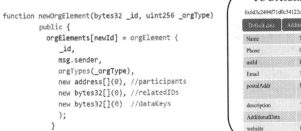
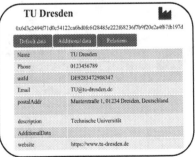

Fig. 2. Excerpt of the smart contract for creating a new organizational element (left) and
exemplary representation of an organizational element (right)

4.2 Application Tests

Most of the potentials, risks, and limitations of BCT have only been studied qualitatively. The limited adoption in existing information systems impedes extensive empirical studies. Therefore, the developed artifact offers an opportunity to assess the scalability and economic feasibility of MDM based on BCT. With the Ethereum-based smart contracts, testing can be done in different test networks based on different consensus algorithms and allows for a statement about permissioned vs. permissionless network suitability. There is a growing debate about the criticality of network accessibility, which we aim to support through our quantitative analysis. The results allow stakeholders to assess the extent to which the blockchain solution can be implemented in a resource-efficient manner. We chose the permissioned test network of *evan.network* with PoA consensus (*Aura* on *Parity* nodes) using Eve as the integrated currency and the permissionless *Ropsten* test network of the Ethereum main net (imitating its behavior) with PoW consensus. The two networks were chosen for their popularity and comparability. Smart contracts in *Solidity* can be executed on both networks while ensuring reproducibility of results.

The node.js based script's flow is as follows (refer to Table 2 for the full list) and has been conducted in the same way in both test nets: The test is initialized with the required blockchain accounts being passed to the *web3js* object. Then, 50 organization elements are randomly created (similar to the element shown in Fig. 2) and given pseudo-data. Next, 30 participants are set up and 20 of them are granted admin rights. Then, some participants are removed and new owners are set for 20 of the organizational elements. Relations between the elements are created and finally, data attributes are changed, rated and signed for 50 elements. This flow is intended to emulate real-world processes in collaborative MDM and allow the comparison of blockchain configurations.

4.3 Results

The results of the application tests are shown in Table 2. The computing operations in the Ethereum-based test networks are settled with a certain amount of *gas* (1 Gwei = 10^{-9} Ether/Eve). For each transaction, the gas consumption was recorded and converted in Ether/Eve and €. We also recorded the time in milliseconds (ms) for transaction execution. The gas price in the *Ropsten* network can be freely determined by the transaction's sender, influencing the execution time. The chosen gas price of 125 Gwei was the average gas price in the *Ropsten* network at the time of testing. The gas price in the *evan.network* is fixed at 20 Gwei, with each transaction treated equally. The fourth and the sixth column contain the converted costs per transaction in €.

5 Discussion

It is evident from Table 2 that the permissioned *evan.network* with PoA consensus has significantly lower average execution times per gas, which means improved scalability compared to the *Ropsten* test network, which mimics the Ethereum mainnet. Besides, costs per transaction and smart contract deployments are considerably lower in *evan.network*. While there are arguments for a permissionless (and public) network like

Table 2. Results of the test runs in *evan.network* and *Ropsten*

Functions of the smart contract	Number of TX with function calls	gas consumption / time in ms *evan.network*	Ø cost per TX in € *evan.network*	gas consumption / time in ms *Ropsten*	Ø cost per TX in € *Ropsten*
newOrgElement()	50	6877532/3357	0,0028	6710794/94489	4,44
setData()	~ 450	86064055/35870	0,0038	83061475/323967	5,96
addParticipant()	30	3312161/2795	0,0022	3108329/12015	3,43
addAdmin()	20	1335070/2674	0,0013	1406242/49849	2,33
rmParticipant()	10	358120/2866	0,0007	355398/87890	1,18
rmAdmin()	10	677655/2805	0,00135	660575/35766	2,19
setOwner()	20	1790043/2866	0,0018	1556626/50380	2,58
addRelation()	50	50524099/3115	0,0035	8117831/182267	5,37
rmRelation()	25	1254523/2801	0,001	1250291/21264	1,65
changeData()	50	5707374/1538	0,0023	6392227/257651	4,23
rateData()	50	2099752/1820	0,00085	2143254/27573	1,42
addSignature()	50	6326825/1753	0,0025	6153900/351221	4,07
rmSignature()	25	729642/2296	0,0006	639293/45135	0,85

gas price for *evan.network* in Gwei: 20, eve price in €: 1 | gas price for *Ropsten* in Gwei: 125, Ether price in €: 264,71 | 1 Gwei = 10^{-9}

auditability and open accessibility to third parties, permissioned systems with consensus mechanisms other than PoW are more cost-effective and scalable for data-intensive MDM processes. Other risks in public and permissionless networks include the volatility of cryptocurrencies, which complicates reliable cost planning. Besides, as many other network partners are active in the public networks, there is no certainty regarding the costs and the execution times of transactions. It should still be emphasized that increased costs will be incurred compared to centralized solutions. There is also greater demand for initial alignment among network participants. Here, stakeholders need to balance the desired distribution of decision-making power, trust-less collaborative efforts, and resource efficiency (costs) to decide on the suitability of a blockchain solution. BCT's strength is minimizing and automating underlying processes and providing higher data quality by avoiding isolated data silos.

Although BCT is particularly useful once the network reaches a certain size, for critical processes that require increased access security and traceability, there is added value even in small networks. It is reasonable to consider the proportion of data to be stored and shared via the blockchain in light of the high cost in permissionless networks compared to permissioned networks. Data creation and modification as the most critical functionalities should be handled off-chain and only referenced on-chain (e.g. hashed). To some extent, this consideration also applies to permissioned networks, as structured master data can be stored on-chain. In contrast, large-size unstructured master data can be referenced and handled off-chain.

We revisit the quality criteria of Sect. 2 to answer the first research question: On the *data accuracy* level, BCT supports the correctness and timeliness of data through the smart contract functionalities and the network-wide distribution of the ledger. Combined with the high failure and access security of blockchain systems, data completeness is ensured even in the event of technical failures. Signatures make it easy to trace changes and increase the trustworthiness of the system. *Data accessibility* is similar to a centralized database. Users can use standardized interfaces to retrieve data directly from the network. Editing data objects directly in the blockchain is costly due to the on-chain writing processes. However, blockchain systems provide increased access and failure security. Democratic processes limit flexibility. If new or changed requirements arise, adjustments cannot be enforced by a central instance. Besides, adaptations are limited concerning the "blockchain trilemma" of security vs. decentralization vs. scalability [26]. Permissioned networks perform well on security and scalability at a lower level of decentralization, whereas permissionless networks perform better on security and decentralization. Turning to *data representation*: The use of digital signatures and persistent transaction storage creates reliable metadata in blockchain systems. If rights are managed with the help of smart contracts, the scope and trustworthiness of this metadata can be increased even further. The integrity of the data is not based on a central authority but arises from the consensus-based trust. Redundancy is not limited but an inherent feature of blockchain, with inconsistencies largely eliminated by fast synchronization.

The technology also influences MDM. Blockchain enables secure, scalable and inter-organizational user management with consensus-based trust and increased transparency. Especially for new international business relationships, blockchain can offer an alternative to the DUNS standard [7]. However, firms can still decide which data to make accessible and manage critical business data off-chain. BCT can be a beneficial option for hybrid MDM configurations. Automatic archiving of records and transactions increases the security of the system. Data can also be exchanged with companies that were previously not trusted. However, further standards for collaborative MDM based on blockchain are needed to exploit the technology's potential fully. Besides, the interoperability of blockchain protocols needs to be improved. It must be noted here that the potentials, risks, and limitations depend on the blockchain's respective configurations. Examining these in detail is beyond the scope of this article.

6 Conclusion

We assess blockchain technology for cross-organizational master data management in this study. Design science research is conducted to develop a concept, which allows an economic evaluation of the technology's usability. This study addresses the need for focused studies on applying BCT in SCM while ensuring practical utility through the developed concept. Answering the research questions concisely, BCT can improve MDM in supply chains through its transparency features, promoting collaborative decentralization, enhanced security and automation potential through smart contracts. Important stakeholder decisions involve the choice of network type, the scope of data to be shared, and the user base. This article offers both quantitative and qualitative statements for these management decisions and provides insights on implications, chances and risks of using BCT for collaborative MDM in SCM.

Limitations of this study include the focus on a specific subarea of SCM. Thus, results for MDM cannot be easily generalized to other business domains, e.g. financial transactions. Further, the derived results of the DSR artifact are based on specific test networks and pseudo-data for transactions. Nevertheless, several implications can be derived from the results of this study. First, as a theoretical implication, the use of BCT for MDM may open a new research area in decentralized data storage and sharing. This study takes initial steps in this direction and can serve as a starting point for further studies to qualitatively and quantitatively assess the usability of the technology. Second, the findings indicate a technological fit of the technology and promising economic results regarding transaction costs. Besides, we substantiate previous qualitative statements with reliable numerical data and confirm the proposition that permissioned networks with PoA consensus are more scalable than permissionless networks.

Future research should include a more sophisticated proof-of-concept in a complex supply network to assess the application's technical fit and scalability for real-life processes. In the context of MDM, hybrid configurations using BCT are significant and should be assessed. Besides, exploring the concept of sidechains seems reasonable to facilitate solutions that combine the real decentralization of permissionless networks with the low costs and scalability of permissioned networks. Open issues also arise concerning the governance of supply chains and the trust-free implications of BCT. How do decentralized equality of partners and "code-is-law" features affect collaboration? A potential trend toward increased short-term business relationships and even more fragmented supply chains should be explored. Data sharing based on BCT also provides leeway for innovative solutions in supply chain finance or revenue sharing based on compensation for real-time data sharing by upstream partners [15].

References

1. Vanpoucke, E., Boyer, K.K., Vereecke, A.: Supply chain information flow strategies: an empirical taxonomy. Int. J. Oper. Prod. Manage. **29**, 1213–1241 (2009). https://doi.org/10.1108/01443570911005974
2. Knolmayer, G.F., Röthlin, M.: Quality of material master data and its effect on the usefulness of distributed ERP systems. In: Roddick, J.F., et al. (eds.) ER 2006. LNCS, vol. 4231, pp. 362–371. Springer, Heidelberg (2006). https://doi.org/10.1007/11908883_43
3. Vilminko-Heikkinen, R., Pekkola, S.: Master data management and its organizational implementation: an ethnographical study within the public sector. J. Enterp. Inf. Manage. **30**, 454–475 (2017). https://doi.org/10.1108/JEIM-07-2015-0070
4. Silvola, R., Jaaskelainen, O., Kropsu-Vehkapera, H., Haapasalo, H.: Managing one master data - challenges and preconditions. Ind. Manage. Data Syst. **111**, 146–162 (2011). https://doi.org/10.1108/02635571111099776
5. Loshin, D.: Master Data Management. Morgan Kaufman, Burlington (2009)
6. Lohmer, J., Lasch, R.: Blockchain in operations management and manufacturing: potential and barriers. Comput. Ind. Eng. **149**, 106789 (2020). https://doi.org/10.1016/j.cie.2020.106789
7. Banerjee, A.: Blockchain technology: supply chain insights from ERP. In: Advances in Computers, pp 69–98. Elsevier (2018). https://doi.org/10.1016/bs.adcom.2018.03.007

8. Otto. B., Hüner, K.M.: Functional reference architecture for corporate master data management (2009)
9. White, A., Radcliffe, J.: Four Dimensions of MDM: Understanding the Complexity. CT, USA, Stanford (2007)
10. Schemm, J.: Zwischenbetriebliches Stammdatenmanagement. Springer, Heidelberg. https://doi.org/10.1007/978-3-540-89030-0
11. Swan, M.: Blockchain: Blueprint for a New Economy, 1st ed. O'Reilly Media, Sebastopol (2015)
12. Kurpjuweit, S., Schmidt, C.G., Klöckner, M., Wagner, S.M.: Blockchain in additive manufacturing and its impact on supply chains. J. Bus. Logist. 1–25 (2019). https://doi.org/10.1111/jbl.12231
13. Babich, V., Hilary, G.: Distributed ledgers and operations: what operations management researchers should know about blockchain technology. Manuf. Serv. Oper. Manage. 22, 223–240 (2020). https://doi.org/10.1287/msom.2018.0752
14. Jain, G., Singh, H., Chaturvedi, K.R., Rakesh, S.: Blockchain in logistics industry: in fizz customer trust or not. J. Enterp. Inf. Manage. 33, 541–558 (2020). https://doi.org/10.1108/JEIM-06-2018-0142
15. Wang, Z., Zheng, Z., Jiang, W., Tang, S.: Blockchain-enabled data sharing in supply chains: model, operationalization, and tutorial. Prod. Oper. Manage. 1–21 (2021). https://doi.org/10.1111/poms.13356
16. Casino, F., Dasaklis, T.K., Patsakis, C.: A systematic literature review of blockchain-based applications: current status, classification and open issues. Telematics Inf. 36, 55–81 (2019). https://doi.org/10.1016/j.tele.2018.11.006
17. Lohmer, J., Bugert, N., Lasch, R.: Analysis of resilience strategies and ripple effect in blockchain-coordinated supply chains: an agent-based simulation study. Int. J. Prod. Econ. 228, 107882 (2020). https://doi.org/10.1016/j.ijpe.2020.107882
18. Kamble, S., Gunasekaran, A., Sharma, R.: Modeling the blockchain enabled traceability in agriculture supply chain. Int. J. Inf. Manage. 52, 1–16 (2020). https://doi.org/10.1016/j.ijinfomgt.2019.05.023
19. Röck, D., Sternberg, H.S., Hofmann, E.: Distributed ledger technology in supply chains: a transaction cost perspective. Int. J. Prod. Res. 58, 2124–2141 (2020). https://doi.org/10.1080/00207543.2019.1657247
20. Wang, Y., Singgih, M., Wang, J., Rit, M.: Making sense of blockchain technology: how will it transform supply chains? Int. J. Prod. Econ. 211, 221–236 (2019). https://doi.org/10.1016/j.ijpe.2019.02.002
21. Lohmer, J., Ribeiro da Silva, E., Lasch, R.: Blockchain technology in operations & supply chain management: a content analysis. Logistics Res. (2021)
22. Redman, T.: Data quality for the information age. Artech House, Boston (1996)
23. Wang, R.Y., Strong, D.M.: Beyond accuracy: what data quality means to data consumers. J. Manage. Inf. Syst. 12, 5–34 (1996). https://doi.org/10.1080/07421222.1996.11518099
24. Hevner, A.R., March, S.T., Park, J., Ram, S.: Design science in information systems research. MIS Q. 28, 75 (2004). https://doi.org/10.2307/25148625
25. Peffers, K., Tuunanen, T., Rothenberger, M.A., Chatterjee, S.: A design science research methodology for information systems research. J. Manage. Inf. Syst. 24, 45–77 (2007). https://doi.org/10.2753/MIS0742-1222240302
26. Zhou, Q., Huang, H., Zheng, Z., Bian, J.: Solutions to scalability of blockchain: a survey. IEEE Access 8, 16440–16455 (2020). https://doi.org/10.1109/aCCESS.2020.2967218

Blockchain for Product Authenticity in the Cannabis Supply Chain

Sven Januszek$^{(\boxtimes)}$ ⓘ, Andreas Siegrist ⓘ, and Torbjørn H. Netland ⓘ

ETH Zürich, Weinbergstr. 56/58, 8050 Zürich, Switzerland
sjanuszek@ethz.ch

Abstract. Cannabis is an emerging industry and like other strictly regulated products prone to fraud. Its medical application and increased regulatory pressure call for secure supply chains and product authenticity. Blockchain's capability to strengthen end-to-end traceability in supply chains has the potential to provide the required levels of assurance. In this study, we describe effective ways of how to integrate Blockchain technology within the cannabis supply chain and other required technologies to ensure product authenticity. Our results show that blockchain is a powerful and promising technology that can effectively improve supply chain transparency and support regulatory compliance. Nevertheless, blockchain alone can only ensure data security and does not capture the linkage between the physical product and its data, which is an important consideration regarding product fraud. For this reason, we conclude that blockchain is an enabling technology that still needs to be supported by further supplementary technologies, such as nuclear magnetic resonance-based screening technology, Internet of Things, and communication standards. Used together, these technologies can ensure product authenticity in cannabis supply chains.

Keywords: Blockchain · Supply chain · Product authenticity

1 Introduction

Product fraud, especially in the pharmaceutical sector, is happening worldwide in high numbers. The global market of substandard (failing to meet quality standards) or falsified (deliberate misrepresentation of composition, identity, or source) medicines is estimated to be worth up to 200 billion USD [1]. The World Health Organization estimated that more than 10% of the global drug supply is counterfeit [2], threatening not only economic stability but also public health.

Medical cannabis is a fast-growing industry that is not excluded from product fraud. Like any crop, it can be tainted by natural (e.g., microbial toxins in soil) or artificial (e.g., pesticides, miticides, and fungicides) adulterants. Studies have shown that cannabidiol (CBD) products are subject to mislabeling and contamination indicating safety issues for consumers (Evans, 2020). For example, a study conducted by the U.S. Food and Drug Administration (FDA) analyzed 108 CBD products and found significant discrepancies between the claimed and tested CBD and tetrahydrocannabinol (THC) amounts [3].

© IFIP International Federation for Information Processing 2021
Published by Springer Nature Switzerland AG 2021
A. Dolgui et al. (Eds.): APMS 2021, IFIP AICT 633, pp. 62–69, 2021.
https://doi.org/10.1007/978-3-030-85910-7_7

To protect consumers from exposure to drugs that may be fraudulent or otherwise harmful, US Congress has enacted the Drug Quality and Security Act, which requires pharmaceutical companies to establish an electronic and interoperable system to trace prescription drugs throughout their entire supply chains by 2024. To enhance the security of drug supply chains further, another requirement is to notify the FDA and other trading partners within 24 h after identifying an illegitimate product.

Despite the regulatory pressure to develop effective ways of tracking, sharing, and reporting information, pharmaceutical supply chains still lack enough traceability to meet the new requirements. Blockchain's immutability and tracking capabilities could change that [cf. 4, 5]. In this study, we, therefore, set out to discuss applications of blockchain in the cannabis supply chain to minimize fraud and ensure product authenticity.

2   Fraud in the Cannabis Supply Chain

2.1   Product Fraud

Fraud, in general, is the intentional deception, trickery, or misrepresentation of facts by one person alone or acting on behalf of an organization. Product fraud in particular is often economically motivated and can be classified into seven types (see Table 1). The higher the product value is, representing a popular brand, a quality label, or a specific health claim, the more it is prone to fraudulent activities. Product fraud can destroy consumer trust and has the potential, dependent on the nature of the fraud, to even risk human health and life [6, 7].

Table 1. Seven types of product fraud (Spink and Moyer, 2011).

Type	Definition
Adulteration	A component of the finished product is fraudulent
Tampering	Legitimate product and packaging are used in a fraudulent way
Over-Run	Legitimate product is made in excess of production agreements
Theft	Legitimate product is stolen and passed off as legitimately procured
Diversion	The sale or distribution of legitimate products outside of intended markets
Simulation	An illegitimate product is designed to look like the legitimate product
Counterfeit	All aspects of the fraudulent product and packaging are fully replicated

2.2   Cannabis Supply Chain

The medical cannabis supply chain is governed by strict standards for safety and consistent quality. All participants of the supply chain, therefore, need to be licensed and the distribution of products requires a specialized, controlled distribution channel. Furthermore, all products must undergo a series of several tests and investigations before they are sold. Many laboratories and testing centers are even run by the government, but there is an increasing number of licensed private laboratories to handle quality control. Figure 1 shows a typical example of the Cannabis supply chain, for simplicity without any regulatory authorities.

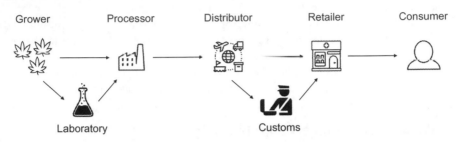

Fig. 1. Example of a cannabis supply chain.

Despite being highly regulated and controlled, fraud is still happening in the cannabis supply chain—as in many food supply chains [8]. Examples include unlicensed growers selling cannabis to processors, adulterated test reports, and false labeling of the sold goods [9, 10].

Today's global and complex supply chains, having multiple national and regulatory boundaries, make it more difficult to trace products, especially where products change hands several times on paper or physically [11]. In addition to the supply chain complexity, there is also a lack of visibility and trust, and the potential of data swamping retailers, businesses, and their employees [12]. Hence, the need for technological support to enhance traceability and control in the cannabis supply chain calls for further research.

3   Blockchain Technology

3.1   Blockchain Definition

Blockchain is a distributed ledger technology (DLT), which means it is a digital dataset being shared and synchronized without any central administrator. It consists of a series of connected blocks, which contain a cryptographic signature of the previous block, a timestamp, and transaction data (see Fig. 2). A peer-to-peer network continuously solves cryptographic puzzles and validates transactions, this way adding new blocks to the chain [4, 5, 13].

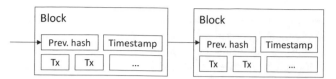

Fig. 2. Linking of blocks [13].

3.2 Blockchain Characteristics

Since all blocks are time-stamped and cryptographically connected to the previous block, it is impossible to retroactively alter previous transactions without alteration of all subsequent blocks in the chain. This chained structure of the blockchain and the collective computational power of the network make it therefore a generally immutable and tamper-proof technology [14].

Another important aspect of the blockchain is its distributed nature. The complete blockchain is a database file, which is replicated between all nodes on the network so that every node shares the same data. These networked copies create decentralization and shared responsibility. Since the classic blockchain is a shared open database of linked blocks, it provides a view of the full transaction history to all nodes. Any member can access it and see the available transactions. This creates traceability of assets over their lifetimes.

3.3 Blockchain Structures

Blockchains can be set up in different ways. The structure depends on their intended application [4, 15]. Generally, a *public blockchain* is open, decentralized, and fully visible to the public. It is not owned by a single entity, but any node can join or leave the blockchain. Any participant can also verify and add data to the blockchain.

A *private blockchain* is controlled by a centralized entity. Only nodes that are authenticated and permitted can join the network. The same applies to adding records to the blockchain and verifying them. Private blockchains do not offer the same decentralized security as public blockchains, which is why entries can be more easily altered by their owner.

In a *consortium* or *hybrid blockchain*, different stakeholders (e.g., suppliers, governments, regulators, producers, processors, retailers, etc.) build a group (a consortium) and operate the blockchain together. Interactions are performed within a limited group of entities that share a common goal. The validation process is often controlled by known, trusted users. The database of the blockchain is only distributed among entitled participants, which makes the network only partly decentralized.

4 Proposing a Framework for Cannabis Authenticity Based on Blockchain Technology

4.1 Blockchain Implementation

Hybrid blockchains are entirely customizable, as they allow granting special permissions to each participant of the network, such as reading, accessing, or writing information.

This way, it is possible to control each participant's activities depending on their role. In the cannabis supply chain, the grower cultivates the plant, the processor manufactures the final product, laboratories test the product for various specifications (e.g., for fungal growth or THC amounts), distributors ship the product, customs authorities clear the product for entrance to their respective nation, and retailers sell the product. Each party plays a vital but specific role in the supply chain, so that a hybrid blockchain may offer the best fit.

Once, the blockchain technology has been implemented in the supply chain, each supply chain member represents a node in the blockchain and is known by the other participants. Depending on their permissions, each node can add product-related information to the blockchain. This can be location information, time, or any other product details as weight or volume. As scalability is an issue for blockchains, big data files should not be put directly on the chain, but off-chain in a separate repository. The only information stored on the ledger for such data can be a cryptographic token, which contains the data reference and a pointer to the off-chain data. With this approach, the ledger can then provide access authorization to members who need access to the data.

4.2   Linking Data to the Physical Product

While blockchains enable greater transparency and data integrity, they cannot ensure data accuracy and correct data entry [e.g., 8]. Data still can get collected on paper or in a spreadsheet and then be manually entered into a blockchain. Therefore, supplementary technologies are needed to ensure the proper linking of information about physical goods to the data stored on the blockchain.

First, a standard for product identification needs to be set up. The GS1 standardization is a potential solution, which provides systematic coding of the Global Location Number for all companies and their locations in the supply chain and their Global Trade Item Number (GTIN) for products [cf. 16]. Each production batch and every packing unit could be assigned its own GTIN, which can then be uniquely referred to in the blockchain ledger.

As individual products get mixed, processed, or divided along the supply chain, single events of the product flow along the supply chain need to be captured. GS1 again provides a solution for this with their Electronic Product Code Information Services (EPCIS) system. Each event keeps a record of product IDs entering a process and the IDs at the output. This also allows the exact tracking of product-related information (e.g., weight or volume) entering and leaving at each process step. As this information is immutably stored on the blockchain, tracing of material addition or removal is facilitated, and easy to verify for any involved player.

Next, to ensure that the product is always linked to the correct digital dataset on the blockchain, additional traceability systems need to be integrated. The GTIN can, for instance, be implemented as a barcode, QR code, or Electronic Product Code in a radio-frequency identification device (RFID). RFID is widely used for simplified digital tracking of products in supply chains and can be enhanced when integrated with blockchain [17]. Walmart and IBM together successfully use blockchain combined with RFID to track consumer products [18]. Using integrated NFC chips in the package, and an NFC reader (e.g., smartphone) makes it possible to directly read information about the product and authorize access to its traceability data stored in a blockchain. As NFC chips use unique identities, they cannot be copied as opposed to simple QR codes. IoT devices, which collect and enter data autonomously and automatically to the blockchain, can further enhance safety and build another level of trust in the product's supply chain [19].

Marking the product package, however, cannot guarantee that the *product* is untampered and original. For that, a promising approach is to integrate molecular screening technologies into the cannabis supply chain and put the molecular identity onto the blockchain ecosystem. For example, nuclear magnetic resonance-based (NMR) screening instruments could be installed between single supply chain participants as gateways that test the authenticity of the product and ensure it by being directly linked to the blockchain and automatically saving the test results onto the blockchain. To provide an example of such a technology, a suitable device is FoodScreener™ by Bruker Corporation, which allows testing origin authenticity, false labeling, and species purity among other factors [20]. Cannabis has—like humans—a unique molecular fingerprint. With reference to an original sample or a statistical model, the FoodScreener™ could detect inconsistencies in the molecular structure of the Cannabis. It would then indicate that the material or product has been altered and thus might have been subject to fraud.

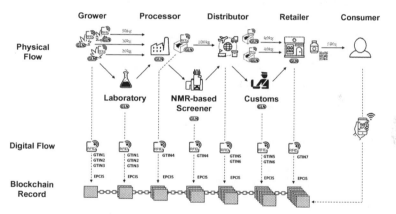

Fig. 3. Blockchain-enabled technological supply chain framework for product authenticity.

Smart active devices locked to the physical product, accompanying it along the supply chain, offer an additional benefit that goes beyond mere protection. They can also monitor the product during idle states in warehouses or shelves for example. Active sensor devices can be placed in product containers, which record time, location, temperature, or other environmental parameters. Such devices can directly interact online with the blockchain, store data, and generate immediate alerts. They also allow communication about the content with the outside world without opening the package. Retailers and consumers immediately can detect whether a critical value (e.g., time or temperature) has been exceeded. A packaging label could change its color to indicate a cold chain interruption, a leaking package, or the unwanted presence of certain bacteria.

With the described standards and technologies in place (see Fig. 3), the consumer or any other supply chain participant can easily back-trace products by using a unique product ID. The information gained can also help to improve the safety of products, as the collected environmental conditions are a source for deciding on the product quality. Adding location tracking enables to see instantly where a product currently is located or to identify at which GLN a potential recorded issue occurred.

5 Conclusion

The purpose of this study was to develop a technological framework to support product safety and authenticity in the cannabis supply chain. The supply chain transparency framework presented in this paper contains many technical elements, which combined provide powerful security against fraudsters and almost guarantee product integrity. Although such a framework with its numerous and detailed security elements remains a high aim, the technical foundation is available already today with the blockchain as a fundamental element.

The advantage of blockchain is that it can bring trust to a network of users through transparency and tamper-evidence. The distributed nature of the platform allows for greater oversight and control of products while real-time tracking via smart devices gives supply chain stakeholders the flexibility to make rapid decisions and update inventory levels continuously, thereby reducing working capital inactivity.

Despite the bright outlook, certain issues, such as interoperability of blockchains, remain and demand future research. Organizations that need to deal with several blockchains in different supply chains would highly benefit from the ability to see and access information across various blockchain systems.

References

1. Ozawa, S., et al.: Prevalence and estimated economic burden of substandard and falsified medicines in low-and middle-income countries: a systematic review and meta-analysis. JAMA Netw. **1**(4), 1–22 (2018). https://doi.org/10.1001/jamanetworkopen.2018.1662
2. World Health Organization: Counterfeit medicines: the silent epidemic (2006). https://www.who.int/mediacentre/news/releases/2006/pr09/en/. Accessed 5 Mar 2021
3. Food and Drug Administration: Sampling Study of the Current Cannabidiol Marketplace to Determine the Extent That Products are Mislabeled or Adulterated, Report to the U.S. House (2020). https://hempindustrydaily.com/wp-content/uploads/2020/07/CBD-Marketplace-Sampling_RTC_FY20_Final.pdf. Accessed 5 Mar 2021
4. Babich, V., Hilary, G.: Distributed ledgers and operations: what operations management researchers should know about blockchain technology. Manuf. Serv. Oper. Manage. **22**(2), 223–240 (2020). https://doi.org/10.1287/msom.2018.0752
5. Schmidt, C.G., Wagner, S.M.: Blockchain and supply chain relations: a transaction cost theory perspective. J. Purchasing Supply Manage. **25**(4), 1–13 (2019). https://doi.org/10.1016/j.pursup.2019.100552
6. Johnson, R.: Food fraud and economically motivated adulteration of food and food ingredients. Congressional Research Service (2014)
7. Walker, M., Gowland, H.: Deadly fraud–food allergen substitution in the food chain. Clin. Transl. Allergy **5**(3), 1 (2015). https://doi.org/10.1186/2045-7022-5-s3-p137

8. McKenzie, J.: Why blockchain won't fix food safety—yet (2018). https://newfoodeconomy. org/blockchain-food-traceability-walmart-ibm/. Accessed 11 Mar 2021

9. Evans, D.G.: Medical fraud, mislabeling, contamination: all common in CBD products. Mo. Med. **117**(5), 394–399 (2020)

10. Food and Drug Administration: Statement from FDA Commissioner Scott Gottlieb, M.D., on signing of the Agriculture Improvement Act and the agency's regulation of products containing cannabis and cannabis-derived compounds (2018). https://www.fda.gov/news-events/press-announcements/statement-fda-commissioner-scott-gottlieb-md-signing-agricu lture-improvement-act-and-agencys. Accessed 5 Mar 2021

11. Manning, L., Smith, R., Soon, J.M.: Developing an organizational typology of criminals in the meat supply chain. Food Policy **59**, 44–54 (2016). https://doi.org/10.1016/j.foodpol.2015. 12.003

12. Sarpong, S.: Traceability and supply chain complexity: confronting the issues and concerns. Eur. Bus. Rev. **26**(3), 271–284 (2014). https://doi.org/10.1108/ebr-09-2013-0113

13. Nakamoto, S.: Bitcoin: A peer-to-peer electronic cash system (2008). https://bitcoin.org/bit coin.pdf. Accessed 5 Mar 2021

14. Queiroz, M.M., Telles, R., Bonilla, S.H.: Blockchain and supply chain management integration: a systematic review of the literature. Supply Chain Manage. An. Int. J. **25**(2), 241–254 (2019). https://doi.org/10.1108/scm-03-2018-0143

15. Mougayar, W.: The Business Blockchain: Promise, Practice, and Application of the Next Internet Technology. John Wiley & Sons, Hoboken (2016)

16. Myhre, B., Netland, T.H., Vevle, G.: The footprint of food-a suggested traceability solution based on EPCIS. In: 5th European Workshop on RFID Systems and Technologies, pp. 1–6 (2009)

17. Sidorov, M., Ong, M.T., Sridharan, R.V., Nakamura, J., Ohmura, R., Khor, J.H.: Ultra-lightweight mutual authentication RFID protocol for blockchain enabled supply chains. IEEE Access **7**, 7273–7285 (2019). https://doi.org/10.1109/access.2018.2890389

18. Reddy, V.P.V.: Emerging of blockchain technology in business industry. Int. J. Innov. Res. Technol. **6**(6), 227–230 (2019)

19. Khare, A.A., Mittal, A.: Blockchain: embedding trust in organic products' supply chain. J. Comput. Theor. Nanosci. **16**(10), 4418–4424 (2019). https://doi.org/10.1166/jctn.2019.8535

20. Bruker: NMR & EPR Food Analysis Solutions – FoodScreener. https://www.bruker.com/en/ products-and-solutions/mr/nmr-food-solutions/food-screener.html. Accessed 17 Mar 2021

A Blockchain-Based Manufacturing Service Composition Architecture for Trust Issues

Qianhang Lyu[(✉)] [iD], Yunqing Rao, Jiawei Wang, and Peng Qi

Huazhong University of Science and Technology, Wuhan 430074, China

Abstract. Cloud platform is found to be an appropriate way to meet the need to improve the performance of information sharing among manufacturing companies. However, there is still a huge gap to be bridged for collaboration among different stakeholders due to interest conflict or distrust. Especially when the whole system is firmly controlled by centralized third parties. Blockchain is a technology based on cryptography, distributed system and consensus mechanism, which is meant to be a critical method used in value convergence to strengthen connections among enterprises and effectively solve trust issues to a certain extent. Obviously it would benefit for platform performance to elevate operational transparency as well as immutability, which are precisely the comprehensive properties of blockchain. This paper proposes a blockchain-based cloud platform manufacturing services composition architecture and elaborates the business collaboration system in detail. Manufacturing resources on the cloud platform are in the form of services to be accessed by any registered users in the system. The blockchain stores and broadcasts transaction and matches results generated in the core cloud services layer. Furthermore, a quality of service (QoS) attribute model is built to evaluate the service composition problem and genetic algorithm is adopted to solve it. Finally, a simulation experiment is presented as the application of proposed system.

Keywords: Cloud platform · Blockchain technology · Quality of service · Manufacturing service composition

1 Introduction

As a manufacturing resource sharing platform, cloud has attracted more and more attention in dealing with optimal resources allocation problems. The internal information delivering is quite mature due to the development of the Internet to this day. The competitive pressure is largely focused on the cooperation with external enterprises. Researchers and practitioners have created plenty of works in the manufacturing field of information sharing and sources configuration.

Cloud platform can provide computing, networking and storage capabilities based on services of hardware and software resources, which is quite an efficient and economical way where every enterprise upload its information, data, solution schemes, service abilities and so on. It does not need any extra costs of time, labor or purchase on software deployment, but sends orders directly to the cloud platform to obtain information or services in different types of all stages of a product lifecycle when enterprise users need a specific application. Though cloud platform is a useful way to deal with this kind of problem, most of companies lack enough trust in their partners, and in most cases refuse to share internal information and data in the cloud, which brings restrictions and obstacles to the cooperation, making it even harder in value convergence at the industry level.

Therefore, it is natural to consider using a particular technique to solve the trust problem in enterprise collaboration. While trust has long been a highly subjective human consensus, the biggest innovation of blockchain is that it provides a way for humans to build trust using rational technological means. Blockchain is a distributed ledger technology that uses a consensus mechanism to activate nodes to keep accounts together. In order to ensure the reliability of information, blockchain usually takes a chain structure and uses cryptographic technology to store information. The blocks obtained by mining are connected by storing the hash of the previous block. Once a new block is added to the chain, it would be extremely hard to delete or change it, which reflects its immutable property [1]. Furthermore, it is decentralized because data is automatically shared among all nodes without third-party interruption. Since every single node has a copy of the blockchain, each participant can get access to transfer records, which makes it transparent. With these superior features of blockchain technology, it can effectively eliminate the concerns among users and thus deal with the trust issues. And it has grabbed wide attention in more and more fields [2]. The authors in [3] constructed a precast supply chain information management framework based on blockchain to realize automatic information sharing, traceability, and transparency in the construction field. Li Z. et al. [4] utilize blockchain technology to optimize power distribution system and manage energy and capital flow among micro grids in a manner with high reliability. In addition, experts and scholars have also carried out deeply exploration in regions of financial, medical [5], healthcare [6], supply chain [7], manufacturing and so on. Abraham Z. [8] built a blockchain-based LCA framework to complete life cycle assessment system. X.L. Liu [9] proposed an blockchain-based PLM architecture. Literatures on the combination of blockchain and cloud have also emerged in recent years. Yuankai Z. [10] studied the application of blockchain technology to cloud manufacturing on consensus protocols. However, the previous literature and research have not addressed the obstacles to cooperation caused by trust among the participants in cloud platform, nor have they been targeted by business collaboration planning. Therefore, this paper combines the blockchain technology with the cloud platform to make up for the defects of the traditional architecture, so as to further implement the resource sharing and value convergence in the industry scope.

Now that the services from providers and demands published by users have converged on the cloud platform. What still remains an issue is the matching problem between requirements which needs to be decomposed and services. Hence, optimization of manufacturing service composition that is regarded as NP-hard problem is to be settled by choosing appropriate candidates for requirements from service pool by the certain rules, the result of which is the core content of proposed system. This kind of service combination process had been studied by many scholars [11]. Among these literatures, service composition results were evaluated through quality of service (QoS) attributes. Genetic algorithm is convenient to be employed in this kind of problem and its performance of global and local search can be effectively achieved through parameter adjustment. The purpose of this research is to establish a blockchain-based manufacturing service composition architecture and clarify its business collaboration system. Meanwhile, the related manufacturing service composition model operated automatically in the cloud platform is proposed. The optimization solutions will be recorded and broadcasted on the blockchain. Finally, Evolutionary genetic algorithm (GA) is adopted to solve the model.

2 Architecture of Blockchain-Based Manufacturing Service Composition

Based on the background mentioned above, an architecture of blockchain-based manufacturing service composition is introduced. Furthermore, the system workflow of the architecture is established in order to demonstrate the business process.

2.1 Architecture of the Proposed System

On the cloud platform, manufacturing resources are visualized in the form of services and so are requirements from customers which need to be decomposed in to subtasks. This

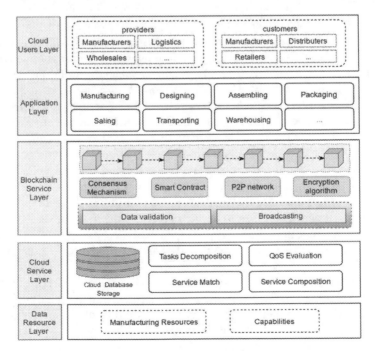

Fig. 1. Architecture of blockchain-based manufacturing service composition

paper proposed an architecture of blockchain-based manufacturing service composition which contains five layers including cloud users layer, application layer, blockchain service layer, cloud service layer and data resource layer, as shown in Fig. 1. A detailed description of this architecture is illustrated as follows.

The cloud users layer. The cloud users layer provides interactive interface for platform users made up of customers and providers. The same user may play different roles in different transactional relationships. For instance, the manufacturer is on the demand side when purchasing while it also could be the service provider when dealing with the distributor. Customers have access to all information from the service provider about the content of the services and the manufacturing capabilities, which is highly credible and reliable stored in blocks.

The application layer. The application layer contains series of related services that meet the needs of demanders including each stage of the product lifecycle from raw materials to finished products, as well as other tradable processes that can be used to resources-sharing among enterprises.

The blockchain service layer. The blockchain service layer plays an important role in the whole architecture. The hash values of service information, transactions and manufacturing service composition results are to be stored permanently and published in this layer after data validation and broadcasting. It contains several basic components of blockchain. Smart contract is a computer protocol that technically facilitates the verification or enforcement of the execution of a contract in order to achieve the specific functions. Meanwhile, smart contract needs the support of consensus mechanism, which was defined as initial state of the system, establishing the process for reaching an agreement among network nodes. P2P network refers to the distributed network environment where blockchain operates. The encryption algorithm is widely used in data protection and digital signature so as to identify the certain user.

The cloud service layer. As the core layer of proposed architecture, the cloud service layer is planned to optimize service matching and to form the service composition as reasonable as possible. The process begins with manufacturing task decomposition, followed by service matching in service pool to subtasks, ended by an optimal composition scheme evaluated by QoS attributes. In order to avoid the storage capacity issues of the blockchain, huge amounts of original data are stored in cloud databases.

The data resource layer. This layer is meant to collect data about services, such as resource description, manufacturing capabilities, providers, function of components and so on. Manufacturing services or idle ones are gathered in this layer.

2.2 System Process of Proposed Architecture

According to the proposed architecture of blockchain-based manufacturing service composition, this sector introduces the system workflow to present the operation process. As shown in Fig. 2. When users publish a task demand on the cloud platform, the system will respond immediately and search for the optimal service composition. After the task assignment is completed, the system will broadcast the result (encrypted or not) to the blockchain through network intermediary, attached by executable smart contract in digital form. The provider promptly gets the notification through the similar process. Once accepting the task, contact with the user will immediately be generated to further complete the requirement task. Otherwise, the system continues to look for the next service provider. In other words, with the confirmation of service provider, the cloud platform ensures the collaboration relationship among them and updates the signed connection to the blockchain, in case of breach of contract and other dishonest circumstances. In addition, if the user refuses to accept the result, the system will re-execute the above process and remove the previous scheme. All records or indexes are permanently stored on the blockchain, because all nodes on a distributed network share the same data. Shortly, cloud platform is responsible for acquiring credible variations from the blockchain network, and in turn hashes stored in blockchains can be used as data integrity and authenticity proof. This mode effectively protects the rights and interests of both demander and provider, reflecting the great potential of blockchain technology to solve the trust issues in the process of transaction and cooperation in manufacturing field.

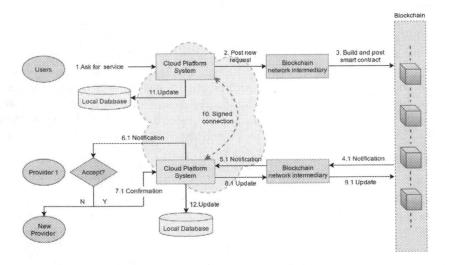

Fig. 2. System workflow of proposed blockchain-based architecture

3   Modeling of Manufacturing Service Composition

This section formulates a model to deal with the matching problem between tasks and services on the cloud platform. The evaluation criterion for the manufacturing service composition problem is based on comprehensive QoS attributes.

3.1   Problem Statement and QoS Attributes

Assuming that task demands received within a certain period of time arrive at the same time on the cloud platform, with uncertainty of its composition and type. The system combined these tasks into a batch and break them down in sequential order. The subtasks obtained by decomposing the task requirements of the system have corresponding service candidate sets in the cloud's resource pool. Concretely, K task requests arrive in a certain period of time, described as $TR = \{tr_1, tr_2,..., tr_K\}$. Each of them contains i_k subtasks, and $tr_K = \{str_k{}^1, str_k{}^2,..., str_k{}^{ik}\}$. When the system starts to process these task requests, it rearranges the subtasks into a new sequence of combination according to predefined logical rules, donated as $TR' = \{str_1, str_2,..., str_N\}$, where str_n represents the nth subtask of the new task sequence TR'. Let $SP = \{sp_1, sp_2,..., sp_M\}$ be the providers combination set corresponding to different subtasks that need to be satisfied, where sp_m refers to the mth service set which gives a bunch of service candidates for subtask str_m. The problem presents the service set $sp_m = \{sp_m{}^1, sp_m{}^2,..., sp_m{}^{Nj}\}$ to describe service candidates sets for the single subtask. Thus, the purpose of optimization is to find an expectedly satisfactory combination as $SP^* = \{sp_1{}^*, sp_2{}^*,..., sp_M{}^*\}$.

QoS attribute value is an ideal comprehensive criterion to evaluate the utility of a composition of manufacturing services, describing qualitative concept of the components in a quantitative way. Basic parameters of QoS attribute mainly include: cost, time, availability and reliability. Cost is the fee that users need to spend on material and execution, which is a pretty critical concern to make decisions. Time contains manufacturing period provided by suppliers and responding time determined by the system. Availability refers to whether the service is accessible to use when allocated a request. Reliability is reflected by failure rate, representing the ability to perform required functionality. This paper also take throughput into account which is the capability and operational efficiency of the system. Since this research combines blockchain technology with cloud platform to build a trusted collaborative system. In addition to the first five factors, number of defaults which implies the compliance records in smart contract is also considered to enhance the objectivity and integrity of the assessment.

As each QoS attributes is quantified into numeric property values, it is necessary to normalize them whose range vary greatly. We use Eq. (1) shown below for both positive and negative attributes. q and q' refer to the original and normalized values for continence which involve maximum and minimum QoS values.

$$q' = \begin{cases} \frac{q-q_{min}}{q_{max}-q_{min}}\left(q'_{max} - q'_{min}\right) + q'_{min} & \text{if } q \text{ is positive} \\ \frac{q_{max}-q}{q_{max}-q_{min}}\left(q'_{max} - q'_{min}\right) + q'_{min} & \text{if } q \text{ is negaitive} \\ 1 & \text{otherwise} \end{cases} \tag{1}$$

where $q_{max} \neq q_{min}$. In the formula, q'_{max} and q'_{min} represent the new maximum and minimum values after interval normalization respectively.

3.2 Expression of Manufacturing Service Composition Model

In order to acquire the optimal service composition and provider combination scheme to meet the needs from request tasks. There comes a comprehensive mathematical model based on the QoS attributes explained above shown as:

$$F(x) = \left\{\sum_{j=1}^{M} C(sp_j), \sum_{j=1}^{M} T(sp_j), \prod_{j=1}^{M} Ava(sp_j), Rel(sp_j)\right\} \tag{2}$$

$$s.t.(Thr(sp_j)) \geq Const\_Thr \qquad (3)$$

$$(Nod(sp_j)) \leq Const\_Nod \qquad (4)$$

Where *Const_Thr* and *Const_Nod* are predefined rated throughput and number of defaults, respectively. If number of defaults exceeds a certain amount, this provider will be of low credit and customers will refuse to accept service. To ensure the user experience, the system must be able to withstand a certain throughput to ensure normal operation. Aim to find an optimal solution from all feasible results, QoS attributes of cost and time need to be minimized and availability and reliability need to be maximized simultaneously. Herein, we use an aggregated function of the comprehensive utility expressed as follows:

$$f(sp_j) = \omega_1\left(q'_{max} - C(sp_j)\right) + \omega_2\left(q'_{max} - T(sp_j)\right) + \omega_3 Ava(sp_j) + \omega_4 Rel(sp_j) \quad (5)$$

In this equation, ω_1, ω_2, ω_3, ω_4 represent the weights of mentioned four QoS properties and $\sum \omega_i = 1$. We use this formula as objective function later to evaluate performance of service composition and further take its inverse as fitness value to do comparison among service candidates.

4   Algorithm and Simulation Experiment

The mathematical problem described in the previous section is a typical discrete optimization problem. Many existing evolutionary optimization algorithms can be used to solve it. Compared with other algorithms like particle swarm optimization (PSO), simulated annealing (SA) and so on, genetic algorithm has superior comprehensive performance in terms of convergence speed, global search and operationality. And the effectiveness of GA has been demonstrated in many previous studies. Therefore, GA is adopted in this paper to solve the service composition model, and a simulation experiment is designed to verify the effectiveness of the proposed system.

4.1   GA for the Proposed Composition Model

This research used real-coded method in genetic algorithm. For a manufacturing task request *TR'* that includes a sequence of *M* subtasks, we code the optional viable services corresponding to all subtasks as integers. One single individual or one chromosome stands for an alternative composition scheme *SP*. Each gene represents the selected service candidate for related subtask. Then, set the number of the population *NP* and generate the initial chromosomes. The fitness function of the *j*th chromosome is defined as Eq. (6).

$$fitness(sp_j) = f(sp_j) + f_{const}(sp_j) \qquad (6)$$

Herein, $f\left(\vec{sp_j}\right)$ is the aggregate objective function illustrated in detail in the previous section and $f_{const}\left(sp_j\right)$ is measurement of service sp_j's feasibility, defined as follows:

$$f_{const}\left(sp_j\right) = N_{\_const} * \sum_{j=1}^{M}\left(max\left(0, \frac{N\left(sp_j\right) - N_0}{N_0}\right)\right)$$
$$+ Thr\_const * \sum_{j=1}^{M}\left(max\left(0, \frac{Thr_0 - Thr\left(sp_j\right)}{Thr_0}\right)\right) \tag{7}$$

where $i = 1, 2, \ldots, \prod_{j=1}^{M} N_j$, N_const and $Thr\ const$ are two fairly large constants. Obviously, the fitness value is better when smaller. The goal of optimization is to select the chromosome with the smallest possible fitness function value.

4.2 Experimental Results and Analysis

Simulation experiment assumes that there are three users initiated demands on the cloud platform in a certain time range. In order to have an advantage in terms of overall system utility, treats it as a task sequence $TR = \{tr_1, tr_2, tr_3\}$. The tasks are decomposed depending on their characteristics as $\{\{tr_1^1, tr_1^2, tr_1^3\}, \{tr_2^1\}, \{tr_3^1, tr_3^2\}\}$ to form a new executed sequence TR', which includes six subtasks to be processed by services provided by suppliers. We present it in the form of $TR' = \{str_1, str_2, str_3, str_4, str_5, str_6\}$ that its subtasks correspond sequentially to each other. It is assumed that the candidate service pool corresponding to each subtask contains 10 service instances with different QoS attribute values. For the datasets of QoS attributes, cost and time are assigned in $[10^2, 10^3]$ respectively; availability and reliability are generated randomly between $[0.8, 1]$; number of defaults is set to be $[0, 60]$ and should be no more than 50 ineffective nodes; the flow size of throughput is between $[0, 10^2]$ and need to be larger than 2 Mbps. All these attribute values are located in the interval $[0, 1]$ after unified standardization. We design the weights of cost, time, availability and reliability are all 0.25. For the genetic algorithm, the parameters $Pc, Pm, Ps, NP, MAXGEN$ are set to be 0.8, 0.1, 0.9, 100, 100, respectively. Finally, we performed simulation experiments on the clarified manufacturing service composition scenario and obtain the convergence curve shown as Fig. 3. It converges quickly to a constant value after iteration and comes the optimal composition scheme (5, 9, 7, 5, 10, 8) with a minimum fitness value 1.7824. More specifically, $sp^* = \{sp_1^5, sp_2^9, sp_3^7, sp_4^5, sp_5^{10}, sp_6^8\}$ is the optimal blockchain-based manufacturing service composition scheme and the three task requirements should match the service $\{5, 9, 7\}, \{5\}, \{10, 8\}$ respectively. On the one hand, this optimization solution proves the validity of the algorithm in terms of computation time and results. A usable optimization result was obtained after an 18-step iteration. On the other hand, it also implies the usability of the proposed framework and system in the whole product lifecycle process of manufacturing enterprises.

In the proposed blockchain-based manufacturing service composition system, information about QoS attributes can be submitted by the service provider, or obtained through user feedback. The optimal composition scheme will then be formed after the service composition model which is calculated with GA. As illustrated in Sect. 2, once the service provider accepts the manufacturing task, a new block generated to record the cooperation information whose function could be defined by collaboration smart contract. Then the block will be published on the network, which is verified by the nodes and then broadcasted to the blockchain. At this point, the deal cannot be retracted or broken. After the completion of the manufacturing task, in the case that both customers and services providers fulfill their corresponding obligations, a new block containing the payment information with the functions defined by payment smart contract is created, which is also verified by the nodes and recorded on the blockchain. So far a complete transaction procedure ended, and system will update the QoS attribute information for the next evaluation.

The traditional information service system is based on the independent and centralized system provided by software operators. And the manufacturing information of products is difficult to integrate and share along the value chain. The Blockchain-based manufacturing service composition architecture proposed in this paper creates a new manufacturing paradigm based on blockchain technology. It can help users to carry out their own data sharing/service exchange in an open environment. Meanwhile, in order to protect the security of internal data of enterprises, the application of cryptography and the design of decentralized consensus mechanism effectively eliminate the concerns of enterprise users and solve the biggest trust barrier that limits the wide implementation of existing third-party information sharing systems. In addition, all peer-to-peer nodes in distributed network are consensus-oriented, and the mining mechanism allows more users with different roles to make contributions to the system and gain new value. In the real world scenario, the system proposed in this paper is especially suitable for the core enterprises that plays a leading role in industry. On the one hand, the huge scale of core enterprises makes their upstream and downstream industrial chains involved numerous and complex. Therefore, a manufacturing information service platform covering all types of users is urgently needed. On the other hand, core enterprises often have high requirements on the confidentiality of data information, which is the biggest obstacle for core enterprises to establish collaborative sharing system. Which is exactly what blockchain technology is inherently capable of solving this security issue.

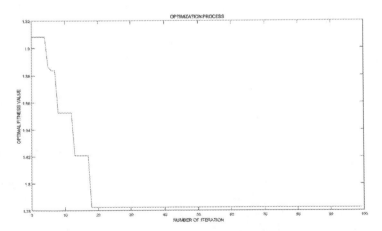

Fig. 3. Optimization process of composition model

5   Conclusion and Future Work

This paper proposed a system that combined cloud platform to work with blockchain technology, which not only preserve the unchanged transactions or events permanently, but also makes information accurately traceable. The introduced architecture makes full use of the advantages of cloud platform in resource allocation and gets rid of the centralized controller, which contributes advanced development to manufacturing industry in terms of fairness and credibility. In this way, the proposed method is quite useful for distrusting among enterprises and strength business synergy. Additionally, due to the mining process of blockchain itself and the verification mechanism based on consensus algorithm, the system not only can safeguard the interests of users, but also enables all nodes to obtain extra benefits. On the basis of the architecture, this research establishes a combinatorial optimization model of manufacturing services on cloud platform and tackles it by genetic evolutionary algorithm. Evaluation criteria are acquired from the QoS attributes, and the optimization results of the model will in turn update the QoS datasets recorded in the blockchain. Moreover, simulation experiment shows that the whole process of blockchain-based manufacturing service composition architecture is effective and owns enough ability to select optimal composite schemes to handle the task requests.

In future work, this kind of framework should be applied in more practical scenarios, where there will be more unexpected problems to be solved, e.g. the design of smart contracts and the agreement of consensus mechanism, etc. In the meantime, it is also necessary to develop more accurate models and algorithms to tackle service composition optimization problems in order to further improve its performance.

Acknowledgment. The research was supported by the National Key R&D Program of China (2018YFB1701400) and the Foundational Research Funds for the Central Universities under Grant 2019kfyXKJC043.

References

1. Hakimi, S.M., Hasankhani, A., Shafie-Khah, M., et al.: Blockchain technology in the future smart grids: a comprehensive review and frameworks. Int. J. Electr. Power Energy Syst. **129**, 106811 (2021). https://doi.org/10.1016/j.ijepes.2021.106811
2. Maesa, D., Mori, P.: Blockchain 3.0 applications survey. J. Parallel Distrib. Comput. **138**, 99–114 (2020)
3. Wang, Z., Wang, T., Hu, H., Gong, J., Ren, X., Xiao, Q.: Blockchain-based framework for improving supply chain traceability and information sharing in precast construction. Automat. Constr. **111**, 103063.1–103063.13 (2020). Blockchain for decentralized transactive energy management system in networked microgrids. Electr. J. (2019)
4. Yong, B., Shen, J., Liu, X., Li, F., Chen, H., Zhou, Q.: An intelligent blockchain-based system for safe vaccine supply and supervision. Int. J. Inf. Manage. **52** (2020)
5. Benil, T., Jasper, J.: Cloud based security on outsourcing using blockchain in E-health systems. Comput. Netw. **178** (2020). https://doi.org/10.1016/j.comnet.2020.107344
6. Wang, Y., Singgih, M., Wang, J., Rit, M.: Making sense of blockchain technology: how will it transform supply chains? Int. J. Prod. Econ. **211**, 221–236 (2019). https://doi.org/10.1016/j.ijpe.2019.02.002

7. Zhang, A., Zhong, R.Y., Farooque, M., Kang, K., Venkatesh, V.G.: Blockchain-based life cycle assessment: an implementation framework and system architecture. Resour. Conserv. Recycl. **152** (2020)
8. Liu, X.L., Wang, W.M., Guo, H., Barenji, A.V., Li, Z., Huang, G.Q.: Industrial blockchain based framework for product lifecycle management in industry 4.0. Robot. Comput.-Integr. Manufact. **63** (2020)
9. Zhang, Y., Zhang, L., Liu, Y., Luo, X.: Proof of service power: a blockchain consensus for cloud manufacturing. J. Manuf. Syst. **59**(1), 1–11 (2021)
10. Chen, F., Dou, R., Li, M., Wu, H.: A flexible QoS-aware web service composition method by multi-objective optimization in cloud manufacturing. Comput. Ind. Eng. **99**, 423–431 (2016). https://doi.org/10.1016/j.cie.2015.12.018
11. Zhang, W., Yang, Y., et al.: A new three-dimensional manufacturing service composition method under various structures using improved Flower Pollination Algorithm. Enterp. Inf. Syst.-UK **12**(5), 620–637 (2018)

An Approach for Creating a Blockchain Platform for Labeling and Tracing Wines and Spirits

Sotiris P. Gayialis(✉) ⓘ, Evripidis P. Kechagias ⓘ, Grigorios D. Konstantakopoulos ⓘ, Georgios A. Papadopoulos, and Ilias P. Tatsiopoulos

School of Mechanical Engineering, National Technical University of Athens, Iroon Polytechniou 9, 15780 Athens, Greece
sotga@central.ntua.gr, {eurikechagias,gkonpoulos, gpapado}@mail.ntua.gr, itat@centra.ntua.gr

Abstract. The traceability and labeling of products have been issues faced for decades in various industrial and commercial sectors. One of the most important product categories that require effective traceability and, at the same time, anti-counterfeit labeling are wines and spirits. The ineffective traceability of such products poses extremely serious risks both to the national economy and consumers' health. This paper aims to propose an approach for creating a blockchain traceability and labeling platform in order to ensure the origin, quality and authenticity of wines and spirits. The platform will combine a number of advanced technologies, namely blockchain, anti-counterfeit labels, and smart contracts and sensors, to offer effective traceability at all stages of the supply chain of wines and spirits. The paper starts by presenting the research's background and continues with analyzing the methodological approach for the development of the platform, its functionality, and the expected benefits from its implementation.

Keywords: Traceability · Supply chain 4.0 · Blockchain · Internet of Things · Labeling · Wines · Spirits · Research project

1 Introduction

The need for effective traceability in the food and beverage industry has greatly increased in recent years due to the growing consumer awareness for the safety and the quality of products they buy [1]. Traceability can be defined as the ability to track and detect the origin of a product during its production and distribution [2]. The loss of visibility as to the origin of a product can cause significant disruptions in the production and distribution of goods, but also poses serious risks for consumers. More specifically, products that endanger consumers' health may be produced and marketed when they can't be effectively traced at all stages. The same can happen when transporting products along the entire supply chain, either due to deviations from the intended transport conditions (e.g., temperature, humidity) or possibly due to product sabotage (replacing packaging

© IFIP International Federation for Information Processing 2021
Published by Springer Nature Switzerland AG 2021
A. Dolgui et al. (Eds.): APMS 2021, IFIP AICT 633, pp. 81–89, 2021.
https://doi.org/10.1007/978-3-030-85910-7_9

contents, forgery of labels, etc.). In addition to the negative effects on consumer health, adverse economic consequences may also arise for the producer, and his credibility may be damaged. Therefore, eventually, consumer confidence can be irreparably shaken [3].

According to the World Health Organization, 25–30% of wines and spirits consumed worldwide suffer from some form of deterioration each year. It is characteristic that between 2017 and 2019, 306 mass cases of beverage adulteration with methanol were recorded worldwide, resulting in 7,104 people becoming ill and 1,888 dying [4]. Such a case is stated by Europol, who reported that in March 2017, in Greece, the Economic Crime Unit of the Ministry of Finance discovered two illegal alcohol storage areas. All seized bottles were about to be transported illegally, mainly to Bulgaria, avoiding duties and taxes. Nearly 1,300 L of adulterated alcohol (vodka and whiskey) were seized, and five people were arrested [5, 6]. Similar illegal trading and adulterations of wines and spirits may occur with a variety of means. Such activities in the economy are enormous as non-effective traceability in the wines and spirits industry results in billions of euros and thousands of jobs being lost every year. In fact, according to the European Union Intellectual Property Office (EUIPO), in the EU, 2.3 billion euros are lost in direct sales each year due to the trading of counterfeit wines and spirits. In addition, 5,681 jobs are lost each year. Overall, however, taking into account the knock-on effect in other sectors, 5.2 billion euros and 31,858 jobs are lost each year [7].

On the other hand, through an effective traceability system, the producer can improve the production quality of his products and reduce or even eliminate the financial damage from the sale of products that do not meet the required specifications. At the same time, the produced products can be transported safely, and the consumer can be able to validate that the product he buys has not undergone any kind of alteration or counterfeiting [8]. Furthermore, an effective traceability system can allow products to be inspected, individually or in batches, so that they can be relatively easily isolated if safety or quality issues arise. Such a system also allows the quick identification of the source of a problem to be addressed immediately and be avoided in the future. Finally, an efficient traceability system provides strong transparency in the production and supply chain, allowing all info related to the supply chain of products to be located at any time [9].

The most common challenge faced when trying to trace products is the incomplete or non-functional labeling they have. The weakness of most labeling systems currently found on food and beverages lies not only in the lack of information on labels but also in their ease of counterfeiting [10]. Most of the labels contain basic information such as the product name, production/expiration dates, origin, and ingredients. In this way, a plethora of data concerning the production and distribution of the product cannot be not visible to consumers [11]. Over the years, various technologies have been applied to deal with these weaknesses of labels. Most of these applications, however, were limited to only creating technologically advanced and non-copyable labels (e.g., Barcodes, QR codes, RFID tags, NFC tags, Holograms, colorhift Inks, Embedded images, digital watermarks, invisible printing, watermarks, Chemical and biological tags, microtaggants), without addressing the problem of traceability holistically [12].

The novel aspect of this research is the holistic approach that is followed, combining both advanced technologies and non-copyable labels and integrating them into an effective traceability platform that will help secure the wine supply chain and lead to more efficient operations. In fact, the application of the blockchain technology in the supply chain is relatively new and only during the last three years research studies started to address related issues [1, 13–19]. As for the wine supply chain, that is the focus of our research, to the best of our knowledge, no such research attempt has been made combining the aforementioned advanced technologies and non-copyable labels into a single software solution.

2   Advanced Technologies for Effective Traceability

Advances in technology can enable companies to monitor, in real time, the conditions, the production, and the distribution of their products through smart sensors via the Internet of Things (IoT) [20]. These sensors are able to record and send events in a secure and inviolable way when aided by the blockchain technology. This technology, which has started to be widely used in many new industrial applications in recent years, can be combined with the technologically advanced labels as well as with smart sensors (location, humidity, temperature, vibration) and smart contracts (self-executing contracts with the terms of the agreement between buyers and sellers) in order to enable wide traceability in the supply chain of food and beverages from their production to their final disposal to consumers [21].

Blockchain can be essentially considered as a seamless distributed digital transaction data chain that is constantly authenticated with each new transaction that is added. This blockchain structure eliminates the possibility of data processing and alteration by third parties while providing data transparency and security for suppliers, distributors, and all counterparties in products' production and supply chain [19]. Blockchain allows the immediate detection of problems or deviations in relation to the specifications and enables the use of quick measures for reducing their impact. At the same time, by collecting information (transactions) from every step in the food and beverage and supply chain, blockchain can offer transparency and protection against the falsification of information on labels and the alteration of products.

Eventually, by combining all the aforementioned advanced technologies into a single functional platform, the consumer will be able to verify the origin and the quality of the goods he buys. Thus, he will be able to find whether the goods suffered any sabotage as well as the point at which it occurred [22]. All these technologies are part of the Industry 4.0 which is the ongoing trend for the automation of traditional manufacturing and industrial practices, using today's technological advances. Additionally, during the last few years, these technologies have started to gain increasing popularity in supply chain activities and have led to the formation of the Supply Chain 4.0. This next-generation supply chain uses advanced technologies such as the Internet of Things (IoT), Blockchain, Big Data Management, etc. in order to achieve more effective and efficient operations within the supply chain.

In the remainder of this paper, the conceptual approach for creating an advanced platform for labeling and traceability of wines and spirits will be presented. The platform will combine a number of advanced technologies, such as blockchain and advanced labels to offer effective traceability at all stages of the supply chain of wine and spirits. The research focuses on wines and spirits as their ineffective traceability poses extremely serious risks both to consumer health and the economy in general.

3   The Blockchain Platform

The need for a clear and safe wines and spirits supply chain led us to the formulation of an approach for creating a platform that enables the end consumer to detect all the information related to each individual wine or spirit he buys while also being able to validate that the product has no type of counterfeit. In other words, the platform will be able to provide reverse control to each counterparty from the producer to the final consumer, presenting all the authentic information related to the product and ensuring faster and safer transactions. Furthermore, the exchange of all information between the different counterparties throughout the supply chain will take place through blockchain technology without compromising privacy and security.

3.1   Platform's Methodology of Development

The methodology proposed to be followed includes two main phases. The first phase is to find and evaluate the requirements of the platform as well as the technologies and methods that will be implemented for the effective traceability of wines and spirits. The second phase concerns the development and testing of the platform in the wine and spirits industry's production and transport companies.

More specifically, during the first phase, wide research needs to be conducted focusing on the inefficient traceability of the wine and spirits supply chain. Advanced methods and technologies that will enable the labeling, identification, and monitoring of each individual bottle along the entire length of the supply chain will also be investigated. At the same time, the methods of integrating blockchain and IoT technologies for data management and sharing will be explored. Afterwards, real scenarios of production and distribution of wines and spirits will be examined, the followed procedures will be recorded, and they will be adapted according to internationally recognized standards. Next, the advanced methods and technologies that are most suitable for implementing the platform will be selected.

In the second phase, all the selected advanced methods and technologies will be integrated into the traceability platform. Finally, the platform will be offered as a BaaS (Blockchain as a Service) service and, before its commercial release, will be tested in production and transportation companies of wine and spirits. Essentially, through the conducted tests, it will be determined whether the platform offers an effective traceability service, while possible weaknesses and failures will be identified and corrected before the platform's final release to the market.

3.2   Platform's Functionality

The blockchain platform, as already stated, is aiming at the effective traceability of wines and spirits. Therefore, internationally recognized standards will be used to identify the products, record the locations, and share data. These standards are effective procedures followed in practice and will effectively manage all data on the platform. In fact, as these standards are universally accepted, they can be used in any kind of product traceability system.

More specifically, to achieve effective traceability, each wine or spirit that needs to be tracked will be recognized by unique codes, allowing access to all data related to its history, use, or location. In addition to identifying this info, the platform will also record all the critical events from the production to the final distribution of the product to consumers. The platform will be able to record all the events of the supply chain of wine and spirits regardless of their origin and the possible inhomogeneities of the entities that will send the events (Fig. 1). In addition, all required codes will be recorded on state-of-the-art labels that cannot be reused, counterfeited, or copied. The blockchain database will contain data shared between the cooperating entities (e.g., producers, distributors, resellers) and data on transactions and verify the authenticity, origin, and possible loss of product quality (Fig. 2). In this way, at any time and in a completely safe way, the products will be able to be checked without making the information available for copying or counterfeit to third parties.

The use of smart non-copyable labels and smart sensors is a significant advancement as they will communicate with the platform sending necessary data (e.g., location, temperature, time, shock or validation). Therefore, there is a need for measurements to ensure that the labels and the smart sensors will not be fiddled. Furthermore, as already mentioned, the platform will operate in the blockchain network, which provides increased security against fraudulent attempts. For this reason, advanced blockchain tools and protocols will be implemented into the system, and each stakeholder will have a set of public and private keys. The data will be inserted into the platform only with the combination of the above keys and will be validated each time a change is made. Therefore, third parties aiming to fiddle the data sent to the system will have no access to perform such activities.

Despite the fact that advanced technologies will be implemented for the effective traceability of products, the platform's interface will be user-friendly both for the stakeholders and the end-customers, requiring basic knowledge of web usage and no advanced programming skills. The stakeholders will feed the platform with their data requiring no knowledge of the blockchain technology. Furthermore, the platform will automatically execute the smart contracts and validate the aforementioned data. Finally, the end-customer will only scan the product's advanced label to view and validate the authenticity, quality, and origin of the products, requiring no registration and personal data provision.

3.3 Expected Benefits from the System's Implementation

When successfully developed and implemented in real-life cases, the blockchain platform can offer a plethora of benefits. First of all, it will strengthen the competitiveness, extroversion, and productivity of all parties involved in the wine and spirits supply chain. Additionally, it will contribute effectively to reducing economic losses and protecting the jobs in Greece and consequently the European Union due to inefficient traceability of food and beverages. The platform may also enhance the efficiency of food and beverage companies, as any deviation from the specifications will be detected directly by the system, and parties will be able to take faster corrective actions.

Moreover, the platform could also serve as a reference point for creating similar software solutions for product traceability. Therefore, through the successful combination of today's technological advances, the platform could be extended and proven to be useful

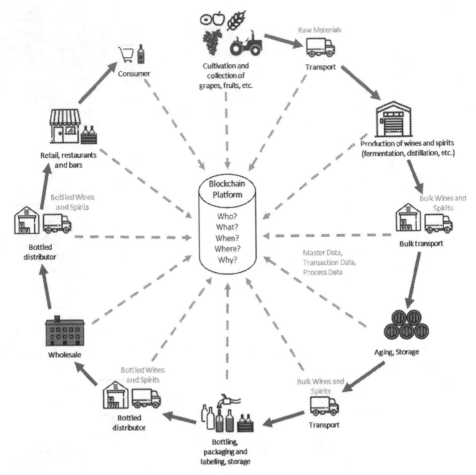

Fig. 1. Blockchain traceability platform's data collection

in all supply chain activities. In this way, all parties of the supply chain will be able to work more efficiently, and the consumer will be able to check the origin, quality, and authenticity of each product he buys. This will ultimately increase the participants' trust in the supply chain, proving the products' origins and providing secure supply chain data management.

Who	What	When	Where	Why
Cultivator	Grape Varieties, Quantities	Harvest Completion Date	Vineyard	Grape Production
Carrier	Vehicles, Boxes of Grapes, Quantities	Boxes Receipt & Delivery Dates	Vineyard - Winery	Transport to Winery
Wine Producer	Wine Varieties, Wine Containers, Lots, Quantities	Wine Production Completion Date	Winery	Wine Production
Carrier	Vehicles, Wine Containers, Lots, Quantities	Container Receipt & Delivery Dates	Winery - Cellar	Transport to Cellar
Ageing Cellar	Barrels, Wine Varieties, Lots, Quantities	Ageing Start & End Dates	Cellar	Aging, Storage
Carrier	Aged Wine Barrels, Lots, Quantities	Barrel Receipt & Delivery Dates	Cellar-Bottler	Transport to a Bottle
Bottler	Bottles, Wine Varieties, Lots, Quantities	Bottling Date	Bottler	Bottling, Packaging, Marking, Storage
Carrier	Boxes with Bottles, Quantities	Boxes Receipt & Delivery Dates	Bottler - Wholesale Warehouse	Transport to Wholesaler
Wholesaler	Boxes with Bottles, Quantities, Orders	Ordering, Receiving & Sending Boxes Dates	Wholesale Warehouse	Retail sale
Carrier	Boxes with Bottles, Quantities	Boxes Receipt & Delivery Dates	Wholesale Warehouse - Retail Stores	Transport to Retail Stores
Retailer	Bottles, Quantities, Orders	Order, Receipt & Shipping of Bottles Dates	Retail Stores or Other Points of Sale	Sale to Consumers
Consumer	Bottles	Bottle Purchase Date	Anywhere	Check of Origin, Quality, Authenticity

Fig. 2. Data received from wines and spirits supply chain

4 Conclusions

This paper presented an approach for creating a blockchain-based platform for labeling and tracing wines and spirits. The research focused on this specific industry as, according to statistics, it belongs to the five industries with the largest loss of sales due to adulteration and counterfeit and doesn't only cause huge financial losses but also poses very serious risks to the health of consumers. However, the proposed platform can strongly contribute to the creation of a visible and safe wines and spirits supply chain making use of today's state of the art technologies such as blockchain, IoT, and advanced labels.

The key advantages offered by the platform include the protection against data counterfeiting, reduction of production and distribution costs, transparency, holistic control, and finally, the guarantee of authenticity and quality of each individual product. The platform will operate in a decentralized manner and allow the secure sharing of data since it will be offered through the BaaS (Blockchain as a Service) model. In this way, parties involved in the wine and spirits supply chain will have no need for back-end users who need advanced computer skills and powerful servers and avoid expensive setup and maintenance costs.

As it becomes clear, the benefits for society will be significant. In fact, the more stakeholders decide to participate in this effort, the more transparent and safer will the traceability platform become. More specifically, the production, the distribution companies, and the retailers will have the ability to immediately be alerted about any deviations from the planned supply chain operations and take proper actions on time. Finally, the end-customers will have the ability to validate the authenticity, the quality, and the origin of the products they buy.

Having concluded the first step of this research, which focused on the conceptualization of the blockchain labeling and traceability platform, the next phase will concern research methods for integrating blockchain and IoT technologies in the platform. This next step of our research is essential as it will include the requirements analysis and the specification of the advanced technological solutions that will be integrated into the platform.

Acknowledgments. The present work is co-funded by the European Union and Greek national funds through the Operational Program "Competitiveness, Entrepreneurship and Innovation" (EPAnEK), under the call "RESEARCH - CREATE – INNOVATE" (project code: T2EDK - 00508 and Acronym: COUNTERBLOCK).

References

1. Behnke, K., Janssen, M.F.W.H.A.: Boundary conditions for traceability in food supply chains using blockchain technology. Int. J. Inf. Manage. **52**(1), 101969 (2020)
2. Olsen, P., Borit, M.: How to define traceability. Trends Food Sci. Technol. **29**(2), 142–150 (2013)
3. Ene, C.: The relevance of traceability in the food chain. Ekon. Poljoprivrede **60**(2), 287–297 (2013)
4. Systech: What's All the Buzz About Counterfeit Wine and Spirits?. https://blog.systechone.com/blog/whats-all-the-buzz-about-counterfeit-wine-and-spirits. Accessed 21 Feb 2021
5. Europol: EUR 230 Million Worth of Fake Food and Beverages Seized in Global Opson Operation Targeting Food Fraud. https://www.europol.europa.eu/newsroom/news/eur-230-million-worth-of-fake-food-and-beverages-seized-in-global-opson-operation-targeting-food-fraud. Accessed 22 Feb 2021
6. Soon, J.M., Manning, L.: Developing anti-counterfeiting measures: the role of smart packaging. Food Res. Int. **123**(1), 135–143 (2019)

7. EUIPO: 2020 Status Report on IPR Infringement: Why IP Rights are Important, IPR Infringement, and the Fight Against Counterfeiting and Piracy. https://euipo.europa.eu/ohimportal/web/observatory/status-reports-on-ip-infringement. Accessed 22 Feb 2021
8. Chhikara, N., Jaglan, S., Sindhu, N., Anshid, V., Charan, M.V.S., Panghal, A.: Importance of traceability in food supply chain for brand protection and food safety systems implementation. Ann. Biol. **34**(2), 111–118 (2018)
9. Freitas, J., Vaz-Pires, P., Câmara, J.S.: From aquaculture production to consumption: freshness, safety, traceability and authentication, the four pillars of quality. Aquaculture **518**(1), 734857 (2020)
10. Tessitore, S., Iraldo, F., Apicella, A., Tarabella, A.: The link between food traceability and food labels in the perception of young consumers in Italy. J. Food Syst. Dyn. **11**(5), 425–440 (2020)
11. Ingrassia, M., Bacarella, S., Columba, P., Altamore, L., Chironi, S.: Traceability and labelling of food products from the consumer perspective. Chem. Eng. Trans. **58**(1), 865–870 (2017)
12. Yu, M.-D. (Mandel), Devadas, S.: Pervasive, dynamic authentication of physical items. Commun. ACM **60**(4), 32–39 (2017)
13. Wamba, S.F., Queiroz, M.M.: Blockchain in the operations and supply chain management: benefits, challenges and future research opportunities. Int. J. Inf. Manage. **52**(1), 102064 (2020)
14. Rodríguez Bolívar, M.P., Scholl, H.J., Pomeshchikov, R.: Stakeholders' perspectives on benefits and challenges in blockchain regulatory frameworks. In: Reddick, C.G., Rodríguez-Bolívar, M.P., Scholl, H.J. (eds.) Blockchain and the Public Sector. PAIT, vol. 36, pp. 1–18. Springer, Cham (2021). https://doi.org/10.1007/978-3-030-55746-1_1
15. Guerpinar, T., Harre, S., Henke, M., Saleh, F.: Blockchain technology - integration in supply chain processes. In: Kersten, W., Blecker, T., Ringle. C.M. (eds.) Proceedings of the Hamburg International Conference of Logistics, HICL, Hamburg, vol. 29, pp. 153–185. ECONSTOR (2020)
16. Dolgui, A., Ivanov, D., Potryasaev, S., Sokolov, B., Ivanova, M., Werner, F.: Blockchain-oriented dynamic modelling of smart contract design and execution in the supply chain. Int. J. Prod. Res. **58**(7), 2184–2199 (2020)
17. Pournader, M., Shi, Y., Seuring, S., Koh, S.C.L.: Blockchain applications in supply chains, transport and logistics: a systematic review of the literature. Int. J. Prod. Res. **58**(7), 2063–2081 (2020)
18. Bumblauskas, D., Mann, A., Dugan, B., Rittmer, J.: A blockchain use case in food distribution: do you know where your food has been? Int. J. Inf. Manage. **52**(1), 102008 (2020)
19. Saberi, S., Kouhizadeh, M., Sarkis, J., Shen, L.: Blockchain technology and its relationships to sustainable supply chain management. Int. J. Prod. Res. **57**(7), 2117–2135 (2019)
20. Kan, C., Yang, H., Kumara, S.: Parallel computing and network analytics for fast Industrial Internet-of-Things (IIoT) machine information processing and condition monitoring. J. Manuf. Syst. **46**(1), 282–293 (2018)
21. Zhao, Y., Cao, N.: Research on traceability of agricultural products based on Internet of Things. In: 2017 IEEE International Conference on Computational Science and Engineering (CSE) and IEEE International Conference on Embedded and Ubiquitous Computing (EUC) Proceedings, Guangzhou, China, pp. 414–417. IEEE (2017)
22. Sander, F., Semeijn, J., Mahr, D.: The acceptance of blockchain technology in meat traceability and transparency. Br. Food J. **120**(9), 2066–2079 (2018)

Blockchain Design for Digital Supply Chain Integration

Kari Korpela[1], Petr Novotny[2], Alevtina Dubovitskay[3], Tomi Dahlberg[4],
Mika Lammi[1], and Jukka Hallikas[5(✉)]

[1] DBE Core, Helsinki, Finland
{kari.korpela,mika.lammi}@dbecore.com
[2] IBM T.J. Watson Research Center, Ossining, USA
P.Novotny@ibm.com
[3] Lucerne University of Applied Sciences and Arts, Luzern, Switzerland
alevtina.dubovitskaya@hslu.ch
[4] University of Turku, Turku, Finland
tkmdah@utu.fi
[5] LUT University, Lappeenranta, Finland
jukka.hallikas@lut.fi

Abstract. The supply-chain process involves multiple actors and intermediary companies that need to coordinate but often lack interoperability and do not fully trust each other. Supply-chain digitalization, including the use of cloud services and domain-specific standards, enables significant improvements in efficiency throughout the entire process. We conduct a case study by collecting and analyzing data from a large business consortium represented by experts in the fields of industry, logistics, banking, and information and communications technology (ICT). Based on the case study's outcomes, we propose the architecture of a blockchain-based system for use in a practical intermodal logistics project and discuss future research directions regarding it.

Keywords: Digitalization · Supply chains · Blockchain · Integration

1 Introduction

Supply-chain process involves multiple actors and intermediary companies that need to sequentially interact with each other. With the objective of maximizing customer value and providing a profit for each supply chain member, stakeholders form heterogeneous network, interconnected with financial, information, and product/service flows [1]. Heterogeneity of the supply network incurs the following challenges that have been extensively discussed from different perspectives in literature [2]. Digitalization aims at addressing the technical challenges to make an and-to-end supply-chain process efficient, fast, and compliant. The business processes and data models are thus company specific and not interoperable with the systems in the other companies. While it is possible to deploy intra-organizational system integrations through ERP systems, e.g., by

© IFIP International Federation for Information Processing 2021
Published by Springer Nature Switzerland AG 2021
A. Dolgui et al. (Eds.): APMS 2021, IFIP AICT 633, pp. 90–98, 2021.
https://doi.org/10.1007/978-3-030-85910-7_10

SAP and Oracle [3], it is extremely challenging to achieve end-to-end information integration through supply networks and the complex interrelationships among multiple organizations.

Emerging blockchain technology has the potential to drastically change the environment in which inter-organizational processes operate by offering a way to execute processes in a trustworthy manner even in a network without any mutual trust between nodes [4]. To date, several research studies have already indicated that blockchain technology can enable secure decentralized transactions between the actors in the supply network [5–7]. This paper adopts qualitative research to investigate applicability of blockchain technology in heterogeneous supply networks.

2 Blockchain Technology and Its Application to Supply Chain Processes

Blockchains are a type of distributed ledger technology (DLT). Blockchain platforms such as Bitcoin [8], Ethereum [9], Hyperledger [10, 11], and others enable secure, decentralized transactions between various parties without the involvement of intermediaries or third parties. Blockchains integrate several methods of trusted and reliable record-keeping, such as timestamping of transactions, smart contracts, and the storage of transactions in an immutable distributed ledger. A blockchain network [5] consists of a set of independent peers (e.g., software agents), which together form the blockchain network. The peer architecture provides a high degree of resiliency, allowing the blockchain network to operate even if some of the peers become unavailable or corrupted (for example from malicious attacks or faults). Each blockchain peer maintains a copy of an immutable ledger. The ledger consists of a series of ordered and timestamped transactions organized into cryptographically connected blocks. This cryptographic connection allows for verification that the ledger was not tampered with and that none of the transactions were modified since being recorded.

The transactions are generated by a smart contract, which is a business-logic component (such as a software code) that is agreed upon by the participants of the blockchain network. An identical copy of the smart contract is hosted by each peer of the blockchain network. When a client submits a request for a transaction into the network, the peers invoke the smart contract and calculate the transaction. Smart contracting code is software written in a programming language. The code acts as a software agent, or as the delegate of the party that employed it, with the intention of fulfilling certain obligations or exercising certain rights. The code may take control of assets within a distributed ledger in an automated way. Thus, the code takes on tasks and responsibilities in the distributed ledger realm by executing code that models or emulates the contract logic of the real world, although the legal justification for this may be unclear [12]. Permissioned blockchains, such as Hyperledger Fabric or Corda, are in contrast, designed as closed-access networks of distributed peers. In such blockchains, identities of the users and the rights to participate in the consensus (right to write to the ledger and/or validate the transactions) are controlled by a membership service. Figure 1 shows general architecture of permissioned blockchain technology with an example of Hyperledger Fabric.

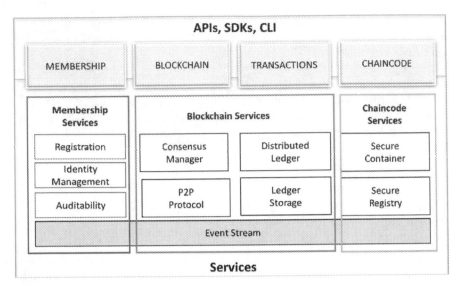

Fig. 1. General architecture of permissioned blockchain, Hyperledger Fabric example.

Similarly to permissionless blockchains, trust and immutability are established by combining a smart contract with a configurable consensus protocol, as well as by the redundancy of the network nodes the stakeholders operate. Unlike in permissionless blockchains, the consensus protocol is custom defined, reflecting the needs of the specific types of transactions involved and of the network itself. From an operational point of view, one important advantage of permissioned blockchains is the high performance available from the optimized software and hardware used for such blockchains [13], which provide several-magnitude faster processing of transactions than is possible with permissionless blockchains.

The use of blockchains in the DSC in most cases requires private blockchain technologies, since one requirement is that the identity of the transacting parties must be known. The transactions recorded into the ledger contain the identities of those who have submitted the transactions into the ledger as well as those who have validated and endorsed those transactions. This type of information serves as a retrospective audit trail and allows further development of various analytical and operational solutions—such as "know your customer" (KYC) and anti-money laundering (AML) processes for financial transactions—as well as various types of audit and compliance solutions [14]. To conduct DSC transaction and document exchange using blockchains, parties must first agree on how this will be done, which is where smart contracts enter the picture [15]. Smart contracts are extremely flexible and can be used to automate DSC transactions at a very detailed level.

Abeyratne and Monfared [1] note several key technological advantages of Blockchain relevant to the supply-chain processes, such as durability, transparency, immutability and process integrity. There exist also several conceptual designs aiming to address the question "Whether blockchains have a disruptive effect on supply chains". These works are based on case-studies conducted either in the specific domain: such as a manufacturing supply chain for cardboard boxes [1], alimentary supply-chain [17], or in supply-chain in general [12, 13], and attempt to draw a map of further research. An empirical investigation of the main drivers of Blockchain adoption and related challenges were recently conducted [11]. The authors claim that despite some existing findings and the potential of digitalization and use of blockchain technology to promote changes in all types of supply chains in terms of new operation models, the literature about blockchain technology in the SCM field is in its infancy. Sternberg and Baruffaldi [13] also report the lack of successful supply chain implementations can pave the way for doubt about the disruptive role of this technology in supply chains. Therefore, research questions related to the applicability of the blockchain technology remain open and of a high interested to the research community.

3   Blockchain-Based Architecture for an Intermodal Logistics Project

In this section, based on the results of the case study and the summary of the related works (cf. Sect. 3), we present an architecture of a blockchain-based framework for an intermodal logistics project. Prior to this, we first describe the use-case scenario and provide detailed description of Hyperledger Fabric – the blockchain technology implementation – that will be employed in the architecture presented. Our goal is to conduct a proof of concept (POC) evaluation of the usefulness of blockchain in the framework of the specific practical example of the two railway transportation corridors that link Scandinavian exporters to their Central and Southern European customers via the Baltic republics. We aim to develop an open-source solution to be offered to all stakeholders to investigate user experiences and benefits. More specifically, we will investigate how the improved visibility of supply chain information, enabled by blockchain technology, influences each stakeholder company and how the blockchain technology as a whole impact the logistics operations in these two railway transportation corridors. The ultimate objective is to reduce cargo end-to-end transit times.

3.1 Use Case Scenario

In cross-border logistics, the main problems are currently the large proportion of manual work necessary to execute business transactions as well as the lack of communication and information sharing between logistics companies, especially in upstream supply chains. The cornerstones of the logistics industry are transferring cargo units between locations and knowing where each cargo unit is at any given time during transportation. Cargo units can only be transferred as efficiently as the underlying infrastructure allows. Information about logistics transactions is now delivered mostly manually, which makes logistics operations expensive, time consuming, and error-prone. To study a possibility to implement permissioned blockchain technology in logistics business operations, we have chosen as a use case scenario of the intermodal logistics with the following stakeholders: supplier companies that export their products, transportation companies, customers, and value-adding service providers. Figure 2 illustrates the concept of blockchain integration of the intermodal logistics project, which aims to solve these problems.

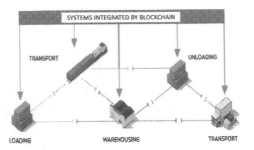

Fig. 2. Multi-modal logistic operations.

Logistics operations use several communication channels and technologies, such as phone calls, text messages, structured and unstructured emails, fax messages, and diverse information systems (IS). Electronic Data Interchange (EDI) messaging is still popular, although company-specific implementations lead to significant integration costs and slowness. Each company purchases and installs its own IS for use in logistics operations. This creates data interoperability challenges with regard to cross-organizational data transfer. In sum, all the necessary logistics information is stored in company-specific ISs, but the lack of data interoperability prevents automated data transfers and integration between companies. We apply blockchain technology for DSC integrations in the environment of multiple stakeholders and various ISs of the logistics companies. In the next section, we present the detailed description of the Hyperledger Fabric - open-source blockchain implementation.

3.2 Hyperledger Fabric Description

Architecture. Within Fabric, nodes are differentiated depending on whether they are clients, peers, or orderers. A client acts on behalf of an end-user and creates transactions, which is also called invoking. Clients communicate with both peers and orderers. Peers maintain the ledger and receive ordered update messages from customers to commit new transactions to the ledger. Endorsers are a special type of peer. Their task is to endorse a transaction by checking whether the transaction fulfills the necessary and sufficient conditions, that is, the five provisions required by the signatures. Ordering service provides a communication channel to clients and peers over which messages containing transactions can be broadcast. During consensus creation in particular, the channels ensures that all connected peers deliver exactly the same messages in exactly the same logical order [10]. Figure 3 shows the communication between the components of Hyperledger Fabric.

Consensus mechanism. Fabric's understanding of consensus is broad and encompasses the entire transaction flow, that is, from proposing a transaction to the network to adding a new transaction block to the ledger. Different nodes assume different roles and tasks in the process of reaching consensus. It is generally known that faults may occur in the delivery of messages when many mutually untrusted orderers are employed. This necessitates the use of a consensus algorithm to reach consensus despite potential

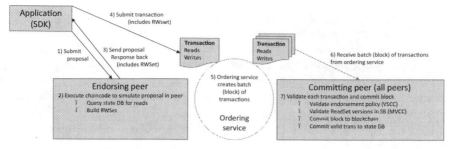

Fig. 3. Hyperledger Fabric communication diagram.

faults, such as the inconsistency of message order. This solution makes the replication of the distributed ledger fault tolerant. Fabric employs a "pluggable" algorithm. This means that various algorithms can be used depending on the application-specific requirements. For example, Byzantine fault-tolerant (BFT) algorithms could be used to deal with random or malicious replication faults. In Fabric, it is an orderer, (which can be implemented as a node, or a cluster of nodes) that participates in the consensus and runs the communication service that implements a delivery guarantee, such as atomic or total order broadcast. This is done by verification and ordering of the transactions. During the verification phase, digital signature of the issuer of the transaction is verified, as well as so-called endorsement policy. Endorsement policy is defined for a chaincode and is used to instruct a peer on how to decide whether a transaction is valid. An example of such a policy can be defined as a requirement that all the peers in the network have to validate (and therefore sign) the transaction. Then the orderer, during the verification, must ensure that the transaction is indeed signed by all the peers, and that the signatures are valid [21].

3.3 SmartLog - Proposed Blockchain-Based Platform for DSC Integration

In this project, we have adopted the latest available (at the moment of the project start) version of Hyperledger Fabric, 1.0, that contains all the necessary components to establish the blockchain environment in the framework of our use case. We used the open-source UBL 2.1 standard to design logistics business processes and business transaction integrations. The aim was to establish full visibility of logistics transactions for all stakeholders in the supply chain. By doing so, we also developed a platform for future Internet of Things (IoT) integrations, with the aim of increasing the data content of logistics data delivered between stakeholders.

The participating companies wanted to obtain real-time information on container locations and automate the business transactions between intra- and inter-organizational ISs. The most important functionality of the blockchain environment is providing an open distributed ledger, which efficiently records transactions between parties in a verifiable and permanent way. Smart contracting components are made up of programmed business rules that automatically trigger transactions.

Verification of the actual movements along the railway corridors is provided via a simple device (a sensor) attached to containers. Access to such real-time sensor data serves several purposes: participating companies are able to analyze and develop their operations and resource management and optimize their route planning. Blockchain technology offers significantly improved visibility and potential for process automation in the investigated case context. The solution presented here is under constant testing and evaluation. The developed solution is highly scalable. When transaction volumes start to grow (exponentially), the processing load can be allocated among the stakeholders so that allocated resources correspond with added value. The creation of a blockchain environment with a large number of participating companies encourages follow-up projects.

The deployment of these technologies makes it possible to deliver the SmartLog platform to practically any infrastructure; it also allows codebases to be maintained with significantly more efficiency than in environment-specific infrastructure compilation and conversion models. Implementation of the blockchain in the logistics context can be beneficial for all the supply chain stakeholders, including suppliers, logistic operators, end customers, and IT service providers.

For the suppliers (manufacturers and exporting companies) the expected benefits are the following:

- Increased information visibility of the supply chain, beginning from the factory gate.
- Increased information visibility of the supply chain enables precise control over manufacturing processes and timely invoicing (accuracy).
- Enhanced off-site inventory management and control.
- The expected benefits for the transportation companies and other logistics operators:
- Both direct and indirect business value is created.
- Full visibility of upstream supply chain operations enables planning and execution of just-in-time logistics instead of tying resources to non-productive events and capacity.
- Automation of manual data entry and decision-making processes, resulting in cost savings.
  The expected benefits for the end customers, buyers:
- Improved inventory control creates business value.
- In retail, increased efficiency and accuracy of annual planning.
- In production, increased efficiency and accuracy of production management and process planning.
  The expected benefits for the IT service providers:
- Enhanced business opportunities resulting from the ability to aggregate information flows and to perform and offer predictive analytics
- All stakeholders have the potential to automate data-dependent processes, thus achieving cost savings.

4   Conclusions and Discussion

Digital supply chains (DSCs) involve the integration of business processes and data regarding products, services, finance, and information flows. The development of intra-organizational system integration is often conducted in global development environments, such as business ecosystems, and digital platforms are used to accelerate development and systems interoperability.

Although several advocates of blockchain technology have emphasized its capability to preclude the use of trusted third-party intermediaries, such avoidance may not be necessary in the digital supply chain integration scenario. By using a business-process model integrated in a smart contract [16], the seller and buyer can mandate a trusted intermediary to "supervise" the execution and flow of transactions, similar to how financial services currently operate. As part of their smart contract and secure transactions, the parties may even agree that a trusted third party will receive one or more security keys necessary to perform its role. In general, blockchains have enabled secure decentralized transactions between parties without the involvement of non–value-adding intermediaries or third parties.

Permissioned blockchain technology (such as Hyperledger Fabric) is developing rapidly and offers automated data exchange within DSCs as a new integration platform. The design of the blockchain system that this project proposes to use for DSC integration promises an integration platform that is cost-effective and flexible. In addition, new services, such as trade finance, can be established based on these trusted transactions.

The business managers participating in this project generated plenty of ideas for integration supported by blockchain technology. They viewed the permissioned blockchain ledger, smart contracting, and consensus elements as the most valuable pieces of functionality. However, transactions need to be standardized. Combining a permissioned blockchain with standardized transactions has the potential to disrupt ecosystem integration and the security of end-to-end interoperability. Public and private cloud integration combined with blockchain integration yield a cost-effective many-to-many integration model.

As pointed out, the literature about blockchain technology in the supply chain management (SCM) field is in its infancy [13]. We advanced it by designing proof of concept (POC) for a blockchain-based platform for DCS integration and by analyzing the potential benefits of such a system for all supply-chain stakeholders, including suppliers, logistics operators, end customers, and IT service providers. Because there are few examples of successful blockchain implementations, the presented SmartLog platform case study adds knowledge to the literature about the potential of this technology to disrupt supply chains. Future research could evaluate cloud applications that can accelerate and simplify DSC integration and examine the advantages and disadvantages for supply chains of various blockchain designs.

References

1. Abeyratne, S.A., Monfared, R.P.: Blockchain ready manufacturing supply chain using distributed ledger. Int. J. Res. Eng. Technol. **5**(9), 1–10 (2016)
2. Androulaki, E., et al.: Hyperledger fabric: a distributed operating system for permissioned blockchains. In: Proceedings of the Thirteenth EuroSys Conference, Porto Portugal, ACM (2018)
3. Brown, R.G.: Introducing r3 corda: a distributed ledger for financial services. R3 (2016)
4. Buterin, V.: A next-generation smart contract and decentralized application platform. White Paper (2014)
5. Di Ciccio, C., et al.: Blockchain-based traceability of inter-organisational business processes. In: Shishkov, B. (ed.) BMSD 2018. LNBIP, vol. 319, pp. 56–68. Springer, Cham (2018). https://doi.org/10.1007/978-3-319-94214-8_4

6. Francisco, K., Swanson, D.: The supply chain has no clothes: technology adoption of blockchain for supply chain transparency. Logistics **2**(1), 2 (2018)
7. Gaur, N., Desrosiers, L., Ramakrishna, V., Novotny, P., Baset, S., O'Dowd, A.: Hands-on Blockchain with Hyperledger: Building Decentralized Applications with Hyperledger Fabric and Composer. Packt Publishing, Birmingham (2018)
8. Hyperledger: Hyperledger Fabric. https://www.hyperledger.org/projects/fabric. Accessed 10 Apr 2021
9. Mendling, J., et al.: Blockchains for business process management-challenges and opportunities. ACM Trans. Manag. Inf. Syst. **9**(1), 4 (2018)
10. Nakamoto, S.: Bitcoin: a peer-to-peer electronic cash system. Decentralized Bus. Rev. 21260 (2008)
11. Queiroz, M.M., Telles, R., Bonilla, S.H.: Blockchain and supply chain management integration: a systematic review of the literature. Supply Chain Manag. Int. J. (2019)
12. Queiroz, M.M., Wamba, S.F.: Blockchain adoption challenges in supply chain: an empirical investigation of the main drivers in India and the USA. Int. J. Inf. Manage. **46**, 70–82 (2019)
13. Sternberg, H., Baruffaldi, G.: Chains in chains–logic and challenges of blockchains in supply chains. In: Proceedings of the 51st Annual Hawaii International Conference on System Sciences, Hawaii, pp. 3936–3943 (2018)
14. Swanson, T.: Consensus-as-a-service: a brief report on the emergence of permissioned, distributed ledger systems. Report (2015)
15. Tapscott, D., Tapscott, A.: Blockchain Revolution: How the Technology Behind Bitcoin is Changing Money, Business, and the World. Penguin (2016)
16. Xu, X., et al.: The blockchain as a software connector. In: Proceedings of the 13th Working IEEE/IFIP Conference on Software Architecture (WICSA), Venice, Italy (2016)
17. Casado-Vara, R., Prieto, J., De la Prieta, F., Corchado, J.M.: How blockchain improves the supply chain: case study alimentary supply chain. Procedia Comput. Sci. **34**, 393–398 (2018)

Data-Based Services as Key Enablers for Smart Products, Manufacturing and Assembly

Customer Order Scheduling in an Additive Manufacturing Environment

Benedikt Zipfel[✉], Janis S. Neufeld, and Udo Buscher

Chair of Business Management, esp. Industrial Management, TU Dresden,
01069 Dresden, Germany
{benedikt.zipfel,janis_sebastian.neufeld,udo.buscher}@tu-dresden.de

Abstract. This paper investigates the customer order scheduling problem on unrelated parallel additive manufacturing machines. The discussed problem comprises the splitting of orders into jobs, the allocation of those jobs to builds and finally the sequencing of builds on 3D printers. A mixed-integer programming model is presented that integrates practical requirements, such as printing profiles and different materials, and minimises total weighted tardiness. Using the GUROBI solver computational results are then given for a comprehensive test bed. It is shown, that medium sized problems can be solved using the proposed model, and that the consideration of printing profiles has a relevant impact on the scheduling task in additive manufacturing.

Keywords: Additive manufacturing · Customer order scheduling · Unrelated parallel machines

1 Introduction and Related Work

Technologies of additive manufacturing (AM) have become the foundation of new on-demand services, such as Factory-as-a-Service and Production-as-a-Service [4]. In the presence of growing amounts of heterogeneous products, that have to be produced in AM facilities, efficient planning and operations management for AM are essential. Due to the customer orientation of the newly emerged on-demand services, we propose a model for customer order scheduling in AM, where multiple types of 3D printers are available. Jobs can be manufactured with different printing profiles, which have an effect on the speed and quality of the production process. This extension to existing scheduling problems for AM is also derived from the customer oriented perspective of additive manufacturing offering a wide palette of materials and various quality levels to their customers. At the same time, it leads to incompatibilities since not all products can be manufactured together. Hence, the main contribution of this paper is the integration of customer orientation into the scheduling problem for AM taking into account new variability regarding materials and quality. To the best of our knowledge,

Published by Springer Nature Switzerland AG 2021
A. Dolgui et al. (Eds.): APMS 2021, IFIP AICT 633, pp. 101–109, 2021.
https://doi.org/10.1007/978-3-030-85910-7_11

this problem configuration has not been addressed before. Due to their leading role in industrial applications of metallic AM, we focus on the technologies selective laser melting (SLM) and direct metal laser sintering (DMLS) [3].

The considered problem combines several aspects of scheduling. Firstly, it comprises the issue of scheduling customer orders, where optimisation objectives shift from a job focus to an order focus. While [1] introduce the problem for a single machine configuration with different job families, [5] recently study order scheduling with the objective to minimise the total weighted completion times of orders for a parallel machine configuration. Secondly, as 3D printers are able to process several products at the same time, the problem can be classified as a batch processing machine scheduling problem (for relevant studies see, e.g. [6,8]). Finally, a growing amount of recent publications can be found focusing on the problems of nesting and scheduling in AM. In [2] three models are presented dealing with the problem of scheduling for AM in single, identical and non-identical parallel machines environments. [7] introduce a model formulation with two objectives of minimising makespan as well as total tardiness and introduce predefined material types. With our model we will expand the perspective of scheduling for AM by combining the stated aspects addressed by previous research, extending the scope by printing profiles and proposing an integrated model formulation.

The remainder of this paper is organized as follows. In Sect. 2 we define the problem and present a mixed-integer programming (MIP) model. Section 3 describes a computational study with 60 randomly generated instances, while Sect. 4 concludes with prospects of future research.

2   Problem Formulation

Before describing the problem, let us give a brief explanation of the examined context. An additive manufacturing company is offering an on-demand 3D printing service to its customers. To process the ordered products, the manufacturer's facility is equipped with several different SLM/DMLS printers. Each product must be made from a specific material $w \in W$ and can be produced in different levels of quality. According to the requested quality a printing profile $d \in D$ must be applied to available 3D printers. Each printer $k \in M$ has a restricted production height, production area and is capable of processing an individual subset of all possible materials. Let a customer order $i \in I$ consist of a subset of products in the manufacturers portfolio with defined quantities, materials, and the desired quality levels.

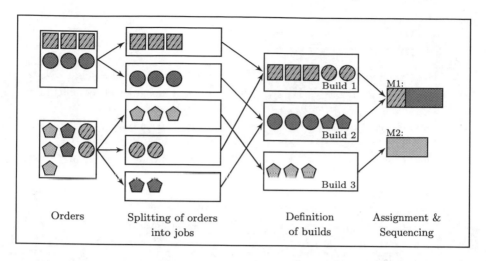

Fig. 1. Schematic description of the optimisation problem

In this context, the considered problem is illustrated in Fig. 1 by an example with two orders. Herein, the shapes indicate different types of products, while the fill colors of the products symbolize the materials. The existence of patterns on the products implies different quality levels, and hence, the need of different printing profiles. An order i can be split into several jobs $j \in J_i$, each of which consists of a defined quantity of products with identical product type, quality level, and material requirement. The described splitting is represented in the second stage of Fig. 1. The objective is to assign all resulting jobs to builds with respect to material and quality similarity, while the splitting of jobs into different builds is allowed. Furthermore, the builds have to be allocated and sequenced on the available printers according to the machine specifications with the objective of minimising the total weighted tardiness of all orders, $\sum_i w_i T_i$. These sub problems are illustrated with the third and fourth stage of Fig. 1.

Due to the focus on SLM/DMLS technology, we allow products only to be placed on the build plate of a printer, i.e., stacking of products within the three-dimensional build space is prohibited. To ensure a valid nesting of products into builds, projections including tolerances are used for the production area of a product type [2]. The notations used for the model are as follows (Table 1):

Table 1. Notation

Sets			
B	Set of builds	S^{J}	Set of incompatible jobs
D	Set of profiles	S^{M}	Set of incompatible combinations of jobs and machines
D_j	Set of profiles of a job j	S^{MW}	Set of incompatible combinations of machines and materials
I	Set of orders	S^{W}	Set of incompatible combinations of jobs and materials
J	Set of jobs	S^{D}	Set of incompatible combinations of jobs and profiles
J_i	Set of jobs of an order i	W	Set of materials
M	Set of machines		

Parameters			
a_j	Production area of the product type of job j	H_k	Maximum production height of machine k
h_j	Height of the product type of job j	HT_{kd}	Processing time for one height unit by machine k with profile d
v_j	Volume of the product type of job j	RT_k	Removal time of processed build on machine k
d_i	Due date of order i	ST_k	Setup time on machine k without changing materials
q_j	Amount of products of job j	ST_k^w	Setup time on machine k with changing materials
w_i	Penalty costs for delay of one time unit of order i	VT_{kd}	Processing time to build one volume unit by machine k with profile d
A_k	Maximum production area of machine k	γ_{bvcw}	Binary matrix to indicate, if setup between build b with material v and build c with material w is necessary
G	Big Number		

Variables			
p_{bk}	Processing time of build b on machine k	CB_{bk}	Completion time of build b on machine k
x_{jbk}	Amount of items of job j in build b on machine k	CI_i	Completion time of order i
y_{bkwd}	1, if build b is scheduled on machine k with material w and profile d, 0 otherwise	HB_{bkd}	Production height of build b on machine k with profile d
z_{jbk}	1, if items of job j are processed in build b on machine k, 0 otherwise	T_i	Tardiness of order i

The studied problem can be classified as an unrelated parallel machine scheduling and nesting problem with batching and incompatible job families. The objective is to minimise the total weighted tardiness of all orders. Inspired by existing models from [2] and [7] we formulate the described problem as a MIP model.

$$\sum_{i \in I} w_i \cdot T_i \to \min \tag{1}$$

s.t.:

$$T_i \geq CI_i - d_i \qquad\qquad \forall i \in I \tag{2}$$

$$CI_i \geq CB_{bk} - G \cdot (1 - z_{jbk}) \qquad \forall i \in I, j \in J_i, \tag{3}$$
$$b \in B, k \in M$$

$$\sum_{b \in B} \sum_{k \in M} x_{jbk} = q_j \qquad\qquad \forall j \in J \tag{4}$$

$$x_{jbk} \leq q_j \cdot z_{jbk} \qquad\qquad \forall j \in J, b \in B, k \in M \tag{5}$$

$$x_{jbk} \geq z_{jbk} \qquad\qquad \forall j \in J, b \in B, k \in M \tag{6}$$

$$\sum_{j \in J}(a_j \cdot x_{jbk}) \leq A_k \qquad\qquad \forall b \in B, k \in M \tag{7}$$

$$z_{jbk} \cdot h_j \leq HB_{bkd} \qquad\qquad \forall j \in J, d \in D_j, \tag{8}$$
$$b \in B, k \in M$$

$$HB_{bkd} \leq H_k \qquad\qquad \forall d \in D, b \in B, \tag{9}$$
$$k \in M$$

$$\sum_{j \in J} z_{jb+1,k} \leq G \cdot \sum_{j \in J} z_{jbk} \qquad \forall b \in B \mid b < |B|, k \in M \tag{10}$$

$$z_{jbk} + z_{lbk} \leq 1 \qquad\qquad \forall (j,l) \in S^{\mathrm{J}} \mid j < l, \tag{11}$$
$$b \in B, k \in M$$

$$z_{jbk} = 0 \qquad\qquad \forall (j,k) \in S^{\mathrm{M}}, b \in B \tag{12}$$

$$\sum_{w \in W} \sum_{d \in D} y_{bkwd} \leq 1 \qquad\qquad \forall b \in B, k \in M \tag{13}$$

$$z_{jbk} \leq y_{bkwd} \qquad\qquad \forall b \in B, d \in D, j \in J, \tag{14}$$
$$k \in M, w \in W,$$
$$(w,j) \notin S^{\mathrm{W}}, (d,j) \notin S^{\mathrm{D}}$$

$$y_{bkwd} \leq 1 \qquad\qquad \forall b \in B, d \in D, k \in M, \tag{15}$$
$$w \in W, (w,k) \notin S^{\mathrm{MW}}$$

$$CB_{bk} \geq \sum_{w \in W} \sum_{d \in D} y_{bkwd} \cdot ST_k^w + p_{bk} \qquad \forall b \in B, k \in M \tag{16}$$

$$CB_{bk} \geq CB_{b-1,k} + p_{bk} + ST_k^w \cdot \gamma_{b-1,vbw} \qquad \forall b \in B \mid b > 0, k \in M, \tag{17}$$
$$+ ST_k \cdot (1 - \gamma_{b-1,vbw}) \qquad\qquad w, v \in W, d, e \in D$$
$$- G \cdot (2 - y_{b-1,kvd} - y_{bkwe})$$

$$p_{bk} = \sum_{d \in D} (HB_{bkd} \cdot HT_{kd})$$

$$+ \sum_{j \in J} \sum_{d \in D_j} (x_{jbk} \cdot v_j \cdot VT_{kd}) + RT_k \qquad \forall b \in B, k \in M \qquad (18)$$

$$x_{jbk} \in \mathbb{N}_0, y_{bkwd} \in \{0,1\}, z_{jbk} \in \{0,1\} \qquad \forall j \in J, b \in B, k \in M, \qquad (19)$$
$$w \in W, d \in D$$

On the basis of a customer oriented scheduling, we consider (1) as the objective function minimising the total weighted tardiness of all orders. (2) computes the tardiness of an order by subtracting the due date from the completion time of the order. By introducing (3) the completion time of an order i is at least equal to the completion time of a build b on machine k if the specific build processes jobs of the respective order. Constraints (4) ensure that the requested order quantity of each job is produced within all scheduled builds. (5) and (6) connect the binary variable z_{jbk} with its integer equivalent x_{jbk}. Furthermore, we adopt the machine restrictions introduced by [2] and adjust them for our purpose in (7), (8) and (9). (7) ensures that the builds fit into the production area of the available printers, while (8) and (9) guarantee that the height of the build does not exceed the maximum production height of the machine. Note that we are not considering a constraint to check for a feasible production volume since the production area of a product is considered as a rectangular projection of the product onto the printing platform as in [2]. With (10) we verify that the builds are filled incrementally one after another. To avoid incompatible job combinations in builds we use (11). The equation allows only one of the jobs j and l to be in a build b on machine k if the tuple (j,l) is in the set S^J. Constraints (12) apply the same logic to incompatible combinations of jobs and machines. With Eq. (13) we specify that a build b on machine k can only be processed using one material w and only one printing profile d. Constraints (14) define the relation between decision variables z_{jbk} and y_{bkwd} using sets of incompatibility. We denote with (15) that a build b on machine k can only be manufactured if the machine is capable of processing the required material w, i.e., the tuple (w,k) is not in the incompatibility set. Inequalities (16) guarantee that the completion time of a build on a certain machine is greater than or equal to the sum of the setup time for a new material and its processing time. For a batch which has at least one predecessor (17) ensures that the completion time is greater than or equal to the sum of the completion time of the predecessor, its own processing time and a required setup time. The latter depends on whether there is a material change between two consecutive builds or not. This is controlled by a binary matrix γ_{bvcw} indicating if a setup with material change is necessary. In addition, we define the processing time of a build as the sum of the time needed to print the height of the build, the printing time for the volume of a build and the time to remove the build from the machine in (18). Finally, (19) defines the ranges of the decision variables.

3   Computational Study

The proposed model has been implemented with GUROBI using the provided PYTHON API. The study has been conducted on an Intel(R) Xenon(R) CPU E5-2630 v2 with 2.6 GHz clock speed and 384 GB RAM. For solving the model the maximum number of threads was set to four and a time limit of 1800 s was chosen. Table 2 describes the structure of the test instances. Six configurations are defined to study the impact of variations concerning materials and profiles as well as the impact of growing problem size. For the first three configurations $config1$ to $config3$ we set the number of available materials and printing profiles to three and two, respectively. For $config4$ to $config6$ these values are increased to five materials and three profiles. For both categories, we choose different numbers of investigated orders, machines and product types. Based on the data set P62 from [2], which provides information for 46 different product types and three unrelated machines, for each test instance the respective number of product types and machines is randomly picked. For each order the number of different products is set between one and 60% of the total number of product types, while the quantities for each product within an order are randomly chosen between one and five. The resulting average number of jobs and products for each configuration that have to be assigned to builds are also displayed in Table 2. As can be seen from this summary the defined structure yields in a test design reaching from small to reasonable problem sizes, i.e., on average from 15.9 products ($config1$) up to 76.0 products ($config6$) and a maximum of five parallel machines. These instances can represent practical scheduling tasks of small on-demand 3D printing service providers.

Table 2. Design of problem instances

	$config1$	$config2$	$config3$	$config4$	$config5$	$config6$
Total instances	10	10	10	10	10	10
Total orders $|I|$	3	5	7	3	5	7
Total machines $|M|$	2	3	5	2	3	5
Total product types	5	7	10	5	7	10
Total profiles $|D|$	2	2	2	3	3	3
Total materials $|W|$	3	3	3	5	5	5
Average total jobs	5.7	15.4	22.4	6.6	14.8	25.2
Average total products	15.9	45.2	66.8	18.3	42.2	76.0

A major factor influencing the computational performance of the proposed model is the upper bound of possible builds $|B|$. As noted by [2], the value must be high enough to ensure that better feasible solutions will not be cut off. In contrast, a large value for $|B|$ results in a much longer computation time. To overcome this issue, instead of setting $|B| = \sum_{j \in J} q_j$, we compute the minimum number of builds to fit in all ordered products by solving a simple bin packing problem in preprocessing. We then use this result as a basis for our tests by iteratively solving the problem instance and increasing $|B|$ until no better solution can be found. This method gradually increases the slackness of the model allowing more builds to be empty.

Table 3. Results of the computational study

	$\varnothing|B|$	# opt. sol.	$\varnothing$ MIPGap (%)	$\varnothing$ Runtime (s)
$config1$	3.6	10/10	0.0	3.6
$config2$	7.6	5/10	38.6	904.1
$config2_{opt}$[a]	6.0	5/10	0.0	8.2
$config3$	10.9	2/10	35.3	1446.0
$config3_{opt}$[a]	9.0	2/10	0.0	30.0
$config4$	4.7	10/10	0.0	0.5
$config5$	8.6	4/10	44.4	1190.1
$config5_{opt}$[a]	7.0	4/10	0.0	275.3
$config6$	9.1	2/10	53.5	1569.9
$config6_{opt}$[a]	7.5	2/10	0.0	649.2

[a] Average values only for instances from those configurations that have been solved to optimality.

The results of the computational study are illustrated in Table 3. The first column of the table shows the average number of builds on each available machine for the optimal (or best found) solution, while the second one denotes the number of instances solved to optimality. The third and fourth column outline the average values of each configuration for MIP gap and runtime of the solver, respectively. All instances of $config1$ and $config4$ can be solved to optimality, while the optimum solution can be found only for about half of the instances with intermediate problem size ($config2$ and $config5$). In each of $config3$ and $config6$ only two instances can be solved to optimality. Instances of reasonable size with up to 27 jobs and 88 products could be solved to optimality. However, quite high MIP gaps exist for instances, where no optimal solution was found within the time limit. This indicates that the solution is highly dependent on the specific characteristics of the considered test problem. With these results, the presented model can already provide helpful decision support for small 3D printing manufacturers. However, for larger real-world problems a heuristic approach would be necessary to ensure high-quality solutions.

Furthermore, the results show a growing computational effort with the increase of variability in material and printing profile options. The gaps to the known lower bounds as well as the runtime of the solver are reasonable lower in $config2$ and $config3$ (low number of printing profiles and materials) in comparison with $config5$ and $config6$ (higher number of printing profiles and materials).

This shows that the integration of the practical requirements of printing profiles and materials is relevant for the scheduling in AM.

4   Conclusion

This paper extended the research on scheduling for AM by combining the premises of order scheduling with the existing model formulations with the aim of minimising total weighted tardiness of customer orders. The problem has been considered in an unrelated parallel machine environment, formulated as MIP model and explored in an computational study with various characteristics. The numerical results in this paper demonstrate the complexity and difficulty of customer order scheduling in an AM environment and the relevance of considering printing profiles and materials in the scheduling. For small to medium problem instances the MIP model can be used by companies to generate optimal schedules. The findings for larger problems demonstrate the need of heuristic algorithms to solve such problem instances efficiently. Apart from this, the proposed model can be adjusted to integrate product geometries by extending the nesting of products from a one dimensional packing problem to a more precise procedure evaluating two or even three dimensions of the products.

References

1. Gupta, J.N., Ho, J.C., van der Veen, J.A.: Single machine hierarchical scheduling with customer orders and multiple job classes. Ann. Oper. Res. **70**, 127–143 (1997). https://doi.org/10.1023/A:1018913902852
2. Kucukkoc, I.: MILP models to minimise makespan in additive manufacturing machine scheduling problems. Comput. Oper. Res. **105**, 58–67 (2019). https://doi.org/10.1016/j.cor.2019.01.006
3. Li, Q., Kucukkoc, I., Zhang, D.Z.: Production planning in additive manufacturing and 3D printing. Comput. Oper. Res. **83**, 157–172 (2017). https://doi.org/10.1016/j.cor.2017.01.013
4. Oh, Y., Witherell, P., Lu, Y., Sprock, T.: Nesting and scheduling problems for additive manufacturing: a taxonomy and review. Addit. Manuf. **36**, 101492 (2020). https://doi.org/10.1016/j.addma.2020.101492
5. Shi, Z., Wang, L., Liu, P., Shi, L.: Minimizing completion time for order scheduling: formulation and heuristic algorithm. IEEE Trans. Autom. Sci. Eng. **14**(4), 1558–1569 (2017). https://doi.org/10.1109/TASE.2015.2456131
6. Shi, Z., Huang, Z., Shi, L.: Customer order scheduling on batch processing machines with incompatible job families. Int. J. Prod. Res. **56**(1–2), 795–808 (2018). https://doi.org/10.1080/00207543.2017.1401247
7. Tavakkoli-Moghaddam, R., Shirazian, S., Vahedi-Nouri, B.: A bi-objective scheduling model for additive manufacturing with multiple materials and sequence-dependent setup time. In: Lalic, B., Majstorovic, V., Marjanovic, U., von Cieminski, G., Romero, D. (eds.) APMS 2020. IAICT, vol. 592, pp. 451–459. Springer, Cham (2020). https://doi.org/10.1007/978-3-030-57997-5_52
8. Zhang, C., Shi, Z., Huang, Z., Wu, Y., Shi, L.: Flow shop scheduling with a batch processor and limited buffer. Int. J. Prod. Res. **55**(11), 3217–3233 (2017). https://doi.org/10.1080/00207543.2016.1268730

A Conceptual Reference Model for Smart Factory Production Data

Giulia Boniotti[1], Paola Cocca[2](✉) ⓘD, Filippo Marciano[2] ⓘD, Alessandro Marini[1] ⓘD,
Elena Stefana[2] ⓘD, and Federico Vernuccio[2]

[1] Quantra S.r.l., BS 25068 Sarezzo, Italy
[2] University of Brescia, 25123 Brescia, BS, Italy
`paola.cocca@unibs.it`

Abstract. As a consequence of the fourth industrial revolution, the data produced by companies' day-by-day activities and the rate at which the transactions occur are growing exponentially. In order to extract business value from those data, they need to be organised under a reference conceptual model facilitating data analysis and decision making. Since no sound reference model for organising digital factory production data has been proposed in the literature, this paper aims at developing and testing a conceptual multidimensional model to support a broad range of data analytics activities for the management and optimisation of production in a smart factory. The testing of the model in a case study company of the printing sector provides insights into the applicability of the model and the connected benefits.

Keywords: Industry 4.0 · Big data · Multi-dimensional modelling · Analytics

1 Introduction

The fourth industrial revolution is fostering the adoption of technological innovations to enhance production processes through the integration of multiple automation, control, and information technologies [1]. As a consequence, the data produced by companies' day-by-day activities and the rate at which the transactions occur are growing exponentially [2]. On one side, this creates the opportunity to shift today's manufacturing paradigm to smart manufacturing [3]. Smart manufacturing (also known as intelligent manufacturing) is a fully integrated, collaborative manufacturing system that responds in real time to meet changing conditions in the factory and in the supply network, and customer needs using advanced information and manufacturing technologies [4, 5]. On the other side, the massive volume of data creates unprecedented challenges in data collection, storage, processing, and analysis [1]. In order to extract business value from those data, they need to be organised under a global unified schema that facilitates data analysis and supports decision making [6]. This reference schema should offer an integrated view of all data sources [7].

The concept of multidimensional data modelling originates from the information system domain [7]. In a data model, the axes are called "dimensions" and represent

© IFIP International Federation for Information Processing 2021
Published by Springer Nature Switzerland AG 2021
A. Dolgui et al. (Eds.): APMS 2021, IFIP AICT 633, pp. 110–118, 2021.
https://doi.org/10.1007/978-3-030-85910-7_12

the different ways of analysing the data [7]. Each dimension corresponds to a business perspective under which facts can be fruitfully analysed and could be organised in a hierarchy of levels [8]. Although a variety of multidimensional data models have recently been proposed by both academic and industrial communities, a consensus on formalism or even a common terminology has not yet emerged [8]. In the information system domain, data models have been primarily intended to support the design of a data warehouse in an implementation-independent way, but based on the needs of the specific context. However, to assure flexibility and re-usability, a model should be specified on a conceptual level, i.e. representing information in an abstract and company-independent way [7, 8].

Despite the importance of the topic, no sound reference firm-independent model for organising and analysing the massive volume of production-related data generated and collected in a smart factory has been proposed in the literature. To overcome this gap, this paper aims at developing and testing a conceptual multidimensional model to support a broad range of data analytics activities for the management and optimisation of production in a smart factory. The model is not developed adopting an information system perspective and does not conform to technical formalisms, because it is not intended to directly support data warehouse design. Neither it is intended to develop an ontology, since the focus is not on knowledge representation or semantic data integration [9]. Rather it is qualitative in nature, because it adopts a managerial point of view and aims at facilitating performance assessment and decision making by plant, process, and production managers.

The remainder of the paper is organised as follows. Section 2 describes the methodology adopted. Section 3 presents the proposed conceptual multidimensional model. An implementation case study is presented and discussed in Sect. 4. Conclusions and possible developments of the present research are outlined in the last section.

2   Methodology

The model has been developed on the basis of literature review and experts' opinions.

The literature review had the objective to identify the types of production-related data generated, collected, and elaborated in a smart factory. First, Web of Science, ScienceDirect, Scopus, and Emerald have been selected as the electronic databases of scientific publications most relevant for the topic under investigation. Then, relevant keywords, e.g. "smart factory data", "industry 4.0 data", "digital factory data", have been used to interrogate those databases. Finally, relevant papers have been analysed to identify possible data dimensions to include in the initial version of the model.

The initial model was then evaluated and improved iteratively based on two expert user review sessions. The experts were a group of 30 people, being entrepreneurs, managers, researchers, or consultants, who were involved in a research project on the topic of factory digitalisation. During the first session the initial model was presented and experts were asked for critical analysis and improvement suggestions. After the first session the improvements identified were introduced, and during the second session the refined model was presented to the experts. Some additional inputs were collected that led to the final version of the model.

The applicability of the conceptual model was then tested in a case study company. Two of the authors of this paper acted as consultants supporting the company over a six-month period in the implementation of the model, specifically with the aim to change the currently adopted cost accounting approach.

3   The Conceptual Model

The multidimensional model proposed in this paper is shown in Fig. 1.

The model comprises of five axes, namely: production, plant hierarchy, process, context, and resources. Each axis is a dimension, i.e. a business perspective under which factory data could be organised and analysed.

In the following a description of each dimension is provided:

- *Production* dimension gathers those data dealing with production management that are usually stored in the Enterprise Resource Planning system (ERP) (e.g. production orders, bills of materials, production cycles, hourly output, production batches) or provided by other manufacturing information systems (e.g. Manufacturing Execution System (MES), Customer Relationship Management (CRM), Supply Chain Management (SCM), and Product Data Management (PDM)). ERP systems still represent the central core of enterprise systems and are considered the backbone for the Industry 4.0 [10, 11].
- *Process* dimension identifies the process data collected by Industrial Internet of Things (IIoT) technologies, which are related to a machine/component functioning state (e.g. real-time performance, operating conditions, rotation speed of a rotor) or specific data detected by sensors monitoring a production process (e.g. pressure, temperature) [3].
- *Plant hierarchy* dimension represents the different hierarchical levels of a factory, adapted from the Reference Architecture Model for Industrie 4.0 (RAMI4.0) [12, 13]: component, station, machinery, work centre, plant. They correspond to the different levels at which factory data could be aggregated. This dimension collects data also on the maintenance history of production equipment (e.g. anomalies, breakdowns, malfunctions, and their causes, occurring to each of the components at the various hierarchical levels in the factory).
- *Context* dimension gathers data related to the external conditions in which machinery operates: environmental conditions in terms of, for example, air temperature, relative humidity, and pressure; and the more general context conditions, for example the personnel on duty in the plant (e.g. in terms of skills, training). Indeed, there is evidence in the literature regarding the relevance of environmental [14–16] and general [17–19] conditions in influencing production. This calls for inclusion of this dimension in the conceptual model.
- *Resources* dimension collects data related to the consumption of resources during production, both in terms of utilities (e.g. electrical energy, methane gas, water) and materials. Indeed, resource consumption monitoring is interesting both from a sustainability point of view, and because the identification of production abnormities can be often anticipated by anomalous material and energy consumption patterns [3, 20, 21].

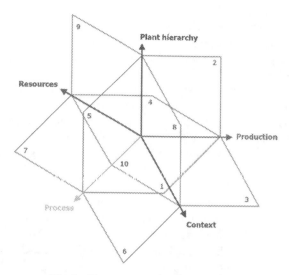

Fig. 1. The conceptual reference model

Two or more axes identify multidimensional spaces interesting for data analysis and performance assessment. Bidimensional spaces (plans) are shown in Fig. 1. Some examples of significant analyses suggested by each plan are described in the following:

1. *Impact of the process on production.* The plan enables analysing the direct impact that process data (e.g. temperature and pressure) have on process compliance, with reference to given production data (e.g. production order, hourly output); this plan can be used, for example, to identify which changes in process conditions have led to the production of a non-conforming batch, or a reduction in production rates.
2. *Impact of the state of production equipment on production.* This plan makes it possible to track the product during the production cycle, with reference to the machinery involved in the various stages of processing, and link all machinery-related events (e.g. anomalies, breakdowns, malfunction) to production orders and all other production-related data.
3. *Impact of context on production.* The plan analyses the direct impact that context data (e.g. environmental conditions, personnel) have on production, with reference to given production data (e.g. production order, hourly output); this plan can be used, for example, to analyse which changes in context conditions have led to the production of a non-conforming batch, or a reduction in production rates.
4. *Resource consumption by production.* This plan enables analysing the specific consumption of different type of resources (e.g. utilities and materials) by each production item (e.g. single product, batch, production order).
5. *Impact of the state of the production equipment on process.* This plan makes it possible to link all the events related to machinery (e.g. anomalies, breakdowns, malfunction) to production process parameters. For example, it allows analysing possible correlations between changes in process parameters and equipment faults in order to implement predictive maintenances approaches.

114   G. Boniotti et al.

6. *Impact of context on process.* This plan enables monitoring the quality of production processes in relation to the personnel involved and environmental conditions; it can be useful for detecting, for example, the role of personnel in determining variations in the process.

7. *Impact of process on resource consumption.* This plan makes it possible to associate resource consumption levels to production process parameters. For example, by cross-referencing energy consumption data with data related to production process, it is possible to carry out effective energy monitoring, which is the basis for energy management, i.e. the management and optimisation of energy consumption.

8. *Impact of context on the state of production equipment.* This plan makes it possible to link all the events related to machinery (e.g. anomalies, breakdowns, malfunction) to context parameters. For example, it allows analysing possible correlations between changes in context parameters and equipment faults in order to implement predictive maintenances approaches.

9. *Resource consumption hierarchy.* This plan allows to make each level of the factory accountable for its resource consumption.

10. *Impact of context on resource consumption.* This plan makes it possible link resource consumption levels to context parameters. For example, it enables analysing the energy impact of ensuring certain operating conditions, particularly in environmental terms.

In order to complement the analyses described above with an economic quantification, an additional axis related to the economic-financial dimension, called *Cost* axis, can be introduced. In this way, five further plans are identified, as shown in Fig. 2:

11. *Production cost.* The plan analyses the costs of production items such as products, production orders, batches.

12. *Process cost.* This plan analyses the cost of each activity carried out to complete the production process.

13. *Cost of plant equipment.* This plan analyses machinery rate, i.e. it includes the cost for machinery ownership (e.g. depreciation) and the operating costs (e.g. fuel, lubrication, maintenance). The costs could be aggregated at different hierarchical levels (e.g. work centre, plant).

14. *Context cost.* This plan analyses the value attributed to the environmental factors affecting the production, and the labour cost.

15. *Cost of resources.* This plan analyses the cost of materials and utilities.

More than two axes identify further multidimensional spaces interesting for data analysis and performance assessment. As an example, the axes Process, Cost, and Resources create a space that makes it possible to analyse the influence of certain process parameters (e.g. processing pressures and temperatures) on the final resource cost of the factory. This allows a precise calculation of the resource costs as a function of process parameters.

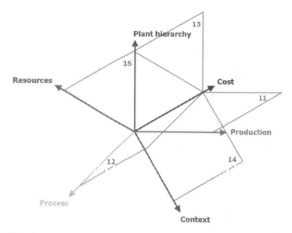

Fig. 2. The conceptual reference model with the cost axis

4 The Case Study

The conceptual model presented in the previous section has been tested in a case study company. The company is an Italian small enterprise operating in the printing sector. The most important piece of equipment in the factory is a Heidelberg printing machine, which is equipped with advanced functionalities that allow the real time collection of data related to operators, jobs, production parameters (e.g. speed, time, energy consumption), productivity, and quality of products. In addition, it is interconnected with the company's information system, allowing the integration of all the data collected by the machine with other information coming from the other interconnected elements of the company.

So far, the production cost used for defining the price, and thus determining the profit margin of the product, was a rough standard cost. It was estimated once a year based on standard values of energy consumption by each work centre and allocation of all the other costs based on the forecasts of total annual operating hours of each centre. Therefore, the company was uncertain about the goodness of such standard cost and needed more reliable cost figures to be able to modulate the price offered based on the strategic importance of each customer or order.

In order to support the organisation of the huge amount of data available and the selection of those data needed to improve cost accounting, and specifically the calculation of the actual hourly production cost, the multidimensional model proposed by this paper was used. The data available were first classified according to the six dimensions of the model. Then, two multidimensional spaces relevant for the analysis have been selected.

The first space is defined by the Cost, Resources, Process, and Production axes. This allows calculating the real time energy consumption for each production order, and thus its specific contribution to the total energy cost. In addition, it allows analysing the relationship between process parameters and energy consumption, thus enabling the optimisation of process parameters for each type of product in order to minimise the consumption.

A second space of analysis is provided by the axes Cost, Context, and Production. Within this space it is possible to integrate information about the influence that different operators and environmental conditions have on the printing process, monitoring the working time, the production speed, the quantity of pieces produced for each production order and their quality. This makes it possible to calculate the performance of operators and to allocate costs based on contextual factors.

All these analyses enabled the calculation of the actual cost of production of a specific product under specific process and context conditions. For example, with reference to one of the most relevant products of the company, it emerged that, based on the actual price, the profit margin determined by the standard costs was 25%, while taking into consideration the actual average product cost, the margin was 37%. The availability of a more accurate product cost enables more informed decisions during the tendering stage. Indeed, the company now knows the maximum reduction of price that still allows covering production cost and could decide for significant discounts in order to win a specific order or to get a new customer.

The company was extremely satisfied of this result. They reported that the multidimensional model has been effective in helping with classification of the huge amount of data available into dimensions, thus transforming raw data into useful information. In addition, the model suggested relevant perspectives for the analysis of those data that have provided new insights into cost accounting.

5   Conclusions

A conceptual reference model for organising and analysing the "big data" related to production available in a smart factory has been proposed in this paper. The testing of the model in a case study company of the printing sector has provided insights on the applicability of the model in real contexts and on the connected benefits. In the specific case, the model has proven useful in increasing the accuracy of product cost calculation, thus facilitating the implementation of data-driven strategies for order winning.

We believe that this paper has both theoretical and practical implications.

From the theoretical point of view, it fills a gap in the literature since it proposes the first multidimensional model for smart production data analysis adopting a managerial point of view. In addition, it could provide useful inputs also to researchers interested in developing a multidimensional model for smart factory data adopting an information system perspective.

From a practical point of view, it could represent a valuable tool to support production-related data analysis and decision making in the complex environment of a smart factory. The use of the model could help managers in the difficult task of organising and exploiting the huge amount of data available in digitalised companies in order to enable data-informed decisions. In addition, it could provide the developers of Information Technology tools for data analytics with useful insights into the multitude of multidimensional spaces relevant for data analysis and performance assessment.

The main limitation of this study concerns the generalisability of results, since only one case study is considered. Further case studies are required for a refinement and full validation of the model.

Acknowledgments. This work was supported by Regione Lombardia (POR FESR 2014–2020), under Grant 236789.

References

1. Santos, M.Y., et al.: A Big Data system supporting Bosch Braga Industry 4.0 strategy. Int. J. Inf. Manage. **37**(6), 750–760 (2017)
2. Niesen, T., Houy, C., Fettke, P., Loos, P.: Towards an integrative Big Data analysis framework for data-driven risk management in Industry 4.0. In: Proceedings of 49th Hawaii International Conference on System Sciences, 5–8 January, Koloa, pp. 5065–5074 (2016)
3. Tao, F., Qi, Q., Liu, A., Kusiak, A.: Data-driven smart manufacturing. J. Manuf. Syst. **48**, 157–169 (2018)
4. Zhong, R.Y., Xu, X., Klotz, E., Newman, S.T.: Intelligent manufacturing in the context of Industry 4.0: a review. Engineering **3**(5), 616–630 (2017)
5. Kusiak, A.: Smart manufacturing. Int. J. Prod. Res. **56**(1–2), 508–517 (2018)
6. Cavalheiro, J., Carreira, P.: A multidimensional data model design for building energy management. Adv. Eng. Inform. **30**, 619–632 (2016)
7. Sapia, C., Blaschka, M., Höfling, G., Dinter, B.: Extending the E/R model for the multidimensional paradigm. In: Kambayashi, Y., Lee, D.-L., Lim, E., Mohania, M., Masunaga, Y. (eds.) ER 1998. LNCS, vol. 1552, pp. 105–116. Springer, Heidelberg (1999). https://doi.org/10.1007/978-3-540-49121-7_9
8. Torlone, R.: Conceptual multidimensional models. In: Rafanelli, M. (ed.) Multidimensional Databases: Problems and Solutions, pp. 69–90. IGI Global, Hershey (2003)
9. Modoni, G.E., Doukas, M., Terkaj, W., Sacco, M., Mourtzis, D.: Enhancing factory data integration through the development of an ontology: from the reference models reuse to the semantic conversion of the legacy models. Int. J. Comput. Integr. Manuf. **30**(10), 1043–1059 (2017)
10. Haddaraab, M., Elragala, A.: The readiness of ERP systems for the factory of the future. Procedia Comput. Sci. **64**, 721–728 (2015)
11. Cocca, P., Marciano, F., Rossi, D., Alberti, M.: Business software offer for Industry 4.0: the SAP case. In: Proceedings of 16th IFAC Symposium on Information Control Problems in Manufacturing (INCOM 2018), Bergamo, Italy, 11–13 Jun (2018)
12. Rojko, A.: Industry 4.0 concept: background and overview. Int. J. Interact. Mobile Technol. **11**(5), 77–90 (2017)
13. Reference Architecture Model Industrie 4.0 (RAMI4.0) (2015). https://www.zvei.org/fileadmin/user_upload/Presse_und_Medien/Publikationen/2016/januar/GMA_Status_Report__Reference_Archtitecture_Model_Industrie_4.0__RAMI_4.0_/GMA-Status-Report-RAMI-40-July-2015.pdf. Accessed 15 June 2021
14. Ye, X., Chen, H., Lian, Z.: Thermal environment and productivity in the factory. ASHRAE Trans. **116**(1), 590–599 (2010)
15. Somanthan, E., Somanthan, R., Sudarshan, A., Tewari, M.: The impact of temperature on productivity and labor supply: evidence from Indian manufacturing. Working paper 244, Centre for Development Economics, Delhi School of Economics (2015)
16. Zhang, P., Deschenes, O., Meng, K., Zhang, J.: Temperature effects on productivity and factor reallocation: evidence from a half million Chinese manufacturing plants. J. Environ. Econ. Manag. **88**, 1–17 (2018)
17. Corvers, F.: The impact of human capital on labour productivity in manufacturing sectors of the European Union. J. Appl. Econ. **29**(8), 975–987 (1997)

18. Syverson, C.: What determines productivity? J. Econ. Literature **49**(2), 326–365 (2011)
19. Backman, M.: Human capital in firms and regions: impact of firm productivity. Pap. Reg. Sci. **93**(3), 557–575 (2014)
20. Mourtzis, D., Vlachou, E., Milas, N., Dimitrakopoulos, G.: Energy consumption estimation for machining processes based on real-time shop floor monitoring via wireless sensor networks. Procedia CIRP **57**, 637–642 (2016)
21. Zuo, Y., Tao, F., Nee, A.Y.C.: An Internet of Things and cloud-based approach for energy consumption evaluation and analysis for a product. Int. J. Comput. Integr. Manuf. **31**(4–5), 337–348 (2018)

Generating Synthetic Training Data for Assembly Processes

Johannes Dümmel$^{(\boxtimes)}$ (ID), Valentin Kostik, and Jan Oellerich

Karlsruher Institut für Technologie (KIT), Institut für Fördertechnik
und Logistiksysteme, Gotthard-Franz-Str. 8, 76131 Karlsruhe, Germany
johannes.duemmel@kit.edu
https://www.ifl.kit.edu/

Abstract. Current assembly assistance systems use different methods
for object detection. Deep learning methods occur, but are not elaborated in depth. For those methods, great amounts of individual training
data are essential. The use of 3D data to generate synthetic training
data is obvious, since this data is usually available for assembly processes. However, to guide through the entire assembly process not only
the individual parts are to be detected, but also all intermediate steps.
We present a system that uses the assembly sequence and the STEP
file of the assembly as input to automatically generate synthetic training
data as input for a convolutional neural network to identify the entire
assembly process. By means of experimental validation it can be demonstrated, that domain randomization improves the results and that the
developed system outperforms state of the art synthetic training data.

Keywords: Object detection · Synthetic training data · Domain
randomization · Assembly assistance systems · Assembly sequence

1 Introduction

Assembly assistance systems (AAS) are key enablers for fully dynamic cross-
company production networks [7]. They assist in manual assembly by guiding
the user step by step through the process. AAS display the individual steps
and control their correct execution. Therefor they need to detect all objects
used in an assembly as accurately as all the steps of the assembly. Current
research activities considering AAS mainly focus on the architecture of the whole
system [31]. However, the different types of object detection still require a certain
amount of manual effort [1].

In the field of machine vision convolutional neural networks (CNNs) efficiently accomplish the task of object detection [2,27,32]. Their main advantage
compared to traditional object detection algorithms is the ability, to automatically extract relevant features of objects from a sufficient amount of training
images. For this CNNs depend on a great number of annotated training data.

A. Dolgui et al. (Eds.): APMS 2021, IFIP AICT 633, pp. 119–128, 2021.
https://doi.org/10.1007/978-3-030-85910-7_13

For the development and testing of the algorithms, developers draw on large databases of annotated images [6,10,18,19]. In industrial applications, however, CNNs must detect individual parts while annotating large numbers of individual images manually is a time consuming process [30]. This results in the motivation to accelerate the process by automation.

In [8] a system is presented that can be used to reduce the time of creating and labeling training images without available 3D data of the object significantly. Here, the object is moved manually under a depth camera to define the objects position while at the same time RGB images of the respective view are created. This process is only applicable for small objects that can be hold in the hand and still requires manual effort. In industrial environments 3D data is available for almost all objects, most often in the form of STEP files [15]. There are several approaches using 3D data to generate synthetic training images to replace the real ones partially or completely [22,23,25].

In this paper we reduce the manual effort of generating training data to detect assemblies by combining synthetic training data from 3D files with the underlying assembly sequence. We automatically generate training images for the individual assembly parts just as for the assembly steps of an entire assembly. Finally, the performance of synthetic images with random backgrounds in comparison to the performance of images with partially application oriented (AO) backgrounds is experimentally evaluated.

2   Related Work

Current AAS use different technologies to identify the individual parts for the assembly steps. Pick-by-light is one of the simpler technologies, as it only marks the corresponding container of the individual parts [16]. This is done by virtually mapping the position of the container [9] or by 1D or 2D barcodes [13,28].

Another possibility of identifying individual parts is the use of image processing algorithms. This involves the use of depth image data [9,17] and RGB data [24]. In current AAS the data for recognizing the objects and the assembly steps are created manually.

THAMM et al. propose in [31] the use of the CNN YOLO [26] for object detection in their AAS. Here, the usage as well as the training methods remain still unexplained. ŽIDEK et al. already use a CNN for object recognition in an AAS [33]. There are also approaches to train a CNN with individual objects using synthetic data from CAD files to detect assembly parts [34].

The generation of synthetic training data for CNNs to recognize individual objects becomes popular in the field of computer vision [22,23,25]. Within this research area, there are two distinct approaches. Domain Adaptation (DA) aims to generate photorealistic training images [4,11,12] which requires a realistic synthetic environment. Furthermore objects will age in industrial environments and therefor wear out or pollute. Recognizing these objects using the DA approach is time consuming due to mapping all possible circumstances.

The second main approach generating synthetic training data is Domain Randomization (DR) [14,21,29]. The idea is to make reality appear as just another

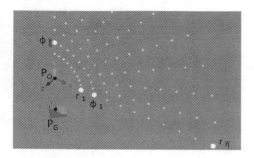

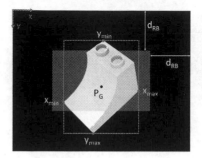

Fig. 1. Camera movement in quarter-circle orbits in the xy-plane around an object

Fig. 2. Random position of the object in an image respecting the constraining distance d_{RB}

synthetic modification of the training images. Random lighting, backgrounds and filters are applied to the initial images. DR is more robust than DA regarding detection under varying circumstances and can be implemented with less manual effort. For this reason our method is using DR.

3   Methodology

In the following section we describe the steps for generating synthetic training images and their corresponding bounding boxes. After that we demonstrate our approach for generating the training data for an entire assembly.

3.1   Synthetic Images

In the further course of the work, the CAD software Autodesk Inventor 2020 is used to read STEP files. They are widely spread in industrial environment and can be opened with any CAD software. In terms of image generating, we use one camera which moves in quarter-circle orbits in the xy-plane around an object. Hereby, the camera always aims at the origin P_O, see Fig. 1. To move the camera around an object and determine its position, we define the following sets

$$\mathbf{\Phi} = [\phi_1, \ldots, \phi_\xi, \ldots, \phi_{\bar{\xi}}]$$
$$\mathbf{R} = [r_1, \ldots, r_\eta, \ldots, r_{\bar{\eta}}]$$

and obtain the corresponding Cartesian coordinates

$$x_{\xi\eta} = r_\eta \cdot \cos\left(\phi_\xi \frac{\pi}{180°}\right), \quad \phi_\xi \in \mathbf{\Phi}, r_\eta \in \mathbf{R} \tag{1}$$

$$y_{\xi\eta} = r_\eta \cdot \sin\left(\phi_\xi \frac{\pi}{180°}\right), \quad \phi_\xi \in \mathbf{\Phi}, r_\eta \in \mathbf{R} \tag{2}$$

(a) Random backgrounds from COCO   (b) AO backgrounds

Fig. 3. Synthetic training images with random (a) and AO backgrounds (b)

where $\mathbf{\Phi}$ describes the angular range between the x- and the y-axis with $\phi_1 \geq 1°$ and $\phi_{\bar{\xi}} \leq 90°$. This enables the adjustment of the training images depending on the use case. The radius of the quarter-circle orbit between origin in the center and camera is defined by the set $\mathbf{R}$. The minimum value r_1 is determined so that the whole object fits in the image. We verify this by finding the minimal surrounding cuboid of the object fitting its biggest extension in the image. Consequently r_1 is variable depending on the size of the object. By defining the increment of the angular range $\mathbf{\Phi}$ by ξ and the increment of the radius range $\mathbf{R}$ by η we calculate the number of images. Consequently the camera position is defined by $P_C(x_{\xi\eta}, y_{\xi\eta})$ for the current step $\xi\eta$.

While the camera moves on a defined path, we select one random orientation of the object for each image. To obtain realistic orientations of the objects we use the software Unity 2019 to drop the objects 45 times and extract the resulting Euler angles. We select one random Euler angle combination to define the orientation of the object and rotate the object around the y-axis by a random angle. The position of the object in the image is defined by the position of the center of gravity P_G. We start with $P_G = P_O$ and move P_G to a random position in each image limited by d_{RB} which is defined as the largest distance between P_G and the minimal surrounding cuboid as shown in Fig. 2. This ensures the whole object being completely visible in the image.

The set of background images consists of 44 AO images and 5 000 random images from the COCO validation dataset [19] (see Fig. 3). For each training image we choose a random background image from the set. In addition we change the lightning of the image by choosing randomly one of the 23 available lightning styles from Inventor. We create two images for each $P_C(x_{\xi\eta}, y_{\xi\eta})$: one RGB training image and one contour image to define the bounding box around the object shown in Fig. 2. After generating the images we apply multiple filters from the ImageFilter module of pillow [5] to each image.

3.2   Data for Entire Assembly

Let an assembly $A = [\mathbf{P}, \mathbf{C}]$ consist of a total amount of parts $\mathbf{P} = [p_1, \ldots, p_k]$ and a certain amount of connecting parts $\mathbf{C} = [c_1, \ldots, c_l]$ such as bolts or shims. In this context, we define that the entire assembly A can be decomposed into single subassemblies where S_0 represents the smallest reasonable subassembly which consists of parts $\mathbf{p_0} \subseteq \mathbf{P}$ and connection parts $\mathbf{c_0} \subseteq \mathbf{C}$. The following greater subassembly S_1 in turn contains S_0 as well as a number of parts $\mathbf{p}_1 \subseteq \mathbf{P}$ and connection parts $\mathbf{c}_1 \subseteq \mathbf{C}$. Considering now that A can be represented by n subassemblies and that each subassembly is related to the corresponding assembly step, we obtain the following recursive relation for a certain subassembly

$$S_i = (\mathbf{p}_i \subseteq \mathbf{P}, \mathbf{c}_i \subseteq \mathbf{C}, S_{i-1}), \quad i = 1, \ldots, n \quad n \in \mathbb{N} \backslash \{0\}. \tag{3}$$

In order to generate synthetic training data for A we first import the corresponding STEP file of the entire assembly. Then, each individual part, i.e. each element of $\mathbf{P}$, is extracted and saved as a separate file. The same applies for the subassemblies S_i. Here, the parts and connection parts which are not included are suppressed. Analogous to the parts, each subassembly is saved as a separate file as well. Finally, we generate synthetic training data based on each of the saved files.

4 Experiments and Validation

In this section, the performance of the developed method is evaluated by means of experimental validation. After describing the results we additionally determine the accuracy of our method by training the CNN CenterNet [32] with synthetic data and evaluating the resulting precision.

4.1 Design of Experiments

Two assemblies are used for the experiments: the Duplo^{TM} and the charger assembly. Both assemblies with all individual parts and all subassemblies are shown in Fig. 4. The Duplo^{TM} assembly possesses form-fit pins and recesses as connections and thus no connection parts. We always connect two components in this assembly, two parts in the first step and in every further step one part to the previous subassembly. With $k = 6$ this results in eleven objects for which synthetic training data must be created.

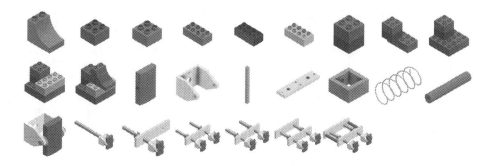

Fig. 4. Objects used in the experiments

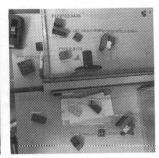

Fig. 5. Results of different test images with varying clutter in the background

The charger assembly has different connection parts like bolts, shims and nuts. Each step consists of two parts or of one part and one subassembly and a varying amount of connection parts. With $k = 7$ and $l = 7$ this results in 14 objects we need to create synthetic training data for. We do not create training data for the connection parts because they are generally delivered in larger quantities and supplied to the assembly workers in these quantities. Therefor the AAS does not need to detect connection parts. We use CenterNet to create one weight file for each assembly. The learning rate is set to $1.5625 \cdot 10^{-5}$. In epoch 90 and 120 we reduce the learning rate by the factor 10 and train 150 epochs.

Our evaluation dataset contains 900 real RGB images captured with the iPhone 5s camera at a resolution of 2448×2448. Here, backgrounds and cluttering in the dataset vary (see Fig. 5). Each object is displayed exactly 100 times on the images while the lightning conditions and the orientation vary as well. Here, all images are labelled manually using LabelImg [20].

4.2 Results

We train five times and vary the parameters for the synthetic training data, see Fig. 6. For the evaluation of our method we use the mean average precision (mAP) at 50% intersection over union (IoU) between the ground truth and the detected labels evaluated with a tool from CARTUCHO et al. [3].

Figure 6 shows the results including standard deviation as error bars. We trained both assemblies separately with 50% AO background images and compared the performance of applying no filters to applying filters to the images. The mAP of the Duplo™ assembly improved by 0.03. The small difference can result from the small variance of the parts of the assembly in size and properties. In order to prove that filtering and thus DR actually provide better results, we compare the charger assembly trained without filters and 50% AO background images and trained with filters and 50% AO background images. Filtering improves the mAP by 0.27. Comparing all objects (see Fig. 4) with and without filter results in an increase of the mAP by 0.16. In another experiment, we verify how the results change by using only random background images. We compare the charger assembly trained with 50% AO and with exclusively random background images. Exclusively random background images result in the declining of the mAP by 0.10. Within the assemblies the standard deviation is declining with increasing randomization.

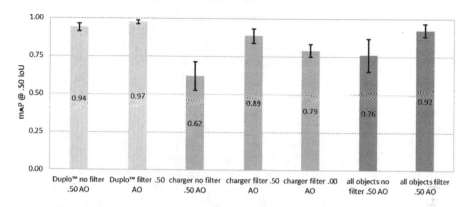

Fig. 6. mAP at .50 IoU for both assemblies and varied parameters

4.3 Discussion

Filtering images results for both assemblies in an increase of mAP. This increase is more visible with the charger assembly due to the higher variance and complexity of the involved assembly parts. The decreasing standard deviation within an assembly with increasing randomization leads to more robust systems. All objects are detected with a similar AP. Removing manual work completely for creating a new dataset by using exclusively random background images decreases the mAP. This could result from the COCO dataset containing everyday object categories in their natural environment. The missing industrial environment leads to a decrease in mAP due to CenterNet confusing industrial backgrounds as industrial objects. Adding the AO dataset increases the variance of backgrounds and leads to improved results for our test images. Whether the variance within the dataset is also sufficient in other industrial environments must be verified in further studies. The mAP for all 25 objects with best performing parameters is 0.92 and outperforms state of the art synthetic training data reaching an mAP @ .50 IoU of 0.89 [14] despite industrial objects being harder to detect due to less features.

5 Conclusion and Future Work

In this paper we describe a system to automatically generate training images from STEP files for an entire assembly. We experimentally demonstrate, that our system outperforms existing approaches of training with synthetic data.

Experiments also show, that randomizing training images leads to less variation in AP within an assembly. Random background images from COCO however do not have sufficient variance. Our AO dataset with industrial backgrounds solves this problem. Further studies should verify whether the variance in our dataset is sufficient and expand it if necessary.

The goal of our future work is to gather the sequence directly from STEP files via simulation. Combining our system with this simulation would lead to the automatic generation of training images for object detection for an entire assembly with just the STEP file of the assembly as input data. This can be offered to companies as a service for AAS but also for the automatic assembly with robots or for remote services enabling customers to assemble or repair complex products without support from the supplier. Using object detection with synthetic training data as a service companies must be willing to share sensitive data. Further research should consider this problem by using encryption techniques or by allowing the software to be used locally on the customers hardware.

Acknowledgements. This research has been funded by the German Federal Ministry of Education and Research (BMBF) under the program "Innovationen für die Produktion, Dienstleistung und Arbeit von morgen" and is supervised by Projektträger Karlsruhe (PTKA). The authors wish to acknowledge the funding agency and all the DPNB project partners for their contribution.

References

1. Bertram, P., Birtel, M., Quint, F., Ruskowski, M.: Intelligent manual working station through assistive systems. IFAC-PapersOnLine **51**(11), 170–175 (2018). https://doi.org/10.1016/j.ifacol.2018.08.253. 16th IFAC Symposium on Information Control Problems in Manufacturing INCOM 2018
2. Bochkovskiy, A., Wang, C.Y., Liao, H.Y.M.: Yolov4: optimal speed and accuracy of object detection (2020). https://arxiv.org/pdf/2004.10934
3. Cartucho, J., Ventura, R., Veloso, M.: Robust object recognition through symbiotic deep learning in mobile robots. In: 2018 IEEE/RSJ International Conference on Intelligent Robots and Systems (IROS), pp. 2336–2341 (2018)
4. Chen, Y., Li, W., Sakaridis, C., Dai, D., Van Gool, L.: Domain adaptive faster R-CNN for object detection in the wild. In: Proceedings of the IEEE Conference on Computer Vision and Pattern Recognition (CVPR) (2018)
5. Clark, A.: Pillow (PIL fork) documentation (2015). https://buildmedia. readthedocs.org/media/pdf/pillow/latest/pillow.pdf. Accessed 15 Mar 2021
6. Deng, J., Dong, W., Socher, R., Li, L.J., Li, K., Fei-Fei, L.: ImageNet: a large-scale hierarchical image database. In: CVPR 2009 (2009)
7. DPNB: Broker für dynamische produktionsnetzwerke (2021). https://www.dpnb. de/. Accessed 19 Mar 2021
8. Dümmel, J., Hochstein, M., Glöckle, J., Furmans, K.: Effizientes labeln von artikeln für das einlernen künstlicher neuronaler netze. In: Logistics Journal: Proceedings. Wissenschaftliche Gesellschaft für Technische Logistik (2019). https://doi.org/10. 2195/lj_Proc_duemmel_de_201912_01

9. Funk, M., Mayer, S., Schmidt, A.: Using in-situ projection to support cognitively impaired workers at the workplace. In: Proceedings of the 17th International ACM SIGACCESS Conference on Computers & Accessibility, ASSETS 2015, New York, NY, USA, pp. 185–192. Association for Computing Machinery (2015). https://doi.org/10.1145/2700648.2809853

10. Geiger, A., Lenz, P., Urtasun, R.: Are we ready for autonomous driving? The KITTI vision benchmark suite. In: Conference on Computer Vision and Pattern Recognition (CVPR) (2012)

11. Georgakis, G., Mousavian, A., Berg, A.C., Kosecka, J.: Synthesizing training data for object detection in indoor scenes (2017). https://arxiv.org/pdf/1702.07836

12. Guo, Y., j. zhang, Cai, J., Jiang, B., Zheng, J.: CNN based real-time dense face reconstruction with inverse-rendered photo-realistic face images. IEEE Trans. Pattern Anal. Mach. Intell. **41**(6), 1294–1307 (2019). https://doi.org/10.1109/TPAMI.2018.2837742

13. Hinrichsen, S., Riediger, D., Unrau, A.: Development of a projection-based assistance system for maintaining injection molding tools. In: 2017 IEEE International Conference on Industrial Engineering and Engineering Management (IEEM), pp. 1571–1575. IEEE (2017)

14. Hinterstoisser, S., Pauly, O., Heibel, H., Martina, M., Bokeloh, M.: An annotation saved is an annotation earned: using fully synthetic training for object detection. In: 2019 IEEE/CVF International Conference on Computer Vision Workshop (ICCVW), pp. 2787–2796. IEEE (2019). https://doi.org/10.1109/ICCVW.2019.00340

15. ISO 10303–21:2016: Industrial automation systems and integration – product data representation and exchange – part 21: Implementation methods: Clear text encoding of the exchange structure (2016)

16. König, M., et al.: MA 2 RA-manual assembly augmented reality assistant. In: 2019 IEEE International Conference on Industrial Engineering and Engineering Management (IEEM), pp. 501–505. IEEE (2019)

17. Kosch, T., Kettner, R., Funk, M., Schmidt, A.: Motioneap - ein system zur effizienzsteigerung und assistenz bei produktionsprozessen in unternehmen auf basis von bewegungserkennung und projektion (2016)

18. Kuznetsova, A., et al.: The open images dataset V4. Int. J. Comput. Vis. **128**(7), 1956–1981 (2020). https://doi.org/10.1007/s11263-020-01316-z

19. Lin, T.Y., et al.: Microsoft COCO: common objects in context (2014). http://arxiv.org/pdf/1405.0312v3

20. Lin, T.: Labelimg. Git code (2015). https://github.com/tzutalin/labelImg. Accessed 02 Aug 2020

21. Mayershofer, C., Ge, T., Fottner, J.: Towards fully-synthetic training for industrial applications. In: 10th International Conference on Logistics, Informatics and Service Sciences (LISS) (2020)

22. Nowruzi, F.E., Kapoor, P., Kolhatkar, D., Hassanat, F.A., Laganiere, R., Rebut, J.: How much real data do we actually need: Analyzing object detection performance using synthetic and real data (2019)

23. Peng, X., Sun, B., Ali, K., Saenko, K.: Learning deep object detectors from 3D models (2014). https://arxiv.org/pdf/1412.7122

24. Quint, F., Loch, F., Orfgen, M., Zuehlke, D.: A system architecture for assistance in manual tasks. In: The 12th International Conference on Intelligent Environments, pp. 43–52 (2016)

25. Rajpura, P.S., Hegde, R.S., Bojinov, H.: Object detection using deep CNNs trained on synthetic images. CoRR abs/1706.06782 (2017). http://arxiv.org/abs/1706.06782
26. Redmon, J., Divvala, S., Girshick, R., Farhadi, A.: You only look once: unified, real-time object detection. In: Proceedings of the IEEE Conference on Computer Vision and Pattern Recognition (CVPR) (2016)
27. Ren, S., He, K., Girshick, R., Sun, J.: Faster R-CNN: towards real-time object detection with region proposal networks. https://arxiv.org/pdf/1506.01497
28. Rüther, S.: Assistive systems for quality assurance by context-aware user interfaces in health care and production. Ph.D. thesis, Universitätsbibliothek Bielefeld (2014)
29. Sarkar, K., Varanasi, K., Stricker, D.: Trained 3D models for CNN based object recognition. In: Proceedings of the 12th International Joint Conference on Computer Vision, Imaging and Computer Graphics Theory and Applications, pp. 130–137. SCITEPRESS - Science and Technology Publications (2017). https://doi.org/10.5220/0006272901300137
30. Sorokin, A., Forsyth, D.: Utility data annotation with amazon mechanical Turk. In: 2008 IEEE Computer Society Conference on Computer Vision and Pattern Recognition Workshops, vol. 51, pp. 1–8 (2008). https://doi.org/10.1109/CVPRW.2008.4562953
31. Thamm, S., et al.: Concept for an augmented intelligence-based quality assurance of assembly tasks in global value networks. Procedia CIRP **97**, 423–428 (2021). https://doi.org/10.1016/j.procir.2020.05.262. 8th CIRP Conference of Assembly Technology and Systems
32. Zhou, X., Wang, D., Krähenbühl, P.: Objects as points (2019). https://arxiv.org/pdf/1904.07850
33. Žídek, K., Hosovsky, A., Piteľ, J., Bednár, S.: Recognition of assembly parts by convolutional neural networks. In: Hloch, S., Klichová, D., Krolczyk, G.M., Chattopadhyaya, S., Ruppenthalová, L. (eds.) Advances in Manufacturing Engineering and Materials. LNME, pp. 281–289. Springer, Cham (2019). https://doi.org/10.1007/978-3-319-99353-9_30
34. Žídek, K., Lazorík, P., Piteľ, J., Pavlenko, I., Hošovský, A.: Automated training of convolutional networks by virtual 3D models for parts recognition in assembly process. In: Trojanowska, J., Ciszak, O., Machado, J.M., Pavlenko, I. (eds.) MANUFACTURING 2019. LNME, pp. 287–297. Springer, Cham (2019). https://doi.org/10.1007/978-3-030-18715-6_24

Data Acquisition for Energy Efficient Manufacturing: A Systematic Literature Review

Henry Ekwaro-Osire[1]([✉]), Stefan Wiesner[1], and Klaus-Dieter Thoben[1,2]

[1] BIBA – Institut für Produktion und Logistik, Hochschulring 20, 28359 Bremen, Germany
eko@biba.uni-bremen.de
[2] University of Bremen, Bibliothekstraße 1, 28359 Bremen, Germany

Abstract. Due to the impending threat of climate change, as well as omnipresent pressures to remain competitive in the global market, manufacturers are motivated to reduce the energy and resource consumption of their operations. Analysis of manufacturing data can enable large efficiency gains, but before the data can be analyzed, it must be acquired and processed. This descriptive literature review assesses existing research on data acquisition and pre-processing in the context of improving manufacturing energy and resource efficiency. A number of insights were derived from the selected literature, based on a specific set of questions. Discrete manufacturing has received more attention than process manufacturing, when it comes to data acquisition and pre-processing methodology. Typically only one or two variables are measured, namely electricity consumption and material flow. Data is most often used for real-time monitoring or for historical analysis, to find opportunities for improving energy efficiency. However, acquisition of meaningful real-time data at a high granularity remains a challenge. There seems to be a lack of robust data acquisition and pre-processing methodologies that are designed and proven applicable across machine, process and plant levels within a factory.

Keywords: Data acquisition · Energy efficiency · Manufacturing

1 Introduction

The industry sector consumes over a third of global energy [1], making increased energy and resource efficiency of the sector an important lever to counter climate change. Analysis of production data is an effective lever to improve these efficiencies. Researchers and industry practitioners state that the most problems in realizing successful production data analytics are at the start of the data pipeline, namely in data acquisition and pre-processing [2–4]. In their recent publication on data-driven energy savings, Teng et al., point out that despite this, academic research on data acquisition and pre-processing is limited, and that most efforts have been focused on modelling and analysis [5]. It is clear that without the proper available data, analysis for energy and resource savings cannot be performed. Making the data available for analysis includes identifying: which variables need to be measured, how to measure the data, how to transmit the data, how

A. Dolgui et al. (Eds.): APMS 2021, IFIP AICT 633, pp. 129–137, 2021.
https://doi.org/10.1007/978-3-030-85910-7_14

to aggregate multiple measurements and how to store the data in a usable form and location. A thorough systematic literature review of this topic was not found among existing publications. Thus, the motivation of this literature review is to identify what this limited research consists of, and what gaps remain.

Objective of this literature review: Determine the current state of research regarding data acquisition and pre-processing for enabling energy and resource efficient manufacturing. Questions that will be addressed: *Question 1)* What types of subjects are examined? E.g., industries, company size, specific processes, etc.; *Question 2)* What types of variables are measured? E.g., electricity consumption, water consumption, CO_2 emissions, etc.; *Question 3)* In what settings is the data acquired? E.g., controlled setting, live production setting, from database, etc.; *Question 4)* How is the data applied once obtained and processed? E.g., basic monitoring, advanced analytics, database of records, etc.

2 Methodology

Since the authors' goal was to assess all available relevant literature on the topic, a descriptive review was conducted. As stated in their information systems article on transparent literature reviews, Templier et al. emphasize that reproducibility of method is critical for ensuring trustworthiness of a review [6]. Thus, one of the most widely used systematic methodologies, PRISMA, was used [7]. Due to the page limitation of this conference paper, the authors plan to elaborate on their methodology and results in a separate journal article. Below follows only a brief summary of the methodology.

The following criteria were defined for literature: type (journal articles and books), language (English and German), and publication status (published and manuscript). Science Direct, SCOPUS and Web of Science were the databases used. As an example, an excerpt of the query used in SCOPUS is shown below:

TITLE-ABS-KEY ((manufactur* OR production) AND ("energy efficiency" OR "energy saving*" OR "resource efficiency" OR "resource saving*") AND ("data acquisition" OR "data collection" OR "data *processing" OR "data availability")).

3 Results

Following the methodology described above, studies were selected as shown in Fig. 1

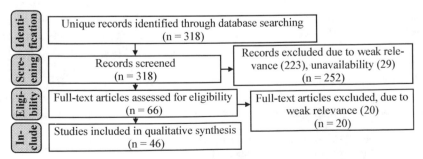

Fig. 1. PRISMA results of each phase of the systematic literature review

Results can be best structured along the initial questions that the review set out to address:

What Types of Subjects are Examined?

43% of the papers concerned discrete manufacturing environments, 35% process manufacturing and 22% both. This is interesting, because discrete manufacturing industries (e.g. machinery, electronics, automotive) are often not as energy intensive as process manufacturing industries (e.g. metals, paper, chemicals), which would imply a higher motivation to optimize energy consumption in process industries [8]. This should be investigated more closely, but a potential explanation could be that discrete manufacturing environments tend to have more machines, creating more dispersed and complex data, making data acquisition and pre-processing a more pressing research topic more. Additionally, process manufacturing processes often have to be monitored more closely, so the issue of data acquisition may have already been addressed extensively in the past, which lowers the need for new research in this area. Small- and medium-sized enterprises (SME) were only mentioned in three papers. Of these, only one considered SME requirements in the development of its methodology, while the others conducted case studies with SMEs.

What Types of Variables are Measured?

Electricity consumption is the most commonly measured variable, as shown in Table 1. In 79% of the papers, at least one further variable is considered, with auxiliary inputs or material flow through the manufacturing process being the most common. Only 35% of papers developed architectures to acquire and process three or more types of variables. This lack of multiple data sources is in line with the findings of Abele et al., who state "not many works develop integration methods of complex data sets from multiple sources" even though this could enable further efficiency gains [9].

Table 1. Variable types measured

Variable type	Papers, n	Papers, %
Electricity	38	83%
Material flow (weight, type, throughput)	18	39%
Auxiliary inputs (fuel, water, gas, compressed air, etc.)	14	30%
Machine parameters (vibrations, temp., pressure, etc.)	11	24%
Manufacturing process (schedule, cut depth and speed)	9	20%
Other (images, material quality, emissions, etc.)	10	22%

In What Settings is the Data Acquired?

As shown in Table 2, 23 papers (55% of the literature) address continuous data acquisition, as this setting is needed for (near) real-time monitoring and meaningful predictive

132   H. Ekwaro-Osire et al.

analytics. In this paper, continuous measurement refers to live production data acquisition on an ongoing basis, as opposed to only acquiring data once. The remaining literature is based on one-time analysis or data from databases, which are both settings with limited applicability beyond historical analysis.

Table 2. Comparison of number of papers per data acquisition method and data granularity

Data Acquisition Method	Data Granularity			Share of papers, compared horizontally
	Low	Med	High	
Continuous measurement	0	15	8	Low
One-time analysis live	3	7	4	
One-time analysis experiment	0	1	4	High
Databases (no measurement)	3	1	0	

Granularity is defined in Table 2 as the manufacturing level at which the data is collected. Continuous measurement and one-time analysis in live settings, mostly provide medium (machine level) granularity data, and occasionally high (component level) granularity data. Zhang et al. and Hu et al. point out that obtaining high granularity real-time data is a challenge [10, 11]. The literature review results indicate that one-time analyses in an experimental environment are used to collect high granularity data, but less for collecting lower granularity data. Woo et al. raise the issue that models based on empirical one-time data are however less reliable than those continuously using historical and real-time data [12]. Databases primarily provide only low (enterprise level) granularity data, and are mostly used for life cycle assessment analysis. Across all data acquisition methods, in 35% of the papers measurements were done on the component level, in 52% at the machine level and in 13% at the enterprise level. Very few papers covered multiple levels, even though research shows that "the extension of an analytical approach to the process and plant levels with multiple machine tools" can lead to further energy savings [13]. Few papers give reasoning for the specific data acquisition architecture, and most describe standalone solutions without significant integration into existing systems or platforms.

How is the Data Applied Once Obtained and Processed?

As shown in Table 3, the majority of literature considers data for (near) real-time, monitoring or historical analysis. However, a trend can be seen towards predictive analytics for energy and resource efficiency, especially in the past three years. A challenge this trend faces is the above-mentioned difficulty of obtaining the high granularity data from continuous measurement, which is needed for flexible predictive models. As Woo et al. explain, high granularity data "leads to precise and flexible modeling because it can decompose and re-compose models dynamically in terms of stratification." E.g. With a dynamic model, unlike with a model based on a smaller data set, energy consumption of a tooling machine could be predicted even when the product geometry is changed [12]. Data is used to build a database of energy-related KPI primarily in the context of life cycle assessment or inventory studies. Such data is most useful for assessing the energy efficiency across multiple enterprises, for example along a supply chain.

Table 3. Comparison of number of papers per data acquisition method and application of data

	Application of Data			
	Database	Historical	Real-time	Predictive
Continuous measurement	0	4	15	4
One-time analysis live	4	9	0	1
One-time analysis experiment	1	2	0	2
Databases (no measurement)	2	2	0	0

Data Acquisition Method

Share of papers, compared vertically
  Low   High

4 Discussion

After evaluation of the results, the following four research gaps were identified:

Research Gap 1: Few papers implement methodology across all machines in the factory, enabling analysis from machine, to process, to plant level. Typically, the analyses are limited to one machine or one process, or only consider the plant in aggregate. However, for example as demonstrated by Kang et al. and Bevilacqua et al. in their integrated machine data analytics approaches, integrating data across these levels can provide valuable insights [13, 14]. Diaz et al. report various analysis that can be done with data from each manufacturing level, and highlight that few studies aim to address data collection to enable analysis across all levels [15]. This integration across levels understandably increases the complexity of the required data acquisition methodology and data architecture, which may be a reason it is rarely attempted. The variety of measurements and data types, especially the spatiotemporal properties [16], increases as more different components and machines are included in the analysis, which increases the difficulty of aggregating the data. A robust architecture is required to manage this data, and these added complexities are likely difficult to address with a single methodology. These challenges should be investigated, and more widely applicable solutions should be developed.

Research Gap 2: Data beyond electricity consumption is rarely incorporated in data acquisition and processing methodologies. At the same time, reasoning for which data is and is not included is often lacking. There are a variety of possible reasons for selecting or omitting certain data, such as technical feasibility of the data acquisition, importance of the data regarding total energy and resource consumption, or external reporting regulations, to name a few. As shown in this literature review, many studies focus solely on electricity consumption. Though this can be a fair prioritization, there are further metrics for energy and resource consumption that can be relevant, as Mani et al. list in their paper on sustainability characterization of manufacturing processes. They mention other secondary energy sources such as fuels, as well as primary sources of the electricity consumed, as noteworthy when measuring energy consumption. They list water, material input and waste, among as relevant metrics when measuring resource consumption [17]. Hence, it would be valuable to research when which data, especially data other than electricity consumption, can provide valuable insights, and how this data can be acquired and processed for analysis.

Research Gap 3: SME are mentioned in less than 7% of the studies. SME production environments typically differ from those of large enterprises, in that they have older machines and less IT infrastructure. Compared to large enterprises, SME face additional challenges in achieving data driven energy savings, including lack of staff to focus on energy efficiency, small budget and need for short return on investments [18], as well as less advanced IT and IoT infrastructure. Rao et al. for example, show a systematic way for companies, especially SME, to assess their sub metering needs and prioritize investments in retrofit electricity sensors [18]. Approaches for data acquisition and pre-processing for energy and resource improvements should likely be differentiated for SME, and require further investigation.

Research Gap 4: Methodologies are rarely tested in multiple settings, and tend to be designed for specific factory and machining processes. This makes it unclear how widely applicable the methodology actually is. Thus, existing methodologies should be tested more, to prove their applicability, or the limitation of their scope should be clearly defined.

5 Conclusion

This literature review fulfills the original objective to determine the current state of research regarding data acquisition and pre-processing, for enabling energy and resource efficient manufacturing. Discrete, not process, manufacturing has received more attention, when it comes to data acquisition and pre-processing methodology. Typically only one or two variables are measured, namely electricity consumption and material flow. Continuous measurement of machine level data is most commonly the subject of study. Data is most often used for (near) real-time monitoring or for historical analysis, to find opportunities for improving energy efficiency. However, collecting (near) real-time energy consumption data at high granularity remains a challenge.

The primary limitation of this study is that database searches were limited to data acquisition and pre-processing methods within the context of energy and resource efficiency. However, methods outside of the energy and resource context could very well be relevant and applied or adapted to the energy and resource context. Initial searches resulted in a very high number of returned documents, going beyond the scope of this conference paper. Thus, in the future, the authors aim to expand this literature review in a journal paper as described above.

Of the multiple gaps identified, the authors will prioritize the lack of data acquisition methods that are applicable across manufacturing levels and different manufacturing setups, in their next research endeavors. In conclusion, data acquisition and pre-processing for sustainable manufacturing is a growing field, in which several challenges remain to be addressed by future research.

Acknowledgements. This research has been funded by the German Federal Ministry for Economic Affairs and Energy (BMWi) through the projects "Mittelstand 4.0 – Kompetenzzentrum Bremen" (01MF17004B) and "ecoKI" (03EN2047A). The authors wish to acknowledge the funding agency and all project partners for their contribution.

References

1. IEA: Tracking Industry 2020 – Analysis - IEA (2021). https://www.iea.org/reports/tracking-industry-2020. Accessed 17 Mar 2021
2. Máša, V., Stehlík, P., Touš, M., Vondra, M.: Key pillars of successful energy saving projects in small and medium industrial enterprises. Energy **158**, 293–304 (2018)
3. Wu, B., Li, J., Liu, H., Zhang, Z., Zhou, Y., Zhao, N.: Energy information integration based on EMS in paper mill. Appl. Energy **93**, 488–495 (2012)
4. Zhang, Y., Ma, S., Yang, H., Lv, J., Liu, Y.: A big data driven analytical framework for energy-intensive manufacturing industries. J. Clean Prod., **197**, 57–72 (2018)
5. Teng, S.Y., Touš, M., Leong, W.D., How, B.S., Lam, H.L., Máša, V.: Recent advances on industrial data-driven energy savings: digital twins and infrastructures. Renew. Sustain. Energy Rev. **135**, 110208 (2021)
6. Templier, M., Paré, G.: Transparency in literature reviews: an assessment of reporting practices across review types and genres in top IS journals. Eur. J. Inf. Syst. **27**(5), 503–550 (2018)
7. PRISMA (2021). http://www.prisma-statement.org/. Accessed 17 Mar 2021
8. IEA: Energy intensity of manufacturing in selected IEA countries, 2000–2018 –Charts – Data & Statistics - IEA (2021). https://www.iea.org/data-and-statistics/charts/manufacturing-and-services-selected-intensities-in-selected-iea-countries-2018. Accessed 3 June 2021
9. Abele, E., Panten, N., Menz, B.: Data collection for energy monitoring purposes and energy control of production machines. Procedia CIRP, **29**, 299–304 (2015)
10. Zhang, C., Ji, W.: Edge computing enabled production anomalies detection and energy-efficient production decision approach for discrete manufacturing workshops. IEEE Access **8**, 158197–158207 (2020)
11. Hu, L., Peng, T., Peng, C., Tang, R.: Energy consumption monitoring for the order fulfilment in a ubiquitous manufacturing environment. Int. J. Adv. Manuf. Technol. **89**(9–12), 3087–3100 (2016)
12. Woo, J., Shin, S.-J., Seo, W., Meilanitasari, P.: Developing a big data analytics platform for manufacturing systems: architecture, method, and implementation. Int. J. Adv. Manuf. Technol. **99**(9–12), 2193–2217 (2018)
13. Kang, H.S., Lee, J.Y., Lee, D.Y.: An integrated energy data analytics approach for machine tools. IEEE Access **8**, 56124–56140 (2020)
14. Bevilacqua, M., Ciarapica, F.E., Diamantini, C., Potena, D.: Big data analytics methodologies applied at energy management in industrial sector: a case study. RFT **8**(3), 105–122 (2017)
15. Diaz C., J.L., Ocampo-Martinez, C.: Energy efficiency in discrete-manufacturing systems: Insights, trends, and control strategies. J. Manuf. Syst. **52**, 131–145 (2019)
16. Yan, J., Meng, Y., Lu, L., Li, L.: Industrial big data in an industry 4.0 environment: challenges, schemes, and applications for predictive maintenance. IEEE Access **5**, 23484–23491 (2017)
17. Mani, M., Madan, J., Lee, J.H., Lyons, K.W., Gupta, S.K.: Sustainability characterisation for manufacturing processes. Int. J. Prod. Res. **52**(20), 5895–5912 (2014)

18. Rao, P., Muller, M.R., Gunn, G.: Conducting a metering assessment to identify submetering needs at a manufacturing facility. CIRP J. Manuf. Sci. Technol. **18**, 107–114 (2017)
19. AlQdah, K.S.: Prospects of energy savings in the national meat processing factory. Int. J. Sustain Energy **32**(6), 670–681 (2013)
20. Chen, E., Cao, H., He, Q., Yan, J., Jafar, S.: An IoT based framework for energy monitoring and analysis of die casting workshop. Procedia CIRP **80**, 693–698 (2019)
21. Deng, C., Guo, R., Liu, C., Zhong, R.Y., Xu, X.: Data cleansing for energy-saving: a case of Cyber-Physical Machine Tools health monitoring system. Int. J. Prod. Res. **56**(1–2), 1000–1015 (2018)
22. ElMaraghy, H.A., Youssef, A.M., Marzouk, A.M., ElMaraghy, W.H.: Energy use analysis and local benchmarking of manufacturing lines. J. Clean Prod. **163**, 36–48 (2017)
23. Emec, S., Krüger, J., Seliger, G.: Online fault-monitoring in machine tools based on energy consumption analysis and non-invasive data acquisition for improved resource-efficiency. Procedia CIRP **40**, 236–243 (2016)
24. Guo, J., Yang, H.: Three-stage optimisation method for concurrent manufacturing energy data collection. Int. J. Comput. Integr. Manuf. **31**(4–5), 479–489 (2018)
25. He, K., Tang, R., Jin, M., Cao, Y., Nimbalkar, S.U.: Energy modeling and efficiency analysis of aluminum die-casting processes. Energ. Effi. **12**(5), 1167–1182 (2018)
26. Herstätter, P., Wildbolz, T., Hulla, M., Ramsauer, C.: Data acquisition to enable research, education and training in learning factories and makerspaces. Procedia Manuf. **45**, 289–294 (2020)
27. Jagtap, S., Rahimifard, S., Duong, L.N.K.: Real-time data collection to improve energy efficiency: a case study of food manufacturer. J. Food Process Preserv. (2019)
28. Kellens, K., Dewulf, W., Overcash, M., Hauschild, M.Z., Duflou, J.R.: Methodology for systematic analysis and improvement of manufacturing unit process life-cycle inventory (UPLCI)—CO2PE! initiative (cooperative effort on process emissions in manufacturing). Part 1: Methodology description. Int. J. Life Cycle Assess **17**(1), 69–78 (2012)
29. Kontopoulos, A., et al.: A hybrid, knowledge-based system as a process control 'tool' for improved energy efficiency in alumina calcining furnaces. Appl. Therm. Eng. **17**(8–10), 935–945 (1997)
30. Krones, M., Müller, E.: An approach for reducing energy consumption in factories by providing suitable energy efficiency measures. Procedia CIRP **17**, 505–510 (2014)
31. Leroy, C.: Provision of LCI data in the European aluminium industry methods and examples. Int. J. Life Cycle Assess (S1), 10–44 (2009)
32. Li, X., Chen, L., Ding, X.: Allocation methodology of process-level carbon footprint calculation in textile and apparel products. Sustainability **11**(16), 4471 (2019)
33. Linke, B.S., Garcia, D.R., Kamath, A., Garretson, I.C.: Data-driven sustainability in manufacturing: selected examples. Procedia Manuf. **33**, 602–609 (2019)
34. Menghi, R., Rossi, M., Papetti, A., Germani, M.: A methodology for energy efficiency redesign of smart production systems. Procedia CIRP **91**, 319–324 (2020)
35. Meo, I., Papetti, A., Gregori, F., Germani, M.: Optimization of energy efficiency of a production site: a method to support data acquisition for effective action plans. Procedia Manuf. **11**, 760–767 (2017)
36. Demichela, M., Baldissone, G., Darabnia, B.: Using field data for energy efficiency based on maintenance and operational optimisation. A step towards PHM in process plants. Processes **6**(3), 25 (2018)
37. Ng, C.Y., Lam, S.S., Choi, S.P.M., Law, K.M.Y.: Optimizing green design using ant colony-based approach. Int. J. Life Cycle Assess **25**(3), 600–610 (2020)
38. Nyamekye, P., Leino, M., Piili, H., Salminen, A.: Overview of sustainability studies of CNC machining and LAM of stainless steel. Phys. Procedia **78**, 367–376 (2015)

39. Palasciano, C., Bustillo, A., Fantini, P., Taisch, M.: A new approach for machine's management: from machine's signal acquisition to energy indexes. J. Clean Prod. **137**, 1503–1515 (2016)
40. Bergaminia, R., Nguyena, T.-V., Bellemoc, L., Elmegaarda, B.: Simplification of data acquisition in process integration retrofit of a milk powder production facility. Chem. Eng. Trans. **76**, 427–432 (2019)
41. Rönnlund, I., et al.: Eco-efficiency indicator framework implemented in the metallurgical industry: part 1—a comprehensive view and benchmark. Int. J. Life Cycle Assess **21**(10), 1473–1500 (2016)
42. Rossi, F., Manenti, F., Pirola, C., Mujtaba, I.: A robust sustainable optimization & control strategy (RSOCS) for (fed-) batch processes towards the low-cost reduction of utilities consumption. J. Clean Prod. **111**, 181–192 (2016)
43. Serin, G., Sener, B., Gudelek, M.U., Ozbayoglu, A.M., Unver, H.O.: Deep multi-layer perceptron based prediction of energy efficiency and surface quality for milling in the era of sustainability and big data. Procedia Manuf., 1166–1177 (2020)
44. Shen, N., Cao, Y., Li, J., Zhu, K., Zhao, C.: A practical energy consumption prediction method for CNC machine tools: cases of its implementation. Int. J. Adv. Manuf. Technol. **99**(9–12), 2915–2927 (2018)
45. Spiering, T., Kohlitz, S., Sundmaeker, H., Herrmann, C.: Energy efficiency benchmarking for injection moulding processes. Robot Comput. Integr. Manuf. **36**, 45–59 (2015)
46. Sucic, B., Al-Mansour, F., Pusnik, M., Vuk, T.: Context sensitive production planning and energy management approach in energy intensive industries. Energy **108**, 63–73 (2016)
47. Tian, J., Shi, H., Li, X., Chen, L.: Measures and potentials of energy-saving in a Chinese fine chemical industrial park. Energy **46**(1), 459–470 (2012)
48. Tokos, H., Pintarič, Z.N., Glavič, P.: Energy saving opportunities in heat integrated beverage plant retrofit. Appl. Therm. Eng. **30**(1), 36–44 (2010)
49. Tristo, G., Bissacco, G., Lebar, A., Valentinčič, J.: Real time power consumption monitoring for energy efficiency analysis in micro EDM milling. Int. J. Adv. Manuf. Technol. **78**(9–12), 1511–1521 (2015)
50. Uluer, M.U., Unver, H.O., Gok, G., Fescioglu-Unver, N., Kilic, S.E.: A framework for energy reduction in manufacturing process chains (E-MPC) and a case study from the Turkish household appliance industry. J. Clean Prod. **112**, 3342–3360 (2016)
51. Waltersmann, L., et al.: Benchmarking holistic optimization potentials in the manufacturing industry – A concept to derive specific sustainability recommendations for companies. Procedia Manuf. **39**, 685–694 (2019)
52. Zhang, Y., Hong, M., Li, J., Liu, H.: Data-based analysis of energy system in papermaking process. Drying Technol. **36**(7), 879–890 (2018)
53. Zhang, C., Jiang, P.: RFID-driven energy-efficient control approach of CNC machine tools using deep belief networks. IEEE Trans. Automat. Sci. Eng. **17**(1), 129–141 (2020)
54. Zhao, H., et al.: Running state of the high energy consuming equipment and energy saving countermeasure for Chinese petroleum industry in cloud computing. Concurr. Comput. Pract. Exp. **2017**(14), e3941 (2017)

Review of Factors Influencing Product-Service System Requirements Along the Life Cycle

Stefan Wiesner[1]([⊠]) [iD] and Jannicke Baalsrud Hauge[1,2] [iD]

[1] BIBA - Bremer Institut für Produktion und Logistik GmbH at the University of Bremen,
Hochschulring 20, 28359 Bremen, Germany
{wie,baa}@biba.uni-bremen.de

[2] KTH – Royal Institute of Technology, Kvarnbergagatan 12, Södertälje, Sweden

Abstract. Rapid technological changes within a highly competitive global market have induced a transformation in the manufacturing industry. A wide range of services is added to the physical product in order to deliver new customized functions and other benefits in the form of Product-Service Systems (PSS). These developments induce a change from quasi-stable and simple socio-technical systems to a more complex and instable dynamic configuration. Various environmental factors also influence the requirements towards the PSS in all life cycle phases. However, such factors have yet to be systematically identified and categorised. Thus, this paper presents the results of a structured literature review on factors influencing the system requirements along the PSS life cycle. The review has classified such factors in three life cycle phases and four categories. Gaps in research have been identified for factors during operation and end of life, especially beyond functional requirements. Thus, future research opportunities have been derived.

Keywords: Product-service system · Life cycle · Requirements engineering · Dynamic system environment

1 Introduction

Rapid technological changes within a highly competitive global market have induced a transformation in the manufacturing industry. Digitalization increases the connectivity between production facilities, products and the customer, while extending their functionality along the whole life cycle [1]. In addition, reduced product cycles demand for reconfigurable manufacturing systems [2]. Following these trends, companies need to consider economic, ecological and functional requirements, in order to make a more sustainable value proposition, to be more efficient and effective on the market, and to satisfy the user needs [3]. As customers increasingly demand support for all phases of the product life cycle, from development over assembly and distribution to operation, a wide range of services is added to the physical product in order to deliver new customized functions and other benefits.

This trend has led to the introduction of Product-Service Systems (PSS) as a promising framework describing the integrated development, realization and offering of specific

A. Dolgui et al. (Eds.): APMS 2021, IFIP AICT 633, pp. 138–145, 2021.
https://doi.org/10.1007/978-3-030-85910-7_15

product-service bundles as a solution for the customer [4]. The growing complexity of these systems, combined with a dynamic environment, creates new challenges for the design process [5].

The system development process needs to handle competing stakeholder demands and dynamically respond to continually changing requirements coming from the environment [6]. In order to secure a comprehensive fulfilment of requirements in such an environment, it needs to be conducted across domains, throughout the whole value network and beyond the development phase. Only by considering such dimensions, it can be ensured that all requirements towards a solution are captured, taken into account when developing system components and that the solution is adaptable to changing requirements in later life cycle phases.

2   Methodology

A descriptive literature review was conducted for identifying factors influencing the PSS requirements along the system life cycle. To systematically screen all relevant literature, the review methodology was oriented on PRISMA, as one of the most widely used frameworks [7]. Due to the limitations of a conference paper, it is intended to describe the methodology and results in an upcoming journal paper in more detail. In summary, the following criteria were applied for the literature review:

- Search terms: *TITLE-ABS-KEY ("*PSS" OR "product-service system*" OR "functional product*" OR "extended product*") AND ("life cycle" OR lifecycle) AND requirements)*
- Database: SCOPUS, limited to journal articles, books and reviews in English or German, in subject areas related to PSS
  The objective is to determine the current state of research on factors influencing PSS requirements along the life cycle. Specifically, two questions are addressed: 1) Which life cycle phase do the articles focus on (from begin to end of life, or across the life cycle)? 2) Which types of influencing factors do the articles consider (PSS functional requirements, or coming from different perspectives of the system environment)?

In order to cluster the papers according to the PSS life cycle stages, we had to define a common framework for categorization. While for PSS the product and service life cycles do often not coincide with each other, or are not linear [8], at high level it can be concluded that PSS have a begin-of-life phase, in which initial requirements are determined and the solution is designed, a middle-of-life phase, in which value is being created for the customer, and an end-of-life phase, in which the PSS is reconfigured or decommissioned. Thus, the papers are classified according to the criteria that they focus on methods, tools or applications for a single, multiple or all of these phases.

Regarding the influencing factors, the clusters were compiled descriptively with criteria derived from the analysed literature. The majority of the papers deals with functional requirements for PSS coming from the customer or user. However, sustainability or decrease of resource consumption has been a core topic of PSS research for a long time. Papers addressing such issues are categorized with an ecological focus. Papers focusing on factors such as servitized business models are clustered with an economic focus. Finally, collaboration of different actors with complementary competences is an important enabler of PSS solutions. Papers dealing with influencing factors from the value network are classified with a network focus.

The life cycle phase and type of influencing factors are especially relevant due to the dynamic nature of PSS. While the functions of traditional products are designed during begin-of-life for the rest of the life cycle, the adaptability of PSS demands for the analysis of influences affecting its requirements during middle- or end-of life as well. Furthermore, due to the variety of stakeholders and the extended value network for PSS, it is necessary to go beyond the functional perspective for the solution. Because PSS also affect business processes and models, as well as answer to societal demands, such as sustainability, these perspectives should be included as well.

3   Literature Review Results

Following the methodology described above, 65 unique records were identified through the database search. After screening the titles, abstracts and keywords, 36 records were excluded due to weak relevance. These papers are apparently not addressing the influencing factors on PSS requirements and could thus not be assigned to any of the mentioned clusters and were not analysed in detail. For seven records, only title, abstract and keywords are open accessible through Scopus, while the full text requires additional subscriptions, which were not available. For the remaining 22 articles, the full text was analysed and included in the qualitative synthesis. The results were structured along the two main issues addressed by the review, PSS life cycle phases and categories of influencing factors on requirements. Percentages add up to a value greater than 100%, as some of the papers are related to more than one category.

Which Life Cycle Phases do the Articles Focus on?
Out of the 22 papers, 17 papers have a focus related to the design phase of PSS. This was expected, as an emphasis is put on requirements engineering during this phase. However, it seems to confirm "traditional" engineering approaches for PSS, where requirements are more or less static and "fixed" after the design phase [9]. While interdisciplinarity between the product, service and software domain is commonly addressed, the view across a dynamic life cycle is missing.

Four papers have a focus on the operational phase of PSS, but mostly in relation to the design phase, in the sense to either anticipate possible maintenance scenarios during development, or derive information from the operational phase for the design of next generation PSS [10].

Two papers focus on the end of life phase of PSS. The low number of papers in this category seems surprising, considering the growing discussions on reuse and sustainability of products. Both papers analysed address the need to identify components and gather information on their condition from a more technical point of view [11, 12].

Seven papers take a cross life cycle phase perspective. The focal points of these papers are mainly frameworks that take into account elements like PSS stakeholders or environmental effects throughout the life cycle [13, 14]. Little attention is given to dynamic environments or changing requirements along the life cycle.

Which Types of Influencing Factors do the Articles Consider?
14 papers mainly consider factors that influence functional requirements of the PSS. This also corresponds to the "traditional" engineering perspective of value being provided by a certain functionality of the PSS [15]. Accordingly, most of these papers are addressing the design phase, but some also cover operations (maintenance), end of life or cross life cycle functionalities. Other factors, such as economic or ecological influences are mostly discussed disconnected from functional requirements.

Four papers cover ecological factors influencing PSS requirements. Here as well, the focus is on the design phase. Naturally however there is a strong cross life cycle perspective and a view on the operational phase [16]. Surprisingly, no paper has put a strong focus on the PSS end of life.

Four papers as well consider economic factors influencing requirements on PSS. A strong focus is on the design phase again, because it is argued the PSS business model is defined here [17], but also cross life cycle effects are discussed [18].

A single paper considers networking as a factor for PSS operations. This seems to be an underrated area to derive PSS requirements in general and the connection to the other articles is weak [19].

The literature review has yielded results published between 2003 and 2020, with an average of two publications per year. There is no clear progressive trend in number of publications. However, comparing the publications related to the life cycle phases and factor categories shows a focus on functional requirements during design, as can be seen in Table 1.

Table 1. Publications related to life cycle phases and factor categories

	Design	Operation	End of Life	Cross LC
Functional	11 [9, 11, 15, 17, 20–26]	2 [15, 21]	2 [11, 12]	3 [13, 17, 27]
Ecological	4 [10, 14, 16, 28]	1 [10]	-	2 [14, 16]
Economic	4 [17, 18, 29, 30]	-	-	3 [17, 29, 30]
Network	-	1 [19]	-	-

The shades of grey in Table 1 indicate the different amount of publications in the topic areas (□ > 4, ▨ 3-4, ▨ 1-2, ■ 0). The uneven distribution suggest the existence of research gaps, which are discussed in detail in the next section.

4 Discussion

The analysis of the 22 papers included in this study on factors that influence the requirements on PSS along the life cycle shows that there is a clear imbalance, both in terms of articles focusing on the different phases as well as in what factors they actually address. 17 out of 22 papers related to the design phase seem at first sight quite naturally, since this is how complex systems have been designed for decades. If these systems are to be used in a stable environment, it can be expected that the requirements will not change too much over time. However, today technology changes rapidly in a dynamic environment and thus also changing the customer requirements. It seems problematic that there is so little published research on the factors that influence the requirements in the operational phase and above all in the end of life phase. This will impact the sustainability of PSS and also the expected life time of the systems, since it is difficult to adapt to a changing environment as long as it is not known which factors to observe. Therefore, PSS require a stronger focus on detecting influences in later phases of the life cycle. This could be e.g. changes in the behaviour of the customer or user of the PSS, indicating a different application scenario. Changes in regulations regarding resource consumption or replacement of problematic materials and changes in the PSS providers' business model, e.g. shifting from a use-oriented to a result-oriented value proposition that also require a more holistic consideration of requirements during the PSS life cycle. Such changes could be detected based on the operational data recorded by the PSS, as well as business intelligence platforms relying on the analysis of big data coming from the PSS environment.

The second part of the analysis was related to what categories of factors have been examined in which life cycle phase. The overwhelming number of articles have focussed on the functional requirements, which is typically for systems that need to meet customer expectations and demand. Thus, most research for functional requirements is located in the design phase, and only three papers look at the whole life cycle process.

In terms of ecological and economic factors, it is visible that even if these are less investigated, there is a better balance of works looking across the life cycle, but surprisingly none that explore specifically the end of life with regard to ecological factors and neither operational nor end of life in terms of economic factors. This lack of published knowledge on how the requirements change over time can lead to a sub-optimal understanding of the systems behaviour and the requirements on it and thus shorten the life time of the PSS in addition to give a chance to consider economic and ecological factors in a proper way. Thus, new methods and tools supporting the monitoring of changes of ecological regulations or business model evolution during PSS operation or end-of-life would be required, e.g. supported by text mining approaches. Since only one article on network factors was identified, it is too early to conclude anything in this area.

5 Conclusions and Future Work

The imbalance of identified articles assessing factors influencing requirements across the life cycle, as well as the focus on functional requirements in existing literature, indicates that there is a need for a more holistic approach. As only 22 relevant papers were identified in this first systematic review, the significance of the findings is still limited.

In a next step, the scope of the review will be extended and the results are discussed in more detail. In order to get a better understanding on how researchers understand the topic of factors influencing requirements on PSS along the life cycle, it is intended in addition to design a survey to be administrated among the IFIP WG5.7 community. The findings shall be published in a journal paper and provide the basis to close the identified gaps during the life cycle and between the categorised factors.

It is expected that based on the analysis and needs of the manufacturing industry, especially monitoring of variations in PSS customer or user behaviour, respectively PSS application could be a major source of changing requirements. Furthermore, the inclusion of new ecological regulations and industry-related business trends through artificial business intelligence solutions could help to adapt a PSS solution proactively.

Acknowledgements. This research has been funded by the German Federal Ministry for Economic Affairs and Energy (BMWi) through the project "Mittelstand 4.0 – Kompetenzzentrum Bremen" (01MF17004B). The authors wish to acknowledge the funding agency and all project partners for their contribution.

References

1. Kagermann, H., Helbig, J., Hellinger, A., Wahlster, W.: Umsetzungsempfehlungen für das Zukunftsprojekt Industrie 4.0. Deutschlands Zukunft als Produktionsstandort sichern; Abschlussbericht des Arbeitskreises Industrie 4.0. Forschungsunion; Geschäftsstelle der Plattform Industrie 4.0, Berlin, Frankfurt/Main (2013)
2. Koren, Y., Gu, X., Guo, W.: Reconfigurable manufacturing systems: principles, design, and future trends. Front. Mech. Eng. **13**(2), 121–136 (2017). https://doi.org/10.1007/s11465-018-0483-0
3. Kaihara, T., et al.: Value creation in production: reconsideration from interdisciplinary approaches. CIRP Ann. **67**(2), 791–813 (2018). https://doi.org/10.1016/j.cirp.2018.05.002
4. Baines, T., Ziaee Bigdeli, A., Bustinza, O.F., Shi, V.G., Baldwin, J., Ridgway, K.: Servitization: revisiting the state-of-the-art and research priorities. Int. J. Oper. Prod. Manage. **37**(2), 256–278 (2017). https://doi.org/10.1108/IJOPM-06-2015-0312
5. Hellenbrand, D.: Transdisziplinäre Planung und Synchronisation mechatronischer Produktentwicklungsprozesse. Zugl.: München, Techn. Univ., Diss., 2013. Produktentwicklung. Dr. Hut, München (2013)
6. Ncube, C.: On the engineering of systems of systems: key challenges for the requirements engineering community. In: 2011 Workshop on Requirements Engineering for Systems, Services and Systems-of-Systems (RES^4), Trento, Italy, pp. 70–73 (2011). https://doi.org/10.1109/RESS.2011.6043923
7. PRISMA. http://www.prisma-statement.org/ (2021)
8. Westphal, I., Freitag, M., Thoben, K.-D.: Visualization of interactions between product and service lifecycle management. In: Umeda, S., Nakano, M., Mizuyama, H., Hibino, H., Kiritsis, D., von Cieminski, G. (eds.) APMS 2015. IAICT, vol. 460, pp. 575–582. Springer, Cham (2015). https://doi.org/10.1007/978-3-319-22759-7_66
9. Liu, C., Jia, G., Kong, J.: Requirement-oriented engineering characteristic identification for a sustainable product-service system: a multi-method approach. Sustainability **12**(21), 8880 (2020). https://doi.org/10.3390/su12218880

10. Amaya, J., Lelah, A., Zwolinski, P.: Design for intensified use in product–service systems using life-cycle analysis. J. Eng. Des. **25**(7–9), 280–302 (2014). https://doi.org/10.1080/095 44828.2014.974523
11. Sundin, E., Lindahl, M., Ijomah, W.: Product design for product/service systems. J. Manuf. Tech. Manage. **20**(5), 723–753 (2009). https://doi.org/10.1108/17410380910961073
12. Bindel, A., Rosamond, E., Conway, P., West, A.: Product life cycle information management in the electronics supply chain. Proc. Inst. Mech. Eng. Part B J. Eng. Manuf. **226**(8), 1388–1400 (2012). https://doi.org/10.1177/0954405412448780
13. Papinniemi, J., Fritz, J., Hannola, L., Denger, A., Lampela, H.: Lifecycle-based requirements of product-service system in customer-centric manufacturing In: Fukuda, S., Bernard, A., Gurumoorthy, B., Bouras, A. (eds.) PLM 2014. IAICT, vol. 442, pp. 435–444. Springer, Heidelberg (2014). https://doi.org/10.1007/978-3-662-45937-9_43
14. Neramballi, A., Sakao, T., Willskytt, S., Tillman, A.-M.: A design navigator to guide the transition towards environmentally benign product/service systems based on LCA results. J. Cleaner Prod. **277**, 124074 (2020). https://doi.org/10.1016/j.jclepro.2020.124074
15. Nilsson, S., Sundin, E., Lindahl, M.: Integrated product service offerings – challenges in setting requirements. J. Cleaner Prod. **201**, 879–887 (2018). https://doi.org/10.1016/j.jclepro.2018.08.090
16. Maxwell, D., van der Vorst, R.: Developing sustainable products and services. J. Cleaner Prod. **11**(8), 883–895 (2003). https://doi.org/10.1016/S0959-6526(02)00164-6
17. Wiesner, S., Thoben, K.-D.: Cyber-physical product-service systems. In: Biffl, S., Lüder, A., Gerhard, D. (eds.) Multi-Disciplinary Engineering for Cyber-Physical Production Systems, pp. 63–88. Springer, Cham (2017). https://doi.org/10.1007/978-3-319-56345-9_3
18. Corti, D., Fontana, A., De Santis, M., Norden, C., Ahlers, R.: Life cycle assessment and life cycle costing for PSS. In: Cattaneo, L., Terzi, S. (eds.) Models, Methods and Tools for Product Service Design. SAST, pp. 83–100. Springer, Cham (2019). https://doi.org/10.1007/978-3-319-95849-1_6
19. Harrington, T.S., Srai, J.S.: Defining product-service network configurations and location roles: a current and future state analysis framework for international engineering operations. IJPD **17**(3/4), 228 (2012). https://doi.org/10.1504/IJPD.2012.052103
20. Belkadi, F., et al.: A knowledge-based collaborative platform for PSS design and production. CIRP J. Manuf. Sci. Technol. **29**, 220–231 (2020). https://doi.org/10.1016/j.cirpj.2018.08.004
21. Wan, S., Li, D., Gao, J., Roy, R., Tong, Y.: Process and knowledge management in a collaborative maintenance planning system for high value machine tools. Comput. Ind. **84**, 14–24 (2017). https://doi.org/10.1016/j.compind.2016.11.002
22. Bertoni, A., Bertoni, M., Isaksson, O.: Value visualization in product service systems preliminary design. J. Cleaner Prod. **53**, 103–117 (2013). https://doi.org/10.1016/j.jclepro.2013.04.012
23. Berkovich, M., Leimeister, J.M., Krcmar, H.: Requirements engineering for product service systems. Bus. Inf. Syst. Eng. **3**(6), 369–380 (2011). https://doi.org/10.1007/s12599-011-0192-2
24. Isaksson, O., Larsson, T.C., Rönnbäck, A.Ö.: Development of product-service systems: challenges and opportunities for the manufacturing firm. J. Eng. Des. **20**(4), 329–348 (2009). https://doi.org/10.1080/09544820903152663
25. Lagerstedt, J., Luttropp, C., Lindfors, L.-G.: Functional priorities in LCA and design for environment. Int. J. LCA **8**(3), 160–166 (2003). https://doi.org/10.1007/BF02978463
26. Kerttula, M.: Virtual Design: A Framework for the Development of Personal Electronic Products. VTT Publications (2006)
27. Abramovici, M., Michele, J., Neubach, M.: Erweiterung des PLM-Ansatzes für hybride Leistungsbündel. ZWF **103**(9), 619–622 (2008). https://doi.org/10.3139/104.101335

28. Vezzoli, C., Sciama, D.: Life cycle design: from general methods to product type specific guidelines and checklists: a method adopted to develop a set of guidelines/checklist handbook for the eco-efficient design of NECTA vending machines. J. Cleaner Prod. **14**(15–16), 1319–1325 (2006). https://doi.org/10.1016/j.jclepro.2005.11.011
29. Sholihah, M., Mitake, Y., Nakada, T., Shimomura, Y.: Innovative design method for a valuable product-service system: concretizing multi-stakeholder requirements. JAMDSM **13**(5), JAMDSM0091–JAMDSM0091 (2019). https://doi.org/10.1299/jamdsm.2019jamdsm0091
30. Rese, M., Karger, M., Strotmann, W.-C.: The dynamics of Industrial Product Service Systems (IPS2) – using the Net Present Value Approach and Real Options Approach to improve life cycle management. CIRP J. Manuf. Sci. Technol. **1**(4), 279–286 (2009). https://doi.org/10.1016/j.cirpj.2009.05.001

Data-Driven Methods for Supply Chain Optimization

Data-Driven Solutions for the Newsvendor Problem: A Systematic Literature Review

Thais de Castro Moraes[1]([⊠]) [iD] and Xue-Ming Yuan[2] [iD]

[1] National University of Singapore, Singapore 117576, Singapore
thais.moraes@u.nus.edu
[2] Agency for Science, Technology and Research - A*STAR, Singapore 138634, Singapore

Abstract. The newsvendor problem captures the trade-off between ordering decisions, stocking costs and customer service level when the demand distribution is known. Nonetheless, in real case scenarios, it is unlikely that the decision maker knows the true demand distribution and its parameters, encouraging the use of datasets for empirical solutions that will achieve more precise results and reduce misleading decisions. Motivated by the availability of large amount of quality datasets, advances in machine learning algorithms and enhancement of computational power, the development of data-driven approaches has been emerging over the recent years. However, it is still unclear in which settings these data-driven solutions outperform the traditional model-based methods. In this paper, a systematic literature review is conducted for the descriptive analysis and classification of the most relevant studies that addressed the newsvendor problem and its variations under the data-driven approaches. The methods developed to solve the problems with unknown demand distribution are categorized and assessed. For each category, our paper discusses the relevant publications in detail and how they evidence the data-driven performance better. By identifying the gaps in the available literature, the future research directions are suggested.

Keywords: Newsvendor · Distribution-free · Nonparametric methods · Data-driven · Inventory optimization · Systematic literature review

1 Introduction

Decision making under uncertainty is a major inventory management challenge that has been addressed in the literature over the past decades. Within this topic, the newsvendor problem (NVP) is a well-known inventory model that captures the decision maker trade-offs between overstocking and understocking of goods. In practice, it can be employed in a variety of industries, with different cost structures and uncertainty levels, such as travel tickets, fashion goods, textbooks, and bakery products.

Traditionally, according to [15], the retailer aims to satisfy a stochastic demand d for a single product in a single period. A cost of C is incurred at the end of this period, which is comprised of an overage cost o for unsold products, and an underage cost u

for stockouts. The NVP intends to minimize the total expected cost, as depicted in (1), where $a^+ := \max\{a, 0\}$.

$$\min_{q \geq 0} C(q), \text{ where } C(q) \triangleq E\big[u(d - q)^+ + o(q - d)^+\big] \tag{1}$$

The stochastic demand d is represented by a cumulative distribution function F(.). The optimal order quantity $q*$ can be achieved by calculating (2).

$$q^* \triangleq \inf\{q : F(q) \geq \frac{u}{u + o}\} \tag{2}$$

This representation holds for when the demand distribution is known, which is unlikely to happen in real life scenarios. If F(.) is unknown, then the optimal order quantity $q*$ cannot be directly evaluated [15]. Estimating a probability distribution is challenging and may result in misleading solutions, which is enhanced in settings with very little demand data to estimate market response to new products, such as the launch of medical devices or equipment by a start-up company [10].

In this context, there are two large groups of methods to solve the unknown demand distribution in inventory decisions: the parametric and nonparametric approaches. The first assumes that the distribution pertains to a parametric family of distributions, but the values of its parameters are unknown [12]. Within this group, the Bayesian approach corresponds to the earliest solutions that were developed. Readers may refer to [25] as the prominent study. Besides that, Operational Statistics is a parametric approach that was designed to perform demand estimation and inventory optimization simultaneously, readers may refer to [16].

In contrast, the nonparametric family of methods requires no assumptions regarding the demand distribution or its parameters and might be referred as data-driven in the literature since they rely on empirical information instead of assumptions to reach the solutions [6]. These methods can be executed in a single stage or in a separated parameters estimation and optimization steps, and can use contextual information, named data features, to enhance the predictive analytics models.

There is a recent surge on the interest in developing data-driven solutions, highlighting the novelty and early-stages of this topic. However, it could not yet be concluded to what extent the data-driven approaches are more accurate and applicable than their model-based counterparts, and in what scenarios the single-stage solutions outperform the two-steps methods [1, 11].

Therefore, our focus will be on the data-driven nonparametric solutions. A systematic literature review filters the publications with the aim to answer the following questions: (RQ 1) What are the data-driven approaches developed to solve the NVP in distribution-free settings? (RQ 2) How do these methods outperform the model-based approaches? (RQ 3) What are the advantages of single stage over two-steps solutions? (RQ 4) What are the research directions that remain unexplored?

The remainder of the paper is structured as follows. Section 2 details the steps executed in the review. Section 3 provides a descriptive analysis and classification of the selected papers with further evaluation and discussion of the findings, highlighting the future research directions. Lastly, Sect. 4 presents the conclusions of this review.

2   Methodology of the Systematic Literature Review

This research is based on the Systematic Literature Review method proposed by [26]. The procedure generally consists of a) identification of the need for a review and formulation of a research question, which was described in Sect. 1; b) elaboration of a research protocol, with establishment of search strings and selection criteria, which is illustrated in Table 1; and c) selection, assessment of relevant studies and discussion of findings as it is detailed in Sect. 3.

Table 1. Research protocol for the systematic literature review

Variable	Description
Databases	Scopus and Web of Science
Publication type	Peer-review journal articles, book chapters and technical reports
Language	Only articles written in English
Date range	All papers published until June 2021
Search fields	Advanced search in titles, abstracts, and keywords
Search terms	("data driven" OR "distribution free" OR "demand uncertainty" OR "nonparametric") AND ("newsvendor" OR "single period inventory" OR "stochastic inventory")
Deselection criterion I: Semantic relevance	Title, abstract, keywords or scanning the full paper was executed to determine the fitting of the paper to the topic
Deselection criterion II: Relevance to data-driven NVP	Full text was reviewed to determine the relevance of the paper to data-driven solutions in the NVP

Scopus showed 306 results, whereas Web of Science provided 357. Those studies that did not focus on the NVP demand uncertainty or adopted parametric methods were removed from the list. The significant papers that did not appear in the results but were frequently cited by the relevant studies were considered. Overall, 24 papers were thoroughly analyzed and will be discussed in Sect. 3.

3   Analysis and Discussion of the Findings

3.1   Descriptive Analysis of Selected Studies

Tables 2 and 3 present the selected studies that are relevant to the review, and facilitate the paper categorization and research trend identification. The categorization was made in terms of the main methods applied to solve the problem of unknown demand distribution. The publications were divided in four groups of methods that were largely adopted and one class for the miscellaneous techniques.

Table 2. Main topics addressed on the selected studies

Paper	Main topic
Scarf (1958) [24]	Min-Max solution for the demand uncertainty in a single period NVP with partial information available
Gallego and Moon (1993) [7]	Compact proof of [24] and extension to several settings
Godfrey and Powell (2001) [8]	Nonparametric adaptive algorithm with censored demand considering a sequence of piecewise linear functions
Powell et al. (2004) [20]	Extension of [8] algorithm that achieves an asymptotically optimal solution
Bertsimas and Thiele (2005) [2]	Data-driven optimization for the NVP and its extensions
Levi et al. (2007) [14]	Bounds in the sampling-based policies for solving the single and multi-period NVP
Perakis and Roels (2008) [19]	Min-Max regret solution in the NVP with partial demand information available
Huh et al. (2011) [12]	Nonparametric adaptive data-driven inventory control with censored demand based on Kaplan-Meier estimator
Lee et al. (2012) [13]	Newsvendor-type models with empirical distributions used as the quantile estimator
Beutel and Minner (2012) [4]	Single-step linear programming model for the NVP
Sachs and Minner (2014) [23]	Extension of [4] in a censored demand distribution and price-dependent settings
Levi et al. (2015) [15]	Extension of [14] with tighter bounds on the relative regret of the sampling-based solutions of the NVP
Wang et al. (2016) [27]	Use of likelihood function to build the distribution uncertainty set in data-driven robust optimization
Methan and Thiele (2016) [17]	Correction term to account for rare events in data-driven robust optimization
Ban and Rudin (2019) [1]	Empirical risk minimization and kernel-weights optimization as machine learning solutions for the NVP
Cheung and Simchi-Levi (2019) [6]	Polynomial time approximation scheme for the sample average approximation solution of the data-driven NVP
Hu et al. (2019) [10]	Functionally robust optimization as a data-driven approach for pricing and ordering decisions
Huber et al. (2019) [11]	Machine learning algorithms along with quantile regression and sample average approximation to solve the NVP
Cao and Shen (2019) [5]	Neural network model to forecast quantiles of stochastic inventory models
Oroojlooyjadid et al. (2020) [18]	Deep learning algorithm for the single-step optimization of the multi-feature NVP
Halman (2020) [9]	Development of approximation schemes for the non-linear and sample based NVP
Punia et al. (2020) [21]	Machine learning algorithm along with quantile regression to solve the NVP and a heuristics for capacity constraint
Qiu et al. (2020) [22]	Support vector clustering-based data-driven robust optimization to solve the multi-product NVP

(continued)

Table 2. (*continued*)

Paper	Main topic
Bertsimas and Koduri (2021) [3]	Global machine learning algorithms for approximating the function and the optimizer based on kernel Hilbert spaces

Table 3. Overview of journals and methods applied on the selected studies

Paper	Journal	RDO	SAA	QR	ML	Other
Scarf (1958)	Book chapter	✓				
Gallego & Moon (1993)	J. Oper. Res. Soc.	✓				
Godfrey & Powell (2001)	Manag. Sci.					✓
Powell et al. (2004)	Math. Oper. Res.					✓
Bertsimas & Thiele (2005)	Technical Report	✓				
Levi et al. (2007)	Math. Oper. Res.		✓			
Perakis & Roels (2008)	Oper. Res.	✓				
Huh et al. (2011)	Oper. Res.					✓
Lee et al. (2012)	Math. Meth. Oper. Res.		✓			
Beutel & Minner (2012)	Int. J. of Prod. Econ.			✓		
Sachs & Minner (2014)	Int. J. of Prod. Econ.			✓		
Levi et al. (2015)	Oper. Res.		✓			
Wang et al. (2016)	Comput. Manag. Sci.	✓				
Methan & Thiele (2016)	Comput. Manag. Sci.	✓				
Ban & Rudin (2019)	Oper. Res.			✓	✓	
Cheung & Simchi-Levi (2019)	Math. Oper. Res.		✓			
Hu et al. (2019)	Oper. Res.	✓				
Huber et al. (2019)	Eur. J. Oper. Res.		✓	✓	✓	
Cao & Shen (2019)	Oper. Res. Lett.			✓	✓	
Oroojlooyjadid et al. (2020)	IISE Trans.				✓	
Halman (2020)	IJOC		✓			
Punia et al. (2020)	Decis. Support Syst.			✓	✓	
Qiu et al. (2020)	Soft Comput.	✓				
Bertsimas and Koduri (2021)	Oper. Res.				✓	

RDO: Robust and Data-Driven Optimization; *SAA*: Sample Average Approximation; *QR*: Quantile Regression; *ML*: Machine Learning

3.2 Evaluation and Findings

Robust and Data-Driven Optimization (RDO)

Scarf [24] was the pioneer in developing a solution for the NVP when the demand information is uncertain. The author established a Min-Max approach to the single product and single period NVP with knowledge about the mean and standard deviation of the distribution. Gallego and Moon [7] extended this model to the recourse, fixed ordering cost, random yields, and multi-item cases.

Bertsimas and Thiele [2] were the first to investigate how to use demand observations as a direct input in data-driven optimization instead of assuming knowledge of the mean and standard deviation. Similarly to [7], the authors studied the NVP with several extensions and showed that these data-driven models could be reformulated as linear programming problems. Perakis and Roels [19] proposed an algorithm to minimize the NVP maximum regret when there is partial demand information available.

Wang et al. [27] addressed the drawbacks of the parametric and Distributionally Robust Optimization approaches by elaborating a new method named Likelihood Robust Optimization that chooses a function in a way that the observed data in the distribution achieve a certain level of likelihood. Hu et al. [10] proposed a modification named Functionally Robust Optimization that achieves a joint pricing and ordering decision under function form uncertainty to address the problem of model misspecification.

Moreover, Methan and Thiele [17] highlighted the weakness of data-driven approaches that rely solely on empirical demand distributions, since they may not consider rare occurrences. Their solution was the first to merge empirical distributions and range forecasts in robust optimization. To account for these tail events, a correction term was aggregated to the solution of the NVP. Recently, Qiu et al. [22] solved a multi-product NVP adopting a Support Vector Clustering based data-driven robust optimization method, which yields less conservative and better performance solutions than the traditional box and ellipsoid uncertainty sets.

Sample Average Approximation (SAA)

Levi et al. [14] considered the single and multi-period NVP to analyze the precision of the SAA method and to establish probabilistic bounds on the number of observations required to achieve a near-optimal solution without considering data features. By using the relative regret, Levi et al. [15] extended this procedure and derived a tighter bound for the probability that the solution exceeds a limit.

Similarly, Cheung and Simchi-Levi [6] evaluated the SAA performance by establishing an upper bound on the number of samples required to achieve a near-optimal solution that is independent of the demand distribution. They proposed a polynomial-time approximation scheme and established the sample lower bounds comparable to that by [15] to solve both single period and multi period NVP.

The SAA was one of the methods executed in Huber et al. [11] to demonstrate that data-driven approaches outperform model-based methods in most of the NVP settings. Halman [9] complemented the results from [6, 14, 15] by extending the SAA to set bounds on the number of observations required in nonlinear cost functions.

Quantile Regression (QR)

It is shown in a large body of literature that the solution for newsvendor-like problems is given by a particular quantile of the cumulative demand distribution [13]. By using an empirical distribution as estimator and QR for reaching optimal decisions in the NVP, Lee et al. [13] showed that erroneous decisions are made if the decision maker adopts an inappropriate model that overlooks or incorrectly considers the dependence of distributions on decisions.

Cao and Shen [5] were the first in the data-driven literature to handle an unknown form general autoregressive demand process by developing a single-step nonparametric method for quantile forecasting. Their model does not need previous quantile values as input and can deal with both stationary and nonstationary time series, outperforming the present neural network-based solutions for quantile prediction.

QR was also one of the methods executed in Huber et al. [11], Ban and Rudin [1] and Punia et al. [21]. The authors demonstrated that their proposed single-step data-driven NVP solution is equivalent to a high-dimensional QR and yields the satisfactory results when there is a large amount of data available.

Machine Learning (ML)

Beutel and Minner [4] designed the optimal inventory levels in a single-step procedure as the decision variables of a linear programming. The data-driven approach was compared with other benchmark methods and underperformed when the data sample was small. Sachs and Minner [23] extended this approach by studying the censored demand and price-dependent scenarios.

Ban and Rudin [1] highlighted that the demand estimation and optimization in separated steps are problematic in high-dimensional settings since it mainly relies on the performance of the demand estimation specifications in the first step. If there is an error, it will be amplified in the optimization. The authors developed algorithms based on the Empirical Risk Minimization principle and Kernel-weights Optimization.

Huber et al. [11] executed several combinations of single and two-steps methods with different target service levels to reach the optimal solution for the multi-feature NVP. Artificial Neural Networks and Decision Trees were adopted as ML forecasting methods. They concluded that in the two-steps method, the choice of the estimation procedure is a key decision to produce optimal results. They highlighted that the data-driven methods outperform because they could identify patterns across products and stores from contextual data, but they present the drawback that the reliable outcomes depend on the availability of a large amount of data.

Next, Cao and Shen [5] complemented the current neural network literature by developing the Double Parallel Feedforward Network-Based QR, a method capable of dealing with nonstationary time series that does not need past quantile values as input.

Oroojlooyjadid et al. [18] addressed the issue mentioned in [11] regarding the necessity of large quantities of historical data by developing a single-step Deep Learning solution for the multi-feature NVP. The model indeed outperforms other ML approaches and provides the solutions that could be achieved even with a small number of data points or high fluctuations in demand. Punia et al. [21] presented a study similar to [11], but with the novelty of addressing a multi-item NVP with a capacity constraint. They developed a heuristics that considers the hierarchies of the retail products, adopted Random Forest and Deep Neural Networks as forecasting methods and proposed a ML based QR for the single-step non-linear optimization.

Bertsimas and Koduri [3] reproduced a kernel Hilbert space to propose a global ML method to predict the objective and optimizer. Global ML predicts by choosing a functional form of the prediction that minimizes the loss function, whereas local ML predicts by measuring closeness to the existing data. They were the first to develop a general and asymptotically optimal approach based on loss function minimizing.

Other Approaches

Some of the studies were concentrated in censored demands settings, which means that there is only sales data available instead of the actual demand information. In this scenario, Godfrey and Powell [8] developed the Concave Adaptive Value Estimation algorithm to approximate the NVP cost function with a sequence of piecewise linear functions but did not provide convergence proof. Powell et al. [20] extended this procedure and demonstrated that an asymptotically optimal solution is achieved.

Huh et al. [12] proposed the first nonparametric adaptive data-driven policy for stochastic inventory models based on the product-limit form of the Kaplan-Meier estimator. Their proposed KM-myopic policies converge to the set of optimal solutions in the case of discrete demand distributions.

3.3 Research Directions

The data-driven methods for solving the NVP and other stochastic inventory models are a recent and active field of research that can be extended in several directions. It is noticed a surge in Machine Learning based approaches for uncertainties in inventory. It is suggested to improve and extend their applications in the development of tractable and accurate solutions in hyper-parameter and higher service level scenarios.

A meaningful downside of ML is the model with lack of interpretability. Building interpretable black-box models is a very important and applicable research direction. In addition, incorporating contextual information from both supply and demand sides will assist in understanding their influence in sales and customer behavior.

For the separated parameter estimation and inventory optimization solutions, exploring different newsvendor situations that have little or no historical sales data will require new approaches for forecasting such as adoption of hybrid demand estimation methods. In the case of single-step methods, Reinforcement (Deep) Learning has shown to be capable of dealing with higher degrees of uncertainty and processing larger datasets, hence this potential can be further extended to solve complex multi-echelon problems or evaluate the relationships in multi-period and multi-product settings.

Another opportunity to investigate is modifications of the loss function in Quantile Regression-Machine Learning based solutions for considering the impact of costs in problems with substitution, capacity, time, space, or budget constraints. Moreover, data-driven robust optimization might be further studied for developing assertive solutions that are protected from rare occurrences without being overly conservative.

4 Conclusions

This review identified and discussed about the major data-driven approaches for the distribution-free newsvendor problem, which have been developed over the past years. The main advantage of data-driven methods over their model-based counterparts is their adaptability in solving complex models with non-linear parameters and processing larger amounts of contextual information along with the demand. However, fully data-driven solutions present the disadvantages of being vulnerable to unusual events, model overfitting if not carefully tunned, lack of interpretability, or requiring large datasets.

RQ 1 in Sect. 1 was addressed in Subsect. 3.1, with five groups of methods that were largely applied in the NVP. The studies discussed in Subsect. 3.2, especially the ones that developed a Machine Learning-based solution, showed how the data-driven methods outperform model-based techniques, and the advantages of single-step over the two-step solutions, answering both RQ 2 and 3. The possible research directions that were suggested in Subsect. 3.3 answered RQ 4.

This study achieved its objectives by executing a systematic literature review about the studies in data-driven solutions to uncertainties in inventory decisions, more specifically in a Newsvendor Problem setting, which is a recent and promising research area. With the discussion of the major methodologies, their performance and identification of the gaps in the literature, it was possible to suggest the future research directions.

References

1. Ban, G., Rudin, C.: The big data newsvendor: Practical insights from machine learning. Oper. Res. **67**(1), 90–108 (2019). https://doi.org/10.1287/opre.2018.1757
2. Bertsimas, D., Thiele, A.: A data-driven approach to newsvendor problems. Technical report, Massachusetts Institute of Technology, Cambridge (2005)
3. Bertsimas, D., Koduri, N.: Data-driven optimization: a reproducing kernel Hilbert space approach. Oper. Res. (2021). https://doi.org/10.1287/opre.2020.2069
4. Beutel, A., Minner, S.: Safety stock planning under causal demand forecasting. Int. J. Prod. Econ. **140**(2), 637–645 (2012). https://doi.org/10.1016/j.ijpe.2011.04.017
5. Cao, Y., Shen, Z.M.: Quantile forecasting and data-driven inventory management under non-stationary demand. Oper. Res. Lett. **47**(6), 465–472 (2019). https://doi.org/10.1016/j.orl.2019.08.008
6. Cheung, W.C., Simchi-Levi, D.: Sampling-based approximation schemes for capacitated stochastic inventory control models. Math. Oper. Res. **44**(2), 668–692 (2019). https://doi.org/10.1287/moor.2018.0940
7. Gallego, G., Moon, I.: The distribution free newsboy problem: review and extensions. J. Oper. Res. Soc. **44**(8), 825–834 (1993). https://doi.org/10.1057/jors.1993.141
8. Godfrey, G.A., Powell, W.B.: An adaptive, distribution-free algorithm for the newsvendor problem with censored demands, with applications to inventory and distribution. Manage. Sci. **47**(8), 1101–1112 (2001). https://doi.org/10.1287/mnsc.47.8.1101.10231
9. Halman, N.: Provably near-optimal approximation schemes for implicit stochastic and sample-based dynamic programs. INFORMS J. Comput. **32**(4), 1157–1181 (2020). https://doi.org/10.1287/ijoc.2019.0926
10. Hu, J., Li, J., Mehrotra, S.: A data-driven functionally robust approach for simultaneous pricing and order quantity decisions with unknown demand function. Oper. Res. **67**(6), 1564–1585 (2019). https://doi.org/10.1287/opre.2019.1849
11. Huber, J., Müller, S., Fleischmann, M., Stuckenschmidt, H.: A data-driven newsvendor problem: from data to decision. Eur. J. Oper. Res. **278**(3), 904–915 (2019). https://doi.org/10.1016/j.ejor.2019.04.043
12. Huh, W.T., Levi, R., Rusmevichientong, P., Orlin, J.B.: Adaptive data-driven inventory control with censored demand based on Kaplan-Meier estimator. Oper. Res. **59**(4), 929–941 (2011). https://doi.org/10.1287/opre.1100.0906

13. Lee, S., Homem-de-Mello, T., Kleywegt, A.J.: Newsvendor-type models with decision-dependent uncertainty. Math. Methods Oper. Res. **76**(2), 189–221 (2012). https://doi.org/10.1007/s00186-012-0396-3

14. Levi, R., Roundy, R.O., Shmoys, D.B.: Provably near-optimal sampling-based policies for stochastic inventory control models. Math. Oper. Res. **32**(4), 821–839 (2007). https://doi.org/10.1287/moor.1070.0272

15. Levi, R., Perakis, G., Uichanco, J.: The data-driven newsvendor problem: new bounds and insights. Oper. Res. **63**(6), 1294–1306 (2015). https://doi.org/10.1287/opre.2015.1422

16. Liyanage, L.H., Shanthikumar, J.G.: A practical inventory control policy using operational statistics. Oper. Res. Lett. **33**(4), 341–348 (2005). https://doi.org/10.1016/j.orl.2004.08.003

17. Metan, G., Thiele, A.: Protecting the data-driven newsvendor against rare events: a correction-term approach. CMS **13**(3), 459–482 (2016). https://doi.org/10.1007/s10287-016-0258-1

18. Oroojlooyjadid, A., Snyder, L.V., Takáč, M.: Applying deep learning to the newsvendor problem. IISE Trans. **52**(4), 444–463 (2020). https://doi.org/10.1080/24725854.2019.1632502

19. Perakis, G., Roels, G.: Regret in the newsvendor model with partial information. Oper. Res. **56**(1), 188–203 (2008). https://doi.org/10.1287/opre.1070.0486

20. Powell, W., Ruszczynski, A., Topaloglu, H.: Learning algorithms for separable approximations of discrete stochastic optimization problems. Math. Oper. Res. **29**(4), 814–836 (2004). https://doi.org/10.1287/moor.1040.0107

21. Punia, S., Singh, S.P., Madaan, J.K.: From predictive to prescriptive analytics: A data-driven multi-item newsvendor model. Decis. Support Syst. **136** (2020). https://doi.org/10.1016/j.dss.2020.113340

22. Qiu, R., Sun, Y., Fan, Z.-P., Sun, M.: Robust multi-product inventory optimization under support vector clustering-based data-driven demand uncertainty set. Soft. Comput. **24**(9), 6259–6275 (2019). https://doi.org/10.1007/s00500-019-03927-2

23. Sachs, A., Minner, S.: The data-driven newsvendor with censored demand observations. Int. J. Prod. Econ. **149**, 28–36 (2014). https://doi.org/10.1016/j.ijpe.2013.04.039

24. Scarf, H.: A min-max solution of an inventory problem. Studies in the Mathematical Theory of Inventory and Production, pp. 201–209. Stanford University Press, Stanford (1958)

25. Scarf, H.: Bayes solutions of the statistical inventory problem. Ann. Math. Stat. **30**(2), 490–508 (1959)

26. Tranfield, D., Denyer, D., Smart, P.: Towards a methodology for developing evidence-informed management knowledge by means of systematic review. Br. J. Manag. **14**(3), 207–222 (2003). https://doi.org/10.1111/1467-8551.00375

27. Wang, Z., Glynn, P.W., Ye, Y.: Likelihood robust optimization for data-driven problems. CMS **13**(2), 241–261 (2015). https://doi.org/10.1007/s10287-015-0240-3

An Information Sharing Framework for Supply Chain Networks: What, When, and How to Share

Eunji Lee$^{(\boxtimes)}$ ⑩ and Stefan Minner

Technical University of Munich, 80333 Munich, Germany
eunji.lee@tum.de

Abstract. In decentralized supply chains, firms often deal with asymmetric information. One company's private information can be relevant for the other company to make better decisions. Therefore, what to share, when to reveal, and how to share the information are of interest. There has been an increasing interest in supply chain coordination issues under asymmetric information in the past two decades. However, few of them consider strategic information sharing among the supply chain members. Thus, this paper aims to review the development of information sharing in supply chain management. We classify the existing literature into three categories, namely (i) supply chain coordination under information asymmetry, (ii) information sharing technologies, and (iii) a strategic information sharing framework regarding what, when, and how to share. The related supply chain literature is reviewed based on the different focuses when dealing with information asymmetry. We report the research development and gaps of each category. Further, we propose some future research directions based on the findings from the literature review.

Keywords: Information sharing · Game theory · Asymmetric information · Information sharing technologies · Literature review

1 Introduction

Nowadays, companies can access abundant data and share precise information with their supply chain members. As competition and interaction are intensified across horizontal and vertical supply chains, the decision to share information is more intricate than ever [50]. In a decentralized supply chain, asymmetric information can lead to a significant efficiency loss [37]. Hence, the right use of available information has become an indispensable factor for a company to sustain its competitiveness [23].

Even though empirical evidence shows that information sharing can be a means of supply chain coordination, strategic information sharing is still challenging for supply chain members [13]. The main reason is the reluctance of

© IFIP International Federation for Information Processing 2021
Published by Springer Nature Switzerland AG 2021
A. Dolgui et al. (Eds.): APMS 2021, IFIP AICT 633, pp. 159–168, 2021.
https://doi.org/10.1007/978-3-030-85910-7_17

the members to share information due to the threat of information leakage and opportunistic behaviors [28]. Further, supply chain members possess different types of private information such as demand, costs, capacity, and inventory. This private information is rarely accessible to the other supply chain members; however, it still directly or indirectly influences each member's performance [34].

Due to its importance but challenging nature, information sharing issues have gained significant attention in the supply chain management (SCM) area [8, 13, 50, 53]. Their focus is mainly on coordination mechanism designs such as a menu of contracts and side payments, given that one member in the supply chain has prior access to certain information. Most of the literature in this field knows what to be shared and investigates how to make the party that possesses the private information reveal it with contractual agreements.

Another way of dealing with information sharing issues is advanced information sharing technology such as cryptographic techniques [18]. In this field, actors focus on secure sharing or even cooperation without revealing private information to each other. The literature on information sharing technologies aims to develop collaboration supporting applications/environments among actors willing to share information (even if it is not truthful) [53]. This stream of literature knows what to share and focuses on how to (securely) share the information.

While increasing attention has been given to information sharing, few authors focus on the impact of different sharing behaviors on performance. However, in many cases, a decision requires different sets of another member's private information, and the decision eventually influences the other's performance. Thus, a strategic information sharing framework that answers what, when, and how to share information is highly relevant. To better understand strategic information sharing issues, we review the development of information sharing in SCM with respect to the three categories of information sharing: (i) supply chain coordination under information asymmetry, (ii) information sharing technologies, and (iii) strategic information sharing framework regarding what, when, and how to share.

2   Literature Review

For a systematic literature review, we followed [52] and employed the keywords: information sharing, asymmetric information, incomplete information, secure sharing, information security, private information, strategic sharing, and supply chain. The sources of data included Google Scholar, Springer, ScienceDirect.

2.1   Coordination Under Asymmetric Information

We refer to [8, 13, 28, 50, 53] for general reviews. We classify the literature depending on asymmetric information types, the two most common being demand and cost information. Even though other types of asymmetric information such as quality, capacity, and effort level exist, the number of literature is significantly lower than that on demand and cost information [50]. Therefore, we focus on these two types.

Demand information of retailers often influences the capacity decision of suppliers. [9] consider a single supplier and multiple retailers who compete for scarce supplier capacity. The private information is the demand-based order quantities of the retailers. They demonstrate that the truth-telling mechanisms may not result in maximum profits for the supplier and the retailers. Later, [10] suggest two capacity compliance contracts that realize truthful demand forecast sharing. Unlike [9], they consider a monopolistic setting with one supplier and one manufacturer. [43] also consider a supplier who makes a capacity decision and a manufacturer who possesses precise demand forecast information. Compared to the previous literature mainly focusing on the screening mechanisms for truth-telling, they develop both signaling (advance purchase) and screening (capacity reservation) mechanisms for credible information sharing.

[49] extend a single period incentive alignment problem to multiple periods. Over repeating selling seasons, the supplier offers a simple contract if the demand information is observed. Otherwise, the supplier designs a truth-telling contract for the manufacturer. He concludes that the manufacturer is worse-off when a simple contract is offered. While most of the literature decides either price or quantity based on the available information, [17] propose a dual decision-making contract where the manufacturer decides both the capacity and the wholesale price. The dual decisions that are influenced oppositely by the demand information reduce the retailer's incentive to distort the information. While most of the literature considers an intra-firm relationship, [3,14,36,45] study inter-firm situations where a manager tries to incentivize salesforces to disclose market information.

Asymmetric cost information has received as much attention as demand information [50]. [21] consider asymmetric cost information and develop a quantity discount contract under asymmetric cost information. They extend to two-part linear schemes and two-part nonlinear schemes introduced earlier by [20]. Quantity discounts are the most frequently applied mechanisms to achieve supply chain coordination between one member who possesses private information and the other who offers the contract [32,51,60]. Another common mechanism is the menu of contracts. The conceptual foundation of both contracts lies in the revelation principle [11,24,33,39,41,56]. To model asymmetric information, [11,39] apply a two-point distribution. On the other hand, [24,33,41,56] assume that the belief in cost follows a certain distribution. While the contract design is an effective means of coordinating supply chains [7,31,40,53] introduce auctions as a coordination mechanism.

Whereas most literature considers a single source of asymmetric information, [6,38] consider two or more sources. [38] use a menu of contracts for the supplier, where the disruption risks of demand and cost are the retailer's private information. [6] consider multiple suppliers with private capacity information and multiple retailers with private demand information. Instead of introducing a contract design mechanism, they compare two bargaining power structures between downstream (pooling systems) and upstream (distribution system) members. They conclude that multilateral information asymmetry only harms the efficiency of the supply chain if the upstream principal distributes resources across multiple downstream agents. [34] study a supplier and an original equipment manufacturer (OEM) relationship where the OEM has two private information sets: demand and production cost. Interestingly, they find that the conventional contract design, such as the menu of contracts, cannot incentivize the retailer to reveal truthful information when there are two sets of asymmetric information.

2.2   Information Sharing Technologies

The technical perspective of secure sharing attracts growing attention while entering the era of big data and leaves future research directions integrated with the classic information asymmetric issues. Companies nowadays actively search for new technologies to share information on time and synchronize information flows with other companies [26]. At the same time, the companies' concerns about privacy and information security grow. In this study, we specifically investigate cryptographic technology such as blockchain and secure multiparty computation (SMC), the main concern of which is secure information sharing.

Blockchain technology gained popularity in computer science after [42] introduced the cryptocurrency Bitcoin. Whilst the most commonly known application of blockchain technology is cryptocurrency, blockchain technology for commodity trading and asset tracking shows its promising future [29]. Despite the slow adaptation of technology in the SCM field, [35] assert that blockchain can improve the transparency, traceability, and efficiency of sharing information. [12,55] give a review of blockchain and propose several future agendas in SCM. For instance, [55] suggest the integration of blockchain technology with IoT-based supply chains. As the number of IoT devices rises, blockchain can be a solution to store an excessive amount of generated data from IoT. On the other hand, [12] highlight technical challenges of blockchain application such as trustfulness, lack of standards, and interoperability.

Even though most papers are conceptual reviews and examine future potentials [46,47], a few quantify the benefit of blockchain technology for supply chain performance. [58] apply the technology in a global trade context with air and ocean shipping. They introduce mathematical models where the benefit of blockchain comes with the accuracy of prediction and reduced operational costs. Further, [22] use a game theoretic framework. They demonstrate that blockchain is not always preferred to the traditional platform as they have to consider the tradeoffs between implementation costs of blockchain and gained efficiency. However, with the help of two smart contracts (wholesale price and revenue sharing), the blockchain application can lead to better performance. [22,58] consider blockchain technology in their economic models. [15] suggest a blockchain protocol, b_verify (a Bitcoin network), and present an implementation that measures the signaling costs of a firm's quality and demonstrate that, due to the transparency, the company can secure lower signaling costs.

Whereas the main benefit of blockchain is the transparency of the information, SMC emphasizes privacy protection. [57] propose a mechanism for secure function evaluation by using garbled circuits. The garbled circuit is one of the first and best-known SMC methods aligned with secret sharing [48] and homomorphic encryption (HE) [16]. A given condition of these three methods is the assumption of honest-but-curious (semi-honest) players. In the SCM field, we find several attempts at applying SMC concepts to share private information. [2], for example, introduce SMC algorithms based on Yao's protocol [57] to allocate the capacity in e-commerce. [1] develop a protocol for secure collaborative forecasting and replenishment (SCPFR) decisions. They both use secret sharing and HE approaches. They are the first to consider inverse optimization issues in SMC. [18] propose a secure mechanism to optimize task swaps of independent trucking companies reluctant to share their current pick-up and delivery schedules. The suggested method allows truck companies to exchange their pick-up and delivery tasks without revealing more information than necessary to execute the exchanged task. [44] also use the garbled circuit to solve the Joint Economic Lot-Sizing (JELS) problem and show the efficiency of SMC to share profits.

2.3 Strategic Information Sharing Framework

The literature on strategic information sharing is relatively scarce. While information sharing itself is a rising topic in the SCM area, only a few offer information exchange strategies for scenarios where the others also share/do not share. [54] investigate the ramification of sharing a retailer's private information with a supplier with prior knowledge from a subjective distribution. They elaborate on the advantages and disadvantages that the retailer faces under different contract schemes by letting the supplier improve knowledge. However, they assume that the private information is held by the retailer only; hence, the information exchange between the supply chain members is not considered. [59] consider both a retailer and a supplier that possess partial demand information. Under a wholesale price contract, they find that sharing occurs based on the variance and the correlation of demand information between the companies and the other company's sharing behavior. Besides, they suggest that a revenue sharing contract can coordinate the system while ensuring information sharing from both firms. [27] investigate sharing behavior of retailers who possess private demand information. They include two competing channels and analyze the impact of competition on the sharing strategy. They propose an information sharing framework that suggests when to share the information with their upstream manufacturers to induce lower wholesale prices. However, they, too, are limited in that they only consider unilateral private information.

3   Results and Implications

From the literature regarding information sharing, we observe the following:

- What to share is exogenously given in the problems
- How to share unilateral information is comprehensively investigated. However, the literature on how to share bi/multilateral information is scarce
- When to share throughout the relationship in a supply chain network is rarely covered

In the information sharing literature, as the type of asymmetric information is set exogenously, the question of what to share is often disregarded. The most common consideration of asymmetric information in the existing literature is either cost or demand. The reason is that most analytical models seek to maximize profit or minimize cost. Having demand or cost as private information facilitates the analysis to observe the impact of asymmetric information on the supply chain performance. However, supply chain members can learn which type of information to reveal over some periods. As most of the literature considers unilateral (bilateral) asymmetric information and the rest of the information in supply chains as common knowledge, endogenizing what to share can be a future research direction.

Further, there is a lack of dual (multiple) information sharing in SCM. A significant proportion of the problems is modeled under a Stackelberg game framework where a leader needs to decide under unilateral information asymmetry. However, it is questionable whether the existing mechanisms can still be efficient under multiple asymmetric information [34]. Moreover, the multilateral/bilateral exchange of information itself can impact the performance of the supply chain members. For example, a manufacturer's capacity decision is often based on the market demands that are the private information of retailers and the production cost of manufacturers. Since the manufacturer's capacity level directly affects the retailer's performance, the retailer is eager to know how and based on what available information the capacity is set. From the supplier's perspective, the more precise he knows demand, the better he can plan. Knowing that the retailer is interested in his capacity decision, he can strategically reveal which information he knows. In this regard, more attention is needed to answer when and how to exchange information under consideration of bilateral or multilateral asymmetric information.

Whereas mechanism designs seek to answer how to make private information be shared, the information sharing technology aims to answer how to securely and efficiently share private information. Especially, blockchain technology is promising because it can be a solution for truthful information sharing. At the same time, SMC can provide a new opportunity by encouraging reluctant supply chain members to cooperate securely. However, reverse optimization and technical security problems still need to be solved before further applications can be realized. Lastly, the research on information sharing technologies often assumes honest-but-curious players. However, this assumption does not take the impact of information distortion into account. Hence, another research direction can integrate truth-telling mechanisms from the supply chain coordination literature and cryptographic technologies. With the right use of information mechanisms, firms can secure private information and avoid suboptimal decisions from information asymmetry.

References

1. Atallah, M., Blanton, M., Deshpande, V., Frikken, K., Li, J., Schwarz, L.: Secure collaborative planning, forecasting, and replenishment (SCPFR). In: Multi-Echelon/Public Applications of Supply Chain Management Conference, pp. 165–180 (2006)
2. Atallah, M., Elmongui, H.G., Deshpande, V., Schwarz, L.B.: Secure supply-chain protocols. In: 2003 EEE International Conference on E-Commerce, CEC 2003, pp. 293–302. IEEE (2003)
3. Atkinson, A.A.: Incentives, uncertainty, and risk in the newsboy problem. Decis. Sci. **10**(3), 341–357 (1979)
4. Babich, V., Li, H., Ritchken, P., Wang, Y.: Contracting with asymmetric demand information in supply chains. Eur. J. Oper. Res. **217**(2), 333–341 (2012)
5. Bagchi, P.K., Ha, B.C., Skjoett-Larsen, T., Soerensen, L.B.: Supply chain integration: a European survey. Inte. J. Logist. Manag. **16**(2), 275–294 (2005)
6. Belloni, A., Lopomo, G., Wang, S.: Resource allocation under demand uncertainty and private information. Manage. Sci. **63**(12), 4219–4235 (2017)
7. Budde, M., Minner, S.: First-and second-price sealed-bid auctions applied to push and pull supply contracts. Eur. J. Oper. Res. **237**(1), 370–382 (2014)
8. Cachon, G.P.: Supply chain coordination with contracts. In: Graves, S., de Kok, T. (eds.) Supply Chain Management: Design, Coordination and Operation, vol. 11, Chap. 10, pp. 227–339. Elsevier (2003)
9. Cachon, G.P., Lariviere, M.A.: Capacity choice and allocation: strategic behavior and supply chain performance. Manage. Sci. **45**(8), 1091–1108 (1999)
10. Cachon, G.P., Lariviere, M.A.: Contracting to assure supply: how to share demand forecasts in a supply chain. Manage. Sci. **47**(5), 629–646 (2001)
11. Cakanyıldırım, M., Feng, Q., Gan, X., Sethi, S.P.: Contracting and coordination under asymmetric production cost information. Prod. Oper. Manag. **21**(2), 345–360 (2012)
12. Chang, Y., Iakovou, E., Shi, W.: Blockchain in global supply chains and cross border trade: a critical synthesis of the state-of-the-art, challenges and opportunities. Int. J. Prod. Res. **58**(7), 2082–2099 (2020)
13. Chen, F.: Information sharing and supply chain coordination. In: Graves, S., de Kok, T. (eds.) Supply Chain Management: Design, Coordination and Operation, vol. 11, Chap. 3, pp. 341–421. Elsevier (2003)
14. Chen, F.: Salesforce incentives, market information, and production/inventory planning. Manage. Sci. **51**(1), 60–75 (2005)
15. Chod, J., Trichakis, N., Tsoukalas, G., Aspegren, H., Weber, M.: On the financing benefits of supply chain transparency and blockchain adoption. Manage. Sci. **66**(10), 4378–4396 (2020)
16. Choi, J.I., Butler, K.R.: Secure multiparty computation and trusted hardware: examining adoption challenges and opportunities. Secur. Commun. Netw. **2019**, 1–28 (2019)

17. Chu, L.Y., Shamir, N., Shin, H.: Strategic communication for capacity alignment with pricing in a supply chain. Manage. Sci. **63**(12), 4366–4388 (2017)
18. Clifton, C., Iyer, A., Cho, R., Jiang, W., Kantarcıoğlu, M., Vaidya, J.: An approach to securely identifying beneficial collaboration in decentralized logistics systems. Manuf. Serv. Oper. Manag. **10**(1), 108–125 (2008)
19. Cohen, M.A., Ho, T.H., Ren, Z.J., Terwiesch, C.: Measuring imputed cost in the semiconductor equipment supply chain. Manage. Sci. **49**(12), 1653–1670 (2003)
20. Corbett, C.J.: Stochastic inventory systems in a supply chain with asymmetric information: cycle stocks, safety stocks, and consignment stock. Oper. Res. **49**(4), 487–500 (2001)
21. Corbett, C.J., De Groote, X.: A supplier's optimal quantity discount policy under asymmetric information. Manage. Sci. **46**(3), 444–450 (2000)
22. De Giovanni, P.: Blockchain and smart contracts in supply chain management: a game theoretic model. Int. J. Prod. Econ. **228**, 107855 (2020)
23. Eymann, T.: The uncertainty of information systems: cause or effect of VUCA? In: Mack, O., Khare, A., Kramer, A., Burgartz, T. (eds.) Managing in a VUCA World, pp. 227–240. Springer, Cham (2016). https://doi.org/10.1007/978-3-319-16889-0_15
24. Fang, X., Ru, J., Wang, Y.: Optimal procurement design of an assembly supply chain with information asymmetry. Prod. Oper. Manag. **23**(12), 2075–2088 (2014)
25. Fawcett, S.E., Magnan, G.M., Williams, A.J.: Supply chain trust is within your grasp. Supply Chain Manag. Rev. **8**(2), 20–26 (2004)
26. Gu, M., Yang, L., Huo, B.: The impact of information technology usage on supply chain resilience and performance: an ambidexterous view. Int. J. Prod. Econ. **232**, 107956 (2021)
27. Guo, L., Li, T., Zhang, H.: Strategic information sharing in competing channels. Prod. Oper. Manag. **23**(10), 1719–1731 (2014)
28. Ha, A.Y., Tang, C.S.: Handbook of Information Exchange in Supply Chain Management. Springer Series in Supply Chain Management, Springer, Cham (2017). https://doi.org/10.1007/978-3-319-32441-8
29. Hellwig, D., Karlic, G., Huchzermeier, A.: Build Your Own Blockchain. Springer, Cham (2020). https://doi.org/10.1007/978-3-030-40142-9
30. Iyer, G., Villas-Boas, J.M.: A bargaining theory of distribution channels. J. Mark. Res. **40**(1), 80–100 (2003)
31. Jin, M., Yu, A.J.: Procurement auctions and supply chain performance. Int. J. Prod. Econ. **162**, 192–200 (2015)
32. Kayış, E., Erhun, F., Plambeck, E.L.: Delegation vs. control of component procurement under asymmetric cost information and simple contracts. Manuf. Serv. Oper. Manag. **15**(1), 45–56 (2013)
33. Kim, S.H., Netessine, S.: Collaborative cost reduction and component procurement under information asymmetry. Manage. Sci. **59**(1), 189–206 (2013)
34. Kostamis, D., Duenyas, I.: Purchasing under asymmetric demand and cost information: when is more private information better? Oper. Res. **59**(4), 914–928 (2011)
35. Kouhizadeh, M., Saberi, S., Sarkis, J.: Blockchain technology and the sustainable supply chain: theoretically exploring adoption barriers. Int. J. Prod. Econ. **231**, 107831 (2021)
36. Lee, C.Y., Yang, R.: Compensation plan for competing salespersons under asymmetric information. Eur. J. Oper. Res. **227**(3), 570–580 (2013)
37. Lee, H.L., Padmanabhan, V., Whang, S.: Information distortion in a supply chain: the bullwhip effect. Manage. Sci. **43**(4), 546–558 (1997)

38. Lei, D., Li, J., Liu, Z.: Supply chain contracts under demand and cost disruptions with asymmetric information. Int. J. Prod. Econ. **139**(1), 116–126 (2012)
39. Li, X., Li, Y.: Optimal service contract under cost information symmetry/asymmetry. J. Oper. Res. Soc. **67**(2), 269–279 (2016)
40. Lorentziadis, P.L.: Pricing in a supply chain for auction bidding under information asymmetry. Eur. J. Oper. Res. **237**(3), 871–886 (2014)
41. Mukhopadhyay, S.K., Zhu, X., Yue, X.: Optimal contract design for mixed channels under information asymmetry. Prod. Oper. Manag. **17**(6), 641–650 (2008)
42. Nakamoto, S.: Bitcoin: a peer-to-peer electronic cash system. Technical report, Manubot (2008)
43. Özer, Ö., Wei, W.: Strategic commitments for an optimal capacity decision under asymmetric forecast information. Manage. Sci. **52**(8), 1238–1257 (2006)
44. Pibernik, R., Zhang, Y., Kerschbaum, F., Schröpfer, A.: Secure collaborative supply chain planning and inverse optimization-the JELS model. Eur. J. Oper. Res. **208**(1), 75–85 (2011)
45. Porteus, E.L., Whang, S.: On manufacturing/marketing incentives. Manage. Sci. **37**(9), 1166–1181 (1991)
46. Pournader, M., Shi, Y., Seuring, S., Koh, S.L.: Blockchain applications in supply chains, transport and logistics: a systematic review of the literature. Int. J. Prod. Res. **58**(7), 2063–2081 (2020)
47. Saberi, S., Kouhizadeh, M., Sarkis, J., Shen, L.: Blockchain technology and its relationships to sustainable supply chain management. Int. J. Prod. Res. **57**(7), 2117–2135 (2019)
48. Shamir, A.: How to share a secret. Commun. ACM **22**(11), 612–613 (1979)
49. Shamir, N.: Asymmetric forecast information and the value of demand observation in repeated procurement. Decis. Sci. **44**(6), 979–1020 (2013)
50. Shen, B., Choi, T.M., Minner, S.: A review on supply chain contracting with information considerations: information updating and information asymmetry. Int. J. Prod. Res. **57**(15–16), 4898–4936 (2019)
51. Sucky, E.: A bargaining model with asymmetric information for a single supplier-single buyer problem. Eur. J. Oper. Res. **171**(2), 516–535 (2006)
52. Tranfield, D., Denyer, D., Smart, P.: Towards a methodology for developing evidence-informed management knowledge by means of systematic review. Br. J. Manag. **14**(3), 207–222 (2003)
53. Vosooghidizaji, M., Taghipour, A., Canel-Depitre, B.: Supply chain coordination under information asymmetry: a review. Int. J. Prod. Res. **58**(6), 1805–1834 (2020)
54. Wang, J.C., Lau, H.S., Lau, A.H.L.: How a retailer should manipulate a dominant manufacturer's perception of market and cost parameters. Int. J. Prod. Econ. **116**(1), 43–60 (2008)
55. Wang, Y., Han, J.H., Beynon-Davies, P.: Understanding blockchain technology for future supply chains: a systematic literature review and research agenda. Supply Chain Manag. Int. J. **24**(1), 62–84 (2019)
56. Xu, H., Shi, N., Ma, S.h., Lai, K.K.: Contracting with an urgent supplier under cost information asymmetry. Eur. J. Oper. Res. **206**(2), 374–383 (2010)
57. Yao, A.C.: Protocols for secure computations. In: 23rd Annual Symposium on Foundations of Computer Science (SFCS 1982), pp. 160–164. IEEE (1982)

58. Yoon, J., Talluri, S., Yildiz, H., Sheu, C.: The value of blockchain technology implementation in international trades under demand volatility risk. Int. J. Prod. Res. **58**(7), 2163–2183 (2020)
59. Zhang, J., Chen, J.: Coordination of information sharing in a supply chain. Int. J. Prod. Econ. **143**(1), 178–187 (2013)
60. Zissis, D., Ioannou, G., Burnetas, A.: Supply chain coordination under discrete information asymmetries and quantity discounts. Omega **53**, 21–29 (2015)

A Robust Data Driven Approach
to Supply Planning

Benoit Loger[✉], Alexandre Dolgui, Fabien Lehuédé, and Guillaume Massonnet

IMT Atlantique, LS2N, 4 rue Alfred Kastler - La Chantrerie, 44307 Nantes, France
`benoit.loger@imt-atlantique.fr`

Abstract. We develop two robust optimization models to plan the supply operations of an assembly line when the latter are subcontracted to an external service provider. The uncertainty sets are constructed from available information on picking times both in a classical budget-based robust approach and by using Support Vector Clustering. Numerical experiments are conducted on test instances derived from a practical case to illustrate the effectiveness of the proposed approach. The results show that the robust optimization approach is efficient to reduce the impact of picking time uncertainties on production and that the SVC-based model outperforms the classical budget-based model.

Keywords: Supply chain · Data-driven optimization · Robust optimization

1 Introduction

We focus on a problem derived from a practical case encountered in the aircraft industry, in which a single assembly line manufactures several products in order to satisfy the needs that are planned over a discrete and finite planning horizon. Each final product has its own bill of material (BOM) that involves different components. The components are stored in a remote warehouse and their picking and delivery to the production line are handled by a third party logistic provider (TPL) following the manufacturer's orders. In a sense, this problem is closely related to the class of assemble-to-order systems, which are often encountered in the inventory control literature. The need to define both component replenishment and production policies makes assemble-to-order systems particularly challenging. Large surveys of this topic have been presented in [1] and more recently in [2] where authors established that the general case of multiple final products and multiple periods have not been solved to optimality yet. However, the recent work of [3] appear like a significant step forward towards this objective. Their method is based on a two stage stochastic program which decomposes the original problem considering the component replenishment problem as the first stage of decision and the assignment problem as second stage decisions.

In this paper, we investigate the planning of picking orders when the available information related to picking times at the TPL is uncertain. Several approaches have been developed in the literature to deal with uncertainty in optimization

Published by Springer Nature Switzerland AG 2021
A. Dolgui et al. (Eds.): APMS 2021, IFIP AICT 633, pp. 169–178, 2021.
https://doi.org/10.1007/978-3-030-85910-7_18

problems (see [4] for a recent survey of these techniques). Stochastic programming and stochastic dynamic programming are two examples of optimization tools that are frequently applied when some parameters of the problem under study are random. These methods relies on the assumption that the random variables of the problem are characterized by a known probability distribution. The main issue with this paradigm is that in most real-life applications this knowledge is not available. To overcome the lack of accurate information, researchers from the operations research community have dedicated considerable efforts in the past decade to develop optimization methods that are robust to imprecision in the modeling assumptions.

The concept of robust optimization was introduced by [5] who considers that unknown parameters belong to a finite *uncertainty set* without making any assumption on their distribution. The objective is then to find a solution that is optimal when the uncertain parameters take their worst values in the uncertainty set. To avoid over-conservatism, [6] and [7] introduce an ellipsoidal uncertainty set controlled by a size parameter and derive a second-order cone robust program. In [8], the authors propose an alternative approach that constructs a polyhedral uncertainty set whose size is controlled by a so-called budget of uncertainty, which also limits over-conservatism. The major advantage of the latter is that when the original problem is formulated as a linear (or mixed integer) program, its robust counterpart remains of the same nature, which is convenient in terms of tractability. The design of the uncertainty sets have been in the center of researchers considerations since the early developments of robust optimization. One major restriction on these uncertainty sets is that they assume that uncertain parameters are symmetrically and independently distributed. Few works have proposed ways to reduce the effects of these drawbacks. For example, [9] modifies the definition of the polyhedral uncertainty set to improve their average performances and [10] integrates correlations between parameters to improve the accuracy of the robust models in this case.

The first application of RO to inventory management is due to [11], the authors apply the model of [8] to tackle uncertainty on the demand for a multi-period inventory management problem. On similar topics, [12] considered a production planning problem with uncertain costs and demands and [13] considered uncertain returns and demands. In [14], the authors proposed a robust model for an integrated production planning with order acceptance problem where customer demands is uncertain. The RO approach have been extended to uncertainty on raw material availability in [15] to schedule the production of a sawmill with uncertainty on products demand and raw material availability and in [16] where the authors proposed a robust approach to tackle lead-time uncertainty.

The growing volume of data available at the operational level recently became a focal point for researchers in order to better incorporate uncertainty into optimization methods. We now witness the emergence of the so-called *Data-Driven Robust Optimization* (DDRO) models in the literature, where uncertainty sets are designed directly from the data available. Among the different DDRO approaches, [17] and [18] use coherent risk measure to construct uncertainty sets

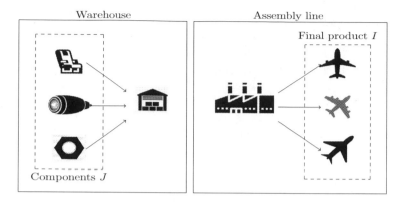

Fig. 1. Diagram of the problem

for linear optimization problems. [19] proposed and uncertainty set based on a support vector clustering algorithm to avoid over conservatism. They introduced a piecewise linear kernel function to derive a polyhedral uncertainty set and a tractable reformulation of linear optimization problem. Their uncertainty set give a better description of random variables in the case of asymmetric distribution and lead to less conservative solution than traditional uncertainty set. Their approach have been applied with success to a multi-product inventory management problem by [20] and to energy system optimization by [21].

The remainder of this paper is organized as follows. Section 2 presents the supply planning problem that motivates this study, along with a deterministic mathematical formulation. In Sect. 3 we derive two tractable robust formulations of the problem from the budget-based and the SVC-based uncertainty sets, respectively. Finally Sect. 4 presents the experimental protocol and the numerical results obtained with both robust formulations, while Sect. 5 contains our concluding remarks and some perspective for future research directions.

2   Problem Statement and Deterministic Formulation

We study the case of a single assembly line that combines different components into several final products over a finite planning horizon discretized into T periods. We denote I and J the set of products and components, respectively. In each period $t = 1, \ldots, T$, the system faces a demand d_{it} for product $i \in I$ that is assembled on demand, i.e. it is impossible to manufacture a product in advance, then store it to satisfy a future demand. For all product $i \in I$ and component $j \in J$, let r_{ij} be the number of components j required to produce one unit of product i.

All components are assumed to be available at all time in a remote warehouse managed by a TPL provider, who is in charge of delivering the assembly line based on its orders for components, as represented on Fig. 1. For each picking operation for component $j \in J$, the quantity collected by an operator is limited to a maximum batch size of m_j units. Note that several batches of the same components can be scheduled in the same period. The picking time for a particular batch of component j of size x_j can be divided into two main parts. First, we consider a fixed time p_j that corresponds to the travel time between the shipping point and the zone where components j are stored, which is spent regardless of the quantity that is transported. In addition, we consider a per-unit picking time τ_j. For all period $t = 1, \ldots, T$, the total picking time spent by the TPL provider to collect all the components delivered to the assembly line in period t cannot exceed a maximum work capacity C_t.

Any demand for product i that is not satisfied immediately is backlogged until the corresponding product is assembled in a subsequent period. Each unit of product i incurs a backlogging penalty cost b_i during each period it is backlogged. Whenever a component j is available on the assembly line but is not immediately used to manufacture an end product, it disturbs the production process by interfering with people and other goods moving nearby. We model this situation with a per-unit, per-period obstruction cost o_j. The problem consists in planning the quantity of each component delivered to the assembly line by the TPL in each period such that the sum of the obstruction and backlogging costs is minimized. We declare decision variables, x_{jt} as the quantity of components $j \in J$ that should be brought to the assembly line during period t. These variables are closely related to variables v_{jt} representing the number of distinct picking operations of components $j \in J$ performed during period t. Variables s_{jt} represent the number of component $j \in J$ held on the border of the assembly line at the end of period t. Variables u_{it} denotes the number of final product $i \in I$ produced during period t and finally, variables P_t and O_t respectively denotes penalty costs caused by the backlogging of final product demand and the total obstruction cost for period t.

We formulate the problem with the following MIP:

$$\min \sum_{t=1}^{T} O_t + P_t \tag{1}$$

$$\text{s.t.} \qquad s_{jt} = s_{j1} + \sum_{k=1}^{t-1} x_{jk} - \sum_{i \in I} r_{ij} u_{ik} \quad \forall j \in J, \forall t = 2, \ldots, T \tag{2}$$

$$\sum_{i \in I} u_{it} r_{ij} \leq s_{jt} + x_{jt} \qquad \forall j \in J, \forall t = 1, \ldots, T \tag{3}$$

$$\sum_{k=1}^{t} u_{ik} \leq \sum_{k=1}^{t} d_{ik} \qquad \forall i \in I, \forall t = 1, \ldots, T \tag{4}$$

$$v_{jt} \geq x_{jt}/m_j \qquad \forall j \in J, \forall t = 1, \ldots, T \tag{5}$$

$$\sum_{j \in J} v_{jt} p_j + \tau_j x_{jt} \leq C_t \qquad \forall t = 1, \ldots, T \tag{6}$$

$$O_t \geq \sum_{j \in J} o_j \left(s_{jt} + x_{jt} - \sum_{i \in I} u_{it} r_{ij} \right) \quad \forall t = 1, \ldots, T \qquad (7)$$

$$P_t \geq \sum_{i \in I} b_i \left(\sum_{k=1}^{t} d_{ik} - u_{ik} \right) \qquad \forall t = 1, \ldots, T \qquad (8)$$

$$x_{jt}, s_{jt}, P_t, O_t \in \mathbb{R}_+ \qquad \forall j \in J, \forall t = 1, \ldots, T \qquad (9)$$

$$u_{it}, v_{jt} \in \mathbb{N}_+ \qquad \forall i \in I, \forall j \in J, \forall t = 1, \ldots, T \qquad (10)$$

The objective (1) aims at minimizing the total cost incurred over the planning horizon. The inventory balance constraints (2) update the stock levels in each period. Constraints (3) ensure that the quantity of component $j \in J$ available in period t are sufficient to perform the planned assembly operations. Constraints (4) impose that the system never manufactures more units of product $i \in I$ than the expressed demand. The minimum number of picking batches corresponding to the quantity of components j ordered in each period t is defined in constraints (5). Constraints (6) ensure that the total picking time does not exceed the picking capacity of the TPL provider in any period t. Constraints (7) and (8) define the components holding costs and final product backlogging costs incurred in each period t, respectively. Finally, constraints (9) and (10) define the domain of the decision variables.

3   Robust Models for Uncertain Setup Times

In practice, the manufacturer often has incomplete or imprecise knowledge on the picking times. As a consequence, some combinations of her orders may exceed the picking capacity of the TPL provider, forcing the latter to postpone some operations to subsequent periods. This delay in some components delivery induces two types of inefficiencies on the assembly line. Indeed, missing components (i) prevent the manufacturer to assemble some of the products, leading to backlogging penalty costs and (ii) leave the other components in the BOM on the border of the line, disturbing other production operations This double effect strongly incentivizes the planner to protect her decisions against uncertain setup times.

In what follows, we assume that we have at our disposal a set of historical setup times $\mathcal{P} = \{\mathbf{p}^{(1)}, \ldots, \mathbf{p}^{(N)}\}$ and we investigate the performance of two robust optimization models in this context.

3.1   Interval Based Robust Model

As a first robust approach, we consider the classical uncertainty set of [8] defined by:

$$\mathcal{U}_t = \left\{ \mathbf{p} \, \middle| \, p_{jt} = \bar{p}_j + \hat{p}_j z_{jt}, \; \sum_j |z_{jt}| \leq \Gamma_t, \; \forall j \in J \right\} \qquad (11)$$

where $\bar{p}_j$ is called the nominal value of p_j and $\hat{p}_j$ is a maximal deviation. The scaled deviation coefficient $z_{jt} = (p_j - \bar{p}_j)/\hat{p}_j \in [-1, 1]$ ensures that $p_{jt} \in [\bar{p}_j - \hat{p}_j, \bar{p}_j + \hat{p}_j]$ for all components $j \in J$ and period t and that the total scaled deviation of $\mathbf{p}$ never exceeds the budgets of uncertainty $\boldsymbol{\Gamma}$. The robust counterpart of the capacity constraint is then obtained thanks to duality theory (see [8] for details), where constraints (6) are replaced with:

$$\sum_{j \in J} v_{jt}\bar{p}_j + x_{jt}\tau_j + q_t\Gamma_t + \sum_{j \in J} w_{jt} \leq C_t \quad \forall t = 1, \dots, T \tag{12}$$

$$q_t + w_{jt} \geq \hat{p}_j v_{jt} \,\, \forall j \in J, \forall t = 1, \dots, T \tag{13}$$

where $\mathbf{q} \geq 0$ and $\mathbf{w} \geq 0$ are additional real variables obtained from the dual formulation of the left-hand side of constraints (6).

3.2   Support Vector Clustering Based Model

We now consider an alternative, data-driven approach introduced in [19] to construct uncertainty sets directly from $\mathcal{P}$. This method rely on the Support Vector Clustering algorithm introduced in [22] and results in a polyhedral uncertainty set that gives a more precise description of $\mathcal{P}$. By using the SVC algorithm we obtain a vector $\alpha = \{\alpha_k, \,\, k = 1, ..., N\}$ that defines whether a given sample $\mathbf{p} \in \mathcal{P}$ resides in the uncertainty set $\mathcal{U}$. More precisely, samples with $\alpha_k = 0$ are strictly contained in $\mathcal{U}$. Samples $\mathbf{p}^{(k)}$ with positive α_k are called *support vectors (SV)*. Points for which $0 < \alpha_k < 1/N\nu$ lie exactly on the boundary of $\mathcal{U}$ and are referred to as *boundary support vectors (BSV)*. In addition, the samples contained in $SV\backslash\{BSV\}$ with $\alpha_k = 1/N\nu$ are considered as outliers and are located outside of $\mathcal{U}$. The regularization parameter $\nu \in [0, 1]$ is used to control the portion of samples in $\mathcal{P}$ covered by $\mathcal{U}$. In practice when $N \to \infty$, the latter portion tend to be $1 - \nu$ (see [19] and [22] for details).

Similar to the robust framework of [8] the capacity constraint can be reformulated as

$$\sum_{k \in SV} (\boldsymbol{\mu}_{kt} - \boldsymbol{\lambda}_{kt})^T \mathbf{Q}\mathbf{p}^{(k)} + \eta\theta + \sum_{j \in J} x_{jt}\tau_j \leq C_t \,\,, \,\, \forall t = 1, \dots, T \tag{14}$$

with the additional constraints :

$$\sum_{k \in SV} \mathbf{Q}(\boldsymbol{\lambda}_{kt} - \boldsymbol{\mu}_{kt}) + \mathbf{v}_t = \mathbf{0} \tag{15}$$

$$\boldsymbol{\lambda}_{kt} + \boldsymbol{\mu}_{kt} = \eta\alpha_k\mathbf{1} \,\, \forall k \in SV \tag{16}$$

where $\mathbf{Q}$ is called the weighting matrix and is defined by $\mathbf{Q} = \Sigma^{-\frac{1}{2}}$ with Σ the covariance matrix of $\mathbf{p}$, $\theta = \min\limits_{k' \in BSV} \left(\sum_{k \in SV} \alpha_k \| \mathbf{Q}(\mathbf{p}^{(k')} - \mathbf{p}^{(k)}) \|_1 \right)$ and $\boldsymbol{\lambda}_{kt} > 0$, $\boldsymbol{\mu}_{kt} > 0$, $\eta > 0$ are additional real variables obtained from the dual formulation of the left-hand side of constraints (6) (see [19] for details).

4   Experimental Results

We first describe several rules that we apply to generate the instances we use to evaluate the performances of the different models presented above. The specific assumptions we consider are listed below, with the objective reflect the framework of application cases: r_{ij} is chosen randomly from an interval $[\underline{r}_j, \bar{r}_j]$, the smallest interval is [2,4] and the widest is [10,25]. Each product i requires a subset $J_i \subset J$ of components. o_j is chosen randomly in $[0,1]$, $b_i = \rho \sum_{j \in J} r_{ij} o_j$, where ρ represents a ratio between the penalty incurred for backlogging a demand for product i versus the maximum obstruction cost of its components. In our numerical experiments, we use $\rho = 5$, but this value can be adjusted depending on the context. In order to primarily focus on the impact of the setup times uncertainty, we disregard the linear part of picking times and set $\tau_j = 0$ and $m_j = 3 \max_{i \in I} r_{ij}$ for all $j \in J$. Demands are deterministic with values drawn from a normal distribution whose parameters vary among products. We compute the capacity of the TPL C_t from the average time needed to pick the required components in each period, that we increase by a given percentage to ensure that it is not always saturated.

4.1   Evaluation of the Solution

To conclude on the performance of the models we need to evaluate how these solutions performs in the face of uncertainty. To do that we first generate a set $\mathcal{P}$ of $N = 400$ historical setup times to define the models. We then generate a set of 10 000 setup time scenarios $\mathcal{S}$ following the same distribution than $\mathcal{P}$. Each scenario is composed of one setup time for each component $j \in J$ and each period $t = 1, \ldots, T$. Finally we evaluate the real cost of each scenario for the given solution in three steps. For each scenario: we simulate the picking operations to obtain the realized quantity of each components delivered in each period; we compute the optimal production plan for the quantities delivered; and we evaluate the cost of the obtained production plan.

4.2   Setup Time Distribution

We assume that the TPL provider organizes the storage of the components in order to optimize the picking operations. Specifically, components are stored in such a way that their accessibility improves with their order frequency. We consider three types of components and separate them based on their storage area. We assume that both the mean and the variability of the setup times decrease with component accessibility. In our instances, we thus we generate setup times using Gamma distributions with three different shape parameters, one for each type of component.

In practice, setting the budget parameter Γ_t is hard and the performance obtained for a given parameter value heavily depends on the characteristics of the instance. In order to compare both models, we set Γ_t to cover a certain portion of $\mathcal{P}$, by iteratively increasing its value until we reach the desired coverage.

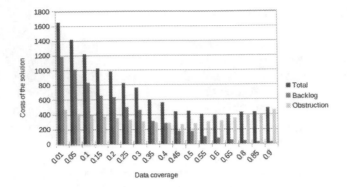

Fig. 2. Evolution of the average costs for different data coverage

4.3 Results

Figure 2 shows the mean value of the total, obstruction and backlogging costs obtained by the SVC based model with different data coverage. The instance considered is composed of 8 components and 4 products and the ratio between the obstruction and backlogging cost parameters o_j and b_i are set to reflect a high preference to avoid backlogging. We observe that the backlogging cost strictly decreases as the data coverage increases which corresponds to the preference based on the costs. The obstruction cost decreases when the data coverage is lower than 0.45 and increases otherwise. The total cost decreases to reach its lowest value for 60% of data coverage. Beyond that point, the reduction in backlogging costs do not compensate the increase of obstruction costs, which leads to a slow increase in the total cost. We also observe that the obstruction costs are nearly the same for 1% and 90% of data coverage while the backlogging costs decrease from 1195 to 26 in this interval.

Figure 3 presents the average backlogging and obstruction costs obtained by the classical and SVC based robust models. The considered instance is composed of 8 components and 4 products, the planning horizon is 5 periods. Each point corresponds to a different value of data coverage in [1%,50%]. We observe that for the same backlogging cost, the SVC based model leads to a smaller obstruction cost than the classical robust model. For example, when both backlogging costs are equal to 288, the obstruction cost of the SVC based solution is 259 whereas it is 317 for the classical robust solution. We also observe that the SVC based model can lead at the same time to a lower obstruction cost and a lower backlogging cost. For example, the SVC based model leads to a backlogging cost of 251 with an obstruction cost of 273 whereas the classical robust model leads to a backlogging cost of 260 with an obstruction cost of 346.

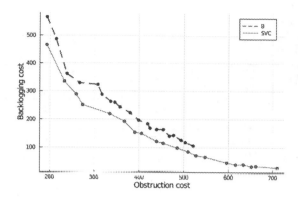

Fig. 3. Comparison of backlogging and obstruction costs obtained with different data coverage

5   Conclusion

In this paper, we considered a data driven robust optimization approach to plan the picking operations of an assembly line when the latter are subcontracted to an outside service provider. Experimental results show that the proposed method efficiently reduces the impact of uncertainties on the performance of the assembly line. By controlling the level of robustness of the model, good tradeoffs can be found between reducing the backlog of assembly operations and minimizing the quantity of components stored on the border of the assembly line. In comparison with a classical budget based robust optimization model, the data driven model yields better performance on the test instances. The proposed robust approach aims at respecting the maximum picking time capacity of the service provider and ignore the consequences of robustness on the solution cost. Hence, it is difficult to define the robustness level in order to find the optimal tradeoff. Future research may consider a multi-stage data-driven robust optimization approach to overcome this drawback. However, such methods generally lead to more complex formulations and make their application to large-scale industrial cases impossible.

References

1. Song, J.S., Zipkin, P.: Supply chain operations: assemble-to-order systems. Handb. Oper. Res. Manag. Sci. **11**, 561–596 (2003)
2. Atan, Z., Ahmadi, T., Stegehuis, C., de Kok, T., Adan, I.: Assemble-to-order systems: a review. Eur. J. Oper. Res. **261**(3), 866–879 (2017)
3. Reiman, M.I., Wang, Q.: Asymptotically optimal inventory control for assemble-to-order systems with identical lead times. Oper. Res. **66**(3), 716–732 (2015)
4. Keith, A.J., Ahner, D.K.: A survey of decision making and optimization under uncertainty. Ann. Oper. Res. **300**(2), 319–353 (2019). https://doi.org/10.1007/s10479-019-03431-8

5. Soyster, A.L.: Technical note - convex programming with set-inclusive constraints and applications to inexact linear programming. Oper. Res. **21**(5), 1154–1157 (1973)
6. El Ghaoui, L., Oustry, F., Lebret, H.: Robust solutions to uncertain semidefinite programs. SIAM J. Optim. **9**(1), 33–52 (1998)
7. Ben-Tal, A., Nemirovski, A.: Robust convex optimization. Math. Oper. Res. **23**(4), 769–805 (1998)
8. Bertsimas, D., Sim, M.: The price of robustness. Oper. Res. **52**(1), 35–53 (2004)
9. Poss, M.: Robust combinatorial optimization with variable budgeted uncertainty. 4OR **11**(1), 75–92 (2013). https://doi.org/10.1007/s10288-012-0217 9
10. Jalilvand-Nejad, A., Shafaei, R., Shahriari, H.: Robust optimization under correlated polyhedral uncertainty set. Comput. Ind. Eng. **92**, 82–94 (2016)
11. Bertsimas, D., Thiele, A.: A robust optimization approach to inventory theory. Oper. Res. **54**(1), 150–168 (2006)
12. José Alem, D., Morabito, R.: Production planning in furniture settings via robust optimization. Comput. Oper. Res. **39**(2), 139–150 (2012)
13. Wei, C., Li, Y., Cai, X.: Robust optimal policies of production and inventory with uncertain returns and demand. Int. J. Prod. Econ. **134**(2), 357–367 (2011)
14. Aouam, T., Brahimi, N.: Integrated production planning and order acceptance under uncertainty: a robust optimization approach. Eur. J. Oper. Res. **228**, 504–515 (2013)
15. Varas, M., Maturana, S., Pascual, R., Vargas, I., Vera, J.: Scheduling production for a sawmill: a robust optimization approach. Int. J. Prod. Econ. **150**, 37–51 (2014)
16. Thorsen, A., Yao, T.: Robust inventory control under demand and lead time uncertainty. Ann. Oper. Res. **257**, 207–236 (2017). https://doi.org/10.1007/s10479-015-2084-1
17. Bertsimas, D., Brown, D.: Constructing uncertainty sets for robust linear optimization. Oper. Res. **57**(6), 1483–1495 (2009)
18. Bertsimas, D., Thiele, A.: Robust and data-driven optimization: modern decision making under uncertainty. In: Tutorial on Operations Research, pp. 95–122. INFORMS (2014)
19. Shang, C., Huang, X., You, F.: Data-driven robust optimization based on kernel learning. Comput. Chem. Eng. **106**, 464–479 (2017)
20. Qiu, R., Sun, Y., Shu, P., Sun, M.: Robust multi-product inventory optimization under support vector clustering-based data-driven demand uncertainty set. Soft Comput. **24**, 6259–6275 (2019). https://doi.org/10.1007/s00500-019-03927-2
21. Shen, F., Zhao, L., Du, W., Zhong, W., Qian, F.: Large-scale industrial energy systems optimization under uncertainty: a data-driven robust optimization approach. Appl. Energy **259**, 114199 (2020)
22. Ben-Hur, A., Horn, D., Siegelmann, H., Vapnik, V.: Support vector clustering. J. Mach. Learn. Res. **2**, 125–137 (2001)

Responsible Manufacturing with Information Disclosure Under Regulatory Inspections

Yifan Cao and Bin Shen[✉]

Donghua University, Shanghai, China
binshen@dhu.edu.com

Abstract. Different legislations are enacted to monitor and promote social sustainability performance. If any unsustainable manufacturing practice is found by the regulatory body, the firm will suffer from huge loss. As pressured by socially responsible purchasing and regulatory pressure, some manufacturing firms have begun to disclose social sustainability in their manufacturing process in audit reports periodically. In this paper, we examine how should a manufacturing firm choose its optimal socially-sustainable manufacturing effort, and how should the manufacturing firm set prices to successfully transmit social sustainability signals to first-stage consumers. We conduct a two-stage game-theoretic analysis to examine a manufacturing firm's socially-sustainable manufacturing effort and dynamic pricing decisions under regulatory pressure. Consumers are classified into socially conscious and non-socially conscious consumers. We find that when the gap of consumer's attitude towards responsibility is moderate, if the manufacturing firm insists on targeting both socially conscious and non-socially conscious consumers in the first period, consumers will believe that the firm is of low responsibility in manufacturing. Then in the second period when socially-sustainable manufacturing effort becomes a symmetric information, the belief that the manufacturing firm is irresponsible will hurt the manufacturing firm's profit. Thus, it is beneficial to target at socially conscious consumers in the first period so as to transfer quality information to consumers. Our findings help a firm to wisely make socially-sustainable manufacturing effort decisions and set an informative price so as to transfer responsible manufacturing information to early consumers.

Keywords: Price signaling · Social responsibility · Sustainable manufacturers · Information sharing · Regulatory inspections · Manufacturing

1 Introduction

The International Labour Organization (ILO) estimates that modern slavery may affect over 40 million individuals around the world (ILO 2017). Social misconduct in a supply chain comprises forced labor, child labor, poor working condition, low payment, worker treatment, and gender inequality, etc. Such social misconduct cut down the production cost and enable firms to set a more competitive price. However, modern slavery not only does harm to workers' interests, but also significantly affects both firm's long-term

© IFIP International Federation for Information Processing 2021
Published by Springer Nature Switzerland AG 2021
A. Dolgui et al. (Eds.): APMS 2021, IFIP AICT 633, pp. 179–188, 2021.
https://doi.org/10.1007/978-3-030-85910-7_19

profitability and brand image. For example, stressful working condition and low payment in Foxconn factories led to workers' suicides in 2016 (Forbes 2016). Nike's scandals related to social misconduct severely affected its profitability, hurt its brand image and disrupt consumers' trust (Tang and Zhou 2012). Modern slavery is found to be the cause of stagnant economic growth and leads to perpetuating the poverty zone (ILO Report 2014).

Although social responsibility is difficult to quantify, consumers nowadays are paying more attention to firms' social responsibility in manufacturing. It has been widely acknowledged that socially conscious consumers are willing to pay a premium for responsible products. In reality, consumers are usually at information disadvantage about manufacturing firms' social sustainability at the time of purchase. Price commonly is the signal about a product's socially-sustainable manufacturing effort (Shao et al. 2020). A high price can transfer the information of high social sustainability to consumers (Jiang and Yang 2019). Information asymmetry provides reasons for unsustainable manufacturing firms pretend to be responsible by setting misleading high prices and defeating consumers. By doing so, they can be profitable in the single period transaction by investing not sufficiently in manufacturing sustainability while charging a high price.

Regulatory inspections put supply chains under scrutiny. Different legislations are enacted to monitor and promote social sustainability performance, such as the US-California Transparency Act (2010), the UK Modern Slavery Act (2015), the Australian Modern Slavery Act (2018). More recently, the leading fashion brand Boohoo is accused to be involved with forced labor and is currently being investigated by US Customs and Border Protection. Although the timeline for investigation has not been decided yet, it will suffer from huge loss (i.e., such as import bans, damaged brand images) if any unsustainable societal practice is found.

As pressured by socially responsible purchasing and regulatory inspection, some manufacturing firms have begun to disclose their socially-sustainable manufacturing effort. With the advance of publicizing social sustainability information in audit reports, consumers can learn the true socially responsible level periodically (Sodhi and Tang 2019). Therefore, in the multi-period setting, firms are motivated to increase socially-sustainable manufacturing effort to earn higher profits from the informed consumers coming at the later period. In this way, firms need to balance the gain by deceiving early consumers and the loss through revealing true responsibility to the late consumers.

We conduct a two-stage game-theoretic analysis to examine a manufacturing firm's socially-sustainable manufacturing effort and dynamic pricing decisions under regulatory pressure. A monopoly manufacturing firm holds private socially-sustainable manufacturing effort information which is invisible to consumers. The firm decides on the optimal social sustainability effort in manufacturing which remains unchanged in the two periods and decides on the optimal selling price in two selling periods. At the first stage, consumers come at an early stage do not have knowledge about product's social sustainability information prior to purchase. Knowing that the firm has incentives to invest in social sustainability in manufacturing to attract later consumers, a rationale consumer will deduce socially-sustainable manufacturing effort information based on the charged price. In the second stage, the firm publicizes audit reports to share socially-sustainable manufacturing effort information with late consumers. Then consumers can make purchase decision based on the knowledge of product's societal attribute. At the end of the second stage, regulator inspects on firm's societal conduct in the manufacturing process and the firm will occur a loss if any misconduct is found. To maximize profits in two periods, how should a firm make pricing and sustainable manufacturing decisions remain questionable. We examine the following questions: In the presence of regulatory pressure in monitoring supply chain social sustainability in manufacturing, how should a firm choose its optimal socially-sustainable manufacturing effort? How should the firm set prices to successfully transmit sustainable manufacturing signals to first-stage consumers?

2   Literature Review

Our paper relates to two stream of the literature: the socially responsible operations and price signaling.

In the stream of socially responsible operations literature, Gallear et al. (2012) empirically find that the decrease in profitability is a main obstacle in motivating socially responsible investment. Gong et al. (2019) suggest that higher social sustainability effort may or may not induce economic growth. Heyes and Martin (2017) claim that greater effort in social sustainability may conditionally hurt consumers' welfare. Cho et al. (2019) investigate the effect of both internal and external audit on firm's decisions of using child labor. Shao et al. (2020) examine the pricing and disclosure decisions of a retailer who can either source from a high or low socially responsible supplier. The above studies assume social sustainability investment exogenously. In our paper, we consider the manufacturing firm could invest more or less on social responsibility. Therefore, we assume the responsible effort is endogenous for the manufacturing firm. We conduct a two-stage game-theoretic analysis to examine a firm's optimal social sustainability effort under regulatory pressure. For more detailed information in this domain, please refer to the review paper Tang and Zhou (2012) and Sodhi and Tang (2019). The former one reviews sustainable operations under the principle of triple bottom line and the latter one discusses the role of information disclosure in socially responsible operations.

In the stream of price signaling, Jiang and Yang (2019) consider consumer to consumer quality-information sharing in two periods. They assume that the first-period consumers who bought the product will learn the true quality and reveal it to later consumers. However, they do not consider the inspection of regulatory body. We follow Jiang and Yang (2019) to model information sharing model. Differently, we tie firm's social sustainability effort decision with regulatory pressure, which induces firms to improve social sustainability effort to lower the probability of violation. However, as consumers enter the market over two periods, increasing the social sustainability effort reduces firm's profitability in the first stage. It could have provided low effort and deceive early consumers into believing the products are of high quality. Therefore, the firm has the trade-off for the payoff between two different periods. Our paper is also motivated by Shao et al. (2020) and Chen et al. (2019). They both examine supply chain decisions under NGO scrutiny. Shao et al. (2020) consider a static one-period price-signaling and cost information asymmetry. Chen et al. (2019) examine disclosure strategy facing regulatory body's uncertain inspection level. Differently, we consider both the capability and social sustainability effort information asymmetry and the firm maximizes profits in two periods. For more detailed information in this domain, please refer to the review paper Shen et al. (2019), which has conducted the comprehensive review about information asymmetry in terms of price signals.

3 The Model

Consider a supply chain model consisting of a monopoly manufacturing firm (we abbreviate it as firm) and its downstream consumers. To meet the growing needs of sustainable development, the firm makes an effort in social sustainability performance in the process of manufacturing, such as providing workers health and safe working conditions, resisting the recruitment of child labor and forced labor, giving workers' a decent pay, etc. Production cost is normalized to zero as we mainly focus on investment in social sustainability. The firm's social sustainability performance is jointly determined by two factors: cost efficiency and social sustainability effort. The firm can be of two types in terms of cost efficiency. We use $i = \{1, 2\}$ to denote high efficiency type and low efficiency type respectively. Cost efficiency and true sustainability effort are denoted by c_i and γ_i respectively where $c_1 < c_2$ (i.e., the type-1 firm has higher efficiency and spends a lower marginal cost than the type-2 firm). Then, the firm's quadric socially-sustainable manufacturing cost function is given by $c_i \gamma_i^2$ (Jiang and Yang 2019). Consumers' prior probability of the firm's type satisfies $Pr(c_i = c_1) = \beta$ and $Pr(c_i = c_2) = 1 - \beta$.

With the popularity of the concept of social sustainability, more consumers are becoming conscious of sustainable development. Socially conscious consumers care about social sustainability and are willing to pay a higher price for social sustainable products. Considering heterogeneity of consumers attitudes towards socially-sustainable manufacturing effort, we use $j = \{H, L\}$ to label consumer's type and θ_j to represent consumer's willingness to pay (WTP). Socially conscious consumers (i.e. H-type) has higher WTP than non-socially conscious consumers (i.e. L-type), which gives $\theta_H > \theta_L$. Consumer's net utility is modeled as $U_j = \theta_j \gamma_i - p$, where p is the price of the product. A consumer will buy the product if her expected utility is larger than zero. Without loss of generality, the number of consumers is normalized to 1. The proportion of H-type consumers accounts for $\alpha \in (0, 1)$, whereas L-type consumers accounts for the remaining $1 - \alpha$. We denote H-type and L-type consumer's maximum willingness-to-pay as $\overline{p_H}$ and $\overline{p_L}$. By denoting market demand as N, if the firm charges the first-period price at $\overline{p_H}$, then only H-type consumers will be targeted and the market demand $N_i^{(1)}$ equals to α. If the firm charges the first-period price at $\overline{p_L}$, then both types of consumers will be targeted and the market demand $N_i^{(1)}$ equals to 1. Utility of non–socially conscious consumers will not be affected by violation. In contrast, socially conscious consumers' WTP will change from θ_H to θ_L if violation occurs. The probability of violation relates to firm's socially-sustainable manufacturing effort γ_i. Greater effort reduces the possibility of being involved with social misconduct. Thus, the expected utility of socially conscious consumers is $E(U_H) = \gamma_i(\theta_H \gamma_i - p) + (1 - \gamma_i)(\theta_L \gamma_i - p)$.

New consumers come into the market over two different selling periods. In the first period, the firm will decide the first-period's price, which will be a signal of socially-sustainable manufacturing effort to consumers. A high price would indicate a higher socially-sustainable manufacturing effort. As the audit report has not been published yet, consumers who come at an early stage do not have knowledge about product's social sustainability information prior to purchase. A rationale consumer deduces such information based on the first-period's price and makes purchase decisions. Whether the firm's efficiency type as public knowledge will influence consumer's expectations. In the second stage, the firm goes through a periodical audit, which will be released in public. Then, consumers can learn about product's true societal attributes and make purchase decisions. Following Shao et al. (2020), consumers make their purchase decisions before they know whether a violation has occurred. A higher effort can decrease the probability of violation of social sustainability. If the violation is discovered and revealed by the regulator body, the firm will suffer from a penalty cost κ, which includes either a penalty, a reputation damage or the cost of remediation. In this stage, consumers can learn about the product's true societal attribute and make purchase decisions. We can derive the profit function as follows: $\pi_i = \left(p_i^{(1)} - c_i\gamma_i^2\right)N_i^{(1)} + \left(p_i^{(2)} - c_i\gamma_i^2\right)N_i^{(2)} - (1 - \gamma_i)\kappa$.

Socially-sustainable manufacturing effort and cost efficiency are firm's private information which are invisible to consumers. We analyze symmetric and asymmetric capability information respectively in Sect. 4. Game sequence is shown in Fig. 1. First, nature decides firm's type of capability (i.e. c_i) and consumers have prior belief about the firm's type. Second, the firm endogenously decides on the social sustainability effort which is firm's private information. All other parameters are common knowledge. Third, the firm sets selling price $p^{(1)}$ in the first stage. In the second period, the firm's socially-sustainable manufacturing effort is published in the periodical audit report, then later consumers can know the true social sustainability effort of the products and make the purchase decision. Lastly, the regulatory body inspects the firm's socially-sustainable manufacturing effort which may last for a quite long time. If the firm violates regulations, it should pay for its social misconduct. The firm sets selling price $p^{(2)}$ in the second stage.

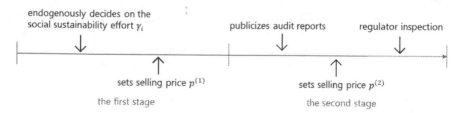

Fig. 1. Game sequence.

4   Equilibrium Analysis

The pros and cons of enhancing effort are the major trade-off. On the one hand, making more socially-sustainable manufacturing effort lowers the possibility of being punished from violation. It can also earn higher profits from the informed socially conscious consumers in the second period. On the other hand, the firm has incentives to provide low quality in the first period to profit from early ignorant consumers. Therefore, the firm will make socially-sustainable manufacturing effort and price decisions to maximize total profits in two periods.

We use the abbreviation H to represent target only H-type consumers and HL to represent target both two types of consumers. We first examine the second period targeting decisions. Results are shown in Lemma 1.

Lemma 1. *Regardless of the type of the equilibrium,*

(i)   *When* $\theta_H > \theta_L + \frac{(1-\alpha)c_i[2\kappa\theta_L+(1+2\alpha)\theta_L^2-\kappa^2]}{\alpha(\kappa+\theta_L)^2}$, *the firm targets at only H-type consumers in the second period;*

(ii) *When* $\theta_L + \frac{(1-\alpha)c_i[\alpha\theta_L(2\kappa+(2+\alpha)\theta_L)-\kappa^2]}{\alpha(\kappa+\theta_L)^2} < \theta_H \leq \theta_L + \frac{(1-\alpha)c_i[2\kappa\theta_L+(1+2\alpha)\theta_L^2-\kappa^2]}{\alpha(\kappa+\theta_L)^2}$, *the firm targets at the same type of consumers in the second period as in the first period;*

(iii) *When* $\theta_H \leq \theta_L + \frac{(1-\alpha)c_i[\alpha\theta_L(2\kappa+(2+\alpha)\theta_L)-\kappa^2]}{\alpha(\kappa+\theta_L)^2}$, *the firm targets at both H-type and L-type consumers in the second period.*

Lemma 1 summarizes the second period targeting decisions with asymmetric social sustainable effort. We list the optimal social sustainable effort and the corresponding profit in Table 1.

Figure 2 shows the firm's second-period targeting sales given the targeting decision in the first-period. From Fig. 2, we can observe that with the increase in consumer's heterogeneity in social sustainable awareness, the incentive of targeting H-type consumers grows. This result is well-acknowledged as the firm would have higher motivations to make the consumers recognize their high responsibility level and earn substantial profits from the high social-awareness consumers. If the gap between consumers' valuation of social responsibility is sufficiently low, then it is trivial to differentiate the firm to build a high responsible image. It will be more profitable to set a lower price which is affordable to both types of consumers. The increase in market demand outweighs the drop in the sales price.

Now we turn to the targeting decisions in the first period. In equilibrium, the price signal is convincing to consumers only if the firm cannot make extra profits from deviating its claim. The firm can claim that it is of high social responsibility by charging $\gamma_i[\gamma_i\theta_H + (1 - \gamma_i)\theta_L]$ and targeting only H-type consumers; Or the firm can set prices at $\gamma_i\theta_L$ to target both types of consumers. According to the second period decisions shown in Lemma 1, we investigate the following three different parameter regions. Results are shown in Lemma 2.

Lemma 2. *When the firm's cost efficiency is common knowledge, its optimal quality and prices are:*

(i)   *When* $\theta_L < \theta_H < min\left\{\theta_L + \frac{(1-\alpha^2)c_i(\theta_L-\kappa)}{2\alpha(\kappa+\theta_L)}, \theta_L + \frac{(1-\alpha)c_i[\alpha\theta_L(2\kappa+(2+\alpha)\theta_L)-\kappa^2]}{\alpha(\kappa+\theta_L)^2}\right\}$, *the firm will target at both types of consumers in two periods (i.e. (HL, HL)) and* $\tilde{\gamma}_i^* = \frac{\kappa+\theta_L}{4c_i}, \tilde{p}_i^{(1)*} = \tilde{p}_i^{(2)*} = \frac{\theta_L(\kappa+\theta_L)}{4c_i}, \tilde{\pi}_i^* = \frac{\kappa^2-8\kappa c_i+4\kappa\theta_L+3\theta_L^2}{8c_i}$.

Table 1. Conditional social sustainability effort and second-period targeting.

θ_H		$\left(\theta_L + \dfrac{(1-\alpha)c_i[2\kappa\theta_L + (1+2\alpha)\theta_L^2 - \kappa^2]}{\alpha(\kappa+\theta_L)^2}, \infty\right)$	$\left(\theta_L + \dfrac{(1-\alpha)c_i[\alpha\theta_L(2\kappa+(2+\alpha)\theta_L) - \kappa^2]}{\alpha(\kappa+\theta_L)^2}, \theta_L + \dfrac{(1-\alpha)c_i[2\kappa\theta_L + (1+2\alpha)\theta_L^2 - \kappa^2]}{\alpha(\kappa+\theta_L)^2}\right)$	$\left(\varepsilon_L, \theta_L + \dfrac{(1-\alpha)c_i[\alpha\theta_L(2\kappa+(2+\alpha)\theta_L) - \kappa^2]}{\alpha(\kappa+\theta_L)^2}\right)$
$N_i^{(1)} = \alpha$	$N_i^{(2)}$	α	α	1
	y_i	$\dfrac{\kappa+\alpha\theta_L}{2\alpha(2c_i-\theta_H+\theta_L)}$	$\dfrac{\kappa+\alpha\theta_L}{2\alpha(2c_i-\theta_H+\theta_L)}$	$\dfrac{\kappa+\theta_L}{2(1+\alpha)c_i}$
	π_i	$\alpha\overline{p_H} - \kappa + \dfrac{\kappa^2+\alpha\theta_L(2\kappa+\alpha\theta_L)}{4\alpha(2c_i-\theta_H+\theta_L)}$	$\alpha\overline{p_H} - \kappa + \dfrac{\kappa^2+\alpha\theta_L(2\kappa+\alpha\theta_L)}{4\alpha(2c_i-\theta_H+\theta_L)}$	$\alpha\overline{p}_{2,H} + \dfrac{(\kappa+\theta_L)^2}{4(1+\alpha)c_i} - \kappa$
$N_i^{(1)} = 1$	$N_i^{(2)}$	α	1	1
	y_i	$\dfrac{\kappa+\alpha\theta_L}{2(c_i+\alpha c_i-\alpha\theta_H+\alpha\theta_L)}$	$\dfrac{\kappa+\theta_L}{4c_i}$	$\dfrac{\kappa+\theta_L}{4c_i}$
	π_i	$\overline{p_L} - \kappa + \dfrac{\kappa^2+\alpha\theta_L(2\kappa+\alpha\theta_L)}{4[(1+\alpha)c_i-\alpha(\theta_H-\theta_L)]}$	$\overline{p_L} + \dfrac{(\kappa+\theta_L)^2}{8c_i} - \kappa$	$\overline{p_L} + \dfrac{(\kappa+\theta_L)^2}{8c_i} - \kappa$

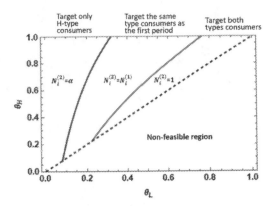

Fig. 2. Conditional targeting in the second period.

(ii) When $min\left\{\theta_L + \frac{(1-\alpha^2)c_i(\theta_L-\kappa)}{2\alpha(\kappa+\theta_L)}, \theta_L + \frac{(1-\alpha)c_i[\alpha\theta_L(2\kappa+(2+\alpha)\theta_L)-\kappa^2]}{\alpha(\kappa+\theta_L)^2}\right\} < \theta_H < \theta_L +$

$\frac{(1-\alpha)c_i[\alpha\theta_L(2\kappa+(2+\alpha)\theta_L)-\kappa^2]}{\alpha(\kappa+\theta_L)^2}$, *the firm will target at H-type consumers in the first period and both types of consumers in the second period (i.e. (H, HL)) and*

$\widetilde{\gamma}_i^* = \frac{\kappa+\theta_L}{2(1+\alpha)c_i}$, $\widetilde{p}_i^{(1)*} = \frac{(\kappa+\theta_L)(\theta_H(\kappa+\theta_L)-\theta_L(\kappa-2(1+\alpha)c_i+\theta_L))}{4(1+\alpha)^2c_i^2}$, $\widetilde{p}_i^{(2)*} = \frac{\theta_L(\kappa+\theta_L)}{2(1+\alpha)c_i}$,

$\widetilde{\pi}_i^* = \frac{\kappa^2-8\kappa c_i+4\kappa\theta_L+3\theta_L^2}{8c_i}$.

(iii) When $\theta_H > \theta_L + \frac{(1-\alpha)c_i[\alpha\theta_L(2\kappa+(2+\alpha)\theta_L)-\kappa^2]}{\alpha(\kappa+\theta_L)^2}$, *the firm will target at H-type consumers in both periods (i.e. (H, H))*

and $\widetilde{\gamma}_i^* = \frac{\kappa+\alpha\theta_L}{2\alpha(2c_i-\theta_H+\theta_L)}$, $\widetilde{p}_i^{(1)*} = \widetilde{p}_i^{(2)*} = \frac{(\kappa+\alpha\theta_L)[\theta_H(\kappa-\alpha\theta_L)+\theta_L(4\alpha c_i+\alpha\theta_L-\kappa)]}{4\alpha^2(2c_i-\theta_H+\theta_L)^2}$,

$\widetilde{\pi}_i^* = \frac{-8\alpha\kappa c_i^2+c_i(\kappa^2+8\alpha\kappa\theta_H-4\alpha\kappa\theta_L+3\alpha^2\theta_L^2)-\alpha(\theta_H-\theta_L)[2\kappa\theta_H+\theta_L(-\kappa+\alpha\theta_L)]}{2\alpha(2c_i-\theta_H+\theta_L)^2}$.

The findings in Lemma 2 are depicted in Fig. 3. From Lemma 2 we can also easily derive corollary 1.

Corollary 1. *The firm has more tendency to apply a niche responsible strategy (i.e. target at only H-type consumers in two periods) if consumers have higher valuation heterogeneity.*

It is natural that higher consumer heterogeneity increases firm's incentives in targeting at only H-type consumers. The firm can make profit from the higher premium from the socially-responsible consumers although the non-socially-responsible consumers are not its targeting objectives any more. Moreover, the firm's optimal sustainable investment also increases in consumers' different attitudes towards social sustainability (i.e.

supported by $\frac{\partial \widetilde{\gamma}_i^*}{\partial \theta_L} = -\frac{\kappa-2\alpha c_i+\alpha\theta_H}{2\alpha(2c_i-\theta_H+\theta_L)^2} < 0$ and $\frac{\partial \widetilde{\gamma}_i^*}{\partial \theta_H} = \frac{\kappa+\alpha\theta_L}{2\alpha(2c_i-\theta_H+\theta_L)^2} > 0$). If the socially-responsible consumers have small difference of valuation compared with non-socially-responsible one, it is better to serve both types consumers without the need to inform consumers of its responsibility information. When the gap of consumer's attitude towards responsibility is moderate, we can see that the first period targeting decisions shifts to be only H-type consumers. The reason is that if the firm insists on targeting at both types of consumers in the first period, consumers will believe that the firm is of low responsibility. Then in the second period when social responsibility effort becomes a symmetric information, profit will be hurt by holding the belief that the firm is irresponsible. Thus, it is beneficial to target H-type in the first period so as to transfer quality information to consumers.

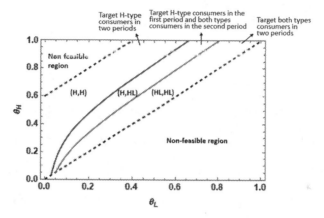

Fig. 3. Firm's optimal targeting decisions.

From Lemma 2, it is also obvious that a high-efficiency firm has more tendency to target H-type consumers. It makes higher social sustainable efforts, sets higher retail prices and earns higher profits. Meanwhile, the higher amount of penalty induces the firm to invest more in social sustainability and target at only H-type consumers in two periods.

5 Conclusion

In recent decades, managing supply chains in a socially responsible manner has become an important and appealing issue (Tang and Zhou 2012). The growing consciousness of CSR from both consumers and regulatory bodies has placed pressure on firms to cope with social challenges. An increasing number of consumers are willing to pay a premium for products' social sustainability. Different legislations are enacted to monitor and promote social sustainability performance. If any unsustainable societal practice is found by the regulatory body, the firm will suffer from huge loss. As pressured by socially responsible purchasing and regulatory pressure, some firms have begun to disclose their social sustainability in audit report periodically. We conduct a two-stage game-theoretic analysis to examine a firm's social sustainability effort and dynamic pricing decisions under regulatory pressure. We find that the extent of consumers' heterogeneity is critically important in firm's responsibility and pricing decisions. Our findings help a firm to wisely make social sustainability effort decisions and set an informative price so as to transfer responsibility information to early consumers. The effects of cost efficiency and the amount of penalty are analyzed as well.

References

Chen, S., Zhang, Q., Zhou, Y.P.: Impact of supply chain transparency on sustainability under NGO scrutiny. Prod. Oper. Manag. **28**, 3002–3022 (2019)

Cho, S.H., Fang, X., Tayur, S., Xu, Y.: Combating child labor: incentives and information disclosure in global supply chains. Manuf. Serv. Oper. Manag. **21**(3), 692–711 (2019)

Forbes. https://www.forbes.com/sites/bensin/2016/08/22/the-real-cost-of-the-iphone-7-more-foxconn-worker-deaths/?sh=27a439fa5560. Accessed 22 Aug 2016

Gallear, D., Ghobadian, A., Chen, W.: Corporate responsibility, supply chain partnership and performance: an empirical examination. Int. J. Prod. Econ. **140**(1), 83–91 (2012)

Gong, Y., Liu, J., Zhu, J.: When to increase firms' sustainable operations for efficiency? A data envelopment analysis in the retailing industry. Eur. J. Oper. Res. **277**(3), 1010–1026 (2019)

Heyes, A., Martin, S.: Social labeling by competing NGOs: a model with multiple issues and entry. Manage. Sci. **63**(6), 1800–1813 (2017)

ILO Report. https://www.ilo.org/global/topics/forced-labour/publications/WCMS_243391/lang–en/index.htm. Accessed 20 May 2014

ILO Report. https://www.ilo.org/global/publications/books/WCMS_575479/lang–en/index.htm. Accessed 17 Sept 2017

Jiang, B., Yang, B.: Quality and pricing decisions in a market with consumer information sharing. Manage. Sci. **65**(1), 272–285 (2019)

Sodhi, M.S., Tang, C.S.: Research opportunities in supply chain transparency. Prod. Oper. Manag. **28**(12), 2946–2959 (2019)

Shao, L., Ryan, J.K., Sun, D.: Responsible sourcing under asymmetric information: Price signaling versus supplier disclosure. Decis. Sci. **51**(5), 1082–1109 (2020)

Shen, B., Choi, T.M., Minner, S.: A review on supply chain contracting with information considerations: information updating and information asymmetry. Int. J. Prod. Res. **57**(15–16), 4898–4936 (2019)

Tang, C.S., Zhou, S.: Research advances in environmentally and socially sustainable operations. Eur. J. Oper. Res. **223**(3), 585–594 (2012)

Understanding Supply Chain Visibility Through Experts' Perspective: A Delphi Based Approach

Tarun Kumar Agrawal[1]([✉]) [iD], Ravi Kalaiarasan[1] [iD], Jan Olhager[1,2] [iD],
and Magnus Wiktorsson[1] [iD]

[1] Department of Sustainable Production Development, KTH Royal Institute of Technology,
Södertälje, Sweden
tkag@kth.se
[2] Department of Industrial Management and Logistics, Lund University, Lund, Sweden

Abstract. Visibility in production logistics and across the supply chain has become a key concern for organizations. Its need has been further emphasized due to the current COVID 19 crisis. Organizations find it challenging to prepare the internal logistics and supply chain, and quickly respond to such unexpected events, due to low visibility. Against this backdrop, the paper, which is a work-in-progress, systematically documents different factors influencing supply chain visibility and crucial information that should be collected and shared among supply chain partners for better visibility. A Delphi analysis is being conducted with twenty-six supply chain experts from various globally recognized enterprises with manufacturing units located worldwide. The study starts with a short open-ended questioner to collect a comprehensive list of antecedents, drivers, barriers, effects, and visibility information based on the qualitative response from the experts. The preliminary results from the first round of the Delphi analysis indicate that risk management, environmental sustainability, and supply chain control are some of the key drivers. Lack of IT infrastructure and maturity are some of the barriers, integrated systems, and technology maturity are among the key antecedents and gaining planning capability and better customer service are some of the positive effects of supply chain visibility as per the experts' opinion. In addition, information related to planning, supplier location, and deviation are among the crucial ones that require the collection and sharing for better supply chain visibility. This research study is among the few that empirically explores factors influencing supply chain visibility and generates new insights as to why the barriers can be difficult to overcome in complex supply chain settings.

Keywords: Supply chain · Visibility · Delphi analysis

1 Introduction

Supply chain visibility (SCV) refers to "management efforts to gather information about operations upstream and downstream in their supply chains" [1]. A simplified conceptualization of SCV – including external and internal visibility – is demonstrated in Fig. 1.

A. Dolgui et al. (Eds.): APMS 2021, IFIP AICT 633, pp. 189–196, 2021.
https://doi.org/10.1007/978-3-030-85910-7_20

Internal visibility management refers to the gathering and sharing of information within a business's processes. It includes all the methods, procedures, and elements needed to collect, record, and share data. Internal tracking takes place when goods or raw materials are received, processed internally, and then the product is delivered to third parties. It involves an intra-site real-time visualization system for material management including dynamic synchronization, takt, and resource planning. External visibility, on the other hand, refers to the product outside of a business entity, in the entire supply chain, and concerns dynamic status and prediction of supply network status among companies and countries. For external SCV to be effective, it relies on the existence and appropriate design of internal visibility of each entity [2].

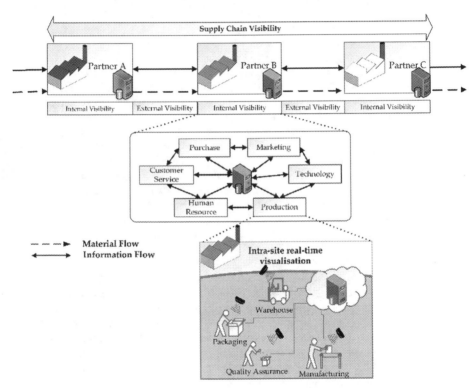

Fig. 1. A simplified conceptualization of Supply Chain Visibility (SCV)

Presently, owing to low SCV, firms are facing numerous challenges and risk those results in huge losses [3]. One of the major risks currently faced by supply chains across the globe is the event risk - for instance, COVID-19 virus - resulting in a long-term disruption in supply chains. These unexpected events lead to material shortages, delay in deliveries, a decrease in productivity, and fall in revenue for manufacturing companies across the globe [4]. Organizations find it challenging to prepare the internal logistics and supply chain, and quickly respond to such unexpected events, due to low inter and intra-site visibility [5]. Due to low SCV, partners usually act upon incomplete information that results in wrong forecasts and the Bullwhip effect. Additionally, because of low SCV focal firms find it difficult to efficiently monitor all the involved actors. As a result, the focal firms are at supply chain sustainability risk, and any sustainability-related violation on part of irresponsible suppliers reflects on the focal firm, leading to reputational loss, financial losses due to costly legal obligations, and negative publicity [6].

Besides risks, the current supply chains are facing challenges due to low visibility in internal production processes. Collecting and sharing real-time data related to the order process, inventory, delivery, and potential supply chain disruptions is still not a well-adopted practice in production units [7]. Parts of the department work independently and do not share crucial information. This makes the whole production process quite opaque and even a small issue leads to huge disturbance. In addition to this, there is a significant demand for transparency and product traceability from customers, assuring ethical practices and sustainable sourcing [8].

Hence, visibility in production logistics and across supply chains has become a key concern for organizations all over the globe. Significant research has been done in past to analyze the state of visibility in different supply chains and exploring new digital technology tools that can enhance visibility throughout the supply chain [9, 10]. It is also observed that though SCV encompasses both internal and external visibility, the concept of visibility and factors influencing its implementation are mostly explored and analyzed in the context of external supply chain - involving buyer-supplier interaction and information asymmetry in the network. It is also evident that most of the studies collect these factors using secondary data through a review of literature, for instance [2]. In the past, little attention has been paid to practitioners' views on SCV, especially after the introduction and wide acceptance of disruptive technologies like blockchain, artificial intelligence, etc.

To bridge this gap, the current study adopts a Delphi-based approach to understand practitioners' views on SCV, the factors influencing its implementation, and crucial information requiring collection in sharing for SCV. It is among the few that empirically explores and rank the barrier, drivers, and antecedents for SCV through a multi-stage analysis that is iterated until a common consensus is reached among the experts. The study is a work-in-progress and describes the first round of Delphi analysis, the results of the full study will be communicated through a journal article in few months.

2 Methodology

2.1 Delphi-Based Approach

Delphi was developed at Rand Corporation in 1968 and since then it is a well-established methodology followed in various literature to explore and attain consensus on multi-faceted and multidisciplinary issues [11]. It is a systematic approach where a group of experts – having extensive experience on the topic under study – communicates and interacts anonymously in multiple rounds. Responses from each Delphi round forms the basis for the input to the following round in terms of the aggregate response from the group, and the respondents can reflect on and change their response. Such an approach helps to avoid adverse effects related to dominating personalities, interpersonal biases, defensive attitudes, and unproductive disagreements [12]. The rounds continue until a saturation point is reached. A Delphi study creates opportunities to gain valuable insights from practicing managers and is suitable for exploratory theory building [13]. In the past, Delphi-based approaches have been adopted in various research studies for needs assessments, policy development, and forecasting [11, 13]. In supply chain management, applications of the Delphi approach are found in studies investigating factors influencing decision-making; see e.g. [8, 14, 15].

2.2 Expert Selection

We followed the general guidelines for Delphi studies [13, 14] for setting up an appropriate panel to ensure the validity of the results. The experts should have extensive experience and knowledge related to the specific issue under study. We invited senior supply chain executives from large and medium-sized industrial firms, operating from northern Europe, with global supply chains and manufacturing locations across the globe. These experts were primarily drawn from, or recommended by, industry contacts and research partners. All invited executives had at least ten years of experience in global SCM. Overall, 34 SCM practitioners were invited, and 26 agreed to participate in the Delphi expert panel. They represent a variety of industries: Aerospace, automotive, fast-moving consumer goods, food and beverage, forest & garden equipment, furniture, heat transfer, heavy industrial goods, optoelectronics, packaging, steel, and telecommunication. The number of participants (26) is in the recommended range for Delphi studies. The panel should include at least 20 respondents to reduce potential individual biases, and larger groups than 30 tend to generate few additional insights and might limit the exploration of insights that emerge [8, 11].

2.3 First Round

The first round consists of four open-ended questions: (i) "Please describe in your own words what supply chain visibility means to you, your company, and your supply chains. Please provide examples." The first question helps us to understand the experts' definition of SCV and the effects SCV can have on a company's internal and external logistics processes. (ii) "Why is supply chain visibility important to your company and your supply chains?" The second question helps us to understand the potential outcome of implementing SCV. (iii) "What factors affect visibility of your supply chains and how?", The third question on other hand helps us to understand the inputs for implementing SCV, for instance, the potential the drivers, barrier and challenges (iv) "Is there anything else that you think is important in the context of supply chain visibility that you would like to add?" This fourth question helps to understand possible contingencies. Experts were given three week times to respond and they could choose to respond directly on the mail or through attached word documents. Reminders were sent after every week and full contact details of the researchers were provided in case the experts had any query. The responses were analyzed individually by the four researchers (one Ph.D. student, one postdoc and two professors), to identify potential themes and categories. Coding was compared and in most cases, there was full agreement among the researchers. Differences in interpretations were thoroughly reexamined and resolved jointly.

3   Results and Discussions

In the first round, we identified five categories within the responses: drivers, barriers, antecedents, effects, and information. Furthermore, effects could be divided into two sub-categories: capabilities, and performance effects, while information was sub-divided into three: (i) market and products, (ii) internal, and (iii) supply. The specific factors in each category are listed in Table 1.

Table 1. Factors influencing SCV and list of crucial information

Factors		
Drivers	**Barriers**	
Risk management	IT infrastructure (lack of …)	
Environmental sustainability	IT maturity (lack of …)	
SC control	Standardization (lack of …)	
Managing deviations	Organizational culture (e.g. silos, conflict of interest)	
Customer service	Risks with sharing sensitive information (IPR)	
Transparency	Information sharing (lack of willingness)	
Operational excellence	IT competence (lack of …)	
Decision-making support	SC competence (lack of …)	
	SC complexity	
	Factors	
Antecedents	**Effects: Capabilities**	**Effects: Performance**
Integrated systems	Planning capability	Customer service
Technology maturity	Decision-making support	Profitability
Information sharing	Advanced analytics capability	Environmental impact
Standardization	Predictive capability	Cost
Inter-organizational collaboration	Risk management	Lead time
Trust	Traceability	
Data quality	SC Control	
	Forecasting	
	Information	
Market & product	**Internal**	**Supply**
Demand	Production plans	Purchasing plans
Forecasts	Inventory levels	Supply
Orders	Capacity	Supplier location
Deliveries	Lead times	Supplier capabilities
Deviations	Safety stocks	Track and trace
Customer service		
Country of origin		
Product in use information		

3.1 Drivers

According to the experts, one of the main driving forces for SCV is risk management and mitigating risk. As one of the experts mentioned in describing the importance of SCV: "To know and understand the full value chain gives you the possibility to make proactive initiatives instead of reactive. Increasing importance of Supply Chain Risk Management, given recent years development with trade barriers, pandemic, natural disasters, etc." Controlling supply chain operations, transparency, and decision-making support are among other mentioned drivers.

3.2 Barriers

Many of the experts state that the main barriers of SCV are lack of IT infrastructure and maturity. One of the experts highlighted it by mentioning: "If visibility means being able to 'see' the supplier's supply chain, or my order's position against plan in it, then that possibility is today greatly affected by existing IT systems that are rarely/never created for visualization in this dimension". Lack of standardization is another crucial factor restricting the adaptation of SCV systems. As the product traverse through stages of the global supply chain standardization becomes a crucial element especially for effective data sharing and technology integration. IPR and fear of losing information advantage (willingness to share information) are some of the other mentioned barriers.

3.3 Antecedents

As per the experts, integration of systems and technology maturity level are some of the prerequisites or enablers for SCV. One of the experts mentioned: "The amount of different systems that drive the supply chains and how easy/difficult it is to load/share data from these systems and the level of integration between these systems. The level of integration between our systems and our suppliers' and customers' systems". Among other factors, quality of data, trust, and collaboration are some of the other antecedents for SCV. One expert mentioned: "The degree of visibility affects our ability to plan and collaborate effectively, and our ability to detect trends and changes in the supply chain at an early stage. This, in turn, affects our ability to grow profitably and our ability to build trust and loyalty with our partners and customers".

3.4 Effects

Some of the effects concerning capabilities are better planning, informed decision-making, advanced analytics and predictive analysis. As one expert state: "part of visibility in supply chains is about making information about demand, capacity, order volume and inventory development visible by creating better processes for demand planning, capacity planning, phasing in and phasing out, etc. Much of this visibility is about making the information visible internally within the company and that everyone functions share the same information in order to make better decisions about the material supply." Traceability is another major effect for which the experts mentioned: "we see with increased Supply Chain Visibility we can secure traceability and chain of custody, certification schemes of raw material for instance." On the other hand, some of the mentioned major performance-based effects of SCV are better customer service, profitability, and decreased lead-time. As per an expert through SCV, the involved actors can get "the ability to see what our customers are asking for (volumes of different products), but also to have a picture of our suppliers' ability to meet our needs."

3.5 Information

Finally, we also identified from the responses, various information that the experts perceive crucial for SCV. This information is worth capturing and sharing among actors through a common database, to get desired effects of SCV. One of the experts mentioned, "Visibility is also about having the same information as your partners in the SC at the same time. It is also about having good tooling to visualize forecasts, plans and orders. A good BI tool with the same information is key to analyze the current status and the future. Common SC master data is important." Some of the crucial information are those regarding demand, forecast, planning, inventory, purchase. As per one expert: "part of visibility in supply chains is about making information about demand, capacity, order volume and inventory development visible by creating better processes for demand planning, capacity planning, phasing in and phasing out, etc. Another dimension of visibility in supply chains is about making information available/visible internally within the company and to other stakeholders in the supply chain, e.g. suppliers, carriers, etc."

4 Conclusions

The study presents the initial results of a Delphi analysis with the aim to understand SCV from practitioners' perspectives. It systematically explores different drivers, barriers, effects, antecedents, and crucial information for SCV. It was found that risk management, environmental sustainability, and supply chain control are some of the key drivers, lack of IT infrastructure and maturity are some of the barriers, integrated systems and technology maturity are among the key antecedents and gaining planning capability and better customer service are some of the positive effects of supply chain visibility as per the experts' opinion. In addition, information related to planning, supplier location, and deviation are among the crucial ones that require collection and sharing for better supply chain visibility. To the best of our knowledge, this research study is among the few that empirically explores factors influencing supply chain visibility and generates new insights as to why the barriers can be difficult to overcome in complex supply chain settings. It also lay the foundation for the development for technological solutions, by providing the required inputs for development of decision support systems (DSS) that can enhance visibility in the supply chain.

Abovementioned, the study is work-in-progress and presents only the results from the first Delphi round. In the subsequent rounds, the experts will revisit the aggregate results, rank the factors and information on basis of their experience – while providing commentary inputs explaining their choices. This process will be repeated until consensus and the full analysis results are available, it would be also meaningful to approach the SCV problem predictively/prescriptively not just descriptively (understand why). Finally, a workshop will be organized with experts, towards the end of the Delphi, around June 2021, to share the findings and collect additional commentary inputs to understand why the top-ranked factors are so important. We expect to have a full paper ready by August 2021.

Acknowledgement. We gratefully acknowledge the funding from Produktion2030 and Vinnova for this research, as part of the research project Production Logistic Visibility (LOVIS).

References

1. Sodhi, M.S., Tang, C.S.: Research opportunities in supply chain transparency. Prod. Oper. Manag. **28**, 2946–2959 (2019)
2. Somapa, S., Cools, M., Dullaert, W.: Characterizing supply chain visibility – a literature review. Int. J. Logist. Manag. **29**, 308–339 (2018)
3. Yu, M.-C., Goh, M.: A multi-objective approach to supply chain visibility and risk. Eur. J. Oper. Res. **233**, 125–130 (2014)
4. Caridi, M., Crippa, L., Perego, A., Sianesi, A., Tumino, A.: Do virtuality and complexity affect supply chain visibility? Int. J. Prod. Econ. **127**, 372–383 (2010)
5. Srinivasan, R., Swink, M.: An investigation of visibility and flexibility as complements to supply chain analytics: an organizational information processing theory perspective. Prod. Oper. Manag. **27**, 1849–1867 (2018)
6. Kalaiarasan, R., Olhager, J., Wiktorsson, M., Jeong, Y.: Production Logistics Visibility – perspectives, principles and prospects. Presented at the Swedish Production Symposium, Jönköping, Sweden, October 2020
7. Bregman, R., Peng, D.X., Chin, W.: The effect of controversial global sourcing practices on the ethical judgments and intentions of U.S. consumers. J. Oper. Manag. **36**, 229–243 (2015)
8. Agrawal, T.K., Pal, R.: Traceability in textile and clothing supply chains: classifying implementation factors and information sets via Delphi study. Sustainability. **11**, 1698 (2019)
9. Cao, X., Li, T., Wang, Q.: RFID-based multi-attribute logistics information processing and anomaly mining in production logistics. Int. J. Prod. Res. **57**, 5453–5466 (2019)
10. Pfahl, L., Moxham, C.: Achieving sustained competitive advantage by integrating ECR, RFID and visibility in retail supply chains: a conceptual framework. Prod. Plan. Control **25**, 548–571 (2014)
11. Ogden, J.A., Petersen, K.J., Carter, J.R., Monczka, R.M.: Supply management strategies for the future: a Delphi study. J. Supply Chain Manag. **41**, 29–48 (2005)
12. Lummus, R.R., Vokurka, R.J., Duclos, L.K.: Delphi study on supply chain flexibility. Int. J. Prod. Res. **43**, 2687–2708 (2005)
13. Melnyk, S.A., Lummus, R.R., Vokurka, R.J., Burns, L.J., Sandor, J.: Mapping the future of supply chain management: a Delphi study. Int. J. Prod. Res. **47**, 4629–4653 (2009)
14. Kembro, J., Näslund, D., Olhager, J.: Information sharing across multiple supply chain tiers: a Delphi study on antecedents. Int. J. Prod. Econ. **193**, 77–86 (2017)
15. Hassan, M., Ali, M., Aktas, E., Alkayid, K.: Factors affecting selection decision of auto-identification technology in warehouse management: an international Delphi study. Prod. Plan. Control **26**, 1025–1049 (2015)

Digital Twins Based on Systems Engineering and Semantic Modeling

STARdom: An Architecture for Trusted and Secure Human-Centered Manufacturing Systems

Jože M. Rožanec[1,2,3]([✉])(iD), Patrik Zajec[1,2], Klemen Kenda[1,2,3](iD),
Inna Novalija[2], Blaž Fortuna[2,3], Dunja Mladenić[2], Entso Veliou[5](iD),
Dimitrios Papamartzivanos[4], Thanassis Giannetsos[4], Sofia Anna Menesidou[4],
Rubén Alonso[6], Nino Cauli[7], Diego Reforgiato Recupero[6,7],
Dimosthenis Kyriazis[8](iD), Georgios Sofianidis[8], Spyros Theodoropoulos[8,9],
and John Soldatos[10]

[1] Jožef Stefan International Postgraduate School, Jamova 39,
1000 Ljubljana, Slovenia
joze.rozanec@ijs.si
[2] Jožef Stefan Institute, Jamova 39, 1000 Ljubljana, Slovenia
[3] Qlector d.o.o., Rovšnikova 7, 1000 Ljubljana, Slovenia
[4] Ubitech Ltd., Digital Security & Trusted Computing Group, Athens, Greece
[5] Department of Informatics and Computer Engineering, University of West Attica,
Agiou Spyridonos Street, 12243 Egaleo, Athens, Greece
[6] R2M Solution Srl, Pavia, Italy
[7] Department of Computer Science, University of Cagliari, Cagliari, Italy
[8] Department of Digital Systems, University of Piraeus, Piraeus, Greece
[9] Department of Electrical and Computer Engineering,
National Technical University of Athens, Athens, Greece
[10] INTRASOFT International, 19.5 KM Markopoulou Ave.,
19002 Peania, GR, Greece

Abstract. There is a lack of a single architecture specification that addresses the needs of trusted and secure Artificial Intelligence systems with humans in the loop, such as human-centered manufacturing systems at the core of the evolution towards Industry 5.0. To realize this, we propose an architecture that integrates forecasts, Explainable Artificial Intelligence, supports collecting users' feedback and uses Active Learning and Simulated Reality to enhance forecasts and provide decision-making recommendations. The architecture security is addressed at all levels. We align the proposed architecture with the Big Data Value Association Reference Architecture Model. We tailor it for the domain of demand forecasting and validate it on a real-world case study.

Keywords: Industry 4.0 · Smart manufacturing · Explainable Artificial Intelligence (XAI) · Active learning · Demand forecasting

© IFIP International Federation for Information Processing 2021
Published by Springer Nature Switzerland AG 2021
A. Dolgui et al. (Eds.): APMS 2021, IFIP AICT 633, pp. 199–207, 2021.
https://doi.org/10.1007/978-3-030-85910-7_21

1   Introduction

The increasing digitalization of manufacturing has enabled the transition to the fourth industrial revolution (Industry 4.0). Based on Cyber-Physical Systems (CPS) and technologies such as cloud computing, the Industrial Internet of Things (IIoT), and Artificial Intelligence (AI), Industry 4.0 enables flexible production lines and supports innovative functionalities such as mass customization, predictive maintenance, zero-defect manufacturing, and digital twins [20]. State-of-the art AI systems in industrial plants operate in controlled environments. Nevertheless, industrial plants' AI systems must be safe, trusted, and secure, even when operating in dynamic, unstructured, and unpredictable environments. Ensuring these systems' safety and reliability is a key prerequisite for deploying them at scale and fully leveraging AI's benefits in manufacturing [8].

The increasing AI adoption in manufacturing has prompted researchers and digital manufacturing communities to research solutions that boost the development of secure and trusted AI systems in production lines and their compliance to ethical principles. A prominent example is the surge of research on Explainable AI (XAI), a field of AI concerned with building models transparent to users or techniques that provide insights on key factors influencing the model's forecast. Such insights help to assess the soundness of given forecasts and aid human decision-making. In the particular manufacturing case, XAI boosts AI solutions' transparency and increases human workers' acceptance. Though much research was done regarding XAI techniques, there is still little research on how the forecast explanations affect human decision-making. To assess their impact, human feedback is required. Human feedback collection regarding AI models and forecast explanations can be addressed as an Active Learning (AL) problem. AL enables AI systems to operate in the absence of enough labeled data and consult an authoritative source (e.g., query a human expert) to obtain the required annotations. Focusing knowledge acquisition only on the most promising data instances accelerates knowledge acquisition and increases industrial systems' robustness.

The increasing digitalization and the development and deployment of AI models have increased vulnerabilities to cyber-attacks. In particular, AI models are vulnerable to attacks in the training phase (e.g., poisoning) and operational phase (e.g., evasion). AI models and XAI techniques must be robust against adversarial attacks.

The development, deployment, and operation of efficient industrial systems that combine advanced AI systems with appropriate cyber-defense strategies must be grounded in well-structured architectures. The latter boost the scalability and efficiency of the systems while at the same time facilitating their integration. In recent years, standards-development organizations, industrial associations, and research groups have introduced reference architecture models for industrial systems. For instance, the Reference Architecture Model for Industry 4.0 (RAMI 4.0) [17] illustrates the main building blocks of Industry 4.0 systems and presents how to develop an industrial system in a structured way. As another example, the Industrial Internet Consortium (IIC) has introduced the Industrial

Internet Reference Architecture (IIRA) [2] that specifies a common architecture framework for developing interoperable IoT systems for different industry verticals, including manufacturing. These architectures do not directly address the security and safety aspects of industrial systems. Complementary architectural frameworks were developed to address them, such as the Industrial Internet Security Framework (IISF) [3]. Likewise, these architectures do not address the structuring principles of AI systems (e.g., the building blocks of machine learning pipelines). These principles are also addressed separately in specifications like the Big Data Value Association (BDVA) Reference Architecture. Overall, there is no single architecture specification that addresses the needs of trusted and secure AI systems with humans in the loop, such as human-centered manufacturing systems at the core of the evolution towards Industry 5.0 [1,13]. In our proposed architecture, human in the loop functionalities are provided making use of active learning and providing decision-making recommendations.

This paper aims to alleviate this gap based on the description and initial validation of an architecture for trusted and human-centered AI systems in production environments. The architecture aims to serve as a blueprint for realizing manufacturing systems that support AI models, XAI, and AL while providing security guarantees. It provides structuring principles for integrating these modules. It creates synergies between them, aligned with some of the above-listed reference models, such as the BDVA reference architecture model and the IISF. Specifically, the introduced architecture leverages layering concepts and components from these architectures towards providing a blueprint for developing trusted AI systems. Leveraging on these blueprints, we also illustrate how cybersecurity components for industrial AI systems are combined with XAI and AL to enable trusted, human-centered AI. The architecture is instantiated and validated on a real-world use case regarding demand forecasting.

The rest of this paper is structured as follows: Sect. 2 presents related work, and Sect. 3 describes the proposed architecture and its application to demand forecasting. Finally, in Sect. 4, we discuss an implementation, provide our conclusions and outline future work.

2   Related Work

The increasing digitalization of manufacturing enables the creation of AI models for multiple use cases. When decisions are made based on forecasts, they should be accompanied with explanations on how those forecasts were reached by the model [10,15]. Such explanations can help the user understand the model reasoning, evaluate the soundness of the forecasts and explanation provided, increasing trust in the model, and avoid costly mistakes. Explanations must be contextual to the user [7]. They can inform key factors influencing the forecast, emphasize the actionable aspects and provide examples of how changes in certain variables can change the forecast outcome. Forecast explanation's quality is a matter of ongoing research, where user feedback can be crucial. To realize it, [21] proposed a framework with three components: a forecasting engine, an explanation engine, and a feedback loop to learn from the users.

Two core ideas drive research in AL: (i) the learner can benefit from asking questions, and (ii) unlabeled data is available or easily obtained [18]. AL strategies can selectively choose the items to be presented to the user, for which feedback is expected. Since users are usually reluctant to provide it, AL strategies enable to identify a small set of items on which users' input can convey the system valuable information [5]. In particular, AL can collect feedback for given forecasts, forecast explanations, and decision-making options.

While AL is concerned with selecting the most informative unlabeled data instances and querying labels for them, simulated reality provides the capability to generate synthetic data in a supervised setting. Such data augmentation is valuable, e.g., in the context of imbalanced datasets, such as infrequent demand items or visual quality inspection [22]. Simulated reality is also a key component for reinforcement learning (RL). Simulations enable RL agents to explore many episodes of trial and error to explore and learn efficient policies. By envisioning the consequences of an action, simulations can help to validate desired outcomes in a real-world setting [4].

The richness and connectivity enabled by the increased manufacturing digitalization and IoT-based *Systems-of-Systems* pose a significant risk regarding malware. Malware can target the network layer and edge devices to extract sensitive information (impacting confidentiality) or alternate data originated by those devices (impacting trustworthiness). AI models are also subject to cyber-attacks, such as poisoning and evasion [23]. The goal of such attacks is to disrupt the AI model forecasts to mislead dependent systems and decision-making. Poisoning consists of altering the training data to disrupt AI models learning and their later performance. Evasion, on the other side, aims to produce wrong forecasts on already trained models by providing a carefully perturbed input that confuses the AI model. XAI techniques were successfully applied to identify such cases, either by supporting the exploration of model vulnerabilities [9,11] or identifying perturbed samples, which usually have different *XAI signatures* [6].

The development of conversational multimodal interfaces can enhance human-machine interactions [12]. While an output interface can be provided through different modes, conversational interactions allow obtaining complementary information from the user, who can provide locally observed collective knowledge [14] not captured by other means.

To realize the components and interactions listed above, an architecture model must be developed, following the best practices introduced by reference architectures described in Sect. 1. We introduce such an architecture in Sect. 3.

3   Proposed Architecture

We propose a modular architecture to enable efficient industrial systems that combine advanced AI systems with appropriate cyber defense strategies. The architecture integrates predictions, gathers insights on relevant features, incorporates domain knowledge and context to each prediction, and provides a forecast explanation and decision-making options to the end-user. Cyber-security is considered across all modules. The architecture (see Fig. 1) comprises the following components:

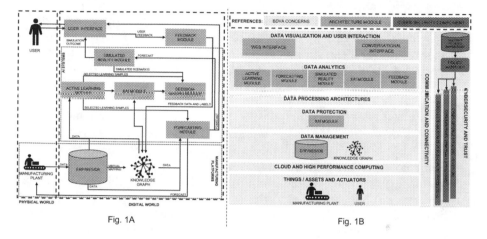

Fig. 1A

Fig. 1B

Fig. 1. Proposed architecture. Figure 1A displays physical and digital components and their interactions. Cyber-security permeates all levels, and thus not expressed as a single module. Figure 1B shows how components in Fig. 1A relate to the BDVA reference architecture model.

- **Knowledge Graph:** receives data from Manufacturing Execution Systems (MES), Enterprise Resource Planning (ERP) software, and other systems and from the *Feedback module*, which is mapped into a graph considering relevant concepts and relationships between them. The knowledge graph can be extended for specific use cases, leveraging existing knowledge and enriching it with new domain knowledge and data specific to that case.
- **Forecasting Module:** provides forecasts based on AI and simulation models. Different models are developed regarding the task to be solved (classification, regression, clustering, or ranking). The models require past data to learn patterns and predict future outcomes based on them. Inputs can be obtained from the knowledge graph, databases, and external systems, such as ERP and MES.
- **XAI Module:** receives input from the *Forecasting module* to assess which features are most relevant to a given forecast. Based on them, an explanation is created for the user, considering their profile, to ensure relevant information is display and confidentiality protected. The *XAI module* also receives input from the *Feedback module*, through which the users assess the goodness of explanations provided and gather knowledge on actions yet unknown to the system. Such feedback can be used to measure forecast explanation's quality, detect biases in the forecasting model, explainability algorithms, and be used

to correct and tailor future explanations and detect potential poisoning and evasion attacks.

Decision-Making Module: envisioned as a recommender system. The decision-making module considers inputs from the *Forecasting, XAI, Simulated reality*, and *Feedback* modules, to provide decision-making advice to users based on their profile and context. Based on inputs from the *XAI module* can create directive explanations [19], suggesting decision-making options that lead to a desired outcome.

- **Simulated Reality Module:** receives input from the *Forecasting module*, which could be either a set of predictions or candidate actions. This input is used to generate alternative scenarios, either through the generation of synthetic data or the reconfiguration of an RL agent environment. These scenarios are evaluated, and the confidence of the algorithm's predictions is assessed. The human operator is an active participant in this process, verifying the simulated scenarios' plausibility and monitoring the algorithm's reactions to them. The output of the component consists of plausible, novel, or low confidence scenarios provided to the *Decision-making module* as a means of robustifying the algorithm's predictive capacity and covering its blind spots before an action is taken in the real world. The algorithm can use the simulation component, either as a means of data augmentation or for readjusting to novel or anomalous inputs.
- **Active Learning Module:** monitors existing knowledge and labeled data to suggest which data instances will be displayed to users to get their feedback and labels. It prioritizes unlabeled data for data instances expected to contain interesting information. Collected feedback and new labeled instances are consumed by the *Forecasting, XAI*, and *Decision-making* modules.
- **Feedback Module:** collects feedback from the users regarding forecasts, forecast explanations, and the decision-making options provided. Feedback can be explicit or implicit, and can be used by the *Forecasting, Active Learning, XAI* and *Decision-making* modules to enhance their operation.
- **User Interface:** enables users' multimodal interactions with the system, e.g., interact through the use of their voice, complemented by other modalities, such as on-screen forms. It enables the machine to provide information to the user through audio, natural language, or other means such as visual information.

The IISF provides a guide for understanding and implementing security for systems that comply with the IIRA. In particular, the IISF provides guidelines for securing each component of the IIRA while at the same time binding these components together in a trustworthy system. They emphasize means to secure the traditional Operation Technology (OT), as conventional IT security solutions do not apply directly to OT systems and services. The IISF specifies a range of functionalities applied across all industry components in a horizontal approach, i.e., a cross-cutting function. These functionalities include protecting data, protecting (edge/cloud) endpoints, protecting communications and connectivity, security configuration, management, monitoring and analytics. Our proposed architecture aligns with IISF. It defines a cyber-defense layer destined to protect AI systems from cybersecurity attacks such as poisoning and evasion attacks.

As depicted in Fig. 1B, the proposed architecture is well aligned with the BDVA reference architecture model and thus can be directly utilized in various additional domains, even beyond the Industry 4.0 domain. The BDVA architecture exploits as a backbone Cloud, High-Performance Computing environments, and data sources and devices in the IoT and edge spaces. These will be exploited in the proposed architecture's scope to deploy the corresponding modules and the diverse data stores – including the Knowledge Graph and the data processing that needs to be performed on top of them. Aligning on that level of the BDVA reference models facilitates the direct deployment of the architecture modules described above and presented in Fig. 1A. Of major importance are the components on the data analytics layer of the BDVA reference model, also addressing the *BDVA Reference Model Verticals* in terms of time series, IoT, media, and other datasets. Thus, the modules placed on the data analytics layer of BDVA tackle the various types of data and can be utilized in combination with analytics models and techniques in various domains to provide additional information (e.g., explainability outcomes). Additionally, the proposed architecture enhances the BDVA reference model in Data Visualization and User Interaction by delivering a conversational interface to obtain feedback from the users and utilize it in the data analytics scope.

We partially validated this architecture with an implementation based on EU HORIZON 2020 FACTLOG and STAR partners' real-world data. The implementation comprised demand forecasting models providing daily forecasts. We created forecast explanations based on LIME [15] implemented decision-making recommendations regarding manufactured goods transportation [16]. Finally, we implemented a knowledge graph to link existing data semantically and an interface to collect implicit and explicit feedback regarding forecasts, forecast explanations, and decision-making options[1]. While a productive version of the demand forecasting models exists, the latest forecasting models and the remaining components were not deployed into production environments. AL and simulated reality modules were not implemented.

4   Conclusions

This research introduces an architecture that integrates different components to enable trusted and human-centered AI. In particular, we align the architecture with the BDVA Reference Model to be directly utilized in additional domains beyond the Industry 4.0 domain. Most architecture components were instantiated and validated on a real-world use case. Future work will focus on developing AL and simulated reality modules and cyber-security enhancements. This architecture will be applied to multiple use cases, such as defect detection towards the Quality 4.0 paradigm, in the EU H2020 STAR project.

---

[1] A video of the application was published in https://youtu.be/ysD2oXQO98I.

Acknowledgement. This work was supported by the Slovenian Research Agency and the European Union's Horizon 2020 program projects FACTLOG and STAR under grant agreements numbers H2020-869951 and H2020-956573.

This document is the property of the STAR consortium and shall not be distributed or reproduced without the formal approval of the STAR Management Committee. The content of this report reflects only the authors' view. The European Commission is not responsible for any use that may be made of the information it contains.

References

1. European commission, enabling technologies for industry 5.0, results of a workshop with Europe's technology leaders, September 2020. https://op.europa.eu/en/publication-detail/-/publication/8e5de100-2a1c-11eb-9d7e-01aa75ed71a1/language-en
2. The industrial internet of things volume g1: Reference architecture, version 1.9 19 June 2019. https://www.iiconsortium.org/pdf/IIRA-v1.9.pdf
3. Industrial internet of things, volume g4: Security framework, industrial internet consortium. IIC:PUB:G4:V1.0:PB:20160926, September 2016
4. Amodei, D., Olah, C., Steinhardt, J., Christiano, P., Schulman, J., Mané, D.: Concrete problems in AI safety. arXiv preprint arXiv:1606.06565 (2016)
5. Elahi, M., Ricci, F., Rubens, N.: A survey of active learning in collaborative filtering recommender systems. Comput. Sci. Rev. **20**, 29–50 (2016)
6. Fidel, G., Bitton, R., Shabtai, A.: When explainability meets adversarial learning: detecting adversarial examples using shap signatures. In: 2020 International Joint Conference on Neural Networks (IJCNN), pp. 1–8. IEEE (2020)
7. Henin, C., Le Métayer, D.: A multi-layered approach for tailored black-box explanations (2021)
8. AI HLEG: High-level expert group on artificial intelligence: ethics guidelines for trustworthy AI. European Commission, 09.04 (2019)
9. Lapuschkin, S., Wäldchen, S., Binder, A., Montavon, G., Samek, W., Müller, K.R.: Unmasking Clever Hans predictors and assessing what machines really learn. Nat. Commun. **10**(1), 1–8 (2019)
10. Lundberg, S., Lee, S.I.: A unified approach to interpreting model predictions. arXiv preprint arXiv:1705.07874 (2017)
11. Ma, Y., Xie, T., Li, J., Maciejewski, R.: Explaining vulnerabilities to adversarial machine learning through visual analytics. IEEE Trans. Visual Comput. Graphics **26**(1), 1075–1085 (2019)
12. Maurtua, I., et al.: Natural multimodal communication for human-robot collaboration. Int. J. Adv. Rob. Syst. **14**(4), 1729881417716043 (2017)
13. Nahavandi, S.: Industry 5.0–a human-centric solution. Sustainability **11**(16), 4371 (2019)
14. Preece, A., et al.: Sherlock: simple human experiments regarding locally observed collective knowledge. Technical report, US Army Research Laboratory Aberdeen Proving Ground, United States (2015)
15. Ribeiro, M.T., Singh, S., Guestrin, C.: "Why should i trust you?" explaining the predictions of any classifier. In: Proceedings of the 22nd ACM SIGKDD International Conference on Knowledge Discovery and Data Mining, pp. 1135–1144 (2016)
16. Rožanec, J.: Explainable demand forecasting: A data mining goldmine. In: Companion Proceedings of the Web Conference 2021 (WWW 2021 Companion), Ljubljana, Slovenia, 19–23 April 2021 (2021). https://doi.org/10.1145/3442442.3453708

17. Schweichhart, K.: Reference architectural model Industrie 4.0 (rami 4.0). An Introduction, I **40** (2016). https://www.plattform-i40.de
18. Settles, B.: Active learning literature survey (2009)
19. Singh, R., et al.: Directive explanations for actionable explainability in machine learning applications. arXiv preprint arXiv:2102.02671 (2021)
20. Soldatos, J., Lazaro, O., Cavadini, F., Boschi, F., Taisch, M., Fantini, P.M., et al.: The Digital Shopfloor: Industrial Automation in the Industry 4.0 Era. Performance Analysis and Applications. River Publishers Series in Automation, Control and Robotics (2019)
21. Tulli, S., Wallkötter, S., Paiva, A., Melo, F.S., Chetouani, M.: Learning from explanations and demonstrations: a pilot study. In: 2nd Workshop on Interactive Natural Language Technology for Explainable Artificial Intelligence, pp. 61–66 (2020)
22. Yun, J.P., Shin, W.C., Koo, G., Kim, M.S., Lee, C., Lee, S.J.: Automated defect inspection system for metal surfaces based on deep learning and data augmentation. J. Manuf. Syst. **55**, 317–324 (2020)
23. Zhang, J., Li, C.: Adversarial examples: opportunities and challenges. IEEE Trans. Neural Netw. Learn. Syst. **31**(7), 2578–2593 (2019)

Semantic Modeling Supports the Integration of Concept-Decision-Knowledge

Yili Jin[1], Jinzhi Lu[2(✉)], Guoxin Wang[1(✉)], Ru Wang[1], and Kiritsis Dimitris[2]

[1] Beijing Institute of Technology, Beijing 100089, China
[2] EPFL SCI-STI-DK, Station 9, CH-1015 Lausanne, Switzerland
jinzhi.lu@epfl.ch

Abstract. The semantics of product design enables to visualize the function of the product and promote communications between the products and the designers. However, the existing theories and methods of product design are lack research on the integration of modeling concepts, domain-specific knowledge, and decision-making. For this reason, this paper proposes a C-D-K theory which is supported by a semantic modeling approach. Firstly, KARMA modeling language, which is a semantics modeling approach, is used to support the formalization of concept space (C) and decision space (D), in which space C is expanded based on the RFLP design framework, and space D is based on PEI-X decision workflow to realize decision problem modeling. Then based on the Open service lifecycle collaboration (OSLC) specification, domain-specific knowledge is represented based on the unified expression of resources in the knowledge space (K), which is used to integrate knowledge to semantics models constructed by KARMA language. Finally, the feasibility and effectiveness of the proposed semantic modeling approach are verified by the case of an unmanned detection vehicle design. From the result, we find the semantics modeling approach enables to integrate semantic models and knowledge based on the C-D-K theory.

Keywords: Semantic modeling · C-D-K theory · MBSE · KARMA

1 Introduction

In the context of Industry 4.0 and intelligent manufacturing, product design is challenged when developing a solution based on existing knowledge and make decisions for the different solutions [1], because of different data structures and lack of design tools. Currently, semantic modeling is the basis of describing product information using models and shareable data [2]. It often contributes to integrating domain-specific knowledge and development solutions with design frameworks. These frameworks are mainly used to identify concept and decision-making elements for product design.

To construct a design framework for the concept development and decision-making for product development, design theories are often used to capture and frame the topologies between concepts, decision-making, and knowledge across different domains. Currently, C-K theory has received wide attention for integrating concept design and domain

© IFIP International Federation for Information Processing 2021
Published by Springer Nature Switzerland AG 2021
A. Dolgui et al. (Eds.): APMS 2021, IFIP AICT 633, pp. 208–217, 2021.
https://doi.org/10.1007/978-3-030-85910-7_22

knowledge. However, when implementing the trade-off between different concept solutions, due to the lack of research on the digitization and modeling representation of decision-making and design knowledge, there is still a challenge for C-K theory to support product design with decision-making.

This paper proposes a semantic modeling approach that supports C-K theory and makes use of a case study to verify its feasibility. The main scientific contributions of this paper include:

1. To support Decision-Based Design for product design, C-K theory is extended to C-D-K theory [3, 4].
2. The semantic modeling method of concept - decision - knowledge integration is proposed, KARMA is used which is a general modeling language based on the GOPPRR method [5], for realizing the formal description of heterogeneous concepts, decision-making, and knowledge of the product.
3. Open Services for Lifecycle Collaboration (OSLC) supports unified knowledge representations which is integrated into KARMA models referring to concept models and decision-making models [6].

In the following chapters, we will introduce in detail our proposed semantic modeling approach that supports the integration of Concept-Decision-Knowledge of product development. Section 2 describes the literature review. Section 3 describes the proposed approach, including the C-D-K theory, semantic modeling using KARMA language, and three specific formal expressions of C-D-K. Section 4 introduces a case study of an unmanned detection vehicle design to verify the feasibility of our proposed method.

2 Literature Review

C-K theory has received extensive attention since it was proposed. To understand and apply C-K theory, the existing literature extends C-K theory from different perspectives. Masson [7] focus on the process of collective creation for product development and puts forward the KCP theory based on the C-K theory. Besides, Kazakci [8] tried to apply C-K theory to the development of computer-aided design tools and developed a new C-K-E theory, which is more explanatory to the design process in a specific field. In the field of design, more and more scholars believe that decision is the basic structure of product design. To support the decision-making of concept models based on the existing knowledge, a C-D-K theory is proposed to integrate concept design, decision-making, and specific knowledge [3].

Semantic modeling is the most important part of the computer-aided design method based on C-D-K theory. In terms of semantic modeling, many methods have been proposed for different purposes. For example, System Modeling Language (SysML), Business Process Modeling Language (BPMN), semantic Web Modeling, and so on. These languages are always developed with different tools, which have their syntax. However, when integrating heterogeneous models in spaces of concepts, decision-making, and knowledge, there are not researchers proposing a semantic modeling approach based on C-D-K theory.

In summary, to support product design from the perspectives of concept design, decision-making, and domain-specific knowledge, a semantics modeling approach is investigated in this paper. Semantic modeling approach based on the previous research [5] is proposed to support C-D-K theory (previous research [3, 4]). Through this approach, concepts and decision-makings are formalized which are integrated with web services of knowledge graph represented based on OSLC specification.

3   Semantic Modeling for Integrating Concept-Decision-Knowledge

3.1   Overview

Aiming at the characteristics of product design with domain-specific knowledge, decision-making process, and conceptual solutions, a C-D-K theory and its semantic modeling method are proposed. In the C-D-K theory, Decision Space (D) is defined as the bridge between Concept Space (C) and Knowledge Space (K) during the whole design process. The semantic modeling approach that supports C-D-K theory is shown in Fig. 1. Due to the heterogeneity of information in these three spaces, this paper uses the KARMA unified modeling language to support the formal description of the C-D-K three-dimensional heterogeneous space. KARMA language [5] is a semantic language with textual grammar based on GOPPRR-E approach. The purpose of Space C is to obtain a satisfactory solution through the product design process. Thus, the concept models are developed using KARMA libraries based on Requirement, Function, Logical and Physical (RFLP) design processes and SysML specifications [9]. Space D aims to formalize the decision-making processes when implementing the trade-off processes of the product concept selections. Thus, the decision-making models are developed using KARMA libraries based on decision support problem (DSP) and PEI-X diagram model [10], for describes the decision-making process across RFLP. Space K represents the existing specific knowledge for support concept development and decision-making. Thus, OSLC specifications is used to transform the heterogeneous knowledge data to a

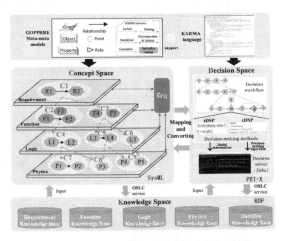

Fig. 1. Semantic Modeling method of C-D-K Theory

unified description of web services. Such web services can be integrated with KARMA models presenting Space C and Space D.

3.2   C-D-K Theory

C-D-K theory is an extension of C-K theory by introducing an extra Space D. It refers to an entire product design framework that contains the perspectives of concept design, decision-making, and existing knowledge. The three spaces are defined as follows.

- **Space C**

Space C refers to multiple alternative models based on the RFLP modeling process, which have a series of attributes: $A1$, $A2$, ..., An. Thus, Space C can be expressed as:

$$ConceptSpace = \sum OptionalSolution_{i,j}\left(\sum Attribute_{i,j,n}\right) \tag{1}$$

Where the $\sum OptionalSolution_{i,j}$ represents the set of alternative concept solutions based on the RFLP workflow which is described using KARMA language and SysML specification. The i refers to the design processes of RFLP ($i \in \{R, F, L, P\}$). The j refers to the jth concept solution ($j \in \{1, 2, ... j\}$), The $\sum Attribute_{i,j,n}$ represents the nth attribute set of the jth concept solution of phase i ($n \in \{1, 2, ... n\}$).

- **Space D**

Space D refers to the decision process based on DSP. DSPs mainly includes selection decision, compromise decision, so Space D can be expressed as:

$$DecisionSpace = \sum (sDSP, cDSP) \tag{2}$$

Where the $sDSP$ is a generic class of multi-attribute decision making, which evaluates and ranks the performance of all feasible options quantitatively to determine the most tendentious options. $cDSP$ is a generic class of multi-objective decision-making, which is a mixed multi-optimal solution based on mathematical programming and goal programming.

- **Space K**

Space K contains all kinds of existing knowledge resources to support the concept solutions of Space C and the decision-making processes of Space D. When constructing the product concepts and decision-making processes, the previous knowledge is considered as the reference models. Therefore, Space K can be expressed as:

$$KnowledgeSpace = \sum (RK, FK, LK, PK, DK) \tag{3}$$

Where the RK represents the existing requirement models and related reference resources; the FK represents existing function models and related reference resources; the LK represents existing logical models and related reference resources; the PK represents existing physical models and related reference resources; the DK represents existing decision-making models and related reference resources.

3.3   Semantic Modeling of the C-D-K Theory

This paper uses KARMA language to construct the models related to the formal expressions based on C-D-K theory. As shown in Fig. 2, the KARMA language is a semantic modeling language based on the GOPPRR method including the meta-meta models, meta-models, and models in an M3-M0 modeling framework. The details are as follows:

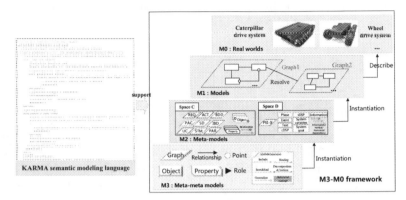

Fig. 2. M3-M0 modeling framework

- **M3:** Meta-meta models are the basic elements for constructing meta-models. KARMA language is developed based on the GOPPRR meta-meta models. The six key meta-meta models of GOPPRR are introduced based on the related definitions proposed by Kelly et al. [11].

a. Graph is a collection of *Objects*, *Relationships*, and their connections which refers to the diagram of the model.
b. *Object* refers to one entity in *Graphs* (for example, one class concept in SysML), which represents a model composition.
c. *Property* refers to one attribute of the other five meta-meta models describing its characteristics.
d. *Point* refers to one port in *Objects*.
e. *Relationship* refers to one connection between the different *Points* of *Objects* or *Objects*.
f. *Role* is at both ends of the *relationship*, which is used to indicate how *objects* are connected.

- **M2:** Meta-models refers to the model compositions which construct the model library, such as KARMA SysML library. The developed meta-models are used to represent the compositions of concept solutions and activities of decision-making processes.
- **M1:** Models are developed based on the meta-model.
- **M0:** Architectural views in the real world described by models.

(1) Semantic Modeling for Space C

When developing the concept models for product design, requirement models, functional models, logical models, and physical models enable to define one concept solution for one product using KARMA SysML library [12]. In KARMA SysML library, there are nine graphs developed based on SysML specification including requirement diagram (REQ), package diagram (PAC), use case diagram (UC) and activity diagram(ACT), sequence diagram (SD), and state machine diagram(STM), block definition diagram(BDD), internal block diagram(IBD) and parameter diagram (PAR). Through these graphs, requirement, functional, logical, and physical models are constructed in order to define the product concepts. The details of the SysML meta-model library based on the GOPPRR approach are shown in Table 1.

Table 1. Space C meta-model library (*C_graph* refers to *graph* for concept modeling)

C_graph	C_object	C_relationship	Description
REQ	Package, Test case, Constraint modules, Comments, Requirements	Include, Trace, Reuse, Improve, Satisfy, verify	**Requirement:** Used to describe the requirements of product design, such as functional requirements
PAC	Package, Module, Interface module, Model, Model base, Feature, Constraint module, Value type	Generalization, Association, Introduction, Combination	**Functional:** Used to realize the functional analysis of the product, such as functional division, interaction between stakeholders, and the system
UC	Package, Participant, Interface module, Module, Use case	Include, Generalize, Associate, Extend	
ACT	Packet, Action, Send action, Shunt, Fork, Node, Accept event, Select, Start, Terminate, End	Object flow, Control flow	
SD	Modules, Operator, Lifeline object, Selection, Cycle	Deliver message, Reply message, Create message	**Logical:** Used to realize the logical analysis of the product, such as the time interaction of the activities in the system and the expression of the system state
STM	Fork, Start, End, Selection, Status, Historical mark	Conversion	

(*continued*)

Table 1. (*continued*)

C_graph	C_object	C_relationship	Description
BDD	Package, Interface block, Block, Constraint block, Value type, Comment	Generalization, Association, Project flow, Composition	**Physical:** Used to describe the physical implementation structure of the product, such as the module composition of the product, the internal elements and relationships of the module
IBD	Interface block, Internal block, Comment	Object stream	
PAR	Parameter, Interface block, Constraint block	Parameter flow	

(2) Semantic Modeling for Space D

There are mainly two kinds of decisions involved in engineering design, namely, selection decision and compromise decision. To formalize the decision-making processes for the trade-off of product concept solution, a domain-specific modeling language, the PEI-X diagram, is used to describe the decision analysis process within Space D. The details of the Space D meta-model library based on the GOPPRR method are shown in Table 2.

Table 2. Space D meta-model library (*D_graph* refers to *graph* for decision-making modeling)

D_graph	D_object	D_relationship	Description
PEI-X diagram	Phase, Event, Text, cDSP, sDSP, System variables, System alternative, System goal, System constraint, System boundary, Information	Information Dependency, Vertical Dependency, Horizontal Dependency	Describe the decision workflow in Space D

(3) Integrating Semantic Models with Space K

Knowledge in Space K is represented as RFLP and decision-making models and related materials. When developing the models of Space C and Space D, knowledge can be used to develop or be integrated into concept and decision-making models. As shown in Fig. 3, models and related resources are transformed to OSLC services through the developed OSLC adaptors. Such OSLC services have their URIs which are presented as OSLC RDF. Through service discovery, OSLC services can be input into concept and decision-making models. Through OSLC services, related knowledge information can be configured into different models. For example, when developing the REQ model, the property of one model composition can be configured as knowledge information through OSLC services.

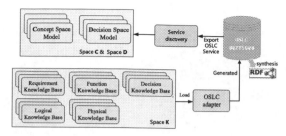

Fig. 3. OSLC service generation

4 Case Study

A case study of an unmanned detection vehicle design is used to evaluate the proposed approach. The vehicle is constructed by mechanical components, electronics, and an embedded system. Its design process is a knowledge-intensive and complex decision-making process. Traditional design methods cannot achieve a unified description of product conceptual schemes, design decisions and design knowledge, resulting in difficulties in design information transmission and low design efficiency. Therefore, the concept-decision-knowledge integrated modeling method proposed in this paper is used to model and digitize the design process of unmanned vehicles.

As shown in Fig. 4, based on KARMA language, requirement models, function models, logic models, and physical structure models are developed based on SysML specifications. The vehicle has different concept solutions as shown in Table 3. Different motor and battery construct different vehicle concepts which lead to different KARMA models for each concept solution. The decision-making processes for the trade-off of the given different concept solutions are formalized using the KARMA language based on PEI-X specification. When developing such concept models and decision-making models, the previous KARMA models are referenced to configure the property values through OSLC services. And the decision-making algorithms used in the decision-making processes are created in JULIA [13]. The developed JULIA script enables to capture of property values in concept solution models and decision-making models. Then after the JULIA script implementation, the optional concept solution model can be selected based on the results obtained from JULIA script implementation.

As shown in Fig. 4, the semantic model of the Space C and Space D is built using a domain modeling tool MetaGraph (http://www.zkhoneycomb.com/). The OSLC adapter for Space K is designed and built by an OSLC designer tool DataLinks (http://www.zkh oneycomb.com/). As shown in Table 3, different components construct different solutions. Thus, all the solutions are developed based on KARMA language in MetaGraph. Moreover, the sDSP decision model is built to formalize the decision-making processes in MetaGraph. Associated with the sDSP models, JULIA algorithms are developed and solved using the Julia solver in the MetaGraph tool. Through the decision-making algorithm results generated after JULIA implementation, the assessment results of all the alternatives are obtained as shown in Table 3. From the result, we can find the concept solution 1 can be accepted.

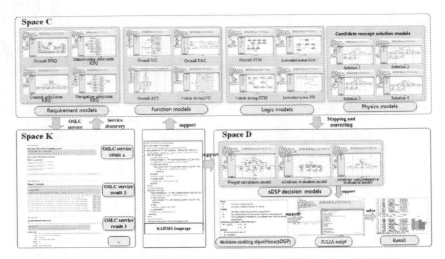

Fig. 4. The design process of unmanned detection vehicle based on C-D-K Theory

Table 3. Alternative concept solutions and their trade-off results

Solution	Power battery	Motor	Drive system	Performance value
1	Lithium-ion battery	Permanent magnet brushless DC motor	Crawler type	0.74329
2	Lithium-ion battery	Permanent magnet brushless DC motor	Wheel type	0.59169
3	Lithium-ion battery	Switched reluctance motor	Crawler type	0.66742
4	Lithium-ion battery	Switched reluctance motor	Wheel type	0.51582

5 Discussion

The C-D-K theory provides a basic framework to integrate product concept, decision-making for concept trade-off, and specific knowledge. Using semantic modeling with KARMA language and OSLC, product concept solutions are developed as different sets of KARMA models. Moreover, decision-making processes are also developed as KARMA models. When developing such models, OSLC services representing resources of knowledge can be load to configure the KARMA models automatically. To select the optimized concept solution, JULIA scripts are used to develop the decision-making algorithm used in the decision-making processes described by the KARMA models. Then an optimized solution can be selected after implementing the JULIA scripts. Compared with the existing research, the contributions of this paper are as follows:

- The proposed semantic modeling approach enables to formalize candidate concept solutions and decision-making processes using a unified semantic representation through KARMA language.
- OSLC specifications are used to capture the information from knowledge that is used to configure the KARMA models.
- Through all the semantics modeling techniques, the C-D-K theory is realized to support the product concept development and decision-making based on the given knowledge.

6   Conclusion

In this paper, a C-D-K theory is proposed to support the integration of concept design, decision-making, and knowledge, which provides a theoretical framework to support product development with semantic modeling. A KARMA language is used to develop concept and decision-making models and OSLC is used to construct web services of domain knowledge. Through OSLC services, concept and decision-making models can be configured automatically. The feasibility of this approach is verified by an unmanned detection vehicle design case.

References

1. Chen, J., et al.: Ebanshu: an interactivity-aware blended virtual learning environment (2014)
2. Chen, Z., Guo, S., Wang, J., Li, Y., Lu, Z.: Toward fpga security in iot: a new detection technique for hardware trojans. IEEE Internet Things **6**, 7061–7068 (2019)
3. Ru, W.A., Abn, B., Gw, A., Yan, Y.C., Jka, D., Fm, E.: A process knowledge representation approach for decision support in design of complex engineered systems. Adv. Eng. Inform. **48** (2021)
4. Wang, R., Milisavljevic-Syed, J., Guo, L., Huang, Y., Wang, G.: Knowledge-based design guidance system for cloud-based decision support in the design of complex engineered systems. J Mech. Design. **143**, 1–22 (2021)
5. Lu, J., Wang, G., Ma, J., Kiritsis, D., Zhang, H., Törngren, M.: General modeling language to support model-based systems engineering formalisms (part 1). In: INCOSE International Symposium, vol. 30, pp. 323–338 (2020)
6. Online OOP: Open services for lifecycle collaboration (2020)
7. Hatchuel A, Masson PL, Weil B: Design theory and collective creativity: a theoretical framework to evaluate kcp process (2009)
8. Kazak, A.O., Tsoukias, A.: Extending the c–k design theory: a theoretical background for personal design assistants. J Eng. Design. **16**, 399–411 (2005)
9. Friedenthal, S.: A practical guide to sysml: the systems modeling language. A Practical Guide to SysML: The Systems Modeling Language (2015)
10. Wang, R., et al.: Ontology-based representation of meta-design in designing decision workflows. J. Comput. Inf. Sci. Eng. **19**, 11001–11003 (2019)
11. Kelly, S.T.J.P.: Domain-specific modeling: enabling full code generation: IEEE Xplore (2008)
12. Bonnet, S., Voirin, J.L., Exertier, D., Normand, V.: Modeling system modes, states, configurations with arcadia and capella: method and tool perspectives. In: INCOSE International Symposium, vol. 27, pp. 548–562 (2017)
13. Bezanson, J., Karpinski, S., Shah, V.B., Edelman, A.: Julia: a fast dynamic language for technical computing. Comput. Sci. (2012)

Model-Based Systems Engineering Supporting Integrated Modeling and Optimization of Radar Cabin Layout

Shiyan She[1], Jinzhi Lu[2(✉)], Guoxin Wang[1(✉)], Jie Ding[1], and Zixiang Hu[3]

[1] Beijing Institute of Technology, Beijing 100000, China
[2] EPFL SCI-STI-DK, Station 9, CH-1015 Lausanne, Switzerland
jinzhi.lu@epfl.ch
[3] China Electronic Technology Group Corporation No.38 Research Institute,
Hefei 230088, China

Abstract. The equipment layout optimization of a UAV (Unmanned Aerial Vehicle) radar cabin can decrease cable length in order to promote the quality of radar and UAV system. Model-based Systems Engineering (MBSE) is widely used for UAV development, particularly for the layout design of UAV radar cabin. In this paper, a semantic modeling approach based on KARMA language is proposed to create the system model of the radar cabin layout based on an MBSE approach for formalizing Requirement, Function, Logical and Physical structure (RFLP). Moreover, the KARMA models for UAV radar cabin layout modeling are transformed to the Genetic Algorithm (GA) in MATLAB toolkit for radar cabin layout optimization by code generation. Based on the layout information generated from the KARMA models, the optimized layout solution is generated by the MATLAB toolkit. From the case study, we find the KARMA language enables to formalize the radar cabin design based on nine diagrams of SysML specification. And optimizations can be executed automatically after getting data generated from KARMA models. Thereby, the proposed semantic modeling approach improves design efficiency and quality during radar cabin design.

Keywords: MBSE · RFLP · KARMA · Radar cabin layout

1 Introduction

Model-Based System Engineering (MBSE) is an emerging technology that supports the development of complex systems and has been widely used in academia and industry. MBSE formalizes requirements, design, analysis, verification, validation, and other specific development activities involved in the entire lifecycle based on a formal modeling approach [1, 2]. Before the physical prototype of the UAV radar cabin is formally put into use, through MBSE formalisms, simulations, and optimizations, design risks can be captured as early as possible. MBSE is proposed to reduce the iterations during product development, to reduce costs, to shorten the development lifecycle [3], and to improve

© IFIP International Federation for Information Processing 2021
Published by Springer Nature Switzerland AG 2021
A. Dolgui et al. (Eds.): APMS 2021, IFIP AICT 633, pp. 218–227, 2021.
https://doi.org/10.1007/978-3-030-85910-7_23

the efficiency of product design. Moreover [4], the use of optimization algorithm can improve the capability to find the optimal solution across optional product alternatives during product design [5].

UAV radar is a complex system, and the design of the UAV radar cabin is challenged because its design process is involved with many layout configuration parameters and constraints. At present, there are three main problems when designing the layout of the radar cabin: (1) The document-centric radar layout design increases the designer's difficulty in understanding the architecture of radar layout and gaps among radar engineers and UAV engineers; (2) The layout design of the radar cabin is based on an empirical approach which lacks capabilities for generating layout automatically and rapidly. (3) During the iterative design of UAV radar cabin among UAV engineers and radar engineers, consistency management between radar cabin design and radar layout simulation cannot be supported in an appropriate way.

In this paper, we adopt MBSE to support UAV radar cabin layout design and optimization. Some researchers proposed related works on this topic. Youguang et al. [6] studied the specific application of the MBSE method for radar systems to improve the entire radar development process based on MBSE. The authors suggest making use of MBSE to support radar design to improve development efficiency and eliminate the gaps across radar designers. When designing the radar layout, Yang et al. [7] identified equipment consistency, color consistency, and space utilization optimization are important to radar layout. Mcdonald et al. [8] analyzed the antenna layout of an improved super-dual-auroral radar network (SuperDARN) high-frequency radar. To handle the high technical risks and rapid new technology application needs in MBSE process, Yao et al. [9] proposed a parallel Verification approach for new technology application in complex radar system. In general, there are a few studies on radar system or radar layout design using MBSE approach, so we adapt a new way to design radar layout using semantics modeling and MBSE approach.

This paper mainly proposes an MBSE approach for the layout design of the radar cabin system: (1) KARMA [10] language-based semantic modeling, and RFLP approach for formalizing the radar designer's understanding of the radar layout. (2) GA analysis for optimizing the radar cabin layout through simulations. (3) Code generation is used to support consistency management across MBSE models and optimization models in order to realize a fast and efficient layout, and improve design efficiency. First, radar design information is expressed through a graphical system model which is based on the KARMA language. The system model captures the aspects of the radar cabin layout from requirement, function, logical, and physical structure [11]. Then the system models are transformed into a GA toolkit for optimizing the layout of the radar cabin through code generation. The GA toolkit enables the generation of the optimal solutions of the radar cabin layout.

The rest of this article is organized as follows. In Sect. 2, the existing problems of radar layout design are introduced. In Sect. 3, descriptions of the semantic modeling and optimization of radar cabin layout are presented. Finally, we discuss our proposed approach in Sect. 4, and the conclusion is given in Sect. 5.

2 Problem Statement

When designing a radar cabin for UAV, it is one of the main carriers of radar equipment and operators. Its interior can be simplified to a cube of 7992 × 1100 × 1400 mm, which is divided into 12 cuboid spaces. The fuel tank has occupied the space in the middle four cuboid spaces, which leads to that the cables can be only allowed for being routed. The two sides of each frame of the fuselage are equipped with antenna arrays, each of which is 333 × 350 mm, and each frame has 2 × 4 collections on one side. There are 96 antenna arrays on one side of the fuselage (see Fig. 1a), the required layout of the device in the engine room, and the logical relationship of the device (see Fig. 1b). "A, B, C..." indicates the type of device. Each device has the characteristics of quantity, length, width, and height.

In the current radar cabin layout, the document-centric radar layout design increases the designer's difficulty in understanding the architecture of radar cabin layout and gaps among radar engineers and UAV engineers. In terms of simulation optimization, the radar cabin's layout design is based on empirical approach, which lacks capabilities for generating layout automatically and rapidly. During the iterative design of UAV radar cabin among UAV engineers and radar engineers, consistency management between radar cabin design and radar cabin layout simulation cannot be supported in an appropriate way.

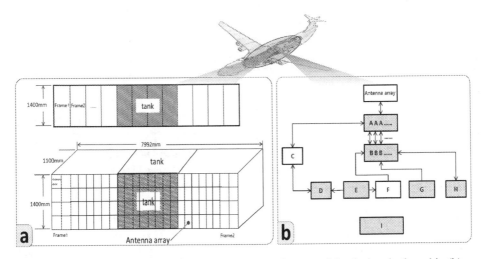

Fig. 1. Radar cabin (a) and the logical relationship diagram of the devices in the cabin (b)

In the design of radar nacelle layout in this paper, the cable length of all equipment A to the antenna array is r and the same length. And the length between device I and other devices are required to be as short as possible.

Through the above content, this paper makes uses of the MBSE approach and semantic modeling to support the radar cabin layout optimization and takes the model as the primary reference to manage consistency across design parameters of all devices. By integrating with the simulation optimization algorithm, an optimal layout can be generated. The optimization results can be configured to the MBSE models in order to manage consistency between design models and optimization models.

3 Semantic Modeling and Optimization of Radar Cabin Layout

3.1 Meta-modeling and Modeling of Radar Cabin Layout Using KARMA

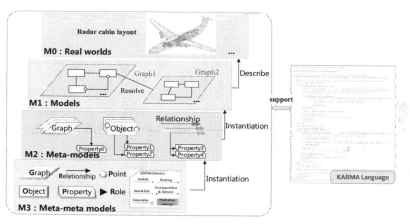

Fig. 2. M0-M3 Domain-specific modeling and GOPPRR

In order to support the MBSE process for radar cabin design, the framework of M0-M3 describes meta-meta models, meta-models, models, and the real world, as shown in Fig. 2. Meta-meta models refer to the six key elements, including Graph, Object, Port, Property, Relationship, and Role [12, 13], which are used to construct meta-models. In this paper, Meta-models are constructed based on the SysML specification. Meta-models are the model compositions for developing models. The models are used to describe the real world. Based on the GOPPRR meta-meta models and M0–M3 framework, the KARMA language is a semantic modeling language to describe meta-meta model, meta-mode, and models. In the KARMA language, it provides concrete syntax and abstract syntax to describe meta-models and models using a textual semi-formal approach.

Through KARMA language, meta-models are developed based on the SysML specification to support an RFLP (requirement function logical physical) MBSE approach. RFLP allows the definition of product elements and their relationships at different levels of abstraction [14]. Using the RFLP approach, requirements (R) refer to requirements associated with systems and subsystems. In order to support requirement formalism, we construct the meta-models, including the Requirement Diagram based on SysML specification as shown in Table 1. Function (F) is a function used to meet the defined requirements [15]. As shown in Table 1, we construct the meta-models, including the Use Case Diagram and the Activity Diagram based on SysML specification. Logic (L) is used to define logical components that can describe the radar cabin layout. Based

Table 1. Summary table of the radar system general layout modeling analysis

Meta Model: Graph	Model	Purpose
Requirement Definition		
Requirement Diagram	Radar system overall requirements diagram	Describe the functional & performance requirements of the radar system. (see Fig. 4a)
Function definition		
Use Case Diagram	Radar detection use case diagram	Describe the functional interaction of signal interception, tracking, and recognition during the detection process of the radar system. (see Fig. 4b)
Activity Diagram	Radar detection activity diagram	Describe the activity flow of the radar system to perform detection functions based on the environment. (see Fig. 4c)
Logical definition		
State Machine Diagram	Radar detection state machine diagram	Describe the state transition between radar detection signal, capture signal, and signal report. (see Fig. 4d)
Sequence Diagram	Radar detection sequence diagram	Describe the interaction of the radar system processor, sensors, and detectors overtime during the radar detection process. (see Fig. 4e)
Physical definition		
Block Definition diagram	Radar cabin layout block definition diagram	Describe the relationship between the components of the radar system and the constraint blocks between the components. (see Fig. 4f)
Internal block diagram	Radar cabin layout internal block diagram	Describe the internal components of the radar cabin and the topologies between the components. (see Fig. 4g)
Parameter Diagram	Radar cabin layout parameter diagram 1	Describe the parameters of devices (including length, width, height, quantity) (see Fig. 4h)
	Radar cabin layout parameter diagram 2	Describe device layout parameters (space coordinates of the devices) (see Fig. 4i)

on SysML specification, we construct the meta-models, including the State Machine Diagram and the Sequence Diagram, as shown in Table 1. Physical (P) is used to set up real physical components, focusing on design parameters about the radar cabin layout. Table 1 shows the Parameter Diagram, Internal block diagram, and the Block Definition Diagram based on SysML specification.

3.2 Optimized Algorithm Design

MATLAB optimization toolbox provides a commercial off-the-shelf library for optimization. The radar cabin layout optimization is implemented by MATLAB's built-in genetic algorithm toolkit. Users can freely adjust the values of parameters (individual, number of iterations, genetic mutation crossover operations, etc.) and intuitively observe the results of dynamic iterations.

According to the problem statement, this paper summarizes three optimization goals of the radar cabin layout: (1) the connection length between equipment A and the antenna array surface is the shortest. (2) the connection length difference between device A and the antenna array surface is the smallest. (3) the shortest connection length between device I and other devices. Through the optimization algorithm, the input information -- device characteristics (length, width, height, quantity) and the optimization targets can be output as the space coordinates of the devices.

3.3 Data Transmission Between KARMA Models and Optimization

As shown in Fig. 3a, code generation [16] is used to support the automatic generation of input files for the layout optimization model from the system model for describing radar cabin layout. In addition, after the layout optimization model is executed by the GA toolkit, the results are input to the MBSE models (the space coordinates of each device) to ensure the consistency of the system model information and the layout optimization model information.

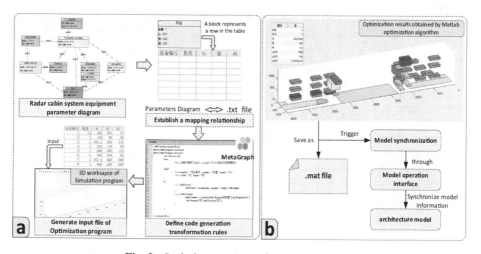

Fig. 3. Optimize process and parameter passing

As is shown in Fig. 3a, we adopt MetaGraph (MetaGraph is a multi-architecture modeling tool developed by Z.K. fc http://www.zkhoneycomb.com/) to construct KARMA language library for meta-models in Table 1. Moreover, in MetaGraph, the KARMA script for defining code-generation rules is developed, as shown in Fig. 3a. When defining the code generation script, mappings between model elements and the expected output table elements are created. Based on the above mappings, the KARMA script for code generation is compiled by the KARMA compiler and is executed by the code-generator. Then, the expected output tables are generated. Finally, the genetic algorithm toolkit in MATLAB is executed by loading the input table.

After obtaining the optimization results, referring to an optimal layout (including the space coordinate of each device), a mat file with such information is generated. Then a developed model synthesis tool kit load the information in the mat file and configure the parameters in the KARMA model through MetaGraph APIs. In the KARMA model, devices's property of the device space coordinate are null in the Radar cabin layout parameter diagram 2 (see Fig. 4i). After optimization, null values are changed to concrete spatial coordinates. Through the model synthesis toolkit, the property value in the KARMA model is synchronized from the optimization results (see Fig. 3b).

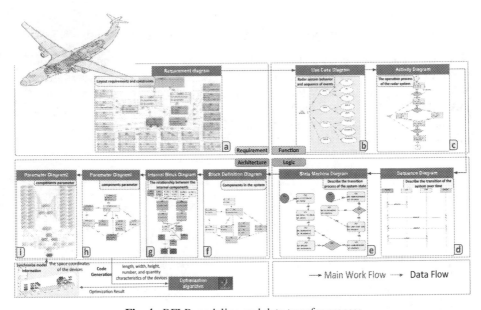

Fig. 4. RFLP modeling and data transfer process

4   Case Study and Discussion

In this paper, a UAV radar cabin case is proposed to evaluate our proposed semantic modeling approach. As shown in Fig. 4, the RFLP (Requirements-Functional-Logical-Physical) approach is used to build the KARMA models for the UAV radar cabin layout

MetaGraph. Requirement diagram model is created to describe the functional and per-formance requirements of radar cabin (Fig. 4 a). The use case diagram and activity diagram models are created to describe the use case and function flow of radar detec-tion (Fig. 4b and c). State machine diagram and Sequence diagram models are created to describe data processing workflow for radar detection (Fig. 4 d and e). Then Block definition diagram and Internal block diagram models are developed to describe the physical structure of the radar compositions, particularly for radar cabin (Fig. 4 f and g). Moreover, one Parameter diagram 1 model is used to define each device's parameters (including length, width, height, quantity), referring to one object instance in the internal block diagram model (Fig. 4 h). Another parameter diagram model is used to define the space coordinate parameter of each device referring to one object instance in the internal block diagram model (Fig. 4 i).

After code generation from KARMA models, the table file is load into the MATLAB optimization toolkit, which implements the optimization and provides results, as shown in Table 2. Before the optimization, the coordinates of devices are null. Then through the model synchronization toolkit, the parameter diagram models are configured based on the optimization results.

Table 2. Summary table of the part of the optimization results

Divice	X coordinate	Y coordinate	Z coordinate
A	600	0	93
C	1998	400	798
D	333	800	798
F	2331	300	798
H	5328	200	393

For the case study, we create 8 Graph meta-models, using 649 lines of KARMA language, and 9 models using 6932 lines of KARMA language, presented in Table 3. We find through the KARMA semantics, and all the model information is described by semantics modeling. Moreover, through code-generation and model synchronization, the data between KARMA models and optimization models can be integrated. In summary, the contribution of this paper is to use the semantic modeling based on KARMA language and the RFLP approach to formalize the radar layout and to implement optimization for radar layout automatically through the code generation and model synchronization.

Table 3. Summary table of models information

Model type	Number	Lines of code in the Karma language
Graph meta-models	8	649
Models	9	6932

5 Conclusion

This article mainly makes use of MBSE to optimize the layout of the radar cabin and to support consistency management of design parameters across MBSE models and optimization models. We adopt KARAM language to support semantics modeling for the radar cabin layout from the perspectives of requirement, function, logical and physical structure. Then by using code-generation, KARMA models are transformed to optimization models, which are executed by MATLAB optimization toolkit. From the GA algorithm, the optimal layout is obtained and synchronized with the KARMA model. From the case study, we find the KARMA language enables to formalize the radar cabin design based on 9 diagrams of SysML specification. Moreover, optimizations can be executed automatically after getting data generated from KARMA models. Finally, the optimization results enable to synchronize with KARMA models. Thereby, the proposed semantic modeling approach improves design efficiency and quality during radar cabin design.

Acknowledgments. This paper was supported by the China Electronic Technology Group Corporation No.38 Research Institute.

References

1. INCOSE Website 2012: Website des International Council on Systems Engineering', Guide for Writing Requirements. INCOSE (2012). http://www.incose.org/
2. Graignic, P., Vosgien, T., Jankovic, M., et al.: Complex system simulation: proposition of a MBSE framework for design-analysis integration. Procedia Comput. Sci. **16**(1), 59–68 (2013)
3. Kaslow, D., et al.: Integrated model-based systems engineering (MBSE) applied to the simulation of a CubeSat mission. In: IEEE Aerospace Conference IEEE (2014)
4. Chen, J., et al.: A blockchain-driven supply chain finance application for auto retail industry. Entropy. 22, 1, 95 (2020)
5. Jian, W., Lu, Z., Li, Y., Fu, Y., Guo, J.: A high-level thermal model-based task mapping for cmps in dark-silicon era. IEEE Trans. Electron. Dev. **63**(9), 3406–3412 (2016)
6. Youguang, F., Xiaobin, C., Ming, L.: A method for radar system lever digital research and development based on MBSE. Modern. Radar. **039**(005), 1–7 (2017)
7. Yang, H.Y.: Considerations on layout design of radar shelter. Electro-Mech. Eng. (2008)
8. Mcdonald, A.J., et al.: Elevation angle-of-arrival determination for a standard and a modified superDARN HF radar layout. Radio Sci. **48**(6), 709–721 (2013)
9. Yao, W., Ming, H., Zhiyong, L.: A parallel verification approach for new technology application in complex radar system. In: Krob, D., Li, L., Yao, J., Zhang, H., Zhang, X. (eds.) Complex Systems Design & Management, pp. 65–72. Springer, Cham (2021). https://doi.org/10.1007/978-3-030-73539-5_6
10. Jinzhi, L., Wang, G., Wang, H., et al.: General modeling language for supporting model-based systems engineering formalisms (Part 1). In: 30th Annual INCOSE International Symposium. John Wiley & Sons, Ltd. (2020)
11. Liguo, J., Chunjing, S., Xiang, L.: Application of MBSE in nuclear engineering design. Tech. Rev. **37**(7), 62–67 (2019)
12. Kern, H., Hummel, A., Kühne, S.: Towards a comparative analysis of meta-meta models. ACM **7** (2011)

13. Kelly, S.T.: Domain-Specific Modeling: Enabling Full Code Generation. Wiley-IEEE. Wiley-IEEE Computer Society Press (2008)
14. Chadzynski, P.Z., Brown, B., Willemsen, P.: Enhancing automated trade studies using MBSE, SysML and PLM. In: INCOSE International Symposium, vol. 28, no. 1, pp. 1626–1635 (2018)
15. Taha, J., Salehi, V., Abraham, F.: Development of a low powered wireless IoT sensor network based on MBSE. In: IEEE International Systems Engineering Symposium (2018)
16. Guo, J., et al.: General modeling language supporting model transformations of MBSE (Part 2). In: INCOSE International Symposium John Wiley & Sons, Ltd. (2020)

Supporting Digital Twin Integration Using Semantic Modeling and High-Level Architecture

Han Li[1], Jinzhi Lu[2(✉)], Xiaochen Zheng[2], Guoxin Wang[1(✉)], and Dimitris Kiritsis[2]

[1] Beijing Institute of Technology, Beijing 100081, China
wangguoxin@bit.edu.cn
[2] EPFL SCI-STI-DK, Station 9, 1015 Lausanne, Switzerland
jinzhi.lu@epfl.ch

Abstract. Digital twin (DT) provides a solution for supporting the interconnection between the physical world and the virtual world. When implementing DT integration, it is challenging to implement interface definition, information and service integration across DTs. This paper proposes a semantic modeling approach with a High-Level Architecture (HLA) to support the DT integration. The semantic modeling approach based on Graph-Object-Property-Point-Role-Relationship (GOPPRR) meta-meta models is used to realize the integrated formalisms of heterogeneous DTs. HLA is used to support interface definition and service integration between virtual entities of DT. Finally, a case of an unmanned aerial vehicle (UAV) landing on ship is used to verify the flexibility of this approach. From the results, we find the GOPPRR ontology and HLA specification enables to provide a unified formalism of the DTs of UAV and the ship, and to implement data exchange during the distributed simulation execution.

Keywords: Digital Twin · Semantic Model · Ontology · Distributed Simulation

1 Introduction

In the context of Industry 4.0, Cyber Physical Systems (CPSs) have become priority issues and core technologies in the manufacturing industry [1, 2]. Computation, Communication and Control (3C) technologies are three main compositions in CPS aiming to realize deep integration and organic collaboration across domains. They are also expected to create the interconnection and interoperability between the virtual world and the physical world. Currently, Digital Twin (DT) is considered as one way to integrate the physical space and virtual space. DT essentially include simulation models related to physical things in the real world. It provides the mappings of the physical systems to the digital models in cyberspace from the perspective of geometry, physics, behavior, etc., ensuring the coordination of the virtual world and physical world. It can also realize real-time monitoring, data collection, simulation, analysis and reasoning of physical objects based on digital models [3].

When building a DT for a CPS, it is necessary to integrate virtual entities in different domains which is a challenging task due to the high heterogeneity. This challenge

© IFIP International Federation for Information Processing 2021
Published by Springer Nature Switzerland AG 2021
A. Dolgui et al. (Eds.): APMS 2021, IFIP AICT 633, pp. 228–236, 2021.
https://doi.org/10.1007/978-3-030-85910-7_24

includes interface definition, data and information integration and service integration. When integrating the heterogeneous models across domains, the interface specifications should be defined in a standardized approach to enable the development of APIs for data exchange between DTs. Data and information integration is the basis to the integration of DT. For example, Singh et al. summarized the five challenges about DT, of which data integration is the most important aspect [4]. The end users expect to arrange different DTs according to their own requirements regardless the DT is developed for such business or not. This brings new challenges to the use of existing DTs for the additional purposes and business.

This paper proposes a semantic modeling approach with High-Level Architecture (HLA) standard to support the integration of DTs. A semantic modeling approach based on Graph-Object-Property-Point-Role-Relationship (GOPPRR) is used to construct DT ontology model, which can realize the integrated descriptions of heterogeneous DT, such as DT creators and descriptions. HLA is a standard for the modeling and simulation of distributed, heterogeneous processes. HLA provides standard interfaces to facilitate the integration of service and interface. The main contribution of this paper is to adapt a semantic modeling approach for DT integration based on HLA.

The rest of this paper is organized as follows. We discuss the related work in Sect. 2. In Sect. 3, we specifically introduce the semantic modeling approach using HLA, including ontology design and semantic modeling of DT and DT integration implemented based on HLA. Then Sect. 4 describes the case study to clarify and validate the proposed approach. Finally, we offer the conclusions and future work in Sect. 5.

2 Related Work

The concept of DT can be traced back to Grieves's speech on product lifecycle management (PLM) in 2003. Then NASA defines DT as "an integrated multi-physics, multi-scale, probabilistic simulation of a vehicle or system that uses the best available physical models, sensor updates, fleet history, etc., to mirror the life of its flying twin" [5]. A basic Digital Twins consists of three aspects: physical space, virtual space, and the connection between them for exchanging data and information [6]. In CPS, the DT can be understood as a digital model inside the CPS, which is a virtual representation that contains all physical information and knowledge [7, 8].

DT involve different systems during the development process, which makes the integration of heterogeneous data difficult [4, 9]. However, semantic modeling technologies provide solutions for data integration of DT [10]. At present, existing studies have attempted to combine semantic models with DT through ontologies. The combination of UML and ontology is proposed to find a common system-level semantic model. The authors of [11] proposed a method of communicating through human-readable text and computer-readable models, which is very important for engineering experts, software developers, and decision makers. The authors of [12] proposed an ontology that represents a DT in the context of CPS and embedded systems, which solves the problem of fusion of physical space and virtual space. In addition, knowledge graphs have been applied to acquire and integrate information into an ontology and utilize a reasoner to derive new knowledge [13]. For example, a query language based on the knowledge graph is used to enhance the manufacturing process management with reasoning ability [14].

Semantic modeling is important for the construction of DT, but it still lacks a unified architecture, and cannot solve the integration problem of model information in different domains. For this reason, more research work is needed.

3   Digital Twin Integration Using Semantic Model and HLA

In this section, the semantic modeling approach based on HLA is first introduced. Then ontology definition to represent DT information is introduced. Finally, distributed simulation based on HLA for DT interaction and service integration is proposed. Ontologies can be used to represent domain knowledge for an agreed understanding between different applications, and it contributes to semantics descriptions and models. Thus ontology is used as the supporter of semantic modeling in this paper.

3.1   Semantic Modeling Method Using HLA

In order to solve the challenges of interface integration, data integration, and service integration in the process of DT integration, this paper proposes an approach to support DT integration using HLA and semantic modeling, as shown in Fig. 1.

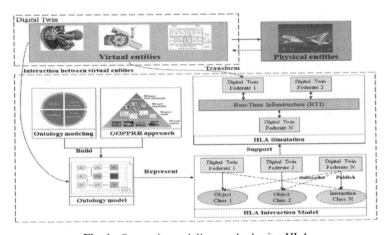

Fig. 1. Semantic modeling method using HLA

A semantic modeling approach is used to describe the topologies between virtual entities for information integration. The GOPPRR meta-modeling approach provides standardized and semantic expressions for different data structures, which is used as the basis of ontology definition and semantic modeling using Ontology Web Language (OWL). DT Information can be described according to Class, Object Property, Data Property and Instance by OWL.

In order to define standardized interfaces of heterogeneous DT, the distributed simulation is used based on HLA. HLA provides specifications, which effectively define interfaces across DT. In HLA, federate is the basic component for the distributed simulation. When integrating DT and HLA, Federate and virtual entities construct Digital Twin Federate (DTF). Thus, each DT has its related DTF referring to a standardized interface. Semantic models can express the interactions between DTFs and are used to generate the compiled codes for executing co-simulations. Thus, DT exchange information through Run-time Infrastructure (RTI), to implement simulation processes for service integration.

3.2 Semantic Modeling for Digital Twin

The ontology is modeled based on the GOPPRR approach which is a modeling framework based on a M0-M3 framework. The M0 layer represents the physical entities of DT in the real world; the M1 layer represents the domain model or virtual entities of DT. The M2 layer represents meta-models, which usually represents the model compositions as a domain specific modeling language. The M3 layer represents the meta-meta model, including six elements of Graph, Object, Relationship, Property, Role, and Point. Table 1 lists a specific definition of GOPPRR.

Table 1. The description of meta-meta model

Meta-meta model	Description
Graph	A collection of objects, relationships, roles, points and their relationships which refers to a model diagram
Object	An object type, it is the basic element in the diagram
Point	It describes the port connected to the relationship in the object
Property	It is used to describe their characteristics and is different from system properties which cannot exist alone
Relationship	It is used to indicate how objects are connected, and each "relationship" is connected to objects through roles
Role	It is used to represent the end of the relationship connecting objects and relationships

OWL can completely express the information in the semantic modeling process and support the exchange of information across virtual entities [15]. This paper uses OWL to describe the GOPPRR information. The ontology using OWL is shown in Fig. 2. Class is used to define GOPPRR meta-meta model, and its subclasses are used to describe meta-model. The Object-property is used to represent the interaction relationship among the six meta-meta models, such as inclusion, binding, etc. The Individual represents models referring to the information of specific DT virtual entities.

Through the GOPPRR modeling approach, meta models are used for constructing models for representing DT. In order to transform GOPPRR models to HLA models,

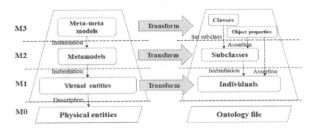

Fig. 2. Ontology supports GOPPRR method

the meta-models are developed based on HLA specifications. The details of HLA are introduced in the next section.

3.3 HLA Supports Digital Twin Integration

HLA is a universal standard protocol for distributed simulation. It consists of three parts: Interface Specification, Object Model Template (OMT) and HLA Rules. Interface Specification defines the services that support interoperability among federates during the simulation run. OMT defines a set of components that describe the HLA object model. HLA rules are the basic guidelines that must be followed in simulation design. HLA provides a set of rules based on the following main concepts to achieve interoperability and reusability when constructing the standardized interfaces for DT:

- *Federation*: A simulation application composed of a set of simulation components.
- *Federate*: One simulation component that represents the basic elements of HLA.
- *Run-time Infrastructure (RTI)*: Simulation-oriented middleware for managing alliance interaction.

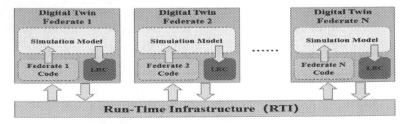

Fig. 3. A Digital Twin Federation based on HLA

Figure 3 shows a Digital Twin Federation based on HLA. The federation contains a number of DTFs based on HLA Interface Specification and OMT. DTF is composed of simulation model referring to virtual entities of DT, federate code and local RTI component (LRC). The simulation model consists of federate objects that meet the HLA standard aiming to construct the data exchange interface of each virtual entity into the request and response to RTI using the HLA Interaction Specification. Federate code is an application program that performs local DT executions and defines interactions to RTI. The LRC is the API component for the DTF to communicate with the RTI.

The semantic models mentioned in Sect. 3.2 are used to transform the HLA model. The concept of GOPPRR is used to describe the interactive information between different virtual entities based on HLA. Therefore, it is necessary to define meta-models using the HLA concept. As shown in Table 2, different meta-models are developed to support HLA concept formalisms. In details, DTFs are mainly composed of HLA OMT, in which Publish and Subscribe mechanism is used to describe the interaction between federates: Publish object class of a federate means that this member can generate an instance of the object class and modify its attributes, and Subscribe interaction class means that this member can receive information with parameters.

Table 2. The mappings between HLA concepts and GOPPRR meta-models

Meta-metamodel	Meta-model
Graph	Federation Object Model(FOM)
Object	Federation, Federate, PathSpace, ObjectClass, ObjectClassAttribute, InteractionClass, InteractionClassParameter
Point	
Property	DeliveryMechanism, DeliveryOrder, UpdateType, TimeConstrained, TimeRegulating, ect
Relationship	Publish, Subscribe, Join, Have
Role	PublishFrom, PublishTo, SubscribeFrom, SubscribeTo, JoinFrom, JoinTo, HaveFrom, HaveTo

The HLA Interface Specification provides a unified standard for DT integration as interface definitions, enabling different simulation components to interact effectively. The co-simulation between different DT can be realized through RTI, and the integration of simulation services can be realized for different business and purposes.

4   Case Study

Here we use the system simulation scenario of unmanned aerial vehicle (UAV) landing to verify our DT semantic modeling method using HLA. As shown in Fig. 4-A, a system consisting of one UAV, one warship and one radar is demonstrated. The simulation scenario is specifically described as follows: the UAV has executed the mission and is planning to land on the warship. Both the UAV and warship have their own initial location (x, y, z) and the warship has a fixed acceleration (dx2, dy2, dz2). When the UAV is landing on the warship, the radar obtains the UAV and warship location informations in real time, and calculates the best trajectory of the UAV and sends it, so the UAV can obtain its own acceleration (dx1, dy1, dz1). This paper simplified the UAV and the warship, assuming that they are mass points without volume, and does not consider the specific navigation algorithm used.

In this case, we focus on whether our method supports DT integration, rather than simulation results. The UAV, the warship and the radar are considered as the DTFs and RTI is the medium of communication. First, the ontology model is constructed using the semantic modeling method in Sect. 3, the meta-models in Table 2 are used to generate the individuals, which represent the information of DT. Then each federate simulation code is developed, and the initial locations and acceleration of warship are provided to initialize the simulation.

Figure 4-B shows the ontology model of this case. The ontology model includes instances of Graph, Object, Property, Point, Role, and Relationship according to the UAV landing scene. The ontology model records the attributes of DT virtual entities and all the interactions between them. The ontology contains three Federate object instances, two ObjectClass object instances, one InteractionClass object instance, two ObjectClassAttribute object instances, and one InteractionClassParameter object instance. Through owl: ObjectProperty, the relationship between different instances can be established to represent the interactive information between federates.

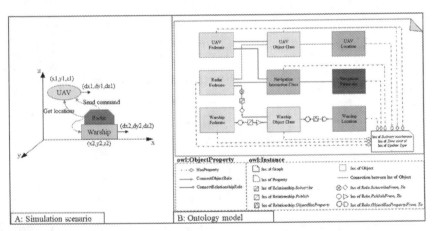

Fig. 4. UAV automatic landing simulation A: The simulation scenario; B: Ontology model of UAV landing Federation

Figure 5-A shows the simulation execution process and result of the DT federation in RTI, where the RTI software is CERTI, an open source RTI software. The co-simulation includes three federate simulation applications and a RunTime Infrastructure Gateway (RTIG). RTIG is the process of coordinating HLA federates with CERTI, and a federation must have at least one RTIG process. Each federate simulation application is developed based on the ontology model shown in Fig. 4-B, and uses CERTI's related APIs. The simulation results is shown in Fig. 5-B.

The application execution shows that the ontology model can completely, accurately and clearly express the DT models in different domains, so as to achieve information integration. And HLA can effectively solve the problems that different hardware, memory or interface specifications of heterogeneous systems make it impossible to realize the DT model in a stand-alone or integrated manner. The service of DT is the purpose of

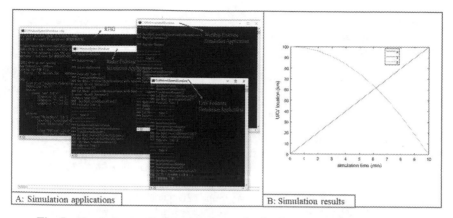

Fig. 5. Simulation applications work together by CERTI and simulation results

using DT, and DT should support the integration of simulation services of each system. HLA realizes the co-simulation between independent models through RTI, which not only meets the simulation requirements of a single virtual entity, but also realizes the overall simulation service integration.

5   Conclusion

This paper proposes a semantic modeling approach to support the integration of DT using HLA. First, a unified semantic modeling approach is established through GOP-PRR, which integrates DT information of heterogeneous data structures into a unified ontology. Then through transformation from GOPPRR ontology model to HLA model, the distributed simulation is executed across DT based on HLA RTI. Finally, a case is used to verify the feasibility of the proposed approach.

The ontology models using HLA support DT integration. However, the related spec-ifications of HLA are more complicated, and the simulation federation development process often requires a significant expertise and a considerable effort. This has led to greatly reduced development efficiency and increased development costs when building complex DT. Since the ontology model has the characteristics of being recognized by the computer, it can be considered to automatically generate simulation application pro-grams through the ontology model to reduce the complexity of simulation application development. In the future, a complete tool kit for ontology modeling, distributed simula-tion and visualization, will be developed to support the automatic distributed simulation executions for DT integration.

References

1. Lee, E.: Cyber physical systems: design challenges. In: 2008 11th IEEE Symposium on Object/Component/Service-Oriented Real-Time Distributed Computing, Orlando (2008)
2. Chen, Z., Guo, S., Wang, J., Li, Y., Lu, Z.: Toward FPGA security in IoT: a new detection technique for hardware trojans. IEEE Internet Things J. **6**(4), 7061–7068 (2019)

3. Foivos, P.: A generic methodology and a digital twin for zero defect manufacturing (ZDM) performance mapping towards design for ZDM. J. Manuf. Syst. (2021)

4. Qi, Q., Tao, F., Hu, T., et al.: Enabling technologies and tools for digital twin. J. Manuf. Syst. (2019)

5. Glaessgen, E., Stargel, D.: The digital twin paradigm for future NASA and U.S. Air Force Vehicles. Aiaa/asme/asce/ahs/asc Structures, Structural Dynamics & Materials Conference Aiaa/asme/ahs Adaptive Structures Conference Aiaa (2012)

6. Grieves, M.: Digital twin: manufacturing excellence through virtual factory replication. A Whitepaper by Dr. Michael Grieves. White Paper, pp. 1–7 (2014)

7. Rosen, R., von Wichert, G., Lo, G., Bettenhausen, K.D.: About the importance of autonomy and digital twins for the future of manufacturing. IFAC Papersonline **48**(3), 567–572 (2015)

8. Tao, F., Zhang, M., Cheng, J., Qi, Q.: Digital twin workshop: a new paradigm for future workshop. Jisuanji Jicheng Zhizao Xitong/Comput. Integr. Manuf. Syst. CIMS (2017)

9. Guo, L., Liu, Q., Shi, K., Gao, Y., Luo, J., Chen, J.: A blockchain-driven electronic contract management system for commodity procurement in electronic power industry. IEEE Access **9**, 9473–9480 (2021)

10. Cho, S., May, G., Kiritsis, D.: A semantic-driven approach for Industry 4.0. In: 2019 15th International Conference on Distributed Computing in Sensor Systems, pp. 347–54 (2019)

11. Rzevski, G., Lakhin, O., Skobelev, P., Mayorov, I., et al.: Ontology-driven multi-agent engine for real time adaptive scheduling. In: 2018 International Conference on Control, Artificial Intelligence, Robotics & Optimization (2018)

12. Steinmetz, C., Rettberg, A., Ribeiro, F.G.C., et al.: Internet of Things ontology for digital twin in cyber physical systems. In: 2018 Viii Brazilian Symposium on Computing Systems Engineering. Brazilian Symposium on Computing System Engineering, pp. 154–9 (2018)

13. Lu, J., Zheng, X., Gharaei, A., Kalaboukas, K., Kiritsis, D.: Cognitive twins for supporting decision-makings of Internet of Things systems. In: Wang, L., Majstorovic, V.D., Mourtzis, D., Carpanzano, E., Moroni, G., Galantucci, L.M. (eds.) Proceedings of 5th International Conference on the Industry 4.0 Model for Advanced Manufacturing. LNME, pp. 105–115. Springer, Cham (2020). https://doi.org/10.1007/978-3-030-46212-3_7

14. Banerjee, A., Dalal, R., Mittal, S., Joshi, K.P.: Generating digital twin models using knowledge graphs for industrial production lines. In: Proceedings of the 2017 Acm Web Science Conference (2017)

15. Wang, H., Wang, G., Lu, J., Ma, C.: Ontology Supporting model-based systems engineering based on a GOPPRR approach. In: Rocha, Á., Adeli, H., Reis, L.P., Costanzo, S. (eds.) WorldCIST'19 2019. AISC, vol. 930, pp. 426–436. Springer, Cham (2019). https://doi.org/10.1007/978-3-030-16181-1_40

Digital Twin-Driven Approach for Smart City Logistics: The Case of Freight Parking Management

Yu Liu[1]([✉]), Pauline Folz[2], Shenle Pan[1], Fano Ramparany[2], Sébastien Bolle[2], Eric Ballot[1], and Thierry Coupaye[2]

[1] Centre de Gestion Scientifique - I3 - UMR CNRS 9217, MINES ParisTech, PSL Research University, 60 boulevard Saint-Michel, 75006 Paris, France
{yu.liu,shenle.pan,eric.ballot}@mines-paristech.fr
[2] Orange Labs, Paris, France
{pauline.folz,fano.ramparany,sebastien.bolle,
thierry.coupaye}@orange.com

Abstract. According to the United Nations' prediction, the world is expected to have 43 megacities that host more than 10 million inhabitants by 2030. City logistics for freight distribution is a challenging and crucial problem for these cities. Recent disruptive approaches such as *Smart City* provide us a new perspective to investigate the problem as well as for decision making. It creates a pervasive and mobile computing environment that allows the city itself to be overlaid with sensing and actuation, embedded with "smart things" to develop an "ambient intelligence." By choosing this angle, this work investigates the problem of freight parking management for last-mile delivery in smart city, called *Smart City Logistics Parking (SCLP)*. A use case is conceptualized and modeled via a bottom-up approach. The bottom-layer aims to represent the structure of the SCLP, i.e., the physical elements constituting the SCLP physical infrastructure into a digital representation, a.k.a a Digital Twin of the SCLP. Property Graph modeling is applied at this step as a meta-model to formulate the object relationships with properties. The upper-layer makes use of associated ontologies to add semantics to the structural description of the SCLP. The built model is then implemented into a Digital Twin experimental platform, namely *Thing in the Future (Thing'in in short)* from *Orange Labs*. The modeling work presented in this paper encourages future works on simulation of the decision-making processes based on the Digital Twin platform.

Keywords: City Logistics · Smart City · Digital Twin · Sustainability · Freight parking management · Last-Mile Delivery · Property Graph · Ontology · Semantics

1 Introduction

City logistics is concerned with freight distribution in the urban area, aimed at sustainability and livability while managing the inbound, outbound, and inner urban freight. Its

© IFIP International Federation for Information Processing 2021
Published by Springer Nature Switzerland AG 2021
A. Dolgui et al. (Eds.): APMS 2021, IFIP AICT 633, pp. 237–246, 2021.
https://doi.org/10.1007/978-3-030-85910-7_25

performance not only results in operational cost but in other external factors, like noise pollution, air pollution, congestion, accidents, etc. [1]. Research shows that depending on the pollutant considered, commercial vehicles (for goods movement) are responsible for 20–30% of total vehicle kilometers, and for 16%–50% of air pollutants generated by all transport activities in cities [2]. Hence, for a sustainable and livable city, many city logistics solutions are provided, such as adopting green vehicles to reduce emissions, using urban consolidation centers for the higher loading rate of vehicles, and optimizing delivery routes to reduce transport cost and congestion. However, the efficiency and effectiveness of these solutions rely more and more on the technologies that provide (real-time) information assisting in the decision-making processes, such as Information and Communication Technologies (ICT) and Internet of Things (IoT), data analytics, and visualization.

In this context, the paradigm of *Smart City* (or *Smart Cities*) provides a new research angle to the problem of city logistics [3]. Generally speaking, smart city "is a place where traditional networks and services are made more efficient with digital and telecommunication technologies for the benefit of its inhabitants and business" [4]. To this end, IoT and ICT technologies are applied to converge the physical infrastructure (or means) and digital computational environment. An emerging associated concept, explored in this work, is the *Digital Twin*. Digital Twin was a concept come from the practice when NASA created a duplicated physical system at ground level to twinning the systems in space in 1960s. Until 2010, NASA officially proposed Digital Twin as *a multi-physics, multi-scale, probabilistic simulation of a vehicle or system that uses the best available physical models, sensor updates, fleet history, etc., to mirror the life of its flying twin* [5]. In order to advance the use of the concept in other industries, Digital Twin is more generally defined as *a virtual representation of real-world entities and processes, synchronized at a specified frequency and fidelity* in [6]. With this trend, there are some applications in logistics and supply chain management, for instance, supply chain network mapping and visulizing for disruptive risk management [7], production logistics synchronization with digital twin system for the real-time monitor, decision and control [8].

Choosing the angle of Smart City, this paper investigates the concept of *Smart city logistics* via studying an important practical issue that is the *freight parking management* in last-mile delivery [9]. This work considers Smart city logistics as a self-cognitive and self-organized system to transport freight in an urban area, with mobility, safety, and sustainability. As part of such a system, freight parking management focuses on parking space utilization and efficiency. Smart parking was well studied for passenger vehicles, like WSN (Wireless Sensor Networks)-Based System for Parking Garages environment monitor and management [10], smartphone's sensors for detecting parking events and providing real-time parking availability [11]. However, recent studies also show that the parking problem is equally critical for commercial vehicles for freight distribution (e.g., heavy or light-duty vehicles, motors). For example, cruising for parking takes 28% of the trip time for commercial vehicles in Seattle downtown, and around 1.1h per commercial vehicle tour [12]. The Smart logistics parking is therefore put forward to emphasize the efficiency of logistics distribution and last-mile delivery, by highlighting the need for infrastructure and various information demands related to freight parking management.

Following this, we study a case called *Smart City Logistics Parking* (SCLP), through conceptualization, modeling, and implementation. The research intends to discover the essential information that is needed from urban infrastructure for freight parking management. It can be considered among the first contributions that propose to use Digital Twins of the urban facilities, where the multi-source data are well organized in multilevel scale, from single objects to complex systems structure and semantics.

Our research questions are as follows: first, what kind of data and objects are (the sources of data) needed to solve the SCLP problem? Second, how to model the data and shape the objects in the digital world? Third, how to implement this model to display the interconnection of the data sources and the physical entities?

The paper is structured as follows. Section 2 clarifies the research methodology used in this research, Sect. 3 conceptualizes the SCLP in the context of smart logistics distribution schemes, Sect. 4 presents the bottom-up modeling approach for the SCLP scenario, Sect. 5 delivers the implementation and visualization of the model in *Thing'in*, and Sect. 6 summarizes the novel discoveries of the present work and points out the perspectives for future work.

2 Methodology

To investigate the SCLP problem, the work applies the conceptual modeling for the simulation approach [13]. A simplified real-life scenario of last-mile delivery is first conceptualized in which the freight parking management should be addressed with the support of interconnected data and objects. Next, this scenario is modeled with a bottom-up approach that includes all the scenario-related objects and depicts their relationship accurately (i.e., the contents in the simulation), see Fig. 2. At the bottom layer, Property Graph modeling is applied to model the relationships of objects with properties, i.e., to describe the structure of the physical logistic system considered. In the upper layer, the semantics of objects and relationships is added by associating ontologies to them. Finally, we inject the constructed model into a digital twin-based platform, *Thing in the Future* (*Thing'in* in short), for establishing these interconnections between objects and data for decision making. Additionally, the necessary information can be queried from the platform for decision-making and simulation. Apart from the simulation section, all the modeling procedures will be described step by step and in detail in this paper.

3 Conceptualization of Smart City Logistics Parking

The last-mile delivery problem is generally defined as shipping cargo from origin A to destination B within the city. Being part of it, the Smart City Logistics Parking (SCLP) problem is concerned with finding the best parking place for last-mile delivery. This problem is a good junction of parking, final destination delivery, and transportation from infrastructure, as shown in Fig. 1.

We first identify the key elements of effective planning in last-mile delivery, including multiple transportation means, destination alternatives, real-time transit points, parking place selection, and dynamic route planning. Second, we determine the four categories of data sources and the related objects or concepts as follows: 1) vehicles that include the information of logistics vehicles and cargo, 2) transportation network such as roads, paths, and highways, 3) stops to pause for logistics activities like transit or delivery, which especially refer to parking places in this use case, and 4) destinations where the end-customer is located. The sources will provide the real-time condition of the infrastructure, namely dynamic traffic, destination information, and the occupancy of logistics facilities. Besides, digital twins act as the counterparts of their physical objects can conserve required information of real-time status. In this way, the digital twin of all the relevant objects will be interconnected to explore the potential of an open logistics network.

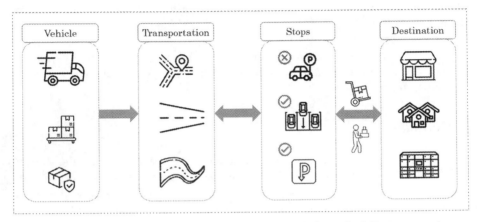

Fig. 1. Illustration of smart logistics parking in last-mile delivery.

4 Modeling

4.1 Bottom-Up Modeling Approach

Due to the complexity of the problem, a bottom-up modeling approach is adopted in this work. We start modeling based on the four types of data sources above. There are two major difficulties at this stage. On the one hand, the number of objects in each data source category is high; on the other hand, there are multiple and complex relationships among objects and among their categories. Considering these two aspects, we start modeling one data source (i.e., an object) and then integrating it upward to identify and define the data source categories. The overall modeling approach is shown in Fig. 2.

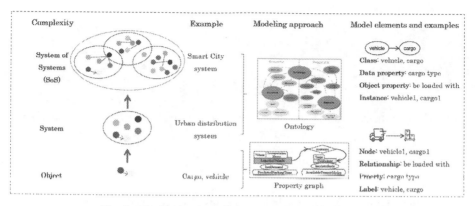

Fig. 2. The illustration of bottom-up modeling approach.

4.2 Bottom-Layer Modeling – Property Graph (PG)

We first model a physical object based on the Property Graph (PG) formalism. A PG is a graph model to orderly organizes data or information. It is composed of nodes, labels, properties, and relationships. In a PG, *nodes* represent the physical entities, and they can hold any number of *properties* and their values expressed with key-value pairs. Nodes can be tagged with *labels*, describing their different roles in the domain. *Relationships* provide directed, named, semantically-relevant connections between two nodes. A relationship has a direction, a type, a start node, and an end node. Like nodes, relationships can also have properties. For example, "loadedWith" has the property "hasTimestamp" (Fig. 3). The advantage of a PG is that it is descriptive as it conforms to the human mindset. It originates from Graph Database (GD) technology, and indeed, manages and stores the data in a GD in a way that mirrors the relationships that hold in the real world. As a result, the PG can organize large amounts of complex data, which can later be retrieved and queried by users. Eventually, responses to these queries may be displayed graphically.

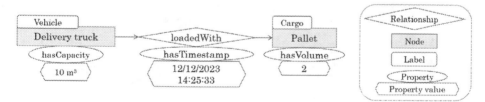

Fig. 3. The sensed information of parking state organized by Property Graph.

By combining the multiple data sources using the Property Graph formalism (Fig. 3), we can then model each object whatever its category. For instance, cargo and logistics delivery trucks in the "vehicle" category and shops in the "destination" category (Fig. 4).

Fig. 4. Property Graph organizes data sources from different categories with their relationships.

4.3 Up-Layer Modeling – Ontology

An ontology is a shared vocabulary to represent and define a domain area. It defines concepts and relationships between those concepts [14]. We used the W3C Web Ontology Recommendation (OWL) [15] and the tool Protégé [16] to design our ontology. OWL allows to define Classes to type an object (e.g. "UndergroundParkingLot"), Data properties to define properties of a Class (e.g. "availableSpace") and Object Properties to define a relationship between Classes (e.g. "accessVia").

After determining all the objects and their related information, ontology modeling proceeds following these steps (Fig. 5): (1) Find the similar classes, object properties, and data properties in the existing and most popular ontologies and catalogs, e.g. the "store," "parking space," etc. from which have been defined in the ontologies like Km4city [17], Schema [18], and Mobivoc [19]. The upper ontology, such as Industrial Ontologies Foundry (IOF) [20], is not involved here since the level is too high to find the suitable ontological elements; (2) Import all the ontologies found into the ontology editor Protégé; (3) For the rest of the elements in the model, as we did not find any ontology that provides elements satisfying our need, we create them using Protégé. That was the case for the concepts of "delivery frequency" and "delivery time window"; (4) Double-check the ontology model with a visual display to ensure that the classes and their properties conform with our scenario. Figure 6 shows the ontology model, the classes and their subclasses (the yellow dots nodes), and the classes come from the existed ontologies are signed with the blue frame.

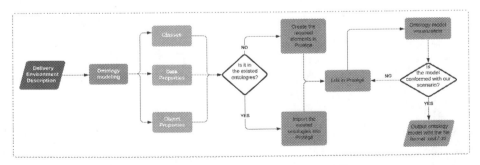

Fig. 5. Working processes in ontology modeling.

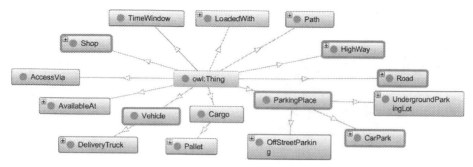

Fig. 6. Relation between classes (classes in the blue frame are from other ontologies).

5 Implementation

5.1 *Thing in the Future (Thing'in)* Platform

Thing'in is an experimental Digital Twin platform. It provides a generic and extensible technological support for the construction of digital twin services. The Thing'in core exposes, through APIs, a graph of digital twins (i.e., a set of nodes and links between nodes). Users can create and manipulate these digital twins and the associated information (function, properties, state, location, shape, etc.), as well as the physical objects to which they are linked (e.g. access to sensors and actuators), but also and above all the structural and semantic relationships between these objects. Thing'in core model is natively property graph and implements the NGSI-LD standard.

Thing'in provides a common informational substrate that homogeneously describes states of the physical world (buildings, factories, cities, roads, and rails…) and therefore allows for the management of digital twins in different and possibly interconnected vertical domains (building, city, manufacturing, transport, etc.). Based on this informational substrate, more complex functions such as simulation or prediction can be developed.

5.2 Model Injection of a Simple Use Case

First, the ontology defined in the previous section was injected into Thing'in. Next, we defined a model for a simple use case named Smart City Logistics Parking. Then Protégé was used to create the instances of the model, where the instances represent objects of the domain of interest. The full model is displayed in Fig. 7, where purple diamonds are instances and yellow circle is the classes defined in the ontology. Finally, those instances were injected into Thing'in to create digital twins of physical objects and facilities. In Fig. 8, all the digital twins of the use case are displayed, and the shop is presented in detail, including information related to itself, like the delivery frequency is three times per month and the address of the delivery entrance. It also indicates the relationship between itself and other digital twins, for instance, connected to parking places via "AvailableAt" (blue arrow), linked to the delivery truck and cargo respectively through the relationship "hasDestination" (orange arrow).

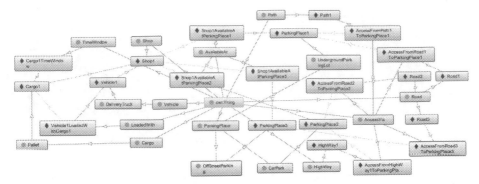

Fig. 7. Ontology model injected in Thing'in depicting the physical world of the use case.

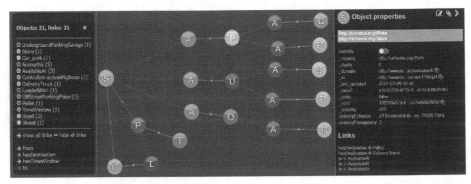

Fig. 8. Avatars created in *Thing'in* corresponding to the ontology model injected.

5.3   Reasoning in the Use Case

In this case, the vehicle loaded with the cargo queries to Thing'in platform for a suitable parking place. It will recieve the response of the parking place candidates with sufficient cargo handling space based on the cargo type. For example, if the cargo is only one pallet, the responded parking place should have a loading bay to unload the pallet. When cargo is larger than this scale, more cargo handling space and infrastrcutre are needed, the response will provide the specific surface area for the delivery man to check the accessibility. However, the material handling constraints will be weaken for light parcel delivery. An example of the process expressed with Thing'in query language is demonstrated in Fig. 9.

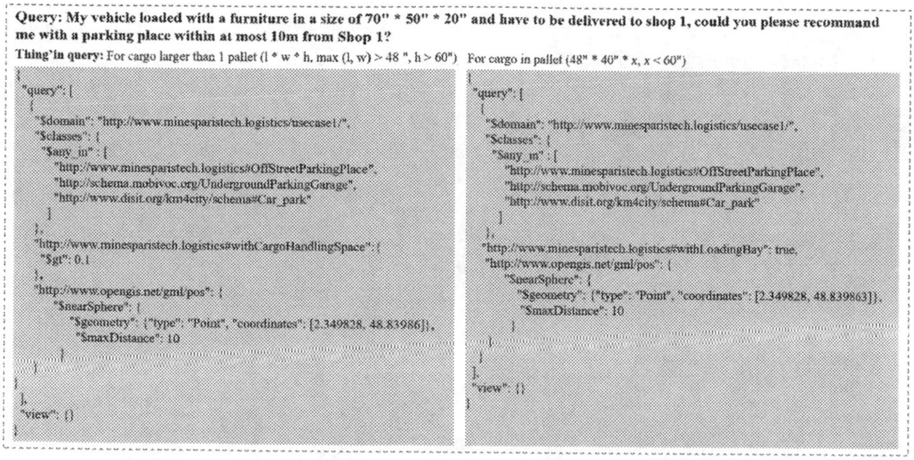

Fig. 9. Demonstration of the query of a parking space based on cargo type.

6   Conclusion and Future Work

This paper presents the first step of the ongoing research work that focuses on modeling the smart city logistics scenario, and more specifically, the freight parking management problem called Smart City Logistics Parking. We first conceptualized a use case in last-mile delivery, then modeled it via a bottom-up approach. In the bottom-layer, property graph helps organize the key information into a Digital Twin, which represents in the digital world its physical counterpart. In the up-layer, the use case's ontology shows validity in defining concepts to clarify the semantic environment of the scenario. Then, the built model was injected into the digital-twin-based platform Thing'in. Founded on the model and the platform, the next step is to assess the value of the connected data and objects by investigating supportive information from the platform for decision-making. Simulation work can be done here to investigate decision quality and decision accuracy according to different levels of data connectivity.

Acknowledgements. This work is supported by the Physical Internet Chair at Mines ParisTech - PSL University, and the project ASAP (Awaken Sleeping Assets Project) which has received funding from the European Union's Horizon 2020 research and innovation programme under grant agreement No 875022.

References

1. Schroten, A., et al.: Handbook on the external costs of transport: version 2019. In: European Commission (2019)
2. Dablanc, L.: Goods transport in large European cities: difficult to organize, difficult to modernize. Transp. Res. Part A Policy Pract. **41**, 280–285 (2007)
3. Pan, S., Zhou, W., Piramuthu, S., Giannikas, V., Chen, C.: Smart city for sustainable urban freight logistics. Int. J. Prod. Res. **59**, 2079–2089 (2021)

4. European Commission. Smart cities (2019). https://ec.europa.eu/info/eu-regional-and-urban-development/topics/cities-and-urban-development/city-initiatives/smart-cities_en
5. Shafto, M., et al.: DRAFT modeling, simulation, information technology & processing roadmap - technology area 11. Natl. Aeronaut. Sp. Adm. **27** (2010)
6. The Definition of a Digital Twin | Digital Twin Consortium®. https://www.digitaltwincons ortium.org/initiatives/the-definition-of-a-digital-twin.htm
7. Ivanov, D., Dolgui, A.: A digital supply chain twin for managing the disruption risks and resilience in the era of Industry 4.0. Prod. Plan. Control **32**, 775–788 (2021)
8. Pan, Y.H., Qu, T., Wu, N.Q., Khalgui, M., Huang, G.Q.: Digital twin based real-time production logistics synchronization system in a multi-level computing architecture. J. Manuf. Syst. **58**, 246–260 (2021)
9. Jaller, M., Holguín-Veras, J., Hodge, S.: Parking in the city - challenges for Freight traffic. Transp. Res. Rec. 46–56 (2013). https://doi.org/10.3141/2379-06
10. Lin, Y.C., Cheung, W.F.: Developing WSN/BIM-based environmental monitoring management system for parking garages in smart cities. J. Manag. Eng. **36**, 1–17 (2020)
11. Krieg, J.G., Jakllari, G., Toma, H., Beylot, A.L.: Unlocking the smartphone's sensors for smart city parking. Pervasive Mob. Comput. **43**, 78–95 (2018)
12. Dalla Chiara, G., Goodchild, A.: Do commercial vehicles cruise for parking? Empir. Eviden. Seattle. Transp. Policy **97**, 26–36 (2020)
13. Liu, C., Lu, M., Johnson, S.: Simulation and optimization of temporary road network in mass earthmoving projects. In: Proceedings of the 2013 Winter Simuliation Conference - Simuliation Maketing Decision a Complex World, WSC 2013 3181–3190 (2013). https://doi.org/10.1109/WSC.2013.6721684
14. Ontologies - W3C. https://www.w3.org/standards/semanticweb/ontology
15. OWL Web Ontology Language Overview. https://www.w3.org/TR/owl-features/
16. protégé. https://protege.stanford.edu/
17. km4city, the DISIT Knowledge Model for City and Mobility. http://wlode.disit.org/WLODE/extract?url=http://www.disit.org/km4city/schema
18. Schema.org - Schema.org. https://schema.org/
19. Open Mobility Vocabulary — MobiVoc. https://www.mobivoc.org/
20. Supply Chain WG – IOF Website. https://www.industrialontologies.org/supply-chain-wg/

Digital Twins in Companies First Developments and Future Challenges

The Advent of the Digital Twin: A Prospective in Healthcare in the Next Decade

Jorge Luis Rojas-Arce$^{(\boxtimes)}$ ⓘ and Eduardo Cassiel Ortega-Maldonado

Facultad de Ingeniería, Departamento de Ingeniería en Sistemas Biomédicos,
Universidad Nacional Autónoma de Mexico, Mexico City, Mexico
{jorge.rojas.arce,cassiel.ortega}@comunidad.unam.mx

Abstract. Industry 4.0 is facing a fast–development in its technologies, automatizing and restructuring processes in order to make them data–driven. However, its uses are not exclusive for the industry as its name suggests, since it can be extended to health sector. In the next decade, the Digital Twin (a digital replica of a physical asset) is going to face a spread into mainstream market due to its potential applications in the healthcare sector, such as a 24/7 monitoring of the evolution of cancer and its treatment, a heart based on cloud–computing, an even receive medical treatment that adapts to every person. But before seeing this as a reality, there are several obstacles that the researchers need to overcome for the proposed Digital Twins to reach its full–potential.

Keywords: Digital twin · Healthcare · Prospective

1 The Digital Twin and its Common Misconceptions

As a result of the upcoming Industry 4.0, technologies are being quickly developed and growing their popularity in both specialized fields and mainstream media alike, being these technologies are the Internet–of–Things (IoT), cloud computing, big data and the automation that does not require the human intervention as a consequence of the implementation of machine learning algorithms and artificial intelligence. As it has been stated, their potential applications are not only limited to the industry, but can be extended and successfully implemented into the healthcare systems around the world, modifying how we understand and work with them [7].

The state–of–the–art of this revolution is known as the Digital Twin (DT), a concept that uses and encompasses all the previously mentioned technologies to develop a living model in the form of a digital instance that represents and mirrors in real time its physical asset or system. However, this term is so broad that most of the time it may lead to false impressions of what it really is, aspect that will be addressed up–ahead, being the main distinction between them how the data flows from the physical to the digital object and vice–versa [5].

© IFIP International Federation for Information Processing 2021
Published by Springer Nature Switzerland AG 2021
A. Dolgui et al. (Eds.): APMS 2021, IFIP AICT 633, pp. 249–255, 2021.
https://doi.org/10.1007/978-3-030-85910-7_26

1.1   Digital Twin

Summarizing, a DT can be described as a virtual replica of a physical object with the virtue of fully–automated data acquisition [7]. In other words, a change that is made in the digital asset is reflected immediately in its physical counterpart, and vice–versa. The main difference of the DT, is that there is no need for a manual data input [5].

1.2   Digital Shadow

This instance, as its name may suggest, is only a digital representation of a physical object, meaning that data is only automated in a one–way flow from the physical to the digital object [6]. It is mostly used to gather and integrate information from different sources to facilitate real–time analysis [12].

1.3   Digital Model

This is where the majority of the misconceptions are centred. This case is a virtual replica of the physical object and it requires a full–time manual input of the data [7]. They are used for the most part in the industry to understand how a change in the digital object would affect its counterpart if implemented [6].

1.4   Digital Terms Summary

To synthesize the presented information, and as way to clarify any possible doubts that may appear, Table 1 is presented as a mean to understand the flow of the data between the physical and digital objects, as well their most common applications.

Table 1. Differences between the digital terms

Digital term	Flow of data	Applications
Digital twin	Fully automatic between the physical and digital asset, and vice–versa [7]	Real–time changes in an object are manifested in the other as well [5]
Digital shadow	Automatic from the physical to the digital counterpart; manual from the digital to the physical asset [6]	Used for information gathering and eventual analysis [12]
Digital model	Completely manual between the physical and digital asset, and vice–versa [7]	Used to describe possible changes [6]

2   Challanges to Overcome

Before seeing these DTs as a reality and as a part of our daily lives, there are some obstacles that need to be dealt with. The first, and most challenging one, is to design them to be identical to their physical self, to be indistinguishable from each other; that is, a real–time exchange of information that is both easy to be operated by its user, and at the same time to be complex enough to model and answer sudden changes in real time [11].

2.1   IT Infrastructure

For this proposal to be successful, then it is mandatory to have the means that will ensure the optimal performance of the system. Both Artificial Intelligence and Machine Learning are expected to be the key–players [11], and both require high–performing hardware and software to be in a constant analysis of data, aspect that becomes obvious in the high–running costs, as well in its subsequent environmental impact [5].

From the IoT point–of–view, the main issue is the flow of data, problem that is enlarged with the rise of big data, which means that a gargantuan volume of data is in constant transit. However, this data, most of the time, is in a "raw" state that needs to be prepared, sorted and organized before being useful for any research [5]. In the healthcare sector, there exists a high–natural variability, which is explained by the innate differences of the human body, such as age, height, or response to medical treatments; parameters that need to be understood by the sensors implemented in the DT to prevent false-positives [9].

As a result, before a personalized, data–driven healthcare becomes a reality, the IT infrastructure needs to be leveraged. This new architecture needs to comply with different standards that ensure the well–being of the patient and continuous function of the DT, its design must entail a hybrid platform: Centralized for a straightforward management and effortless data sharing, yet distributed enough to ensure real–time deployment [7].

2.2   Data Privacy and Security

In the recent years, the threat of cyberattacks has been increasing, compromising personal data that ranges from personal keywords to paralyze whole communities' finances. In the case of the DT, the data used is both sensitive and confidential, and it must be only accessed by the patient and by qualified personnel, such as physicians or nurses. In the case of IoT, interconnected devices are an easy target for denial–of–service attacks (DDoS) that can take offline a healthcare system, temporarily freezing its infrastructure and even pose a threat to the lives of the patients [8]. As ludicrous as it might sound, in the next decades the idea of hijacking a organ can become a reality if cybersecurity is not guaranteed.

An important factor to be consolidated in both DT and Industry 4.0 is law regulation, governments need to define the scope of the Artificial Intelligence and ensure that the data is at all–times protected [5]. As a byproduct of the massive amount of information generated by the big data, cyber–attacks are prone to happen, compromising sensitive data [7], meaning that cybersecurity analysis and protocols are mandatory, and security frameworks are to be adopted as a design paradigm known as "Security by Design" [8].

2.3 Data Quality

As expected for a complex system that integrates and coordinates multiple engineering fields, the DT needs to work with noise–free and high–quality data to perform as expected [5].

In the case of the DT, data are crucial, and they come from multiple sources and need to be integrated as a whole. The sources of this information are many, some is obtained from the digital–physical asset, other from the digital–models that support the DT performance, and a small yet crucial part is provided by experts in the fields of health and engineering. In the end, all of them need to be merged together (applying different AI methods) to give as a result the "fusion data", core of the DT performance [10].

2.4 Ethics

A downside of introducing a data–driven healthcare system, is the that the boundaries of medicine need to be posed once more. The use of the DT, at the beginning, raises the possibility of a new kind of patient, ones that have a digital enhancement of themselves. Of course, personalized medicine highly exceeds the cost of off–the–shelf treatments, meaning that only people with the enough resources can access to this opportunity. As a result of both these situations, a segmentation of the population and which medical treatment they receive is prone to occur if the technologies used do not lower costs [3].

Another issue that needs to be addressed before the DT can go mainstream, is the ownership of the data used, being the most important ones "Who will be the rightful owner? The patient or a health institution?", "Who will play the bigger role, the government or the private sector and for what purpose they will use personal data? Will all they have a share?"

Although these questions at first sound like science–fiction, the truth is that they need to be answered as soon as possible, the DT is around the corner and its development must not be left stray [3].

2.5 Expectations

Albeit the potential applications of the DT, it is expected to change how the problems are solved in the healthcare sector. Instead, caution is needed to really understand that the implementation of the DT can take its time to become a reality, due to the fact that all the supporting technologies and the DT itself is in a developing phase where the real applications remain uncertain [13].

Another important aspect to take into consideration, is that current trends may not be the same for the next decade, meaning that the DT applications in health-care may stem from what is proposed and described in this paper [5] (Table 2).

2.6   Challenges Summary

Table 2. Summary of the challenges that the DTs need to overcome

Challange	Description	Possible solution
IT infrastructure	-Need of high–performing hardware and software [5] -Volume of data in a "raw" state [5] -Natural variability in each patient [9]	IT infrastructure needs to be leveraged and comply with different standards [7]
Data privacy and security	-Threat of cyberattacks, specially DDoS [8] -Unregulated technology [5]	Adopt protocols and security frameworks [8]
Data quality	-High–grade of prepared data [5] -Data integration from multiple sources [10]	Data merge using AI methods [10]
Ethics	-Question the current boundaries of medicine [3] Inequality between patients [3] -Ownership of the data	Lower costs and define the roles of all the involved parties [3]
Expectations	Change of current trends [5]	Adapt and understand the technological limits [5]

3   Future Applications

Although the applications in both products and services seem endless, it is time to focus solely on what can be made in the next decade with this brand–new technology. At the time being, the DT has already been successfully implemented at the healthcare sector. Its first use was in medical devices for preventive maintenance and for the optimization of its capabilities [1]. However, the asset potential can be exploited to disrupt how we understand and perceive human healthcare and lifestyle and make a fully–functional device of ourselves, thus creating a new paradigm in health [5].

3.1   Non-invasive Treatment

The most realistic application for the next decade of non–invasive treatments is not the whole human body, but the development of physiological models of organs or systems. For example, Dassault Systèmes in 2015 released its "Living Heart" project, which is the first digital representation of the organ that works as the real one: The electrical impulses that are translated into mechanic contractions and expansions and control the blood flow [1].

For the 5G/6G communications era, the previous application is expected to improve and to be capable to replicate a disease and its effects in a DT. As a result, research is being made to develop the DT of lung cancer in all of its stages and the damage that these organs undergo, and is expected for this approach to benefit from the enormous amount of data that circulates between the digital and physical organ, then made understandable for the physicians and finally choose the best medical treatment for this patient; process that is also known as personalized medicine [14].

3.2   Personalized Medicine

As a result of the fast–development that the DTs are showing in the healthcare sector, the old paradigm of "one size fits all", i.e. assume the people's physiology is exactly the same for everybody, is meant to disappear. Instead, personalized medicine is the next standard, as it can monitor all day long the patient and gather data on how the treatment performs: If the dose needs to be modified, which side–effects are expected in the patient, and even if the treatment will be effective or not [4].

As it has been stated, data from multiple sources are collected by the DT need to be concealed in order to perform as desired. In turn, this is the biggest obstacle for the personalized medicine, since it deals with multiple degrees of complexity in a single individual, that ranges from the molecular to even the environmental levels. Another benefit of this brand–new approach, is that some diseases can be diagnosed in early stages in which damage and symptoms to the patient are yet to occur, giving physicians the enough time to reverse the disease, if it is the case [2].

3.3   Telemedicine

Subsequent from the IoT and Cloud computing of the DT, another application for it is the telemedicine. Using the data that is always flowing and being analyzed, it can allow for a real–time monitoring and prediction of the health–status of the patient, meaning that face–to–face interactions between patient and physician can be reduced.

As a result of this characteristic, healthcare platforms are almost certain to occur in the next decade, a digital landscape where different services can be offered: Medication reminder, crisis warning, and the disease prevention or the early detection of them. Of course, the data used is confidential, and it needs to be protected by security frameworks and protocols at all times, and as discussed previously, data leakage must be prevented [7].

4   Conclusions

As history shows, when a revolutionary technology is first presented, most of the people fear the unknown until they saw the potential and benefits in their lifestyles. It is expected that during the next decade, healthcare is most likely to face severe changes on how we understand it, due to the advent of the Digital Twin, a concept that is currently undergoing a continuous research and development process to bring together health specialists and engineers, as part of the Fourth Industrial Revolution.

Whilst there are serious obstacles to overcome before seeing this as a public technology, the benefits that it offers for the healthcare greatly exceed the costs. For the next decade, biomedical engineering is expected to make bigger developments and become a key player in the redefinition of medicine, one that is personalized and solely data–driven.

References

1. Barricelli, B.R., Casiraghi, E., Fogli, D.: A survey on digital twin: definitions, characteristics, applications, and design implications. IEEE Access **7**, 167653–167671 (2019)
2. Björnsson, B., et al.: Digital twins to personalize medicine. Genome Med. **12**(1), 1–4 (2020)
3. Bruynseels, K., Santoni de Sio, F., van den Hoven, J.: Digital twins in health care: ethical implications of an emerging engineering paradigm. Front. Genet. **9**, 31 (2018)
4. Feng, Y., Chen, X., Zhao, J.: Create the individualized digital twin for noninvasive precise pulmonary healthcare. Significances Bioeng. Biosci. **1**(2), 2–5 (2018)
5. Fuller, A., Fan, Z., Day, C., Barlow, C.: Digital twin: enabling technologies, challenges and open research. IEEE Access **8**, 108952–108971 (2020)
6. Gochhait, S., Bende, A.: Leveraging digital twin technology in the healthcare industry-a machine learning based approach. Eur. J. Mol. Clin. Med. **7**(6), 2547–2557 (2020)
7. Liu, Y., et al.: A novel cloud-based framework for the elderly healthcare services using digital twin. IEEE Access **7**, 49088–49101 (2019)
8. Lou, X., Guo, Y., Gao, Y., Waedt, K., Parekh, M.: An idea of using digital twin to perform the functional safety and cybersecurity analysis. In: INFORMATIK 2019: 50 Jahre Gesellschaft für Informatik-Informatik für Gesellschaft (Workshop-Beiträge). Gesellschaft für Informatik eV (2019)
9. Patrone, C., Lattuada, M., Galli, G., Revetria, R.: The role of Internet of Things and digital twin in healthcare digitalization process. In: Ao, S.-I., Kim, H.K., Amouzegar, M.A. (eds.) WCECS 2018, pp. 30–37. Springer, Singapore (2020). https://doi.org/10.1007/978-981-15-6848-0_3
10. Qi, Q., et al.: Enabling technologies and tools for digital twin. J. Manuf. Syst. **58**, 3–21 (2019)
11. Rasheed, A., San, O., Kvamsdal, T.: Digital twin: values, challenges and enablers from a modeling perspective. IEEE Access **8**, 21980–22012 (2020)
12. Riesener, M., Schuh, G., Dölle, C., Tönnes, C.: The digital shadow as enabler for data analytics in product life cycle management. Procedia CIRP **80**, 729–734 (2019)
13. Singh, M., Fuenmayor, E., Hinchy, E.P., Qiao, Y., Murray, N., Devine, D.: Digital twin: origin to future. Appl. Syst. Innov. **4**(2), 36 (2021)
14. Zhang, J., Li, L., Lin, G., Fang, D., Tai, Y., Huang, J.: Cyber resilience in healthcare digital twin on lung cancer. IEEE Access **8**, 201900–201913 (2020)

Reviewing the Application of Data Driven Digital Twins in Manufacturing Systems: A Business and Management Perspective

Ehsan Badakhshan$^{(\boxtimes)}$ [ID] and Peter Ball [ID]

University of York Management School, York, UK
{ehsan.badakhshan,peter.ball}@york.ac.uk

Abstract. Simulation modelling has been a widely used tool for analyzing manufacturing systems and improving their performance. Although, little attention has been paid to the application of data-driven simulation modelling of the manufacturing systems. With the development of new-generation information and digitalization technologies, more data can be collected from the manufacturing shop floor. This has paved the way for employing data-driven simulation of manufacturing systems knows as a digital twin. This paper reviews the literature and practice on digital twins in manufacturing systems from a business and management perspective to identify the gaps and recommend avenues for future research. The results show that 2018 has been a turning point in the literature with small scale case studies of digital twins emerging independent of commercial practice. Since 2018 the digital twin literature has moved on from descriptions and conceptual frameworks to focus on one product lifecycle phase with any reference to sustainability advance being confined to energy and resource efficiency. Practice has been advanced by manufacturers and IT vendors however the definition of digital twins lacks precision for ease comparison with the literature. Future avenues for research are identified in the areas of lifecycle phases and digital model fidelity.

Keywords: Digital twin · Manufacturing systems · Production · Industry 4.0 · Literature review

1 Introduction

In today's highly competitive markets, increasing product variants and individualized demands are presenting new challenges to the manufacturing industry. Digitalization in manufacturing is seen as a promising solution to increase productivity and quality. The digital technologies also known as Industry 4.0 technologies enable real-time monitoring and control of intelligent components in the shopfloor by integrating and synchronizing the physical and virtual worlds [1]. The digital twin is one of the Industry 4.0 technologies that help optimize business performance.

The concept of the digital twin was first introduced by Grieves in an industry presentation in 2003 [2]. A digital twin is a virtual representation of a physical system

© IFIP International Federation for Information Processing 2021
Published by Springer Nature Switzerland AG 2021
A. Dolgui et al. (Eds.): APMS 2021, IFIP AICT 633, pp. 256–265, 2021.
https://doi.org/10.1007/978-3-030-85910-7_27

developed as an independent entity. The digital twin contains the information embedded within the physical system and would have real-time communication with the physical system throughout its lifecycle [3]. Therefore, the digital twin provides crucial insights into the physical twin's performance, leading to actions such as a change in product design or manufacturing process design or control in the physical world.

Recent significant reductions in computing, storage and bandwidth costs have made data-driven technology such as digital twins economically feasible. Digital twin development provides cost saving and revenue generation opportunities for the companies across the lifecycle of their products and processes. For instance, reducing the time to market for a new product, reduced defects, cost saving opportunities and maintenance service business model opportunities for revenue generation. Such cost saving and revenue generation opportunities have attracted manufacturing companies to invest in digital twin technology. The digital twin market is forecasted to grow from its current market value of more than \$4 billion to over \$35 billion by 2026 [4].

Similar to the industry community, digital twins have drawn the attention of the academic community. The number of digital twin papers published in academic journals and conferences has risen significantly. Using a structured literature review, this paper discusses the concept and application of the digital twin in manufacturing systems. It provides a holistic overview of lifecycle phases in which a digital twin is implemented, modelling techniques applied, and solutions offered by vendors. This paper guides future work on the application of digital twins in manufacturing systems by identifying the gaps in the literature and contrasts with practice.

The paper is organized as follows. Section 2 presents the review methodology and a visualization of the literature. Section 3 classifies the literature based on publication type, lifecycle phases, research scope, and modelling techniques. Section 4 discusses the digital twin solutions offered by the digital twin vendors. Finally, a concluding discussion is presented in Sect. 5.

2 Literature Review Methodology

A structured review was conducted to evaluate the body of literature on the application of digital twins in manufacturing systems from a business and management perspective. This systematic review was performed in accordance with the methodology presented by [5] and [6]. First, a search in Scopus was carried out to identify the relevant papers. The literature search was carried out using Boolean keywords combinations "(digital twin OR digital twins) AND (manufacturing OR manufacturing systems OR cyber physical production systems)". The search process led to 94 papers by limiting the search scope to the subject area 'Business, Management, and Accounting' and selecting papers in English published from 2018 until 2021. The reason for limiting the search to papers published from 2018 until 2021 is that Kritzinger et al. (2018) [7] and Negri et al. (2017) [1] have thoroughly reviewed the literature before 2018. The papers identified were reviewed and irrelevant ones excluded. The exclusion criteria were: (1) "digital twin" phrase is used without bidirectional data flow between the physical and digital entities; (2) Industry 4.0 technologies proposals for which digital twins is not the focus. This led to 55 papers for review.

2.1 Literature Review Analysis

The initial analysis was conducted to establish what keywords capture the field and which journals and conferences are publishing such work.

A co-occurrence analysis of the literature using VOS viewer [8] identified keyword clusters. The results show industry 4.0, embedded systems, and cyber-physical systems are the most common keywords used in digital twin manufacturing systems papers.

International Journal of Production Research, IEEE International Conference on Industrial Engineering and Engineering Management, Journal of Cleaner Production, and International Conference Management of Large-Scale System Development are the top four contributors to digital twins in manufacturing systems literature. Operations research (OR) journals have not published studies on digital twins in manufacturing systems showing that OR techniques are in their infancy and more research is needed.

3   State of the Art Literature

In this section, the literature review on digital twins in manufacturing systems is classified by publication type, lifecycle phases, research scope, and modelling techniques.

3.1   Publication Type Classification

Kritzinger et al. (2018) [7] reported that the majority of the studies published between 2014 and 2017 focused on developing the conceptual frameworks. Since then, case studies represent 55% of works, outstripping conceptual frameworks at 41% and dwarfing review papers at 4%. Most cases are from academic laboratories with limited research on physical implementations. Interestingly, Kritzinger et al. (2018) [7] reported that up to 2017 a few studies discussed the definition but since this review shows no studies, indicating a consensus on the definition of the digital twins has been reached hence focus is now on small scale applications.

3.2   Life-Cycle Phase Classification

A physical twin's lifecycle is characterized by four phases: (1) Design phase that contains not just the product design but the process and plant design as well; (2) Manufacturing phase that comprises the production and relevant internal plant logistics; (3) Service phase that includes distribution, use, repair, and maintenance; (4) Retirement phase that refers to operations such as disassembling, remanufacturing, reusing, disposal [9].

Table 1 illustrates the share of different lifecycle phases in the literature on digital twins in manufacturing systems. A few studies in the literature examined more than one life cycle phase of the physical twins. In this case, the main studied life cycle phase was considered for classification. 16% of the reviewed papers studied digital twins in the design phase of the physical twin's lifecycle. In the design phase of the physical twin, the digital twin provides designers with complete digital footprints of products and processes, thereby shortening the design cycle and reducing rework cost.

As shown in Table 1, more than half of the studies in the literature are related to the manufacturing phase of the physical twin's lifecycle. In the manufacturing phase, digital twins provide real-time monitoring of the manufacturing process, therefore reducing the defects and improving resource efficiency. Many manufacturing applications such as identifying the optimal machine sequencing and production schedule [19], minimizing the geometrical deviations [21], process planning [27], and efficient energy and resource planning [24, 25] were reported.

The service phase is the second most studied lifecycle phase in the literature, more than the design phase. Here the digital twin enhances the performance of the physical twin by monitoring the real-time operating state and providing predictive maintenance and fault diagnosis [50, 51], representing the supply chain network in real-time to provide complete end-to-end visibility [6, 52, 53, 55, 56].

Table 1. Literature on digital twins for the lifecycle of manufacturing systems

Phase	Share	Refs	Business outcome
Design	16%	[10–17]	Reducing design cost, reducing design cycle, increasing the geometrical quality of final product, improving product performance
Manufacturing	52%	[18–48]	Reducing production cost, increasing production efficiency, increasing quality and throughput, reducing the geometrical deviations, reducing mean throughput time, increasing resource and energy efficiency
Service	29%	[6, 49–62]	Reducing maintenance cost, reducing bullwhip effect and ripple effect, increasing supply chain resilience
Retirement	3%	[63, 64]	Reducing the uncertainty in remanufacturing process, reducing electrical and electronics equipment waste

The retirement phase of the product lifecycle is the least studied phase in the literature. Here the digital twin supports the recovery and remanufacturing process [63, 64]. In cases where the physical twin is not suitable for remanufacturing, the digital twin supports less environmental impact on disposal.

3.3 Research Scope Classification

Digital twins are developed to represent a detailed visualization of parts of the life cycle of physical products and processes. One of the most common areas of study is planning and control problems. Manufacturing system digital twins enable an order-based and automated production planning and control system by real-time monitoring of the production shop floor. 18% of the reviewed papers studied the application of digital twins in the manufacturing environment in general rather than focusing on a particular area within manufacturing. Product and process design is the third most studied problem. These studies aimed to reduce the design cost and design cycle of the new and existing products using digital twin technology. 14% of the studies in the literature are related to applying digital twins for predictive maintenance and fault diagnosis. Supply chain planning is the fifth most studied problem in literature, these studies aim to increase the efficiency of the supply chains as well as increase the resilience to disruption. Only 7% of the reviewed papers applied digital twins to increase the efficiency of the energy and resource planning in manufacturing systems. Finally, recovery and remanufacturing of the retired products is the least studied problem in the literature, indicating there is significant potential for further work in this area.

3.4 Modelling Techniques Classification

Digital twins are simulation models built using the real-time or near real-time data received from their physical twins [47]. Therefore, simulation is the main pillar of building digital twins. 38% of the literature on digital twins developed simulation models to represent the physical twins in different phases of the lifecycle and predict the future status of the physical twins. 29% of the studies incorporated optimization into simulation models to transform the digital twins from predictive models to prescriptive models. 15% of the papers integrated simulation and data analytics in digital twin models. In these studies, the data collected from physical twins are firstly analyzed by data analytics techniques such as machine learning that provide predictive analytics and are then input into the simulation models. Applying the data analytics techniques reduces the computational burden on simulation models and therefore run time of this combination is less than that for simulation models alone. 18% of the studies in the literature incorporated optimization into integrated simulation and data analytics models to improve the performance of the physical twins.

3.5 Literature Findings

Reviewing the literature on digital twins in manufacturing systems since 2018 reveals many gaps: (1) Much of the literature presents laboratory case studies. The literature lacks industrial cases to show the implementation of the digital twin in real-world manufacturing systems; (2) Much of the literature study digital twins in one life cycle phase of the physical twin. Few studies consider the more than one lifecycle of the physical twin, none considers the whole lifecycle; (3) Among the lifecycle phases of the physical twins, the retirement phase is the least studied phase. More studies on digital twins in the retirement phase are needed to address the challenges of the return cycle; (4) Sustainability is poorly addressed, only a few papers consider the narrow scope of energy and resource efficiency. The literature reviewed does not go beyond this; (5) Modellers develop high fidelity real-time data-based simulation models, however, there are computational burdens in identifying optimal manufacturing decisions. There is a lack of work on multi-level modelling to consider variation in fidelity; (6) Data analytics has potential for reducing the computational time of simulation-optimization (including for high fidelity models) however frameworks for this lack development for wider application; (7) A limited number of studies employed machine learning techniques and more research on their use in the various life cycle phases is needed; (8) Humans are one of the main resources in the manufacturing systems. There is limited research on considering humans in the digital twins of the manufacturing systems.

4   Digital Twin Software

The digital twin market is forecasted to grow at a compound annual growth rate of over 30% from 2021 to 2026 [4]. This market growth opportunity has attracted many companies to invest in developing digital twin solutions. The digital twin solutions can be classified into commercial solutions and cloud-based solutions.

The commercial solutions are provided by the manufacturers of IoT-connected industrial products to create a digital twin of the manufacturing assets, processes, and systems. General Electric, Dassault Systemes, Siemens, and Bosch are the key players in providing commercial solutions. The cloud-based solutions are provided by IT companies to create digital twins of the assets, places, processes and people. Microsoft, Oracle, and IBM are the key players in providing cloud-based solutions.

The competitive advantage of the commercial digital twin solutions offered by the industrial equipment manufacturers is the availability of the ready to use digital twins of industrial equipment. The competitive advantage of the cloud-based digital twin solutions offered by IT companies is the seamless integration of these solutions with other cloud-based services such as AI and analytics. Industrial equipment manufacturers and IT companies are collaborating to integrate the advantages of the commercial and cloud-based digital twin solutions. The partnership between IBM and Siemens is an example of such collaborations.

Reviewing practice on digital twins in manufacturing systems against the gaps found in the earlier literature review reveals: (1) The peer reviewed literature lags industry application; (2) Little can be discerned about the dominant application of digital twins (e.g. manufacturing, service, etc.) and whether applications span across multiple stages of the lifecycle; (3) Vendors do not explicitly address the fidelity versus computation time found to be an issue in the academic literature; (4) The potential for and mechanism of data analytics to reduce computation burden are unclear; (5) There is little evidence of environmental sustainability as a potentially valuable focus as identified by the literature; (6) Finally, the use of the term digital twin is dominant in practice but it is unclear if applications compise a bidirectional data flow between physical and digital twins. This lack of definition and clarity of what is being reported on industry application makes comparison with the academic literature difficult.

5   Conclusions

This paper reviewed manufacturing system digital twins in literature and from vendors. It is clear that most academic work has been on conceptual frameworks or case studies to address planning problems in the manufacturing phase of the physical twins. Simulation modelling is the inseparable element of the digital twins but appears only as high-fidelity analysis with its associated computational burden. The literature shows computational time can be reduced through data analytics but there is an absence of guidance on appropriate model fidelity. The literature lacks studies on digital twins addressing problems across the physical twin lifecycle as well as considering sustainability challenges beyond energy and resource efficiency. Similarly, there is a lack of work on manufacturing systems for end of life products. Studies are needed that consider humans in the digital twins of manufacturing systems. The industrial equipment manufacturers and IT companies that are the main vendors of digital twin solutions are collaborating to enrich their digital twin solutions. The commercial solutions reported are ahead in application in practice, however, most of the above research challenges remain.

References

1. Negri, E., Fumagalli, L., Macchi, M.: A review of the roles of digital twin in CPS-based production systems. Procedia Manuf. **11**, 939–948 (2017)
2. Grieves, M.: Digital twin: manufacturing excellence through virtual factory replication. White Pap. **1**, 1–7 (2014)
3. Grieves, M., Vickers, J.: Digital twin: mitigating unpredictable, undesirable emergent behavior in complex systems. In: Kahlen, F.-J., Flumerfelt, S., Alves, A. (eds.) Transdisciplinary Perspectives on Complex Systems, pp. 85–113. Springer, Cham (2017). https://doi.org/10.1007/978-3-319-38756-7_4
4. Digital Twin Market Statistics | Global Size Forecasts 2026. https://www.gminsights.com/industry-analysis/digital-twin-market
5. Hosseini, S., Ivanov, D., Dolgui, A.: Review of quantitative methods for supply chain resilience analysis. Transp. Res. Part E Logist. Transp. Rev. **125**, 285–307 (2019)
6. Dolgui, A., Ivanov, D., Sokolov, B.: Reconfigurable supply chain: the X-network. Int. J. Prod. Res. **58**, 4138–4163 (2020)
7. Kritzinger, W., Karner, M., Traar, G., Henjes, J., Sihn, W.: Digital twin in manufacturing: a categorical literature review and classification. IFAC-PapersOnLine. **51**, 1016–1022 (2018)
8. van Eck, N.J., Waltman, L.: How to normalize cooccurrence data? An analysis of some well-known similarity measures. J. Am. Soc. Inf. Sci. Technol. **60**, 1635–1651 (2009)
9. Kiritsis, D., Bufardi, A., Xirouchakis, P.: Research issues on product lifecycle management and information tracking using smart embedded systems. Adv. Eng. Inform. **17**, 189–202 (2003)
10. Tao, F., et al.: Digital twin-driven product design framework. Int. J. Prod. Res. **57**, 3935–3953 (2019)
11. Liu, Q., Zhang, H., Leng, J., Chen, X.: Digital twin-driven rapid individualised designing of automated flow-shop manufacturing system. Int. J. Prod. Res. **57**, 3903–3919 (2019)
12. Aderiani, A.R., Wärmefjord, K., Söderberg, R., Lindkvist, L.: Developing a selective assembly technique for sheet metal assemblies. Int. J. Prod. Res. **57**, 7174–7188 (2019)
13. Huang, S., Wang, G., Yan, Y.: Building blocks for digital twin of reconfigurable machine tools from design perspective. Int. J. Prod. Res. 1–15 (2020)
14. Eisentrager, M., Adler, S., Kennel, M., Moser, S.: Changeability in engineering. In: 2018 IEEE International Conference on Engineering, Technology and Innovation, ICE/ITMC (2018)
15. Strelets, D.Y., Serebryansky, S.A., Shkurin, M.V.: Concept of creation of a digital twin in the uniform information environment of product life cycle. In: 2020 13th International Conference Management of Large-Scale System Development, MLSD (2020)
16. Zheng, P., Lin, T.J., Chen, C.H., Xu, X.: A systematic design approach for service innovation of smart product-service systems. J. Clean. Prod. **201**, 657–667 (2018)
17. He, B., Cao, X., Hua, Y.: Data fusion-based sustainable digital twin system of intelligent detection robotics. J. Clean. Prod. **280**, 124–181 (2021)
18. Zhang, Z., Guan, Z., Gong, Y., Luo, D., Yue, L.: Improved multi-fidelity simulation-based optimisation: application in a digital twin shop floor. Int. J. Prod. Res. 1–20 (2020)
19. Ding, K., Chan, F.T.S., Zhang, X., Zhou, G., Zhang, F.: Defining a digital twin-based cyber-physical production system for autonomous manufacturing in smart shop floors. Int. J. Prod. Res. **57**, 6315–6334 (2019)

20. Zhou, G., Zhang, C., Li, Z., Ding, K., Wang, C.: Knowledge-driven digital twin manufacturing cell towards intelligent manufacturing. Int. J. Prod. Res. **58**, 1034–1051 (2020)
21. Polini, W., Corrado, A.: Digital twin of composite assembly manufacturing process. Int. J. Prod. Res. **58**, 5238–5252 (2020)
22. Ait-Alla, A., Kreutz, M., Rippel, D., Lütjen, M., Freitag, M.: Simulated-based methodology for the interface configuration of cyber-physical production systems. Int. J. Prod. Res. 1–16 (2020)
23. Lin, T.Y., et al.: Efficient container virtualization-based digital twin simulation of smart industrial systems. J. Clean. Prod. **281**, 124443 (2020)
24. Leiden, A., Herrmann, C., Thiede, S.: Cyber-physical production system approach for energy and resource efficient planning and operation of plating process chains. J. Clean. Prod. **280**, 125–160 (2020)
25. Ma, S., Zhang, Y., Liu, Y., Yang, H., Lv, J., Ren, S.: Data-driven sustainable intelligent manufacturing based on demand response for energy-intensive industries. J. Clean. Prod. **274**, 123–155 (2020)
26. Park, K.T., Lee, D., Do Noh, S.: Operation procedures of a work-center-level digital twin for sustainable and smart manufacturing. Int. J. Precis. Eng. Manuf. - Green Technol. **7**, 791–814 (2020)
27. Zhang, C., Zhou, G., Hu, J., Li, J.: Deep learning-enabled intelligent process planning for digital twin manufacturing cell. Knowl.-Based Syst. **191**, 105247 (2020)
28. Kusiak, A.: Convolutional and generative adversarial neural networks in manufacturing. Int. J. Prod. Res. **58**, 1594–1604 (2020)
29. Uhlenkamp, J.-F., Hribernik, K., Wellsandt, S., Thoben, K.-D.: Digital twin applications: a first systemization of their dimensions. In: 2019 IEEE International Conference on Engineering, Technology and Innovation (ICE/ITMC), pp. 1–8. IEEE (2019)
30. Catarci, T., Firmani, D., Leotta, F., Mandreoli, F., Mecella, M., Sapio, F.: A conceptual architecture and model for smart manufacturing relying on service-based digital twins. In: 2019 IEEE International Conference on Web Services, ICWS (2019)
31. Horváthová, M., Lacko, R., Hajduová, Z.: Using Industry 4.0 concept – digital twin – to improve the efficiency of leather cutting in automotive industry. Qual. Innov. Prosper. **23**, 1–12 (2019)
32. Raza, M., Kumar, P.M., Hung, D.V., Davis, W., Nguyen, H., Trestian, R.: A Digital twin framework for Industry 4.0 enabling next-gen manufacturing. In: ICITM 2020 (2020)
33. Lin, W.D., Low, M.Y.H.: Concept and implementation of a cyber-physical digital twin for a SMT line. In: IEEE International Conference on Industrial Engineering and Engineering Management, pp. 1455–1459 (2019)
34. Vijayakumar, K., Dhanasekaran, C., Pugazhenthi, R., Sivaganesan, S.: Digital twin for factory system simulation. Int. J. Recent Technol. Eng. **8**, 63–68 (2019)
35. Negri, E., Assiro, G., Caioli, L., Fumagalli, L.: A machine state-based digital twin development methodology. In: XXV Summerschool Francesco Turco (2019)
36. Agostino, Í.R.S., Broda, E., Frazzon, E.M., Freitag, M.: Using a digital twin for production planning and control in Industry 4.0. In: Sokolov, B., Ivanov, D., Dolgui, A. (eds.) Scheduling in Industry 4.0 and Cloud Manufacturing. ISORMS, vol. 289, pp. 39–60. Springer, Cham (2020). https://doi.org/10.1007/978-3-030-43177-8_3
37. Assawaarayakul, C., Srisawat, W., Ayuthaya, S.D.N., Wattanasirichaigoon, S.: Integrate digital twin to exist production system for Industry 4.0. In: 4th Technology Innovation Management and Engineering Science International Conference (2019)
38. Lin, W.D., Low, Y.H., Chong, Y.T., Teo, C.L.: Integrated cyber physical simulation modelling environment for manufacturing 4.0. In: IEEE International Conference on Industrial Engineering and Engineering Management, pp. 1861–1865 (2019)

39. Santos, R., Basto, J., Alcalá, S.G.S., Frazzon, E., Azevedo, A.: Industrial IoT integrated with simulation-a digital twin approach to support real-time decision making. In: International Conference on Industrial Engineering and Operations Management, pp. 23–26 (2019)
40. Zhang, Y.F., Shao, Y.Q., Wang, J.F., Li, S.Q.: Digital twin-based production simulation of discrete manufacturing shop-floor for onsite performance analysis. In: IEEE International Conference on Industrial Engineering and Engineering Management, pp. 1107–1111(2020)
41. Lin, W.D., Low, M.Y.H.: Concept design of a system architecture for a manufacturing cyber-physical digital twin system. In: IEEE International Conference on Industrial Engineering and Engineering Management, pp. 1320–1324 (2020)
42. Protic, A., Jin, Z., Marian, R , Ahd, K., Campbell, D., Chahl, J.: Implementation of a bi-directional digital twin for industry 4 labs in academia: a solution based on OPC UA. In: International Conference on Industrial Engineering and Engineering Management (2020)
43. Guo, D., Li, M., Zhong, R., Huang, G.Q.: Graduation intelligent manufacturing system (GiMS): an Industry 4.0 paradigm for production and operations management. Ind. Manag. Data Syst. **121**, 86–98 (2020)
44. Makarov, V.V., Frolov, Y.B., Parshina, I.S., Ushakova, M.V.: MES systems as an integral part of digital production. In: 13th International Conference Management of Large-Scale System Development, MLSD (2020)
45. Golovina, T., Polyanin, A., Adamenko, A., Khegay, E., Schepinin, V.: Digital twins as a new paradigm of an industrial enterprise. Int. J. Technol. **11**, 1115 (2020)
46. Yildiz, E., Møller, C., Bilberg, A.: Virtual factory: competence-based adaptive modelling and simulation approach for manufacturing enterprise. In: Lecture Notes in Business Information Processing, pp. 197–207 (2020)
47. Rodič, B.: Industry and the new simulation modelling paradigm. Organizacija **50**, 193–207 (2017)
48. Amos, H.C., Bandaru, S.: Virtual factories with knowledge-driven optimization as a new research profile (2020)
49. Wang, K.-J., Lee, Y.-H., Angelica, S.: Digital twin design for real-time monitoring–a case study of die cutting machine. Int. J. Prod. Res. 1–15 (2020)
50. Wang, J., Ye, L., Gao, R.X., Li, C., Zhang, L.: Digital twin for rotating machinery fault diagnosis in smart manufacturing. Int. J. Prod. Res. **57**, 3920–3934 (2019)
51. Ardanza, A., Moreno, A., Segura, Á., de la Cruz, M., Aguinaga, D.: Sustainable and flexible industrial human machine interfaces to support adaptable applications in the Industry 4.0 paradigm. Int. J. Prod. Res. **57**, 4045–4059 (2019)
52. Park, K.T., Son, Y.H., Do Noh, S.: The architectural framework of a cyber physical logistics system for digital-twin-based supply chain control. Int. J. Prod. Res. 1–22 (2020)
53. Ivanov, D., Dolgui, A., Das, A., Sokolov, B.: Digital supply chain twins: managing the ripple effect, resilience, and disruption risks by data-driven optimization, simulation, and visibility. In: Ivanov, D., Dolgui, A., Sokolov, B. (eds.) Handbook of Ripple Effects in the Supply Chain. International Series in Operations Research & Management Science, vol. 276. Springer, Cham (2019). https://doi.org/10.1007/978-3-030-14302-2_15
54. Aivaliotis, P., Georgoulias, K., Arkouli, Z., Makris, S.: Methodology for enabling digital twin using advanced physics-based modelling in predictive maintenance. Procedia CIRP **81**, 417–422 (2019)
55. Baruffaldi, G., Accorsi, R., Manzini, R.: Warehouse management system customization and information availability in 3PL companies. Ind. Manag. Data Syst. (2019)
56. Ivanov, D., Dolgui, A.: A digital supply chain twin for managing the disruptions risks and resilience in the era of Industry 4.0. Prod. Plan. Control **32**, 1–14 (2020)
57. Navas, M.A., Sancho, C., Carpio, J.: Disruptive maintenance engineering 4.0. Int. J. Qual. Reliab. Manag. **37**, 853–871 (2020)

58. Yevgenievich Barykin, S., Aleksandrovich Bochkarev, A., Vladimirovna Kalinina, O., Konstantinovich Yadykin, V.: Concept for a supply chain digital twin. Int. J. Math. Eng. Manag. Sci. **5**, 1498–1515 (2020)
59. Jharko, E.: Some aspects of creation of flexible modeling software package for NPP. In: International Conference Management of Large-Scale System Development, MLSD (2020)
60. Perno, M., Hvam, L.: Developing a framework for scoping digital twins in the process manufacturing Industry. In: the Swedish Production Symposium (2020)
61. Chen, Q., Zhu, Z., Si, S., Cai, Z.: Intelligent maintenance of complex equipment based on blockchain and digital twin technologies. In: IEEE International Conference on Industrial Engineering and Engineering Management, pp. 908–912 (2020)
62. Chakrabortty, R.K., Rahman, H.F., Mo, H., Ryan, M.J.: Digital twin-based cyber physical system for sustainable project scheduling. In: IEEE International Conference on Industrial Engineering and Engineering Management, pp. 820–824 (2019)
63. Wang, X.V., Wang, L.: Digital twin-based WEEE recycling, recovery and remanufacturing in the background of Industry 4.0. Int. J. Prod. Res. **57**, 3892–3902 (2019)
64. Wang, Y., Wang, S., Yang, B., Zhu, L., Liu, F.: Big data driven hierarchical digital twin predictive remanufacturing paradigm: architecture, control mechanism, application scenario and benefits. J. Clean. Prod. **248**, 119299 (2020)

Improving a Manufacturing Process using Recursive Artificial Intelligence

Jose Antonio Marmolejo-Saucedo[1]([✉]) [iD], Roman Rodriguez-Aguilar[2] [iD],
Uriel Abel Romero Perea[1] [iD], Manuel Garrido Vaqueiro[1] [iD],
Regina Robredo Hernandez[1] [iD], Fernando Sanchez Ramirez[1] [iD],
and Ana Paula Martinez[1]

[1] Facultad de Ingenieria, Universidad Panamericana, Augusto Rodin 498,
03920 Ciudad de Mexico, Mexico
jmarmolejo@up.edu.mx
[2] Facultad de Ciencias Economicas y Empresariales, Universidad
Panamericana, Augusto Rodin 498, 03920 Ciudad de Mexico, Mexico
rrodrigueza@up.edu.mx

Abstract. This work explores the improvements that can be made in the process of parametrization of discrete-event simulation models. A manufacturing process is modeled through queuing systems and alternative decisions to perform production, transport, and merchandise handling tasks. The use of recursive artificial intelligence is suggested to improve the quality of the parameters used in the simulation model. Specifically, a vector support machine is used for statistical learning. A relevant characteristic of the proposed model is the integration of different information technology platforms so that the simulation can be recursive.

Keywords: Discrete event simulation · Digital twins · Support vector machines

1 Introduction

Typically, manufacturing processes have been the target of multiple strategies for optimization. From the classic techniques of process improvement, through the optimization and simulation techniques among others. In recent years, artificial intelligence has taken off and is one of the most used techniques to improve repetitive processes such as a manufacturing process. Some examples range from logistics and other areas such as health services.

In these cases, Emergency Medical Services faces significant challenges due to the complex nature of pre-hospital events, coordinating several resources according to the collected information in a short time. In this context, both agent-based and discrete event simulation seem to be excellent approaches to find

Supported by Universidad Panamericana.

new strategies for facing this complexity. Our general process benefits from an intensive exchange with a multi- disciplinary group of experts from medicine, including practitioners, paramedics, coordination center managers, and stakeholders, among others. Furthermore, we validated our simulation model using real-world data from an emergency coordination center from North Germany.

The accelerated evolution of Information and Communication Technologies has allowed the use of mobile communication devices has increased in the last two decades. Becoming a luxury to a need, allowing the diversification of its costs to access people of any kind social, opening unlimited communication channels (voice, video, and data), constant access to various social networks, joining the daily life of the vast majority of people in the world, moving from a specific operating team to one that can be used as a camera, for the management of bank accounts, such as GPS, personal agenda, email, e-book reader, music and video player, videogames, texting, etc.

2   Literature Review

According to Monostori's research, [5] since the beginning of the Century, researchers began asking what would it be the application of artificial intelligence (AI) and machine learning (ML) in the future, which benefits they could bring combining AI, ML and simulation into manufacturing? The answer was divided into three main fields: production processes and process chains, flexible manufacturing systems (FMS's) and holonic manufacturing systems (HMS). To achieve this EU implemented a project name "Zero defect manufacturing of composite parts in the aerospace industry" which consists in the combination of information acquired from a fibre orientation sensor and data taken from a laser profile scanner, in order to made a simulation that serves to optimize the movement of the production and the inspections only do it make quality inspections at key points so that operating costs are saved and quality is equal or higher [8]. Moving forward, at the beginning of 2021 we found out that more than 20 years later, AI and ML haven't placed themselves as a standard in manufacturing, even more, making emphasis on the car manufacturing, one of the most important sectors worldwide, this is not a reality, new laws and regulations, customers demanding self-driving cars and the global SARS-CoV-2 (COVID-19) pandemic led into high investments and the ROI has not waged it, as Fiat Group World posted on their website, as is shown in [13], vehicle sales fell a 43% in April. Despite that, Demlehner [3] found key areas in which AI may be implemented, contrasting realizability and business value, as is shown in Fig. 1.

3   Application of Machine Learning Methods for the Estimation of Strategic Variables

The parameter prediction problem is a central issue in the design and analysis of production systems. By integrating simulation methods and artificial intelligence

Fig. 1. Realizability vs business value of AI application in car manufacturing. See [3]

in the process analysis, the need arises to feed the models in a first stage with historical data, later to integrate information from the real operation, and in a prospective analysis to make projections on key indicators of the operation of the system. In a production system, demand is a fundamental variable for production planning, financial prospects as well as company management. There are various methods commonly used to make demand projections, depending on the particular objective of the projections [2, 7, 9, 12].

The integration of simulation methods with machine learning methodologies allows the construction of innovative and comprehensive strategies that allow improving the estimates made in the operation of companies. In the case of demand as a key variable, the classic methods for estimating demand, such as exponential smoothing methods or time series analysis, have shown some limitations in reference to the need for sufficient historical information, forecasting capacity, as well as problems with the treatment of non-linear behavior presented in the variables. One of the drawbacks in estimating demand forecasts using traditional methods is the non-linear treatment since the margin of error in the predictions increases in those variables that present non-linear behaviors. In

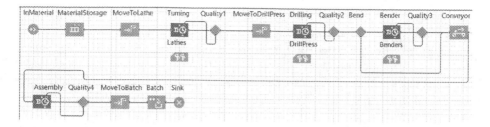

Fig. 2. Discrete event simulation model

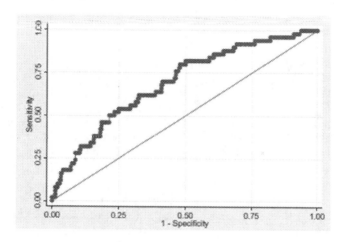

Fig. 3. ROC for SVM model (Area under ROC curve 0.71450)

practice, the assumption of linearity in many cases is far from reality. Therefore, this work proposes the use of the support vector machine (SVM) method that allows considering the non-linear treatment in the variables as well as using a smaller amount of data as inputs for the estimates. It is proposed to integrate into the simulation model of the system the interaction with a machine learning model that allows integrating the prediction of demand in different horizons as a key input for the simulation (Figs. 2 and 3).

3.1 Support Vector Machines for Non-linear Treatment

The Support Vector Machines (SVM) method consists of finding the separation hyperplane with the greatest margin of separation between the classes. That is the linear discriminant function:

$$g(x) = w^T x + b \tag{1}$$

With the widest margin to ensure a robust generalization resistant to outliers. The vectors formed by the points closest to the hyperplane are called support vectors. Generally, SVM is used to solve classification problems, however since

the objective is to build a separation hyperplane that is determined by a set
of variables, it is also possible to use the methodology to perform prediction.
Among all the possible separation hyperplanes, finding the one with the widest
margin becomes an optimization problem. Sometimes the data are separable
but noisy. This can generate a poor solution for the maximal margin classifier
so is possible use a soft margin by adding a regularization parameter C (cost
parameter) [4].

$$MaxM[\beta_0, \beta_1, ..., \beta_p] \tag{2}$$

Subject to

$$\sum_{j=1}^{p} \beta_j^2 = 1 \tag{3}$$

$$y_i \left(\beta_0 + \beta_1 x_{i1} + ... + \beta_p x_{ip} \right) \geq M \left(1 - \varepsilon_i \right) \tag{4}$$

$$\varepsilon_i \geq 0, \sum_{i=1}^{n} \varepsilon_i \leq C \tag{5}$$

The cost parameter is also established, which refers to the acceptable number of erroneously classified observations and the smaller the number of support
vectors increases, making it more precise. In the case in which the separation
hyperplane with the highest margin cannot be found with the linear discriminant function, we would seek to smooth the separation and expand the space
of functions with non-linear curves through Kernel functions with the projection of the information to a larger-dimensional feature space to find the optimal
spacing hyperplane in the original dimension. The most used types of kernel
functions are linear, polynomial, radial, exponential, and perceptron multilayer.
The process of integrating kernel functions through transformations to the variables used allows projecting the data to a p-dimensional space to a $M > p$.
This allows SVM to fit in the enlarged space, this implies being able to generate
non-linear borders in the original space. The SVM in the enlarged space solves
the problem in the lower dimensional space. Using the concept of inner product
between vectors, it is possible to express the SVM alternatively as the sum of
inner products of the observations with new data. For a new observation x, the
SVM with kernel functions would be [4]:

$$f(x) = \beta_0 + \sum_{i \in S} \hat{\alpha_i} \langle x, x_i \rangle \tag{6}$$

This last specification of SVM allows the use of the method for prediction,
thus being the variable to predict the new observation and the explanatory
variables used as part of the support vectors. In the same way, this allows the
generated prediction or the adjustment made for the prediction to consider the
non-linear behavior of the variable to be predicted.

3.2   Demand Prediction Using an SVM

SVMs were originally conceptualized to solve non-linear classification problems [1,2]. But in recent years they have been applied to regression problems [7,11] as well as time series prediction [6,10]. In this work demand data are used for a company of agricultural products, the tons demanded per year are considered and a period from 1990–2020 is analyzed (Fig. 4).

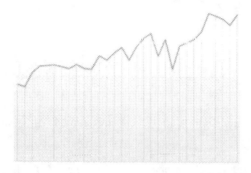

Fig. 4. Historical demand (thousands of tons)

Based on these historical data, we want to build the forecast for the next five years using a comparison of different kernel functions for SVM and using an ARIMA model as a reference methodology. The estimation of the SVM models was carried out by cross-validation in order to optimize the hyperparameters of the model: a) kernel function, b) Cost function, c) Gamma and d) Epsilon. In the case of the ARIMA model, the AIC was considered as a model selection criterion and an ARIMA model (0, 1, 1) was estimated. The selection criterion between the different forecasting models is the square root of the mean square of the error (RMSE). Table 1 shows the results of the contrasted models.

Table 1. Model of statistical learning proposed

Model	Specification/kernel	RSME
ARIMA	(0,1,1)	1,748
SVM1	Radial	1,031
SVM2	Linear	1,678
SVM3	Polynomial	3,396

According to the performance of the forecast of the compared models, it can be observed that the non-linear behavior of the series is better captured through the SVM with radial kernel function, this allows generating a lower RMSE, the second-best model it is the SVM with kernel and linear and in third place the ARIMA model (Fig. 5).

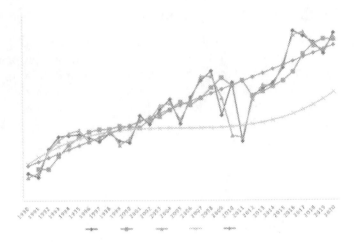

Fig. 5. Comparison of the forecast between the different models

It is observed that the fit of the SVM model with radial kernel is the clos-est to the real behavior of the series. However, it should be noted that it is a semi-parametric method, so it is not possible to estimate confidence inverts in the estimates as in the case of the ARIMA models, in the same way, the fore-cast horizon is short-term. Based on the selected model, forecasts with a 3-year horizon were estimated, which will be updated according to the frequency of the information (Fig. 6). The proposed model will be one more component of the simulation model, through an interface the simulation data will be updated as well as the forecasts in real-time and at the desired frequency when required.

The integration of machine learning methodologies, especially SVM, have shown great adaptability to real data that present non-linear behavior, likewise the performance of the model as part of a simulation model allows the integration of better quality parameters and constitute an artificial intelligence module that can interact directly with the simulation model, providing feedback for decision-making in real time as well as the evaluation of feasible scenarios in the medium and short term.

4   Results

The process of elaboration of our product, being this furniture's elaborated with wood, consists of two phases; The first being the manufacturing process of the pieces that will later make up an ornamental article, the second process is the one in which the initial inspection of the manufactured pieces is carried out, to later put them together and make a final product (Table 2).

In the first phase of the process, the raw material is required, which is col-lected and transported by means of a forklift vehicle to a lathe, which is the set of machines and tools that allow machining, threading, cutting, drilling, turning,

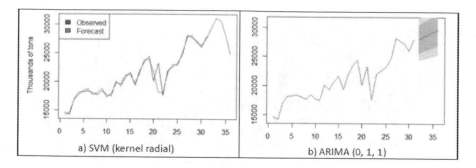

Fig. 6. Forecast SVM (Kernel radial) vs ARIMA (0, 1, 1)

Table 2. Support vector machine

Parameter	Value
Kernel	Kernel
Optimal cost	0.01
Gamma-value	0.005319149
Number of support Vectors	4086
Mean square error	0.2172682

roughing and grooving the pieces in a geometric way by means of their revolution. Once the pieces leave the lathe, they go through the first inspection stage, in which it is verified that the pieces have been made correctly and that they have the size and quality required to continue with the following processes.

Once the piece goes through this inspection process and it has been verified that it is in optimal conditions, it is transferred to the table drill, where the piece is drilled with the help of HSS Drills. At the same time that this happens, in the same table drill, the part goes through a removal process using brushes and sanding discs. Once again, after this process, the part is inspected and if it is in good condition, it goes to the next stage of the process.

If the piece requires a bending process, which refers to the process in which an electric motor is used to power a flywheel, which, adjusted to a clutch, moves the crank that drives the piston up and down, this they exert force on the cylinder with air pressure and thus, the part bends, the procedure is carried out and after this process, it is inspected again to know its state. However, if the part does not require this process, it goes directly to the next stage.

When the piece passes the inspection, it is transferred through a conveyor (conveyor belts), to the second phase of the process, the final inspection of the pieces. In this part, the pieces are valued and inspected to determine if they are in an optimal state to be used as parts of a final piece (furniture) (Figs. 7 and 8).

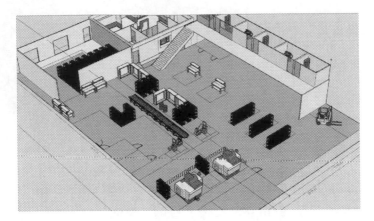

Fig. 7. Plant layout

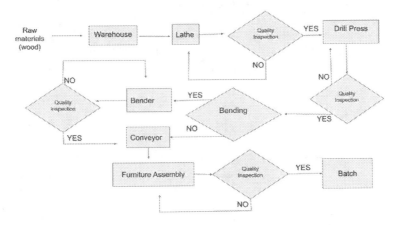

Fig. 8. Manufacturing process flow chart

If the pieces are approved in each of the previous processes, they are used for the assembly of the furniture. In the event that any of the aforementioned inspections do not pass, the pieces are returned to the beginning of the process and reworked.

Once the furniture has been assembled with the pieces made in the initial processes, it goes to the last inspection stage, in which it is verified that it is in the optimal conditions to be used and that it passes all the quality principles.

Finally, the final piece is transferred to a winery, where the batches will be created that will later be marketed.

The results show how product demand can be predicted using a recursive process based on SVM. In this work, an interface was developed to connect the SVM process encoded in Python and the discrete event simulation process in specialized software. This proposal corroborates how it is possible to nest machine learning processes in the simulation and optimization of events.

References

1. Belousov, A., Verzakov, S., Von Frese, J.: A flexible classification approach with optimal generalisation performance: support vector machines. Chemom. Intell. Lab. Syst. **64**(1), 15–25 (2002)
2. Burges, C.J.: A tutorial on support vector machines for pattern recognition. Data Min. Knowl. Discov. **2**(2), 121–167 (1998)
3. Demlehner, Q., Schoemer, D., Laumer, S.: How can artificial intelligence enhance car manufacturing? A Delphi study-based identification and assessment of general use cases. Int. J. Inf. Manag. **58**, 102317 (2021)
4. Hastie, T., Tibshirani, R., Friedman, J.: The Elements of Statistical Learning: Data Mining, Inference, and Prediction. 333. Springer, New York (2009). https://doi.org/10.1007/978-0-387-84858-7
5. Monostori, L., Kádár, B., Viharos, Z., Mezgár, I., Stefán, P.: AI and ML techniques combined with simulation for designing and controlling manufacturing processes and systems. IFAC Proc. Vol. **33**(20), 181–186 (2000). https://doi.org/10.1016/S1474-6670(17)38046-1, https://www.sciencedirect.com/science/article/pii/S1474667017380461, iFAC Symposium on Manufacturing Modelling, Management and Control (MIM 2000), Rio, Greece, 12–14 July 2000
6. Mukherjee, S., Osuna, E., Girosi, F.: Nonlinear prediction of chaotic time series using support vector machines. In: Neural Networks for Signal Processing VII. Proceedings of the 1997 IEEE Signal Processing Society Workshop, pp. 511–520. IEEE (1997)
7. Smola, A.J., Schölkopf, B.: A tutorial on support vector regression. Stat. Comput. **14**(3), 199–222 (2004)
8. Steringer, R., Zörrer, H., Zambal, S., Eitzinger, C.: Using discrete event simulation in multiple system life cycles to support zero-defect composite manufacturing in aerospace industry. IFAC-PapersOnLine **52**(13), 1467–1472 (2019). https://doi.org/10.1016/j.ifacol.2019.11.406, https://www.sciencedirect.com/science/article/pii/S2405896319313874, 9th IFAC Conference on Manufacturing Modelling, Management and Control MIM 2019
9. Tay, F.E., Cao, L.: Application of support vector machines in financial time series forecasting. Omega **29**(4), 309–317 (2001)
10. Thissen, U., Van Brakel, R., De Weijer, A., Melssen, W., Buydens, L.: Using support vector machines for time series prediction. Chemom. Intell. Lab. Syst. **69**(1–2), 35–49 (2003)
11. Vapnik, V., Golowich, S.E., Smola, A., et al.: Support vector method for function approximation, regression estimation, and signal processing. In: Advances in Neural Information Processing Systems, pp. 281–287 (1997)
12. Velásquez, J.D., Olaya, Y., Franco, C.J.: Time series prediction using support vector machines. Ingeniare **18**(1), 64–75 (2010)
13. Vieira, J.F.M.: Global vehicle sales fell 43% in April (2020). https://fiatgroupworld.com/2020/06/03/global-vehicle-sales-fell-43-in-april/

Digital Twin in the Agri-Food Supply Chain: A Literature Review

Letizia Tebaldi🆔, Giuseppe Vignali🆔, and Eleonora Bottani(✉)🆔

Department of Engineering and Architecture, University of Parma, Parco Area delle Scienze 181/A, 43124 Parma, Italy
eleonora.bottani@unipr.it

Abstract. The present manuscript aims at presenting some preliminary results from a literature review carried out on the existing documents dealing with Digital Twin models within the context of agri-food supply chain, in order to assess the state-of-art of such new technology for this promising field. The analysis considers both descriptive metrics (i.e., year of publication, research type, geographical origin and keywords analysis) and qualitative aspects (i.e., subdivision according to the supply chain phase involved and data-driven *versus* physic-based modelling of the Digital Twin solutions presented in the documents).

Keywords: Digital twin · Industry4.0 · Agri-food supply chain · Literature review · Food industry

1 Introduction

As one of the keywords of the Industry4.0 paradigm is "digitalization", recent technologies enabling this digitalization are not missed, of course.

One of these, is the Digital Twin (DT). A DT is basically defined as *a virtual representation of a physical system (and its associated environment and processes) that is updated through the exchange of information between the physical and virtual system* [1], typically involved for real-time prediction, monitoring, control and optimization of the asset for the improved decision-making throughout the life cycle of the asset and beyond [2]. In other words, a DT reflects the physical status of a system in a virtual space [3], thus allowing to describe the process, the product or the service through mathematical models in order to carry out analyses based on data collected from sensors, from experts or from other machines integrated with historical data [4]. According to that, they allow to reply to the question "what happens if…?" without carrying out physical experiments, but just through analyses and simulations.

DTs are implemented in different contexts; for instance, within the field of medicine e.g. for simulating cardiac electrophysiology [5] or for enabling the vision of precision cardiology by building a DT of a patient [6] or even for defining personalized therapies for precision oncology [7]. Within the field of education, for instance for creating a holographic classroom in order to promote the reform and reconstruction of learning

© IFIP International Federation for Information Processing 2021
Published by Springer Nature Switzerland AG 2021
A. Dolgui et al. (Eds.): APMS 2021, IFIP AICT 633, pp. 276–283, 2021.
https://doi.org/10.1007/978-3-030-85910-7_29

spaces and learning modes [8] or for the development of the DT of a smart campus for monitoring the comfort [9]. Again, several applications were developed in the industrial context; in this light, as in this field the DT technology is more spread, the authors recall interesting literature reviews on different specific areas in which the DT turned out to be implementable and relevant, such as that of safety in manufacturing [10], additive manufacturing [11] or maintenance [12]. It follows that DT solutions can be involved for different purposes.

Remaining in the industrial sphere, the aim of this paper is to investigate the state-of-art of literature related to a promising field for DT solutions, namely that of agri-food supply chains (AFSC in the following). Dealing with products, quite often temperature sensitive, having specific constraints (e.g., the shelf-life) and being constituted by different actors having different roles in different supply chains [13], the AFSC has great challenges to face and can offer interesting research insights related to digitalization; however, as it will be highlighted in this manuscript, this technology is still at an embryonic stage in this field as also demonstrated by the limited number of documents found. Indeed, to this end, a literature review was carried out on 14 scientific papers, analyzing both descriptive and qualitative aspects. Despite there are other literature reviews dealing with DT applications such as those already mentioned few lines above, none of them is focused on a specific industrial sector; hence the novelty of the paper, since there are no evidences of previous studies referring to the AFSC.

The remainder of the paper is as follows: Sect. 2 describes the methodology, followed by Sect. 3 in which descriptive parameters are illustrated and Sect. 4 which deals with the contents analysis. Finally, brief conclusions are provided in Sect. 5.

2 Methodology

In August 2020 different queries were launched on respectively Scopus (www.scopus.com), Web of Sciences (www.webofknowledge.com) and Google Scholar (scholar.google.com) databases, including keywords dealing with the topic in question, i.e. "digital twin" AND "food", "digital twin" AND "food industry", "digital twin" AND "cold chain"; note that for exporting results from the Google Scholar, the software Publish or Perish (https://harzing.com/resources/publish-or-perish) was also involved, returning more than 1,000 documents. No constraints on type, year of publication or language were set.

After a careful check on title and abstract, the sample turned out to be constituted of 14 papers; this result is in line with Scopus and Web of Science outcomes (19 papers for the first and 9 for the second), since Publish or Perish allows to access documents in which the selected keywords appear everywhere in the full text (even in the reference lists, for instance), and the number of off topic papers was extremely high. Specifically, the documents included are 6 journal papers and 8 conference papers.

At first, descriptive parameters were investigated, namely year of publication, research type, geographical origin and keywords analysis. Then, the contents analysis follows: papers were firstly divided according to the phase of the supply chain they deal with, and then according to the modelling used in the development of the DT (i.e. physic-based or data-driven). In the following, these aspects will be clearly deepened and better defined.

3 Descriptive Analysis

3.1 Temporal Evolution

The first aspect investigated is the year of publication of the 14 papers constituting the sample. The first document appears in 2017, highlighting the novelty of the topic, and it is the only one published in that year. Two papers were instead written the subsequent year, i.e. 2018, eight in 2019, the most productive year, and finally three in 2020. Note that for this last year four months are missed due to the period in which this study was carried out, and it is reasonable to expect that more papers could have been published.

Hence, the trend can be defined as timidly positive.

3.2 Type of Research

The second descriptive parameter considered is the type of research presented in the 14 papers. This classification is particularly useful for understanding the state-of-art of projects and applications of DT solutions.

Specifically, four types of research were recognized:

- *Review*: documents dealing with literature analysis related on a specific aspect;
- *Technical papers*: papers in which the development and implementation of a DT solution within the food context is treated, however without practical outcomes and implementations (in other words, only dealing with theoretical applications);
- *Partial Experiments*: documents dealing with the preliminary presentation of results or on a specific phase of the development of a DT;
- *Application Papers*: full practical applications and implementation of a DT solution.

Within the sample, two papers were identified as being literature reviews, five technical papers, three partial experiments and finally four full application papers.

It follows that most of the papers do not deal with a full presentation of a DT solution; indeed, most of the documents present partial applications or are limited to the design phase of how the solution could be implemented or illustrated the benefits which could be achieved.

These outcomes gain further value if we consider the type of research linked to the year of publication, shown in Table 1.

Table 1. Type of research related to the year of publication.

Publication year	Reviews	Technical papers	Partial experiments	Application papers
2017	–	1	–	–
2018	–	2	–	–
2019	1	1	3	3
2020	1	1	–	1
Total	2	5	3	4

As it is possible to note, 2019 can be considered a year of considerable development of the technology, both from the point of view of application papers and from the partial experiments side, suggesting that many projects are currently in progress; 2018, instead, is the year presenting most of the technical papers (two). According to that, the subdivision turned out to be consistent with the time trend and the evolution of the topic: the first documents do not enter specifically in full applications and are preliminary presentations, but are progressively oriented towards the implementation of solutions.

3.3 Geographical Distribution

The geographical origin of the documents, aiming at assessing most productive countries or regions, was made according to the affiliation of the first author of the document. Due to the small number of papers constituting the sample, results are presented according to the continents rather than on the specific countries. Specifically, most of the contributions come from Europe (seven documents), followed by America (four), Asia (two) and Africa (one). No papers from Oceania. This could be actually due to the fact that in Europe and America we find the most industrialized countries, having also an intensive food production.

By further deepening, it is worth mentioning the United States with three publications, and Switzerland again with three documents, two of which proposed by the same team of authors and dealing with the mango cold chain, recalled in the content analysis.

3.4 Keywords Analysis

Quite common in studies of this kind among the descriptive parameters, is the keywords analysis [14]. Due to the limited number of papers, only the absolute frequency is considered. A total of 64 keywords was identified, and they were divided into three macro-categories according to the topic they represent: "digitalization", "AFSC" and, finally, "other" in case of particular keywords not belonging to the two previous classes and accordingly off topic compared to the topic of this review.

In the first class we find 27 keywords; due to constraints set on the length of the paper, we only refer to those having frequency equal or greater than two, namely, as expected, digital twin (with a frequency of 9), artificial intelligence (2), internet of things (2) and robotics (2). The relation with artificial intelligence is immediate; indeed, DTs are also defined as artificial intelligent virtual replicas of physical systems [15]. Internet of things as well is quite obvious, since this technology is one of the enabling technologies allowing the development and implementation of DT solutions, while robotics is one of the fields of potential applications of DT.

In the second class, related to the AFSC, all the 13 keywords found have frequency equal to 1; the only one in line with the topic of this study are food equipment, food security, cold chain and food. The remaining (e.g., mangos or livestock disease) are quite far from our specific argument and more niche and specific.

The last class, less important, includes keywords considered off-topic, such as sustainability, pharmaceutical, pandemic, or safety, referring to the content of the papers.

4   Contents Analysis

The most interesting outcomes originate from the contents analysis. For this purpose, the authors decided to divide papers according to the phase of supply chain to which the DT solution is intended to be implemented, or at least studied, and according to the modelling of the DT itself, namely if it is data-driven or physic-based.

As far as the first subdivision, it is worth recalling that in an AFSC, and more in general in a supply chain, three phases are identifiable: the supply stage, the production stage and finally the distribution. In this context, however, by "supply" we mean a phase in which the product is treated as raw material, including activities such as cultivation or farming; the remaining two stages deal with industrial transformation and subsequent distribution. For the second classification, instead, by "data-driven modeling" we mean a DT whose analysis is made on historical and collected data elaborated through Machine Learning tools, while by "physic-based" it is meant a model based on a physics approach, namely relying on the observation of a real phenomenon and then on the formulation of mathematical equations which can describe it and provide for resolutions on the bases of different behaviors. In the below subsections results are illustrated.

4.1   Classification According to the Supply Chain Phase

Overall, we identified 6 papers dealing with the first supply chain phase, 5 with the second and, finally, 3 with the third. It immediately emerges that the most investigated area is that related to the raw materials production, while less attention has been payed towards the distribution stage, despite its relevance above all when dealing with cold chains. This is in line with the spread of the topics of Smart Farming and Precision Farming, as a result of the paradigm of Agriculture 4.0, including DT solutions [16].

For the sake of brevity not all the studies are mentioned, only the most interesting.

Dealing with the first phase, we found the work by [17], who proposed an innovative system for improving irrigation; by [18] who presented a model to implement DTs in sustainable agriculture, specifically through the joint creation of physical and digital layers of IoT-enabled structures for vertical farming; by [19], who discuss the possibility of creating a DT of the planet Earth to determine and quantify the environmental impact of innovations in agriculture; by [20], who developed a DT for replicating and simulating a livestock farming to face livestock disorders; finally, by [21] who studied the implementation of DT for aquaponics in the fisheries sector, with control and monitoring purposes. For a complete overview, finally, we mention the literature review by [22], whose focus is on general DT applications in supply chains, but has a section dedicated to the implementation in food contexts and precision agriculture.

Related to the transformation phase, i.e. the second one, we found five studies, whose attention is shifted to the industrial production. In particular, relating to this phase we found the oldest paper, by [23], in which the DT is implemented for monitoring the variation of CO_2, temperature, humidity and PH in the three steps of the malting process; we also found an application to a whole water bottling line for optimizing production and avoiding bottlenecks [24]; finally, a DT of a pasteurizer was developed for operators' risk prevention [25].

The less debated aspect, as already stressed, is related to the distribution stage; in this case only three studies have dealt with this issue, and among these the already mentioned Swiss papers, [26] and [27], in which a DT of a mango is proposed, in order to study its cooling level and determine its impact on the quality of the fruit during the transportation and storing stages; in the first paper the project and the general architecture are presented (partial experiment), while in the second one, various simulations of the system behavior were carried out (application paper).

4.2   Data-Driven *vs.* Physic-Based Modeling

The second and last qualitative aspect under investigation is the nature of the modelling for developing the DT solutions, with the meaning detailed at the beginning of the present section. Overall, we found 7 data-driven papers and 4 physics-based ones; clearly for the 2 reviews this aspect was not determined, as well as a for a single paper in which different solutions for farming were proposed. Table 2 below summarizes results from this classification, including the linkage with the supply chain phase. It is interesting to note that for the transformation step, exception made for one document, all the DT models are data-driven; indeed, for industrial processes it is easier to collect data, both in terms of input and output.

Table 2. Classification of the modelling linked to the supply chain phase.

Modelling	Phase		
	Supply	Transformation	Distribution
Physics-based	2	–	2
Data-driven	2	4	1
Not available	2	1	–

5   Conclusions

The present paper aimed at presenting some key results from a literature review carried out on 14 papers whose focus was the development or the implementation of Digital Twin solutions in the field of agri-food supply chains, a promising context for solutions of this kind, above all, as emerged, in the agriculture field.

For sure, we are aware of the limited number of papers under investigation; however, this actually can be seen as a symptom of the fact that specific literature and applications of this kind are still lacking and are at an embryonic stage.

However, it can be conjectured that this technology can bring multiple benefits. First of all, it allows monitoring and identifying process anomalies in a timely manner, but above all it makes it possible to make predictions of these anomalies and possible behaviors either through Machine Learning algorithms or by solving complex physical equations. Moreover, an automated management of production systems can be allowed, as well as resource usage optimization, fundamental aspects in the light of the challenges that our planet is currently facing.

Being a recent and innovative technology within the AFSC, several insights can be provided. Specifically, further analyses and studies related to the food industrial production are highly recommended, thus enabling savings and higher efficiency of processes. Moreover, for sure it is in plan to extend the literature review and the sample size by the end of the year, in order to include more recent studies, hopefully numerous.

Finally, note that for those interested readers the full list of reviewed papers can be made available, as well as the Excel spreadsheets used for the analyses.

References

1. VanDerHorn, E., Mahadevan, S.: Digital twin: generalization, characterization and implementation. Decis. Support Syst. **145**, 113524 (2021)
2. Rasheed, A., San, O., Kvamsdal, T.: Digital twin: values, challenges and enablers. Electrical Engineering and Systems Science (2019)
3. Lim, K.Y.H., Zheng, P., Chen, C.-H.: A state-of-the-art survey of digital twin: techniques, engineering product lifecycle management and business innovation perspectives. J. Intell. Manuf. **31**(6), 1313–1337 (2019). https://doi.org/10.1007/s10845-019-01512-w
4. Bevilacqua, M., Bottani, E., Ciarapica, F., Costantino, F., Di Donato, L., et al.: Digital twin reference model development to prevent operators' risk in process plants. Sustainability **12**(3), 1088 (2020)
5. Pagani, S., Dede', L., Manzoni, A., Quarteroni, A.: Data integration for the numerical simulation of cardiac electrophysiology. PACE - Pacing and Electrophysiology (2021)
6. Corral-Acero, J., Margara, F., Marciniak, M., Rodero, C., Loncaric, F., Feng, Y., et al.: The "digital twin" to enable the vision of precision cardiology. Eur. Heart J. **41**(48), 4556-4564B (2020)
7. Schade, S., Ogilvie, L., Kessler, T., Schütte, M., Wierling, C., et al.: A data- and model-driven approach for cancer treatment. Onkologe **25**, 109–115 (2019)
8. Shuguang, L., Lin, B.: Holographic classroom based on digital twin and its application prospect. In: 2020 IEEE 3rd International Conference on Electronics and Communication Engineering, ICECE (2020)
9. Zaballos, A., Briones, A., Massa, A., Centelles, P., Caballero, V.: A smart campus' digital twin for sustainable comfort monitoring. Sustainability **12**(21), 1–33 (2020)
10. Agnusdei, G., Elia, V., Gnoni, M.: A classification proposal of digital twin applications in the safety domain. Comput. Ind. Eng. **154**, 107137 (2021)
11. Zhang, L., Chen, X., Zhou, W., Cheng, T., Chen, L., et al.: Digital twins for additive manufacturing: a state-of-the-art review. Appl. Sci. **10**(23), 1–10 (2020)
12. Errandonea, I., Beltrán, S., Arrizabalaga, S.: Digital Twin for maintenance: a literature review. Comput. Ind. **123**, 103316 (2020)
13. van der Vorst, J., da Silva, C., Trienekens, J.: Agro-industrial supply chain management: concepts and applications. http://www.fao.org/3/a1369e/a1369e.pdf. Accessed 29 Mar 2021
14. Fadlalla, A., Amani, F.: A keyword-based organizing framework for ERP intellectual contributions. J. Enterp. Inf. Manag. **28**, 637–657 (2015)
15. Barricelli, B., Casiraghi, E., Fogli, D.: A survey on digital twin: definitions, characteristics, applications, and design implications. IEEE Access **7**, 167653–167671 (2019)
16. Verdouw, C., Tekinerdogan, B., Beulens, A., Wolfert, S.: Digital twins in smart farming. Agric. Syst. **189**, 103046 (2021)

17. Gomes Alves, R., Souza, G., Filev Maia, R., Tran, A., Kamienski, C., et al.: A digital twin for smart farming. In: IEEE Global Humanitarian Technology Conference (GHTC 2019), Seattle, USA (2019)

18. Monteiro, J., Barata, J., Veloso, M., Nunes, J.: Towards sustainable digital twins for vertical farming. In: 2018 Thirteenth International Conference on Digital Information Management (ICDIM), Berlin, Germany (2018)

19. Delgrado, J., Short, N., Roberts, D., Vandenberg, B.: Big data analysis for sustainable agriculture on a geospatial cloud framework. Front. Sustain. Food Syst. **3**, 54 (2019)

20. Jo, S., Park, D., Kim, S.: Smart livestock farms using digital twin: feasibility study. In: 2018 International Conference on Information and Communication Technology Convergence (ICTC), Jeju, Korea (South) (2018)

21. Ahmed, A., Zulfiqar, S., Ghandar, A., Chen, Y., Hanai, M., Theodoropoulos, G.: Digital twin technology for aquaponics: towards optimizing food production with dynamic data driven application systems. In: Tan, G., Lehmann, A., Teo, Y.M., Cai, W. (eds.) AsiaSim 2019. CCIS, vol. 1094, pp. 3–14. Springer, Singapore (2019). https://doi.org/10.1007/978-981-15-1078-6_1

22. Srai, J., Settanni, E., Tsolakis, N., Aulakh, P.: Supply chain digital twins: opportunities and challenges beyond the hype. In: 23rd Cambridge International Manufacturing Symposium - University of Cambridge, Cambridge, UK (2019)

23. Dolci, R.: IoT solutions for precision farming and food manufacturing: artificial intelligence applications in digital food. In: 2017 IEEE 41st Annual Computer Software and Applications Conference (COMPSAC), Turin, Italy (2017)

24. Gericke, G., Kuriakose, R., Vermaak, H., Mardsen, O.: Design of digital twins for optimization of a water bottling plant. In: IECON 2019 - 45th Annual Conference of the IEEE Industrial Electronics Society (2019)

25. Bottani, E., Vignali, G., Tancredi, G.: A digital twin model of a pasteurization system for food beverages: tools and architecture. In: 2020 IEEE International Conference on Engineering, Technology and Innovation (ICE/ITMC), Cardiff, UK (2020)

26. Defraeye, T., Tagliavini, G., Wu, W., Prawiranto, K., Schudel, S., et al.: Digital twins probe into food cooling and biochemical quality changes for reducing losses in refrigerated supply chains. Resour. Conserv. Recycl. **149**, 778–794 (2019)

27. Tagliavini, G., Defraeye, T., Carmeliet, J.: Multiphysics modeling of convective cooling of non-spherical, multi-material fruit to unveil its quality evolution throughout the cold chain. Food Bioprod. Process. **117**, 310–320 (2019)

A Digital Twin Implementation for Manufacturing Based on Open-Source Software and Standard Control Systems

Christian Dalheim Øien[(✉)], Håkon Dahl, and Sebastian Dransfeld

SINTEF Manufacturing, Enggata 40, 2830 Raufoss, Norway
christian.dalheim.oien@sintef.no

Abstract. The concept of Digital Twins (DTs) can be utilized to solve complex problems in manufacturing based on the principle of Cyber-Physical Systems (CPS). While there are several reference architectures for CPS, there seems to be a knowledge gap between such high-level outlines and actual shopfloor-level implementations. This paper focuses on process control applications of the DT concept and proposes a specific implementation setup using fieldbus communication with a computer, aiming to fulfil a set of defined requirements. The setup is tested in an industrial use-case and the resulting characteristics of the solution are presented. A resulting assertion is that a DT of a process must be as specialized and customized as the system controlling it.

Keywords: Digital twins · Cyber-physical production systems · Smart manufacturing · Process control

1 Introduction

The principle of Cyber-Physical Systems (CPS) is often a desired base for implementing decision-making autonomy and self-adaptiveness of machines in industry. A CPS is the integration of a virtual world that interacts with a physical world [1]. Through interconnection, the computational part of the system can monitor, control and affect the physical process, and vice versa [2]. Lee et al. proposed the 5C reference architecture for implementation of a CPS [3] which describes five necessary functional levels named connection, conversion, cyber, cognition and configuration. This gives a conceptual understanding of the main constituents of a CPS, but they do not correspond specifically to necessary technology or implementation methods.

Another Smart Manufacturing approach that has been given much attention in research recent years is the Digital Twin (DT) concept. While dating back to 2003 as a virtual representation of a physical product or process [4], a consensus of its actual meaning is still not reached. A literature review conducted by Kritzinger et al. [5] categorized Digital Twin-related papers based on data integration level between physical assets and their digital representation. This resulted in the following three-level classification

A. Dolgui et al. (Eds.): APMS 2021, IFIP AICT 633, pp. 284–291, 2021.
https://doi.org/10.1007/978-3-030-85910-7_30

scheme; 1) Digital Models are characterized by manual data transfer, 2) Digital Shadows are characterized by one-way automatic data transfer from physical to digital, and finally that 3) *Digital Twins are characterized by two-way automatic data integration.*

In slight contrast to Kritzinger et al. [5], VanDerHorn and Mahadevan [6] proposed, on the basis of on 46 different definitions found in literature, a generalised definition of a DT as "*a virtual representation of a physical system (and its associated environment and processes) that is updated through the exchange of information between the physical and virtual systems*". Consequently, this definition does not strictly require a two-way data integration and invites for a more open understanding. VanDerHorn and Mahadevan in fact stated that a requirement of two-way data interaction is restrictive and could exclude applications where the output is not intended to be used automatically in a machine-interaction but, for instance, as an operator interaction via a human-machine-interface (HMI). As a contrast, it is an underlying perspective behind this paper that the transition of small and medium-sized enterprises (SMEs) towards digital manufacturing rely on data integration solutions at process level, and specifically, that they need to be cost-effective, use open-source software, need relatively few hardware components, and are based on an easily understandable framework. At the same time, it seems this perspective is little represented in current research.

Regardless of the definition used, several sources found in literature describe CPS and DT as high-level shopfloor integrations that can enhance a large part of a value chain. While such integration can bring significant value to larger companies, it requires complex and expensive solutions that would be inappropriate for most SMEs that, in the sense of digital transformation, are more likely to benefit from process level enhancements. Furthermore, as this section is intended to show, DT concepts and implementations found in literature are often used as simulation models with the purpose of conducting offline studies leading to optimizations of production plans or layouts, and not as a means of process enhancement based on data integration.

1.1 State of the Art of Manufacturing DT Applications

Tao et al. [7] have done a systematic review of the state-of-the-art of industrial DTs and concluded that production control and prognostics and health managements were the most relevant areas covering more than two-thirds of the applications. Out of 50 papers this review points to only one related to an interacting and collaborating DT, i.e., with a data integration focus. That paper, written by Vachálek et al. [8], describes a setup that simulates an assembly line for hydraulic pistons in order to optimize its production plan, using the proprietary software SIEMENS Tecnomatix Plant Simulation [9]. The study does not involve a two-way data integration providing feedback to the physical process, but proposes, however, an enhanced operator feedback based on potential inconsistencies between simulation result and actual measurements.

The aforementioned literature review by Kritzinger et al. [5] covers 43 DT-related papers, out of which 12 describing case-studies, and characterized only one of them as using a two-way data integration. In that study, Bottani et al. [10] implemented a DT in a laboratory setting for independent decision making of an automated guided vehicle (AGV) in the sense that scheduling problems solved by a decision-making algorithm were executed remotely in addition to locally on the AGV microcontroller. The paper, however, does not state which value or enhanced functionality this lead to.

Cimino et al. [11] reviewed and categorized 52 manufacturing related DT applications out of which 19 were classified as aiming to monitor and improve the production process. Only one out of these involved process enhancement, namely Karanjkar et al. [12] who used a DT approach to suggest an enhanced process flow in a Printed Circuit Board (PCB) assembly line that would reduce its energy consumption. In this application, analyses were done offline based on historical data in order to tag machine states and then calculate the energy consumption per state. Based on these state-wise energy consumptions and a discrete-event simulation model made using SimPy [13] the authors identified process flow enhancements. The generated information was, however, neither used for process control via a data connection back to the control system of the production line nor for operator feedback via HMI.

1.2 Research Question and Scope

None of the above three referenced DT applications [8, 10, 12] exemplify an automated use of information generated by the DT. This paper, however, focuses on using the DT concept for enhanced control of manufacturing processes that, due to complexity and varying conditions, cannot be robustly and accurately controlled by a standard process control algorithm using a programmable logic controller (PLC) only. Instead, in such cases, the control accuracy could be increased through a two-way data integration between the PLC and a DT enabling a more advanced process control based on real-time analyses. The research question that this paper seeks to answer is – *What is a viable method for implementing a process control DT in an SME, that ensures the needed functionality while being easy to understand, maintain and adjust?* In order to do this, a set of requirements for such DT implementations is suggested in Sect. 2, as well as an explicit implementation method that fulfils those requirements. An industry use-case is described in Sect. 3 where the resulting DT characteristics and performance is described while a discussion is given in Sect. 4. The use-case itself is not concluded and its specific results are therefore not part of this paper.

2 Method

In an industry use-case related to increasing the process control robustness and accuracy of a machine, a DT with two-way data integration was developed. In the work with defining a suitable implementation setup, the following requirement was defined – *A process Digital Twin implementation should ensure programmability and availability of support through standardized software, without impeding the desired functionality.* An application written in Python running on an industrial PC (IPC) equipped with a high-speed PLC communication interface was consequently chosen as an outline for the DT.

Python is one of the most used general-purpose programming languages and it gives the application a fair chance of being understood by operations or maintenance engineers. Other advantages are a high number of available libraries and easily accessible support from a vast web user community. These were all desired key characteristics of the solution.

In terms of connectivity, the use of a fieldbus interface was chosen. As industrial edge computing solutions are designed to enable fast database interactions and applications with reduced bandwidth consumption, its general area of application is to store and do computations on production data. However, in most cases it is not used for deterministic, millisecond-level, two-way communication with PLCs. Based on the categorization done in [5] one could claim that industrial edge computing is mainly suitable for digital model or digital shadow functionality when it comes to single process applications. In order to achieve a two-way data integration with a PLC and the mentioned communication characteristics, a fieldbus communication interface seemed to be the best option. For practical reasons, PROFINET was chosen.

As a conclusion, the following specific requirements are suggested for SME DT applications related to process control enhancements.

- Uses deterministic, millisecond-level, two-way communication with one PLC
- Facilitates easy visualization and analysis of received PLC data
- Is based on program code that is intended to be easy to maintain and customize
- Is cost-effective

2.1 Industrial Use-Case

The studied use-case focuses on the control of two magnetic induction ovens that pre-heat aluminium extrusion billets. These billets are cast cylinders of aluminium alloy approximately 1 m in length and 0.3 m in diameter. The ovens heat up one billet each from room temperature to about 500 °C with a cycle time of around 4 min. They work by each rotating four separate ring-shaped assemblies of permanent magnets around the billets at about 1500 rpm using an individual electrical motor per magnet assembly. The heating process is intended to ensure a certain temperature profile along the longitudinal direction of the billets which is beneficial for the proceeding extrusion process.

As the magnet rings cover most of the billets their temperatures are only measured on the billet ends during heating, and then measured on several surface positions along the billet length after completion of each process cycle. Process control is ensured by a SIEMENS PLC maintaining rotational speed and longitudinal position of the four magnet rings according to a pre-defined recipe and continues the process until set-point temperatures at the billet ends have been reached. This control method is, however, unable to accurately account for the following characteristics and dependencies.

- The magnetic field from each single magnet is non-uniform.
- The magnetic field strength is dependent on the temperature of the magnets.
- The billet specific heat capacity is dependent on local aluminium temperature.
- An end-effect reduces the magnetic induction in regions close to the billet ends.

Due to the variation resulting from these characteristics the original heating process control leads to an accuracy of around 5% for the temperature profile. This causes an unwanted variability of the main extrusion process leading to suboptimal stability of product quality and overall equipment effectiveness (OEE). The aim of the DT approach is to combine the capabilities of the PLC with the computational power of an IPC and increase the accuracy to around 1%. Based on finite element analysis (FEA) and thermal dynamics calculations, the DT setup will allow for an estimation of the final temperature profile to be regularly updated and returned to the PLC for usage in an improved control routine. Based on initial work with FEA, it is estimated that the temperature profile can be calculated within one or two seconds which makes it possible for the PLC to do 100 logic-based adjustments during a single process cycle.

2.2 Digital Twin Implementation

The DT setup in this use-case facilitates the use of Python-based software to perform estimations and calculations on an IPC, along with a communication interface between the PLC and IPC via PROFINET fieldbus. An Ixxat® INpact PIR Slave PCIe [14] dedicated device card on the IPC was used to send and receive data in the form of struct object instances. The struct types were defined on the PLC in Structured Text (ST) according to IEC 61131-3.

Specifically, three main parts of source code ensure the DT functionality. Firstly, 288 lines of Python code that translates the ST struct definition from the PLC to Python. Secondly, 772 lines of C code and 118 lines of Python code handling the I/O communication between the PLC and the actual DT Python program. This is done by making use of an application programming interface (API) with the device card (which requires the C code). Thirdly, 20 lines of Python code defining a main loop that sets up the connection and works as interface for the user program.

By this setup, the bytes of data that the struct consist of can be sent between the PLC and the IPC without overhead, as the C code receives and forwards them via a socket connection to the Python program which has been provided with identical struct definitions. This communication concept is illustrated in Fig. 1.

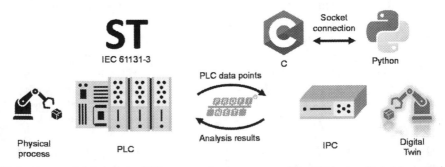

Fig. 1. Process Digital Twin (DT) communication concept. The DT is constituted by a Python program on an IPC where a separate program written in C regularly exchanges data with the PLC over PROFINET fieldbus.

By exchanging data on a predefined, bytewise format there is no need of descriptions or metadata to be sent on every communication cycle. This way the necessary amount of transferred data is reduced to a minimum, and a millisecond-level communication between the DT and PLC is possible, depending on the amount of data. It is due to the identically defined struct datatype that this is achieved. To visualise the concept, example definitions in Structured Text and Python are shown in Fig. 2. This specific struct would require 29 bytes of data.

```
TYPE "Regulator_Data"
VERSION : 0.1
    STRUCT
        Version : Byte;
        timestamp : UDInt;
        alloy : DInt;
        length : Real;
        actual_speed_rpm : Real;
        actual_motor_temperature : Real;
        actual_torque : Real;
        temperature_front : Real;
    END_STRUCT;

END_TYPE
```

```
class RegulatorData(BigEndianStructure):
    _pack_ = 2

    _fields_ = [
        ("version", c_byte),
        ("timestamp", c_uint),
        ("alloy", c_int),
        ("length", c_float),
        ("actual_speed_rpm", c_float),
        ("actual_motor_temperature", c_float),
        ("actual_torque", c_float),
        ("temperature_front", c_float),
    ]
```

Fig. 2. Struct definition code excerpt in Structured Text (left) automatically translated to Python (right). An instance of this struct would require 29 bytes of data.

3   Results

The key result of this study is that the described DT implementation setup enables usage of gathered PLC data points as direct input to an advanced analysis routine, and reversely that it enables the use of the results from that routine as direct input back into the PLC. Generally, any type of analysis could be suitable for this setup, including finite element analysis (FEA), model-based analysis, statistical analysis, and machine learning.

The cycle time for the PROFINET fieldbus was set to 2 ms, which can be handled when sending up to 1440 bytes of data in each direction for each cycle. In a communication test the use-case PLC was set to tag each data package with its internal millisecond clock in order to evaluate jitter. The jitter distribution in Table 1 is based on this test, which had a duration of about 20 min.

Table 1. Number of sent data packages vs. their respective measured cycle time.

	2 ms	3 ms	4 ms	>4 ms
PLC to IPC	543394	14242	247	
IPC to PLC	545187		12692	4

In other words, the set cycle time of 2 ms was achieved for about 97,5% of the sent data packages in both directions. Due to the 2 ms PROFINET cycle time and since new data was only registered at the IPC if the timestamp had changed, we see that occasional packages at 3 ms from the PLC was converted to 4 ms at the IPC. In any case, the IPC-to-PLC communication was shown to be similarly deterministic as the PLC-to-IPC communication. This shows that the setup of C code forwarding data via socket to the Python code handles the 2 ms cycle time well.

For the use-case 446 bytes is sent from PLC to IPC at each cycle, and 182 bytes in the other direction. This is a mix of process parameters that changes sporadically and continuously changing variables. The data is connected to 3 processes, namely the two ovens and a proceeding temperature measuring station. From the aforementioned communication test the sent and received data were stored yielding a total of 174 MB in csv format. However, this was reduced to 9,3 MB by converting the data to Parquet format which is only about 5%. For the single process studied in this use-case it would mean a yearly amount of about 5 TB uncompressed, or 250 GB compressed. On the IPC, reading the csv-data took about 7 s while reading the Parquet-data took about 0.5 s. Hence, the achieved compression ratio makes it realistic to continuously store and analyze data from such systems.

4   Discussion

In this paper it has been intended to substantiate that DT applications meant to be easy to program, customize, and maintain are more likely to succeed than proprietary or turn-key solutions. In other words, as manufacturing processes are predominantly customized for its specific purpose, a DT of a process must be as specialized and customized as the system controlling it. One could say that the specificity required on PLC level, or the 5C connection level [3], will also be required in the higher levels of a CPS framework. Based on this assumption a standardized DT solution with limited configuration possibilities will always yield limited functionality.

The purpose of this study has been to define and evaluate a process level DT setup that achieves a two-way automatic data integration with its physical counterpart. The main motivation for this was to enhance the control of a machine in order to increase product quality and the OEE of the connected production line. It is the authors' understanding that such process level data integration will play an important role in digital transformation of manufacturing SMEs, laying the foundation for higher-level integrations in terms of data, competence, and system ownership. This is a contrast to similar studies found in literature where DT applications do not utilize two-way data integration but instead provide a basis for discrete improvement or enhancement actions.

While the intended usage of FEA is relevant at a second-level communication rate, it was still the wish in the described use-case to establish a millisecond-level two-way communication and a millisecond-level dataset for future analysis. It is not unlikely that other faster analysis methods could be used to further enhance the performance. Furthermore, Parquet compression gave tolerable data amount from continuous logging and does not significantly compromise the reading speed. Keeping a fully detailed dataset for future work was therefore seen as valuable.

Acknowledgements. We wish to thank The Research Council of Norway for their financial contribution to the project *'BIA KPN CPS-Plant'* by which the R&D work in this article was funded.

References

1. Negri, E., Fumagalli, L., Macchi, M.: A review of the roles of digital twin in CPS-based production systems. Procedia Manufact. **11**, 939–948 (2017)
2. Lee, E.A.: Cyber Physical Systems: Design Challenges. IEEE (2008)
3. Lee, J., Bagheri, B., Kao, H.-A.: A cyber physical systems architecture for industry 4.0-based manufacturing systems. Manuf. Lett. **3**, 18–23 (2015)
4. Grieves, M.: Digital Twin: Manufacturing Excellence through Virtual Factory Replication (2015)
5. Kritzinger, W., et al.: Digital twin in manufacturing: a categorical literature review and classification. IFAC-PapersOnLine **51**(11), 1016–1022 (2018)
6. VanDerHorn, E., Mahadevan, S.: Digital twin: generalization, characterization and implementation. Decis. Support Syst. 113524 (2021)
7. Tao, F., et al.: Digital twin in industry: state-of-the-art. IEEE Trans. Industr. Inf. **15**(4), 2405–2415 (2019)
8. Vachálek, J., et al.: The digital twin of an industrial production line within the industry 4.0 concept. In: 2017 21st International Conference on Process Control (PC) (2017)
9. SIEMENS. Plant Simulation & Throughput Optimization. https://www.plm.automation.siemens.com/global/en/products/manufacturing-planning/plant-simulation-throughput-optimization.html
10. Bottani, E., et al.: From the Cyber-Physical System to the Digital Twin: the process development for behaviour modelling of a Cyber Guided Vehicle in M2M logic (2017)
11. Cimino, C., Negri, E., Fumagalli, L.: Review of digital twin applications in manufacturing. Comput. Ind. **113**, 103130 (2019)
12. Karanjkar, N., et al.: Digital twin for energy optimization in an SMT-PCB assembly line. In: 2018 IEEE International Conference on Internet of Things and Intelligence System (IOTAIS) (2018)
13. Overview — SimPy 4.0.2.dev1+g2973dbe documentation. https://simpy.readthedocs.io/en/latest/. Accessed 10 Mar 2021
14. Ixxat®. Industrial Ethernet and fieldbus interface for PCIe, PCIe Mini and M.2. 2021. https://www.ixxat.com/products/products-industrial/inpact-overview/ixxat-inpact—profinet-irt. Accessed 26 Jan 2021

Human-Centered Artificial Intelligence in Smart Manufacturing for the Operator 4.0

Towards Active Learning Based Smart Assistant for Manufacturing

Patrik Zajec[1,2], Jože Martin Rožanec[1,2,3](✉) (iD), Inna Novalija[2] (iD),
Blaž Fortuna[2,3], Dunja Mladenić[2], and Klemen Kenda[1,2,3] (iD)

[1] Jožef Stefan International Postgraduate School,
Jamova 39, 1000 Ljubljana, Slovenia
`joze.rozanec@ijs.si`
[2] Jožef Stefan Institute, Jamova 39, 1000 Ljubljana, Slovenia
[3] Qlector d.o.o., Rovšnikova 7, 1000 Ljubljana, Slovenia

Abstract. Smart assistants in manufacturing can guide and aid on decision-making while also provide means to collect additional insights and information available to the users. A general approach for building a smart assistant that provides users with machine learning forecasts and a sequence of decision-making options is presented in this work. The system provides means for knowledge acquisition by gathering data from users. To minimize interactions and friction with users, we envision active learning can be used to get data labels for most data instances expected to be most informative. The system is demonstrated on a demand forecasting use case in manufacturing. The methodology can be extended to several use cases in manufacturing.

Keywords: Smart assistant · Artificial intelligence · Machine learning · Demand forecasting · Knowledge acquisition · Active learning

1 Introduction

The increasing digitalization of manufacturing has accelerated the information flow. Technologies such as Cyber-Physical Systems (CPS), Industrial Internet of Things (IIoT), and Artificial Intelligence (AI) are bringing an extensive added value into Industry 4.0 value chains [6]. In particular, AI has been successfully researched and applied on several manufacturing tasks (e.g., predictive maintenance, production simulation, and production planning). The advancement of AI and its applications in manufacturing is conditioned by data availability. Though much data is available from software, such as Enterprise Resource Planning (ERP) or Manufacturing Execution Systems (MES), many aspects are not captured by sensors or such software. An example of such information is the collective knowledge, which employees are aware of, but is not captured by existing

---

P. Zajec and J. M. Rozanec—Equal contribution.

© IFIP International Federation for Information Processing 2021
Published by Springer Nature Switzerland AG 2021
A. Dolgui et al. (Eds.): APMS 2021, IFIP AICT 633, pp. 295–302, 2021.
https://doi.org/10.1007/978-3-030-85910-7_31

software integrations. To mitigate this data gap, we propose a software solution with a user interface to collect locally observed collective knowledge [2]. An example of such data acquisition can be feedback collection regarding forecasts, forecast explanations, or decision-making options. Feedback can be provided in an implicit (e.g., by not editing an option) or explicit form (e.g., marking a forecast explanation to be improbable). Another example can be asking the user to input yet unknown data (e.g., a decision taken in a certain context that was not registered in the past). When recommending decision-making options to the user, many decisions must be made: which subset of available decision-making options to display, how to rank them, or how to enable the user to provide useful feedback. We envision active learning to weigh which decision-making options are most informative to the system when users' feedback is provided.

We demonstrate a conceptual design and a developed system that can acquire and encapsulate complex knowledge. The system is based on semantic technologies, considering ontology concepts that are generic and ported to multiple use cases. We demonstrate its usability on demand forecasting, providing recommendations for transport scheduling. The system integrates demand forecasting models, explainable AI (XAI), a decision-making recommender system, and a knowledge graph. The aforementioned components are used to develop decision-making workflows, which are displayed through an interactive user interface. Feedback is collected from users regarding forecasts, forecast explanations, and decision-making options displayed to the users.

2   Related Work

In smart manufacturing, several characteristics (such as context awareness, modularity, heterogeneity, and interoperability) and technologies (such as intelligent control, energy efficiency, cybersecurity, CPS, IoT, data analytics, and IT-based production management) have been identified to play a crucial role [9]. Variety and depth of technologies in Industry 4.0 represent a great potential, and micro-level local units' usage provides the best outcomes [3]. Several risks are associated with the implementation of smart technologies in manufacturing [8] such as i) the perceived risk of novel technologies, ii) the complexity of integration, and iii) the consideration of human factors. As several most accurate AI algorithms (such as gradient boosting or deep neural networks) are difficult to explain and justify, they represent a significant perceived risk of novel technologies in a shop-floor environment.

In the context of manufacturing, explainable AI (XAI) technologies [1] have been tested in several scenarios such as predictive maintenance [7], real-time process management [10] and quality monitoring [5]. One of our research goals is to highlight the explainability of the algorithms and methods used in smart manufacturing processes, aligning XAI technologies with human interaction. We also aim to collect feedback on the quality of such explanations, since there are few validated measurements for user evaluations on explanations' quality [16].

Active Learning (AL) is usually the natural approach to provide human-in-the-loop functionalities in advanced AI systems. Typically, AL attempts to improve learners' performance by asking questions to an expert (e.g., query a human operator) to obtain labels for data instances [14]. Since users are usually reluctant to provide information and feedback, AL is used to identify a set of data instances on which the provided users' input conveys the most valuable information to the system [4]. In a decision-making process in manufacturing, AL can also be implemented in recommender systems. In such cases, it tackles obtaining high-quality data that better represents the user's preferences and improves the recommendation quality. The ultimate goal is to acquire additional feedback that enables the system to generate better recommendations [4]. Collecting feedback from forecast explanations can be realized with a framework of three components: a forecasting engine, an explanation engine, and a feedback loop to learn from the users [15]. We extend this approach to collect feedback from forecasts, forecast explanations and decision-making options we recommend to the users.

3   Proposed Methodology and System

To realize a system described in Sect. 1, we developed a methodology to identify relevant components, decision-making options, information and feedback of interest, and how to collect them. The methodology consists of ten steps:

1. create an AI model, to provide predictions that comply with a given use case;
2. provide local forecast explanations, either by querying a glass-box model or using complementary methods for black-box models;
3. list decision-making options available to the user;
4. create a flow of decision-making options available to the user;
5. list the kind of feedback expected for forecasts, forecast explanations, and decision-making options. Identify opportunities for implicit feedback;
6. create a list of relevant entities related with forecasts, explanations, and decision-making options;
7. extend the ontology [13] to include use-case specific entities and relate them to the entities that model the AI model, forecasts, forecast explanations, and feedback;
8. instantiate a knowledge graph based on the ontology entities;
9. develop a software application binding forecasts, forecast explanations, and decision-making options while enabling decision-making flows and feedback gathering;
10. develop an Active Learning module that receives input from the database and knowledge graph to suggest data instances that are expected to be most informative to the system. This input can be used by the decision-making recommender system;

The system requires at least eight components (see Fig. 1A):

- **Database**, stores operational data from the manufacturing plant. Data can be obtained from ERP, MES, or other manufacturing platforms;

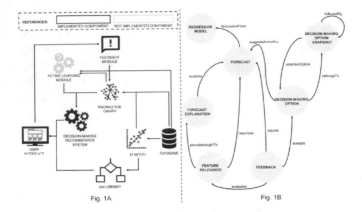

Fig. 1. **A** displays a diagram of the system components and their interaction. **B** shows the main ontology concepts we considered, and their relationships.

- **Knowledge Graph**, stores data ingested from a database or external sources and connects it, providing a semantic meaning. To map data from the database to the knowledge graph, virtual mapping procedures can be used, built considering ontology concepts and their relationships;
- **Active Learning module**, aims to select data instances whose labels are expected to be most informative to the system and thus help enhance AI model's (e.g., predictive model or recommender system model) performance. Obtained labels are persisted to the knowledge graph and database;
- **AI model**, aims to solve a specific task relevant to the use case, such as classification, regression, clustering, or ranking;
- **XAI Library**, provides some insight into the AI model's rationale used to produce the output for the input instance considered at the task at hand. E.g., in the case of a classification task, it may indicate the most relevant features for a given forecast;
- **Decision-Making Recommender System**, recommends decision-making options to the users. Recommended decision-making options can vary depending on the users' profile, specific use case context, and feedback provided in the past;
- **Feedback module**, collects feedback from the users and persists it into the knowledge graph;
- **User Interface**, provides relevant information to the user through a relevant information medium. The interface must enable user interactions to create two-way communication between the human and the system.

The knowledge graph is a central component of the system. Instantiated from an ontology (see Fig. 1B), it relates forecasts, forecast explanations, decision-making options, and feedback provided by the users. To ensure context regarding decision-making options and feedback provided is preserved, different relationships are established. The feedback entity directly relates to a forecast, forecast explanation, and decision-making option. While a chain of decisions can exist for a given forecast, there is a need to model the decision-making options available at each stage and the sequence on which they are displayed. To that end, the decision-making snapshot entity aims to capture a list of decision-making options provided at a given point in time. A relationship between decision-making option snapshots (*followedBy*) provides information on such a sequence. For each decision-making snapshot, a *selectedOption* relationship is created to the user's selected decision-making option. To link the first decision-making options to the forecast, the *suggestsActionFor* relationship is created between the forecast entity and entities that correspond to the first decision-making options displayed for that forecast. Since the decision-making options are linked to decision-making option snapshot and preserve a sequential relationship, all decision-making options can be traced back to the forecast that originated them.

4   Use Case

Demand forecasting is a key component of supply chain management since it directly affects production planning and order fulfillment. Accurate forecasts enable operational and strategic decisions regarding manufacturing and logistics for deliveries. For the evaluation of our methodology, we developed a model to forecast demand on a material and client level daily. The model was trained on three years of data for 516 time-series corresponding to 279 materials and 149 clients of a European automotive original equipment manufacturer's daily demand. To validate the system we developed, a subset of demand forecasts was used. Forecast explanations were generated with the LIME library [11]. The decision-making options recommender system was implemented with a set of simple heuristics that allow to select a new transport or chose among existing ones that satisfy certain criteria (e.g., have enough capacity to satisfy the expected demand for a given client). Finally, a user interface was developed to display forecasts, forecast explanations, and decision-making options (see Fig. 2). In the user interface, we identify four distinct parts:

A **Forecast panel**: given date and material, it displays the forecasted demand for different clients. For each forecast, three options are available: edit the forecast (providing explicit feedback on the forecast value), display the forecast explanation, and display the decision-making options. The lack of editing on displayed forecasts is considered implicit feedback approving the forecasted demand quantities.

B **Forecast explanation panel**: displays the forecast explanation for a given forecast. Our implementation displays the top three features identified by the LIME algorithm as relevant to the selected forecast. If the users considers some of the features displayed do not explain the given forecast, they can provide feedback by removing it from the list.

C **Decision-making options panel**: displays possible decision-making options, that are tied together into a decision-making snapshot, for a given forecast or step in the decision-making process.

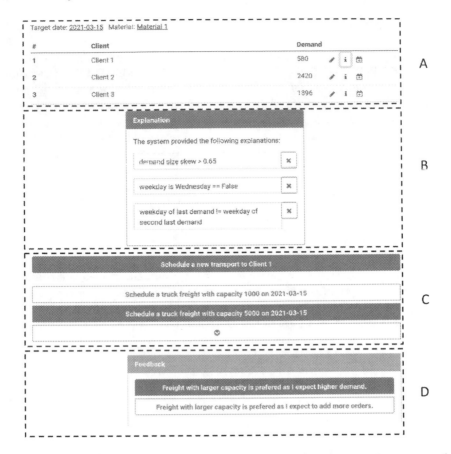

Fig. 2. User interface, displaying forecasts, forecast explanations, and recommended decision-making options.

D **Feedback panel**: gathers feedback from the user to understand the reasons behind the chosen decision-making option. While some pre-defined are shown to the user, we always include the user's possibility to add their own reasons and enrich the existing knowledge base. Such data can be used to expand feedback options displayed to the users in the future.

Though the current decision-making options recommender system is constrained to heuristics, we envision that in the future, more complex models can be developed leveraging data regarding user interactions with the recommendations we currently display.

5   Evaluation and Discussion

To evaluate the proposed methodology and system, empirical evaluations and the development of a concrete use case were utilized [6]. In particular, we applied the methodology outlined in Sect. 3 (except for the Active Learning module implementation) to develop a system that enables displaying forecasts, forecast explanations, and decision-making options, provide a decision-making workflow, and means to collect feedback and knowledge from the users[1]. The system we developed for the particular use case of demand forecasting proves that a semantic approach enables effective and flexible means to solve complex knowledge acquisition and solve interoperability conflicts. Since the system was not deployed to production environments, we cannot assess the perceived quality of the forecast explanations, and the impact of the given forecast explanations and decision-making options provided. The impact of the forecasting models was assessed on data provided by EU H2020 FACTLOG and STAR project partners [12]. The development of an Active Learning module remains the subject of future work.

6 Conclusion and Future Work

The current work presents a system's conceptual design to acquire and encapsulate complex knowledge using semantic technologies and AI. The system was instantiated for the demand forecasting use case in the manufacturing domain, using real-world data from partners from the EU H2020 projects STAR and FACTLOG. In particular, the system provides forecasts, forecast explanations, decision-making options, and the capability to provide implicit and explicit feedback. The system enables the development of an active learning module that can enhance data collection by identifying promising data instances that, when labeled, are expected to be most informative to the system. Future work will focus on implementing an active learning module and explore recommender systems that learn from data to provide decision-making options to the users.

Acknowledgemnts. This work was supported by the Slovenian Research Agency and the European Union's Horizon 2020 program projects FACTLOG under grant agreement H2020-869951 and STAR under grant agreement number H2020-956573.

References

1. Arrieta, A.B., et al.: Explainable artificial intelligence (XAI): concepts, taxonomies, opportunities and challenges toward responsible AI. Inf. Fusion **58**, 82–115 (2020)
2. Bradeško, L., Witbrock, M., Starc, J., Herga, Z., Grobelnik, M., Mladenić, D.: Curious cat-mobile, context-aware conversational crowdsourcing knowledge acquisition. ACM Trans. Inf. Syst. (TOIS) **35**(4), 1–46 (2017)

---

[1] A video demonstrating the application is available at https://youtu.be/Kx5U nE_yTM0.

3. Büchi, G., Cugno, M., Castagnoli, R.: Smart factory performance and industry 4.0. Technol. Forecast. Soc. Change **150**, 119790 (2020). https://doi.org/10.1016/j.techfore.2019.119790
4. Elahi, M., Ricci, F., Rubens, N.: A survey of active learning in collaborative filtering recommender systems. Comput. Sci. Rev. **20**, 29–50 (2016)
5. Goldman, C.V., Baltaxe, M., Chakraborty, D., Arinez, J.: Explaining learning models in manufacturing processes. Procedia Comput. Sci. **180**, 259–268 (2021)
6. Grangel-González, I.: A knowledge graph based integration approach for industry 4.0. Ph.D. thesis, Universitäts-und Landesbibliothek Bonn (2019)
7. Hrnjica, B., Softic, S.: Explainable AI in manufacturing: a predictive maintenance case study. In: Lalic, B., Majstorovic, V., Marjanovic, U., von Cieminski, G., Romero, D. (eds.) APMS 2020. IAICT, vol. 592, pp. 66–73. Springer, Cham (2020). https://doi.org/10.1007/978-3-030-57997-5_8
8. Micheler, S., Goh, Y.M., Lohse, N.: Innovation landscape and challenges of smart technologies and systems - a European perspective. Prod. Manuf. Res. **7**(1), 503–528 (2019). https://doi.org/10.1080/21693277.2019.1687363
9. Mittal, S., Khan, M., Romero, D., Wuest, T.: Smart manufacturing: characteristics, technologies and enabling factors. Proc. Inst. Mech. Eng. Part B J. Eng. Manuf. **233**, 1342–1361 (2019). https://doi.org/10.1177/0954405417736547
10. Rehse, J.R., Mehdiyev, N., Fettke, P.: Towards explainable process predictions for industry 4.0 in the DFKI-smart-lego-factory. KI-Künstliche Intelligenz **33**(2), 181–187 (2019)
11. Ribeiro, M.T., Singh, S., Guestrin, C.: "Why should i trust you?" explaining the predictions of any classifier. In: Proceedings of the 22nd ACM SIGKDD International Conference on Knowledge Discovery and Data Mining, pp. 1135–1144 (2016)
12. Rožanec, J.: Explainable demand forecasting: A data mining goldmine. In: Companion Proceedings of the Web Conference 2021 (WWW 2021 Companion), Ljubljana, Slovenia, 19–23 April 2021 (2021). https://doi.org/10.1145/3442442.3453708
13. Rožanec, J.M., Zajec, P., Kenda, K., Koval, I., Fortuna, B., Mladenić, D.: Ontologies for XAI and decision-making feedback collection (2021)
14. Settles, B.: Active learning literature survey (2009). http://digital.library.wisc.edu/1793/60660
15. Tulli, S., Wallkötter, S., Paiva, A., Melo, F.S., Chetouani, M.: Learning from explanations and demonstrations: a pilot study. In: 2nd Workshop on Interactive Natural Language Technology for Explainable Artificial Intelligence, pp. 61–66 (2020)
16. van der Waa, J., Nieuwburg, E., Cremers, A., Neerincx, M.: Evaluating XAI: a comparison of rule-based and example-based explanations. Artif. Intell. **291**, 103404 (2021)

Human-AI Collaboration in Quality Control with Augmented Manufacturing Analytics

Alexandros Bousdekis[1], Stefan Wellsandt[2], Enrica Bosani[3], Katerina Lepenioti[1], Dimitris Apostolou[1], Karl Hribernik[2], and Gregoris Mentzas[1]([✉])

[1] Information Management Unit (IMU), Institute of Communication and Computer Systems (ICCS), National Technical University of Athens (NTUA), Athens, Greece
{albous,klepenioti,dapost,gmentzas}@mail.ntua.gr
[2] BIBA - Bremer Institut für Produktion und Logistik GmbH at the University of Bremen, Bremen, Germany
{wel,hri}@biba.uni-bremen.de
[3] Whirlpool EMEA, Benton Harbor, USA
enrica_bosani@whirlpool.com

Abstract. Augmented analytics is an emerging topic which deals with the enhancement of analytics with conversational interfaces as well as the exploitation of the human knowledge representation through intelligent digital assistants allowing users to easily interact with data and insights. The communication with the user by voice poses new challenges to the development and execution of data analytics services. In this paper, we outline a framework for implementing quality analytics for decision augmentation through optimized human-AI interaction. Our approach aims to reduce the number of quality issues through fast, mobile, and easy access to quality predictions for products and processes. An application case is the production of white goods is presented.

Keywords: Quality control · Augmented analytics · Human-AI collaboration

1 Introduction

Quality of products and processes concerns more and more the manufacturing firms because negative consequences do not show up until the product is actually produced or worse, until the customer returns it [1]. The acceleration of technological growth in the context of Industry 4.0 does not automatically result in improvements in manufacturing quality. The products' complexity (i.e. number of components and their relations) and variety is continuously increasing, while the traditional quality management practices, such as Material Requirements Planning, Lean Manufacturing, Theory of Constraints and Six Sigma, have lost their effectiveness [2]. The future of quality management is to be proactive: adverse effects of quality flaws have to be prevented before they become evident in the actual use of a product [1, 3] or even before they cause inefficiencies in the production process. This trend is significantly facilitated by the latest advancements

© IFIP International Federation for Information Processing 2021
Published by Springer Nature Switzerland AG 2021
A. Dolgui et al. (Eds.): APMS 2021, IFIP AICT 633, pp. 303–310, 2021.
https://doi.org/10.1007/978-3-030-85910-7_32

in machine learning [4] which dictate that production is gauged based upon the product quality, the process quality, and the quality of the services provided surrounding the product. To this end, predictive quality is an approach that moves beyond traditional quality evaluation methods towards extracting useful insights from various data sources by determining patterns, revealing correlations between products and defects and predicting future outcomes (e.g. product defects and fault localization) [1–3, 5].

Predictive quality approaches can be further enhanced by extending data analytics with augmented analytics. Augmented analytics aims at optimizing the use of data for decision making in order to augment human intelligence and contextual awareness [6]. It brings automation to the complete analytics cycle [7] by leveraging AI algorithms in order to transform how analytics content is developed, consumed and shared. Augmented analytics uses natural language processing and conversational interfaces, allowing all users to interact with AI through spoken and written language, without requiring advanced skills [6], something which has long been a goal of AI researchers [8]. On the other hand, prescriptive analytics moves beyond the provision of meaningful insights about the current or the anticipated states (e.g. prediction of future defects) and aims at prescribing the best decision options within time constraints in order to take advantage of the predicted future, e.g. to eliminate or mitigate the impact of a future undesired event [9, 10]. With augmented analytics, conversational interfaces can provide users fast access to non-intrusive recommendations and real-life feedback from the shop floor. Moreover, intelligent digital assistants allow users to interact with data and insights easily.

In this paper, we focus on Augmented Manufacturing Analytics (AMA). We present a voice-enabled Digital Intelligent Assistant (DIA), which interacts with a prescriptive quality analytics service. The assistant's interface aims to allow workers to access and customize quality predictions and the prescribed mitigating measures. Our approach aims to reduce the number of quality issues through fast, mobile, and easy access to quality predictions for products and processes. The application case is the production of white goods. The next section briefly overviews the current state of the art in business analytics and digital intelligent assistants. Section 3 presents our conceptual framework for augmented quality analytics and highlights some of our innovation objectives. The fourth section outlines the case study in quality management in the home appliances industry, while the fifth section presents the concluding remarks.

2   State of the Art

2.1   Augmented Analytics

Companies have at their disposal staggering amounts of data, which, if analyzed and processed properly, can generate valuable insights and lead to better decisions. The use of advanced techniques that can analyze and process large and diverse data sets that include structured, semi-structured and unstructured data, from different sources, and in different sizes from terabytes to zettabytes, has led to the field of business analytics [11]. The data analytics lifecycle consists of three phases: description, prediction, and prescription. While descriptive analytics analyzes past events, predictive analytics predicts future events – both do not provide direct support for decision-making [12,

13]. Prescriptive analytics, on the other hand, is a newer data analytics type enabling data-driven optimization for decision support and planning [9]. Prescriptive analytics has the potential to provide the greatest benefit for business by providing insights about proactive mitigating actions for the predicted undesired events [14]. Current solutions, however, require that users have higher skills in data science and machine learning, which impairs wide adoption. To address this barrier, combining prescription with augmented analytics can enable users with lower data science and machine learning skills to find and surface the most important insights or changes in the business by interacting through spoken and written language taking advantage of natural language processing and conversational interfaces [15].

2.2 Digital Intelligent Assistants

Digital Intelligent Assistants (DIAs) emerged from fragile niche applications to everyday helpers. Consumers use them for home automation, to schedule appointments, and to search for facts. There are various voice-based assistants such as Amazon Alexa, and text-based assistants (chatbots) [16, 17]. Market researchers expect that AI-based digital assistants will become a key element in the future of work [18, 19]. A voice-enabled DIA processing pipeline has four core components [20, 21]: Speech-to-Text (STT) to transcribe voice inputs, Natural Language Understanding (NLU) to extract intents and entities, Dialog Management (DM) to track dialog states and decide the next actions, and Text-to-Speech (TTS) to generate a computer voice output. Morana et al. classified DIA's along two dimensions: (1) the degree of interactivity enabled by the user assistance, and (2) the degree of intelligence of user assistance [22]. The former characterizes the DIA's capability to support humans in an ongoing dialog and the latter describes its capability to assist the user considering, for instance personal and task characteristics.

Applications in manufacturing include, for instance, smart voice-enabled digital assistants for human-robot communication [23, 24]. Although further research is still needed for a more accurate voice recognition and conversational intelligence, the technology is mature enough for running experiments [25, 26] and building commercial applications in manufacturing, such as Spix[1]. Realizing DIA in this domain is challenging though. Achieving robustness under industrial operating conditions, clarity about an assistant's accountability, acceptance among employees, ethics issues, and data security risks are some examples that slow down wider adoption [27]. Tools and frameworks for building DIAs, however, prosper. Many global IT leaders, such as Google, Amazon, Microsoft, Baidu, or IBM offer tools to design, develop, deploy, and maintain assistants. A noteworthy effort in the Open Source domain is Mycroft[2], which offers a privacy-centred digital assistant framework. Their solution offers exchangeable natural language processing modules, speech-to-text, intent parsing, and text-to-speech.

---

[1] https://www.simsoft-industry.com/en/intelligent-vocal-assistant-for-my-industry/.
[2] https://mycroft.ai.

3 Augmented Manufacturing Analytics Framework for Human-AI Collaboration in Quality Control

Our framework (Fig. 1) implements quality analytics for decision augmentation through optimized human-AI interaction. The framework covers the whole data analytics life-cycle (descriptive, predictive, and prescriptive analytics) aiming at extracting increased value from quality data and prescribing appropriate mitigating actions through a voice-enabled DIA. As such, it can support tasks related to product and process quality control, such as detecting abnormal behaviors and root causes of defects, predicting their conse-quences in terms of product and process quality and prescribing appropriate actions in the form of voice-first advices. Specifically, the framework foresees stream processing to perform real-time data processing for: (i) detecting potential sources of defects and revealing correlations between products and defect rates; (ii) predicting future quality issues and their consequences; and (iii) prescribing mitigating actions to optimize rel-evant manufacturing performance indicators, such as Overall Equipment Effectiveness (OEE), uptime and scrap rate.

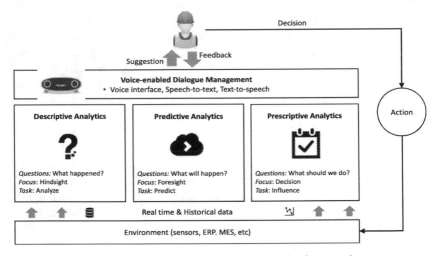

Fig. 1. Augmented manufacturing analytics framework

We use the DIA to recognize worker intents, questions, and instructions in the indus-trial environment. The DIA has to manage typical interaction constraints in manufac-turing, such as factory noise, multiple languages, jargon, and workers wearing earplugs, masks, safety googles, and safety gloves. Its STT component has to be reliable under these conditions, which is a technical challenge. Reliable solutions ground on thousands of hours of audio data and their transcription – each supported language needs its own dataset. Therefore, STT model training is costly and companies, such as Google, Ama-zon, Apple, and Baidu, invested millions of Euros in this field to develop proprietary solutions. Their closed solutions are a cause for ethical concerns because the training data are not transparent and biases hard to identify. Open solutions are not as reliable yet, but projects such as DeepSpeech[3] and CommonVoice[4] develop transparent alternatives. The application of trustworthy STT mechanisms is challenging and it is not clear how successful open state of the art technology can be.

Furthermore, the DIA has to address: i) data security requirements of manufacturing environments through data access management, traceability, and encryption; ii) data privacy requirements derived from the legal frameworks through a privacy-by-design approach with clear data ownership, data processing scope, and user consent management. The assistant needs to operate on mobile devices to be usable wherever and whenever the user needs it. Since time pressure is a typical work condition, the DIA's dialogs must be fast, unambiguous, and easy to use. Voice interactions are inherently fast, potentially hands-free, and we assume they are also easier to learn than interactions via graphical interfaces. For multi-dimensional analytics results (e.g. graphs or tables) voice can be inefficient because of the slower audio processing on the human side. For these cases, the assistant needs access to graphical interfaces. Relevant interaction options include voice-based drill-down, drill-up, and customization options for the analytics processes. Wake words should activate the assistant for hands-free interactions.

4 Case Study on Quality Control

The case study of our approach concerns the quality control procedures of Whirlpool, one of the leading companies in the home appliances industry, with around 92,000 employees and over 70 manufacturing and technology research centers worldwide. The use case will address the end-of-line quality control with human-AI collaboration with the aim to adopt a predictive quality strategy that will link the quality control of the finished product with the design stage and the shop floor.

4.1 As-is Situation

In the Whirlpool production model, the whole white goods production is tested from quality and safety point of view in order to ensure a high standard level of product quality to final customers. These tests are executed in all factories either through the usage of automatic dedicated machines at the end of production line or through automatic, semiautomatic or manual checks in some critical workstation along the production flow (visual quality checks, quality gates). To these testing actions, Whirlpool Production system adds also some statistical quality check actions that are applied both on internal production parts on quality critical processes (statistical process control stations) and on finished goods, after the packaging process. In particular, this last testing, called Zero Hour Testing (ZHT) is referring to the Statistical Quality Control applied in a dedicated laboratory out of production flow on some finished products retrieved from the quantities ready to be delivered to the markets; see Fig. 2.

---

[3] https://github.com/mozilla/DeepSpeech/wiki.

[4] https://commonvoice.mozilla.org/en.

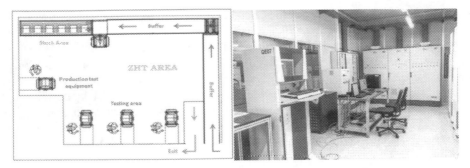

Fig. 2. Zero Hour Testing (ZHT) laboratory at Whirlpool

The main objectives of ZHT are to measure the quality level of the outgoing product from an aesthetic, functional, and normative point and to measure the effectiveness of process control. These tests are executed in dedicated laboratory environment, created in each production site, and following a specific STD operating procedure. This testing method is designed to replicate the customer approach to the product, simulating the normal product usage conditions at final customer first usage. Currently, the procedure is executed manually by a laboratory operator and it is fixed, statically defined during process design phase both for what concerns checklist and reference parameters, and for statistical product withdrawal rate.

4.2   To-be Scenario

With our proposed framework we aim at adopting a predictive quality strategy that will link the quality control of the finished product with the design stage and the shop floor. By integrating all available information sources (e.g. sensor data, historical operation-al data, and expert knowledge), the factory will be able to a) predict low-quality products and b) to plan effective control actions to mitigate the impact. In this way, Whirlpool will be able to effectively capture defects risk and proactively initiate resolution process before it may impact on the final customer level. The support to decision making process in mitigation actions identification and implementation will ensure a prompt reaction of the overall Whirlpool quality network system, ensuring fast and effective reconfiguration with the modification of control points to capture un/conformities. A second important contribution is in the facilitation of root cause analysis that, due to the high complexity of white goods production process (high number of components, several quality-critical processes within production flow, high production pace, high variety of product range), is very often difficult to be executed at shop floor level. An interactive system collaborat-ing with workers and leading into a deep dive analysis, will facilitate the identification of early signal of quality derailing effects and the possibility to consolidate knowledge to be used for the future. An augmented human-AI interaction is of outmost importance to enhance the shop floor workers' capabilities in identifying potential failures, investi-gating root-causes, and addressing the causes effectively, allowing them the opportunity to fully leverage on whole data availability to anticipate the events instead of reacting the events.

5   Conclusions and Further Work

Augmented analytics is an emerging topic which deals with the enhancement of analytics with conversational interfaces as well as the exploitation of the human knowledge representation through intelligent digital assistants allowing users to easily interact with data and insights. The communication with the user by voice poses new challenges to the development and execution of data analytics services. Apart from visualization dashboards, the data analytics outcomes should be structured in a way that can be translated to speech. On the other way around, they should be able to take as input parameters that are derived from the human speech. In this paper, we outlined a framework for implementing quality analytics for decision augmentation through optimized human-AI interaction. The coupling of analytics with augmentation is in line with the overall trend towards human-AI osmosis for Operator 4.0 as a grand challenge [28].

Acknowledgements. This work is partly funded by the European Union's Horizon 2020 project COALA "COgnitive Assisted agile manufacturing for a LAbor force supported by trustworthy Artificial Intelligence" (Grant agreement No 957296). The work presented here reflects only the authors' view and the European Commission is not responsible for any use that may be made of the information it contains.

References

1. Nalbach, O., Linn, C., Derouet, M., Werth, D.: Predictive quality: towards a new understanding of quality assurance using machine learning tools. In: Abramowicz, W., Paschke, A. (eds.) BIS 2018. LNBIP, vol. 320, pp. 30–42. Springer, Cham (2018). https://doi.org/10.1007/978-3-319-93931-5_3
2. Bai, Y., et al.: Manufacturing quality prediction using intelligent learning approaches: a comparative study. Sustainability **10**(1), 85 (2018)
3. Berger, D., et al.: Predictive quality control of hybrid metal-CFRP components using information fusion. Prod. Eng. Res. Devel. **12**(2), 161–172 (2018). https://doi.org/10.1007/s11740-018-0816-1
4. Gunasekaran, A., Subramanian, N., Ngai, W.T.E.: Quality management in the 21st century enterprises: research pathway towards Industry 4.0, pp. 125–129 (2019)
5. Gittler, T., et al.: Towards predictive quality management in assembly systems with low quality low quantity data – a methodological approach. Procedia CIRP **79**, 125–130 (2019)
6. Prat, N.: Augmented analytics. Bus. Inf. Syst. Eng. **61**(3), 375–380 (2019)
7. Gartner Inc.: When and How to Combine Predictive and Prescriptive Techniques to Solve Business Problems. Published: 25 October 2018 ID: G00368423 (2018)
8. Sangaiah, A.K., Thangavelu, A., Sundaram, V.M.: Cognitive computing for big data systems over IoT. Gewerbestrasse **11**, 6330 (2018)
9. Lepenioti, K., Bousdekis, A., Apostolou, D., Mentzas, G.: Prescriptive analytics: literature review and research challenges. Int. J. Inf. Manag. **50**, 57–70 (2020)
10. Bertsimas, D., Kallus, N.: From predictive to prescriptive analytics. Manag. Sci. **66**(3), 1025–1044 (2020)
11. Davenport, T.H.: Competing on analytics. Harvard Bus. Rev. **84**(1), 98 (2006)
12. LaValle, S., Lesser, E., Shockley, R., Hopkins, M.S., Kruschwitz, N.: Big data, analytics and the path from insights to value. MIT Sloan Manag. Rev. **52**(2), 21–32 (2011)

13. Chen, H., Chiang, R.H.L., Storey, V.C.: Business intelligence and analytics: from big data to big impact. MIS Q. 1165–1188 (2012)
14. Frazzetto, D., Nielsen, T.D., Pedersen, T.B., Šikšnys, L.: Prescriptive analytics: a survey of emerging trends and technologies. VLDB J. **28**(4), 575–595 (2019). https://doi.org/10.1007/s00778-019-00539-y
15. Gartner: Augmented Analytics Is the Future of Data and Analytics, Published: 31 October 2018, ID: G00375087 (2018)
16. Maedche, A., Morana, S., Schacht, S., Werth, D., Krumeich, J.: Advanced user assistance systems. Bus. Inf. Syst. Eng. **58**(5), 367–370 (2016)
17. Maedche, A., et al.: AI-based digital assistants: opportunities, threats, and research perspectives. Bus. Inf. Syst. Eng. **61**, 535–544 (2019)
18. Gartner Newroom: Gartner Predicts 25 Percent of Digital Workers Will Use Virtual Employee Assistants Daily by 2021, 9 January 2019. https://www.gartner.com/en/newsroom/press-releases/2019-01-09-gartner-predicts-25-percent-of-digital-workers-will-u. Accessed 02 Mar 2021
19. Bradley, A.: Brace Yourself for an Explosion of Virtual Assistants. Gartner Blog Post, 10 August 2020. https://blogs.gartner.com/anthony_bradley/2020/08/10/brace-yourself-for-an-explosion-of-virtual-assistants/. Accessed 02 Mar 2021
20. Deriu, J., et al.: Survey on evaluation methods for dialogue systems. Artif. Intell. Rev. **54**(1), 755–810 (2020). https://doi.org/10.1007/s10462-020-09866-x
21. Maedche, A., et al.: AI-based digital assistants. Bus. Inf. Syst. Eng. **61**(4), 535–544 (2019)
22. Morana, S., Pfeiffer, J., Adam, M.T.P.: User assistance for intelligent systems. Bus. Inf. Syst. Eng. **62**(3), 189–192 (2020)
23. Ghofrani, J., Reichelt, D.: Using voice assistants as HMI for robots in smart production systems. In: CEUR Workshop Proceedings, vol. 2339 (2019)
24. Longo, F., Padovano, A.: Voice-enabled assistants of the opera-tor 4.0 in the social smart factory: prospective role and challenges for an advanced human–machine interaction. Manuf. Lett. **26**, 12–16 (2020)
25. Abner, B., Rabelo, R.J., Zambiasi, S.P., Romero, D.: Production management as-a-service: a softbot approach. In: Lalic, B., Majstorovic, V., Marjanovic, U., von Cieminski, G., Romero, D. (eds.) APMS 2020. IAICT, vol. 592, pp. 19–30. Springer, Cham (2020). https://doi.org/10.1007/978-3-030-57997-5_3
26. Rabelo, R.J., Zambiasi, S.P., Romero, D.: Collaborative softbots: enhancing operational excellence in systems of cyber-physical systems. In: Camarinha-Matos, L.M., Afsarmanesh, H., Antonelli, D. (eds.) PRO-VE 2019. IAICT, vol. 568, pp. 55–68. Springer, Cham (2019). https://doi.org/10.1007/978-3-030-28464-0_6
27. Wellsandt, S., Foosherian, M., Thoben, K.-D.: Interacting with a Digital Twin using Amazon Alexa. Procedia Manufact. **52**, 4–8 (2020)
28. Bousdekis, A., Apostolou, D., Mentzas, G.: A human cyber physical system framework for operator 4.0–artificial intelligence symbiosis. Manuf. Lett. **25**, 10–15 (2020)

Digital Platform and Operator 4.0 Services for Manufacturing Repurposing During COVID19

John Soldatos[1](✉) (iD), Nikos Kefalakis[1] (iD), Georgios Makantasis[1], Angelo Marguglio[2], and Oscar Lazaro[3]

[1] Research and Innovation Development, INTRASOFT International, Nicolas Bové, 1253 Luxembourg City, Luxembourg
John.Soldatos@intrasoft-intl.com
[2] Research and Innovation Division, Engineering Ingegneria Informatica S.P.A., Rome, Italy
[3] Advanced Manufacturing Systems, Innovalia Association, Bilbao, Spain

Abstract. This paper introduces digital solutions for manufacturing repurposing transformations that address the impact of COVID19 on production operations. The paper outlines how different Industry 4.0 solutions can be combined in a unified platform for manufacturing repurposing. Emphasis is paid on introducing worker and Operator 4.0 related solutions, including tools for plant risk assessment, shifts allocation, context-aware reskilling of employees and remote support processes. The latter are essential elements of a strategy for exploiting automation and Artificial Intelligence (AI) systems during COVID19 times and future healthcare crises.

Keywords: Manufacturing repurposing · Operator 4.0 services · Human centered services · Sustainability · Human machine interaction · COVID19

1 Introduction

1.1 COVID19 and Sustainable Manufacturing

The COVID19 pandemic outbreak has had a severe impact on industrial production [1]. COVID19 impacted the volume of the production, yet it also had other short- and medium-term effects, including: (i) Critical shortages in products like PPE (Personal Protection Equipment) and CCE (Clinical Care Equipment), as a result of supply chain disruptions and a surge in demand for medical products [2]; (ii) Rapid repurposing of supply chains towards confronting disruptions and increasing resilience; (iii) Repurposing capabilities towards new products that were high in demand, such as sanitizers, face masks, and other types of PPE/CCE [3, 4]; (iv) Impacts on the well-being of the workforce that got infected; (v) A stronger emphasis on supply chain security towards trusted exchange of digital Intellectual Property (IP) (e.g., digital models for new products).

Several manufacturers developed rapid responses to COVID19 disruptions, through proper repurposing of manufacturing operations [5]. Despite these responses, there is

A. Dolgui et al. (Eds.): APMS 2021, IFIP AICT 633, pp. 311–320, 2021.
https://doi.org/10.1007/978-3-030-85910-7_33

still a lack of an integrated framework for addressing the implications of this pandemic and of similar future crises. Most of the developed solutions were ad hoc and focused on the issues faced by each specific factory, rather than framed in a more general platform. This paper introduces a structured, integrated approach for manufacturing repurposing during COVID19 and similar crises that may disrupt production operations. Specifically, the paper specifies a pool of digital solutions that address adverse implications of COVID19. The solutions consider best practices and manufacturing response development guidelines provided by organizations like the World Economic Forum (WEF) and the World Manufacturing Forum (WMF). Furthermore, the paper provides a vision for integrating these technologies in a unified platform. Emphasis is paid on presenting a set of Operator 4.0 related solutions for the continuity of plants and production operations. These include for example solutions for identifying COVID19 risks and for allocating shifts in-line with the skills, health status and availability of employees. The rest of the paper is structured as follows: Sect. 2 presents four main manufacturing repurposing scenarios that drive the specification of the manufacturing repurposing platform. Section 3 introduces the building blocks of the platform. Section 4 delves into details about the Operator 4.0 related services that ensure business continuity. Section 5 is the concluding section.

2 Manufacturing Repurposing and Response Scenarios

Following paragraphs present four representative manufacturing repurposing transformations. These scenarios stem from our analysis of many manufacturing repurposing cases during the first wave of the COVID19 pandemic.

Scenario 1: Rapid Reconfiguration and Continuity of Production Line Operation: Following the pandemic outbreak, manufacturers had to re-configure their production lines for two main reasons: (i) Reduction of orders and personnel; (ii) Need for social distancing. In this direction, they had to simulate how their production lines could operate at reduced production capacity and at reduced workforce presence. The above listed capabilities can be provided based on methods and tools for virtual commissioning of safe and secure reconfigured production lines such as digital twins. A pool of Operator 4.0 related services is also required to ensure that flexible, modular, and highly automated production lines can operate with less workers.

Scenario 2: Reliable Repurposing of Production Processes: In this scenario manufacturers had to repurpose their factories to produce different products. This transformation was triggered due to high demand for certain products (e.g., PPE/CCE), as well as due to the lower demand for their original products. The transformation requires digital capabilities for new product design, engineering, simulation as well as increased manufacturing automation, and effective quality management. Likewise, support for certification in-line with medical standards and normative rules is important for products like PPE/CCE.

Scenario 3: Resilient Smart Supply Networks: Several supply chain reconfigurations took place in response to market barriers (e.g., lack of access to certain suppliers in some regions) or due to political sovereignty reasons (e.g., less reliance in suppliers from certain countries). To address supply chain reconfiguration there is a need for trusted digital supply chain networks that share production capacities (e.g., yield and production throughput) to match demand with supply. Such supply chains support Manufacturing as a Service business models within a network of trusted companies which share data in a common/shared space.

Scenario 4: Robust On-demand Remanufacturing Networks: This kind of transformation focuses on the execution of orders through an Additive Manufacturing network. It is based on-demand production networks that share information about their production capabilities, including information on certification levels that they support in cases of medical products. Emphasis is paid on the trusted sharing of IP (e.g., Computer Aided Designs (CAD)) through production networks.

3 Manufacturing Repurposing Platform

3.1 Digital Services for Manufacturing Repurposing

Flexible Production Lines: Flexible Production Lines leverage digital technologies to make their configuration flexibly adaptable to changing needs. Examples of relevant digital components include: (i) **Digital Simulations and Digital Twins** for supporting production flexibility and repurposing (Scenario 1), as well as digital quality management and digital lean manufacturing technologies that support new product design (Scenario 2); and (ii) **Additive Manufacturing solutions**, which boost the flexibility of a production line in the absence of specific materials or parts. This can be useful for several of the presented repurposing scenarios (e.g., Scenarios 1 and 2). It can also enable the provision of on-demand capabilities (Scenario 4).

Flexible and Trusted Supply Chains: Flexible and trusted information sharing across the supply chain boosts the flexibility of supply chain decisions. It also enables smart matching making of supply and demand, which enable manufacturers to take optimal supply chain decisions under constraints. The latter relate to location, time, and cost limitations.

Digital Quality Management (DQM) and Zero-Defect Manufacturing (ZDM): DQM and ZDM services facilitate the rapid discovery of quality issues in the production (e.g., defective products), while empowering relevant remedial actions. Such components are vital for simulating ramp-up times and identifying quality issues during new products design and development (i.e., Scenario 2).

Regulatory and Certification Support: To support regulatory processes there is a need to follow rules, best practices, and regulatory mandates, as part of a multi-level certification framework. The latter provides recommendations for ensuring the compliance of sites, processes, and equipment.

Operator 4.0 Services for Business Continuity: Business continuity must respect applicable restrictions such as COVID19 constraints and related work policies. Services in this direction including plant risk assessment, training, and reskilling resources, COVID19 aware shift allocation strategies, technologies for supporting remote processes, as well as components for financial impact assessment of repurposing scenarios. Such services are important to supporting Scenario 1, yet they are useful for the rest scenarios when factories operate under restrictions.

3.2 Integrated Platform

Table 1 provides a mapping between the four reference scenarios and the Industry 4.0 components and services that were presented in previous paragraphs. The table marks with "M" the services that are mandatory for supporting the scenarios, yet it indicates with an "O" i.e., optional, opportunities for using them in other scenarios.

Table 1. Mapping of manufacturing repurposing scenarios to industry 4.0 components

Repurposing scenarios	Flexible production line	Trusted supply chains	DQM and ZDM	Regulatory and certification	Business continuity services
Scenario 1	M		O		M
Scenario 2	O	O	M	M	O
Scenario 3		M	O		O
Scenario 4		M	O	O	O

Figure 1 Illustrates how the above-listed services are integrated in a unified platform, while breaking down some of them in sub-services. For instance, the regulatory compliance and certification services are analyzed to sub-services for site, equipment, process, and product certification. Likewise, the business continuity services include various services such as plant risk assessment, shifts allocation, context awareness, remote support, training, and reskilling. Some of these services address Operator 4.0 needs. Key to the integration of the various services is the industrial data space [6], which enables the trusted exchange of information across the various stakeholders. Figure 1 also illustrates a semantic interoperability framework, which plays a key role in ensuring that data from different sources adhere to common semantics. This is important to supporting intelligent supply and demand matching for Scenario 2.

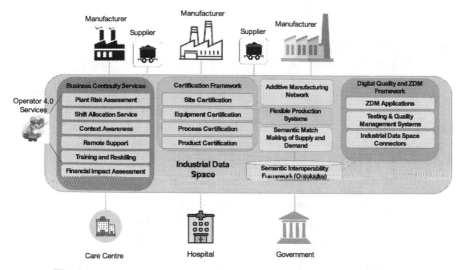

Fig. 1. Integration concept for manufacturing repurposing transformations

4   Operator 4.0 Services for Crises Management

4.1   (COVID19) Plant Risk Assessment: Identifying Operator 4.0 Risks

Manufacturers must identify activities that ease the spreading of the virus and plan for remedial actions to minimize the likelihood of spreading. To this end, they must establish risk assessment processes aimed at: (i) **Identifying and documenting risk factors** that could cause damage to the workforce and the enterprise. These include risk factors concerning the health and safety of the employees, yet there are also other risks that concern supply chain operations and contractors; (ii) **Grading the risks** through assessing their likelihood of occurrence and their potential impact on the enterprise. This is important for prioritizing remedial actions; (iii) **Specifying mitigation actions** for eliminating or controlling the risks. Typical risk control actions are the implementation of social distancing measures, the reengineering of production processes towards a safer direction (e.g., reduce sharing of tools), the implementation of staggering shifts, the exploitation of PPE for workers, and the provision of handwashing facilities. The risk assessment tool of our platform leverages best practices and recommendations specified by health and safety organizations in Europe (e.g., the Health and Safety Executive (HSE) governmental organization in the UK). They also specify mitigation actions such as: (i) **Workplace social distancing**; (ii) **Reduction of physical activities** that can lead to infection (e.g., sharing of tools across workers); (iii) **Support for Remote Work**; (iv) **Special measures for groups of people** that are at higher risk if infected. When compared to the COVID19 risk assessment forms used by many factories, our risk assessment tool provides the following added-value: (i) **On-line data collection and sharing** with other modules that support manufacturing repurposing; (ii) **Provision of actionable recommendations** for each main risk.

4.2   Operator 4.0 Shifts Allocation

Given COVID19 restrictions, ensuring an adequate number of employees with proper skills in the shopfloor is challenging. In this context, shifts allocation must identify mitigation actions that could alleviate production continuity challenges. In this direction, our solution considers the following functionalities: (i) **Assessing employee skillsets**, to identifying shortages in certain skills; (ii) **Identification of retraining requirements**, towards mitigating shift allocation and skills shortage; (iii) **Ensuring conflict avoidance** towards supporting production continuity; (iv) **Management of leaves and time-off**, considering applicable restrictions; (v) **Management of shift coverage**, including scheduling of positions based on the available skills; (vi) **Support for limited capacity operation**, for reasons such as physical distancing rules and unplanned absences due to infections. Baseline shift allocation functionalities are provided by mainstream ERP (Enterprise Resource Planning) systems such as SAP (i.e., SAP's Time and Attendance Management), and Microsoft Navision (i.e., Resources Allocation module). Furthermore, there are various stand-alone tools (e.g., Connectteam (https://connecteam. com/), mHelpDesk (https://www.mhelpdesk.com), Shiftboard (https://www.shiftboard. com), Staffjoy (https://www.shiftboard.com) that solve the shift allocation problem. Nevertheless, these tools fall short when it comes to supporting allocations in the light of COVID19. Most of them do not provide support for defining continuity between departments or defining department areas, so that employees' shifts can be optimized in the light of distancing restrictions. Based on these considerations, our tailored shift allocation services assign available staff workers to shifts per sector in the facility.

To achieve maximum isolation between staff workers, our tool divides them into groups. Each group is assigned to a unique shift in a specific sector of the department. Employees can work in different sectors during their shift. Each shift is configurable (i.e., 8-h by default with 2–3 daily shifts per sector). Personnel is assigned to shifts in each sector according to their profession and skills, i.e., employees that fit the sector's required profession have higher cardinality to be selected. Shift allocation is applied every two weeks. To balance the activities, each group of employees rotate their shift every week. To achieve maximum productivity per sector, a minimum number of working hours is set to our solution model with respect to the maximum contractual number of working hours per week. The key objective function of the solution is to minimize the sum of the deviations from the contractual number of working hours for each worker. Deviations apply additional costs to the organization: Positive deviations will lead to extra costs, while negative ones lead to missing hours in an employee's schedule that need to be paid. The solution model follows the MILP (Mixed-Integer Linear Programming) formulation. Linear dynamic programming solvers are applied to define the optimal solution to the shift allocation problem. The main constraints are reflected in the following equations.

$$\min \Delta : \sum_{e \in E} \sum_{w \in W} \delta_{ew}^{-} + \delta_{ew}^{+} \tag{1}$$

$$\text{s.t.} \sum_{\alpha \in A} \sum_{s \in S} x_{se}^{wa} = 1 \tag{2}$$

$$\sum_{\alpha \in A} \sum_{w \in E} x_{se}^{wa} = 1 \tag{3}$$

$$\sum_{e \in E} y_{se}^{wa} \geq \tau_{sa} \qquad (4)$$

$$\sum_{a \in A} \sum_{s \in S} y_{se}^{wa} + \delta_{ew}^{-} - \delta_{ew}^{+} = h_{e}^{max} \qquad (5)$$

$$x_{se}^{wa} \leq c_{ea} \qquad (6)$$

The six equations [7] are interpreted as follows: (1) The objective function that needs to be minimized. It minimizes the total deviation between the amount of weekly contractual hours of each worker and the actual working hours; (2) Each employee must be weekly assigned to exactly one shift and one sector (A => set of sectors, s => set of shifts); (3) Each employee must work in exactly one sector per shift (A => set of employees); (4) Ensures that the working hours for every shift in each sector are respected; (5) Ensures that the actual working hours per week for a specific employee after subtracting the deviations must be equal to the contractual hours; (6) Ensures that each employee that is selected for a specific shift is aligned with the sectors required qualifications ($C_{ea} \varepsilon \{0,1\}$), where 1 represents that an employee is qualified and 0 represents that the employee does not fill the requested qualifications for a specific sector. The optimization problem is solved using open-source Integer optimization solvers. For this purpose, open source software Google OR-Tools [8] is used for modeling and solving the MILP equations. The data model that supports the provision of the service is depicted in Fig. 2 below.

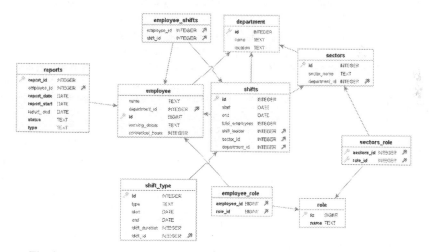

Fig. 2. Outline of the database model supporting the shifts allocation service

MILP problem formulation will lead to deterministic solutions, emergency situations are handled by each solution by assigning emergency personnel in standby to operate the production line of each sector during a shift in case of contagious event.

Each employee is described by the **employee** table. An employee can have multiple roles and is member of a specific department. Also, contractual working hours and his availability to work (working_status) are also persisted. An employee can be assigned to multiple shifts and each shift belongs to a specific sector, **employee_role, employee_shifts** are index tables defining many to many relationships between employee and roles as long as employees and shifts. Each shift is described by the **shift** table, each shift belongs to a sector and includes multiple employees that need to work between timestamps defined by **start** and **end** attributes. Emergency employees are scheduled in each shift so that they can replace colleges in case of infection. All departments consist of multiple sectors and require multiple qualifications in terms of roles from employees in order to be assigned to relative shifts. The **sector** table describes all sectors per department and **sector_role** index table defines many to many relationships between sectors and roles required for each of them during the production stages. Finally, each employee can provide reports regarding his health status and his availability to participate in his assigned shift. All information in each report is included in **reports** table.

In case of an infection during a shift, all employees that were working in the same group are isolated as part of the contact tracing procedure, until they receive a negative test. In the meanwhile, the facility operator decides if the shift will be operated by emergency staff assigned by the MILP formulation solution, or the production line can be adjusted to bypass the sector that the event took place.

4.3 Situational Awareness

COVID19 leads to volatile and dynamic manufacturing contexts. Therefore, manufacturing enterprises and their employees can greatly benefit from (near) real-time monitoring of business continuity parameters [9]. In this direction, trusted data spaces that collect and consolidate information from different sources can provide value as shown in Fig. 3. The data of these spaces are analyzed and exploited to improve the resilience of the monitored digital infrastructures, through the construction of Situational Awareness (SA). SA pictures (i.e., snapshots) provide an understanding of relevant events and offer the ability to observe the state of the systems in an integrated manner. Manufacturing workers and the business management can therefore confront these pictures to objectives, constraints, and acceptable risks.

The proposed modular and incremental approach to Situation Awareness design is grounded on a series of data analysis tools, based on (big) data analytics techniques, Artificial Intelligence, graph intelligence and correlation of information. To this end innovative multi-level situational awareness models may be adopted, to include in an integrated way information relating to all the relevant aspects for the integrated assessment of the digital infrastructures underlying the monitored manufacturing businesses. This information model constitutes the enabling layer to determine, analyze and manage the risk, at the different levels and components of the monitored infrastructures intended as a complex System of Systems.

Furthermore, as part of a situational awareness creation service, for the continuous monitoring of the resilience and business indicators of the monitored ecosystem, techniques and solutions will be integrated in order to obtain an effective early warning in the event of possible accidents or threats. In this sense, a "focusing" and "zooming" mechanism and related intelligent functions will be defined and designed to focus on specific entities. Therefore, this module implements a multi-level surveillance and situational awareness approach in which the monitoring services will be "activated" more on specific areas and data sources/flows according with the perceived level of risks and received high-level signals.

Any manufacturing business ecosystem is, in fact, characterized by multiple components and subsystems highly interconnected from a technical, technological, functional, organizational and process point of view. This interconnection turns into dependencies at the level of vulnerability that can generate cascading threats and accidents (think about the effect of a lack of raw material in a supplier that certainly impacts a multiplicity of its customers). Analysis of the cascading effects between the various elements of the same system or the same business manufacturing ecosystem can be conducted to assess the status and performance whole business ecosystem.

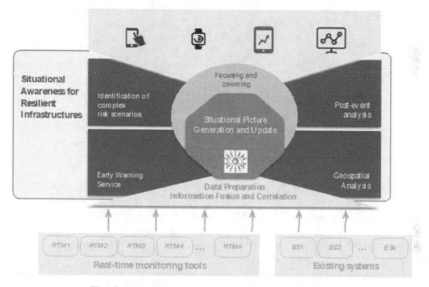

Fig. 3. Situational awareness solution architecture

4.4 Remote Support

COVID19 has added new requirements towards remote reprogramming and support, which eliminates the contact between the operators and ensures the security distances. Work allocation in the factory layout must be organized in the virtual environment, keeping security distances between plant operators, and maximizing productivity. In a limited mobility environment, the virtual environment must provide interactive support through VR (Virtual Reality) and AR (Augmented Reality) technologies. The latter allow the operators to be trained in new production requirements and to safely execute everyday tasks such as asset monitoring, field services and repairs.

5 Conclusions

This paper has specified digital services that alleviate challenges faced by manufacturers during COVID19. It has also illustrated the integration of these services in a unified platform. The latter includes Operator 4.0 related services aimed at ensuring engagement of workers with the proper skills in the plant operations, despite COVID19 restrictions. The presented platform could become a blueprint for manufacturing repurposing in cases of large-scale disruptions to production operations. In this direction, we are currently developing the services of the platform, which we plan to validate in two manufacturing plants that produce PPE/CCE products. The blueprint design and selected components will be made available through the Digital Factory Alliance (DFA) (https://digitalfacto ryalliance.eu/).

Acknowledgements. This work has been carried out in the H2020 Eur3ka project (Grant Agreement Number 101016175), which is co-funded by the European Commission.

References

1. Eurostat, Development of industrial production, January to November 2020. https://ec.eur opa.eu/eurostat/statistics-explained/index.php/Impact_of_Covid-19_crisis_on_industrial_p roduction
2. Policy Link. Covid-19: International Manufacturing Policy Responses - A preliminary review of international approaches to supporting the manufacturing supply chains and workforce. University of Cambridge (2020). https://www.ciip.group.cam.ac.uk/reports-and-articles/covid-19-international-manufacturing-policy-respon/download/2020-04-07-COVID19A.pdf
3. Sean, O.: How GM and Ford Switched Out Pickup Trucks for Breathing Machines. The Verge (2020)
4. Netland, T.: A better answer to the ventilator shortage as the pandemic rages on. Zurich, World Economic Forum, April 2020
5. López-Gómez, C., et al.: COVID-19 Critical Supplies: The Manufacturing Repurposing Challenge. United Nations Industrial Development Organization (2020)
6. Industrial Data Spaces Association, Reference Architecture Model, Version 3.0, April 2019
7. Zucchi, G., Iori, M., Subramanian, A.: Personnel scheduling during Covid 19 pandemic, October 2020. https://link.springer.com/article/10.1007/s11590-020-01648-2.pdf
8. Google Ink: About OR-Tools. https://developers.google.com/optimization/introduction/ove rview. Accessed June 2021
9. Furtado, V., Kolaja, T., Mueller, C., Salguero, J.: Managing a manufacturing plant through the coronavirus crisis. Mckinsey Operational Practice, Report, April 2020

Anatomy of a Digital Assistant

Stefan Wellsandt[1(✉)], Karl Hribernik[1], and Klaus-Dieter Thoben[1,2]

[1] BIBA - Bremer Institut für Produktion und Logistik GmbH at the University of Bremen,
Hochschulring 20, 28359 Bremen, Germany
{wel,hri,tho}@biba.uni-bremen.de

[2] Faculty of Production Engineering, University of Bremen, Badgasteiner Straße 1,
28359 Bremen, Germany

Abstract. Why is it helpful to have a digital assistant? This question's answer is not simple nor easy to find because artificial intelligence (AI) assistants, such as Alexa, Bixbi, or Siri, are amorphous compound technology and multi-purpose tools. Most of an assistant's components provide unique benefits on their own. Mobility, voice interaction, the delegation of administrative tasks, and rapid data analysis are typical benefits, but they are not exclusive to digital assistants. Understanding an assistant's benefits helps assistant designers and decision-makers who need to assess whether an assistant is a suitable workforce enhancement tool. Academic literature often describes an assistant's benefits superficially. This article presents an overview of a preliminary catalog of these benefits in manufacturing. It covers central access, customization, delegation and guidance, eyes-free and hands-free interactions, mobile assistance, the support of multiple interface types, permanent accessibility, and speed. We conclude that the cataloged benefits need more evidence, preferably created during experiments in natural manufacturing environments, to explore and experience the factors that determine the use of a digital assistant. These factors include trust in AI systems, impacts on teams and individuals, training and education, and capabilities of open and closed technologies. Disadvantages, limitations, and risks concern reduced worker autonomy, constrained language understanding, increased dependency on software, and harmful exploitation.

Keywords: Virtual assistant · Conversational AI · Voice interface · Industry 4.0 · Smart Manufacturing

1 Introduction

Why is it helpful to have a digital assistant? This question's answer is not simple nor easy to find because artificial intelligence (AI) assistants, such as Alexa, Cortana, Bixbi, or Siri, are *amorphous compound technology* and *multi-purpose tools*. Most of an assistant's components provide unique benefits on their own. Mobility, voice interaction, the delegation of tasks, and rapid data analysis are typical benefits, but they are not exclusive to digital assistants. Therefore, developing an assistant is challenging because customers can object that they do not benefit from all components immediately. For example, if an

A. Dolgui et al. (Eds.): APMS 2021, IFIP AICT 633, pp. 321–330, 2021.
https://doi.org/10.1007/978-3-030-85910-7_34

organization wants to delegate repetitive tasks to artificial intelligence, its solution may not need a voice interface or run on a mobile device. An assistant's compound nature may overfit in this case.

Answering the question above begins with an assistant's anatomy. Its purpose is to identify the assistant's components, functions, and benefits. Assistant designers and customers can jointly use this knowledge to assess if a digital assistant is a helpful tool. The starting point for this anatomy can be the *business domain*. A digital assistant for employees will likely integrate deeply into the company's information systems to be as helpful as possible. Therefore, such an assistant would be expensive to develop and deploy, and due to the novelty of its technology, it may fail to be helpful initially.

Besides, a failing assistant is often more costly for a business than a consumer. Disruptions of deeply integrated software can propagate and affect many people, machines, processes, and even collaborating organizations. Therefore, businesses are typically more skeptical about digital assistants.

Among the business domain, *manufacturing* is highly relevant for digital assistants. In 2017, the European Union's manufacturing sector had around 2 million enterprises, employed 28.5 million persons, and generated 1,820 billion Euros value-added [1]. The future workforce in the EU will be smaller due to demographic changes, diverse due to immigration, and threatened to be replaced by automation solutions [2]. Enhancing the remaining workforce's skills and capabilities through artificial intelligence offers a way out of this challenging situation. It allows companies to employ people they would otherwise not hire. At the same time, digital assistants provide several opportunities to save employees' time and, consequently, contribute to increasing work efficiency.

This paper aims to summarize the benefits of business-focused digital assistants in manufacturing. Its results may help assistant designers and decision-makers in companies assessing whether an assistant is a suitable tool at work. The remainder of this paper has four sections. Section 2 presents conversational and technology-based agents, digital assistant types, and other related work. Section 3 describes a use case that outlines challenges and problems in manufacturing environments. Section 4 presents the identified benefits that digital assistants could provide, while Sect. 5 concludes the results and suggests future work.

2   Related Work

Academic literature about digital assistants is extensive and heterogeneous. The Scopus database finds more than 12,000 entries that contain digital assistant, virtual assistant, conversational agent, or software robot in the abstract, title, or keywords. These entries belong to computer science (6,500+), engineering (4,300+), medicine (2,400+), mathematics (1,500+), and social sciences (1300+). Scopus indicates 889 entries for 2020 and a peak of 1,332 entries for 2004 – which is the same year Scopus launched. The numbers above demonstrate that the scientific foundation for digital assistants is strong. Literature likely contains critical information to answer why these assistants are useful.

2.1 Conversational and Technology-Based Agents

The main conceptual foundation for this article is the so-called **conversational agent** (CA). Literature mentions various terms describing software with similar functions. Some terms are synonymous with the CA, and others articulate a specific subtle distinction [3]. A CA is a dialog system embedded in personal technologies and devices [3]. It can support spoken and written natural language as input and output. The minimal architecture of a CA provides the following functions [4, 5]:

Speech recognition transcribes voice utterances – the result is a text. *Meaning extraction* uses the transcript to understand intents and entities, i.e., context. *Data queries* acquire additional information to fulfill the intent. The *Dialog manager* tracks the dia logue state and decides how to respond [6]. It uses the dialog state to interpret the final meaning of an utterance. *Response generation* selects or creates the specific response text. Finally, the *speech output* synthesizes voice from that text.

A CA supports task completion in real-time and develops knowledge about the user to act on their behalf. It does not focus on anthropomorphism nor representing a specific person and is, therefore, no human avatar [7].

The second key concept is the **technology-based agent**, a system that observes, interprets, decides, and learns to act upon its environment [8]. This agent interacts with humans and machines to achieve shared goals. Autonomy and capabilities determine how such agents support humans. Less autonomous agents can retrieve information for the user and automate tasks in decision-making. If a user delegates more responsibility to an agent, it can execute various tasks without further human involvement. An agent with limited capabilities uses static patterns to react to the inputs it receives from the environment. Sophisticated agents learn to operate in initially unknown environments and improve their capabilities.

2.2 Digital Assistants

Digital assistants are socio-technical systems and an application class [9]. The former considers individual users, their goals, related tasks, and technology that processes data and allows human-computer interaction. The latter means the assistant is an orchestration of different components that provide specific functions.

Knote et al. [10] investigated 115 assistants and identified 31 design characteristics grouped into ten dimensions. Relevant characteristics include, for instance, communication mode, the direction of interaction, query input, response output, assistance domain, command complexity, adaptivity, and embodiment. Knote et al. [10] used them in a k-means clustering method to identify assistant categories. Table 1 summarizes the results of their investigation.

Table 1. Assistant categories identified through empirical analysis [10]

Category	Features
Adaptive voice assistants	Speech, optical sensors, screen outputs, execute services upon request, general-purpose, adaptive, computer-generated human-like voice
Chatbot assistants	Text, images, videos, screen interaction, task-oriented support, special purpose, present information to users, virtual characters
Embodied virtual assistants	Human-like, speech, screen outputs, virtual characters, special purpose, adjust to user autonomously, anthropomorphism
Passive pervasive assistants	Unobtrusive, collects data from sensors, initiates interaction with user, observes user's tasks and context, autonomous, special purpose
Natural conversation assistants	Speech, imitate human natural language interactions, execute services upon request, static behavior, understands compound commands

The characteristics and categories above provide a first direction for the benefits of digital assistants. *General-purpose* assistants support humans in tasks, such as information retrieval, calendar management, working with communication channels, and controlling smart devices. An assistant with *special-purpose* knowledge supports humans in fulfilling clearly defined tasks, such as filling an issue report. Some assistants are *adaptive* and learn from interactions. They can improve their language understanding and interpretation skills and adjust their behavior to improve user experience. Finally, *embodied* assistants use anthropomorphism to increase user acceptance – a typical feature is generating a human-like voice.

Maedche et al. [9] point out that machines, such as digital assistants, are ideal for repeatable and highly structured tasks. They are good at collecting, storing, and processing data and they make accurate predictions provided the environment is relatively stable. On the other hand, humans are better suited to solve abstract problems and manage fragmented information efficiently. Besides, they are more aware of context and can use intuition, empathy, and ethics in decision-making. Maedche et al. [9] also argue that the desired collaboration level between humans and digital assistants will occur within a continuum of autonomy. On one end, the human decides, and, on the other end, the assistant decides – the space in between covers all possible cases where AI assistants support humans and vice versa.

2.3 Operator 4.0 and Software Robots

Romero et al. [11] introduced the idea of the so-called Operator 4.0. This name summarizes an operator's new roles in Industry 4.0, Smart Manufacturing, and similar visions for future manufacturing. The *Smart Operator* role refers to operators that collaborate with digital assistants in the following areas: a) searching and retrieving from a digital library; b) scheduling and setting reminders for actions or events; c) store and visualize planning data to support humans in problem-solving; d) mobility and location assistance; e) interfacing with connected devices; f) detecting and diagnosing errors and problems; g) suggest troubleshooting tools and strategies; h) track operator and machine behavior to build predictive models; and i) notify about the need for proactive actions.

Rabelo, Romero and Zambiasi [12] demonstrated how operators could benefit from software robots, referred to as softbots. The authors recognized that softbots largely overlap with the software agent concept [13]. Abner et al. [14] argue that a softbot can respond to a user request directly, perform pre-defined scheduled tasks, and proactively communicate the status of fully delegated tasks. Their softbot provides descriptions, diagnostics, predictions, and prescriptions, which users access via sequential workflows or independently.

2.4   Studies on the Use of Voice Assistants

Rzepka [15] investigated when and why users choose speech interaction over traditional user interfaces. She applied the Means-End Chain theory to understand individual decision-making processes. Her findings for a group of 31 users indicate that fundamental objectives are: faster task completion, easy access to the underlying system, joy of the interaction, minimize physical effort, and minimize deliberate thinking. The author points out that her study focused on the private use of digital assistants, and future work should address assistants' use in an organizational context.

3   Use Case

We define a use case in this section to clarify challenges in manufacturing that digital assistants could address. The case outlines the work situation in production with a focus on information-intensive processes. Such processes may naturally benefit from digital assistants. The following description grounds on our experience from two assistant prototypes. Their focus is on predictive maintenance, augmented analytics, and cognitive assistance during on-the-job training in production. We added labels in parentheses to highlight challenges and connection points for digital assistance.

In production environments, workers operate, maintain, and repair machines to manufacture products. These persons work under *time pressure* to meet production performance goals (A). Performing these jobs requires *skills and competencies*. Workers receive vocational and on-the-job training to acquire these – this training is costly, takes weeks, months, or years, and limits the available workforce (B). Beyond their initial training, workers continuously learn and develop their skills and competencies (C).

Workers experience *fatigue* and require *recreation* – physically demanding work or highly repetitive tasks exhaust workers faster. Organizations can use a shift system to guarantee permanent operations. However, shift systems are costly because the organization must employ persons with similar skills, competencies, and knowledge (D).

Besides, reaching the performance goals in complex manufacturing processes typically requires workers to *access information* about machines, products, and processes

(E). Some information is available after time-consuming data processing and analysis only (F). Information differs in complexity, may change quickly, and is accessible through software or printed media; it can be structured, semi-structured, or unstructured. Related software typically has different user interfaces and might be installed on desktop computers. The former requires workers to *learn* using these interfaces (G), and the latter requires them to *move* between the workplace and the computer (H). Both are time-consuming, and moving to access an interface *interrupts and delays tasks* (I).

We describe the following benefits from two perspectives: machine operators and technicians. *Machine operators* are responsible for one or more machines. They operate them, perform simple maintenance tasks, and collaborate with production line managers and technicians to solve problems. *Technicians* are responsible for maintaining and repairing machinery – they are highly mobile and may visit several machines per day. Besides, they analyze the hardware systematically to identify the root causes of problems and address them through repair, replacement, or other on-site measures. Such tasks may require both hands, and technicians must pay attention to avoid injuries or damage to the machine. Typically, they use software for complex analyses, and they collaborate with people from different professions to identify and discuss causes and solutions.

4   Results

The related work above contains various arguments for using a digital assistant in manufacturing. Unfortunately, authors often describe benefits superficially in a single sentence or list them without further justification and explanation. This lack of detail makes it difficult for assistant developers and decision-makers to articulate and identify benefits that solve or partially address specific problems. This section outlines an assistant's benefits and connects them to technology and practical manufacturing challenges. The collection is not comprehensive and represents a work-in-progress.

The order of the following benefits is alphabetical to create a neutral overview. Parentheses with a letter indicate how benefits connect to the challenges in the use case.

Central Access (E, G, H, I). A digital assistant interfacing multiple information systems can become a central access point to these systems from the user's perspective. Users access the assistant via one or more personal devices. Central access minimizes learning different interfaces and moving between workplace and suitable computers.

Customization (A, C). Employees differ in skills, competencies, motivations, physical capabilities, and personality. Providing customized assistance can address individual needs and preferences. It can increase the acceptance of using a digital assistant. Higher acceptance could minimize opportunity costs that emerge when employees reject potential assistance. Furthermore, such costs could incur when provided assistance is inefficient due to an individual's characteristics.

Delegation (A, D, F). Tasks can be highly structured and repetitive. As a result, employees perceive these tasks as boring, and employers seek their delegation to a computer. The former affects an employee's satisfaction with their work situation, while the latter saves time. Companies can use this time-saving in two ways. First, to *increase employees' efficiency* because they can perform more of the remaining tasks in this time. Second, to *empower employees* by assigning them new tasks that focus on solving abstract problems and managing fragmented information efficiently.

Users can delegate a variety of tasks to a digital assistant. The assistant performs the delegated tasks with different degrees of autonomy and can perform synchronously with a user's task or asynchronously. *Synchronous* performance is beneficial during imminent work situations where users and assistants collaborate [16]. *Asynchronous* task performance can be necessary when tasks require a long execution time. An assistant can significantly outperform humans in performing specific tasks.

An example is calendar management, where the user can perform the task easily but may decide to delegate it to have time for more valuable activities. A second example is the delegation of root cause analysis. Skilled employees can analyze failures to identify root causes but decide to leave this task to a digital assistant. The assistant may be significantly more efficient than a human because it can process large amounts of data reliably and quickly.

Eyes-Free (A, I). For many tasks, it can be beneficial if the employee's eyes focus on the objects of interest. Changing this focus may result in oversight, which can have no impact. Sometimes oversight has an impact, though, ranging from minor follow-up costs to severe injuries or death. Employees can use their voice to interact with a digital assistant without switching their eyes' focus. Its impact is difficult to pinpoint, but it includes less oversight due to the avoided shift of eye focus and avoiding the costs of inaccessible information because the eyes focus on the objects of interest.

Guidance (B). Assistants can guide employees through complex tasks, effectively reducing related skill requirements. This reduction would allow producers to hire less skilled people, reduce training costs, and increase the potential workers' supply. Typically, these employees receive lower salaries and, therefore, further cost savings.

Hands-Free (A, I). Performing tasks can require that employees use both hands simultaneously. In these situations, graphical user interfaces are nearly impossible to use.[1] Instead, an employee can use voice to interact with a digital assistant. Its impact is difficult to pinpoint, but it includes aspects such as: saving the time spent on using the graphical interface, increased safety due to avoided work interruptions, and reducing costs of making information accessible while hands are busy. The latter includes, for instance, the time spent by co-workers that must deliver the needed information.

Mobile Assistance (A). Employees may need to move during their work to access different locations. A digital assistant can support these employees either while they move or at the target location. Mobile assistance is beneficial when notifications reach a person quickly to minimize follow-up costs – i.e., actual costs and opportunity costs. It is also beneficial if a person must act quickly for the same reason. Acting includes, for instance, delegating a task. Besides, mobile assistance covers on-site support.

---

[1] Nearly because graphical interfaces may use hands-free technologies, such as eye tracking.

Multiple Interface Types (E). Employees may need specific forms of assistance for tasks and situations. Specific interface types, e.g., voice, text, haptic, or visual elements, can be adequate for some but not all tasks and situations. For instance, an information retrieval task can return a table with measurements. A voice interface conveys the table's contents much slower than an interface that uses visual elements to display the table. A digital assistant can have two or more interfaces to account for the variability among assistances, tasks, and situations.

Permanent Accessibility (D). Human co-workers experience fatigue and require recreation time. Their services are, therefore, not accessible to others at all times. A digital assistant has no downtime provided the infrastructure has energy management[2] and redundancy to compensate for maintenance, repair, overhaul, and breakdown. Users can – at all times – benefit from an assistant, either by requesting support or because the assistant can communicate with the user whenever necessary.

Augmented data analytics is one application for manufacturing that benefits from an assistant's permanent accessibility. For example, users can ask the assistant to perform root-cause analysis any time a factory system fails. Since the assistant has no working hours, it can immediately respond, perform the analysis, and report the result. Besides, an assistant that continuously monitors measurements can notify one or more users about unusual measurements.

Speed (A). Performing tasks faster mostly has the benefit that an employee can spend the saved time on other tasks. Besides, taking less time can minimize follow-up costs, as outlined above. A digital assistant can accelerate task performance in different ways. Speed advantages of functions that involve arithmetic and logical operations are often easy to argue because the time saving is so significant. The benefit of voice interactions is harder to quantify, but Ruan et al. [17] identified that using voice is almost three times faster than typing on a QWERTY keyboard. These results are only indicative because the authors performed their experiments in a controlled environment with little noise. Besides, the error rate in the final transcribed text was higher when using voice. Other areas that can create speed benefits are the flatter navigation structures of voice interfaces and the effects of learning efficient assistance.

5   Conclusion

The results above are our first attempt to answer why digital assistants are helpful in manufacturing. Indeed, they are preliminary, and the remaining vague expressions require evidence and discussion before assistant designers and decision-makers can use them effectively.

Future research should investigate benefits through experiments in *natural work environments* to explore and experience the various factors determining digital assistants' use. These factors are concepts, such as trust in AI systems, impacts on teams and individuals, training and education, and capabilities of open and closed technologies.

---

[2] This includes, for instance, recharge strategies for mobile devices and permanent power supply.

Besides, future work has to clarify the **disadvantages and limitations** of using assistants in manufacturing. There is an inherent risk that workers lose their *autonomy* when assistants influence or take over their tasks. Human-in-the-loop designs could ensure that workers always remain essential for the process and participate in decisions.

An assistant has technological and designed limits *understanding language.* For example, it may not understand the jargon in manufacturing and need human help resolving ambiguity. Worker training must create awareness for these constraints and teach how to talk effectively with a digital assistant. Developing and performing this training may be costly and time-consuming.

When digital assistants contribute substantial work in manufacturing, producers become *dependent.* The assistant must work reliably   sometimes even in extreme situations, such as a blackout or network breakdown. It should be replaceable by another digital assistant (e.g., to avoid vendor lock-in) or by a human to cover situations where the assistant is unavailable.

Finally, every additional information and communication technology in an organization increases the risk that third parties *exploit* it. Scenarios range from industrial espionage through eavesdropping to the corruption of an assistant to disrupt production or harm employees.

Acknowledgments. This work is funded by the European Union's Horizon 2020 research and innovation program via the project COALA "COgnitive Assisted agile manufacturing for a LAbor force supported by trustworthy Artificial Intelligence" (Grant agreement No 957296).

References

1. Eurostat: Manufacturing statistics - NACE Rev. 2 (2020). https://ec.europa.eu/eurostat/statistics-explained/pdfscache/10086.pdf. Accessed 16 Mar 2021
2. Smit, S., Tacke, T., Lund, S., et al.: The future of work in Europe: automation, workforce transitions, and the shifting geography of employment (2020)
3. Luger, E., Sellen, A.: "Like having a really bad PA": The gulf between user expectation and experience of conversational agents. In: Kaye, J. (ed.) Proceedings of the 2016 CHI Conference on Human Factors in Computing Systems. Association for Computing Machinery, New York, pp. 5286–5297 (2016)
4. Wyard, P., Simons, A., Appleby, S., et al.: Spoken language systems - Beyond prompt and response. BT Technol. J. **14**, 187–205 (1996)
5. McTear, M., Callejas, Z., Griol, D. (eds.): The Conversational Interface: Talking to Smart Devices, 1st edn. Springer, Cham (2016). https://doi.org/10.1007/978-3-319-32967-3
6. Harms, J.-G., Kucherbaev, P., Bozzon, A., et al.: Approaches for dialog management in conversational agents. IEEE Internet Comput. **23**, 13–22 (2019). https://doi.org/10.1109/MIC.2018.2881519
7. von der Pütten, A.M., Krämer, N.C., Gratch, J., et al.: "It doesn't matter what you are!" Explaining social effects of agents and avatars. Comput. Hum. Behav. **26**, 1641–1650 (2010). https://doi.org/10.1016/j.chb.2010.06.012
8. Seeber, I., Waizenegger, L., Seidel, S., et al.: Collaborating with technology-based autonomous agents. INTR **30**, 1–18 (2020). https://doi.org/10.1108/INTR-12-2019-0503
9. Maedche, A., et al.: AI-based digital assistants. Bus. Inf. Syst. Eng. **61**(4), 535–544 (2019). https://doi.org/10.1007/s12599-019-00600-8

10. Knote, R., Janson, A., Söllner, M., et al.: Classifying smart personal assistants: an empirical cluster analysis. In: Bui, T. (ed.) Proceedings of the 52nd Hawaii International Conference on System Sciences. Hawaii International Conference on System Sciences (2019)

11. Romero, D., Stahre, J., Wuest, T., et al.: Towards an operator 4.0 typology: a human-centric perspective on the fourth industrial revolution technologies. In: Dessouky, M., Dessouky, Y., Eldin, H.K. (eds.) Proceedings of the 46th International Conference on Computers and Industrial Engineering, pp. 608–618 (2016)

12. Rabelo, R.J., Romero, D., Zambiasi, S.P.: Softbots supporting the operator 4.0 at smart factory environments. In: Moon, I., Lee, G.M., Park, J., Kiritsis, D., von Cieminski, G. (eds.) APMS 2018. IAICT, vol. 536, pp. 456–464. Springer, Cham (2018). https://doi.org/10.1007/978-3-319-99707-0_57

13. Rabelo, R.J., Zambiasi, S.P., Romero, D.: Collaborative softbots: enhancing operational excellence in systems of cyber-physical systems. In: Camarinha-Matos, L.M., Afsarmanesh, H., Antonelli, D. (eds.) PRO-VE 2019. IAICT, vol. 568, pp. 55–68. Springer, Cham (2019). https://doi.org/10.1007/978-3-030-28464-0_6

14. Abner, B., Rabelo, R.J., Zambiasi, S.P., Romero, D.: Production management as-a-service: a softbot approach. In: Lalic, B., Majstorovic, V., Marjanovic, U., von Cieminski, G., Romero, D. (eds.) APMS 2020. IAICT, vol. 592, pp. 19–30. Springer, Cham (2020). https://doi.org/10.1007/978-3-030-57997-5_3

15. Rzepka, C.: Examining the use of voice assistants: a value-focused thinking approach. In: Santana, M., Montealegre, R., Rodriguez-Abitia, G., et al. (eds.) Proceedings of the 25th Americas Conference on Information Systems (AMCIS 2019), pp. 1–10 (2019)

16. Norman, D.: Design, business models, and human-technology teamwork. Res. Technol. Manage. **60**, 26–30 (2017). https://doi.org/10.1080/08956308.2017.1255051

17. Ruan, S., Wobbrock, J.O., Liou, K., et al.: Comparing speech and keyboard text entry for short messages in two languages on touchscreen phones. In: Proceedings of the ACM on Interactive, Mobile, Wearable and Ubiquitous Technologies vol. 1, pp. 1–23 (2018). https://doi.org/10.1145/3161187

Human in the AI Loop in Production Environments

C. Emmanouilidis[✉], S. Waschull, J. A. C. Bokhorst, and J. C. Wortmann

University of Groningen, PO Box 800, 9700 AV Groningen, The Netherlands
{c.emmanouilidis,s.waschull,j.a.c.bokhorst,j.c.wortmann}@rug.nl

Abstract. The integration of Artificial Intelligence (AI) in manufacturing is often pursued as technology push. In contrast, this paper looks upon the AI-human interaction from a viewpoint that considers both to play an important role in reshaping their individual capabilities. It specifically focuses on how humans can play an important role in enhancing AI capabilities. The introduced concepts are tested in an industrial case study of vision-based inspection in production lines. Furthermore, the paper highlights the need to consider relevant implications for work design for AI integration. The contribution can be of practical value for system developers and work designers in how to target at the design stage the human contribution in AI-enabled systems for production environments.

Keywords: Human-in-the-loop · AI · Work design · Industry 4.0

1 Introduction

Modern manufacturing environments are not simply technical systems but complex sociotechnical ones. In sociotechnical systems, human actors hold a key role with implications for system performance, alongside the physical technical systems. However, while the interaction between human and non-human actors in sociotechnical systems has been broadly explored, there is still a lack of understanding regarding the inclusion of Artificial Intelligence (AI) actors within sociotechnical systems. Aiming at narrowing this gap in the literature, this paper critically assesses human engagement with AI. It then proposes a model of human-AI interaction that goes beyond augmentation, and applies that on an industrial case study to show how selected aspects of these interaction can positively affect outcomes. This can be of practical value for system developers and work designers in how to effectively integrate human-centric AI in production environments at the design stage of such a process. This paper is structured as follows. Section 2 analyses related work and the role of human and AI actors in sociotechnical production environments. Section 3 outlines key aspects of integrating human and non-human actors to enhance AI capabilities. Section 4 applies elements of the proposed concepts on an industrial case study. Section 5 outlines work design implications and concludes outlining next steps for the research.

© IFIP International Federation for Information Processing 2021
Published by Springer Nature Switzerland AG 2021
A. Dolgui et al. (Eds.): APMS 2021, IFIP AICT 633, pp. 331–342, 2021.
https://doi.org/10.1007/978-3-030-85910-7_35

2   Human and AI Actors in Sociotechnical Systems

The joint consideration of human and technical actors in sociotechnical systems has been studied for long, going back to the early years of Human System Engineering (HSE). HSE refers to the application of principles, models, and techniques to system design, taking into account human capabilities and limitations [1]. Increasingly literature accepts that human actors can be more effective when they act upon a shared context ("situational awareness") of work activities, which is a "collective activity" view of work environments [2]. A collective activity is not merely the sum of individual parts but is shaped up from interacting actors. The nature of these interactions is now deeply influenced by the introduction of AI in production activities [3]. The integration of human and AI actors in manufacturing can be looked upon as a collective activity. It is therefore justified to consider not only how processes can be automated, or how humans can be augmented by AI [4], but also to capitalize on the emergent outcomes of the evolving human-AI interaction. These outcomes become more powerful when the opportunities offered by humans augmenting the AI [5] or by integrating the human cognitive capabilities in the AI loop are designed-in the systems [6]. Human cognitive capabilities have been part of the design of artificial cognitive system architectures [7] but are not often sufficiently integrated in AI deployments in manufacturing. Human-AI interaction can drive radical changes in the affordances of the human and non-human actors in such environments. The term "affordance" is used in different disciplines and broadly "denotes action possibilities provided to the actor by the environment" [8]. The significant expansion of interaction affordances arising from the human-AI integration has not received sufficient attention when dealing with AI in manufacturing. This adds to the growing acceptance that, since the application of Industry 4.0 technologies in production systems changes the role of workers in unprecedented ways [9], there is a need to address challenges to enhance both operational performance and work design and human effects. As a result, human-centricity, which emphasises the need to pay attention to human workers during the design and adoption of sociotechnical systems, is now pointing towards human-centric design approaches, and human-centered principles in the design of AI, within the view point of work design [10]. While the role of humans regarding changes in work and work organization has received ample attention in the literature in the context of today's technological change [11], for many practitioners the human implications of integrating AI within the technology toolset of their operating environments remains a black box. Part of the difficulty lies with the relative lack of understanding regarding the nature of human-AI interaction. This in turn limits both the effectiveness of the integration of humans in the AI loop, as well as the perspectives of work design towards integrating more effective human-AI synergies in production environments. These are looked upon in further detail next.

3   The Role of Human Actors in Enhancing AI

There is barely a single definition of what constitutes AI, but to the extent that intelligence characteristics are associated with thought processes and behaviours, the expectations for an AI agent would be to exhibit at least some of those characteristics. The thought processes viewpoints are typically looked upon from the cognitive systems and logic viewpoints, while the behavioural ones may result from applying concepts, methods, and practice related to machine learning, knowledge representation and reasoning, natural language processing, and agent-based systems [12]. While AI has the potential to take on human tasks [13], there is a growing consensus to design human-centric technologies which integrate rather than eliminate humans and their capabilities [6, 14, 15]. While the majority of such human-in-the-loop scenarios consider how AI augments humans [16], the opposite (humans aiding AI) also holds significant potential for the success-ful integration of humans and AI in manufacturing [5, 6, 15]. The advances made in the practical application of AI, involving scenarios of automation and augmentation of human work [13], create the need to better understand the interactions between human and AI actors. Human augmentation in manufacturing has benefitted from a range of technology enablers and the established paradigm shift to ubiquitous computing [17]. Contributing enables include multimodal interfaces [18], augmented [19] and virtual [20] reality, context-adaptive computing [21], exoskeletons for physical augmentation [22] and natural interfaces, including speech [23] and brain – computer interfaces [24]. Yet, the potential contribution of humans towards AI agents [5] can be beneficial across the whole process workflow of data-driven machine learning. Considering this from a software-based systems perspective [25], the workflow of activities wherein humans can have a distinct role can be outlined in the waterfall diagram of Fig. 1. The diagram illustrates the five typical phases of such a software engineering process. While the

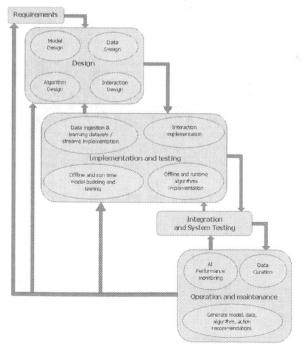

Fig. 1. Machine learning waterfall diagram outlining human actions

requirements and integration and system testing phases are certainly relevant to human involvement, the interest is nonetheless placed on the design, implementation and testing, and operation and maintenance, to outline key human involvement with machine learning, rather than the system or software process.

Table 1 shortlists specific human involvement activities for the design stage, while the corresponding activities for the implementation and operation stages are seen in Table 2 and 3 respectively. Both domain and data/AI experts have distinct roles there.

Table 1. Humans aiding AI actors - design

Activities	Application perspective	Machine learning perspective
Problem definition	Set application targets (e.g. recommend actions, classify states, estimate values)	Translate application to ML targets (ML problem formulation)
Data design	Link aims to data collection Ensure data are representative of the problem domain states Explore and assess veracity of data (visual analytics, statistics) Labeling data records Enrich data with domain-relevant contextual information Domain-specific data attributes	Ensure appropriate statistical representation of data in samples Design data types and structures Determine data quality management (for example missing values policy) Produce recommendations for data management activities Design ML-specific data features Feature selection/extraction for ML
ML model design	Domain-relevant abstract model of problem (for example, time series, spatial or other; decision or recommender system, etc.) Impose constraints/relations on models (for example "forced" associations in relational models according to application specific knowledge)	Select family of ML models to address problem needs (for example a Time-Delayed network for times series, a Convolutional Neural network for vision, an explainable model for model transparency, etc.) Select method for initialising structure of models (for example, how many layers, how many computational nodes per layer, the type of function that nodes perform)

(*continued*)

Table 1. (*continued*)

Activities	Application perspective	Machine learning perspective
ML algorithm design	Consider the "physical" source of knowledge about the data and feedback on ML performance (for example penalty / rewards for reinforcement learning, error estimation through real, model-based, or simulation systems)	Performance metrics selection Training [off line, streaming][unsupervised, supervised, reinforcement, semi-supervised] Method to initialise weights/costs for ML Method to set algorithmic hyperparameters Select how outcomes are derived (activation functions, decision thresholds etc.) Select performance assessment data policy (e.g. sampling/training/test/validation data) ML process flow (i.e. data batch sizes, epochs, algorithm termination criteria etc.)
Interaction design	Data, features, model and algorithms selection	Integrate human interaction designs into ML designs and enable outcomes validation

Table 2. Humans aiding AI actors - Implementation

Activities	Application perspective	Machine learning perspective
Data ingestion	Physical data integration	Link ML models with data sources
Model building	Deploy trained models with operational workflows	Develop different ML models Trained model selection
Algorithm building	Deploy implemented algorithms	Implement selected algorithms
Interaction building	Select recommendations based on domain-specific knowledge	Include interaction interfaces in ML process

The human role in shaping AI is not static. AI-enabled systems and human operators have their affordances reshaped as a result of their interaction, as they benefit from each other's capabilities. The superiority of human cognitive capabilities over AI in performing cross-domain activities is not a controversial statement and the same applies regarding the superiority of AI in repetitive and data-intensive tasks. Efforts to bridge the deficiency of AI to perform only within narrow contexts have been mostly focused on transfer learning [26] aiming to transfer the learned capabilities from the original

Table 3. Humans aiding AI actors – operation and maintenance

Activities	Application perspective	Machine learning perspective
Track performance	Monitor if targets are met	Monitor ML performance
Data generation, curation	Curate/label new data and assign data to cases	Manage and adjust data distributions for ML (e.g. train/test/validate)
Choices and actions	Assess adequacy of assumptions and recommend adjustments Define priorities, utility values Choose 'costs' for outcomes Interpret, select, validate recommendations Select/execute actions	Generate multiple alternative ML models to meet performance targets Evaluation of actions based on defined 'utility values'/predictions Trigger Data, Model, Algorithm revisions

domain of the learning to a new one. There have been various examples of integrating human knowledge to machine learning [27]. Additionally, there is increased interest in the empowering effect that human and AI-driven non-human actors can have on each other [28]. Additionally, the concept of meta-human learning systems [29] has been proposed to refer to emergent "learning" capabilities of a sociotechnical system and this can be seen also from the prism of collective activity mentioned in Sect. 2. Starting from key concepts about humans-AI interaction proposed in [28] and incorporating ideas about introducing human cognitive capabilities in the AI loop [6], the way the two types of actors interact to maximise outcomes of their collective activity is illustrated in Fig. 2. Human actors, capabilities and interaction affordances are marked in green. AI-driven technical actor capabilities are marked with blue.

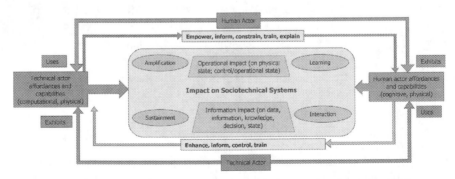

Fig. 2. Human and AI-enabled actors benefiting from each other's capabilities

All actors exhibit capabilities which are expressed in interaction affordances in the operating environment. Technical actors empower humans to expand their capabilities, inform them about relevant processes or knowledge, train them on certain tasks, explain outcomes or recommendations, but also bound their affordances within an admissible range of actions. Human actors can exert control over AI and perform a range of actions listed in Tables 1, 2 and 3, such as labelling or enhancing the knowledge range of the machine learning model. Through their interaction both actors' capabilities are enhanced, resulting in higher added value outcomes as part of collective activity.

4   Humans and AI in Vision-Based Quality Inspection

To illustrate some of the earlier concepts, an industrial use case of vision based quality inspection in consumer goods manufacturer production lines is selected. The manufacturer aims to automate part of the quality inspection via a human-cobot solution. Quality inspection cobots are equipped with digital cameras. AI capabilities aim to distinguish between good and bad quality components. Thus, the vision is to automate the repetitive task of checking each product by a human and instead introduce different human roles to undertake more cognitive demanding tasks. To explore this, tests were conducted with an image pool of labeled samples. The aim was to explore tasks that can be undertaken by AI and assess possibilities offered by integrating the human in the AI loop. The setup comprised 400 samples, equally divided between good and bad quality products. An example is shown in Fig. 3.

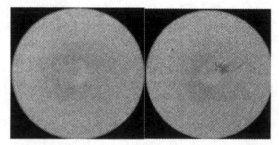

Fig. 3. Vision-based quality inspection showing good (left) and bad (right) quality products. Source: courtesy of Philips, through STAR project, ID: 956573, www.star-ai.eu.

The experiments involved training convolutional neural networks (CNN). Their grid-type structure makes them appropriate for image processing [30]. Defining a kernel of influence in the grid, a CNN is able to process image data in ways that are invariant to unimportant changes in the data, for example the exact position of an object in an image, or the exact angle of view when taking the image. There can be several convolutional processing steps in a CNN. Each step includes a convolution stage (image transformation into a different feature space). Defining the number of kernels of influence (neurons) and their spread (size of kernel) are the key user-specified parameters that define the convolution layer, which transforms the original data into an alternative "feature space" and for that reason the next layer of processing is considered the "feature detector" layer. This layer applies a nonlinear function on the features resulting from the convolution layer. It is possible to have multiple feature detector layers at different abstraction layers.

The final layer is the "pooling" when the processed features are combined to produce the final output. Being one of the earliest examples of deep learning, CNNs have witnessed a renaissance as their computational requirements ceased to be a challenge for computers with standard computing power. The experimental setup emulated active learning interaction tasks [31]:

A.   standard experiment with training, test and validation sets
B.   emulation of data labeling by humans to expand the knowledge pool of the CNN
C.   emulation of human-driven data resampling to emphasise hard to learn cases

These scenarios are now brought into the form of part of the Tables 1, 2 and 3: The achieved performance on each scenario is presented in Table 5, where TP, TN, FP, and FN standing for true positives, true negatives, false positive, and false negative cases. These experiments served the purpose of illustrating that even a basic level of human engagement in the AI loop can lead to notable AI performance enhancements. However, assuming that human engagement in the AI loop is bound to be integrated into future jobs, the next section takes a work design viewpoint of the studied problem.

5   Discussion on Work Design Consequences and Conclusion

The collective activity of human and AI-driven actors may pose certain physical, cognitive and mental demands on humans that may affect the overall performance of the operations [32]. Therefore, it is important to design the interaction in a way that the resulting work characteristics lead to positive outcomes. This requires an analysis based on work design theory. Various streams of work design theory came together in [33] and overview is given in [10], including integrative perspectives that provide links between the earlier streams. Work design theory provides a set of work characteristics that should be considered when (re)designing jobs in response to technological and social changes to achieve different individual and organizational purposes. As such, the design of the human-AI interaction needs to pay attention to these characteristics. The focus is on work characteristics related to the task environment (task and knowledge characteristics) and the social environment (social characteristics), as these are affected when the interaction is redesigned. The work characteristics related to the physical and organizational environment (contextual characteristics) are excluded. Adopting the terminology from [34], key task characteristics to be considered are outlined next. *Autonomy* refers to the amount of freedom that a human has during the work in terms of timing of the work, choice of methods, and the ability to make decisions. Jobs that lack autonomy are considered poorly designed. AI may impact autonomy in positive and negative ways [10]. *Task variety* considers the range of tasks that humans need to perform in their job, while *skill variety* relates to the required skills to perform the job. AI may replace routine cognitive tasks, but also create new tasks, requiring new skills from humans who are interacting with the system. The task and skills variety should match the abilities and needs of individuals. The same holds for *job complexity*: too little and the job lacks challenges; too much creates fatigue and stress. AI may impact job complexity by altering the cognitive demands. *Feedback from the job* i.e. being able to evaluate the quality of work while it

Table 4. Humans aiding AI actors – operation and maintenance

Activities	Application perspective	Machine learning perspective
Problem definition	Classify products quality	Classification machine learning setting
Data design	Image data samples (good/bad) Labeled data available in sample	Sufficient quantities of bad/good images jpg image files (1024×1024 pixels) Standard image preprocessing (RGB) 200 images in training; 100 in test; 100 in validation data sets (scenario A)
ML model design	N/A	CNN initialised structure; sigmoid activation in final layer and relu in other layers
ML algorithm design	Data ground truth available	Confusion matric performance assessment Standard gradient-based CNN training Kernel sizes of 3 and 5 employed Learning rate: 0.0005 Fixed choices for number of epochs (100), batch sizes (20), regularisation (holdout: 0.5)
Interaction design	N/A	Manual choices for ML Model and Algorithm
Interaction implementation	Selection of A; B; C scenarios	Implementation of data policies: (B: labeling of 10 additional data images per class); (C: including 20 worst performing images in training - sampling)

Table 5. Performance without and with Human in the AI Loop

Scenario A		Scenario B		Scenario C	
TP: 93.94%	FP: 6.06%	TP: 100%	FP: 0%	TP: 97.06%	FP: 2.94%
FN: 20.41%	TN: 79.59%	FN: 2.38%	TN: 97.62%	FN: 0%	TN: 100%

is being performed, is another task characteristic. AI may contribute by providing more insightful feedback. Poor tasks division between AI and humans may lead to weakened opportunities for learning and impaired situational awareness. *Specialization* refers to extent to which a job involves the performance of tasks requiring specific knowledge and skill, and AI may empower humans to take on a variety of tasks by supplementing knowledge and enhancing capabilities, but it may also shift human work to focus on a narrow set of specialized tasks. *Problem solving* in the job is a task characteristic which should be challenging, but not too challenging for the individual employee. AI can execute routine problems allowing humans to focus on more complex ones. *Information processing* is a task characteristic which should match the worker's cognitive capabilities and is enhanced by digitization. There are also characteristics related to the social environment that may be impacted by AI. These characteristics reflect relations among workers. However, they may also relate to interactions between humans and AI. *Interdependence* refers to the extent that humans connect to each other, but may also reflect the connection between humans and AI. Integrating humans in the AI-loop implies dependency between both actors. Similarly, AI may facilitate *social support* by providing valuable connections between team members and enhancing their communication. Similar effects may be expected for the enhancement of the amount of *feedback from other humans*. Overall, designing the AI-human collaboration in production environments requires further research to establish methodologies for human-centric designs. The added value of integrating the human in the AI loop was outlined conceptually, as well as through an exploratory industrial case, arguing that to unleash the human-AI interaction benefits, design approaches for the effective integration of human and AI actors in manufacturing are needed (Table 4).

Acknowledgements. The research was supported through H2020 grant ID 956573. Sourcing the image data in the project through Philips Consumer Lifestyle B.V. is gratefully acknowledged.

References

1. DOD: Manpower, personnel, training, and safety (MPTS) in the defense system acquisition process. DoD Directive 5000.53, Washington, DC (1988)
2. Caroly, S., Barcellini, F.: A conceptual framework of collective activity in constructive ergonomics. In: Bagnara, S., Tartaglia, R., Albolino, S., Alexander, T., Fujita, Y. (eds.) IEA 2018. AISC, vol. 822, pp. 658–664. Springer, Cham (2019). https://doi.org/10.1007/978-3-319-96077-7_71
3. Burggräf, P., Wagner, J., Saßmannshausen, T.M.: Sustainable interaction of human and artificial intelligence in cyber production management systems. In: Behrens, B.-A., Brosius, A., Hintze, W., Ihlenfeldt, S., Wulfsberg, J.J. (eds.) WGP 2020. LNPE, pp. 508–517. Springer, Heidelberg (2021). https://doi.org/10.1007/978-3-662-62138-7_51
4. Raisch, S., Krakowski, S.: Artificial intelligence and management: the automation–augmentation paradox. Acad. Manage. Rev. **46**, 192–210 (2021). https://doi.org/10.5465/AMR.2018.0072
5. Grønsund, T., Aanestad, M.: Augmenting the algorithm: emerging human-in-the-loop work configurations. J. Strateg. Inf. Syst. **29**, 101614 (2020). https://doi.org/10.1016/j.jsis.2020.101614

6. Emmanouilidis, C., et al.: Enabling the human in the loop: linked data and knowledge in industrial cyber-physical systems. Annu. Rev. Control. **47**, 249–265 (2019). https://doi.org/10.1016/j.arcontrol.2019.03.004

7. Langley, P., Laird, J.E., Rogers, S.: Cognitive architectures: research issues and challenges. Cogn. Syst. Res. **10**, 141–160 (2009). https://doi.org/10.1016/j.cogsys.2006.07.004

8. Kaptelinin, V., Nardi, B.: Affordances in HCI: toward a mediated action perspective. In: CHI '12: Proceedings of the SIGCHI Conference on Human Factors in Computing Systems, Austin, Texas, USA, pp. 967–976 (2012). https://doi.org/10.1145/2207676.2208541

9. Neumann, W.P., Winkelhaus, S., Grosse, E.H., Glock, C.H.: Industry 4.0 and the human factor – a systems framework and analysis methodology for successful development. Int. J. Prod. Econ. **233**, 107992 (2021). https://doi.org/10.1016/j.ijpe.2020.107992

10. Parker, S.K., Grote, G.: Automation, algorithms, and beyond: why work design matters more than ever in a digital world. Appl. Psychol. (2020). https://doi.org/10.1111/apps.12241

11. Cimini, C., Pirola, F., Pinto, R., Cavalieri, S.: A human-in-the-loop manufacturing control architecture for the next generation of production systems. J. Manufact. Syst. **54**, 258–271 (2020). https://doi.org/10.1016/j.jmsy.2020.01.002

12. Russel, S., Norvig, P.: Artificial Intelligence: A Modern Approach. Pearson, New York (2020)

13. Raisch, S., Krakowski, S.: Artificial intelligence and management: the automation-augmentation paradox. Acad. Manage. Rev. **46**(1), 192–210 (2020). https://doi.org/10.5465/2018.0072

14. Kadir, B.A., Broberg, O.: Human-centered design of work systems in the transition to industry 4.0. Appl. Ergon. **92**, 103334 (2021). https://doi.org/10.1016/j.apergo.2020.103334

15. Romero, D., et al.: Towards an operator 4.0 typology: a human-centric perspective on the fourth industrial revolution technologies. In: CIE 2016: 46th International Conferences on Computers and Industrial Engineering, Tianjin (2016)

16. Raisamo, R., Rakkolainen, I., Majaranta, P., Salminen, K., Rantala, J., Farooq, A.: Human augmentation: past, present and future. Int. J. Hum. Comput. Stud. **131**, 131–143 (2019). https://doi.org/10.1016/j.ijhcs.2019.05.008

17. Lampe, M., Strassner, M., Fleisch, E.: A Ubiquitous computing environment for aircraft maintenance. In: Proceedings of the 2004 ACM Symposium on Applied Computing - SAC 2004, p. 1586 (2004). https://doi.org/10.1145/967900.968217

18. Washburn, C., Stringfellow, P., Gramopadhye, A.: Using multimodal technologies to enhance aviation maintenance inspection training. In: Duffy, V.G. (ed.) ICDHM 2007. LNCS, vol. 4561, pp. 1018–1026. Springer, Heidelberg (2007). https://doi.org/10.1007/978-3-540-73321-8_114

19. Schwald, B., DeLaval, B.: An augmented aeality system for training and assistance to maintenance in the industrial context. In: WSCG 2003, International Conference in Cent. Europe Comput. Graph., Vis. Comput. Vision, pp. 425–432 (2003). https://doi.org/10.1007/119413 54_29

20. Li, J.R., Khoo, L.P., Tor, S.B.: Desktop virtual reality for maintenance training: an object oriented prototype system (V-REALISM). Comput. Ind. **52**, 109–125 (2003). https://doi.org/10.1016/S0166-3615(03)00103-9

21. Papathanasiou, N., Karampatzakis, D., Koulouriotis, D., Emmanouilidis, C.: Mobile personalised support in industrial environments: coupling learning with context - aware features. In: Grabot, B., Vallespir, B., Gomes, S., Bouras, A., Kiritsis, D. (eds.) APMS 2014. IAICT, vol. 438, pp. 298–306. Springer, Heidelberg (2014). https://doi.org/10.1007/978-3-662-44739-0_37

22. Fox, S., Aranko, O., Heilala, J., Vahala, P.: Exoskeletons: comprehensive, comparative and critical analyses of their potential to improve manufacturing performance. J. Manuf. Technol. Manage. **31**, 1261–1280 (2019). https://doi.org/10.1108/JMTM-01-2019-0023

23. Goose, S., Sudarsky, S., Zhang, X., Navab, N.: Speech-enabled augmented reality supporting mobile industrial maintenance. IEEE Pervasive Comput. **2**, 65–70 (2003). https://doi.org/10.1109/MPRV.2003.1186727

24. Zhang, B., Wang, J., Fuhlbrigge, T.: A review of the commercial brain-computer interface technology from perspective of industrial robotics. In: 2010 IEEE International Conference on Automation and Logistics, pp. 379–384 (2010). https://doi.org/10.1109/ICAL.2010.5585311

25. Somerville, I.: Software Engineering. Pearson, Harlow (2016)

26. Zhuang, F., et al.: A comprehensive survey on transfer learning. Proc. IEEE. **109**, 43–76 (2021). https://doi.org/10.1109/JPROC.2020.3004555

27. Deng, C., Ji, X., Rainey, C., Zhang, J., Lu, W.: Integrating machine learning with human knowledge. iScience **23**, 101656 (2020). https://doi.org/10.1016/j.isci.2020.101656

28. James Wilson, H., Daugherty, P.R.: Collaborative intelligence: humans and AI are joining forces. Harv. Bus. Rev. **96**(4), 114–123 (2018)

29. Lyytinen, K., Nickerson, J.V, King, J.L.: Metahuman systems = humans + machines that learn. J. Inf. Technol., 0268396220915917 (2020). https://doi.org/10.1177/0268396220915917

30. LeCun, Y., Bengio, Y.: Convolutional networks for images, speech, and time series. In: The Handbook of Brain Theory and Neural Networks, no. 10, p. 3361 (1995)

31. Monarch, M.: No TitleHuman-in-the-Loop Machine Learning. Manning (2021)

32. Kolus, A., Wells, R., Neumann, P.: Production quality and human factors engineering: a systematic review and theoretical framework. Appl. Ergon. **73**, 55–89 (2018). https://doi.org/10.1016/j.apergo.2018.05.010

33. Oldham, G.R., Richard Hackman, J.: Not what it was and not what it will be: the future of job design research. J. Organ. Behav. **31**, 463–479 (2010). https://doi.org/10.1002/job.678

34. Morgeson, F.P., Humphrey, S.E.: Job and team design: toward a more integrative conceptualization of work design. Res. Pers. Hum. Resour. Manage. **27**, 39–91 (2008). https://doi.org/10.1016/S0742-7301(08)27002-7

Operations Management
in Engineer-to-Order Manufacturing

Value Stream Mapping for Knowledge Work: A Study from Project-Based Engineering-To-Order Organization

Daria Larsson[1,2(✉)], Arne Gildseth[2], and R. M. Chandima Ratnayake[1]

[1] University of Stavanger, 4036 Stavanger, Norway
chandima.ratnayake@uis.no
[2] Blueday Technology AS, Sandnes, Norway
{daria.larsson,arne.gildseth}@blueday.no

Abstract. This paper presents a tailor-made value stream mapping (VSM) methodology for engineering projects with a focus on knowledge work. The VSM is a lean-management method for analyzing value-adding processes through material and information flow mapping. The tool helps organizations to reduce engineering hours, lower project costs and improve project margins. A documented systematic procedure for VSM for an office environment has been identified in the literature; however, there is no universal approach regarding a VSM methodology for knowledge work, specifically engineering design. This paper addresses these issues, by proposing a systematic procedure for conducting VSM for engineering design projects, along with a case study. First, the manuscript describes the examples of VSM attempts in knowledge work reported in the literature. Next, it demonstrates a case study, conducted in a project-based engineering-to-order (ETO) organization, where the main goal was to identify waste through a current project value stream map (CPVSM). Based on the findings, a future project value stream map (FPVSM) was developed and is presented in the article.

Keywords: Lean · Value stream mapping · Knowledge work

1 Introduction

Lean philosophy had its origins in the automobile industry and was later extended to apply to various organizations; it is known for reducing waste, while adding value to products and services [1]. Lean principles have been applied in office-based functional areas such as administration, customer service, and engineering design [1, 2]. Value stream mapping (VSM) is one of the most powerful lean tools [3] that also supports organizations depending on knowledge work [4]. The tool is used to map value-adding processes [5], in order to help organizations to realize the connection between information flow and material flow [1], and to identify wasteful activities. Finally, it helps to reduce or eliminate non-value-adding activities and improve process productivity [5].

© IFIP International Federation for Information Processing 2021
Published by Springer Nature Switzerland AG 2021
A. Dolgui et al. (Eds.): APMS 2021, IFIP AICT 633, pp. 345–353, 2021.
https://doi.org/10.1007/978-3-030-85910-7_36

According to a review of the literature, VSM has been widely used in manufacturing, healthcare, construction, product development and service sectors [6]. The number of publications referring specifically to the approaches of VSM in engineering projects and the office work environment is limited [1, 2, 7, 8]; in addition, the literature does not adequately describe the aspect of VSM in office knowledge work. This paper fills the existing gap in the literature by providing a systematic approach to VSM for knowledge work. It presents the VSM performed for an engineering-to-order organization focusing on a selected engineering project and project stakeholders.

This paper is organized in five sections. Section 1 introduces the subject of VSM. Section 2 presents the methodology used to develop this article, while Sect. 3 provides the relevant literature review related to examples of VSM approaches to knowledge work. In Sect. 4, a VSM for the case study is provided. Finally, Sect. 5 summarizes the main topics discussed in the article.

2 Methodology

The research methodology (Fig. 1) consists of action research and case study-based research. A comprehensive literature review was conducted, focusing on existing examples of VSM approaches related to different industry sectors and engineering knowledge work. Established search criteria for the paper retrieval included: academic journals, books, conference papers. Oria, an academic database, was searched for relevant publications. At the same time, the case study research was conducted based on interviews with employees, performed in the company. Interviews had a standardized format, with each interviewee being asked the same questions. There was one interviewer and ten interviewees; all interviewed people were involved in one specific project selected for case study need.

The detailed methodology for the performance of VSM is presented in Fig. 3, Sect. 4.1 of this paper. The VSM methodology developed in this paper was adapted from the VSM model given by [9]. The basic model contains four main steps: selection of product family, current state map, future state map, and work plan for the implementation of the future state [9]. The data received from VSM has been analyzed and is presented in the graphical form of a current project value stream map (CPVSM) and a future project value stream map (FPVSM), in subsequent sections.

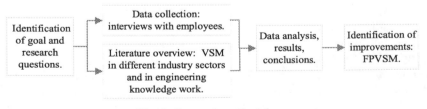

Fig. 1. Research methodology.

3   Literature Overview

3.1   Value Stream Mapping in Knowledge Work

Value Stream (VS) in an Office Environment. VS can be defined as all activities required to fulfill a customer's request, from order to delivery [10]. Depending on the type of VS, two main flows can be recognized: the flow of information and the flow of materials [10]. The information flow in engineering knowledge work is usually defined in a project management communication plan, which specifies interactions between project stakeholders. A material flow in an office environment can be represented by, for example, a digital document sent for a discipline check or an email, which is a form of corporate electronic documented information. According to the literature [11], all daily activities and processes, such as sales, customer service or engineering, can be defined as office VS (Fig. 2).

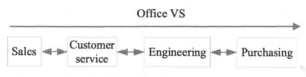

Fig. 2. Office VS adapted from [11].

While material flow is visible in a physical work environment and therefore can be observed and mapped, in the office environment, on the contrary, information and material flow might not be visible (e.g., digital transfer of a document, e-mail). A similar analogy occurs during the identification of non-value-adding activities. Typical waste in manufacturing is transportation, inventory, waiting, defects, over-processing or excessive motion [12]. In the office environment, there is a significant challenge in defining and identifying waste [1]. Tasks are assigned through emails or meetings; thus, it is challenging to track the flow of information [1]. The exact time needed to complete a task is difficult to estimate, as some tasks require confirmation by a manager or a customer [1]. The number of tasks assigned to an employee is not transparent, as some employees can perform multitasking [3]. Moreover, it is hard to tell whether the task was completed successfully or not, due to the many variables included [1].

VSM in Industries. As the lean concept was originally created to support the manufacturing sector, the majority of studies related to VSM focus on the manufacturing industry [6, 13]. Several publications refer to the use of VSM in healthcare service sectors [14–16] and sales processes [17]. VSM has also been used in construction supply chains [18] and product development processes [19–23]. In manufacturing, VSM has contributed to reduced cycle time, reduced waste in the supply chain, increased productivity and reduced lead time [6]. In healthcare, VSM was used in conjunction with queuing modelling, to reduce patient wait time and medical errors [16]. The new process model delivered more efficient service and a reduction in non-value-added activities [16]. As also observed by other authors, the benefits of applying VSM to healthcare were reduced employee overtime and customer complaints in the administrative process, as well as reduced treatment time [6]. VSM application in the service sector contributed to eliminating delays, errors and inappropriate procedures and to improving customer satisfaction [6]. The construction sector used VSM to improve process performance [24] and enable sustainability [25]. VSM was applied to several areas within construction, such as supply chain, administrative management, construction process and designing [6]. The product development sector is the closest one to engineering knowledge work, as the development of products and design is very often included in engineering office activities. According to [26], product development value stream mapping (PDVSM) can lead to excessive complexity in a traditional process flow map, to the point where drawing a process is lost. The author proposes a tool named Design Structure Matrix (DSM), which is a visual representation of a system or project in the form of a square matrix recommended for complex projects or processes [26]. Several benefits have been obtained from using VSM in the product development process, such as reductions in waiting time and iteration [22], development costs, man hours and cycle time [23].

VSM in Knowledge Work. Several publications refer to approaches for using VSM in office work [1, 2, 7, 8], where authors have successfully managed to describe possible ways of conducting VSM in a knowledge work environment; however, the literature does not adequately describe the aspect of VSM in engineering projects with a focus on knowledge work and office activities. Therefore, the aim of this paper is to perform VSM for a case study company, inspired by the existing methodologies described in the literature [1, 2, 6, 7], and to support a systematic approach for the implementation of VSM in knowledge work.

4   Case Study Description

A case study was performed in Blueday Technology AS (BDT), which is a medium-sized engineering-to-order (ETO) organization. BDT provides knowledge work (project management, engineering), service and manufacturing to five industry sectors: shore power, defense, marine, offshore and aquaculture. This paper focuses only on knowledge work and non-manufacturing activities within the company. Based on previously performed studies, it was concluded that, for the majority of projects, final project margins were significantly lower than the estimated project margins. As concluded from earlier analyses, exceeded engineering hours were a main reason for low project margins. Through VSM, the case study aims to identify the exact reasons behind time-consuming engineering hours in projects.

4.1   Value Stream Mapping

The proposed VSM methodology (Fig. 3) provides a systematic approach for implementing lean in engineering projects with a focus on office work. First, the person responsible for VSM selected a project to analyze. The following employees were chosen to join the VSM team: project manager, Vice President (VP) project executive, mechanical engineer, electrical engineer, automation engineer, service technician, purchaser, document controller, and production technician.

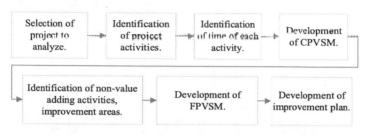

Fig. 3. Methodology for performance of VSM.

The CPVSM was developed while "walking through" the actual pathway of the material and information flow. Due to the complexity of the project, the VSM responsible person conducted separate interviews with VSM team members, in order to collect information about project activities within each discipline. The interviewed persons defined their contribution to the current state of the project process, including problems, based on their experience and improvement ideas. Once the interviews were completed, the person responsible for VSM prepared a complete CPVSM, based on collected data. Next, all improvement propositions and problems identified by team members were added to the graph, through the use of agreed symbols (Fig. 4). Finally, the overall analysis was performed, with a focus on the elimination of waste such as waiting time (Fig. 5). The challenges identified during the CPVSM were replaced by solutions and later presented in the FPVSM (Fig. 6).

Fig. 4. Legend for VSM.

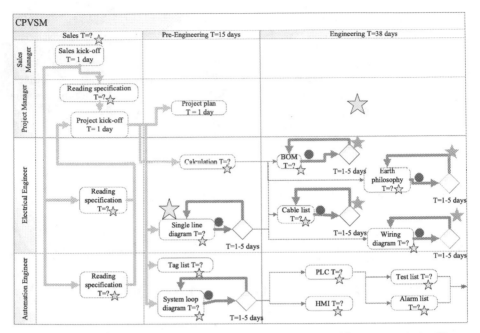

Fig. 5. CPVSM with identified problems and improvement propositions - case study. (Due to large size of the complete map, only a small section is presented.)

In order to ensure that all improvement proposals are documented and implemented, an implementation plan has been developed (Fig. 7). The execution of this plan is expected to start in the coming months in the case study company.

VSM – Findings. One of the main reasons behind the exceeded engineering hours was interviewed persons' inability to identify the exact time needed for various engineering activities. Those activities were related to the creation of design and documentation, such as designing single line diagrams, or the creation of a bill of materials (BOMs). Moreover, insufficient project management control over engineering activities and over documentation development was found to be one of the most important problems (for example, lack of documented project status meetings, lack of document status reports). Other challenges identified based on VSM were as follows: insufficient involvement of document controller in the project process (reflected in lack of control over project document list); undocumented activities related to transfer of knowledge and experience (design reviews); lack of documented project milestones such as design freeze for 3D model.

The findings suggest that improvements are required in the area of engineering control and monitoring. It is very important for the organization to define the time for each engineering activity, to meet delivery milestones. There is also a clear requirement to increase the monitoring of all activities in the pre-engineering and engineering phases (mainly activities related to recurring processes such as creation of document revisions, design changes), in order to improve control over the process.

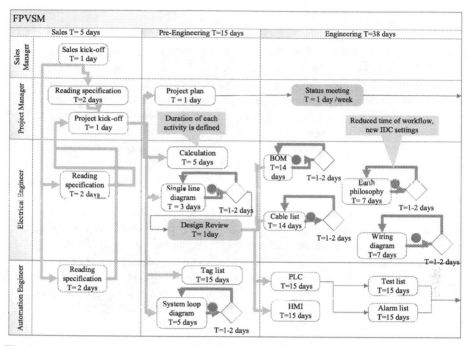

Fig. 6. FPVSM - case study. (Due to large size of the complete map, only a small section is presented.)

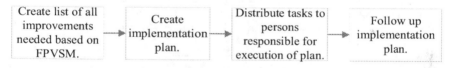

Fig. 7. Implementation plan.

Based on the findings, it can be concluded that future improvements can lead to reduced project time, by eliminating non-value-added activities, reduced project delays, and reduced engineering design errors. In addition, an improvement within administrative routines and the structuring of documentation could potentially improve knowledge sharing among project stakeholders. The potential improvements demonstrate similarities to those improvements achieved in other sectors such as manufacturing, construction, healthcare or product development. In each of these sectors, VSM contributed to improved productivity of lead time and improved process efficiency, by eliminating waste such as long waiting time or man hours. However, the findings and potential improvements from the case study described in this paper can be compared only to case studies related to other sectors and industries, as the literature review related to office knowledge work within engineering companies is very limited. Individual sectors have fundamental differences, and therefore the comparison of findings between different VSM approaches is limited.

5 Conclusions

The paper focuses on improving office VS in engineering knowledge work, achieved through the use of one of the most popular lean tools – VSM. The literature overview identifies several examples of the implementation of VSM in knowledge work; however, research related to the engineering office environment is limited. This article aims to fill the existing gap in the literature, by presenting an approach to VSM in an engineering office environment, based on a case study company. In the presented methodology, the information and document flows were improved by the identification of waste in various project phases such as engineering design, document control, and project management. The proposed FPVSM aims to reduce the total number of engineering hours required to accomplish the project and to lower the final project cost. As presented in the case study findings, the overall project performance can be improved by reducing non-value-adding activities, such as recurring tasks or improved control over duration of engineering assignments. The systematic approach to VSM presented in this paper could be applied to any organization, in order improve the efficiency of the office work environment.

Future research shall be focused on lean tools and techniques supporting VSM in a knowledge work environment, the identification of typical waste in office work, and factors contributing to the successful performance of CPVSM and FPVSM.

References

1. Chen, J.C., Cox, R.A.: Value stream management for lean office - a case study. Am. J. Ind. Bus. Manage. **2**, 17–29 (2012). https://doi.org/10.4236/ajibm.2012.22004
2. Torres, L.A., Souza, M.C.S., Xavier, A.C.B., Melo, R.S.S.: Value stream mapping of the design process in a design-build firm. In: 35th International Symposium on Automation and Robotics in Construction (2018)
3. Wan, H.D., Chen, F.F.: Leanness score of value stream maps. In: Proceedings of the 2007 Industrial Engineering Research Conference, Nashville, vol. 20–23, p. 1515 (2007)
4. Biskupska, D., Chandima Ratnayake, R.M.: On the need for effective lean daily management in engineering design projects: development of a framework. In: 2019 IEEE International Conference on Industrial Engineering and Engineering Management (IEEM), Macao, China, pp. 789–794 (2019). https://doi.org/10.1109/IEEM44572.2019.8978660
5. Silva, S.K.P.N.: Applicability of Value Stream Mapping (VSM) in the apparel industry in Sri Lanka. Int. J. Lean Think. **3**(1), 36–56 (2012)
6. Shou, W., Wang, J., Wu, P., Wang, X., Chong, H.Y.: A cross-sector review on the use of value stream mapping. Int. J. Prod. Res. **55**(13), 3906–3928 (2017). https://doi.org/10.1080/00207543.2017.1311031
7. Stadnicka, D., Chandima Ratnayake, R.M.: Development of a rule base and algorithm for a quotation preparation process: a case study with a VSM approach. In: 2015 IEEE International Conference on Industrial Engineering and Engineering Management (IEEM), Singapore, pp. 1100–1106 (2015). https://doi.org/10.1109/IEEM.2015.7385819
8. Rachman, A., Chandima Ratnayake, R.M.: Implementation of lean knowledge work in oil and gas industry – a case study from a risk-based inspection project. In: 2016 IEEE International Conference on Industrial Engineering and Engineering Management (IEEM), Bali, Indonesia, pp. 675–680 (2016). https://doi.org/10.1109/IEEM.2016.7797961
9. Rother, M., Shook, J.: Learning to See: Value Stream Mapping to Add Value and Eliminate Muda. Lean Enterprise Institute, Brookline (1999)

10. Martin, K., et al.: Profit through simplicity. Value Stream Mapping in non-manufacturing settings. https://www.slideshare.net/AMEConnect/value-stream-mapping-for-non-manufacturingmartinreplacement. Accessed 3 June 2021

11. Keyte, B., Locher, D.A.: The Complete Lean Enterprise: Value Stream Mapping for Office and Services, 2nd edn. CRC Press (2015). ISBN-13: 978-1482206135

12. Ohno, T.: Toyota Production System: Beyond Large-Scale Production. Productivity Press, New York (1988)

13. Yang, T., Hsieh, C.H., Cheng, B.Y.: Lean-pull Strategy in a re-entrant manufacturing environment: a pilot study for TFT-LCD array manufacturing. Int. J. Prod. Res. **49**(6), 1511–1529 (2011)

14. Dogan, N.O., Unutulmaz, O.: Lean production in healthcare: a simulation-based value stream mapping in the physical therapy and rehabilitation department of a public hospital. Total Qual. Manage. Bus. Excell. **27**(1–2), 64–80 (2014)

15. Claire, M., Naik, K., McVicker, M.: Value stream mapping of the Pap test processing procedure: a lean approach to improve quality and efficiency. Am. J. Clin. Pathol. **139**(5), 574–583 (2013)

16. Chadha, R., Singh, A., Kalra, J.: Lean and queuing integration for the transformation of health care processes: a lean health care model. Clin. Gov. Int. J. **17**, 191–199 (2012). https://doi.org/10.1108/14777271211251309

17. Barber, C.S., Tietje, B.C.: A research agenda for value stream mapping the sales process. J. Pers. Sell. Sales Manage. **28**(2), 155–165 (2008)

18. Arbulu, R., Tommelein, I., Walsh, K., Hershauer, J.: Value stream analysis of a re-engineered construction supply chain. Build. Res. Inf. **31**(2), 161–171 (2003)

19. Ali, N.B., Petersen, K., Nicolau de França, B.B.: Evaluation of simulation-assisted value stream mapping for software product development: two industrial cases. Inf. Softw. Technol. **68**, 45–61 (2015)

20. Mayrl, P., McManus, H.L., Boutellier, R.: Eliciting product development knowledge using value stream mapping. Int. J. Prod. Dev. **18**(6), 492–511 (2013)

21. Schulze, A., Schmitt, P., Heinzen, M., Mayrl, P., Heller, D., Boutellier, R.: Exploring the 4I framework of organisational learning in product development: value stream mapping as a facilitator. Int. J. Comput. Integr. Manufact. **26**(12), 1136–1150 (2013)

22. Tyagi, S., Choudhary, A., Cai, X., Yang, K.: Value stream mapping to reduce the lead-time of a product development process. Int. J. Prod. Econ. **160**, 202–212 (2015)

23. Tuli, P., Shankar, R.: Collaborative and Lean new product development approach: a case study in the automotive product design. Int. J. Prod. Res. **53**(8), 2457–2471 (2015)

24. Pasqualini, F., Zawislak, P.A.: Value stream mapping in construction: a case study in a Brazilian construction company. In: Proceedings of the 13th International Group for Lean Construction Conference, pp. 117–125. International Group on Lean Construction (2005)

25. Ogunbiyi, O., Goulding, J.S., Oladapo, A.: An empirical study of the impact of lean construction techniques on sustainable construction in the UK. Constr. Innov. **14**(1), 88–107 (2014)

26. McManus, H.L.: Product Development Value Stream Mapping (PDVSM) Manual Release 1.0. Massachusetts Institute of Technology Lean Aerospace Initiative (MIT) (2005)

A Literature-Based Exploration of Servitization in Engineer-to-Order Companies

Antonio Masi[✉], Margherita Pero, and Nizar Abdelkafi

Politecnico Di Milano, Milano, Italy
antonio.masi@polimi.it

Abstract. Servitization allows manufacturing companies to enrich their value proposition with services. It enables them to differentiate their offers from competitors, while capitalizing more on digital technologies. Servitization practices such as maintenance services, training and advisory, or rental and leasing solutions are widespread among many sectors. In this paper, we focus on the ETO context. We explore the literature to capture how and why servitization has been adopted by ETO companies. Based on our findings, we build a theoretical framework that we partly validate through an analysis of secondary sources. We conclude the paper with possible future research directions.

Keywords: Engineer to Order · Servitization · Product-Service Systems

1 Introduction

For many companies, digitalization is a strategic pillar of the future. It is expected to reshape manufacturing and drive the Fourth Industrial Revolution, also referred to as "Industry 4.0" [1]. Digital technologies are enablers of servitization [2], the process by which industrial companies change their offers from mere products to bundles of products and services, or Product-Service Systems (PSS) [3].

A recent survey that investigates European capital goods manufacturers' transition towards service-oriented business models [4] shows that services are widely adopted by European manufacturers and generate, on average, about 20% of their sales. Nevertheless, PSS is rather limited to product-related services such as repair and spare parts provision. The same study, however, found that most respondents expect that servitisation will become more important in the future, and that there is a lot of unexploited potential for the adoption of digital technologies, especially in small enterprises.

There is a large body of research on servitization, but this paper addresses a particular context, in which servitization can take place: the Engineer-to-Order (ETO) context. In ETO, companies carry out engineering activities according to specific customer requests. Most literature treats engineering in the ETO context as one single compact activity. According to Cannas et al. [5], however, engineering – at the physical product level – consists of many sub-activities: research, develop, design, modify (major changes), modify (minor changes), and combine. Thus, it is possible to define different types of

© IFIP International Federation for Information Processing 2021
Published by Springer Nature Switzerland AG 2021
A. Dolgui et al. (Eds.): APMS 2021, IFIP AICT 633, pp. 354–362, 2021.
https://doi.org/10.1007/978-3-030-85910-7_37

ETO-companies, depending on the sub-activity, at which the customer order enters. Cannas et al. [5] also mention that ETO companies have been traditionally more focused on complex and highly customized products than on servitization. By analogy to products, and by extending engineering sub-activities to services, ETO companies may combine product and service engineering activities to better fit customers' requirements. Conceptually, ETO companies can leverage standardized services or specifically engineered services to enrich their ETO products. Digitalization even increases the possibility that such ETO companies will be more widespread in the future.

To the best of our knowledge, the simultaneous consideration of product and service engineering has not been addressed explicitly. This paper starts by exploring current literature related to how ETO companies adapt to embrace smart PSS. It aims to initiate a discussion on the implications of servitization in ETO companies by dealing with the research question (RQ): "*Why do ETO companies apply servitization? And how?*". To answer this question, we look for literature review and draw on secondary online sources.

2 Methodology

To get a general overview of the topic, the first phase of this research was exploratory, based on a non-systematic scouting of both sources from peer-reviewed journals and from company websites. In particular, we analyzed in detail the website of Biesse S.p.A. (www.biesse.com), since it is the largest machinery producer in Italy by revenue in 2019 – according to the informatic analysis of Italian companies (https://aida.bvdinfo.com/version-2021727/home.serv?product=AidaNeo) – and machinery is a key ETO industry [e.g., 5–7].

Then, we searched relevant articles in the Scopus database. We tried different keywords and refined our query by trial and error. The starting keywords for ETO were derived from the literature review by Gosling and Naim [7], since it is the most cited systematic literature review on this subject. Choosing the keywords related to servitisation was harder, due to the "blurred" [8, p. 261] boundaries between the terms related to it. Eventually, the starting keywords for servitisation were based on those used by Paschou et al. [9] for two main reasons. First, it is one of the most recent literature reviews on the topic. Second, it is based on the keywords used by Baines et al. [3] who, in turn, published the most highly cited review on this subject, and the second most cited article (1188) when searching for "serviti*ation" on Scopus. So, these keywords seemed the best starting point for the literature search.

After several attempts, we refined our starting query into the following search string: (TITLE ABS KEY ("serviti*ation" OR "product service system" OR "inte-grated solution*" OR "service transformation" OR "service infusion" OR "service focused" OR "industrial service") AND TITLE ABS KEY ("engineer to order" OR "design to order" OR "one of a kind" OR "project based")) AND (LIMIT TO (LANGUAGE, "English")).

A possible limitation of this query is the string "project based". This string was the result of refining the keyword "project", which was used by Gosling and Naim [7] but that was leading to too many results to be screened. Actually, by modifying it into "project-based" it was possible to include papers related to "project based organizations" or "project based firms". Although this string led to some irrelevant papers in later stages, its omission would have possibly resulted in neglecting relevant contributions, which is why we included it.

Our string led us to 41 articles we later filtered as follows. First, we screened title, abstract and keywords of the papers, excluding: 8 duplicates, which were collections of conference articles that were also present separately; 4 articles related to "project based learning"; 4 articles related to energy engineering; and, finally, other 11 papers not related to servitisation. For instance, a paper was discussing project-based organizations deeply, but unrelated to servitisation [10]. So, out of 41 papers, only 14 passed this first step.

Second, we went through the full text of the articles to select only those related to ETO contexts. This step was necessary especially for "project based" papers, since this is a subset larger than ETO, as Moretto [11, p. 4] pointed out: "among the possible project-based organizations, we chose engineer-to-order (ETO) companies as the unit of analysis of the study". In this step, more precisely, we were looking for statements in the articles to show that the contexts analyzed by the authors are companies making products that are engineered to order. Here are examples of quotes from the selected articles: "the five solutions that we included in the analysis all have an engineer, procure, construct (EPC)— project delivery followed by long-term O&M [Operations and Maintenance] service contract" [12, p. 963]; "EngCo (a pseudonym) is an original equipment manufacturer which develops, produces and manages engineering products, including through-life support" [13, p. 255]. This step resulted in 9 papers.

Finally, we analyzed the selected papers. In line with the methodological guidelines provided by Grant et al. [14], we firstly characterized the selected papers according to demographics (year of publication, source ranking, citations), methodologies employed and contexts discussed. This was done to identify the least commonly discussed methods and contexts, which would deserve further attention by future research. Then, we dived deeper into the content of the selected papers, looking for answers to our RQ. In particular, with respect to our 'why' RQ, we decided to frame the insights collected from the papers within the Strength, Weaknesses, Opportunities and Threats (SWOT) framework [15]. This framework allowed us to organize the reasons favoring servitisation in four categories, related to internal (Strengths and Weaknesses) and external (Opportunities and Threats) environments, in which firms operate. It is chosen for its clarity and completeness. Moreover, it is widely used by practitioners [15], who may be interested in our study.

3   Results

3.1   Bibliometric Analysis

Demographic Analysis. The final set consists of seven journal articles and two conference papers. Most journal articles (4 papers) were published in the International Journal of Project Management. This can be explained by the project-based nature of ETO manufacturing. All articles were published between 2008 and 2019 without noteworthy peaks. All the sources of the selected articles are placed in the first quartile (Q1) of the Scimago Journal Rank (SJR), except for one, which is classified Q2. Thus, according to SJR, the selected articles have a medium to high quality, which is a good indicator for the reliability of the published results. In addition, the selected articles have, on average, about 25 citations, with 6 papers having more than 10 citations and one [16] with 92 citations. This suggests that the articles in our sample had a relatively good impact on the research community.

Methodology Analysis. All selected articles used a case study methodology. Most of them (six papers) develop single case studies. In three articles, the re-searchers use multiple case study analysis. Most of the papers of our sample recognized the low generalizability of the results they obtained [e.g., 12, 13, 17, 18].

Context Analysis. The companies analyzed in the case studies belong to two main sectors: machinery and construction (Table 1). These sectors are different regarding the size of the product. Machines are smaller than buildings and can be produced off-site, while construction projects produce larger facilities that are built on-site. Construction and machinery are typical industries in the ETO literature [7].

Examples of machinery from the reviewed papers are: computerized numerical controlled machine centers [19]; energy systems [18]; mold-making machines [17]; material handling equipment [21]. Within the construction industry companies deliver products such as power plants [12, 16]; sludge treatment centers [21], and telecom networks [22].

Only two papers develop case studies in both industries: machinery and construction [21, 22], whereas seven papers focus on only one industry. Note, however, that other typical ETO sectors such as shipbuilding [23] and aerospace [6] are not present in our final sample.

Table 1. Characteristics of the case studies reviewed

Reference	Case Study	Machinery	Construction
[19]	Multiple	9	0
[16]	Single	0	1
[18]	Single	1	0
[12]	Single	0	1
[22]	Multiple	4	1
[17]	Single	1	0
[20]	Single	1	0
[13]	Single	1	0
[21]	Multiple	2	1
	TOTAL	19	4

3.2 Content Analysis

How Do ETO Companies Apply Servitization? The papers selected for our re-view describe servitization in ETO companies from different perspectives: an opportunity for certain companies to leverage on new technologies to improve specific services [17, 20], a trend that is involving entire sectors, which are offering more and more complex bundles of products and services [13, 18, 19, 21], or a new business model [12, 16, 22]. More specifically, Kujala [12, 16] notice that, due to the project-based nature of capital goods products, a servitization business model in an ETO context should be seen as "solution specific".

To classify companies, authors use two main taxonomies for servitization: one is focused on product lifecycle, and the other on the characteristics of the services.

Artto et al. [22] use a product lifecycle taxonomy. They distinguish servitization practices implemented before, during, and after project delivery. Because the authors understand engineering as a service, all ETO companies adopt "by definition" at least one servitization practice.

Kujala et al. [12, 16] and Raja et al. [13] use a taxonomy related to the characteristics of service. Based on previous literature, they distinguish between product-oriented offerings, use-oriented offerings, and result-oriented offerings. These categories lead to different types of services and different types of buyer-supplier relationships [16]. For instance, for product-oriented offerings arms-length relationships are enough, while result-oriented offerings require integration of focal firm, buyers, and suppliers.

Supply chain integration and coordination have been discussed not only in Kujala et al. [12, 16], but also in other studies. ETO companies that want to embrace servitization should dramatically improve their inter-firm and intra-firm coordination. For instance, Ivory and Alderman [21] stress the problems of downstream coordination for ETO companies offering PSS, especially because they often have to interact with several stakeholders along a project lifecycle.

Why Should an ETO Company Pursue Servitization? ETO companies adopt servitization for many reasons. We organize the motives for servitization according to the Strengths, Weaknesses, Opportunities, and Threats (SWOT) framework [15].

ETO companies face two external threats: general economic downturn, which can cause demand stagnation, especially in Europe [13, 16] and increasing globalization, which allows manufacturers from low-cost countries to compete with well-established ETO companies by offering lower prices [13, 16, 19]. Servitization can enable companies to deal better with the decreasing domestic demand and increasing competition from overseas suppliers.

To address these threats ETO firms can either cut costs and shift towards mass-customization or become more effective through differentiation [24]. This differentiation can be achieved by offering value-adding services to satisfy the needs of the customers better. In addition, customers of capital-intensive systems have become increasingly interested in the life-cycle costs of their investments [12]. ETO products typically have long lifecycles, high total costs of ownership, and expensive downtimes [19]. Thus, services such as after-sales support, training, advisory, spare parts provision, and maintenance are highly attractive to clients that are aware of the total cost of ownership [21].

Servitization can support ETO companies to achieve two (inter-related) opportunities: digitalization and sustainability. Technologies such as Artificial Intelligence [17] and Augmented Reality [20] can trigger new or improved services, e.g., predictive main-tenance. Servitization can also lead to the production of fewer, but highly value-adding products, thus consuming fewer resources, in line with the "dematerialized solution" paradigm [20, p. 219].

Servitization allows ETO firms to capitalize on a major strength, which is their assets base located in the customers' facilities. The more products ETO companies deliver to their customers, the more services they can sell, an effect that is amplified by the typical long lifecycle of ETO products [13, 16]. The availability of these assets can reduce the impact of a major structural weakness of ETO companies: the "lumpy" demand. "Service revenues from an installed asset base can provide a buffer against fluctuating demand cycles" [13, p. 250].

4   Discussion

The 9 papers reviewed discuss 23 cases of servitisation in ETO and capture different reasons for embarking on it. This answers our 'why' research question. Understanding 'how' ETO companies apply servitisation was more difficult, since there was less information about concerning this aspect on the sources we reviewed. Nonetheless, we found some interesting insights, in particular in Kujala et al. [16].

Kujala et al. [16] describe two types of PSS in ETO contexts. The first is represented by project-led solutions, where an Operations & Maintenance (O&M) contract is offered independently of the product, and the contract is almost standard. The second is represented by life-cycle-led solutions, that are "seamless offering for the customer, consisting of an integrated EPC project and O&M service" [16, p. 101]. The authors also observed that the life-cycle-led solution was more profitable than the project-led one. The distinction made by these scholars highlighted two different levels of service customization in ETO companies offering PSS: PSS with a standardized service component, and PSS with a service highly customized and strictly connected to the product.

This dichotomy between high and low levels of standardized services in PSS should be particularly interesting for ETO companies, since we know from recent developments in the literature [e.g., 5, 6] that within the context of ETO there are different levels of product customization, too. In fact, many ETO companies are pursuing mass customization, by offering less tailor-made products, but still answering to customer orders', thanks to levers such as modularity and technology [6].

Therefore, we elaborated especially on the results in [16] and [5] to propose a theoretical framework that combine the product and service customization levels dimensions (Fig. 1). On the x-axis, we represent the product customization dimension, which can range from low to high (of course, always in the range of ETO products). On the y-axis, we represent the service customization dimension, which also ranges from low to high.

Within this matrix, it is possible to position the two configurations mentioned by Kujala et al. [16], whose article discusses PSS composed by services with different levels of customization and with EPC products. However, it is also possible to position other product families with lower level of product customization as the one of the PSS discussed by the aforementioned work. In this sense, Biesse is an interesting case, which we previously mentioned above. Biesse (www.biesse.com) is a world-leader producer of wood working machines. It claims, in the brochure of one of its products, the ROVER-A16, that "a team of specialized sales engineers can understand production requirements and suggest the optimal machine configuration." This means that this product is likely to be "standard customized", in line with the definition provided in [5]. In addition, Biesse also offers several services, as shown by its 3-years business plan. In particular, their installation and maintenance services are more standardized than the ones described in [16]. Therefore, this case is placed in the bottom left corner of our matrix.

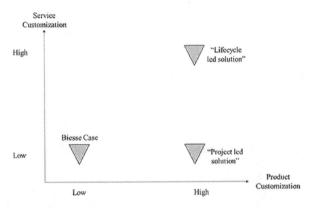

Fig. 1. ETO product-service strategic matrix

The matrix shows that companies can develop different approaches for the integration of products and services, ranging from standardized products and services, that can be designed independently of the customer, to customized products and services that are designed together with the customer. In line with Kujala et al. [16], we believe that the different positions on the matrix can have an im-pact on the level of profitability of ETO companies. For this reason, we propose that this matrix can be used as a strategic tool to map the different options in terms of PSS variety when ETO companies adopt servitisation.

Additionally, we expect that the different quadrants in the matrix have deep implications for operational activities. For instance, when product and service customization are high, higher inter-functional coordination as well as adaptations of the sales, design and delivery processes are required. To be able to confirm this proposition, however, future research is needed.

5   Conclusions

This paper proposes a literature-based exploration of servitization in ETO companies, by investigating why and how ETO companies embrace it. To this aim, based on the results of a systematic literature review and case studies from secondary sources, a SWOT analysis and a strategic matrix have been built. The results suggest that servitization can be a strategic lever, which enables ETO companies to differentiate themselves from other companies, in face of the downsizing of domestic demand and the increasing competition from overseas companies. Servitization allows ETO companies to leverage the opportunity of having the company's asset base located at the customer's site, and coupled with digitalization, to propose sustainable solutions. For ETO companies, thanks to servitization, differentiation can now occur along two axes, i.e., the product and the service.

From a managerial perspective, this paper provides a strategic matrix, which can be used by companies to define their positioning in terms of product and service customization, while comparing their positioning with their competitors. Moreover, the SWOT analysis may clarify to managers in ETO companies the possible reasons to adopt servitisation.

The main theoretical contribution of this paper is to highlight the need to better explore servitization in ETO. Some future research directions emerge from the results of this paper. First, the proposed matrix should be improved and detailed, e.g., with metrics to assess the positioning along the axes. Indeed, one limitation of this study is the limited number of cases and papers included. Therefore, future research can be devoted to enrich the set of cases within the matrix. Then, how to put in practice the different strategies identified with the proposed matrix should be investigated, e.g., in terms of the positioning of the Customer Order Decoupling Point (CODP), software and technologies supporting each strategy, and upstream and downstream coordination along the supply chain. In addition, it is important to diversify the sectors and expand the analysis to cross-sectoral studies, especially to include industries – like shipbuilding and aerospace – which have not been discussed as much in the extant literature. Finally, as we pointed out in the demographic analysis, the articles we reviewed use only the case study methodology, the application of other methodologies can help to refine the results discussed in the reviewed articles.

References

1. Xu, L.D., Xu, E.L., Li, L.: Industry 4.0: state of the art and future trends. Int. J. Prod. Res. **56**(8), 2941–2962 (2018). https://doi.org/10.1080/00207543.2018.1444806
2. Pirola, F., Boucher, X., Wiesner, S., Pezzotta, G.: Digital technologies in product-service systems: a literature review and a research agenda. Comput. Ind. **123**, 103301 (2020). https://doi.org/10.1016/j.compind.2020.103301
3. Baines, T.S., et al.: State-of-the-art in product-service systems. Proc. Inst. Mech. Eng. Part B: J. Eng. Manufact. **221**(10), 1543–1552 (2007). https://doi.org/10.1243/09544054JEM858
4. Adrodegari, F., Bacchetti, A., Saccani, N., Arnaiz, A., Meiren, T.: The transition towards service-oriented business models: a European survey on capital goods manufacturers. Int. J. Eng. Bus. Manage. **10**, 1–10 (2018). https://doi.org/10.1177/1847979018754469
5. Cannas, V.G., Gosling, J., Pero, M., Rossi, T.: Engineering and production decoupling configurations: an empirical study in the machinery industry. Int. J. Prod. Econ. **216**, 173–189 (2019). https://doi.org/10.1016/j.ijpe.2019.04.025
6. Cannas, V.G., Masi, A., Pero, M., Brunø, T.D.: Implementing configurators to enable mass customization in the Engineer-to-Order industry: a multiple case study research. Prod. Plann. Control, 1–21 (2020). https://doi.org/10.1080/09537287.2020.1837941
7. Gosling, J., Naim, M.M.: Engineer-to-order supply chain management: a literature review and research agenda. Int. J. Prod. Econ. **122**(2), 741–754 (2009). https://doi.org/10.1016/j.ijpe.2009.07.002

8. Baines, T., Ziaee Bigdeli, A., Bustinza, O.F., Shi, V.G., Baldwin, J., Ridgway, K.: Servitization: revisiting the state-of-the-art and research priorities. Int. J. Oper. Prod. Manage. 37(2), 256–278 (2017). https://doi.org/10.1108/IJOPM-06-2015-0312

9. Paschou, T., Rapaccini, M., Adrodegari, F., Saccani, N.: Digital servitization in manufacturing: a systematic literature review and research agenda. Ind. Mark. Manage. 89(February), 278–292 (2020). https://doi.org/10.1016/j.indmarman.2020.02.012

10. Koskinen, K.U.: Project-based companies as learning organisations: systems theory perspective. Int. J. Project Organ. Manage. 3(1), 91–106 (2011). https://doi.org/10.1504/IJPOM.2011.038866

11. Moretto, A., Patrucco, A.S., Walker, H., Ronchi, S.: Procurement organisation in project-based setting: a multiple case study of engineer-to-order companies. Prod. Plann. Control, 1–16 (2020). https://doi.org/10.1080/09537287.2020.1837938

12. Kujala, S., Kujala, J., Turkulainen, V., Artto, K., Aaltonen, P., Wikström, K.: Factors influencing the choice of solution-specific business models. Int. J. Project Manage. 29(8), 960–970 (2011). https://doi.org/10.1016/j.ijproman.2011.01.009

13. Raja, J.Z., Chakkol, M., Johnson, M., Beltagui, A.: Organizing for servitization: examining front- and back-end design configurations. Int. J. Oper. Prod. Manage. 38(1), 249–271 (2018). https://doi.org/10.1108/IJOPM-03-2016-0139

14. Grant, M.J., Booth, A.: A typology of reviews: an analysis of 14 review types and associated methodologies. Health Inf. Libr. J. 26(2), 91–108 (2009). https://doi.org/10.1111/j.1471-1842.2009.00848.x

15. Grant, R.M.: Contemporary Strategy Analysis. Wiley, Chichester (2010)

16. Kujala, S., Artto, K., Aaltonen, P., Turkulainen, V.: Business models in project-based firms - towards a typology of solution-specific business models. Int. J. Project Manage. 28(2), 96–106 (2010). https://doi.org/10.1016/j.ijproman.2009.08.008

17. Mourtzis, D., Boli, N., Fotia, S.: Knowledge-based estimation of maintenance time for complex engineered-to-order products based on KPIs monitoring: a PSS approach. Procedia CIRP 63, 236–241 (2017). https://doi.org/10.1016/j.procir.2017.03.317

18. Ståhle, M., Ahola, T., Martinsuo, M.: Cross-functional integration for managing customer information flows in a project-based firm. Int. J. Project Manage. 37(1), 145–160 (2019). https://doi.org/10.1016/j.ijproman.2018.11.002

19. Adrodegari, F., Alghisi, A., Bacchetti, A.: Analysis of servitization in engineering-to-order manufacturing companies: an empirical research. In: Proceedings of the Summer School Francesco Turco, 11–13 September, pp. 127–132 (2013)

20. Mourtzis, D., Angelopoulos, J., Boli, N.: Maintenance assistance application of Engineering to Order manufacturing equipment: a Product Service System (PSS) approach. IFAC-PapersOnLine 51(11), 217–222 (2018). https://doi.org/10.1016/j.ifacol.2018.08.263

21. Ivory, C.J., Alderman, N.: Who is the customer? Maintaining a customer orientation in long-term service-focused projects. Int. J. Technol. Manage. 48(2), 140–152 (2009)

22. Artto, K., Wikström, K., Hellström, M., Kujala, J.: Impact of services on project business. Int. J. Project Manage. 26(5), 497–508 (2008). https://doi.org/10.1016/j.ijproman.2008.05.010

23. Pero, M., Stößlein, M., Cigolini, R.: Linking product modularity to supply chain integration in the construction and shipbuilding industries. Int. J. Prod. Econ. 170, 602–615 (2015). https://doi.org/10.1016/j.ijpe.2015.05.011

24. Porter, M.E.: Competitive Strategy: Techniques for Analyzing Industries and Competitors. Free Press, New York (1980)

The Unexpected Consequences of the Covid 19 on Managing ETO Projects

Kristina Kjersem[1(✉)] and Marte F. Giskeødegård[2]

[1] Møreforsking AS, Molde, Norway
kristina.kjersem@moreforsking.no
[2] NTNU Ålesund, Alesund, Norway
marte.giskeodegard@ntnu.no

Abstract. This paper presents findings of the consequences of the recent Covid 19 pandemic on the shipbuilding industry. Through qualitative interviews with key stakeholder on their experiences, the paper identifies an increased emphasis on contracts as regulative for collaboration. This increased focus on legalism in the shipbuilding industry was already triggered by the recent oil crisis yet escalated to a new level by the rules and regulations imposed by the pandemic. The paper argues that the ramifications of this pandemic cannot be understood without interpreting it in respect to the ongoing market transition the industry was already facing when the pandemic hit the world. The findings of increased formal regulation of collaboration, requires further studies and have implications also for the ETO literature.

Keywords: ETO · Collaboration · Legalism

1 Introduction

Engineer-To-Order (ETO) is a business strategy where each product is delivered through a project-based approach that ensures the level of customization required by each specific customer [1]. One important characteristic of this strategy is that, due to a need for specific components, material, equipment, as well as specialized workers to install these elements on the final product, most ETO companies have implemented an outsourcing policy that gives them flexibility in choosing suppliers that can deliver within the required quality and price [2]. However, this extensive outsourcing of both materials, components, and workers has lately been affected by two major events that together increased the focus on how contracts are written and followed by all parts involved in delivering an ETO product. These two events are the oil crisis that started in 2014 and the Covid 19 global pandemic that started in 2020. The former created an unbalanced relationship, with both customers and suppliers, that was further accentuated by the pandemic constraints. One of the most relevant elements of this changed relationship is the way contracts between project participants are negotiated and applied in practice. The consequences of this change are observed at several working levels as shown throughout our research.

© IFIP International Federation for Information Processing 2021
Published by Springer Nature Switzerland AG 2021
A. Dolgui et al. (Eds.): APMS 2021, IFIP AICT 633, pp. 363–370, 2021.
https://doi.org/10.1007/978-3-030-85910-7_38

This paper presents preliminary findings from a qualitative study exploring the impact of the pandemic on the shipbuilding industry that was already affected by significant changes. A few years ago, most shipyards located in the western part of Norway had to adapt to producing cruise vessels after several decades of delivering specialized vessels for the offshore market. While working with offshore customers and suppliers, these shipbuilding companies had developed relationships based on trust and mutual understanding that ensured a close collaboration between the project partners. Changing markets meant that new suppliers and collaboration strategies had to be identified and the contract took on a more central role in defining the relationships between project participants. This process of transition from one market to the next was on its peak when the Covid 19 pandemic hit the world affecting all kinds of businesses and services including the shipbuilding industry.

To fight the rapid spread of this virus, most governments enforced several restrictions on travelling outside own countries, as well as quarantine rules for people arriving from another country. For the case companies, which are dependent on foreign workers to execute large parts of the project, these restrictions led to a change in the way work processes are managed and planned. Now, team leaders must consider the risk of prolonged quarantine or lack of competent workforce when allocating work packages and activities to be completed by the selected suppliers. All that in a context of projects sold with low profit margins and short project delivery time.

Subsequently, the case companies had to deal simultaneously with two types of challenges: 1) to adapt working with new and unfamiliar customers and suppliers; 2) deal with the constraints imposed by the pandemic rules and regulations. Based on these matters, the main research question is: *How did the recent pandemic affected the collaboration between project participants in ETO shipbuilding companies while transitioning between markets?* This research question addresses the context of transition as an underlying factor that started a "legalism[1]" trend which was accentuated, and later elevated to new levels, by the pandemic rules and regulations.

2   Theoretical Background

ETO products are delivered through a project-based approach where each one of them is designed and engineered according to specific requirements made by the final customer [3]. To accomplish these specifications, each project includes numerous engineering hours and a close collaboration between the project team, the customer, and several specialized suppliers [4, 5]. Most European shipbuilding companies have, over the years, implemented a strategy where about 60–80% of the value added to the final product is externally procured from specialized suppliers. These suppliers offer services and products that varies from simple standard parts to highly complex equipment, materials, and components. They also offer design and engineering services as well as specialized production workers [2]. Such high dependency on suppliers is usually regulated by contracts that during the years have become more detailed, increasing the focus on the legalism aspect of each deal between the shipyard and the supplier [6]. In the project

---

[1] Strict adherence to law or prescriptions, especially to the letter rather than the spirit (www.dic tionary.com).

management literature, contracts are seen as a "glue for good project management and relations, and that they are a good and effective control mechanism, reducing risk for project participants" [7]. Yet, results from the industry show that focus on contracts reduces the likelihood of achieving a good project control since they are usually subject to different interpretations that depend on the economic context. When the economy is booming, securing profit, and ensuring a steady supply of appropriately skilled workers is unproblematic, but the situation changes when the economy is heading for a crash. Thus, the way a contract is interpreted has a huge influence on the profitability of the work specified within this formal document [7], challenging also the collaboration between project participants.

In his article, Emblemsvåg [6] describes the negative effects of increased focus on defining and following contracts in project-based industries by referring to cases from shipbuilding and other similar environments. The author argues that due to limitations imposed by contractual agreements, the collaboration among project participants and the expected product quality are now suffering severe drawbacks that can affect project-based industries on the long-term perspective. Among the drawbacks mentioned in the article were more manual work and reactive quality management that decreased the level of open and constructive cooperation between the project participants. Thus, following contracts to the letter creates an increasing bureaucratic approach to collaboration, resulting often in an adversarial attitude among project participants. On the other hand, detailed contracts makes it easier for incapable suppliers to win bids by offering low prices, but failing to deliver within the agreed budget and time [6].

Relationships based on a legalistic view result often in an attitude where project participants stop inviting each other to discussions on finding the best possible solution for the project as a whole [6]. This approach has negative consequences in the Norwegian context characterized by a cluster culture where companies in the maritime industry are recognized for their collaboration in developing new and advanced technological solutions [8]. Reducing the collaboration possibilities due to more focus on following contracts to the letter, has unwanted consequences on maintaining the competitive advantage brought in by the cluster culture. Moreover, the consequences of increased legalism are high costs and risks for each entity involved in a project [6] in a context where shipbuilding companies and their suppliers are increasingly challenged to deliver highly customized vessels to lower prices.

The negative consequences described above are all observed and discussed during our research project, however, a surprising benefit of more focus on the contractual agreements surfaced through our recent interviews. We discuss these preliminary findings throughout this paper.

Based on the theoretical perspectives presented above, this paper contributes mainly to further develop the literature on ETO as a business model where legalism creates new challenges that limits collaboration and innovation among project participants.

3 Research Methodology

The data presented in this article is primarily from two qualitative interviews with key stakeholders, discussing the experience of dealing with the pandemic from the perspective of a director of the purchasing department at a yard and a managing director at a supplier company. The supplier is an international supplier that delivers products and services to several other shipyards in the region, a situation that gives them the possibility to perform a comparative view on the development and trends within the industry. These interviews should be regarded as pilots, where the authors have ambitions to explore the insights from these interviews by comparing it to experience of other yards and suppliers. However, the two interviews have to be understood as part of an ongoing research project, commencing in 2018, that study the transition from offshore to cruise in shipbuilding. The project combined has an extensive data base, stemming from over 30 qualitative interviews, 2 quantitative surveys in production (a total of 600 participants combined) and participant observations from yard activity as planning and project meetings, production work, and so forth. All interviews conducted throughout the project have been transcribed and coded in NVIVO. This wider source of data is key both to identifying the topic in question, and to the interpretation of how the ramifications of the pandemic cannot be evaluated individually but have to be interpreted as related to the context of an ongoing process of market reorientation.

Due to the pandemic, the interviews took place through Teams. Each one lasted around 1 h and 30 min and were recorded with the consent of the interviewees. The interviews followed a focused semi-structured guide, which specifically targeted their experience with the pandemic. The guide started with fairly broad questions where the interviewees were asked to elaborate on their experiences and lessons learned through the pandemic, following up with more topic specific questions during the interview (the role of the contract of managing the relationship, recruiting, and maintaining workers, dialogue with the yard, outlook to the future and so forth). The topic specific questions were identified through observations and talks at the yard, as well as through issues emerging in the media about the consequences of the pandemic for the maritime industry. The open questions were meant to create a rich dialogue allowing the interviewees to bring to discussion possible information that is not easy to predict in advance [9]. The research team listened through the recordings of interviews in the aftermath then systematized, and compared the insights from the two interviews, interpreting them in the context of the findings within the wider project.

The research question for this paper seeks to understand if the existing theory explains the behavior observed in the studies cases [10]. For that, we used case studies from an industry relevant to the call of the conference. The results presented in this paper are preliminary as the research team plans similar interviews at other shipbuilding companies in the region.

4   Case Companies

Like the European ones, the Norwegian shipbuilding companies produce mainly highly customized vessels that requires customer involvement from the design phase all the way throughout the project. The first case company produces vessels to a large range of industries like offshore, fishing, wind farms, and alike. A few years ago, due to the oil crisis that reduced the number of orders for offshore vessels, the company started to produce vessels for the cruise market. This transition required an adaptation process where the shipyard had to develop new types of relationships with new customers and new suppliers since the scope of a cruise vessel differs to a high extent from the scope of an offshore one. While the offshore customers focus on performance of the equipment on the vessel, the cruise customers focus on design solutions on the interior part of it. New relationships and new demands caused changes in terms of planning, coordination, and work practices [11]. While adapting to these changes, the constraints imposed by the pandemic challenged the newly established working procedures once more. One of the elements that needed a new evaluation was the contractual agreement between the shipyard and the customer, and between the shipyard and its suppliers.

The second case company, an international supplier working with shipyards all over the world, is also an important project partner for the main case company. This company delivers products and customized solutions to both offshore and cruise vessels managing to keep a long-term collaboration with the case shipyard. Thus, they were able to inform the research team on how the wave of changes that started with the oil crisis and continued throughout the pandemic, affected their collaboration with the shipyard. The supplier's perspective on the pandemic rules is showing how local rules imposed by the shipyard on top of the existing national and regional ones, affected their working processes that were already pressured to change due to the oil crisis.

Both companies agreed that the new focus on detailing and interpreting contracts was limiting the open and trustful collaboration experienced during the offshore boom.

5   Findings

The preliminary findings in this research emphasize several categories of consequences created by the pandemic in the context of transition within the shipbuilding industry. One of the first consequences of these two different events was more focus on the way contracts are written and followed by both customers, shipyard, and suppliers. Yet, while the pre-pandemic contracts were reaching a high level of detail and focus on legal issues, the pandemic ones managed somehow to bring to light new types of legal topics that were never an issue before the pandemic. An immediate result of this approach is a significant increased cost of the project especially on the administrative side since both the customer, the shipyard, and the suppliers had to use more hours on solving several types of legal issues. Another result was higher cost for the purchasing of materials, components, equipment, and services from their suppliers, particularly the ones providing specialized workforce. All these unanticipated costs have huge consequences for each project under construction as they were sold with low profit margins on a highly competitive market.

Towards the end of last year, many specialized workers were ready to leave the shipyard since they work in shifts of average one month here and one month in home country. The sudden increase in the number of Covid 19 cases urged the authorities to close the country again, creating a new challenge for the shipyard which is dependent on importing specific disciplines at specific times. Luckily for the case company, these rules landed right after a new shift of foreign workers had arrived at the shipyard after the Christmas vacation. Some of the relevant workers decided to remain for one, max two periods more, but many of them had other issues to solve their home countries. This situation led to another dilemma of how and when to import the needed workers in the context of closed borders at the national level. For the shipyard, a delayed project delivery is way too expensive if the customer decides to follow the existing contractual agreement. Moreover, given the fact that the collaboration between the ship owners and the shipyard was new for both of them, using the contract as a guide in every decision to be made complicated the evolution of the project even more.

Most shipyards outsource a significant part of their activities to specialized suppliers who in turn import these services from other countries or continents. When the Norwegian government imposed severe restrictions on travelling to Norway, most project-based industries had to start finding solutions that would keep projects on schedule without breaching the new rules and regulations. One of the solutions applied by the shipyards was to test people for Covid 19 when they entered the country, then a few days after arriving at the quarantine place at the yard, and a third time at the end of the quarantine period. As the pandemic evolved to be longer and more complicated than expected, new national rules were imposed for companies importing workforce. They had to write applications for each specific worker that would arrive at the shipyard. These applications were sent to a specific governmental institution that would evaluate them and send them back to the company that issued them. The testing process, the time spent in quarantine, and the new documentation process raised questions like who pays for the tests used for each worker? Who pays for the quarantine days? Who pays for the hours used by each company in getting the required workforce to the shipyard? New and unexpected issues had to be debated and introduced in each contract between project participants. Since no one could afford these unplanned costs alone, each of the new agreements added to the official document was seen as limiting the collaboration to the letter of the contract. Thus, workers on each side were asked to discuss every improving initiative with own leaders before it could be brought to the customer or to suppliers, an unusual approach within the Norwegian cluster.

Furthermore, based on requirements from some of the customers, the shipyard had to introduce additional rules for testing people arriving from other shipyards located in the same region. These rules are similar to the ones used for workers arriving from other countries and that created a new debate regarding who will support such additional costs since the national rules did not cover them specifically. Or the cost for keeping local workers in quarantine just because they were coming from another local shipyard. At the time of the interview, there was no clear answer to these questions, but a result of these discussions was a reevaluation of a more general contractual agreement between the shipyard and the suppliers stipulating that "suppliers must follow shipyards rules" (I31). These rules are now becoming even more specific so that they make a better distinction between national and local rules. That created additional project costs and determined clearer responsibilities for each project participant, yet at the expense of the open and trustful collaboration observed in earlier projects.

Another challenge the shipyard and its suppliers had to deal with is related to changes in the delivery of materials, equipment and components from suppliers who have their production facilities located outside Europe. The unexpected stop in sea shipping led to increased cost for transportation due to lack of containers, fewer routes to Europe, reduced inland transport capacity due to pandemic measures, etc. As one of the interviewee states "transporting a batch of walls by plane became more expensive than the product itself" (I31). Consequently, a new discussion surfaced: who will pay for all these special transportation solutions? The customer who wants the vessel delivered on time, the shipyard who is responsible for the project, or the supplier who is bounded by a contract created before the pandemic? Questions like these opened for new types of details in the already detailed contracts. One of the most discussed issue was referring to "force majeure situations" clause that was very much used in the beginning of the pandemic but became a subject to change when companies grew more accustomed with the new rules and regulations. According to the supplier's perspective, this clause has now a new definition and meaning, adding new constraints to the collaboration between the project participants.

When the shipyard had to impose all these additional rules for testing and quarantine, they also had to introduced them as agreements in the contracts with customers and suppliers. Beside all the juridical implications, some positive consequence on planning project activities were noted both by the shipyard and by the supplier. In order to deliver according to the existing plan, the company had to improve the quality of the existing planning process by making sure that each project participant delivers as planned. A more dynamic and proactive communication with the suppliers became necessary and the result was fewer delayed deliveries on each side. However, both companies mentioned that they now follow the plan and the contract much closer, and they perceive the collaboration as more formal than before (I30, I31).

6 Discussion and Conclusions

The focus in this article is on how the recent pandemic affected the collaboration between participants in ETO shipbuilding projects. Based on our preliminary findings, it seems like the contractual agreements existing before the pandemic are now under a very detailed scrutiny. Many of the elements that were quite general and somehow implied as a part of the understanding between the customer, the shipyard, and its suppliers, are now reevaluated and new, more explicit elements are getting added.

Having to deal first with a new market and then with new pandemic triggered rules and regulations, changed the perception on how contracts are written and followed both by all project participants. Before the pandemic, the shipyard and the supplier were preoccupied by the negative consequences of more focus on contractual agreements that would restrict the informal collaboration that existed during the offshore era. When the pandemic arrived, they had to get together and find solutions that imply close collaboration in finding the right formulation on the contractual agreements. How this approach will affect the future collaboration in developing innovative solutions, the trademark of this regional cluster, remain to be seen.

Based on our preliminary findings, it seems like the rules and regulations imposed by the pandemic have changed the attitude and the approach to contracts in the ETO environment. Meanwhile, the same rules exposed the vulnerability of being dependent on imported workforce and many ETO companies must reevaluate their business models and find solutions that would keep projects on schedule despite disturbing events like global pandemics. Thus, the next step of this research is to analyze how a business model based on extensive import of specialized workforce can survive the impact of extremely disruptive events. The research team plans a larger mapping process of how ETO companies have adapted to a new way of managing their projects.

Among the limitations of this paper is that our data is mainly from the shipbuilding industry, and we would probably find different challenges in construction or other similar industries.

Acknowledgement. The research team wants to acknowledge the support received from the Norwegian Research Council by funding this project. We would also like to thank to the companies involved in the project for their dedication and the willingness to share their experiences with us.

References

1. Kjersem, K.: Contributing to resolving a project planning paradox in ETO: from plan to planning, p. 295. in Logistics, Molde University College, Norway (2020)
2. Held, T.: Supplier integration as an improvement driver: An analysis of some recent approaches in the shipbuilding industry. In: Engelhardt-Nowitzki, C., Nowitzki, O., Zsifkovits, H. (eds.) Supply Chain Network Analysis, pp. 369–384 (2010)
3. Pandit, A., Zhu, Y.: An ontology-based approach to support decision-making for the design in ETO (engineer-to-order) products. Autom. Constr. **16**(6), 759–770 (2007)
4. Duchi, A., Schönsleben, P.: A three steps methodological approach to assess the engineer-to-order operations environment. In: Lödding, H., Riedel, R., Thoben, K.-D., von Cieminski, G., Kiritsis, D. (eds.) APMS 2017. IAICT, vol. 514, pp. 251–258. Springer, Cham (2017). https://doi.org/10.1007/978-3-319-66926-7_29
5. Hammervoll, T., Halse, L.L., Engelseth, P.: The role of clusters in global maritime value networks. Int. J. Phys. Distrib. Logist. Manage. **44**(1/2), 98–112 (2014)
6. Emblemsvåg, J.: On Quality 4.0 in project-based industries. Total Qual. Manage. J. (2020)
7. Clegg, S., Bjørkeng, K., Pitsis, T.: Innovating the practice of normative control in project management contractual relations. In: P. Morris, J. Pinto, and J. Sönderlund, Editors. The Oxford Book of Project Management, p. 550. Oxford University Press, UK (2012)
8. Fløysand, A., Jakobsen, S.-E., Bjarnar, O.: The dynamism of clustering: interweaving material and discursive processes. Geoforum **43**(5), 948–958 (2012)
9. Yin, R.K.: Qualitative Research from Start to Finish. ed. T.G. Press (2011)
10. Stuart, I., et al.: Effective case research in operations management: A process perspective. J. Oper. Manage. **20**, 419–433 (2002)
11. Kjersem, K., Giskeødegård, M.F.: Changing markets: implications for the planning process in ETO Companies. In: Ameri, F., Stecke, K.E., von Cieminski, G., Kiritsis, D. (eds.) APMS 2019. IAICT, vol. 566, pp. 554–561. Springer, Cham (2019). https://doi.org/10.1007/978-3-030-30000-5_68

Requirements for Sales and Operations Planning in an Engineer-to-Order Manufacturing Environment

Swapnil Bhalla[1]([⊠]) [iD], Erlend Alfnes[1] [iD], Hans-Henrik Hvolby[2] [iD], and Olumide Emmanuel Oluyisola[1] [iD]

[1] Norwegian University of Science and Technology, Trondheim, Norway
swapnil.bhalla@ntnu.no
[2] Aalborg University, Aalborg, Denmark

Abstract. Sales and Operations Planning (S&OP) is the process through which enterprises develop tactical plans for aligning supply and demand management activities, usually with the objective of maximizing profitability. Demand-supply balancing is particularly complex and challenging in Engineer-to-Order (ETO) manufacturing environments, which are characterized by highly customer-driven order-fulfilment processes, creating a dynamic and uncertain planning environment. Recent studies highlight that ETO environments and their contextual influence on S&OP have been overlooked within extant S&OP research. This paper addresses this by investigating how the characteristics of ETO manufacturing influence the design of S&OP. Through a case study of a maritime equipment manufacturer, the paper identifies requirements that are imposed on the S&OP process by the characteristics of an ETO planning environment. These requirements serve as basis for identifying three main research areas that can support the design of S&OP in ETO environments, namely, customer enquiry management, multi-project management and spare parts management. The findings are summarized in a high-level framework for S&OP in ETO production and related research areas.

Keywords: Sales and operations planning · Tactical planning · Engineer-to-order

1 Introduction

Sales and operations planning (S&OP) refers to the process by which enterprises develop tactical supply and demand management plans [1]. The S&OP process usually aims to maximize revenue and/or profitability by minimizing the imbalance between supply and demand, while operating within the constraints set by strategic decisions [2]. Since its conception, knowledge on S&OP has matured and advanced significantly but unevenly across industrial environments [1, 3], as exemplified by the lack of normative guidance for S&OP design in engineer-to-order (ETO) environments [4].

A. Dolgui et al. (Eds.): APMS 2021, IFIP AICT 633, pp. 371–380, 2021.
https://doi.org/10.1007/978-3-030-85910-7_39

Trends such as digitalization, globalization and increasing global competition force manufacturers to adapt to stay effective and efficient [5, 6], where S&OP can serve as top-management's lever to steer the business [1]. The importance of effective S&OP is further underlined in ETO environments such as shipbuilding supply chains, where markets have undergone dramatic changes in demand, profit margins and competition during the last decade [7]. The high complexity of ETO operations and structural differences between ETO and mass-production environments limit the extent to which extant knowledge can be applied to guide S&OP design in ETO environments, as most of the previous S&OP research was contextualized in high-volume production environments [1, 4]. Therefore, this paper investigates how the characteristics of ETO manufacturing environments create design requirements for the S&OP process.

The remainder of the paper is structured as follows. Section 2 further elaborates on the gap in literature vis-à-vis S&OP in ETO environments, and provides theoretical background for the case study in Sect. 3, which serves to identify the requirements imposed by the characteristics of an ETO manufacturing environment on the design of the S&OP process. Section 4 relates the identified requirements to relevant research areas and bodies of knowledge that can support S&OP design in ETO environments, organizing the findings in a proposed framework. Finally, Sect. 5 concludes the paper, and lists limitations and further research directions.

2   ETO Manufacturing, S&OP, and Strategic Fit

ETO production environments, i.e. companies and/or supply chains operating with an ETO strategy, are typically characterized by big-sized complex products that are produced in low volumes and high variety, with several customer order-driven engineering and production activities [8, 9]. These order-driven activities create substantial planning complexity in ETO environments, which in turn creates the need for using specialized tools and practices in planning processes [4, 10], e.g., advanced planning and scheduling (APS) systems, collaborative planning, etc. Production planning and control (PPC) literature proposes the application of the strategic fit concept in designing planning processes and in selecting and/or developing tools and practices to be used in the planning processes; arguing that planning processes should be designed according to the requirements of the planning environment [5]. Understanding a planning environment and its requirements is essential for using appropriate planning methods, as lack of fit between the planning environment's characteristics and PPC processes negatively affects manufacturing firms' performance [11]. Consequently, as a PPC process, the strategic fit concept has also been applied to the S&OP process.

Kristensen and Jonsson's [1] application of the strategic fit concept and contingency theory in analyzing S&OP literature reveals the shortcomings of extant S&OP literature vis-à-vis ETO manufacturing environments. Their review suggests that most of the S&OP literature has been contextualized in relatively high-volume industrial environments, e.g., retail, food production, pharmaceuticals, etc. As a result, S&OP literature is contextually weak in describing and guiding the S&OP process in ETO environments and lacks a reference framework for researchers and practitioners [4].

Existing S&OP frameworks, such as the widely used five-step process framework for S&OP [12, 13], are aligned with the characteristics of high-volume manufacturing environments and define S&OP as the process of setting inventory levels and production volumes for product families based on demand forecasts and planned capacity levels. However, in ETO environments, where engineering, procurement and production activities are often planned based on customer orders due to low forecast accuracy [9], the role and structure of the S&OP process is not accurately described by existing S&OP process frameworks. Moreover, existing PPC frameworks for ETO environments, such as those found in references [9, 14], provide some insights into how S&OP might support the fulfilment process of individual orders, but do not clarify the ongoing role, inputs, objectives and outcomes of S&OP as a planning process.

3 S&OP Requirements in ETO Manufacturing

This section identifies the requirements imposed on the S&OP process by the characteristics of an ETO manufacturing environment. As described in the Sect. 2, understanding the planning environment and its characteristics is essential for designing PPC processes, to ensure strategic fit between the planning requirements and the features of a PPC process. To identify the requirements imposed on the S&OP process by the characteristics of an ETO manufacturing environment, a case study of a maritime equipment manufacturer was conducted, where data collection focused on describing the planning environment of the case company. The case selection logic is best described as convenience sampling, since the case company itself is the industrial context that motivated the research problem addressed in this paper, while also being a suitable context for conducting research to address the problem, i.e., a typical ETO production environment, as further described in Subsect. 3.1.

The case company is and has been NTNU's industrial partner in research projects, which facilitated access to historical production data and transcripts from various interviews and workshops conducted over the course of several years by other researchers in the research group, including the second author. Based on factory visits (last in March 2020) curated by the master planner, and the insights gained from the archived data, a preliminary description of the characteristics of the company's planning environment was drafted. To validate the characteristics, semi-structured interviews with the master planner and the head of the planning department were conducted remotely between November 2020 and February 2021. These interviews were recorded and transcribed, and the transcripts were verified with the interviewees.

3.1 Characteristics of the Case Company

The case company, which will be referred to as 'SHIPRO' (short for Ship Propulsion - not the real name), is an original equipment manufacturer (OEM) that supplies propulsion and maneuvering equipment (propellers, gearboxes, thrusters, etc.) for ships through a globally dispersed sales network. SHIPRO's target customer segments include offshore vessels, fishing and research vessels, cruise ships, ferries, and naval vessels, and their product portfolio consists of a wide variety of propeller and thruster systems to fit the needs of different ship-types. Table 1 presents the main characteristics of SHIPRO's product, order-fulfilment process and resources, and market environment.

Table 1. Main characteristics of SHIPRO's planning environment

---

Product characteristics:
- customized and standard propeller and thruster systems for ships, consisting of heavy-duty mechanical, hydraulic, and electronic subsystems
- big-sized product with deep and wide bill-of-materials (BOM) with up to 8 levels
- long product life (over 25 years) and maintenance regulations make after-sales maintenance, repair, and spare parts sales an important part of SHIPRO's business

Process & resource characteristics:
- fulfilment of each customer order for new equipment is managed as a project, and several such projects are managed and executed simultaneously
- functionally laid-out job-shop production for fabrication of components and steel-structures; fixed positions for sub-assemblies and final assembly
- customer order-based steel-structure fabrication, sub-assembly, and final assembly
- fabrication of machined components is partly customer order- or project-based, and partly based on spare part demand forecasts
- various specialized single-axis and multi-axis CNC-machines (computer numerical control) for component fabrication – only few components (less than 10%) have alternate routings
- production lead time for the same product varies significantly across different projects due to variations in the composition of the order-book or project-portfolio
- high variability in customization requirements across projects – less than 100 engineering hours typically used for order-specific configuration for standard equipment orders, whereas customized equipment may require twice-thrice the number of engineering hours and multiple iterations before drawings are finalized

Market characteristics:
- high variability in annual demand and production volumes – have varied between 200 and 500 thrusters per year in the last 5 years
- high variability in product mix – depends on demand for types of new vessels
- delivery dates are contractually committed – necessitates reliable estimation of delivery lead time during project sales phase to ensure high delivery precision
- high responsiveness in spare part delivery – promised delivery lead time for spare parts is three weeks with a 95% service level target
- stock-keeping-units (SKUs) with wide range of demand and supply characteristics in spare part portfolio, e.g., low vs. high annual demand; sporadic vs. stable demand; replenishment lead time of few days vs. several weeks, etc.

3.2   S&OP Requirements at SHIPRO

This subsection analyzes the characteristics of the case company's planning environment, as presented in the previous subsection, to identify the implications of the characteristics on the design of the S&OP process. We interpret these implications as requirements that these characteristics impose on the design of the S&OP process. The concept of strategic fit is used as the theoretical fundament to analyze the planning environment's characteristics or attributes, such that each attribute results in one or more requirements for the S&OP design.

Figure 1 shows the five main requirements identified based on SHIPRO's planning environment, where each requirement is linked to one or more planning environment

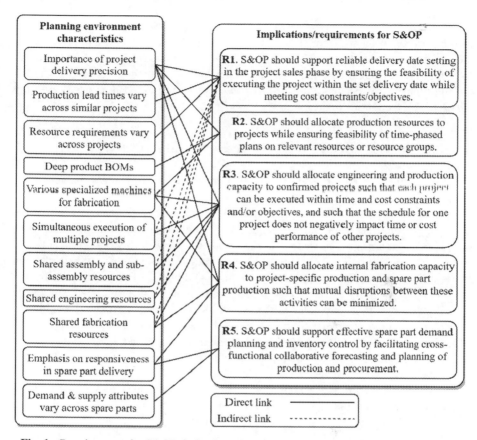

Fig. 1. Requirements for S&OP design based on the case company's planning environment

attributes that generate the requirement. While most of the attribute-requirement links are shown as solid lines, four of the linkages to **R1** (requirement #1) are shown as dashed lines to represent an indirect link. For instance, the fact the SHIPRO executes multiple projects simultaneously on shared resources does not itself generate the requirement that S&OP should support reliable delivery date setting (**R1**). Instead, simultaneous execution of multiple projects on shared resources leads to variability in the production lead time for similar projects, which in-turn necessitates that reliable delivery date setting is supported by S&OP (**R1**).

The S&OP requirements identified in the case study, as shown in Fig. 1, can be associated with the three broad phases of customer-supplier interaction (CSI) associated with each product, i.e., *project-sales* (**R1**), *project-execution* (**R2, R3** and **R4**) and *after-sales service* (**R4** and **R5**). By fulfilling **R1**, S&OP can support effectiveness of the sales process by ensuring that estimated delivery dates are realistic and competitive. By fulfilling **R2, R3** and **R4**, S&OP can support project-execution by increasing the likelihood of achieving delivery and cost targets set and agreed upon with the customer in the sales phase. Finally, by fulfilling **R4** and **R5**, S&OP can maintain customer-satisfaction by supporting responsiveness in spare part delivery while ensuring that the responsiveness is not achieved at the expense of delayed projects and vice-versa. Another insight that can be gained from the attribute-requirement linkages shown in Fig. 1 is that the requirements associated only with the *project-sales* and *project-execution* phases (**R1–R3**) are generated by engineering, fabrication and assembly resources; whereas the requirements associated with the *after-sales service* phase (**R4** and **R5**) are only generated by the fabrication resources.

4   Relating ETO S&OP to Existing Research Areas

Having identified the requirements that an ETO planning environment's characteristics impose on the S&OP process design, the question arises as to how the S&OP process should be designed to fulfil these requirements. Furthermore, the analysis in in Subsect. 3.2 provides the insight that the requirements are associable with different phases of CSI. *Can this insight be used while designing the S&OP process in an ETO environment?* This section explores this question through a discussion of concepts from literature that are considered relevant for the three CSI phases. The purpose of this discussion is not to provide conclusive guidelines for individual design elements of the S&OP process, e.g., meeting and collaboration, organization, information technology and tools, planning parameters, etc. [1]. Instead, the discussion aims to propose possible links between S&OP and other research areas that appear relevant based on the requirements identified in the case. These links can serve to identify relevant tools and/or practices to use within the design of the S&OP process.

Three main research areas within operations management (OM) literature emerge as relevant for S&OP process design in an ETO context based on the requirements identified in Subsect. 3.2, and the CSI phases they are associated with. These are:

1. *Customer Enquiry Management* – linked to project-sales (**R1**),
2. *Multi-Project Management* – linked to project-execution (**R2, R3** and **R4**),
3. *Spare Parts Management* – linked to after-sales service (**R4** and **R5**).

The first two research areas emerged from ETO literature that was identified using backward and cited reference searches, starting from a relatively recent systematic literature review on 'big-sized customized product manufacturing systems' [8]. While we found support for the requirements associated with after-sales service (i.e., **R4** and **R5**) in ETO literature [7], a particular research area that could be related to S&OP did not emerge from this literature. Consequently, keyword searches for terms like 'service parts', 'spare parts', 'after-sales', etc. were used on Scopus to identify relevant literature, from which the third research area emerged process.

These research areas and their overlaps with S&OP in an ETO environment, as seen in the case, have been visualized in a proposed framework shown in Fig. 2. The following three subsections briefly describe the link of each research area with S&OP in ETO environments, thus also serving as descriptions of the elements of the framework.

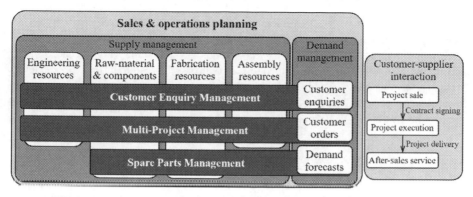

Fig. 2. A framework of S&OP in ETO production and related research areas

4.1 Customer Enquiry Management (CEM)

Customer enquiries and offer-preparation for responding to these enquiries are the first planning triggers for the order-fulfilment process in ETO environments, and serve as precursors to confirmed projects [9, 15]. *Customer enquiry* is used here as an overarching term for enquiries, tender invitations, Requests for Proposal (RFPs), sales leads and any other forms of information through which ETO companies identify potential projects or customer orders. The decision process that takes place in ETO companies between receiving a customer enquiry and the consequent processing of a confirmed order is referred to as CEM [15] or RFP-management [9]. The main decisions and activities within CEM are listed below.

- **Strategic filtering of customer enquiries** (a.k.a. *project selection* or *project portfolio management* [16]): deciding whether management wishes to make an offer for an enquiry, based on factors such as profitability of customer segment, development of core in-house competencies, long-term growth strategy, etc. [4, 15, 16].
- **Preliminary product engineering**: specifying preliminary technical characteristics and features of the product to match customer's requirements [9, 15]. The importance of this process is emphasized by the fact that the features of the technical solution are often the order-winning criteria in many ETO environments [17].
- **Macro process planning (MPP) and rough-cut capacity planning (RCCP)** (a.k.a. *project planning* and *aggregate capacity planning* respectively [9]): identifying main tasks within the order-fulfilment activities, i.e., engineering, procurement, fabrication, etc. and estimating aggregate activity durations and resource requirements for these activities to establish tentative project milestones [9, 16, 18].
- **Specification and negotiation of commercial characteristics of the project**: estimation of project cost and duration based on outputs of MPP and RCCP, e.g., activity durations, type of planned capacity – internal or subcontracted, etc. These estimates are used to quote price and delivery dates for customer enquiries, which may be followed by negotiation and/or replanning [9, 15, 16, 18].

Through CEM, managers and planners can control the selection of projects that are accepted, the delivery dates for accepted projects, and identify the need for any tactical capacity adjustments, e.g., through hiring personnel or subcontracting. Because of the role of CEM in controlling the workload imposed on internal resources on a tactical level, CEM can be considered closely related to S&OP. Moreover, CEM could be integrated as an element of S&OP, and tools and practices from CEM literature [15, 19] can be incorporated into the S&OP process in ETO environments.

4.2 Multi-project Management (MPM)

Hans et al. [16] define a project as a "unique undertaking consisting of a complex set of precedence-related activities that have to be executed using diverse and mostly limited company resources". In ETO environments, projects result in the production of products that are uniquely designed and/or engineered to fit customers' requirements, where each project requires resources for physical processes such as fabrication, assembly, testing, etc., and for non-physical processes such as product design and engineering, process planning, etc. [9]. Furthermore, each project requires material inputs that can be transformed into the finished product by fabrication and assembly processes. The finiteness of available resources and material create the need for MPM in ETO environments that execute multiple projects simultaneously [9, 16].

MPM refers to the ongoing process of creating and managing resource and material plans for multiple projects while ensuring that, firstly, schedules and milestones of individual projects are met, and secondly, mutually conflicting material and resource allocations to projects are avoided [16]. Through this, MPM plays a vital role in ensuring that resources and materials are available in the required quantity at the right time to meet delivery promises made during CEM. Because of this emphasis on ensuring realistic availability and allocation of material and resources, MPM plays a vital role in tactical level demand-supply balancing in ETO environments, emerging as another process that can be integrated with S&OP in ETO environments.

4.3 Spare Parts Management (SPM)

SPM collectively refers to demand management and inventory control for spare parts [20]. Spare parts are independent demand items which pose unique challenges within forecasting and inventory control due to the wide range of part characteristics usually found in OEMs' spare part portfolios [21]. Consequently, specialized tools and practices have been proposed in the SPM literature for SKU-classification, forecasting and inventory control [20], e.g., multi-criteria classification methods, forecasting methods for intermittent demand items, etc. These specialized tools and practices from SPM literature can be used in the S&OP process for tactical planning activities such as spare part demand forecasting, planning raw-material and component inventories, and allocating fabrication resources. Furthermore, integrating tools and practices from SPM, MPM and CEM into S&OP can support planners and managers in avoiding capacity and material conflicts across plans generated by SPM, MPM, and CEM.

5   Conclusions, Limitations, and Further Research

This paper has identified the requirements that are imposed on the design of the S&OP process by the characteristics of an ETO planning environment. The requirements, which were identified from a case study of a maritime equipment manufacturer, have been further linked to three research areas in extant literature, that can serve as relevant bodies of knowledge for guiding the design of the S&OP process in ETO environments. The findings were summarized in a high-level framework (Fig. 2).

The limitations of this study and the abundance of unexplored topics provide several directions for further work. Firstly, the study is based on a single case, which limits the generalizability of the findings across ETO contexts. Therefore, identifying S&OP requirements in other ETO contexts, understanding similarities and differences in S&OP requirements across these contexts and the planning environment attributes that lead to the differences can support development of generalizable and robust frameworks and models for S&OP in ETO environments. Secondly, despite undertaking a detailed single case study, this paper has only addressed S&OP design on a high level, i.e., by identifying design requirements and relevant bodies of knowledge to support the design. Future studies can explore how traditional design elements of S&OP, e.g., meeting and collaboration, organization, information technology and tools, etc. should be designed to fulfil the requirements of ETO contexts. Finally, the study has not exhaustively explored OM literature for concepts and research areas that can support S&OP design in ETO environments. Therefore, applications of other relevant concepts such as customer-order-decoupling-point, capable-to-promise, etc. should also be explored for further development of the proposed framework.

References

1. Kristensen, J., Jonsson, P.: Context-based sales and operations planning (S&OP) research. Int. J. Phys. Distrib. Logistics Manag. (2018)
2. Coker, J., Helo, P.: Demand-supply balancing in manufacturing operations. Benchmarking Int. J. (2016)
3. Ling, R.C., Goddard, W.E.: Orchestrating Success: Improve Control of the Business with Sales & Operations Planning. Oliver Wight Limited Publications (1988)
4. Shurrab, H., Jonsson, P., Johansson, M.I.: A tactical demand-supply planning framework to manage complexity in engineer-to-order environments: insights from an in-depth case study. Prod. Planning Control, 1–18 (2020)
5. Buer, S.-V., Strandhagen, J.W., Strandhagen, J.O., Alfnes, E.: Strategic fit of planning environments: towards an integrated framework. In: Temponi, C., Vandaele, N. (eds.) ILS 2016. LNBIP, vol. 262, pp. 77–92. Springer, Cham (2018). https://doi.org/10.1007/978-3-319-73758-4_6
6. Philipp, R., Gerlitz, L., Moldabekova, A.: Small and medium-sized seaports on the digital track: tracing digitalisation across the south baltic region by innovative auditing procedures. In: Kabashkin, I., Yatskiv, I., Prentkovskis, O. (eds.) RelStat 2019. LNNS, vol. 117, pp. 351–362. Springer, Cham (2020). https://doi.org/10.1007/978-3-030-44610-9_35
7. Strandhagen, J.W., Buer, S.-V., Semini, M., Alfnes, E., Strandhagen, J.O.: Sustainability challenges and how Industry 4.0 technologies can address them: a case study of a shipbuilding supply chain. Prod. Plan. Control, 1–16 (2020)

8. Zennaro, I., Finco, S., Battini, D., Persona, A.: Big size highly customised product manufacturing systems: a literature review and future research agenda. Int. J. Prod. Res. **57**(15–16), 5362–5385 (2019)
9. Adrodegari, F., Bacchetti, A., Pinto, R., Pirola, F., Zanardini, M.: Engineer-to-order (ETO) production planning and control: an empirical framework for machinery-building companies. Prod. Plan. Control **26**(11), 910–932 (2015)
10. Wikner, J., Rudberg, M.: Integrating production and engineering perspectives on the customer order decoupling point. Int. J. Oper. Prod. Manag. (2005)
11. Jonsson, P., Mattsson, S.A.: The implications of fit between planning environments and manufacturing planning and control methods. Int. J. Oper. Prod. Manag. (2003)
12. Grimson, J.A., Pyke, D.F.: Sales and operations planning: an exploratory study and framework. Int. J. Logistics Manag. (2007)
13. Thomé, A.M.T., Scavarda, L.F., Fernandez, N.S., Scavarda, A.J.: Sales and operations planning: a research synthesis. Int. J. Prod. Econ. **138**(1), 1–13 (2012)
14. Nam, S., Shen, H., Ryu, C., Shin, J.G.: SCP-Matrix based shipyard APS design: application to long-term production plan. Int. J. Naval Archit. Ocean Eng. **10**(6), 741–761 (2018)
15. Zorzini, M., Stevenson, M., Hendry, L.C.: Customer enquiry management in global supply chains: a comparative multi-case study analysis. Eur. Manag. J. **30**(2), 121–140 (2012)
16. Hans, E.W., Herroelen, W., Leus, R., Wullink, G.: A hierarchical approach to multi-project planning under uncertainty. Omega **35**(5), 563–577 (2007)
17. Amaro, G., Hendry, L., Kingsman, B.: Competitive advantage, customisation and a new taxonomy for non make-to-stock companies. Int. J. Oper. Prod. Manag. (1999)
18. Carvalho, A.N., Oliveira, F., Scavarda, L.F.: Tactical capacity planning in a real-world ETO industry case: an action research. Int. J. Prod. Econ. **167**, 187–203 (2015)
19. Zorzini, M., Hendry, L., Stevenson, M., Pozzetti, A.: Customer enquiry management and product customization. Int. J. Oper. Prod. Manag. (2008)
20. Bacchetti, A., Saccani, N.: Spare parts classification and demand forecasting for stock control: investigating the gap between research and practice. Omega **40**(6), 722–737 (2012)
21. Bacchetti, A., Plebani, F., Saccani, N., Syntetos, A.: Empirically-driven hierarchical classification of stock keeping units. Int. J. Prod. Econ. **143**(2), 263–274 (2013)

A Systematic Approach to Implementing Multi-sourcing Strategy in Engineer-to-Order Production

Deodat Mwesiumo[1]([✉]), Bella B. Nujen[2], and Nina Pereira Kvadsheim[3]

[1] Faculty of Logistics, Molde University College, Britvegen 2, Molde, Norway
Deodat.E.Mwesiumo@himolde.no
[2] Faculty of Economics, Department of International Business, Norwegian University of Science and Technology, Ålesund, Norway
[3] Møreforsking AS, Britvegen 4, Molde, Norway

Abstract. Engineer-to-order (ETO) manufacturers operate in an increasingly volatile, uncertain, and complex business environment, which has added more complexity to their already complex supply chain operations. As they navigate the ramifications of the COVID-19 pandemic, they need knowledge-based guidance on selecting and implementing approaches to increasing resilience. Based on a clinical management design, this study develops a systematic approach for a case firm that recently transitioned from single sourcing to multi-sourcing. The goal is to strike a balance between the total cost of acquisition and supply chain resilience. The study reveals that effective implementation of multi-sourcing in ETO production requires involving the purchasing and supply function (PSF) right from the design stages. Besides, it is essential to deploy a cloud-based procurement system that facilitates interactions between PSF and the suppliers, as well as other critical organisational functions involved in an ETO project.

Keywords: Multi-sourcing · Single sourcing · Engineer-to-order production · Clinical management research

1 Introduction

The outbreak of the COVID-19 pandemic and the subsequent measures by authorities to stop the spread quickly led to the disruption of supply links, which in turn caused material shortages and delivery delays. A clear message sent by the pandemic is that supply chains need to be more resilient [1], and thus, supply chain recovery scenarios and approaches must be developed [2]. This is understandable because it appears that some of supply chain management "best practices" partly contributed to the heightened vulnerability of supply chains. For instance, it is argued that lean practices, globalised structures, single sourcing, and offshoring strategies made many companies prone to the pandemic [3, 4]. In their report, Kilpatrick and Barter [5] note that "a decades-long focus on supply chain optimisation to minimise costs, reduce inventories, and maximise

© IFIP International Federation for Information Processing 2021
Published by Springer Nature Switzerland AG 2021
A. Dolgui et al. (Eds.): APMS 2021, IFIP AICT 633, pp. 381–389, 2021.
https://doi.org/10.1007/978-3-030-85910-7_40

asset utilisation has removed buffers and flexibility to absorb disruptions, and COVID-19 illustrates that many companies are not fully aware of the vulnerability of their supply chain relationships to global shocks" (p. 14).

As the pandemic is forcing many companies to rethink and transform their supply strategies, various approaches have been proposed to address the repercussions of major supply chain disruptions. The measures include balancing global sourcing with nearshore and local sourcing, increased collaboration with suppliers, the adoption of multiple sources [3], and greater utilisation of supply chain technologies such as the Internet of Things, artificial intelligence, and robotics [5]. Conceivably, navigating through the ramifications of the pandemic requires knowledge-based guidance on the selection and implementation of these strategies. This study develops a systematic approach for implementing a multi-sourcing strategy in the context of engineer-to-order (ETO) production. The study is based on a clinical management research design (CMR) [6], where a framework is developed for an ETO firm that initially relied on a single sourcing strategy but recently decided to implement a multi-sourcing strategy.

The remainder of this chapter is organised as follows. The next section describes single-sourcing versus multi-sourcing, followed by Sect. 3 that describes sourcing in ETO production. Section 4 describes the methodology deployed in the study, while Sect. 5 presents the case firm and its decision to multisource. Section 6 provides the framework, followed by a conclusion.

2 Theoretical Foundation

2.1 Single Sourcing Versus Multi-sourcing

Besides inputs produced internally, firms rely on external sources to obtain other inputs – goods or services - required to make their final product. According to the Chartered Institute of Procurement & Supply (CIPS), sourcing is the process of finding, evaluating and engaging suppliers to achieve cost savings and the best value for goods and services is what we refer to as sourcing [7]. The supply chain operations reference model (SCOR) identifies sourcing as one of the essential elements of supply chain management, along with planning, production, delivering and returning. To be successful, supply chain management must have an effective sourcing strategy that allows it to combat uncertainties in both supply and demand [8]. This is important because lack of an effective sourcing strategy can lead to supply breakdown and excessive downtime of production resources, upstream and downstream supply chain. As such, strategic sourcing – a process that directs all sourcing activities toward opportunities that enable the firm to achieve its long-term operational and organisational performance goals – is highly promoted [9].

One of the decisions made under strategic sourcing is whether to obtain inputs from a single supplier or multiple suppliers. Obtaining supplies from a single supplier has its own advantages. Such advantages include the possibility of forming a long-term relationship with a supplier based on trust and shared benefits, low purchase price due to economies of scale, and increased supplier's commitment. With such deepened relationship, the supplier can even make costly specific investments to maintain the relationship. However, reliance on a single supplier may have negative consequences such as the increased risk of supply disruption, particularly for asset-specific products, and potential opportunistic behaviour due to significant dependency on the supplier [10].

Conversely, sourcing from multiple suppliers provides flexibility to respond to one supplier's inability to supply due to unexpected events. It also increases competition among suppliers, leading to better quality, price, delivery, product innovation and buyer's negotiation power. Nevertheless, multi-sourcing increases transactional costs due to supplier searching costs, negotiation with multiple suppliers, and a greater number of orders [11]. Besides, individual suppliers may reduce their effort to match buyer's requirements due to reduced volume.

Thus, the choice between single versus multiple sourcing calls for a cost-benefit analysis. That is, weighing the advantages and disadvantages of the two approaches, given the circumstances of the buying firm. Burke et al. [8] conclude that single sourcing is a suitable strategy only when supplier capacities are high compared to the product demand and when the buying firm does not obtain benefits through multi-sourcing. Additionally, it works well without natural or man-made disruptions in supply chains [12]. In recent years supply chains have been facing increased vulnerabilities due to trade tensions, natural disasters, and other geo-economic disruptions [13]. Under such circumstances, therefore, single sourcing is quite risky, which is why even before the pandemic, the multi-sourcing strategy had become a significant trend in the contemporary outsourcing landscape [11].

2.2 Sourcing in ETO Production

ETO production strategy involves designing, engineering, and producing a product to meet the needs of a specific customer [14]. Therefore, such products are highly customised and often produced in low volume [15]. Given the high level of customisation, the design of ETO products begins when a customer places an order. This way, ETO production is characterised by complex environments, high demand variability, multifaceted design stages, and intensive project life cycles [14]. Given these characteristics, PSF can play a strategic role in ETO production [16]. However, the PSF working under this strategy faces an entirely different dynamic compared to working in a production system where production volumes are based on sales forecasts. Therefore materials and components can be purchased in advance based on predicted demand. Having an estimate of demand allows PSF to enter long term contracts with suppliers and commit to buy specific volumes.

Conversely, PSF operating under ETO production strategy does not have the possibility of buying all inputs in advance as it is difficult to identify and source all the required materials and components before a customer places an order. Thus, while some standard components can be purchased in advance, PSF can only determine all the requirements after a bill of materials (BOM) for a project has been created following a customer order. This implies that negotiating long-term contracts and committing specific volumes with suppliers is challenging due to demand uncertainty associated with ETO production. To deal with such uncertainty, Moretto et al. [16] suggest that PSF must have a flexible approach that allows it to implement a responsive sourcing strategy. This means that implementing a multi-sourcing strategy in ETO will be different from a multi-sourcing strategy in a forecast-based production system. For PSF in an ETO production, multi-sourcing means having multiple suppliers who can provide the same input(s) required for a specific project. In other words, for each component needed for a particular project, two or more qualified suppliers are boarded, and optimal quantities are allocated between them. Such a system requires striking a balance between the total costs of acquiring inputs and supply risk. The aim is to create a strategy that allows an ETO firm to bounce back from unforeseen disruptions while still minimising costs.

3 Methodology

This study deploys clinical management research (CMR), a method that involves 'observing, eliciting and reporting of data which are available when the researcher is engaged in a helping relationship in the management of change' [17]. The method is suitable because it allows case firms and their management to gain deeper and richer insights into a particular problem [6]. This is because this type of research constitutes both an investigation and a response to a problem faced by the case firm. In principle, CMR operates within the realm of practical knowing where 'knowledge is contextually embedded, and there is a primary concern for the practical and the particular' [18]. Thus, regarding case selection, CMR is not based on random sampling; instead, there must be a firm that has a specific problem to be addressed. Unlike case study design, where a researcher initiates a project to explore or generate theory, CMR is initiated by a firm that has experienced a challenge and wants to solve it. In this study, the firm (henceforth Superprop) is an ETO firm that produces custom-made propulsion, positioning and manoeuvring systems for domestic and international shipyards and ship owners. This study is part of a larger research project where among other things, the purpose is to apply research-based insights in solving logistics-related challenges faced by the case firm and its suppliers. Two of the researchers involved in this project have previously worked with the case firm in projects that addressed other logistics-related problems. This is valuable because the long-term relationship these researchers have had with the case firm has provided a deeper understanding of the circumstances surrounding the current decision to switch to a multi-sourcing strategy. Thus, the analysis conducted in this study is based on current and past data collected through semi-structured interviews, document reviews, and workshops. Informants were managers of critical functional areas. More precisely, interviews were conducted with the procurement manager, the production manager, the design and engineering manager, and a manager from the aftersales and service department. In total, eight hours of interviews were conducted and later analysed. To further enhance our understanding of Superprop operations, the study also involved direct non-participant observations. In terms of analysis, the collected data were synthesised and aggregated to determine an appropriate sequence of activities that would form a systematic approach to multi-sourcing strategy.

4 The Case Firm and the Decision to Multisource

Superprop follows an ETO strategy, where they design, engineer, produce and deliver products to meet customers' unique requirements. Thus, customisation and ultimately value generation is achieved through an iterative engineering design process, whose degree is different for the thruster systems produced. This is because some variants have extensions while others do not. For example, a tunnel is one of the customised components, as it has a complex mechanical interface and integration to the vessel hull, making it impossible to fit in other new projects. Another example is the control system that also has many interfaces and is specified to the vessel's electrical interface and motor starter. Some propeller hubs and blades are also customised, as their designs are optimised for a specific individual ship.

In the past years, Superprop had a stable supply chain, and it mostly implemented a single sourcing strategy where the focus was on forming and maintaining close relationships with suppliers, preferably in close proximities. However, in recent years the firm experienced changes that compelled it to consider multi-sourcing. Competition has increased in the market, and new strategic approaches are needed to increase Superprop's competitiveness. The firm has recognised the potential strategic role that PSF can play to improve competitiveness. The goal is to use this function to maximise value. As an ETO firm, they recognise that maximising value depends not only on delivering customer's perceived value but also on minimising total production costs. Thus, Superprop decided to implement multi-sourcing. Before the pandemic, the main reason for this decision was to avoid potential opportunistic pricing behaviour from single suppliers. Following the pandemic, and its impact on supply chains, Superprop, like other firms across the globe, has realised that they need a multi-sourcing strategy also for hedging against disruptive risks.

Under Superprop's single-sourcing strategy, each externally sourced component or material that goes into a product (e.g., a thruster) is provided by one supplier who covers 100% of the requirements. Examples of such inputs include hydraulic cylinders, electronic components, and toothed rings. Given challenges associated with this strategy, Superprop wants to attain a situation where each externally sourced component or material that goes into their customised products is sourced from two or more suppliers, hence implementing multi-sourcing strategy. However, they are concerned that sourcing materials and components from previously "unknown" suppliers may compromise the quality of their final products and eventually compromise their competitiveness. As such, Superprop is strict on quality and lead time. Therefore all selected suppliers must guarantee high quality and high delivery precision. Thus, the challenge is to optimise two variables: the quantity and total cost of acquiring inputs for each project. For each project, the goal is to meet all input requirements at a lower total cost of acquisition compared to the single-source strategy. It is important to note that the multi-sourcing strategy is intended only for the non-standard inputs that cannot easily be sourced. Figures 1 and 2 summarise Superprop's desired transition from single sourcing to multi-sourcing strategy.

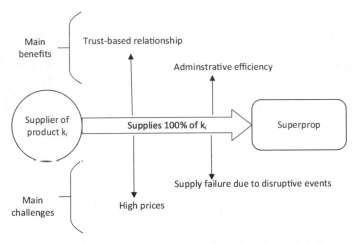

Fig. 1. Superprop's single sourcing strategy, its benefits, and challenges

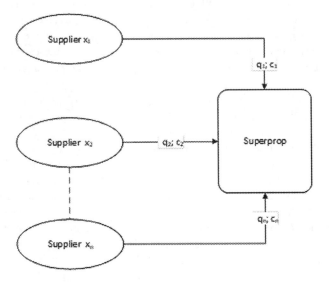

q : Quantity supplied by supplier x

: $q_1 + q_2 + \ldots\ldots + q_n = 100\%$ of product k

c : Total cost of acquiring a given proportion of product k from supplier x

: $c_1 + c_2 + \ldots + c_n < TCO1$

: TCO1 is the total cost of acquiring product k under single sourcing strategy

Fig. 2. Superprop's desired multi-sourcing strategy

5   A Systematic Approach to Multi-sourcing Strategy

Based on the collected data from Superprop, this section provides the framework to guide the transition from single sourcing to multi-sourcing. Figure 3 summarises the proposed approach, and the explanation follows.

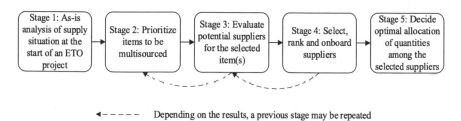

Fig. 3.   Systematic approach to multi-sourcing strategy in ETO production

As-Is Analysis of Supply Situation. This is the first step in the transition to multi-sourcing, where the current supply state is assessed. Two activities are critical. First, all typical materials and components used in the final product must be identified. Second, the specified items must be categorised according to their total cost of acquisition and supply risk. In the case of Superprop, the focus is their main product – propeller. Thus, all externally sourced materials and components used to make it were identified and categorised. As part of this process, product availability, the potential number of alternative suppliers, switching costs, competitive structure, and consequence of delay are assessed [19]. Each of these criteria must be evaluated by assigning a score to show its current state. For instance, for the product availability criterion, one end of the scale represents the easy availability of inputs in the market, and the other end represents a state where inputs are highly customised. Likewise, for the switching cost criterion, one end of the scale represents zero cost of switching to another supplier, and the other end represents a state where Superprop would incur a substantial cost to switch to another supplier. The same evaluation logic is applied to the other criteria. A result of this stage was an overview of Superprop's supply base for the chosen project, positioning procured items according to their overall scores.

Prioritise Items to Be Multi-sourced. Given the information obtained in the first stage, it was quickly realised that Superprop embarking on multi-sourcing for all materials and components would be practically impossible as it would radically increase the complexity of supplier management. Thus, it was essential to prioritise and select which items that would be multi-sourced. The selected items were mainly those that score high on both financial value and supply risk.

Evaluate Potential Suppliers for the Selected Item(s). Once the priority items have been selected, the next stage is to evaluate potential suppliers. For example, one of the items prioritised by Superprop was initially supplied by a local supplier; therefore, the assessment of alternative suppliers included checking price, quality, location of the supplier, the total cost of acquisition, and delivery precision. Each of the potential suppliers is compared with the local supplier.

Select, Rank and Onboard Suppliers. At this stage, suppliers that meet the criteria are selected and ranked accordingly. In cases where none of the potential alternative suppliers beats the incumbent supplier, the next two best suppliers are chosen. Next, all suitable suppliers should be notified that they have fulfilled the selection. Thus, information and necessary documents will then be collected to add the suppliers to the approved vendor list. Contracts with the selected suppliers must be flexible in terms of volumes. Supplier information must also be shared with all key functional areas involved in the projects. For Superprop, these would be product engineering, purchasing, production, logistics, and sales. To be effective, a dedicated cloud-based procurement software (CBPS) must be in place. This will facilitate interaction with suppliers and across the organisation.

Decide Optimal Allocation of Quantities Among the Selected Suppliers. Once an order is received and preliminary BOM is created based on the initial drawings, the procurement must be involved to start estimations from the pool of suppliers through simultaneous requests for information. A CBPS can make this process very efficient and effective. At this stage, Superprop must determine an optimal number of suppliers that minimises the total cost of acquisition without compromising quality and delivery precision. Using information generated in the previous step, Superprop must determine an optimal number of suppliers and their respective quantities. Based on the results, the sales unit can create a final offer to the client. Hence, the allocation of amounts is not subject to a long-term contract; instead, it is tied to the project at hand. This means an evaluation must be conducted for each new project to renew the allocation. However, since Superprop wants to ensure that multi-sourcing is viable in every project, it must maintain relationships with at least two potential suppliers. This can be achieved by assuring at least 20% allocation of supplies in each project. The remaining 60% should be contested between suppliers based on the total cost of acquisition.

6   Closing Remarks

In response to increased uncertainties and competition, firms worldwide seek ways to maximise value through strategies such as multi-sourcing. In this study, a clinical management study guides an ETO firm to implement a multi-sourcing strategy. The study is part of a larger project that aims to address logistics-related challenges faced by the case firm and its suppliers. Based on knowledge derived from previous collaborations with the case company and the data collected from this current project, a systematic approach is developed for implementing multi-sourcing. Of the five stages, the case firm has implemented the first three. Besides, so far, only one major component has been considered. In the next steps of the project, the final two stages will be implemented for the selected component and subsequently extend the approach to other items. Although the study is based on a single case, the developed framework can be applied by other ETO firms when transitioning from single sourcing to multi-sourcing strategy.

Acknowledgement. The authors acknowledge the support of the Research Council of Norway for the research project Respons.

References

1. Linton, T., Vakil, B.: Coronavirus is proving that we need more resilient supply chains. Harvard Bus. Rev. (2020)
2. Lopes de Sousa Jabbour, A.B., Chiappetta Jabbour, C.J., Hingley, M., Vilalta-Perdomo, E.L., Ramsden, G., Twigg, D.: Sustainability of supply chains in the wake of the coronavirus (COVID-19/SARS-CoV-2) pandemic: lessons and trends. Modern Supply Chain Res. Appl. **2**(3), 117–122 (2020)
3. van Remko, H.: Research opportunities for a more resilient post-COVID-19 supply chain – closing the gap between research findings and industry practice. Int. J. Oper. Prod. Manag. **40**, 341–355 (2020)
4. Ivanov, D.: Predicting the impacts of epidemic outbreaks on global supply chains: a simulation-based analysis on the coronavirus outbreak (COVID-19/SARS-CoV-2) case. Transp. Res. Part E Logist. Transp. Rev. **136**, 101922 (2020)
5. Kilpatrick, J., Barter, L.: COVID-19: Managing supply chain risk and disruption. Deloittte (2020)
6. Karlsson, C.: Clinical management research. In: Karlsson, C. (ed.) Research Methods for Operations Management. Routledge, London (2016)
7. CIPS. Sourcing. https://www.cips.org/knowledge/procurement-topics-and-skills/understand-need---market-and-options-assessment/sourcing1/
8. Burke, G.J., Carrillo, J.E., Vakharia, A.J.: Single versus multiple supplier sourcing strategies. Eur. J. Oper. Res. **182**, 95–112 (2007)
9. Formentini, M., Ellram, L.M., Boem, M., Da Re, G.: Finding true north: design and implementation of a strategic sourcing framework. Ind. Mark. Manag. **77**, 182–197 (2019)
10. Costantino, N., Pellegrino, R.: Choosing between single and multiple sourcing based on supplier default risk: a real options approach. J. Purch. Supply Manag. **16**, 27–40 (2010)
11. Lioliou, E., Willcocks, L., Liu, X.: Researching IT multi-sourcing and opportunistic behavior in conditions of uncertainty: a case approach. J. Bus. Res. **103**, 387–396 (2019)
12. Meena, P.L., Sarmah, S.P.: Multiple sourcing under supplier failure risk and quantity discount: a genetic algorithm approach. Transp. Res. Part E Logist. Transp. Rev. **50**, 84–97 (2013)
13. Baumgartner, T., Malik, Y., Padhi, A.: Reimagining industrial supply chains (2020)
14. Willner, O., Powell, D., Gerschberger, M., Schönsleben, P.: Exploring the archetypes of engineer-to-order: an empirical analysis. Int. J. Oper. Prod. Manag. **36**, 242–264 (2016)
15. Mwesiumo, D., Kvadsheim, N.P., Nujen, B.B.: The potential for purchasing function to enhance circular economy business models for ETO production. In: Advances in Production Management Systems. Towards Smart and Digital Manufacturing, pp. 557–64 (2020)
16. Moretto, A., Patrucco, A.S., Walker, H., Ronchi, S.: Procurement organisation in project-based setting: a multiple case study of engineer-to-order companies. Prod. Plan. Control, 1–16 (2020)
17. Coghlan, D.: Interlevel dynamics in clinical inquiry. J. Organ. Chang. Manag. **13**, 190–200 (2000)
18. Coghlan, D.: Toward a philosophy of clinical inquiry/research. J. Appl. Behav. Sci. **45**, 106–121 (2009)
19. Shlopak, M., Rød, E., Oterhals, O.: Developing supplier strategies for eto companies: a case study. In: Nääs, I., et al. (eds.) APMS 2016. IAICT, vol. 488, pp. 911–918. Springer, Cham (2016). https://doi.org/10.1007/978-3-319-51133-7_107

Product and Asset Life Cycle Management for Smart and Sustainable Manufacturing Systems

A Holistic Approach to PLI in Smart Maintenance Towards Sustainable Manufacturing

Harald Rødseth[1](✉) ⓘD, Endre Sølvsberg[2], Anna Steine[1], Per Schjølberg[2], and Espen Henriksen-Polanscak[3]

[1] Oceaneering, Integrity Management and Digital Solutions, No 7452, Trondheim, Norway
HRodseth@oceaneering.com
[2] Department of Mechanical and Industrial Engineering, Norwegian University of Science and Technology, No 7491, Trondheim, Norway
[3] HTS Dynamics, No 3027, Drammen, Norway

Abstract. With the digital transformation of the maintenance function with emerging technology such as machine learning, Smart Maintenance will contribute to increased plant capacity as well as reduced maintenance costs. Profit Loss Indicator (PLI) has been tested for preventive maintenance combined with anomaly detection. Yet, it remains to include PLI into Smart Maintenance processes to ensure standardized application. PLI will also contribute towards sustainability in terms of improved production performance through reduced waste and time losses. This will also contribute to an improved working environment. The aim of this article is therefore to develop a smart maintenance process for PLI. This article demonstrates the main processes of smart maintenance that are harmonized with EN 17007 and sustainability. In addition to PLI, a hybrid approach for anomaly deployment as well as a dynamic FMECA (failure mode, effect and criticality analysis) are included in Smart Maintenance. Also, the result is partly tested where PLI is calculated for a Norwegian use-case. It is concluded that more elements for the smart maintenance processes must be further modelled and tested with industrial use-cases.

Keywords: Smart maintenance · Profit loss indicator · Sustainability

1 Introduction

With more commercial sensor technologies available on the market such as wireless sensors, predictive maintenance (PdM) is considered to contribute to reducing downtime and saving operational costs [1]. It is expected that PdM will digitally reshape several industry branches in terms of deployment of a predictive maintenance strategy [2]. In particular, the indicator profit loss indicator (PLI) has been applied and tested for PdM based on machine learning (ML) application in maintenance planning [3]. The sustainable digitalisation in PdM will require a change in the maintenance function

© IFIP International Federation for Information Processing 2021
Published by Springer Nature Switzerland AG 2021
A. Dolgui et al. (Eds.): APMS 2021, IFIP AICT 633, pp. 393–400, 2021.
https://doi.org/10.1007/978-3-030-85910-7_41

towards Smart Maintenance that includes data-driven decision making with both human and capital resources [4], as well as dynamic failure mode, effect and criticality analysis (FMECA) [5].

In addition to the technology development outlined in the mission statement for digitalization, the sustainability is also clearly elaborated in terms of e.g. better work life as well as climate protection [2]. In fact, Smart Maintenance contributes towards sustainability in e.g. human-machine training [6].

In order to allow for PdM, machines and equipment are monitored for condition and faults [7]. Using sensor data, pattern recognition, failures and events, anomalies are detected using methods such as equipment-specific algorithms (1), ML techniques (2) and small-scale lab collected data (3). Implementing the PdM methodology in an I4.0 environment will require considerable work developing data structure and architecture to allow for near real-time analytics, Big Data methods, data quality, data security and data integration [7, 8]. ML methods are dominant in terms of published papers, but there are some more critical towards ML methods, highlighting areas like "black-boxing", trust issues, data availability and scaling issues [8, 9]. Proposed solutions to AI-method challenges include "Explainable AI" and hybrid methods, using both ML and classical statistical methods [10, 11]. A "toolbox" of classical methods that can be employed in complex, multivariate environments includes Principal Component Analysis (PCA), that can be used to detect anomalies in large, multivariate datasets and as a data reduction strategy [11]. Thus, Smart Maintenance and PdM should also include a toolbox of classical methods in data-driven decision making.

To succeed with Smart Maintenance a "common language" is also required with particular contribution from the standard EN 17007 "Maintenance process and associated indicators" [12]. In PdM, a standardisation roadmap has also been developed and will contribute to standardisation [1]. It remains to investigate how EN 17007 will be aligned with PLI as a tool for Smart Maintenance. Although this standardisation work is expected to be rolled out in Europe, there are still several obstacles that must be evaluated in Norwegian Industry. One fundamental challenge is to have the correct competence, leadership and culture for measuring the losses in maintenance. Relevant challenges and existing initiatives towards Smart Maintenance in Norwegian industry is therefore of importance to address. Among others, the research project CM4Smart aims to develop Smart Maintenance for Norwegian industry.

The aim of this article is to develop Smart Maintenance process for PLI. The future structure in this article is as follows: Sect. 2 first presents the status of Smart Maintenance in Norwegian industry and then proposed smart maintenance process. Section 3 presents some results of Smart Maintenance processes based on an industrial use-case, whereas discussions and concluding remarks are made in Sect. 4.

2   Smart Maintenance

2.1   The Maintenance Function in Norwegian Industry

Despite that some companies in Norway represented by e.g. the smelting industry and manufacturing industry seem to be in front in developing Smart Maintenance, there is still a gap between ambitions and the reality. Traditionally, Norwegian industry has been focusing on corrective maintenance. A challenge may also be the accuracy of data that has been manually collected. Yet, today this industry is more focused on proactive maintenance. Norwegian industry should learn even more from digitalization of maintenance from countries such as Germany [2] and Japan [6].

The Norwegian O&G industry has today implemented preventive maintenance programmes. For some new equipment types such as rotating equipment, a high degree of condition monitoring is applied and can be further used for predictive maintenance. A portion of equipment at ageing facilities have little or no sensors for condition monitoring. Yet, these facilities have long data history of condition parameters that have been manually collected. These condition parameters can support maintenance planning. An example can be inspection results used for prediction calculations for equipment and facilities with low degree of automatic condition monitoring methods. It remains to align this experience in Smart Maintenance processes.

The CM4Smart project aims to develop and implement a Smart Maintenance concept within HTS maskinteknikk. In addition to developing, integrating and testing IoT-technologies, an important part is to align new technologies with a new way of thinking about maintenance. In its essence Smart Maintenance forces and motivates a company like HTS maskinteknikk to become more proactive. This implies that all personnel, from the management to the production employees are faced with the task of thinking more about risks and optimizing specific costs. Having access to real time data and a trustworthy PLI indicator will change maintenance scheduling and hopefully lead to increased uptime and utilization as well as lower overall maintenance cost. An online and connected PLI will help HTS maskinteknikk make faster and better decisions.

2.2 PLI and Smart Maintenance Processes

PLI has its offspring from the "hidden factory" and the need for measuring time losses and e.g. calculation of overall equipment effectiveness (OEE) [13]. Today, an appropriate industry standard for OEE calculations exists [14]. PLI expands this OEE calculation and measures the hidden factory as a monetary indicator and includes ML [3].

Since PLI is founded on measuring time losses and waste in production it has a clear contribution to sustainability. In fact, the production industry with a more efficient production process can significantly reduce pollution and waste and contribute to a better working environment [6]. Figure 1 presents central main elements for sustainability inspired from [15].

Smart Maintenance Parameters	Smart Maintenances elements	Innovation in Sustainable Manufacturing
- Profit Loss Indicator - Innovative education and training - Smart systems & network	- Human-Machine Interface - Human-Machine education and collaboration - Smart prediction with anomaly detection and remaining useful life	- New generation of intelligent manufacturing - Zero losses and waste activity

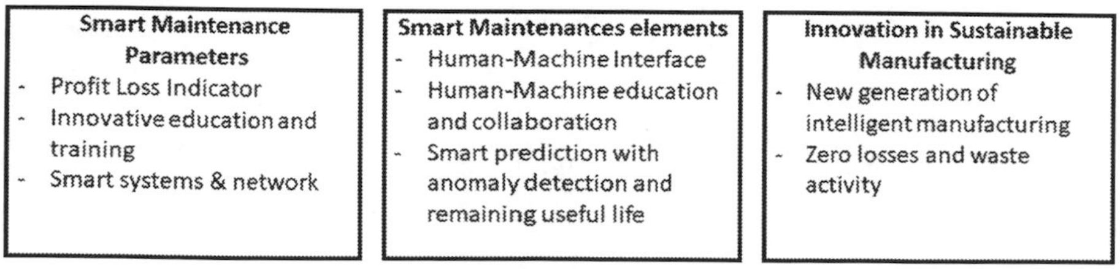

Fig. 1. Key elements for sustainability, inspired from [15]

In addition to PLI in Fig. 1, key elements for sustainability will also include innovation in activities that contribute to e.g. near zero losses and improved human-machine interfaces.

The standard for maintenance processes EN 17007 will provide an aid for the maintenance managers to compare their organisation by a generic description and detect any significant deviation [12]. The Maintenance processes are categorised into the following main categories:

1. *Management process:* Activities for determining the objectives and the policy to be implemented in the organisation.
2. *Realization processes:* These processes contribute directly to achieving the expected result expressed in terms of satisfaction by the customer.
3. *Support processes:* Processes that are essential to the support of the other processes and includes human, financial and material resources.

In Smart Maintenance, all these main processes will be affected. For data-driven maintenance it is of interest to investigate the support process "manage data" (DTA).

Both ML and statistical methods rely on high quality raw data from sensors. Sensor accuracy and drift must be accounted for before data pre-processing. Addressing these inaccuracies might be difficult using either ML methods or mathematical correction [16]. Using classical statistical methods like PCA can be utilized as standalone classical methods, or as part of a hybrid method [16, 17].

A proposed framework for smart maintenance processes using both classical and ML methods is shown in Fig. 2, inspired by [18]. In this framework, processes for deploying anomaly detection as well as activities for PLI are identified.

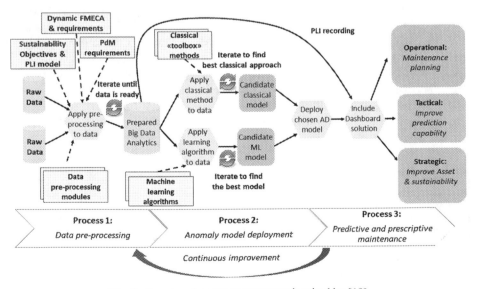

Fig. 2. Smart maintenance processes inspired by [18].

FMECA has a significant contribution in data-driven maintenance [5] and is therefore included in data pre-processing. The criticality can evolve over time due to e.g. usage conditions, the technological evolution or new skills acquired in the organisation [19]. With suitable digital platforms FMECA can support maintenance planning more in real-time instead of only during company-specific revisions. Table 1 further elaborates the Smart Maintenance processes. Predictive maintenance will include forecasts derived from analysis. Yet, Smart Maintenance incorporates several dimensions such as data-driven decision-making, human capital resource, internal integration as well as external integration [4].

Table 1. Description of smart maintenance processes.

Smart maintenance process	Description of smart maintenance process	Elementary process in EN 17007
Process 1: Data pre-processing	– Dynamic FMECA for data-driven maintenance – PdM requirements: required time horizon, accuracy – PLI Model and Sustainability objectives	DTA.2: Evaluate the reliability and maintainability of the items by maintaining an actual state assessment of the items
Process 2: Anomaly model deployment	– Principal Component Analysis – Deep Learning	
Process 3: Predictive and prescriptive maintenance	– PLI recording – Remaining life evaluation – Operative, tactical & strategic decisions	DTA.11: Calculate, save and provide access to performance and monitoring indicators

3   Smart Maintenance Process Result

Figure 3 presents a storyboard for smart maintenance process 3 (predictive and prescriptive maintenance) for HTS maskinteknikk. Starting with PLI recording, it is possible to collect data for future maintenance decisions in terms of avoiding failures as well as improvement of the physical asset. By applying anomaly decision analytics combined with PLI and FMECA, it is possible to evaluate possible future maintenance actions in terms of preventive and corrective maintenance. The further use-case describes the PLI recording at the company.

The use case is a state-of-the-art CNC cell with the following main functions: raw material handling and storage, material transport/movement, CNC-tending, machining/turning, cleaning, measurement and tool correction, monitoring and reporting.

This CNC cell in the use case is executing important work orders for the company and is a strategic implementation of state-of-the-art technologies available on the market. It is a "signal project" within the company, meaning that it represents what can be done

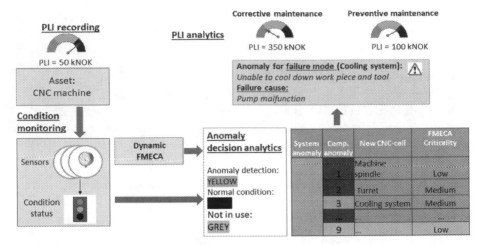

Fig. 3. Storyboard for smart maintenance process

today to increase productivity and efficiency. The CNC-cell is planned to be operated with few to no production technicians due to the level of automation and monitoring implemented. This means that the company must rely on the IoT monitoring systems to notify if something goes wrong or if anomalies are detected. All this to allow the company to act fast and to fix and ensure required output. The ROI demand for this cell is high due to the high acquisitions.

Table 2 summarizes the PLI elements included in the use-case and should illustrate PLI for one arbitrary week. The PLI categories are based on time loss categories from OEE calculations [13].

Table 2. PLI categories measured in use-case

Loss category	Turnover loss content	PLI value [NOK]
Availability	*Shutdown loss (1), Breakdown and failure loss (2), Setup- and adjustment loss (3), Tool replacement loss (4), Start-up loss (5) and other Downtime Losses such as waiting for materials (6)*	11.000
Performance	*Minor stoppages and idling (7) and Speed loss (8)*	4.000
Quality	*Quality defect and rework loss (9)*	3.500
Utilization	*Not scheduled (10) and Unscheduled (11) (Overcapacity)*	75.000
TOTAL PLI		93.500

4 Discussion and Concluding Remarks

This article has developed 3 main processes for Smart Maintenance and partly tested these in Norwegian Industry. To reshape a company towards Smart Maintenance the organisation must still conduct the fundamental maintenance functions where e.g. the time losses are measured before calculating PLI. This will require accurate time loss registration for computation and integration into the digitalized maintenance systems and the IoT system at HTS. The short-term aim for HTS maskinteknikk is to implement smart maintenance including a plant wide FMECA project. The plan long term is to further change the mindset from "have we done some service?" towards "what is the current OEE and PLI in plant? How can we improve it?". Also, this change will shift the focus from measuring breakdowns towards measuring minor stoppages.

For process 1 and 2 different methods have been proposed. Adding a "toolbox" of classical methods that can handle multivariate analysis can be beneficial when utilizing ML methods. A PCA analysis can help reduce the dimensionality of large datasets and help determine critical variables as part of data pre-processing. PCA can also help with detecting anomalies in multivariate processes. Both methods have been applied in a pilot experiment in the QU4LITY EU project in conjunction with ML methods to automate anomaly detection, and the results are promising. Some of this is related to the ability to include expert domain knowledge from the analysed processes and the transparency of utilizing classical methods.

For process 3 PLI has been tested in a use-case. For operational application this PLI recording will be used to measure e.g. significant downtime due to failure and breakdown. This can then be used for future maintenance planning.

Sustainable maintenance should be a holistic perspective on Smart Maintenance, incorporating PLI and Industry 4.0, and ensuring a balanced approach to sustainability through e.g. reduced PLI (economic), reduced use of raw material (environmental) and application of "ethical" AI in anomaly detection (social).

Finally, the closed loop must ensure continuous improvement for the smart maintenance processes. For example, PLI recording can also be used for strategic decisions where the physical asset is improved and PLI reduced.

To conclude, Smart Maintenance must be a holistic approach, and should include PLI, dynamic FMECA, PdM requirements, continuous improvement, sustainability objectives, a dedicated data structure, and a transparent classical statistical approach to support ML activities to improve maintenance planning, prediction capability, sustainability and the asset itself.

Further, HTS maskinteknikk will develop this framework with application of a more generic and dynamic FMECA and PLI. Also, PLI should be included as an indicator for sustainable manufacturing.

Acknowledgement. The authors wish to thank the research project CM4Smart with all its partners for valuable input. The Research Council of Norway is funding CM4Smart.

References

1. Standardization Council Industrie 4.0. The Standardisation Roadmap of Predictive Maintenance for Sino-German Industrie 4.0/ Intelligent Manufacturing. Federal Ministry of Economic Affairs and Energy, Department of Public Relations, Berlin (2018)
2. Standardization Council Industrie 4.0. German Standardization Roadmap Industrie 4.0. DIN, Berlin (2020)
3. Rødseth, H., Schjølberg, P., Andreas, A.: Deep digital maintenance. Adv. Manuf. **5**, 299–310 (2017)
4. Bokrantz, J., Skoogh, A., Berlin, C., Stahre, J.: Smart maintenance: instrument development, content validation and an empirical pilot. Int. J. Oper. Prod. Manag. **40**(4), 481–506 (2020)
5. Sala, R., Pirola, F., Pezzotta, G.: Data-driven maintenance delivery framework: test in an italian company. In: Lalic, B., Majstorovic, V., Marjanovic, U., von Cieminski, G., Romero, D. (eds.) APMS 2020. IAICT, vol. 592, pp. 322–329. Springer, Cham (2020). https://doi.org/10.1007/978-3-030-57997-5_38
6. The European House: Towards the creation of Society 5.0 - Hitachi's contribution to new human-centered and sustainable society in Italy (2020)
7. Sølvsberg, E., Øien, C.D., Dransfeld, S., Eleftheriadis, R.J.: Analysis-oriented structure for runtime data in Industry 4.0 asset administration shells. Procedia Manuf. **51**, 1106–1110 (2020)
8. Yu, W., Dillon, T., Mostafa, F., Rahayu, W., Liu, Y.: A global manufacturing big data ecosystem for fault detection in predictive maintenance. IEE Trans. Ind. Inform. **16**, 183–192 (2019)
9. Rai, R.: Explainable AI: from black box to glass box. J. Acad. Mark. Sci. **48**, 137–141 (2020)
10. Hagenmann, S., Sünnetciogulu, A., Stark, R.: Hybrid artificial intelligence system for the design of highly-automated production systems. Procedia Manuf. **28**, 160–166 (2019)
11. Imayakumar, A.A., Dubey, A., Bose, A.: Anomaly detection for primary distribution system measurements using principal component analysis. In: IEE Texas Power and Energy Conference (TPEC), pp. 1–6 (2020)
12. CEN: EN 17007: Maintenance process and associated indicators. Standard Norge (2017)
13. Rødseth, H., Skarlo, T., Schjølberg, P.: Profit loss indicator: a novel maintenance indicator applied for integrated planning. Adv. Manuf. **3**(2), 139–150 (2015). https://doi.org/10.1007/s40436-015-0113-6
14. Koch, A.: OEE Industry Standard. Blom Consultancy BV, Aarle-Rixtel (2003)
15. Forest, R., Rossi, S., Magnani, M., Bianco, C.G.L., Delmonte, N.: Smart society and artificial intelligence: big data scheduling and the global standard method applied to smart maintenance. Engineering **6**, 835–846 (2020)
16. Sun, L., Westerdahl, D., Ning, Z.: Development and evaluation of a novel and cost-effective approach for low-cost NO2 sensor drift correction. Sensors **17**, 1916 (2017)
17. Boullosa-Falaces, D., Barrena, J.L.L., Lopez-Arraiza, A., Mendendez, J., Solaetxe, M.A.G.: Monitoring of fuel oil process of marine diesel engine. Appl. Therm. Eng. **127**, 517–526 (2017)
18. Chapell, D.: Introducing Azure Machine Learning. Chapell & Associates, San Francisco (2015)
19. Colli, M., Sala, R., Pirola, F., Pinto, R., Calvalieris, S., Wæhrens, B.V.: Implementing a dynamic FMECA in the digital transformation era. IFAC-PapersInLine, pp. 755–760 (2019)

Sustainable Maintenance Performances and EN 15341:2019: An Integration Proposal

Chiara Franciosi[1]([⊠]) [iD], Irene Roda[2] [iD], Alexandre Voisin[3] [iD], Salvatore Miranda[1] [iD], Marco Macchi[2] [iD], and Benoit Iung[3] [iD]

[1] Università degli Studi di Salerno, 84084 Salerno, Italy
{cfranciosi,smiranda}@unisa.it
[2] Politecnico di Milano, 20156 Milan, Italy
{irene.roda,marco.macchi}@polimi.it
[3] Université de Lorraine, CNRS, CRAN, 54000 Lorraine, France
{alexandre.voisin,Benoit.Iung}@univ-lorraine.fr

Abstract. Maintenance is a key process contributing to sustainable manufacturing operations. According to this vision, recent scientific studies underline the need for indicators to assess maintenance sustainable performances. In the normative field, the EN 15341:2019 standard about Key Performance Indicators of the Maintenance Function was recently released covering all major aspects of maintenance and physical assets management, giving more emphasis to sustainability. Nevertheless, a complete set of indicators covering the environmental and social dimensions of maintenance sustainability under the sustainable manufacturing perspective is still missing. Therefore, in this paper the relevant factors to be considered for integrating the existing standard and to achieve a complete maintenance performance measurement system tackling sustainability are identified by analyzing the wider literature and normative frameworks about sustainable manufacturing performances. A validation in the industrial reality is identified as a next step to assess the factors' applicability in terms of measurability.

Keywords: Maintenance · Sustainable performance · Sustainable manufacturing · Performance indicators

1 Introduction

Nowadays, manufacturing organizations are facing the urge to adopt new sustainable strategies to respond to the market and customer's demand for sustainable products, considering the scarcity of the natural resources and the growing pressure coming from governments [1], moving towards sustainable manufacturing practices [2]. In this frame, in recent years maintenance is more and more recognized both in the scientific and normative worlds, as a key process within manufacturing that can strongly contribute to promote sustainable development if properly managed [3]. However, for achieving such goals, it is relevant to define shared indicators to assess sustainable performances of maintenance [4, 5]. The aim of this paper is to provide an overview of the normative

A. Dolgui et al. (Eds.): APMS 2021, IFIP AICT 633, pp. 401–409, 2021.
https://doi.org/10.1007/978-3-030-85910-7_42

and scientific advances as well as the existing gaps on maintenance performance measurement to go towards this direction. In particular, new considerations for building a practical maintenance performance measurement system focusing on sustainability are provided.

The paper is organized as follows. Section 2 presents the state of the art of the advances both in the scientific literature and technical standards, concerning maintenance and sustainable performances. Section 3 provides the factors identified as missing in the EN 15341:2019 technical standard, and relevant for measuring maintenance performance and its impact on sustainability. Section 4 discusses the conclusion and future research steps.

2 Scientific and Normative State of the Art

Despite the maintenance strategic role in manufacturing systems, only in the last years it has started to be more deeply investigated with a sustainable vision that goes beyond the consideration of the merely technical and economic aspects [6]. In fact, maintenance activities have several non-negligible impacts on the technical condition of production systems (e.g. reliability and availability performance as well as on the product quality), but also on the three dimensions of sustainability, i.e. economic, environmental, and social [7]. A recent study conducted by Holgado et al. 2020 [8] showed some advanced and best maintenance practices adopted by few virtuous industrial realities to contribute to sustainable business strategy concluding that maintenance needs to be taken more into consideration and given a more central role in future research and practice addressing sustainability in manufacturing. To achieve such goals, maintenance managers need to understand the relationship among the maintenance processes, including the impact of their realization, and sustainable performance with the aim to assess how they contribute to the achievement of business objectives towards sustainable development. Effectiveness, efficiency, and quality of maintenance must be assessed through specific indicators [5], and technical, economic, environmental, and social factors must be identified with the aim of constructing sensible maintenance sustainable indicators. Scientific literature only recently proposed studies considering sustainability-related factors and indicators for maintenance in different industrial sectors, for automotive companies [9], cement industry [10], or rubber industry [11]. Although few recent papers propose a first classification of sustainable maintenance performance measures, they focused on specific aspects of sustainability connected with maintenance system, not providing an exhaustive framework of factors and indicators for measuring sustainable maintenance performances. Addressing such gap, Franciosi, Voisin et al. 2020 [7] provide factors that were not considered in previous studies, tackling the wider sustainable perspective. For this reason, their paper is considered as reference for this research.

Standardized definitions for best practice for building up a maintenance performance measurement system have been established at international level by the European Federation of National Maintenance Societies (EFNMS) and the Society of Maintenance and Reliability Professionals (SMRP, an American society). Two major standards exist, the European Standards' EN 15341:2019 [12] and the North American SMRP best practice metrics [13–15]. In 2019, the European standard BS EN 15341:2019 was released, replacing the previous version from 2007. The older version of the standard proposed 71 KPIs and only the economic dimension of sustainability was explicitly considered. The environmental dimension was considered in a very global way through the concept of "environmental damage". While the social dimension was indirectly considered through worker safety with the number of personal injuries due to maintenance [16, 17]. A step forward to explicitly consider sustainability indicators was done with the publication of the EN 15341:2019 [12]. With respect to the older version, the recently published standard lists maintenance Key Performance Indicators and gives guidelines to define a set of suitable indicators to appraise and to improve not only effectiveness and efficiency but also some sustainability aspects in the maintenance of physical assets. In particular, the standard still addresses the economical, technical, organizational KPIs of the previous edition but enlarges the vision covering all the major aspects of physical assets management (PHA), structuring the KPIs into 8 groups, one for PHA, six dedicated to maintenance subfunctions (Health – Safety Environment, Maintenance Management, People Competence, Maintenance Engineering, Organization and Support, Administration and Supply), and one for information communication technologies. Nevertheless, despite more importance is given to sustainability, only still few KPIs are introduced addressing the environmental and the social dimensions.

Enlarging the perspective over sustainable manufacturing, a growing number of initiatives and organizations are trying to develop environmental, social and sustainability indicators for companies [18]. Veleva and Ellenbecker, 2001 [18], Marimon et al. 2012 [19], Joung et al. 2013 [20] claim that there is a wide list of sustainability reporting standards, proposing indicator sets that are publicly available and that can be used to measure sustainability in manufacturing processes. Among them, the GRI Standards [21] are most often used by large companies worldwide. Thus, these standards, developed in 1997 and now in their sixth version, deserve particular attention [22] and sustainability aspects here reported should be considered also from the maintenance performance perspective while their primary intention is dedicated to the sustainable performance of an organization as a whole.

3   Performance Indicators for Sustainable Maintenance

Given the current technical and scientific advances on maintenance performance measurement systems, the objective of this paper is to identify gaps in the existing standard EN 15341:2019 for reaching an exhaustive list of indicators addressing maintenance sustainability assessment from a holistic viewpoint. For such a purpose, on one hand, Franciosi, Voisin et al. 2020 [7] proposed an extensive review of the literature and then a reference framework, including a list of indicators. Hence, it will be used as the scientific reference document. On the other hand, as presented in the previous section, the EN 15341:2019 standard [12] is the technical reference document providing an industrial viewpoint. Hence, the list of factors in the EN 15341:2019 [12] to calculate the proposed KPIs, was analyzed and compared with the list of factors proposed by Franciosi, Voisin et al. 2020 [7]. At the end of the process, a list of missing factors in the standard that could bring a more complete perspective over maintenance sustainability is identified, as shown in the next tables (Tables 1, 2, 3, 4 and 5).

In the EN 15341:2019 [12] the sustainability area is explicitly introduced as one of the driven areas related to three KPIs included in the sub-function "Maintenance within physical asset management". Specifically, the economic indicator "PHA1: Maintenance contribution to improve sustainability (%)", is proposed and is defined as the ratio between the cost of maintenance resources spent yearly to improve the sustainability and Physical assets turnover. It is still very general though, not specifying which kind of actions could be considered. Considering the environmental dimension, a section of the standard is dedicated to 22 KPIs of Sub-function "Health-Safety-Environment (HSE)" on Maintenance. This sub-function concerns the implementation of policies and procedures by the maintenance management to prevent injuries and losses and be compliant with laws, rules, and company objectives. The 4 main driven areas of HSE, related to the maintenance performances and the KPIs, are: i) Conformity to Laws and Rules, ii) Statistical Records (relating to injuries and their impact on people and productivity), iii) Maintenance safety practices (including the impact of potential failures to the environment but also safety management practices in place), iv) Prevention-Improvements (relating to prevention actions in place to reduce HSE risks). Looking at the social dimension, 21 KPIs of Sub-function "People Competence" are introduced in the standard, referring to the EN 15628:2014 [23] and relating to the different qualification levels of maintenance personnel addressing education, field experience, skill and training. Concerning the economic dimension of sustainability, although the EN 15341:2019 [12] provides many factors and indicators aimed at assessing the economic impact of maintenance, still economic aspects related to the environmental sustainability are neglected (e.g. cost for maintenance waste treatment and disposal, costs to recycle spare parts or Waste Electric and Electronic Equipment for maintenance).

Tables 1, 2, and 3 show the environmental factors (and associated IDs) directly affected by maintenance performance, as reported in Franciosi, Voisin et al. 2020 [7], but lacking in the new EN 15341: 2019 [12]. These indicators address several aspects of maintenance impact: Land, Materials & Water Resources; Energy; Emissions, Effluents & Wastes, to cite a few. Indeed, while the norm considers materials and spare parts needed for maintenance activities and the cost associated to their purchase and management, no reference to the type of materials adopted, such as renewable and non-renewable materials, virgin, reused, recycled, repurposed, remanufactured, lubricants, cleaners, oils, chemicals (IDs 3, 4 and 5 in Table 1), is found. However, these are fundamental aspects that must be considered and monitored for contributing to the no longer negligible paradigm of the circular economy.

Table 1. Environmental Sustainability dimension: Land, Materials & Water Resources

ID	Factor name
1	Maintenance waste effects on land quality (e.g. indicated by surface integrity, soil nutrients and contaminants, non-fertile land)
2	Land used by maintenance infrastructure, categorized by fertile and non-fertile areas

(continued)

Table 1. (*continued*)

ID	Factor name
3	Materials used for maintenance process (spare parts, documentation) divided in renewable and non-renewable materials and with a breakdown on type of used materials (virgin, reused, recycled, repurposed, remanufactured)
4	Quantity of PBT (persistent, bio accumulative and toxic) chemicals used due to maintenance processes
5	Quantity of auxiliary fluids used by maintenance processes (lubricants, cleaners, oils, …)
6	Volume of water withdrawn for maintenance process with a breakdown by the sources

Concerning the energy aspects in maintenance, the norm only considers very generic factors such as "energy cost" or "number of maintenance actions implemented to improve energy conservation", while the details related to the energy consumption within the organization for maintenance processes (ID 7 in Table 2) and outside the organization (ID 8 in Table 2) are not considered.

Table 2. Environmental sustainability dimension: energy

ID	Factor name
7	Energy consumption within an organization for maintenance processes (fuel, electricity, heating, cooling, steam) through equipment and tools
8	Energy consumption outside the organization for maintenance processes (e.g. transportation and distribution of spare part suppliers)
9	Energy emitted (e.g. heat, vibration) by maintenance processes

Factors related to maintenance wastes, effluents and emissions are totally missing in the norm. However, Table 3 provides several aspects that should be considered. Indeed, evaluating factors such as the amount of wastes generated by maintenance processes specifying the waste type and the disposal method (i.e. hazardous and non-hazardous, recyclable, reusable, remanufacturable, disposable) (ID 10 in Table 3), the maintenance WEEE (ID 13 in Table 3), the Greenhouse Gases Emissions or Ozone-depleting substances or air emissions or noise emissions generated due to maintenance processes (see details in IDs 16, 17, 18, 19, 20, 21 in Table 3), could concretely allow highlighting maintenance environmental impacts on sustainability.

Table 3. Environmental sustainability dimension: emissions, effluents & wastes

ID	Factor name
10	Amount of wastes generated by maintenance processes (e.g. replaced items, used tools, lubricants, oils, documentation) specified by waste type and disposal method (i.e. hazardous and non-hazardous, recyclable, reusable, remanufacturable, disposable)
11	Amount of waste water discharged by maintenance processes specified by quality (e.g. eco-toxic, hazardous, treated, non-treated, reused) and destination
12	Volume of recorded significant spills (i.e. accidental release of hazardous substances that can affect human health, land, vegetation, water bodies, and ground water) derived by maintenance processes
13	Amount of WEEE produced by maintenance processes
14	Transport of hazardous waste generated by maintenance activities
15	Maintenance waste effects on the surface integrity of surrounding buildings and places
16	Direct GHG emissions: CO2-eq due to electricity, heating, cooling and steam consumed by maintenance processes; transportation of materials, spare parts, and maintenance workers on the field
17	Indirect GHG emissions: CO2-eq due to purchased or acquired electricity, heating, cooling, and steam consumed by maintenance processes
18	Reduction of GHG emissions as a direct result of reduction initiatives taken by maintenance processes
19	Ozone-depleting substances produced due to maintenance processes
20	Air emissions (such as NOX, SOX, POP (Persistent Organic Pollutants), VOC (Volatile Organic Compounds), HAP (Hazardous Air Pollutants), PM (Particulate Matter)) deriving from used chemicals, additives for lubricants, waste incineration, transportation and other, due to maintenance activities
21	Noise emissions for maintenance processes
22	Air quality within an organization and in its surrounding areas due to maintenance processes (smog, visibility, odor, GHG concentration, pollutant concentration, etc.)

Furthermore, as reported in Table 4, suppliers of maintenance materials play a role and as such should be assessed through both environmental (ID 23 in Table 4) and social (ID 24 in Table 4) criteria going beyond the merely economic aspects generally considered.

Table 4. Environmental and social sustainability dimensions: supplier assessment

ID	Factor name
23	% Suppliers that were screened using environmental criteria
24	% Suppliers that were screened with social criteria

Concerning the social dimension of sustainability, while maintenance safety issues have traditionally been considered in the maintenance norms and further detailed factors in the new version are provided, what is still missing is the evaluation of maintenance employees involvement and employee suggestions, in terms of quality, social and EHS performance (ID 32 in Table 5), safety measured adopted or safety equipment installed (ID 29 in Table 5), but also in terms of maintenance employees who report complete job satisfaction (ID 31 in Table 5). Assessing social sustainability in maintenance means also evaluating maintenance employees, by gender, who received a regular performance and career development review (ID 30 in Table 5) and number of employee hires and turnover, categorized by age group, gender, and region (ID 25 in Table 5). In addition, although the training of maintenance stakeholders constitutes a relevant part of the existing norm, there is no reference on maintenance employees trained in basic sustainability concepts (ID 27 in Table 5) or maintenance employees' empowerment (ID 34 in Table 5). Table 5 reports details of the factors that should be considered.

Table 5. Social Sustainability dimension: Maintenance employees

ID	Factor Name
25	New employee hires and employee turnover: number and rate of new maintenance employee hires during the reporting period, by age group, gender and region; number and rate of maintenance employee turnover during the reporting period, by age group, gender and region
26	Revitalization of maintenance employee suggestions for improvement and specific effort periods (e.g. One month, one week a month)
27	% Maintenance employees trained in basic sustainability concepts and/or current sustainability initiatives
28	Absentee rate (maintenance employees)
29	Number of safety measures adopted, and safety/fail-safe equipment installed due to maintenance employee suggestions, and improvements in safety performance from these suggestions
30	Maintenance employees by gender who received a regular performance and career development review
31	% Maintenance employees who report complete job satisfaction (e.g. through use of questionnaire, surveys)
32	Number of maintenance employee suggestions in quality, social and EHS performance
33	Education, training, counselling, prevention, and risk-control programs in place to assist maintenance workforce members and their families regarding serious diseases
34	Number or % maintenance employees empowered with the knowledge to make safer choices for themselves and coach their peers to do the same

4 Conclusions and Further Steps

The identified factors allow the development of a maintenance performance measurement system to monitor the activities of the maintenance function as a contributor to a sustainable manufacturing approach. The reference standard to date (EN 15341:2019) neither includes the use of maintenance resources in a circular way nor the wastes, effluents and emissions generated by maintenance function. Moreover, the social dimension of sustainability is still missing mainly in terms of maintenance employees' involvement and satisfaction, and inclusion of diversity related issues (gender, region, age group). Therefore, considering and assessing the factors reported in Tables 1, 2, 3, 4 and 5 allow designing sustainable performance indicators to quantify maintenance impacts on sustainability and taking more "sustainability-aware" maintenance actions and choices for contributing actively and effectively to environmental-conscious and socially responsible performance of manufacturing systems. Following this research, further research steps will have to focus on the following issues:

- Validation of the identified factors in the industrial reality to show their applicability in terms of measurability of the factor itself and of availability of mandatory data to compute it. For this reason, a survey is in the way to be designed to collect opinions from manufacturing companies across Europe.
- Definition of formalized relationships and rules among indicators that are designed based on the identified sustainability factors and conventional technical and economic indicators.
- Integration of the sustainable indicators in maintenance decision-making tools to quantitatively measure maintenance impacts on sustainability aiming at contributing to organizations' sustainability targets.

References

1. Eslami, Y., Dassisti, M., Lezoche, M., Panetto, H.: A survey on sustainability in manufacturing organisations: dimensions and future insights. Int. J. Prod. Res. **57**(15–16), 5194–5214 (2019)
2. Garetti, M., Taisch, M.: Sustainable manufacturing: trends and research challenges. Prod. Plan. Control **23**(2–3), 83–104 (2012)
3. Jasiulewicz-Kaczmarek, M., Żywica, P., Gola, A.: Fuzzy set theory driven maintenance sustainability performance assessment model: a multiple criteria approach. J. Intell. Manuf. **32**(5), 1497–1515 (2021). https://doi.org/10.1007/s10845-020-01734-3
4. Kumar, U., Galar, D., Parida, A., Stenström, C., Berges, L.: Maintenance performance metrics: a state-of-the-art review. J. Qual. Maint. Eng. (2013)
5. Parida, A., Kumar, U., Galar, D., Stenström, C.: Performance measurement and management for maintenance: a literature review. J. Qual. Maint. Eng. (2015)
6. Iung, B., Levrat, E.: Advanced maintenance services for promoting sustainability. Procedia CIRP **22**, 15–22 (2014)
7. Franciosi, C., Voisin, A., Miranda, S., Riemma, S., Iung, B.: Measuring maintenance impacts on sustainability of manufacturing industries: from a systematic literature review to a framework proposal. J. Clean. Prod. **260**, 121065 (2020)

8. Holgado, M., Macchi, M., Evans, S.: Exploring the impacts and contributions of maintenance function for sustainable manufacturing. Int. J. Prod. Res. **58**(23), 7292–7310 (2020)

9. Sari, E., Shaharoun, A.M., Ma'ara Yazidm, A.: Sustainable maintenance performance measures: a pilot survey in Malaysian automotive companies. Procedia CIRP **26**, 443–448 (2015)

10. Ighravwe, D.E., Oke, S.A.: Ranking maintenance strategies for sustainable maintenance plan in manufacturing systems using fuzzy axiomatic design principle and fuzzy-TOPSIS. J. Manuf. Technol. Manag. (2017)

11. Amrina, E., Yulianto, A., Kamil, I.: Fuzzy multi criteria approach for sustainable maintenance evaluation in rubber industry. Procedia Manufacturing **33**, 538–545 (2019)

12. BS EN 15341:2019. Maintenance - Maintenance Key Performance Indicators (2019)

13. SMRP. SMRP Best Practices, 5th Edition (2017)

14. Stenström, C., Parida, A., Kumar, U., Galar, D.: Performance indicators and terminology for value driven maintenance. J. Qual. Maint. Eng. (2013)

15. Lukens, S., Naik, M., Saetia, K., Hu, X.: Best practices framework for improving maintenance data quality to enable asset performance analytics. In: Annual Conference of the PHM Society, vol. 11, no. 1 (2019)

16. Sénéchal, O.: Research directions for integrating the triple bottom line in maintenance dashboards. J. Clean. Prod. **142**, 331–342 (2017)

17. Franciosi, C., Di Pasquale, V., Iannone, R., Miranda, S.: Multi-stakeholder perspectives on indicators for sustainable maintenance performance in production contexts: an exploratory study. J. Qual. Maint. Eng. (2020)

18. Veleva, V., Ellenbecker, M.: Indicators of sustainable production: framework and methodology. J. Clean. Prod. (2001)

19. Marimon, F., del Mar Alonso-Almeida, M., del Pilar Rodríguez, M., Alejandro, K.A.C.: The worldwide diffusion of the global reporting initiative: what is the point? J. Clean. Prod. **33**, 132–144 (2012)

20. Joung, C.B., Carrell, J., Sarkar, P., Feng, S.C.: Categorization of indicators for sustainable manufacturing. Ecol. Ind. **24**, 148–157 (2013)

21. GRI. Global Reporting Initiative. Consolidated Set of GRI Sustainability Reporting Standards, The Netherlands (2016)

22. Bednárová, M., Klimko, R., Rievajová, E.: From environmental reporting to environmental performance. Sustainability (Switzerland) **11**(9), 1–12 (2019)

23. EN 15628. Qualification of maintenance personnel (2014)

System-Level Overall Equipment Effectiveness for Improving Asset Management Performance: A Case Study Application

Alberto Franzini[ID], Adalberto Polenghi[✉][ID], Irene Roda[ID], and Marco Macchi[ID]

Department of Management, Economics and Industrial Engineering, Politecnico di Milano,
Via Lambruschini 4/b, 20156 Milano, Italy
{alberto.franzini,adalberto.polenghi,irene.roda,
marco.macchi}@polimi.it

Abstract. The discipline of Asset Management (AM), which focuses on the management of physical assets in an integrated and holistic way along their life cycle, can be adopted by companies to promote sustainability since it enhances asset reliability and availability for the whole duration of its usage. Within the manufacturing industry, a relevant AM-related performance indicator is the Overall Equipment Effectiveness (OEE), which measures the efficiency of equipment. However, traditionally OEE measures the performance of individual equipment only, while neglecting the system perspective, which is core in AM. Only few contributions propose an extension towards a system-level performance indicator. After the OEE-related system-level indicators from the scientific literature are reviewed, an application of one of them in an industrial case is presented, selected as the indicator best fitting the characteristics of the industrial case itself, which is a disconnected flow manufacturing line. The application of the system-level indicator allows comparing it with the traditional OEE. Results show that a system approach better supports AM since the information carried out by the indicator is more complete and adherent with the actual asset and system characteristics. In turn, the system-level perspective is assumed just as a first step towards a holistic performance improvement as it is required by AM. A step forward to fulfill the sustainable performance is the integration of measurements of other sustainability-related impacts leading to effective asset-related decisions.

Keywords: OEE · OFE · System-level performance · Asset management · Life cycle · Disconnected flow line

1 Introduction

Nowadays, due to the increasing pollution generation and scarcity of resources registered in the last decades, the entire society looks towards sustainable development [1]. Out of all sectors, manufacturing companies are considered among the major responsible sources of materials and energy usage, while undeniably leading also towards the increase

A. Dolgui et al. (Eds.): APMS 2021, IFIP AICT 633, pp. 410–417, 2021.
https://doi.org/10.1007/978-3-030-85910-7_43

in emission generations [2]. The discipline of Asset Management (AM), which focuses on the management of physical assets in an integrated and holistic way along their life cycle [3], could be adopted by companies to promote sustainability [4] since it enhances asset reliability and availability for the whole duration of its usage [2].

AM is defined as "the coordinated activities of an organization to realize value from assets" by ISO 55000 [5]. Despite originating in the context of Maintenance Management (MM), considering both the approaches of Total Productive Maintenance (TPM) and Reliability Centered Maintenance (RCM), it goes beyond the traditional goals of MM. Instead of focusing mainly on the operational phase of an asset, it covers its whole life cycle, from the Beginning of Life (BoL) to the End of Life (EoL) [2]. Therefore, evaluating the performance of a production asset along its life constitutes the foundation for any improvement activity (corrective or preventive). Indeed, this is a relevant approach for the achievement of a sustainable performance.

Considering the improvement activity, since the late 1980s the Overall Equipment Effectiveness (OEE) has been recognized as a fundamental indicator for measuring the performance of production systems and it is now accepted as primary performance metric [6]. However, OEE presents a relevant limitation that should be taken into consideration and further investigated when thinking from an AM standpoint: it focuses on the individual equipment, therefore lacking a system-level perspective [7]. In fact, it is worth remarking that AM claims that "an organization may choose to manage its assets as a group, rather than individually, according to its needs, and to achieve additional benefits" (extract from ISO 55000 [5]). This leads to the need of building a management practice that looks at individual assets, systems of assets and multiple assets portfolio, for effective asset-related decisions.

The present work focuses on OEE and its limitations at system-level perspective. After a brief introduction on OEE, this research work addresses this limitation by reviewing extant system-level indicators developed in the scientific literature. The indicator that better fits the characteristics of a manufacturing company taken as industrial case is selected and applied. Finally, results as well as managerial implications are discussed.

2 Beyond OEE: Review of Existent System-Level Performance Indicators

The OEE was proposed by Nakajima in 1988 as a supporting metric to Total Productive Maintenance (TPM) [8] and it has the dual purpose of discovering hidden losses in production systems and evaluating the effect of improvement actions [9, 10]. Analytically, the OEE can be expressed as the product of three mutually exclusive components: Availability (A), Performance (P), and Quality (Q). Generally, it represents the ratio between what is actually manufactured and what could be ideally manufactured. The inefficiencies that cause the actual production to differ from the ideal production are classified into the so-called Six Big Losses [8]: failures, set up & adjustment, minor stoppages, reduced speed, defects, and reduced yield. Despite the broadly accepted relevance of OEE, Scott and Pisa [11] pointed out also some limitations. Indeed, the OEE is able to measure only the performance of individual equipment, whereas in a factory machines are usually not isolated, but operate jointly in a production line. Another limitation that is closely linked arises when the inefficiencies of a line cannot be easily classified in terms of the Six Big Losses because they are generated at a system-level [8]. This may lead to a misattribution of inefficiencies to the three components of the OEE.

Since the ultimate objective of any factory is to have a highly efficient integrated system and not brilliant individual equipment [9], it is important to take into consideration variables that are outside the perimeter of OEE, such as relationships between machines, material flows, logistics, queues, and the integration of information, decisions and actions across independent systems and subsystems [7].

In the literature there is no evidence of a standard method to measure the overall effectiveness at system or factory level [12], but several studies have tried to expand the application scope of OEE to overcome its main limitation.

Nachiappan and Anantharaman [13] propose the Overall Line Effectiveness (OLE), expressed in Eq. 1, as a metric for performance evaluation in a continuous manufacturing line.

$$OLE = LA \times LPQP \tag{1}$$

Where LA is Line Availability and LPQP is Line Production Quality Performance, a parameter that merges Line Quality and Line Performance in a single metric. The peculiar assumption at the base of this indicator is that only the good output of machine i (where $i = 1...n$, being n the last machine of the line) will be the input of machine $i + 1$, defects and reworks will not reach the downstream process. LA is computed as the Operating Time of machine n (i.e., the last machine in the line) as a percentage of the Loading Time (i.e., the time the line is expected to operate). LPQP can be calculated as the amount of good production realized by machine n times the largest cycle time of the line (i.e., the bottleneck cycle time) over the operating time of the first machine.

Muthiah and Huang [6] develop the Overall Throughput Effectiveness (OTE) as an extension of the definition of OEE to the factory level by comparing the actual and the maximum attainable productivity of the line. The OTE is formulated in Eq. 2.

$$OTE = \frac{Actual\ throughput\ (units)\ from\ factory\ in\ total\ time}{Theoretical\ throughput\ (units)\ from\ factory\ in\ total\ time} \tag{2}$$

The OEE on which the OTE is based is a modified version of the conventional OEE developed by Nakajima and takes the name of Theoretical OEE. What changes is the Performance parameter: in the conventional OEE, P accounts for equipment idle time, which according to [7] can be attributed to poor factory operations such as material-handling problems or factory design flaws rather than the equipment itself. For this reason, it should be captured by factory-level metrics. The manufacturing line is decomposed in subsystems, which can be of four different types, namely series, parallel, assembly and expansion. OTE is computed for each subsystem. The process is repeated until the OTE of the factory (also designated as Overall Factory Effectiveness – OFE) is computed.

Braglia et al. [8] propose the Overall Equipment Effectiveness of a Manufacturing Line (OEEML), expressed by Eq. 3:

$$OEEML = \frac{O_{LM}}{LLT/CT_{BN}} \tag{3}$$

Where O_{LM} is the output of the last machine, CT_{BN} is the ideal cycle time of the bottleneck machine, and LLT is the Line Loading Time (i.e., Calendar Time minus Planned Stops). At the basis of this approach is a modification to the traditional structure of losses that characterizes the OEE, as it is important to separate the losses that can be directly ascribed to an equipment from the losses that are spread in the line. The former takes the name of Equipment Dependent Losses (EDL), the latter Equipment Independent Losses (EIL). Finally, this approach allows to express the OEEML as a function of efficiency reduction components, i.e., reductions due to the shifting of the bottleneck from theoretical to actual, minor inefficiencies upstream of the bottleneck machine, minor inefficiencies downstream of the bottleneck machine, and the quality rate of machines installed downstream from the constraining operation. These components provide additional information on what is actually lowering the performance of the line.

Raja et al. [12] propose the Overall Line Effectiveness (OLE) for continuous flow lines computed with the same logic of the OEE:

$$OLE = A \times P \times Q \tag{4}$$

Availability is computed on the basis of Mean Time Between Failures (MTBF) and Mean Time To Repair (MTTR) and takes into account the relationships between machines (i.e., series and parallel); Performance is based on the number of products realized by the bottleneck machine; finally, Quality not only expresses the rate of good production over total production but also takes into account the number of parameters that are measured in the quality assessment process.

Finally, Roda and Macchi [7] develop the OFE (Overall Factory Effectiveness), which extends from the already mentioned OTE. The OFE is expressed in Eq. 5, where D is a coefficient accounting for deterministic losses, like scheduled maintenance, and TH_{system} is the theoretical throughput of the system. The other terms consider the product output from the factory and the simulation time since the OFE is based on the evaluation of system performance with multi-state machines.

$$OFE = D \times \frac{actual\ product\ output\ from\ factory\ in\ simulation\ time}{TH_{system} \times simulation\ length} \tag{5}$$

3   System-Level Indicator Applied in a Case Study

3.1   Case Study Introduction

The choice of the most suitable system-level indicator cannot disregard the characteristics of the case study whose performance it is supposed to measure. Therefore, a brief introduction of the case study is provided before comparing the metrics.

The system of interest could be classified as a disconnected flow line (see Fig. 1) according to the classification by Hopp and Spearman [14].

In a disconnected flow line, product batches are produced on a limited number of routings and individual stations within lines are not connected by paced material-handling systems, so that inventories can build up between stations.

Specifically, the manufacturing line under examination realizes components for gas turbines and is composed of five stations (see Fig. 1). Products are moved from a station to the next manually through the usage of various types of cranes.

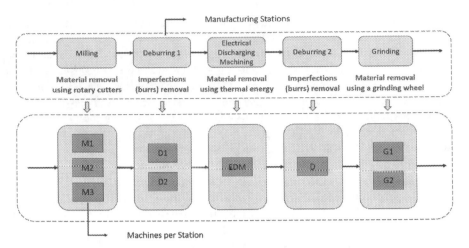

Fig. 1. Schematic representation of the case study manufacturing line.

3.2 Metric Selection

The screening process that is used to select the best fit for the case study can be broken down into two stages.

The first stage excludes the metrics that are not suitable for the line configuration (i.e., disconnected flow lines). OLE from [12] and OLE from [13] were discarded in this way, as they find application in connected flow lines. According to [14], in connected flow lines products are fabricated and assembled along a rigid routing connected by a paced material-handling system, which prevents building up inventories in between stations.

The second stage consists in an evaluation of the complexity of the metric. This can be defined by considering two functional aspects in relationship to the input and output information flows of the metric computation: on one hand, the amount and type of required input data in terms of availability and reliability; on the other hand, the usefulness and coverage of the output information the metric returns to the decision-maker. As for the latter aspect, all the remaining metrics appear as relevant indicators. In fact, OTE/OFE [7] allows to compute performance at system-level based on the type of connection between machines as well as identify inefficiencies down to subsystem-level. OEEML [8] allows to identify the location of inefficiencies regarding the position of the theoretical and actual bottlenecks. And finally, OFE [7], allows to operate an ex-ante system-level performance evaluation as opposed to all the other metrics that are ex-post. As for this last metric, it was discarded due to its intrinsic complexity, as it requires the building of the RBD (Reliability Block Diagram), the modeling of Markov chains and the execution of the simulation. As for the remaining two metrics, despite OEEML provides, to an extent, more specific information on inefficiencies, OTE/OFE is selected based on the aspect of availability of input data. While OTE/OFE only requires modifying the Performance component of OEE by taking into account losses that are directly attributable to the individual machine, OEEML requires a deeper adjustment of the structure of losses. This deeper adjustment is not judged feasible in the real case study.

3.3 Computation of OFE and Results Analysis

Figure 2 summarizes the results of the computation of OEE for each machine and OTE for each subsystem for a given scenario relying on the formulae for the computation of OTE that are reported in [6].

The data required for the computations were provided by the company and were already organized into the items that typically characterize an OEE data collection, which are common to all the lines as regards this company. According to the type of data, some were automatically computed by the information systems, some were automatically retrieved by machines and some other were inserted manually by the operator.

Due to extensive maintenance interventions, the first machine of the milling phase and the EDM are characterized by the lowest OEE in the line. Considering the importance of maintenance interventions, the OEE takes into account the losses measured within the availability. In this work, Performance and Quality are instead both coefficients set to 1.

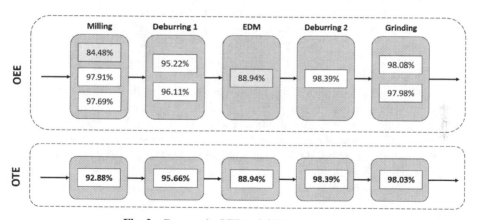

Fig. 2. Case study OEE and OTE computation.

The results allow making two main observations: the first one about the difference between the classic OEE and OTE; the second one about the difference between OFE (as previously said, the OTE of the entire line according to the designation of the authors [7]) and the OEE of the line computed as mathematical average, which is how the company used to compute system-level performances.

Regarding the first observation, according to the conventional OEE priority should be given to the first machine of the milling phase, as 84.48% is the lowest value in the line. However, its low efficiency is dampened by the parallel connection with the other two machines of the phase. This piece of information is taken into consideration by OTE, which is much greater (i.e., 92.88%) than the OEE of the first machine. Instead, the effort should be focused on the subsystem with the lowest efficiency (i.e., EDM – 88.94%), as the five subsystems are connected in series.

Regarding the second observation, not taking into account the connections between machines and between phases when computing system-level performances may result in their overestimation or underestimation. In this specific case, the mathematical average of all the OEE's amounts to 94.98%, which is 6.79% greater than the OFE (i.e., 88.94%). From a factory perspective, knowing the actual performance of a line would prove to be crucial when deciding where to invest and/or focus the effort. This line would probably go overlooked if decisions were made based on the overestimated value of the OEE, when, instead, the actual performance could be deemed as critical form an OFE point of view.

4 Conclusions

The discipline of AM is promising to support companies in pursuing sustainability-related goals given its holistic approach. To this end, a key enabler is having available the right set of indicators to measure the performance of assets comprehensively. This is the reason why it is appropriate to consider OEE but also to go beyond it, as the efficiency of individual equipment only is not sufficient, and a system-level perspective is missed. Despite the absence of a unique standard for measuring system-level performance, in the scientific literature different examples of system-level performance indicators are available, each trying to consider the complexity of the system. It is however not clear enough what is the proper system-level indicator to be used or recommended in a given production context.

Based on the characteristic of an industrial case study, an indicator from the literature is selected. The application helps highlight the differences between an actual system-level indicator, the OTE/OFE, and an indicator whose perimeter is limited to an individual equipment, the OEE. The non-negligible discrepancy of the results shows how important it is to rely on the right key performance indicators for the sake of taking decisions, especially when they entail choosing among different improvement options, considering both investments and operational decisions. By adopting system-level performance, it is possible for companies to focus the effort on the actual major causes of inefficiency and waste that damage the system of assets, rather than individual assets.

It is evident that the system-level perspective herein discussed is a necessary step, but cannot be considered enough to achieve a holistic performance assessment and improvement as it is required by AM. The research direction to extend the current results, entails the integration of measures of other sustainability-related impacts and, moreover, their arrangement in an entire framework that consists of different levels including individual assets, systems of assets and multiple assets portfolio. It will be orienting to the requirements for the AM system as indicated in asset-related norms such as the ISO 55000. As a specific interest of the authors, there is a major insight on the energy efficiency at system level to cover this sustainability aspect; at the same time, it is relevant to evaluate the balance of cost and performance, thus looking at the total cost of ownership or similar economic-related indicators. In turn, these are just a few actions that will set in motion a process of continuous improvement towards a more sustainable production performance.

References

1. OECD: Global Material Resources Outlook to 2060: Economic Drivers and Environmental Consequences. OECD Publishing, Paris (2019). https://doi.org/10.1787/9789264307452-en
2. Franciosi, C., Lambiase, A., Miranda, S.: Sustainable maintenance: a periodic preventive maintenance model with sustainable spare parts management. IFAC-PapersOnLine **50**(1), 13692–13697 (2017). https://doi.org/10.1016/j.ifacol.2017.08.2536
3. Roda, I., Macchi, M.: A framework to embed asset management in production companies. Proc. Inst. Mech. Eng. Part O J. Risk Reliab. **232**(4), 368–378 (2018). https://doi.org/10.1177/1748006X17753501
4. Acerbi, F., Polenghi, A., Roda, I., Macchi, M., Taisch, M.: Exploring synergies between circular economy and asset management. In: Lalic, B., Majstorovic, V., Marjanovic, U., von Cieminski, G., Romero, D. (eds.) APMS 2020. IAICT, vol. 592, pp. 695–702. Springer, Cham (2020). https://doi.org/10.1007/978-3-030-57997-5_80
5. ISO 55000. Asset management-Overview, principles and terminology. BSI Standard Publications (2014)
6. Muthiah, K.M.N., Huang, H.: Overall throughput effectiveness (OTE) metric for factory-level performance monitoring and bottleneck detection. Int. J. Prod. Res. **45**(20), 4753–4769 (2007)
7. Roda, I., Macchi, M.: Factory-level performance evaluation of buffered multi-state production systems. J. Manuf. Syst. **50**, 226–235 (2019)
8. Braglia, M., Frosolini, M., Zammori, F.: Overall equipment effectiveness of a manufacturing line (OEEML): an integrated approach to assess systems performance. J. Manuf. Technol. Manag. **20**(1), 8–29 (2009)
9. Oechsner, R., Pfeffer, M., Pfitzner, L., Binder, H., Müller, E., Vonderstrass, T.: From overall equipment efficiency (OEE) to overall Fab effectiveness (OFE). Mater. Sci. Semicond. Process. **5**, 333–339 (2003)
10. Nakajima, S.: Introduction to TPM: Total Productive Maintenance. Productivity Press, Cambridge (1988)
11. Scott, D., Pisa, R.: Can overall factory effectiveness prolong Moore's law? Solid State Technol. **41**(3), 75–82 (1998)
12. Raja, N., Kannan, S.M., Jeyabalan, V.: Overall line effectiveness – a performance evaluation index of a manufacturing system. Int. J. Prod. Qual. Manag. **5**(1), 38–59 (2010)
13. Nachiappan, R.M., Anantharaman, N.: Evaluation of overall line effectiveness (OLE) in a continuous product line. J. Manuf. Technol. Manag. **17**(7), 987–1008 (2006)
14. Hopp, W.J., Spearman, M.L.: Factory Physics: Foundation of Manufacturing Management, 2nd edn. Irwin/McGraw-Hill, New York (2000)

Semantic Interoperability and Sustainability an Industry 4.0 Product Life Cycle Issue

Yasamin Eslami[1]($\boxtimes$) (ID), Sahand Ashouri[2] (ID), and Mario Lezoche[1] (ID)

[1] Université de Lorraine, CNRS, CRAN, Nancy, France
{yasamin.eslami,mario.lezoche}@univ-lorraine.fr
[2] Politecnico di Milano, Milan, Italy
sahand.ashouri@mail.polimi.it

Abstract. Four concepts stand out in the current landscape of modern industrial production. The product life cycle, sustainability, Industry 4.0 and semantic interoperability. The article will be focused on creating a link between the four and expresses the strong causal relationship between them in order to optimise production processes. To that point, a 3D model will be developed to bridge sustainability and product life cycle inside an organization. Then, knowledge formalisation techniques will be discussed for constructing a mutual understanding of the semantics in the context on Industry 4.0 throughout the developed model.

Keywords: Product life cycle · Semantic interoperability · Knowledge formalization · Big data · Data mining · Sustainability models · Industry 4.0

1 Introduction

The concept of the Product Life Cycle (PLC) has been introduced since the 1950s [1], and it is a biological metaphor that describes every phase a product goes through, from the first initial requirement until it is retired and disposed.

Product lifecycle management (PLM) expresses the engineering point of view of product life-cycle concept and integrates the aspects of people, processes, and data to manage the entire life cycle of the product. It is also defined as a set of capabilities that enable an enterprise to effectively and efficiently innovate and manage its product and related service throughout the entire Product lifecycle (PLC) [1]. PLM offers a shared platform through which the process of capturing, representing, retrieving and reusing knowledge is supported to collate various enterprise system at each stage of PLC. The knowledge concerning a product along its life cycle, which is named as PLC-related knowledge, has become one of the essential concepts in a PLM solution [2]. Therefore, abilities like knowledge discovery, data cleansing and inferencing must be inactivated through the PLM solutions to exchange information, data and knowledge in a meaningful way.

Knowledge brings to its owner the capability of grasping the meaning (Semantics) from the received information. Semantic interoperability is the ability to ensure that the

© IFIP International Federation for Information Processing 2021
Published by Springer Nature Switzerland AG 2021
A. Dolgui et al. (Eds.): APMS-2021, IFIP AICT 633, pp. 418–426, 2021.
https://doi.org/10.1007/978-3-030-85910-7_44

exchanged information has got the same meaning considering the point of view of both the sender and the receiver [3]. In order to have a more connected and thus sustainable organization, the systems inside have to work together on the exchanged information and take decisions based on this information. They have different procedures, backgrounds, unique knowledge, particular needs and specific practices, which increase the difficulty to achieve the semantic interoperability [4]. The same problem goes for PLM, as its stakeholders, who operate on the information systems, have different traits which itself increases the difficulty to achieve semantic interoperability. This situation interferes in achieving a mutual understanding between all the systems, and so does in the coopera-tion across the enterprises. To overcome the obstacle, the implicit knowledge should be brought to the surface and be formalized explicitly with the help of knowledge formaliza-tion techniques so that it is mutually and semantically understood by all parties. This way semantic interoperability and consequently cooperation can be achieved inter and intra systems in an organization and throughout PLC. Putting altogether, the present study will be mainly focused on the issue of mutual understanding of the semantics for supporting knowledge management in the context of PLC inside an organization through modelling and knowledge formalisation techniques, all aiming at achieving sustainability inside an organization.

2 Product Life Cycle and Sustainability

PLM evolves around data visualization and transformation, a context in which ICT (Information and Communication Technology) plays an important role. Together with ICT, there are two other important levels that establish PLM: Process and Methodology. The former points at the data flow among the actors/resources while the latter is practice and techniques adopted along the processes, using and generating product data [8]. The

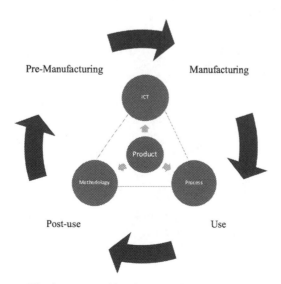

Fig. 1. PLM and its elements [inspired by [8]]

three elements move through the life cycle of the product to reach a better connectedness in all the stages (see Fig. 1).

Enterprises are forced by several increasing challenges such as resource depletion, economic stagnation, human being pursuing higher life quality and stricter regulations and banning policies. Sustainability has intended to empower the companies to cope with such challenges and guide them to stand out in the competitive market today. Due to [3], there are main aspects to be considered in terms of sustainability to help enterprises cope with the challenges they are faced. The study shows that, sustainability should be looked at in a holistic way inside the enterprise and the big picture must be considered to avoid ad hoc solutions. The Triple Bottom Line (TBL: economic, environment and social) must be considered at the three associated levels that matter in an enterprise namely product, process and system. In addition to that, no product life cycle stage is excluded from sustainability concerns, therefore another aspect would be to visualize and standardize the relationships and links between activities needs to be performed throughout the life of a product.

The closed loop life cycle of the product consists of four main stages: Pre-manufacturing, Manufacturing, Use and Post-use. In addition, attempts to close the material loop and to transform the life cycle have been made to support product and material reutilization and product end-of-life management. Many works like [5] accomplished the task by using 3R (Reduce, Reuse and Recycle) or the 6R (Reduce, Reuse, Recover, Redesign, Remanufacture and Recycle) throughout the manufacturing cycle and the product life cycle. On the other hand, based on the analysis [5] and [6] made, the concept "6R" was announced as the one factor that plays the most important role in reaching environmental sustainability, and the one with the highest influential level in sustainable manufacturing respectively. Therefore, to understand thoroughly the content of sustainability of a product, it is necessary to have a total analysis of the life cycle of the product and it's imperative to have all the 4 stages plus the 6R in any new evolutionary sustainability methods [7].

3   The Life Cycle and Industry 4.0 Issue of the Semantic Interoperability

PLC can be classified into five main phases[6] from production point of view (shown in the Fig. 2): (1) Imagination phase, in which, a product only exists as an idea in human's mind; (2) Definition phase, in which, the idea of product is formulated by various kinds of description; (3) Realization phase, in which, an actual product is manufactured following the description; (4) Using and Supporting phase, in which, a product is used by a customer and benefits the supports from the enterprise; (5) Retiring and Disposing of phase, in which, a product is no longer used by a customer and needs to be recycled or disposed of. In fact, this categorization is at a high abstraction level. Actual PLC models are always represented in a more complete way through extending more details in one or several of these phases. The Computer Aided Design systems appears in the early 1980s, along with its evolution , the problems of locating the required data and losing control of change process associated with these data become increasingly intense [7]. The needs of easy, quick and secure access to valid data during the product design phase became the primary motivation to the development of a Product Data Management (PDM) solution [8].

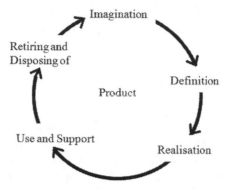

Fig. 2. Product life cycle [3]

However, due to the limited scope and the initial design of PDM solution, it is usually restricted to handling the product data in the engineering domain, but it remains inadequate with the non-engineering data, such as sales, planning, after sale services and so on. To be more specific, unlike the comprehensive supports to Computer Aided Design (CAD), Computer Aided Engineering (CAE), Computer Aided Process Planning (CAPP) and Computer Aided Manufacturing (CAM), PDM solutions cannot provide all the necessary supports to Enterprise Resource Planning (ERP), Supply Chain Management (SCM) and Customer Relationship Management (CRM).

In order to further extend the functionalities of a PDM solution and to fill the gap between the PDM proposal and the enterprise business activities, during the 1990s, the concept of Product Lifecycle Management (PLM) is proposed. Different from a PDM solution that only focuses on managing product data, a PLM solution focuses on managing all the PLC-related knowledge throughout the different phases of the PLC [8]. It aims at providing a shared platform for facilitating the process of capturing, representing, organizing, retrieving and reusing the knowledge concerning the related product in or across enterprises, and to provide the integration strategies and technological supports to bring together all existing enterprise systems that dealt with the product [9].

More and more enterprises adopted the PLM solutions and discovered the benefits for their complex engineered products in the last decade. According to the market research in IT enterprises, PLM became one of the fastest growing markets and the total revenues of PLM in 2006 is projected to increase by$5.5 billion compared with the corresponding period in 2001 [8]. Presently, an increasing number of commercial PLM solutions have been developed, for example, to mention only a few, Agilie PLM solutions, Siemens PLM Software, Arena PLM solution, SAP PLM, PTC Windchill. Based on their functions, the existing PLM solutions can be classified into three groups [10]: (1) Information management, which provides methods to identify, structure, store, retrieve and share product, process and project-related data. (2) Process management, which provides methods for modelling and operating formal and semi-formal processes. (3) Application integration, which defines and manages the interfaces between the PLM platform and the variety of enterprise systems (such as CAD, CAM, CAE, ERP, MES, CRM, etc.).

Though, all existing PLM solutions try to propose an efficient and powerful collaboration environment for the variety of enterprise systems, they are still obstructed by various kinds of issues. From the collaboration point of view, due to multiplicity of formats, standards and versions, [9] considered the information sharing and exchange as one of the main challenges in PLM. From the implementation point of view, CIM data concluded that the cost, the quality, the time-to-market and the innovation are the four main challenges for a PLM solution [7]. Hewett indicated six main directions for improving the current PLM solutions: data exchange, design collaboration, enterprise-centric view, scale to reality, standard and technique for engineering processes, information and knowledge representation [11]. Among all these issues, one of the main drawbacks of existing solutions draws our attention: they are mainly focusing on dealing with the syntax but rarely the semantics of the objects that are produced, transformed, exchanged during the PLC. One of the first purpose of this research is to propose a way for assisting the mutual understanding of the semantics that embedded inside the shared and exchanged objects for further supporting the knowledge management processes in the context of PLC.

Industry 4.0 reflects a combination of digital and manufacturing technologies, Specifically the new technological transformation embraces technological advances that concern the production process (i.e., advanced manufacturing systems, autonomous robots, additive manufacturing), the use of smart products and/or data tools and analytics [12]. The increasing multiplication and complexity of the information necessary for the management of production processes pushes to the structuring of knowledge to accelerate its passage and optimize the interoperability of systems. In Fig. 3 we can see all the different steps where the implicit knowledge of the systems is a brake to the knowledge passage itself between the various systems.

In the face of this new epochal change, two characterizations were highlighted:

- The importance of knowledge as a means of development and evolution. The information needed to manage production processes is increasingly numerous, more heterogeneous, more volatile and more distributed. This implies the use of business information systems increasingly linked to real processes in a continuous way in order to retrieve and process data, contextualize them into information and apply knowledge to improve performance.
- The key role that some technologies, such as cyber-physical systems, are playing in the restructuring of dominant roles in society.

The exploitation of the knowledge accumulated in the various systems involves two different issues. The first is the need to model systems so that they can semantically interoperate without problems of meaning. The second is to highlight methods to formalize and extract knowledge from all systems that are part of the value creation chain.

The two issues are discussed in the following:

Industry – Product Life Cycle

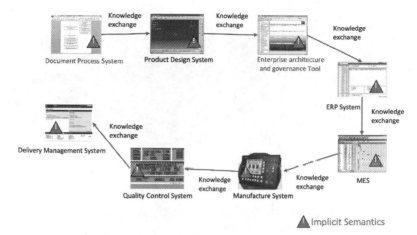

Fig. 3. Implicit semantics and semantic interoperability problem [3]

3.1 Modelling

Due to the aforementioned, connectedness and interoperability in terms of data, meaning and process between life cycle stages is prominent to characterize sustainability. Otherwise, information from not connected parts can be lost and knowledge cannot be formalized correctly. Therefore, there would be the risk to have missed or incomplete knowledge and the process of knowledge formalization gets into a repeated loop which can be both time and resource consuming. That itself misleads the enterprise form the context of sustainability, the very first goal all the attempts were put for.

To cover the discussed issues above, a 3D model (see Fig. 4) is introduced here to make help reach sustainability in an organization. The reference model aims at sustainability in diverse aspects in a holistic view. It combines the functional level inside the enterprise with the life cycle of the product in line with the TBL. The reference model maximum traceability of information is provided as it clarifies description, implementation and accessibility to sustainability in each intersection of dimensions inside the model. It looks at the big picture while it maintains the awareness of the interconnectedness of the components of the picture; its combination of hierarchical level inside an enterprise (product, process and system) with the life cycle of the product (pre-manufacturing, manufacturing, use and post-use) for the three main dimensions of sustainability (economic, social and environmental). In addition, and due to the derived essence of sustainability, the 6R concept (Redesign, Remanufacture, Reuse, Recover, Recycle and Reduce) will be considered inside the life cycle of the product at the "post-use" stage.

To employ sustainability in the context of life cycle, all activities belonging to the life cycle of the product should be optimized to reach an efficient management of information and process. As mentioned before, the lifecycle sustainability approach, means to deal with product or service evaluation from material extraction (pre manufacturing) to manufacturing and use and ends it by recycle in post use stage. Going through all

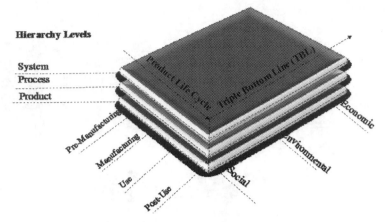

Fig. 4. 3D model for sustainability in an enterprise [13]

the stages, information is generated and needs to be analysed and formalized to create knowledge.

3.2 Knowledge Formalization

As already has been discussed above, Cooperation is achieved inside an information system if the information is physically exchanged, is understood and is used for the purpose for which it has been produced. Therefore, an obstacle towards having the systems cooperate to reach sustainability inside the model described in Fig. 4, is the semantic interoperability [14] issue. To overcome that, two important obstacles are on the way:

- The implicit semantics that is necessary for understanding a knowledge representation that is not made explicit.
- The lack of mechanisms to verify the correctness of explicit semantics in the exchanged knowledge representation.

A mutual understanding of the semantics inside the shared and exchanged knowledge representations is the cornerstone in the quest for semantic interoperability. To achieve this goal is crucial to formalize the knowledge exchanged between the systems inside the organization. This way, semantic explication of the exchanged knowledge is represented and is mutually understood while cooperation.

Formal concept analysis (FCA) [15] has been proven as a versatile framework for Knowledge discovery from data (KDD) [16] in many practical applications [17]. It extracts knowledge as a compact set of association rules. Relational concept analysis (RCA) [18] is MRDM extension of FCA. However, straightforwardly defined relational association rules may easily contain circular references or references from conclusion to premise, thus preventing a meaningful interpretation. FCA [15] is an algebraic approach for eliciting the conceptual structure of a dataset. Input data format is a triple $K = (O, A, I)$ called a (formal) context. O is a set of objects, A is a set of attributes and $I \subseteq O \times A$ an incidence relation listing valid pairs (o, a) (object o has the attribute a). FCA reveals all pairs of sets $(X, Y) \in \wp(O) \times \wp(A)$ strongly correlated, meaning that all objects having the attributes in Y are in X and vice-versa. Such pair is a (formal) concepts with an extent X and intent Y. Relational concept analysis assumes datasets are made of several contexts, one per type of object, and context-to-context relations. Any relational intent can be described with only non-relational attributes. Such expansion avoids circular dependencies, even if one may exist between full intents.

4 Conclusion

The product life cycle is one of the pillars of modern industry. The advent of the industry 4.0 paradigm has introduced the possibility of using data, information and above all knowledge to optimize production and introduce the concept of sustainability in an extremely important way. These three concepts are made cohesive by a fourth and central concept which is semantic interoperability. In this article, the strong link between these four concepts is highlighted, through a developed model and knowledge formalization inside the model to reach semantic interoperability. This way, semantic explication of the exchanged knowledge throughout PLC is represented in forms of lattices and is mutually understood while all defined dimension of the model will cooperate inside the organization. Accordingly, the link among the four concept is quantified by the help of clustering techniques as FCA in order to create an automated process for structuring automated industrial production.

References

1. Rink, D.R., Swan, J.E.: Product life cycle research: a literature review. J. Bus. Res. **7**, 219–242 (1979). https://doi.org/10.1016/0148-2963(79)90030-4
2. Gupta, S., Dangayach, G.S., Singh, A.K.: Key determinants of sustainable product design and manufacturing. Procedia CIRP **26**, 99–102 (2015). https://doi.org/10.1016/j.procir.2014.07.166
3. Liao, Y.X., Lezoche, M., Rocha Loures, E., et al.: A semantic annotation framework to assist the knowledge interoperability along a product life cycle. In: Advanced Materials Research, vol. 945–949, pp. 424–429 (2014). https://doi.org/10.4028/www.scientific.net/AMR.945-949.424
4. Etienne, A., Guyot, E., van Wijk, D., Roucoules, L.: Specifications and development of interoperability solution dedicated to multiple expertise collaboration in a design framework. Int. J. Prod. Lifecycle Manag. **5**, 272–274 (2011)
5. Lu, T., Gupta, A., Jayal, A.D., et al.: A framework of product and process metrics for sustainable manufacturing. In: Seliger, G., Khraisheh, M., Jawahir, I. (eds.) Advances in Sustainable Manufacturing, pp. 333–338. Springer, Heidelberg (2011). https://doi.org/10.1007/978-3-642-20183-7_48
6. Stark, J.: Product Lifecycle Management: 21st Century Paradigm for Product Realisation, 2nd edn. Springer, London (2011). https://doi.org/10.1007/978-0-85729-546-0
7. PDM to PLM: growth of an industry. Conteúdo/Home - Portal de Conhecimentos. http://www5.eesc.usp.br/portaldeconhecimentos/index.php/por/content/view/full/11623/(relations)/all. Accessed 11 Apr 2021

8. Ameri, F., Dutta, D.: Product lifecycle management: closing the knowledge loops. Comput.-Aided Des. Appl. **2**, 577–590 (2005). https://doi.org/10.1080/16864360.2005.10738322
9. Ball, A., Ding, L., Patel, M.: An approach to accessing product data across system and software revisions. Adv. Eng. Inform. **22**, 222–235 (2008)
10. Abramovici, M.: Future trends in product lifecycle management (PLM). In: Krause, F.-L. (ed.) The Future of Product Development, pp. 665–674. Springer, Heidelberg (2007). https://doi.org/10.1007/978-3-540-69820-3_64
11. Hewett, A.: Product lifecycle management (PLM): critical issues and challenges in implementation. In: Nambisan, S. (ed.) Information Technology and Product Development, pp. 81–105. Springer, Boston (2009). https://doi.org/10.1007/978-1-4419-1081-3_5
12. Porter, M.E., Heppelmann, J.E.: The operations and organizational structure of firms are being radically reshaped by products' evolution into intelligent, connected devices, 19 p. (2015)
13. Eslami, Y.: A Modelling-Based Sustainability Assessment in Manufacturing Organizations. Phdthesis, Politecnico di Bari (2019)
14. Panetto, H.: Towards a classification framework for interoperability of enterprise applications. Int. J. Comput. Integr. Manuf. **20**, 727–740 (2007)
15. Džeroski, S.: Multi-relational data mining: an introduction. SIGKDD Explor. Newsl. **5**, 1–16 (2003). https://doi.org/10.1145/959242.959245
16. Porter, M.E., Heppelmann, J.E.: How smart, connected products are transforming competition. Harvard Bus. Rev. **92**(11), 64–88 (2014)
17. Baader, F., Ganter, B., Sertkaya, B., Sattler, U.: Completing description logic knowledge bases using formal concept analysis. In: Proceedings of the 20th International Joint Conference on Artifical Intelligence, pp. 230–235. Morgan Kaufmann Publishers Inc., San Francisco (2007)
18. Rouane-Hacene, M., Huchard, M., Napoli, A., Valtchev, P.: Relational concept analysis: mining concept lattices from multi-relational data. Ann. Math. Artif. Intell. **67**, 81–108 (2013)

The Concept of Sustainable Maintenance Criteria Assessment

Małgorzata Jasiulewicz-Kaczmarek[1]([ID]) [ID] and Katarzyna Antosz[2] [ID]

[1] Faculty of Management Engineering, Poznan University of Technology, Rychlewskiego 2,
60-965 Poznań, Poland
malgorzata.jasiulewicz-kaczmarek@put.poznan.pl
[2] Faculty of Mechanical Engineering and Aeronautics, Rzeszow University of Technology,
Al. Powstancow Warszawy 12, 35-959 Rzeszów, Poland

Abstract. In recent years, companies have had to change their approach to the production and consumption of goods in order to meet the requirements of sustainable development. These companies, by changing the way products are manufactured, strive to increase its efficiency, while reducing the consumption of raw materials, reducing costs and reducing their impact on the environment. An inherent element supporting such activities is the implementation of an appropriate maintenance processes. Maintenance as a business function is a crucial part in achieving the status of a sustainable company. Keeping in view the importance of maintenance, in this study the concept of sustainable maintenance criteria assessment is presented. The development of the criteria assessment method requires consideration of two aspects. First, one should determine the way data will be obtained and the method of their evaluation (e.g. index, descriptive, point). Secondly, the way in which aggregations of partial assessment should be defined within each criterion. To solve this problem the maturity matrix was used.

Keywords: Maturity matrix · Assessment model · Sustainable maintenance

1 Introduction

The goal of maintenance sustainability assessment is to provide information on the current maintenance performance and support decision-makers in the decision-making process regarding future directions of operations [1–3]. This information should be synthetic, and thus show the result of the assessment in an aggregated way, and at the same time enable decomposition to lower levels showing the impact of each of the assessed criteria on the result.

One of the methods of developing performance measurement models most frequently mentioned in the literature, from the perspective of sustainable development is a balanced scorecard (BSC) developed by [4]. From the point of view sustainability assessment this model has four important features: (1) combines the strategy with the objectives and measures of their implementation; (2) includes and links financial

A. Dolgui et al. (Eds.): APMS 2021, IFIP AICT 633, pp. 427–436, 2021.
https://doi.org/10.1007/978-3-030-85910-7_45

and non-financial measures; (3) considers links between internal effectiveness of processes and their external efficiency; and in addition; (4) enables inclusion of dimensions of sustainable development. Since the BSC was introduced, many authors have proposed modifications for adapting the initial BSC to other models that are specific to different areas or industrial environments. The application of the balanced scorecard in tracking maintenance action plan effectiveness was reported in [5], who mentions in his study the use of the balanced scorecard as a medium for educating maintenance personnel on the organization's maintenance strategy. Adapting from the original BSC, [6] coined the term "maintenance scorecard" (MSC). He defined the MSC as an approach used to develop and implement strategies for the area of asset management in both short and long terms, and defined six areas of importance of asset management: (1) Productivity Perspective; (2) Cost Effectiveness Perspective; (3) Safety Perspective; (4) Quality Perspective; (5) Environmental Perspective; (6) Learning Perspective. The MSC is used to develop and implement a strategy in the area of asset management. It also serves to identify strategic improvement initiatives, along with the areas they focus on, early in the process. The extended BSC presented in [7] incorporates performance measures based on seven perspectives: corporate business (financial), society, consumer, production, support functions, human resources, and supplier perspectives. In [8] the authors suggest a performance management framework based on the BSC model and a list of key indicators for a project for the Norwegian oil and gas industry. The framework considers cost, operation, HSE, and organization perspectives. Maintenance and employee satisfaction are not included. However, in the work [9] a multi-criteria hierarchical framework for MPM that consists of multi-criteria indicators for each level of management, i.e. strategic, tactical and operational is proposed. These multi-criteria indicators are categorized as equipment/process related (e.g. capacity utilization, OEE, availability, etc.), cost related (e.g. maintenance cost per unit production cost), maintenance task related (e.g. ratio of planned and total maintenance tasks), customer and employee satisfaction, health, safety and environment (HSE). Indicators are proposed for each level of management in each category. In the work [10] authors developed a maintenance performance measurement model using three reference models - the Cost of Poor Maintenance Model, the Malcolm Baldrige National Quality Award and the Context-Input-Process-Product assessment model. Based on their research results, they identified the most important factors affecting the results of maintenance and assigned them to four classic BSC perspectives: learning and growth, internal process, customer, and finance, and then identified the corresponding indicators. The developed model was validated on the basis of a case study in a real company. In the paper [11] authors based on the BSC model, developed an original structure for evaluating sustainable maintenance performance for automotive companies which consists of eight perspectives assigned to three dimensions of TBL: (1) economic: cost effectiveness perspective, quality perspective, productivity perspective; (2) environmental: environmental perspective; (3) social: learning and growth perspective, health and safety perspective, employee satisfaction perspective, stakeholder's satisfaction perspective.

The analysis of different models of maintenance results assessment from the point of view of sustainable development presented in the literature indicates that:

1. Most frameworks attempt to address economic performance, but they are still using traditional economic indicators that are not the true measure of sustainability (e.g. spare parts stock price, profitability).
2. Social issues receive the least attention in the existing performance measurement framework. In only a few cases when workers issues are included, they cover mainly health and safety but not worker well-being or job security.
3. Although there are dependencies between assessment perspectives (economic, environmental and social) and indicators, in most of the works links between them are not analyzed.
4. BSC method does not include any techniques for quantifying the synthetic value of all perspectives. This problem could be solved by using for example Choquet integral [12] Moreover BSC method does not include any techniques for quantifying the contribution of each perspective, or criteria/indicators within the same perspective.

The aim of this paper is to proposed maturity model to solve the problem with assessment of each perspective of maintenance sustainability BSC model. This paper is a continuation of the previously undertaken work presented in [12, 13].

Given the purpose above, the paper is organised as follows: in Sect. 2 the overall methodology for aggregate maintenance assessment is presented. Then, in Sect. 3 the maintenance assessment procedure according developed methodology is described. Finally, the conclusions and direction of the future research are presented.

2 Maintenance Sustainability Assessment Model

The maintenance contribution in the realization of sustainability challenges is dependent on the operational and business context of a company. Therefore, in order to support maintenance decision makers in attaining sustainability and to point out the way of maintenance function contribution to sustainable manufacturing, main maintenance factors affecting sustainable manufacturing should be identified and analysed. Due to the need for simplicity and clarity in decision-making support, the information provided to decision-makers in the form of recommendations needs to be unequivocal, logical and easy to interpret. The answer to this problem was given in the form of the Composite Maintenance Sustainability Index (CMSI) [12]. In this paper authors developed performance assessment model, which integrate three sustainability dimensions (economic, social, and environmental) with four Kaplan and Norton's balance scorecard perspectives (financial, client, internal processes and learning & growth). The model consists of two inference levels, the first one encompassing the assessment perspectives and the other including the assessment criteria (Fig. 1). The detailed description of the perspectives and respective criteria can be found in [12]. The result is a synthetic indicator of performance, based on the paradigm of aggregate assessment. The above-mentioned model approaches the problem of aggregation function, for which its mathematical properties point to formally correct aggregation of criteria and behavioural properties express relationships between criteria including, for example, synergy and redundancy.

The general scheme of methodology for aggregate maintenance assessment includes three main stages: (1) Assessment criteria selection, (2) Selection of criteria assessment methods, and (3) Development of Composite Maintenance Sustainability Index (CMSI) (Fig. 2).

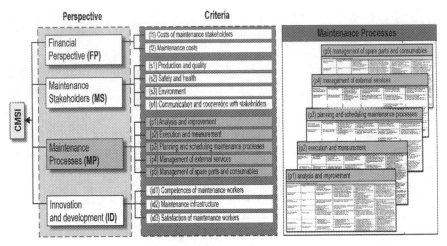

Fig. 1. Hierarchical model for maintenance sustainability assessment [8]

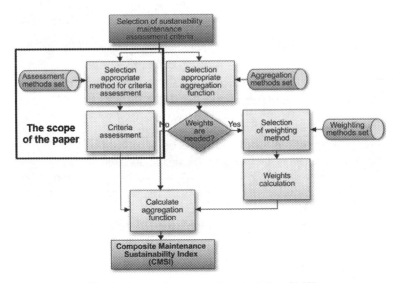

Fig. 2. A generic process for calculating CMSI

The model of sustainable maintenance performance assessment developed according to the three stages scheme (Fig. 2) should help maintenance managers put the strategy into action and offer predictive measures for future performance. To apply the model, it is needed to collect data and assess each of the criterion. The assessments are then aggregated using the Choquet integral [12]. The calculated CMSI value can be then used to determinate the relative importance between perspectives and criteria. Such procedure of calculation of CMSI value can be helpful for decision-makers to pay their attention to the areas that need improvements.

In this paper the stages of the criteria assessment method will be detail presented. The development of the criteria assessment method (Fig. 1) requires consideration of two aspects. First, one should determine the way data will be obtained and the method of their evaluation (e.g. index, descriptive, point). Secondly, the way in which aggregations of partial assessment should be defined within each criterion.

3   Method of Maintenance Criteria Assessment

Because the result of maintenance assessment is a function of quantitative and qualitative variables, in the process of evaluating each criterion, it is necessary to use information and data acquisition tools such as: review of documents, databases and methods of their collection and supervision, direct observation of events, interview with staff (in the assessment process, information from people involved in technical support is very important if they are properly confirmed by objective records). An adequate tool for obtaining data to assess criteria in the model is, therefore, a maintenance audit. In the paper [14] authors defined a maintenance audit as an 'examination of the maintenance system to verify if the maintenance management is carrying out its mission, meeting its goals and objectives, following proper procedures, and managing resources effectively and efficiently'. According to [15], a maintenance audit enables the integration of two different assessment methods, namely quantitative and qualitative. From the quantitative point of view, it makes it possible to assess the measures and indicators used in mainte-nance, the purposes of their application and the current status, and thus to examine the difference between the target value and the current one. On the other hand, the qualitative method allows to assess the effectiveness level of activities that are being carried out.

Audit programs consist of key elements that are examined through a set of statements or questions. Each statement or question has a score and a weight. Then based on the audit, a total weighted score is compiled and compared to an ideal score. The scores serve as a foundation for an improvement action plan. The process is repeated periodically to ensure continuous improvement. Considering the above, it is necessary to specify: (*1*) The scope of the audit program; (*2*) The subject of research within the scope of the audit; (*3*) The method of evaluating the subject of research; (*4*) The method for the aggregation of partial assessment.

(1)   *The scope of the audit program.*

From the point of view of the data obtaining method for calculating the CSMI index value, the scope of the audit program is defined by four perspectives of the sustainable maintenance assessment model and by the criteria describing them (see Fig. 2).

(2)   *The subject of research within the scope of the audit*

The subjects of research within the defined audit program are detailed issues characteriz-ing each of the criteria of the sustainable maintenance assessment model. Detailed issues were identified based on the analysis of sustainable production requirements, principles of sustainable maintenance and a criteria. An example of the issues under consideration in the 'Maintenance processes' perspective are:

- *Analysis and improvement* – assessment subject: Improvement system; Analytical methods; Failure investigation; Failure mode analysis; Oil analysis program; Equipment modification; Resource utilization analysis.
- *Implementation and measurement* – assessment subject: Reporting procedure (PMn and emergency); Lubrication reporting; Measuring schedule compliance; Quality of PMn inspection; PMn prioritization; PdM work orders creation; Lubrication KPIs; Work Order Closeout.
- *Planning and scheduling* – assessment subject: Design of maintenance plan; Identification of E&S requirements; PMn content and procedures; PMn scheduling; Lubrication selection; Lubrication program design; Identification of equipment criticality; Work orders.
- *Management of external service providers* – assessment subject: Outsourcing activities; Risk analysis of contractors; Performances of service providers; Principles of cooperation with suppliers.
- *Management of spare parts and consumables* – assessment subject: Risk analysis of spare parts suppliers; Performance of spare parts suppliers; Determination of required spare parts; Ordering spare parts and consumables; Storage of spare parts and consumables.

Individual criteria differ in the number of issues assessed, but it seems unreasonable to strive for the harmonization of the number of issues applied to each criterion. Each criterion, because of the scope to which it applies, requires the collection of a different scope of information and data.

(3) **The method of evaluating the subject of research.**

In general, the issues being investigated can be assessed using one of the following methods: indicative, descriptive or a point method. The most popular and internally diversified groups of methods are quantitative indicator methods. They enable the identification, measurement and evaluation of economic and non-economic effects. A large part of the literature proposes useful indicators and metrics for the performance of assessment [11, 16, 17], but does not deal with the problem of data collection. The second group of methods are descriptive methods which are devoid of any formalization elements. They recognize and value qualitative/quantitative characteristics of the assessed phenomena by way of logical analysis and presentation of the test result in a descriptive form. The third group of methods is point methods. Their use identifies measures and values both measurable and verbal qualities.

In the proposed model of sustainable maintenance assessment, a point method was selected to assess the issues describing individual criteria. In comparison with the other two methods (indicative and descriptive), this method has three basic advantages. Firstly, is simple to use. Secondly, the values of features in the point method are expressed in homogeneous, non-quantified numbers (grades of the adopted point scale), which makes it possible to aggregate partial grades into a synthetic evaluation, without the need for their prior normalization and standardization. Thirdly, the point method, apart from the main objective, which is the valuation, provides additional information on the level of implementation of requirements for a given issue. This information may constitute a significant support for the designers of improvement activities. Nevertheless, this method has also its drawbacks. Many problems appear when choosing the right span of the point scale. Literature studies indicate that the spread of the rating scale should not be less than three levels and not more than ten. With regard to the assessment of maintenance, this scale should express levels of maturity adequate to each of the issues assessed. Therefore, in order to assess the issues that characterize each perspective, appropriate maturity models should be built. Maturity models can be used both as an assessment tool and as an improvement tool [18]. Maturity models allow to evaluate the maintenance system and its processes in accordance with good practices. That models are focused on behaviours and thanks to this, allow to identify the next steps that should be taken to reach higher maturity levels [19, 20]. The identification and characterization of maturity models and maturity levels have been discussed in [20–24]. Taking the above and that the data are obtained by maintenance audit, the issues to be assessed will be represented by statements or questions, and answers may take one of the following forms: (1) selecting 'yes' or 'no' or (2) putting an item on the Likert-type scale to reflect different levels of meeting the requirement. Both forms of response representation require the development of an adequate point scale. Based on [14], a 5-point scale (maturity levels) was adopted, where '0' means that no action was taken, while '4' means that the issue is fully implemented. If the issues are formulated in the form of a question, and the evaluators will be able to choose the answer 'yes' or 'no', the answer 'yes' will be the highest possible number of points, i.e. '4', whereas the answer 'no' the lowest '0'. In other cases, the evaluators will have to choose one of the ordered and uniquely characterized categories (standard values) by assessing the issue (statement or question). A specific number of points from the scale will be assigned to the categories. The reference values will be described using qualitative characteristics for each of the proposed issues. Figure 3 presents the developed assessment matrix for the 'Maintenance processes' perspective on the example of analysis and improvement criterion. The structure of assessment defined in the above manner will allow for a common language of communication while discussing the current situation and planning the future development of the maintenance system amongst interested professionals from various departments in the company (for example, amongst mechanical engineers, production engineers and managers).

(4) *The method for the aggregation of partial assessment.*

The general assessment of each criterion is calculated by the aggregation of partial assessments of issues describing them. Based on the literature analysis, the method used by the Australian Maintenance Excellence Awards [25] was adopted, according to which the general assessment of the criterion is calculated as the ratio of the sum of points obtained for all issues being assessed to the sum of all possible points under the criterion. The value obtained in this way are, on the one hand, input data for calculating the CMSI index (Fig. 4), and on the other hand, they are analytical measures allowing for an in-depth analysis of the maintenance results in individual assessment criteria.

Perspective: Maintenance Processes					
Criterion: Analysis and improvement					
	0	1	2	3	4
Improvement system	None	Occasionally undertaken improvement activities; however, not documented	There is a formal procedure for reporting improvements; however, it functions to a limited extent; some of the activities documented	Formal procedure, documented activities, analysis of the effectiveness of the actions taken is carried out	Regular flow of employees' suggestions is evaluated, implemented and the resulting outcome is fed back to employees
Analytical methods	None	Informal, based on experience	Conducted to a limited extent based on cost trends and execution of orders (work orders)	Integration of operational measurements, asset health and RCM completed for all critical assets	Applying OEE, Life Cycle Cost, RCM used to update service plans and parts criticality
Failure investigation	None	Analysis carried out sporadically, rarely documented	Some formal RCA based on high cost failure	Formal analysis of failure causes including costs, environmental impact and safety	Specified indicators for assessing the effectiveness of actions taken + all actions from level 3
Failure Mode Analysis	None	Informal FMEA analyses for selected critical machines	Informal FMEA analyses for most critical machines	Informal FMEA analyses for all critical machines	FMEA utilized on critical equipment and integrated with Life Cycle Cost
Oil Program Analysis	Not used	No consistent analysis performed, only utilized when there is a problem	Routine testing of critical compartments only (regardless of compartment size)	Plant-wide routine testing, some tailoring of frequency and test slate to meet equipment needs	Analysis strategy takes into account equipment criticality, failure modes and symptoms, primary and secondary detection techniques, and test effectiveness, all equipment considered

Fig. 3. The developed assessment matrix for the 'Maintenance processes' perspective on the example of analysis and improvement criterion

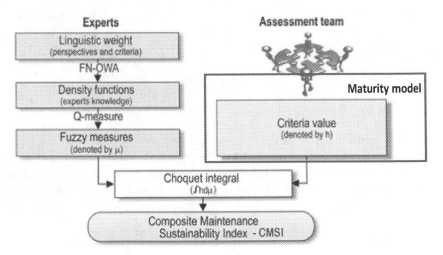

Fig. 4. Construction process of the non-additive fuzzy integral for CMSI

4   Conclusion

The criteria of maintenance sustainability assessment BSC model can be assessed by an maturity model. The result is a measure of maturity level of each maintenance assessment perspective in BSC model. The main goal is to provide an improvement activities in the maintenance management to achieve sustainability outcomes. In other words, it is a measure of the organizational understanding of, and application of the sustainability challenges of maintenance key-processes or how compliant the maintenance key-processes are with the best practices.

The criteria assessment method presented above meets two functions in the company. First, cognitive, by providing knowledge and possibility of using it for organizational learning. Second, utilitarian, as it allows to create directions of improvement adequate to the current context of the enterprise, paying attention to maintaining balance be-tween economic benefits and environmental and social requirements.

References

1. Franciosi, C., Voisin, A., Miranda, S., Riemma, S., Iung, B.: Measuring maintenance impacts on sustainability of manufacturing industries: from a systematic literature review to a framework proposal. J. Cleaner Prod. **260**, 121065 (2020)
2. Holgado, M., Macchi, M., Evans, S.: Exploring the impacts and contributions of maintenance function for sustainable manufacturing. Int. J. Prod. Res. **58**(23), 7292–7310 (2020)
3. Jasiulewicz-Kaczmarek, M., et al.: Application of MICMAC, fuzzy AHP, and fuzzy TOPSIS for evaluation of the maintenance factors affecting sustainable manufacturing. Energies **14**(5), 1436 (2021)
4. Kaplan, R.S., Norton, D.P.: The Balanced Scorecard: Translating Strategy into Action. Harvard Business Press, Harvard (1996)
5. Tsang, A.H.C.: A strategic approach to managing maintenance performance. J. Qual. Maint. Eng. **4**(2), 87–94 (1998)
6. Mather, D.: The Maintenance Scorecard: Creating Strategic Advantage. Industrial Press, New York (2005)
7. Alsyouf, I.: Measuring maintenance performance using a balanced scorecard approach. J. Qual. Maint. Eng. **12**(2), 133–149 (2006)
8. Kumar, U., Ellingsen H.P.: Design and development of maintenance performance indicators for the Norwegian oil and gas industry. In: Proceedings of the 15th European Maintenance Congress: Euromaintenance 2000, Gothenburg, Sweden, March 2000, pp. 224–228 (2000).
9. Parida, A., Chattopadhyay, G.: Development of multi-criteria hierarchical framework for maintenance performance measurement (MPM). J. Qual. Maint. Eng. **13**(3), 241–258 (2007)
10. Chopu-inwai, R., Diaotrakun, R., Thaiupathump T.: Key indicators for maintenance performance measurement: the aircraft galley and associated equipment manufacturer case study. In: 2013 10th International conference Service systems and service management (ICSSSM), Hong Kong, China, 17–19 July, pp. 844–849 (2013)
11. Sari, E., Shaharoun, A.M., Maaram, A., Yazid, A.M.: Sustainable maintenance performance measures: a pilot survey in Malaysian automotive companies. Procedia CIRP **26**, 443–448 (2015)
12. Jasiulewicz-Kaczmarek, M., Żywica, P.: The concept of maintenance sustainability performance assessment by integrating balanced scorecard with non-additive fuzzy integral. Eksploatacja i Niezawodnosc Maintenance Reliability **20**(4), 650–661 (2018)
13. Jasiulewicz-Kaczmarek, M., Żywica, P., Gola, A.: Fuzzy set theory driven maintenance sustainability performance assessment model: a multiple criteria approach. J. Intell. Manuf. 1–19 (2021)
14. Galar, D., Sandborn, P., Kumar, U.: Maintenance Cost and Life Cycle Cost Analysis. CSR Press (2017)
15. Kumar, U., Galar, D., Parida, A., Stenström, C.: Maintenance audits using balanced scorecard and maturity model. Maintworld **3**, 34–40 (2011)

16. Amrina, E., Yulianto, A.: Interpretive structural model of key performance indicators for sustainable maintenance evaluatian in rubber industry. IOP Conf. Ser. Mater. Sci. Eng. **319**(1), 012055 (2018)
17. Maletič, D., Maletič, M., Al-Najjar, B., Gomišček, B.: Development of a model linking physical asset management to sustainability performance: an empirical research. Sustainability **10**(12), 4759 (2018)
18. Maier, A.M., Moultrie, J., Clarkson, P.J.: Assessing organizational capabilities: reviewing and guiding the development of Maturity grids. IEEE Trans. Eng. Manag. **59**(1), 138–159 (2012)
19. Oliveira, M., Lopes, I., Figueiredo, D.: Survey on maintenance area of companies of Manaus industrial pole. In: Kim, H.K., Amouzegar, M.A., Ao, S. (eds.) Transactions on Engineering Technologies, pp. 501–514. Springer, New York (2015). https://doi.org/10.1007/978-94-017-7236-5_35
20. Fernandez, O., Labib, A.W., Walmsley, R., Petty, D.J.: A decision support maintenance management system: development and implementation. Int. J. Qual. Reliability Manag. **20**(8), 965–979 (2003)
21. Cholasuke, C., Bhardwa, R., Antony, J.: The status of maintenance management in UK manufacturing organisations: results from a pilot survey. J. Qual. Maint. Eng. **10**(1), 5–15 (2004)
22. Chemweno, P., Pintelon, L., Van Horenbeek, A., Muchiri, P.N.: Asset maintenance maturity model: structured guide to maintenance process maturity. Int. J. Strateg. Eng. Asset Manag. **2**(2), 119–135 (2015)
23. Oliveira, M.A., Lopes, I.: Evaluation and improvement of maintenance management performance using a maturity model. Int. J. Product. Perform. Manag. **69**(3), 559–581 (2020)
24. Schmiedbauer, O., Biedermann, H.: Validation of a lean smart maintenance maturity model. Tehnički glasnik **14**(3), 296–302 (2020)
25. SIRF Roundtables AMEA criteria and applications guidelines (2013). http://www.sirfrt.com.au/sirfrt_new/images/content/AMEA-Criteria_and_Application_Guidelines.pdf. Accessed 5 Oct 2017

Cost Projections for the Product Life Cycle at the Early Stages of Product Development

Marcin Relich[1]([⊠]) [iD], Grzegorz Bocewicz[2] [iD], and Zbigniew Banaszak[2] [iD]

[1] Faculty of Economics and Management, University of Zielona Gora, Zielona Gora, Poland
m.relich@wez.uz.zgora.pl
[2] Faculty of Electronics and Computer Science,
Koszalin University of Technology, Koszalin, Poland
{grzegorz.bocewicz,zbigniew.banaszak}@tu.koszalin.pl

Abstract. The paper is concerned with predicting the total cost of a new product and searching for cost reduction at the early stages of product development. The costs of a new product development project, product promotion, production and after-sales service are predicted using parametric models. The identified relationships are also used to searching for possibilities to reduce the cost of faulty products and after-sales service through increasing prototype tests. As a result, the trade-off between the cost of a product development project and costs of production and after-sales service are sought. Company resources and product specification are formulated in terms of variables and constraints that constitute the systems approach for a problem related to cost optimization. This problem is described in the form of a constraint satisfaction problem and implemented using constraint programming techniques. An example shows the applicability of the proposed approach in the context of searching for the desirable level of the cost related to prototype tests, faulty products and after-sales service. This study develops previous research in the context of adding the cost of after-sales service to a model of total costs of a new product. Moreover, the proposed method of predicting cost has been developed towards using the similarity value to data selection.

Keywords: Product data management · New product development · Production cost · Decision support system · Constraint programming

1 Introduction

Cost management is one of the most important business activities, affecting the sales revenue, profits and competitiveness. The effective cost management maintains a company growth and survival. However, its effectiveness depends on a stage of the product life cycle. The earlier total product costs are predicted, the more chance to obtain benefits of predictions. These benefits refer to the timing of price changes, product withdrawal, impacting strategies of product lifecycle management. Generally, total product costs are related to new products development (NPD), product promotion, manufacturing, and after-sales service. Manufacturing is usually the longest stage in the product life cycle.

© IFIP International Federation for Information Processing 2021
Published by Springer Nature Switzerland AG 2021
A. Dolgui et al. (Eds.): APMS 2021, IFIP AICT 633, pp. 437–446, 2021.
https://doi.org/10.1007/978-3-030-85910-7_46

Consequently, production cost has the largest share in the total product costs. However, the costs related to production and after-sales service depend on the quality of product design created in the NPD process. This process is therefore one of the most important activities in today's companies, also taking into account shortening product life cycles and competitive markets. Moreover, shorter time for developing new products and the limited resources impel companies towards greater effort and attention in managing the NPD projects. Increasing competition and customers' requirements impose more often product launches on the market within the acceptable cost that is prerequisite for the product success. If predictions of the total product costs do not satisfy the company's top management team, then there are sought possibilities to reduce costs. This paper is concerned with developing an approach to cost projection and searching for the trade-off between costs at the early stages of the product life cycle (product design and prototype tests) and in the later stages (production and after-sales service).

The NPD costs are related to market research, generating concepts of a new product, its design and prototype tests. Specially, the latter cost is often a long-term process which absorbs the majority of the NPD budget. However, prototyping costs are usually low (if not negligible) in comparison to the overall cost of production [1]. Moreover, the number of prototype tests affects product reliability, and finally, the costs related to faulty products in manufacturing and the after-sales stage. The low product reliability can reduce customer satisfaction and increase the warranty cost. Companies usually tend to seek the trade-off between the prototyping cost and costs related to production and after-sales service. Cost projections can be based on relationships between variables that are identified by parametric models. These relationships can also be used to the search for possibilities to reduction of the number of faulty products and return of goods, and the trade-off between different type of costs.

The identification of possibilities for reducing the costs variants requires the specification of variables, their domains and constraints, including the mentioned relationships between variables. This specification can be formulated in terms of a constraint satisfaction problem (CSP). In the context of product development, the CSP paradigm has been mainly applied to product design [2]. Taking into account cost projections and simulations, the CSP paradigm has been used in the context of the NPD cost [3], and production and advertising cost [4]. The contribution of this study is the development of previous research in the context of using the CSP paradigm to find the trade-off between the mentioned costs. Moreover, a method of cost estimation is proposed using databases of project-oriented enterprises, in order to identify the possibility of cost reduction of the total product cost. The proposed method includes a step related to using the similarity value to data selection. Finally, this study presents the use of constraint programming (CP) techniques to identify possible variants of cost reduction. The paper is organised as follows: Sect. 2 presents problem formulation in terms of a CSP. A method of projecting cost and searching for possible variants of cost reduction is shown in Sect. 3. An illustrative example of the proposed approach is presented in Sect. 4. Finally, conclusion is shown in Sect. 5.

2   Problem Formulation

The proposed approach allows the decision maker to identify prerequisites, by which an NPD project can obtain the trade-off between costs related to prototype tests, production and after-sales stage. The number of possible variants of cost reduction depends on constraints, domains related to variables, and their granularity. Relationships between variables can be identified using previous experiences related to the similar completed projects. The identified relationships are used to cost projections and verification of the existence of such changes, by which the target cost could be reached.

The application of the proposed approach requires the specification of variables, their domains, and constraints that can be described in terms of a CSP in the following form: $((V, D), C)$, where V is a finite set of n variables $\{v_1, v_2, ..., v_n\}$, D is finite and discrete domains $\{d_1, d_2, ..., d_n\}$ of variables V, and C is a finite set of constraints $\{c_1, c_2, ..., c_m\}$. Constraints can link variables and restrict their values. The solution of a CSP is a set related to the value of each variable that satisfies all constraints C.

Problem formulation in terms of a CSP includes the variables and constraints regarding an NPD project and company resources. The selection of variables is performed in an arbitrary way, taking into account the impact of a specific variable on the cost of NPD, production, and after-sales service. The specification of a cost model as a CSP enables the search for a set of values of decision variables, for which cost reduction is possible, if any. The problem solution is related to possible changes in NPD project performance that satisfy all specified constraints, including the desirable level of costs.

There are the following variables regarding cost estimation of a new product:

V_1– the cost of an NPD project (product design and prototype tests),
V_2– the cost of product promotion,
V_3– the unit production cost,
V_4– the cost of after-sales service,
V_5– the number of employees involved in an NPD project,
V_6 – the number of prototype tests,
V_7 – the number of product components,
V_8 – the period of an advertising campaign (in weeks),
V_9 – the number of target clients in an advertising campaign (in thousands),
V_{10}– the amount of materials used to produce a unit of a new product (in kilograms),
V_{11}– the number of components in a product for assembling,
V_{12}– the number of components in a product for processing,
V_{13}– the number of faulty products in manufacturing (in each 1,000 final products).

The set of constraints is as follows:

C_1 – the budget of an NPD project,
C_2 – the budget of product promotion,
C_3 – the maximal unit production cost,
C_4 – the minimal number of product components,
C_5 – the minimal number of prototype tests,
C_6 – the total number of employees who may be involved in NPD,

C_7 – the maximal amount of materials needed to produce a unit of a new product,
C_8 – the maximal cost of faulty products in manufacturing.

The model specification in terms of a CSP integrates technical parameters of a new product, parameters regarding the NPD project performance, estimated costs of a new product, and available resources in a company. The solution of the above-described problem can be referred to the answers to the following questions:

- what is the cost related to an NPD project, product promotion, its production, and after-sales service?
- what values should have the variables related to prototype tests to reach the desirable level of total costs of a new product?

The answer to the second question refers especially to the problem formulation in terms of a CSP and its declarative programming paradigm. Using this paradigm all possible solutions are identified, if any. This often requires the verification of a large space of solutions, especially if there are many decision variables and highly differentiated domains. Consequently, there is a need to use the effective techniques of space search reduction, such as constraint programming.

3   A Method of Cost Projections and Searching for Possible Variants of Cost Reduction

The proposed method includes the following steps: collecting data from existing products that are similar to a new product, identifying relationships between input and output variables, predicting costs related to a new product, and searching for possible variants to obtain the desirable level of costs. A framework of the proposed method is presented in Fig. 1.

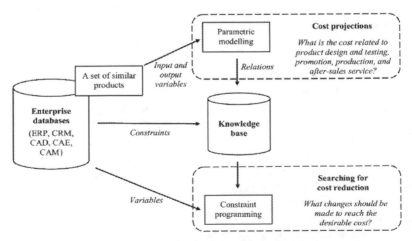

Fig. 1. A framework of the proposed method

The data is collected from enterprise databases stored in information systems that support product data management in a company. These information systems can include systems related to enterprise resource planning (ERP), customer relations management (CRM), computer-aided design (CAD), computer-aided engineering (CAE), or computer-aided manufacturing (CAM). The data stored in these systems is used in product lifecycle management.

Information of the product life cycle is acquired from specifications of past or existing products that are in the same product line as a new product. The most similar products to a new product are retrieved from the enterprise database using the similarity function (1) and similarity value – SV (2) that are calculated as follows:

$$sim\left(f_i^P, f_i^R\right) = 1 - \frac{\left|f_i^P - f_i^R\right|}{max(f_i)} \tag{1}$$

$$SV = \frac{\sum_{i=1}^{n} w_i \times sim\left(f_i^P, f_i^R\right)}{\sum_{i=1}^{n} w_i} \tag{2}$$

where:

- $sim\left(f_i^P, f_i^R\right)$ – the similarity function of the i-th product features (e.g. weight, size) between the value of the new product f_i^P and the value of the retrieved product f_i^R; it ranges from 0 to 1.
- w_i – the weight of the i-th product features.

The costs of a new product can be estimated using analogical and parametric methods. Analogical methods estimate the cost using similarity to previous products. The comparison between the new and existing products can refer to cost reduction in different areas, for example, product design [5]. In turn, parametric methods estimate the cost from parameters that significantly affect the cost.

The proposed method uses cause-and-effect relationships to cost estimation within prototype tests of a new product, faulty products in manufacturing, and return of goods in the after-sales stage. Product reliability affects the number of faulty products and return of goods, increasing the total cost of production and after-sales service. Product reliability can be measured by the number of product usage to the first failure that directly depends on the number of prototype tests.

The variables to cost estimation are selected taking into account their impact on the specific cost and their controllability. For example, a company can manage the number of prototype tests, project team members, and product components. A set of variables, their domains, and constraints constitutes a CSP that is a framework for obtaining answers to the questions about the value of the cost, and if it is non-acceptable, about the values of variables that enable the desirable level of the specific cost.

The proposed method is based on parametric estimation models that include an analytical function of a set of variables. These variables are usually related to some features of a new product (e.g. the number of components, dimensions, materials used) and an NPD project (e.g. the number of prototype tests, project duration, project team members) that are supposed to have a significant impact on NPD project performance and the cost of a new product. Parametric estimation techniques often base on regression analysis [6, 7], artificial neural networks [8, 9] or hybrid systems (e.g. neuro-fuzzy and genetic fuzzy systems). The identified relations are stored in a knowledge base and used to search for possible variants of designing and manufacturing a new product.

The last step of the proposed method refers to the search for possible solutions to reach the desirable cost of prototyping, promotion, production and after-sales service. The search space depends on the number of variables chosen to the analysis, their domains, and constraints that can link variables and limit possible solutions. An exhaustive search always find a solution if it exists but its performance is proportional to the number of admissible solutions. Therefore, an exhaustive search tends to grow very quickly as the size of the problem increases, what limits its usage in many practical problems. Consequently, there is a need to develop more effective methods for searching the space and finding possible solutions. As CP uses the specific search methods and constraint propagation algorithms, it enables a significant reduction of the search space. Consequently, CP is suitable to model and solve complex problems [10]. CP includes search strategies that are crucial for improving search efficiency of solving a wide range of problems, for instance, planning and scheduling [11, 12], manufacturing [13, 14], and resource allocation [15, 16].

4   A Case Study

4.1   Calculating the Similarity Between New and Past Products

The first stage of the proposed method is related to data selection, namely selection of a set of the most similar existing products to a new product. The similarity between products is calculated for products belonging to the same product line. There are 22 products from the same product line as a new product. The following set of features has been chosen to evaluate the similarity between products: the number of parts, product size, product weight, and the amount of materials used. Table 1 presents the similarity function (SF) and similarity value (SV) for the most similar past product and new product.

Table 1. Similarity functions and similarity value.

Features	f^P	f^R	SF
Number of parts	42	45	93.3%
Product size	0.65	0.68	95.6%
Product weight	0.71	0.73	97.3%
Amount of materials used	0.77	0.81	95.1%
$SV = (93.3\% + 95.6\% + 97.3\% + 95.1\%)/4$ $= 95.3\%$			

There are 15 similar products with the similarity value above the assumed threshold of 85%, which are considered in the further analyses.

4.2 Predicting Product Development Costs

The total cost of a new product mainly consists of costs related to product design, promotion, production, and after-sales service. These costs are further estimated using an arithmetic average that is calculated for a set of the most similar product to a new product, and a parametric approach, where the costs are identified using several independent variables. The relationships of the cost of product design and testing (3), promotion (4), production (5), and after-sales service (6) are as follows:

$$V_1 = f(V_5, V_6, V_7) \tag{3}$$

$$V_2 = f(V_8, V_9) \tag{4}$$

$$V_3 = f(V_7, V_{10}, V_{11}, V_{12}) \tag{5}$$

$$V_4 = f(V_6, V_7, V_{13}) \tag{6}$$

The relationships (1)–(4) have been identified using linear regression, and the results have been compared with the average of output variables to illustrate to what extent the parametric models outperform the arithmetic average. The dataset for analysis includes 15 cases that has been divided into training set (12 cases) and testing set (3 cases) to evaluate the quality of an estimation model. The experiments were performed using 5-fold cross validation, and the results were determined as the average of these folds. The identified relationships have the following form:

$$V_1 = 5.28V_5 + 0.64V_6 + 0.46V_7 + 64.04 \tag{7}$$

$$V_2 = 0.94V_8 + 3.70V_9 + 70.56 \tag{8}$$

$$V_3 = 0.50V_7 + 247.80V_{10} + 0.36V_{11} + 0.01V_{12} + 14.88 \tag{9}$$

$$V_4 = 0.41V_6 + 0.52V_7 + 15.73V_{13} - 17.69 \tag{10}$$

Table 2 presents the mean absolute percentage square error (MAPE) in the training set (TR_S) and testing set (TE_S) for the cost of an NPD project (V_1), the cost of product promotion (V_2), the unit production cost (V_3), and the cost of after-sales service (V_4). The results indicate that parametric models (PM) produce the less error than the arithmetic average, both in training and testing dataset.

Table 2. Comparison of MAPE for the parametric model and average.

Variable	Model	MAPE for TR_S in (%)	MAPE for TE_S in (%)
V_1	PM	1.00	1.56
	Average	6.05	10.16
V_2	PM	6.27	4.44
	Average	14.38	17.45
V_3	PM	2.62	5.48
	Average	23.69	17.73
V_4	PM	5.14	5.33
	Average	12.23	13.44

As the parametric models have been generated in the testing set smaller MAPE than the arithmetic average, they have been used to cost estimation. The cost of an NPD project (V_1) has been estimated at 310 thousand €, taking into account the following values of input variables: $V_5 = 5$, $V_6 = 300$, $V_7 = 60$. The cost of product promotion (V_2) has been predicted at 320.9 thousand € for the following input variables: $V_8 = 30$, $V_9 = 60$. The unit production cost (V_3) has been estimated at 218.7 €, taking into account the input variables such as: $V_7 = 60$, $V_{10} = 0.65$, $V_{11} = 35$, $V_{12} = 15$. In turn, the after-sales service cost (V_4) has been estimated at 183.7 € per 1,000 sold products, taking into account the input variables such as: $V_6 = 300$, $V_7 = 60$, $V_{13} = 3$. The values of input variables (V_5, ..., V_{13}) are acquired from specification of a new product, including product design and testing, product promotion, production process, and after-sale stage. Specification of a new product is elaborated on the basis of experiences from the implementation of previous products.

The budget of an NPD project reaches 350 thousand €, so this constraint is fulfilled. In turn, the unit production cost, which is related to faulty products, and after-sales service is too high for senior managers, and they decided that these costs should be reduced to 210 € and 175 € for each 1,000 sold products, respectively. In the next step, the possibility of fulfilling these expectations is sought.

4.3 Searching for Possibilities of Cost Reduction

The solution of the above-described problem is sought using constraint programming that requires the specification of decision variables, their domains, and constraints, including relationships between variables. Scenario analysis is carried out for three variables: the number of employees involved in an NPD project, the number of prototype tests, and the amount of materials used to produce a unit of a new product. Domains of these variables are as follows: $D_5 = \{4, 5, 6\}$, $D_6 = \{300, ..., 400\}$, $D_{10} = \{0.60, ..., 0.70\}$.

The criterion for selecting the best variant of cost reduction (SC) is as follows:

$$\min SC = V_3 + V_4 \tag{11}$$

Table 3 presents a few possible solutions for the specified variables, their domains, and constraints. The increment of prototype tests results in increasing the NPD cost but at the same time it reduces the costs of production and after-sales service.

Table 3. A set of possible solutions.

Values of variables	V_3	V_4	SC
$V_5 = 5$, $V_6 = 399$, $V_{10} = 0.65$	210.0	174.9	384.9
$V_5 = 5$, $V_6 = 400$, $V_{10} = 0.65$	209.8	174.9	384.7
$V_5 = 5$, $V_6 = 389$, $V_{10} = 0.60$	209.9	173.3	383.2
...	...	...	...
$V_5 = 5$, $V_6 = 400$, $V_{10} = 0.60$	207.2	172.3	379.5
$V_5 = 6$, $V_6 = 375$, $V_{10} = 0.60$	210.0	172.7	382.7
...	...	...	...
$V_5 = 6$, $V_6 = 400$, $V_{10} = 0.60$	208.8	173.8	382.6

Table 3 illustrates an example of changes in three variables. The increasing number of NPD project team members enlarges the cost of prototype tests but also can increase the quality of a new product, and consequently, reduce the cost of production and after-sales service. Moreover, this kind of analysis can be an advice for the decision maker about directions of changes that can lead to reach the trade-off between the cost of prototyping, production and after-sales service.

5 Conclusion

The presented approach supports the decision makers in cost projections for all costs related to the product life cycle, and in searching for possibilities of reaching the desirable level of the cost related to production and after-sales service at the early stage of product development. The approach is dedicated for project-oriented enterprises that register their product specification and develop NPD projects within the similar product line. This study presents the use of parametric modelling to identify the relationships for predicting the cost of a new product. Moreover, the identified relationships can be used to search variants of increasing the quality of a new product, and reduce the cost of faulty products and warranty. If these costs are unacceptable for the decision makers, then the identified variants can support them in identifying the impact of input variables on the specific cost within the assumed constraints. The proposed model encompasses the product specification and company's resources, and it is formulated in terms of a CSP. The application of CP techniques reduces computational time compared to an exhaustive search, what is especially useful in the case of a vast space of possible solutions. Constraint programming techniques enables the use of strategies related to constraint propagation and variable distribution, significantly reducing a set of admissible solutions and the average computational time, what improves interactive properties of a decision support system. Drawbacks of the proposed approach can be seen from the perspective of collecting enough amounts of data of the existing similar products. Future research directions include identification of the impact of the number of decision variables (including granularity of their domains) and constraints on the time needed to obtain solutions, and the effectiveness of using constraint programming techniques. Moreover, future research could specify the adjustment of weights related to the similarity value, and their impact on data selection, and finally, on cost projections.

References

1. Rayna, T., Striukova, L.: From rapid prototyping to home fabrication: how 3D printing is changing business model innovation. Technol. Forecast. Soc. Chang. **102**, 214–224 (2016)
2. Yang, D., Dong, M.: A constraint satisfaction approach to resolving product configuration conflicts. Adv. Eng. Inform. **26**, 592–602 (2012)
3. Relich, M., Nielsen, I., Bocewicz, G., Banaszak, Z.: Constraint programming for new product development project prototyping. In: Nguyen, N.T., Jearanaitanakij, K., Selamat, A., Trawiński, B., Chittayasothorn, S. (eds.) ACIIDS 2020. LNCS (LNAI), vol. 12034, pp. 26–37. Springer, Cham (2020). https://doi.org/10.1007/978-3-030-42058-1_3
4. Relich, M., Świć, A.: Parametric estimation and constraint programming-based planning and simulation of production cost of a new product. Appl. Sci. **10**, 6330 (2020)
5. Harlalka, A., Naiju, C.D., Janardhanan, M.N., Nielsen, I.: Redesign of an in-market food processor for manufacturing cost reduction using DFMA methodology. Prod. Manuf. Res. **4**(1), 209–227 (2016)
6. Liu, H., Gopalkrishnan, V., Quynh, K.T., Ng, W.K.: Regression models for estimating product life cycle cost. J. Intell. Manuf. **20**(4), 401–408 (2009)
7. Nielsen, P., Jiang, L., Rytter, N.G., Chen, G.: An investigation of forecast horizon and observation fit's influence on an econometric rate forecast model in the liner shipping industry. Marit. Policy Manag. **41**(7), 667–682 (2014)
8. Wang, Q.: Artificial neural networks as cost engineering methods in a collaborative manufacturing environment. Int. J. Prod. Econ. **109**, 53–64 (2007)
9. Relich, M.: Computational intelligence for estimating cost of new product development. Found. Manag. **8**, 21–34 (2016)
10. Apt, K.R.: Principles of Constraint Programming. Cambridge University Press, Cambridge (2003)
11. Booth, K.E., Tran, T.T., Nejat, G., Beck, J.C.: Mixed-integer and constraint programming techniques for mobile robot task planning. IEEE Robot. Autom. Lett. **1**(1), 500–507 (2016)
12. Bocewicz, G., Nielsen, I., Gola, A., Banaszak, Z.: Reference model of milk-run traffic systems prototyping. Int. J. Prod. Res. 1–18 (2020). https://doi.org/10.1080/00207543.2020.1766717
13. Soto, R., Kjellerstrand, H., Gutiérrez, J., López, A., Crawford, B., Monfroy, E.: Solving manufacturing cell design problems using constraint programming. In: Jiang, He., Ding, W., Ali, M., Wu, X. (eds.) IEA/AIE 2012. LNCS (LNAI), vol. 7345, pp. 400–406. Springer, Heidelberg (2012). https://doi.org/10.1007/978-3-642-31087-4_42
14. Sitek, P., Wikarek, J.: A multi-level approach to ubiquitous modeling and solving constraints in combinatorial optimization problems in production and distribution. Appl. Intell. **48**(5), 1344–1367 (2017). https://doi.org/10.1007/s10489-017-1107-9
15. Hladik, P.E., Cambazard, H., Déplanche, A.M., Jussien, N.: Solving a real-time allocation problem with constraint programming. J. Syst. Softw. **81**(1), 132–149 (2008)
16. Zeballos, L.J.: A constraint programming approach to tool allocation and production scheduling in flexible manufacturing systems. Robot. Comput. Integr. Manuf. **26**(6), 725–743 (2010)

Robotics Technologies for Control, Smart Manufacturing and Logistics

Redundancy Resolution in Kinematic Control of Serial Manipulators in Multi-obstacle Environment

Wanda Zhao[1($\boxtimes$)], Anatol Pashkevich[1,2], and Damien Chablat[1,3]

[1] Laboratoire des Sciences du Numérique de Nantes (LS2N), UMR CNRS 6004, Nantes, France
Wanda.Zhao@ls2n.fr
[2] IMT Atlantique Bretagne Pays de la Loire, Nantes, France
Anatol.Pashkevich@imt atlantique.fr
[3] Centre National de la Recherche Scientifique (CNRS), Nantes, France
Damien.Chablat@cnrs.fr

Abstract. The paper focuses on the redundancy resolution in kinematic control of a new type of serial manipulator composed of multiple tensegrity segments, which are moving in a multi-obstacle environment. The general problem is decomposed into two sub-problems, which deal with collision-free path planning for the robot end-effector and collision-free motion planning for the robot body. The first of them is solved via discrete dynamic programming, the second one is worked out using quadratic programming with mixed linear equality/non-equality constraints. Efficiency of the proposed technique is confirmed by simulation.

Keywords: Serial manipulator · Tensegrity mechanisms · Kinematic control · Redundancy resolution · Obstacle-avoidance

1 Introduction

In robotics, kinematic control of compliant serial manipulators attracted much attention recently [1–3]. Because of their specific design including not only rigid components but also elastic elements, such manipulators allow achieving excellent flexibility and ability of shape-changing in under the environment. However, kinematic control of such manipulators is not a trivial problem, which requires redundancy resolution considering possible collisions of the robot end-effector and its body with the obstacles.

The considered manipulator is composed of multiple tensegrity segments, each of which contains two rigid triangle parts connected by a passive joint and two elastic edges with controllable preload [4]. In practice, to achieve the desired target location of the end-effector, both the end-effector and the manipulator body must avoid touching the obstacles. The latter imposes very essential constraints on the redundancy resolution, which is usually resolved via the kinematic model linearization and the classical quadratic programming with the linear equality constraint applied to the end-effector [5, 6]. In this paper, it is proposed to solve the problem sequentially, generating the

© IFIP International Federation for Information Processing 2021
Published by Springer Nature Switzerland AG 2021
A. Dolgui et al. (Eds.): APMS 2021, IFIP AICT 633, pp. 449–456, 2021.
https://doi.org/10.1007/978-3-030-85910-7_47

collision-free path for the robot end-effector first, and collision-free motion for the robot body at the second stage. Relevant techniques are based on the discrete dynamic programming and the quadratic programming with mixed equality constraints applied to the end-effector, and the non-equality constraints applied to the manipulator segments.

2   Problem Statement

Let us consider a serial manipulator composed of n similar segments based on dual-triangle tensegrity mechanisms, composed of rigid parts connected by passive joints whose rotation is constrained by two linear springs as shown in Fig. 1. It is assumed that the mechanism geometry is described by two triangle parameters (a, b), and the mechanism shape is defined by the central angle q, which is adjusted through two control inputs influencing on the lengths of the springs L_1 and L_2. More details concerning the manipulator kinematics is given in our previous paper [4], here we concentrate on the control issues and the redundancy resolution.

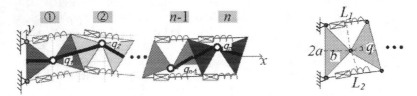

Fig. 1. Kinematic structure of the multi-segment serial manipulator.

For this manipulator, the direct kinematics equations can be written as follows

$$x_i = b + 2b \sum_{j=1}^{i-1} \left(\cos(\sum_{i=1}^{j} q_i) \right); \quad y_i = 2b \sum_{j=1}^{i-1} \left(\sin(\sum_{i=1}^{j} q_i) \right); \quad i = 1, ..., n$$

$$x_e = x_n + b \cos(\sum_{i=1}^{n} q_i); \qquad y_e = y_n + b \sin(\sum_{i=1}^{n} q_i)$$

(1)

where q_i are the joint angles, (x_i, y_i) denote the position of the ith joint center and (x_e, y_e) is the end-effector position. Corresponding Jacobians involved in the differential kinematics can be presented in the following way

$$\mathbf{J}_i = 2b \cdot \begin{bmatrix} -\sum_{k=1}^{i-1} \left(\sin \sum_{s=1}^{k} q_s \right) & -\sum_{k=2}^{i-1} \left(\sin \sum_{s=1}^{k} q_s \right) & \cdots & -\sum_{k=n}^{i-1} \left(\sin \sum_{s=1}^{k} q_s \right) \\ \sum_{k=1}^{i-1} \left(\cos \sum_{s=1}^{k} q_s \right) & \sum_{k=2}^{i-1} \left(\cos \sum_{s=1}^{k} q_s \right) & \cdots & \sum_{k=n}^{i-1} \left(\cos \sum_{s=1}^{k} q_s \right) \end{bmatrix}_{2\times n}$$

(2)

$$\mathbf{J}_e = \mathbf{J}_n + b \cdot \begin{bmatrix} -\sin \sum_{i=1}^{n} q_i & -\sin \sum_{i=1}^{n} q_i & \cdots & -\sin \sum_{i=1}^{n} q_i \\ \cos \sum_{i=1}^{n} q_i & \cos \sum_{i=1}^{n} q_i & \cdots & \cos \sum_{i=1}^{n} q_i \end{bmatrix}_{2\times n}$$

(3)

Obviously, for $n > 2$ this manipulator is kinematically redundant since the desired end-effector location can be achieved in an infinite number of ways. So, **the principle problem** considered here is how efficiently to use this kinematic redundancy in a multi-obstacle environment, i.e. to ensure the end-effector displacement to the given end-effector location (x_e^d, y_e^d) with minimum joint motions $\Delta q_i, i = 1, ..., n$ while avoiding possible collisions of the manipulator body and the end-effector with the obstacles. In this paper, it is proposed to decompose these general problems into two sub-problems sequentially dealing with (i) collision-free path planning for the robot end-effector and (ii) collision-free motion planning for the robot body. More strict formalization of these problems and their solutions are presented in the following chapters.

3   Path Generation for the Manipulator End-Effector

To find the best **collision-free path for the end-effector** let us apply the discrete dynamic programming technique allowing to generate the shortest trajectory in the obstacle-dense task space, which connects the initial and target points $\mathbf{p}^0$, $\mathbf{p}^g$ and avoids collisions with the obstacles. To apply this technique, let us discretize the task space (x, y) and present it as a two-dimensional set of nodes defined in the following way

$$\mathbf{L}(i,j) = \left(x^0 + \Delta x \cdot j, \ y^0 + \Delta y \cdot i \right), \quad i = 0, 1, ...m, j = 0, 1, ...n \tag{4}$$

where Δx, Δy are the discretization steps such that the index $j = 0$ corresponds to the initial point $\mathbf{p}^0$ and the index $j = n$ corresponds to the target point $\mathbf{p}^g$. Using such presentation the desired trajectory can be presented as the sequence of the nodes

$$\mathbf{L}(i_0, 0) \rightarrow \mathbf{L}(i_1, 1) \rightarrow \ ... \ \rightarrow \mathbf{L}(i_{n-1}, n-1) \rightarrow \mathbf{L}(i_n, n) \tag{5}$$

with the purely geometric definition of the distances between the successive nodes as

$$dist\{\mathbf{L}(i,j), \ \mathbf{L}(i',j+1)\} = \sqrt{\Delta y^2 \cdot (i' - i)^2 + \Delta x^2} \tag{6}$$

To take into account possible collisions between the robot end-effector and the workspace obstacles, let us also define the binary matrix B of size $m \times n$ whose elements $\mathbf{B}(i,j) \in \{0, \ 1\}$ are equal to zero if there is no collision between the manipulator end-effector and the workspace obstacles at the node $\mathbf{L}(i,j)$, (otherwise, it is equal to one). It is worth mentioning that the above presentation neglects the robot end-effector dimensions and presents it as a point. For this reason, while computing the matrix $\mathbf{B}$ it is reasonable to modify slightly the obstacle models and increase their dimensions by the value of $\sqrt{a^2 + b^2}$, where a, b are the geometric parameters of the manipulator segments (see Fig. 1).

Such formalization operating with the discretized task space $\{\mathbf{L}(i,j)\}$, which includes the obstacles defined by the binary matrix $\mathbf{B}$, allows us to present the original problem of the collision-free path planning for the manipulator end-effector as the classical shortest-path searching on the graph: *find the optimal path* (5) *on the graph connecting adjacent columns of* $\{\mathbf{L}(i,j)\}$, *which* (i) *connects the given nodes* $\mathbf{L}(i_0, 0)$ *and* $\mathbf{L}(i_n, n)$, (ii) *passes through allowable nodes only* $\mathbf{B}(i,j) = 0$ *and* (iii) *satisfies the optimization criterion*

$$\sum_{j=0}^{n-1} dist\{\mathbf{L}(i_j, j), \quad \mathbf{L}(i_{j+1}, j+1)\} \rightarrow \min_{\{i\}} \tag{7}$$

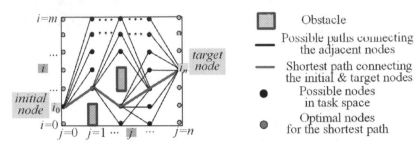

▢	Obstacle
—	Possible paths connecting the adjacent nodes
—	Shortest path connecting the initial & target nodes
●	Possible nodes in task space
◉	Optimal nodes for the shortest path

Fig. 2. Generation of the obstacle-free path using discrete dynamic programming

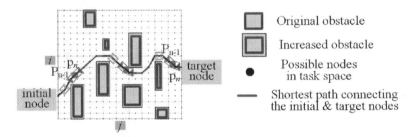

▢	Original obstacle
▢	Increased obstacle
●	Possible nodes in task space
—	Shortest path connecting the initial & target nodes

Fig. 3. Example of obstacle-free path generation for the robot end-effector.

It should be noted that for such presentation the desired trajectory is defined by the sequence of the row indices $\{i_0, i_1, ..., i_n\}$, where both i_0 and i_n are given (they are defined by the initial and target points). It is clear that this shortest-path problem can be solved via the discrete dynamic programming that is based on the following expression

$$d_{j+1}^*(i') = \min_i \left\{ d_j^*(i) + dist\{\mathbf{L}(i,j), \quad \mathbf{L}(i', j+1)\} \right\}, \quad \forall i' = 0, 1, ..., m \tag{8}$$

where $d_j^*(i)$ denotes the shortest distance between the initial node $\mathbf{L}(i_0, 0)$ and the node $\mathbf{L}(i,j)$ corresponding to the optimization of the lower dimension ($j \leq n$). This expression is applied sequentially starting from $j = 1$ and ending with $j = n\text{-}1$, and memorizing the row indices $\{i_1^*, ..., i_{n-1}^*\}$ obtained from (5) and corresponding to all intermediate optimal paths. At the final step, a single node $\mathbf{L}(i_n^*, n)$ corresponding to the desired endpoint is selected, and the desired solution is obtained through the backtracking allowing to find the remaining row indices $\{i_1^*, ..., i_{n-1}^*\}$ describing the optimal path. Geometric explanation of this technique is given in Fig. 2, where the spatial location of the initial and target points corresponds to the motion "from left to right".

The efficiency of this technique has been confirmed by the simulation study. An example of obstacle-free path generation with the discretization of 20×20 is presented in Fig. 3. It should be mentioned that here, to take into account the end-effector size, the obstacles were slightly increased. As follows from this study, for such relatively rough discretization the algorithm is very fast. However, for finer discretization the computing time may increase significantly.

To overcome this difficulty, a two-step modification of the path-generation algorithm was also proposed. The basic idea of the proposed modification (leading to the algorithm speed-up) is to find first an initial solution with the rough discretization, and to improve it further using a relatively small discretization step (and applying at both steps the same numerical technique based on the discrete dynamic programming). Geometric explanation of this approach is presented in Fig. 4, where at the first step the task space is divided into several big areas $\mathbf{S}(u, v)$, $u \subset \{0, 1, ...m\}$, $v = \{0, 1, ...n\}$.

Then after applying the proposed technique, the confident areas in every column in the task space could be found, which contain the possible points for connecting the shortest path, and the corresponding trajectory could be obtained with the indices expressed as $\mathbf{S}(u_0, 0) \rightarrow \mathbf{S}(u_1, 1) \rightarrow ... \rightarrow \mathbf{S}(u_{n-1}, n-1) \rightarrow \mathbf{S}(u_n, n)$. As the second step, it is only necessary to search for the points $\mathbf{L}(i_v, v) \in \mathbf{S}(u_v, v)$ inside of the confident areas obtained from the first step. It is clear that this approach allows us to increase significantly the computing speed.

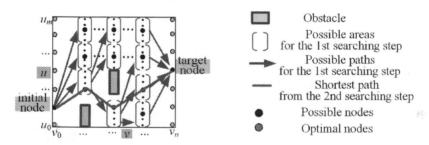

Fig. 4. Speed-up of the algorithm for obstacle-free path generation for the robot end-effector

4   Motion Generation for the Manipulator Body

To generate motions for the manipulator body it is necessary to use the best way of the manipulator redundancy, which in our case can be treated as simultaneous achievement of two goals: (i) *minimization of the joint motions for the desired end-effector location*; (ii) *ensuring safe distances between the manipulator segments and the obstacles*. The first of them can be presented as the minimization of the joint increments $\Delta \mathbf{q}$

$$\sum_{i=1}^{n} \Delta \mathbf{q}_i^{\mathrm{T}} \cdot \Delta \mathbf{q} \rightarrow \min_{\Delta \mathbf{q}} \qquad (9)$$

subject to the geometric constraint

$$\Delta \mathbf{p} = \mathbf{J}_e \cdot \Delta \mathbf{q} \tag{10}$$

arising from the desired end-effector displacement $\Delta \mathbf{p}$ computing via the kinematic Jacobian $\mathbf{J}_e$ of the manipulator end-effector. It is known that these constraint optimization problems can be easily solved analytically via the Jacobian pseudo-inverse

$$\Delta \mathbf{q} = \mathbf{J}_e^T \left(\mathbf{J}_e \mathbf{J}_e^T \right)^{-1} \Delta \mathbf{p} \tag{11}$$

However, to take into account the second goal (collision avoidance), it is necessary to impose some additional constraints arising from the safety distances between the obstacles and the manipulator intermediate segments. It can be proved that these distances can be computed in the following way

$$d_{ij} \triangleq dist(\mathbf{p}_i, {}^0\mathbf{p}_j) \geq d_j^0, \qquad \forall i = 1, 2, ...n; \quad \forall j = 1, 2, ..., m \tag{12}$$

where d_{ij} denotes the distance between the ith joint center and the jth obstacle, and d_j^0 is the allowable minimum value for the jth obstacle that takes into account its size (equivalent radius). In more detail, these definitions are explained in Fig. 5, where the joint axis locations are described by the points $\{\mathbf{p}_i, \forall i\}$ and the obstacles are approximated by the circles with the centers $\{{}^0\mathbf{p}_j\}$ and radiuses $\{r_j\}$.

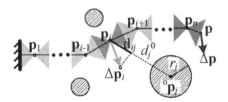

Fig. 5. Computing the distances dij between the robot joints and obstacles.

To present these additional constraints more conveniently, let us use the linearized expression $\Delta \mathbf{p}_i = \mathbf{J}_i \cdot \Delta \mathbf{q}$ for the manipulator joints, where $\mathbf{J}_i$ is computed from (2). Such linearization allows us to present $dist(\mathbf{p}_i, {}^0\mathbf{p}_j)$ as the projection of the displacement vector $\Delta \mathbf{p}_i$ onto the line segment connecting the points $\mathbf{p}_i$ and ${}^0\mathbf{p}_j$ (see Fig. 5), i.e.

$$d_{ij} = \mathbf{e}_{ij}^T \cdot \mathbf{J}_i \cdot \Delta \mathbf{q} \tag{13}$$

where the unit vector $\mathbf{e}_{ij}$ is computed as $\mathbf{e}_{ij} = (\mathbf{p}_i - {}^0\mathbf{p}_j)/\|\mathbf{p}_i - {}^0\mathbf{p}_j\|$.

So finally, for the n segment manipulator with m different task space obstacles, the $m \times n$ collision-free constraints can be rewritten as the following way

$$\mathbf{e}_{ij}^T \cdot \mathbf{J}_i \cdot \Delta \mathbf{q} - d_j^0 \geq 0, \quad i = 1, 2, ...n; \quad j = 1, 2, ..., m \tag{14}$$

where the safety parameter $d_j^0 = r_j + \sqrt{a^2 + b^2}$ is computed taking into account both the obstacle equivalent radius r_j and the manipulator geometric parameters a, b.

Curved line motion with (x, y, φ) control

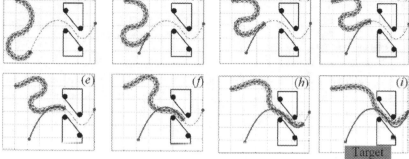

Fig. 6. Example of collision-free motion control for the multi-segment manipulator.

Hence, the original optimization problem with the quadratic objective (9) and linear equality constraint (10) is transformed to a more general one, which includes both the linear equality constraint (10) and a number of linear non-equality constraints (14). The main particularity of this mixed optimization problem is related to the influence of the non-equality constraints. In particular, some of them can be stronger than the other ones, leading to the situation when a limited number of non-equalities are active. In this work, it is proposed the following technique to solve this optimization problem:

1. First, try to release all non-equality constraints and find the optimal solution $\Delta \mathbf{q}^*$ of this reduced problem from (11).
2. For the obtained solution $\Delta \mathbf{q}^*$, verify all non-equality constraints (14) and find those that are violated. If no one of the constraints is violated, the final solution is obtained.
3. If some of the non-equality constraints are violated, the strongest of them is selected for each joint and transformed into the equality constraint.
4. Then the problem is solved for the extended set of equality constraints and the obtained new optimal solution $\Delta \mathbf{q}^*$ is evaluated by starting from step 2.

To find the optimal solution for the extended optimization problem at step 4, the Lagrange technique can be applied dealing with the minimization of the function

$$L(\Delta \mathbf{q}, \lambda, \mu) = \Delta \mathbf{q}^T \Delta \mathbf{q} + \lambda^T \cdot (\mathbf{J} \cdot \Delta \mathbf{q} - \Delta \mathbf{p}) + \sum_{active} \mu_{ij} \left(\mathbf{e}_{ij}^T \cdot \mathbf{J}_i \cdot \Delta \mathbf{q} - d_j^0 \right) \rightarrow \min$$

$$(15)$$

which leads to the following linear system

$$\Delta \mathbf{q} - \lambda^T \cdot \mathbf{J} - \mu^T \cdot \mathbf{J}_a = \mathbf{0}; \quad \mathbf{J} \cdot \Delta \mathbf{q} - \Delta \mathbf{p} = \mathbf{0}; \quad \mathbf{J}_a \cdot \Delta \mathbf{q} - \mathbf{d}_a = \mathbf{0} \quad (16)$$

where the matrix $\mathbf{J}_a$ and the vector $\mathbf{d}_a$ are composed of elements $\mathbf{e}_{ij}^T \cdot \mathbf{J}_i$ and d_j^0 corresponding to the active constraints, and λ and μ are the Lagrange multipliers. It is clear that this system can be solved in a usual way via the matrix pseudo-inverse. The efficiency of the develop technique is confirmed by the simulation results presented in Fig. 6, where the manipulator end-effector must follow the curved path located inside of the narrow gap between the obstacles.

5 Conclusion

The paper proposes a new method of redundancy resolution in kinematic control of a new type of serial manipulator, which is moving in the multi-obstacle environment. Because of their specific design including not only rigid components but also elastic elements, such manipulators allow achieving excellent flexibility and ability of shape-changing in accordance with the environment. However, kinematic control of such manipulators requires redundancy resolution taking into account possible collisions of the robot end-effector and its body with the obstacles. To find the desired robot motion, the general problem is decomposed in two sub-problems, which deal with collision-free path planning for the robot end-effector and collision-free motion planning for the robot body. The first of them is solved via discrete dynamic programming, the second one is worked out using quadratic programming with mixed linear equality/non-equality constraints. The efficiency of the proposed technique is confirmed by simulation. In the future, this technique will be extended for the 3D manipulator with similar tensegrity segments.

References

1. Arsenault, M., Gosselin, C.M.: Kinematic, static and dynamic analysis of a planar 2-DOF tensegrity mechanism. Mech. Mach. Theory **41**, 1072–1089 (2006)
2. Furet, M., Lettl, M., Wenger, P.: Kinematic analysis of planar tensegrity 2-X manipulators. In: Lenarcic, J., Parenti-Castelli, V. (eds.) ARK 2018. SPAR, vol. 8, pp. 153–160. Springer, Cham (2019). https://doi.org/10.1007/978-3-319-93188-3_18
3. Wenger, P., Chablat, D.: Kinetostatic analysis and solution classification of a class of planar tensegrity mechanisms. Robotica **37**, 1214–1224 (2019)
4. Zhao, W., Pashkevich, A., Klimchik, A., Chablat, D.: Stiffness analysis of a new tensegrity mechanism based on planar dual-triangles. Presented at the 17th International Conference on Informatics in Control, Automation and Robotics, pp. 402–411 (2020)
5. Cai, B., Zhang, Y.: Different-level redundancy-resolution and its equivalent relationship analysis for robot manipulators using gradient-descent and zhang 's neural-dynamic methods. IEEE Trans. Industr. Electron. **59**, 3146–3155 (2012)
6. Tanaka, M., Matsuno, F.: Modeling and control of head raising snake robots by using kinematic redundancy. J. Intell. Rob. Syst. **75**(1), 53–69 (2013). https://doi.org/10.1007/s10846-013-9866-y

Automatic Drones for Factory Inspection: The Role of Virtual Simulation

Omid Maghazei$^{(\boxtimes)}$ ⓘ, Torbjørn H. Netland ⓘ, Dirk Frauenberger,
and Tobias Thalmann

ETH Zürich, Zürich, Switzerland
omaghazei@ethz.ch

Abstract. Manufacturers experiment with the use of drones for various processes such as surveillance, inspection, cycle counting, and intralogistics, but implementation into routine operations remains rare. One reason for low adoption rates relates to the manual control requirements of most drone systems. This paper studies the use of automatic drones in manufacturing. A virtual simulation of drone flights in a manufacturing facility was developed to identify and evaluate the potential of automatic drones for thermal inspection of injection molding machines. This paper reports the implementation of the virtual simulation and discusses how such simulations can inform the use of automatic drones for factory inspections.

Keywords: Unmanned aerial vehicles · Automatic drones · Virtual simulation

1 Introduction

Unmanned vehicles, such as automated guided vehicles (AGV), can take over routine tasks previously done by humans. Automated vehicles require advanced algorithms to detect and avoid static and moving obstacles [1], as well as systems for path planning and traffic management [2]. Mobility becomes an order of magnitude more difficult when the vehicle moves through the air. Yet unmanned aerial vehicles (UAVs)—popularly known as drones—have high potential in both outdoor and indoor manufacturing environments [3].

Indoor industrial applications of drones are much less common than outdoor applications [3]. For example, drones are already finding applications in emergency operations [4], infrastructure maintenance [5], logistics [6], and warehouse management [7]. Indoor drone flights pose additional challenges compared to outdoor flights, such as navigation, obstacle detection, explosion risk, and collision avoidance in the three-dimensional (3D) factory space [8]. There is also a considerable risk to both humans and assets involved when drone systems fail in indoor environments. Other limiting factors are noise and privacy concerns. Most importantly, established alternatives to drones such as floor-based AGVs, conveyor belts, and wall- or roof-mounted cameras and sensors can do many of the tasks usually attributed as potential applications of drones (e.g., surveillance, inspection, or intralogistics).

Published by Springer Nature Switzerland AG 2021
A. Dolgui et al. (Eds.): APMS 2021, IFIP AICT 633, pp. 457–464, 2021.
https://doi.org/10.1007/978-3-030-85910-7_48

From an industrial management perspective, the challenge is to identify niche applications where drones can outcompete existing technologies in terms of accessibility, speed, safety, cost, or accuracy—or do tasks not previously carried out by any other technology. To address this challenge, the authors engaged in field research with a leading manufacturer of products for household construction, Household Inc. The authors identified several potential use cases and employed piloted drones to test the use cases' feasibility. High potential was found in using drones in routine inspections of thermal losses in injection molding machines, which would normally require manual inspection. However, with piloted drones, the return on investment would be marginal because a human operator would still be needed. It was concluded that the use case is viable, but only with automated drones.

It is not without reason that most reported drone implementations in manufacturing use piloted drones [9]. Automated drone technology is still subject to basic research [10] and—at the time of writing—is only used for "simple" tasks such as cycle counting in warehouses. This paper seeks to address this limitation using the simulation of automated drone inspection flights in the factory floor environment of Household Inc. The purpose is to demonstrate the role of simulation for automated drones and identify challenges and opportunities for real implementation in manufacturing.

2   Simulation of Automatic Drone Flights

Automation is defined as the partial or full replacement of a human operator's intended task (e.g., decision selection) with a machine agent, usually a computer [11]. There are various approaches to classify the 'level of automation' of drones. This study uses a framework that classifies drone automation in five levels based on the level of involvement of drone pilots (see Table 1) [12, 13]. The literature recommends step-wise automation. This paper's primary focus is to examine the operational and technological challenges of moving from level 0, 'no automation,' to automatic drones indoors with level 2, 'partial automation.'

Table 1. Five levels of automation for drones (adapted from [12, 13])

Level 0	Level 1	Level 2	Level 3	Level 4	Level 5
None	Low	Partial	Conditional	High	Full
Entirely manual flight	Piloted flight with autopilot assistance	Automated flights with predefined waypoints, pilot supervision when necessary	Automated flight with waypoints and adaptive safety systems but with pilot involvement	Automated flight with failsafe systems, with no pilot involvement	Autonomous flight

Simulation is an established method in industrial engineering and management. It is a practical approach when field implementation is costly, risky, or impossible [14, 15].

Simulation can 'extend our understanding into the realm of possibility, imagination, and projection of future possibilities for pretesting yet-to-be-implemented possibilities' [16, p. 1196]. There is a wide range of simulation approaches, such as virtual simulation, system dynamics, discrete event simulation, Monte Carlo simulation, agent-based simulation, and intelligent simulation [see, 17]. This paper focuses on virtual simulation.

Virtual simulations can be used to visualize and test digital copies of smart factories (e.g., digital twins). It can help optimize current factory processes or avoid future failures. For instance, virtual simulations can allow for optimizing planning and maintenance decisions concerning the operations of a manufacturing system or assist in layout and factory planning. Virtual simulation also has potential in the study of intelligent robotics and industrial automation [18] by simulating and visualizing operations at the micro level using 3D graphics models [19].

3 Implementation of Drone Flight Simulation

In this study, a simulation was used to explore the potential of automated drones for the inspection of injection molding machines in Household Inc. The simulation model was based on an area of Household Inc.'s shop floor with nine injection molding machines. A simulation model mirroring the real shop floor was developed. The simulation model was implemented in five steps.

The first step was to simulate drone operations. The research team used Gazebo, an open-source '3D dynamic simulator with the ability to accurately and efficiently simulate populations of robots in complex indoor and outdoor environments' [20]. Gazebo was installed on a Linux operating system (OS) with a Ubuntu OS that supports the robot operating system (ROS)—a collection of tools, libraries, and conventions that helps software developers to build robot applications [21, 22]. Then RotorS, a modular drone simulation framework, was used to assemble a drone in Gazebo [22]. Figure 1 shows the real AscTec Firefly hex-rotor drone from Ascending Technologies (owned by Intel) and the simulated Firefly drone in Gazebo.

(a)   (b)

Fig. 1. (a) Real AscTec Firefly drone; (b) Simulated Firefly hex-rotor drone in Gazebo.

The modular framework included drone components, namely, a body, a fixed number of rotors, and sensors attached to the body (e.g., inertial measurement unit, a generic odometry sensor, a visual-inertial sensor, and sensors developed by the user), all of which were 'designed to be analogous to its real-world counterparts' [22, p. 595]. The framework also included a position controller to access various levels of commands and a state estimator to obtain information about the drone state [22]. The RotorS simulator provided a fully functional trajectory tracking controller, which allowed for implementing higher-level tasks such as collision avoidance, path planning, and vision-based problems [22].

The second step was to simulate the environment for drone operations by building a virtual factory. Dimensions, appearance, and positions were measured and noted in the same production area, where the human-assisted drone experiment had been conducted [23]. The digital model of the shop floor was created in Fusion 360 software. Having knowledge about the operating environment helped better determine the drone path for precise navigation in a global positioning system–denied environment [see 24].

The third step was to define feasible airspace areas or corridors for the safe operation of automatic drones in factories, in part due to the air turbulence generated around drones. In this study, a safe area was defined by following the suggested flying space boundary [see, 8], allocating a 50 cm safety distance around the drone. An area was designated for safe take-off and landing for the automatic drone. Figure 2 shows the 3D model of the safe flight zone in the factory.

Fig. 2. 3D model of the safe flight zone in the shop floor by Fusion 360.

The fourth step was to develop flight scenarios. In this study, two scenarios were defined based on a trade-off between drone flight duration and coverage. Each scenario consisted of a flight trajectory with predefined waypoints for thermal inspection of the nine injection molding machines. The scenarios considered obstacles in the indoor physical environments that limited the maneuverability of automatic drone flights. The scale and duration of drone operations were also limited by current battery technologies. The first scenario was described as 'quick and limited' and designed to collect data from restricted angles (see Fig. 3a) through 49 waypoints. The second scenario was described as 'slow and detailed' and designed to collect more data from each machine from multiple available angles in the safe zone, most notably by going on top of the machines with movable robotic arms (see Fig. 3b) through 163 waypoints.

The final step was to launch the simulation of drone flights in the virtual factory in Gazebo. Figure 4 shows the file structure of the simulation model that combines the files from RotorS, including both unchanged and changed libraries, Gazebo files, waypoints from Microsoft Excel software, and a 3D model of the shop floor from Fusion 360 software. Having combined the various files in Gazebo allowed for the development of AscTec drone flights in the 3D model of the company's shop floor.

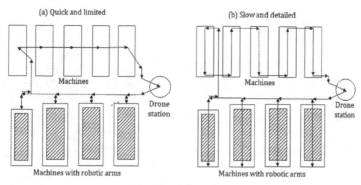

Fig. 3. A schematic representation of the (a) quick and limited scenario and (b) slow and detailed simulated drone flight scenarios.

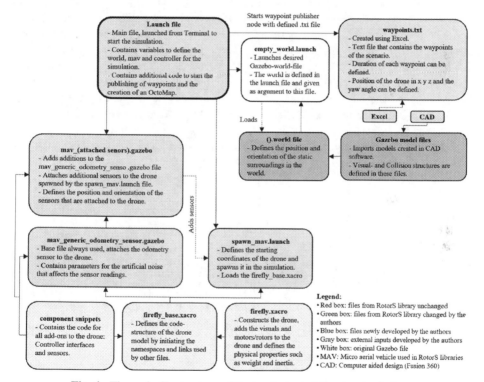

Fig. 4. The main file structure of the implemented Gazebo simulation.

4   Results and Discussion

The virtual model simulated drone flights close to the real behavior of automated drones. It allowed for no-risk virtual tests and exploration of technological and operational opportunities and challenges of using automatic drones indoors. In this study, the simulation runs were evaluated on the basis of speed and safety.

The quick and limited model, with 49 waypoints, took 3 min and 52 s. The slow and detailed scenario, with 163 waypoints, required 5 min and 47 s. In the case of Household Inc., both these durations were acceptable and considerably faster than manual inspections, which were estimated to on average 90 min for 9 machines (10 min per machine including preparations and breaks). Household Inc.'s production plant in Switzerland has 80 injection molding machines that are currently manually inspected four times a year. In a scenario with automated drones, inspections could be run much more frequently.

Concerning the safety assessment, a 50 cm flying-space boundary was considered the minimum safety requirement by Household Inc. For some automatic drone flights, particularly for the inspection of machines with movable robotic arms, this safety distance was classified as risky. To assess potential risks for the two scenarios, an analysis of the minimum distance of the drone from three particularly critical machines with robotic arms was conducted (i.e., the three first machines in Fig. 3(a) and 3(b)). The drone's minimum distance to any object in the area 90° straight down and 45° to the front was measured. This view resembled the effective coverage area of the thermal camera. A Python script was written that read the depth sensor data published by the drone over the ROS channels. This sensor provided a point cloud, each point representing an observation of a surface. The script iterated for each published set (i.e., frame) through each point and determined the one closest to the drone. This minimal distance was then logged in a text file. Figure 5 shows the result of this test. It compares the two scenarios according to potential risks, defined as any flight position closer than 1 m from an object. The horizontal axis represents the flight completion percentage, and the vertical axis shows the minimum distance measures of the down-view to objects. The quick and limited and slow and detailed scenarios had 0 and 13 potential risks, respectively.

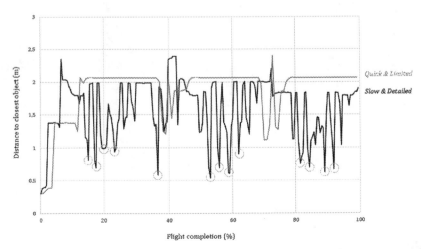

Fig. 5. Minimum distance measures for the two scenarios.

The results demonstrated that the virtual simulation helped Household Inc. evaluate the potential of automatic drones for thermography inspection and could quickly be adapted for different use cases and scenarios. The potential implementation of automated, routine thermal inspection of injection molding machines could help increase productivity at Household Inc. The company could discover heat losses and irregularities earlier than it can now, which could (1) reduce defective parts produced or improve the material quality of products, (2) increase machine uptime, (3) reduce maintenance time (e.g., by reducing time to search for undetected heat losses, sources of oil leakages, and defective band heaters, isolations, and cooling systems), and (4) reduce energy costs. The potential savings to maintenance costs alone were estimated to be USD 24,000 annually by Household Inc. managers. Given that the technology would be available, safe, and cost-efficient to implement and operate, there should be a positive business case for automated drone flights for inspection. With the current development of drone technology, such implementation could be possible within the next few years.

5 Conclusions

Automatic drones can improve indoor manufacturing processes, particularly repetitive tasks such as inspection operations, intralogistics for small parts, cycle counting in warehouses, security monitoring, ergonomic monitoring, risk monitoring, and building-information modeling. Implementing automatic drones involves considerable technological and operational challenges. This paper showed that virtual simulations can animate automatic drone flights in 3D and help better understand the technological and operational challenges of using new technologies in real manufacturing environments and support decision-making and problem-solving processes. For instance, factory planners can use simulation models to evaluate, allocate, and design airspace for drone flights. Virtual simulation of automatic drones also helps set and define safe flight zones for indoor airspace, which helps quickly evaluate various scenarios, such as trade-offs between coverage, speed, and risks. Furthermore, factory managers can use 3D models to communicate and collaborate with drone technology developers, as well as sensor manufacturers and robotics companies, by virtually presenting the technological requirements of using automatic drones with embedded sensors/technologies in their settings. For instance, primary metal companies would require drones and thermal cameras that can cope with high temperatures, petrochemical companies require explosion-proof drone systems, and e-commerce warehouses may benefit from collaborative drone technologies (i.e., swarming) with advanced path planning and fleet management systems.

References

1. Franke, J., Lütteke, F.: Versatile autonomous transportation vehicle for highly flexible use in industrial applications. CIRP Ann. **61**(1), 407–410 (2012)
2. Gyulai, D., Bergmann, J., Váncza, J.: Adaptive network analytics for managing complex shop-floor logistics systems. CIRP Ann. **69**(1), 393–396 (2020)
3. Maghazei, O., Netland, T.: Drones in manufacturing: exploring opportunities for research and practice. J. Manuf. Technol. Manag. **31**(6), 1237–1259 (2019)
4. Park, Y., Moon, I.: UAV set covering problem for emergency network. In: Ameri, F., Stecke, K.E., von Cieminski, G., Kiritsis, D. (eds.) APMS 2019. IAICT, vol. 567, pp. 84–90. Springer, Cham (2019). https://doi.org/10.1007/978-3-030-29996-5_10

5. Maghazei, O., Steinmann, M.: Drones in railways: exploring current applications and future scenarios based on action research. Eur. J. Transp. Infrastr. Res. **20**(3), 87–102 (2020)
6. Herrera, S., Cervantes, A.: The Drones Are Coming! How Amazon, Alphabet and Uber Are Taking to the Skies. https://www.wsj.com/articles/the-drones-are-coming-11571995806. Accessed 30 September 2019
7. Wawrla, L., Maghazei, O., Netland, T.: Applications of Drones in Warehouse Operations. Whitepaper, D-MTEC, ETH Zurich (2019)
8. Khosiawan, Y., Nielsen, I.: A system of UAV application in indoor environment. Prod. Manuf. Res. **4**(1), 2–22 (2016)
9. Mazur, M., Wiśniewski, A.: Clarity from Above. https://www.pwc.pl/en/publikacje/2016/clarity-from-above.html. Accessed 22 July 2019
10. Floreano, D., Wood, R.J.: Science, technology and the future of small autonomous drones. Nature **521**(7553), 460–466 (2015)
11. Parasuraman, R., Riley, V.: Humans and automation: use, misuse, disuse, abuse. Hum. Fact. **39**(2), 230–253 (1997)
12. Nanduri, A.: Building the Autonomous Future. https://nari.arc.nasa.gov/sites/default/files/attachments/6%20Nanduri-Building%20the%20Autonomous%20Future.pdf. Accessed 18 July 2020
13. Radovic, M.: Tech Talk: Untangling the 5 Levels of Drone Autonomy. https://www.droneii.com/project/drone-autonomy-levels. Accessed 20 Mar 2019
14. Shafer, S.M., Smunt, T.L.: Empirical simulation studies in operations management: context, trends, and research opportunities. J. Oper. Manag. **22**(4), 345–354 (2004)
15. Negahban, A., Smith, J.S.: Simulation for manufacturing system design and operation: literature review and analysis. J. Manuf. Syst. **33**(2), 241–261 (2014)
16. Burton, R.M., Obel, B.: Computational modeling for what-is, what-might-be, and what-should-be studies—and triangulation. Organ. Sci. **22**(5), 1195–1202 (2011)
17. Jahangirian, M., Eldabi, T., Naseer, A., Stergioulas, L.K., Young, T.: Simulation in manufacturing and business: a review. Eur. J. Oper. Res. **203**(1), 1–13 (2010)
18. Posada, J., et al.: Visual computing as a key enabling technology for Industrie 4.0 and industrial internet. IEEE Comput. Graph. Appl. **35**(2), 26–40 (2015)
19. Orady, E.A., Osman, T., Bailo, C.P.: Virtual reality software for robotics and manufacturing cell simulation. Comput. Ind. Eng. **33**(1–2), 87–90 (1997)
20. Gazebo. Why Gazebo? http://gazebosim.org/. Accessed 08 Mar 2020
21. ROS, Documentation. http://wiki.ros.org/. Accessed 28 Feb 2020
22. Furrer, F., Burri, M., Achtelik, M., Siegwart, R.: Rotors—a modular Gazebo Mav simulator framework. In: Koubaa, A. (ed.) Robot Operating System (ROS). SCI, vol. 625, pp. 595–625. Springer, Cham (2016). https://doi.org/10.1007/978-3-319-26054-9_23
23. Zhong, Y., Shirinzadeh, B.: Virtual factory for manufacturing process visualization. Complex. Int. **12**(1), 1–22 (2008)
24. De Croon, G., De Wagter, C.: Challenges of autonomous flight in indoor environments. In: IEEE/RSJ International Conference on Intelligent Robots and Systems (IROS), Madrid, Spain, pp. 1003–1009 (2018)

Geometric Error Modeling and Sensitivity Analysis of a Laser Pipe-Cutting System Based on Lie Group and Sobol Method

Yuze Jiang, Wenyu Yang[(⊠)], Liang Qin, and Tong Ding

School of Mechanical Science and Engineering, Huazhong University of Science and Technology, Wuhan 430074, China
mewyang@hust.edu.cn

Abstract. Laser pipe-cutting system, a special machine tool, has been widely used in the precision machining of metal pipe. The geometric errors remarkably affect the machining accuracy of products. Error modeling and sensitivity analysis are key issues to improve the product quality. In this paper, the geometric error model of the laser pipe-cutting system which contains 70 geometric errors is established based on multi-body theory and Lie group. The coupling effects caused by two chucks are considered as the spatial angular deviation in modeling. The sensitivity analysis for the geometric error model is conducted to identify the essential sensitivity errors based on an improved Sobol method with quasi-Monte Carlo algorithm. The results show that not only the linear positioning errors, but also the squareness errors and parallelism errors play crucial roles in the machining accuracy. Based on the result, the essential sensitivity errors are calibrated and the machining accuracy is improved.

Keywords: Lie group · Geometric error model · Sobol method · Error sensitivity analysis

1 Introduction

Precision pipes produced by laser cutting are widely used in medical equipment, aerospace and other fields. The feeding accuracy of the pipe feeding system plays an important role in the product quality. Considered as a multi-body system, the geometric error model of the laser pipe-cutting system needs to be established to predict the deviation between the desired and actual position of the working point.

Over the past decades, scholars have employed many approaches in the geometric error modeling, and got many noteworthy achievements. Abbaszadeh-mir [1] used homogeneous transform matrix (HTM) to build the geometric error model of a five-axis machine tool, and identified the sensitive errors based on the sensitivity Jacobian matrix. Zhu [2] established the geometric error model of a five-axis machine tool considered of the PIGEs and PDGEs based on HTM. To express the kinematic chain more clearly, the Lie group [3] is introduced to formulate the geometric error model which only needs to

© IFIP International Federation for Information Processing 2021
Published by Springer Nature Switzerland AG 2021
A. Dolgui et al. (Eds.): APMS 2021, IFIP AICT 633, pp. 465–472, 2021.
https://doi.org/10.1007/978-3-030-85910-7_49

establish the reference frame and end effector frame. Cheng [4] studied the geometric error model of a five-axis machine tool based on POE model and identified the essential errors with Morris sensitivity analysis. Xiang [5] established a novel method to represent PIGEs and PDGEs using POE model, which was applied to the five-axis machine. Also, the Lie group describes the motion according to its geometric property. Hence, the Lie group theory is suitable for solving kinematic problems of multi-degree-of-freedom complex machinery, and is widely used.

Based on the geometrical error model, sensitivity analysis can estimate the influences of each errors on machining accuracy and identify the critical errors. Common sensitivity analysis methods can be determined as local sensitivity analysis and global sensitivity analysis. As a well-known global sensitivity analysis approach, Sobol method [6] is applied to the sensitivity analysis for complex multi-body system, which can estimate the contribution and coupling effect of errors in the whole workspace. Zou [7] applied the Sobol method to a three-axis diamond turning machine, and identified the crucial errors between 18 geometric errors. Xia [8] established the geometric error model of a gear grinding machine tool and analyzed the error sensitivity based on Sobol method, which reduced the tooth surface errors by 68.75%.

Few researches of geometrical error modeling have been made about the machine tools with two chucks or two spindles, except Liu [9]. In [9], he considered the dual-spindle ultra-precision drum roll lathe as a combination of a five-axis machine tool and a virtual C' axis which was ignored in the error modeling. Therefore, the aim of this paper is (I) to establish the geometrical error model of the laser pipe-cutting system considering the coupling effect between two chucks, (II) to identify the essential sensitivity errors for the calibration.

The rest of the paper is organized as follows. In Sect. 2, the geometrical error model of the laser pipe-cutting system is established based on the topological structure and Lie group. The global sensitivity analysis of the error model is implemented to identify the essential sensitivity errors using an improved Sobol method in Sect. 3. Finally, the conclusions are presented in Sect. 4.

2   Geometric Error Modeling Based on Lie Group

The pose of the multi-body system with respect to the base frame can be described by Lie group theory. For an open chain with n-dof, the forward kinematic can be written as:

$$T = e^{\hat{\xi}_1 \theta_1} \cdots e^{\hat{\xi}_n \theta_n} \cdot T(0) \tag{1}$$

where ξ_n and θ_n represent the twist and joint variable of the nth joint. $T(0)$ is the initial transformation matrix. The Eq. (1), which is known as POE model, can be used in error modeling of multi-body system. More details can be referenced to Dai [10].

In classical machine tool modeling, the two open-chain kinematic loops, which are workpiece and tool kinematic loop, are closed at the tool-workpiece contact point. The geometric error model is established based on the relative position and orientation of the contact point between two loops. The schematic diagram of the laser pipe-cutting system is illustrated in Fig. 1. In the system we introduced, the main chuck and feeding chuck clamp the pipe simultaneously, which means the workpiece kinematic loop is not a serial chain. According to the characteristics above, the workpiece kinematic model is divided in two levels. The first level is the transformer from the bed to the jaws, named as $0\text{-}1\text{-}2\text{-}3.N$ and $0\text{-}4\text{-}5.N$, which computes the clamping concentricity of two chucks. Based on the concentricity errors, the pose of pipe is deduced to estimate the actual location of the working point as the second level.

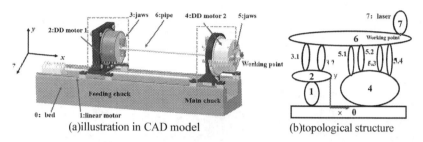

(a)illustration in CAD model   (b)topological structure

Fig. 1. Structural diagram of the laser pipe-cutting system

As Fig. 1 shown, the main chuck with 4 orthogonal jaws is fixed on the bed. The feeding chuck with only 2 jaws is located on a linear motor which provides the motion in X-direction as the feeding process. The jaws move to the central axis until the pipe is clamped by two chucks simultaneously. The twists of each part related to the machine frame are as follow:

$$\xi_{01} = \begin{bmatrix} 0\ 0\ 0\ 1\ 0\ 0 \end{bmatrix}^{T}$$
$$\xi_{12} = \begin{bmatrix} 1\ 0\ 0\ 0\ 0\ 0 \end{bmatrix}^{T}$$
$$\xi_{23.1} = \xi_{23.2} = \begin{bmatrix} 0\ 0\ 0\ 0\ 1\ 0 \end{bmatrix}^{T}$$
$$\xi_{04} = \begin{bmatrix} 1\ 0\ 0\ 0\ 0\ 0 \end{bmatrix}^{T} \qquad (2)$$
$$\xi_{45.1} = \xi_{45.2} = \begin{bmatrix} 0\ 0\ 0\ 0\ 1\ 0 \end{bmatrix}^{T}$$
$$\xi_{45.3} = \xi_{45.4} = \begin{bmatrix} 0\ 0\ 0\ 0\ 0\ 1 \end{bmatrix}^{T}$$

where $\xi_{23.1}$, $\xi_{23.2}$ are the twists of jaws on the feeding chuck. $\xi_{45.1}, \xi_{45.2}, \xi_{45.3}, \xi_{45.4}$ are the twists of jaws on the main chuck. Based on the design of opposing-jaw linkage, the relationships between jaw motion variables are $Y_{23.1} = -Y_{23.2}$, $Y_{45.1} = -Y_{45.2}$, $Z_{45.3} = -Z_{45.4}$.

According to Dai [10], the ideal POE models of each jaws are obtained as:

$$P_{03.1} = e^{\hat{\xi}_{01}X_{01}} \cdot e^{\hat{\xi}_{12}X_{12}} \cdot e^{\hat{\xi}_{23.1}Y_{23.1}} \cdot P_{03.1}(0)$$

$$P_{03.2} = e^{\hat{\xi}_{01}X_{01}} \cdot e^{\hat{\xi}_{12}\theta_{12}} \cdot e^{\hat{\xi}_{23.2}Y_{23.2}} \cdot P_{03.2}(0)$$

$$P_{05.1} = e^{\hat{\xi}_{04}\theta_{04}} \cdot e^{\hat{\xi}_{45.1}Y_{45.1}} \cdot P_{05.1}(0)$$

$$P_{05.2} = e^{\hat{\xi}_{04}\theta_{04}} \cdot e^{\hat{\xi}_{45.2}Y_{45.2}} \cdot P_{05.2}(0) \qquad (3)$$

$$P_{05.3} = e^{\hat{\xi}_{04}\theta_{04}} \cdot e^{\hat{\xi}_{45.3}Y_{45.3}} \cdot P_{05.3}(0)$$

$$P_{05.4} = e^{\hat{\xi}_{04}\theta_{04}} \cdot e^{\hat{\xi}_{45.4}Y_{45.4}} \cdot P_{05.4}(0)$$

According to the definition from both ISO 230-1 and ISO 230-7, 70 error components of PIGEs (position-independent geometric errors) and PDGE (position-dependent geometric errors) are taken into consideration, as shown in Table 1.

Table 1. Error components of pipe feeding system

Adjacent bodies	PDGEs	PIGEs	
		Squarenes errors	Parallelism errors
0–1	$\delta_{xX01}, \delta_{xY01}, \delta_{xZ01}$ $\varepsilon_{xX01}, \varepsilon_{xY01}, \varepsilon_{xZ01}$	–	
1–2	$\delta_{xX12}, \delta_{xY12}, \delta_{xZ12}$ $\varepsilon_{xX12}, \varepsilon_{xY12}, \varepsilon_{xZ12}$	–	$\kappa_{xZ12}, \kappa_{xY12}$
2–3.1	$\delta_{yX23.1}, \delta_{yY23.1}, \delta_{yZ23.1}$ $\varepsilon_{yX23.1}, \varepsilon_{yY23.1}, \varepsilon_{yZ23.1}$	$\beta_{yX23.1}, \beta_{yZ23.1}$	–
2–3.2	$\delta_{yX23.2}, \delta_{yY23.2}, \delta_{yZ23.2}$ $\varepsilon_{yX23.2}, \varepsilon_{yY23.2}, \varepsilon_{yZ23.2}$	$\beta_{yX23.2}, \beta_{yZ23.2}$	–
0–4	$\delta_{xX04}, \delta_{xY04}, \delta_{xZ04}$ $\varepsilon_{xX04}, \varepsilon_{xY04}, \varepsilon_{xZ04}$	–	$\kappa_{xZ04}, \kappa_{xY04}$
4–5.1	$\delta_{yX45.1}, \delta_{yY45.1}, \delta_{yZ45.1}$ $\varepsilon_{yX45.1}, \varepsilon_{yY45.1}, \varepsilon_{yZ45.1}$	$\beta_{yX45.1}, \beta_{yZ45.1}$	–
4–5.2	$\delta_{yX45.2}, \delta_{yY45.2}, \delta_{yZ45.2}$ $\varepsilon_{yX45.2}, \varepsilon_{yY45.2}, \varepsilon_{yZ45.2}$	$\beta_{yX45.2}, \beta_{yZ45.2}$	–
4–5.3	$\delta_{zX45.3}, \delta_{zY45.3}, \delta_{zZ45.3}$ $\varepsilon_{zX45.3}, \varepsilon_{zY45.3}, \varepsilon_{zZ45.3}$	$\beta_{zX45.3}, \beta_{zY45.3}$	–
4–5.4	$\delta_{zX45.4}, \delta_{zY45.4}, \delta_{zZ45.4}$ $\varepsilon_{zX45.4}, \varepsilon_{zY45.4}, \varepsilon_{zZ45.4}$	$\beta_{zX45.4}, \beta_{zY45.4}$	–

With the errors in Table.1, the actual POE models of the jaws can be written as [4]:

$$P^e_{03.1} = e^{\hat{\xi}_{01}}_{PDGE} e^{\hat{\xi}_{01}X_{01}} \cdot e^{\hat{\xi}_{12}}_{PIGE} e^{\hat{\xi}_{12}}_{PDGE} e^{\hat{\xi}_{12}\theta_{12}} \cdot e^{\hat{\xi}_{23.1}}_{PIGE} e^{\hat{\xi}_{23.1}}_{PDGE} e^{\hat{\xi}_{23.1}Y_{23.1}} \cdot P_{03.1}(0)$$

$$P^e_{03.2} = e^{\hat{\xi}_{01}}_{PDGE} e^{\hat{\xi}_{01}X_{01}} \cdot e^{\hat{\xi}_{12}}_{PIGE} e^{\hat{\xi}_{12}}_{PDGE} e^{\hat{\xi}_{12}\theta_{12}} \cdot e^{\hat{\xi}_{23.2}}_{PIGE} e^{\hat{\xi}_{23.2}}_{PDGE} e^{\hat{\xi}_{23.2}Y_{23.2}} \cdot P_{03.2}(0)$$

$$P^e_{05.1} = e^{\hat{\xi}_{04}}_{PIGE} e^{\hat{\xi}_{04}}_{PDGE} e^{\hat{\xi}_{04}\theta_{04}} \cdot e^{\hat{\xi}_{45.1}}_{PIGE} e^{\hat{\xi}_{45.1}}_{PDGE} e^{\hat{\xi}_{45.1}Y_{45.1}} \cdot P_{05.1}(0) \qquad (4)$$

$$P^e_{05.2} = e^{\hat{\xi}_{04}}_{PIGE} e^{\hat{\xi}_{04}}_{PDGE} e^{\hat{\xi}_{04}\theta_{04}} \cdot e^{\hat{\xi}_{45.2}}_{PIGE} e^{\hat{\xi}_{45.2}}_{PDGE} e^{-\hat{\xi}_{45.2}Y_{45.1}} \cdot P_{05.2}(0)$$

$$P^e_{05.3} = e^{\hat{\xi}_{04}}_{PIGE} e^{\hat{\xi}_{04}}_{PDGE} e^{\hat{\xi}_{04}\theta_{04}} \cdot e^{\hat{\xi}_{45.3}}_{PIGE} e^{\hat{\xi}_{45.3}}_{PDGE} e^{\hat{\xi}_{45.3}Z_{45.1}} \cdot P_{05.3}(0)$$

$$P^e_{05.4} = e^{\hat{\xi}_{04}}_{PIGE} e^{\hat{\xi}_{04}}_{PDGE} e^{\hat{\xi}_{04}\theta_{04}} \cdot e^{\hat{\xi}_{45.4}}_{PIGE} e^{\hat{\xi}_{45.4}}_{PDGE} e^{-\hat{\xi}_{45.4}Z_{45.1}} \cdot P_{05.4}(0)$$

Based on the Eqs. (3) and (4), the position error of each jaw can be obtained as:

$$E_{0N} = \begin{bmatrix} E_{xN} & E_{yN} & E_{zN} & 0 \end{bmatrix}^T = P^e_{0N} - P_{0N} \qquad (5)$$

where N represents the number of N-th jaw. E_x, E_y, E_z stand for the position errors in each direction. According to Eq. (5), the concentricity error can be deduced. As for the feeding chuck, a pair of opposite jaws, with the errors $E_{03.1}$, $E_{03.2}$, clamp the pipe. The concentricity error of the feeding chuck is deduced as:

$$E_{x03} = \frac{E_{x03.1} + E_{x03.2}}{2}; E_{y03} = \frac{E_{y03.1} + E_{y03.2}}{2}; E_{z03} = \frac{E_{z03.1} + E_{z03.1}}{2} \qquad (6)$$

As for the main chuck, two pairs of opposite jaws orthogonally, with the errors $E_{05.1}$, $E_{05.2}$, $E_{05.3}$, $E_{05.4}$, clamp the pipe. The tips of the main chuck jaws are bearings, which can not apply constraints in X-direction to the pipe. The concentricity error of the main chuck is:

$$E_{y05} = \frac{E_{y05.1} + E_{y05.2}}{2}; E_{z05} = \frac{E_{z05.3} + E_{y05.4}}{2} \qquad (7)$$

According to (6) and (7), the spatial angular deviations of the pipe along Y- and Z-axis can be written as:

$$\theta_y = \frac{E_{z05} - E_{z03}}{L_{04} - L_{23} - L_{01} - X}; \theta_z = \frac{E_{y05} - E_{y03}}{L_{04} - L_{23} - L_{01} - X} \qquad (8)$$

Then the actual position of working point is:

$$P'_W = Trans\left(E_{x03}, E_{y03}, E_{z03}\right) \cdot e^{\hat{\xi}_z \theta_z} \cdot e^{\hat{\xi}_y \theta_y} \cdot P_W \qquad (9)$$

The geometric error model of the laser pipe-cutting system can be formulated as:

$$E = P'_W - P_W = \left[E_x \ E_y \ E_z \ 0 \right]^T \qquad (10)$$

The geometric error model established in this section is the theoretical basis for the sensitivity analysis and error calibration.

3   Error Sensitivity Analysis Based on Improved Sobol Method

Sobol method is one kind of global sensitivity analysis method, which is suitable for not only linear model but also nonlinear model. In this section, an improved Sobol method based on quasi-Monte Carlo sampling is applied to identify the essential error components for the laser pipe-cutting system. As defined in [11], the computation process can be formulated as:

$$V_i = \frac{1}{k} \sum_{m=1}^{k} f(B)_m \left(f\left(A_B^{(i)}\right)_m - f(A)_m \right)$$

$$V_{Ti} = \frac{1}{2k} \sum_{m=1}^{k} \left(f(A)_m - f\left(A_B^{(i)}\right)_m \right)^2$$

$$V = \frac{1}{k} \sum_{m=1}^{k} f(A)_m^2 - \left[\frac{1}{k} \sum_{m=1}^{k} f(A)_m \right]^2 \qquad (11)$$

$$S_i \approx \frac{V_i}{V}, \ S_{Ti} \approx \frac{V_{Ti}}{V}$$

where A, B are the sampling matrices needed for the quasi-Monte Carlo algorithm which represent the random input of geometric errors. f $(A$ or $B)$ is the output function based on the error model established in Sect. 2. V_i and V_{Ti} represent the variance of the first-order and total effect of the i-th geometric error component, respectively. S_i and S_{Ti} are the first order and total sensitivity coefficient of the volumetric error model.

The geometric errors are divided into five types, and the sample ranges of each type are given in Table 2. The number of sampling point for each error is set to 20000. Hence, A and B are constructed as 20000 × 70 sampling matrics. Based on the assumption of small displacement, the sum of first-order sensitivity coefficient is close to 1. For 70 errors, the average sensitivity coefficient is $1/70 \approx 0.015$. In our analysis, we define the essential sensitivity error as the component whose sensitivity coefficient is larger than 0.03.

Table 2. The ranges of all geometric error components

Error types	Error ranges
Linear positioning errors	$[-10 \, \mu m, 10 \, \mu m]$
Straightness errors	$[-1 \, \mu m, 1 \, \mu m]$
Angular errors	$[-5 \, \mu rad, 5 \, \mu rad]$
Squareness errors	$[-5 \, \mu rad, 5 \, \mu rad]$
Parallelism errors	$[-5 \, \mu rad, 5 \, \mu rad]$

The sensitivity analysis of geometric errors will be discussed under the conditions below. The distances of jaws' motion are set as, $Y_{23.1} = 20$, $Y_{45.1} = 20$, $Z_{45.3} = 20$, which represent the jaws clamping the pipe. The DD motors are fixed at the initial degree, $\theta_{12} = \theta_{04} = 0$. The position of feeding truck is varied considered as the feeding motion, $X = 100, 450, 800$ mm.

The results of sensitivity analysis of the feeding system are shown in Fig. 2. According to the Fig. 2, S_{Ti} of each error component is slightly larger than S_i but almost equal. The result above means that the coupling effect between various errors is small and can be ignored. So, the discussion about sensitivity is based on the analysis of S_i.

The first, second and last three columns show the sensitivity coefficients of each error component along X, Y and Z direction when $X = 100, 450, 800$ mm. For E_X, the linear positioning error of the linear motor plays an absolutely important role which the sensitivity efficient is above 0.40. The reason is that the linear motor controls the feeding along X direction directly, and the main chuck can not apply the constraint to the pipe in axis direction. The straightness errors of feeding-chuck jaws are also essential errors, which represent the clamp error of the feeding chuck.

E_Y and E_Z, which are considered as the radial errors, depend on the distance between the pipe surface and the laser. As the second and last three columns of Fig. 2 shown, the linear positioning errors of jaws are the main errors. This is clearly because the pipe pose is depended on the jaws in YoZ plane. Also, the straightness and angular errors of jaws are essential sensitivity errors because the jaws are arranged orthogonally. Compared with E_X, the squareness and parallielism errors of E_Y and E_Z are important factors. As the feeding process continued (X = 100,450,800 mm), the sensitivity coefficients of linear positioning and angular errors of jaws, the squareness and parallelism errors between aligned axis are increased. The distance between main chuck and feeding chuck is closer, and higher accuracy of the clamp is needed.

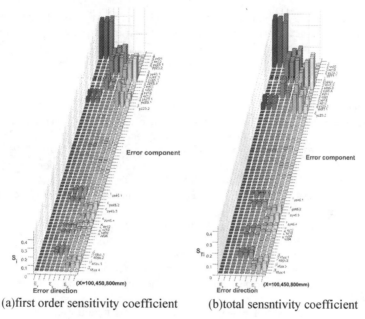

| (a)first order sensitivity coefficient | (b)total sensntivity coefficient |

Fig. 2. Sensitivity coefficient of each error component along X direction motion (X = 100,450,800 mm)

Based on the geometric error model and sensitivity analysis, we choose the linear motors with higher feed accuracy. The transmission mechanism of the jaws is redesign, including the feeding accuracy of actuators, the tolerance between the jaws and the slideway. The parts are assembled with multiple adjustments to guarantee the squareness and parallelism errors at a minimum value. As a consequence, the machining quality of the laser cutting system is improved.

4   Conclusion

In this paper, the geometric error model of a laser pipe-cutting system based on Lie group is established. The coupling effect of clamps by two chucks are involved in modeling considered as the angular deviation. To identify the essential sensitivity errors, an improved Sobol method is imposed to compute the sensitivity coefficients of 70 errors along the feeding direction. The results indicate that the concentricity of each chucks caused by jaws play an important part in the position deviation of pipe. The squareness and parallelism errors are also essential which can not be ignored.

Based on the analysis, the accuracy of product is improved. In the future, the optimization of the clamping force and stiffness will become the research topic considering the deformation of pipe.

References

1. Abbaszadeh-Mir, Y., Mayer, J.R.R., Cloutier, G.: Theory and simulation for the identification of the link geometric errors for a five-axis machine tool using a telescoping magnetic ball-bar. Int. J. Prod. Res. **40**(18), 4781–4797 (2002)
2. Zhu, S., Ding, G., Qin, S.: Integrated geometric error modeling, identification and compensation of CNC machine tools. Int. J. Mach. Tools Manuf **52**(1), 24–29 (2012)
3. Murray R., Sastry, S., Li, Z.: A Mathematical Introduction to Robotic Manipulation. CRC Press, Inc. (1994)
4. Cheng, Q., Feng, Q., Liu, Z., Gu, P., Zhang, G.: Sensitivity analysis of machining accuracy of multi-axis machine tool based on POE screw theory and Morris method. Int. J. Adv. Manuf. Technol. **84**(9–12), 2301–2318 (2015). https://doi.org/10.1007/s00170-015-7791-x
5. Xiang, S., Altintas, Y.: Modeling and compensation of volumetric errors for five-axis machine tools. Int. J. Mach. Tools Manuf. **101**, 65–78 (2016)
6. Sobol, I.M.: Sensitivity analysis for non-linear mathematical models. Math. Modeling Comput. Exp. **1** (1993)
7. Zou, X., Zhao, X., Li, G., Li, Z., Sun, T.: Sensitivity analysis using a variance-based method for a three-axis diamond turning machine. Int. J. Adv. Manuf. Technol. **92**(9–12), 4429–4443 (2017). https://doi.org/10.1007/s00170-017-0394-y
8. Xia, C., Wang, S., Sun, S.: An identification method for crucial geometric errors of gear form grinding machine tools based on tooth surface posture error model. Mech. Mach. Theory **138**, 76–94 (2019)
9. Liu, Y., Fei, D., Li, D.: Machining accuracy improvement for a dual-spindle ultra-precision drum roll lathe based on geometric error analysis and calibration. Precis. Eng. **66**, 401–416 (2020)
10. Dai, J.: Screw Algebra and Kinematic Approaches for Mechanisms and Robotics. Springer, London (2019)
11. Sobol, I.M.: Global sensitivity indices for nonlinear mathematical models and their Monte Carlo estimates. Math. Comput. Simul. **55**(1–3), 271–280 (2014)

Tensegrity Morphing: Machine Learning-Based Tensegrity Deformation Predictor for Traversing Cluttered Environments

Eduard Zalyaev(iD) and Sergei Savin[(✉)](iD)

Innopolis University, Innopolis 420500, Russia
{e.zalyaev,s savin}@innopolis.ru

Abstract. In this paper we introduce a neural network-based approach to tensegrity morphing: the task of actively changing the shape of a tensegrity structure to "fit" between obstacles in a cluttered environment. We specifically focus on a class of forming tasks, when the robot is required to pass between two parallel plate-like obstacles, and develop a robust solution both for generating dataset and for training predictor. Proposed predictor is able to predict both the shape of the tensegrity structure and the desired rest lengths of the actuated elastic elements, which can serve as motor commands when a quasi-static configuration-space trajectory tracking is used. We demonstrate high accuracy on validation dataset, and show the conditions when predictor overfits.

Keywords: Deformation of a tensegrity structure · Supervised learning · Dataset generation

1 Introduction

Tensegrity structures are based on a connection of a discontinuous set of compressive structural elements (struts) and a continuous set of tensile elements (cables); actuated tensegrity structures, used in robotics applications, are actuated by motors controlling rest lengths of the elastic elements. Such structures are relatively cheap t manufacture, foldable and resilient to impact which makes them useful for exploration and other impact-rich tasks.

Control of such structures poses a new set of challenges when compared to conventional robots, as even basic control approaches for tensegrity mechanisms are still being actively developed. Many of the commonly used control strategies involve the manipulation of cables in order to generate gaits. Control policies are often found by involving a such methods as genetic algorithms [5],

The research is supported by grant of the Russian Science Foundation (project No: 19-79-10246).

© IFIP International Federation for Information Processing 2021
Published by Springer Nature Switzerland AG 2021
A. Dolgui et al. (Eds.): APMS 2021, IFIP AICT 633, pp. 473–480, 2021.
https://doi.org/10.1007/978-3-030-85910-7_50

reinforcement learning-based policy search for motor actions [3,11] and neural network-based and Bayesian optimization of central pattern generators (CPG) [2,6]. These methods cover the case when environment does not require a deformation of the structure to "fit in" or "fit through", which would often be the case when a relatively large and highly deformable structure moves through a cluttered environment. Here we propose a method for automatically predicting correct shape of the robot and high-level motor commands, indicating desired rest lengths of the actuated elastic elements, in order to fit through a particular gap between the obstacles. The method is based on collecting a specially formatted dataset and training a neural network to predict configurations of the tensegrity structure based on the type of a gap between the obstacles that the robot encounters (Fig. 1).

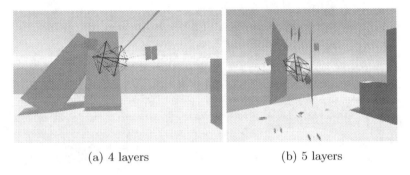

(a) 4 layers   (b) 5 layers

Fig. 1. Visualization of a flying tensegrity structure, fitting between narrow plate-like obstacles

To the best of our knowledge, this is the first time a neural network-based predictor of the desired form and desired rest lengths of the actuated elastic elements was proposed. Our experiments (for building a dataset and validating the results in simulation) are performed with a six-bar tensegrity structure.

The rest of the paper is organized as follows. Section 2 describes how tensegrity structure is modelled, including the questions of finding static equilibrium configurations under different constraints, and with different actuation patterns. Section 3 outlines the dataset generation procedure and the assumptions made for the simulation-based dataset generation. Section 4 presents our regression strategy, and Sect. 5 gives an analysis of the effects different types of dense neural networks have on the training dynamics of the proposed dataset.

2   Tensegrity Model

Tensegrity robot can be described as a graph consisting of n nodes. Connectivity between nodes is characterized by the type of forces acting between the nodes (tensile or compressive). The type of forces defines the physical implementation of the connection, which is a cable for tensile forces, and a strut for compressive ones.

Connections between the nodes can be represented using symmetric binary-valued adjacency matrix $\mathcal{C}$. This matrix describes which node is connected to which: if element $\mathcal{C}_{ij} = 1$, then the i-th node is connected to the j-th node; $\mathcal{C}_{ij} = 0$, they are not connected.

Elastic properties of the connections can be described using stiffness coefficient matrix $\mathcal{M}$ and rest length matrix $\mathcal{R}$. Elements of $\mathcal{M}$ are denoted as μ_{ij} and define scalar coefficients of the linear elastic force generated between the two nodes. Elements of $\mathcal{R}$ are denoted as ρ_{ij} and define the rest length of the elastic element between i-th and j-th nodes. Note that:

$$\mathcal{M} = \mathcal{M}^\top \quad \mathcal{R} = \mathcal{R}^\top \quad \mu_{ii} = 0 \quad \rho_{ii} = 0 \tag{1}$$

Also $\mathcal{C}_{ij} = 0$ implies $\mu_{ij} = 0$, i.e. $(1 - \mathcal{C}_{ij})\mu_{ij} = 0$. Assuming linear elastic force model, we can define the force $\mathbf{f}_{ij}$ acting between i-th and j-th nodes as follows:

$$\mathbf{f}_{ij} = \mu_{ij}(\|\mathbf{r}_i - \mathbf{r}_j\| - \rho_{ij})\frac{\mathbf{r}_i - \mathbf{r}_j}{\|\mathbf{r}_i - \mathbf{r}_j\|}. \tag{2}$$

where $\mathbf{r}_i$ and $\mathbf{r}_j$ are the positions of the nodes i and j in Cartesian space.

Tensegrity robot achieves an *equilibrium position* when the resulting elastic forces acting on each node are equal to zero:

$$\sum_{j=1}^{n} \mathbf{f}_{ij}(\mathbf{r}_i, \mathbf{r}_j, \rho_{ij}) = 0, \ \forall i \tag{3}$$

We define *forward kinematics* as a problem of finding such $\mathbf{r}_i$, that for given ρ_{ij} condition (3) holds. Let us define node position matrix $\mathbf{R}$ given as a horizontal concatenation of the column-vectors $\mathbf{r}_i, \forall i$. Then we can define *output vector* for the tensegrity structure as:

$$\mathbf{y} = \mathbf{Cr}; \quad \mathbf{r} = \text{vec}(\mathbf{R}) \tag{4}$$

where $\text{vec}(\cdot)$ is a vectorization of a matrix (performed by stacking its columns to obtain a column-vector), and $\mathbf{C}$ is an output matrix. Assuming that we are given desired value of the output vector denoted as $\mathbf{y}^*$, we can define *inverse kinematics* as a problem of finding such ρ_{ij} and $\mathbf{r}_i$ that both (3) and (4) hold.

In general, only a subset of the cables are actuated, i.e., capable of changing their rest lengths. We can capture this fact by defining *tensegrity control input* as follows:

$$\mathbf{u} = \mathbf{B}\rho; \quad \rho = \text{vec}(\mathcal{R}) \tag{5}$$

where $\mathbf{B}$ is the control matrix, determining which cables are actuated. This implies that

$$\mathbf{N}\rho = \text{const}; \quad \mathbf{N} = \text{null}(\mathbf{B}) \tag{6}$$

where $\text{null}(\cdot)$ is an operator returning an orthonormal basis in the null space of the input matrix. Then inverse kinematics becomes a problem of finding such control input $\mathbf{u}$ that output vector $\mathbf{y}$ approaches its desired value $\mathbf{y}^*$, and conditions (1), (3), (4), (5) and (6) hold.

As a rule, it is computationally easy to generate a dataset of a stable tensegrity configurations by solving forward kinematics for a randomly generated matrix $\mathcal{R}$. Even though forward kinematics is not a convex problem, its geometry corresponds to the geometry of the potential energy of the structure, and its local minima represent stable configurations, i.e. viable solutions. Methods for solving forward kinematics for tensegrity structures are presented in [8,9].

3   Tensegrity Deformation as a Data Collection Problem

Tensegrity structures can deform by changing values of $\rho = \text{vec}(\mathcal{R})$. Once a value of ρ is chosen, the corresponding values of $\mathbf{r} = \text{vec}(\mathbf{R})$ are found via forward kinematics. We will describe a configuration of a tensegrity structure as $\langle \mathbf{r}, \rho \rangle$. Having that description, we can formulate questions regarding the shape of the structure.

3.1   Direct Fitting

Let us consider a problem of fitting a tensegrity structure into an allocated area. Assuming the area is described an H-polytope (inequality representation of a polytope) $H = \{\mathbf{x} : \mathbf{Ax} \leq \mathbf{b}\}$, with matrix $\mathbf{A}$ and vector $\mathbf{b}$ representing the inequalities, we can define the problem as follows:

$$\text{find}\quad \mathbf{x}, \mathbf{T}$$
$$\text{s.t.}\quad \begin{cases} \mathbf{AT}(\mathbf{r}_i + \mathbf{x}) \leq \mathbf{b}, \forall i \\ \mathbf{TT}^\top = \mathbf{T}^\top\mathbf{T} = \mathbf{I} \end{cases} \tag{7}$$

where $\mathbf{x} \in \mathbb{R}^3$ is a displacement vector and $\mathbf{T} \in SO(3)$ is a rotation matrix. Searching over the space of rotation matrices is computationally difficult; here we propose to freeze the orientation of the structure, making the computations simple, but introducing additional challenges and limitations that are discussed further in this section. Without the search over possible orientations of the structure, the optimization problem becomes convex:

$$\text{find}\quad \mathbf{x}$$
$$\text{s.t.}\quad \mathbf{A}(\mathbf{r}_i + \mathbf{x}) \leq \mathbf{b}, \forall i \tag{8}$$

If (8) has a solution, tensegrity configuration $\langle \mathbf{r}, \rho \rangle$ can fit into a given polytope H without rotations.

There is a special case of this problem that can be solved without the use of quadratic programming. Assume that the allocated area is restricted by two parallel planes, given by their normal vector $\mathbf{a}$, the distance between the planes is h. We will call such area an *opening*. Openings can be used to describe tall narrow doors and windows, spaces under wheeled vehicles, space between trees, buildings, cables and other structural element in an industrial sites, bridges, power lines, etc.

Configuration $\langle \mathbf{r}, \rho \rangle$ can fit into an opening described by a unit vector $\mathbf{a}$ and width h can formulated as:

$$w = \max(\mathbf{a}^\top \mathbf{R}) - \min(\mathbf{a}^\top \mathbf{R})$$
$$w \leq h \tag{9}$$

where w is a measure of the width of the configuration with respect to the opening's direction. Condition (9) is can be checked very fast. If we have a dataset of stable configurations, we can pose questions such as which configuration is the "best fit" for the given opening. This can lead to an optimization problem

$$\underset{\mathbf{k}}{\text{minimize}} \quad ||\mathbf{R}_k - \mathbf{R}^*||$$
$$\text{s.t.} \qquad \max(\mathbf{a}^\top \mathbf{R}_k) - \min(\mathbf{a}^\top \mathbf{R}_k) \leq h \tag{10}$$

where $\mathbf{R}^*$ is a preferred configuration. Solving the problem (10) we can match an opening $(\mathbf{a}, h)$ with the best-fit configuration $\langle \mathbf{r}, \rho \rangle$. This allows us to build a labeled dataset, which can later be used to train a predictor, which could propose a configuration suitable for a given opening.

3.2 Inverse Fitting Problem

Let us consider the following problem: given configuration $\langle \mathbf{r}, \rho \rangle$, find the narrowest opening in which it can fit; we will call it an *inverse fitting problem*.

This problem can be approximately solved using SVD decomposition. Let matrix $\mathbf{R}$ have the following decomposition: $\mathbf{R} = \mathbf{U} \Sigma \mathbf{V}^\top$, where Σ is a matrix with singular values of $\mathbf{R}$ on its diagonal, sorted in descending order, and $\mathbf{U} = [\mathbf{u}_1, \mathbf{u}_2, \mathbf{u}_3]$. Then $\mathbf{u}_3$ gives us an approximation of the direction in which the structure has the least width. Then we can construct the opening $(\mathbf{a}, h)$, which current configuration would fit in as:

$$\mathbf{a} = \mathbf{u}_3$$
$$h = \max(\mathbf{u}_3^\top \mathbf{R}) - \min(\mathbf{u}_3^\top \mathbf{R}) \tag{11}$$

This inverse approach to pairing opening with configurations also allows us to generate a dataset to train a predictor. The major difference between the direct and inverse fitting is that the first allows us to focus on typical openings geometries, where as the second allows us to pair each configuration with an opening that fits it "tightly".

In the following section we discuss the use of the proposed dataset in training a stable configuration predictor, given an opening as an input.

4 Predictor Structure and Regression Strategy

Our prior studies of ML-based forward kinematics for tensegrity robots [10] have shown that dense neural networks (DNN) demonstrated the best possible results

Table 1. Mean error and accuracy on validation dataset

Layer sizes	MSE	Accuracy(%)
[10]	2.652e−3 ± 2.0e−7	72.9 ± 0.072
[20]	2.155e−3 ± 2.6e−7	76.4 ± 0.14
[30]	1.730e−3 ± 1.3e−7	78.7 ± 0.093
[40]	1.726e−3 ± 1.2e−7	79.0 ± 0.11
[80]	1.291e−3 ± 2.9e−8	81.6 ± 0.034
[10 10]	1.250e−3 ± 2.4e−7	83.0 ± 0.22
[20 20]	6.570e−4 ± 4.8e−8	87.7 ± 0.13
[30 30]	5.949e−4 ± 7.1e−8	88.4 ± 0.11
[40 40]	5.203e−4 ± 4.5e−8	88.5 ± 0.21
[80 80]	4.113e−4 ± 1.0e−8	89.9 ± 0.16
[10 10 10]	8.097e−4 ± 1.365e−7	86.5 ± 0.15
[20 20 20]	5.475e−4 ± 1.1e−7	89.3 ± 0.15
[80 40 40]	3.695e−4 ± 1.257e−8	92.2 ± 0.035
[80 80 60 50]	3.477e−4 ± 1.865e−8	92.3 ± 0.031
[80 80 80 80]	4.194e−4 ± 1.207e−7	91.1 ± 0.092
[80 80 80 80 80]	4.585e−4 ± 8.812e−8	92.2 ± 0.033

compared to the linear models such as Linear Regression (LR) and Support Vector Machines (SVM) as well as kernel-based SVM. With that in mind, this study is focused exclusively on application of NN to a regression problem.

To determine which NN configuration fits our dataset best, we had to test it in the fashion of increasing complexity for both hidden layer sizes as well as for the number of such layers. Each network structure had ReLU [4] activation functions to prevent vanishing gradient problem from occurring on deeper model structures. The training was performed on 1500 epochs, batch size of 512 and learning rate of 10^{-3} with RMSprop Gradient Descent algorithm. Each model configuration was tested 20 times with the aim of providing more descriptive results that would include ranges for the appropriate metrics.

4.1 Dataset Description

The dataset used in this study is generated for a six-bar tensegrity structure, well known for its use in NASA's SUPERball [1,7]. The structure includes six rods, giving us total of 12 nodes, with $\mathbf{R} \in \mathbb{R}^{3 \times 12}$. Forward kinematics is solved with the algorithm proposed in [8] with a non-convex optimization solver based on interior-point method.

The dataset included of $5 \cdot 10^4$ samples collected with the direct fitting method. Training and validation sets were divided in a ratio of 1 to 5.

5   Evaluation of Different DNN Structures

To evaluate the performance of the regression model we used mean squared error (MSE). However, the error rates may not always be indicative of the accuracy of the model since the amount of possible configurations that can fit into the opening is not fixed to a single rest length vector. So we additionally test the accuracy of the regression by checking whether or not out estimated rest lengths indeed produce robot configurations that will fit into the desired opening. In order to do that we have take our predicted $\hat{\rho}$ and solve forward kinematics to find corresponding for $\hat{\mathbf{r}}$. Thus found $\hat{\mathbf{r}}$ is then checked against the 9 criterion; if the check succeeds, the prediction is deemed accurate. The results of the evaluation can be seen in the Table 1.

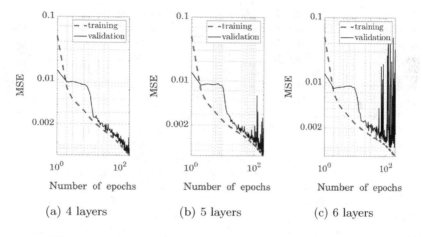

(a) 4 layers   (b) 5 layers   (c) 6 layers

Fig. 2. Training and validation error curves for a regressor

It can be seen that the accuracy and error rates are improving with the increase of the model's complexity. To better understand the training dynamics, we plot MSE for three different cases: network with 4, 5 and 6 layers. Figure 2a shows low variances in error rates as well as error convergence, indicating that the training did not lead the model to overfit. Figure 2b suggests no improvement with the increased number of layers, and finally Fig. 2c shows overfitting. In order to visualize the performance of the designed method we built an obstacle course with way points, tasking the six-bar structure to pass through a number of parallel plates (assuming the structure has enough control authority to move along the given path, as a tensegrity drone would, for example), which were given to the robot as openings, described by their normal vector and width. The robot used pre-trained predictor to find appropriate stable configuration that fits through the opening.

6   Conclusions

In this paper we introduced an approach to formalize the cluttered environment traversal scenario for a tensegrity robot by introducing trajectory consisting of a set of openings that a robot has to fit in. A neural network model for robot stable state prediction from opening parameters was proposed and tested using a six strut tensegrity robot dynamics. Said model achieved 92% accuracy on a validation set while not showing any signs of overfitting. Unfortunately, our method is not universal and requires extensive testing on each individual robot configuration with accuracy validation that may take up a lot of time.

References

1. Bruce, J., et al.: Superball: exploring tensegrities for planetary probes. In: 12th International Symposium on Artificial Intelligence, Robotics and Automation in Space (i-SAIRAS) (2014)
2. Hustig-Schultz, D., SunSpiral, V., Teodorescu, M.: Morphological design for controlled tensegrity quadruped locomotion. In: 2016 IEEE/RSJ International Conference on Intelligent Robots and Systems (IROS), pp. 4714–4719. IEEE (2016)
3. Luo, J., Edmunds, R., Rice, F., Agogino, A.M.: Tensegrity robot locomotion under limited sensory inputs via deep reinforcement learning. In: 2018 IEEE International Conference on Robotics and Automation (ICRA), pp. 6260–6267. IEEE (2018)
4. Nair, V., Hinton, G.E.: Rectified linear units improve restricted Boltzmann machines. In: Fürnkranz, J., Joachims, T. (eds.) Proceedings of the 27th International Conference on Machine Learning (ICML 2010), pp. 807–814 (2010)
5. Paul, C., Roberts, J.W., Lipson, H., Cuevas, F.V.: Gait production in a tensegrity based robot. In: 2005 Proceedings of 12th International Conference on Advanced Robotics, ICAR 2005, pp. 216–222. IEEE (2005)
6. Rennie, C.M.: Designing and learning CPG gaits for spherical tensegrity robots using Bayesian optimization. Ph.D. thesis, Rutgers University-School of Graduate Studies (2018)
7. Sabelhaus, A.P., et al.: System design and locomotion of superball, an untethered tensegrity robot. In: 2015 IEEE International Conference on Robotics and Automation (ICRA), pp. 2867–2873. IEEE (2015)
8. Savin, S., Balakhnov, O., Klimchik, A.: Energy-based local forward and inverse kinematics methods for tensegrity robots. In: 2020 Fourth IEEE International Conference on Robotic Computing (IRC), pp. 280–284. IEEE (2020)
9. Savin, S., Balakhnov, O., Maloletov, A.: Linearization-based forward kinematic algorithm for tensegrity structures with compressible struts. In: Ronzhin, A., Shishlakov, V. (eds.) Proceedings of 15th International Conference on Electromechanics and Robotics "Zavalishin's Readings". SIST, vol. 187, pp. 293–303. Springer, Singapore (2021). https://doi.org/10.1007/978-981-15-5580-0_24
10. Zalyaev, E., Savin, S., Vorochaeva, L.: Machine learning approach for tensegrity form finding: feature extraction problem. In: 2020 4th Scientific School on Dynamics of Complex Networks and their Application in Intellectual Robotics (DCNAIR), pp. 265–268. IEEE (2020)
11. Zhang, M., et al.: Deep reinforcement learning for tensegrity robot locomotion. In: 2017 IEEE International Conference on Robotics and Automation (ICRA), pp. 634–641. IEEE (2017)

Seed-and-Prune Approach for Rapid Discovery of Tensegrity-Like Structures of the Desired Shape

Sergei Savin[(✉)] [ID]

Innopolis University, Innopolis 420500, Russia
s.savin@innopolis.ru

Abstract. In this paper, a new tensegrity generation method, based on a combination of a random search, quadratic programming and connection pruning is proposed. The method exploits the structure of the static equilibrium equations of tensegrity structures with static nodes, allowing to form linear equality constraints. By abandoning the requirement of struts being disconnected we arrive at a simple convex program, where the existence of solution represents the existence of the sought structure. We propose a way to generate node positions and to prune the connections in order to shape the resulting tensegrity-like structures in the desired form.

Keywords: Generation of tensegrity structures · Force density method · Convex optimization

1   Introduction

Tensegrity structures are often defined as a collection of structural elements, where each element experiences axial forces: compression or tension. Elements experiencing only tension can be referred to as cables, while compressed elements are called struts [5]. These structures are of interest for a number of applications, but especially in robotics, where their properties are highly desirable. Those properties include folding, a good stiffness-to-mass ratio, collision resilience, and many others [2,13]. Tensegrity structures have already been proposed for planetary exploration, underwater robotics, humanoid robotics, collaborative and other applications [1,7,9,10].

Design of tensegrity structures is an especially interesting issue. The design process is significantly from the traditional engineering, allowing less freedom in "adding together" known structural elements, and instead requiring a generation of the entire structure, explicitly and simultaneously taking into account force balance and position of elements withing the structure. This process if often referred to as form finding [8,12].

The research is supported by grant of the Russian Science Foundation (project No:19-79-10246).

© IFIP International Federation for Information Processing 2021
Published by Springer Nature Switzerland AG 2021
A. Dolgui et al. (Eds.): APMS 2021, IFIP AICT 633, pp. 481–487, 2021.
https://doi.org/10.1007/978-3-030-85910-7_51

Form finding, and a related forward and inverse kinematics problem (finding stable element positions for the given element lengths, or finding element lengths to achieve a given element position) can be of interest for a number of design-related tasks. One of those tasks is generation of a customized tensegrity structures. Those can be structures with a given shape, given number of elements, given limits on the tensile or compressive forces, etc. We will refer to it as a *form-finding design problem*. Existing methods already allow us to approach this problem. In this paper we show that with a new formulation, we can radically speed-up parts of the computational process, and facilitate the use of random search as a part of tensegrity design process. We use this methodology as a basis to build a pipeline for generation of shape-specific tensegrity structures, accounting for limits in terms of tensile and compressive forces, number of cables and connectivity patterns. Our main contributions are:

- Convex representation of a form-finding design problem with fixed nodes position, with a natural extension to include constrained modes and external forces.
- Seed-and-prune algorithm for generating connectivity patterns in accordance with constraints on the number of structural element, and on the relative connections between struts.
- A method for rapidly generating tensegrity structures of a specific shape, taking into account limits on the tensile or compressive forces.

The rest if the paper is organized as follows: Sect. 2 gives a description of the state of the art, Sect. 3 provides a description of static equilibrium conditions of the tensegrity structure, written as a linear constraint, and Sect. 4 presents seed-and-prune algorithm. Finally, Sect. 5 demonstrates an example of the generated structure and its connectivity matrix.

2   State of the Art

Form finding for tensegrity structures has long become a diverse field of study with a number of sub-domains. There are works on general conditions of stability of tensegrity structures of certain class, such as [3] where group symmetry was used to define conditions for stability of tensegrity structures with dihedral symmetry. Another domain is building algorithms for finding connectivity patterns and the lengths of the structural elements for which tensegrity structure can remain stable. That problem is generally referred to as "form finding" [11], making it difficult to address other sub-domains in the field. Another set of problems can be presented as forward and inverse position problems; in the first, the task is to find stable position of the nodes while cable and strut lengths are known, and in the second the task is to find lengths of either cables or struts or both or of a subset of those [16]. Similar forward and inverse problems can be formulated for stiffness design and static force distribution for a given pose of the robot [14,15].

Form finding has been addressed a number of times before. A classification of methods provided in [17] includes two major categories: kinematic and static methods, different in the choice of variables; first category permits the strut lengths to change, while the second does the same for the cable lengths. Reviewed methods include two special-case analytical solutions, one method relying on a non-convex optimization, two equivalent force density methods and a dynamics simulation-like method. Force density methods are of particular interest, since they yield an algebraic formulation of the problem.

Paper [6] introduced a way to generate tensegrity structures in a systematic way by solving a mixed-integer convex program. This method has a number of advantages, including the ability to limit the connections between the struts, following the definition of a tensegrity structure as a set of disconnected compressive elements (struts); however, if such a requirement is not of necessity, then there is a possibility to significantly simplify the generation process by eliminating integer variables from the problem design. Mixed-integer convex programs are solved using branch-and-bound methods, which limits the possibility of predicting the computational load and termination time of the algorithm. This may lead to the imitations to the size of the problems tackled by such algorithm.

In this paper it is proposed to use a quadratic programming-based approach to tensegrity generation, abandoning the requirements for the discontinuity of the set of struts, but compensating for that in the ability to solve the generation problems for large numbers of nodes, and use a pruning method for shaping the resulting tensegrity structure.

3   Static Equilibrium of a Tensegrity Structure as a Constraint

We will model tensegrity structure as a set of nodes $\mathbf{r}_i$, where $1 \leq i \leq n$. In order to arrive at a description of the static equilibrium of a tensegrity structure as a linear constraint, we need to consider direction matrices $\mathbf{D}_i$ that indicate from which directions can the forces act on the node $\mathbf{r}_i$:

$$\mathbf{D}_i = \left[(\mathbf{r}_1 - \mathbf{r}_i), (\mathbf{r}_2 - \mathbf{r}_i), ..., (\mathbf{r}_n - \mathbf{r}_i) \right] \tag{1}$$

With that, we can formulate the static equilibrium condition as a question of the existence of the vectors $\mathbf{f}_i$ that deliver equality to the constraints:

$$\mathbf{D}_i \mathbf{f}_i = \mathbf{f}_i^{ext} \tag{2}$$

where $\mathbf{f}_i^{ext}$ is the sum of external forces acting n the node. Assuming that $\mathbf{F} = \left[\mathbf{f}_1, \mathbf{f}_2, ..., \mathbf{f}_n \right]$, we can add an additional constraint, respecting the fact that action equal reaction with the opposite sign:

$$\mathbf{F} = \mathbf{F}^\top \tag{3}$$

where the opposite sign should be encoded in the matrix (1).

Additionally, we note that some nodes do not have a connection between them. That can be integrated into the constraint as:

$$\mathbf{D}_i = \left[(\mathbf{r}_1 - \mathbf{r}_i)c_{1,i}, \ (\mathbf{r}_2 - \mathbf{r}_i)c_{2,i}, \ ..., \ (\mathbf{r}_n - \mathbf{r}_i)c_{n,i} \right] \tag{4}$$

where $c_{j,i}$ is a binary variable, which equals 0 if there is no connection between the nodes, and 1 otherwise. The matrix formed by there variables is called connectivity matrix, and is denoted as $\mathbf{C}$.

Together expressions (2) and (3) form constraints for a convex optimization problem. If the problem has a solution, the structure with the given nodes $\mathbf{r}_i$ is possible, and the sign of $f_{j,i}$ (elements of $\mathbf{F}$) determines whether each particular connection is a strut or a cable.

In order to chose some of the nodes as fixed (which can represents connective elements of a mounted structure), an additional decision variable can be added, acting as a reaction force. Assuming first w elements are fixed, the equation(2) for them becomes:

$$\mathbf{D}_i \mathbf{f}_i = \mathbf{f}_i^{ext} + \lambda_i, \ 1 \leq i \leq w \tag{5}$$

where λ_i is the reaction force implementing the imposed constraints. We should note that this type of additional constraints actually is a relaxation of the problem, as it increases its domain; it also provides the possibility to reduce the number of decision variables during a resolve stage, if a solver wrapper like CVX is used to automatically re-shape the problem [4].

4 Seed-and-Prune Algorithm

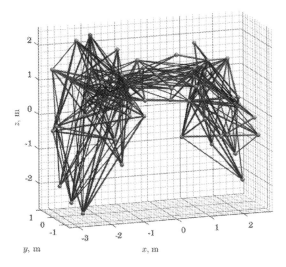

Fig. 1. Example of a tensegrity-like structure, generated using proposed method; the nodes are shown in purple, cables are shown in black and struts are shown in blue

Given m areas described by ellipsoids $\mathcal{E}_k = \{\mathbf{x} : \|\mathbf{E}_k\mathbf{x}\| \leq 1\}$, chosen such that their union represents a connected set, we generate P nodes, randomly distributed in the union of the ellipsoids. This stage represents *seeding*.

If a line segment between two points lies entirely in one of the ellipsoids, we set the connection between the points as active $c_{j,i} = 1$, otherwise it is set to 0:

$$c_{j,i} = \begin{cases} 1 & \text{if } \exists k, \ \|\mathbf{E}_k\mathbf{r}_i\| \leq 1, \ \|\mathbf{E}_k\mathbf{r}_j\| \leq 1 \\ 0 & \text{otherwise} \end{cases} \tag{6}$$

Next stage is pruning. Given number of connections p to prune, we chose p unique (irrespective of permutations) pairs of numbers (v_1, v_2), and set corresponding connections to zero.

$$c_{v_1(j),v_2(j)} = 0, \quad c_{v_2(j),v_1(j)} = 0, \quad j = 1,...,p \tag{7}$$

Choosing the number of connections to prune we can control the complexity of the resulting structure.

After pruning we can formulate and solve quadratic program in order to find if the requested tensegrity structure is feasible:

$$\begin{aligned} \underset{\mathbf{x}}{\text{minimize}} \quad & \|\mathbf{F}\| \\ \text{subject to} \quad & \begin{cases} \left[(\mathbf{r}_1 - \mathbf{r}_i)c_{1,i}, (\mathbf{r}_2 - \mathbf{r}_i)c_{2,i}, ..., (\mathbf{r}_n - \mathbf{r}_i)c_{n,i}\right] \mathbf{f}_i = \mathbf{f}_i^{ext} \\ \mathbf{F} = \mathbf{F}^\top \end{cases} \end{aligned} \tag{8}$$

If there is no solution, the previous steps can be repeated for a different set of randomly distributed nodes.

5   Resulting Structures

In this section we present example of a structure that can be discovered using proposed method. It is obtained using three ellipsoids, forming a Π-shaped structure. Figure 1 shows an example of resulting structure. The elements that experience compressive loads are shown in blue, the elements that experience tensile loads are drawn as black lines. Nodes are drawn in red, except for fixed nodes that are yellow.

We can also demonstrate the connectivity matrix for the found structure. Figure 2 shows the color map for the found structure. We can see blocks on the diagonal, that represent connections inside each of the three ellipsoids mentioned previously. We can notice that there are interconnections between the ellipsoids, represented by the off-diagonal connections. This example did not include pruning, allowing to see dense number of connection formed inside each ellipsoid. This density is well-represented in the shape of the resulting structure, with a numerous elastic elements running close to one another, which in practice means a low volume work space, as the densely packed cables and struts will likely intersect as the structure deforms.

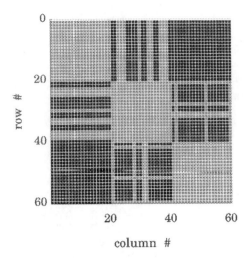

Fig. 2. Color map for the connectivity matrix of the tensegrity-like structure, generated using proposed method; blue correspond to no connection, yellow to a connection

6   Conclusions

In this work it was demonstrated that tensegrity generation problem can be formulated as a random search problem, solving a single quadratic program in order to identify the existence of the structure. The main advantage of the method is the low computational cost associated with solving quadratic programs, allowing for fast experimentation with the structure generation. The main downsides are the lack of constraint on the connectivity patterns, notably on the disconnectedness of the compressed elements; this is the result of the trade-off made to rid the problem of the integer variables, necessary to encode such a constraint. Also, same as other tensegrity topology generation methods shown in the literature, this one is based around the requirements of the existence of a static equilibrium under a possible pre-stress; however, there is also a separate issue of the stiffness of the resulting system, which needs not only to be sufficient for the chosen application, but also to allow the structure to avoid collapse under bounded external forces. It is of further interest to investigate stiffness-aware tensegrity generation, where structures that do not exhibit sufficient stiffness properties are discarded.

References

1. Bliss, T., Iwasaki, T., Bart-Smith, H.: Central pattern generator control of a tensegrity swimmer. IEEE/ASME Trans. Mechatron. **18**(2), 586–597 (2012)
2. Caluwaerts, K., et al.: Design and control of compliant tensegrity robots through simulation and hardware validation. J. R. Soc. Interface **11**(98), 20140520 (2014)
3. Connelly, R., Terrell, M.: Globally rigid symmetric tensegrities. Struct. Topol. 1995 núm 21 (1995)

4. Grant, M., Boyd, S., Ye, Y.: CVX: Matlab software for disciplined convex programming (2008)
5. Guest, S.D.: The stiffness of tensegrity structures. IMA J. Appl. Math. **76**(1), 57–66 (2011)
6. Kanno, Y.: Exploring new tensegrity structures via mixed integer programming. Struct. Multidiscip. Optim. **48**, 95–114 (2013)
7. Kim, K., et al.: Rapid prototyping design and control of tensegrity soft robot for locomotion. In: 2014 IEEE International Conference on Robotics and Biomimetics (ROBIO 2014), pp. 7–14. IEEE (2014)
8. Kim, K., Agogino, A.K., Toghyan, A., Moon, D., Taneja, L., Agogino, A.M.: Robust learning of tensegrity robot control for locomotion through form-finding. In: 2015 IEEE/RSJ International Conference on Intelligent Robots and Systems (IROS), pp. 5824–5831. IEEE (2015)
9. Lessard, S., Bruce, J., Jung, E., Teodorescu, M., SunSpiral, V., Agogino, A.: A lightweight, multi-axis compliant tensegrity joint. In: 2016 IEEE International Conference on Robotics and Automation (ICRA), pp. 630–635. IEEE (2016)
10. Lessard, S., et al.: A bio-inspired tensegrity manipulator with multi-DOF, structurally compliant joints. In: 2016 IEEE/RSJ International Conference on Intelligent Robots and Systems (IROS), pp. 5515–5520. IEEE (2016)
11. Paul, C., Lipson, H., Cuevas, F.J.V.: Evolutionary form-finding of tensegrity structures. In: Proceedings of the 7th Annual Conference on Genetic and Evolutionary Computation, pp. 3–10 (2005)
12. Paul, C., Roberts, J.W., Lipson, H., Cuevas, F.V.: Gait production in a tensegrity based robot. In: ICAR'05. Proceedings, 12th International Conference on Advanced Robotics, pp. 216–222. IEEE (2005)
13. Paul, C., Valero-Cuevas, F.J., Lipson, H.: Design and control of tensegrity robots for locomotion. IEEE Trans. Robot. **22**(5), 944–957 (2006)
14. Sabelhaus, A.P., et al.: Inverse statics optimization for compound tensegrity robots. arXiv preprint arXiv:1808.08252 (2018)
15. Savin, S., Balakhnov, O., Klimchik, A.: Convex optimization-based stiffness control for tensegrity robotic structures. In: 2020 28th Mediterranean Conference on Control and Automation (MED), pp. 990–995. IEEE (2020)
16. Savin, S., Balakhnov, O., Maloletov, A.: Linearization-based forward kinematic algorithm for tensegrity structures with compressible struts. In: Ronzhin, A., Shishlakov, V. (eds.) Proceedings of 15th International Conference on Electromechanics and Robotics "Zavalishin's Readings". SIST, vol. 187, pp. 293–303. Springer, Singapore (2021). https://doi.org/10.1007/978-981-15-5580-0_24
17. Tibert, A., Pellegrino, S.: Review of form-finding methods for tensegrity structures. Int. J. Space Struct. **18**(4), 209–223 (2003)

Serious Games Analytics: Improving Games and Learning Support

Experiencing the Role of Cooperation and Competition in Operations and Supply Chain Management with a Multiplayer Serious Game

Matteo Galli, Davide Mezzogori, Davide Reverberi,
Giovanni Romagnoli(✉), and Francesco Zammori

University of Parma, Viale delle Scienze 181/A, 43124 Parma, Italy
giovanni.romagnoli@unipr.it

Abstract. We present an innovative, cooperative, and competitive multiplayer serious game, suited for the educational needs of supply chain and operation management post-graduate students. Hence, the objective is to satisfy the ever-increasing requirement of students to have the ability to experience and practice the theory learned in traditional ways, for active knowledge acquisition. To cope with such needs, we designed and implemented a multiplayer online serious game, that provides players with a realistic industrial experience, and teaches them how to take a whole range of day-to day and medium-term challenging decisions. Learners are divided into teams, each one representing an Original Equipment Manufacturer (OEM), in every team the students will collaborate and will compete in the same market, and sharing a limited set of suppliers. To this aim they have to define a strategy to target the best market segmentation. Teachers have the possibility to investigate the decision patters of the learners, analyze KPIs and learning analytics, to better understand the learning process and guide the learners in their educational journey. By means of a preliminary questionnaire, the interest in using the serious game to study operation management was confirmed. In addition, the game was tested by a small group of students, who acknowledged the effectiveness of the game's dynamics as a tool to complement traditional teaching methods.

Keywords: Serious game · Supply chain · Operations management ·
Competitive · Cooperative

1 Introduction

Serious games in the education of both engineering students and professional have been proposed and implemented since a couple of decades, but especially in the first years, they have not been taken very seriously [1]. Nonetheless, with the rise of virtual-labs, distance learning and on-line services for continuous education, a renewed interest for innovative, immersive, and even entertaining ways of learning calls for a reconsideration of such learning tools. Moreover, for many teachers and pedagogues, learning by doing

A. Dolgui et al. (Eds.): APMS 2021, IFIP AICT 633, pp. 491–499, 2021.
https://doi.org/10.1007/978-3-030-85910-7_52

is considered one of the most effective teaching styles to close the gap between theory and practice, as it gives learners the opportunity to experience, explore and understand the context in which they will be operating, through an effective simulation. Indeed, an intrinsic characteristic of Serious Games is that of being simulations of real-world environments and to reflect everyday practical processes. For these reasons, Serious Games are ideal tools to teach and learn Operations Management [2].

Nowadays is possible to find Serious Games developed either for single or multiplayer usage. The first approach definitely helps the learner to accelerate his or her training path, but it cannot deliver the augmented experience that multiplayer games have [3]. Indeed, many researchers investigated the added benefits of multiplayer serious games, and concluded that multiplayer solutions teach team-working, collaboration and cooperation in a very effective way [4, 5], and they can be successfully implemented for game-based collaborative learning [3]. Multiplayer Serious Games, such as the one represented in this paper, can be conceptually seen as virtual laboratories that enable distance learning through online services, if the multiplayer is accessible remotely through, for example, the Internet. So, they can perfectly fit with the necessity to have distance learning and on-line services [2].

This work belongs to this stream of research and presents a multiplayer serious game that allows learners to experience the day-to-day workings activities and the dynamics of managing a business in a competitive environment, both at the operational and strategic levels, together with the correct coordination with different supply chain actors. The paper also presents the ongoing evaluation of the proposed serious game, which will be firstly targeted to bachelor's degree students of industrial engineering courses.

The rest of the paper is organized as follows: Sect. 2 provides a quick overview of the literature review on the most relevant papers on serious games with a strong focus on studies concerning existing Operation Management/Supply Chain Management serious games. Section 3 presents the design of the serious game, describing the educational features implemented. Finally, Sect. 4 provides the mid-term results, extracted from the questionnaires distributed to students in order to have a feedback on the preliminary design of the Serious Game, as well as on provided didactical support during the game sessions.

2   Literature Review on Operations and Supply Chain Management Serious Games

Nowadays, the studies on Serious Games are numerous. Briefly, Serious Games can be defined as "an application with three components: experience, entertainment, and multimedia" [6]. During their research, [7] discovered that different outcomes of the adoption of Serious Games can be identified by empirical evidence, like the acquisition of knowledge but also the improvement of motivational, social, physiological behaviors. Moreover, Serious Games are main focused on the improvement of the learners' performances, the motivational features are usually of secondary interest. Nonetheless, [8] showed that games can promote intrinsic motivation, encouraging and sustaining learning, of both academic and non-academic skills, motivating learners to collaborate and share information effectively, thus improving soft skills. However, to achieve that, additional mechanisms need to be implemented.

Recently there has been a spike of interest in the popularity of applying gamification to teach supply chain and operations management. Indeed, having powerful and representative simulations help students to experience and apply learned theory, in a timely and cost-effective way. Although engineering education has traditionally focused on the so-called hard or technical skills, modern curricula are changing to expand core engineering competences and to deliver up-to-date knowledge in a fast-changing world, as well as broader professional skills [9]. Moreover, many researchers highlighted the need to enrich engineering curriculum with design-build-test projects, helping scholars to practice soft skills such as collaboration, team building, communication, leadership, through active and experiential learning, and constantly improve [10].

To better contextualize the multiplayer serious game object of this study, the most relevant supply chain and operations management serious games will be briefly discussed. Relatively to the first group, the Beer Game [11], originally designed as a multiplayer card game, is probably the most known and used one. Players represent different tiers of a supply chain and interact with each other to fulfill customer's demand; in doing so, they experience naturally arising dynamics of a supply chain, such as the bullwhip effect. Also, AUSUM [12] is a supply chain serious game, but the focus is on the dynamics of an automobile supply chain and the aim is to investigate the interconnection and dependencies among players' decisions. Finally, the Fresh Connection [13] is about value chain learning. This game gives players the opportunity to experience the importance of cross-functional alignment and inter-company collaboration (i.e., internal, and external coordination), in terms of both strategy and actions. Players, indeed, should avoid maximizing personal objectives, and are driven by the goal of maximizing the Return on Investments (ROI) of the whole supply chain.

Learn2Work [14] is one of the main examples of serious games in the field of operation management. It delivers three main scenarios, each one designed to help the player to embark, from different starting points, in the journey of an entrepreneur trying to bring the company to success. In doing so, the learner has to deal with a variegated set of entrepreneurial challenges, from hiring staff and expanding production capacity, to managing customer relations. Finally, Practice operations [15] is presented as a 3D, single-player, interactive game that allows students to control the operational management of a clothing company. To assure the success of the company, players have to cover different corporate roles, and deal with tasks such as: placing offers for orders, managing physical and human resources, managing the procurement of raw materials, transforming them into finished products and organizing shipment to the customer.

3   Overview of an Innovative Multiplayer Serious Game on Operations and Supply Chain Management

The serious game is aimed at bachelor students of supply chain and operation management courses. An extension for master students is planned for the future. The aim is to address different learning habits (i.e. Self-Directed Learning, lectures, etc.) of learners and to motivate them in different ways. To increase the effectiveness of the proposed

Serious Game, we followed the ARCS model. The ARCS model [16] is a method to improve the appeal of learning/instructional material, and it is composed of three different features: (i) it details four conceptual categories, which address specific variables and concepts, to try and characterize human motivation; (ii) it suggests a set of strategies to increase the appeal of instructions from the educational point of view; (iii) it suggests an approach called "motivational design" that can be successfully applied to instructional design models [16]. This model is one of the first theory that addresses the question of how to motivate the stimulation to learn, and it is often referred to in Serious Games design (see for example [17]).

Concretely, users will face various real-life and real-time dilemmas that naturally occur during the daily management of a manufacturing company. Also, to improve both hard and soft skills, the game was designed as a multiplayer environment and implemented as a web application. In this regard is worth noting that the only requirement for participants is to have a computer/tablet/smartphone with any common web browser software. In each match, players are grouped into teams (of two or three students at most), and each team represents an Original Equipment Manufacturer (OEM). OEMs are e-bikes manufacturers that compete in the same market niche, sharing suppliers and customers. At the beginning the product portfolio is fixed, but during the gameplay (at precise moments dedicated to strategic decisions) it can be extended or modified, if the players within the same company agree to do so. Each company compete for the satisfaction of a limited number of customer agents, which model the overall market demand dynamics, in terms of quantities, qualities, due dates, and price. To this aim they must define a strategy to target the best market segmentation.

Each player performs a specific role within the company, with a precise scope and a pre-defined set of tasks to be accomplished for an effective and efficient management. Roles are the following ones: purchasing manager (PM), operations manager (OM), and sales manager (SM). PM is in charge of managing the procurement of raw materials, managing raw materials stock levels, and correctly selecting the best suppliers/material combination, planning orders timely, both in terms of quantity, quality, and due date. OM is in charge of effectively and efficiently schedule production orders, to satisfy demand, correctly exploiting the equipment at disposal. SM is in charge of dealing with customers' requests and managing customer deliveries.

For an effective management, players must cooperate and coordinate their daily activities, and they are also required to make shared and consensual decisions, concerning the supply chain management strategy. Indeed, teamwork, cross-functional understanding and collaboration are key issues to turn the company around, toward success.

In Fig. 1 is depicted the simplified flow chart of operation and interconnectedness and dependencies between the different main call to actions of each role. In particular, the flow chart shows one of the main approaches to deal with market demand, namely make to order (MTO). In this strategy, players react to the successful acquisition of a customer request made by the SM. Indeed, as soon as the acquisition is successful, the SM should alert the OM which in turn should check and plan shop floor activities accordingly, in coordination with the PM which is in charge of checking and managing future raw materials availability. Such strategy is one of the many that players can explicity or implicity adopt. Many others can be evaluated and chosen. Indeed, by design, not only one specific strategy must be followed in order to successfully play the game. So, in order to successfully apply this strategy, the SM has to learn how to analyze the market demand, and negotiate with each customer, as well as managing the outbound logistics. The OM has to learn and apply classical scheduling methodologies by considering the overall productive capacity. The PM must learn how to handle the inventory, by managing the raw materials supply chain, using well known inventory management policies.

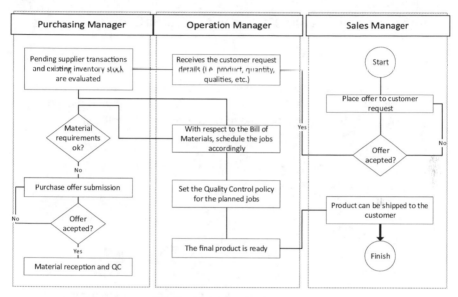

Fig. 1. Make to order flow chart

One of the most prominent examples is the market segmentation analysis. Indeed, the demand dynamics are modeled in a way that, depending on the selected difficulty level, more than a single market segment could exist. Thus, the players should discover these segments, and tailor their production and distribution strategy to perfectly meet the needs and expectations of the customers they decided to serve. Quality management in another prominent issue that players have to deal with, both at the operational and strategic level. Indeed, anytime a customer's enquiry is received, SM should analyze it not only in terms of quantity, price, and delivery dates, but also in terms of quality requirements. These parameters, in fact, can be negotiated with the customer, and choosing a right trade-off is crucial for success. These decisions also impact the manufacturing process because, in turn, the OM must schedule production accordingly and decide whether is economical convenient to plan detailed quality controls in one or more points of the production process. Similarly, also the PM must operate accordingly when submitting order requests to potential suppliers and he or she must decide if which, if any, quality controls policies should be applied when goods are received.

Finally, the game is designed to teach the value of communication as a necessary means of coordination among different departments and/or corporate functions. To force an active communication among partners, in fact, the game interface, designed to mimic a simplified ERP, does not allow players to have full visibility of the actions taken by their teammates. Specifically, the interface hides the information at disposal of the other members or, at the most, it offers a partial and very aggregated information about the targets achieved in other processes. So, the players are strongly encouraged to communicate with each other, and must establish effective communication protocols for better coordination.

4   Students' Opinions and Preliminary Evaluation

To confirm the growing interest in serious games, and to assess the quality of our solution, a total of 176 bachelor-degree students (enrolled in industrial engineering courses held at two Italian-speaking universities) were interviewed. The same students will be asked to use the serious game during the next semester, and a second questionnaire will be submitted to register their perceptions and their satisfaction about the game.

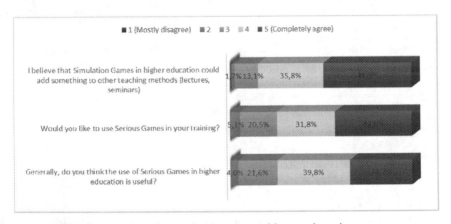

Fig. 2. Questionnaire results about general interest in serious games

Results, concerning the first questionnaire used to measure the general interest in serious games are summarized in Fig. 2.

We note that the questionnaire also included questions to measure the students' previous knowledge on the subject. Nonetheless, these results are not included herein, as they will be part of a future work, aimed to compare the learning performance of a group of students who used the game, relatively to a control group who only attended standard theory lessons.

Since the courses are ongoing at the time of writing, we present interim results obtained on a demo session, during which a cohort of nine bachelor students tested the serious game. At the end of the demo session, that lasted around eight hours, a questionnaire was administered. The aim of the questionnaire was to measure different aspects of user engagement and playability, and to collect general comments about the experience of the participants during the serious game, however due to the limited game time, it was not possible to evaluate the learning outcomes. All nine students were at the last semester of their bachelor-degree, and they have already attended and passed the operation management module.

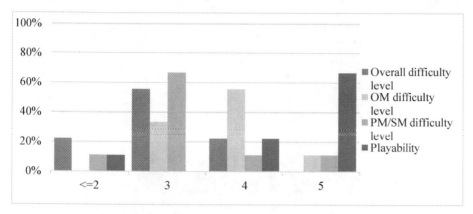

Fig. 3. Results about perceived game difficulty and playability

As it can be seen in Fig. 3, in terms of perceived difficulty, most of them (56%) felt the game was properly calibrated (i.e., right level of difficulty or slightly lower), according to their knowledge and limited time to learn the game. However, perceptions of the students who played as Operations Manager were slightly worse. Indeed, 66% reported a difficulty level higher or equal to 4 (on a scale ranging from 1 very easy to 5 very difficult). However, such results were expected, since the role of the OM is more demanding and the player experiences more operational pressure, even more during a short demo session. Vice versa, player engaged either as PM or SM reported a less demanding and less stressful gaming experience and 66% of them quantify in three point (i.e., adequate) the perceived difficulty level. To minimize this unavoidable unbalance (among roles) a full gameplay foresees roles turnover, to equalize the effort of the players and to better balance their experience. This turnover is supposed to lead to a better understanding of a production company's whole environment. Moreover, the learners will better understand how to interact according with the company's function they are representing. Also, as already showed before (Fig. 3), the difficulty perceived for the company functions is not equal, so a more balanced learning environment for the trainee to interact with is provided.

Moreover, as shown in Fig. 4, all, but one student, reported a very high correlation between the game mechanics and the theory they studied.

This is one of the main results, given that one of goals of such preliminary survey was for the authors to measure how well the game have been designed to make tangible for students the application of theory in the simulated environment. Indeed, such results have been collected from experienced students, which have already successfully studied operation management.

Competition awareness was overall high, with almost 90% of students reporting a level higher of equal to four. All of them agreed that the game is enjoyable, if not exciting, but noted that an integrated chat system could be beneficial, as the communication among players in a company was considered a key issue for a successful business management. Finally, 77% of interviewee found the user interface easy enough, while the remaining 23% reported full satisfaction of the user interface.

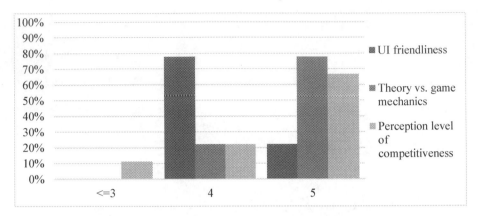

Fig. 4. Results about perception of key game design choices

5   Conclusions and Future Works

The present work describes an innovative multiplayer serious game aimed at the education of supply chain and operation management learners.

The game is built upon several innovative design choices: first, it is meant to be played by many students at the same time, both cooperating with each other within the same OEM, as well as competing for optimizing the market share. Moreover, within the same company, players have the opportunity to experience different roles, which enable them to better understand both at the operational level as well as the strategic level the implications of several business units' functionalities. These game dynamics enables learners to directly experience and learn the importance of a well-established framework of communication, which, if planned and executed well, should give them a competitive advantage over the competitors.

Early-stage testing have been conducted to confirm the game design and mechanics. Results attest to the correct design of the game, especially in terms of workload balance of the different players, as well as in the general interest of the students in the use of an advanced educational tool within the relevant curriculum with respect to covered topics. While the analysis tested a relatively small cohort of bachelor's degree students, shortly the analysis will be conducted over a bigger sample. Such analysis will be the subject of a future work. Moreover, a questionnaire administered to a cohort of undergraduate students showed notable interest in the use of serious game for operation management which further strength the exploitability of such learning method for teaching operation management and supply chain management courses.

In addition, other future developments could include the ability for players to play roles at different levels of the supply chain, or the creation of computer-managed virtual players to allow one team, or even multiple human teams to compete with computer-managed companies.

References

1. Hauge, J.M.B., Pourabdollahian, B., Riedel, J.C.K.H.: The use of serious games in the education of engineers. In: Emmanouilidis, C., Taisch, M., Kiritsis, D. (eds.) Advances in Production Management Systems Competitive Manufacturing for Innovative Products and Services, pp. 622–629. Springer, Heidelberg (2013). https://doi.org/10.1007/978-3-642-40352-1_78
2. Reese, H.W.: The learning-by-doing principle. Behav. Dev. Bull. **17**(1), 1 (2011)
3. Wendel, V., Konert, J.: Multiplayer serious games. In: Dörner, R., Göbel, S., Effelsberg, W., Wiemeyer, J. (eds.) Serious Games, pp. 211–241. Springer, Cham (2016). https://doi.org/10.1007/978-3-319-40612-1_8
4. Wendel, V., Gutjahr, M., Steinmetz, R.: Designing collaborative multiplayer serious games Escape from Wilson Island — a multiplayer 3D serious game for collaborative learning in teams. Educ. Inf. Technol. **18**, 287–308 (2013). https://doi.org/10.1007/s10639-012-9244-6
5. Wendel, V., Hertin, F., Göbel, S., Steinmetz, R.: Collaborative learning by means of multiplayer serious games. In: Luo, X., Spaniol, M., Wang, L., Li, Q., Nejdl, W., Zhang, Wu. (eds.) ICWL 2010. LNCS, vol. 6483, pp. 289–298. Springer, Heidelberg (2010). https://doi.org/10.1007/978-3-642-17407-0_30
6. Laamarti, F., Eid, M., El Saddik, A.: An overview of serious games. Int. J. Comput. Games Technol. **2014** (2014)
7. Connolly, T.M., Boyle, E.A., Macarthur, E., Hainey, T., Boyle, J.M.: A systematic literature review of empirical evidence on computer games and serious games. Comput. Educ. **59**(2), 661–686 (2012)
8. Felicia, P.: Motivation in games: a literature review
9. Buyurgan, N., Kiassat, C.: Developing a new industrial engineering curriculum using a systems engineering approach. Eur. J. Eng. Educ. **42**(6), 1263–1276 (2017)
10. Despeisse, M.: Games and simulations in industrial engineering education: a review of the cognitive and affective learning outcomes, no. Cedefop, pp. 4046–4057 (2018)
11. Kaminsky, P., Simchi-Levi, D.: A new computerized beer game: a tool for teaching the value of integrated supply chain management. Glob. Supply Chain Technol. Manage. **1**(1), 216–225 (1998)
12. Crowe, J.: Learning by gaming: Supply chain application, pp. 3935–3946 (2011)
13. De Leeuw, S., Schippers, M.C., Hoogervorst, S.J.: The fresh connection: cross-functional integration in supply chain management. In: The Handbook of Behavioral Operations Management. Oxford University Press, New York (2015)
14. Van Learnwork, D.: De waarde van leerproject Learn2Work
15. Practice Operations. https://www.mhpractice.com/products/Practice_Operations
16. Keller, J.M.: The use of the ARCS model of motivation in teacher training. Asp. Educ. Technol. **17**, 140–145 (1984)
17. Gunter, G., Kenny, R.F., Vick, E.H.: A case for a formal design paradigm for serious games. J. Int. Digit. Media Arts Assoc. **3**(1), 93–105 (2006)

Towards a Serious Game on Data Sharing in Business Ecosystems

Ulriikka Järvihaavisto[✉], Mikael Öhman, and Riitta Smeds

Department of Industrial Engineering and Management, School of Science, Aalto University,
P.O. Box 15500, 00076 Aalto, Finland
ulriikka.jarvihaavisto@aalto.fi

Abstract. In this paper we develop design principles for a serious game on data sharing in business ecosystems. Even though data has been said to be the new fuel of the economy, we have not seen much large-scale data trading in industrial settings. The purpose of the game is to experimentally study the dynamics of data trading in simulated business ecosystems, particularly under different kinds of governance structures: in centralized and decentralized ecosystems. The objective of the game is also to support the learning of MBA and university students. Through the game, the students can experience the risks and benefits of sharing data in ecosystems, an emerging and increasingly important topic in business life.

Keywords: Data sharing · Business ecosystems · Simulation · Teaching game · Design principles

1 Introduction

Over the past couple of decades, there has been an increasing interest in different streams of literature towards 'ecosystems'. Ecosystems are a heterogeneous set of actors that are organized around a shared goal, such as a customer-facing value proposition, core technology, or another important strategic goal shared by the actors. By specializing in compatible offerings to deliver the shared goal, ecosystem participants bind themselves together through interdependencies. Together they co-create an ecosystem-level value offering while ensuring ecosystem benefits for each stakeholder [1, 2]. To reach the shared goal in ecosystems, data sharing has become an essential part of value co-creation. However, even though the value of data sharing is in principle widely understood in different ecosystem contexts, we do not see datasets openly and transparently traded on a large scale in praxis [3].

Indeed, sharing organizational data is one of the key challenges for established industrial firms in their transition towards platforms and ecosystems [3]. Organizations strive to tightly control their proprietary data, as they are afraid of losing ownership and the

A. Dolgui et al. (Eds.): APMS 2021, IFIP AICT 633, pp. 500–509, 2021.
https://doi.org/10.1007/978-3-030-85910-7_53

potential benefits from their own data. However, research has shown that openness in data sharing fosters generativity in value creation in ecosystems [4]. Thus, industrial organizations need to find a balance between openness and control of their proprietary data.

There are two different types of governance structures that guide the sharing of data between ecosystem actors: centralized and decentralized ecosystem governance models. Extant ecosystem research has focused mostly on centralized ecosystems, where a central ecosystem orchestrator also determines the rules for data sharing [5, 6]. These ecosystem orchestrators, or "hub" firms, actively promote and guide the direction of the ecosystem to enhance their own competitive advantage [7]. Research has paid less attention to understanding governance dynamics in decentralized ecosystems, where the ecosystem actors share data without the governance of a central hub.

We are developing a data sharing game to empirically study, albeit in a simulated game setting, the decision making dynamics of data sharing in centralized versus decentralized ecosystems. Through concrete experience in the ecosystem simulation game, we aim to improve the game participant's understanding of the risks and benefits of their data sharing decisions in a simulated case ecosystem. The aim of the game is to improve the awareness of the participants concerning the transparency and openness of data trading in business ecosystems, in general, and to sensitize the participants to the differences of data sharing in centralized versus decentralized ecosystems, in particular.

Our game aims to give to the participants first-hand experience on data sharing in an ecosystem. At the same time, we collect data from the participants' decisions in the game to study the dynamics of data sharing in the simulated ecosystem. The game thus serves two synergistic objectives:

1) Educational objective: Developing the participants' understanding about the risks and benefits of sharing data in centralized versus decentralized ecosystems.
2) Research objective: Developing through empirical simulation-based research a theoretical interpretation of the dynamics of data sharing in ecosystems and of the impact of the ecosystem governance structure on this data sharing dynamics.

In this paper we explore the suitable game design principles that would meet the educational and research objectives set for the game.

2 Data Sharing in Business Ecosystems

In this chapter, we describe the characteristics of centralized and decentralized ecosystems, and examine the underlying risks and benefits of data sharing.

2.1 Centralized and Decentralized Business Ecosystems

Business ecosystems are usually structured around some kind of platform, often a technological architecture that ensures interoperability and modularity of different ecosystem members [4]. Ecosystem researchers have mostly considered centralized ecosystems, where a hub-firm owns the platform where the ecosystem operates [1, 2, 8, 9]. The ecosystem hub can determine who can access the platform and the principles of how the data is shared in the ecosystem. We call data sharing ecosystems that operate under centralized governance as data monopolies.

An alternative model for ecosystem coordination is a decentralized governance structure, where the decision making for platform structure and data sharing is jointly operated by the ecosystem participants [3]. However, no decentralized platforms have yet emerged in industrial settings. Koutroumpis et al. [3] believe that the reason for this is the difficulty to collectively design technical and contractual structures that would guide appropriate behavior in the ecosystem.

Nevertheless, distributed ledger technologies (DLTs) could open up possibilities to collective data trading without a centralized intermediary [3]. DLTs are distributed databases that automatically track transactions in a data trading system and provide a reliable record for the origins, i.e. provenance, of the traded data. The blockchain that underlies cryptocurrency Bitcoin is one of the most known DLT. A decentralized context can also be a collective marketplace, a data collective, where the ecosystem participants establish clear rules through different contracts and bylaws. The data collective should have transparent procedures to collectively change the rules, and to monitor and audit data trading in the ecosystem [3].

We are curious to explore the opportunities of decentralized governance systems for data trade in an industrial context. Since there are no existing decentralized ecosystems for data trading, we see this game as a great opportunity to study data sharing dynamics experimentally in simulated ecosystems with different governance structures [10].

2.2 Benefits and Risks of Data Sharing in Ecosystems

Data are rarely valuable alone. In order to become final goods and useful for ecosystem actors, data need to be shared, further processed and combined with analytics [3]. Thus, data are intermediate goods that are produced to be combined and transformed to become information goods [3]. The more data are shared in an ecosystem, the more possibilities there are to combine available data, which increases the generativity of the ecosystem. The increasing volume of data sharing also attracts new members to the ecosystem where data are shared, thus creating positive network effects [11].

By nature, data are experience goods. This means that the value and quality of data is only observable after data has been consumed. Hence, the quality assessment of data is difficult, which can lead to an increase of low-quality goods in the market [3, 12]. Data sharing ecosystems can be thus vulnerable to opportunism and free riding [13]. In addition, data appropriability is weak. The copyright of databases usually protects the empty shell of the structure and the organization of the database, not the data itself. Thus, the provenance of data becomes an important aspect for assessing data quality. High quality data need to have detailed metadata on its origin, characteristics, and history [3].

The difficulty in evaluating the value of data creates barriers for data sharing in ecosystems. Ecosystem actors need to learn how to appropriately evaluate the value of data they wish to sell and buy. They need to understand the kind of data they have in order to protect the core of their business. Furthermore, the actors need to trust the ecosystem governance structure for providing correct information on data provenance. The data sharing game provides an excellent opportunity to study these behaviors and dynamics of data sharing in ecosystems.

3 Translating Educational and Research Objectives into Game Design

In this section we explain the background of the game and elaborate educational and research objectives based on the reviewed literature above. We also explain how these objectives are translated to the game design decisions, and how we can analyze the data generated in the game for the purpose of research.

3.1 Background of the Game

The game will be built upon a paper-based data sharing game we created and piloted together with Cornell University in 2017. In the paper-based game, data creation, ownership, and trading was modeled in a hypothetical dyadic data market in a workshop setting. A simulation of data buying and -selling was done through a "text-scraping" exercise. Players could trade and exploit text-based data during the workshop. We found out that sellers (who could see the full sentences with all words) showed slightly higher valuations of open source data than buyers (who only saw the "scraped" sentences). These initial findings of the game were interesting. However, the game model with English language sentences, and data as words, was perceived as confusing by the participants. Thus, in the new version of the game we focus to increase the approachability of the data sharing game through developing a more intuitive business ecosystem case. Furthermore, in the new version, we explore different governance systems of data ecosystems.

3.2 Educational Objectives

Given the unfolding nature of the topic, our target audience for the game is twofold. First, the game is intended for industry experts, for example in MBA programs, that are currently struggling with decisions related to data sharing. For this audience, the game provides a sandbox where they can test their understanding of data sharing dynamics, and how they are affected by governance structures. The game should also enable profiling of the players, providing them with insight on their behavior (e.g. risk aversiveness/benefit optimism), which would be of personal benefit to the players.

Second, the game is also intended for university students for supporting learning in courses that relate to the ecosystem/platform economy. The game would provide students with an environment where they can test the theories that are being taught and get to experience the effects of their decisions first-hand [14]. Considering this target audience, a modular game structure, or preset scenarios would be important. Also in-game tips and explanations could be added to support the students' in their independent study.

3.3 Research Objectives

Our research objectives are to develop a theoretical interpretation of the dynamics of data sharing in ecosystems and of the impact of the ecosystem governance structure on these dynamics. We analyze the data valuation and trading behavior of the players in an ecosystem context: how valuable they see their own data, and for what price the other players are prepared to buy the data in question. The basis for this analysis is the "bidding data" that is generated by the players when they agree upon compensation for gaining access to the data. We are also interested in the effects of different types of available data [3], which we could study e.g. through varying the amount of publicly available data between games.

One of our research interests is to study the data sharing behavior in centralized and decentralized ecosystem governance structures. Centralized ecosystem in this game means that there is a hub firm in the ecosystem that creates the rules and opportunities for data trading for other ecosystem members; this would create a data monopoly. Decentralized ecosystem in this game could mean that the platform is operated through distributed ledger technologies (DLTs) that would ensure the collective trading of data.

We have two alternatives for how to study and analyze this contextual difference on data sharing behavior. In the first alternative, the ecosystem governance structure is given to the player in the beginning of the game. At first the players trade data in a centralized ecosystem, and after the first game they play the same game again in a decentralized ecosystem. In the second alternative, players choose their data trading mechanisms by themselves, and we see whether a centralized or decentralized ecosystem emerges during the game. Analyzing the results from the first scenario would be easier from a research perspective, whereas the second scenario would better support the learning of the player, as the player would have first-hand experience of the rationale behind joining/proposing either a centralized or a decentralized ecosystem.

Over time, the game accumulates information about the overall value created by ecosystems during game rounds, and how the co-created value is captured by each ecosystem player. We want to analyze how ecosystem governance affects co-creation and capture of value; do ecosystems create more value under centralized or decentralized governance, and how do differences in governance structures affect sharing of co-created value? After each game round, we also feed some of the results from the game analytics for the players to support their learning from the game. We also plan to run a debriefing with the players after they have finished the game. Debriefing topics are e.g. the perceived fairness of value capture in the ecosystem, and the satisfaction of the players towards their individual results and their ecosystem's results.

Implications for Game Design

In providing the players with a reflective learning experience, the game should embody an experiential learning cycle of experiencing, reflecting, thinking and acting [15]. In terms of game progression this means that a turn-based game with discrete time would probably be advantageous compared to a continuous, real-time game clock. In terms of organizing game sessions, discrete time would allow asynchronous decision making during the game, which may be advantageous considering the target audience of the game, as it would relax requirements on finding a time that suits potentially busy and geographically dispersed players. Asynchronous games could also enable bigger games, which would in the best case enable emergence of several competing ecosystems.

This leads us to the great question of whether ecosystem emergence is achievable in a game setting. If implementable, the players would get to experience the emergence of an ecosystem first-hand, understanding the rationale of the emergence from the perspective of their ecosystem roles. Implementing this in the game, however, would require an approachable operationalization and flexible implementation of the ecosystem governance mechanisms. Further, allowing ecosystem emergence could benefit from an open game source code. The other alternative, where the ecosystem and its governance mechanisms would be given, and the player would play subsequent games in centralized and decentralized ecosystems, is probably easier to implement. However, it would not offer data nor learning effects on the emergence of ecosystems. Based on the focal phenomena identified in literature, we propose the following game design principles (Table 1):

Table 1. Game design principles derived from the focal phenomena

Phenomenon	Educational objective	Research objective	Game design principle
Data valuation	1. Understand own cognitive biases related to the valuation of data 2. Reflect upon what affects own perception of data value, both as a seller and a buyer	1. Understand how risk aversiveness and benefit estimation affects perception of the counterpart's risk/benefit 2. Understand the effect of behavioral aspects on ecosystem formation	– The price of data/access should be determined based on negotiation/bidding – There should be data/decision uncertainty – Data should be related to both cost and profit – All playable positions can both buy and sell data
Types of data	1. Become aware of how she evaluates different types of data 2. Understand how the availability of different types of data affects ecosystem formation	1. Understand how the existence of different forms of data affects the formation of data ecosystems	– There should be different types of data in the game, e.g. private, public, and open data – There should be both substituting and complementing data

(continued)

Table 1. (*continued*)

Phenomenon	Educational objective	Research objective	Game design principle
Data sharing mechanism	1. Be able to relate the data sharing mechanism to issues such as trust and valuation	1. Understand how distributed ledger technology affects governance structures of sharing	– There should be different options for how data is shared (1st tier), e.g. inclusive, exclusive – It should be possible to control access to data
Governance structures of sharing	1. Understand how different governance structures are evaluated by stakeholders	1. Understand how different governance structures emerge 2. Comparing competitive performance of different governance structures	– The governance structures in the game should be malleable to some extent – Ideally governance structures should emerge within the game, initiated by a player

4 A Tentative Game Design in the Context of Gold Mining

In order to simulate an ecosystem, and perhaps even its emergence, we need to have at least three different, but co-dependent roles in the game. Each role signifies a type of economic actor of which there can exist multiple playable instances that compete and cooperate with each other. Together the different players are expected to maximize the ecosystem-level value offering (i.e. pursue the shared goal), while each player needs to ensure their own value capture.

The game roles are Equipment Manufacturers, Gold Miners, Surveyors and Environmental Consultants. There could also be other possible roles such as Gold Brokers and Key Component Suppliers. We also might want to include a number of non-profit (non-playable) organizations, such as an environmental agency, and some sort of land registrar. Each game role has a focal decision concerning the mining for gold. This decision has a degree of uncertainty and is directly tied to their economic outcome. The decision-related uncertainty can be reduced by having access to other player's data, either within the same role, or from another role. The game world consists of a large number of mineable terrain grids, that have different properties (making them more tempting to some miners, compared to other miners) and mining them will produce different payoffs. A table of the actor's focal decisions are included below (Table 2).

Table 2. Game roles and associated focal decisions

Role	Focal decision	Uncertainty	Data needs
Gold miners	Which grid(s) to mine	Expected grid payoff?	Survey data Environmental impact data
Equipment manufacturers	What equipment capability to develop	What direction do the miners prefer?	Data from mining operations
Surveyors	Which grid(s) to survey	What type of grids are the miners interested in?	Environmental knowledge
Environmental consultants	Which grid type competence to develop	What type of grids are the miners interested in?	Equipment capability data

When making the focal decision, the impact of having information is visible to the player - e.g. through displaying a probability distribution of the expected outcome with and without a given piece of information, providing the player with an idea of what the benefit of having information is. Further, each player has access to options of being dishonest (e.g. selling the information to other players, ignoring agreed terms), along with likelihoods of being caught in the act. Together, these two aspects serve as the basis for the players perception of risk and benefit in data negotiations.

Both bidding and forming of ecosystem governance structures would have to be at least semi-structured processes to ensure fluent gameplay. The former is realized through giving ballpark alternatives for starting bids, and limited options for bargaining. The latter is presented as a configuration task, where the player (in case of emergent ecosystems) or the game facilitator (in case of given ecosystems) chooses the preferred alternatives on issues such as conditions for joining the ecosystem, contribution requirements, methods for enforcing rules and procedures for changing them, etc. For the less versed player, implications of the different options would be available as expandable info-boxes.

The game is round-based, where the mining-season is interrupted by winter, when the ground freezes over, making mining impossible. This creates a natural rhythm for experiential learning [15], where players make their decisions, observe the outcomes of these decisions, which in turn affects their next season decisions. Each round would have two types of decisions - the focal business decision, which is linked to actor profitability, and the data market decisions, which result in extra profits when selling data, and presumably improved focal decision (and of course additional cost) when buying data. After each season the players would see their financial result, and every five(?) seasons there is a bidecadal industry conference, where players get to see their performance relative to other players and the whole ecosystem (Fig. 1).

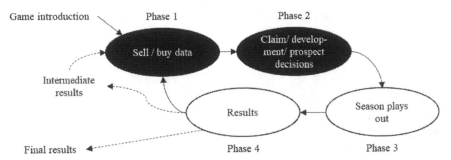

Fig. 1. Each game round consists of four phases, including two types of decisions.

Being a business game, the ultimate measure of success is financial performance. Comparability of performance creates competition, which in turn (along with the built-in possibility of being dishonest - e.g. through allowing arbitrage [16]) would create player emotional engagement, which is beneficial for learning [17]. However, in order to create variance in player behavior, there are predefined player competences (e.g. a miner might be specialized on one type of grid, and thus be able to extract more from this type of grids) and additional incentives (e.g. a prestigious and lucrative environmental award at every industry conference). At the game conclusion, there is a thorough run-through and recap of game events, which secures learning objectives.

5   Conclusions and Next Development Steps

In this paper we develop design principles for a serious game on data sharing in business ecosystems. Once materialized, the simulation game would create a fruitful opportunity to study data sharing in a business context, something which has been proven to be difficult in real life. The game would also serve the educational purpose of increasing understanding of the challenges and opportunities of data sharing among students and industry professionals. As highlighted by prior research, there is a need for understanding the different governance models for such data ecosystems [3], to which our game would be able to contribute to.

We expect that our paper will serve as a starting point for other game developers as well as researchers that are interested in data sharing in business ecosystems as a complex decision making problem, but approachable through serious games. After finalizing the game design principles, we start building a minimum viable version (MVP) of the game together with a software company partner. Then we proceed into piloting, and iteratively develop the research game based on user experiences and recorded game behavior. After piloting, we start intensive promotion of the game and launch the game to the public.

Our vision is that the game will establish itself as a platform for research related to data ecosystems, forming a link between researchers and practitioners. As a boundary object, we see that the game would be able to connect fellow academics and industry professionals to think and discuss the dynamics of data sharing and explore opportunities for successful and fair data sharing in business ecosystems.

References

1. Adner, R.: Ecosystem as structure: an actionable construct for strategy. J. Manage. **43**(1), 39–58 (2017)
2. Jacobides, M.G., Cennamo, C., Gawer, A.: Towards a theory of ecosystems. Strateg. Manage. J. **39**, 2255–2276 (2018)
3. Koutroumpis, P., Leiponen, A., Thomas, L.D.: Markets for data. Ind. Corp. Chang. **29**(3), 645–660 (2020)
4. Dattée, B., Alexy, O., Autio, E.: Maneuvering in poor visibility: how firms play the ecosystem game when uncertainty is high. Acad. Manage. J. **61**(2), 466–498 (2018)
5. Gawer, A., Cusumano, M.A.: Platform Leadership: How Intel, Microsoft, and Cisco Drive Industry Innovation, vol. 5, pp. 29–30. Harvard Business School Press, Boston (2002)
6. Lusch, R.F., Nambisan, S.: Service innovation: a service-dominant logic perspective. MIS Q. **39**(1), 155–176 (2015)
7. Williamson, P.J., De Meyer, A.: Ecosystem advantage: how to successfully harness the power of partners. Calif. Manage. Rev. **55**(1), 24–46 (2012)
8. Moore, J.F.: Predators and prey: a new ecology of competition. Harv. Bus. Rev. **71**(3), 75–86 (1993)
9. Iansiti, M., Levien, R.: The Keystone Advantage: What the New Dynamics of Business Ecosystems Mean for Strategy, Innovation, and Sustainability. Harvard Business Press, Boston (2004)
10. Harrison, J., Carroll, G., Carley, K.: Simulation modeling in organizational and management research. Acad. Manage. Rev. **32**(4), 1229–1245 (2007)
11. Ghazawneh, A., Henfridsson, O.: Balancing platform control and external contribution in third-party development: the boundary resources model. Inf. Syst. J. **23**(2), 173–192 (2013)
12. Akerlof, G.A.: The market for "lemons": quality uncertainty and the market mechanism. Quart. J. Econ. **84**(3), 488–500 (1970)
13. Dhanaraj, C., Parkhe, A.: Orchestrating innovation networks. Acad. Manage. Rev. **31**(3), 659–669 (2006)
14. Geithner, S., Menzel, D.: Effectiveness of learning through experience and reflection in a project management simulation. Simul. Gaming **47**(2), 228–256 (2016)
15. Kolb, A.Y., Kolb, D.A.: Learning styles and learning spaces: enhancing experiential learning in higher education. Acad. Manage. Learn. Educ. **4**(2), 193–212 (2005)
16. Koutroumpis, P., Leiponen, A.: Understanding the value of (big) data. In: IEEE International Conference on Big Data, pp. 38–42. IEEE (2013)
17. Burguillo, J.C.: Using game theory and competition-based learning to stimulate student motivation and performance. Comput. Educ. **55**(2), 566–575 (2010)

Accessibility Considerations in the Design of Serious Games for Production and Logistics

Jannicke Baalsrud Hauge[1,2](✉) (iD), Ioana Andreea Stefan[3] (iD), Niina Sallinen[4] (iD), and Jakob A. H. Baalsrud Hauge[1] (iD)

[1] BIBA – Bremer Institut für Produktion und Logistik GmbH, Hochschulring 20, 28359 Bremen, Germany
{baa,hau}@biba.uni-bremen.de
[2] Royal Institute of Technology, Kvarnbergagt. 12, 15181 Södertälje, Sweden
jmbh@kth.se
[3] Advanced Technology Systems, Str. Tineretului Nr 1, 130029 Targoviste, Romania
ioana.stefan@ats.com.ro
[4] LAB University of Applied Sciences, Mukkulankatu 19, 15210 Lahti, Finland
niina.sallinen@lab.fi

Abstract. Digital accessibility has been the focus of initiatives, policies and standards at European and international level in the last decade. However, adoption of accessibility guidelines and the development of accessible resources and applications remain limited and education is a primary example of the multiple challenges that must be addressed. This research has highlighted the main barriers that should be overcome in order to make digital educational games accessible for learners with disabilities and it has brought forward the critical need of personalizing the game contexts and analytics to meet specific profiles of learners with disabilities. Building upon the outcomes of two case studies, the authors propose a game analytics framework for learners with disabilities, in an effort to streamline game design processes that target accessibility.

Keywords: Accessibility · Digital educational games · Design considerations · Engineering education

1 Serious Games and Accessibility

Using Digital Educational Games for teaching aspects on logistics and production has a long tradition in engineering education [1, 2]. Many of the games have been used for many years with good results [3, 4], however hardly any of these are, to our knowledge, designed with a focus on accessibility. With an increased focus on different students' needs and with an increasing number of students with disabilities enrolling into higher education [5], there is a need to ensure that these students have access to the teaching material in a way that serves their rights of adapted teaching and corresponding materials [6–10], in order to avoid exclusions [11]. This has become more a more a topic as online

© IFIP International Federation for Information Processing 2021
Published by Springer Nature Switzerland AG 2021
A. Dolgui et al. (Eds.): APMS 2021, IFIP AICT 633, pp. 510–519, 2021.
https://doi.org/10.1007/978-3-030-85910-7_54

education has been increasingly growing [12], forcefully accelerated during the COVID pandemics [13].

Much has already happened in the field of online material including the Web Content Accessibility Guidelines (WCAG) and there is a wide range of assistive technologies and alternative methods of interaction that enable people with disabilities to use digital documents, as well as web and mobile applications [14]. Research has revealed the complexity of accessibility [15] and efforts have been made to tackle this multifaced issue [16]. A primary goal of applying web accessibility standards is improving the user experience (UX), by balancing the interplay between accessibility objectives and UX [17, 18], extending the availability of multimedia leaning content [19] or applying filtering option to make information on websites more accessible for visually impaired and blind users [20]. In addition to this, as educational institutions within EU, we need to bear in mind that we as public sector bodies need to implement the Directive (EU) 2016/2102 on the accessibility of the websites and mobile applications of public sector bodies. Therefore we have to follow the regulatory framework for the adoption of the accessibility guidelines [21] also for our teaching materials.

The objective of this article is therefore firstly to investigate the situation of games and accessibility in higher education, using an online survey, and secondly, to analyse a set of existing games (case studies A and B) in relation to their accessibility. In case study A, we assess three educational games. In case study B, we explain how we, following the EU directive, have started to improve the accessibility of a digital twin that we use in a gamified way to teach students. The last part of our work addresses some considerations on how we could use game analytics to identify the accessibility needs of students and to adapt the games to meet the students' needs while playing, and not as currently, in the pre-settings of the game.

2 Methodology

The objective of this paper is related to the knowledge and take-up of accessibility standards in higher education. In order to address these research questions, we have used a blended research method:

- A literature review in order to identify the relevant standards
- A survey with 22 questions administrated to teachers that teach in higher education. This survey was distributed in two existing consortia between January and March 2021. The questionnaire comprised 22 questions and was divided in five sections. The questionnaire was created in English and Romanian. It was completed by a number of 27 respondents from nine countries.
- An analysis of existing games that are used for educational purposes and their fulfilment of the current EU directive
- A design consideration on how accessibility requirements will have to be considered in the re-design of gaming applications that do not fulfil the requirements.

3 Analysis Results

This section describes first the online survey results, then the analysis of existing games and gamified applications on how well these meet the requirement given by the EU directive.

3.1 Online Survey Results

The distributed survey is part of two projects. Thus, it addresses more questions on accessibility than just those related to games, and also other fields than production and logistics as teaching topic. The 26 respondents represent: Universities – 9 (35%), Training centers – 5 (19%), University of Applied Science – 5 (19%), Higher education – 2 (11%), Vocational education – 1 (4%), NGO – 1 (4%) and Other – 3 (11%).

Regarding their area of expertise, the respondents come mostly from Computer Science 8 (31%), followed by Business and economics 7 (27%), to which also the field of logistics is counted. Most respondents are highly experienced in their field, with 48% reporting more than 10 years of experience (2 respondents above 20 years) and 52% between 1 and 10 years.

In the survey section that dealt with games and accessibility, 19 (73%) respondents answer that they hardly use digital games for teaching. Thus, 27% have more experience in using games at least monthly, as follows: four (15%) use games monthly, one (4%) use games weekly and two (8%) use games daily in their activities.

From 26 respondents only six (23%) use digital games as learning activities for students with special needs, but for the other part of the respondents who gave a negative answer 20 (77%) it is possible that there it may be a high risk that they have students with special needs which they are not aware of, due to the privacy restrictions and lack of access to the students records.

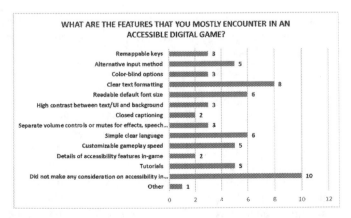

Fig. 1. Features the respondents mostly encounter in an accessible digital game

Regarding the greatest challenges in using digital games, eleven respondents mention insufficient time, followed by nine being unfamiliar with the technology, and eight answering that they lack accessible games that fit their teaching purpose. Only four respondents mention costs as their greatest challenge, and one mentions lack of administrative support.

When asked about the accessibility features that the respondents encounter in a game, 38% of them did not consider these features of a game at all, while 63% chose one or more feature from the list provided to them, as shown in Fig. 1.

3.2   Case Study A

This section describes the outcome of the assessment of existing games that are used for teaching purposes. Four research assistants not involved in the teaching activities carried out the assessment concerning to what extent these games fulfil the accessibility guidelines given in the EU directives.

RUEU? [22]: This game is used to let students explore different perspectives to a topic. One scenario is related to transport of goods across EU. The design and implementation part of the RUEU? game did not involve any design considerations concerning accessibility. Even though RUEU? is targeted to regular students, this game has potential for re-design to support players with disabilities. Below we present a list of design improvements that we think are relevant:

- *Visual impairment.* RUEU? is a text-based game and involves intensive reading. It is not possible for a visually impaired person to play it. Being able to see the screen and the layout of the buttons involved is crucial to the game-playing actions. This situation can be improved with a text-to-speech functionality with voice command.
- *Auditory impairment:* People with auditory impairment should not have any problem to play the game, given they do not have other difficulties. The music/sound in the game is not a mandatory part for the playability.
- *Silent/Mute:* People who are silent or mute can also play this game if they are able to read.
- *Physical impairment:* People who are physically impaired, in this case the people without fingers and/or hands will have difficulty playing the game. Other than extensive reading, RUEU? game is progressed through clicking the mouse. It could be resolved with implementing a voice command option.
- *ADHD/Autism:* Some of the texts/questions/statements in the game have a time constrain. For people with ADHD and/or Autism or similar impairment, the game could be tweaked to have no or longer time limitation for reading/answering to facilitate better participation.

Beaconing [23]: Beaconing's target is to break barriers in education through serious games and this project has facilitated a few accessibility options mainly related to sight and hear impairment as well as dyslexia. The game interface for both teachers and students have possibilities to be disability-friendly. The focus is mostly on visually impaired people in terms of adjustment options, but other disabilities are addressed as well:

- *Visual impairment:* Beaconing has text-to-speech functionality implemented for people who require oral feedback on the screen. The user can use a read-aloud function. Such a feature helps visually impaired as well as people with dyslexia to play the games. The font size, style and text colour can be changed according to the user needs. This is helpful for people who have lower degree of visual impairment, cognitive disabilities and Dyslexia. There is an option to use a magnification tool, which has adjustable magnification levels like a regular magnifying lens. The lens window can be moved around over the screen as desired. This platform also has the option to use screen tinting which is helpful with Dyslexia and other associated conditions. The access bar of the interface is equipped with different background theme options to facilitate certain eye conditions, acuteness to colour, colour blindness and other visual impairments. The options of having a reading bar that allows tracking of the position on the page with an underlining bar is also available. This feature can be helpful for people who have Dyslexia, ADHD, Down syndrome or other cognitive disabilities. There is another option called an Overlay Bar, which blackens out the content of the page except what the user is focusing on. The colour of the overlay bar can also be tinted when necessary.
- *Auditory impairment:* Beaconing has limited options in this respect. In the settings tab of Access Bar, the users have options to adjust text-to-speech voices, pitch and speed of the narration. This is for people with lower auditory impairment. For complete deaf people, the platform is still usable, as the visual inputs suffice to enable the gameplay and learning experience.
- *Silent/Mute:* People who are silent or mute can also participate in the games, as the interface is friendly enough for them. The games do not mandatorily require voice command to enable any feature.
- *Physical impairment:* Speech recognition has been implemented in the platform to facilitate people with physical impairment. People, who have limited physical abilities, have difficulties in putting information to the platform and in navigating around the page. Voice recognition, however, has over 40 different languages, which is a ground-breaking achievement. Dictated speech is transcribed into text and put into the Beaconing interface. The accuracy of speech to text is fantastic. Physically impaired people who have difficulties in terms of using a keyboard and/or a mouse benefit the most from this feature.
- *ADHD/Autism:* People with cognitive impairment can benefit from this platform as it ensures more inclusiveness for them. Text to speech, different background themes, various options regarding fonts, reading bar and overlay bar are beneficial for them. The lessons designed in different minigames can be changed in terms of time constrains according to user needs. The interface enables the teachers to copy and create another version of the same lesson to facilitate different impaired pupils. This option ensures that the teachers have options to reuse an existing lesson plan without requiring too much time.

Sumaga Island [24] - a co-operative game used for teaching the bullwhip effect. It is not designed with any accessibility considerations, but has good UI that is clear structured and fulfil the general recommendation for good design.

Visual Impairment: People with visual impairment are unable to use the game as the player is required to see the interface and interact with it. Potential improvement that can be relatively easily implemented: voice over everything and prepare for voice-recognition input; this makes the system a little bit like an answering machine. Sumaga Island is a text-based game and it has discrete steps (round based). Conclusion: The game can only be suitable for visual impaired people if voice recognition and corresponding actions on screen might be involved using different sensors etc.

Auditory Impairment: As described in the previous section, Sumaga Island is text based, so in this case people who have auditory impairments can play the game. However, depending on the group settings, the students often discuss while playing. This would reduce the suitability for this user group. A work around should be developed in this case.

Physically Impaired: The players need to be able interact with the interface and currently this is only possible through a mouse or touchscreens. A possible extension could be to implement eye-tracker options. Again, if the voice recognition and eye sensing is involved in the game, it can be possible for the player to play this game.

Silent/Mute Impairment: People who are silent or mute can also play this game if they are able to read.

ADHD/Autism: Sumaga per-se is not time sensitive; all players have to wait for the slowest one. Time management is not very good in the game because everyone has to wait for the other player to do his task/activity. The infrastructure of the game can be changed from server-client model to standalone entity in which each player performs her duties for a certain period of time and then leaves the game.

In the end, we can conclude by saying that these games have attributes that facilitate different impairments on different levels. There are options to include various features to make the games more inclusive, and thus to improve the accessibility of the games to people with disabilities. As long as these games serve as tools for education, the suggested improvements could be implemented to ensure barrier-free education for all.

3.3 Case Study B

Case study B is about creating a more accessible Digital Twin for logistic operation. The digital twin described in this section is used for problem based and explorative learning on the topics of technology assessment in logistics [25, 26]. This digital twin environment was originally developed for teaching and research purposes, but due to the pandemic, we needed to shift from laboratory-based teaching to online teaching. Different educational modules were included into the digital twin environment, related to technology usage in production logistics. The environment is adapted to fit the needs of sight impaired students and teachers. The application is used in a gamified way when it is used for teaching purposes and mirrors logistical operations.

An analysis of the original digital twin showed that it did not conform to the EU accessibility directive. Since the teaching modules for which it was planned to be used was finished after September 2020, the directive was already in force and we needed to fulfil its requirements.

As a first step, we therefore selected one of our regular target groups - a group of people with sight impairment, to test with us the digital twin environment. An analysis of the User Interface showed that the following functionalities could be added: a) Font size b) Subtitles c) Audio Assistance. These functionalities were implemented by March 2021, and even though the first experiments show an increased accessibility for sight impaired users, the current tests have shown that we need to improve the contrast in data visualisation. In addition, the system also has a replay function, which can be used for its original purpose of analysing different logistics operations, but also for a sight impaired person to investigate the operations with reduced speed. This function might also be used at a later stage for supporting students with minor learning difficulties.

The digital twin has the capability to start different physical operations via the user interface. This opens up the possibility for carrying out experiments in risk areas. The mixed-reality digital twin environment is in its prototypical implementation phase and the results are preliminary. We still need more testing with sight impaired people.

4   Design Considerations

The analysis presented in Sect. 3 reveals that there is still much work to do in order to meet the EU directive on accessibility for the games and gamified applications we are currently using in our classes. A main issue is however related to how we can identify what we need to change, both while playing or as in case study B, as pre-selection option before starting. Research on learning analytics has shown that original assessment designs require adaptations [27] and when it comes to accessibility, Gilbert [14] stated that "design is much more likely to be the source of exclusion than inclusion". Based on our collective experience in game re-design, re-purposing and adaption, we have made a first draft of a 'Game Analytics Framework for learners with disabilities' which we will

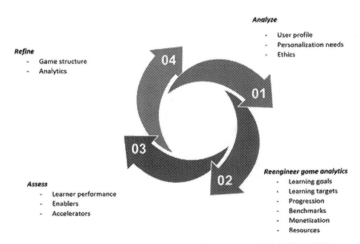

Fig. 2. Game Analytics Framework for learners with disabilities

apply for the games in case studies A and B for verification. The framework consists of four steps, illustrated in Fig. 2 and the associated text below.

01) Analyse: User profile: The user data represents the reference point for reengineering game analytics; Personalization needs: Specific user needs are identified; Ethics: User data has to be subject to data protection. **02) Reengineer game analytics:** Learning goals: The standard learning goals are analysed against the personalization needs; Learning targets: Obtainable performance levels are defined; Progression: Game progression is optimized based on specific needs; Benchmarks: Game benchmarks are adapted to match user personalization needs; Resources: Game resources are optimized to stimulate engagement and motivation. **03) Assess:** Learner performance: The player performance is evaluated and a summary of recommendations is made; Facilitators: The assessment identifies components that stimulate the learner and motivate learning processes; Accelerators: the assessment identifies adaptations that were successfully applied. **04) Refine:** The game structure: Further adaptations are implemented to enhance the player experience; Game analytics: Analytics are reviewed to maximize learning outcomes.

5 Conclusion and Next Steps

Just like content or web performance, accessibility represents a core consideration not only for creating websites [28], but for creating any type of educational resource or application [12, 29, 31, 32], including digital games [30].

Efforts towards establishing guidelines for game accessibility [31] have shown that rearrangement in the game design can help make games more accessible for people with disabilities [32]. However, such guidelines have not addressed the challenge of adapting game analytics to learners with disabilities.

Acknowledgment. This work has been partly funded by the EU projects Unilog (CB743), Includeme (No. 621547-EPP-1-2020-1-RO-EPPA3-IPI-SOC-IN), and by the German Federal Ministry of Education and Research (BMBF) through the project DigiLab4U (No. 16DHB2113).

References

1. Liu, C.-L.: Using a video game to teach supply chain and logistics management. Interact. Learn. Environ. **25**(8), 1009–1024 (2017). https://doi.org/10.1080/10494820.2016.1242503
2. Baalsrurd Hauge, J., Meyer-Larsen, N., Müller, R.: Improving the understanding of supply chain interaction through the application of business games. LDIC **2014**, 533–542 (2014)
3. Baalsrud Hauge, J., Riedel, J.C.K.H.: Evaluation of simulation games for teaching engineering and manufacturing. VS-GAMES **2012**, 210–220 (2012)
4. Hauge, J.M.B., Pourabdollahian, B., Riedel, J.C.K.H.: The use of serious games in the education of engineers. In: Emmanouilidis, C., Taisch, M., Kiritsis, D. (eds.) APMS 2012. IAICT, vol. 397, pp. 622–629. Springer, Heidelberg (2013). https://doi.org/10.1007/978-3-642-40352-1_78

5. Ismail, A., Kuppusamy, S.: Web accessibility investigation and identification of major issues of higher education websites with statistical measures: a case study of college websites. J. King Saud Univ. Comput. Inf. Sci. (2019). ISSN 1319-1578. https://doi.org/10.1016/j.jksuci.2019.03.011

6. Gelineau-Morel, R., Dilts, J.: Virtual education during COVID-19 and beyond. Pediatr. Neurol. **119**, 1–2 (2021). ISSN 0887-8994

7. Liu, C.H., Lin, H.Y.H.: The impact of COVID-19 on medical education: experiences from one medical university in Taiwan. J. Formos. Med. Assoc. (2021). ISSN 0929-6646. https://doi.org/10.1016/j.jfma.2021.02.016

8. Ratten, V., Jones, P.: Covid-19 and entrepreneurship education: implications for advancing research and practice. Int. J. Manage. Educ. **19**(1), 100432 (2021). ISSN 1472-8117

9. Haslam, M.: What might COVID-19 have taught us about the delivery of Nurse Education, in a post-COVID-19 world? Nurse Educ. Today **97**, 104707 (2021). ISSN 0260-6917. https://doi.org/10.1016/j.nedt.2020.104707

10. Jamalpur, B., Kafila, Chythanya, K.R., Kumar, K.S.: A comprehensive overview of online education – impact on engineering students during COVID-19. Mater. Today Proc. (2021). ISSN 2214-7853

11. Madhesh, A.: Full exclusion during COVID-19: Saudi Deaf education is an example. Heliyon **7**(3), e06536 (2021). ISSN 2405-8440

12. Lee, K.: Rethinking the accessibility of online higher education: a historical review. Internet High. Educ. **33**, 15–23 (2017). ISSN 1096-7516

13. Oyedotun, T.D.: Sudden change of pedagogy in education driven by COVID-19: perspectives and evaluation from a developing country. Res. Glob. **2**, 100029 (2020). ISSN 2590-051X

14. Gilbert, R.: Inclusive Design for a Digital World: Designing with Accessibility in Mind. Apress, New York (2019)

15. Michailidou, E., Eraslan, S., Yesilada, Y., Harper, S.: Automated prediction of visual complexity of web pages: tools and evaluations. Int. J. Hum. Comput. Stud. **145**, 102523 (2021). ISSN 1071-5819

16. Barroso, P.D.M., Pimenta, F.A., Pontin de Mattos Fortes, R.:: Accessibility and software engineering processes: a systematic literature review. J. Syst. Softw. **171**, 110819 (2021). ISSN 0164-1212

17. Aizpurua, A., Harper, S., Vigo, M.: Exploring the relationship between web accessibility and user experience. Int. J. Hum. Comput. Stud. **91**, 13–23 (2016). ISSN 1071-5819

18. Rodríguez, G., Pérez, J., Cueva, S., Torres, R.: A framework for improving web accessibility and usability of Open Course Ware sites. Comput. Educ. **109**, 197–215 (2017). ISSN 0360-1315

19. Rodriguez, D.: Increasing accessibility of audiovisual materials in the institutional repository at Florida State University. J. Acad. Libr. **47**(1), 102291 (2021). ISSN 0099-1333. https://doi.org/10.1016/j.acalib.2020.102291

20. Giraud, S., Thérouanne, P., Steiner, D.: Web accessibility: filtering redundant and irrelevant information improves website usability for blind users. Int. J. Hum. Comput. Stud. **111**, 23–35 (2018). ISSN 1071-5819

21. Yanyue, S.Y.: A review of the accessibility of ACT COVID-19 information portals. Technol. Soc. **64**, 101467 (2021). ISSN 0160-791X

22. Boyle, E.A., et al.: Linking learning outcomes and game mechanics in the early stages of the RU EU? Project. GALA **2018**, 191–200 (2018)

23. Hauge, J.B., Judd, N., Stefan, I.A., Stefan, A.: Perspectives on accessibility in digital games. In: Clua, E., Roque, L., Lugmayr, A., Tuomi, P. (eds.) ICEC 2018. LNCS, vol. 11112, pp. 402–406. Springer, Cham (2018). https://doi.org/10.1007/978-3-319-99426-0_51

24. Stefan, I.A., Baalsrud Hauge, J., Haase, F.: Using serious games and simulations for teaching co-operative decision-making. ITQM **2019**, 745–753 (2019). Own work

25. Hauge, J.B., Zafarzadeh, M., Jeong, Y., Li, Y., Khilji, W.A., Wiktorsson, M.: Digital and physical testbed for production logistics operations. In: Lalic, B., Majstorovic, V., Marjanovic, U., von Cieminski, G., Romero, D. (eds.) APMS 2020. IAICT, vol. 591, pp. 625–633. Springer, Cham (2020). https://doi.org/10.1007/978-3-030-57993-7_71

26. Hauge, J.B., Zafarzadeh, M., Jeong, Y., Li, Y., Khilji, W.A., Wiktorsson, M.: Employing digital twins within production logistics. ICE/ITMC **2020**, 1–8 (2020)

27. Ipperciel, D., ElAtia, S., Zaïane, O.R.: Data Mining and Learning Analytics. Wiley, Hoboken (2016)

28. Kalbag, L.: Accessibility for Everyone. A Book Apart, New York (2017)

29. LaSala, K.B., Polyakova-Norwood, V., Starnes-Ott, K.: Initiation of a nursing education curriculum with accessibility to all learners. J. Prof. Nurs. **36**(2), 24–28 (2020). ISSN 8755-7223

30. Stefan, I.A., Baalsrud Hauge, J.M., Sallinen, N., Stefan, A., Gheorghe, A.F.: Accessibility and education: are we fulfilling state of the art requirements? In: The 17th International Scientific Conference eLearning and Software for Education 2021, eLse, Bucharest (2021)

31. Kulkarni, M.: Digital accessibility: challenges and opportunities. IIMB Manage. Rev. **31**(1), 91–98 (2019). ISSN 0970-3896

32. Pereira, A.F.: Game accessibility guidelines for people with sequelae from macular chorioretinitis. Entertain. Comput. **28**, 49–58 (2018). ISSN 1875-9521

Smart and Sustainable Production and Supply Chains

Achieving Circular and Efficient Production Systems: Emerging Challenges from Industrial Cases

Mélanie Despeisse[1]([⊠]) [iD], Arpita Chari[1] [iD], Clarissa Alejandra González Chávez[1] [iD], Xiaoxia Chen[1] [iD], Björn Johansson[1] [iD], Víctor Igelmo Garcia[2] [iD], Anna Syberfeldt[2] [iD], Tarek Abdulfatah[3], and Alexey Polukeev[4] [iD]

[1] Chalmers University of Technology, Gothenburg, Sweden
{melanie.despeisse,arpita,clarissa.gonzalez,xiaoxia.chen,
bjorn.johansson}@chalmers.se
[2] University of Skövde, Skövde, Sweden
{victor.igelmo.garcia,anna.syberfeldt}@his.se
[3] Volvo Group Trucks Operations, Gothenburg, Sweden
tarek.abdulfatah.2@volvo.com
[4] Lund University, Lund, Sweden
alexey.polukeev@chem.lu.se

Abstract. As the need for more responsible production and consumption grows quickly, so does the interest in the concepts of eco-efficiency and circularity. To make swift progress towards sustainability, solutions must be developed and deployed at scale. It is therefore critical to understand the challenges faced by industry to accelerate the uptake of best practices for circular and efficient production systems. This paper presents the emerging issues from three industrial pilots in an on-going collaborative project. We discuss and suggest further work around crucial questions such as: How to deploy circular solutions from lab to industrial scale? How can digitalization support efficient circular processes?

Keywords: Sustainable development · Circular economy · Resource efficiency · Recycling · Remanufacturing · Reuse

1 Introduction

1.1 Background

Circular economy (CE) is an umbrella concept [1] promoting the retention of economic and environmental value of materials. The aim is to keep products in productive use for longer or to recapture materials in loops to give them a new life as products. Ideally, waste should systematically be seen as a resource and source of value [2]. Consequently, the benefits of CE align with the UN Sustainable Development Goals focusing on environmental impact reduction [3]. Several circular strategies were proposed to define the practices associated with different loops and targeting different parts of the value chain

© IFIP International Federation for Information Processing 2021
Published by Springer Nature Switzerland AG 2021
A. Dolgui et al. (Eds.): APMS 2021, IFIP AICT 633, pp. 523–533, 2021.
https://doi.org/10.1007/978-3-030-85910-7_55

[4, 5]. CE is well-defined [4, 6] and typically focuses on products' end-of-life; e.g. reuse, repair and remanufacturing to retain the value embedded in materials for as long as possible. They further include industrial waste management strategies, such as industrial symbiosis [7], and regenerative approaches, such as biomimicry [8, 9]. These strategies offer opportunities to decouple the environmental impact from the value delivered to customers and captured by businesses.

1.2 Knowledge Gap, Project Aim and Research Question

As the literature and examples of CE grow, the feasibility and benefits are becoming clearer. But our society is still largely linear and circular solutions are still the exceptions rather than the industrial norm. While inspiring CE ideas exist, they are often theoretical, experimental, isolated cases, or difficult to replicate [10, 11]. Transitioning towards CE requires a paradigm shift [12, 13], complex structures often relying on collaboration between organizational functions and between stakeholders along the value chain. This complexity presents additional challenges to create procedures to formalize and coordinate collaborative efforts. Many researchers have recognized different types of barriers, such as technological, financial, organizational, operational, etc. [14–16].

To support companies in their sustainability efforts, the project presented in this paper aims to identify and overcome the challenges they face in adopting circular and eco-efficient solutions. Accordingly, the overarching research question for this project was: How can technology development support efficient circular solutions and enable their uptake from lab to industrial scale?

1.3 Project Structure and Study Designs

This paper presents empirical findings from three case studies exploring novel circular solutions as part of a collaborative project between industry and academia: Enabling REuse, REmanufacturing and REcycling Within INDustrial systems (REWIND). The project structure is described in Fig. 1. Each case study employed different study designs and empirical methods to address the specific needs and conditions of each case. Pilot 1 was exploratory, qualitative business research. Pilot 2 was applied research focusing on technology development in a robot lab. Pilot 3 was an early-stage techno-economic analysis based on experimental research in a chemistry lab.

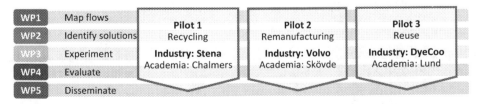

Fig. 1. Project structure and study design.

The next section presents the findings from the pilots (WP1-2) and the barriers encountered in developing circular solutions (WP3-4). We then discuss these barriers and suggest further work to realize, scale-up and systematize these solutions (WP5).

2   Emerging Issues from Industrial Pilots

2.1   Business Case for High-Value Recycling of Cooling Appliances

The first industrial pilot focused on recycling Waste from Electrical and Electronic Equipment (WEEE). Today, Stena Recycling handles a wide range of WEEE products. If managed improperly, WEEE can negatively affect the environment and human health [17]. In Sweden, it is the responsibility of end users to transport end-of-life refrigerators to collection centers. The WEEE collected from Sweden, Denmark and Norway is then transported to Stena Nordic Recycling Center. The current collection system does not promote value-retention, as the refrigerators are stored outdoors, where valuable components can be damaged or stolen, depleting the products of their potential value. Retaining the value of end-of-life refrigerators requires better integration across the supply chain, along further development and improvement of the collection centers.

At the Stena Nordic Recycling Center, the preparation processes for treating refrigerators are cleaning (removal of fridge contents), separation (removal of cables) and evaluation (registering of missing pieces such as doors and/or compressors). Today, the refrigerators are manually marked to identify the required recovery processes. Then cooling agents and oil are extracted from the system. The compressor is removed, drilled and drained in a mostly manual process. Finally, the refrigerator skeleton is fed to a shredding machine and materials sent for recycling. Advanced technologies could support operators directly in the more complex or dangerous processes. Stena is currently exploring the potential of physical and cognitive automation (e.g. robotics, machine vision and learning) to aid recovery processes. For example, compressors are valuable components but collecting them is labor intensive (high levels of know-how and physical efforts). Physical automation could prevent injuries and accidents while increasing the efficiency of and value recovered from the dismantling process.

All the refrigerators arriving at Stena's facilities are considered as end-of-life products. However, the intention to transition towards a more CE has led to interesting discussions suggesting that refrigerators could be remanufactured and refurbished as alternatives to recycling for value recovery. Implementing these alternatives requires operators' upskilling. Thus, alternative sources of value for social sustainability exist at organizational level through the use of digital training tools, such as AR/VR [18].

Finally, capturing data from end-of-life products as a source of value (e.g., brand, model, and product lifetime) could be appealing to manufacturers. This possibility was explored in similar studies attempting to achieve traceability for producers as a potential business model for post-consumer recycling [19]. However, commercializing data from products and enabling collaboration along the value chain also present a number of challenges for Stena. For instance, the placement of the compressor and information labels are not standardized between different brands and models of refrigerators, thereby hindering data capture and process automation. As of today, the process of identifying the product and its components requires extensive manual intervention. The data required to teach AI to recognize the product and assist in automating the compressor removal would require a database of at least 100,000 images. Gathering this data is demanding and the benefits still unclear.

Stena continuously strives to innovate and achieve more sustainable recycling processes. However, efforts are currently limited to an organizational level. Collaboration with manufacturers, collection centres and other logistics actors is still difficult in the absence of incentives to promote it (e.g. regulations, standards or market forces). CE is gaining attention, but the supporting information flows for collaboration are not yet in place. For example, leading manufacturers, such as Electrolux, focus on new product designs using recycled materials; but efforts to tackle problems at the products' end-of-life are comparatively low, especially considering that the majority of refrigerators reaching recyclers today were designed and manufactured a decade ago or more. This delay between design improvements for end-of-life management and their benefits present a major barrier for collaboration between manufacturers, collection centres, recyclers and other actors in circular value chains to tackle today's WEEE at scale.

2.2 Operator Support for Remanufacturing Truck Components

The second industrial pilot targeted remanufacturing operations at Volvo focusing on "giving a new lifecycle" to components from their previously manufactured truck engines. Remanufacturing begins with an order from customers. The product previously collected is taken into the remanufacturing line consisting of five major processes: disassembly, cleaning, machining, reassembly, and quality control. In the disassembly process, all components are removed and classified. Some components are systematically discarded (e.g. wiring harnesses, air harnesses, sensors, camshafts). The main parts are cleaned and assessed whether they can be reused or must be replaced. Parts that must be reprocessed to meet quality standards are sent to machining stations. The components are then reassembled using reprocessed parts and new parts. Finally, the product goes to a quality control station before being delivered to the customer.

Remanufacturing is a highly variable and complex operation at the task level. Most of the remanufacturing-related knowledge is tacit. However, analysis and evaluation are usually more effective and meaningful when knowledge is explicit [20]. This pilot aims to convert this tacit knowledge into digitalized, explicit knowledge. Once transformed, this knowledge can be standardized in content and form, and presented to the worker using head-mounted augmented reality (AR) devices.

The central piece of this solution is an industrial internet of things (IIoT) platform used as a scalable medium. It retrieves up-to-date information for the operation at hand from the product lifecycle management platform and sends it to the AR device. This information (dis/assembly instructions) is displayed in AR as overlayed 3D objects, animations, text, audio or a combination of them. The IIoT creates dependencies between connected industrial equipment or retrieve worker's feedback for future improvements. Moreover, the IIoT platform can be used to perform data analytics enabling data-driven CE-related improvements. Ideally, this AR solution will offer benefits related to increased efficiency and effectiveness [21] as well as new opportunities enabled by data continuity and cloud-based systems [22, 23] including improvements on scalability, adaptability, and cybersecurity. Furthermore, data continuity can provide a systematic approach to standardize critical operations that have high environmental impacts when performed sub-optimally.

An *ex-ante* evaluation identified technical challenges hindering successful implementation, including the implications of a foundational change in tools used in the process; for instance, considerable investment, implementation ramp-up, or human implications. Furthermore, several technology-related challenges have become apparent in this pilot. For instance, the complexity introduced from a data and information perspective requires upskilling of the IT department. In addition, few companies have developed feasible AR and IIoT products and their maturity in industrial environments is still limited. Complementary technologies, such as object tracking or environment understanding in AR, need to be improved to further exploit the potential of this solution.

2.3 Efficiency and Reuse in Textile Dyeing Processes

The third pilot explored a novel process to dye natural fibers. Textile production is a major contributor to water pollution as water is the most common dyeing medium. Although end-of-pipe technologies progressed well to prevent effluents and chemicals from entering the environment (e.g. zero liquid discharge and zero discharge of hazardous chemicals), equipment price and running costs can be expensive. Besides, zero-liquid discharge processes are energy-intensive and increase energy-related emissions. Moreover, solid wastes are still produced and difficult to treat.

A new dyeing process was introduced in the 1980s using a supercritical fluid as a dyeing medium [24]. It provides easy separation from chemicals, further allowing recirculation and reuse of the supercritical fluid and dyes at a low energy cost. Carbon dioxide is frequently used as supercritical fluid for dyeing because of its low critical point (31 °C, 73.8 bar), safety (non-toxic, non-flammable), low cost and high availability (by-product produced in large volume from different sources) [25]. Synthetic fibers, in particular polyester, are perfectly compatible with supercritical carbon dioxide ($scCO_2$) and the respective $scCO_2$ dyeing process was commercialized by DyeCoo in 2012. In a typical setting, solution of a dye in $scCO_2$ is pumped through a roll of textile at high temperature and pressure (80–120 °C and 200–250 bar) until dye absorption is complete. Evaporation of $scCO_2$ gives dry textile and dye leftovers in a separate vessel. Environmental benefits are 40–60 l/kg water savings, 0.2–0.3 kg/kg process chemical savings, smaller dye leftovers (1% vs 10% for water) and lower energy consumption. Additionally, $scCO_2$ dyeing allows freedom in factory location since it is not reliant on water sources and has lower machine operational costs.

However, dyeing of natural fibers is more complicated. While $scCO_2$ is a good solvent for dyeing polyester (hydrophobic solvent and substrate), water is a good solvent for dyeing natural fibers (hydrophilic solvent and substrate) [26]. In contrast to polyester, $scCO_2$ does not promote swelling and plasticization of natural fibers, and dyes do not readily diffuse into them. Cotton is an especially challenging substrate due to a hydrogen-bonded cross-linked framework which remains nearly intact in $scCO_2$. Therefore, either natural fibers must be modified for the dye to adhere to the fabric, or process chemicals must be added to promote dye uptake. Fiber modifications in their present state seem too chemicals-intensive for an eco-friendly solution and also require an additional water-based pre-treatment step. Medium modifications hold considerable promise, but a feasibility study is needed to find out to what extent environmental benefits of $scCO_2$ dyeing will be preserved. While the dyeing itself can still be more energy-efficient (comparable dyeing conditions, for example), recycling of process chemicals raises some concerns. Main implementation barriers are the same as for other supercritical fluid technology applications, and are associated with high equipment price compared to traditional setup. More specifically with respect to natural fibers, studies are needed to confirm expected process benefits and the possibility to reach the desired dyeing quality at an acceptable environmental cost.

3 Discussion

Building on prior published work [14–16], this section presents the issues emerging in the industrial pilots by categorizing them and suggesting ways to overcome the barriers encountered. The pilots connecting to each barrier are annotated as lettered superscripts (a: recycling; b: remanufacturing; c: reuse) in Table 1 for engineering challenges, Table 2 for business challenges, and Table 3 for other legal and societal challenges.

Table 1. Barriers and recommendations from an engineering perspective.

Barriers	Recommendations
The material heterogeneity and contamination make it difficult to reprocess[a]	Avoid mixing incompatible materials and establish standards to define "sustainable" composite materials
The technology or processes for separation, decontamination, recycling and/or reprocessing do not exist due to lack of R&D[a,b,c]	Create a strong research community for scientific and technical development to explore solutions for material reprocessing
Recovery solutions exist but are not widely available[a,b,c]	Deploy recovery solutions and the necessary infrastructure to ensure accessibility
The recycled material does not have the characteristics (aesthetic value, quality or performance) required for its reuse[a]	Ensure that reprocessing does not degrade the material quality, that the material properties are known and stable to enable reuse in new products
The processes for material reprocessing is too complex or too inefficient to be attractive[a,b,c]	Develop materials which can be reprocessed with minimal mechanical, thermal and chemical treatment
The complexity of the component (its structure and assembly) makes it difficult to repair and disassemble[a,b]	Design products and components for longevity, non-destructive disassembly, reparability and remanufacturability
The materials are difficult to transport and store (e.g. time-sensitive, condition-critical, voluminous, needs monitoring)[a,b]	Develop storage solutions and local reprocessing infrastructure

(continued)

Table 1. (*continued*)

Barriers	Recommendations
The material is hazardous with adverse health and environmental effects[a,c]	Engineer materials which are inert or non-toxic when handled adequately so they can be reprocessed safely
The resources required and environmental impacts generated by recovery processes offset in part or completely the benefits (compared to linear disposal)[b,c]	Evaluate the potential environmental trade-offs in the waste management system and develop alternative solutions to increase the net benefits of recovery

Table 2. Barriers and recommendations from a business perspective.

Barriers	Recommendations
Economic viability	
Virgin materials are cheap and abundant resulting in low incentives for recovery despite high "environmental and social costs"[a,b]	Integrate externalities as an economic cost (tax or penalty) to balance the economic competitiveness of sustainable alternatives
The inherent economic value of the end-of-life products, components or materials is insufficient to justify the investments required for their recovery[a,b]	Create a market pull (demand) for recycled materials to incentivize the development of adequate infrastructure for cost-efficient recovery and reprocessing of recyclate
There is too much diversity in material composition and product design to allow for efficient and economically viable recovery[a,b]	Standardize key aspects of material, product and component design so the recovery solutions are applicable industry-wide and benefit from economies of scale
It is too difficult to evaluate and compare circular and linear solutions, especially considering returning material flows' uncertainty[a]	Develop evaluation methods to highlight trade-offs between short- and long-term effects, thus better supporting decision makers
Organizational context and governance	
Top management does not integrate sustainability in the business strategy[a,c]	Prioritize sustainability as a core value in the business strategy
Top management is resistant to deviation from business-as-usual (risk aversion) which limits their ability to innovate[a,c]	Encourage green innovations and show willingness to change through top management commitment and support (CSR)
The company focuses on operating within a fixed model (high reliance on given constraints)[a,b,c]	Develop and test new ideas continuously to increase agility around constraints and build resilience capabilities to operate flexibly under uncertain conditions

(*continued*)

Table 2. (*continued*)

Barriers	Recommendations
Industry stakeholders and value chain configurations	
The current linear model of production and consumption is the norm in a given sector despite its environmental and social impacts[a,b,c]	Increase the visibility of impacts caused by the current linear model
There is no interest in shifting for CE and no awareness about the benefits of doing so[a,c]	Advocate for circular solutions by showcasing the benefits through examples of best practices relevant this sector
There are no clear responsibilities for handling the end-of-life materials[a]	Create a chain of responsibility and accountability for the impacts generated at each step of the supply chain by the actors with control over the materials
The materials and products are distributed and difficult to locate[a,b]	Define central locations for collection and inform relevant stakeholders
There is insufficient information sharing to develop efficient circular solutions[a,b]	Connect relevant stakeholders along the value chain to feedback information necessary for continuous improvement of material recovery processes
There are no established structures to develop the necessary industry-wide solutions for CE and the benefits of value recovery are distributed between stakeholders in ways that do not encourage investing in such infrastructure[a,b]	Promote collaboration to generate and share benefits with all stakeholders involved in the circular value chain

Table 3. Barriers and recommendations from a non-industrial stakeholder perspective.

Barriers	Recommendations
Regulatory framework	
There are no government incentives to tackle problematic material flows[a,b]	Offer subsidies and support to stimulate the transition to CE
There are no consequences for wrongful handling and disposal of materials[a,b,c]	Impose substantial fines and strict control of wrongful handling and disposal of materials
Old regulations are preventing the shift to alternative waste management systems[a]	Remove regulatory barriers by adapting legal requirements to BAT
Public perception and consumption habits	
End-users/consumers are not aware of the problems caused by the current linear model and has accepted is as the status quo[a,b,c]	Educate end-users/consumers about the impacts of the current linear model and share examples of best practice to inspire change

(*continued*)

Table 3. (*continued*)

Barriers	Recommendations
There is no information available to end-users/consumers about the impact of product and materials life cycle to influence their purchase decision[a,b,c]	Increase transparency about the impact of product and materials provenance and end-of-life management through clear communication solutions (e.g. eco-labels)
There are no public discussions or media coverage about the disposal of problematic materials due to discomfort or taboo[a,b,c]	Raise public awareness and interest in tackling these issues through sensible communication media and sensible solutions

4 Conclusion

This paper presented three pilots exploring circular solutions within industrial systems. We discussed arising issues to extract lessons learnt based on the barriers encountered (technical, economic, organizational, structural, legal and societal). Some of the circular solutions explored make use of digital technologies (automation, information sharing, operator support, computer vision and machine learning). We also identified and evaluated trade-offs between achieving circular processes and reducing the net environmental impact of these processes. We went on to make recommendations to overcome the barriers identified. Some of the key messages are summarized below:

- Recovery processes are often too complex or too inefficient to be attractive when products and materials are not designed to fit in a CE. Product complexity (its structure and component assembly) makes it difficult to disassemble in a non-destructive manner. Efficient and automated reprocessing technologies are sometimes available or can be developed to overcome such barriers. However, integrating environmental considerations in early stages of the product design remains a priority.
- In some cases, the environmental impacts generated by circular processes offset some of the benefits compared to traditional processes and linear disposal. Trade-offs must be evaluated between the benefits and additional impacts of the waste management system. Alternative solutions must be explored to increase the net benefits of recovery and make them more attractive economically and environmentally.
- End-of-life materials or products can be difficult to transport and store. When adequate infrastructure and transport solutions are not in place, products may lose some of their value before reaching the stage where it can be recovered. This is especially the case when the benefits of value recovery are distributed between stakeholders in ways that do not incentivize investments in such infrastructure. Collaboration across the supply chain is therefore necessary to promote value retention.
- When the materials and processes have adverse health and environmental effects, standardized procedures must be in place to ensure they are handled and reprocessed safely. Automation is often an attractive solution; however, material and product diversity hinder technical feasibility and economically viability. Key aspects of material, product and component design should be standardized so the recovery solutions can be applied industry-wide and benefit from economies of scale.

- Information sharing between end-of-life (recyclers and remanufacturers) and beginning-of-life stakeholders (designers and manufacturers) is often missing, thus limiting the ability to develop efficient circular solutions in the future. Relevant stakeholders along the value chain must be connected to feedback information necessary to develop circular solutions and to enable their continuous improvement. Such information flows can be supported by value chain digitalization; e.g. digital thread.
- When the recovery processes are handled by the original manufacturer, lack of information is less of an issue, although the product complexity and variability remain a challenge. The tasks require high levels of skills and knowledge; thus operator support and training (reskilling and upskilling) are needed. Digital solutions can provide an enabling platform for knowledge transfer and information flows to and from the process to support continuous improvement of circular processes.

Further work aims to implement the recommendations and scale up the solutions proposed to demonstrate their economic feasibility and environmental benefits, and showcase inspiring examples of circular industrial processes.

Acknowledgements. The authors wish to acknowledge Magnus Johnson, Ernst Siewers, Henrik Jilvero, Märta Bergfors, Farshid Harandi, Rasmus Johansson, Johanna Reimers, Geoffrey Blanc, and Johan Kronholm for their contribution to the project. With thanks to the Swedish innovation agency Vinnova and the Strategic Innovation Programme Produktion2030 (funding number 2019-00787). The work was carried out within Chalmers' Area of Advance Production; the support is gratefully acknowledged.

References

1. Blomsma, F., Brennan, G.: The emergence of circular economy: a new framing around prolonging resource productivity. J. Ind. Ecol. **21**(3), 603–614 (2017)
2. den Hollander, M.C., Bakker, C.A., Hultink, E.J.: Product design in a circular economy: development of a typology of key concepts and terms. J. Ind. Ecol. **21**(3), 517–525 (2017)
3. Schroeder, P., Anggraeni, K., Weber, U.: The relevance of circular economy practices to the sustainable development goals. J. Ind. Ecol. **23**(1), 77–95 (2019)
4. Kalmykova, Y., Sadagopan, M., Rosado, L.: Circular economy - from review of theories and practices to development of implementation tools. Resour. Conserv. Recycl. **135**, 190–201 (2018)
5. Saidani, M., Yannou, B., Leroy, Y., Cluzel, F., Kendall, A.: A taxonomy of circular economy indicators. J. Clean. Prod. **207**, 542–559 (2019)
6. Kirchherr, J., Reike, D., Hekkert, M.: Conceptualizing the circular economy: an analysis of 114 definitions. Resourc. Conserv. Recycl. **127**, 221–232 (2017)
7. Benedetti, M., Holgado, M., Evans, S.: A novel knowledge repository to support industrial symbiosis. In: Lödding, H., Riedel, R., Thoben, K.-D., von Cieminski, G., Kiritsis, D. (eds.) APMS 2017. IAICT, vol. 514, pp. 443–451. Springer, Cham (2017). https://doi.org/10.1007/978-3-319-66926-7_51
8. Benyus, J.M.: Biomimicry: Innovation Inspired by Nature. William Morrow, New York (1997)
9. Byrne, G., Dimitrov, D., Monostori, L., Teti, R., van Houten, F., Wertheim, R.: Biological-isation: biological transformation in manufacturing. CIRP J. Manuf. Sci. Technol. **21**, 1–32 (2018)

10. Ehrenfeld, J., Gertler, N.: Industrial ecology in practice: the evolution of interdependence at Kalundborg. J. Ind. Ecol. **1**(1), 67–79 (1997)
11. Chertow, M., Ehrenfeld, J.: Organizing self-organizing systems: toward a theory of industrial symbiosis. J. Ind. Ecol. **16**(1), 13–27 (2012)
12. Gladwin, T.N., Kennelly, J.J., Krause, T.-S.: Shifting paradigms for sustainable development: implications for management theory and research. Acad. Manag. Rev. **20**(4), 874–907 (1995)
13. Geisendorf, S., Pietrulla, F.: The circular economy and circular economic concepts—a literature analysis and redefinition. Thunderbird Int. Bus. Rev. **60**(5), 771–782 (2018)
14. Ritzén, S., Sandström, G.Ö.: Barriers to the circular economy - integration of perspectives and domains. Procedia CIRP **64**, 7–12 (2017)
15. Halse, L.L., Jæger, B.: Operationalizing industry 4.0: understanding barriers of industry 4.0 and circular economy. In: Ameri, F., Stecke, K.E., von Cieminski, G., Kiritsis, D. (eds.) APMS 2019. IAICT, vol. 567, pp. 135–142. Springer, Cham (2019). https://doi.org/10.1007/978-3-030-29996-5_16
16. Dieckmann, E., Sheldrick, L., Tennant, M., Myers, R., Cheeseman, C.: Analysis of barriers to transitioning from a linear to a circular economy for end of life materials: a case study for waste feathers. Sustainability **12**(5), 1725 (2020). https://doi.org/10.3390/su12051725
17. Jang, Y.-C.: Waste electrical and electronic equipment (WEEE) management in Korea. J. Mater. Cycles Waste Manag. **12**(4), 283–294 (2010)
18. Kerin, M., Pham, D.T.: A review of emerging industry 4.0 technologies in remanufacturing. J. Clean. Prod. **237**, 117805 (2019)
19. Tong, X., Tao, D., Lifset, R.: Varieties of business models for post-consumer recycling in China. J. Clean. Prod. **170**, 665–673 (2018)
20. Johannesson, P., Perjons, E.: An Introduction to Design Science. Springer, Cham (2014). https://doi.org/10.1007/978-3-319-10632-8
21. Egger, J., Masood, T.: Augmented reality in support of intelligent manufacturing – a systematic literature review. Comput. Ind. Eng. **140**, 106195 (2020)
22. Babiceanu, R.F., Seker, R.: Big Data and virtualization for manufacturing cyber-physical systems. Comput. Ind. **81**, 128–137 (2016)
23. Oztemel, E., Gursev, S.: Literature review of Industry 4.0 and related technologies. J. Intell. Manuf. **31**(1), 127–182 (2018). https://doi.org/10.1007/s10845-018-1433-3
24. Bach, E., Cleve, E., Schollmeyer, E.: Past, present and future of supercritical fluid dyeing technology. Rev. Prog. Color. Relat. Top. **32**(1), 88–102 (2002)
25. Banchero, M.: Supercritical fluid dyeing of synthetic and natural textiles – a review. Color. Technol. **129**(1), 2–17 (2013)
26. Sawada, K., Takagi, T., Jun, J.H., Ueda, M., Lewis, D.M.: Dyeing natural fibres in supercritical carbon dioxide using a nonionic surfactant reverse micellar system. Color. Technol. **118**(5), 233–237 (2002)

Value Stream Mapping (VSM) to Evaluate and Visualize Interrelated Process-Chains Regarding Circular Economy

Jeff Mangers[✉], Meysam Minoufekr, and Peter Plapper

University of Luxembourg, Luxembourg City, Luxembourg
jeff.mangers@uni.lu

Abstract. The concept of circular economy (CE) aims to close and slow resource loops without neglecting the goals of sustainable development. Recently, the concept received encouraging attention among researchers and business experts to be a convenient solution to move away from the finite linear economy concept to a more sustainable solution. However, this change of paradigm is only possible if we consider systems in a holistic manner and can localize the preventing hurdles.

Value stream mapping (VSM) is a commonly known lean method, used to develop current state visualization of product and information flows within organization, helping to seek weaknesses and improve process flows. The motivation of this paper is a new C-VSM model, which enables its users to evaluate and visualize connected process-chains regarding CE on different levels in a holistic manner. For this purpose, the traditional VSM model was adapted towards the needs and requirements of CE through the application of a new representation method, additional indicators, and an appropriated evaluation system. C-VSM is in line with the current political and industrial objectives to apply CE principles by enabling a holistic reflection and consideration of supply-chains (SCs) on different levels. The model itself is validated through an extensive cross-company case study.

Keywords: Value stream mapping (VSM) · Circular-economy · Process-chains · Supply-chain · Company

1 Introduction

The concept of circular economy is attracting more and more attention and is currently a highly debated topic within scientific, political, and industrial communities. CE promotes the responsible and cyclical use of resources [1], the longevity of products [2], the minimization of waste [3] and this without neglecting sustainability [4]. CE is seen as a way to overcome the current dominant economic development model, the so called 'take, make and dispose' [5] model, by promoting the adoption of closed and slowed resource loops [1]. A major critique of CE is the missing uniformly accepted definition [6], which may lead to the concept ultimately collapsing or remaining in a deadlock [7].

© IFIP International Federation for Information Processing 2021
Published by Springer Nature Switzerland AG 2021
A. Dolgui et al. (Eds.): APMS 2021, IFIP AICT 633, pp. 534–542, 2021.
https://doi.org/10.1007/978-3-030-85910-7_56

Furthermore, it complicates the circularity assessment and measurement of products or process-chains, resulting in a wide range of circularity indicators [8], which may lead to different or even incoherent conclusions [1].

The change in production systems leads to new logistical needs related to resources and waste, as well as to the distribution and recovery of products, thus influencing the current SCs [9]. A SC consists of all parties involved, directly or indirectly, fulfilling a customer request [10]. The change towards circular supply chain management (CSCM) comes up with new challenges, concerning resource efficiency, life management strategies, reverse network management and sustainability [11]. One possibility to visualize and map supply-chains is VSM [12], even with regard to sustainability [13] and CE [14]. The VSM method was made popular by Rother and Shook [15] and was standardized due to a variety of different approaches leading to misunderstanding and conflicts within supply networks [16] within ISO 22468 [17]. VSM is one of the more common lean methods, which is used to develop current state visualizations of product and information flows within organizations [18].

This paper extends the VSM application towards the evaluation and visualization of process-chains regarding CE on macro (supply-chain) and micro (company) level. In doing so, it is possible to analyze SCs in a top-down manner regarding CE with the help of VSM. The macro level allows for a holistic view and evaluation, and the micro level provides a more detailed perspective on the individual resource flows. The different micro VSMs are added up to one overall macro level VSM.

2   Literature Review

This chapter reviews the current applicability of VSM within the scientific literature. In this research, 'value' refers to the 9R-framework and the waste hierarchy [6, 19].

Typically, VSM visualizes material and information flows within companies and focuses on time. Over time, this has been extended by further applications. The integration of CE aspects into VSM has already been done recently by other researchers. Edtmayer et al. [20] included three re-utilization cycles for waste material into VSM. Galvão et al. [21] mainly focused on connecting value streams within circular business models and their ecosystems and not on measuring the circularity of value streams. Hedlund et al. [14] investigated how companies and industrial systems and networks might use value stream mapping as a tool to enhance sustainability and accelerate change towards an eco-friendly, circular economy.

In addition, a lot of focus lately lay on combining VSM with sustainability [20, 22–27]. In this context, additional assessment ladders with new indicators were added to the time assessment. The added indicators are related to materials [22], environment [28], energy [29], water [24], emissions [22], transport [26], waste [13], efficiency (OEE) [30], physical work index [24], noise level [25] and life-cycle-assessment [25]. Other interesting fields of application for VSM are discrete event simulation [31], industry 4.0 with dynamic value streams [32], information flows [18, 33] and multi-layer VSMs [34].

As shown, a research gap concerning the holistic applicability of VSM within interrelated SCs based on CE is missing. None of the listed studies can evaluate the circularity of related process-chains and visualize the connection between different partners. This essential gap is filled by the results presented in the following sections.

3   Research Methodology and Findings

This chapter explains the research methodology and discusses the findings, so the new C-VSM evaluation and visualization for macro- (Fig. 1) and micro-level (Fig. 2).

The research methodology is analytical and the case study structure is based on the Yin methodology [35]. The data collection was done during 10 different company visits, which are all part of PET-bottle SC-network in Luxembourg. The logic behind C-VSM is to first map the overall resource flow throughout the SC, by starting at the OEM on a macro level with as main information the determination of the resource flow value. This helps to get a general overview and understanding of the SC. Afterwards, the different SC-partners are analyzed more in detail on a micro-level and the respective data for each process are collected. This implies the information exchange as well between different SC partners. The visualization itself is based on ISO 22468:2020 and on other mentioned VSM use cases. The evaluation with the respective indicators is taken either from a list of indicators already integrated in sustainable VSMs or from a systematic literature review coming up with 181 circularity measurement indicators (not yet published). The indicators are divided into direct (related to circularity, so the resource flow) and indirect indicators (related to sustainability, so environmental, economic, and social aspects). In another study [36], three main CE goals (close & slow loops [1], minimized waste [37] and sustainability [6]) and two areas with a need for action (identifying the needed collection, sorting and R-infrastructure & developing circular product guidelines) were determined on which the indicators are dependent.

The C-VSM model uncovers overarching problems within SCs, which are only visible through the holistic applicability. The practical application was validated by the PET-bottle case study, which highlighted the close dependencies between the end-of-life (EOL) and the beginning-of-life (BOL). In the future, the study should be extended to other products and sectors.

3.1   Macro-level

The macro C-VSM visualization differs significantly from traditional VSMs. The main questions were how to depict a circular flow of resources and how to add a value depiction into the framework. Both were achieved by referring to the swim lane alternative [17] and the inclusion of the 9R-framework [6]. Each level of the swim lane diagram represents a certain CE value, whereas the lowest level defines the overall value of a SC. The 9R-framework is included as a vertical value-hill on the right side of the diagram, ranging from R0 (highest) to R9 (lowest). Since the three highest Rs (refuse, rethink, and reduce) are only reachable trough an adapted design, they are depicted collectively on the design level. The second value is the actual use-phase, during which the product has its highest value. All other Rs are subsequently included except for the last one, namely 'disposal' which has no CE value and should be avoided.

Each SC-partner is visualized as a process-box with a respective data-box, which contains information from the micro analysis. The OEM is visualized as ISO 22468 customer and the direct (e.g., PET-bottle, HDPE-cap) and indirect (e.g., additional packaging foil) supplier are visualized as ISO 22468 supplier. The user has a completely new symbol. Depending on the respective stage, different information is shown within the data-boxes (see Fig. 1 and 2). Since the overall value is defined during the collection and sorting process (compare a glass and PET-single use bottle), this process is ranging from R3 to disposal. The resource flows between two SC-partners are color coded and completed by a respective transportation symbol. A last addition is the inclusion of two information flows, D- (active in the product/ process design) and R-info flow (active in the resource retake), and the inclusion of certain basic product-characteristics (e.g., material, fu, etc.), defining the product in question.

3.2 Micro-level

The micro C-VSM differs slightly from traditional VSM. Main differences are the newly included indicators and the visualization of additional material flows. The material flows, the same as the suppliers are divided into 4 different groups, which are color coded. The first group represents the actual product (e.g., water; green), the second group represents direct inputs (e.g., bottle, cap, and label; blue), the third indirect inputs (e.g., additional foil packaging; red) and auxiliary materials (e.g., glue; black). The output flows and customers are similarly divided into three groups, resources staying in the same loop (e.g., packed bottles; black), resources going to other loops (e.g., PET-scrap; blue) and waste (e.g., foil wraps; red). The traditional information flow is kept and the D- and R-info flow are added to see if a link between both exists.

The used indicators are shown in Fig. 1 and Fig. 2 and the meaning of the abbreviations can be found in Table 1 (appendix). Relations between micro- and macro data exist and the indicators are mostly based on a functional unit. The CO_2-equivalents are calculated with national conversion factors and serve as rough indication. The data itself and the names are fictive to avoid sharing any critical information from companies.

4 Discussion and Conclusion

This paper introduces a new VSM visualization and evaluation on macro and micro level regarding CE. This is of importance for other researchers and industrials, who benefit from the holistic applicability of C-VSM and the insights of the case study. Thus, the results not only help to advance the applicability of VSM but are interesting for everyone interested in better understanding the connections and dependencies within SCs and economic systems in general. A future publication will discuss the used indicators.

Currently, C-VSM was only applied within one extensive packaging use case, focusing on the main resource flow. In the future, it needs to be verified in further use cases. At present, MS-Visio is used to draw the VSM and a connection to MS-Excel is included for the data handling. Since this is not an ideal solution, mainly regarding the analysis (potential improvement VSM) and optimization (future state VSM [17]) as well as the short-, medium-, and long-term perspectives for sustainability, this should be made more interactive, allowing for the simulation of different scenarios.

A valuable extension of the current VSM applicability was presented in this paper, which highlighted the necessity of holistic approaches to solve current CE problems.

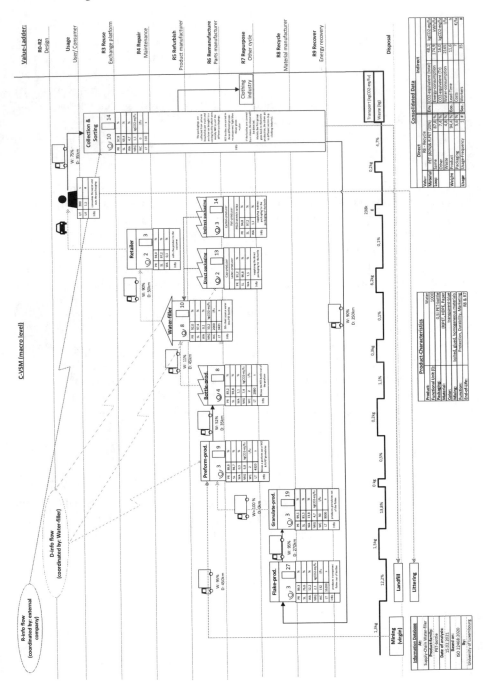

Fig. 1. C-VSM, macro level

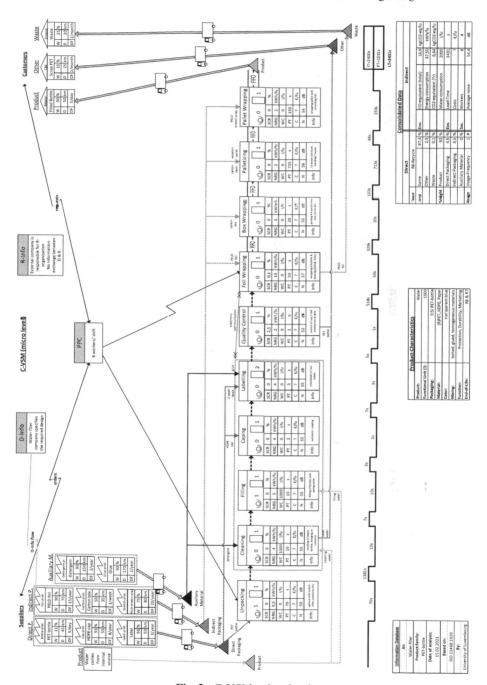

Fig. 2. C-VSM, micro level

Appendix
See Table 1.

Table 1. Abbreviations of the different indicators

Abbreviation:	Meaning:
C	costs
D	distance
DF	deliver frequency
fu	functional unit
IT	idle time
LT	lead time
N	noise
NRG	energy-consumption
PR	product-weight
PT	process-time
SCR	scrap-rate
SL	same-loop
W	weight
WA	waste
WC	water-consumption
☺	number of operators
☐	macro: number of process, micro: number of machines

Funding. This research was funded by the Di-Plast project, which is supported by Interreg NWE. The project aims to improve the uptake of recycled plastic material (rPM) within the packaging and building sectors. Di-Plast aims to improve processes for a more stable rPM material supply and quality.

Find more details about Di-Plast at https://www.nweurope.eu/projects/project-search/di-plast-digital-circular-economy-for-the-plastics-industry/.

References

1. Moraga, G., et al.: Circular economy indicators: what do they measure? Resour. Conserv. Recycl. **146**(March), 452–461 (2019). https://doi.org/10.1016/j.resconrec.2019.03.045
2. Kristensen, H.S., Mosgaard, M.A.: A review of micro level indicators for a circular economy – moving away from the three dimensions of sustainability? J. Clean. Prod. **243**, 118531 (2020). https://doi.org/10.1016/j.jclepro.2019.118531
3. Di Maio, F., Rem, P.C., Baldé, K., Polder, M.: Measuring resource efficiency and circular economy: a market value approach. Resour. Conserv. Recycl. **122**, 163–171 (2017). https://doi.org/10.1016/j.resconrec.2017.02.009
4. Elia, V., Gnoni, M.G., Tornese, F.: Measuring circular economy strategies through index methods: a critical analysis. J. Clean. Prod. **142**, 2741–2751 (2017). https://doi.org/10.1016/j.jclepro.2016.10.196
5. Bocken, N.M.P., Olivetti, E.A., Cullen, J.M., Potting, J., Lifset, R.: Taking the circularity to the next level: a special issue on the circular economy. J. Ind. Ecol. **21**(3), 476–482 (2017). https://doi.org/10.1111/jiec.12606

6. Kirchherr, J., Reike, D., Hekkert, M.: Conceptualizing the circular economy: an analysis of 114 definitions. Resour. Conserv. Recycl. **127**(April), 221–232 (2017). https://doi.org/10.1016/j.resconrec.2017.09.005

7. Blomsma, F., Brennan, G.: The emergence of circular economy: a new framing around prolonging resource productivity. J. Ind. Ecol. **21**(3), 603–614 (2017). https://doi.org/10.1111/jiec.12603

8. Saidani, M., Yannou, B., Leroy, Y., Cluzel, F., Kendall, A.: A taxonomy of circular economy indicators. J. Clean. Prod. **207**, 542–559 (2019). https://doi.org/10.1016/j.jclepro.2018.10.014

9. González-Sánchez, R., Settembre-Blundo, D., Ferrari, A.M., García-Muiña, F.E.: Main dimensions in the building of the circular supply chain: a literature review. Sustainability **12**(6), 1–25 (2020). https://doi.org/10.3390/su12062459

10. Chopra, S., Meindl, P.: Supply Chain Management - Strategy, Planning, and Operation, 5th edn., vol 53, no. 9. Pearson Education (2013)

11. Lahane, S., Kant, R., Shankar, R.: Circular supply chain management: a state-of-art review and future opportunities. J. Clean. Prod. **258** (2020). https://doi.org/10.1016/j.jclepro.2020.120859

12. Suarez-Barraza, M.F., Miguel-Davila, J., Vasquez-García, C.F.: Supply chain value stream mapping: a new tool of operation management. Int. J. Qual. Reliab. Manag. **33**(4), 518–534 (2016). https://doi.org/10.1108/IJQRM-11-2014-0171

13. Megayanti, W., Anityasari, M., Ciptomulyono, U.: Sustainable supply chain value stream mapping (Ssc-Vsm) the application in two bottle drinking water companies. In: Proceedings of the International Conference on Industrial Engineering and Operations Management, vol. 2018-March, pp. 3573–3585 (2018)

14. Hedlund, C., Stenmark, P., Noaksson, E., Lilja, J.: More value from fewer resources: how to expand value stream mapping with ideas from circular economy. Int. J. Qual. Serv. Sci. **12**(4), 447–459 (2020). https://doi.org/10.1108/IJQSS-05-2019-0070

15. Rother, M., Shook, J.: Learning to See: Value Stream Mapping to Add Value and Eliminate Muda (Lean Enterprise Institute), Lean Enterprise Institute Brookline (1999).https://doi.org/10.1109/6.490058

16. Mangers, J., Oberhausen, C., Minoufekr, M., Plapper, P.: Creation of an ISO standard at the example of value stream management method. In: Jakobs, K. (ed.) Shaping the Future Through Standardization. IGI Global, pp. 1–26 (2020)

17. ISO 22468, Value stream management (VSM) (2020)

18. Mangers, J., Thoussaint, L., Minoufekr, M., Plapper, P.: Multi-level information value stream mapping, pp. 147–156 (2020)

19. EMF, Towards a Circular Economy: Business Rationale for an Accelerated Transition, p. 20. Ellen MacArthur Foundation (2015)

20. Edtmayr, T., Sunk, A., Sihn, W.: An approach to integrate parameters and indicators of sustainability management into value stream mapping. Procedia CIRP **41**, 289–294 (2016). https://doi.org/10.1016/j.procir.2015.08.037

21. Galvão, G.D.A., Homrich, A.S., Geissdoerfer, M., Evans, S., Scoleze Ferrer, P.S., Carvalho, M.M.: Towards a value stream perspective of circular business models. Resour. Conserv. Recycl. **162**(June 2019), 105060 (2020). https://doi.org/10.1016/j.resconrec.2020.105060

22. Paju, M., et al.: Framework and indicators for a sustainable manufacturing mapping methodology. In: Proceedings - Winter Simulation Conference, no. December, pp. 3411–3422 (2010). https://doi.org/10.1109/WSC.2010.5679031

23. Roosen, T.J., Pons, D.J.: Environmentally lean production: the development and incorporation of an environmental impact index into value stream mapping. J. Ind. Eng. **2013**, 1–17 (2013). https://doi.org/10.1155/2013/298103

24. Faulkner, W., Badurdeen, F.: Sustainable Value Stream Mapping (Sus-VSM): Methodology to visualize and assess manufacturing sustainability performance. J. Clean. Prod. **85**, 8–18 (2014). https://doi.org/10.1016/j.jclepro.2014.05.042

25. Vinodh, S., Ben Ruben, R., Asokan, P.: Life cycle assessment integrated value stream mapping framework to ensure sustainable manufacturing: a case study. Clean Technol. Environ. Policy **18**(1), 279–295 (2015). https://doi.org/10.1007/s10098-015-1016-8

26. Garza-Reyes, J.A., Torres Romero, J., Govindan, K., Cherrafi, A., Ramanathan, U.: A PDCA-based approach to Environmental Value Stream Mapping (E-VSM). J. Clean. Prod. **180**, 335–348 (2018). https://doi.org/10.1016/j.jclepro.2018.01.121

27. Jamil, N., Gholami, H., Saman, M.Z.M., Streimikiene, D., Sharif, S., Zakuan, N.: DMAIC-based approach to sustainable value stream mapping: towards a sustainable manufacturing system. Econ. Res. Istraz. **33**(1), 331–360 (2020). https://doi.org/10.1080/1331677X.2020.1715236

28. Lorenzon dos Santos, D., Giglio, R., Helleno, A.L., Campos, L.M.S.: Environmental aspects in VSM: a study about barriers and drivers. Prod. Plan. Control **30**(15), 1239–1249 (2019). https://doi.org/10.1080/09537287.2019.1605627

29. Müller, E., Stock, T., Schillig, R.: A method to generate energy value-streams in production and logistics in respect of time- and energy-consumption. Prod. Eng. **8**(1–2), 243–251 (2013). https://doi.org/10.1007/s11740-013-0516-9

30. Dadashnejad, A.A., Valmohammadi, C.: Investigating the effect of value stream mapping on overall equipment effectiveness: a case study. Total Qual. Manag. Bus. Excell. **30**(3–4), 466–482 (2019). https://doi.org/10.1080/14783363.2017.1308821

31. Helleno, A.L., Pimentel, C.A., Ferro, R., Santos, P.F., Oliveira, M.C., Simon, A.T.: Integrating value stream mapping and discrete events simulation as decision making tools in operation management. Int. J. Adv. Manuf. Technol. **80**(5–8), 1059–1066 (2015). https://doi.org/10.1007/s00170-015-7087-1

32. Huang, Z., Kim, J., Sadri, A., Dowey, S., Dargusch, M.S.: Industry 4.0: development of a multi-agent system for dynamic value stream mapping in SMEs. J. Manuf. Syst. **52**(April), 1–12 (2019). https://doi.org/10.1016/j.jmsy.2019.05.001

33. Meudt, T., Metternich, J., Abele, E.: Value stream mapping 4.0: Holistic examination of value stream and information logistics in production. CIRP Ann. - Manuf. Technol. **66**(1), 413–416 (2017). https://doi.org/10.1016/j.cirp.2017.04.005

34. Lourenço, E.J., Pereira, J.P., Barbosa, R., Baptista, A.J.: Using multi-layer stream mapping to assess the overall efficiency and waste of a production system: a case study from the plywood industry. Procedia CIRP **48**, 128–133 (2016). https://doi.org/10.1016/j.procir.2016.04.086

35. Yin, R.K.: Case Study Research and Applications: Design and Methods, 6th edn. SAGE Publications Inc., Thousand Oaks (2018)

36. Mangers, J., Minoufekr, M., Plapper, P., Kolla, S.: An innovative strategy allowing a holistic system change towards circular economy within supply-chains. Energies **14**, 4375 (2021). https://doi.org/10.3390/en14144375

37. Morseletto, P.: Targets for a circular economy. Resour. Conserv. Recycl. **153**(October 2019), 104553 (2020). https://doi.org/10.1016/j.resconrec.2019.104553

Research on a Preannounced Pricing Policy in a Two-Period Dual-Channel Supply Chain

Haijiao Li[1,2(✉)], Kuan Yang[1], and Guoqing Zhang[2]

[1] School of Business Administration, Hunan University, Changsha 410082, Hunan, China
haijiaoli@hnu.edu.cn
[2] Supply Chain and Logistics Optimization Research Centre, Department of Mechanical, Automotive & Materials Engineering, University of Windsor, Windsor, ON N9B 3P4, Canada

Abstract. The development of the e-commerce and the fast update of the product have an incentive to widespread attempts at multi-channel with multi-period sales. Prior studies have been mainly focused on revenue management issue in a multi-period traditional channel or a single-period multi-channel. This paper extends these studies by exploring the issue in a multi-period multi-channel context. We propose a two-period dual-channel supply channel model, where the manufacturer sells its product in each period through its direct channel and an independent retail channel. Both channels implement preannounced pricing. The results show that the selling prices of both channels in the first period is higher than those in the second period, and the price rate of change in the retail channel is higher than that in the direct channel. It implies that the manufacturer adopts a deeper discount in the direct channel than the retailer does in the retail channel. The numerical analysis reveals that the impact of channel substitutability on the price rate of change in the retail channel is more significant than the direct channel. In addition, the channel substitutability is harmful for the retailer and the manufacturer.

Keywords: Dual-channel supply chain · Preannounced pricing · Game theory

1 Introduction

Due to the rapid development of economy and technology, products update speed gets faster and the product life cycle increasingly becomes shorter. More products are being sold in multi-period instead of single-period. Therefore, multi-period pricing has drawn attention to researchers and practitioners, among which preannounced pricing is one of the most popular pricing methods. Preannounced pricing represents that the firm announces the future market prices to consumers before the selling period [1]. In practice, preannounced pricing is common in industry applications, such as Costco, Sam's Club and Filene's Basement. The issue of preannounced pricing usually arises from literature on strategic consumer, where the pricing policy can mitigate strategic waiting behavior [2–4]. In contrast to prior studies, this paper considers the seller's perspective and aims to explore the impact of the preannounced pricing on the dual-channel supply chain.

© IFIP International Federation for Information Processing 2021
Published by Springer Nature Switzerland AG 2021
A. Dolgui et al. (Eds.): APMS 2021, IFIP AICT 633, pp. 543–549, 2021.
https://doi.org/10.1007/978-3-030-85910-7_57

The development of e-commerce increasingly encourages the manufacturer to introduce a direct online channel besides a traditional retail channel. A data shows that the number of online shopping users in China has reached 782 million by December 2020. Hence, adding an online channel helps the manufacturer to increase the consumer traffic. Meanwhile, such a strategy also adds the channel's flexibility. For instance, consumers can buy product online and pick up in store to examine the fit and quality [5], read the online reviews and purchase in physical store [6], or buy online and return in physical store or online [7]. Therefore, adopting dual-channel increases the consumer loyalty and satisfaction. Although a substantial body of literature discusses the dual-channel performance, they ignore a critical issue of a multi-period selling, which is filled the gap in this paper.

We develop a two-period dual-channel model, where the manufacturer sells its product via both manufacturer's direct channel and an independent retail channel to end market in two periods. The manufacturer adopts a static wholesale price and a preannounced pricing plans in two-period model. In the first period, both players announce the selling prices of both direct channel and retail channel to the market. We use a two-period Stackelberg game between the manufacturer and the retailer to derive a unique Stackelberg equilibrium, and find that the retail price and the direct channel price in the first period is higher than those in the second period. Meanwhile, the price rate of change in the retail channel is higher than that in the direct channel, implying that the manufacturer provides a deeper discount for consumers in the direct channel than the retailer does in the retail channel.

This paper is organized as follows. The related literature is reviewed in Sect. 2. Section 3 analyzes the model and a sensitivity analysis is presented in Sect. 4. Conclusion is presented in Sect. 5.

2 Literature Review

The research on dual-channel has been a hot topic from different aspects. One of the most focused research is competition between direct channel and retailer channel, including price competition [8], inventory competition [9] and service competition [10], and others. However, this competition relationship between chains inevitably brings new challenge. The introduction of direct channel may harm the benefits of manufacturer or retailer, and thus the total supply chain [11]. As a result, some researchers embark study various coordination mechanism to mitigate the channel conflict, such as revenue-sharing contract [12], quantity discount contract [13] and buyback contract [14]. Based on prior studies that mostly focus on a dual-channel supply chain in a single period, this paper extends their investigation by considering a multiple- period selling.

The literature on pricing strategy in multi-period operations management is mainly based on preannounced pricing. Stokey [1] was the first to discuss the preannounced pricing in multiple periods when consumers are rational. Aviv and Pazgal [2] compare preannounced pricing with dynamic pricing, and find that the former outperforms the latter with revenue improvement up to 8.32% when consumers are strategic. Correa et al. [4] use a gradient-based method to solve a class of preannounced pricing policies where the price path depends on the available inventory. Mersereau and Zhang [15] propose a robust pre-announced pricing policy, where the proportion of strategic consumers is uncertain. Different from these literatures that investigate the preannounced pricing in a single echelon or a traditional supply chain, this paper explores the impact of preannounced pricing on the multi-channel environment.

3 Model Analysis

We consider a two-period dual-channel supply chain, where the manufacturer sells its product through its own direct channel and an independent retail channel in each period.

A two-period model could be applied by industry practices. For instance, Apple sells the two latest generations of products on official channels and the selling period of each generation iPhone is about two years. Let D_{tj} and p_{tj} denote demand and price of the j channel in period t, where $t = \{1, 2\}$ and $j = \{r, m\}$. Here r and m denote retail channel and direct channel, respectively. To characterize demand functions of the two channels in each period, we use a utility function of a representative consumer, which has been widely utilized in the field of marketing and operations management [16–18]. The utility function contains the classical economic characteristics of diminishing marginal substitution rate and diminishing marginal utility, and the representative consumer setup is better than the Hotelling model where the consumers have a preference heterogeneity. Based on these literatures, we present the representative consumer utility in the first period as

$$U_1 = D_{1r} - \frac{D_{1r}^2}{2} + D_{1m} - \frac{D_{1m}^2}{2} - \delta D_{1r} D_{1m} - (p_{1r} D_{1r} + p_{1m} D_{1m}), \qquad (1)$$

where δ ($0 \le \delta < 1$) denotes channel substitutability, namely, the competition between retail channel and direct channel. A larger δ indicates more instense competition between the two channels. Maximizing Eq. (1) with respect to D_{1r} and D_{1m} gets

$$
\begin{aligned}
D_{1m} &= \frac{1}{1+\delta} + \frac{\delta p_{1r}}{1-\delta^2} - \frac{p_{1m}}{1-\delta^2}, \\
D_{1r} &= \frac{1}{1+\delta} + \frac{\delta p_{1m}}{1-\delta^2} - \frac{p_{1r}}{1-\delta^2}.
\end{aligned}
\qquad (2)
$$

Since the realized demand of the two channels in the first period are D_{1m} and D_{1r}, the utility function for a representative consumer in the second period is given by

$$U_2 = (1 - D_{1r})D_{2r} - \frac{D_{2r}^2}{2} + (1 - D_{1m})D_{2m} - \frac{D_{2m}^2}{2} - \delta D_{2r} D_{2m} - (p_{2r} D_{2r} + p_{2m} D_{2m}) \qquad (3)$$

Correspondingly, the demand function for each channel in the second period is

$$
\begin{aligned}
D_{2m} &= \frac{\delta}{(1+\delta)^2} + \frac{(1+\delta^2)}{(1-\delta^2)^2} p_{1m} - \frac{2\delta}{(1-\delta^2)^2} p_{1r} - \frac{1}{(1-\delta^2)^2} p_{2m} + \frac{\delta}{(1-\delta^2)^2} p_{2r}, \\
D_{2r} &= \frac{\delta}{(1+\delta)^2} + \frac{(1+\delta^2)}{(1-\delta^2)^2} p_{1r} - \frac{2\delta}{(1-\delta^2)^2} p_{1m} - \frac{1}{(1-\delta^2)^2} p_{2r} + \frac{\delta}{(1-\delta^2)^2} p_{2m}.
\end{aligned}
\qquad (4)
$$

In the two-period model, the manufacturer adopts the static wholesale price strategy, i.e., the wholesale prices in two periods are set the same. This is common in practice. For example, when there is no major technological innovation in smart phones, the wholesale price will keep unchanged in whole selling period. Without loss of generality, product cost in this paper is normalized to zero. The assumption can be relaxed easily. However, such a relaxation cannot bring substantive result. Hence, the retailer's and manufacturer's profits are obtained by

$$\Pi_r = (p_{1r} - \omega)D_{1r} + (p_{2r} - \omega)D_{2r}, \tag{5}$$

$$\Pi_m = \omega D_{1r} + p_{1m}D_{1m} + \omega D_{2r} + p_{2m}D_{2m}. \tag{6}$$

To assure the concavity of profit functions, our analysis is carried out with a reasonable assumption of $\delta \leq 0.5$ to consider a weak the substitutability between the direct channel and the retail channel in reality. For instance, with in-store shopping restricted during the COVID-19 pandemic, most consumers can purchase online to reduce human-to-human contact. On the other hand, for some high-price products, such as cars and luxury goods, consumers tend to examine the product in person at physical stores and choose their favorite style.

The sequence of events under preannounced pricing is summarized as follows. The manufacturer announces firstly all its price decisions in the first period including wholesale prices (ω) and direct channel prices (p_{1m}, p_{2m}). Then the retailer reveals all its retail prices (p_{1r}, p_{2r}). Using a backward induction approach, we can obtain the following results.

Theorem 1. The optimal wholesale price, direct channel prices and retail prices in two periods are obtained as follows:

$$\omega = \frac{1}{2}, p_{1m} = \frac{6\delta^4 + 3\delta^3 - 22\delta^2 - \delta + 12}{2(6\delta^4 - 17\delta^2 + 9)}, \quad p_{1r} = \frac{9\delta^4 - 2\delta^5 + 6\delta^3 - 26\delta^2 - 4\delta + 15}{2(6\delta^4 - 17\delta^2 + 9)},$$
$$p_{2m} = \frac{6\delta^4 - 3\delta^3 - 12\delta^2 + \delta + 6}{2(6\delta^4 - 17\delta^2 + 9)}, \quad p_{2r} = \frac{9\delta^4 - 2\delta^5 + 4\delta^3 - 23\delta^2 - 2\delta + 12}{2(6\delta^4 - 17\delta^2 + 9)}. \tag{7}$$

Proof. The Hessian matrix of (5) is negative definite because $\frac{\partial^2}{\partial p_{1r}^2}\Pi_r = \frac{\partial^2}{\partial p_{2r}^2}\Pi_r = \frac{2}{\delta^2-1} < 0$ and $\Delta_2 = \frac{3\delta^4 - 10\delta^2 + 3}{(1-\delta)^4(1+\delta)^4} > 0$ (note $\delta \leq 0.5$). Therefore, the retailer's profit function is jointly concave in (p_{1r}, p_{2r}). Solving the first order necessary conditions for optimality, that is $\frac{\partial \Pi_r}{\partial p_{1r}} = 0$ and $\frac{\partial \Pi_r}{\partial p_{2r}} = 0$, we get the reaction function as

$$p_{1r} = \frac{(2p_{1m} - p_{2m} - 1)\delta^5 + 3\omega\delta^4 + 6(1 - p_{1m})\delta^3 - (6 + 4\omega)\delta^2 + (p_{2m} - 1)\delta + 2 + \omega}{3\delta^4 - 10\delta^2 + 3},$$
$$p_{2r} = \frac{(2p_{2m} - p_{1m} - 1)\delta^5 + 3\delta^4 + 4(p_{1m} - p_{2m})\delta^3 - (4 + 6\omega)\delta^2 + (-3p_{1m} + 2p_{2m} + 1)\delta + 1 + 2\omega}{3\delta^4 - 10\delta^2 + 3}. \tag{8}$$

Substituting (8) into (6), we still find that the profit function of the manufacturer is joint concave in (ω, p_{1m}, p_{2m}). Hence, there is a unique optimal solution for the wholesale price and direct channel prices, which is given by Theorem 1.

Correspondingly, substituting (7) into (5) and (6), the manufacturer's and the retailer's profits are given by

$$\Pi_m = \frac{4\delta^4 + 12\delta^3 - 29\delta^2 - 8\delta + 18}{4(6\delta^4 - 17\delta^2 + 9)}, \quad \Pi_r = \frac{(1 - \delta^2)(3\delta^4 - 7\delta^2 + 3)(3 - 2\delta)^2}{4(6\delta^4 - 17\delta^2 + 9)^2}. \tag{9}$$

Based on Theorem 1, we discuss the comparison of the first-period equilibria and the second-period equilibria as follows, where the price rate of change (ROC) in two channels are defined as $\frac{p_{2r}-p_{1r}}{p_{1r}}$ in the retail channel and as $\frac{p_{2m}-p_{1m}}{p_{1m}}$ in the direct channel.

Corollary 1. (1) the retail price and the direct channel price decrease over time; (2) ROC in the retail channel is higher than that in the direct channel.

Proof. Since $\delta \le 0.5, p_{1r}-p_{2r} = \frac{(1-\delta^2)(3-2\delta)}{2(6\delta^4-17\delta^2+9)} \ge 0, p_{1m}-p_{2m} = \frac{(\delta-1)(3\delta^2-2\delta-3)}{6\delta^4-17\delta^2+9} \ge 0;$

$$\frac{p_{2r}-p_{1r}}{p_{1r}} - \frac{p_{2m}-p_{1m}}{p_{1m}} = \frac{(\delta-1)(12\delta^7-50\delta^6-12\delta^5+169\delta^4-33\delta^3-171\delta^2+27\delta+54)}{(6\delta^4+3\delta^3-22\delta^2-\delta+12)(2\delta^5-9\delta^4-6\delta^3+26\delta^2+4\delta-15)} \ge 0.$$

Corollary 1 indicates that the retailer and the manufacturer set higher retail price and direct channel price in the first period than they do in the second period, which means that the ROC in both channels are negative. Moreover, the ROC in the retail channel is higher than that in the direct channel, which suggests that the direct channel provides a deeper discount than the retail channel.

4 Sensitivity Analysis

We investigate the impact of channel substitutability (i.e., δ) on: (1) retail prices and direct channel prices in two periods; (2) the price rate of change in two channels; (3) the profits of the retailer and the manufacturer.

Figure 1(a) shows that when the channel substitutability increases, the retail prices in two periods decrease, while the first-period (second-period) direct channel price first decreases (increases) and then increases (decreases). The selling prices of both channels in the first period are higher than those in the second period, which is consistent with Corollary 1(1). The result leads to the ROCs of both channels are negative as shown in Fig. 1(b), which means that the discount in the direct channel is deeper than that in the retail channel. The impact of the channel substitutability on the ROCs in both channels is not monotonic. The ROCs first increase and then decrease as the competition between retail channel and direct channel becomes more intense. In other words, the retailer and the manufacturer adopt the same pace of discount policies to make profits. The channel substitutability has more significant effect on the retail channel than the direct channel because the impact degree of the channel substitutability on the retail channel is higher than that on the direct channel. Finally, the fierce competition is harmful for the players' profits as shown in Fig. 1(c). Correspondingly, we can get that the competition between the two channels has a negative impact on the total profit of dual-channel.

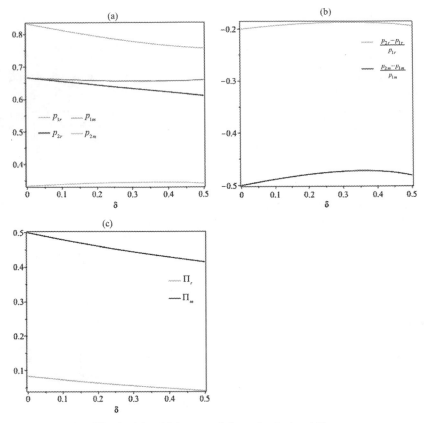

Fig. 1. (a) ~ (c) Impact of channel substitutability.

5 Conclusion

This paper investigates a two-period dual-channel supply chain where the manufacturer's products are sold via a dual-channel in each period. We develop a two-period model, and analyze a leader-follower game framework for each period, where the manufacturer determines his wholesale price and direct channel price and the retailer then decides on her retail price. The results derive a unique Stackelberg equilibrium for each period. The finding reveals that the retail price and the direct channel price decrease over time and that the ROC in the retail channel is higher than that in the direct channel. The impact of channel substitutability on the retail channel is higher than that on the direct channel.

Acknowledgments. This work was supported by Natural Sciences and Engineering Research Council of Canada discovery grant (Grant No. RGPIN-2014-03594, RGPIN-2019-07115), Hunan Thinktank Project (No. 16ZWC60) and China Scholarship Council (No. 201806130044).

References

1. Stokey, N.: Intertemporal price discrimination. Q. J. Econ. **93**(3), 355–371 (1979)

2. Aviv, Y., Pazgal, A.: Optimal pricing of seasonal products in the presence of forward-looking consumers. Manuf. Serv. Oper. Manag. **10**(3), 339–359 (2008)
3. Zhang, Q., Zaccour, G., Zhang, J., Tang, W.: Strategic pricing under quality signaling and imitation behaviors in supply chains. Transp. Res. Part E: Logist. Transp. Rev. **142**(2020), 102072 (2020)
4. Correa, J., Montoya, R., Thraves, C.: Contingent preannounced pricing policies with strategic consumers. Oper. Res. **64**(1), 251–272 (2016)
5. Gao, F., Su, X.: Omnichannel retail operations with buy-online-and-pick-up-in-store. Manage. Sci. **63**(8), 2478–2492 (2017)
6. Gu, Z., Tayi, G.: Consumer pseudo-showrooming and omni-channel product placement strategies. Manag. Inf. Syst. Q. **41**(2), 583–606 (2017)
7. Radhi, M., Zhang, G.: Optimal cross-channel return policy in dual-channel retailing systems. Int. J. Prod. Econ. **210**(2019), 184–198 (2019)
8. Zhou, J., Zhao, R., Wang, W.: Pricing decision of a manufacturer in a dual-channel supply chain with asymmetric information. Eur. J. Oper. Res. **278**(3), 809–820 (2019)
9. Alawneh, F., Zhang, G.: Dual-channel warehouse and inventory management with stochastic demand. Transp. Res. Part E: Logist. Transp. Rev. **112**(2018), 84–106 (2018)
10. Chen, K., Kaya, M., Özer, Ö.: Dual sales channel management with service competition. Manuf. Serv. Oper. Manag. **10**(4), 654–675 (2008)
11. Chen, J., Zhang, H., Sun, Y.: Implementing coordination contracts in a manufacturer Stackelberg dual-channel supply chain. Omega **40**(5), 571–583 (2012)
12. Xu, G., Dan, B., Zhang, X., Liu, C.: Coordinating a dual-channel supply chain with risk-averse under a two-way revenue sharing contract. Int. J. Prod. Econ. **147**(2014), 171–179 (2014)
13. Modak, N., Kelle, P.: Managing a dual-channel supply chain under price and delivery-time dependent stochastic demand. Eur. J. Oper. Res. **272**(1), 147–161 (2019)
14. Wu, D.: Coordination of competing supply chains with news-vendor and buyback contract. Int. J. Prod. Econ. **144**(1), 1–13 (2013)
15. Mersereau, A., Zhang, D.: Markdown pricing with unknown fraction of strategic customers. Manuf. Serv. Oper. Manag. **14**(3), 355–370 (2012)
16. Cai, G.: Channel selection and coordination in dual-channel supply chains. J. Retail. **86**(1), 22–36 (2010)
17. Wu, H., Cai, G., Chen, J., Sheu, C.: Online manufacturer referral to heterogeneous retailers. Prod. Oper. Manag. **24**(11), 1768–1782 (2015)
18. Yang, X., Cai, G., Ingene, C., Zhang, J.: Manufacturer strategy on service provision in competitive channels. Prod. Oper. Manag. **29**(1), 72–89 (2020)

Sustainable and Resilience Improvement Through the Design for Circular Digital Supply Chain

Abla Chaouni Benabdellah$^{(\boxtimes)}$, Kamar Zekhnini, and Anass Cherrafi

L2M3S Laboratory, ENSAM, Moulay Issmaïl University, Meknes, Morocco

Abstract. Resilient and sustainable supply chain management (SCM) practices have been established in recent decades to reduce the likelihood and consequences of disruptions and the negative environmental effects along the supply chain. To deal with such issues, it's important to be able to quantify the effectiveness of all supply chain processes in a circular economy model while taking technological revolution into account. Furthermore, Design for X (DFX) approaches show significant potential for improving product and service functionality from a variety of perspectives X. In this respect, the aim of this paper is first to propose a circular digital SCOR model that depicts the impact of digital technology on various circular SCOR processes. Second, using DFX techniques, a conceptual model, called Design for circular digital Supply chain (DFCDSC), has been proposed that includes the key design factors for the development and implementation of the circular digital supply chains. Since it highlights the main lines of research in the area, the proposed framework will provide crucial managerial perspectives for practitioners and managers.

Keywords: Resilience · Sustainability · Supply chain management · Design for X · Circular economy · Digital technologies

1 Introduction

In the current global scenario and increasingly complex, digital world, supply chains (SC) are faced various events that interrupt SC operational processes and successful performance. Furthermore, consumers, regulators, and other stakeholders around the world are pushing corporations to conduct their activities responsibly to boost their economic, social and environmental efficiency [1]. Thus, organizations were forced to adjust their activities and take a constructive position in creating safer and more resilient systems to meet the needs of all stakeholders while improving sustainability outcomes [2]. In this context, Circular economy (CE) and emerging technologies have emerged as key elements of the sustainability and resilience response to assist organizations in being more successful [3].

Through the achievement of collaboration, transparency, resiliency, responsiveness, and flexibility across all SC processes, DSC can have clear sight in real time [4]. Besides,

A. Dolgui et al. (Eds.): APMS 2021, IFIP AICT 633, pp. 550–559, 2021.
https://doi.org/10.1007/978-3-030-85910-7_58

organizations that consider CE gain from material saving, reduced manufacturing and supply costs, improved customer loyalty, and the ability to keep products and parts in use for a longer time [3]. Moreover, when SC is influenced by changes in the operational and environmental conditions, resilience capabilities allow adaptation and recovery [4]. Furthermore, a successful transition to sustainability dependent on a variety of social, economic, legal, cultural, and political factors, and it necessitates fundamental changes, not only at the company level but also across the product and service activities [5]. Methods and tools to enable the systematic integration of all products and services concerns from a digital and circular and perspective, however, are still being developed. From a particular X viewpoint, the Design for X (DFX) approach is used to increase the quality of the product and SC processes [6, 7].

Many authors explored and explained how to perceive the CE transition through the use of DFX approaches [3, 8]. Other researchers have created new DFX methods as part of the introduction of Industry 4.0 by DFX techniques [9]. Therefore, no paper dealing specifically with the incorporation of the CE and digitalization to achieve sustainable and resilient concerns in the SC based on the DFX perspective can be found among all the advances made and research contributions. In this respect, the aim of this paper is first to develop a circular-digital SCOR model which serves as a reference model for the enhancement of SCs. Then, by considering the prominent DFX techniques needed in each circular-digital SCOR model, a series of design factors have been enumerated to integrate circular and digital concerns in SC to reach resiliency and sustainability enhancement. The conceptual framework, design for circular digital supply chain (DFCDSC), will provide crucial and managerial implications for both practionners and managers to develop dynamics capabilities theory.

This paper is structured as follows; Sect. 2 presents an analysis of the literature review. Section 3 elaborates the proposed circular digital SCOR model for the integration of circular and digital impacts on the SC. Section 4 proposes the theoretical elements of our integrated model DFCDSC. The key design factors needed to implement DFCDSC fir resilient & sustainable purpose is established. Section 5 presents implications for both practitioners and researchers. The conclusions and future works are drawn in the final section.

2   Literature Review

Considering the high competition atmosphere and technological transition (Industry 4.0), organizations have begun to concentrate on sustainable practices to resolve environmental, social, and economic issues, forming an agenda that aims to promote resilience, digitalization, and circularity along the SC.

2.1   Circular Supply Chain

The CE is characterized as an economic model in which resources are used for as long as possible while extracting maximum value. By reducing (or delaying) unintended negative environmental impacts, the principles of CE broaden the boundary of green, resilience and sustainable SCM [3, 10]. In this regard, as the world moves toward a CE,

SCs players are paying more attention to their environmental effects, and opportunities to generate value through minimizing, preserving, and recovering natural resources. "Open-loop SC", "circular SC", and "closed-loop SC", are all terms used to describe SCs in a CE [3, 8]. More clearly, CSCM includes a vision of a zero-waste economy, restorative and regenerative cycles planned using circular thinking. Motivated by all these benefits, several researchers have contributed significantly to the literature on the CE.

Several authors have suggested a complete rethinking of the way products, processes and SC are designed by using DFX Techniques [3, 11]. Further ones have studied drivers, barriers and enable for the integration of CE in SCM [12, 13]. Researchers have also focused on elaborating frameworks for the CSCM [1, 12, 14] with the integration of green, reverse logistics, industrial ecology with CE concerns. Other ones have included the benefits of using Industry 4.0 technologies such as Additive manufacturing with circular SC [15, 16].

2.2 Digital Supply Chain

Technological and computing advancements have led to a rapidly evolving environment in recent decades [17]. Companies need a digital supply chain (DSC) based on sustainability, visibility, efficiency and flexibility to help them solve the challenges of volatility, resiliency, uncertainty, and transparency [18]. According to [18], DSC can be defined as "an intelligent best-fit technological system that is based on the capability of massive data disposal and excellent cooperation and communication for digital hardware, software, and networks to support and synchronize interaction between organizations by making services more valuable, accessible and affordable with consistent, agile and effective outcomes". This implies a collection of advanced technologies that companies must integrate with human capital to transform their SCs from a traditional to instrumented, integrated and intelligent one [19]. Therefore, DSC is about how SCs are handled; how both digital and physical flows help to achieve visibility and quality enhancement as well as real-time feedback at all levels [20].

DSC implementation has gotten high attention from many practionners and academicians. Among the contributions to this research field, few research papers have attempted to implement DSC [1, 18]. Several authors have used systematic reviews to concentrate on advanced technologies effect on SCs, such as "Big Data", "Internet of Things", "Cyber Security" and "Augmented Reality". Other ones have contextualized IT in a SC 4.0 [21, 22]. Further, established a structure for understanding DSC based on an overview of key advantages and limitations [18, 19].

3   Circular-Digital SCOR Model

The SCOR model is a known structure that divides SC processes into six sub-processes ("plan, source, make, deliver, return, and enable") that serve as the foundation to describe any SC [23]. To achieve sustainability, it is important to assess the actual efficiency of all SC processes in a circular context. To do so, two processes have been added to the standard SCOR model: (1) Use that represents the end-consumption users of the products as well as maintenance and repair activities to the extent the product lifespan and (2) Recover that represents the remanufacture, reuse, recycle, repair and redesign activities. Furthermore, since the conventional SC is made up of a series of siloed steps, incorporating digital technology may be able to break down these barriers and turn them into a seamless system [18, 19]. Figure 1 represents the circular and digital SCOR (CDSCOR) model that depicts the effect of digital technologies on the various circular proposed processes.

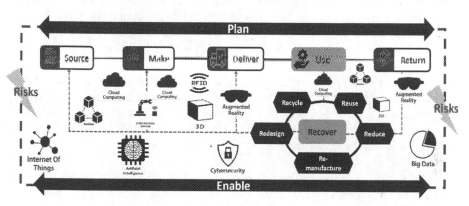

Fig. 1. Proposed Circular-Digital SCOR model (CDSCOR)

For the Make, Deliver, and Return processes, 3D printing aids in the development of product prototypes for evaluation, as well as mass customization [24]. Cloud Computing encourages collaboration among SC participants, improves connectivity, and adaptability in the Use, Make, and Source processes [25]. In both Deliver and Return processes, AR increases their efficiency and visibility [26]. The CPS, which is primarily used in the Make process, through the use of interconnected computers, physical processes and networks assess agility by contributing to production and inventory optimization [27]. Besides, RFID allows real-time detection and tracking, which helps to improve data quality [20]. Whereas, Blockchain technology enables the real-time enhancement and monitoring of products and actors, especially for Use and Source processes [28]. In contrast, other techniques such as BD, Cybersecurity, IoT and AI have positive impacts on the entire SC processes. BD gives better forecast, increase SC visibility and strong relationships [20]. IoT help increasing warehouse operations productivity, and unnecessary procedures. In addition to all of these advantages, risk management and control in a DSC would concentrate primarily on cybersecurity, as it is required to identify security incidents, enforce the appropriate safeguarding tools, react to attacks in real-time [19]. Furthermore, AI improves the efficiency of SC drivers by developing a great understanding of their interactions [29]. As a result, by considering CDSCOR model, we connect SC actors to create reliability, transparency, resiliency, and effectiveness in the end-to-end sustainable value chain by including the Use and Recover processes and incorporating Industry 4.0 technologies.

4 Design for Circular Digital Supply Chain

Given the high level of concurrence, SC must meet new digital and circular features, as well as ensure the integration of resilience and sustainable practices with multiple conventional functionalities. Furthermore, mastering the management of an organization's intellectual resources is critical. As a result, successful SCs have a strong vision and use structures and roadmaps to drive them forward. In this regard, the original structure depicted in Fig. 2 presents a roadmap for better understanding the problem of SC sustainability and resilience when taking into account an integrated vision that involves circularity, industry 4.0, and DFX techniques capabilities. More clearly, the framework, called Design for Circular Digital Supply Chain (DFCDSC), defines a set of over 300 design factors that must be considered for each of the proposed CDSCOR processes to achieve sustainability and resilience efficiency outcomes. Therefore, it's important to note that the design factors within each process come from a variety of sources, including applications, guidelines, papers, books, and real design projects and the main DFX techniques used in each process are based on the categorization of [5]. In the following, a discussion of each process is presented.

- The **Plan** process purpose is to define SC needs and align them against available assets and resources. Environmental limits, such as the environment's assimilative potential and resource extraction relative to yield, are primarily considered in a CE context. Using Industry 4.0 technologies capabilities, we obtain a synchronized & digital planning with a real-time inventory & disruption prediction.
- The **Source** process aims to organize product deliveries, obtain and validate the product, pass the product, and approve payment to the supplier. Sourcing is linked to all resource principles in the CE model, including sustainable, exhaustible, and renewable resources. Besides, to achieve resilience, back-up suppliers should be incorporated, component replacement and supplier communication portals should be used. Using Industry 4.0 technologies capabilities, we obtain intelligent supply and predictive analysis sourcing.
- The **Make** process aims to organize manufacturing activities, issue materials, manufacture and test, deliver products, and stage products while taking into account waste disposal and packaging limitations. Make covers tasks such as maintenance, recovery, recycling, and material transformation from a circular perspective. Furthermore, flexible manufacturing lines and the application of postponement concepts are regarded as critical drivers of demand resilience and responsiveness. Using Industry 4.0 technologies capabilities, we establish a smart factory and a proactive risk sensing to adjust manufacturing capabilities.
- The **Deliver** process describes the tasks associated with building loads, routing packages, selecting carriers, receiving products, picking, packing, documenting, shipping, installing the product, and fulfilling customer orders. Deliver can also coordinate the supply of replacement parts for repair during usage of the product in a circular context to prolong the product's lifespan. Besides, omnichannel delivery, decentralized logistics, disturbance monitoring, and real-time transportation control are some of the

other ways to easily and efficiently use resilience assets. Using Industry 4,0, technologies capabilities we obtain dynamic fulfillment with full inventory transparency and dynamic/predictive routing.

- The **Use** process includes the end-usage user's or use of the product, as well as repair and maintenance to extend the product's lifespan. In a CE, end-users need to return their goods at the end of their useful lives, as these goods are 'after recovery' inputs for the manufacturing process. Besides, using Industry 4.0, we obtain a connected & responsiveness customer.

- The **Return** process to return material from the end-user to the SC return material. Moreover, resource-related practices which specifically include the return of a faulty or unnecessary product can be linked to the CE's consumer product construct. Recycled products, closed-loop SC tools and constructive procurement dependent plans are all examples of ways to use resilience assets for creating value in the return process. Using Industry 4.0 capabilities, we obtain End to end transparency for customers.

- The **Recovery** process includes the processes of Remanufacturing, recycling, reusing, reducing and redesigning. As a fully circular operation, it takes into account all aspects of assembly, disassembly, remanufacture, and recycling policies, as well as CO_2 emissions, hazardous effects, and essential materials. Using the Industry 4.0 technologies capabilities, we obtain intelligent traceability, collaborative value capture and zero landfills.

- The **Enable** process refers to the SCM process, which involves business regulations, facility efficiency, data resources, contracts, enforcement, and risk management, among other things. In a circular perspective, the enablers that were not evident in a linear business model are taken into account. Materials would be sourced not only from manufacturers but also from end-users who are disposing of their obsolete goods. Furthermore, DSC twins and Industry 4.0 technologies enable several vital resilience capabilities, including coordination, visibility and collaboration.

In a summary, by considering the proposed DFCDSC, a specific set of performance objectives such as agility, flexibility, visibility, transparency, security, proactivity, adaptability can be reached. In addition to that, by considering both internal (Errors made by humans, computer malfunctions, and product consistency) and external risks (natural disasters, pandemics, exchange rates, legislations) resiliency can be achieved. There are also several sustainability advantages to be gained. From an economic standpoint, expenses are decreased while sales and profitability are improved. From an ecological standpoint, there is a reduction in carbon footprint, resource depletion, pollution and toxicity. Finally, on a social level, wages, workplace safety and health, social justice, life expectancy, and education are all enhanced, whereas excessive working hours, severe poverty, and child labor are reduced. In this respect, the proposed system can give insights into the consideration of circular, digital, and DFX techniques to have a SC that is both sustainable and resilient.

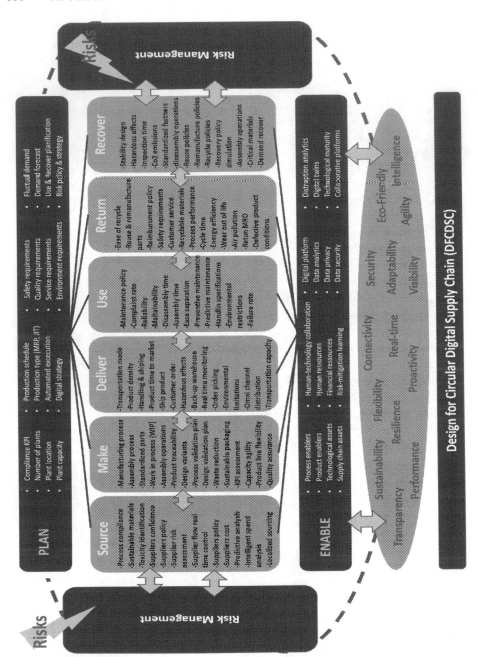

Fig. 2. Design for Circular Digital Supply Chain (DFCDS)

5   Managerial and Practionners Implications

From a managerial and practical perspective, the proposed DFCDSC framework will provide important insights for practionners, decision-makers, and anyone interested in acquiring a more in-depth understanding when incorporating DFX strategies, circularity, and digitalization in SC. More clearly, from a practionners point of view, this paper can help them to facilitate the adaptation to a circular-digital SC while using DFX techniques. Second, in light of significant influential papers in digital [18, 19] and circular SC [3], our paper contributes significantly by proposing a SCOR categorization model that incorporates both digitalization and circularity into the SC processes. Besides, a conceptual model for the development and implementation of CDSC has been suggested, which includes the main design factors needed to enhance sustainability and resiliency. This is as far as we know, the first attempt to establish the DFCSSC definition. It is then considered as a significant contribution to theory as it adds a solid structure that combines cutting-edge technologies with DFX techniques to gain a deeper understanding of digital complexities in a CSC. From the Managers point of view, the proposed framework assists them in ensuring that CSC operations are more environmentally aware and offers a roadmap in terms of economic, financial, social, logistical, organizational and operational activities to successfully implement CSC models. Furthermore, the proposed structure emphasizes that in the digital age, managers are continuously forced to strengthen their understanding of cutting-edge technology to promote the adoption, deployment, and dissemination of the key technologies that help SCM sustainability and resiliency. In summary, we conclude that the proposed structure, as well as the CDSCOR model, will serve as a useful guide for DSC project managers, consultants, and practitioners. Furthermore, the DSCC structure can be enhanced in terms of SC participant engagement and appropriate to the needs and skills of a particular organization.

6   Conclusion and Future Works

The current competitive environment requires companies to be innovative in their production systems and to rethink the current use of resources and waste management by integrating, CE, digital technologies and DFX techniques into their SCs. However, to resolve all of these problems at once, much of the study has concentrated on the technical side. This means that products should be designed not only with an emphasis on how SC concepts enable products to adapt into a CE or digitalization framework but also with a focus on how products adapt to people's desires, needs and behavioral trends. To achieve sustainability and resiliency, we need strategies to help in the implementation of both digital and circular supply chain architecture, according to this viewpoint. To do so, first, we have proposed a new categorization of the SCOR model that incorporates circular and depicts the impact of emerging technology on each process. We've added the recovery and use processes, as well as the effect of various technologies on SC efficiency, such as BD, Cybersecurity, IoT, and AR. Second, we suggested a set of design factors to DFCDSC to boost resilience and sustainability issues while taking into account an integrated view of circular, digital, and DFX techniques in SC. As mentioned in Sect. 5, this framework offers different insights for practitioners and managers. Nonetheless, there are some drawbacks to this article. To evaluate the applicability of these findings, further research is necessary. More precisely, there is a need to delve deeper into not only the direct connection between CSC processes while integrating circular and digital concerns, but to test the design factors in different scenarios. The ability to fully map the interrelationships between various design factors and their impact on the efficiency of the CDSC will be crucial in making realistic suggestions for maximizing return on investment. We propose also to regroup the design factors into homogenous modules to facilitate the implementation of this framework by using classification or clustering algorithms.

References

1. Jabbour, C.J.C., Fiorini, P.D.C., Ndubisi, N.O., et al.: Digitally-enabled sustainable supply chains in the 21st century: a review and a research agenda. Sci. Total Environ. **725**, 138177 (2020)
2. Siegel, R., Antony, J., Garza-Reyes, J.A., et al.: Integrated green lean approach and sustainability for SMEs: from literature review to a conceptual framework. J. Cleaner Prod. **240**, 118205 (2019)
3. Sassanelli, C., Urbinati, A., Rosa, P., et al.: Addressing circular economy through design for X approaches: a systematic literature review. Comput. Ind. **120**, 103245 (2020)
4. Ivanov, D.: Viable supply chain model: integrating agility, resilience and sustainability perspectives—lessons from and thinking beyond the COVID-19 pandemic. Annals of Operations Research (2020). https://doi.org/10.1007/s10479-020-03640-6
5. Benabdellah, A.C., Benghabrit, A., Bouhaddou, I., Benghabrit, O.: Design for relevance concurrent engineering approach: integration of IATF 16949 requirements and design for X techniques. Res. Eng. Des. **31**(3), 323–351 (2020). https://doi.org/10.1007/s00163-020-003 39-4
6. Benabdellah, A.C., Bouhaddou, I., Benghabrit, A., Benghabrit, O.: A systematic review of design for X techniques from 1980 to 2018: concepts, applications, and perspectives. Int. J. Adv. Manuf. Technol. **102**(9–12), 3473–3502 (2019). https://doi.org/10.1007/s00170-019-03418-6
7. Liverani, A., Caligiana, G., Frizziero, L., Francia, D., Donnici, G., Dhaimini, K.: Design for Six Sigma (DFSS) for additive manufacturing applied to an innovative multifunctional fan. Int. J. Interact. Des. Manuf. (IJIDeM) **13**(1), 309–330 (2019). https://doi.org/10.1007/s12 008-019-00548-9
8. Bovea, M.D., Pérez-Belis, V.: Identifying design guidelines to meet the circular economy principles: a case study on electric and electronic equipment. J. Environ. Manage. **228**, 483–494 (2018)
9. Pereira Pessôa, M.V., Jauregui Becker, J.M.: Smart design engineering: a literature review of the impact of the 4th industrial revolution on product design and development. Res. Eng. Des. **31**(2), 175–195 (2020). https://doi.org/10.1007/s00163-020-00330-z
10. Bag, S., Gupta, S., Foropon, C.: Examining the role of dynamic remanufacturing capability on supply chain resilience in circular economy. Management Decision (2019)
11. Wastling, T., Charnley, F., Moreno, M.: Design for circular behaviour: considering users in a circular economy. Sustainability **10**, 1743 (2018). https://doi.org/10.3390/su10061743
12. Farooque, M., Zhang, A., Thürer, M., et al.: Circular supply chain management: a definition and structured literature review. J. Clean. Prod. **228**, 882–900 (2019). https://doi.org/10.1016/j.jclepro.2019.04.303

13. Vegter, D., van Hillegersberg, J., Olthaar, M.: Supply chains in circular business models: processes and performance objectives. Resour. Conserv. Recycl. **162**, 105046 (2020). https://doi.org/10.1016/j.resconrec.2020.105046

14. Li, Q., Guan, X., Shi, T., Jiao, W.: Green product design with competition and fairness concerns in the circular economy era. Int. J. Prod. Res. **58**, 165–179 (2020). https://doi.org/10.1080/00207543.2019.1657249

15. Rahito, W.D., Azman, A.: Additive manufacturing for repair and restoration in remanufacturing: an overview from object design and systems perspectives. Processes **7**, 802 (2019). https://doi.org/10.3390/pr7110802

16. Nascimento, D.L.M., Alencastro, V., Quelhas, O.L.G., et al.: Exploring Industry 4.0 technologies to enable circular economy practices in a manufacturing context: a business model proposal. J. Manuf. Technol. Manag. **30**, 607–627 (2019). https://doi.org/10.1108/JMTM-03-2018-0071

17. Benabdellah, A.C., Zekhnini, K., Cherrafi, A., et al.: Design for the environment: an ontology-based knowledge management model for green product development. Business Strategy and the Environment

18. Büyüközkan, G., Göçer, F.: Digital supply chain: literature review and a proposed framework for future research. Comput. Ind. **97**, 157–177 (2018). https://doi.org/10.1016/j.compind.2018.02.010

19. Zekhnini, K., Cherrafi, A., Bouhaddou, I., et al.: Supply chain management 4.0: a literature review and research framework. Benchmarking: An International Journal (2020)

20. Ivanov, D., Dolgui, A.: A digital supply chain twin for managing the disruption risks and resilience in the era of Industry 4.0. Production Planning & Control, pp. 1–14 (2020). https://doi.org/10.1080/09537287.2020.1768450

21. Tao, F., Cheng, J., Qi, Q., Zhang, M., Zhang, H., Sui, F.: Digital twin-driven product design, manufacturing and service with big data. Int. J. Adv. Manuf. Technol. **94**(9–12), 3563–3576 (2017). https://doi.org/10.1007/s00170-017-0233-1

22. Wu, K.-J., Liao, C.-J., Tseng, M.-L., et al.: Toward sustainability: using big data to explore the decisive attributes of supply chain risks and uncertainties. J. Clean. Prod. **142**, 663–676 (2017). https://doi.org/10.1016/j.jclepro.2016.04.040

23. Müller, J.M.: Contributions of Industry 4.0 to quality management - a SCOR perspective. IFAC-PapersOnLine **52**, 1236–1241 (2019). https://doi.org/10.1016/j.ifacol.2019.11.367

24. Shree, M.V., Dhinakaran, V., Rajkumar, V., et al.: Effect of 3D printing on supply chain management. Mater. Today Proc. **21**, 958–963 (2020)

25. Novais, L., Maqueira, J.M., Ortiz-Bas, Á.: A systematic literature review of cloud computing use in supply chain integration. Comput. Ind. Eng. **129**, 296–314 (2019)

26. Merlino, M., Spro\'ge, I.: The augmented supply chain. Procedia Eng. **178**, 308–318 (2017)

27. Da Silva, V.L., Kovaleski, J.L., Pagani, R.N., et al.: Implementation of Industry 4.0 concept in companies: empirical evidences. Int. J. Comput. Integr. Manuf. **33**, 325–342 (2020). https://doi.org/10.1080/0951192X.2019.1699258

28. Tönnissen, S., Teuteberg, F.: Analysing the impact of blockchain-technology for operations and supply chain management: an explanatory model drawn from multiple case studies. Int. J. Inform. Manag. **52**, 101953 (2020)

29. Benabdellah, A.C., Bouhaddou, I., Benghabrit, A.: SmartDFRelevance: a holonic agent based system for engineering industrial projects in concurrent engineering context. In: International Conference on Artificial Intelligence & Industrial Applications. Springer, pp. 103–123 (2020)

A Literature Review on Smart Technologies and Logistics

Xingwei Lu[1]([✉]), Xianhao Xu[1], and Yeming Gong[2]

[1] School of Management, Huazhong University of Science and Technology, Wuhan, China
[2] EMLYON Business School, 23 avenue Guy de Collongue, 69134 Ecully Cedex, France

Abstract. The emergence of smart technologies has brought substantial changes in logistics. Hence, understanding smart technologies applied in logistics has become critical for practitioners and scholars to make smart technologies better empower logistics activities. Because research on this issue is new and largely fragmented, it will be theoretically essential to evaluate what has been studied and derive meaningful insights through a literature review. In this study, we conduct a mixed-method literature review of smart technologies in logistics. We classify these studies by topic modeling and identify important research domains and methods. More importantly, we draw upon the task-technology fit theory and logistics activities process to propose a multi-level theoretical framework in smart technologies in logistics for understanding the current status in research. We believe that this framework can provide a valuable basis for future logistics research.

Keywords: Literature review · Topic modelling · Logistics · Smart technologies · Multi-level framework

1 Introduction

With the rapid development of artificial intelligence (AI), AI application in logistics has become more and more extensive. There are three main reasons for the realization of the value of AI in logistics: first, the cost reduction of information technology (cloud computing, RFID, etc.) has made the cost of perception, processing, and learning of logistics data popular. Second, logistics operations often involve many links, complex relationships between entities, and a large number of physical objects, funds, information, complex network structure, and large data volume characteristics make logistics suitable for AI application scenarios. Third, the current AI application ratio in logistics enterprises is less than 10%, which has a great development prospect [1].

Taking predictive logistics as an example, the aviation industry uses machine learning algorithms to analyze 50–60 parameters, which can accurately predict the delay time of flights to arrange goods, personnel, consumables, and other elements more reasonably, and reduce the cost of air transportation. Ernst & Young has applied image recognition processing technology to the audit of import and export documents. Its recognition accuracy rate can reach 97%, which can significantly shorten the time for import and export

© IFIP International Federation for Information Processing 2021
Published by Springer Nature Switzerland AG 2021
A. Dolgui et al. (Eds.): APMS 2021, IFIP AICT 633, pp. 560–567, 2021.
https://doi.org/10.1007/978-3-030-85910-7_59

customs clearance and make logistics operations smoother. To maintain competitiveness, practitioners in the logistics industry have to keep up with the trend and explore how AI can empower the logistics industry and scholars.

AI research has a long history since the creation of the Turing Test in 1950. Early AI mainly only refers to expert systems or decision support systems. Until 2012, increasing computing power and advances in big data and machine learning research have led to renewed interest in AI. After carefully studying the existing literature in AI and logistics, we find some related literature reviews. The first category summarizes current research on the combination of supply chain and big data [2, 3]or machine learning [4]. The second category is focused on combining AI technology with specific industry research, such as apparel [5] and agriculture [6]. The third category is a general analysis of the status quo and future trends in applying AI in the supply chain [7–11]. Despite valuable contributions to the previous literature reviews, when observed, none of the reviews studied the overall status of AI in the logistics industry. Besides, it has raised the need to have a broader outlook of AI techniques employed for improving efficiency in different logistics stages. To address the concerns from both industry and academia, we propose two research questions for conducting this literature review:

1. Since the new generation of AI (i.e. Since 2012), what is the trend and application of AI in logistics?
2. How to understand and exploitation of AI techniques employed at various logistics stages?

To achieve the two objectives mentioned above, we collect the literature related to AI application in logistics. In particular, we use the topic modeling algorithm to classify the literature. After the systematic literature review of each topic, we synthesize the findings and propose a multi-level theoretical framework.

2 Literature Identification and Collection

Many studies focus on the respective fields of logistics and AI. Still, the study that combines the two is limited, presenting challenges for constructing good research and review strategy, as it can be difficult to distinguish between relevant and non-relevant research in the paper collection. On the one hand, in AI, where the number of keywords is high and ranges from specific technology to the strategic level. When including many keywords in a search, the search will likely return a large number of researches, many of which may not be relevant. On the other hand, some studies use words such as "smart" in logistics but do not involve specific AI concepts or technologies.

We employed a systematic approach to identifying relevant articles for our literature review. We selected the Scopus database as it encompasses a wide range of refereed journals belonging to major publishing houses such as Elsevier, Taylor and Francis, IEEE, Emerald, and Springer. The papers' search applied the "AND" operator between both AI and logistics areas and an "OR" operator within each area. This ensures that at least one keyword of each area is present. An overview of the search words is depicted in Table 1. The search was conducted on Title and Keywords where applicable. The

Subarea was limited to "decision sciences", "social sciences", "business, management and accounting", "economics, Econometrics and finance". After excluding the book chapters, edited, conference review, note, and short survey, we collected 397 studies in total. Due to AI's rapid development in recent years and the rapid update and iteration, we did not exclude conference articles.

Table 1. Search words in AI and logistics

Research domain	Search words
Logistics	Logistics; shipping; reverse logistics; shipment; transport*; storing; warehous*; package*; inventory
AI	Machine learning; deep learning; artificial intelligen*; big data; smart; robot*

3   Topic Modeling

Topic modeling refers to the generation probability model that automatically extracts its implicit semantic topics from discrete data. Topic modeling is used to grouped related papers into topics, enabling an overview of the main research topics. The advantage of topic modeling is that it allows replicability and transparency. Other researchers can run the same code to verify the results or run the analysis when more papers have been published, providing an updated overview of the research. Based on the outcome of topic modeling, relevant papers on the same topic can be selected for a systematic literature review.

We use the topic modeling algorithm - Latent Dirichlet Allocation (LDA) for an exploratory review and classification of relevant papers. The model regards documents as a collection of words and is not affected by the position and order of words. After the group features are learned, topics are generated in the form of the vocabulary probability distribution to describe the data set.

The topic modeling process begins with loading and cleaning the abstract of papers, where words are converted to lower case and stemmed. We use the stop words of the NLTK (natural language toolkit) corpus to remove the stop words. Besides, to ensure the readability of the LDA results, we expand the stop words which are common and highly appeared in most papers such as "use", "paper", "research", "propose," etc. After the papers are cleaned, we set the parameters and conduct the iterative experiment to select the correct number of topics.

Having grouped the study into five different topics, each topic must have its topic named. The naming of the topic is based on the most frequent words in each topic group, taking the title and abstract into account. The result is presented in Table 2. Topic 1 can be named "AI in logistics system design". It studies how the logistics system could be configured physically and as far as the infrastructure is concerned. Topic 2 and 3 are about improving the efficiency or performance in inventory/warehouse management and transportation respectively by specific AI tools or models. Topic 4 is labeled as AI in logistics performances, whose literatures are about exploring the dimensions and indicators of logistics performance evaluation in the AI context. Topic 5 is named "Trends and framework of AI in logistics," whose primary focus is to analyze the current situation and future AI trends applied in the logistics field from a strategic level.

Table 2. Overview of topics

Topic Label	Ten most frequent words
AI in logistics system design	Design; urban; system; city; model; management; improve; industry; interaction; adoption
AI in warehouse and inventory management	Inventory; replenishment; pick; demand; model; decision; policy; time; control; forecasting
AI in transportation	Transport; freight; time; route; optimization; delivery; vehicle; local; speed; decision
AI in logistics performance	Performance; maturity; implementation; approach; level; process; dimension; facility; evaluation; combine
Trends and frameworks of AI in logistics	Trend; present; technology; efficiency; outbound; framework; potential; enhance; organizational; review

4   A Theoretical Multi-level Framework for AI in Logistics

Through the results of topic modeling, we can identify several critical stages of studying AI in logistics. To provide a coherent picture of the steps in this context, we propose an integrated multi-level framework based on the LDA results and task-technology fit (TTF) theory.

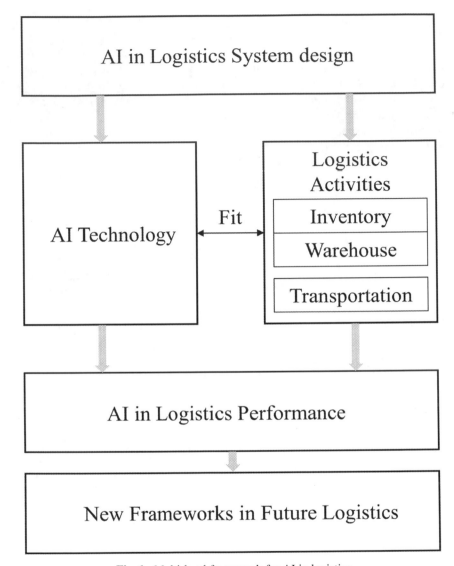

Fig. 1. Multi-level framework for AI in logistics.

The Fig. 1 depicts an overview of the framework. We divide the entire logistics activities into five stages: Topic 1 - AI in logistics system design. This stage's primary purpose is to design a logistics system and propose a specific implementation plan for logistics activities. Topic 2 - AI in warehouse and inventory management and Topic 3 - AI in transportation are based on TTF theory's perspective. We explore how AI technologies can empower specific logistics processes. Topic - 4 concerns how to evaluate the efficiency of the entire logistics activities. The final stage is topic 5 - the future trends of AI in logistics. Details of its theoretical background and essential components and factors are discussed below.

4.1   AI in Logistics System Design

Logistics system design refers to completing the conception of the logistics system hardware and software structure, thus forming the logistics system design and technical roadmap. From a macro perspective, according to the scope of the logistics system, the logistics system design can be classified into regional logistics system design, industry, logistics system design, city logistics system design, and port logistics system design. From a micro perspective, logistics system design can be classified into node design and link design.

4.2   AI in Warehouse and Inventory Management

AI and big data have disruptively changed the industry as the barriers to its implementation disappear. A subject profoundly discussed in logistics management is warehouse and inventory planning, which is the essential activity of many logistics enterprises.

4.3   AI in Transportation

The innovation in transportation can be classified into five main categories: new vehicles, proximity stations or points, collaborative and cooperative urban logistics, optimization of transport management, and routing. All these innovations can be applied in both long and short-distance transportation. From our perspective, we divide the research on this topic into the application of AI in long-haul freight transportation and short-haul freight transportation.

4.4   AI in Logistics Performance

As we all know, it is bound to pursue the quality and efficiency of logistics performance when its development reaches a certain level. Especially in the modern logistics network, after the penetration of AI gets higher and higher, the previous logistics evaluation dimensions and indicators will change and iterate accordingly.

4.5   Trends and Frameworks of AI in Logistics

AI has received increasing attention because of its popular and prominent role in logistics in improving the overall supply chain performance. The academic literature within this topic has revealed the emergence of two sub-topics: the first one is identifying opportunities for logistics research by analyzing the current research status and trends from different perspectives. The second one is proposing definitions and a framework for new conceptions.

Finally, we summarize each logistics stage's details by providing a detailed framework for AI in logistics. Building upon Fig. 1, a holistic view of our complete theoretical frame is depicted in Fig. 2.

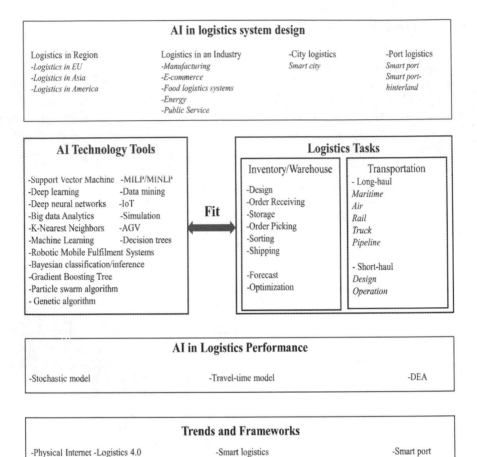

Fig. 2. Complete multi-level framework for AI in logistics.

5 Discussion

The purpose of this study is to conduct a systematic review of the literature on AI in logistics. AI has been shown to exercise a significant influence on modern logistics, while research on this issue is new and largely fragmented. We focus on reviewing the state-of-the-art research to propose a multi-level framework. The collected literature shows an increasing publication trend in the emerging area of AI in logistics. We also use the topic modeling algorithm (LDA) to classify the papers. In our review, we categorize the studies into five groups, summarized in three stages. Further, we discuss what important themes and technology have been studied combined with the TTF theory. Finally, we propose an integrative multi-level framework to understand the current status of AI in logistics, enabling us to achieve a holistic understanding in the setting of AI in logistics.

We believe that the findings of this study carry several important implications. First, to the best of our knowledge, this is the first study to conduct a thorough literature review on AI in logistics. While existing studies in this area are emerging, their findings are fragment and in their infancy. Thus, it isn't easy to obtain conclusive insights regarding how AI empowers logistics activities. In this respect, we provide an overview of the literature's current state and uncover the research contexts and methods. More importantly, we propose a multi-level theoretical framework to show and integrate the three stages of logistics activities. It can advance our knowledge of how AI is applied in logistics in different tasks and provide a notable theoretical foundation for future research.

Second, our research is one of the very few studies that conceptualize logistics activities with various stages. This broad view directs us to achieve a more comprehensive understanding of AI and to examine logistics activities occurring in different stages in this context. As shown in figure 13, our findings reveal that different research emphases are placed on different stages. For instance, in the topic 1,4 and 5, research focus on the overall design and implementation of AI in logistics, rather than the specific technologies in the topic 3 and 4.

References

1. Queiroz, M.M., Telles, R.: Big data analytics in supply chain and logistics: an empirical approach. Int. J. Logist. Manag. **29**(2), 767–783 (2018). https://doi.org/10.1108/IJLM-05-2017-0116
2. Kuo, Y.H., Kusiak, A.: From data to big data in production research: the past and future trends. Int. J. Prod. Res. **57**(15–16), 4828–4853 (2019). https://doi.org/10.1080/00207543.2018.1443230
3. Wang, G., Gunasekaran, A., Ngai, E.W.T., Papadopoulos, T.: Big data analytics in logistics and supply chain management: certain investigations for research and applications. Int. J. Prod. Econ. **176**, 98–110 (2016). https://doi.org/10.1016/j.ijpe.2016.03.014
4. Asmussen, C.B., Møller, C.: Enabling supply chain analytics for enterprise information systems: a topic modelling literature review and future research agenda. Enterp. Inf. Syst. **14**(5), 563–610 (2020). https://doi.org/10.1080/17517575.2020.1734240
5. Giri, C., Jain, S., Zeng, X., Bruniaux, P.: A detailed review of artificial intelligence applied in the fashion and apparel industry. IEEE Access **7**, 95376–95396 (2019). https://doi.org/10.1109/ACCESS.2019.2928979
6. Sharma, R., Kamble, S.S., Gunasekaran, A., Kumar, V., Kumar, A.: A systematic literature review on machine learning applications for sustainable agriculture supply chain performance. Comput. Oper. Res. **119**, 95–106 2020. https://doi.org/10.1016/j.cor.2020.104926
7. Lamba, K., Singh, S.P.: Big data in operations and supply chain management: current trends and future perspectives. Prod. Plan. Control **28**(11–12), 877–890 (2017). https://doi.org/10.1080/09537287.2017.1336787
8. Min, H.: Artificial intelligence in supply chain management: theory and applications. Int. J. Logist. Res. Appl. **13**(1), 13–39 (2010). https://doi.org/10.1080/13675560902736537
9. Wu, L., Yue, X., Jin, A., Yen, D.C.: Smart supply chain management: a review and implications for future research. Int. J. Logist. Manag. **27**(2), 395–417 (2016). https://doi.org/10.1108/IJLM-02-2014-0035
10. Yudhistyra, W.I., Risal, E.M., Raungratanaamporn, I.S., Ratanavaraha, V.: Exploring big data research: a review of published articles from 2010 to 2018 related to logistics and supply chains. Oper. Supply Chain Manag. **13**(2), 134–149 (2020). https://doi.org/10.31387/OSCM0410258
11. Zhong, R.Y., Newman, S.T., Huang, G.Q., Lan, S.: Big data for supply chain management in the service and manufacturing sectors: challenges, opportunities, and future perspectives. Comput. Ind. Eng. **101**, 572–591 (2016). https://doi.org/10.1016/j.cie.2016.07.013

A Robust Optimization Model for a Community Healthcare Service Network Design Problem

Congke Wang[1], Yankui Liu[1], Jinfeng Li[1], and Guoqing Yang[2(✉)]

[1] College of Mathematics and Information Science, Hebei University,
Baoding 071002, Hebei, China
[2] School of Management, Hebei University, Baoding 071002, Hebei, China
ygq@hbu.edu.cn

Abstract. In this paper, we present a robust model for the community healthcare service network design problem. The community healthcare service network can determine the location of central hospitals and the allocation of the community medical service stations in order to minimize that cost of the whole network. Beside, we employ the Box+ellipsoidal set to deal with the objective which obtain the uncertain parameter. In addition, we reformulate the proposed model into a computationally tractable robust counterpart form under Box+ellipsoidal set. Finally, we verify the validity of the model by a case study.

Keywords: 2-service network · Community healthcare service network · Robust optimization

1 Introduction

In recent years, community health service networks have become an increasing research hot spot for scholars. It is necessary to establish a reasonable and efficient community health care network to meet the health care needs of the community. The community healthcare service network is a typical facility location problem. [1] first proposed the study of location-allocation in the field of healthcare facilities, and many scholars have since conducted extensive research on the issue of healthcare facilities different perspectives [2–4]. [5] put forward that some healthcare facility location models are based on p-median model. Based on the 2-allocation p-hub model proposed in [6], this paper proposes a community medical service network model with 2-service structure. The community healthcare network with 2-service structure that needs to decided p central hospitals and each community medical service station is served by exactly two central hospitals. We conduct a 2-service community healthcare network that can effectively immunize against unforeseen circumstances and reduce the risk of uncertainty. For example, the emergence of covid-19 is an unexpected and unforeseen event

© IFIP International Federation for Information Processing 2021
Published by Springer Nature Switzerland AG 2021
A. Dolgui et al. (Eds.): APMS 2021, IFIP AICT 633, pp. 568–573, 2021.
https://doi.org/10.1007/978-3-030-85910-7_60

that requires specialized designated hospital to test. Our proposed 2-service community healthcare network that indicates a designated hospital is served by two central hospitals has a stronger ability to cope with the outbreak of the epidemic.

Our primary concern with this study also contains uncertain factors in the service network. In recent years, the research on uncertainty in medical field has attracted more and more attention from scholars. [7] studied a stochastic optimization of primary health care network to deal with random variables in the network, and proposed a random model of integer nonlinear programming to improve the service level of the whole service network. In practice, the precise probability of the realization of uncertain variables is difficult to obtain. Distributionally robust optimization approach is an alternative to address this defect. Distributionally robust optimization [8–10] is an emerging approach to deal with uncertainty by limiting uncertain variables through an uncertainty set with certain characteristics. [11] proposed a new hybrid robust possibility programming for hierarchical health network design based on input parameter uncertainty. In this paper, we propose a distributionally robust model for the proposed 2-service network problem and use Box+ellipsoid uncertain set to deal with the uncertain demand in medical network.

2 Problem Statement of CHSN

In this section, we introduce structure of the community health care service network. As shown in Fig. 1, the community health care service network design problem includes a fixed central hospitals, a group of community medical service stations and the allocation structure between them. In particular, we assumed that any community health service station was assigned to exactly two central hospitals for service. We believe that the identified central hospitals serve the community medical service stations allocated to them and that medical resources are shared among the central hospitals.

3 The Robust Healthcare Service Network Model

In this section, we introduce the robust model for the community health care service network.

$$
\min_{\mathbf{h}, \mathbf{Y}, \mathbf{x}} \sum_{k \in [N]} F_k h_k + \sum_{i,k \in [N]} C_{ik} Y_{ik} +
$$
$$
\max_{\mathbb{P} \in \mathscr{F}} \mathbf{E}_{\mathbf{u} \sim \mathbb{P}} [\sum_{i,k \in [N]} u_i x_{ik} d_{ik} \beta + \sum_{k \in [N]} P_k (\sum_{i \in N} u_i x_{ik} - Q_k)] \tag{1}
$$

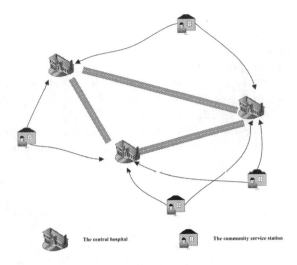

The central hospital   The community service station

Fig. 1. The network of community medical service design problem

$$\text{s.t.} \sum_{k \in [N]} Y_{ik} + (2 - p)h_i = 2 \qquad \forall i \in [N] \tag{2}$$

$$Y_{kk} = h_k \qquad \forall k \in [N] \tag{3}$$

$$\sum_{k \in [N]} h_k = p \tag{4}$$

$$Y_{ik} \le h_k \qquad \forall i \in [N], k \in [N] \tag{5}$$

$$m_{kl} \le h_k \qquad \forall k \in [N], l \in [N] \tag{6}$$

$$m_{kl} \le h_l \qquad \forall l \in [N], k \in [N] \tag{7}$$

$$m_{kl} \ge h_l + h_k - 1 \qquad \forall l \in [N], k \in [N] \tag{8}$$

$$x_{ik} \le Y_{ik} \qquad \forall i \in [N], k \ne i \in [N] \tag{9}$$

$$\sum_{k \in [N]} x_{ik} = 1 \qquad \forall i \in [N] \tag{10}$$

$$x_{ik} \ge 0, h_k, Y_{ik}, m_{kl} \in \{0,1\} \quad \forall i \in [N], k \in [N], l \in [N] \tag{11}$$

The purpose of objective (1) is to minimize all the fixed cost and the maximum of the expected operating cost by limiting the distributions of the uncertain variables to Box+ellipsoidal sets. Constraint (2) indicates that one community medical service station is assigned to two central hospitals. Constraint (3) implies that community medical service stations can only be allocated to central hospitals. Constraint (4) ensures that P central hospitals are selected. Constraint (5) shows that a community medical service station can only be assigned to an open central hospital. Constraints (6)–(8) indicate the contact of the central hospital. Constraint (9) implies that community service stations can only be assigned to open links. Constraint (10) requires that all demands be served by the central hospital. Constraint (11) is standard binary and non-negative integral constraint.

For the objective with uncertain parameters, we use the Box+ellipsoidal uncertain set to process. We assume that the uncertain parameter $E_{\mathbb{P}}[u]$ has the following form: $E_{\mathbb{P}}[u] = E_{\mathbb{P}}^{0}[u] + \sum_{l \in L} \zeta_l E_{\mathbb{P}}^{l}[u]$. In this study, we assume that the first moment $E_{\mathbb{P}}[u]$ is subject to a Box+ellipsoidal set, which can be depicted by the following distributional set $\mathscr{F}$: $\mathscr{F} = \{\zeta_l \in \mathbf{R}^l : -1 \leq \zeta_l \leq 1, l \leq L, \sqrt{\sum_{l \in [L]} \zeta_l^2 / \sigma_l^2} \leq \Omega, l \in L\}$, where σ_l is the given parameter, and Ω is the adjustable safe parameter controlling the size of the distributional set. Finally, we obtain the computationally processable form of the robust community health-care service network.

$$\min \sum_{k \in [N]} F_k h_k + \sum_{i,k \in [N]} C_{ik} Y_{ik} + \sum_{k \in [N]} P_k Q_k + 2t$$

$$\text{s.t.} \sum_{l \in [L]} |z_l| + \Omega \sqrt{\sum_{l \in [L]} w_l^2 \sigma_l^2} \leq t - (E_p^0[u])^T \mathbf{x} \mathbf{d}^T \beta$$

$$z_l + w_l = -(E_p^l[u])^T \mathbf{x} \mathbf{P}^T \quad \forall l \in [L]$$

$$\sum_{l \in [L]} |s_l| + \Omega \sqrt{\sum_{l \in [L]} v_l^2 \sigma_l^2} \leq t - (E_p^0[u])^T \mathbf{x} \mathbf{d}^T \beta$$

$$s_l + v_l = -(E_p^l[u])^T \mathbf{x} \mathbf{P}^T \quad \forall l \in [L]$$

$$(2)\text{--}(11)$$

where t, z, w, s, v are auxiliary decision variables.

4   Case Study

In this section, we apply our model to a small-scale case. We selected ten community medical service stations as shown in Fig. 2 for experimental study. Figure 3

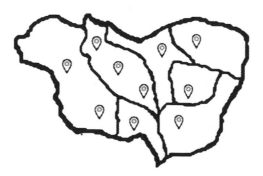

Fig. 2. The network of community medical service design problem

and Table 1 show our experimental results. As shown in Fig. 3, the optimal solution of the robust model selects community medical service stations 2,7 and 9 as central hospitals, and gives the corresponding demand allocation. The topology of the robust model shows that the demand of each district service station is served by two central hospitals, thus improving the overall service level of the medical service network.

Table 1. The result of robust model

	Optimal value	Hubs	Routes
Robust Model	863939.2	2,7,9	$3,4,6 \rightarrow (2,7)$ $1,10 \rightarrow (2,9)$ $5,8 \rightarrow (7,9)$

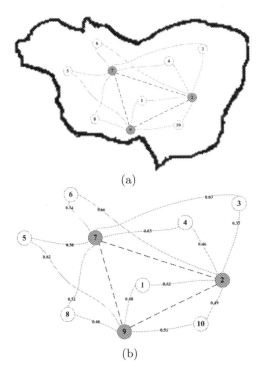

(a)

(b)

Fig. 3. Topology analysis of the robust model.

5   Conclusions

In this paper, we aimed to minimize the total cost of service network, and proposed a community healthcare network system to enable markers to make an effective location-allocations decision. For the uncertain parameters in the community healthcare network, we use robust optimization to deal with the objective with uncertain parameters, and obtain a exact model which can be processed. We also provide an illustrative example and highlight the impact of uncertain parameters on the model. The results show that the robust community healthcare network model proposed by this paper can well resist the uncertainty of the uncertain parameters.

References

1. Rahman, S.-U., Smith, D K : Use of location allocation models in health service development planning in developing nations. Eur. J. Oper. Res. **123**(3), 437–52 (2000)
2. Rais, A., Viana, A.: Operations research in healthcare: a survey. Int. Trans. Oper. Res. **18**(1), 1–31 (2011)
3. Zhang, Y., Berman, O., Verter, V.: The impact of client choice on preventive healthcare facility network. OR Spectrum **34**, 349–370 (2012)
4. Ahmadi-Javid, A., Seyedi, P., Syam, S.S.: A survey of healthcare facility location. Comput. Oper. Res. **79**, 223 263 (2017)
5. Daskin, M.S., Dean, L.K.: Location of health care facilities. In: Brandeau, M.L., Sainfort, F., Pierskalla, W.P. (eds.) Operations Research and Health Care, pp. 43–76. Springer, NewYork (2004)
6. Mokhtar, H., Krishnamoorthy, M., Ernst, A.T.: The 2-allocation p-hub median problem and a modified Benders decomposition method for solving hub location problems. Comput. Oper. Res. **104**, 375–393 (2019)
7. Ahmadi-Javid, A., Ramshe, N.: A stochastic location model for designing primary healthcare networks integrated with workforce cross-training. Oper. Res. Health Care **24**, 100–226 (2020)
8. Ben-Tal, A., Hochman, E.: More bounds on the expectation of a convex function of a random variable. J. Appl. Prob. **9**(4), 803–812 (1972)
9. Ben-Tal, A., Nemirovski, A.: Robust solutions of linear programming problems contaminated with uncertain data. Math. Program. **88**, 411–424 (2008)
10. Bertsimas, D., Sim, D.: The price of robustness. Oper. Res. **52**(1), 1–22 (2004)
11. Mousazadeh, M., Torabi, S.A., Pishvaee, M.S., Abolhassani, F.: Health service network design: a robust possibilistic approach. Int. Trans. Oper. Res. **25**, 337–373 (2018)

A Review of Explainable Artificial Intelligence

Kuo-Yi Lin[1,2] , Yuguang Liu[1], Li Li[1,2], and Runliang Dou[3(✉)]

[1] College of Electronics and Information Engineering,
Tongji University, Shanghai 201804, China
[2] Shanghai Institute of Intelligent Science and Technology,
Tongji University, Shanghai 201804, China
[3] School of Management, Tianjin University, Tianjin 300072, China
drl@tju.edu.cn

Abstract. Artificial intelligence developed rapidly, while people are increasingly concerned about internal structure in machine learning models. Starting from the definition of interpretability and historical process of interpretability model, this paper summarizes and analyzes the existing interpretability methods according to the two dimensions of model type and model time based on the objectives of interpretability model and different categories. With the help of the existing interpretable methods, this paper summarizes and analyzes its application value to the society analyzes the reasons why its application is hindered. This paper concretely analyzes and summarizes the applications in industrial fields, including model debugging, feature engineering and data collection. This paper aims to summarizes the shortcomings of the existing interpretability model, and proposes some suggestions based on them. Starting from the nature of interpretability model, this paper analyzes and summarizes the disadvantages of the existing model evaluation index, and puts forward the quantitative evaluation index of the model from the definition of interpretability. Finally, this paper summarizes the above and looks forward to the development direction of interpretability models.

Keywords: Explainable · Machine learning · Classification · Application

1 Introduction

The deep learning model fits well in the era of big data, but its accuracy and efficiency are based on the improvement of algorithm efficiency and the combination of huge parameter space. This also means that efficient machine learning algorithms are difficult to directly understand or explain. At present, the existing interpretable machine learning methods are mostly classified according to the original model of the interpretation model. Therefore, this paper summarizes the definition, scope, nature and categorizes the interpretation model more comprehensively and discusses the interpretation issues faced in the digital manufacturing process and proposes some suggestions.

The paper is organized into the following sections. Section 2 provides a review of the related research pertaining to the definition of interpretability and explainable model.

© IFIP International Federation for Information Processing 2021
Published by Springer Nature Switzerland AG 2021
A. Dolgui et al. (Eds.): APMS 2021, IFIP AICT 633, pp. 574–584, 2021.
https://doi.org/10.1007/978-3-030-85910-7_61

Section 3 describes the explainable model from the aspects: aims, scope, implementation and classification, especially in the last part, the classification of explainable models has been reorganized in a clearer way. Section 4 discusses the application and problems of explainable models, as well as proposes the feasible solutions. In the Conclusion, the paper looks forward to the development prospects the research trends of explainable models.

2   Related Works

Historically speaking, since the 1970s, there has been sporadic interest in explanations itself, which began with attention on expert systems. In the following thirty years, the attention of related research shifted to neural networks and recommendation systems, as shown in Fig. 1. Nonetheless, progress on these issues slowed about a decade ago. This is because the focus of AI research has shifted to implementing algorithms and models that focus on predictive power, while the ability to interpret decision processes has taken a back seat.

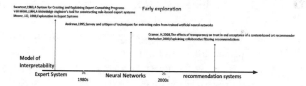

Fig. 1. Early exploration of explainability model and definition

The interpretive definition has improved over time, for example, Gunning [1] adopts that explainable artificial intelligence enables human users to understand, appropriately trust, and effectively manage the emerging generation of artificially intelligent partners. Molnar [2] considers that interpretable machine learning refers to methods and models that make the behavior and predictions of machine learning systems understandable to humans. Miller [3] regards interpretability as the degree to which a human can understand the cause of a decision. The details and the reasons used to explain or even whether the explanation is easy to understand are completely dependent of the audience while these definition neglects the role of the audience. So the definition must reflect the dependence of the explainable model on audience.

Aimed at above problems, [4] gives the definition of explanation that given a certain audience, explainability refers to the details and reasons a model gives to make its functioning clear or easy to understand. At this point, we can define the interpretability model as given an audience, an explainable Artificial Intelligence is one that produces details or reasons to make its functioning clear or easy to understand (Fig. 2).

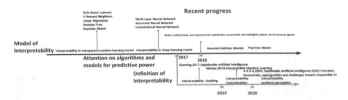

Fig. 2. Recent progress of explainability model and explainability definition

3 Explainable Model

3.1 Scope of Explainable Model

Algorithm transparency is only responsible for answering the question of creating a model without data or learning models [2], but the focus of interpretable machine learning is prediction rather than algorithm [5]. Decomposability refers to the ability of the model to explain each part, which can ensure that the model obtains the interpretation of the input or parameters from the existing conditions. Simulability is the ability to simulate in a more complex environment, within which the model can obtain simulation equations from known conditions.

The global interpretability model starts from the training data and the entirety of each part of the model. The interpretability of the global model can be divided into the overall level and the modular level. The overall level of global interpretability can be realized conceptually [6], but this requires a trained model and corresponding algorithms and data [5], which is difficult to complete in practice [2]. Although the global interpretability at the overall level is difficult to achieve, the interpretability at the module level can be achieved [5]: For example, the interpretable part of a linear model is its weight; the interpretable part of a decision tree is its node splitting and analysis [5, 2]. It is worth noting that the various parameters of the linear model are related to the whole, and feature decoupling may be involved when considering feature interaction [7].

The idea of explaining the prediction of a single sample is to enlarge a single sample and try to understand how the model achieves the prediction [5]. For the black box model, using a simpler interpretability model to approximate a smaller target area can maintain interpretability while maintaining high accuracy. This is because under the assumption that local predictions are linearly or monotonically dependent on certain features, local explanations may be more accurate than global explanations [2]. For the interpretation of a certain type of sample prediction, there are essentially two methods: treating the target sample group as the entire data set for prediction and interpretation; or summarizing the above-mentioned partial interpretation of the prediction of a single sample to achieve the prediction of the sample group [2].

3.2 Implementation of Explainable Model

The interpretability of the model can be divided into the interpretation model and the interaction with the audience. As stated in the previous definition of interpretability, interpretability is not limited to models, it is for specific audiences. For interaction with users, it may involve prototype interpretation interfaces and visualization of models; or the use of psychological knowledge to explain machine learning principles, etc.

The interpretation model can be realized by simplifying or imposing constraints on transparent or other specific models; it can also be realized by establishing post interpretable models for existing models. Specifically, for a deep interpretation model that aims to explain deep learning, improved deep learning techniques can be used to learn its interpretable functions. For example, Cheng [8], etc. look for evidence of scene judgment in pictures and learn semantic association. Cheng [8] trains the network to associate semantic attributes with hidden layer nodes and associates labeled nodes with known ontology, which makes it have explanatory power. Researchers at the University of California, Berkeley [9] use the idea of generating image captions and generating visual interpretations to generate visual interpretations, which associate image descriptions with class definitions, identify objects in the image through the CNN model, and use the RNN model to convert the features in CNN model into words and titles.

Interaction modules that enhance audience understanding can be divided into psychology (or humanities) and human-computer interaction (HCI) parts. Specifically, we should first study and model how humans produce and understand explanations, and what attributes can make humans perceive explanations to achieve human interpretability, which belongs to the category of psychology or humanities. In addition, the way and process of interaction between users and entities greatly affects users' understanding and trust in them.

4 Classification of Explainable Model

The interpretability model can be summarized into three categories according to its training sequence with the original model: pre-model, in-model, and post-model, which is shown in Fig. 3.

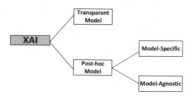

Fig. 3. Current status of interpretable model research

Solvability models can be divided into specific model-specific interpretation models and model-independent interpretation models according to whether they are restricted to specific models, which is shown in Fig. 3. Because model-specific interpretation methods are based on the internal characteristics of certain specific models, they are limited to specific model classes; relatively, interpretation models that have nothing to do with the original model can be applied to a wider range of model interpretation.

4.1 Scope of Explainable Model

The transparent model refers to a model that is understandable by itself. The range of interpretability can be described by the transparency, decomposability and emulation of the above algorithm. The interpretability of a transparent model can be achieved by imposing constraints on the model, such as sparsity, monotonicity, causality, or physical constraints in the professional field. The current status of interpretable transparent model is shown in Fig. 4.

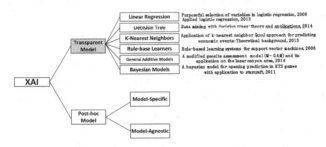

Fig. 4. Current status of interpretable transparent model

Logistic regression model is essentially a classification model, and a logistic regression model with continuous dependent variables is a linear model. There is a linear dependence between the predictors and predictors of this type of model, so it reduces the flexibility of data fitting while giving the model interpretability. Decision tree is a decision-making hierarchy used to solve classification and regression problems, and it satisfies the constraints of model transparency. K-Nearest Neighbors (K-Nearest Neighbors) makes decisions on test samples by coordinating the prediction results of K-nearest neighbors. The key to the interpretability of this model is the distance and similarity between K neighbors, which is similar to the human decision-making process. Enhancing the interaction between the user and the model [4]. Rule learning is a general term for a certain type of model, which refers to a model that can obtain corresponding rules from training data. The rules can be simple if-then conditional rules or more complex rules combined by simple rules. The number and nature of the rules in the model have a greater impact on the performance and interpretability of the model. The generalized additive model is a linear model that makes predictions or decisions through a combination of smooth functions defined by predictor variables. The Bayesian model adopts the form of probability directed acyclic graph to express the conditional dependence between a group of variables. These models above can be applied to production scenarios with small data but high requirements for real-time and model transparency.

4.2 Post-hoc Explainable Models

The post-hoc interpretable model refers to the model that explains the existing initial model. Its purpose is to explain the opaque black box machine learning model. The post-hoc interpretability model can be divided into an explanation model for a specific machine learning model and an explanation model independent of the model.

4.2.1   Model-Specific methods in Shallow ML

Machine learning models include a variety of supervised learning models, many of which are complex algorithms. For example, extracting interpretation rules from LSTM or distilling neural networks into soft decision trees belong to this type of interpretation model method. The current status of interpretable shallow ML model is shown in Fig. 5.

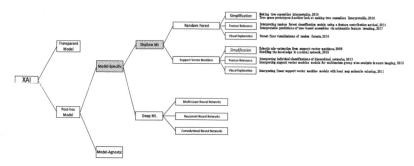

Fig. 5. Current status of interpretable shallow ML model

The interpretation method for this model can be summarized as model simplification and variable importance analysis. Subsequently, Deng [10] created a simplified tree set learning model (STEL). But the simplification of the model inevitably means the loss of efficiency. S. Hara et al. [11] proposed to use the simplified model for model interpretation while maintaining the original complex model for decision-making. Based on the above problems, Breiman [12] first proposed to use the importance of features in random forests as an explanation basis. Subsequently, Tolomei et al. [13] proposed a method to measure the importance of features by changing the prediction category.

The support vector machine model completes tasks such as classification by constructing one or more hyperplanes in a high-dimensional space. Support vector machines have high generalization performance, and their commonly used model visualization methods include: model simplification, visualization, and local interpretation. In terms of model simplification, [4] divided it into the following four categories according to the depth of the model: 1) Extract a more explanatory rule learning model from the support vector machine; 2) [14] established additional hyperplanes for the support vector machine and constructed a rule learning model to complete the model simplification; 3) trained with the original interpretation model; 4) There are still studies [15] that have created statistics that explicitly explain the margins of support vector machines and specifically explain the multi-factor patterns shown in neuroimaging. The above models are suitable for production scenarios with more data and more complex models required. In this scenario, the interpretability of the model can be enhanced by imposing limiting factors on it.

4.2.2   Model-Specific Methods in Deep Learning Models

Although deep neural networks are black box models, their good accuracy makes them widely used in various industries. Explanatory research has always been a hot issue in the industry. As shown in Fig. 6, common interpretation methods include, simplified models, feature correlation models, visual interpretation models, text interpretation models, sample interpretation models, partial interpretation models, etc.

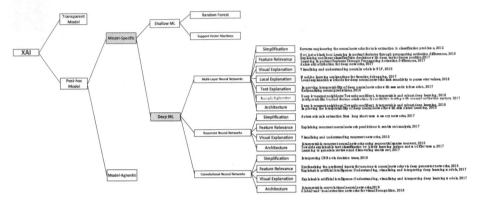

Fig. 6. Current status of interpretable Deep ML Model

Multi-layer neural network is one of the most common black box models, and the explanation of the black box model is a necessary condition to realize its application value. There are few studies on the simplified interpretation of multi-layer networks directly, such as the Deep-RED algorithm [16]. [17] et al. treat model simplification as a Post-hoc interpretability method independent of the model. [16] interprets the original model through a gradient boost tree, and [17] reduces the multi-layer model to a model. However, for complex multilayer neural networks with deep layers, the feature correlation model is more suitable. [17] proposed on the basis of the Deep-LIFT algorithm of [18] to explain the original model by correlating the output result with the contribution of the input.

RNN network is widely used in original data with inherent order such as natural language processing and time series because of its ability to store data relationships. [19] et al. proposed a specific propagation rule that works with RNN multiplicative connection to explain the knowledge of RNN neural network. [20] combined the hidden Markov model with the RNN model to ensure the interpretability and accuracy of the model, [21] et al. changed the model itself to understand the process of model decision-making.

The CNN network is widely used in computer vision, and its ability to visualize data essentially strengthens human understanding of the model. By constructing a global average pooling layer between the last convolutional layer of CNN and the fully connected layer of the predicted object, the weight projection of the output layer in the convolutional feature is realized, and the important image for a specific object class is identified by this Area and improve the mapping quality [22]. [23] uses the method of feature correlation analysis, using the loss of each filter in the high-level convolutional layer to force it to learn a specific object. [24] adopted a visual interpretation method and proposed the Grad-CAM algorithm to highlight the interpretation area of the predicted target in the image. [25] combined the CNN network with the RNN network and the LSTM model, and explained the pictures by analyzing the text information. In addition to the above method of explaining the decision-making process by mapping the output in the input space, [26] explained how the CNN network makes decisions by going deep into the network and through the middle layer. [27] combined the above-mentioned deep model internal method with the input-output mapping method to explore the decision-making process of CNN. In addition, [28] and [29] used LIME algorithm and bio-confrontation detection interpretation method to explain CNN network respectively. The above models are suitable for production scenarios with extremely large data and high accuracy requirements. This scenario usually trains the model in an offline state, but simply imposing constraints on the model cannot balance the performance of the model and its interpretability. Therefore, for such production scenarios, a separate interpretable model is usually trained to explain the original model.

4.2.3   Model-Agnostic Methods Divided by Explainable Scope

The model diagnosis interpretation method does not depend on the original model to be explained. Under certain circumstances, model-specific interpretation methods are better than model-independent interpretation methods, but the advantage of the latter is that it is completely independent of the original model, which guarantees the reusability of the model to a certain extent.

   This paper will classify and summarize this type of interpretation model within the scope of its interpretation. Specifically, it can be divided into a local interpretability model, a global interpretability model, and a local/global interpretability model, which is shown in Fig. 7.

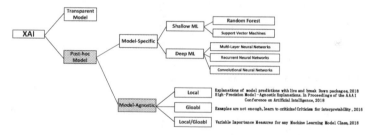

Fig. 7. Current status of interpretable deep ML model

5   Problems and Development

The problems of interpretability models include the trade-off between model interpretability and performance, the evaluation indicators of interpretability models, and other problems or other unresolved problems in existing interpretability models. However, the emergence of ex post interpretability models and mixed interpretation models may provide interpretability while maintaining the performance of the original model. The evaluation index of an interpretability model refers to a measurement system that evaluates the pros and cons of the model from the definition, nature and goals of the model. Starting from the definition of the interpretability model, comprehensibility needs to consider the understanding ability of the audience, so it is a relatively subjective nature. But from an objective point of view, a relatively simple model is easier to understand. Based on the expansion of this definition, Doshi-Velez and Kim [30] proposed three levels of interpretability of evaluation models according to the interpretation cost and the effectiveness of the interpretation results: application-based evaluation, model audience-based evaluation and application evaluation method. Interpretability is essential to promote learning. Humans do not need to explain everything, but when dealing with a specific event, human curiosity will drive them to explore the reasons for the event and update their environmental thinking models in the process of exploring the reasons. Therefore, the interpretability model does not have a mandatory goal. Its main goal is to develop the original artificial intelligence model toward responsibility, fairness, privacy and data fusion while maintaining a high level of predictive performance.

6   Conclusions

This paper defines the interpretability model and describes the aims, scope, implementation and classification of the explainable model. The paper discusses the application and problems of explainable models, as well as proposes the feasible solutions. Aiming at the contradiction between the interpretability of the interpretability model and the accuracy of the original model, the ex post interpretability model can be used to solve the above contradiction; and for the problem of the evaluation index of the interpretability model, this article considers the nature of interpretability and starting from the definition, put forward a method route that can quantitatively evaluate the model. Follow-up research can do more in-depth exploration of this method.

Progress	Details
Model	Summarize the definition, scope and nature for interpretability model and categorize the interpretability model
Applications	Analyze the applications in industrial fields and discuss the interpretation issues faced in the digital manufacturing process
Development	Propose suggestions based on the existing interpretability model

References

1. Gunning, D.: Explainable artificial intelligence (xAI), Technical report, Defense Advanced Research Projects Agency (DARPA) (2017)
2. Molnar, C.: Interpretable machine learning (2019). https://christophm.github.io/interpretable-ml-book/. Accessed 22 Jan 2019
3. Miller, T.: Explanation in artificial intelligence: insights from the social sciences. Artif. Intell. **267**, 1–38 (2018). [CrossRef]
4. Arrieta, A.B., et al.: Explainable artificial intelligence (XAI): concepts, taxonomies, opportunities and challenges toward responsible AI. Inf. Fusion **58**, 82–115 (2020)

5. Carvalho, D.V., Pereira, E.M., Cardoso, J.S.: Machine learning interpretability: a survey on methods and metrics (2019)
6. Lipton, Z.C.: The mythos of model interpretability. arXiv 2016. arXiv:1606.03490
7. Bengio, Y., Courville, A., et al.: Representation learning: a review and new perspectives. IEEE Trans. Pattern Anal. Mach. Intell. **35**(8), 1798–1828 (2013)
8. Cheng, H., et al.: SRI-Sarnoff AURORA at TRECVID 2014: multimedia event detection and recounting (2014)
9. Hendricks, L.A, Akata, Z., Rohrbach, M., Donahue, J., Schiele, B., Darrell, T.: Generating Visual Explanations. arXiv:1603.08507v1 [cs.CV], 28 Mar 2016
10. Deng, H.: Interpreting tree ensembles with intrees (2014). arXiv:1408.5456
11. Hara, S., Hayashi, K.: Making tree ensembles interpretable (2016). arXiv:1606.05390
12. Breiman, L.: Classification and Regression Trees. Routledge (2017)
13. Tolomei, G., Silvestri, F., Haines, A., Lalmas, M.: Interpretable predictions of tree-based ensembles via actionable feature tweaking. In: Proceedings of the 23rd ACM SIGKDD International Conference on Knowledge Discovery and Data Mining, pp. 465–474. ACM (2017)
14. Fu, X., Ong, C., Keerthi, S., Hung, G.G., Goh, L.: Extracting the knowledge embedded in support vector machines. In: IEEE International Joint Conference on Neural Networks, vol. 1, pp. 291–296. IEEE (2004)
15. Gaonkar, B., Shinohara, R.T., Davatzikos, C., Initiative, A.D.N., et al.: Interpreting support vector machine models for multivariate group wise analysis in neuroimaging. Med. Image Anal. **24**(1), 190–204 (2015)
16. Zilke, J., Loza Mencía, E., Janssen, F.: DeepRED – rule extraction from deep neural networks. In: Calders, T., Ceci, M., Malerba, D. (eds.) DS 2016. LNCS (LNAI), vol. 9956, pp. 457–473. Springer, Cham (2016). https://doi.org/10.1007/978-3-319-46307-0_29
17. Traoré, R., Caselles-Dupré, H., Lesort, T., Sun, T., Cai, G., Rodríguez, D. Filliat, DisCoRL: continual reinforcement learning via policy distillation (2019).
18. Shrikumar, A., Greenside, P., Shcherbina, A., Kundaje, A.: Not just a black box: learning important features through propagating activation differences (2016)
19. Arras, L., Montavon, G., Müller, K.-R., Samek, W.: Explaining recurrent neural network predictions in sentiment analysis (2017)
20. Krakovna, V., Doshi-Velez, F.: Increasing the interpretability of recurrent neural networks using hidden Markov models (2016)
21. Choi, E., Bahadori, M.T., Sun, J., Kulas, J., Schuetz, A., Stewart, W.: RETAIN: an interpretable predictive model for healthcare using reverse time attention mechanism, In: Advances in Neural Information Processing Systems, pp. 3504–3512 (2016)
22. Zhou, B., Khosla, A., Lapedriza, A., Oliva, A., Torralba, A.: Learning deep features for discriminative localization. In: IEEE Conference on Computer Vision and Pattern Recognition, pp. 2921–2929 (2016)
23. Zhang, Q., Nian Wu, Y., Zhu, S.-C.: Interpretable convolutional neural networks, In: Proceedings of the IEEE Conference on Computer Vision and Pattern Recognition, pp. 8827–8836 (2018)
24. Selvaraju, R.R., Cogswell, M., Das, A., Vedantam, R., Parikh, D., Batra, D.: Grad-CAM: visual explanations from deep networks via gradient-based localization. In: Proceedings of the IEEE International Conference on Computer Vision, pp. 618–626 (2017)
25. Dong, Y., Su, H., Zhu, J., Zhang, B.: Improving interpretability of deep neural networks with semantic information. In: IEEE Conference on Computer Vision and Pattern Recognition, pp. 4306–4314 (2017)
26. Bau, D., Zhou, B., Khosla, A., Oliva, A., Torralba, A.: Network dissection: quantifying interpretability of deep visual representations. In: Proceedings of the IEEE Conference on Computer Vision and Pattern Recognition, pp. 6541–6549 (2017)

27. Olah, C., et al.: The building blocks of interpretability, Distill (2018)
28. Ribeiro, M.T., Singh, S., Guestrin, C.: Model-agnostic interpretability of machine learning (2016)
29. Papernot, N., McDaniel, P.: Deep k-nearest neighbors: towards confident, interpretable and robust deep learning (2018)
30. Doshi-Velez, F., Kim, B.: Towards a rigorous science of interpretable machine learning. arXiv (2017). arXiv:1702.08608

The Impact of the Number of Regulated Suppliers in Green Supply Chain Action on Financial Performance

Xuanchang Qi[iD] and Hanhui Hu[(✉)]

Southeast University, Nanjing 211189, Jiangsu, China
huhh@seu.edu.cn

Abstract. In recent years, with the gradual attention to environmental pollution and the deep understanding of sustainability theory, the supply chain of the real estate industry has begun to change to a green and sustainable development approach. In 2016, Society of Entrepreneurs and Ecology and other real estate industry alliance organizations, together with Vanke and other industry leaders, launched the "Green Supply Chain Action" to establish a green procurement whitelist by testing the environmental performance of building materials suppliers in various categories. This paper focuses on the impact of the number of suppliers regulated by the company on the financial performance of the company in the sustainable supply chain. The empirical results show that the number of suppliers under corporate supervision is negatively related to financial performance. In response to the findings, this paper puts forward development suggestions for real estate green supply chain management.

Keywords: Sustainable supply chain management · Green Supply Chain Action · Supplier management · Financial performance

1 Research Background and Problem Formulation

In recent years, the positive development of economy in China has attracted world attention, but at the same time more and more environmental pollution problems have been exposed by the media, and it is imperative to deepen the supply-side reform and promote the green development of the whole industry. The real estate industry has always been one of the highly polluting enterprises in China. In the past, real estate enterprises mainly made profits with the real estate development model and took profit maximization as their primary goal, ignoring the management control of environmental pollution. In the whole life cycle of real estate, the enterprises involved in each link are fragmented, the development of standards in the industry still needs to be improved, and the real estate supply chain urgently needs to be regulated and managed [1]. In recent years, with the gradual attention to the problem of environmental pollution and the deep understanding of the theory of sustainable development, the supply chain of the real estate industry has

A. Dolgui et al. (Eds.): APMS 2021, IFIP AICT 633, pp. 585–590, 2021.
https://doi.org/10.1007/978-3-030-85910-7_62

begun to embark on the transformation to a green and sustainable development approach [2].

In 2016, Society of Entrepreneurs and Ecology (hereinafter referred to as the SEE) joined hands with industry alliances such as Zhongcheng United Investment, as well as industry leaders such as Vanke and Landsea, to jointly launch the "Green Supply Chain Action In The Real Estate Industry" (hereinafter referred to as the GSC). Unlike the previous sustainable transformation of a single enterprise, GSC is the first attempt to implement a green supply chain in the whole real estate industry in the form of an industry coalition. The GSC Working Group established a partnership with a third-party testing organization to establish a green procurement whitelist by testing the environmental performance of building materials suppliers in various categories. Until now, the number of product categories included in the testing has gradually increased, and the number of supplier companies that have been tested and added to the whitelist has also increased.

Therefore, based on study of environmental management in supply chains, this paper will focus on industry federated supply chain regulation, using real estate companies that have joined the GSC action as the subject of the study, to investigate the impact of the number of suppliers subject to corporate regulation in sustainable supply chains on corporate financial performance. The findings of this study will provide recommendations for the future development of environmental regulation in the supply chain of the real estate industry.

2   Theoretical Analysis and Research Hypothesis

On the one hand, according to the performance evaluation theory that considers the environment, assessing suppliers' environmental performance and implementing green procurement can help motivate suppliers to improve their production processes, reach environmental cooperation between upstream and downstream enterprises, and improve the environmental performance of green supply chains. At the same time, the study shows that the supervision of suppliers by enterprises has a positive impact on both environmental and social performance of suppliers, and cooperation with suppliers has a positive impact on suppliers' environmental performance. Suppliers' performance improvement on environmental and social responsibility has a positive impact on corporate performance [3]. At the same time, supplier and customer relational capital improve financial performance indirectly through supplier and customer green management [4]. Therefore, the expansion of regulated supplier is likely to have a positive impact on corporate financial performance.

On the other hand, drawing on Porter's hypothesis, suppliers are likely to innovate technologically or even undergo a general renewal of product production processes or industrial transformation when they are under pressure from environmental regulation [5]. It can be inferred that suppliers will increase their financial performance by using new technologies to shrink production costs or increasing the selling price of products, the latter of which will lead to an increase in procurement costs for real estate firms. Joining the GSC requires real estate firms to supervising suppliers to complete relevant testing steps and oversee their rectification, and the increase in the number of supervised suppliers is likely to lead to an increase in corporate management costs. In recent years, the internal competition in the real estate industry has intensified and the external government regulation and supervision has become stricter. The level of return on investment of real estate enterprises has decreased and the profit level has fallen, so the cost in supervising suppliers may have a negative impact on the profitability of enterprises instead.

Therefore, based on the above theoretical studies and inferences, increasing the number of regulated supplier firms may have two different effects on firms' financial performance, and the following two hypotheses are proposed.

Ha: The number of regulated suppliers is positively associated with corporate financial performance.

Hb: The number of regulated suppliers is negatively associated with corporate financial performance.

3 Empirical Analysis

3.1 Sample Selection and Data Sources

This paper examines the impact of the growth in the number of regulated suppliers on the financial performance of the companies, using all listed companies in the first 48 companies that joined the GSC as a sample. According to the screening, there were five listed companies that joined the GSC at the beginning of the action, and none of them have been ST from 2016 to date, and their financial data are sourced from Juchao Information Network and each company's public annual report.

The source of supplier whitelist data is the official website of GSC (http://www.cura.cn/) and the official WeChat official account. According to statistics, the number of supplier companies in the whitelist updated every year are 159, 575, 3491 and 3841.

3.2 Model Setting

Referring to the studies of Zhou, Li and Hua [6, 7], the model is set as follows.

$$NPG_{it} = \beta_0 + \beta_i CGR_t + \sum \lambda_i Control_{it} + \varepsilon_{it} \tag{1}$$

i takes values from 1 to 5 and refers to the five listed companies that are the subject of the study. t is the number of years since joining the GSC action. β is the slope of the regression line, indicating the correlation between NPG and CGR, and λ indicates the correlation between the dependent variable and the control variable.

The detailed definition of each variable is shown in Table 1.

Table 1. Main variables and definitions.

Variable type	Variable name	Variable symbols	Variable description
Main Variables	Net profit growth rate	NPG	Total net income for the current period/ Total net income for the previous period
	Growth rate of regulated suppliers	CGR	Number of regulated suppliers in year t/Number of regulated suppliers in the first year
Control variables	Ratio of liabilities	lev	Average total liabilities/ Average total assets
	Current ratio	CR	Total current assets/ Total current liabilities
	Total assets turnover ratio	TAT	Sales revenue/ Average total assets

3.3 Regression Results

Regression analysis of the data according to the above model yields the following results.

$$\{\beta i\} = \{0.395, -1.98, -5.538, -32.827, 0.046\}.$$

The regression results of the data related to Vanke Group and Suzhou Golden Mantis Construction & Decoration Co., Ltd. are positively correlated and the independent variable has little effect on the dependent variable, while the results of the remaining three listed companies are negatively correlated. Therefore, it can be tentatively concluded that hypothesis Hb holds that the number of regulated suppliers is negatively correlated with corporate financial performance. The more upstream supplier companies in the industry are evaluated and supervised by real estate firms, the greater the negative impact on profitability is.

3.4 Conclusion Analysis

In recent years, with the government's proposition of "stabilizing expectations, housing prices, and land prices", real estate policies have been strengthened and financial regulation has become stricter, and real estate companies have encountered more difficulties in their development. Especially after 2018, real estate companies have scaled down their core businesses to maintain a good cash flow position. Vanke, Landsea, Longhu and other core firms of the GSC have actively transformed to carry out diversified businesses [8]. While the leading companies in the industry have entered the transition period, the companies joining the GSC still need to maintain continuous monitoring of suppliers and increase the number of tested product categories and suppliers year by year. The increase of costs and expenses in the property business has a negative impact on the economic performance of the companies.

4   Development Suggestions

4.1   Establishment of Intelligent Data System for Real Estate Industry

In the background of cloud computing, Internet of Things, big data and other information technologies are widely used, in order to control the management costs consumed by the assessment and supervision, the GSC action intelligent data system can be established. Enterprises supervise upstream suppliers to report environmental indicators and financial indicators such as product prices truthfully into the system and update them regularly. Real estate companies will use the system to intelligently work out the upstream suppliers with the greatest performance gains in all aspects, thus optimizing green procurement solutions and saving procurement costs.

4.2   Comprehensive Performance Appraisal

The sustainability of an organization does not only lie in one aspect of economic performance, but should be considered from three dimensions of economic, environmental and social performance. According to relevant studies, enterprises can more effectively improve their environmental performance by proactively implementing green supply chain management practices [5]. Therefore, the environmental performance assessment index of real estate green supply chain can be comprehensively established based on the industry characteristics of the real estate industry and the main pollutant measurement index, using performance assessment methods such as lifecycle assessment (LCA), multi-attribute utility and balanced scorecard [9]. Based on this index, the impact of upstream supplier monitoring on the economic and environmental performance of enterprises is analyzed comprehensively to further clarify the future development direction of enterprises involved in GSC action.

5   Conclusion and Outlook

This paper examines the impact of the number of regulated suppliers on the economic performance of companies, using the example of already listed companies participating in the GSC action. The result shows that the number of upstream suppliers in the industry supervised by the firm has a negative impact on economic performance. Through the analysis, the author believes that this is due to the increasing cost of supervising suppliers in the context of government policies regulating the real estate industry.

At present, GSC action is in a positive development stage, and its influence in the industry is increasing year by year, while it has effectively made outstanding contributions to the real estate industry in reducing pollution emissions. As the first industry organization to jointly implement green supply chain, the impact it will bring to the development of enterprises, industry and society after its long-term development still needs further observation and research. The real estate industry continues to play an economic pillar role in China, and only if the real estate supply chain practices sustainable production and actively optimizes economic and environmental performance can it achieve greater development space and make the real estate industry develop in a more healthy and reasonable direction.

References

1. Wang, T.: Research on barriers and solutions to the development of green supply chain in real estate. Hous. Real Estate (21), 9–10(2019)
2. Wang, Q.: Research on green supply chain management and its supplier selection in construction industry. M.S. Thesis, Xi'an Engineering University(2018)
3. Dai, J.: Sustainable supply chain management for Chinese enterprises. M.S. Thesis, University of International Business and Economics (2015)
4. Yubing, Y.: The impact of relational capital on green supply chain management and financial performance. Prod. Plan. Control 32(10), 861–874 (2021)
5. Zhou, L.: Research on the impact of corporate green supply chain management on its environmental performance. M.S. thesis, Jiangsu University (2020)
6. Zhou, X.: Research on the factors influencing the performance of listed real estate companies in China. M.S. thesis, Northern Polytechnic University (2017)
7. Li, T.: Research on factors influencing the performance of China's real estate listed companies based on micro perspective. J. Inner Mongolia University Finance Econ. 16(06), 63–67 (2018)
8. Feng, K.: Research on the development trend of real estate industry. Hous. Real Estate (36), 1–2 (2019)
9. Jing, H.: A review of sustainable supply chain performance evaluation. J. Shenyang University Aeronautics Astronautics 35(06), 1–13 (2018)

Digitalization for Resilience and Sustainability During the Covid-19 Pandemic: An Explorative Event Study

Seyoum Eshetu Birkie[(⊠)] [ID]

KTH Royal Institute of Technology, Stockholm, Sweden
seyoume@kth.se

Abstract. This paper reports on an initial explorative investigation on the relationship among resilience, digitalization, sustainability practices, and operations performance following the outbreak of Covid-19. It builds on literature survey and event study based on news items from international outlets. The findings indicate the need for holistic perspectives to leverage from different efforts in manufacturing firms to drive competitiveness with as little impact on other measures especially considering manufacturing companies.

Keywords: Digital transformation · Disruption · Industrial sustainability

1 Introduction

The financial and social burden of the Covid-19 pandemic has been felt by manufacturing companies globally. Despite government support, a large number of SMEs are in the verge of or have already been out of business, leaving millions jobless. Only those that could leverage some form of resilience in managing the disruptive consequences of the pandemic seem to be able to continue their operations. There are reports that emission levels during the pandemic have decreased in many parts of the world. Likely causes include- reduced transportation and mobility of people as well as reduction in manufacturing activities. However, we need to understand if such reductions on environmental impact is spontaneous consequence or related to established sustainability practices in manufacturing firms.

Use of digital technologies has been intensified in the fight against the pandemic. The competitive implications of such efforts both in relation to the pandemic as well as in relation to other aspects of interest such as resilience and sustainability. Embarking on digitalization, building resilience capabilities to keep or recover performance affected by disruption and having better sustainability all require investment and consume valuable and limited company resources. If we are able to identify possible synergies between practices towards resilience against disruptive events, and sustainability achievement it could help us devise ways of enhancing operational performance over time with limited compromise on other objectives and resource consumption.

© IFIP International Federation for Information Processing 2021
Published by Springer Nature Switzerland AG 2021
A. Dolgui et al. (Eds.): APMS 2021, IFIP AICT 633, pp. 591–600, 2021.
https://doi.org/10.1007/978-3-030-85910-7_63

This paper is primarily concerned with understanding the existence and nature of relationships among the constructs: digitalization, disruption management capabilities, and subsequent possible impact on manufacturing competitiveness following the Covid-19 outbreak. The paper sets to answer the research questions:

RQ1: What relationships exist among resilience, sustainability, and digitalization upon prevalence of unanticipated disruption?

RQ2: Are there differences among these relationships for SMEs and other manufacturing companies?

2   Theoretical Background

In this section, a brief presentation of the conceptual underpinnings of the constructs of interest in this study is provided.

2.1   Digitalization

Digitalization refers to enabling, improving, and transforming operations, functions, models, processes, or activities by leveraging digital technologies [1].

It can also be understood as the application of digital information and means to fundamentally change intra- and inter-organizational decision structure, processes, and architectures [2]. Digitalization is changing the way data and communication flows in the workplace including manufacturing shop floor. "Almost real-time" data is providing possibilities for more proactive decisions, augmented reality and human robot collaboration is being experimented in manufacturing setting.

Digital technologies enabling industry 4.0 are regarded to provide immense opportunities for better value creation, that SMEs could advance manufacturing productivity, flexibility and competitiveness [3–5]. For example, the most dominant benefits reported in literature include better quality measured as reduction in errors, better logistics and time saving [4]. Famously mentioned challenges of digitalization include data security issues and the commitment to keep up with high technical requirements.

2.2   Disruption Management – resilience

Disruptions can be triggered by unanticipated incidents that critically affect the normal flows (materials, information or cash flow) in a manufacturing setting [6], leading to severe unwanted consequences. A disruption can be an outcome of a chain of events. Natural disasters, supply shortages, financial crises demand shifts, quality problems and labour disputes have been mentioned as popular triggering events for disruptions of manufacturing supply chains [7]. The negative financial and social consequences from Covid-19 disruption have been felt globally. It revealed flaws of system interdependencies, disrupted logistics flows, and forced manufacturers to downsize operations.

Risk management literature suggests that companies, big or small need to build proactive and reactive capabilities to be resilient in managing unpredictable disruptions which they will inevitably experience somehow in some form [8, 9]. Creating different flexibilities and redundant assets and capabilities are generally regarded to enhance resilience of firms to disruptions [9, 10]. A key element in the discussion of resilience in manufacturing enterprises is how different organisations make synergistic arrangements not only to deal with disruptions but also to positively influence different performance dimensions, be it environmental sustainability or operational output, [11] during "normal" circumstance [12, 13].

2.3 Sustainability Practices

Sustainability can be viewed from either a practice or a performance perspective. When sustainability is viewed as practice, it is about initiatives, structures, routines, or even strategic items such as awareness improvement and sustainability management system that are actively undertaken by a company [14, 15]. Most of these practices are internally focused while others could be induced from external pressure such as customers or regulators [16]. Companies seem to better engage in sustainability practices when they perceive associated competitive advantage.

Sustainability as performance [e.g. 17] is essentially a set of metrics to measure what has been achieved in terms of important targets ex-post (i.e. items under the triple bottom line). Typically, part of the economic sustainability is captured in traditional operations performance measures such as cost. Distinction can be made between local (e.g. manufacturing plant) and global sustainability measures. Manufacturing firms with better competences are likely to use more (sustainability) practices successfully and subsequently drive better competitive performance [18].

3 Methodology

3.1 Literature Review

The study started with a systematic literature review. Using Scopus® database, the search query shown in Table 1 has been used. The query included aspects of sustainability, digitalization, operational performance and prevailing context. In this search context has been prescribed as a form of disruption or pandemic having implication on business activities. The intent is to explore if extant literature has identified some relationship among the parameters of interest in prevalence of pandemic or disruption.

The search resulted in an initial list of 181 papers (as of 22 February 2021). Manual picking by reading titles enabled to identify 38 papers. By skimming through the abstract, a shortlist of 20 relevant papers has been produced for more detailed review. These papers have been published in the years 2018 (3 papers), 2020 (13) and 2021 (4).

Some of the reviewed papers from the shortlist are presented in Table 2 with synthesized relationships among constructs.

Table 1. Literature search query

Subject	String (*search in title, abstract, keywords*)
Sustainability:	(*Sustainab** AND (*economic* OR *environment** OR *social*) AND
Digitalization: Performance:	Digital* OR *innovation* OR "*advanced manufacturing*" OR *technolog**) AND ("*operation* Performance*" OR *quality* OR *cost* OR *flexibility* OR *dependability*) AND
Context:	(*disruption* OR *pandem** OR *outbreak* OR *lockdown*)
Include only:	Articles, chapters, reviews, books, editorials; written in English

3.2 Event Study in the Covid-19 Context

The potential relationships among the constructs of interest identified in extant literature have been synthesised through the literature review. A subsequent event study based on news items published about businesses in relation to the pandemic in international media has been employed. The event study aimed at empirical exploration for possible relationships among the four parameters of interest in the context of Covid-19 that is considered the preliminary trigger of decisions and actions by comapnies.

Initially Financial Times®, Reuters® and a few local business news outlets have been the primary considerations. Integrated search capabilities and easier classification of business news items in FT was a main reason for the choice. More than 100 news items have been collected in the initial round. Almost half have been excluded after reading each item for the lacked attributable relationships at least between two constructs. Each news item could have addressed multiple relationships between constructs or even multiple companies and industry sectors exhibiting possibly different relationships that were accounted for in the study.

Coding of the constructs followed measurement items identified from the literature review. For example, operational performance has been coded using 9 items such as operating cost, revenue, flexibility, lead time/speed, quality, and productivity, see [e.g. 19]. Resilience has been coded using 14 proactive and reactive capability practices as proposed in Dabhilkar *et al.*, [9]. Sustainability has been captured using items that reflect social (e.g. fair working conditions, equal opportunity, work-social life balance), environmental (e.g. efficient energy and material use, recycling, decarbonisation, afforestation actions) and economic (e.g. fair economic gain/income) dimensions. There were two issues here: (1) some of economic sustainability items have been covered in operational performance that duplication had to be avoided, (2) differentiating between sustainability as performance and as practice has been somehow difficult. Digitalization was coded using items of technology and organisation including robotics and artificial intelligence (AI), work place automation, use of data connectivity and e-commerce platforms, digital technology as core business. The trigger event of Covid-19 has been captured using major observable indicators as identified in public media and government other organisational communications (9 items). These included movement restrictions/logistics hindrance, work from home, limited service availabilities, infection spread and so on. This way, it was possible to establish relationships among items prescribed under each of the constructs brought together in the study.

4   Findings

4.1   Findings from Literature

Extant literature provides some episodes of relationships among the constructs represent by the three sub-domains mentioned. The empirical sources for these relationships have mainly been big companies.

Table 2. Summary of findings in extant literature

Ref.	Identified/implied findings	Relation
[20, 21]	Digitalization (industry 4.0) leads to better sustainability in the covid-19 lockdown situation	DIG → SUS
[22]	Covid-19 lockdown leads to carbon emission reduction	DIS → SUS
[23]	Digitalization helps to foster business networking which is enabler for improving operational performance during global technological shift	DIG → PER
[12]	Recovery of operations performance can be coupled well with sustainability improvement; Business model redesign is forced by the Covid-19 pandemic	RES → SUS
[24]	Infrastructural innovation (and digitalization) helps to foster post-pandemic green economy	DIG → SUS
[25]	Digitalization as a means to drive flexibility	DIG → PER
[26]	Performance in health care should adapt to accommodate for resilience and sustainability	(RES, SUS) → PER
[27]	Sustainable supply chain network (closed loop supply chain) should help to deal with disruption situations	SUS → RES
[13]	Covid-19 as opportunity to improve TBL; learning from covid-19 in energy sector for better resilience	DIS → (SUS, RES)
[28]	Flexibility and social aspects of sustainability become communication focus points after pandemic	SUS ←→ PER
[29, 30]	Positive environmental impact observed after Covid-19 lockdown; (better) waste management strategies observed in developing countries during Covid-19	DIS → SUS
[31]	Sustainability to reduce impact from future pandemic	SUS → RES
[32]	Covid-19 situation motivated more digital services	DIS → DIG

Note: DIG = Digitalization; DIS = Disruption; SUS = Sustainability; PER = Operational performance; RES = Resilience

Here are a few example relationships as compiled from extant literature (compilation presented in Table 2):

(1) Digital transformation complements innovative capabilities leading to better sustainability performance achievement [e.g. 20]. However, the detail aspects of this relationship remains under-researched for manufacturing SMEs [33].
(2) Sustainability can drive realisation of innovative approaches [34], including digitalization. Obviously, the conceptual abstraction of sustainability here is different from the aforementioned one.
(3) Recent studies argue that digitalization implemented both in manufacturing core processes as well as across support organisation is more likely to create and channel superior or augmented value across a value chain [2].
(4) Studies have contended that resilience practices and sustainability (either as practice or performance) could be positively correlated [e.g. 11].

Combining all these relationships of the three constructs of interest brings in a new perspective to look at prevailing circumstances that could help us better understand how manufacturing firms, continue to remain economically viable and keep on improving environmental impact from manufacturing activities post-pandemic.

One can notice that pandemic/disruption as context is the starting point/trigger for all actions or consequences. One directional relation is discussed in literature among most of the constructs, all leading to operational performance implications (except sustainability that could be affected due to changes in operations performance).

4.2 Findings from Event Study

The preliminary empirical exploration sheds light on some relationships noticed during the Covid-19 pandemic. Figure 1 shows a depiction of initial analysis. In the figure, arrows represent the direction of causality as interpreted from analysed descriptions. The numbers in bold represent positive relationship while those in parenthesis represent negative relationship in the direction indicated by the corresponding arrow. The existence and the relative strength of relationships is more important than the actual number of reported events. The figure shows that empirical relations identified appeared to be on directional. This has not been prescribed except that of Covid-19 as the triggering event of disruption. Furthermore, while both positive and negative relationships could have been likely, only a few relations have shown both.

One can clearly observe that the pandemic has fostered or expedited the need for more digital integration in some form in several businesses. Dominant part of the digitalization related to either digital technology as core business (e.g. technological companies) or digital augmentation to sales and delivery aspects of business. Only a few companies reported on the application of robotics and AI in a manufacturing context.

The impact of the pandemic reported on performance has been mixed. In many cases, reduction in performance has been reported. This applies to, for example, reduction in revenue, increase in costs of manufacturing, and delays. On the other hand, a few sectors have reported pronounced increase in their revenue streams or demand for their products/services. Typical ones include the technology companies, logistics service providers

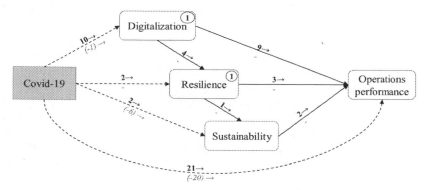

Fig. 1. Empirically identified relationships

and pharmaceuticals. It is also interesting to note that the increase in revenue streams has been coupled with increases in some form of digitalization.

The need and motivation for enhancing resilience capabilities of businesses has increased following the outbreak of the pandemic. Therefore, many companies scrambled to do something to get their affected business out of crisis.

Out of the items under each construct compiled from literature for observing the relationships, a portion have been over represented. For example, out of fourteen practices under resilience only four items were represented in the empirics. Most items in digitalization observed, indicating the strong potential it has to address several issues. Except for Covid-19 as trigger of disruption, the other constructs seemed to have positive influence on operational performance and among each other. Compared to wat the literature review suggested, the empirical finding so far did not capture the possible link from operational performance to sustainability in the scope if this study.

5   Discussion

Consistent with the conceptual discussions, the economic benefits of digitalization during the pandemic have been apparent. The stress the pandemic put on existing technical and regulatory structures have revealed the need for improvement and changes. The (limited) environmental sustainability gains obtained did not seem to have resulted from systematically established practices. They came rather as "conjoint" effects. Despite the potential benefits understood, establishment of sustainability as systematic practice seems limited.

Even though uni-directionality of relations needs to be further explored, it has been noted that manufacturers and other businesses could exercise sustainability and resilience practices to keep up performance in multiple dimensions. In terms of social sustainability, multiple news items reported that productivity seemed to increase despite deteriorating social-work conditions due to lockdowns, which could be worrying from long-term perspective.

Large companies often report achievements in sustainability performance. And continued achievement of sustainability performance improvement requires employment of sustainability practices. Large companies impose demands for some sustainability performance on their suppliers, some of which may be SMEs. However, not every supplier SME is able to effectively address sustainability issues through implementation of coherent and comprehensive processes and practices. However, the implications of digital technology application in manufacturing cannot be just extrapolated from earlier studies. SMEs are often mentioned as lagging in extent of digitalization [35]. Even those that managed to do so, prioritize small scope technical solutions such as factory shop floor technologies [36, 37]. At the same time, changing industry circumstances seem to favour towards pursuit of flexibility and digital transformation even in small companies [11, 38]. The empirical analysis seems to suggest that even with the limited resources, SMEs seem to be able to leverage synergies between resilience and sustainability when affected by the pandemic.

In terms of resilience, mostly reactive capabilities were exploited during the pandemic. Even so, companies that had the agility to take swift measures in response to the disruption situations gained prime-mover advantages. In line with the resilience discussion in earlier studies [9], empirics indicate that proactive resilience capabilities can support better reaction resilience upon disruptions.

6 Concluding Remarks

The preliminary findings illustrate that it is possible and beneficial to create comprehensive view that jointly looks at resilience, sustainability and digitalization efforts in a manufacturing setting. Variations in the observed relations among the constructs (e.g. SMEs versus large firms) imply that more focused investigation is needed to understand underlying phenomena better.

With financial downturn following the Covid-19 pandemic, it is very likely that an increased number of SMEs may go bankrupt; besides, the ones that survive will have tough time to keep up practices and initiatives for better economic, social and environmental sustainability [16, 17]. These issues are cyclically connected in crisis situations: financial well-being of SMEs implies better social conditions; if social conditions deteriorate, people may take less (if not destructive) roles in combating environmental sustainability; and so on. This calls for further exploration.

As part of the limitation, more work is needed to scrutinise this initial event study through expanded database as well as a further structuring of content analysis from the news items. Statistical analysis on larger sample size could also help to identify areas of more significant relationship and impact for better sustainability and competitiveness of manufacturing organisations belonging to different size and sectors.

References

1. Gürdür, D., El-khoury, J., Törngren, M.: Digitalizing Swedish industry: what is next?: Data analytics readiness assessment of Swedish industry, according to survey results. Comput. Ind. **105**, 153–163 (2019)
2. Holmström, J., Holweg, M., Lawson, B., Pil, F.K., Wagner, S.M.: The digitalization of operations and supply chain management: theoretical and methodological implications. J. Oper. Manag. **65**, 728–734 (2019)

3. Sjödin, D.R., Parida, V., Leksell, M., Petrovic, A.: Smart Factory Implementation and Process Innovation. Res. Technol. Manag. **61**, 22–31 (2018)
4. Brozzi, R., Forti, D., Rauch, E., Matt, D.T.: The advantages of industry 4.0 applications for sustainability: Results from a sample of manufacturing companies. Sustain. **12** (2020)
5. Nagy, J., Oláh, J., Erdei, E., Máté, D., Popp, J.: The role and impact of industry 4.0 and the internet of things on the business strategy of the value chain-the case of Hungary. Sustain. 10, (2018). https://doi.org/10.3390/su10103491.
6. Kleindorfer, P.R., Saad, G.H.: Managing disruption risks in supply chain. Prod. Oper. Manag. **14**, 53–68 (2005)
7. Chopra, S., Sodhi, M.S.: Reducing the risk of supply chain disruptions. MIT Sloan Manag. Rev. **55**, 73–80 (2014)
8. Kusiak, A.: Open manufacturing: a design-for-resilience approach. Int. J. Prod. Res. **58**, 4647–4658 (2020)
9. Dabhilkar, M., Birkie, S.E., Kaulio, M.: Supply-side resilience as practice bundles: a critical incident study. Int. J. Oper. Prod. Manag. **36**, 948–970 (2016)
10. Talluri, S., Kull, T.J., Yildiz, H., Yoon, J.: Assessing the efficiency of risk mitigation strategies in supply chains. J. Bus. Logist. **34**, 253–269 (2013)
11. Ivanov, D.: Revealing interfaces of supply chain resilience and sustainability: a simulation study. Int. J. Prod. Res. **56**, 3507–3523 (2018)
12. Bhattacharyya, S.S., Thakre, S.: Coronavirus pandemic and economic lockdown; study of strategic initiatives and tactical responses of firms. Int. J. Organ. Anal. (2021)
13. Chiaramonti, D., Maniatis, K.: Security of supply, strategic storage and Covid-19: which lessons learnt for renewable and recycled carbon fuels, and their future role in decarbonizing transport? Appl. Energy. **271** (2020)
14. Maletič, M., Maletič, D., Gomišček, B.: The impact of sustainability exploration and sustainability exploitation practices on the organisational performance: a cross-country comparison. J. Clean. Prod. **138**, 158–169 (2016)
15. Jacobsen, P., Pedersen, L.F., Jensen, P.E., Witfelt, C.: Philosophy regarding the design of production systems. J. Manuf. Syst. **20**, 405–415 (2001)
16. Tsvetkova, D., Bengtsson, E., Durst, S.: Maintaining sustainable practices in SMEs: Insights from Sweden. Sustain. **12** (2020). https://doi.org/10.3390/su122410242
17. Fagerlind, T., Stefanicki, M., Feldmann, A., Korhonen, J.: The distribution of sustainable decision-making in multinational manufacturing enterprises. Sustain. **11** (2019)
18. Demeter, K., Szász, L., Boer, H.: Plant role and the effectiveness of manufacturing practices. Int. J. Oper. Prod. Manag. **37**, 1773–1794 (2017)
19. Birkie, S.E.: Operational resilience and lean: in search of synergies and trade-offs. J. Manuf. Technol. Manag. **27**, 185–207 (2016)
20. Barcaccia, G., D'Agostino, V., Zotti, A., Cozzi, B.: Impact of the SARS-CoV-2 on the Italian agri-food sector: An analysis of the quarter of pandemic lockdown and clues for a socio-economic and territorial restart. Sustain. **12** (2020)
21. Acioli, C., Scavarda, A., Reis, A.: Applying Industry 4.0 technologies in the COVID-19 sustainable chains Applying Industry 4.0 technologies in COVID. Int. J. Product. Perform. Manag. (2021)
22. Bera, B., Bhattacharjee, S., Shit, P.K., Sengupta, N., Saha, S.: Significant impacts of COVID-19 lockdown on urban air pollution in Kolkata (India) and amelioration of environmental health. Environ. Dev. Sustain. (2020)
23. Pellicelli, M.: Gaining flexibility and innovation through offshore outsourcing. Sustain. **10** (2018)
24. Barbier, E.B.: Greening the post-pandemic recovery in the G20. Environ. Resource Econ. **76**(4), 685–703 (2020). https://doi.org/10.1007/s10640-020-00437-w

25. Ivanov, D., Das, A., Choi, T.M.: New flexibility drivers for manufacturing, supply chain and service operations (2018)
26. Vainieri, M., Noto, G., Ferre, F., Rosella, L.C.: A performance management system in healthcare for all seasons? (2020)
27. Babagolzadeh, R., Rezaeian, J., Khatir, M.V.: Multi-objective fuzzy programming model to design a sustainable supply chain network considering disruption. Int. J. Ind. Eng. Prod. Res. **31**, 217–229 (2020)
28. Chevtaeva, E., Guillet, B.D.: A review of communication trends due to the pandemic: perspective from airlines. Anatolia. (2020)
29. Praveena, S.M., Aris, A.Z.: The impacts of COVID-19 on the environmental sustainability: a perspective from the Southeast Asian region. Environ. Sci. Pollut. Res. (2021)
30. Belhadi, A., Kamble, S.S., Khan, S.A.R., Touriki, F.E., Kumar M, D.: Infectious Waste Management Strategy during COVID-19 Pandemic in Africa: an Integrated Decision-Making Framework for Selecting Sustainable Technologies. Environ. Manage. **66**, 1085–1104 (2020)
31. Coccia, M.: How (Un)sustainable environments are related to the diffusion of COVID-19: the relation between coronavirus disease 2019, air pollution, wind resource and energy. Sustain. **12** (2020)
32. Drljača, M., Štimac, I., Bračić, M., Petar, S.: The role and influence of industry 4.0. in airport operations in the context of COVID-19. Sustain. **12** (2020)
33. Enyoghasi, C., Badurdeen, F.: Industry 4.0 for sustainable manufacturing: Opportunities at the product, process, and system levels. Resour. Conserv. Recycl. **166** (2021)
34. Stål, H.I., Babri, M.: Educational interventions for sustainable innovation in small and medium sized enterprises. J. Clean. Prod. **243** (2020)
35. Buer, S.V., Strandhagen, J.W., Semini, M., Strandhagen, J.O.: The digitalization of manufacturing: investigating the impact of production environment and company size. J. Manuf. Technol. Manag. (2020)
36. Bosman, L., Hartman, N., Sutherland, J.: How manufacturing firm characteristics can influence decision making for investing in Industry 4.0 technologies. J. Manuf. Technol. Manag. **31**, 1117–1141 (2020)
37. Harland, C.M., Caldwell, N.D., Powell, P., Zheng, J.: Barriers to supply chain information integration: SMEs adrift of eLands. J. Oper. Manag. **25**, 1234–1254 (2007)
38. Gölzer, P., Fritzsche, A.: Data-driven operations management: organisational implications of the digital transformation in industrial practice. Prod. Plan. Control. **28**, 1332–1343 (2017)

Smart Methods and Techniques for Sustainable Supply Chain Management

Minimising Total Costs of a Two-Echelon Multi-Depot Capacitated Vehicle Routing Problem (2E-MD-CVRP) that Describes the Utilisation of the Amsterdam City Canal Network for Last Mile Parcel Delivery

Bartje Alewijnse and Alexander Hubl[✉]

Industrial Engineering and Management, University of Groningen,
Groningen, The Netherlands
a.hubl@rug.nl

Abstract. An increase in e-shopping and (last mile) parcel deliveries has contributed to a rapid growth of urban freight transportation. This generates major impacts on city sustainability and liveability. Current solutions for urban logistics concern road traffic, but multiple Dutch cities have an extensive range of city canals that could be used for freight transportation over water. It was investigated how the city canal network of Amsterdam can be utilised for last mile parcel delivery, and what the related effects are. A MILP formulation of a Two-Echelon, Multi-Depot, Capacitated Vehicle Routing Problem (2E-MD-CVRP) was developed. The model describes a network in which ships transport parcels to pre-determined satellite locations in the city centre, where the parcels are transferred to cargo e-bikes for the last mile of the delivery to the customer. The model was optimised by minimising the total costs, using the Genetic Algorithm (GA). The algorithm was able to find solutions but could not always stay within the constrained search space. Different possible network scenarios were evaluated, describing the consequences with respect to emissions, costs, and traffic flows. The results show promising economic, social, and environmental outcomes for a network with ships and cargo e-bikes instead of delivery vans. A daily and investment cost reduction of 16% and 36% respectively and a CO_2 emission reduction of 78.26% can be realised.

Keywords: Vehicle routing problem · Genetic algorithm · Urban logistics · Last mile parcel delivery · City canal network · Cargo bikes

1 Introduction

During the last few years, urban logistics and last mile parcel delivery have become issues of great importance. The amount of city inhabitants is increasing,

© IFIP International Federation for Information Processing 2021
Published by Springer Nature Switzerland AG 2021
A. Dolgui et al. (Eds.): APMS 2021, IFIP AICT 633, pp. 603–612, 2021.
https://doi.org/10.1007/978-3-030-85910-7_64

and people tend to order more goods online every day. In the Netherlands, one out of six vehicles in city centres is driving around for the transportation of goods. As a result, many cities are currently facing social, environmental, and economic problems caused by transport and traffic [3]. When travelling through a city centre, one will almost always experience traffic congestion. In addition, cities become more polluted, and the number of accidents is increasing [5,7]. Consequently, new solutions are needed to enhance urban transport while decreasing the negative impacts described above.

Many of the current regulations and solutions for urban logistics concern land traffic, mainly on roads. However, multiple Dutch cities have an extensive range of city canals that could possibly be used for freight traffic over water. It has already been proven that (electric) waterway transport can contribute to sustainable logistics, so why not use this in urban areas as well [14]? In fact, the initial purpose of city canals was to serve as a waterway network for the transportation of goods and people [10,16].

Amsterdam, the capital of the Netherlands, has one of the most extensive city canal networks in the world. The aim of this paper is to evaluate a Vehicle Routing Problem (VRP) that describes a network which utilises ships in the city canals of Amsterdam, in combination with cargo e-bikes, for last mile parcel delivery. The goal is to investigate to what extent this solution would result in economic, environmental, and social benefits. A VRP is a combinatorial optimisation problem that calls for the optimal set of routes for a fleet of vehicles to deliver the demand of a given set of customers. In this case, the problem is divided into two levels or echelons. The first level consists of electric ships that leave the distribution centre at the Port of Amsterdam and drive through the city canals as a depot. These ships supply the cargo(e-)bikes that deliver the parcels to the customers in the second level. All locations where transfer of the packages between the vehicles of the two different levels is possible are called satellites. These satellites are located at docks in the city centre.

Section 2 elaborates on the case study that was conducted and the different scenarios that were evaluated. There exist many different variants of the Two-Echelon (2E) VRP [2]. In Sect. 3.1, the mathematical formulation of the applied 2E-VRP is given. Next, Sect. 3.2 focuses on the Genetic Algorithm that was used to optimise the model. Lastly, the results are presented in Sect. 4 and the final conclusion is given in Sect. 5.

2   Case Study

A numerical analysis was executed in Python 3.7. The data set that was used represents the average daily parcel demand in Amsterdam for one transportation party. The effects were evaluated with respect to three different KPIs: costs (euros), CO_2 emissions, and traffic flows (given by the amount of vehicles per day).

Two different scenarios were analysed. In Scenario 1, it is assumed that all city canals and appointed (un)loading docks are available during the day. However, it is currently not allowed to transport goods through the canals in the inner part of the Amsterdam city centre between 10am and 8pm. Even though it is possible to receive a permit if one has a concrete plan which the municipality supports, this might not always be the case. Therefore, Scenario 2 only includes availability of the canal network outside the city centre. In Scenario, 31 satellites (docks indicated by the municipality) are available for the (un)loading of the parcels. In Scenario 2, this was decreased to 11.

Furthermore, increasing portions or percentages of the total daily demand were used. This was called the delivery performance, which ranges from 25% to 130%. I.e. it was investigated what the effects are if x% of the current daily demand was delivered via the proposed network. The remaining parcels would then be delivered as usual, with electric vans. In order to compare the outcomes to this current situation, the effects when using electric delivery vans were evaluated too, using the same model (Sect. 3.1).

3 Model

3.1 MILP Formulation

This problem can be defined as a Two-Echelon, Multi-Depot, Capacitated Vehicle Routing Problem (2E-MD-CVRP) [13]. Both levels of the problem are represented separately by the model that is formulated below. In other words, there are two MD-CVRPs. First, the routes of the second level fleet of cargo bikes should be determined, where the demand is given by the customer demand, and the (pre-determined) satellites in the city centre serve as depots. The outcome will then include the amount of parcels that should be distributed from every satellite, i.e. the demand for the ships. After that, the routes of the ships in the first level can be determined, where hubs at the Port of Amsterdam are the depots, and the satellites from where the cargo bikes should depart are the customers.

The mathematical formulation of these MD-CVRPs is defined on a graph $G = (V, A)$, where $V = \{1, \cdots, n + w\}$ is the set of nodes and $A = \{(i, j) : i, j \in V, i \neq j\}$ the set of edges. V consists of two subsets: the set of n customers $V_c = \{1, \cdots, n\}$ and the set of w depots $V_d = \{n + 1, \cdots, n + w\}$. At every depot, a fleet of vehicles, K with each a maximum capacity Q_k and fixed cost h_k is available. All vehicles are restricted to a maximum work time T. For every customer i, a non-negative demand p_i and service time r_i is given. The travel cost and time between node i and j is given by $c_{i,j}$ and $t_{i,j}$ respectively.

The decision variable for this problem is given by the binary variable $x_{i,j}^k \in \{0, 1\}$, which is equal to 1 if vehicle k travels from node i to node j, and 0 if otherwise. The MILP formulation of the model is given below.

$$min \sum_{i \in V} \sum_{j \in V} \sum_{k \in K} x_{i,j}^k c_{i,j} + \sum_{i \in V_d} \sum_{j \in V} \sum_{k \in K} x_{i,j}^k h_k \tag{1}$$

s.t.

$$\sum_{i \in V} \sum_{k \in K} x_{i,j}^k = 1 \qquad \forall j \in V_c \tag{2}$$

$$\sum_{j \in V} \sum_{k \in K} x_{i,j}^k = 1 \qquad \forall i \in V_c \tag{3}$$

$$\sum_{i \in V} x_{i,h}^k - \sum_{j \in V} x_{h,j}^k = 0 \qquad \forall k \in K, \forall h \in V \tag{4}$$

$$\sum_{i \in V_c} \sum_{j \in V} p_i x_{i,j}^k < Q_k \qquad \forall k \in K \tag{5}$$

$$\sum_{i \in V} \sum_{j \in V} t_{i,j} x_{i,j}^k + \sum_{i \in V} \sum_{j \in V} r_j x_{i,j}^k \le T \qquad \forall k \in K \tag{6}$$

$$\sum_{j \in V_c} x_{i,j}^k \le 1 \qquad \forall k \in K_i, \forall i \in V_d \tag{7}$$

$$\sum_{i \in V_c} x_{i,j}^k \le 1 \qquad \forall k \in K_j, \forall j \in V_d \tag{8}$$

$$\sum_{j \in V_c} x_{i,j}^k = 0 \qquad \forall i \in V_d, \forall k \in K_i \tag{9}$$

$$\sum_{i \in V_c} x_{i,j}^k = 0 \qquad \forall j \in V_d, \forall k \in K_j \tag{10}$$

$$\sum_{i \in S} \sum_{j \in S} x_{i,j}^k \le |S| - 1 \qquad S \subseteq V_c, 2 \le |S| \le n, \forall k \in K \tag{11}$$

$$x_{i,j}^k \in \{0,1\} \qquad \forall i \in V, \forall j \in V, \forall k \in K \tag{12}$$

The objective function (1) aims to minimise the total costs. Constraints (2) assure that only one vehicle arrives at every customer exactly once, and Constraints (3) ensure that this single vehicle also leaves the customer once. Constraints (4) are flow conservation constraints, such that a vehicle leaves a customer after delivering. Constraints (5) state that every vehicle cannot be loaded beyond its capacity. Constraints (6) make sure that the total duration of the route does not exceed the defined work-day. Constraints (7) and (8) ensure that the vehicles also arrive and leave their home depots at most once. Constraints (9) states that a vehicle can only depart from its assigned home depot. In addition, Constraints (10) ensure that the vehicles may also only return to this assigned home depot, however, these are only applicable to the first level of the 2E-VRP. The ships should return to their home depot to spend the night and be re-loaded for the next day, but cargo bikes are finished as soon as they served the last customer of their route. Constraints (11) are sub-tour elimination constraints. Lastly, Constraints (12) define the binary variable that can either be equal to 1 or 0, depending on whether the vehicle travels along that arc. Solving this model will give a network including a required fleet size per depot, routes for the first and second echelon, and an applicable schedule.

The values assigned to the parameters of the mathematical model are given in Table 1 below.

Table 1. Parameter values mathematical model.

Parameter	Ships	Cargo e-bikes	Delivery vans
Speed $[km/h]$	6	24	30
Capacity $[parcels]$	1517	40	184
Work day $[hours]$	9	4	8
Service time $[hours]$	0.5	0.05	0.05
Wages $[euros/hour]$	70	40	55
Operational costs $[euros/100km]$	20.92	0.15	10
Fixed costs $[euros/vehicle/day]$	19.17	3.30	28.50
Investment costs $[euros/vehicle]$	200,000	4,000	60,000
Emissions $[kgCO_2/km]$	0.582	0.00417	0.278

3.2 Genetic Algorithm

The VRP is an NP-hard optimisation problem. Therefore, meta-heuristics should be used to guide the process of searching for solutions and approximate a sufficient solution. The Genetic Algorithm (GA) was used most often to successfully solve VRPs in general [1,4,6,8,12,15]. Also, it was found that the GA was able to optimise problems similar to the one introduced earlier. In the past, the algorithm accomplished to obtain high quality solutions for the 2E-CVRP [17]. In addition, the GA has proven to be a successful approach to optimise several MD-CVRPs [11]. However, it has not been applied yet to the specific 2E-MD-CVRP defined before. Therefore, the GA was implemented to solve this paper's VRP. Operators were applied that allow crossover, inversion and insertion mutation, and to merge routes. In addition, elite solutions were selected to be passed on to the next generation without alternations. The GA parameter values are given in Table 2. Different test-runs have shown that in general, the solution does not improve significantly anymore after approximately 200 generations.

Table 2. Parameter values genetic algorithm.

Parameter	Value	Parameter	Value
Number of generations	250	Insertion mutation rate	0.1
Population size	50	Merge routes rate	0.05
Crossover rate	0.05	Elite selection size	4
Inversion mutation rate	0.05		

4   Results

In Figs. 1, 2, 3 and 4 the outcomes per KPI (i.e. emissions, costs, traffic flows) are visualised in bar charts. In every chart, both Scenario 1 and 2 are indicated, and the earlier introduced delivery performance changes over the x-axis. Red represents the effects caused by the electric ships, and yellow the cargo e-bikes. In addition, the blue bars show the outcomes if (only) electric vans would be used.

When executing the experiments to find routes for the ships in Scenario 2, no feasible solutions were found. Only when the vehicle capacity was increased to 2000 parcels, the search space of possible solutions was found. Therefore, these results include this relaxation of the capacity constraint.

Also, the algorithm was not able to find feasible solutions for the delivery vans serving a demand of 50% or 100%. Consequently, the corresponding results were extrapolated using the solutions for the cargo e-bikes.

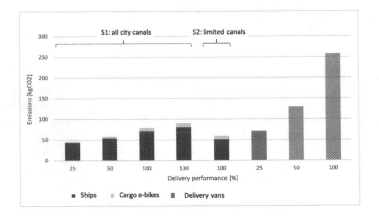

Fig. 1. Emissions per scenario.

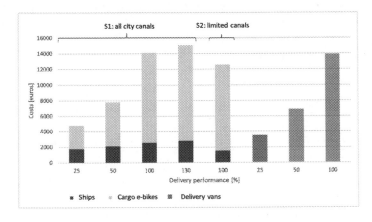

Fig. 2. Daily costs per scenario.

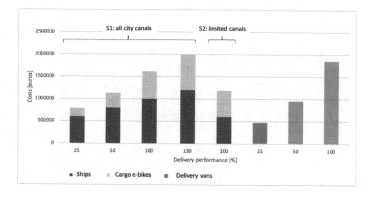

Fig. 3. Investment costs per scenario.

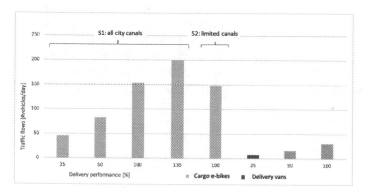

Fig. 4. Road traffic flows per scenario.

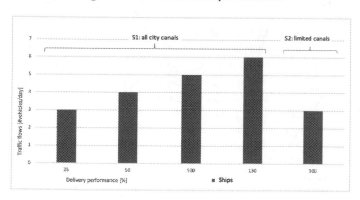

Fig. 5. Traffic flows on water per scenario.

In addition, the solutions showed that the vehicle capacity was used up to almost 100% in every case. However, a utilisation of less than 50% of the total work-day capacity for the bicycle couriers was given. The route duration stayed under 2 h, while their work-day was set to 4.

Furthermore, the algorithm was not always able to find feasible solutions. For Scenario 1, a relatively small percentage (between 8% and 21.2%) of the 250 generations offered feasible solutions for ship routes. However, in Scenario 2, after increasing the ship capacity from 1517 to 2000, this was almost equal to 100%. For the cargo bike routes the number of generations with feasible solutions was higher (between 7.2% and 100%). When considering this limited amount of successful generations, it can be stated that the current constraints are quite strict, and make it difficult for the GA to find sufficient solutions. Therefore, additional constraints such as traffic jams, multiple trips, and uniting the two levels, might make it impossible to find feasible solutions. Despite the experienced difficulties, it can be argued that the performance of the algorithm has shown to be sufficient in order to find an optimal set of routes for the vehicles. There are feasible solutions available that were optimised over at least 30 generations. Moreover, all solutions follow similar and constant trends, and show no significant outliers. However, even though previous research has shown much promise, the Genetic Algorithm applied to the mathematical model was not validated using another algorithm or meta-heuristic to compare it with. It could be possible that in this specific case, another algorithm shows different, e.g. more favourable, solutions.

Several conclusions can be drawn from the results. First of all, as the relative amount of customers that were served increases from 25% to 100%, the generated emissions, costs, and traffic flows rise as well (Figs. 1 to 5). This applies mostly to the second level of the network, where cargo e-bikes are used, and less to the ships.

The generated emissions stay below 100 $kgCO_2$ per day for the proposed network (Fig. 3). On the other hand, if delivery vans would be utilised this number goes up to more than 250 $kgCO_2$ per day, which means that employing ships and cargo e-bikes is more environmentally friendly.

When meeting 100% of the daily parcel delivery demand, the proposed network of ships and cargo e-bikes requires at best only 84% and 64% of the daily and investment costs respectively needed for delivery vans (Figs. 1 and 2).

Regarding the traffic flows, the outcomes show that (at least) 3 ships are needed to meet 100% of the demand (Fig. 5). This amount can be considered to be low, which means that no inconveniences will be caused in the city canals. In addition, around 150 cargo e-bikes are required to execute the last mile of the delivery (Fig. 4). However, the bicycle couriers are assigned to routes that last on average less than 2 h, while their work-day duration is set to 4. Therefore, it seems possible to let the bicycle couriers work two shifts. As a result, only half of the cargo e-bikes have to be acquired, which also significantly lowers the investment costs. In both cases, on a daily basis, 75 cargo e-bikes will drive around for 4 h each, thereby replacing 8 delivery vans that occupy the streets for

8 h each. Since cargo bikes can be passed by easily and park on the pavement, this results in less traffic congestion which has several social, economic, and environmental advantages.

The favourable outcomes for Scenario 2 (limited canals) compared to Scenario 1 (all city canals) at first appear to be unexpected. This difference can be explained by the order of optimising the two levels of the VRP. First, the routes for the cargo e-bikes are determined. The availability of a larger amount of depots divides the pick-up or start locations of the cargo e-bikes over more satellites. As a result, the number of customers or stops for the ships increases as well. Therefore, a higher amount of ships and longer routes are required in Scenario 1. Uniting both levels and optimising them as one would solve this drawback and may lead to more optimal solutions.

5   Conclusion

A GA was used to optimise a 2E-MD-CVRP that describes a network of ships and cargo e-bikes for (last mile) parcel delivery in Amsterdam. When meeting a demand of 100%, favourable outcomes for a network with ships and cargo e-bikes compared to one with delivery vans were obtained. On a daily basis, 56.13 instead of 258.22 $kgCO_2$ will be emitted. Also, the daily and investment costs equal 11,627.95 and 1,192,000 euros, which saves 16% and 36% respectively compared to employing delivery vans. Moreover, the daily traffic flows are represented by 3 ships and 150 cargo e-bikes or 8 delivery vans. However, the bicycle couriers only work for a route duration of less than 2 h, which means they could execute two trips. This could halve the number of cargo bikes to 75 and the related investment costs from 592,000 to 296,000 euros. Due to the current constraints, the algorithm was not always able to stay within the search space of feasible solutions. However, due to its constant behaviour it can be concluded that the solutions that were obtained sufficiently optimise the network. In the future, the solutions of the optimiser could be tested using discrete event simulation including stochastic effects [9].

References

1. BoussaïD, I., Lepagnot, J., Siarry, P.: A survey on optimization metaheuristics. Inf. Sci. **237**, 82–117 (2013)
2. Cuda, R., Guastaroba, G., Speranza, M.G.: A survey on two-echelon routing problems. Comput. Oper. Res. **55**, 185–199 (2015)
3. Demir, E., Huang, Y., Scholts, S., Van Woensel, T.: A selected review on the negative externalities of the freight transportation: modeling and pricing. Transp. Res. part E Logistics Transp. Rev. **77**, 95–114 (2015)
4. Deng, P., Amirjamshidi, G., Roorda, M.: A vehicle routing problem with movement synchronization of drones, sidewalk robots, or foot-walkers. Transp. Res. Procedia **46**, 29–36 (2020)

5. Ducret, R.: Parcel deliveries and urban logistics: changes and challenges in the courier express and parcel sector in Europe-The French case. Res. Transp. Bus. Manag. **11**, 15–22 (2014)
6. Elshaer, R., Awad, H.: A taxonomic review of metaheuristic algorithms for solving the vehicle routing problem and its variants. Comput. Ind. Eng. **140**, 106–242 (2020)
7. European Commission: Clean Transport, Urban Transport. https://ec.europa.eu/transport/themes/urban/urban_mobility_en. Accessed 22 Oct 2020
8. Ghoseiri, K., Ghannadpour, S.F.: Multi-objective vehicle routing problem with time windows using goal programming and genetic algorithm. Appl. Soft Comput. **10**(4), 1096–1107 (2010)
9. Hübl, A., Altendorfer, K., Jodlbauer, H., Gansterer, M., Hartl, R.F.: Flexible model for analyzing production systems with discrete event simulation. In: Proceedings of the 2011 Winter Simulation Conference (WSC), pp. 1554–1565 (2011)
10. Johnsen, L., Duarte, F., Ratti, C., Xiaojie, T., Tian, T.: A fleet of autonomous boats for Amsterdam. Landscape Architecture Frontiers **7**(2), 100–110 (2019)
11. Karakatič, S., Podgorelec, V.: A survey of genetic algorithms for solving multi depot vehicle routing problem. Appl. Soft Comput. **27**, 519–532 (2015)
12. Kumar, S.N., Panneerselvam, R.: A survey on the vehicle routing problem and its variants (2012)
13. Ramos, T.R.P., Gomes, M.I., Póvoa, A.P.B.: Multi-depot vehicle routing problem: a comparative study of alternative formulations. Int. J. Logistics Res. Appl. **23**(2), 103–120 (2020)
14. Rohács, J., Simongati, G.: The role of inland waterway navigation in a sustainable transport system. Transport **22**, 148–153 (2007)
15. Stodola, P.: Using metaheuristics on the multi-depot vehicle routing problem with modified optimization criterion. Algorithms **11**(5), 74 (2018)
16. Tussenbroek, G.: De grachten van Amsterdam. 400 jaar bouwen, wonen, werken en leven. De Zeventiende Eeuw. Cultuur in de Nederlanden in interdisciplinair perspectief **30**(1) (2014)
17. Wang, K., Lan, S., Zhao, Y.: A genetic-algorithm-based approach to the two-echelon capacitated vehicle routing problem with stochastic demands in logistics service. J. Oper. Res. Soc. **68**(11), 1409–1421 (2017)

Evaluating the Deployment of Collaborative Logistics Models for Local Delivery Services

Andrea Bari[1], Fabio Salassa[1] (ID), Maurizio Arnone[2] (ID), and Tiziana Delmastro[2](✉) (ID)

[1] DIGEP, Politecnico di Torino, Corso Duca degli Abruzzi 24, 10129 Torino, Italy
fabio.salassa@polito.it
[2] LINKS Foundation - Leading Innovation and Knowledge for Society, via Pier Carlo Boggio 61, 10138 Torino, Italy
{maurizio.arnone,tiziana.delmastro}@linksfoundation.com

Abstract. The current pandemic situation and lockdowns have given rise to various problems not only of public health but also of organization of daily activities, especially in the purchase and delivery of goods. As a response to newly generated needs for customers' demand, in this work, we try to evaluate several aspects for the deployment of collaborative logistics models aimed at the optimization of local delivery services.

Keywords: Collaborative logistics · Pickup and delivery · Optimization

1 Introduction

The current pandemic situation in Italy has given rise to various problems not only of public health, but also of organization of daily activities. Prolonged lockdowns implemented not only in Italy, but also in many countries have often radically changed the habits of most of the citizens. The purchase of food and non-food consumer goods is certainly an aspect that has changed in daily life due to the difficult access to shops for many people, for example, the elderly and all those who, for reasons of contagion, have been placed in quarantine.

During 2019, business-to-consumer e-commerce in Italy has reached a turnover of 31.6 billion euros, with the biggest increase ever, compared to the previous year (+15%). As in the past, consumers buy online more products than services (products accounted for 18.1 billion euros). Moreover, the first quarter of 2020 has registered a further boom in e-commerce sales due to the COVID19 outbreak: during the third week of March the online consumer goods sales increased by 142.3% compared to the same week in 2019 [8–10]. In this period, many large-scale retailers have organized themselves to enhance their home delivery services of consumer goods. Despite this, in many cases, this was not enough to cover the rising demand and it was not unusual that, during periods of total lockdown, the waiting times for deliveries increased dramatically. In addition, the emergency has pushed many small retailers toward e-commerce and local shops have undergone changes to carry out delivery services for their customers.

Published by Springer Nature Switzerland AG 2021
A. Dolgui et al. (Eds.): APMS 2021, IFIP AICT 633, pp. 613–621, 2021.
https://doi.org/10.1007/978-3-030-85910-7_65

B2C e-commerce entails, however, high complexity of logistic activities in the supply chain. As the most complicated segment of the logistic chain, last-mile delivery seems to account for about 30% of total transport costs (up to 50 in some cases) [7].

The study carried out in this paper was born in this context. The purpose is in fact to respond to the need on the one hand of customers to be able to buy not only through large-scale distribution platforms but also from local neighborhood shops. On the other hand to allow local merchants to save delivery costs and time in a collaborative logistics framework for goods delivery. The main idea of the project is to study if and under what conditions a collaborative delivery system, in which several local retailers share a (private or outsourced) delivery service, is sustainable from an economic and operational perspective. The collaborative system will pursue an optimised organization of deliveries and a reduction in the number of circulating vehicles, empty miles and, consequently, in traffic and air pollution, thus also trying to achieve environmental sustainability. To the best of authors' knowledge, we introduce a new variant of the Vehicle Routing Problem with Pickups and Deliveries, which models this particular delivery service.

The studied problem belongs to the broader class of *Pickup&Delivery* problems (PDP) [2]. We focus here on a variant that allows for multiple visits to locations where we consider that local shops and customers are set. Specifically, the routing problem can have multiple location visits as resulting from divisible pickups and deliveries. Other variants of the classic problem may include single commodity problems with split loads, that is, everything that is to be picked up from (delivered to) a location has the same destination (origin) (e.g. [4]). For divisible pickups and deliveries, each location can serve as a pickup and/or delivery point for multiple commodities (e.g. [6]). That is, every location may require transportation of loads to and/or from multiple other locations. Our problem classifies as a problem with divisible pickups and deliveries. Moreover, we restrict the problem to a maximum length for each route as a result of a working shift for drivers and capacitated vehicles. Very recent papers on similar variants with single and multiple vehicles of PDP are [1, 3, 5].

The remainder of the paper is as follows. Section 2 is dedicated to the description of the optimization problem that has to be managed for the depicted collaborative logistics delivery service. In Sect. 3 a solution approach for the presented problem is proposed. Finally, in Sect. 4 and 5, results and conclusions are given.

2   Problem Description

The project that is the subject of this work aims to support, in various ways, collaborative commerce enterprises through the use of optimization technologies to achieve greater competitiveness in the management of specific aspects of business such as logistics, home deliveries, orders management etc.

The problem is defined on a graph, $G = (V, A)$, in which the set of vertices $V = P \cup D \cup \{0\}$. $P = \{1, ..., p\}$ is the set of pickup nodes, and $D = \{p + 1, ..., p + n\}$ is the set of delivery nodes where $|D| = n$ and $p \leq n$. The node 0 in G defines the starting and ending depot. Let $R = \{r_1, ..., r_m\}$ be the set of requests to be routed where $|R| = m$ and $m \geq n$: every customer can make an order to one or multiple stores, thus each customer can make multiple requests and each shop is assigned to multiple requests from multiple customers. Each request $r \in R$ is represented by one pick-up node $p_r \in P$ and one delivery node $d_r \in D$ with a volume quantity, q_r. All the pick-up nodes must be visited before the delivery nodes for each request, $r \in R$. K is the set of identical capacitated vehicles that can be used located at the depot 0, with $|K| = p$. The set of arcs is $A = V \times V$, each arc $(i, j) \in A$ has an associated travel time $t_{ij} \geq 0$. It is assumed that the travel times satisfy the triangular inequality: $t_{ij} \leq t_{il} + t_{lj} \forall i, j, l \in V$. Each node $n_i \in N$ has a service time s_i for loading or unloading at that node. Each node $p_i \in P$ has a quantity of requests to load onto the vehicle, $Q_i \geq 0$, which is the sum of quantities of all the requests having node i as the pick-up node. The sum of the volumes loaded on the vehicle is constrained by the capacity of the vehicle, C_k. All the orders loaded on the vehicles must be delivered in the T_k hours slot time, so every vehicle $k \in K$ can do a tour of at most T_k. The objective is to minimise the total distance travelled by the vans and also to minimise the number of used vans.

In the current situation, every retailer carries out the deliveries for his customers with a distinct (privately owned) vehicle, without any coordination among the different shops. This situation is used as a benchmark for the proposed business model of collaborative deliveries.

3 Solution Approach

Algorithm 1 depicts main algorithmic ingredients used to solve the proposed problem.

Algorithm 1 Heuristic Algorithm
1: **procedure** Creation routes
2:      **for** each shop **do**
3:          TSP (Input: Nodes, Output: Path)
4:          Add Path in Best
5:          Add Path in Bench
6:      Calculate Centroids (Input: Nodes; Output: Distance Matrix Centroids)
7:      **for** c in C **do**
8:          Merge Relaxed Routes (Input: Bench, c, Distance Matrix Centroids; Output: Elite Routes)
9:          **for** each route in Elite Routes **do**
10:             Reconstruct Route (Input: route; Output: Route)
11:             Improved Route (Input: Route; Output: Improved Route)
12:             Add Improved Route in Sol
13:         **if** All Improved Route are feasible AND Objective value ≤ Best **then**
14:             Best = Sol
15:             Sol = 0
16:     Return Best

Hereafter a more detailed description of each step of the algorithm:

- *TSP*: To solve the route of each shop we used the TSP mathematical model in order to use these results as benchmark for the algorithm's solution;
- *Calculate Centroids*: We found the distance matrix of the centroids in order to consider the location in the map of each shop with the relative customers and to merge the routes;

- *Merge Relaxed Routes*: We merged routes with a Bin packing mathematical model through the relaxation of the constraints using factors (C) from 1 to 2.5, which multiply the capacity and time constraints. It also keeps in count of the Centroids to merge the shops in the same area, with maximum execution time: 12 s;
- *Reconstruct Route*: For each vehicle using at most 500 order's permutations. We reconstructed the route for each permutation solving the TSP of the first 2 shops with depot and unique customers of the first shop, then putting as constraints all the nodes until shop 2. After that we redo the TSP with shop 3 and unique customers of shop 2 with the constraints found before. We repeat these steps until we found the route;
- *Improved Route*: We improve some of these permutations through the Relocate 1–0 moving the customers ahead in the path if the time decreases and if the capacity constraint is satisfied.

The instances used to test the algorithm have a maximum route time of 6 h per vehicle and each request order has a volume between 27 dm^3 and 33 dm^3. The instances are classified according to different properties:

- Number of nodes, which include depot, customers, and shops: 50, 100, 150, 200;
- Map size: 15 min × 15 min, 30 min × 30 min, and 45 min × 45 min;
- Percentage of shops out of all nodes: 10%, 20%;
- Percentage of repeated orders: 0%, 15%, 30%;
- Vehicle capacities: Small (625 dm^3), Medium (1250 dm^3), Large (2500 dm^3).

By percentage of repeated orders, we mean the probability for all customers to have overlapping orders at the same shops. For each combination of these characteristics, there are 5 different simulations for the position of the nodes and the requests (orders). For the position of the nodes, we assumed that the depot can have (x, y) coordinates in the map between 0.3 and 0.7 the map size, in order to have it in the center of the area, instead, customers and shops are random points in the map. The orders are also generated randomly, associating a customer with a shop and random quantity described above. A total of 1080 tests have been performed.

4   Results

The experiments reported have been performed on a 1, 4 GHz Quad-Core Intel Core i5 CPU with RAM 8 GB. The algorithm is coded in Python 3 and the mathematical model of the algorithm is solved by GUROBI solver. The maximum execution time for all the tests is, in the worst case, 105 s.

In Table 1 all instance classes used to test the algorithm for each node size (50, 100, 150, 200) are presented. The first two columns represent the label of each analyzed instance, the first one with all instances having 10% of shops and the second one with 20% of shops.

These labels, i.e. instance's names, help to read the next graphs: label 1 is the instance with 10% of shops, 15 min map size, 0% of repeated orders and vehicle capacity 625 dm^3. For each instance there are 5 random simulations in order to get the average values of the algorithm's results.

Table 1. Instances used to test the algorithm.

10% shops	20% shops	Map size (min)	% order repetition	Capacity (dm^3)
1	28	15	0	625
2	29	15	0	1250
3	30	15	0	2500
4	31	15	15	625
5	32	15	15	1250
6	33	15	15	2500
7	34	15	30	625
8	35	15	30	1250
9	36	15	30	2500
10	37	30	0	625
11	38	30	0	1250
12	39	30	0	2500
13	40	30	15	625
14	41	30	15	1250
15	42	30	15	2500
16	43	30	30	625
17	44	30	30	1250
18	45	30	30	2500
19	46	45	0	625
20	47	45	0	1250
21	48	45	0	2500
22	49	45	15	625
23	50	45	15	1250
24	51	45	15	2500
25	52	45	30	625
26	53	45	30	1250
27	54	45	30	2500

In Fig. 1 there is an example of two maps showing the initial routes (a) in comparison with the final routes (b) of the instance 10 (map size 30 × 30 min).

Figure 2 shows a graph of the average percentage decrease of vehicles used for all instances described in Table 1 with 4 distinct lines for 50, 100, 150 and 200 nodes. The x axis represents the instances from 1 to 54. The percentage decrease of used vehicles has a similar trend for all the 4 lines, proving that the algorithm gives an output regardless the number of nodes.

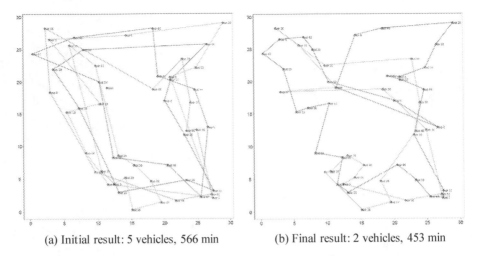

(a) Initial result: 5 vehicles, 566 min   (b) Final result: 2 vehicles, 453 min

Fig. 1. Maps of instance 10 with 50 nodes.

In the left part of the plot there are the instances with 10% of shops, here results show that there is a much larger gap between the minimum and maximum decrease of used vehicles compared to the second half of the graph (20%). Another important element in the first half of the graph, is that increasing the map size, from 15 to 45 min, the decrease percentage drops, which is also present in the second half with a lower gradient. This relationship is important to understand that this problem is strictly affected by the dimension of the map in case the shops and customers are randomly distributed in the map when the ratio between customers and shops is about 10%. Again, in the left half of the graph it is possible to observe that the line with 50 nodes has some lower values with respect to the other lines for small vehicle instances (7, 10, 13, 16), this is because with more shops it is not straightforward to have vehicles saved. In the second part of the graph instead there is no evidence that vehicles capacity strongly affects results since there are less customers assigned to a shop thus having more chance to decrease the load of the vehicle during the route passing to the customers.

Figure 3 shows a graph of the average percentage decrease of route time represented in the same way as in Fig. 2.

As in the previous graph, it is notable the fact that in the first part of the graph (10%) the percentage decrease of the global route time has an higher interval of oscillation with respect to the right part (20%). Apparently, there is also the same trend with the maps size and the percentage decrease of the routes time, in particular with 45 min map size the results do not clearly improve compared to the initial solution. Instead, on the second part of the graph there is an higher linearity for all the instances, which may imply that for instances with low daily orders per shop the algorithm finds a considerable improved solution.

We point out that tests performed in this work were mainly dedicated to the assessment of the economic and operational feasibility of the proposed collaborative delivery business model rather than on stressing the algorithmic performances of the approach.

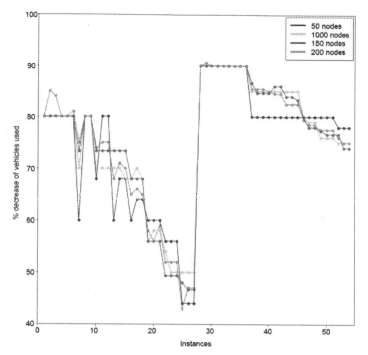

Fig. 2. Percentage decrease of vehicles used

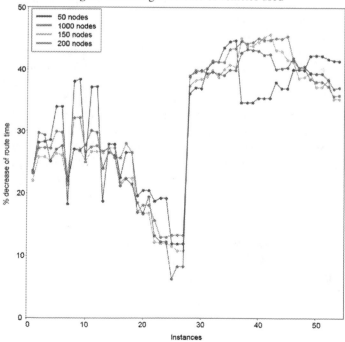

Fig. 3. Percentage decrease of route time

To sum up, instances with 20% of shops (roughly 5 daily orders per shop) have the best improvements in all map sizes, when the shared delivery service can be implemented. Instead, when there are roughly 9 daily orders per shops (10% of shops) it is preferable to have 15 min map size or at most 30 min map size in order to achieve relevant improvements. Another relevant aspect is that the small vehicles have comparable results with the other vehicle sizes in 80% of the cases, except for 4 instances with 10% of shop out of 18 instances (54 divided by the number of vehicle sizes). This somehow confirms that a local collaborative delivery service can be set up also with small vehicles.

5 Conclusions

In this paper, we have defined and analysed a new variant of the VRP for *Pickup&Delivery* class, allowing for multiple visits to local retails and customers, in relation to the deployment of a collaborative logistics model for local delivery services.

The purpose of the study is to understand whether a collaborative delivery system, in which several local retailers share their (private or outsourced) shipping services, allows local merchants to save delivery costs and time by reducing the number of needed vehicles and the driven empty miles, thus enhancing their competitiveness against large-scale distribution as well as improving environmental sustainability. We designed and implemented a heuristic algorithm testing it on a large instance set. The results proved that for a local collaborative delivery service there is a relevant decrease in used vehicles and in travelled kilometers and time under specific conditions, in particular, for instances with low daily orders per shop (roughly 5 daily orders per shop). This may be a great benefit for small local shops, allowing them to reduce distribution costs but also to serve customers that they may not reach in other ways. Moreover, with low numbers of daily orders, there is no evidence that vehicle capacity affects the variation in the percentage decrease of used vehicles. This means that in these scenarios few smaller vehicles can be used saving fixed vehicle costs, fuel consumption and pollutant emissions volumes, thus improving the environmental sustainability and the urban liveability without reducing the retails' competitiveness and delivery performances.

The algorithm has just been tested with simulated data; however, the simulation of a real case study (with data on current volumes of home-deliveries and on shops and customers' locations within an urban neighborhood) would be needed. This would provide a more precise estimate of delivery costs reduction (in relation to the reduced number of needed vehicles and of driven kilometers and trip time) in a collaborative framework with respect to the current scenario (where local shops deliver their goods autonomously with their own vehicles). Moreover, it would support the assessment of future distribution scenarios and potential business models for collaborative delivery services depending on the neighbourhood conditions.

References

1. Aziez, I., Coté, J.-F., Coelho, L.C.: Exact algorithms for the multi-pickup and delivery problem with time windows. Eur. J. Oper. Res. **284**, 906–919 (2020)

2. Berbeglia, G., Cordeau, J.-F., Gribkovskaia, I., Laporte, G.: Static pickup and deliveryproblems: a classification scheme and survey. TOP **15**, 1–31 (2007)
3. Bruck, B.P., Iori, M.: Non-elementary formulations for single vehicle routing problems with pickups and deliveries. Oper. Res. (65), 1597–1614 (2017)
4. Haddad, M.N., et al.: Large neighborhood-based metaheuristic and branch-and-price for the pickup and delivery problem with split loads. Eur. J. Oper. Res. **270**, 1014–1027 (2018)
5. Jargalsaikhan, B., Romeijnders, W., Roodbergen, K.J.: A compact arc-based ILPFormulation for the pickup and delivery problem with divisible pickups and deliveries. Transp. Sci. **55**, 336–352 (2021)
6. Nagy, G., Wassan, N.A., Speranza, M.G., Archetti, C.: The vehicle routing problem with divisible deliveries and pickups. Transp. Sci. **49**, 271–294 (2015)
7. Xiao, Z., Wang, J.J., Liu, Q.: The impacts of final delivery solutions on e-shopping usage behaviour: the case of Shenzhen. China. Int. J. Retail Distrib. Manag. **46**, 2–20 (2018)
8. Report Osservatorio eCommerce B2c: L'eCommerce B2c: il motore di crescita e innovazione del Retail! (2019). https://blog.osservatori.net/reportecommerce?hsCtaTracking=1b8915c1-7a7e-4209-a329-c36db1fd6d87%7C5d9392aa-cadc-4586-a370-43378da6e5e4 (in Italian). Accessed 18 Mar 2021
9. Report Casaleggio Associati: E-COMMERCE IN ITALIA 2019 (2019). https://www.casale ggio.it/wp-content/uploads/2019/04/Report_E-commerce-in-Italia_2019-1.pdf (in Italian). Accessed 18 Mar 2021
10. Report Nielsen: MarketTrack, Iper+Super+Liberi Servizi+Discount+Specialisti Drug. Vendite a valore per categoria nella settimana 12 del 2020 vs. la stessa settimana del 2019 (2019). https://nielseniq.com/global/it/insights/analysis/2020/coronavirus-la-spesa-in-quarantena/ (in Italian). Accessed 18 Mar 2021

Suppliers Selection Ontology for Viable Digital Supply Chain Performance

Kamar Zekhnini[✉], Anass Cherrafi, Imane Bouhaddou,
and Abla Chaouni Benabdellah

L2M3S Laboratory, ENSAM, Moulay Ismail University, 50500 Meknes, Morocco
kamar.zekhnini@gmail.com, a.cherrafi@ensam.umi.ac.ma

Abstract. Unprecedented challenges have confronted the contemporary era with serious negative effect on supply chain management performance. As known, organizations performance is dependent on their suppliers. For this reason, organizations have to improve their practices in suppliers' selection process considering resilience, sustainability and digitalization capabilities to retain competitive and ensure viable performance. In this context, this paper aims to propose an ontology-based model for suppliers' selection criteria with consideration of digitalization, sustainability and resilience capabilities. The incorporation of those paradigms while selecting appropriate suppliers enables the exploration of viable supply chain performance in regard to disruptions. The proposed method is useful to both academics and professionals because it addresses the prominent criteria taxonomy for an effective suppliers' selection in the disruption and digital era.

Keywords: Suppliers selection · Viable digital supply chain · Resilience · Sustainability · Ontology · Knowledge management

1 Introduction

With the spread of globalization and the evolution of industries, there is a crucial need for effective and reliable supply chain systems [1]. A more interconnected environment certainly holds both benefits and risks [2, 3]. For instance, disruptions affect the daily flow of goods or services within a system. Besides, organizations today are more exposed to increased and various disruptive events (unexpected exchange rates, supply fluctuations, dynamic markets, geopolitical tensions, volatile demand, and natural disasters) that have a direct impact on SC performance [4]. More clearly, this implies that there is an increased need for enhanced supply chain viability practice and study.

One of the supply chain management (SCM) challenges that have piqued the interest of many researchers is supplier selection [5]. In other words, the supplier is an important actor in the end-to-end value chain [6]. Because one of the most important factors to achieve an organizations' performance is the selection of relevant suppliers. Therefore, there has been an increased interest in the selection of reliable and robust suppliers [7]. In this context, to remain competitive and improve their performance, organizations

© IFIP International Federation for Information Processing 2021
Published by Springer Nature Switzerland AG 2021
A. Dolgui et al. (Eds.): APMS 2021, IFIP AICT 633, pp. 622–631, 2021.
https://doi.org/10.1007/978-3-030-85910-7_66

need to consider and include the viable capability in suppliers' selection criteria. More clearly, the selected suppliers should have the capacity to adapt to the difficulties and function in a changing world. Besides, they should "react agilely to positive changes, be resilient to absorb negative events and re-cover after the disruptions and survive at the times of long-term" [8]. This means that organizations should take into consideration the 'digitalization', 'resilience', and, 'sustainability criteria in the supplier's selection.

Several studies focused on the suppliers' selection process methods and techniques [9–11]. However, little consideration is given to determining and selecting the right evaluation criteria. Whereas, choosing appropriate criteria determines the quality and accuracy of the developed model [12]. For this reason, it is widely recommended to exploit and develop suppliers' selection knowledge assets. Especially that spreading knowledge in supplier selection while considering resilience, sustainability, and digi talization capabilities, as well as a lack of proper knowledge about criteria describing them, create an evident necessity to have a comprehensive solution for gathering and sharing knowledge, and underlining the interrelationships between them. To overcome this research challenge, the capitalization of knowledge in an ontology for supporting supplier selection and assessment criteria is recommended. In this respect, this paper aims to provide an ontology-based model for supporting suppliers' selection for viable supply chain (VSC) performance. It analyses and organizes knowledge about suppliers' selection criteria including so-called digitalization and resilience capabilities. Moreover, it helps to share information about currently used supplier selection criteria to allow semantics-driven knowledge processing.

This article is organized as follows: in the following section, we present the related works. Section 3 illustrates the research methodology. Section 4 presents the developed ontology supporting the viable-oriented suppliers' selection. And finally, Sect. 5 presents the managerial and practical implications.

2   Related Works

Previous research explored and analyzed supplier selection in the digital supply chain using a variety of methods such as Multi-Criteria Decision-Making Methods, Mathematical Programming models, AI approaches for the development of decision support systems [9–11, 13]. However, every robust decision-making system requires a variety of context data to support the assessment process. To handle the massive amount of information in suppliers' selection process, it is valuable to use knowledge management tools [14]. Ontologies refer to a hierarchical conceptual model representing and capitalizing knowledge that provides definitions of relations and classes (concepts) that incorporate domain knowledge in an integrated manner [15, 16].

The reviewed literature also presented a range of supplier selection criteria approaches, evolving from standard data gathering methods for text analysis to more advanced semantic-matching-oriented methods based on ontologies [17]. In this context, some ontological models aimed at addressing suppliers' selection criteria have been developed. On the one side, [18, 19] suggest an ontology-based negotiating decision protocol to support the suppliers' selection. Reference [15] established a Supplier Segmentation Ontology based on knowledge derived from the literature on behavioral operations in the supply chain from 1934 to 2013. On the other side, references [12, 20] provide a conceptual context for collecting and maintaining knowledge about green supplier selection criteria, as well as formal guidance for their proper acquisition.

These ontologies have proved to expand the knowledge, but they have a restricted scope. More clearly, these ontologies have covered the green aspect or the sustainable aspect of suppliers' selection criteria. And as far as we know, there is no paper dealing with developing an ontology-based model considering the resilience and digitalization capabilities. For this reason, this paper aims to cover the three capabilities namely resilience, digitalization, and sustainability in one ontology to ensure the SC viability performance.

3   Research Methodology

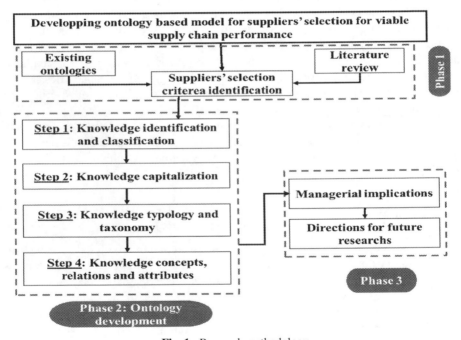

Fig. 1. Research methodology

Figure 1 outlines the research methodology used in this study. It presents the conceptual steps used to address the study's aim. The proposed approach is divided into 3 interconnected phases. The first phase is about searching relevant documents and existing ontologies to identify and classify suppliers' selection criteria. Only relevant manuscripts have been reviewed. That is to say that the collected documents and examined ontologies are revised to produce appropriate data in the light of viable-oriented supplier selection and evaluation criteria. This phase resulted in a set of clusters with identified criteria. The second phase refers to the development of an ontology-based model to support suppliers' selection based on the previously identified set of criteria. For doing so, there are four steps to follow: (1) Knowledge identification and classification; (2) Knowledge capitalization; (3) Knowledge typology and taxonomy; and (4) Knowledge concepts, relations, and attributes. Each of these steps is described in the following section. The final phase consists of discussing managerial and practical implications and presenting future research directions.

4 Development of Ontology-Based Model for Supporting Viable-Oriented Suppliers' Selection

4.1 Knowledge Identification and Classification

Our ontology-based model is built on the identification and classification of knowledge via a structured approach to modeling the criteria required for supplier selection while considering three complex capabilities: "resilience", "sustainability," and "digitalization." Concepts and relations are the principal component of our model. Thus, the first step to be taken when defining the relations is to define the domain and range. For doing so, through the literature review, the unstructured data obtained from a wide variety of scientific articles have been reincorporated into semi-structured form. Besides, the collection of criteria and sub-criteria was conceptualized based on the given set of clusters and items allocated to them. More clearly, we defined five classes (Resilience Criteria, Sustainability Criteria, Digitalization Criteria, Primary Criteria, and Profile Criteria) representing the criteria ensuring the viable selection of suppliers. Besides, several sub-criteria were defined for each criterion considering also circular economy (use and recovery).

4.2 Knowledge Capitalization

The analysis of literature and existing ontologies enables one to specifically define knowledge that is used and elaborated. With this analysis, we have written a series of knowledge which we have attributed to criteria. They were then verified and validated by an expert to finally can be capitalized on the taxonomy. We may build a list of knowledge that has been established as important for capitalization.

4.3 Knowledge Typology and Taxonomy

We generated an information classification to present a Knowledge classification for the supplier selection criteria. We also defined five Knowledge classes (Table 1). Each class reflects a particular type of knowledge. Hence, we developed a taxonomy to organize the Knowledge. In other words, it provides a hierarchical classification of data entities based on the implied connections of the real-world entities that they represent. Besides, the grouping is based on the resemblance of the knowledge entities known as concepts. This taxonomy illustrates the layout of the necessary criteria for selecting viable suppliers (Fig. 2). More clearly, the suggested taxonomy aims to hierarchize knowledge about resilient-digital-sustainable suppliers' selection criteria that characterize viable suppliers. After identifying knowledge to capitalize, we have analyzed and studied existing ontologies that we can re-use. Among ontologies-based models for suppliers' selection, we have used [12, 21, 22]. Some of the concepts presented aided us in conceptualization, especially concerning the primary criteria, profile criteria, and sustainability criteria. The [12] ontology is veritable in selecting green suppliers. However, its concepts don't cover the resilience and digitalization capabilities. Therefore, using the presented ontologies above, we conceptualized the viable-oriented suppliers' selection criteria model and defined attributes and relationships between the concepts related to ensuring viability.

Table 1. Knowledge classification

Name of the knowledge type	Knowledge
ResilienceCriteria	Knowledge presenting the criteria related to ensuring resilience
SustainabilityCriteria	Knowledge related to sustainability criteria
DigitalizationCriteria	Knowledge presenting the suppliers digital abilities
ProfileCriteria	Knowledge defining the general information of suppliers
PrimaryCriteria	knowledge related to the basic criteria for suppliers selection

4.4 Knowledge Concepts, Relations and Attributes

This step of the ontology consists of specifying concepts and relations of suppliers' selection criteria. More clearly, this phase consists of attributing a unique name for concepts, a concept ID, the inheritance ID, and a natural language definition of the concept (Table 2). Besides, it attributes potential relations name, the domain, and range (Table 3). To sum up, the proposed ontology has 399 concepts and 70 relations.

Table 2. Extract from the original concepts table

ConceptID	ParentID	Natural language definition
Economic_Risks	Risks	Risks that may affect an investment or a business
Technological_Capability	DigitalizationCriteria	Capabilities related to novel technologies
Material_Cost	Cost	Costs of materials
Risks_Identification	Risks_solutions	a step that identifies risks

Table 3. Extract from the original relations table

Relation	Relation ID	Domain	Range
Avoid	Avoid	Cybersecurity	Itrisks
Can Lead To	Can_Lead_To	Digitalizationcriterea	Resiliencecriterea
Ensure	Ensure	AI	Forecastingcapabilities
Has For Challenge	Has_For_Challenge	Information	Datasecurity
Has For Issue	Has_For_Issue	Profilecriteria	Resiliencecriterea
Improve	Improve	Digitalizationcriterea	Primarycriterea
Prevent	Prevent	Technologies	Risks
Secure	Secure	Blockchain	Communicationcapability

4.5 Viable-Oriented Suppliers Selection Ontology Implementation with Protégé

After extracting the concepts defining a set of criteria and sub-criteria, and, defining properties and relations between them, the core ontology model is formed. The main structure of the proposed ontology is modeled using Protégé software (see Fig. 2). Protégé software is a tool allowing to visualizing, validating and building the proposed ontology in the OWL language respecting W3C recommendations [23]. Each of the presented classes contains a set of sub-classes. We have five classes namely ResilienceCriteria, SustainabilityCriteria, DigitalizationCriteria, PrimaryCriteria, and ProfileCriteria, and 394 subclasses. Each class has many sub-classes. For instance, the DigitalizationCriteria has the following sub-classes: Innovation, Process_Quality, Product_Quality, Ressources, Security, Technological_Capability, Technologies. For ResilienceCriteria class, it has 3 sub-classes namely Actions, Performance, and Risks.

In a summary, our ontology offers a structured model for storing knowledge related to relevant criteria for selecting suitable suppliers considering the viability performance. Thanks to the proposed ontology, the domain definition of viable-oriented supplier selection criteria, its attributes, and relations with other concepts may be queried, inferred, or interpreted using the formal, explicit, and rich semantics to enable efficient viable suppliers' selection.

5 Practical and Managerial Implications

The developed ontology reflects current knowledge of the viable-oriented supplier selection domain criteria. It allows many benefits. It helps to systematize knowledge of the selected set of criteria and to represent knowledge structurally. Besides, it offers the opportunity of transdisciplinary conditions to collaboration between systems. The ontology's hierarchical structure enables rigorous thinking regarding domain concepts. That is to say, that managers will have the ability to rebuild the model and replenish it with information systems data. Furthermore, it can provide a dynamic mechanism for building or integrating information and other component-based information systems. It may also contribute to the development of information systems for the evaluation

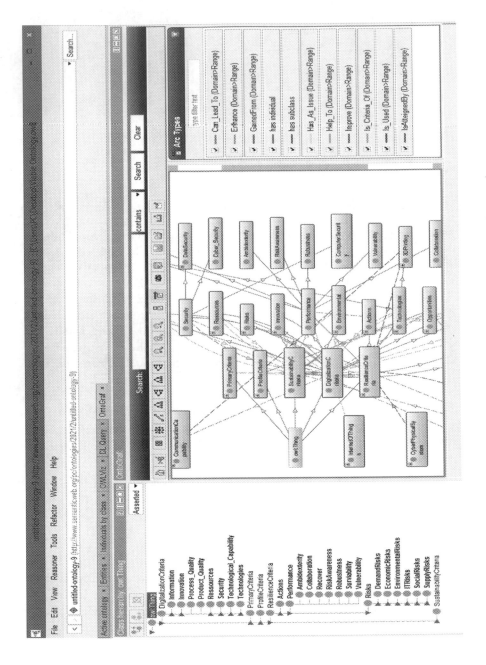

Fig. 2. Viable-oriented suppliers selection ontology implementation

of the whole domain, enabling automatization, visibility, and transparency. The proposed ontology's practical implications involve efforts to implement a large amount of knowledge covering resilience, digitalization, and sustainability dynamic capabilities that define viable-oriented supplier selection criteria. In other words, it is referencing the literature source metadata. These criteria knowledge could be used to interoperate with any knowledge base or database, or information systems. Furthermore, the proposed ontology unifies the scattered knowledge regarding viable-oriented supplier selection criteria and categorizes them into a comprehensive hierarchy.

6   Conclusion

With an increasingly global consciousness of resilience, viable-oriented cooperation in end-to end supply chains has emerged as a key feature. Because of the international changes that have arisen as a result of market globalization, technological advancements, or natural disasters [7]. Therefore, a successful viable-oriented supplier selection strategy will help reduce risks and disruptions effect while increasing organizations' competitiveness. For doing so, several sets of criteria were established to strengthen this process. While there are numerous studies on supplier selection, there is no comprehensive study considering viability issue in the suppliers' selection process.

Exchanging and transparently sharing information and knowledge represents a challenge for organizations to remain viable. To meet this challenge, this paper aims to present a new ontology-based-model for supporting suppliers' selection considering the viability performance. More clearly, the viable-oriented suppliers' selection is based on resilience, digitalization, and sustainability capabilities criteria. Thus, acquiring these criteria knowledge in an ontology is cost-effective and flexible to have access to needed information. It allows also to capitalize knowledge related to suppliers selection which can be considered as an important contribution for viable suppliers selection knowledge performance. In this article, to implement the viable-oriented suppliers' selection, the first step consisted of retrieving criteria from the literature. After that, we have identified, classified, and capitalized knowledge to draw up the taxonomy and define knowledge concepts, relations, and attributes. Then, we have implemented and visualized the proposed ontology using Protégé software.

This ontology-based-model supporting viable-oriented suppliers' selection can be pursued in further work. This ontology can promote the standardization and sharing of knowledge by qualified actor-assisted tools such as the Multi-Agent System. This paper has some limitations that provide the opportunity for potential research. In other words, there is always the potential of enhancing the veracity of data collection and enriching knowledge while implementing an ontology. Moreover, future ontologies can consider disruption phases (pre-disruption, post-disruption, and disruption) knowledge to enhance the supply chain viability. Furthermore, we can introduce fuzzy logic theory in the proposed ontology to handle the concept of the decision subjectivity.

References

1. Zekhnini, K., Cherrafi, A., Bouhaddou, I., Benghabrit, Y., Garza-Reyes, J.A.: Supply chain management 4.0: a literature review and research framework. Benchmarking: Int. J. **28**(2), 465–501 (2021). https://doi.org/10.1108/BIJ-04-2020-0156
2. Zekhnini, K., Cherrafi, A., Bouhaddou, I., Benghabrit, Y.: Supply chain 4.0 risk management: bibliometric analysis and a proposed framework. In: Saka, A., et al. (eds.) CPI 2019. LNME, pp. 322–332. Springer, Cham (2021). https://doi.org/10.1007/978-3-030-62199-5_29
3. Zekhnini, K., Anass, C., Bouhaddou, I., Benghabrit, Y., Belhadi, A.: Supply chain 4.0 risk management: an interpretive structural modelling approach. International J. Logistics Syst. Manag. **1**, 1 (2020) https://doi.org/10.1504/IJLSM.2020.10037750
4. Zekhnini, K., Cherrafi, A., Bouhaddou, I., Benghabrit, Y.: Analytic Hierarchy Process (AHP) for supply chain 4.0 risks management. In: Masrour, T., Cherrafi, A., El Hassani, I. (eds.) A2IA 2020. AISC, vol. 1193, pp. 89–102. Springer, Cham (2021). https://doi.org/10.1007/978-3-030-51186-9_7
5. Mesmer, L., Olewnik, A.: Enabling supplier discovery through a part-focused manufacturing process ontology. Int. J. Comput. Integr. Manuf. **31**, 87–100 (2018). https://doi.org/10.1080/0951192X.2017.1357837
6. Jaskó, S., Skrop, A., Holczinger, T., Chován, T., Abonyi, J.: Development of manufacturing execution systems in accordance with Industry 4.0 requirements: a review of standard- and ontology-based methodologies and tools. Comput. Ind. **123,** 103300 (2020). https://doi.org/10.1016/j.compind.2020.103300
7. Zekhnini, K., Cherrafi, A., Bouhaddou, I., Benghabrit, Y., Garza-Reyes, J.A.: Supplier selection for smart supply chain: an adaptive fuzzy-neuro approach (2020)
8. Ivanov, D.: Lean resilience: AURA (Active Usage of Resilience Assets) framework for post-COVID-19 supply chain management. IJLM Ahead-of-print (2021). https://doi.org/10.1108/IJLM-11-2020-0448
9. Parmar, D., Wu, T., Callarman, T., Fowler, J., Wolfe, P.: A clustering algorithm for supplier base management. Int. J. Prod. Res. **48**, 3803–3821 (2010). https://doi.org/10.1080/00207540902942891
10. Che, Z.H.: A genetic algorithm-based model for solving multi-period supplier selection problem with assembly sequence. Int. J. Prod. Res. **48**, 4355–4377 (2010). https://doi.org/10.1080/00207540903049399
11. Ghadimi, P., Ghassemi Toosi, F., Heavey, C.: A multi-agent systems approach for sustainable supplier selection and order allocation in a partnership supply chain. Eur. J. Oper. Res. **269**, 286–301 (2018). https://doi.org/10.1016/j.ejor.2017.07.014
12. Konys, A.: Green supplier selection criteria: from a literature review to a comprehensive knowledge base. Sustainability **11**, 4208 (2019).https://doi.org/10.3390/su11154208
13. Stević, Ž., Pamučar, D., Puška, A., Chatterjee, P.: Sustainable supplier selection in healthcare industries using a new MCDM method: measurement of alternatives and ranking according to COmpromise solution (MARCOS). Comput. Ind. Eng. **140,** 106231 (2020). https://doi.org/10.1016/j.cie.2019.106231
14. Yu, C., Wong, T.N.: An agent-based negotiation model for supplier selection of multiple products with synergy effect. Expert Syst. Appl. **42**, 223–237 (2015). https://doi.org/10.1016/j.eswa.2014.07.057
15. Kundu, A., Jain, V.: On development of supplier segmentation ontology using latent semantic analysis for supplier knowledge management in supply chain. In: 2013 IEEE International Conference on Industrial Engineering and Engineering Management, pp. 1007–1011. IEEE, Bangkok (2013)

16. Benabdellah, A.C., Zekhnini, K., Cherrafi, A., Garza-Reyes, J.A., Kumar, A.: Design for the environment: an ontology-based knowledge management model for green product development. Bus. Strategy Environ. (2021)
17. Ameri, F., Dutta, D.: A matchmaking methodology for supply chain deployment in distributed manufacturing environments. J. Comput. Inf. Sci. Eng. **8** (2008)
18. Achatbi, I., Amechnoue, K., Aoulad Allouch, S.: An ontology based approach to organize supplier and transportation provider selection negotiation in multi-agent system model. In: Ezziyyani, M., Bahaj, M., Khoukhi, F. (eds.) AIT2S 2017. LNNS, vol. 25, pp. 129–137. Springer, Cham (2018). https://doi.org/10.1007/978-3-319-69137-4_13
19. Achatbi, I., Amechnoue, K., Haddadi, T.E., Allouch, S.A.: Advanced system based on ontology and multi agent technology to handle upstream supply chain: intelligent negotiation protocol for supplier and transportation provider selection, 337–354 (2020). https://doi.org/10.5267/j.dsl.2020.5.002
20. Wątróbski, J.: Ontology supporting green supplier selection process. Procedia Comput. Sci. **159**, 1602–1613 (2019). https://doi.org/10.1016/j.procs.2019.09.331
21. Singh, S., Ghosh, S., Jayaram, J., Tiwari, M.K.: Enhancing supply chain resilience using ontology-based decision support system. Int. J. Comput. Integr. Manuf. **32**, 642–657 (2019). https://doi.org/10.1080/0951192X.2019.1599443
22. Zaoui, F., Souissi, N.: Onto-digital: an ontology-based model for digital transformation's knowledge. IJITCS **10**, 1–12 (2018). https://doi.org/10.5815/ijitcs.2018.12.01
23. Monticolo, D., Hilaire, V., Koukam, A., Gomes, S.: Ontodesign; a domain ontology for building and exploiting project memories in product design projects **6** (2007)

Green Supply Chain Management: A Meta-analysis of Recent Reviews

Eleonora Bottani[1](✉) [iD] and Teresa Murino[2] [iD]

[1] Department of Engineering and Architecture, University of Parma, Parco Area delle Scienze 181/A, 43124 Parma, Italy
eleonora.bottani@unipr.it
[2] Department of Chemical, Materials and Production Engineering, University of Naples, "Federico II" – Piazzale V. Tecchio 80, 80125 Naples, Italy

Abstract. This paper provides a meta-analysis of the review papers targeting the theme of green supply chain management (GSCM). The chosen topic is of central interest among researchers in supply chain and logistics, and a number of review papers have appeared on that theme. Using a combination of bibliographic and bibliometric analyses, this paper makes an attempt to delineate the most debated topics in GSCM, the most prominent themes and the need for future research in the field.

Keywords: Meta-analysis · Systematic literature review · Green supply chain

1 Introduction

Green supply chain management (GSCM) describes the concept of integrating sustainable environmental processes into the traditional supply chain management processes, such as product design, material sourcing and selection, manufacturing and production, operation, logistics, up to end-of-life management [1, 2]. It is therefore a holistic approach that incorporates environmental concerns in the supply chain [3] and aids firms to improve their footprint on sustainability [4]. Greening operations by reducing air, water and waste pollution, enhances firms' performance in terms of less waste, reuse/recycling of products, decrease in manufacturing costs, enhanced assets efficiency, positive image, and higher customer satisfaction.

GSCM has recently gained increasing importance, as reducing air, water and environmental pollution is one of the key challenges of the 21st century [5]. GSCM also has a mediating role in achieving Sustainable Development Goals (SDGs) [6, 7], which is a main target of companies worldwide. This increased interest towards GSCM has led to many papers published on this topic, and, consequently, to the publication of review papers on GSCM as well. Starting from the pioneer state-of-the-art review on GSCM (i.e. [1]), many researchers have carried out reviews on specific topics of GSCM (e.g. [8–10] or [11]). In the light of the wide number of review papers available on GSCM and of the various topics that have been addressed in these reviews, this paper proposes a meta-analysis of the review papers on GSCM. This methodology has been chosen as it typically allows researchers to arrive at conclusions that are more accurate and reliable than those presented in a single study or review paper [12].

The remainder of the paper is structured as follows: Sect. 2 describes the methodology used in carrying out this study. Section 3 shows the main results of the meta-analysis. Section 4 highlights the conclusions, limitation and implications of the study.

2 Methodology

A meta-analysis is a quantitative statistical analysis grounded on the results of multiple scientific studies, all addressing the same topic, with each individual study reporting specific aspects or measurement [12]. The quantitative procedures of meta-analysis help to address some of the challenges introduced by the existence of multiple answers to a given research question. Meta-analyses allow combining numerical results from various studies, accurately estimating the resulting statistics [13] and explaining inconsistencies (if any) in the research findings. The meta-analysis carried out in this study targets review papers in the field of GSCM and, in particular, systematic literature reviews (SLRs). Being SRL a structured approach, this choice ensures that homogeneous data can be retrieved from the papers analyzed. Indeed, a requirement of SLRs is to follow a clearly defined and replicable protocol, where the criteria for reviewing the literature are clearly stated. Moreover, SLRs involve planning a well thought out search strategy which has a specific focus or answers a defined question [14].

For retrieving the pertinent studies, different queries were made on the Scopus database (www.scopus.com) on November 2020. The queries were made using search terms linked to the theme of GSCM, namely: "green supply chain management", "green supply chain" and "sustainable supply chain". These terms were searched for in the "abstract/title/keyword" (TITLE-ABS-KEY) of the document. Moreover, in line with the scope of this paper, the query results were limited to "review" as article type. The timespan of the studies was limited as well, and it was set from 2007 to 2020. Indeed, one of the first reviews on GSCM (i.e. [1]) was carried out exactly in 2007, which is a robust justification for starting in that year for retrieving the pertinent studies; moreover, at the time of the query, only a preliminary amount of studies of 2021 were available online, meaning that year 2021 could not be evaluated in full and this is why it was excluded from the analysis. Therefore, the query settings were PUBYEAR > 2006 AND PUB-YEAR < 2021 AND (LIMIT-TO (DOCTYPE, "re")). The queries made returned 300 documents in total: 67 documents using "green supply chain management", 92 using "green supply chain" and 141 using "sustainable supply chain".

For the three groups of papers, some key pieces of information (i.e. the paper's metadata, the number of citations and the author's keywords) were directly downloaded in .csv file format using the "export" function of Scopus and imported in Microsoft Excel™ for creating the full dataset of useful studies. The database was thus used for removing papers for which the author name was not available (i.e. that returned "[No author name available]" or a blank cell in the corresponding field of Scopus). Despite the query settings, indeed, these papers typically are not scientific papers (nor review papers): they could be editorials, prefaces of conferences, papers published in non-scientific magazines or something similar; in any case, these documents should be excluded from any elaboration. Four papers with this characteristic were thus removed from the database. Duplicated studies, i.e. studies that resulted from more than one query, were then identified, by simply comparing the articles' title using the "IF" function of Microsoft Excel™. This check involved 85 papers to be removed from the sample. The fulltexts of the remaining 211 papers were retrieved and checked to ensure that each study meets the criterion of being a SLR and not a mere review paper. This led to 106 documents that matched this criterion and that were taken as the final sample of papers to be analyzed.

The analyses made on the 106 papers were of both bibliographic and bibliometric nature. Bibliographic analyses mainly aim at providing an overview of the sample of papers; examples of these analyses include the number of publications per year, the trend of publications in time or the publication outlet. Bibliometric analyses instead are more structured elaborations that apply quantitative tools to the evaluation of a sample of papers [15]. Among the possible elaborations, citation analyses and keyword analyses [16] were carried out in this study. All these analyses were made exploiting appropriate functions available on Microsoft Excel™.

3   Results

The first aspect investigated is the trend of publications in time (Fig. 1). The first SLR on topics related to GSCM appeared in 2011, despite the fact that review papers on this theme were published even before that year. However, this outcome could be expected as SLR started gaining attention in engineering research in recent years only, while being a known methodology in medicine and social sciences since the late '90s [17]. This is also confirmed by the almost constant increase in the number of SLRs published since that date, with a peak of 30 papers in 2019; overall, 55 papers (51.8% of the sample) were published in the last two years of the timespan. The 106 SLRs of the sample were found to be published, overall, on 51 different sources. Looking at those journals that published at least two studies (Fig. 2), the *Journal of Cleaner Production* emerges as the source in which the greatest number of studies has been published (19 out of 106, 17.9%), followed by *Sustainability* (12 out of 106, 11.3%) and *Supply chain management* (11 out of 206, 10.4%). This outcome is consonant with the theme under examination; indeed, both *Journal of Cleaner Production* and *Sustainability* target expressively the topics of green and environment, while *Supply chain management* has a broader focus, targeting, more in general, studies that investigate the supply chain under various perspectives.

A quite well-known tool for mapping the research trends on a given topic is the keywords analysis [16] by means of their frequency (i.e. the number of occurrences of a keyword) and persistency (i.e. the number of years elapsed since the keyword was used for the first time). This analysis was made using the "author's keywords" field of Scopus. In this respect, for four papers of the sample, the keywords were not available; therefore, these studies were excluded from the analysis, leading to a sample of 102 usable papers. The keywords of these papers were elaborated using Microsoft Excel™, with the aim first of all to identify terms which needed to be grouped into a single keyword. In fact, it is frequent that the different authors use slightly different terms with the same meaning;

this is for instance the case of keywords written in full or using acronyms (e.g. supply chain management *vs.* SCM), or of the same terms written in singular or plural form (e.g. supply chain *vs.* supply chains). Some preliminary adjustments were therefore made to fix these small inconsistencies. The number of keywords resulting after these adjustments was 564. Because of the still high number of outcomes, each keyword was examined singularly to identify a macro-theme to which it could be associated. For example, "green" as a keyword can be easily associated to a macro-theme like "green supply chain". Approximately 60 keywords could not be associated to any macro-theme, either because they represented terms appearing just once or because they expressed very specific concepts.

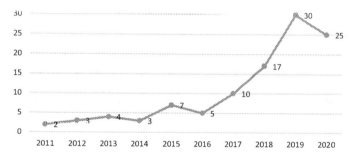

Fig. 1. Trend of publications in time.

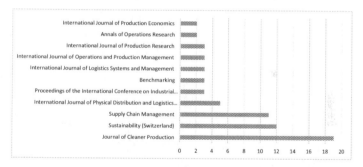

Fig. 2. Top journals.

The results of this analysis, limited to those keywords that appeared at least twice and excluding the keyword that were not classified, are proposed in Table 1. From Table 1 it can be seen that the most recurrent macro-theme is the wide topic of "sustainable supply chain management" (SSCM, frequency: 65), which includes 4 keywords that appeared at least twice. The next most recurrent macro-themes are "Systematic literature review" (frequency: 48), "sustainability" (frequency: 46) and "green supply chain" (frequency: 45), which are all in line with the focus of the sample of papers reviewed. It should be mentioned that keywords related to "literature review" (as opposed to SLR) occur a significant lower number of times (frequency: 19), which once again denotes appropriateness of the sample of papers. Interestingly, a macro-theme relating to the usage of specific tools for "bibliometric analyses" has also been found (frequency: 11).

It is also interesting to see that "supply chain management" and "logistics" are quite recurrent as well (frequencies: 38 and 20, respectively), suggesting that these themes are often investigated in GSCM literature. The three pillars of sustainability, i.e. the economic, social and environmental ones [18], are all covered among the macro-themes identified; the most frequent one is environmental sustainability (frequency: 18), followed by social sustainability (frequency: 9) and economic sustainability (frequency: 5). Various themes related to sustainability have also been identified, including sustainable development, circular economy or corporate social responsibility.

Table 1. Frequency of keywords and macro-themes.

Macro-theme	Frequency	Appearance	Keywords	Frequency
SSCM	65	2011	Sustainable supply chain management	31
			Sustainable supply chain	20
			Supply chain sustainability	3
			Sustainable operations	2
Systematic literature review	48	2012	Systematic literature review	40
			Systematic review	3
			PRISMA	2
			Structured literature review	2
Sustainability	46	2012	Sustainability	30
			Triple bottom line	2
			Sustainability performance	2
Green supply chain	45	2013	Green supply chain management	20
			Green supply chain	6
			Green	2
Supply chain management	38	2011	Supply chain management	13
			Supply chain	13
			Multi-tier supply chain	2
Logistics	20	2012	Logistics service provider (LSP)	3
			Logistics	2
			Freight transport	2
			Vehicle routing	2
Performance measurement	19	2015	Performance measurement	4
			Performance measures	2
			Supply chain performance measurement	2
			Green supply chain performance measurement	2
			Performance	2
Literature review	19	2013	Literature review	16

(continued)

Table 1. (*continued*)

Macro-theme	Frequency	Appearance	Keywords	Frequency
Environmental sustainability	*18*	2011	Environment	5
			Environmental sustainability	4
			Environmental management	3
Supplier selection	*14*	2011	Supplier selection	4
			Third-party logistics (3PL)	3
			Sustainable sourcing	2
			Partner selection	2
Circular economy	*14*	2017	Circular economy	9
Corporate social responsibility	*12*	2011	Corporate social responsibility	5
			Social responsibility	2
Bibliometric analysis	*11*	2016	Content analysis	4
			Bibliometric analysis	3
			Quantitative methods	2
Industry 4.0	*11*	2018	Industry 4.0	3
			Big data analytics	2
			Blockchain	2
Developing countries	*11*	2017	Developing countries	4
			Guanxi	2
			Asian emerging economies	2
MCDM	*10*	2011	Multi criteria decision making	3
			AHP	3
			Topsis	2
Social sustainability	*9*	2014	Social sustainability	3
Sustainable development	*7*	2012	Sustainable development	6
Innovation	*6*	2017	Innovation	3
Framework	*6*	2015	Conceptual framework	2
Collaboration	*5*	2019	Collaboration	3
Closed-loop supply chain	*5*	2017	Closed-loop supply chain	5
Economic sustainability	*5*	2011	Economic performance	3
			Economic sustainability	2
Reverse logistics	*5*	2011	Recycling	2
Research methodology	*4*	2012	Interpretive structural modeling	2
Agility/leannes	*4*	2018	Lean	2
Electronic	*4*	2012	Electrics and electronics industry	2
Construction industry	*3*	2019	Construction industry	3
Knowledge	*2*	2019	Knowledge	2
Fuzzy	*2*	2011	Fuzzy	2
Manufacturing sector	*2*	2017	Manufacturing sector	2

A second interesting aspect is the persistency of keywords, which allows for identifying the new themes *vs.* the well-established ones. As the first SLR about GSCM appeared in 2011, the persistency of the keywords can range from 1 for a keyword appearing in 2020, to 10 for a keyword appearing in 2011. Because of the high number of keywords found, the macro-themes were used for the determination of the persistency (all data can be seen in columns 2 and 3 of Table 1). The results are shown in Fig. 3, which correlates the persistence (*y*-axis) and the frequency (*x*-axis) of each macro-theme. To be more effective, the graph in Fig. 3 was divided into 4 quadrants, obtained by distinguishing high *vs.* low values of persistency and frequency. As persistency is computed on a range of 10 years, it is quite immediate to label the resulting values as "high" if they range from 6 to 10 (corresponding to a study published between 2011 and 2015) or "low" if they range from 1 to 5 (corresponding to a study published after 2015). For frequencies, the median value (i.e. 5) was taken as the boundary to separate the "high" and "low" values.

The outcomes show that macro-themes such as Industry 4.0, agility/leanness, circular economy, or innovation started being explored in review papers concerning GSCM in recent times only. On the contrary, the first SLRs about GSCM have targeted themes like performance measurement, environmental sustainability, sustainable development, corporate social responsibility, supplier selection or reverse logistics. This outcome highlights the maturity of these themes compared to the more recent ones. Moreover, for a SLR to be carried out on a given topic, it is evident that a relevant amount of studies on that topic should have been published; for newer themes, such as Industry 4.0 or circular economy, it is reasonable to suppose that the number of studies useful for a review has been reached in recent years only.

The last analysis presented tries to evaluated the relevance of the macro-themes by taking into account the average number of citations received by the papers falling into that macro-theme. The number of citations per year (instead of the absolute number of

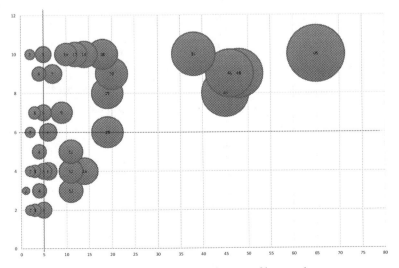

Fig. 3. Frequency vs. persistency of keywords.

citations) was used in carrying out the analysis, to normalize the resulting values. Table 2 shows the results obtained, limited to those macro-themes that received more than 10 citations/year on average. As Table 2 and Fig. 3 show, macro-themes that appeared in earlier studies are also more cited in literature, suggesting that over the years they have become well-established topics on which many authors are working. It is interesting to see, nonetheless, that some more recent topics (e.g. sustainable development or research methodologies) have also received a relevant number of citations, meaning that are attracting the attention of researchers.

Table 2. Average number of citations per year vs. macro-theme.

Macro-theme	Citations/year	Macro-theme	Citations/year
Economic sustainability	31.6	Research methodology	13.0
Manufacturing sector	26.0	Developing countries	12.2
Processes	21.3	Supplier selection	12.1
Organization	18.5	Sustainable development	11.6
Closed-loop supply chain	18.5	Electronic	11.4
Corporate social responsibility	17.5	Supply chain management	11.2
Circular economy	16.8	Environmental sustainability	11.1
Literature review	15.0	SSCM	10.5
Decision science	13.5	Agility/leannes	10.3

4 Conclusions

This paper has presented a meta-analysis of systematic literature reviews focusing on the topic of GSCM. A set of 106 papers was retrieved from the Scopus database and the relevant pieces of information were exported to allow their elaboration on Microsoft Excel™. Out of the numerous analyses that can be made on a set of papers using bibliographic and bibliometric tools, this paper has focused on some descriptive statistics, keyword analysis and citation analysis. These analyses were used to provide a preliminary investigation of the topic and to identify the most prominent themes. For sure, the analyses presented could be deepened and complemented by additional elaborations intended to confirm the results obtained and highlight further specific facets. As an example, all the data relating to the systematic literature reviews (e.g. the number of papers examined, the timespan of the review, the database used etc.) could be retrieved from the set of papers and compared. The correlation between the number of papers reviewed and the specific topic of the review is a further point worth of investigation.

References

1. Srivastava, S.: Green supply-chain management: a state-of-the-art literature review. Int. J. Manag. Rev. **9**(1), 53–80 (2007)

2. Khan, S.: Introductory Chapter: Introduction of Green Supply Chain Management. Green Practices and Strategies in Supply Chain Management (2018)
3. Malviya, R., Kant, R.: Green supply chain management (GSCM): a structured literature review and research implications. Benchmark Int. J. **22**(7), 1360–1394 (2015)
4. Bhatia, M.S., Gangwani, K.: Green supply chain management: scientometric review and analysis of empirical research. J. Cleaner Prod. **284**, Article No. 124722 (2021)
5. Balasubramanian, S., Shukla, V.: Green supply chain management: the case of the construction sector in the United Arab Emirates (UAE). Prod. Plan. Control **28**(14), 1116–1138 (2017)
6. Badi, S., Murtagh, N.: Green supply chain management in construction: a systematic literature review and future research agenda. J. Clean. Prod. **223**, 312–322 (2019)
7. Ilyas, S., Hu, Z., Wiwattanakornwong, K.: Unleashing the role of top management and government support in green supply chain management and sustainable development goals. Environ. Sci. Pollut. Res. **27**(8), 8210–8223 (2020). https://doi.org/10.1007/s11356-019-07268-3
8. Sarkis, J., Zhu, Q., Lai, K.: An organizational theoretic review of green supply chain management literature. Int. J. Prod. Econ. **130**(1), 1–15 (2011)
9. Seuring, S.: A review of modeling approaches for sustainable supply chain management. Decis. Support Syst. **54**(4), 1513–1520 (2013)
10. Luthra, S., Garg, D.H.A.: Green supply chain management: implementation and performance: a literature review and some issues. J. Adv. Manag. Res. **11**(1), 20–46 (2014)
11. Fahimnia, B., Sarkis, J., Davarzani, H.: Green supply chain management: a review and bibliometric analysis. Int. J. Prod. Econ. **162**, 101–114 (2015)
12. Greenland, S., O'Rourke, K.: Meta-Analysis (2008)
13. Rosenthal, R.: Meta-Analytic Procedures for Social Research - Revised Edition. Sage Publications (1991)
14. Dewey, A., Drahota, A.: Introduction to systematic reviews: online learning module. https://training.cochrane.org/interactivelearning/module-1-introduction-conducting-systematic-reviews
15. Ball, R.: An Introduction to Bibliometrics - New Development and Trends. Elsevier Science (2017)
16. Fadlalla, A., Amani, F.: A keyword-based organizing framework for ERP intellectual contributions. J. Enterp. Inf. Manag. **28**, 637–657 (2015)
17. Petticrew, M., Roberts, H.: Systematic Reviews in the Social Sciences: A Practical Guide. Blackwell Publishing (2006)
18. Elkington, J.: Towards the sustainable corporation: win-win-win business strategies for sustainable development. Calif. Manag. Rev. **36**(2), 90–100 (1994)

Development of an Eco-efficiency Distribution Model: A Case Study of a Danish Wholesaler

Malte Herold Jeberg[1], Simon Hummelshøj Sloth[1], Janus Haslund Løgtved[1], Hans-Henrik Hvolby[1] (iD), and Kenn Steger-Jensen[1,2(✉)] (iD)

[1] Department of Materials and Production, Aalborg University, Aalborg, Denmark
kenn@mp.aau.dk
[2] Department of Maritime Operations, University of South-Eastern Norway, Vestfold, Norway

Abstract. A decision model is presented to support selecting the best distribution to optimise earnings and minimise environmental impact. The model has been tested on a Danish wholesaler that wants to sell its goods on the Norwegian market. In this connection, they must therefore choose how the goods are to be distributed. Via the decision model, it is possible to choose the distribution and mode of transport they need for the individual markets, as it is not always the same modes of transport that are optimal for all markets. Thus, the model supports and shows that it is possible to optimise the company's earning capacity and minimise environmental impact by choosing the proper distribution. Furthermore, national requirements for reducing carbon can be expected to affect taxes and duties, which is why a sensitivity analysis has been prepared, which shows the effect of increasing carbon taxes on the contribution margin in the optimal modes of transport.

Keywords: Eco-efficiency · Distribution model · Sustainable distribution

1 Background

An eco-efficiency approach is needed to address environmental challenges such as climate change, acidification, eutrophication, etc. The concept of eco-efficiency was first introduced in the 1970s as the concept of environmental efficiency by Freeman et al. [1] and eco-efficiency as a business link to sustainable development in the 1990s by Schaltegger and Sturm [2].

According to Verfaillie and Bidwell [3], eco-efficiency brings together economic and environmental aspects to foster economic prosperity with more efficient use of resources and lower emissions.

However, it is well known that carbon dioxide emissions are directly proportional to the car fuel consumption rate affected by factors such as speed, load, acceleration, road gradient and traffic congestion [4]. Chang and Morlok [5] studied the Green Vehicle Routing Problem (GVRP) and proposed the impact of vehicle speed on fuel consumption. The characteristic of GVRP is to harmonise environmental and economic costs

A. Dolgui et al. (Eds.): APMS 2021, IFIP AICT 633, pp. 641–648, 2021.
https://doi.org/10.1007/978-3-030-85910-7_68

by planning effective routes to maximise benefits and meet environmental concerns. Raeesi and Zografos [6] used the Chicago road network as an example to introduce a realistic urban freight distribution model. They included flexible time windows and departure times, crowded city road network, random vehicle number, and instantaneous acceleration and deceleration of trucks in fuel consumption estimation.

Besides the transportation behaviour, the utilisation of payload and scale of business is essential to minimise carbon footprint per ton-mils. Tsoulfas and Pappis [7] suggested incorporating environmental factors and product recovery in transportation network decisions. Data envelopment analysis (DEA) can be used as a support tool to establish a relative eco-efficiency measure for the different bioethanol transportation modes and prioritising different modes according to these figures [8].

From an eco-efficiency perspective, intermodal transport has a lower environmental impact than competing modes [9]. For example, intermodal transport has, on average, 20–50% less CO_2 emissions than all-road transport on 19 tested European routes [10].

Studies in modelling eco-efficiency in intermodal or multimodal transportation system are not fully exploited. The benefit of integrating ships advantage of low emissions per ton-km with truck advantage as last mils delivery to customers has not between presented, which is the focus in this paper.

2 Model

To reduce the carbon footprint, models must be developed that support choosing the right distribution method that optimises both earnings and minimises environmental impact simultaneously. It can be expected that the national requirements for reducing carbon will mean that taxes and duties on carbon will increase to realise the goals and thus affect earnings negatively proportionally if the choice of distribution is not chosen wisely.

When estimating the potential revenue of a new market and the transport cost of distribution, numerous variables and influencing factors must be considered. A model is thus developed, which can dynamically measure the profitability and eco-efficiency of distributing to a given market with goods. One objective of the model is to estimate the transport cost and environmental impact, as this will directly affect the profitability and eco-efficiency. The advantage of a model is the ability to test different scenarios and measure the different variables' sensitivity. The developed model has three main functionalities: 1) measuring the potential revenue in a given market, 2) calculating the cost of transporting the goods, and 3) measuring the environmental impact. The model structure and its steps are displayed in Fig. 1.

The **first** step addresses the potential revenue by identifying the relevant markets, followed by determining the sales potential for each market. Next, competitive factors must be evaluated. Finally, if necessary, the sales potential should be scaled according to these factors by introducing a competitive parameter into the model, e.g. scaling the revenue based on the number of competitors.

In the **second** step, the frequency and volume of deliveries are estimated and included as a variable in the model, making it possible to test the impact on total transport cost. Furthermore, the distance from the company base to each of the identified markets is fetched, which can be used to calculate the total transport cost to each market once prices

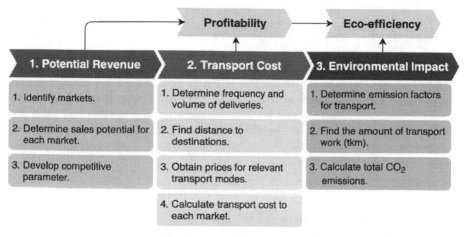

Fig. 1. Model structure

from shipping companies have been obtained. Hereafter, the profitability is estimated by subtracting the transport cost from the potential revenue in each of the potential markets.

In the final step, an emission factor is determined for each mode used in the second step. The choice of transport mode will significantly influence the environmental impact of supplying goods to each market due to different emission factors. The total distance and volume of each delivery can be transformed into a total amount of transport work, measured in tonnes-kilometres (tonnes-km), multiplied with the emission factor resulting in the total amount of CO_2 emitted. The profitability from step 2 of the model is used to calculate the eco-efficiency denoted as profit per ton CO_2 emitted.

3   Case Study: A Danish Wholesaler

The model's applicability will be showcased through a case study using a Danish wholesaler as an example. The company seeks to enter the Norwegian market, which might be beneficial to supply with goods by sea along the west coast rather than with truck from the Oslo region due to a logistical imbalance. Which modes of transport, and if alternative routes should be considered, will vary depending on the preferences of the case company and the location of the target market. The case study will follow the structure in Fig. 1.

3.1   Potential Revenue (Step 1)

In step 1.1, an analysis of the case company's overall strategy is performed to set requirements for the target market. The analysis led to the identification of 397 towns with strategical relevance for the case company. The revenue consists of the cost of goods sold and gross profit. For step 1.2, a simple linear regression of the cost of goods sold in a current market with strategical similarities to the target market was used as a basis for estimating the revenue. To estimate the gross profit margin range, a sales analysis was made of the current market.

Although the cost of goods sold is constant and independent of the location within the target market, the gross profit margin is not. Therefore, in Step 1.3, a competitive parameter was introduced to address the discrepancies between a currently serviced market and the target market. It is strategically important for the case company that the target market has a significant degree of isolation; hence the distance to larger cities was reflected in the competitive parameter. The gross profit margin is scaled with the competitive parameter, alternating the potential revenue depending on the strategic fit of each town, which yields the gross profit, enabling an estimation of the expected yearly revenue of a target market (town) as seen in Eq. 1.

$$\text{Revenue} = P \times \frac{\text{CP} \times \text{COGS}}{1 - (\text{CP} \times \text{GPM})} \qquad (1)$$

where P is the target market population, COGS is the cost of goods sold, CP is the competitive parameter, and GPM is the gross profit margin.

The potential revenue was calculated for all of the 397 towns. An example of an identified town is Vaksdal, with a population of 1335 people. Using Eq. 1, a yearly estimated cost of goods sold of € 51 per person, scaled by a competitive parameter of 0.91 and a scaled gross profit margin of 18.59%, yielding an estimated potential annual revenue for Vaksdal of around € 76K.

3.2   Transport Cost (Step 2)

In **step 2.1**, the annual volume per area in the target market was approximated from the potential sales, assuming that the value-density (value in € per m^3) is the same within the two markets. As the estimated volume is based on annual demand, a yearly delivery frequency (shipments per year) is needed to determine the volume per shipment. However, the price per unit of volume is highly dependent on the space utilisation of the shipping trailer. The volume demand of a single town is only a fraction of a full trailer, driving up the price and reducing the contribution margin. Therefore, it is beneficial to aggregate several towns to bring down transport costs. For this case, clustering analysis was used in conjunction with a short iterative manual process to refine the clusters and ensure no volume demand of a cluster violates the maximum capacity of a trailer. This yielded a total of 29 clusters in Norway, and a fragment of these can be seen in Fig. 2.

In **step 2.2**, the distance to the market must be identified before estimating the total transportation cost. If several towns are to be visited, determining the shortest route can be categorised as a travelling salesman problem. To solve a travelling salesman problem, a distance matrix is needed. In a country with many remote areas, such as Norway, it is recommended to use the driving distance between towns instead of the Euclidian distance. A distance matrix of driving distances can be obtained from e.g. the Google API, which extracts the distance between any two destinations from Google Maps.

In **step 2.3**, the prices for the relevant transport modes must be found. The Norwegian market calls for a comparison between road and ship transport to be made, and therefore two alternative routes will be calculated. The first will use road transport (through the port of Kristiansand) directly to the customers, whereas the other will employ ship transport to the nearest port of the cluster. After consulting shipping companies that currently supply the target market, price sheets for transporting goods the relevant distance were obtained.

Finally, in **step 2.4** the transportation prices to supply each cluster can be found by extrapolating or interpolating the prices to the final destination. The mode of transportation will influence the applicability of linear extrapolation, and road transport prices are more likely to be accurately estimated using this method. Therefore, specific prices for as many of the target destinations as possible should be obtained.

When estimations of transportation costs have been obtained, they are subtracted from the revenue to obtain the profitability of a given cluster, as shown in Eq. 2.

$$\text{Profitability} = R - (C \times F) \tag{2}$$

where R is the annual revenue of a cluster, C is the stated cost of transportation, and F is the yearly frequency of deliveries.

Prices of transportation for the two alternative routes to each of the 29 clusters were obtained. The profitability of a cluster (highlighted in Fig. 2, including previously mentioned Vaksdal) is calculated using Eq. 2 and yielded a profit of € 142K and € 143K for road transport and sea transport, respectively.

3.3   Environmental Impact (Step 3)

Step 3.1 requires determining the emission factors for the chosen modes of transport. Several studies have been made regarding which emission factor is most suitable, and for this case, a factor of 62g CO_2 per tonnes-km of road transport is used. For ship transport, a factor of 16g CO_2 per tonnes-km is used [11].

Step 3.2 requires a calculation of the amount of transport work (tonnes-km) to be carried out, which can be calculated by combining the weight of the supplied goods by the travelled distances. The amount of yearly pallets distributed is known from the calculation of the transport costs. Moreover, the average weight of a pallet of goods can be found from the strategically similar market. Therefore, it is possible to calculate a total weight for the supplied goods, which in combination with the distances returns the total tonnes-km.

In **step 3.3**, the total tonnes-km is multiplied by the emission factors to estimate the total CO_2 emission for each of the chosen transportation routes. Note that inventory logic can be used for the last (mile) distribution by dividing this distance by two if making several stops for delivering goods. This assumes equal distances between the target towns and equal distribution of supply between the towns.

Finally, the eco-efficiency of the market can be calculated as shown in Eq. 3:

$$\text{Profit per ton } CO_2 = \frac{\text{Profitability}}{(TK \times SEF \times SP) + TK \times REF \times (1 - SP)} \tag{3}$$

where TK is the total tonnes-km, SEF is the emission factor for ship, REF is the emission factor for road transport, and SP is the proportion of ship transport.

For the case company, the eco-efficiency was calculated for all clusters. For the example cluster, using Eq. 3, it was calculated to be € 13.5K and € 22K profit per ton CO_2 emitted for road transportation and sea transportation, respectively.

Figure 2 (next page) depicts an extract of Norway and some of the clusters contained within. In picture 1, an overall higher contribution margin is achieved by road transport rather than by sea transport, as seen in picture 2. There are, however, some clusters that are as good or even slightly better when using sea transport. These are often clusters located close to a port, for example, the three clusters in the red circle close to the port of Bergen. On the contrary, these clusters have a significantly higher eco-efficiency, averaging 75% higher using sea transport.

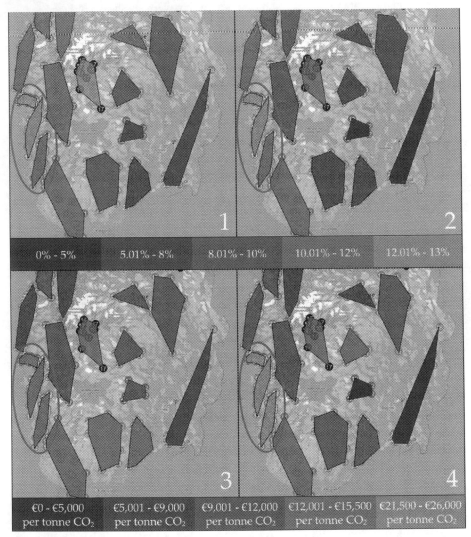

Fig. 2. The juxtaposition of the contribution margin and eco-efficiency of different areas in Norway. Picture 1 and 2 illustrates the contribution margin for road and sea transport, whereas picture 3 and 4 illustrate the eco-efficiency for road and sea transport.

4   Concluding Remarks

This model provides the case company with the possibility to test different scenarios before moving into a new market. It can help to make decisions not only based on profitability but also taking eco-efficiency into account. For the calculated example cluster, it becomes clear that even though the profitability is very similar regarding which mode of transportation to choose, the eco-efficiency of a solution using sea transportation can be employed with significantly less emission of CO_2. Furthermore, as shown in Fig. 3, a future expected increase of CO_2 tax will further impact the profitability of different modes of transport. This framework should be applicable to similar cases when important exporting decisions are to be made.

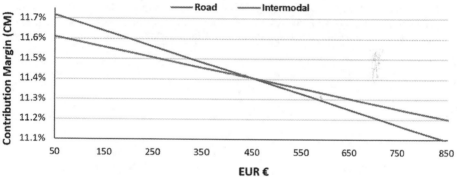

Fig. 3. The effect of increasing CO_2 tax on the contribution margin (CM) for both road and sea scenario. The CO_2 tax in Norway is currently € 53.5 per ton.

Acknowledgements. We want to thank the ØKS-Interreg program for supporting the Value2Sea project, which this article is a part of.

References

1. Freeman III, A.M., Haveman, R.H., Kneese, A.V.: The economics of environmental policy. Am. J. Agric. Econ. **55**(4-Part-1), 687–687 (1973)
2. Schaltegger, S., Sturm, A.: Environmental rationality (Ökologische Rationalität in German). Die Unternehmung **4**, 117–131 (1990)
3. Verfaillie, H., Bidwell, R.: Measuring Eco-Efficiency - a Guide to Reporting Company Performance (2000)
4. Suzuki, Y.: A dual-objective metaheuristic approach to solve practical pollution routing problem. Int. J. Prod. Econ. **17**, 143–153 (2016)
5. Chang, D.J., Morlok, E.K.: Vehicle speed profiles to minimize work and fuel consumption. J. Transp. Eng. **131**(3), 173–182 (2005). ISSN (print): 0733-947X I ISSN (online): 1943-5436

6. Raeesi, R., Zografos, K.G.: The multi-objective Steiner pollution-routing problem on congested urban road networks. Transp. Res. Part B: Methodol. **2019**(122), 457–485 (2019)
7. Tsoulfas, G.T., Pappis, C.P.: Environmental principles applicable to supply chains design and operation. J. Clean. Prod. **14**, 1593–1602 (2006)
8. Leal, I.C., de Almada Garcia, P.A., Márcio de Almeida, D.A.: A data envelopment analysis approach to choose transport modes based on eco-efficiency. Environ. Dev. Sustain. **14**(5), 767–781 (2012). https://doi.org/10.1007/s10668-012-9352-x
9. Kreutzberger, E., Macharis, C., Vereecken, L., Woxenius, J.: Is intermodal freight trans-port more environmentally friendly than all-road freight transport? A review. In: Bijdragen Vervo-erslogistieke Werkdagen 2003 (deel 1), pp. 169–197 (2003). Secretariaat Vervoerslogistieke Werkdagen p/a Connekt. https://research.tudelft.nl/en/publications/is-intermodal-transport-more-environmentally-friendly-than-all-ro. Accessed 18 June 2021
10. IRU, International RoadTransportation Union: Comparative Analysis of Energy Consumption and CO2-Emissions of Road Transport and Combined Transport Road/Rail (2002). https://www.iru.org/sites/default/files/2016-01/en-co2.pdf. Assessed 18 June 2021
11. McKinnon, A., Piecyk, A.: Measuring and Managing CO2 Emissions of European Chemical Transport, p. 20 (2010). https://cefic.org/library-item/measuring-and-managing-co2-emission-of-european-chemical-transport/. Accessed 18 June 2021

The New Digital Lean Manufacturing Paradigm

The Automation of Lean Practices: Digitalized or Digitally Wasted?

Jamila Alieva[1](✉) and Daryl Powell[2,3]

[1] Faculty of Engineering and the Environment, University of Gävle, Gävle, Sweden
jamila.alieva@hig.se
[2] SINTEF Manufacturing AS, Horten, Norway
daryl.powell@sintef.no
[3] Norwegian University of Science and Technology, Trondheim, Norway

Abstract. Lean manufacturing has experienced massive changes under the influence of Industry 4.0, with the automation of lean practices becoming common among manufacturing companies in many countries and different industries. Automating lean practices promises a number of opportunities for growth and competitiveness. One of the key advantages of lean automation has been acknowledged to be the significant reduction of waste. Meanwhile, there is also discussion of a new form of waste: *digital waste*. However, do companies consider digital waste a part of production waste? It is also unclear if automation of lean practices is a trigger for digital waste with a negative impact on value creation. This paper aims to investigate companies with automated lean practices and the particular case of digital waste in automated processes. The research is based on case studies of manufacturing based in Sweden.

Keywords: Lean · Digitalization · Digital waste · Automation · Manufacturing · Sweden

1 Introduction

Industry 4.0 is pushing the automation of lean practices [1–5]. The study of manufacturing process automation has increased spectacularly within the last few years, corresponding to the expected improvements in production, quality, and safety [6–8]. Substantial reduction of waste under the control of technologies is one of the key benefits attracting manufacturing practitioners [3, 4, 9, 10]. Lean automation leads to manufacturing transformation, with cheaper, smarter, and more adaptable processes [11]. "Industrial IT and automation have annual sales of over SEK 70 billion in Sweden, of which the Stockholm region accounts for 70%" [12]. The Norwegian Research Council initiated the project to promote small and medium enterprise (SME) cooperation and flexibility by automating the manufacturing processes within the Norwegian SMEs to help them stay competitive in global competition [13]. Two definitions of lean automation are the networking of equipment and people for rapid communication with the aid of digitalization [14], or the establishment of the platform and connective mechanisms to utilize data analytics from the real world [15]. Lean automation is also associated with a disruptive digital technology from Industry 4.0. It emphasizes the importance of adoption levels of technologies based on the performance of the companies, as well as how advanced the adoption of their lean practices is [4]. Research findings also indicate the positive correlation between Industry 4.0 technologies and lean practices, with a high potential to overcome traditional barriers and challenges of the lean management approach [3, 16].

Indeed, while the potential benefits that adoption of lean automation can bring are discussed by researchers [2–5, 8–10], studies investigating potential risks associated with automating lean practices are lacking. The topic of digital waste is relatively new in the field of lean manufacturing [17, 18]. We need a deeper discussion of digital waste in the context of lean automation.

2 Literature Review

2.1 Lean, Waste and Industry 4.0

The elimination of waste (muda) was discussed in 1990 in The Machine that Changed the World [19] through a five-stage process: specification of value, identification of value stream, creation of flow, pulling the product as needed, and aiming for perfection. Often, lean production was primarily associated with elimination of waste as excess inventory or excess capacity to impact the variability in supply, processing time, or demand [20].

In the digital era, a new way of lean thinking integrated with digital technologies— sensors, CPS, Internet of Things (IoT), and social networks—has arisen [21]. Industry 4.0 and lean methodology have a strong correlation while sharing similar priorities of waste reduction and efficiency gains [22]. The new concept of digital lean manufacturing involves human capabilities and strategic digital technologies, as well as quality planning, control, and improvement [23]. Industry 4.0 should not be treated as a single technology. Instead, it integrates product, process, and system levels to reveal its potential for advance manufacturing competitiveness [24].

Manufacturers need to systematically combine lean thinking and practices with advanced industry 4.0 technologies to build competitive advantage in the digital era and implement successful lean transformation through improved performance and capability. By applying "lean and learn" as a lens for strategic lean practice automation, learning can play a vital role in the continuous improvement process [25]. Learning in combination with an automation approach would improve the efficiency of manufacturing processes and develop the workforce skills to adopt advanced automation solutions [25–27].

The topic of digital waste is sensitive in the context of growing volumes of data in close to real time. A "lean data approach" was developed for information aggregation to derive machine-based knowledge [28]. Digital waste has been discussed as buffer waste in the context of the cyber-physical production system from four interdependent perspectives: physical to physical, physical to digital, digital to physical, and digital to digital [18]. It has also been defined as any non-value-adding digital activity to women/men, materials, machines, methods, measurements and it can appear due to lost digital opportunities and/or overuse of the digital capabilities of new digital manufacturing technologies [29]. In this paper, we follow the definition of digital waste as uncollected, unprocessed, or misinterpreted data in the production process [17].

2.2 Industry 4.0 and Technology

Among a number of resources tested as essential for Industry 4.0 adoption, production systems (product and process traceability), and big data analytics (big data processing capability) were recognized as key [30]. Production data employing servers, sensors, and cloud computing have impacted data exchange procedures that became more complex. Lean manufacturing and the decision-making process are likely to be improved on the process level with the integration of data analytics and IoT [31]. The increased amount of production data requires autonomous monitoring, control, and optimization of value creation processes through the lean-data approach. There is a need for new, process-based technological solutions, such as decentralized sensor systems dealing with growing volumes of data at close to real time with an accuracy of more than 95% [32, 33].

Industry 4.0 offers technologies for product improvement and innovation of manufacturing operations. It is important not to dismiss the focus on smart products through simulation, additive manufacturing, and augmented reality [34]. 3D printing is one of the examples of smart product concept early in the product life cycle, as the foundation for building multifunctional structures as smart products with integrated sensors in the manufacturing process chain [35]. Big data analytics, additive manufacturing, and sustainable smart manufacturing technologies are beneficial to manufacturing enterprises to make better decisions for the beginning-of-life stage of the product life cycle [36, 37].

The lean method can integrate new technologies and allow better support of continuous improvement in the world of increasing product complexity. Smart products are connected to sensors and able to store a large amount of data, self-process, and communicate with industrial systems throughout their in-service life [38]. Data prediction has increased popularity in the manufacturing sector for the planning and control forecasting and covering the entire life cycle of a product. Service-oriented and cloud-based technologies are implemented throughout the supply chain to ensure secure data access for testing, prototyping, and factory optimization [39]. Additive manufacturing, augmented reality, and 3D simulation of product/service development and production processes are promising technologies in the Industry 4.0 environment. They disruptively change supply chains, business models, and business processes through interoperability, virtualization, decentralization, real-time capability, service orientation, and modularity [40]. A study at an auto-parts manufacturing firm [2] discovered the combination of lean manufacturing and Industry 4.0, where the positive influence of smart production control and cyber-physical systems optimized lead times, non-value-added time, and value-added time by 25.60%, 56.20% and 24.68%, respectively.

2.3 Internally Related Lean Practice

Production scheduling involves continuous flow processes that provide support for achieving production of standardized products, and control of product flow forecasting approaches and monitoring take time [41]. The synergy between quality and lean practices leads to an improved flow process [42]. For increased productivity and a better working environment for the operator, a one-piece flow technique is used to manufacture product components. The flow describes the sequence of transient activities in a process within a single stage of production within a certain time frame. It increases the number of products through the process steps simultaneously [43].

Identification of techniques for setup time reduction is listed as one of the biggest challenges faced by automobile component manufacturing firms while implementing lean [44]. Some of the reasons for increased setup time are underutilization of creel, lack of tools, improper scheduling [45]. The single-minute exchange of dies is a lean technique that involves separation and conversion of internal setup operations into external operations. The goal of the technique is to achieve a setup time of less than ten minutes [46]. Advanced manufacturing is moving towards mass customization, where long setup times between variants are unacceptable for the competitive priority through process technology [47].

2.4 Supplier and Customer Related Lean Practices

Supplier management was highlighted as one of the most important social factors for successful lean implementations along with employee involvement, internal technical practices, and customer management. It requires long-term relations with suppliers; feedback on quality and delivery performance; close contact with suppliers, especially senior management on the most important issues related to suppliers' involvement [48]. The just-in-time (JIT) lean purchasing approach is very convenient for long-term relations with suppliers. It can be optimized in three dimensions: management, financial, and technological. Technological dimension improvement expects partners to be more willing to share/give access to technology. It can also motivate partners to participate in product design based on knowledge and commitment to the other partner. Supplier involvement in design could lead to improved quality and reduced time to market [49]. Supplier integration is positively associated with the speed of new product introduction, but it does not support lean practices for operational performance indicators. Lean practices are positively associated with operational performance indicators, but not with delivery [50].

Companies widely consider customer involvement to help with issues such as quality standards, facilitating customer participation in product development processes, and technical assistance [51]. Customer focus was recognized as one of the key success (external) factors for lean manufacturing, along with government intervention [52]. Customer focus addresses emerging customer requirements and expectations, manages customer relationships, and defines customer satisfaction [53]. The relationship between lean and customer-focused performance is mediated by process improvement. Lean is positively related to customer-focused performance in an environment where customer effectiveness is considered important [54]. The level of lean maturity is related to customer focus, especially regarding external customer involvement in product development [51]. Attention to customer satisfaction, customer relationships, and customer involvement are discussed in the context of indicators of soft lean practices and have an impact on quality. Among the hard lean practices, total quality management is an indicator for the delivery to customers [55].

2.5 Theoretical Framework

A summary of our theory can be seen in Fig. 1:

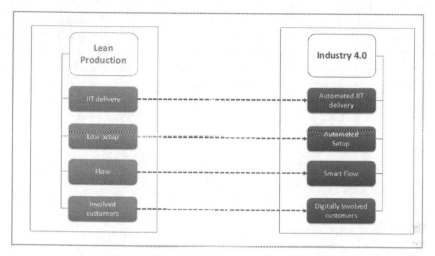

Fig. 1. Theoretical framework of this study.

3 Method

Qualitative study was conducted through two case studies. The data was collected through the semi-structed interviews with plant managers [56]. There were several criteria in selection of cases [57]. The first, both companies are following lean principles. The second, both companies are the same size – SME. The third, both companies engaged with technologies in their production.

4 Results

Company A, based in Gävle, Sweden, has 20 years of experience in customized switchboard production for private companies. There are 22 people employed by the company, with an average age of 40 years and approximately 95% of employees are males. Each switchboard is assembled by one employee within approximately 24 h at one working desk. Consequently, there is no need for automated setup or smart flow, due to the nature and simplicity of the tasks. Daily interactions with customers are time-consuming and often require middle management involvement to negotiate delivery, price discounts, or order specifications. All the information is saved on the company's drive and is not sorted or processed systematically for continuous improvements. However, Company A has very automated relations with their suppliers. About 60% of orders are packed by robots, with zero human interaction. In cases when the order formulation is done by robot, it is possible to receive wrong items inside the box. The items are accompanied by packing slips. In the case of a robot mistake, the description on paper is correct (matching the order), but the items inside the box are wrong.

Company B, established in Sweden in 2013, works closely with three sister companies. There are 16 male employees with an average age of 35 years working one shift at the plant, which is based in Gävle. The company produces stairs and railings made from steel, with a focus on firefighting stairs. Their standard portfolio of stairs allows assembly of one order within 20 h from the half-finished items supplied by their partners. Communication with suppliers is dominantly digital, via ERP systems and emails. About 30% of orders are packed by robots, leading to a problem like that faced by Company A. The supplier might also delay the delivery due to poor digital order management and uncollected orders attached to emails from Company B. As a result, delivery to customers of company B can be delayed. It is outsourced to a post company and all the communication is fully digital. Often, delays can't be fixed without personal interaction between management and the outsource company.

5   Discussion

We suggest that the automation of supplier-related lean practices can lead to digital waste in product- and service-oriented technologies. The case company managers reflected that the number of mistakes caused by robots during automated JIT delivery is very small (1% of orders). Yet it is important to recognize the mistakes done by robots and associate this with digital waste, specifically misinterpreted data. There is evidence of digital waste in supplier-related lean practices with service-oriented technologies. Suppliers might miss or ignore emails with attached orders unless they receive a phone call or personal confirmation. There is no evidence of digital waste in internal lean practices, due to the absence of automation processes, which can be associated with the small size of the enterprise and the lack of need to automate setup time or the flow of manufacturing processes. In customer-related lean practices on service-oriented technologies, the delivery service that outsources to a third party and misleading information of delivery address can cause delay and digital waste. A summary of our results can be seen in Table 1. The digital waste is 'not available' when the lean practice is not automated, consequently it cannot generate the digital waste at any product, process or service levels. The digital waste is 'not detected' when lea practice it is automated, but it is not causing any obvious digital waste.

Table 1. Digital waste detection.

Underlying Construct	Lean Practice	Product oriented technology	Service oriented technology	Process oriented technology
Supplier related	Automated JIT delivery	DIGITAL WASTE	DIGITAL WASTE	Not detected
Internally related	Automated setup	Not available	Not available	Not available
	Smart flow	Not available	Not available	Not available
Customer related	Digitally involved customers	Not available	DIGITAL WASTE	Not available

6 Conclusion and Further Work

Digital waste was detected in product- and service-oriented technologies through automation of supplier- and customer-related lean practices. There was no digital waste detected in the process-oriented technologies. Internal lean practices were not automated in the cases investigated in this paper, so no digital waste potentially could be investigated in those technologies. The study contributes to the discussion of both production waste [19, 20] and digital waste [17, 18, 29] under the influence of Industry 4.0. It also contributes to the discussion of automating lean practices [3, 4] at the product, process, and system levels [24]. This study aims to encourage practitioners to detect digital waste and work on reducing it. Practitioners might also be motivated to consider digital waste as part of production waste and include it in value stream mapping. This study discussing the digital waste only in the context of lean manufacturing. The study is also limited to SME companies, where internally related lean practices are not automated. This study is limited to Swedish manufacturing plants located in the Gävle region. The study is also limited to only four lean practices. The technologies discussed in the study are limited by robots. Further research could investigate digital waste in automated lean practices such as: smart suppliers' development, automated pull, digitally controlled processes, employee involvement in digital technologies, and smart productive maintenance outside of Sweden.

Acknowledgements. The authors would like to acknowledge support from the Research Council of Norway for the project Lean Digital and the Center for Logistics and Innovative Production research group at the University of Gävle for the project Lean and Digitalization.

References

1. Jasperneite, J., Sauter, T., Wollschlaeger, M.: Why we need automation models: handling complexity in Industry 4.0 and the Internet of Things. IEEE Ind. Electron. Mag. **14**(1), 29–40 (2020)
2. Amjad, M., Rafique, M., Hussain, S., Khan, M.: A new vision of LARG manufacturing — a trail towards Industry 4.0. CIRP J. Manuf. Sci. Technol. **31**, 377–393 (2020)
3. Tortorella, G., Sawhney, R., Jurburg, D., de Paula, I.C., Tlapa, D., Thurer, M.: Towards the proposition of a Lean Automation framework: integrating Industry 4.0 into lean production. J. Manuf. Technol. Manag. (2020)
4. Tortorella, G.L., Narayanamurthy, G., Thurer, M.: Identifying pathways to a high-performing lean automation implementation: an empirical study in the manufacturing industry. Int. J. Prod. Econ. **231**, 107918 (2021)
5. Shahin, M., Chen, F.F., Bouzary, H., Krishnaiyer, K.: Integration of lean practices and Industry 4.0 technologies: smart manufacturing for next-generation enterprises. Int. J. Adv. Manuf. Technol. **107**(5–6), 2927–2936 (2020). https://doi.org/10.1007/s00170-020-05124-0
6. Lazai, M., et al.: Automated system gains in lean manufacturing improvement projects. Procedia Manuf. **51**, 1340–1347 (2020)
7. Frontoni, E., Rosetti, R., Paolanti, M., Alves, A.: HATS project for lean and smart global logistic: a shipping company case study. Manuf. Lett. **23**, 71–74 (2020)
8. Pantano, M., Regulin, D., Lutz, B., Lee, D.: A human-cyber-physical system approach to lean automation using an Industrie 4.0 reference architecture. Procedia Manuf. **51**, 1082–1090 (2020)
9. Purushothaman, M., Seadon, J., Moore, D.: Waste reduction using lean tools in a multicultural environment. J. Cleaner Prod. **265**, 121681 (2020)
10. Ejsmont, K., Gladysz, B., Corti, D., Castaño, F., Mohammed, W., Martinez Lastra, J.: Towards "lean Industry 4.0" – current trends and future perspectives. Cogent Bus. Manag. **7**(1), 1781995 (2020)
11. Tilley, J.: Automation, robotics, and the factory of the future (2017). https://www.mckinsey.com/business-functions/operations/our-insights/automation-robotics-and-the-factory-of-the-future
12. Sharp rise of industrial IT and automation. https://www.investstockholm.com/news/sharp-rise-of-industrial-it-and-automation/. Accessed Feb 2021
13. Wadhwa, R.: Flexibility in manufacturing automation: a living lab case study of Norwegian metalcasting SMEs. J. Manuf. Syst. **31**(4), 444–454 (2012)
14. Palange, A., Dhatrak, P.: Lean manufacturing: a vital tool to enhance productivity in manufacturing. Materials Today (2021)
15. Abd Rahman, M.S.B., Mohamad, E., Abdul Rahman, A.A.B.: Development of IoT—enabled data analytics enhance decision support system for lean manufacturing process improvement. Concurr. Eng. (2021)
16. Buer, S., Semini, M., Strandhagen, J., Sgarbossa, F.: The complementary effect of lean manufacturing and digitalisation on operational performance. Int. J. Prod. Res. **59**(7), 1976–1992 (2020)
17. Alieva, J., Haartman, R.: Digital muda – the new form of waste by Industry 4.0. Oper. Supply Chain Manag. Int. J. **13**(3), 269–278 (2020)
18. Romero, D., Gaiardelli, P., Thürer, M., Powell, D., Wuest, T.: Cyber-physical waste identification and elimination strategies in the digital lean manufacturing world. In: Ameri, F., Stecke, K.E., von Cieminski, G., Kiritsis, D. (eds.) APMS 2019. IAICT, vol. 566, pp. 37–45. Springer, Cham (2019). https://doi.org/10.1007/978-3-030-30000-5_5
19. Womack, J., Jones, D.: The Machine that Changed the World. Rawson, New York (1990)

20. Shah, R., Ward, P.: Defining and developing measures of lean production. J. Oper. Manag. **25**, 785–805 (2007)
21. Cattaneo, L., Rossi, M., Negri, E., Powell, D., Terzi, S.: Lean thinking in the digital era. In: Ríos, J., Bernard, A., Bouras, A., Foufou, S. (eds.) PLM 2017. IAICT, vol. 517, pp. 371–381. Springer, Cham (2017). https://doi.org/10.1007/978-3-319-72905-3_33
22. Pavlovic, D., Milosavljevic, P., Miladenovic, S.: Synergy between Industry 4.0 and lean methodology. J. Mechatron. Autom. Identif. Technol. **5**(4), 17–20 (2020)
23. Romero, D., Gaiardelli, P., Powell, D., Wuest, T., Thürer, M.: Total quality management and quality circles in the digital lean manufacturing world. In: Ameri, F., Stecke, K.E., von Cieminski, G., Kiritsis, D. (eds.) APMS 2019. IAICT, vol. 566, pp. 3–11. Springer, Cham (2019). https://doi.org/10.1007/978-3-030-30000-5_1
24. Enyoghasi, C., Badurdeen, F.: Industry 4.0 for sustainable manufacturing: opportunities at the product, process, and system levels. Resour. Conserv. Recycl. **166**, 105362 (2021)
25. Bäckstrand, J., Powell, D.: Enhancing supply chain capabilities in an eto context through "lean and learn." Oper. Supply Chain Manag. **14**(3), 360–367 (2021)
26. Romero, D., Gaiardelli, P., Powell, D., Wuest, T., Thürer, M.: Rethinking jidoka systems under automation & learning perspectives in the digital lean manufacturing world. IFAC-PapersOnLine **52**(13), 899–903 (2019)
27. Solheim, A.B., Powell, D.J.: A learning roadmap for digital lean manufacturing. In: Lalic, B., Majstorovic, V., Marjanovic, U., von Cieminski, G., Romero, D. (eds.) APMS 2020. IAICT, vol. 592, pp. 417–424. Springer, Cham (2020). https://doi.org/10.1007/978-3-030-57997-5_48
28. Küfnera, T., Schönigb, S., Jasinskic, R., Ermer, A.: Vertical data continuity with lean edge analytics for industry 4.0 production. Comput. Ind. **125**, 103389 (2021)
29. Romero, D., Gaiardelli, P., Powell, D., Wuest, T., Thürer, M.: digital lean cyber-physical production systems: the emergence of digital lean manufacturing and the significance of digital waste. In: Moon, I., Lee, G.M., Park, J., Kiritsis, D., von Cieminski, G. (eds.) APMS 2018. IAICT, vol. 535, pp. 11–20. Springer, Cham (2018). https://doi.org/10.1007/978-3-319-99704-9_2
30. Bag, S., Yadav, G., Dhamija, P., Kataria, K.: Key resources for industry 4.0 adoption and its effect on sustainable production and circular economy: an empirical study. J. Cleaner Prod. **281**, 125233 (2021)
31. Soufhwee, M., Effendi, M., Azwan, A.: Development of IoT-enabled data analytics enhance decision support system for lean manufacturing process improvement. Concurr. Eng. Res. Appl. (2021). https://doi.org/10.1177/1063293X20987911
32. Küfnera, T., Schönigb, S., Jasinskic, R., Ermerc, A.: Vertical data continuity with lean edge analytics for industry 4.0 production. Comput. Ind. **125**, 103389 (2021)
33. Schmidt, D., Diez, J.V., Ordieres-Meré, J., Gevers, R., Schwiep, J., Molina, M.: Industry 4.0 lean shopfloor management characterization using EEG sensors and deep learning. Sensors **20**(10), 2860 (2020)
34. Powell, D., Romero, D., Gaiardelli, P., Cimini, C., Cavalieri, S.: Towards digital lean cyber-physical production systems: industry 4.0 technologies as enablers of leaner production. In: Moon, I., Lee, G.M., Park, J., Kiritsis, D., von Cieminski, G. (eds.) APMS 2018. IAICT, vol. 536, pp. 353–362. Springer, Cham (2018). https://doi.org/10.1007/978-3-319-99707-0_44
35. Lenz, J., MacDonald, E., Harik, R., Wuest, T.: Optimizing smart manufacturing systems by extending the smart products paradigm to the beginning of life. J. Manuf. Syst. **57**, 274–286 (2020). https://doi.org/10.1016/j.jmsy.2020.10.001
36. Majeed, A., et al.: A big data-driven framework for sustainable and smart additive manufacturing. Robot. Comput.-Integr. Manuf. **67**, 102026 (2021). https://doi.org/10.1016/j.rcim.2020.102026

37. Yang, Y., Dong, Z., Meng, Y., Shao, C.: Data-driven intelligent 3D surface measurement in smart manufacturing: review and outlook. Machines **9**(1), 13 (2021). https://doi.org/10.3390/machines9010013
38. Saxby, R., Cano-Kurouklis, M., Viza, E.: An initial assessment of lean management methods for Industry 4.0. TQM J. **32**(4), 587–601 (2020). https://doi.org/10.1108/TQM-12-2019-0298
39. Caiado, R., Scavarda, L., Gavião, L., Ivson, P., Nascimento, D., Garza-Reyes, J.: A fuzzy rule-based industry 4.0 maturity model for operations and supply chain management. Int. J. Prod. Econ. **231**, 107883 (2021)
40. Marcucci, G., Antomarioni, S., Ciarapica, F., Bevilacqua, M.: The impact of operations and IT-related Industry 4.0 key technologies on organizational resilience. Prod. Plan. Control (2021). https://doi.org/10.1080/09537287.2021.1874702
41. Yadav, G., Luthra, S., Huisingh, D., Mangla, S., Narkhede, B., Liu, Y.: Development of a lean manufacturing framework to enhance its adoption within manufacturing companies in developing economies. J. Cleaner Prod. **245**, 118726 (2020). https://doi.org/10.1016/j.jclepro.2019.118726
42. Onofrei, G., Fynes, B., Nguyen, H., Azadnia, A.: Quality and lean practices synergies: a swift even flow perspective. Int. J. Qual. Reliab. Manag. **38**(1), 98–115 (2020). https://doi.org/10.1108/IJQRM-11-2019-0360
43. Ioana, A., Maria, E., Cristina, V.: Case study regarding the implementation of one-piece flow line in automotive company. Procedia Manuf. **46**, 244–248 (2020). https://doi.org/10.1016/j.promfg.2020.03.036
44. Sahoo, S.: Assessing lean implementation and benefits within Indian automotive component manufacturing SMEs. Benchmarking Int. J. **27**(3), 1042–1084 (2020). https://doi.org/10.1108/BIJ-07-2019-0299
45. Mohan Prasad, M., Dhiyaneswari, J., Ridzwanul Jamaan, J., Mythreyan, S., Sutharsan, S.: A framework for lean manufacturing implementation in Indian textile industry. Mater. Today Proc. **33**(7), 2986–2995 (2020). https://doi.org/10.1016/j.matpr.2020.02.979
46. Gomero-Campos, A., Mejia-Huayhua, R., Leon-Chavarri, C., Raymundo-Ibañez, C., Dominguez, F.: Lean manufacturing production management model using the Johnson method approach to reduce delivery delays for printing production lines in the digital graphic design industry. IOP Conf. Ser. Mater. Sci. Eng. **796**, 012002 (2020). https://doi.org/10.1088/1757-899X/796/1/012002
47. Omoush, M.: An integrated model of lean manufacturing techniques and technological process to attain the competitive priority. Manag. Sci. Lett. **10**(13), 3107–3118 (2020). https://doi.org/10.5267/j.msl.2020.5.012
48. Malik, M., Abdallah, S.: The relationship between organizational attitude and lean practices: an organizational sense-making perspective. Ind. Manag. Data Syst. **120**(9), 1715–1731 (2020). https://doi.org/10.1108/IMDS-09-2019-0460
49. Taghipour, A., Hoang, P., Cao, X.: Just in time/lean purchasing approach: an investigation for research and applications. J. Adv. Manag. Sci. **8**(2), 43–48 (2020). https://doi.org/10.18178/joams.8.2.43-4
50. Bento, G.S., Schuldt, K.S., Carvalho, L.C.: The influence of supplier integration and lean practices adoption on operational performance. Gestão Produção **27**(1), e3339 (2020). https://doi.org/10.1590/0104-530X3339-20
51. Bento, G., Tontini, G.: Maturity of lean practices in Brazilian manufacturing companies. Total Qual. Manag. Bus. Excellence **30**(1), S114–S128 (2019). https://doi.org/10.1080/14783363.2019.1665827
52. Alefari, M., Almanei, M., Salonitis, K.: Lean manufacturing, leadership and employees: the case of UAE SME manufacturing companies. Prod. Manuf. Res. **8**(1), 222–243 (2020). https://doi.org/10.1080/21693277.2020.1781704

53. Bento, G., Tontini, G.: Developing an instrument to measure lean manufacturing maturity and its relationship with operational performance. Total Qual. Manag. Bus. Excell. **29**(9–10), 977–995 (2018). https://doi.org/10.1080/14783363.2018.1486537
54. van Assen, M.: Lean, process improvement and customer-focused performance. The moderating effect of perceived organisational context. Total Qual. Manag. Bus. Excell. **32**(1–2), 57–75 (2021). https://doi.org/10.1080/14783363.2018.1530591
55. Sahoo, S.: Lean manufacturing practices and performance: the role of social and technical factors. Int. J. Qual. Reliab. Manag. **37**(5), 732–754 (2019). https://doi.org/10.1108/IJQRM-03-2019-0099
56. Yin, R.: Case Study Research: Design and Methods. Sage Publications, Thousand Oaks (2014)
57. Voss, C., Johnson, M., Godsell, J.: Case research. In: Karlsson, C. (ed.) Research Methods for Operations Management, 2nd edn., pp. 165–193. Routledge, London (2016)

Study of the Predictive Mechanism with Big Data-Driven Lean Manufacturing and Six Sigma Methodology

Hong Chen$^{(\boxtimes)}$ ⓘ, JianDe Wu ⓘ, Wei Zhang, Qing Guo, and HuiFeng Lu

College of Electrical Engineering, Zhejiang University, 310027 Hangzhou,
People's Republic of China
chenhonghz@zju.edu.cn

Abstract. In order to achieve the sustainable development, the predictive mechanism with big data-driven Lean Manufacturing and Six Sigma methodology is proposed in this paper. The sustainable development for serious competition is often studied, however, the predictive mechanism with big data-driven Lean Manufacturing and Six Sigma methodology is seldom mentioned in publications. This paper reports the predictive mechanism from the perspective of big data-driven Lean Manufacturing. The key techniques including PLC communication, DMAIC roadmap, SPC technique and Hypothesis Testing are utilized to eliminate the waste and obtain continuous improvement. The demonstration of calculator production indicates the predictive mechanism can effectively eliminate the waste and improve the output by 60% with the sufficient capability of $Cp > 1.33$ and $Cpk > 1$.

Keywords: Predictive mechanism · Lean manufacturing · Six sigma · DMAIC · Statistical process control · Hypothesis testing

1 Introduction

It is very important for the industrial company to achieve the sustainable development for the increased competition. The increased competition is based on the sustainable development. The sustainable development roots in the forecast and the current capability. The variation in current capability can cause the unacceptable output in technology, management, operation and production. If the variation can be predicted and eliminated at the first occurrence, the remedy cost can be saved. So it is necessary to set up the Predictive Mechanism (PM) to prevent the potential out of control accident from happening. The Big Data and the Internet of Things (IoT) are often studied in Industry 4.0. However, the PM with big data-driven Lean Manufacturing is seldom emphasized in publications.

In the 21st century the industrial revolution starts with the automation and the IoT to bring the new production scheme and the smart products. The big data is the outcome of IoT [1]. Digitalization-based manufacture is often referred to as Industry 4.0 [2]. The

© IFIP International Federation for Information Processing 2021
Published by Springer Nature Switzerland AG 2021
A. Dolgui et al. (Eds.): APMS 2021, IFIP AICT 633, pp. 662–672, 2021.
https://doi.org/10.1007/978-3-030-85910-7_70

data from IoT in manufacturing site is big volume, real-time, variety in operation, pure and practical digitals, which is called as Big Data. In this research the Big Data is the base of PM with Lean Manufacturing (LM) and Six Sigma methodology.

The LM corresponds to a system that addresses a range of practical management applications [3]. Increased competition means that lean paradigms are increasingly employed to reduce waste and improve productivity: to reduce non-value-added activities and create value for the customer [4]. Lean origins are linked to the Toyota production system, which was a manufacturer's principle, attributed to engineers from Japan [5]. Now LM becomes popular in industry for its reducing waste. The waste are caused by variance in process. One method to analyze process issues and variance is Six Sigma and was developed in the 1980s by Motorola and is analogous to previous improvement techniques, such as, total quality management [4]. From a business point of view, it is used to improve the effectiveness and efficiency of all operations to meet or exceed the customers' needs and expectations [6]. The waste often cause the quality out of control. The Big Data can be analyzed by Six Sigma methodology to find and reduce the variation of process for the quality control and continuous improvement. PM can ensure LM and LM can help to achieve high productivity and sustainable development. In this research, the Echelon company's LonWorks technology is utilized to get the real-time Big Data and the data is analyzed by Six Sigma methodology to find the source of variations, which drive and achieve LM in PM.

The paper is structured as follows. This first section presented the initial considerations and the aim of this research. Section 2 presents the systematic literature review and PM workflow. Section 3 introduces the case study. Section 4 performs a general discussion and then conclude in Sect. 5.

2 Literature Review and PM Design

2.1 Literature Review

Lean Manufacturing
LM is a business concept and philosophy in management to minimize the amount of time and resources used to get the customer satisfaction. The lean principles provide perfect quality to satisfy the customer's demand and at the same time minimize the non-value-adding activities [7]. The minimum non-value-activities means the maximum customer satisfaction. The LM tools includes JIT, Kanban, Poka-Yoke, VSM, Kaizen and TPM [8]. The LM with eliminating waste is to achieve customer satisfaction, on time delivery, cost reduction and quality assurance. Both Total Productive maintenance (TPM) and Six Sigma are key business process strategies to enhance manufacturing performance [9]. As Six Sigma adopts a data driven philosophy, the opportunities provided by big data environments would be a natural fit [10].

Six Sigma Methodology
Six Sigma is a data-driven approach using specific tools and methodologies that lead to fact-based decision-making. This is a continuous improvement to reduce process variability and eliminate waste [11]. The data-driven nature of Six Sigma applied in

a big data environment can provide competitive advantages by implementation of the problem solving strategy – define, measure, analyze, improve and control (DMAIC) [6]. DMAIC is a systematic and scientific method, based on facts that contribute to the improvement of processes [12].

Since variability is often a major source of poor quality, statistical techniques, including Statistical Process Control (SPC) and designed experiments are the major tools of quality control and improvement [13]. When the quality characteristics of the process distributes with the specification limit at three standard deviation σ either side of the mean, the variability in this process are at least six standard deviation from the mean [13]. The Process Capability Indices of SPC indicates the statistical characteristics of process. The Process Capability Indices include the process potential index Cp and the process performance index Cpk. The equation of double-sided distribution is in (1) [14].

$$Cp = \frac{USL - LSL}{6\sigma}$$
$$Cpk = \min\left(\frac{USL - \mu}{3\sigma}, \frac{\mu - LSL}{3\sigma}\right) \tag{1}$$

Where USL and LSL are the upper and the lower specification limits, μ and σ are the average value and the standard deviation. The process potential ability is sufficient when Cp > 1.33 and the process performance ability is sufficient when Cpk > 1 [14]. The Cp will increase as the mean of the process measurement center to the target with high potential. The Cpk is the distance of the process mean and the specification limit.

A Hypothesis Testing was applied to understand the process performance for the real data [15]. Hypothesis Testing can check either modified input could improve the process outcome or not [15]. The null hypothesis and the alternative hypothesis are set up by checking the P-Value of 0.05.

2.2 PM Design

The research of PM is to eliminate the non-value-activities and keep the process control in supply chain management. The PM is set up based on the big data-driven LM and Six Sigma Methodology (see Fig. 1).

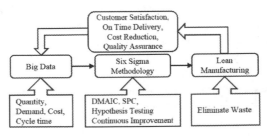

Fig. 1. Predictive mechanism

The idea of Industry 4.0 pivots around extensive automation, intelligization and digitization of the processes in a data-driven environment [16]. Industry 4.0 is driven by data and the rapid development of Industry 4.0 technologies has led to the explosive growth of data in almost every industry and business area [17]. The Power Line Carrier Communication (PLC) is suitable for the data acquisition and machine to machine talking in manufacturing site. Narrowband PLC (NB-PLC) technology is a data communication via LV electric power grids which operates in the frequency bandwidth of 0–500 kHz and provides data rates of tens of kb/s [18]. If compared to the broadband PLC (BPL, 1.7–250 MHz), which commonly requires a number of repeaters with a shorter distance among devices, NB-PLC has been considered the technology with best tradeoff among communication distance range, low data rate requirement, and implementation cost [18]. The LonWorks technology of Echelon company is utilized to set up the acquisition of Big Data. Routing is realized by tunneling LonTalk protocol telegrams in IP standard frames [19]. The software in control layer is programmed by C language in LonWorks (see Fig. 2).

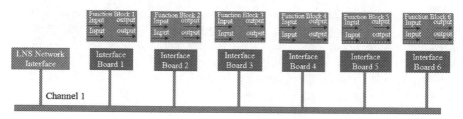

Fig. 2. Software design for IoT

The Function Block in Fig. 2 is programmed according to the hardware connection in LonWorks field bus with input ports and output ports. The hardware of interface board is designed (see Fig. 3).

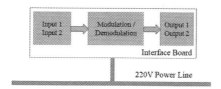

Fig. 3. Structure of interface board

The interface board get the data and the power supply by 220 V power line in blue color. The signal is modulated and demodulated in the interface board.

3 Case Study

The PM is implemented in the calculator manufacturing. DMAIC roadmap is utilized to implement PM. The manufacturing process includes PCB Printing, PCBA Testing, LCD Assembly, Housing Assembly, Function Testing, Cosmetic Checking, Quality Checking, and then pack to ship out (see Fig. 4).

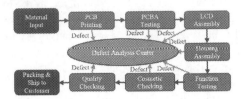

Fig. 4. Manufacturing process of calculator

All of the parts in "Pass" status stay on production line to send to next station with green arrows. All of the defects are sent to the Defect Analysis Center (DAC) to be repaired with brown arrows. The data of facility running and material quantity are supervised with the output of production line every day. PM is used in this case study to predict and eliminate the variation with DMAIC roadmap. The target output is 400 pieces of finished goods every day. However, the maximum quantity of the finished goods is 250 pieces.

Define
The material is input and the finished goods is the output of production line. The output quantity has 37.5% less than the target output every day. The data of material quantity and the finished goods within ten days are plotted (see Fig. 5).

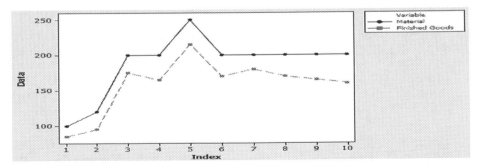

Fig. 5. Ten days' data of material qty. and finished goods qty.

The analysis indicates that the material quantity in black color is much higher than the quantity of the finished goods in red color, which indicates the defects and failure rate are high.

Measure

The quantity of the material and Working-In-Progress (WIP) are accumulated on each station in production line. The working station on production line are listed by number as PCB Printing as 1, PCBA Testing as 2, LCD Assembly as 3, Housing Assembly as 4, Function Testing as 5, Cosmetic Checking as 6, Quality Checking as 7 (see Fig. 6).

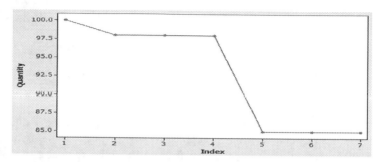

Fig. 6. Material and WIP quantity measurement on production line

The quantity changes on the stations of No. 2 and No. 5. The No. 2 indicates PCBA Testing and the No. 5 indicates Function Testing station. The reduced quantity means that the defect is sent to Defect Analysis Center.

Analyze

The defect from the PCBA Testing station is analyzed that LCD connector on PCBA is skewed. The defect from the Function Testing station is analyzed and the LCD flex cable dropped out of skewed connector so as to cause No Display issue. The flex cable dropped out is caused by the skewed connector. Thus the SMT printing need be checked from the solder, the connector material, the SMT printing machine to the stencil. It is found out that the connector layout and the connector position on stencil are different (see Fig. 7).

Fig. 7. Connector Layout (left) in green color and Connector hole on stencil (right) in black color

The connector hole on the stencil in black color is unfit for the connector layout. The solder on the PCB is less than expectation, which causes the connector skewed and flex cable dropped out. The stencil need get the same size as connector layout. At the same time the repairing of No Display issue causes the housing material scrap in DAC.

Improve

The root causes of the defects are found and the corrective action plan can be considered to set up. Firstly the new stencil same as connector layout need be made. Secondly the LCD Assembly is advised to combine with the PCBA Testing in order to reduce the housing scrap. The new process is analyzed (see Fig. 8).

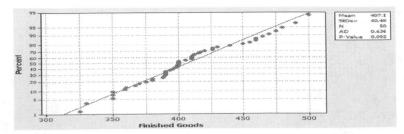

Fig. 8. Probability plot for finished goods in improved process

The null hypothesis and the alternative hypothesis in Hypothesis Testing are set up with checking P-Value of 0.05. The P-Value of the finished goods per day is 0.092 in the probability plot, which is larger than the hypothesis checking value 0.05 and the null hypothesis cannot be rejected. Thus the data of finished goods is in normality distribution. The output with new stencil and improved process can reach the maximum 520 pieces and average 407 pieces per day, which meets the target and the non-value-activities are effectively eliminated. The process capability is analyzed (see Fig. 9).

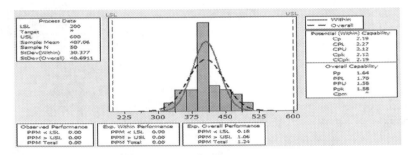

Fig. 9. Capability analysis of new process

The Process Capability means the ability of process to produce the output that are centered on the target and a very high percentage of the measurement fall within the specification. The Process Capability is sufficient with Cp > 1.33 and Cpk > 1 in Capability Analysis of new process, which meet the criteria and the corrective action plan is effective. The quantity of input material and output are analyzed to check the quality control with minimum failures (see Fig. 10).

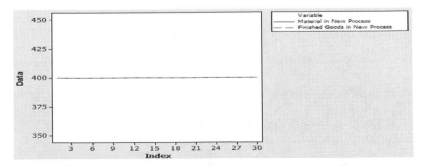

Fig. 10. Material qty. and finished goods qty. by improved process

The 30 days' input material quantity are same as the data of the finished goods, which shows the defect drops to zero.

Control

The process performance is improved with new stencil and updated process. The improved process become the Working Instruction (see Fig. 11).

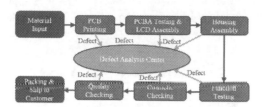

Fig. 11. Improved process with big data-driven LM

The PCBA Testing station combines with LCD Assembly to reduce the cycle time. The scrap of housing material is dropped to zero. The non-value-activities of manufacturing process is eliminated and 60% improvement for output with sufficient capability of Cp > 1.33 and Cpk > 1.

4   Discussion

4.1   Practical Contribution

In this research, the research of PM starts from the Big Data, moves to find the waste in production process, then focuses on quality control and ends at LM to achieve sustainable development. The purpose of this research is to set up the PM to maintain the sustainable development and competition enhancement in Industry 4.0.

IoT make the automation in Industry 4.0, which can make the every step in process stable and repeatable with data record. The recorded data can be analyzed by Six Sigma methodology and predict the potential waste. It is the reducing variation that the waste can be eliminated for LM and the continuous improvement can be achieved. Thus PM is very necessary to avoid that the minor variation become the big remedy cost and the loss of productivity in Industry 4.0.

PM implementation is both the continuous improvement and the sustainable development in supply chain management by three contributions. Firstly the research utilizes PLC communication with the LonWorks technology to realize the Big Data real-time acquisition in IoT operation. And the Big Data can be used for variation's real-time monitoring. Secondly the variation is the source of waste on the cost and the productivity. The Six Sigma methodology can find the source of variation by analysis of Big Data in IoT. Thirdly PM that can reduce the variation and maintain the quality control for the continuous improvement and the sustainable development with the Big Data-driven LM and Six Sigma Methodology. The continuous improvement and the sustainable development are ensured by PM with the reduced variation and the achieved LM. The case study demonstrates the effective PM workflow, which can effectively eliminate the waste and improve the output by 60% with the sufficient capability of Cp > 1.33 and Cpk > 1.

4.2 Theoretical Contribution

The research has the following theoretical values. Firstly PM set up the connection between sustainable development and the Big Data in Industry 4.0. IoT provide the automation and the real-time data acquisition, which have been reported widely for Industry 4.0 technologies. However, how to gain the value of Big Data in sustainable development and competition enhancement in Industry 4.0 is seldom discussed. It is PM that can make the Big Data drive LM in Industry 4.0 with Six Sigma Methodology which is effective in setting up the close loop for the sustainable development (see Fig. 12).

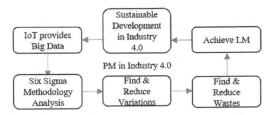

Fig. 12. PM in industry 4.0

Secondly PM can indicate the trend of development by Big Data-driven LM and Six Sigma Methodology in advance. The business decision is often made for sustainable development and the competition enhancement by business management level. PM provide the predictive operation status to business management level before their making correct decision, which is very important for industrial operation.

4.3 Limitation and Future Research

The PM is effective in sustainable development and competition enhancement in Industry 4.0. But the research has limitations. Firstly the Big Data come from the PLC network and the power supply is very important for PLC communication. The data will miss when the power supply is cut off. Secondly PM workflow need the manufacturing staff's involvement. The related function team members must be trained with the knowledge of LM and Six Sigma Methodology. The unskilled technicians are not suitable for PM.

The research of the PM is verified to be effective for calculator manufacturing. In future, the research of PM in different industries that provide other products or services may reveal different valuable results.

5 Conclusion

PM with Big Data driven LM and Six Sigma methodology is proposed in this paper to achieve sustainable development and survival in serious competition of Industry 4.0. The automation of IoT provide the data to monitor the process. The Six Sigma methodology provide the analysis to find and reduce the variation and waste to reach LM for the sustainable development in Industry 4.0.

The PM demonstrates that it is effective to improve the output by 60% with the sufficient capability of Cp > 1.33 and Cpk > 1 by Six Sigma methodology. The process output is measured with null hypothesis and alternative hypothesis by checking P-Value of 0.05 on the normality status before SPC analysis. The Process Capability of SPC is utilized to verify the improvement of the process with the acceptance criteria. The LM is obtained by the waste elimination and improved status with Big Data. The research demonstrates that PM has the practical contribution and theoretical value in sustainable development in Industry 4.0.

References

1. Roy, M., Roy, A.: Nexus of internet of things (IoT) and big data: roadmap for smart management systems (SMgS). IEEE Eng. Manag. Rev. 47(2), 104–117 (2019)
2. Vasilieva, V.A., Aleksandrovaa, S.V., Aleksandrova, M.N., Velmakinaa, Y.: Possibilities for the integration of quality management tools and methods with digital technologies. Russian Metall. 2020(13), 1649–1652 (2020)
3. Salvador, R., Barros, M.V., dos Santos, G.E.T., van Mierlo, K.G., Piekarski, C.M., de Francisco, A.C.: Towards a green and fast production system: Integrating life cycle assessment and value stream mapping for decision making. Environ. Impact Assess. Rev. 87, 106519 (2021)
4. Hardy, D.L., Kundu, S., Latif, M.: Productivity and process performance in a manual trimming cell exploiting Lean Six Sigma (LSS) DMAIC – a case study in laminated panel production. Int. J. Qual. Reliab. Manag. (2021). ISSN 0265-671X
5. Alhuraish, I., Robledo, C., Kobi, A.: The effective of lean manufacturing and six sigma implementation. In: Framinan, J.M., Gonzalez, P.P., Artiba, A. (eds.) International Conference on Industrial Engineering and Systems Management 2015, IESM, Seville, Spain, pp. 1–8. IEEE Publisher (2015)
6. Sony, M., Antony, J., Park, S., Mutingi, M.: Key criticisms of six sigma: a systematic literature review. IEEE Trans. Eng. Manag. 67(3), 950–962 (2020)
7. Singh, J., Singh, H., Singh, A., Singh, J.: Managing industrial operations by lean thinking using value stream mapping and six sigma in manufacturing unit: Case studies. Manag. Decis. 58(6), 1118–1148 (2019)
8. Valamede, L.S., Akkari, A.C.S.: Lean 4.0: a new holistic approach for the integration of lean manufacturing tools and digital technologies. Int. J. Math. Eng. Manag. Sci. 5(5), 851–868 (2020)
9. Sharma, R.K., Sharma, R.G.: Integrating six sigma culture and TPM framework to improve manufacturing performance in SMEs. Qual. Reliab. Eng. Int. 30(5), 745–765 (2014)
10. Koppel, S., Chang, S.: MDAIC – a six sigma implementation strategy in big data environments. Int. J. Lean Six Sigma 2040–4166 (2020)
11. Bucko, M., Schindlerova, V., Hlavaty, I.: Application of six sigma tools in the production of welded chassis frames. MM Sci. J. 12, 4188–4193 (2020)
12. Mendes, F.S., Soares, J.M.: Financial KPI analysis in the implementation of DMAIC in a pharmaceutical organization - a case study. Int. J. Qual. Res. 15(1), 189–208 (2021)
13. Montgomery, D.C., Borror, C.M.: Systems for modern quality and business improvement. Qual. Technol. Quant. Manag. 14(4), 343–352 (2017)
14. Kaya, İ, Kahraman, C.: Process capability analyses based on fuzzy measurements and fuzzy control charts. Expert Syst. Appl. 38(4), 3172–3184 (2011)
15. Rubel Ahammed, M., Hasan, Z.: Humming noise reduction of ceiling fan in the mass production applying DMAIC-six sigma approach. World J. Eng. 18(1), 106–121 (2021)

16. Amjad, M.S., Rafique, M.Z., Khan, M.A.: Modern divulge in production optimization: an implementation framework of LARG manufacturing with Industry 4.0. Int. J. Lean Six Sigma 1–25 (2021)
17. Abd Rahman, M.S.B., Mohamad, E., Abdul Rahman, A.A.B.: Development of IoT-enabled data analytics enhance decision support system for lean manufacturing process improvement. Concurrent Eng. Res. Appl. 1–13 (2021)
18. de M.B.A. Dib, L., Fernandes, V., Filomeno, M.D.L., Ribeiro, M.V.: Hybrid PLC/wireless communication for smart grids and internet of things application. IEEE Internet Things J. 5(2), 655–667 (2018)
19. Andrzej, O., Jakub, G.: Energy saving in the street lighting control system-a new approach based on the EN-15232 standard. Energ. Effi. 10(3), 563–576 (2017)

Industry 4.0: Expectations, Impediments and Facilitators

Sergio Miele Ruggero[1](✉) ⓘD, Nilza Aparecida dos Santos[1,2](✉) ⓘD,
Antonio Carlos Estender[1](✉) ⓘD, and Marcia Terra da Silva[1](✉) ⓘD

[1] Programa de Engenharia da Produção – Universidade Paulista, São Paulo, SP 04026-002,
Brazil
[2] FATEC, Cotia, SP 06702-155, Brazil

Abstract. Industry 4.0 encompasses the main technological innovations transforming the physical, digital and biological pillars and promoting changes that
affect the economy as a whole. In each company, the transition to the use of
new technologies is established in a different way and the diagnosis of strategic
objectives in the medium and long term to understand the organizational scenario
can facilitate this process. The philosophy of Lean Manufacturing appears in the
literature and in this research as an important facilitator. The methodology used
to carry out this article was exploratory, qualitative and quantitative, through a
survey applied to 51 managers in the industrial area of companies in the automotive segment in Brazil. The main results showed that the increase in productivity
and cost reduction are expected gains, that the low level of use of new technologies, connectivity, knowledge about the theme, among others, are configured as
impediments to the transition, highlighting that the association of Lean Manufacturing and the technologies of Industry 4.0, can accelerate this process, minimize
possible risks and facilitate solutions for implementation.

Keywords: Lean manufacturing · Technology · Automotive segment

1 Introduction

The concept of Industry 4.0 encompasses the main technological innovations in the
fields of automation, control, and information technology [1] emerging as an opportunity
towards competitiveness. Part of the fourth industrial revolution, it is configured as a
technological trend based on cyber-physical systems, the internet of things, big data, and
cloud computing, which are technologies that seek to serve an advanced manufacturing
system transforming the physical, digital and biological pillars and promoting changes
that affect the economy as a whole [2].

The transition to Industry 4.0 is not restricted to the use of technological resources,
but also to information systems, organizational structure, and culture. Establishing itself
differently in each company leads to the need for diagnosis of strategic objectives in the
medium and long term for a better understanding of the organizational scenario [3].

Published by Springer Nature Switzerland AG 2021
A. Dolgui et al. (Eds.): APMS 2021, IFIP AICT 633, pp. 673–680, 2021.
https://doi.org/10.1007/978-3-030-85910-7_71

Although there is no broad knowledge about the consequences for manufacturing operations, the transition appears to be inevitable, leading companies to define their manufacturing model and plan a program for transformation [4]. Knowledge about Industry 4.0 is an important requirement for the use of new technologies, but in Brazil, industry users, in general, have low knowledge on the subject, requiring greater dissemination on the subject [5].

Another issue to highlight in relation to the transition refers to the philosophy of Lean Manufacturing, since the association of lean concepts and technologies of Industry 4.0, can accelerate this process, minimize possible risks and facilitate solutions for implementation [6].

Although the cost of the technologies needed for digital transition is decreasing, in Brazil, companies still face many obstacles, such as tax burden, logistical costs, and obtaining financial and intellectual capital [7]. Despite the difficulties in making this transition, the technologies covered by Industry 4.0 appear not as an obligation to implement, but as a real possibility of expectations of gains.

In this context, the most varied segments are affected by this scenario, and the automotive sector stands out for its relevance in the national economy. Considering the pillars of Industry 4.0, the competitiveness, and requirements of companies in the automotive segment, the question studied in this article is: How is the automotive industry in Brazil preparing for the transition to Industry 4.0? Aiming to identify and analyze the impediments, expectations of gains, and facilitators for this transition.

2   Literature Review

Industry 4.0 based on nine pillars: big data, autonomous robots, simulation, vertical and horizontal integration systems, internet of things, cyber-physical systems, cloud, additive manufacturing or 3D printing, and augmented reality [8], is based on the use of technologies that drive the transformation of the manufacturing process into digitized and intelligent [9].

New technologies and intelligent systems with advanced standards of human-machine interaction allow specificity and communication for each component of the value chain. The use of these technologies offers more comprehensive impacts in the productive sector and indirectly in other departments and can also lead to productivity gains [10]. It is noteworthy that communication in the productive chain occurs through the connectivity between devices, sensors, machines, and software [11].

The information obtained and the analysis of data between machines, streamlining, and flexibility in the production environment can make the processes more efficient with increased manufacturing productivity, leading to the production of higher quality goods at lower cost, changing the profile of the company. Workforce, with a consequent improvement in competitiveness [12]. In this way, the diversity of technologies can provide more intelligent, productive, and efficient factories that stimulate economic growth and development [13].

There are many changes in the production environment caused by the use of technologies that enable production planning in a more dynamic way and the use of techniques for market analysis [14]. In the automotive industry, the development of different technologies for the production of intelligent vehicles was propitiated by the paradigm shift from high-performance vehicles to safe and comfortable vehicles, a standard of comfort and safety that can be obtained by autonomous cars, which perceive environments driving and carry out the planning and control of the route without human intervention. The development of autonomous cars aggregates technologies from the automotive industry and mobile robots, creating reliable mechanical and electrical platforms [15].

In Brazil, studies indicate that the use of digital technologies impacts the value chain of products, business models, and commercial integration, leading to important gains in productivity, providing national and international competitiveness [16, 17].

In the literature, references were found to elements that facilitate the implementation of Industry 4.0: culture of innovation and change, and the lean manufacturing management philosophy. The latter, also known as Toyota production system, is considered a method of improving manufacturing with a focus on the customer and one of the most used business strategies in the last three decades [14, 18]. Thus, Industry 4.0 associated with lean manufacturing provides benefits for companies in general, facilitating the transition process [19].

3   Method

The method used to carry out this article was of a qualitative and quantitative nature and the segment chosen was the automotive, composed of automakers and auto parts.

The primary data were obtained by the survey method, with 60 questionnaires being sent in January 2020, to directors, managers, supervisors, and leaders, who carry out activities in the areas of manufacturing and industrial engineering in companies in that segment.

The form consisted of 12 questions, presented at random, to be filled in via the electronic platform, with 2 questions being for the qualification of the sample. In the elaboration of the other questions, relevant aspects about Industry 4.0 were considered, such as the use of new technologies, impediments, expectations of gains, and facilitators for the transition. In constructing the questions, the theoretical framework on the subject was taken as the base [3] and based on the professional experience of the authors.

Of the 60 questionnaires sent, 51 returned answered and 9 did not justify their absence. The surveyed sample corresponds to 75% of small and medium-sized auto parts companies and 25% of automakers. Secondary data were obtained from bibliographic references and in the analysis of the results, the professional experience and participation of the authors in the segment were also considered.

4   Results e Discussions

The results found were reported in the tables based on the responses of the research participants. Table 1 identifies the current scenario of the companies surveyed in relation to the use of new technologies, making investments, knowledge about Industry 4.0 and data connectivity.

Table 1. Portrait of companies in relation to transition to Industry 4.0

Questions	View of the participants
Knowledge about Industry 4.0	100% consider the topic important and claim to have some knowledge
Making investments	Last 2 years: 25% made large investments, 3% small investments and 72% no investment; Next 5 years: 16% intend to make large investments, 80% small investments and 4% no investment
Data connectivity	94% report a low level of data connectivity between their company, suppliers and customers
Use of sensors in production machines and equipment	49% indicate that the machines do not have sensors, but installation is possible; 51% claim that the machines have sensors that provide partial data
Control level of the machines (IT network)	80% report that the level is low or nonexistent; 20% indicate that the level is medium/high
Communication level between machines	78% indicate that the level is low or nonexistent; 22% claim that the level is medium/high

Source: (Prepared by the authors)

The research participants claim to have knowledge on the topic (Table 1), however, in the analysis of the responses, it was noticed that the level of knowledge of the participants in relation to Industry 4.0 is embryonic since they indicate the lack of knowledge as bottleneck to the transition as described in Table 3, as it occurs in industries in general [5].

Investments in new technologies appear to be insufficient, as in the last 2 years 72% of the companies surveyed have not made any investments and for the next 5 years 80% intend to make small investments, a situation that is configured as an obstacle to Industry 4.0, considering that regardless of the transition stage of each company, it is necessary to make investments [20]. It is worth mentioning that the share of high investments mentioned refers only to the automakers corroborating with secondary research in which the automakers, in Brazil, represent the share of companies with a greater possibility of investing [7].

The difficulty in relation to connectivity pointed out by 94% of the participants is in line with research in Brazil [21], in which 91% of the companies are not connected. Thus, the low level of use of digital technologies, equipment infrastructure and sensors for data collection shown in the results (Tables 1 and 2) may justify the mentioned connectivity difficulties.

The use of sensors in production machines and equipment and especially the level of control and communication between machines was reported by the participants as low level, which added to the lack of connectivity and the low level of investments may explain part of the difficulties for use of new technologies as shown in Table 2, which presents the use of technologies related to Industry 4.0, considering the perception of the survey respondents.

Table 2. Use of technologies

Technologies	Not applicable	Null	Low	Medium	High
Big data analytics	6%	58%	10%	6%	20%
Cloud computing	6%	62%	6%	6%	20%
Communication between machines	2%	45%	25%	8%	20%
Robots	12%	60%	2%	10%	16%
Communication with machines via cell phone	4%	60%	10%	10%	16%
Real-time location system	4%	62%	8%	10%	16%
Process simulation	8%	66%	2%	8%	16%
3D printing	0%	39%	33%	16%	12%
Artificial intelligence	6%	66%	8%	10%	10%
Use of RFID to tag products and components	2%	66%	8%	22%	2%

Source: (Prepared by the authors)

In the analysis of Table 2, it can be seen that the use of new technologies in most of the companies surveyed is still low and/or null in all modalities. However, in the details of the data, it was found that the percentages classified as medium and mainly high refer to the responses of the participants in the assemblers.

The scenario shown in Tables 1 and 2 supports the bottlenecks depicted in Table 3 which identifies, in addition to the impediments, the facilitator and the expectations of earnings of the referred companies.

In Table 3, the bottlenecks indicated by the respondents were the lack of connection, low investments, lack of qualification of manpower and little interest from managers. These impediments that are reported in secondary research [22] that point beyond the mentioned bottlenecks, others such as high logistical costs and precarious infrastructure, highlighting that some companies are in a more advanced stage of technological development and have more abundant financial resources.

The managers' lack of interest in making the transition may be related to the low knowledge, already mentioned, about Industry 4.0, as well as the respondents' perception that the gains with the transition are limited. It is noteworthy that secondary research also classified the knowledge of the industries in general as superficial when compared to the real qualification needs of the people involved [5, 23].

Considering that studies in Brazil [17, 24] point out that the level of investment is guided by the search for cost reduction and productivity gains and that the respondents of the research identified these searches as earnings expectations, the low level of investment indicated in Table 1 and referred to as an impediment in Table 3, it can hinder the transition process due to the lack of investments.

Table 3. Impediments, facilitators and expectations of gains

Questions	Expectations/impediments
Bottlenecks that hinder the transition	Lack of connection between participants in the business chain; unavailability of financial resources; lack of indicators to measure return on investment; economic crisis or other external factors; restricted knowledge, lack of interest in the transition and qualified labor to use new technologies
Importance of lean manufacturing with facilitator for transition to Industry 4.0	96% of respondents consider the use of Lean to be important for the transition to Industry 4.0
Gains to be obtained from the transition to Industry 4.0	Agility in production processes; greater availability of information; cost reduction and product quality improvement

Source: (Prepared by the authors)

Despite the identified obstacles, 96% of the research participants highlighted Lean Manufacturing as an important factor in the transition to Industry 4.0, as well as highlighted in the literature that places Lean as one of the most applied and used business strategies as a basis for the implementation of new technologies [18], offering benefits to companies in general [14, 19].

It is important to mention that Lean focuses on eliminating waste, segregating what does not add value, that is, it optimizes the production process, confirming the proposal in the literature in which the association of technology and lean manufacturing can streamline the process and minimize possible risks, facilitating the implementation of Industry 4.0 [6]. That said, it can be said that the management philosophy of Lean Manufacturing and the technologies of Industry 4.0, in addition to walking together, complement each other, being more than an association becoming a synergy.

5   Conclusions

The objective of this study was to identify and analyze the impediments, gains and facilitators so that companies in the automotive segment can make the transition to Industry 4.0. Based on the results, it was possible to understand that the researched companies have been conducting this transition process at a slow pace, considering the low use of new technologies, caused by impediments such as low level of investment, connectivity and knowledge on the subject. The most cited earnings expectations were the increase in productivity and cost reduction, however this opportunity is still distant, for these companies, given the scenario portrayed in the present research.

Despite the mentioned obstacles, Lean Manufacturing appears as an important facilitator for the transition process, both in the literature and in the opinion of the research participants. Thus, the association of Lean with the technologies of Industry 4.0 opens the way to structure and streamline the transition process in the automotive segment in Brazil.

The main contribution of this article was to point out the means to facilitate the access of companies in the automotive segment to the process of transition to Industry 4.0, detecting the main impediments that need to be resolved so that the expectations pointed out are converted into gains.

Like all research, this study has limitations related to nature, especially due to the sample size, not concluding conclusions. Thus, other studies in different segments or times may present different results. As a proposal for future studies, it is recommended to further detail the development conditions for the use of Industry 4.0 technologies adapted to the Brazilian reality.

Acknowledgment. "This study was financed in part by the Coordenação de Aperfeiçoamento de Pessoal de Nível Superior - Brasil (CAPES) - Finance Code".

References

1. Lee, J., Bagheri, B., Kao, H.A.: A cyber-physical systems architecture for Industry 4.0-based manufacturing systems. Manuf. Lett. **3**, 18–23 (2015)
2. Schwab, K.: The Fourth Industrial Revolution. 1st edn., World Economic Forum. Crown Business, New York (2016). ISBN: 9781524758869
3. Schuh, G., Anderl, R., Gausemeier, J., Hompel, M., Wahlster, W.: Industrie 4.0 Maturity Index. Managing the Digital Transformation of Companies (acatech STUDY). Herbert Utz Verlag, Munich (2017)
4. Almada-Lobo, F.: The Industry 4.0 revolution and the future of manufacturing execution systems (MES). J. Innov. Manag. **3**(4), 16–21 (2016)
5. CNI: Confederação Nacional da Indústria. Industry 4.0. Special poll. Brasília, n. 66 (May 2016)
6. Kolberg, D., Zuhlke, D.: Lean automation enabled by Industry 4.0 technologies. IFAC **48**, 1873 (2015)
7. CNI: Centro Nacional da Indústria. Indicadores Industriais. São Paulo (2019). http://www.portaldaindustria.com.br/estatisticas/indicadores-industriais. Accessed 10 Apr 2020
8. Motyl, B., Baronio, G., Uberti, S., Speranza, D., Filippi, S.: How will change engineer's skills in the Industry 4.0 framework? A questionnaire survey. Procedia Manuf. **11**, 1501–1509 (2017)
9. Pilloni, V.: How data will transform industrial processes: crowdsensing, crowdsourcing and big data as pillars of Industry 4.0. Future Internet **10**, 24 (2018)
10. Schuh, G., Potente, T., Wesch-Potente, C., Weber, A.R., Prote, J.P.: Collaboration mechanisms to increase productivity in the context of Industrie 4.0. Procedia CIRP **19**, 51–56 (2014). Robust Manufacturing Conference (RoMaC 2014)
11. Büyüközkan, G., Göçer, F.: Digital supply chain: literature review and a proposed framework for future research. Comput. Ind. **97**, 157–177 (2018)
12. Rüßmann, M., et al.: Industry 4.0: the future of productivity and growth in manufacturing industries. Boston Consult. Group **9**(1), 54–89 (2015)
13. Brettel, M., Friederichsen, N.: How virtualization, decentralization and network building change the manufacturing landscape: an Industry 4.0 perspective. Int. J. Mech. Aerosp. Ind. Mechatron. Manuf. Eng. **8N**(1), 37–44 (2014)
14. Sanders, A., Elangeswaran, C., Wulfsberg, J.: Industry 4.0 implies lean manufacturing: research activities in Industry 4.0 function as enablers for lean manufacturing. Journal of Industrial Engineering and Management, 9(3), 811–833 (2016)

15. Kichun, J., Kim, J., Kim, D., Jang, C., Sunwoo, M.: Development of autonomous car-part I: distributed system architecture and development process. IEEE Trans. Industr. Electron. **61**(12), 7131–7140 (2014). https://doi.org/10.1109/TIE.2014.2321342
16. FIRJAN: Federação das Indústrias do Estado do Rio de Janeiro. Industry 4.0 in Brazil: opportunities, perspectives and challenges, FIRJAN, SENAI, FINEP, Rio de Janeiro (2019)
17. CNI: Confederação Nacional da Indústria – CNI. Industry 2027 Risks and Opportunities for Brazil in the face of disruptive innovations, Brasília (2018)
18. Sony, M.: Industry 4.0 and lean management: a proposed integration model and research propositions. Prod. Manuf. Res. **6**(1), 416–432 (2018). https://doi.org/10.1080/21693277. 2018.1540949
19. Zhong, R.Y., Xu, X., Klotz, E., Newman, S.T.: Intelligent manufacturing in the context of Industry 4.0: a review. Engineering **3**(5), 616–630 (2017)
20. Lorenz, M., Küpper, D., Rüβmann, M., Heidemann, A., Bause, A.: Time to Accelerate in the Race Toward Industry 4.0. Boston Consulting Group, Boston (2016)
21. ABIMAQ: Associação Brasileira de Máquinas e Equipamentos. Full General Report. São Paulo (2018). http://abimaq.org.br/COMUNICACOES/2018/PROJETOS. Accessed 20 Feb 2020
22. Santos, N.A., Ruggero, S.M., Sacomano, J.B.: A transição para a Indústria 4.0: um estudo sobre a natureza dos investimentos em montadoras e autopeças. ENEGEP (2019)
23. Ruggero, S.M., Santos, N.A., Estender, A.C., Sacomano, J.B.: A Transição para a Indústria 4.0: Impedimentos e Ganhos para a Indústria. In: Anais do XII CASI - Congresso de Administração, Sociedade e Inovação. Anais, Palhoça (SC) FATENP - Unigranrio (2019)
24. IEDI: https://iedi.org.br/media/site/artigos/20190311indústria_do_futuro_no_brasil_ e_no_mundo.pdf. Accessed 10 Nov 2020

Implementation of Digital Tools for Lean Manufacturing: An Empirical Analysis

Bassel Kassem[✉] and Alberto Portioli Staudacher

Politecnico Di Milano, 20156 Milan, Italy
{bassel.kassem,alberto.portioli}@polimi.it

Abstract. Purpose: The literature on Lean Manufacturing and Industry 4.0 has identified a strong link between the two paradigms and a positive impact on operational performances. Industry 4.0 offers digital tools to support LM tools and practices. However, empirical and in-depth analyses to validate such propositions are still scarce in the literature. Therefore, the observation of the implementation of Industry 4.0 tools for Lean Manufacturing with a focus on the factors needed for properly introducing them in firms is the next logical step to further strengthen this area of research. This study aims to understand the required factors needed to take into consideration for a successful implementation of the tools in the manufacturing process. **Methodology:** We rely on multiple case studies performed in 6 Italian Manufacturing companies that adopt digital tools for Lean Manufacturing. **Findings:** Our findings highlighted the central role of skills, the need for a specialized team to oversee the implementation in addition to better formulation of the tool's offerings by the suppliers through successful case studies. We also tried to connect individually each tool with the operational performance it aims at improving .

Keywords: Lean · Digital tool · Implementation · Industry 4.0

1 Introduction

The literature on Lean Manufacturing (LM) and Industry 4.0 (I4.0) has started to pay increasing attention to their combined effect rather than to each one individually. Academicians and practitioners have identified a strong link between LM and I4.0 and a positive impact on operational performances [1]. The combination of these two paradigms in the industrial field in practice is represented by the challenge of implementing I4.0's technologies into existing LM systems, with the necessary adjustments to business processes. However, the expected performance improvements seem to justify this effort, even if not all firms are still aware of that. In evaluating the main challenges of the implementation of I4.0, according to [2], academicians should put their efforts to better understand "how I4.0 technologies impact processes, products, and services of firms".

The implementation of digital tools for LM as a part of the digital transformation process is a challenge in the digital era. Many enterprises seem reluctant to start a digital

© IFIP International Federation for Information Processing 2021
Published by Springer Nature Switzerland AG 2021
A. Dolgui et al. (Eds.): APMS 2021, IFIP AICT 633, pp. 681–690, 2021.
https://doi.org/10.1007/978-3-030-85910-7_72

transformation process. It is becoming increasingly important to understand the needed requirements for the adoption of digital tools.

To fill this knowledge gap, this study aims at understanding empirically:

"What are the factors needed for properly introducing the digital tools in manufacturing companies?". In addition, we try to answer the knowledge gap highlighted by [3] that called for associating digital tools to corresponding operational performances.

2   Theoretical Background

The literature review confirms that when applied together, I4.0 and LM improve greatly operational performances [4–6]. It is also shown empirically in the work of [4, 7] who surveyed companies in European and Brazilian contexts about the level of implementation of both LM and I4.0 and how this contributes to their performances. High adopters of lean are the ones most likely to apply I4.0 technologies, whereas low adopters of lean are less inclined to adopt I4.0 technologies, and former ones achieve greater operational performances compared to the latter ones.

Those studies confirm the support I4.0 gives to LM in improving operational performances but do not dwell on how this is possible. Empirical case studies were done in this context postulating that I4.0 offers digital tools for Lean, and through them, performances are improved. Those studies, however, focus on few lean digital tools such as the e-kanban [8, 9] and VSM 4.0 [10, 11]. The literature emphasizes heavily the role of sculpting skills whether technical ones or analytical ones to face the new era of I4.0 and its rapidly growing technologies [12–17]. With this research, we will try to see empirically whether this is the main factor for companies or there are other factors as well.

Based on the literature, a list of a more comprehensive set of tools was developed: E-Kanban, E-Poka Yoke, E-Andon, Value Stream Mapping software (VSM 4.0), OEE software, Computerised Maintenance Management Software (CMMS), KPI dashboard, Root Cause Analysis software, Cause and Effect Diagram software, S.M.A.R.T. Goals software, Mind Mapping software, RFID trackers, Handsfree Radio Data Terminals, 3D Factory Simulation software, Collaborative Manufacturing, GPS fleet tracking, Real-Time Production Monitoring software, Collaborative Robots, Virtual Reality, Real-Time Machine Monitoring, Real-Time Inventory tracking, and I-bin.

3   Research Methodology

We decided to conduct an explanatory multiple case study. The scope here is the identification of relationships and relevant variables in a limited number of realities. This allows us to create initial knowledge for academicians and practitioners who are facing the challenge of digitization.

The selection of cases was made among the Italian participants of a survey developed by the Lean Excellence Center at Politecnico di Milano (reference omitted for peer-review) which showed a particular commitment to digital tools adoption. We have grouped the participants into high and low implementers based on the number of tools they implement. The case study follows a holistic approach, which considers a single unit of analysis corresponding to the implementation process of digital tools.

We followed a theoretical sampling approach, thus collecting information that will support the results of our survey analysis and refine them by identifying "polar types" from the different firms of the initial survey sample. Indeed, this approach generally reinforces the generalization of results and enables a comparative analysis of findings. Using the "heterogeneity approach" for the selection of cases, we searched for different cases representative of different sizes, different sectors (all belonging to the manufacturing environment) but at the same time, we selected homogeneous cases as in Italian manufacturing companies. Though it might reduce the possibility to generalize findings, it assures that confounding variables do not cause variation [18] (Table 1).

We have designed semi-structured interviews based on a set of pre-determined questions. All the interviews were recorded (after receiving permission from respondents) and then transcribed. The transcripts, together with notes taken during and after each interview, were collected and stored in a dedicated database. We have archived this information in a well-organized structure to make it ready for the coding phase. This process mainly involved content analysis performed to identify relations or patterns or to contribute to the development of the theory. Indeed, transcripts together with the team's observations, external documents, notes, and precedent survey answers, ensured data triangulation. The coding process has been conducted manually by the authors, to ensure inter-code reliability [19]. We followed a two-steps coding procedure. In the first-round coding, the authors have done the coding of each text interview separately, and then a comparison was done between the coders. The interview model has been divided into 6 main sections:

1) Organization structure description that includes the role of the interviewees in the company, their definition of I4.0, and whether their company's culture is "just Lean", or "just I4.0" or "Lean 4.0" exploiting the relationship between the two paradigms.
2) Digital tools adoption level: it was asked whether company size, sector and type of process affect the digital tool implementation process and the reasons why they implemented the digital tools they are using
3) Guidelines for digital tools implementation and the decisional process and feasibility analyses undertaken by the company before implementing a specific digital tool.
4) Obstacles to digital tools implementation process we asked the interviewees the reasons why their company did not decide to implement the digital tools.
5) Performances impacted by digital tools adoption: both positive, neutral, and negative of each of the implemented digital tools on the various operational performances
6) Insights for future development: we asked the interviewees to share, based on their experience, some insights to improve digital tools providers' offer

Table 1. Interviewees information sum-up

Implementers	Case	Size	Sector	Operating model	Production type	Role of interviewee	Tools currently implemented	Tools to be implemented
High	A	Small	Packaging	B2B	High volume, Low variety	Lean Six Sigma Improvement Facilitator	5	7
High	B	Medium	Healthcare	B2B	High volume, High variety	Head of Continuous Improvement	4	5
High	C	Medium	Furniture	B2C	Low volume, High variety	Lean Specialist	13	8
High	D	Large	Automotive	B2B	Low volume, High variety	Digital Manufacturing specialist	8	2
Low	E	Small	Machining	B2B	Low volume, High variety	Quality Manager	3	3
Low	F	Small	Pressure equip	B2C	Low volume, High variety	Operations Director	1	3

4   Discussion

The first finding of case study analysis is the confirmed bi-directional relationship between LM and I4.0 discussed in the existing academic literature. All the practitioners have confirmed both the enabling effect of Lean on I4.0 implementation [7, 20, 21] and the empowering effect of I4.0 on Lean [8, 9]. We report in Table 2 a summary of the factors that companies take into consideration to properly implement the digital tools according to the various interviewees. All the investigated case studies in this work confirmed the agreed statement of LM as a prerequisite of I4.0 confirming the corresponding academicians' theory [7, 22, 23] also in the practitioners' field.

Table 2. Implementation factors for digital tools

Implementation factors	Company					
	A	B	C	D	E	F
Change of mentality	x	x	x		x	x
Suppliers involvement	x	x	x		x	x
Freedom in decision making					x	
Investment in personal knowledge		x	x		x	
Incremental change	x	x	x			
Adequate information system			x	x		
Ad hoc division for LM	x	x		x		
Presence of cross-functional team to foster digitalization		x		x		
People Involvement	x	x	x			

   Moreover, most of the interviewed firms started using the traditional Lean tools (such as Kanban, Andon, and Poka-Yoke) and then updated them with the corresponding digital version.

4.1   Contributing Factors and Decision Making

Given the fact that LM provides the right culture to the company to embrace the digital transformation, a very important element is the people factor. Indeed, one commonality that emerged among the high implementers, but not among the low implementers, is the presence of an ad hoc division inside the company fully dedicated to digitization projects. In some cases, the team was composed of the previous LM team, while in other cases, it was created in recent years using an interdisciplinary approach of young profiles. This peculiarity is aligned with [18], who observed a case in which a new business division was created to provide I4.0 solutions based on LM competencies. Also, Kaizen and Multifunctional Team are often considered as "soft" LM techniques [1, 24], however, the analyzed case studies prove that their contribution to I4.0 adoption can be very effective, confirming the hypothesis of [18]. Therefore, future research can also concentrate the attention on the enabling effect of "soft" Lean practices on companies' digitization process.

Seeing the digital tools for LM as resources, we can use the Resource-Based-View [25] according to which these two types of resources can bring a positive synergistic effect to operational performances. However, because of the case studies analysis, an additional resource should be introduced in this model: this third resource is represented by the people factor. For all the interviewed firms, skilled people are seen both as the main facilitator and as the main difficulty for the implementation of digital tools. Therefore, the central role of people emerged both as a well-known pillar of the Lean paradigm but also as a basis for I4.0 adoption. Indeed, I4.0 technologies aim to support people's work rather than replace them [26, 27] by converting workers' activities without value-added into value-added ones [21]. Considering this concept and the Resource-Based-View by [28], skilled people within the company fit all the requirements of the resources which are: valuable, rare, imperfectly imitable, and un-substitutable/unique. We can conclude that the commitment of people is more evident among high implementers than low ones, and its effect seems to have a positive contribution to the digitization intensity, as observed by [29] stating: "The change can only come with the involvement of the operational staff".

Moreover, the perception of the contextual factors' impact (especially company size, sector, and type of process) among the interviewed firms is various. Indeed, it is not possible to find a different perception on contextual factors' impact between high and low implementers or between SMEs and large companies interviewed. Most interviewees (both high and low implementers) have stated that the type of process had an impact on the selection of type and number of digital tools to be implemented.

While the existing literature investigating the possible barriers for non-implementation of digital tools [26, 30] is mainly focused on the SMEs which seem the most vulnerable in this sense, none of the small-medium firms has cited the limited financial availability as a reason for non-implementation, while the most common reason was represented by the internal resistance to change showed by workers, confirming the perspectives of [26, 31, 32].

Both high and low implementers agree on the importance of people training to successfully introduce new technologies. The training should be both technical and cultural, a very important aspect to introduce digital tools is the understanding of the "importance of data" [29] and thus the creation of "Digital Culture cultivation" [33].

In particular, the low-experienced firm in Lean 4.0 (Company E) perceived that the main barriers to the introduction of I4.0 in manufacturing firms are related to internal challenges such as lack of skilled operators and culture for the change, while the digital transformation of Company F is mainly limited by strategic and operative issues [33, 34]. On the contrary, the most cited barrier among high implementers is the uncertainty of such investments that usually do not have reliable ROI values.

Therefore the maturity stage in the digitization rather than the company size or sector is relevant, confirming the independence of contextual factors in the adoption of the digital tools [2, 4, 9].

To start the digitization process, an internal "Digital Culture" should be developed [33]. Modern company processes require a certain degree of maturity in innovation methods and tools for digitization and companies usually need external help to explore these possibilities [32]. This support is not only related to the knowledge of the existence of available technologies but mainly related to the knowledge of how to make them functional in real production systems.

Indeed, low implementers seem not to be able to sustain this cultural change alone, therefore, they ask the support of external entities (first the digital tools providers, but also universities and consultants) in the implementation and installation of the digital tools, but also the training of the employees affected by the change.

4.2 Supplier Side

Both families of implementers asked for a revision of current digital tools offerings, by changing the structure of the product, marketing strategy, and price. The increased modularity of software will help firms in the gradual adoption of digital solutions starting from strategic modules to then integrate all other systems. Moreover, the possibility to customize the offer concerning the characteristics and operations of the firm seems to be a value-added for most companies interviewed by avoiding buying systems that the company does not truly need, negatively influencing the company's perception of digitization. Finally, all interviewees recognized great benefits in receiving case study examples dealing with similar context applications and highlighting the results obtained from the implementation of digital tools, to assess the effects of the digital projects in advance.

4.3 Tools and Operational Performances

We report in a tree (see figure below) a tree associating the tools with the operational performance it tackles. In general terms, we can see that Productivity is recognized as the most positively impacted performance. Regarding the individual relations between performances and used instruments, this observation is necessary to, we can see that almost all the performances have at least one association; in particular, the positive ones are the most noticeable, suggesting a general performance satisfaction of digital tools users.

A positive association has emerged between the E-Kanban adoption and the reduction of Lead Time by Company C, between the OEE software and the Real-Time Production monitoring adoption by Companies A, D, and E, with a significant increase in Productivity and between the Real-Time Inventory tracking adoption and an improvement in warehouse management, by Company C.

Many manufacturers indicate that the integrated systems of MES (Manufacturing Execution System) and ERP (Enterprise Resource Planning) can immediately communicate anomalies or breakdowns as well as calculate KPIs.

This is in line with the scientific works by [8, 35] who show that Smart Machines empower the production capability using displays with graphical user interfaces connected to the production line and the MES.

It is remarkable the positive effects observed by Company D due to the usage of RFID to reduce human errors as well as to increase the traceability of items in the Warehouse Management, aligned with the concept of Poka-Yoke 4.0 by [36].

In addition, Company B has notified the benefit of 3D Factory simulation and Virtual Reality to allow the company to try out different layout configurations through a virtual walk in the simulated environment, already observed by [18, 37].

5   Conclusion, Future Research, and Limitations

In conclusion, this research sheds the light on the three main areas the academic and practitioners' fields should focus on for the proper implementation of digital tools for LM. The first is sculpting the skills of the operators for the use of the digital tools and limiting their resistance to change and this could direct governments and companies into investing in education and skills formation. The second is dedicating a team in the company to oversee the implementation of the tools. The third one instead is the effort digital tools suppliers should put on to modify their product offerings in such a way to highlight empirically how the tools could be used and implemented through successful case studies. This result confirms the academic request for empirical validations of the use of digital tools [1]. In addition, the research sets the first step into answering the gap identified by [4] that calls for associating each performance to each tool to guide the company into adopting the tools according to the needed improvement. This research surely presents some limitations. Having relied on only 6 Italian manufacturing companies, the results are neither enough to be generalized nor can they be in their current form extended to other industries. Future research of ours will try to expand on those limitations to ensure more generalizability of the results (Fig. 1).

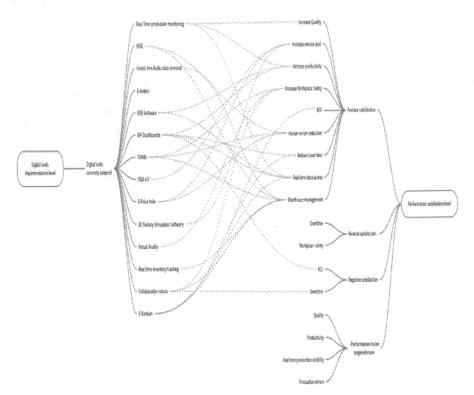

Fig. 1. Association performance-tool

References

1. Buer, S.V., Strandhagen, J.O., Chan, F.T.S.: The link between industry 4.0 and lean manufacturing: mapping current research and establishing a research agenda. Int. J. Prod. Res. **56**, 2924–2940 (2018)
2. Kipper, L.M., Furstenau, L.B., Hoppe, D., Frozza, R., Iepsen, S.: Scopus scientific mapping production in industry 4.0 (2011–2018): a bibliometric analysis. Int. J. Prod. Res. **58**, 1605–1627 (2020)
3. Tortorella, G.L., Miorando, R., Mac Cawley, A.F.: The moderating effect of Industry 4.0 on the relationship between lean supply chain management and performance improvement. Supply Chain Manag. **24**, 301–314 (2019)
4. Rossini, M., Costa, F., Tortorella, G.L., Portioli-Staudacher, A.: The interrelation between Industry 4.0 and lean production: an empirical study on European manufacturers. Int. J. Adv. Manuf. Technol. **102**, 3963–3976 (2019)
5. Hoellthaler, G., Braunreuther, S., Reinhart, G.: Digital lean production an approach to identify potentials for the migration to a digitalized production system in SMEs from a lean perspective. Procedia CIRP **67**, 522–527 (2018). https://doi.org/10.1016/j.procir.2017.12.255
6. Rossini, M., Cifone, F.D., Kassem, B., Costa, F., Portioli-Staudacher, A.: Being lean: how to shape digital transformation in the manufacturing sector. J. Manuf. Technol. Manag. **32**, 239–259 (2021)
7. Tortorella, G.L., Rossini, M., Costa, F., Portioli-Staudacher, Alberto Sawhney, R.: A comparison on Industry 4.0 and Lean Production between manufacturers from emerging and developed economies. Total Qual. Manag. Bus. Excell. (2019)
8. Kolberg, D., Knobloch, J., Zühlke, D.: Towards a lean automation interface for workstations. Int. J. Prod. Res. (2017)
9. Sanders, A., Elangeswaran, C., Wulfsberg, J.: Industry 4.0 implies lean manufacturing: research activities in industry 4.0 function as enablers for lean manufacturing. J. Ind. Eng. Manag. **9**, 811–833 (2016)
10. Hartmann, L., Meudt, T., Seifermann, S., Metternich, J.: Value stream method 4.0: holistic method to analyse and design value streams in the digital age. Procedia CIRP, 249–254 (2018)
11. Lugert, A., Batz, A., Winkler, H.: Empirical assessment of the future adequacy of value stream mapping in manufacturing industries. J. Manuf. Technol. Manag. **29**, 886–906 (2018)
12. Whysall, Z., Owtram, M., Brittain, S.: The new talent management challenges of Industry 4.0. J. Manag. Dev. **38**, 118–129 (2019)
13. Flores, E., Xu, X., Lu, Y.: Human Capital 4.0: a workforce competence typology for Industry 4.0. J. Manuf. Technol. Manag. **31**, 687–703 (2020)
14. Nabilah, F., et al.: The emerging challenges of industrial revolution 4.0: a students' perspective. Int. J. Adv. Sci. Technol. **29**, 1215–1225 (2020)
15. Johansson, J., Abrahamsson, L., Kåreborn, B.B., Fältholm, Y., Grane, C., Wykowska, A.: Work and organization in a digital industrial context. Manag. Revu. **28**, 281–297 (2017)
16. Bruno, G., Antonelli, D.: Dynamic task classification and assignment for the management of human-robot collaborative teams in workcells. Int. J. Adv. Manuf. Technol. **98**, 2415–2427 (2018)
17. Powell, D., Romero, D., Gaiardelli, P., Cimini, C., Cavalieri, S.: Towards digital lean cyber-physical production systems: Industry 4.0 technologies as enablers of leaner production. In: Moon, I., Lee, G.M., Park, J., Kiritsis, D., von Cieminski, G. (eds.) APMS 2018. IAICT, vol. 536, pp. 353–362. Springer, Cham (2018). https://doi.org/10.1007/978-3-319-99707-0_44
18. Ciano, M.P., Dallasega, P., Orzes, G., Rossi, T.: One-to-one relationships between Industry 4.0 technologies and Lean Production techniques: a multiple case study. Int. J. Prod. Res. 1–25 (2020)

19. Duriau, V.J., Reger, R.K., Pfarrer, M.D.: A content analysis of the content analysis literature in organization studies: research themes, data sources, and methodological refinements. Organ. Res. Methods **10**, 5–34 (2007)

20. Rossini, M., Portioli-Staudacher, A., Cifone, F.D., Costa, F., Esposito, F., Kassem, B.: Lean and sustainable continuous improvement: assessment of people potential contribution. In: Rossi, M., Rossini, M., Terzi, S. (eds.) ELEC 2019. LNNS, vol. 122, pp. 283–290. Springer, Cham (2020). https://doi.org/10.1007/978-3-030-41429-0_28

21. Rüttimann, B.G., Stöckli, M.T.: Lean and Industry 4.0—twins, partners, or contenders? A due clarification regarding the supposed clash of two production systems. J. Serv. Sci. Manag. **09**, 485–500 (2016)

22. Rossini, M., Costa, F., Portioli-Staudacher, A., Tortorella, G.L.: Industry 4.0 and lean production: an empirical study. IFAC-PapersOnLine **52**, 42–47 (2019)

23. Kassem, B., Portioli, A.: The interaction between lean production and Industry 4.0: mapping the current state of literature and highlighting gaps. In: Proceedings of the Summer School Francesco Turco, pp. 123–128 (2019)

24. Kassem, B., Costa, F., Portioli-Staudacher, A.: JIT implementation in manufacturing: the case of Giacomini SPA. In: Rossi, M., Rossini, M., Terzi, S. (eds.) ELEC 2019. LNNS, vol. 122, pp. 273–281. Springer, Cham (2020). https://doi.org/10.1007/978-3-030-41429-0_27

25. Khanchanapong, T., Prajogo, D., Sohal, A.S., Cooper, B.K., Yeung, A.C.L., Cheng, T.C.E.: The unique and complementary effects of manufacturing technologies and lean practices on manufacturing operational performance. Int. J. Prod. Econ. **153**, 191–203 (2014)

26. Cimini, C., Pirola, F., Pinto, R., Cavalieri, S.: A human-in-the-loop manufacturing control architecture for the next generation of production systems. J. Manuf. Syst. **54**, 258–271 (2020)

27. Romero, D., Gaiardelli, P., Powell, D., Wuest, T., Thürer, M.: Digital lean cyber-physical production systems: the emergence of digital lean manufacturing and significance of digital waste. IFIP Adv. Inf. Commun. Technol. **535**, v–vi (2018)

28. Barney, J.: Firm resources and sustained competitive advantage. J. Manage. **17**, 99–120 (1991)

29. Moeuf, A., Lamouri, S., Pellerin, R., Tamayo-Giraldo, S., Tobon-Valencia, E., Eburdy, R.: Identification of critical success factors, risks and opportunities of Industry 4.0 in SMEs. Int. J. Prod. Res. **58**, 1384–1400 (2020)

30. Chiarini, A., Belvedere, V., Grando, A.: Industry 4.0 strategies and technological developments. In: An Exploratory Research from Italian Manufacturing Companies. Taylor & Francis (2020)

31. Mittal, S., Khan, M.A., Romero, D., Wuest, T.: A critical review of smart manufacturing & Industry 4.0 maturity models: implications for small and medium-sized enterprises (SMEs). J. Manuf. Syst. **49**, 194–214 (2018)

32. Kaartinen, H., Pieska, S., Vahasoyrinki, J.: Digital manufacturing toolbox for supporting the manufacturing SMEs. In: Proceedings of the 7th IEEE International Conference Cognitive infocommunications, CogInfoCom 2016, pp. 71–76 (2017)

33. Romero, D., Flores, M.: Five management pillars for digital transformation integrating the lean thinking philosophy. In: Proceedings of the 2019 IEEE International Conference on Innovations in Engineering and Technology ICE/ITMC 2019 (2019)

34. Ghobakhloo, M., Fathi, M.: Corporate survival in Industry 4.0 era: the enabling role of lean-digitized manufacturing. J. Manuf. Technol. Manag. **31**, 1–30 (2020)

35. Kolberg, D., Zühlke, D.: Lean automation enabled by Industry 4.0 technologies. IFAC-PapersOnLine **28**, 1870–1875 (2015). https://doi.org/10.1016/j.ifacol.2015.06.359

36. Mayr, A., et al.: Lean 4.0-A conceptual conjunction of lean management and Industry 4.0. In: Procedia CIRP, pp 622–628. Elsevier B.V. (2018)

37. Rosin, F., Forget, P., Lamouri, S., Pellerin, R.: Impacts of Industry 4.0 technologies on Lean principles. Int. J. Prod. Res. **58**, 1644–1661 (2020)

Reflections from a Hybrid Approach Used to Develop a Specification of a Shopfloor Platform for Smart Manufacturing in an Engineered-to-Order SME

Yann Keiser[1] , Shaun West[2(✉)] , and Simon Züst[2]

[1] School of Computer Science and Information Technology, Lucerne University of Applied Sciences and Arts, Rotkreuz, Switzerland
[2] School of Technology and Architecture, Lucerne University of Applied Sciences and Arts, Horw, Switzerland
{shaun.west,simon.zuest}@hslu.ch

Abstract. This paper describes the steps that an engineered-to-order SME firm took to identify their requirements for a shopfloor Manufacturing Execution System (MES). The firm had limited experience and followed a hybrid Design Thinking/Lean approach to develop and test use cases that could be reviewed with stakeholders in the factory to confirm their value in supporting the critical economical outcomes of single piece flow in the factory. The firm created a set of requirements based on use cases and a roadmap for the further development of the MES. During the investigation, the foundation work necessary to develop a shopfloor platform was supported by a digital maturity assessment tool. The higher-level analytical micro-services were dependent on easily accessible transactional data from the system. The work's limitations are that implementation is not part of this study and that the approach taken must be compared with more traditional approaches.

Keywords: Smart manufacturing · Design Thinking · Lean · Manufacturing Execution Systems · SME

1 Introduction

Shopfloor materials and work planning can now be automated using Manufacturing Execution Systems (MES) that allow firms to track and document raw materials' transformation to finished goods [1]. Today it is possible to integrate MES with other digital technologies to move to predictive planning environments [2]. This enables the MES to provide information to help decision-makers to optimize and improve production output [3]. A gap remains, with many firms continuing to use Excel-based planning processes without the integration of more advanced digital tools [4].

This paper's motivation comes from the desire to understand how an SME in an engineered-to-order (ETO) environment can design and specify a shopfloor platform

Published by Springer Nature Switzerland AG 2021
A. Dolgui et al. (Eds.): APMS 2021, IFIP AICT 633, pp. 691–701, 2021.
https://doi.org/10.1007/978-3-030-85910-7_73

that provides advanced monitoring, diagnostics, and prediction to be integrated into the business. Planning on both an operational and strategic basis requires the controlling MES to be connected to systems that support production optimization. An ETO environment requires agile planning and replanning to adapt to the dynamic production environment; for example, workers may be absent, machines may require maintenance, or the sales team may request variations to orders. This occurs in a complex environment with multiple perspectives, where adaptations to the production plan need to be integrated into the day-to-day operations.

This study follows a firm in an ETO environment using a hybrid approach based on Design Thinking and a traditional Lean approach to develop a concept to future-proof their MES implementation. The research question for this study is: *"how can an SME with limited experience successfully specify the requirements for a smart manufacturing shopfloor platform that integrates with an MES, supporting the operation and strategic optimization?"*

2 Literature Review

Production needs to evolve to continuously meet customer expectations [5], and to fulfill individual customer requirements, integrated business solutions are needed. The flexibility and service orientation required can be achieved through digital manufacturing [6]. Under the term "Industry 4.0" the German government initiated a strategy in 2011 to address such changes [7]. A holistic approach in terms of driving the transformation into tomorrow's production paradigms is necessary [8]. This review will consider Smart Manufacturing and how it has been integrated into manufacturing businesses.

Through the application of Industry 4.0 technologies, a high level of process integration in human-machine collaboration can be achieved with respect to shopfloor equipment [9]. To attain flexibility and adaptability within the digitization of manufacturing, not just technological, but also organizational and cultural aspects are relevant [10, 11]. Schuh et al. [10] proposed an Industry 4.0 maturity index which leads to a roadmap encompassing tailored actions within these aspects. According to the maturity index, computerization and connectivity must first be created in the context of digitization, so that smart factory initiatives can progress. In other words, to achieve the objective of smart factories, the collecting and processing of data gathered within the value stream is crucial [12]. Techniques such as simulation, data analytics, and optimization will help to build a better understanding of manufacturing processes, as well as creating transparency throughout the value stream on the shopfloor [9]. This is possible today for single production lines, but the major challenge is accomplishing this along the value stream [13].

Many companies have monolithic IT-structures, based on Enterprise Resource Planning (ERP) systems which can make shopfloor digitization difficult [8]. According to Fend and Hofmann [14] platform models are standards, which provide a basis for the further development of application programs. For the production floor, a tool that can assist such a paradigm shift in operation technologies is the MES [15]. Many systems are built based on standards as ISA 95, VDI 5600, MESA or similar [1], within those are functions for resource management, quality management, and manufacturing control, and often customer requirements are defined based on these standards [1]. Today, MES are mainly task oriented and lack the forward-looking tools for analytics and prediction [1, 10, 16], but as we move towards smart manufacturing, information systems within the cyber world will have new requirements to use shopfloor data to achieve more flexible production [13]. Besides more advanced analytical functions, future requirements can be summarized in horizonal and vertical integration, decentralization, and connectivity [15]. Althoughthe adoption of MESs in companies is increasing [17], currently an approach is missing to define requirements for driving data-enabled decisions within the smart factory environment to realize its potential benefits [13]. However, the focus should not solely rely on technological aspects but should be arranged in a holistic approach focusing also on organizational structures and business process reengineering [17]. Especially in manufacturing companies, Lean tools are seen as a foundation to start with, prior to the commencement of digitization activities [11, 18].

3   Methodology

A single case with structured analysis and reflection provides the foundation from which we may start to generalize a solution [19, 20]. In this instance, the subject is the development of a concept for the system within the firm, which was defined by the research question. The purpose is exploratory, to test the theoretical approach of Design Thinking (Fig. 1) using a retrospective case in which one of the authors was embedded [21]. The Design Thinking approach was enhanced by Lean tools, as Lean is a relevant foundation to increase manufacturing performance and therefore build the basis for a highly integrated system [11]. Each of the major steps was stated, and the purpose of each documented, the tasks undertaken were described, and an analysis of the outcome with reflections/reviews was offered at the end of each task. Detailed interview data, use case and workshop output were all documented and archived as part of the case study investigation. A timeline of the study was constructed and represented the anchor for the subsequent results describing the period of data collection. Data collected was confirmed with the participants following the initial analysis and interpretation.

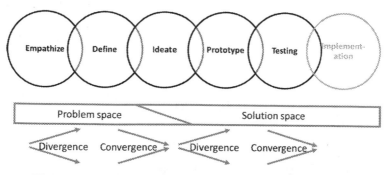

Fig. 1. Design thinking approach based on Fleischmann et al. [22]

4 Results

Project work was undertaken during the period October 2020 to April 2021, and the findings are presented based on Design Thinking based methodology, with Lean tools added to support new perspectives. The results focus on the first five phases, as the aim of the work was to create an implementation plan or roadmap.

4.1 Case Description

The company investigated operates within the furniture industry in Switzerland. Product and service quality at a competitive price-performance ratio are essential for customers. Therefore, the company does not release production orders until the products have been configured and ordered by the customer. Hence, the company does not produce into a distribution center as products are manufactured in a single piece flow, sequenced to the customer's delivery requirements. A consistent data flow starting in sales and going into production helps the company to ensure economic efficiency, while maintaining flexibility of products. Some individual Lean tools are used within the company however, a holistic implementation of Lean does not exist. The Design Thinking process is not yet established within the company.

4.2 Empathize

The purpose of this step was to generate a common understanding of stakeholder problems and to investigate the needs within the company. Table 1 presents the three major tasks and the insights generated.

Table 1. Empathize phase – approach, insights, and reflections

Task	Purpose	Insights and reflections
Literature research	Insights in state-of-the-art research, concepts and methodologies	- Paradigm change in manufacturing based on digitally-enabled manufacturing versus task/transactional orientation of MES - Important to focus on flexibility and efficiency while complexity increases
Value stream map	Understand the production process and philosophy	- Provided an overview of the processes, material flows and information flows within the factory - The basis for further investigation and stakeholder identification
Gemba walks ($\geq$1/week)	Understand the actual job of the workforce today	- Excessive use of paper forms and Excel sheets - Lack of accessibility to information - Wide range of technologies in use
Interviews (7)	Identify the pain points with current manufacturing philosophy	- Some data on orders is available, but poorly used for KPIs as well for analytics and prediction - Problems need to be solved in a holistic approach using data for decisions

The literature review described the necessity of digital tools in manufacturing to stay competitive. Such tools already exist within the firm but are not used to their full potential. The value stream mapping provided an overview of production processes as well as material and information flows within the factory. Gemba walks confirmed that the company has a wide range of technologies and automation in use. Data for the main processes are generated automatically and are provided directly to machines. Nevertheless, paper systems are primarily used to provide employees with information for production tasks. The interviews provided additional depth to the information obtained from the Gemba walks. The interviewees provided insights into the current problems in the production and supply chain. This was consolidated using a cause-effect diagram to provide a holistic view of the current situation, clearly showing that data was not being used for decision-making, as obtaining the relevant data was a fundamental problem.

4.3   Define

After divergence in the first phase, convergence of the pain points was needed. Therefore, information was consolidated in a cause-effect diagram built on the eight-dimensions: machine, material, method, manpower/mind power, management, measurement, milieu, and money (8Ms), which focus on relevant aspects of a production environment [17]. Table 2 highlights the major tasks performed within this phase.

Consolidating the information collected, the 162 pain points identified were aggregated into 55. Clustering using the 8Ms increased acceptance by stakeholders and also provided a useful overview. The summary of the pain points using a cause-effect diagram identified the need for improvements in all eight areas, but especially with operational dashboards and production planning. The root causes of these pain points showed that most of the workforce are aware of the problems and their possible causes. Having them clearly documented was supported by the stakeholders.

Table 2. Define phase – approach, insights, and reflection

Task	Purpose	Insights and reflections
Consolidation of pain points	Aggregation and summarization of pain points across multiple actors	- Grouping in 8Ms provides different perspectives on the pain points - Correct use of information leads to faster decisions with less effort
Root-causes analysis	Deepen/broaden understanding of pain points and their causes	- Take time on reflection and ask why performing this task is necessary - Analysis and documentation were supported by stakeholders and delivered new insights to them

4.4 Ideate

Awareness of the current problems allows abstract solutions to be generated to address them [23]. As described in Table 3, the ideas developed were examined to determine whether they could also use digital means to create a positive effect for production.

Discussing pain points with practitioners not only reduces misunderstandings, but often delivers practical ideas that might be included in abstract solutions. These show that a reactively managed production could be transformed into a more actively managed production, which might allow more flexibility. The rating of the solution approaches developed showed that it makes sense to address some topics without digital integration. On the other hand, it also became clear that a lot of data is already available in the MES, but that it is currently not used, or only used to a limited extent.

Table 3. Ideate phase – approach, insights, and reflection

Task	Purpose	Insights and reflections
Abstract solution	Identify ideas on possible solutions	- Change from reactive production environment to a more proactive environment via the use of data - When asking *"how can I do better?"* practitioners have valuable insights
Rating on digital shopfloor solutions	Search for matching solutions that can be realized with digital tools	- Most of the data-handling needed for the shopfloor services is handled through the MES - MES (as described in VDI 5600) lacks functions in advanced analytics, prediction, and simulation

4.5 Prototype

The aim of the prototype phase is to visualize issues through low fidelity prototypes, storyboards, wireframes, or other tools to further test, develop and discuss ideas [22]. For the creation of concrete use cases, visualization methods were used here. These are summarized in Table 4.

Detailed use cases were developed based on the abstract solutions from the ideation phase. Visualization supported the use case development and aided the classification of the use cases based on their type, in the form of a diagram. Selected scenarios were rated using the Industry 4.0 maturity index [10], which allowed detailed mapping of the scenarios, and in parallel, the development of a roadmap. The five use case scenarios are presented in Fig. 2.

Table 4. Prototype phase – approach, insights, and reflection

Task	Purpose	Insights and reflections
Use case development (21)	Grouping, use case identification, ideation	- Enabling data processing through analytics, prediction and simulation in production is crucial. This is missing in current MES requirements - It is about empowering employees to make informed decisions, not to remove them
Consolidation of scenarios (5)	Complementary use of use cases	- Model of Porter and Heppelmann and Schuh et al., delivered a good basis for developing a roadmap of use cases

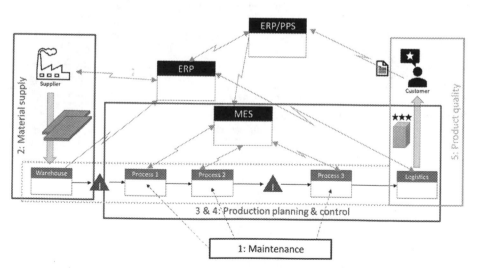

Fig. 2. Developed use case scenarios illustrated on the value stream

4.6 Testing

The purpose was to evaluate the results from the prototyping critically, and the approach, *"Prototype as if you know you're right, but test as if you know you're wrong"* [22, p. 170] was taken. Testing was completed on early paper-based prototypes, Table 5 summarizes the approach taken.

A slide deck of use cases was prepared to support the interviews. The internal and external interviews provided feedback on the cases and confirmation (or otherwise) of the assumptions used when creating the use cases. The interviewees' perspectives were summarized according to Mayring [24] so that results could be easily compared. A mind map was created to visualize the findings and to support the linking between input and subcategorization.

Table 5. Testing phase – approach, insights, and reflection

Task	Purpose	Insights and reflections
Preparation	Develop the interview case book	- Visual descriptions support the prototypes
Internal interviews (5)	Verification of use cases with stakeholders	- Opportunities and risk to implement use cases - Interview insightful but provided no uniform opinion on the prototypes
External interviews (5)	Investigate and verify foundation and confirm assumptions	- Very different understanding of terms e.g., digital twin, smart factory, Industry 4.0. Process first, digitization second, & start small - Practitioners having a hard time to define terms differentiating digital representations
Summarization and revision	Summarize learnings and obtain confirmation	- Content analysis and categorization - The categorization generated insights from the interviews and thus improved the prototype

5 Discussion

The firm had limited experience in MES and smart manufacturing technologies, but more importantly, they lacked maturity in Lean manufacturing and process optimization which are the foundations of a successful manufacturing system implementation. Consequently, it was decided to capture the requirements by focusing on the apparent problems met in operational.

During the study, the foundations necessary to develop a shopfloor platform were supported by using an Industry 4.0 maturity index to assess the solutions developed. The higher-maturity, analytical micro-services [10] were found to be based on easily accessible transactional data from the system. Although some of the firm's operational technologies provide data, they are rarely used, as accessing the data was difficult. Developing and testing prototypes showed that a different understanding of terms exists, making it hard to derive precise requirements. However, testing the prototypes provided valuable feedback and overcame the differences in understanding. Following detailed evaluation of the needs, the firm decided to prioritize and phase the implementation by defining a roadmap that supported their ongoing needs. An important aspect to consider is potential future needs, to ensure that the chosen solution can scale with the firm and provide industrial agility. Further, this approach, when coupled with kaizen thinking, encourages suggestions for ongoing improvement at an operational level.

This work shows a possible approach to how Design Thinking [22] can be adapted and applied successfully within a ETO environment of an SME that has limited understanding of their requirements for Smart Manufacturing. It also confirmed that following a hybrid Design Thinking approach with the integration of Lean tools, which are well integrated into a production environment [11], allowed the firm to build a roadmap to further build and evolve such an MES. A properly applied MES then also facilitates the identification and elimination of waste which helps to increase operational efficiency further [18]. The integration of different perspectives gives the firm the opportunity to develop targeted and suitable solutions for a range of stakeholders. This was particularly important in the area of planning, advanced analytics, simulation and prediction, where digital tools can add even more value in the future [13]. The iterative approach and conscious expansion and contraction of the problem space as well as the solution space was a new approach for the firm. The study confirms that MES requires customization to individual businesses, and that MES must provide the shopfloor platform for additional Industry 4.0 functionality [1].

Reflecting on the research question, in this case an SME with limited experience in smart manufacturing can specify their requirements for a Smart Manufacturing system that integrates operational, tactical, and strategic requirements. The application of a hybrid Design Thinking/Lean approach supported the process of discovery and allowed an adaptable roadmap to be created forming the basis of the plan for the firm's Smart Manufacturing program.

The limitation of the work is that it was limited to one case and was reported before the implementation phase. A review should be made post implementation over a longer period to understand the value created. A multi-case study of firms using more traditional approaches should be undertaken.

6 Conclusions

This is only the first step for the firm in the digitalization journey to lead to Smart Manufacturing and ultimately to a Smart Factory. Using the hybrid approach, the firm has a roadmap that focuses on the short-term adoption of an MES and a longer-term version with increased levels of optimization and automation. This approach helps to understand the challenges faced and gain consensus. Missing from the approach was identifying the key metrics that can be used to measure the success of the implementation. This will help prove the value and confirm the initial requirements were covered allow the firm to build a solid foundation for the digitalization of their manufacturing process.

It is recommended that an action-research project is embedded within the digitalization to allow a longitudinal case study to be built up following the digitization efforts over two years. This would enable a detailed set of the lessons learnt to be abstracted from digitalization.

References

1. Wiendahl, H.-H., Kluth, A., Kipp, R.: Fraunhofer-Institut für Produktionstechnik und Automatisierung IPA, and Trovarit AG, Marktspiegel Business Software - MES - Fertigungssteuerung 2017/2018 (2017)
2. Urbina Coronado, P.D., Lynn, R., Louhichi, W., Parto, M., Wescoat, E., Kurfess, T.: Part data integration in the shop floor digital twin: mobile and cloud technologies to enable a manufacturing execution system. J. Manuf. Syst. **48**, 25–33 (2018). https://doi.org/10.1016/j.jmsy.2018.02.002
3. Åkerman, M.: Implementing shop floor IT for Industry 4.0. Chalmers University of Technology, Göteborg (2018)
4. Bartoszewicz, G., Wdowicz, M.: Automation of the process of reporting the compliance of the production plan with its execution based on integration of SAP ERP system in connection with Excel spreadsheet and VBA application. Digitalization of Supply Chains, RILEM Publications SARL, pp. 101–116 (2020). https://doi.org/10.17270/B.M.978-83-66017-86-3.8
5. Bauernhansl, T.: Die Vierte Industrielle Revolution – Der Weg in ein wertschaffendes Produktionsparadigma. In: Bauernhansl, T., ten Hompel, M., Vogel-Heuser, B. (eds.) Industrie 4.0 in Produktion, Automatisierung und Logistik, pp. 5–35. Springer, Wiesbaden (2014). https://doi.org/10.1007/978-3-658-04682-8_1
6. Ivanov, D., Sokolov, B., Dolgui, A.: Introduction to scheduling in Industry 4.0 and cloud manufacturing systems. In: Sokolov, B., Ivanov, D., Dolgui, A. (eds.) Scheduling in Industry 4.0 and Cloud Manufacturing. ISORMS, vol. 289, pp. 1–9. Springer, Cham (2020). https://doi.org/10.1007/978-3-030-43177-8_1
7. BMBF: Industrie 4.0 - BMBF. Bundesministerium für Bildung und Forschung - BMBF. https://www.bmbf.de/de/zukunftsprojekt-industrie-4-0-848.html. Accessed 22 Feb 2021
8. Gausemeier, J., Wiendahl, H.-P. (eds.) Wertschöpfung und Beschäftigung in Deutschland. Springer, Heidelberg (2011). https://doi.org/10.1007/978-3-642-20204-9
9. Kamble, S.S., Gunasekaran, A., Gawankar, S.A.: Sustainable Industry 4.0 framework: a systematic literature review identifying the current trends and future perspectives. Process Saf. Environ. Prot. **117**, 408–425 (2018). https://doi.org/10.1016/j.psep.2018.05.009
10. Schuh, G., Anderl, R., Dumitrescu, R., Ten Hompel, M., Krüger, A. (eds.): Industrie 4.0 Maturity Index: die digitale Transformation von Unternehmen gestalten – UPDATE 2020. Herbert Utz Verlag, München (2020). https://www.acatech.de/wp-content/uploads/2020/04/aca_STU_MatInd_2020_de_Web-1.pdf
11. Rüttimann, B.G., Stöckli, M.T.: Lean and Industry 4.0—twins, partners, or contenders? A due clarification regarding the supposed clash of two production systems. JSSM **09**(06), 485–500 (2016). https://doi.org/10.4236/jssm.2016.96051
12. Abele, E., et al.: Effiziente Fabrik 4.0: Einzug von Industrie 4.0 in bestehende Produktionssysteme. ZWF **110**(3), 150–153 (2015). https://doi.org/10.3139/104.111293

13. Dittmann, S., Zhang, P., Glodde, A., Dietrich, F.: Towards a scalable implementation of digital twins - a generic method to acquire shopfloor data. Procedia CIRP **96**, 157–162 (2021). https://doi.org/10.1016/j.procir.2021.01.069
14. Fend, L., Hofmann, J. (eds.): Digitalisierung in Industrie-, Handels- und Dienstleistungsunternehmen. Springer, Wiesbaden (2018). https://doi.org/10.1007/978-3-658-21905-5
15. Almada-Lobo, F.: The Industry 4.0 revolution and the future of Manufacturing Execution Systems (MES). JIM **3**(4), 16–21 (2016). https://doi.org/10.24840/2183-0606_003.004_0003
16. MPDV Mikrolab: Smart Factory Elements. Whitepaper (March 2019). https://www.mpdv.com/en/innovation-vision/mes-industry-40/smart-factory-elements/. Accessed 09 Apr 2021
17. Invernizzi, D., Gaiardelli, P., Arica, E., Powell, D.: MES implementation: critical success factors and organizational readiness model. In: Ameri, F., Stecke, K.E., von Cieminski, G., Kiritsis, D. (eds.) APMS 2019. IAICT, vol. 567, pp. 493–501. Springer, Cham (2019). https://doi.org/10.1007/978-3-030-29996-5_57
18. Perico, P., Arica, E., Powell, D.J., Gaiardelli, P.: MES as an enabler of lean manufacturing. IFAC-PapersOnLine **52**(13), 48–53 (2019). https://doi.org/10.1016/j.ifacol.2019.11.306
19. Yin, R.K.: Case Study Research: Design and Methods, 4th edn. Sage Publications, Los Angeles (2009)
20. Thomas, G.: Case Study. In: SAGE Research Methods Foundations. SAGE Publications Ltd., London (2020). https://doi.org/10.4135/9781526421036812890
21. Dugdale, D.: Understanding design thinking, lean and agile. https://www.wdoinnovation.com/design-thinking-lean-agile/. Accessed 07 Apr 2021
22. Fleischmann, A., Oppl, S., Schmidt, W., Stary, C.: From Modeling to Digitalization. In: Contextual Process Digitalization, pp. 151–177. Springer, Cham (2020). https://doi.org/10.1007/978-3-030-38300-8_5
23. Lee, J.S., Pries-Heje, J., Baskerville, R.: Theorizing in design science research. In: Jain, H., Sinha, A.P., Vitharana, P. (eds.) DESRIST 2011. LNCS, vol. 6629, pp. 1–16. Springer, Heidelberg (2011). https://doi.org/10.1007/978-3-642-20633-7_1
24. Mayring, P.: Qualitative Inhaltsanalyse. In: Mey, G., Mruck, K. (eds.) Handbuch Qualitative Forschung in der Psychologie. Wiesbaden: VS Verlag für Sozialwissenschaften, pp. 601–613 (2010). https://doi.org/10.1007/978-3-531-92052-8_42

The Role of Emerging Technologies in Disaster Relief Operations: Lessons from COVID-19

Shelter Location-Allocation Problem with Vulnerabilities of Network and Disruption of Shelter During the Response Phase of Disaster

Sweety Hansuwa[1,2]([⊠]), Usha Mohan[1]([⊠]), and Viswanath Kumar Ganesan[2]([⊠])

[1] Department of Management Studies, Indian Institute of Technology Madras, Chennai, India
ushamohan@iitm.ac.in
[2] Tata Consultancy Services, IITM Research Park, Chennai, India
{sweety.hansuwa,viswanath.ganesan}@tcs.com

Abstract. In this paper, we define and formulate the shelter location-allocation problem considering both the network vulnerability of the affected area and the shelter's disruption during the disaster management's response phase. We capture the vulnerability metric using the traveling cost and location vulnerability for shelter disruption using the shelter's operating cost. We formulate the problem as a mixed-integer linear programming (MILP) model and present an evacuee-allocation plan considering vulnerable network connectivities between the populated areas and the shelter locations. We finally apply and solve the problem using real-life case data obtained during the Nepal earthquake in 2015 and compare our models with Rahman's same data [10]. We demonstrate using the case example the usefulness of our modelling approach and show that we can achieve better results compared to a simulation study.

Keywords: Shelter location-allocation · Mixed-integer linear programming · Earthquake

1 Introduction

The year 2020 has witnessed more than 200 natural disasters [4]. The rise in the number of events is 27% in the first half of 2020 compared to 2019. Earthquakes are considered one of the worst natural disasters in the last 30 years. An example of a disaster is the 2004 earthquake and Tsunami and the Haiti earthquake that killed around 220,000 people and 159,000 people, respectively [3]. After a disaster strikes, many organizations need to respond to save peoples' lives and their needs in the affected areas. The selection of shelter locations is essential to relocate the people to a safer place as quickly as possible.

Operations research models have played an extensive role in all phases of disaster management. In particular, a class of models referred to as shelter-location-allocation models is instrumental in disaster management's planning and response stages. In the work, we attempt to answer the following questions:

© IFIP International Federation for Information Processing 2021
Published by Springer Nature Switzerland AG 2021
A. Dolgui et al. (Eds.): APMS 2021, IFIP AICT 633, pp. 705–713, 2021.
https://doi.org/10.1007/978-3-030-85910-7_74

1. Can we develop and use operation research models for real-life disaster relief and response requirements?
2. Can we improve the quality of the results from a mathematical model evaluating with practical data sets?
3. Is it feasible to build a decision model that can be relevant to practical needs as well as computationally fast?

The answers to the above questions are demonstrated in this work by formulating the problem as a MILP Model for the shelter location-allocation problem with the objectives of minimizing unmet demand, the travelling cost and the travel time. The problem of allocation of shelter locations (or relief centers) to relocate people (or important resources/materials) safely from vulnerable areas in a geography is presented in this work and real life case data has been used to validate the proposed model.

2 Literature

The literature has addressed the problem of the selection of candidate shelters using mathematical models. Allocation of evacuees to shelters has been studied using the p-median problem, the p-center model, and the maximal covering model using single objectives [5]. Alçada-Almeida et al. [1] proposed the multi-objective approach to solve the p-median model to select the number of shelters for the evacuation route plans in significant fire incidents. The objectives include minimizing the total distance, the people's risk to reach the shelters using the primary route, the shelters' risk, and the evacuation time from shelters to hospitals. Kilci et al. [7] discussed a mixed-integer model to locate temporary shelters and minimize the shelter area's minimum weight after the occurrence of an earthquake. Cavdur et al. [3] have discussed the temporary facilities' location problem under the demand's uncertainty and proposed the stochastic programming model in two-stage to decide the number of facility's need to open in the first decision, and service decisions next. They discuss the case study by taking up an earthquake event to test the model. Mostajabdaveh et al. [9] have addressed the shelter location for disaster preparedness that considers the efficiency and equity using the Gini index in the objective function. They proposed a mixed-integer programming formulation and a genetic algorithm to compare the performance of the proposed model. Rahman et al. [10] have discussed the post-disaster facility location problem and proposed the simulation approach and analysis between decisions and uncertainty. Yahyaei et al. [11] have discussed the robust relief network design under uncertainty and risk in the shelter and supply facility location. They have proposed the mathematical model and robust optimization programming model while considering the disruption of facility locations and network performance. In our research work, we discuss the shelter-location and allocation problem for the response phase. We consider the disruption of shelter location and the vulnerability of network connectivity. We also discuss the result analysis with real-life data on the Nepal earthquake 2015.

This paper's contribution introduces the vulnerability metric in the traveling cost and another metric for shelter's disruption and shelter's operating cost. The first metric evaluates the network vulnerability that considers a network's susceptibility between locations and the shelters during response. The traveling cost computes based on distance, and the network vulnerability captures the actual condition among locations and evaluates the total travel cost between locations. The second metric discussed is the shelter's operating cost that considers shelter conditions after a disaster and computes the actual operating cost to open a shelter.

3 Problem Description and Assumptions

This section discusses the problem statement and assumptions for the shelter-location and allocation problem for a disaster response phase. Also, we present the mixed-integer linear programming model, along with the descriptions of parameters, variables, constraints, and objective function.

Sets and indexes	
I	a set of affected locations that require evacuation
i	index for affected locations
J	a set of potential shelter locations
j	index for potential shelter locations
N	a set of nodes ($I \cup J$)
L	a set of capacity level of shelter locations
Parameters	
D_i	number of affected people at location i
$d_{i,j}$	distance between location i to shelter j before disaster
$d'_{i,j}$	distance between location i to shelter j after a disaster
$cap_{j,l}$	the capacity of a shelter j with capacity level l
$f_{j,l}$	the operating cost of a shelter j with capacity level l
$c_{i,j}$	the travel cost between location i to shelter j per kilometer
$penalty_i$	the penalty cost on unmet demand at location i
$v_{i,j}$	the vulnerability between location i to location j, i.e. $v_{i,j} \in [0,1]$
r_j	disruption level of shelter j, i.e. $r_j \in [0,1]$
M	positive big number

The shelter location and allocation problem in the evacuation planning is defined and considering the network's vulnerability and shelter's disruption for the disaster response phase. Network vulnerability concepts are captured in our model as opening up shelter locations near the affected location is not feasible. The evacuation process becomes critical when a network is most susceptible to travel between two nearest locations, affecting travel costs. The actual shelter situation is known after the disaster strikes, and it may not be the same as considered during the planning stage. To operate at the total capacity, consider the additional operational cost. We present the model and first discuss the definition of network vulnerability. Mattsson and Jenelius [8] have studied vulnerability based on topology-based and system-based metrics. Topology-based vulnerability indices discuss the transportation network in terms of connectivity and efficiency without considering its congestion. Gu et al. [6] discuss the topology-based efficiency indices (*TEI*) between two points i and j for a network by Eq. (1).

$$TEI = \frac{1}{|N|(|N-1|)} \frac{\sum_{i \neq j \in N} \left(\frac{1}{d_{i,j}} - \frac{1}{d'_{i,j}} \right)}{\sum_{i \neq j \in N} \frac{1}{d_{i,j}}} \tag{1}$$

We compute the network vulnerability among locations in terms of the topology-based efficiency indices as discussed in Eq. (1). Hence, the network vulnerability $v(i,j)$ between location i to location j as defined in the following equation.

$$v(i,j) = \frac{\left(\frac{1}{d_{i,j}} - \frac{1}{d'_{i,j}} \right)}{\frac{1}{d_{i,j}}} \quad \forall i \in I, j \in J \tag{2}$$

The list of assumptions considered for our problem definition is:

1. A set of shelters with location definitions and their available capacities (in terms of the number of people) with associated operating costs are known.
2. A set of connectivity between various locations and the shelter locations and their vulnerabilities are available and computed using Eq. (2).
3. The number of people to be evacuated from each affected location is known.
4. The disruption level of each shelter is known.

Decision Variables

$x_{j,l}$ is a binary variable, and its value equal to 1 if a shelter j with the capacity level l is selected to open, 0 otherwise.

$y_{i,j}$ is a binary variable, and its value equal to 1 if affected location i is assigned to shelter j, 0 otherwise.

$z_{i,j}$ is an integer variable and represents the number of people evacuated from location i to shelter j.

w_i is an integer variable and represents the unmet demand at location i.

$t_{i,j}$ is a continuous variable and represents the traveling cost between location i to location j.

3.1 Mixed-Integer Linear Programming (MILP)

The first term of the objective function is to minimize the total cost of operating a shelter while considering the disruption level of shelter. The operating cost is increased by $(1 + r_j)$ with a level of shelter disruption. The second term is to minimize the total transportation cost that depends on the distance and the network's vulnerability between locations i and j. The third term is to minimize the total penalty cost on unmet demands.

$$\text{Minimize} \sum_{j \in J} \sum_{l \in L} f_{j,l}(1 + r_j) \times x_{j,l} + \sum_{i \in I} \sum_{j \in J} t_{i,j} + \sum_{i \in I} penalty_i \times w_i \tag{3}$$

subject to the constraints presented in Eqs. (4) to (12).

Constraint (4) ensures only one type of capacity level to be selected when a shelter is opened.

$$\sum_{l \in L} x_{j,l} \leq 1 \quad \forall j \tag{4}$$

Constraint (5) ensures that maximum p facilities are opened.

$$\sum_{j \in J} \sum_{l \in L} x_{j,l} \leq p \tag{5}$$

Constraint (6) ensures each location should be allocated to exactly one shelter.

$$\sum_{j \in J} y_{i,j} = 1 \quad \forall i \tag{6}$$

Constraint (7) ensures that location's assignment to shelter only if it is open.

$$y_{i,j} \leq \sum_{l \in L} x_{j,l} \quad \forall i, \forall j \tag{7}$$

Constraint (8) ensures that the demand of the number of people to evacuate should be satisfied.

$$\sum_{j \in J} z_{i,j} + w_i = D_i \quad \forall i \tag{8}$$

Constraint (9) allocation of demand to the shelter if location i is allocated to shelter j.

$$z_{i,j} \leq M \times y_{i,j} \quad \forall i, \forall j \tag{9}$$

Constraint (10) the total evacuated people allocated to the shelter should be less than shelter capacity.

$$\sum_{i \in I} z_{i,j} \leq \sum_{l \in L} cap_{j,l} \times x_{j,l} \quad \forall j \tag{10}$$

Constraints (11), (12) computes the transportation cost if location i is allocated to shelter j while considering the vulnerability of the network between location i to shelter j. The vulnerability of the network increases the additional cost of transportation cost by $(1 + v_{i,j})$.

$$t_{i,j} \geq c_{i,j} \times d_{i,j} \times (1 + v_{i,j}) - M \times (1 - y_{i,j}) \quad \forall i, \forall j \tag{11}$$

$$t_{i,j} \leq c_{i,j} \times d_{i,j} \times (1 + v_{i,j}) + M \times (1 - y_{i,j}) \quad \forall i, \forall j \tag{12}$$

4   Results and Case Study

This study uses the data discussed by Rahman et al. [10]. Rahman et al. [10] formulate the problem to minimize the unmet demand, uncovered demand points, and the maximum travel time. A simulation study has been performed using the post-disaster operational scenario on Nepal Earthquake in 2015 in their work. This study used data with 30 demand points/locations, 20 facilities as shelter locations (or facilities), and disruption factors for all nodes. The disruption factor is computed for each node based on the distance to the epicenter, and the range of factors is defined between 1 to 2. The distance between various locations before a disaster is computed using the open-source routing machine (OSRM-open street map) as data of latitude and longitude given by Rahman et al. [10]. The operating cost is the same across all shelters, and definitions are taken from the Cap_61 instance of Mostajabdaveh et al. [9]. The travel cost is considered among locations based on the data provided by Rahman et al. [10]. We consider the best estimate of transport cost of 10 USD per 1000 kg per hour. The penalty cost for unmet demand is defined as equal to ten thousand times the operating cost of a shelter in our experimental results.

The MILP model has been implemented in OPL CPLEX 12.8, and the models have been executed using a computing processor with Intel Xeon 2.4 GHz (dual core) and 64 GB RAM. The solution obtained with the data as mentioned earlier using the MILP model is presented in Table 1 for different p-values. The p-values indicate the number of shelter locations chosen from the defined data sets on Nepal Earthquake data 2015. We observe that the objective function value decreases with increased p-values. The objective function value includes the transportation cost, shelter operating cost, and penalty cost. The results in Table 1 observe that the transportation cost has decreased and shelter operating cost increased with increased p-values. The objective function becomes constant at maximum p-values equal to 7 (chosen six locations of facilities in solution) and same with the transportation cost and shelter operating cost for Nepal Earthquake data 2015. We further discuss the MILP model solution for the maximum p-values equal to 10 in Table 2 for the increased demand of location from the nominal value. We consider the five levels (10%, 30%, 50%, 70%, 90%) for increased demands of locations and discuss the results in Table 2. We observe that the objective function values increased with the increased demands and the same with the transportation cost and shelter operating cost.

Table 1. Results obtained using MILP formulation with various number of shelter locations

p-value	Objective function value	Transportation cost	Shelter operating cost	Facilities chosen
3	231632.6	196895.2	34737.3	8, 10, 18
4	200548	155879.9	44668.03	8, 10, 12, 18
5	189974.2	132344.9	57629.34	8, 10, 12, 13, 18
6	187778.7	120273.8	67504.88	8, 9, 10, 13, 14, 18

Table 2. Results obtained using MILP formulation with p value = 10

# of facilities open	Demand increased (in %)	Objective function value	Transport-ation cost	Shelter operating cost	Facilities chosen
6	10	199806.1	132301.2	67504.8	8, 9, 10, 13, 14, 18
6	30	223860.9	156356	67504.8	8, 9, 10, 13, 14, 18
7	50	247815.8	170380.2	77435.6	8, 9, 10, 12, 13, 14, 18
7	70	270533.2	193097.6	77435.6	8, 9, 10, 12, 13, 14, 18
7	90	293250.5	215814.9	77435.6	8, 9, 10, 12, 13, 14, 18

We compare the solution on the data sets considering the unmet demand, travel costs, and travel time as given in Rahman et al. [10] using the constraints defined in our MILP model. The data used for our experimentation for comparison of results consists of the logistics requirements for transportation of relief materials post-disaster in Nepal. First, we compute the objective function values for the facilities chosen by Rahman et al. [10] and then compare them with the MILP model. Table 3 presents the comparison against results obtained using both models. We observe that the first objective function of the unmet demand solution has improved for the MILP model compared to Rahman et al. [10].

The second objective function, the travel/transportation cost solution of MILP, increases as compared to the objective function value of Rahman et al. [10]. Still, the unmet demand for Rahman et al. [10] solution is 7205910, which means that the solution is satisfied only 62.096% of the total demand. The MILP solution has met 99.90% of total demand. The third objective function, the travel time, is comparable with Rahman et al. [10], and the difference between the total travel time of both models is 9.3%. The MILP model satisfied 99.69% of total demand, and Rahman et al. [10] met 98.60%. It is observed that the MILP formulation solved using CPLEX Solver provides significantly better values for the selection of facilities. Table 4 gives the disruption indices of the 20 locations, and we can see that the MILP model chooses the locations with low vulnerability.

Table 3. Compare the MILP with the same objective function of Rahman et al. [10]

Objective function ($p = 4$)	Objective values from (Rahman et al.)	Facility chosen (Rahman et al. 2019)	Objective values form MILP Model	Facility chosen
Unmet demand	115940.00	4, 8, 12, 13	50360.0	3, 8, 13, 16
Travel cost	87937.89	2, 4, 15, 17	245673.1	8, 10, 12, 18
Travel time	186978.00	4, 8, 13, 20	204423.3	8, 12, 13, 20

Table 4. Facility location's disruption (Rahman et al. [10])

Facility	1	2	3	4	5	6	7	8	9	10
Disruption	0.9	0.49	0.19	0.46	0.88	0.39	0.10	0.35	0.21	0.8
Facility	11	12	13	14	15	16	17	18	19	20
Disruption	0.86	0.32	0.73	0.43	0.46	0.34	0.47	0.46	0.12	019

5 Conclusion

This paper presents a shelter location-allocation problem for the response phase to mini-mize operating cost, travel cost, and penalty cost on unmet demand. This paper introduces the vulnerability metric in the traveling cost and shelter's disruption metric for shelter's operating cost. We proposed a MILP model, and evaluate the results of the model using case data from Nepal earthquake occurred in 2015. We do evaluate the performance of the proposed MILP model with the results of simulation study [10] based on the post-disaster facility location decisions for the Nepal earthquake. Our future research is exploratory, and the current study can be extended to study multi-period dimensions thus leveraging the dynamic nature of the real-life requirements for planning and deployment needs. There is a potential need to leverage heuristic approaches to solve large instances and study the uncertainty parameters using robust optimization.

References

1. Alçada-Almeida, L., Tralhão, L., Santos, L., Coutinho-Rodrigues, J.: A multi-objective app-roach to locate emergency shelters and identify evacuation routes in urban areas. Geogr. Anal. **41**(1), 9–29 (2009)
2. Cavdur, F., Kose-Kucuk, M., Sebatli, A.: Allocation of temporary disaster response facilities under demand uncertainty: an earthquake case study. Int. J. Disaster Risk Reduct. **19**, 159–166 (2016)
3. Downearth Organization (2020). https://www.downtoearth.org.in/news/natural-disasters/new-study-can-help-improve-earthquake-prediction-72275. Accessed 1 Apr 2021
4. Global Catastrophe Recap: First Half of 2020. AON Solutions, https://www.downtoearth.org.in/news/climate-change/more-than-200-natural-disasters-across-world-in-1st-half-of-2020-72445. Accessed 30 Mar 2021

5. Hakimi, S.L.: Optimum locations of switching centers and the absolute centers and medians of a graph. Oper. Res. **12**(3), 450–459 (1964)
6. Gu, Y., Fu, X., Liu, Z., Xu, X., Chen, A.: Performance of transportation network under perturbations: reliability, vulnerability, and resilience. Transp. Res. Part E: Logist. Transp. Rev. **133**, 1–16 (2020)
7. Kilci, F., Kara, B.Y., Bozkaya, B.: Locating temporary shelter areas after an earthquake: a case for Turkey. Eur. J. Oper. Res. **243**(1), 323–332 (2015)
8. Mattsson, L.G., Jenelius, E.: Vulnerability and resilience of transport systems - a discussion of recent research. Transp. Res. Part A Policy Pract. **81**, 16–34 (2015)
9. Mostajabdaveh, M., Gutjahr, W.J., Sibel Salman, F.: Inequity-averse shelter location for disaster preparedness. IISE Trans. **51**(8), 809–829 (2019)
10. Rahman, M.T., Majchrzak, T.A., Comes, T.: Deep uncertainty in humanitarian logistics operations: decision-making challenges in responding to large scale natural disasters Int. J. Emerg. Manage. **15**(3), 276–297 (2019)
11. Yahyaei, M., Bozorgi-Amiri, A.: Robust reliable humanitarian relief network design: an integration of shelter and supply facility location. Ann. Oper. Res. **283**(1–2), 897–916 (2018). https://doi.org/10.1007/s10479-018-2758-6

Technologies Helping Smart Cities to Build Resilience: Focus on COVID-19

Helton Almeida dos Santos[1]([✉]) [ID], Emerson da Silva Santana[1] [ID],
Robson Elias Bueno[2] [ID], and Silvia Helena Bonilla[1] [ID]

[1] Graduate Studies in Production Engineering, Universidade Paulista, Sao Paulo, Brazil
[2] Graduate Studies in Technological Innovation, UNIFESP, São Paulo, Brazil

Abstract. Sustainable development goal #11 (SDG#11) deals with making cities inclusive, safe, resilient, and sustainable. SDG#3 deals with "Strengthen the capacity of all countries, in particular developing countries, for early warning, risk reduction and management of national and global health risks" So, the COVID-19 pandemic can be included within the targets of SDG#11 and #3 targets. It is reiterated the necessity of disaster and emergency health risk reduction and the building of resilience within the context of sustainable development concerns. Resilience is a concept also contemplated within the paradigm of smart planning and smart cities. The urban domain is selected to explore the tools used to cope with the current COVID-19 pandemic and that contribute to building resilience. Innovation and the relevance of SDG#9 are clear since the urgency of improvements in general and domestic technology and access to universal and affordable internet have to be guaranteed to achieve the objective of building resilience. A categorized vision of the main technologies, applications, and functionalities within the Smart City domain are discussed to identify the way those technologies support COVID-19 and integrate with the three SDGs fundamentals for resilience building. We hope that this work will contribute for practitioners, policymakers, academics, and citizens to be better prepared for future outbreaks.

Keywords: COVID-19 · Smart cities · SDG · Resilience · Resilience building · Disrupting technologies

1 Introduction

The United Nations' Sustainable Development Goal #11 (SDG#11) deals with turning cities inclusive, safe, resilient, and sustainable. It is a fact that urbanization is exerting pressure on the living environment (fresh water supply, sewage discharge) and public health. In the current situation of the coronavirus pandemic, the high demographic density in urban environments is acting as an enabler for virus dissemination.

Due to the lack of consensually effective drug therapy and incomplete vaccination, interventions in terms of virus spread prevention are mandatory. The measures to prevent the dissemination of viral infections in communities include maintaining social distancing combined with different degrees of lockdown [1]. According to Shoruzaman et al.

A. Dolgui et al. (Eds.): APMS 2021, IFIP AICT 633, pp. 714–723, 2021.
https://doi.org/10.1007/978-3-030-85910-7_75

[2], the social distancing protocols include country wide lock downs, travel bans, and limiting access to essential businesses. People face the challenge of meeting the needs in total or partial isolation whereas the continuity of essential services is ensured.

Among the targets included in SDG#11, two are explicitly applicable to the current situation of the pandemic. In this way, target 11.5 deals with reduction of the number of deaths and the number of people affected by disasters and target 11.B deals with increasing the number of cities adopting and implementing integrated policies and plans towards resilience to disasters in line with the Sendai Framework for Disaster Risk Reduction (SFDRR) [3]. The SFDRR reiterates the necessity of disaster and emergency health risk reduction and the resilience building within the context of sustainable development, being resilience defined as "The ability of a system, community or society exposed to hazards to resist, absorb, accommodate, adapt to, transform and recover from the effects of a hazard in a timely and efficient manner, including through the preservation and restoration of its essential basic structures and functions through risk management" [4].

As stated by Wright et al. [5] the SFDRR recognizes health at the heart of disaster risk management. Thus, target 3.D of SDG#3 dealing with "Strengthen the capacity of all countries, in particular developing countries, for early warning, risk reduction and management of national and global health risks" [6] is aligned with the SFDRR. So, the COVID-19 pandemic can be undoubtedly considered a matter of concern of SDG#11 and #3.

The transboundary characteristics of the pandemic lead to a multilevel necessity of management, at the global, national, regional, and city levels. The approach of SDG#11, more specifically its focus on resilience, offer the approach to explore the tools used to cope with the COVID-19 pandemic at the urban level and consequently, to help in building resilience.

Resilience is a concept also contemplated within the paradigm of smart planning and smart cities [7, 8]. The smart city (SC) concept although broad and still open to new approaches, converges into two fundamentals: new technology-based applications (based on information and communication technologies (ICT) and data-driven smart applications) providing an added value to the human/environment binomial.

The main function of innovation is related to the role to develop, test, and implement new solutions through the building, sharing, and continuously enhancing practical knowledge in response to the goals, strategies, policies, and visions of the city [9]. The relevance of SDG#9 is evident since the urgency of improvements in technology and access to universal and affordable internet have to be guaranteed to achieve the objective of building resilience.

The present paper aims to discuss how the information and communication technologies within the smart city environment could contribute to building resilience during the COVID-19 pandemic in an integrated way with SDG#11, #9 and #3. There is little discussion on smart city technology devoted to support urban resilience in the context of Sustainable Development paradigm. It is expected this paper will shed light to identifying ways of operationalizing the SDGs (in this case, three of them) with a well-focused goal of resilience construction within pandemic. We hope discussion will help practitioners and academic researchers.

2 Literature Review

This brief review organizes literature according to three classes. Some papers deal with technologies adopted to fight against pandemics without identification of the domain of action and application. Others explicitly express the focus on SC. And it is found an incipient research approach which deals with SC network.

Among the first class of papers in mitigating the spread of COVID-19 [10], cover the role of smart technology with specific focus on advancement in the field of drone, robotics, artificial intelligence (AI), mask, and sensor technology [11] explore three initiatives: COVID-19 focused datasets; Artificial intelligence-powered search tools and contact tracing based on mobile communication technology [12] analyses the different technological response to control the transmission of the pandemic adopted by China and Western democracies, concluding that the impact of smart technologies is potentially moderated by the social and political contexts in which they are implemented. Among the research explicitly concerning technologies within SC domain [13], discuss extensive use of SC technology in South Korea [14] discuss the heterogeneous impact of smart cities on COVID-19 prevention and control from different phases and city population size in China. The relevance of SC networks is represented by Allam and Jones (2020) [15] who address how smart city networks should work towards enhancing standardization protocols for increased data sharing in the event of outbreaks or disasters, leading to better global understanding and management.

3 Methodology

3.1 Bibliographic Research

Instead of engaging in an orthodox systematic review, a review at different levels was conducted, searching for representative cases of technologies within the smart city approach showing the current or potential use in building resilience during the pandemic. Journals retrieved from the World Health Organization open database were used to identify representative technologies. Some combinations of keywords were adopted.

In addition to COVID-19 or coronavirus, these other terms were included: ICT, "smart cities", "smart city", IoT, Artificial Intelligence, Bigdata, traceability, tracking, Cloud, technologies, disrupting technologies, apps, among others. A subsequent stage of filtering was conducted to retrieve only those initiatives related to the urban environment. As the pandemic is still in course the sources consulted also include, when necessary, divulgation journals or media. Cases dealing with specific medical applications such as drug therapy, artificial intelligence to develop the synthesis of novel drugs, or vaccine development, were discarded since they do not belong to the research scope.

On the other hand, health-related technologies that integrate ICT are included if they deal with the following tasks: allow communication between patients and health staff, remote support to diagnose, and distant provision of care since they support measures that minimize virus spreading.

3.2 Outlining the Smart City Approach Adopted

It was mentioned above that SC presents various definitions and that two principles are extracted as fundamentals to define SC: i) adoption of ICT technologies and, ii) inhabitants/environment improvement through identifying and solving problems.

In the present paper, the services delivered by ICT contribute to the containment of the pandemic, thus contributing at different levels to building resilience. To organize and categorize the representative technological applications, the structural model of SC defined by Calvillo et al. [16] and Chamoso et al. [17] is adopted. The structure of a SC is composed of different layers and it can be represented as a three-level platform, where hardware is the base, the communication mechanism represents the middle layer and the top layer is represented by the intelligent software [16]. This structural approach based on the necessary layers to support and allow technologies operationalization (and consequently service delivering to citizens) was chosen as the framework to discuss and categorize the technologies. The technologies are classified within the specific layer based on the service that is currently delivering to society.

3.3 Outlining the Approach of Resilience Adopted

In the present case, the selected approach is not focused on its definition but on the stages necessary for its building. To build resilience the technological-based interventions have to fulfill abilities capable of contributing at one or more of the following stages:

1) Planning or anticipation to mitigate or prevent risks.
2) Preparedness in order to further ensure that capacities are in place for effective response.
3) Responsiveness in order to ensure a rapid and effective reaction to the occurrence of a catastrophic disaster or emergency.
4) Recovery in order to restore critical community functions.
5) Strengthening of resilience capabilities: continuous improvement.

3.4 Line of Thought Adopted

The technologies against COVID-19 relevant to building resilience are explored through two aspects: the layer they belong to, as discussed in Sect. 3.2 and at which stage, they support building resilience (Sect. 3.3). Figure 1 shows the line of thought in an illustrative way. The collection of data that feed the first block is extracted from considerations explained in Sect. 3.1.

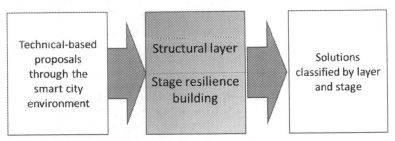

Fig. 1. Line of thought adopted and the relationships among the different elements and blocks. The first block represents the technical-based solutions inherent to Smart city; the second represents the two classification criteria explored, whereas block 3 displays the results classified according to block 2.

4   Results

Results are organized according to the structural layer.

Layer 1. Infrastructure
The first or lower layer (here termed the infrastructure layer) is represented by the city infrastructure. It corresponds to both the connected objects of the city and the sensor network in addition to the technology used to gather or exchange information. In this case, equipment and devices play the role of substituting a person or acts as an enabler to turn a function more efficient and effective with less risk and without human intervention. Among them, robots and drones were used to clean and disinfect, measure patient's temperature, deliver medicine and food [18]. Robots can measure patients' parameters and allow communication between patients and medical staff, reducing direct contact [19]. In the transport domain, according to Kanda and Kivimaa [20], electric vehicles (EV) will decrease health risks by reducing human contact in the absence of human drivers.

Robots and drones also are used to disinfect [21] [22] avoiding workforce mobilization and decreasing exposure risk to personnel.

Robots with the ability to track or detect high-risk areas are gaining importance in busy public areas as well as playing an important role in tracking the disease, say the researchers [21]. Tables 1 show in a categorized form the main contributions.

Table 1. Main applications at the infrastructure layer, functions, benefits and relation with SDGs and stage of resilience

Layer	Functions	Benefits		
	Substitute humans	Decrease risk More efficient More effective		
	Acquire data/collect data	Aid in decision-making after proper analysis (in upper layers)		
	Application	**Examples**	**SDG integration**	**Resilience stage**
Infrastructure	Health care	Robots with biosensors	Contributes to SDG#3. Aligned with SDG#9	Response
	logistic	Robots/drones/EV	Contributes to SDG#3/SDG#11. Aligned with SDG#9	Response
	Capture of geolocation (risk area/crowds)	drones	Contributes to SDG#3/SDG#11. Aligned with SDG#9	Preparedness
	Community services	Disinfection robots/cleaning robots	Contributes to SDG#3/SDG#11. Aligned with SDG#9	Response
	Sensing	Heterogeneous sensors	Aligned with SDG#9	Necessary for posterior Planning.
	Physiological data sensing	Biosensors/ Biometric terminals	Contributes to SDG#3. Aligned with SDG#9	Response

Layer 2. Communication

The data collected at layer 1 has to be exchanged with the system and the functionalities used to configure the sensor networks integrated into the objects located in the middle layer, namely Communication Layer. Tables 2 show in a categorized form the main contributions supported by this layer and their functions, benefits, alignment with SDGs, and at which stage they support resilience building.

Layer 3. Intelligence

The third layer is associated with data analysis and managed to deliver to the citizens/city/institutions/governmental the most appropriate information and services. Results from this layer allow more accurate decision-making and provide information from prediction models.

Table 2. Main applications at the Communication layer, functions, benefits and relation with SDGs and stage of Resilience

Layer	Functions	Benefits		
	Allow exchange data	Ensure real time exchange among devices		
	Ensure remotely communication between persons or persons/devices	Allow establishing real time communication among people. Allow information integration Allow real time communication among devices (robots, platforms) and people.		

Layer	Application	Examples	SDG integration	Resilience stage
Communication	Health	telemedicine	Contributes to SDG#3. Aligned with SDG#9	Response
	Contact tracing	Apps (supported by Bluetooth, internet, GPS)	Contributes to SDG#3/ SDG#11. Aligned with SDG#9	Response
	Real-time exchange data/information	IoT network/internet/ 5G	Contributes to SDG#3/SDG#11. Aligned with SDG#9	Preparedness
	Care	tele-care services for elderly people	Contributes to SDG#3. Aligned with SDG#9	Response

AI-supported robots can perceive emotional states and can aid when isolation is imperative [23]. AI technologies, as well as Big Data analytics, are the main supportive technologies of this layer's functionalities. The alignment with innovation and the necessity of real-time transference of data and information is imperative to support proper outcomes from this layer, namely the adherence to SDG # 9 is imperative. Table 3 show in a categorized form the main outcomes, their functions, benefits, integration with SDGs, and at which stage they support resilience building.

Table 3. Main outcomes at the Intelligent layer, functions, benefits and relation with SDGs and stage of Resilience

Layer	Functions	Benefits
	Data treatment and processing	Simplify decision-making
		Enable autonomous decision-making
		Enable anticipation/prevention
		Perception of existing patterns and relations
	Delivering of applications for citizens/city/institutions	Improvement of services.

	Application	Examples	SDG integration	Resilience stage
Intelligent	Health	Chatbot/socially assistive robots	Contributes to SDG#3. Aligned with SDG#9	Recovery
	Disease surveillance	monitor trends in the disease where human-to-human transmission occurs	Contributes to SDG#3/ SDG#11. Aligned with SDG#9	Preparedness
	Mask wearing recognizing	Intelligent drones/intelligent robots	Contributes to SDG#3/SDG#11. Aligned with SDG#9	Response
	Contagious prediction	Algorithm identifies hotspots for exposure and vulnerability	Contributes to SDG#3/SDG#11. Aligned with SDG#9	Preparedness
	virtual reality for training purpose	Virtual platforms	Contributes to SDG#3/SDG#11. Aligned with SDG#9	Preparedness

5 Discussion

Some questions arise from the results and although they are not addressed in the present paper, they deserve some comments. The identification and organization of technologies according to their contribution on different stages of building resilience, will help practitioners and policy makers to decision making in administration, organization and planning. However, the paper does not address the challenges and barriers, legal, normative or even due to societal and cultural differences among countries and cities. It is worth noticing that vulnerable sectors are not expected to benefit from the technologies (depending on which one) at the same level. Or elderly people who are less familiar with apps or internet access. These niches may serve as starting points for future research.

Present results show alignment with results from other papers, although the models of SC or the organization of technologies differ. Thus, comparison with Bragazzi et al. (2020) [24] shows points in common with the categories they defined as a) Short-Term Applications and b) Long-Term Applications. SC technologies classified by Costa and Peixoto (2020) [25] in solutions for detection, alerting, mitigation shows points of adherence with our results. The paper of Jaiswal et al. (2020) [26] classifies solutions into smart technology, smart healthcare, and smart delivery system. Our results, although having adopted other approach show alignment with theirs.

6 Conclusions

An overview although categorized, of the main technologies, applications, and functionalities within the SC domain is discussed to identify the way they support COVID-19 and integrate with three SDGs that were considered fundamentals for resilience building. Results show a starting point to define and implement an accessible strategy of defensive measures against COVID-19 and/or other types of natural disaster situations within the Agenda 2030 and focused on turning the cities more resilient. We hope that this work will contribute to governance systems and citizens to be better prepared for future outbreaks. Some challenges arise from the technologies proposals among them the individual rights related to personal data. However, it is undeniable that pandemic accelerates innovation thus strengthen the role of SC against COVID-19 spread.

References

1. Fong, M.W., et al.: Nonpharmaceutical measures for pandemic influenza in nonhealthcare settings—Social distancing measures. Emerg. Infect. Dis. **26**(5), 976–984 (2020). https://doi.org/10.3201/eid2605.190995
2. Shorfuzzaman, M., Hossain, M.S., Alhamid, M.F.: Towards the sustainable development of smart cities through mass video surveillance: a response to the COVID-19 pandemic. Sustain. Cities Soc. **64**, 102582 (2021)
3. UNDRR, United Nations office for disaster Risk Reduction. https://www.undrr.org/terminology/resilience. Accessed July 2020
4. UNISDR: Terminology on Disaster Risk Reduction, Geneva, Switzerland (2009)
5. Wright, N., et al.: Health emergency and disaster risk management: five years into implementation of the Sendai framework. Int. J. Disaster Risk Sci. **11**(2), 206–217 (2020). https://doi.org/10.1007/s13753-020-00274-x
6. UN: United Nations Sustainable Development Summit 2015, New York, 25–27 September. The United Nations (2015)
7. Moraci, F., Errigo, M.F., Fazia, C., Burgio, G., Foresta, S.: Making less vulnerable cities: resilience as a new paradigm of smart planning. Sustainability **10**, 755 (2018)
8. Tzioutziou, A., Xenidis, Y.: A study on the integration of resilience and smart city concepts in urban systems. Infrastructures **6**, 24 (2021). https://doi.org/10.3390/infrastructures6020024
9. Bibri, S.E.: A novel model for data-driven smart sustainable cities of the future: the institutional transformations required for balancing and advancing the three goals of sustainability. Energy Inform. **4**(1), 1–37 (2021). https://doi.org/10.1186/s42162-021-00138-8
10. Khan, H., Kushwah, K.K., Singh, S., Urkude, H., Maurya, M.R., Sadasivuni, K.K.: Smart technologies driven approaches to tackle COVID-19 pandemic: a review. 3 Biotech **11**(2), 1–22 (2021). https://doi.org/10.1007/s13205-020-02581-y
11. Kricka, L.J., Polevikov, S., Park, J.Y., et al.: Artificial intelligence-powered search tools and resources in the fight against COVID-19. EJIFCC **31**(2), 106–116 (2020)
12. Kummitha, R.K.R.: Smart technologies for fighting pandemics: the techno- and human- driven approaches in controlling the virus transmission. Gov. Inf. Q. **37**(3), 101481 (2020). ISSN 0740-624X, https://doi.org/10.1016/j.giq.2020.101481
13. Sonn, J.W., Lee, J.K.: The smart city as time-space cartographer in COVID-19 control: the South Korean strategy and democratic control of surveillance technology. Eurasian Geogr. Econ. **61**(4–5), 482–492 (2020). https://doi.org/10.1080/15387216.2020.1768423

14. Yang, S., Chong, Z.: Smart city projects against COVID-19: quantitative evidence from China. Sustain. Cities Soc. **70**, 102897 (2021). ISSN 2210-6707, https://doi.org/10.1016/j.scs.2021.102897

15. Allam, Z., Jones, D.S.: On the Coronavirus (COVID-19) outbreak and the smart city network: universal data sharing standards coupled with Artificial Intelligence (AI) to benefit urban health monitoring and management. Healthcare **8**(1), 46 (2020). https://doi.org/10.3390/healthcare8010046

16. Calvillo, C.F., Sánchez-Miralles, A., Villar, J.: Energy management and planning in smart cities. Renew. Sustain. Energy Rev. **55**, 273–287 (2016). https://doi.org/10.1016/j.rser.2015.10.133

17. Chamoso, P., De La Prieta, F.: Smart cities simulation environment for intelligent algorithms evaluation. ADCAIJ: Adv. Distrib. Comput. Artif. Intell. J. **4**, 87 (2016). https://doi.org/10.14201/ADCAIJ2015438796

18. Zeng, Z., Chen, P.J., Lew, A.A.: From high-touch to high-tech: COVID-19 drives robotics adoption. Tour. Geogr. **22**, 724–734 (2020). https://doi.org/10.1080/14616688.2020.1762118

19. Romero, M.E.: Tommy the robot nurse helps Italian doctors care for COVID-19 patients, April 2020. https://www.pri.org/stories/2020-04-08/tommy-robot-nurse-helps-italian-doctors-care-covid-19-patients

20. Kanda, W., Kivimaa, P.: What opportunities could the COVID-19 outbreak offer for sustainability transitions research on electricity and mobility? Energy Res. Soc. Sci. **68**, 101666 (2020). https://doi.org/10.1016/j.erss.2020.101666

21. Yang, G.Z., et al.: Combating COVID-19—the role of robotics in managing public health and infectious diseases. Sci. Robot. **5**, eabb5589 (2020). https://doi.org/10.1126/scirobotics.abb5589

22. Murphy, R.R.: Robots and pandemics in science fiction. Sci. Robot. **5**(42), eabb9590 (2020). https://doi.org/10.1126/scirobotics.abb9590

23. Scassellati, B., Vázquez, M.: The potential of socially assistive robots during infectious disease outbreaks. Sci. Robot. **5**(44), eabc9014 (2020). https://doi.org/10.1126/scirobotics.abc9014

24. Bragazzi, N.L., Dai, H., Damiani, G., Behzadifar, M., Martini, M., Wu, J.: How big data and artificial intelligence can help better manage the COVID-19 pandemic. Int. J. Environ. Res. Public Health **17**(9), 3176 (2020). https://doi.org/10.3390/ijerph17093176

25. Costa, D.G., Peixoto, J.P.J.: COVID-19 pandemic: a review of smart cities initiatives to face new outbreaks. IET Smart Cities **2**(2), 64–73 (2020). https://doi.org/10.1049/iet-smc.2020.0044

26. Jaiswal, R., Agarwal, A., Negi, R.: Smart solution for reducing the COVID-19 risk using smart city technology. IET Smart Cities **2**, 82–88 (2020). https://doi.org/10.1049/iet-smc.2020.0043

Key Success Factors for Supply Chain Sustainability in COVID-19 Pandemic: An ISM Approach

Surajit Bag[1], Peter Kilbourn[1], Noleen Pisa[1], and Mihalis Giannakis[2(✉)]

[1] University of Johannesburg, Johannesburg, South Africa
[2] Audencia Business School, Nantes, France
mgiannakis@audencia.com

Abstract. The COVID-19 pandemic has resulted in major disruptions to businesses, supply chains and economies alike. The negative effects of the pandemic are yet to be fully realised. In this study, we aimed to reflect on and explore strategies for supply chain sustainability in the face of business downturn caused by the COVID-19 pandemic. The focus of this study is the heavy engineering industry in South Africa as it relies on a global supply chain network. The paper begins with a brief introduction of negative effects of COVID-19 on supply chains followed by the research questions that drives this study. We used a literature review to select the critical success factors which were further refined using experts' opinion. These factors subsequently, were used as input to an interpretive structural modeling (ISM) technique. The ISM model yielded some interesting findings that can aid organizations in building resilient supply chains that are sustainable in nature. We conclude that organizations need to develop a culture of collaboration; since greater collaboration among value chain members is required to create a more resilient supply chain.

Keywords: COVID-19 · Pandemic · Critical success factors · Supply chain · Sustainability · ISM

1 Introduction

Supply chains are dynamic processes with multifaceted operations and associated disruption risks [1]. Disruption risks can evolve naturally or artificially with or without forewarning [2]. Pandemic outbursts are extraordinary disruptive circumstances, which significantly contribute towards supply chain management risk with endured presence, prolonged proliferation and elevated ambiguity [3]. The outbreak of COVID-19 is one of the biggest examples in the history of pandemics that has extensively contributed towards supply chain management disruptions globally [4, 5]. It is pertinent to understand that the existing management processes are mostly not equipped to sustain COVID-19 pandemic disruptions [1, 6]; instead hold worrying weaknesses. Organizations are facing various challenges such as failing to optimise supply and demand gaps and developing resilient

© IFIP International Federation for Information Processing 2021
Published by Springer Nature Switzerland AG 2021
A. Dolgui et al. (Eds.): APMS 2021, IFIP AICT 633, pp. 724–733, 2021.
https://doi.org/10.1007/978-3-030-85910-7_76

supply chains that can recover fast after disruptions. Lastly, organizations are facing challenges to develop sustainable supply chains [7]. COVID-19 has not only caused health care crises [8]; but caused severe economic downturn that shifted attention of organizations towards business continuity and sustainability [9]. The health and safety aspects of employees and community are at stake. Organizations are assisting employees to adapt to new systems [7]. The whole world is experiencing effects of COVID-19 for the first time and many new strategies and practices have evolved since March 2020 to cope up with this situation. To extend the knowledge base we aim to answer the below research question.

RQ1: What are the critical success factors for enhancing supply chain sustainability amid COVID-19 pandemic?

The relation between each set of critical success factors and outcomes of the interaction can provide rich insights which can be useful in redesigning the supply chain to cope up in this pandemic. Since COVID-19 is a completely new phenomenon facing supply chain managers; understanding the interrelationships between critical success factors of supply chain sustainability can add great value [10]. However, literature on COVID-19 is mainly limited to medical studies and thus highlights the need for investigation in the supply chain sustainability context. We therefore, aim to address the second research question namely;

RQ2: What is the interrelationship between the critical success factors that can empower supply chain resilience amid the COVID-19 pandemic?

The rest of the sections are organized as follows. Section 2 presents literature review followed by Sect. 3 that presents the ISM methodology and data analysis. The discussion is presented in Sect. 4 and conclusions are drawn in Section 4.

2 Literature Review

Critical success factors for supply chain sustainability amid COVID-19 pandemic were identified from literature review and presented below.

a) Technology readiness of organizations - Technology readiness is essential to cope with supply chain disruptions such as the COVID-19 pandemic [7]. Advanced information and communication technologies do more than assisting in making timely decisions but also aid in factory automation; and thus, connecting the factory shop floor to the top floor (i.e., top management level) [11]. The COVID-19 pandemic and the resultant national lockdowns and social distancing have impacted the normal factory operations; which can be overcome by factory automation and use of digital systems to run production, quality checking and packing [12]. Technologies such as big data powered artificial intelligence can enhance sustainable manufacturing [13].

b) Historical disruption data analysis - It has clearly been demonstrated that healthcare supply chains have not learned any lessons from previous epidemics such as Middle East Respiratory Syndrome (MERS) and Severe Acute Respiratory Syndrome (SARS) [14]. However, Ivanov and Dolgui [15] have argued that the analysis of historical disruption data can help in managing disruption risks.

c) Availability of real-time disruption data - It is not possible for any supply chain to become fully immune from global shocks created by COVID-19; however, availability of real-time data can reduce the risks. Supply chain executives can collect real-time data, infer insights and take immediate actions. This will reduce the response times significantly and lower incidents of customer complaints. It is a necessity during a pandemic to access real-time disruption data and keep updated on the latest trends. China is considered a powerhouse of the global economy as they have shown ability to manufacture and supply products at low costs. However, with the onset of the novel coronavirus, thousands of factories had to shut their production units [16]. Consequently, supply chain managers need real time disruption data to assess the supply chain status and change strategies accordingly. Real-time disruption data thus proves to be an important agility mechanism for supply chain managers [15].

d) Ensure end-to-end visibility - Supply chain managers must have end-to-end visibility to identify problems in the supply chain and take immediate actions. This has been recently confirmed by Ivanov and Dolgui [15] where they opined that end-to-end visibility is important for companies operating in international markets. Visibility in supply chains has reduced significantly during this COVID-19 pandemic [7]. Ivanov and Dolgui [15] emphasized on supply chain visibility to enhance end-to-end supply chain visibility and avert risks. Advanced supply chain visualizations can uncover the relationships behind big data sets. Other benefits include: data validation, chain-of-custody reporting, supplier benchmarking, supply chain planning and optimization, risk heat maps and alerts, emergency response and control tower-like visibility [21].

e) Derive values from technology deployment - In this Industry 4.0 era harnessing the power of technology such as big data and artificial intelligence, automation, IoT, blockchain, edge computing, deep learning, advanced computing power, application programming interfaces and high-power satellites can help an organization become cautious about supply chain challenges and an organization can change strategies and practices to mitigate the same [7].

f) Prevent exploitation of workers - It has been found that COVID-19 has triggered modern slavery. The pandemic has resulted in severe job losses in the last six months and existing employees fear job losses and thereby ready to overwork even after getting pay cuts/suffering from other mal-treatments. Trautrims et al. [17] cautioned that organizations need to prevent exploitation of workers in COVID-19 pandemic. Sharma et al. [7] opined that organizations need to take care of the health and wellbeing of their own employees and also need to consider the health and wellbeing of tier one and tier two suppliers' employees to gain sustainability.

g) Consider the value of flexibility - Remko [18] suggested organizations to consider the value of flexibility. For example, Sub-Saharan African countries need to put in place flexible but effective policies and legislation approaches that harness and formalise the informal trade and remove supply chain barriers. This could include strengthening cross-border trade facilities such as adequate pro-poor, gender-sensitive, and streamlined cross-border customs, tax regimes, and information flow [19]. Additive manufacturing has proven to enhance flexibility in COVID-19 pandemic and organizations need to adopt flexibility to gain sustainability [20].

h) Short response times - It is essential that organizations devise strategies to ensure short response times to changes in their business environment [18]. The more agile an organization is, the better its chances for survival during the COVID-19 pandemic [1].

i) Adoption of multiple supply sources - Adoption of multiple supply strategy has become more important for managing supply risks [18]. In the current pandemic, some suppliers may be located in red zones (high spread of infection) resulting in restricted business operations and supply shortages Therefore, dependency on a few of suppliers is no longer a viable option for organizations; instead, organisations are increasingly adopting multiple supplier sourcing strategies to ensure continuity of timely supplies for production [18].

j) Near shore and local sourcing - Near shore and local sourcing is suggested by Remko [18] as another strategy to ensure supply chain sustainability in the face of a global pandemic. The closure of international borders resulting from national lockdowns amid the COVID-19 pandemic, necessitates near shore and local sourcing of raw material in order to sustain business operations. Most importantly, the sustainability standards need to be checked [17].

k) Greater utilization of information technology - It was suggested by Remko [18] that supply chain managers need to undertake greater utilization of information technology to drive more complete and immediate information availability for quality decision making and that too in a timely manner.

l) Collaboration with external stakeholders - Collaboration with external stakeholders results in supply chain sustainability and enhances competences to sustain business operations particularly during a pandemic such as the COVID-19 pandemic [7]. Literature indicates that more intensive information exchange and collaboration with unions, NGOs, and other expert stakeholders increases supply chain transparency and allows for a proactive detection of early warning signals on deteriorating conditions even when physical audits are disrupted [17].

m) Develop a collaborative culture - A collaborative organizational culture is a very important factor in ensuring collaboration with suppliers and customers to make timely production and dispatches. Literature indicates that greater collaboration among value chain members is required to create a more resilient supply chain [7].

n) Synchronize strategic processes - is essential that organizations focus on synchronization of strategic processes [7]. If an organization mechanizes processes by converting into intelligent workflows—starting from managing demands to dispatch strategies, organizations will provide a platform to processes, people and technology to interact. This will bridge the current gap in a firm's ability to feel the changes in the environment, respond to that with the help of intelligent workflows, and generate required businesses [7].

o) Supply chain resilience - Supply chain disruptions can result in significant economic downturn. Resilience is the ability to deal with sudden changes in business environment while retaining the organization's basic functions [22]. Supply chain resilience has turned out to be one of the key factors amid COVID-19 pandemic for managing risks and enhancing supply chain sustainability [23].

3   Research Method

3.1   Interpretive Structural Modelling (ISM)

The ISM methodology is used in this study to develop the structural model. This technique was popularized by Sushil [24, 25]. The critical success factors (CSFs') for enhancing supply chain sustainability amid COVID-19 pandemic are identified from the literature review and further refined using two experts' opinion. Therefore, the CSFs' are validated in context to South Africa. The final list of Critical success factors (CSFs') is presented in Table 1.

Table 1. CSF refined through experts' opinion

Sl No	Variables
1	Technology readiness
2	Historical disruption data analysis
3	Availability of real-time disruption data
4	Ensure end-to-end viability
5	Derive values from technology deployment
6	Prevent exploitation of workers
7	Consider the value of flexibility
8	Short response times
9	Adoption of multiple supply sources
10	Nearshore and local sourcing
11	Greater utilization of information technology
12	Collaboration with external stakeholders
13	Develop a culture of collaboration
14	Synchronize strategic processes
15	Supply chain resilience

The second step in ISM involves examining the contextual relationship between pairs of critical success factors/elements. A questionnaire was used to collect the responses from five referees, who are working in the heavy engineering sector for more than 20 years. We applied the statistical function "mode" to develop the aggregate structural self-interaction matrix (SSIM).

The aggregate structural self-interaction matrix (SSIM) in Table 2, is based on the notations below which denote the direction of relationships between variables (i and j):

V: i lead to j but j does not lead to i
A: i do not lead to j but j lead to i
X: i lead to j and j lead to i
O: i and j are unrelated to each other

The SSIM has been converted into a binary matrix, i.e., the reachability matrix (Table 3) by substituting V, A X and O by 1 and 0. The substitution rule is explained below:

- If the (i, j) entry in the SSIM is V, then the (i, j) entry in the reachability matrix becomes '1' and (j, i) entry becomes '0'

Table 2. Aggregate structural self interaction matrix

	XV	XIV	XIII	XII	XI	X	IX	VIII	VII	VI	V	IV	III	II	I
I	V	X	A	A	A	O	O	V	V	O	V	V	V	V	
II	V	V	O	O	A	A	A	O	O	O	A	O	A		
III	V	V	A	A	A	O	O	O	O	O	A	A			
IV	V	V	A	A	A	O	O	V	V	O	A				
V	V	V	V	A	A	O	O	O	O	O					
VI	V	O	A	A	V	O	O	O	O						
VII	V	A	A	A	A	V	V	V							
VIII	V	A	A	A	A	A	A								
IX	V	A	A	A	A	A									
X	V	V	A	A	A										
XI	V	V	A	A											
XII	V	V	A												
XIII	V	V													
XIV	V														

- If the (i, j) entry in the SSIM is A, then the (i, j) entry in the reachability matrix becomes '0' and (j, i) entry becomes '1'
- If the (i, j) entry in the SSIM is X, then the (i, j) entry in the reachability matrix becomes '1' and (j, i) entry also becomes '1'
- If the (i, j) entry in the SSIM is O, then the (i, j) entry in the reachability matrix becomes '0' and (j, i) entry also becomes '0'

Table 3. Initial reachability matrix

	I	II	III	IV	V	VI	VII	VIII	IX	X	XI	XII	XIII	XIV	XV
I	1	1	1	1	1	0	1	1	0	0	0	0	0	1	1
II	0	1	1	0	0	0	0	0	0	0	0	0	0	1	1
III	0	0	1	0	0	0	0	0	0	0	0	0	0	1	1
IV	0	0	1	1	0	0	1	1	0	0	0	0	0	1	1
V	0	1	1	1	1	0	0	0	0	0	0	0	0	1	1
VI	0	0	0	0	0	1	0	0	0	0	1	0	0	0	1
VII	0	0	0	0	0	0	1	1	1	1	0	0	0	0	1
VIII	0	0	0	0	0	0	0	1	0	0	0	0	0	0	1
IX	0	1	0	0	0	0	0	1	1	0	0	0	0	0	1
X	0	1	0	0	0	0	0	1	1	1	0	0	0	1	1
XI	1	1	1	1	1	0	1	1	1	1	1	0	0	1	1
XII	1	0	1	1	1	1	1	1	1	1	1	1	0	1	1
XIII	1	0	1	1	1	1	1	1	1	1	1	1	1	1	1
XIV	1	0	0	0	0	0	1	1	1	0	0	0	0	1	1
XV	0	0	0	0	0	0	0	0	0	0	0	0	0	0	1

The transitivity principle is checked in this step. If element i leads to element j and element j leads to element k, then element i should lead to element k. By transitivity embedding, the final reachability matrix is obtained as shown in Table 4.

Table 4. Final reachability matrix

Variables	I	II	III	IV	V	VI	VII	VIII	IX	X	XI	XII	XIII	XIV	XV	Driving Power (Y)
I	1	1	1	1	1	1*	1	1	1*	1*	0	0	0	1	1	12
II	1*	1	1	1*	0	1*	1*	1*	1*	1*	0	0	0	1	1	11
III	1*	0	1	1*	0	1*	1*	1*	1*	1*	0	0	0	1	1	10
IV	1*	0	1	1	0	0	1	1	1*	1*	0	0	0	1	1	9
V	1*	1	1	1	1	1*	1*	1*	1*	1*	0	0	0	1	1	12
VI	1*	1*	1*	1*	1*	1	1*	1*	1*	1*	1	0	0	1*	1	13
VII	0	1*	0	0	0	0	1	1	1	1	0	0	0	1*	1	7
VIII	0	0	0	0	0	0	0	1	0	0	0	0	0	0	1	2
IX	0	1	1*	0	0	0	0	1	1	0	0	0	0	1*	1	6
X	1*	1	1*	0	0	0	1*	1	1	1	0	0	0	1	1	9
XI	1	1	1	1	1	1*	1	1	1	1	1	1*	0	1	1	14
XII	1	1*	1	1	1	1	1	1	1	1	1	1	0	1	1	14
XIII	1	1*	1	1	1	1	1	1	1	1	1	1	1	1	1	15
XIV	1	1*	1*	1*	1*	0	1	1	1	1*	0	0	0	1	1	11
XV	0	0	0	0	0	0	0	0	0	0	0	0	0	0	1	1
Dependence Power (X)	11	11	12	10	7	8	12	14	13	12	4	3	1	13	15	

The level partitioning is done in this stage. After the first iteration, the variable classified to level 1 are discarded and the partitioning process is repeated on the remaining variable to determine the level 2. These iterations are continued until the level of each variable is completed. The results for iterations 1 to 9 are summarised in Table 5.

Table 5. Level partitioning

Variables	Reachability set	Antecedent set	Intersection set	Level
I	1,2,3,4,5,6,7,8,9,10,11,15	1,2,3,4,5,6,7,11,12,13,14,15	1,2,3,4,5,6,7,11,15	V
II	1,2,3,4,5,7,8,9,10,11,15	1,2,3,6,7,8,10,11,12,13,14,15	1,2,3,7,8,10,11,15	VI
III	1,2,5,7,8,9,10,11,15	1,2,3,4,5,6,7,10,11,12,13,14,15	1,2,5,7,10,11,15	V
IV	1,2,4,5,8,9,10,11,15	1,2,3,4,5,6,7,11,12,13,14	1,2,4,5,11	V
V	1,2,3,4,5,6,7,8,9,10,11,15	1,6,7,12,13,14,15	1,6,7,15	VIII
VI	1,2,3,4,5,6,7,8,9,10,11,12,15	1,2,3,4,6,7,12	1,2,3,4,6,7,12	VI
VII	3,8,9,10,11,15	1,2,3,4,5,6,7,8,11,12,13,14,15	3,8,11,15	IV
VIII	9	1,2,3,4,5,6,7,8,9,10,11,12,13,14,15	9	II
IX	2,3,4,9,10,15	1,2,3,4,5,6,7,8,10,11,12,13,14,15	2,3,4,10,15	III
X	1,2,3,4,8,9,10,11,15	1,2,3,4,5,6,7,8,11,12,13,14,15	1,2,3,4,8,11,15	IV
XI	1,2,3,4,5,6,7,8,9,10,11,12,13,15	2,7,12,13,14	2,7,12,13	VIII
XII	1,2,3,4,5,6,7,8,9,10,11,12,13,15	12,13,14	12,13	VIII
XIII	1,2,3,4,5,6,7,8,9,10,11,12,13,14,15	14	14	IX
XIV	1,2,3,4,5,6,8,9,10,14,15	1,2,3,4,5,6,7,8,10,11,12,13,14,15	1,2,3,4,5,6,8,10,14,15	IV
XV	15	1,2,3,4,5,6,7,8,9,10,11,12,13,14,15	15	I

The structural model is developed using nodes and lines of edges. The digraph is presented in Fig. 1.

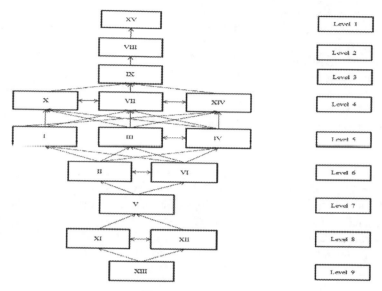

Fig. 1. ISM digraph

From ISM digraph we developed the ISM model (refer Fig. 2).

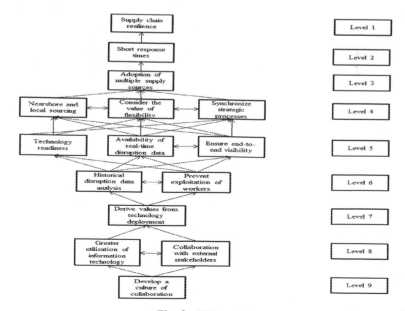

Fig. 2. ISM model

4 Conclusion

Byron and Thatcher [26] indicated that one of the more intimidating challenges researchers face is in understanding theory and theory-building. The following questions circle on the mind of researchers such as (a) What is (and isn't) theory? (b) Should we care about theory? (c) Where do new theories come from? (d) How do you build a good theory? and lastly (d) How do you get your theory published?

Referring back to the building blocks of theory suggested by Whetten [27] which articulates theory as consisting of following fundamental things: What and How (description), Why (explanation), and Who, Where, When (boundary conditions) we further explain our research findings to extend the knowledge base.

In the current study which is exploratory in nature; we have used ISM technique to build theory and answer two key questions- What, and How. We have answered as to what are the critical success factors for supply chain sustainability amid COVID-19 pandemic. Second, we have also answered-how these critical success factors been interrelated. The bottom level CSF i.e., development of collaborative culture is very important and more attention is required on this element as it influences the final outcome i.e., supply chain resilience. Figure 2 provides a clear understanding about how to use this model as it demonstrates the interrelationships between all variables.

References

1. Ivanov, D.: Predicting the impacts of epidemic outbreaks on global supply chains: a simulation-based analysis on the coronavirus outbreak (COVID-19/SARS-CoV-2) case. Transp. Res. Part E: Logistics Transp. Rev. **136**, 101922 (2020a)
2. Basole, R.C., Bellamy, M.A.: Supply network structure, visibility, and risk diffusion: a computational approach. Decis. Sci. **45**(4), 753–789 (2014)
3. Ivanov, D., Dolgui, A.: New disruption risk management perspectives in supply chains: digital twins, the ripple effect, and resileanness. IFAC-PapersOnLine **52**(13), 337–342 (2019)
4. Kırılmaz, O., Erol, S.: A proactive approach to supply chain risk management: shifting orders among suppliers to mitigate the supply side risks. J. Purch. Supply Manag. **23**(1), 54–65 (2017)
5. Lai, Y., Sun, H., Ren, J.: Understanding the determinants of big data analytics (BDA) adoption in logistics and supply chain management. The International Journal of Logistics Management (2018). https://doi.org/10.1108/IJLM-06-2017-0153
6. Giannakis, M., Papadopoulos, T.: Supply chain sustainability: a risk management approach. Int. J. Prod. Econ. **171**, 455–470 (2016)
7. Sharma, A., Adhikary, A., Borah, S.B.: Covid-19's impact on supply chain decisions: strategic insights for NASDAQ 100 firms using Twitter data. J. Bus. Res. **117**, 443–449 (2020)
8. Liu, Y., Lee, J.M., Lee, C.: The challenges and opportunities of a global health crisis: the management and business implications of COVID-19 from an Asian perspective. Asian Bus. Manag. **19**, 277–297 (2020)
9. Queiroz, M.M., Ivanov, D., Dolgui, A., Wamba, S.F.: Impacts of epidemic outbreaks on supply chains: mapping a research agenda amid the COVID-19 pandemic through a structured literature review. Annals of Operations Research, pp. 1–38 (2020)
10. Sarkis, J.: Supply chain sustainability: learning from the COVID-19 pandemic. Int. J. Oper. Prod. Manag. **41**(1), 63–73 (2021)

11. Telukdarie, A., Buhulaiga, E., Bag, S., Gupta, S., Luo, Z.: Industry 4.0 implementation for multinationals. Process Safety Environ. Prot. **118**, 316–329 (2018)
12. Malik, A.A., Masood, T., Kousar, R.: Repurposing factories with robotics in the face of COVID-19. Science Robotics, vol. 5, no. 43 (2020). https://doi.org/10.1126/scirobotics.abc 2782
13. Bag, S., Pretorius, J.H.C.: Relationships between industry 4.0, sustainable manufacturing and circular economy: proposal of a research framework. International Journal of Organizational Analysis (2020). https://doi.org/10.1108/IJOA-04-2020-2120
14. Peeri, N.C., et al.: The SARS, MERS and novel coronavirus (COVID-19) epidemics, the newest and biggest global health threats: what lessons have we learned?. Int. J. Epidemiol. **49**(3), 717–726 (2020). https://doi.org/10.1093/ije/dyaa033
15. Ivanov, D., Dolgui, A.: A digital supply chain twin for managing the disruption risks and resilience in the era of Industry 4.0. Production Planning & Control, pp. 1–14 (2020)
16. Wang, J., Wang, Z.: Strengths, weaknesses, opportunities and threats (Swot) analysis of china's prevention and control strategy for the covid-19 epidemic. Int. J. Environ. Res. Public Health **17**(7), 2235 (2020)
17. Trautrims, A., Schleper, M.C., Cakir, M.S., Gold, S.: Survival at the expense of the weakest? managing modern slavery risks in supply chains during COVID-19. J. Risk Res. **23**(7-8), 1–6 (2020)
18. Remko, V.H.: Research opportunities for a more resilient post-COVID-19 supply chain– closing the gap between research findings and industry practice. Int. J. Oper. Prod. Manag. **40**(4), 341–355 (2020)
19. Renzaho, A.: The need for the right socio-economic and cultural fit in the COVID-19 response in sub-saharan Africa: examining demographic, economic political, health, and socio-cultural differentials in COVID-19 morbidity and mortality. Int. J. Environ. Res. Public Health **17**(10), 3445 (2020)
20. Ivanov, D.: Viable supply chain model: integrating agility, resilience and sustainability perspectives—lessons from and thinking beyond the COVID-19 pandemic. Annals of Operations Research, pp. 1–21 (2020b)
21. Sourcemap white paper: End-to-End supply chain visualization. https://static1.squarespace.com/static/56ad86dffd5d088a88b8a425/t/5d2cdef8dd52da000123cca1/1563221752511/End-toEnd%2BSupply%2BChain%2BVisualization%2Bby%2BSourcemap.pdf
22. Holling, C.S.: Resilience and stability of ecological systems. Annu. Rev. Ecol. Syst. **4**(1), 1–23 (1973)
23. Ivanov, D., Das, A.: Coronavirus (COVID-19/SARS-CoV-2) and supply chain resilience: a research note. Int. J. Integr. Supply Manag. **13**(1), 90–102 (2020)
24. Sushil. Interpretive ranking process'. Glob. J. Flexible Syst. Manag. **10**(4), 1–10 (2009)
25. Sushil. Interpreting the interpretive structural model. Glob. J. Flexible Syst. Manag. **13**(2), 87–106 (2012)
26. Byron, K., Thatcher, S.M. (Eds) Comments: "What I know now that I wish I knew then"— teaching theory and theory building. Academy of Management Review, vol. 41, no. 1 (2016). https://doi.org/10.5465/amr.2015.0094
27. Whetten, D.: What constitutes a theoretical contribution? Acad. Manag. Rev. **4**, 490–495 (1989)
28. Golan, M.S., Jernegan, L.H., Linkov, I.: Trends and applications of resilience analytics in supply chain modeling: systematic literature review in the context of the COVID-19 pandemic. Environ. Syst. Decis. **40**(2), 222–243 (2020). https://doi.org/10.1007/s10669-020-09777-w

Author Index